Ethical Theory

Classical and Contemporary Readings

Jacques Louis David, *The Death of Socrates*. Courtesy the Metropolitan Museum of Art, Wolfe Fund, 1931.

Ethical Theory

Classical and Contemporary Readings
Second Edition

LOUIS P. POJMAN
University of Mississippi

I(T)P™ Wadsworth Publishing Company
An International Thomson Publishing Company

Belmont • Albany • Bonn • Boston • Cincinnati • Detroit • London • Madrid • Melbourne
Mexico City • New York • Paris • San Francisco • Singapore • Tokyo • Toronto • Washington

Philosophy Editor: Tammy Goldfeld
Editorial Assistant: Kelly Zavislak
Production: Ruth Cottrell
Print Buyer: Randy Hurst
Permissions Editor: Robert Kauser
Interior Designer: Andrew Ogus
Copy Editor: Sandra Beriss
Cover Designer: Laurie Anderson
Compositor: ColorType, San Diego
Printer: Arcata Graphics/Fairfield

For more information, contact Wadsworth Publishing Company.

Wadsworth Publishing Company
10 Davis Drive
Belmont, California 94002
USA

International Thomson Publishing
Berkshire House 168-173
High Holborn
London, WC1V7AA
England

Thomas Nelson Australia
102 Dodds Street
South Melbourne 3205
Victoria, Australia

Nelson Canada
1120 Birchmount Road
Scarborough, Ontario
Canada M1K 5G4

International Thomson Editores
Campos Eliseos 385, Piso 7
Col. Polanco
11560 México D.F. México

International Thomson Publishing GmbH
Königswinterer Strasse 418
53227 Bonn
Germany

International Thomson Publishing Asia
221 Henderson Road
#05-10 Henderson Building
Singapore 0315

International Thomson Publishing-Japan
Hirakawacho Kyowa Building, 3F
2-2-1 Hirakawacho
Chiyoda-ku, Tokyo 102
Japan

*This book is printed on
acid-free recycled paper.*

Library of Congress Cataloging-in-Publication Data
Pojman, Louis P.
   Ethical theory: classical and contemporary readings / [edited by]
   Louis P. Pojman. —2nd ed.
      p. cm.
   Includes bibliographical references.
   ISBN: 0-534-21636-6
   1. Ethics.   I. Pojman, Louis P.
BJ1012.E8839   1994
170—dc20

To
Ruth and Paul

Contents

*For advanced courses

Contents

Preface to the Second Edition

I am grateful for the good reception that the first edition of this work has had, allowing me to put together a new edition. Responding to several suggestions and the reviews of the original work, I have made several changes in this edition that enhance it. While I have kept the same format and core readings, I have added several articles (13 in all), while deleting others, bringing the number of selections from 69 to 73. The introductions and bibliographies have been brought up to date. I have commissioned two essays on the emerging topic of interest, evolutionary ethics, by two leading philosophers in that area, Michael Ruse and Elliott Sober. I have revised the Nietzsche selection in Part IV. I have added three contemporary selections on consequentialist ethics in Part V (by Nozick, Foot, and Scheffler). I have added Walter Schaller's excellent defense of virtue ethics to Part VII and Evan Jobe's critique of Sturgeon's version of moral realism to Part IX. Perhaps the most important addition to this work is David Hume's discussion of reason and emotion and the fact/value distinction in Part VIII. I had considered including this in the first edition but didn't feel confident in editing Hume's work. Since then, I've spent considerable time studying Hume's moral theory, and I am happy to be able to include a substantial selec-tion. In that same section, I have replaced the selection on Hare's prescriptivism with a more recent, fuller account. In Part XII, I have included Wallace Matson's challenging essay "Justice: A Funeral Oration" and Thomas Nagel's thoughtful "Equality." Needless to say, I keenly regret having to drop some very good essays in order to bring together this final set. Some anguish was involved, but I was guided by reviewers' and readers' comments. The final decisions rest with me.

I am grateful to the following reviewers for their helpful suggestions for improving this work: Sheralee Brindell, University of Colorado, Boulder; Richard Fumerton, University of Iowa; Patricia Hanna, University of Utah; and Michael Potts, Kennesaw State College. Mane Hajdin supplied a penetrating and thorough critique that caused me to make several alterations. Thanks are due to Sandra Beriss, the copy editor, and to Ruth Cottrell for the production.

As the first edition was, this edition of the work is dedicated to my daughter and son, Ruth Freedom and Paul, two of the most wonderful children parents could be blessed with having.

Louis Pojman

Preface to the First Edition

The goal of this anthology is to combine classical and contemporary ethical readings to provide a fruitful basis for discussion of perennial problems in ethical theory. It is modeled after Paul Taylor's excellent *Problems of Moral Philosophy,* which I used until it went out of print a few years back. In fact, the first step in putting together this anthology was my request that Taylor's anthology be revised and updated. Only when I realized that this wasn't feasible did I accept editorial responsibility for *Ethical Theory: Classical and Contemporary Readings.*

Like Taylor, I have included works representing the main ethical traditions in Western thought. In addition, I have expanded the number of topics—organizing the readings around thirteen major theoretical issues in contemporary ethics: (1) what is ethics, (2) ethical relativism, (3) ethical egoism, (4) value, (5) utilitarianism, (6) Kantian and deontological systems, (7) virtue-based ethical systems, (8) fact/value problem, (9) moral realism, (10) morality and self-interest, (11) religion and ethics, (12) justice, and (13) rights.

The major problem in compiling an anthology in ethical theory is one of selection—deciding which issues, points of view, and articles to include. Currently, the field of ethical theory exists in a state of anarchy. It isn't simply that there are problems with existing ethical theories, there is also a plethora of coherent theories that are mutually inconsistent. Some ethicists (for example, Alasdair MacIntyre and Bernard Williams) are extremely dubious about the prospect of a viable ethical theory arising out of the Anglo-

American analytic tradition. Others (for example, Derek Parfit, Thomas Nagel, and Philippa Foot), while recognizing the difficulties involved, are more hopeful.

This perspective has been given clearest expression by Thomas Nagel:

> The best reasons for skepticism about ethical theory are the meagerness and controversiality of its results and the lack of agreement over methods. There is of course disagreement and uncertainty in science and mathematics, but there is also an enormous body of incontestable discoveries, which make the rejection of realism in those domains nothing but a philosophical fantasy. Ethics is different, and the attempt to give it premature definition can result in disengaged moralizing. However, nothing in the primitive current state of ethical theory requires us to give up hope for the possibility of eventual progress and for the retrospective validation of the modest apparent progress that some of us believe has already been made. This optimism is best combined with the view that ethical theory, if there is such a thing, is in its infancy.
> (Review of Bernard Williams's "Ethics and the Limits of Philosophy," in *The Journal of Philosophy,* vol. 83:6, 1986, p. 360)

Although my bias is with the latter group (those that remain hopeful despite the difficulties in development of a viable ethical theory), I am disturbed by the cogency of some of the considerations set forth by the former group, especially as they are set forth in *After Virtue* and *Ethics and the Limits of Philosophy.* Material from the historicist (MacIntyre) and skeptical (Williams) traditions are included in this work, but so are articles representing both the mainstream of the Western tradition (Plato, Aristotle, Hobbes, Hume, Kant, Mill, Moore, and Ross) and the mainstream of the analytic tradition (Ayer, Feinberg, Foot, Frankena, Hare, Harman, Mackie, Nielsen, Nagel, Nozick, Rawls, Rescher, Russell, and others, including some very promising younger ethicists). These essays should be valuable even for those who find themselves rejecting the main tradition, since the antagonists are unintelligible without understanding the background of the tradition.

Organization of This Anthology

I have made the selections of the contemporary readings on the basis of current relevance of the problem considered, clarity and cogency of the argument presented, as well as accessibility of the essay to students. Economy of space is a limiting factor in a work of this sort; hence, many important articles were regrettably omitted. Nevertheless, the sixty-nine articles included should provide ample material for discussion.

Each section opens with an introductory essay by the editor and closes with suggestions for further reading. I have kept most of the introductions brief, but Parts VIII and XIII required a somewhat longer treatment. Except for one very contemporary section (Part IX), each set of readings begins with a classical article and is followed by contemporary works. Wherever feasible, I have presented the articles in a dialectical fashion, *pro et contra,* exhibiting opposite points of view. In other places (Part VIII, for example) a historical sequence seemed more appropriate. Sometimes these two approaches are compatible and are set forth as such.

This anthology is designed for both lower- and upper-division ethical theory courses. To enable the instructor to use this work for a basic introductory ethics course, a sufficient number of basic readings, which are accessible to the average university student, are included. This text also contains more than twenty-five advanced-level readings, suitable for philosophy majors and graduate students. (I have used this material for both 200- and 500-level courses. Instructors who wish to use it for a basic ethics course at the 100 or 200 level can spend more time with those readings that are marked with an asterisk in the table of contents.)

Acknowledgments

Several people have provided special assistance in compiling and writing this anthology. David Brink, Greogry Kavka, Roger Rigterink, Jim Sterba, and Steven Sverdlik provided helpful suggestions at various times during production of this text. Bruce Russell was especially generous, offering helpful criticisms throughout the entire project. Several academic colleagues reviewed the manuscript and provided commentary that greatly enhanced the finished text. These reviewers include Joseph Des Jardins, Villanova University; Daniel Farrell, Ohio State University; Walter Obriant, University of Georgia; Jeff Olen, University of Wisconsin; Edward Sankowski, University of Oklahoma; Joe Schuler, University of Wisconsin; Edward Walter, University of Missouri; and Morton Winston, Trenton State University.

I am deeply grateful for the support of my editor, Ken King, who encouraged me to begin this work and carry it through to the end. Michael Oates, production editor, Alan Titche, copy editor, and Andrew Ogus, designer, did an excellent job of correcting and designing the manuscript to bring this work to its present form.

My wife, Trudy, as always, provided sustaining love, and my children, Ruth and Paul, served as an inspiration for the thought that the youth of our day may yet create a more moral world than my generation has.

Louis Pojman

Ethical Theory

Classical and Contemporary Readings

Part I

What Is Ethics?

We are discussing no small matter, but how we ought to live.

SOCRATES
in Plato's *Republic*

Ethics, or moral philosophy as it is sometimes called, is the systematic endeavor to understand moral concepts and justify moral principles and theories.* It undertakes to analyze such concepts as 'right,' 'wrong,' 'permissible,' 'ought,' 'good,' and 'evil' in their moral contexts. It builds and scrutinizes arguments setting forth large-scale theories on how we ought to act, and it seeks to discover valid principles (for example, never kill innocent human beings) and the relationship between those principles (for example, does saving a life in some situations constitute a valid reason for breaking a promise?).

Whereas much of philosophy is concerned with the knowledge of what is (for example, metaphysics, philosophy of science, philosophy of religion, and philosophy of the mind), ethics is concerned with action and practice. It is concerned with values—not what is, but what ought to be. How should I live my life? What is the right thing to do in this situation? Should one

*In this book, the terms 'ethics' and 'morality' (and their cognates) are used synonymously.

always tell the truth? Ought a woman ever to have an abortion? Ethics has a distinct action-guiding aspect, and, as such, belongs to the group of practical institutions that includes religion, law, and etiquette.

A good way to grasp the distinctive features of ethics is to compare it with these other practical institutions that set standards of behavior (namely, law, religion, and etiquette). Consider the following illustration. Recently I heard a Presbyterian missionary tell of a remarkable spiritual experience in rural Brazil. A well-to-do farmer in his church was not paying his workers, who complained about this to the missionary. He and the workers prayed that the farmer would pay them. Then the missionary went to the farmer and told him that it was God's will that he pay his people for their work, and that the farmer was sinning against the Lord. The farmer departed in anger. A week later he reappeared. To the missionary's amazement he gave the missionary a huge hug and told him that the Lord had spoken to him (through his conscience). He said he would obey the Lord, and he paid all of his workers, plus interest.

What probably would have happened in urban America? If workers are not paid, what do they usually do? They get a lawyer and go to court to demand reparations with punitive damages.

In neither of these cases is morality brought directly into the discussion. In the first case a sin against God is committed, and in the second a law is broken. But morality is not necessarily the same as either of these.

How would this case be handled morally? The injured parties or their representatives would approach the farmer and reason with him. In essence they would appeal to his sense of justice. "Look, you've broken your promise to us. That's morally wrong, isn't it? What's more, you're causing great suffering. You can see that this is against the moral law (or against moral principles), can't you?"

Implied in this appeal is the suggestion that the farmer is not entirely a good person, and that character judgment will be the main sanction used against him. He has lost respect from his fellows. They hope he has some moral sensitivity, and that his conscience will bother him and motivate him to make reparations.

Morality makes reference to right/wrong/permissible behavior with regard to basic values. Moral theories differ on the scope of morality (does it include all and only human beings, or rational beings, or sentient creatures?), and they differ on the exact hierarchy of values (how does one rank survival, justice, happiness, freedom, and other good qualities?), but in general they have in common a concern to alleviate suffering and promote well-being.

Morality can be closely bound up with religion, and moral behavior is typically held to be essential to the practice of religion. But neither the practices nor the precepts of morality should be identified with religion. The practice of morality need not be motivated by religious considerations. And moral precepts need not be grounded in revelation or divine authority, as religious teachings invariably are. The most salient characteristic of ethics—by which I mean both philosophical morality (or morality, as I will simply refer to it) and moral philosophy—is that it is grounded in reason and human experience.

To use a spatial metaphor, secular ethics is horizontal, omitting a vertical or transcendental dimension, while religious ethics is vertical, being grounded in revelation or divine authority, although generally using reason to supplement or complement revelation. These two differing orientations often generate different moral principles and standards of evaluation, but they need not do so. Some versions of religious ethics, which posit God's revelation of the moral law in nature or conscience, hold that reason can discover what is right or wrong even apart from divine revelation. We shall discuss this subject in Part XI.

Morality is also closely related to law, and some people equate the two practices. After all, law can promote well-being and social harmony, and resolve conflicts of interest, just as morality does. Yet there are crucial differences. Ethics may judge some laws to be immoral without denying that they are valid *as laws*. For example, I would judge laws that permit slavery or discrimination against people on the basis of race or sex to be legally valid but immoral. An antiabortion advocate may believe that the laws permitting abortion are immoral.

In a recent television series, "Ethics in America," James Neal, a trial lawyer, was asked what he would do if he discovered that, some years back, his client had committed a murder for which another man had been convicted and would soon be executed.[1] Mr. Neal said that he would have a legal obligation to keep the information confidential and that if he divulged it, he would be disbarred. It is arguable that he would have a moral obligation that overrides his legal obligation and demands that he take action to protect the innocent man from being executed.

Furthermore, some aspects of morality are not covered by law. For example, while it is generally agreed that lying is usually immoral, there is no law against it (except under special conditions, such as in cases of perjury or falsifying income tax returns). Sometimes college newspapers publish advertisements for "research assistance," where it is known in advance that the companies will aid and abet plagiarism. Publishing such ads is legal, but it is doubtful that it is moral, since it promotes cheating.

There is one other major difference between law and morality. In 1351 King Edward of England promulgated a law against treason that made it a crime merely to think homicidal thoughts about the king. But, alas, the law could not be enforced, for no tribunal could search the heart or fathom the intentions of the mind. It is true that *intention,* such as malice aforethought, is considered during the legal process in deter-

mining the character of an act once the act has been committed. But preemptive punishment of people presumed to have bad intentions is illegal. If having malicious intentions (called in law *mens rea*) was illegal, would we not all deserve punishment? And even if it were possible to detect intentions, when should the punishment be administered? As soon as the subject has the intention? But how do we know that he or she will not have a change of mind? And to make the issue even more complex, is there not a continuum between imagining some harm to X, wishing harm to X, desiring harm to X, and then, finally, intending harm to X?

While it is impractical to have laws against bad intentions, such intentions are still bad, still morally wrong. Suppose I buy a gun with the intention of using it to kill Uncle Charlie in order to inherit his wealth, but never get a chance to fire it (Uncle Charlie moves to Australia). While I have not committed a crime, I have committed a moral wrong.

Finally, law differs from morality in that there are physical and financial sanctions to enforce the law but only the sanctions of conscience and reputation to enforce morality.

Morality also differs from etiquette and mere social custom, which concern form and style rather than the essence of social existence. Etiquette determines whether behavior is polite rather than whether behavior is right in a deeper sense. Custom represents society's decisions about how we are to dress, greet one another, eat, celebrate festivals, carry out social transactions, and dispose of the dead.

Whether we greet one another with a handshake, a bow, a hug, or a kiss on the cheek differs in different social systems, but none of these rituals has any moral superiority. People in England hold their forks in their left hands when they eat, whereas people in other countries hold them in their right hands or in whichever hand they prefer. In India, people usually eat without a fork at all; they simply use their right forefinger. None of these practices has any moral superiority. Etiquette helps social transactions flow smoothly, but it is not concerned with the substance of those transactions. The observance of customs graces our social existence, but it is not what social existence is about.

Yet it can be immoral to disregard or flaunt etiquette. A cultural crisis recently developed in India when American tourists went to the beaches clad in skimpy bikini bathing suits. This was highly offensive to the Indians, and an uproar erupted.

There is nothing intrinsically wrong with wearing skimpy bathing suits—or with wearing nothing at all, for that matter—but people get used to certain behavioral patterns and it's extremely insensitive to flaunt those customs, especially when you are a guest in their home or country. It is not the bathing suits themselves but the insensitivity that is morally offensive.

Law, etiquette, and religion are all important institutions, but each has limitations. Limitations of the law are that you can't have a law for every social malady and you can't enforce every desirable rule. The limitation of etiquette is that it doesn't get to the heart of what is of vital importance for personal and social existence. Whether one eats with one's fingers seems unimportant compared with whether one is honest or trustworthy or just. Etiquette is a cultural invention, but morality claims to be a discovery.

The limitation of the religious injunction is that it rests on authority, and we are not always sure of or in agreement about the credentials of the authority nor on how the authority would rule in ambiguous or new cases. Since religion is founded not on reason but on revelation, you cannot use reason to convince someone who does not share your religious views that yours are the right ones. I hasten to add that when moral differences are caused by disagreements about fundamental moral principles, it is unlikely that philosophical reasoning will settle the matter. Often, however, our moral differences turn out to be rooted in worldviews, not in moral princi-

ples. For example, antiabortion and pro-choice advocates often agree that it is wrong to kill innocent persons but differ on specifics. The antiabortion advocate may hold a religious view that states that the fetus has an eternal soul and thus a right to life, while the pro-choice advocate may deny that anyone—let alone a fetus—has a soul and maintain that only self-conscious, rational beings have a right to life.

In summary, morality distinguishes itself from law and etiquette by going deeper into the essence of our social existence. It distinguishes itself from religion by seeking reasons, rather than authority, to justify its principles. The central purpose of moral philosophy is to secure valid principles of conduct and values that can be instrumental in guiding human actions and producing good character. As such it is the most important activity known to humans, for it has to do with how we are to live.

Domains of Ethical Assessment

It might seem at this point that ethics concerns itself only with rules of conduct based only on an evaluation of acts. However, the situation is more complicated than this. Most ethical analysis falls into one, or some, of the following domains:

DOMAIN	EVALUATIVE TERMS
1. Action	Right, wrong, obligatory, optional
2. Consequences	Good, bad, indifferent
3. Character	Virtuous, vicious, neutral
4. Motive	Good will, evil will, neutral

Let us examine each of these domains.

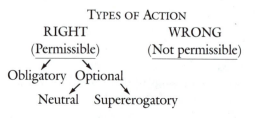

TYPES OF ACTION

RIGHT
(Permissible)

WRONG
(Not permissible)

Obligatory   Optional

Neutral   Supererogatory

Action

The most common classification of actions may be as right or wrong, but the term "right" is ambiguous. Sometimes it means "obligatory" (as in "*the* right act"), but sometimes it means "permissible" (as in "*a* right act" or "it's all right to do that"). Usually, philosophers define "right" as permissible, including under that category what is obligatory.

(i) A "right act" is an act that is permissible. It may be either (a) optional or (b) obligatory.

(a) An "optional act" is an act that is neither obligatory nor wrong to do. In other words, it is not one's duty to do it; nor is it one's duty not to do it—neither would be wrong.

(b) An "obligatory act" is one that morality requires one to take, an act that it is not permissible to refrain from doing.

(ii) A "wrong act" is an act that one has an obligation or duty to refrain from; it is an act one ought not to do, an act that is not permissible.

Let us briefly illustrate these concepts. The act of lying is generally seen as a wrong act (and therefore not permissible), whereas telling the truth is generally seen as obligatory. But some acts seem to be neither wrong nor obligatory. Whether you decide to take a course in art history or in Asian literature and whether you write your friend a letter with a pencil or a pen—all of these acts seem morally neutral. They are optional (hence, permissible).

Consider the decision to marry. Admittedly, this is a decision of great moral significance. It is, after all, an important decision about how one lives one's life. Under most circumstances, however, the act of getting married is neither obligatory nor wrong, because being married, in itself, is considered morally neutral. To marry is therefore an optional act. You are not required to marry. Neither are you required not to marry.

Within the range of permissible acts are "supererogatory" acts. These highly altruistic acts go beyond the call of duty. They are not obligatory, and they exceed the requirements of morality. You may have an obligation to give a donation to strangers in dire need, but you are not obligated to sell your house or car, let alone to become destitute yourself, in order to help them. To help such people by selling your house or car or by becoming destitute yourself would be supererogatory.

Theories that place the emphasis on the nature of the act are called "deontological" (from the Greek word for duty). These theories hold that there is something inherently right or good about such acts as truth-telling and promise-keeping and something inherently wrong or bad about such acts as lying and promise-breaking. We shall study deontological theories in Part VI.

Consequences

We have said that lying is generally seen as wrong and that telling the truth is generally seen as right. But consider this situation: You are hiding in your home an innocent woman named Laura, who is fleeing gangsters. Gangland Gus knocks on your door, and when you open it, he asks if Laura is in your house. What should you do? Should you tell the truth or lie? Those who believe that morality has something to do with the consequences of actions would prescribe lying as the morally right thing to do. Those who believe that we should not consider the consequences of our acts in the face of a clear and absolute rule of action would say that we should either keep silent or tell the truth. When no other rule is at stake, of course, the rule-oriented ethicist allows the foreseeable consequences to determine a course of action. Theories that focus primarily on consequences in determining moral rightness and wrongness are called "teleological" ethical theories (from the Greek *telos,* meaning goal-directed). The most famous of these theories is utilitarianism, which we shall study in Part V.

Character

While some ethical theories emphasize principles of actions for themselves and some emphasize principles involving consequences of actions, other theories, such as Aristotle's ethics, emphasize character or virtue. According to Aristotle, it is most important to develop virtuous character, for if and only if we have good people can we ensure habitual right action. While the virtues are not central to other types of moral theories, most moral theories include the virtues as important. Different moral systems emphasize different virtues and emphasize them to different degrees. We shall study virtue ethics in Part VII.

Motive

Finally, practically all ethical systems, and especially Kant's system, accept the relevance of motive. It is important to the full assessment of any action that the intention of the agent be taken into account. Two acts may be identical, but one may be judged morally culpable and the other excusable. Consider John's pushing Joan off a ledge, causing her to break her leg. In situation A he is angry and intends to harm her, but in situation B he sees a knife flying in her direction and intends to save her life. In situation A what he did was clearly wrong, whereas in situation B he did the right thing. In contrast, two acts, while equally good on the basis of intention, may have opposite results. For example, two soldiers try to cross the enemy line to communicate with an allied force, but one gets captured through no fault of his own and the other succeeds. In a full moral description of any act, motive will be taken into consideration as a relevant factor.

A few more distinctions need to be made before we embark on our study of ethical theory. The first is the distinction between descriptive and normative ethics. Anthropology and sociology, as descriptive sciences, examine the ethical beliefs and practices of given societies or of people as such (e.g., sociobiologists claim that human nature exhibits a common set of moral practices). They tell us what *is* in different cultures. But, while moral philosophy may take into account the results of science, it is distinctly normative rather than descriptive. It is about ideal behavior, about what should be, even though it is not a present reality, and it seeks to justify sets of principles pointing toward those ideals.

Secondly, we need to note that the term 'moral' is ambiguous and has two possible opposites: 'nonmoral' and 'immoral.' We may use the term 'moral' in discussing whether some issue is within the scope of moral consideration. Deciding whether to write with a pen or a pencil or whether to wear a white shirt rather than a blue one is not normally a moral issue at all. Some issues in etiquette may not be moral issues. They are nonmoral. On the other hand, when we normally speak of some deed as moral, we use the term as shorthand for the morally right thing to do, as opposed to the morally wrong thing to do or the immoral act.

Finally, we said that morality had to do with value judgments. However, not all value judgments are within the scope of moral considerations. Some value judgments are prudential, others are aesthetic. When we say, "That is good," we need to pay attention to the context, for we may mean either that an act is the most fitting one if we want to reach our goal, or that an object described is beautiful or aesthetically satisfying, or, speaking morally, that an act is the morally correct deed.

Our first reading, Plato's dialogue called the *Crito,* is a classic example of ethical thinking. Written in the fourth century B.C., it is one of the earliest surviving treatises on philosophical ethics. It represents an acutely self-conscious attempt to use reasoning to decide what is the right course of action in a particular situation.

The year is 399 B.C., the place, an Athenian jail. Socrates, a 70-year-old philosopher, has been condemned to death by an Athenian court for not believing in the Greek gods and for corrupting the youth. In fact, he has been unjustly condemned, but his refusal to compromise with the powers-that-be has provoked extreme behavior.

Now his friends, led by Crito, have planned his escape and have arranged passage to Thessaly, where Socrates has been assured of a tranquil retirement among admirers. The moral issue is: Should Socrates escape? Should he avail himself of Crito's help and attempt to free himself from prison? In other words, should he engage in civil disobedience?

Crito and Socrates engage in a moral argument. As you read this dialogue, identify Crito's arguments and Socrates's counterarguments. Try to identify the major principles that each holds and decide how valid the arguments are. Note especially the relationship between law and morality. In another treatise, the *Apology,* Socrates seems to put one principle above the law. He says that if the law commands him to refrain from teaching, he will not obey it. In fact, some years before the events in the *Crito,* he refused to obey the leaders of Athens when they commanded him to arrest an admiral whom he considered innocent of any crime. Do these actions affect his argument in the *Crito*? Was Socrates correct in his arguments? Did he do the right thing? What would you have done in his position, and why?

A good discussion of civil disobedience may be found in Ronald Dworkin's "Taking Rights Seriously" in Part XIII.3 of this book.

Endnote

[1]"Ethics in America," produced by Fred Friendly. *PBS, 1989.*

I.1 *Socratic Morality: Crito*

PLATO

Plato (428–348 B.C.) was born in Athens and studied under Socrates. In this dialogue he describes the death of Socrates and the moral arguments given by Socrates against escaping from prison.

CRITO: I come to bring you a message which is sad and painful; not, as I believe, to yourself, but to all of us who are your friends, and saddest of all to me.

SOCRATES: What? Has the ship come from Delos, on the arrival of which I am to die?

CR.: No, the ship has not actually arrived, but she will probably be here to-day, as persons who have come from Sunium tell me that they left her there; and therefore to-morrow, Socrates, will be the last day of your life.

SOC.: Very well, Crito; if such is the will of God, I am willing; but my belief is that there will be a delay of a day.

CR.: Why do you think so?

SOC.: I will tell you. I am to die on the day after the arrival of the ship.

CR.: Yes; that is what the authorities say.

SOC.: But I do not think that the ship will be here until to-morrow; this I infer from a vision which I

Reprinted from *Dialogues of Plato,* translated by Benjamin Jowett, Oxford, 1896.

had last night, or rather only just now, when you fortunately allowed me to sleep.

CR.: And what was the nature of the vision?

SOC.: There appeared to me the likeness of a woman, fair and comely, clothed in bright raiment, who called to me and said: O Socrates,

> 'The third day hence to fertile Phthia shalt thou go.'[1]

CR.: What a singular dream, Socrates!

SOC.: There can be no doubt about the meaning, Crito, I think.

CR.: Yes; the meaning is only too clear. But, oh! my beloved Socrates, let me entreat you once more to take my advice and escape. For if you die I shall not only lose a friend who can never be replaced, but there is another evil: people who do not know you and me will believe that I might have saved you if I had been willing to give money, but that I did not care. Now, can there be a worse disgrace than this — that I should be thought to value money more than the life of a friend? For the many will not be persuaded that I wanted you to escape, and that you refused.

SOC.: But why, my dear Crito, should we care about the opinion of the many? Good men, and they are the only persons who are worth considering, will think of these things truly as they occurred.

CR.: But you see, Socrates, that the opinion of the many must be regarded, for what is now happening shows that they can do the greatest evil to any one who has lost their good opinion.

SOC.: I only wish it were so, Crito; and that the many could do the greatest evil; for then they would also be able to do the greatest good — and what a fine thing this would be! But in reality they can do neither; for they cannot make a man either wise or foolish; and whatever they do is the result of chance.

CR.: Well, I will not dispute with you; but please to tell me, Socrates, whether you are not acting out of regard to me and your other friends: are you not afraid that if you escape from prison we may get into trouble with the informers for having stolen you away, and lose either the whole or a great part of our property; or that even a worse evil may happen to us? Now, if you fear on our account, be at ease; for in order to save you, we ought surely to run this, or even a greater risk; be persuaded, then, and do as I say.

SOC.: Yes, Crito, that is one fear which you mention, but by no means the only one.

CR.: Fear not — there are persons who are willing to get you out of prison at no great cost; and as for the informers, they are far from being exorbitant in their demands — a little money will satisfy them. My means, which are certainly ample, are at your service, and if you have a scruple about spending all mine, here are strangers who will give you the use of theirs; and one of them, Simmias the Theban, has brought a large sum of money for this very purpose; and Cebes and many others are prepared to spend their money in helping you to escape. I say, therefore, do not hesitate on our account, and do not say, as you did in the court, that you will have a difficulty in knowing what to do with yourself anywhere else. For men will love you in other places to which you may go, and not in Athens only; there are friends of mine in Thessaly, if you like to go to them, who will value and protect you, and no Thessalian will give you any trouble. Nor can I think that you are at all justified, Socrates, in betraying your own life when you might be saved; in acting thus you are playing into the hands of your enemies, who are hurrying on your destruction. And further I should say that you are deserting your own children; for you might bring them up and educate them; instead of which you go away and leave them, and they will have to take their chance; and if they do not meet with the usual fate of orphans, there will be small thanks to you. No man should bring children into the world who is unwilling to persevere to the end in their nurture and education. But you appear to be choosing the easier part, not the better and manlier, which would have been more becoming in one who professes to care for virtue in all his actions, like yourself. And indeed, I am ashamed not only of you, but of us who are your friends, when I reflect that the whole business will be attributed entirely to our want of courage. The trial need never have come on, or might have been managed differently; and this last act, or crowning folly, will seem to have occurred through our negligence and cowardice, who might have saved you, if we had been good for anything; and you might have saved yourself, for there was no difficulty at all. See now, Socrates, how sad and discreditable are the consequences, both to us and you. Make up your mind then, or rather have your mind already made up, for the time of deliberation is over, and there is only one thing to be done, which must be done this very night, and if we delay at all will be no longer practicable or possible; I beseech you therefore, Socrates, be persuaded by me, and do as I say.

SOC.: Dear Crito, your zeal is invaluable, if a right one; but if wrong, the greater the zeal the greater the danger; and therefore we ought to consider whether I shall or shall not do as you say. For I am and always have been one of those natures who must be guided by reason, whatever the reason may be which upon reflection appears to me to be the best; and now that this chance has befallen me, I cannot repudiate my own words: the principles which I have hitherto honoured and revered I still honour, and unless we can at once find other and better principles, I am certain not to agree with you; no, not even if the power of the multitude could inflect many more imprisonments, confiscations, deaths, frightening us like children with hobgoblin terrors. What will be the fairest way of considering the question? Shall I return to your old argument about the opinions of men? — we were saying that some of them are to be regarded, and others not. Now were we right in maintaining this before I was condemned? And has the argument which was once good now proved to be talk for the sake of talking — mere childish nonsense? That is what I want to consider with your help, Crito: — whether, under my present circumstances, the argument appears to be in any way different or not; and is to be allowed by me or disallowed. That argument, which, as I believe, is maintained by many persons of authority, was to the effect, as I was saying, that the opinions of some men are to be regarded, and of other men not to be regarded. Now you, Crito, are not going to die tomorrow — at least, there is no human probability of this — and therefore you are disinterested and not liable to be deceived by the circumstances in which you are placed. Tell me then, whether I am right in saying that some opinions, and the opinions of some men only, are to be valued, and that other opinions, and the opinions of other men, are not to be valued. I ask you whether I was right in maintaining this?

CR.: Certainly.

SOC.: The good are to be regarded, and not the bad?

CR.: Yes.

SOC.: And the opinions of the wise are good, and the opinions of the unwise are evil?

CR.: Certainly.

SOC.: And what was said about another matter? Is the pupil who devotes himself to the practice of gymnastics supposed to attend to the praise and blame and opinion of every man, or of one man only — his physician or trainer, whoever he may be?

CR.: Of one man only.

SOC.: And he ought to fear the censure and welcome the praise of that one only, and not of the many?

CR.: Clearly so.

SOC.: And he ought to act and train, and eat and drink in the way which seems good to his single master who has understanding, rather than according to the opinion of all other men put together?

CR.: True.

SOC.: And if he disobeys and disregards the opinion and approval of the one, and regards the opinion of the many who have no understanding, will he not suffer evil?

CR.: Certainly he will.

SOC.: And what will the evil be, whither tending and what affecting, in the disobedient person?

CR.: Clearly, affecting the body; that is what is destroyed by the evil.

SOC.: Very good; and is not this true, Crito, of other things which we need not separately enumerate? In questions of just and unjust, fair and foul, good and evil, which are the subjects of our present consultation, ought we to follow the opinion of the many and to fear them; or the opinion of the one man who has understanding? ought we not to fear and reverence him more than all the rest of the world: and if we desert him shall we not destroy and injure that principle in us which may be assumed to be improved by justice and deteriorated by injustice; — there is such a principle?

CR.: Certainly there is, Socrates.

SOC.: Take a parallel instance: — if, acting under the advice of those who have no understanding, we destroy that which is improved by health and is deteriorated by disease, would life be worth having? And that which has been destroyed is—the body?

CR.: Yes.

SOC.: Could we live, having an evil and corrupted body?

CR.: Certainly not.

SOC.: And will life be worth having, if that higher part of man be destroyed, which is improved by justice and depraved by injustice? Do we suppose that principle, whatever it may be in man, which has to do with justice and injustice, to be inferior to the body?

CR.: Certainly not.

SOC.: More honourable than the body?

CR.: Far more.

SOC.: Then, my friend, we must not regard what the many say of us: but what he, the one man who has understanding of just and unjust, will say, and what the truth will say. And therefore you begin in error when you advise that we should regard the opinion of the many about just and unjust, good and evil, honourable and dishonourable.—'Well,' some one will say, 'but the many can kill us.'

CR.: Yes, Socrates; that will clearly be the answer.

SOC.: And it is true: but still I find with surprise that the old argument is unshaken as ever. And I should like to know whether I may say the same of another proposition—that not life, but a good life, is to be chiefly valued?

CR.: Yes, that also remains unshaken.

SOC.: And a good life is equivalent to a just and honourable one—that holds also?

CR.: Yes, it does.

SOC.: From these premises I proceed to argue the question whether I ought or ought not to try and escape without the consent of the Athenians: and if I am clearly right in escaping, then I will make the attempt; but if not, I will abstain. The other considerations which you mention, of money and loss of character and the duty of educating one's children, are, I fear, only the doctrines of the multitude, who would be as ready to restore people to life, if they were able, as they are to put them to death—and

with as little reason. But now, since the argument has thus far prevailed, the only question which remains to be considered is, whether we shall do rightly either in escaping or in suffering others to aid in our escape and paying them in money and thanks, or whether in reality we shall not do rightly; and if the latter, then death or any other calamity which may ensue on my remaining here must not be allowed to enter into the calculation.

CR.: I think that you are right, Socrates; how then shall we proceed?

SOC.: Let us consider the matter together, and do you either refute me if you can, and I will be convinced; or else cease, my dear friend, from repeating to me that I ought to escape against the wishes of the Athenians: for I highly value your attempts to persuade me to do so, but I may not be persuaded against my own better judgment. And now please to consider my first position, and try how you can best answer me.

CR.: I will.

SOC.: Are we to say that we are never intentionally to do wrong, or that in one way we ought and in another we ought not to do wrong, or is doing wrong always evil and dishonourable, as I was just now saying, and as has been already acknowledged by us? Are all our former admissions which were made within a few days to be thrown away? And have we, at our age, been earnestly discoursing with one another all our life long only to discover that we are no better than children? Or, in spite of the opinion of the many, and in spite of consequences whether better or worse, shall we insist on the truth of what was then said, that injustice is always an evil and dishonour to him who acts unjustly? Shall we say so or not?

CR.: Yes.

SOC.: Then we must do no wrong?

CR.: Certainly not.

SOC.: Nor when injured injure in return, as the many imagine; for we must injure no one at all?

CR.: Clearly not.

SOC.: Again, Crito, may we do evil?

CR.: Surely not, Socrates.

SOC.: And what of doing evil in return for evil, which is the morality of the many — is that just or not?

CR.: Not just.

SOC.: For doing evil to another is the same as injuring him?

CR.: Very true.

SOC.: Then we ought not to retaliate or render evil for evil to any one, whatever evil we may have suffered from him. But I would have you consider, Crito, whether you really mean what you are saying. For this opinion has never been held, and never will be held, by any considerable number of persons; and those who are agreed and those who are not agreed upon this point have no common ground, and can only despise one another when they see how widely they differ. Tell me, then, whether you agree with and assent to my first principle, that neither injury nor retaliation nor warding off evil by evil is ever right. And shall that be the premise of our argument? Or do you decline and dissent from this? For so I have ever thought, and continue to think; but, if you are of another opinion, let me hear what you have to say. If, however, you remain of the same mind as formerly, I will proceed to the next step.

CR.: You may proceed, for I have not changed my mind.

SOC.: Then I will go on to the next point, which may be put in the form of a question: — Ought a man to do what he admits to be right, or ought he to betray the right?

CR.: He ought to do what he thinks right.

SOC.: But if this is true, what is the application? In leaving the prison against the will of the Athenians, do I wrong any? or rather do I not wrong those whom I ought least to wrong? Do I not desert the principles which were acknowledged by us to be just — what do you say?

CR.: I cannot tell, Socrates; for I do not know.

SOC.: Then consider the matter in this way: — Imagine that I am about to play truant (you may call the proceeding by any name which you like), and the laws and the government come and interrogate me: Tell us, Socrates, they say; what are you about? are you not going by an act of yours to overturn us — the laws, and the whole state, as far as in you lies? Do you imagine that a state can subsist and not be overthrown, in which the decisions of law have no power, but are set aside and trampled upon by individuals?' What will be your answer, Crito, to these and the like words? Any one, and especially a rhetorician, will have a good deal to say on behalf of the law which requires a sentence to be carried out. He will argue that this law should not be set aside; and shall we reply; yes; but the state has injured us and given an unjust sentence? Suppose I say that?

CR.: Very good, Socrates.

SOC.: 'And was that our agreement with you?' the law would answer; or were you to abide by the sentence of the state?' And if I were to express my astonishment at their words, the law would probably add: 'Answer, Socrates, instead of opening your eyes — you are in the habit of asking and answering questions. Tell us, — What complaint have you to make against us which justifies you in attempting to destroy us and the state? In the first place did we not bring you into existence? Your father married your mother by our aid and begat you. Say whether you have any objection to urge against those of us who regulate marriage?' None, I should reply. 'Or against those of us who after birth regulate the nurture and education of children, in which you also were trained? Were not the laws, which have the charge of education, right in commanding your father to train you in music and gymnastic?' Right, I should reply. 'Well then, since you were brought into the world and nurtured and educated by us, can you deny in the first place that you are our child and slave, as your fathers were before you? And if this is true you are not on equal terms with us; nor can you think that you have a right to do to us what we are doing to you. Would you have any right to strike or revile or do any other evil to your father or your master, if you had one, because you have been struck or reviled by him, or received some other evil at his hands? — you would not say this? And because we think right to destroy you, do you think that you have any right to destroy us in return, and your country as far as in you lies? Will you, O professor of true virtue, pretend that you are justified in this? Has a philosopher like you failed to discover that our country is more to be valued and higher and holier far than mother or father or any ancestor, and more to be regarded in the eyes of the gods and of men of understanding? also to be soothed, and gently and reverently entreated when angry, even more than a father, and either to be persuaded, or if not persuaded, to be obeyed? And when we are punished by her, whether with imprisonment or stripes, the punishment is to be endured in silence; and if she leads us to wounds or death in battle, thither we follow as is right; neither may any one yield or retreat or leave his rank, but whether in battle or in a court of law, or in any other place, he must do what his city and his country order him; or he must change their view of what is just: and if he may do no violence to his father or mother, much less may he do violence to his country? What answer shall we make to this, Crito? Do the laws speak truly, or do they not?

CR.: I think that they do.

SOC.: Then the laws will say, 'Consider, Socrates, if we are speaking truly that in your present attempt you are going to do us an injury. For, having brought you into the world, and nurtured and educated you, and given you and every other citizen a share in every good which we had to give, we further proclaim to any Athenian by the liberty which we allow him, that if he does not like us when he has become of age and has seen the ways of the city, and made our acquaintance, he may go where he pleases and takes his goods with him. None of us laws will forbid him or interfere with him. Any one who does not like us and the city, and who wants to emigrate to a colony or to any other city, may go where he likes retaining his property. But he who has experience of the manner in which we order justice and administer the state, and still remains, has entered into an implied contract that he will do as we command him. And he who disobeys us is, as we maintain, thrice wrong; first, because in disobeying us he is disobeying his parents; secondly, because we are the authors of his education; thirdly, because he has made an agreement with us that he will duly obey our commands; and he neither obeys them nor convinces us that our commands are unjust; and we do not rudely impose them, but give him the alternative of obeying or convincing us; — that is what we offer, and he does neither.

'These are the sort of accusations to which, as we were saying, you, Socrates, will be exposed if you accomplish your intentions; you, above all other Athenians.' Suppose now I ask, why I rather than anybody else? they will justly retort upon me that I above all other men have acknowledged the agreement. 'There is clear proof,' they will say, 'Socrates, that we and the city were not displeasing to you. Of all Athenians you have been the most constant resident in the city, which, as you never leave, you may be supposed to love. For you never went out of the city either to see the games, except once when you went to the Isthmus, or to any other place unless when you were on military service; nor did you travel as other men do. Nor had you any curiosity to know other states or their laws: your affections did not go beyond us and our state; we were your special favourites, and you acquiesced in our government of you; and here in this city you begat your children, which is a proof of your satisfaction. Moreover, you might in the course of the trial, if you had liked, have fixed the penalty at banishment; the state which refuses to let you go now would have let you go then. But you pretended that you preferred death to exile, and that you were not unwilling to die. And now you have forgotten these fine sentiments, and pay no respect to us the laws, of whom you are the destroyer; and are doing what only a miserable slave would do, running away and turning your back upon the compacts and agreements which you made as a citizen. And first of all answer this question: Are we right in saying that you agreed to be governed according to us in deed, and not in word only? Is that true or not?' How shall we answer, Crito? Must we not assent?

CR.: We cannot help it, Socrates.

SOC.: Then will they not say: 'You, Socrates, are breaking the covenants and agreements which you made with us at your leisure, not in any haste or under any compulsion or deception, but after you have had seventy years to think of them, during which time you were at liberty to leave the city, if we were not to your mind, or if our covenants appeared to you to be unfair. You had your choice, and might have gone either to Lacedaemon or Crete, both which states are often praised by you for their good government, or to some other hellenic or foreign state. Whereas you, above all other Athenians, seemed to be so fond of the state, or, in other words, of us her laws (and who would care about a state which has no laws?), that you never stirred out of her; the halt, the blind, the maimed were not more stationary in her than you were. And now you run away and forsake your agreements. Not so, Socrates, if you will take our advice; do not make yourself ridiculous by escaping out of the city.

'For just consider, if you transgress and err in this sort of way, what good will you do either to yourself or to your friends? That your friends will be driven into exile and deprived of citizenship, or will lose their property, is tolerably certain; and you yourself, if you fly to one of the neighbouring cities, as, for example, Thebes or Megara, both of which are well governed, will come to them as an enemy, Socrates, and their government will be against you, and all patriotic citizens will cast an evil eye upon you as a subverter of the laws, and you will confirm in the minds of the judges the justice of their own condemnation of you. For he who is a corrupter of the laws is more than likely to be a corrupter of the young and foolish portion of mankind. Will you then flee from well-ordered cities and virtuous men? and is existence worth having on these terms? Or will you go to them without shame, and talk to them, Socrates? And what will you say to them? What you say here about virtue and justice and institutions and laws being the best things among men? Would that be decent of you? Surely not. But if you go away from well-governed states to Crito's friends in Thessaly, where there is great disorder and licence, they will be charmed to hear the tale of your escape from prison, set off with ludicrous particulars of the manner in which you were wrapped in a goatskin or some other disguise, and metamorphosed as the manner is of runaways; but will there be no one to remind you that in your old age you were not ashamed to violate the most sacred laws from a miserable desire of a little more life? Perhaps not, if you keep them in a good temper; but if they are out of temper you will hear many degrading things; you will live, but how? — as the flatterer of all men, and the servant of all men; and doing what? — eating and drinking in Thessaly, having gone abroad in order that you may get a dinner. And where will be your fine sentiments about justice and virtue? Say that you wish to live for the sake of your children — you want to bring them up and educate them — will you take them into Thessaly and deprive them of Athenian citizenship? Is this the benefit which you will confer upon them? Or are you under the impression that they will be better cared for and educated here if you are still alive, although absent from them; for your friends will take care of them? Do you fancy that if you are an inhabitant of Thessaly they will take care of them, and if you are an inhabitant of the other world that they will not take care of them? Nay; but if they who call themselves friends are good for anything, they will — to be sure they will.

'Listen, then, Socrates, to us who have brought you up. Think not of life and children first, and of justice afterwards, but of justice first, that you may be justified before the princes of the world below. For neither will you nor any that belong to you be happier or holier or juster in this life, or happier in another, if you do as Crito bids. Now you depart in innocence, a sufferer and not a doer of evil; a victim, not of the laws but of men. But if you go forth, returning evil for evil, and injury for injury, breaking the covenants and agreements which you have made with us, and wronging those whom you ought least of all to wrong, that is to say, yourself, your friends, your country, and us, we shall be angry with you while you live, and our brethren, the laws in the world below, will receive you as an enemy; for they will know that you have done your best to destroy us. Listen, then, to us and not to Crito.'

This, dear Crito, is the voice which I seem to hear murmuring in my ears, like the sound of the flute in the ears of the mystic; that voice, I say, is humming in my ears, and prevents me from hearing any other. And I know that nothing more which you may say will be vain. Yet speak, if you have anything to say.

CR.: I have nothing to say, Socrates.

SOC.: Leave me than, Crito, to fulfill the will of God, and to follow whither he leads.

Endnote

[1]Homer, II, ix. 363.

Suggestions for Further Reading

Baier, Kurt. *The Moral Point of View.* Cornell University Press, 1958. An abridged edition of this fine work is available in paperback from Random House, 1965. The work sees morality primarily in terms of social control.

Brandt, Richard. *Ethical Theory: The Problems of Normative and Critical Ethics.* Prentice-Hall, 1959. A thorough and thoughtful treatment of ethical theory.

Feldman, Fred. *Introductory Ethics.* Prentice-Hall, 1978. A clear, concise, critical analysis of the major ethical theories.

Frankena, William K. *Ethics.* 2d ed. Prentice-Hall, 1973. A succinct, insightful account of ethics.

Gert, Bernard. *Morality: A New Justification of the Moral Rules.* 2d ed. Oxford, 1988. A clear and comprehensive discussion of the nature of morality.

MacIntyre, Alasdair. *A Short History of Ethics.* Macmillan, 1966. A lucid, if uneven, survey of the history of Western ethics.

Mackie, J. L. *Ethics: Inventing Right and Wrong.* Penguin, 1976. A brilliant critique of moral realism.

Pojman, Louis. *Ethics: Discovering Right and Wrong.* 2d ed. Wadsworth, 1994.

Singer, Peter. *The Expanding Circle: Ethics and Sociobiology.* Oxford University Press, 1983. A fascinating attempt to relate ethics to sociobiology.

Taylor, Paul. *Principles of Ethics.* Dickenson, 1975. This work covers many of the same topics as my book, usually from a different perspective. The author's discussion of the principle of universalizability (pp. 95–105) is especially useful.

Taylor, Richard. *Good and Evil.* Prometheus, 1970. A lively, easy to read work that sees the main role of morality to be the resolution of conflicts of interest.

Warnock, G. J. *The Object of Morality.* Methuen, 1971. A clearly written, well-argued analysis of the nature of morality.

Wilson, James Q. *The Moral Sense.* Free Press, 1993. An argument for an underlying moral nature as a fundamental part of our humanity. Well worth reading.

Part II

Ethical Relativism

We see neither justice nor injustice which does not change its nature with change in climate. Three degrees of latitude reverse all jurisprudence; a meridian decides the truth. Fundamental laws change after a few years of possession; right has its epoch; the entry of Saturn into the Lion marks to us the origin of such and such a crime. A strange justice that is bounded by a river! Truth on this side of the Pyrenees, error on the other side. . . . Theft, incest, infanticide, parricide, have all had a place among virtuous actions. Can anything be more ridiculous than that a man should have the right to kill me because he lives on the other side of the water, and because his ruler has a quarrel with mine, though I have none with him?

BLAISE PASCAL
Pensées #294, 17

Ethical relativism is the notion that there are no universally valid moral principles, but that all moral principles are valid relative to cultural or individual choice. It is to be distinguished from moral skepticism, the view that there are no valid moral principles at all (or at least that we cannot know whether there are any), and from moral objectivism, the view that there are universally valid moral principles.

Two forms of ethical relativism suggest that morality is either a matter of individual preference or social choice. We will call the first form

subjectivism. Subjectivism views morality as a personal decision. "Morality is in the eyes of the beholder," as one of my students put it. You and I may have two opposite moralities, and both of us may be right. You may affirm that premarital sex is permissible and I may deny it, and each position would be right for each of us. Who's to judge between us?

The second form of ethical relativism states that an act or principle is morally permissible if and only if it is permitted by one's society or culture. We will call this form of relativism *conventionalism* because what makes a principle moral is simply the decision or convention of the social order, not something independent of individual societies. If society A chooses to condemn abortion, but society B chooses to permit abortion, abortion is morally wrong in society A but morally permissible in society B. If society A viewed abortion as wrong before 1973, but permissible after 1973, then abortion has changed its moral status since 1973.

Ethical relativism (especially conventionalism) must be distinguished from *cultural relativism,* which is an anthropological thesis that simply states that there is enormous variety in the mores and morals of people in different climes and times. Cultural relativism is a descriptive thesis, whereas ethical relativism is a normative thesis. That is, cultural relativism merely describes a social fact about people's behavior and beliefs, but ethical relativism grants ultimate validity to those traits. Cultural relativism neither entails ethical relativism, nor vice versa. Cultural relativism could be the true description of things, while ethical relativism could still be a false thesis. And conversely, cultural relativism could be false (that is, there could be more actual uniformity than anthropologists suspect), while ethical relativism could be true.

The contrary of ethical relativism is ethical objectivism, the view that some moral principles are universally valid, whether or not a culture or individual chooses them. An ethical principle may be valid without being an absolute principle. An absolute moral principle cannot be overridden by any other principle, but some objective ethical principles may be overridden by other ethical principles.

Suppose that you have two ethical principles that you consider universally valid, principles A and B. Principle A states that one should keep one's promises and principle B that one should save innocent people from death whenever the occasion arises and the cost is not enormous. Suppose that you have promised to meet me in my office at 3 P.M. today, but while you are driving over to see me, you come upon a person who is in need of medical attention and may die without it. What should you do? You cannot obey both moral principles A and B, but only one. Which one?

Most people will say that in this case, the principle to save human life overrides the principle to keep promises. If this is so, then the principle of promise-keeping is not an absolute moral principle. It has objective validity, but it is not always the applicable principle when it conflicts with another moral principle. W. D. Ross calls it a prima facie duty (that is, a principle that has obligatory force without actually obligating in the specific situation) that becomes one's actual duty only if no other higher duty is present.

Is principle B (the duty to save lives) an absolute principle? If there are absolute principles, are there very many of them? Remember, absolute principles cannot be overridden by any other principles, not even other absolute principles. In most moral systems there are only one or a very few absolute duties. For example, act utilitarianism, which we shall examine in Part V, has only one absolute principle: Always do that which will bring about the most good.

Given this background, which is the correct viewpoint: a version of ethical relativism or a version of ethical absolutism or objectivism?

The following table may help clarify these and other positions:

I. Moral absolutism is the view that there is one true morality with a consistent set of moral principles that never conflict and thus need not be overridden. Kantian ethics, which we will explore in Part VI, is an example of this type of system, and act utilitarianism seems to be an example of this view as well.

II. Moral objectivism holds that moral principles have universal objective validity, but it admits that many (if not all) of its principles may be overridden by other principles on various occa-

POSITIONS

Propositions Asserted	I Absolutism	II Objectivism	III Subjective Universalism	IV Conventionalism	V Subjectivism	VI Moralism	VII Skepticism
Moral principles cannot be overridden.	+	−	−	−	−	−	?
Moral principles are objectively valid.	+	+	−	−	−	−	?
Moral principles must be universalizable.	+	+	+	−	−	−	?
Moral principles are interpersonal.	+	+	+	+	−	−	?
Moral principles apply to oneself.	+	+	+	+	+	−	?
We can know whether there is moral truth.	+	+	+	+	+	+	−

Adapted from J. Fishkin, *Beyond Subjective Morality,* Yale University Press, 1984. p. 17.

sions. W. D. Ross's intuitionism is an instance of this view (Part VI). Geoffrey Warnock (Part VIII.7) holds this sort of position, and it is the view that I defend in my paper in this part of this book.

III. Subjective universalism denies that moral principles are objectively valid, for they must be chosen by rational agents to have any validity. In a sense, we create morality through our choices. The important thing about morality is that it must have universal application, so that we must be willing to universalize any moral principle that we choose. R. M. Hare (Part VIII.5) holds this sort of position, as does Jean-Paul Sartre (in his book *Existentialism is a Humanism*). Subjective univeralism is a type of relativism. We could designate it universalizable relativism.

IV. Conventionalism is the classic form of ethical relativism that we mentioned earlier. It holds that moral principles depend not on individual choice, but on social choice or interpersonal agreement. William Graham Sumner

and Gilbert Harman defend this position in this part of the book.

V. Subjectivism is the view that moral principles are applicable to the agent alone. What's morally right for me may differ radically from what's right for you. As we said earlier, "Morality is in the eye of the beholder." Friedrich Nietzsche (Part IV.4) seems to hold to something like this in some instances, and I have met many people who claim to hold this position.

VI. Amoralism is the view that there is no such thing as moral truth at all, that morality is completely a fiction, so that all our moral claims are false. J. L. Mackie seems to hold a view similar to this (Part IX.1), but he then calls on us to invent right and wrong. Sometimes this view is called moral nihilism, and it too has been attributed to Nietzsche.

VII. Moral skepticism is the view that we cannot know whether there are moral truths. It is dubious about the whole enterprise. Sometimes skeptics call on us to act as if there were moral truths because we will be happier if we do so. Gilbert Harman (Part IX.3) seems to hold this sort of position.

We shall encounter all of these positions in this book, but it is important at this juncture that we distinguish among them so that we can analyze the arguments for and against each of them.

Our first reading is a brief segment from the ancient Greek historian Herodotus's *Histories*. It illustrates cultural relativism and may suggest that ethical relativism is the correct view ("custom is king"). Whether or not we can draw a normative conclusion from Herodotus, we certainly can from the eminent anthropologist, William Graham Sumner, who views morality as dependent on the varying histories and environments of different cultures. Sumner assembles an impressive amount of data from which he draws his conclusion that conventionalism is the correct view of moral principles.

My article follows Sumner's. In it I argue that both subjectivism and conventionalism have serious problems and that there is something to be said for moral objectivism.

The fourth article, Gilbert Harman's "Moral Relativism Defended," provides a careful attempt to reconstruct relativism, viewing morality as a social agreement whereby the parties intend to cooperate with each other. Harman's view is relativist in that there need be no common content among various forms of agreement. It may be moral for a criminal gang to kill a third party simply because the members have contracted to do so.

A central feature of Harman's position is his *internalism*. Traditionally, ethical theories have assumed that moral agents could be said to have acted rightly or wrongly, depending on objective standards, regardless of whether the agent was motivated at the moment of action by those standards. That is, the criteria of moral assessment of action are *external* to the agent. This view is sometimes referred to as *externalism*. Internalism, on the other hand, claims that an agent must have a motivating reason to do an act in order to have an obligation to do that act. Unless the agent has a motive for doing his duty, it is incoherent to speak of him as having a duty.

Internalism arose, largely, as a reaction to highly rationalist and intuitionist systems, such as Kant's (Part VI.1), utilitarianism (Part V), and the intuitionism of G. E. Moore (Part VIII.2) and William Ross (Part VI.2), who provide justifying grounds for moral duty that underemphasize the causal relationships between reasons and actions. These systems seem, according to the internalists, to lack an adequate answer to the question, "Why should I be moral?" The internalist solves this problem by beginning moral assessment by stressing motivation, so that the question cannot properly arise. An action is right or obligatory for an agent A only if A has a reason that motivates him or her to do the action.

Harman combines internalism with relativism and contractualism, producing an ingenious version of moral relativism that seems to escape many of the standard objections to relativism. The reader will want to ask whether this version does successfully escape these objections.

The discussion of justifying moral principles will continue in other parts of this anthology, specifically in Parts VIII (facts and values) and IX (moral realism). The articles in Part II should set the stage for these future discussions.

II.1 *Custom Is King*

HERODOTUS

In this brief passage from his *Histories,* Herodotus (485–430 B.C.), a Greek and the first Western historian, illustrates cultural relativism and may suggest that ethical relativism is the better view.

Thus it appears certain to me, by a great variety of proofs, that Cambyses was raving mad; he would not else have set himself to make a mock of holy rites and long-established usages. For if one were to offer men to choose out of all the customs in the world such as seemed to them the best, they would examine the whole number, and end by preferring their own; so convinced are they that their own usages far surpass those of all others. Unless, therefore, a man was mad, it is not likely that he would make sport of such matters. That people have this feeling about

Excerpted from the *History of Herodotus,* Book 3, Chapter 38, translated by George Rawlinson (D. Appleton and Co., 1859–61).

their laws may be seen by very many proofs: among others, by the following. Darius, after he had got the kingdom, called into his presence certain Greeks who were at hand, and asked—"What he should pay them to eat the bodies of their fathers when they died?" To which they answered, that there was no sum that would tempt them to do such a thing. He then sent for certain Indians, of the race called Callatians, men who eat their fathers, and asked them, while the Greeks stood by, and knew by the help of an interpreter all that was said—"What he should give them to burn the bodies of their fathers at their decease?" The Indians exclaimed aloud, and bade him forbear such language. Such is men's wont herein; and Pindar was right, in my judgment, when he said, "Custom is the king o'er all."

II.2 *Folkways and Ethical Relativism*

WILLIAM GRAHAM SUMNER

William Graham Sumner (1840–1910) was an Episcopalian minister and an anthropologist. Among his works are *Science of Society* (1927) and *Folkways* (1907), from which this selection is taken.

Sumner argues that societies are shaped by "folkways," behavior practices that spontaneously arise from basic needs and interests. Folkways become the *mores* that legitimate the society. They are based on faith, unlike laws, which have a rational and utilitarian basis. Thus, there is no universal standard of right conduct. "Immorality" simply means contrary to the mores of the society.

1. *Definition and mode of origin of the folkways.* If we put together all that we have learned from anthropology and ethnography about primitive men and primitive society, we perceive that the first task of life is to live. Men begin with acts, not with thoughts. Every moment brings necessities which must be satisfied at once. Need was the first experience, and it was followed at once by a blundering effort to satisfy it. It is generally taken for granted that men inherited some guiding instincts from their beast ancestry, and it may be true, although it has never been proved. If there were such inheritances, they controlled and aided the first efforts to satisfy needs. Analogy makes it easy to assume that the ways of beasts had produced channels of habit and predisposition along which dexterities and other psychophysical activities would run easily. Experiments with newborn animals show that in the absence of any experience of the relation of means to ends, efforts to satisfy needs are clumsy and blundering. The method is that of trial and failure, which produces repeated pain, loss, and disappointments. Nevertheless, it is a method of rude experiment and selection. The earliest efforts of men were of this kind. Need was the impelling force. Pleasure and pain, on the one side and the other, were the rude constraints which defined the line on which efforts must proceed. The ability to distinguish between pleasure and pain is the only psychical power which is to be assumed. Thus ways of doing things were selected, which were expedient. They answered the purpose better than other ways, or with less toil and pain. Along the course on which efforts were compelled to go, habit, routine, and skill were developed. The struggle to maintain existence was carried on, not individually, but in groups. Each profited by the other's experience; hence there was concurrence towards that which proved to be most expedient. All at last adopted the same way for the same purpose; hence the ways turned into customs and became mass phenomena. Instincts were developed in connection with them. In this way folkways arise. The young learn them by tradition, imitation, and authority. The folkways, at a time, provide for all the needs of life then and there. They are uniform, universal in the group, imperative, and invariable. As time goes on, the folkways become more and more arbitrary, positive, and imperative. If asked why they act in a certain way in certain cases, primitive people always answer that it is because they and their ancestors always have done so. A sanction also arises from ghost fear. The ghosts of ancestors would be angry if the living should change the ancient folkways.

3. *Folkways are made unconsciously.* It is of the first importance to notice that, from the first acts by which men try to satisfy needs, each act stands by

From William Graham Sumner, *Folkways* (Chicago: Ginn and Company, 1906).

itself, and looks no further than the immediate satisfaction. From recurrent needs arise habits for the individual and customs for the group, but these results are consequences which were never conscious, and never foreseen or intended. They are not noticed until they have long existed, and it is still longer before they are appreciated. Another long time must pass, and a higher stage of mental development must be reached, before they can be used as a basis from which to deduce rules for meeting, in the future, problems whose pressure can be foreseen. The folkways, therefore, are not creations of human purpose and wit. They are like products of natural forces which men unconsciously set in operation, or they are like the instinctive ways of animals, which are developed out of experience, which reach a final form of maximum adaptation to an interest, which are handed down by tradition and admit of no exception or variation, yet change to meet new conditions, still within the same limited methods, and without rational reflection or purpose. From this it results that all the life of human beings, in all ages and stages of culture, is primarily controlled by a vast mass of folkways handed down from the earliest existence of the race, having the nature of the ways of other animals, only the topmost layers of which are subject to change and control, and have been somewhat modified by human philosophy, ethics, and religion, or by other acts of intelligent reflection. . . .

28. *Folkways due to false inference.* Furthermore, folkways have been formed by accident, that is, by irrational and incongruous action, based on pseudo-knowledge. In Molembo a pestilence broke out soon after a Portuguese had died there. After that the natives took all possible measures not to allow any white man to die in their country. On the Nicobar islands some natives who had just begun to make pottery died. The art was given up and never again attempted. White men gave to one Bushman in a kraal a stick ornamented with buttons as a symbol of authority. The recipient died leaving the stick to his son. The son soon died. Then the bushmen brought back the stick lest all should die. Until recently no building of incombustible materials could be built in any big town of the central province of Madagascar, on account of some ancient prejudice. . . . Soon after the Yakuts saw a camel for the first time small pox broke out amongst them. They thought the camel to be the agent of the disease. A woman amongst the same people contracted an endogamous marriage. She soon afterwards became blind. This was thought to be on account of the violation of ancient customs. A very great number of such cases could be collected. In fact they represent the current mode of reasoning of nature people. It is their custom to reason that, if one thing follows another, it is due to it. A great number of customs are traceable to the notion of the evil eye, many more to ritual notions of uncleanness. No scientific investigation could discover the origin of the folkways mentioned, if the origin had not chanced to become known to civilized men. We must believe that the known cases illustrate the irrational and incongruous origin of many folkways. In civilized history also we know that customs have owed their origin to "historical accident"—the vanity of a princess, the deformity of a king, the whim of a democracy, the love intrigue of a statesman or prelate. By the institutions of another age it may be provided that no one of these things can affect decisions, acts, or interests, but then the power to decide the ways may have passed to clubs, trades unions, trust, commercial rivals, wire-pullers, politicians, and political fanatics. In these cases also the causes and origins may escape investigation.

29. *Harmful folkways.* There are folkways which are positively harmful. Very often these are just the ones for which a definite reason can be given. The destruction of a man's goods at his death is a direct deduction from other-worldliness; the dead man is supposed to want in the other world just what he wanted here. The destruction of a man's goods at his death was a great waste of capital, and it must have had a disastrous effect on the interests of the living, and must have very seriously hindered the development of civilization. With this custom we must class all the expenditure of labor and capital on graves, temples, pyramids, rites, sacrifices, and support of priests, so far as these were supposed to benefit the dead. The faith in goblinism produced other-worldly interests which overruled ordinary worldly interests. Foods have often been forbidden which were plentiful, the prohibition of which injuriously lessened the food supply. There is a tribe of Bushmen who will eat no goat's flesh, although goats are the most numerous domestic animals in the district. Where totemism exists it is regularly accompanied by a taboo on eating the totem animal. Whatever may be the real principle in totemism, it overrules the interest in an abundant food supply. "The origin of the sacred regard paid to the cow must be sought in the primitive nomadic life of the Indo-European race," because it is common to Iranians and Indians of Hindostan. The Libyans ate oxen but not cows. The same was true of the Phoenicians and Egyptians. In some cases the sense of a food taboo is not to be learned. It may have been entirely capricious. Mohammed would not eat lizards, because he thought them the offspring of a metamorphosed clan of Israelites. On the other hand, the protective taboo which forebade killing crocodiles, pythons, cobras, and other animal enemies of man was harmful to his interests, whatever the motive. "It seems to be a fixed article of belief throughout southern India, that all who have willfully or accidentally killed a snake, especially a cobra, will certainly be punished, either in this life or the next, in one of three ways: either by childlessness, or by leprosy, or by ophthalmia." Where this faith exists man has a greater interest to spare a cobra than to kill it. India furnishes a great number of cases of harmful mores. "In India every tendency of humanity seems intensified and exaggerated. No country in the world is so conservative in its traditions, yet no country has undergone so many religious changes and vicissitudes." "Every year thousands perish of disease that might recover if they would take proper nourishment, and drink the medicine that science prescribes, but which they imagine that their religion forbids them to touch." . . .

30. *How "truth" and "right" are found.* If a savage puts his hand too near the fire, he suffers pain and draws it back. He knows nothing of the laws of the radiation of heat, but his instinctive action conforms to that law as if he did know it. If he wants to catch an animal for food, he must study its habits and prepare a device adjusted to those habits. If it fails, he must try again, until his observation is "true" and his device is "right." All the practical and direct element in the folkways seems to be due to common sense, natural reason, intuition, or some other original mental endowment. It seems rational (or rationalistic) and utilitarian. Often in the mythologies his ultimate rational element was ascribed to the teaching of a god or a culture hero. In modern mythology it is accounted for as "natural."

Although the ways adopted must always be really "true" and "right" in relation to facts, for otherwise they could not answer their purpose, such is not the primitive notion of true and right.

31. *The folkways are "right." Rights. Morals.* The folkways are the "right" ways to satisfy all interests, because they are traditional, and exist in fact. They extend over the whole of life. There is a right way to catch game, to win a wife, to make one's self appear, to cure disease, to honor ghosts, to treat comrades or strangers, to behave when a child is born, on the warpath, in council, and so on in all cases which can arise. The ways are defined on the negative side, that is, by taboos. The "right" way is the way which the ancestors used and which has been handed down. The tradition is its own warrant. It is not held subject to verification by experience. The notion of right is in the folkways. It is not outside of them, of independent origin, and brought to them to test them. In the folkways, whatever is, is right. This is because they are traditional, and therefore contain in themselves the authority of the ancestral ghosts. When we come to the folkways we are at the end of our analysis. The notion of right and ought is the same in regard to all the folkways, but the degree of it varies with the importance of the interest at stake. The obligation of conformable and cooperative action is far greater under ghost fear and war than in other matters, and the social sanctions are severer, because group interests are supposed to be at stake. Some usages contain only a slight element of right and ought. It may well be believed that notions of right and duty, and of social welfare, were first developed in connection with ghost fear and otherworldliness, and therefore that, in that field also, folkways were first raised to mores. "Rights" are the rules of mutual give and take in the competition of life which are imposed on comrades in the in-group, in order that the peace may prevail there which is essential to the group strength. Therefore rights can never be "natural" or "God-given," or absolute in any sense. The morality of a group at a time is the sum of the taboos and prescriptions in the folkways by which right conduct is defined. Therefore morals can never be intuitive. They are historical, institutional, and empirical.

World philosophy, life policy, right, rights, and morality are all products of the folkways. They are reflections on, and generalizations from, the experience of pleasure and pain which is won in efforts to carry on the struggle for existence under actual life conditions. The generalizations are very crude and vague in their germinal forms. They are all embodied in folklore, and all our philosophy and science have been developed out of them.

15. *Ethnocentrism* is the technical name for this view of things in which one's own group is the center of everything, and all others are scaled and rated with reference to it. Folkways correspond to it to cover both the inner and the outer relation. Each group nourishes its own pride and vanity, boasts itself superior, exalts its own divinities, and looks with contempt on outsiders. Each group thinks its own folkways the only right ones, and if it observes that other groups have other folkways, these excite its scorn. Opprobrious epithets are derived from these differences. "Pig-eater," "cow-eater," "uncircumcised," "jabberers," are epithets of contempt and abomination. The Tupis called the Portuguese by a derisive epithet descriptive of birds which have feathers around their feet, on account of trousers. For our present purpose the most important fact is that ethnocentrism leads a people to exaggerate and intensify everything in their own folkways which is peculiar and which differentiates them from others. It therefore strengthens the folkways.

16. *Illustrations of ethnocentrism.* The Papuans on New Guinea are broken up into village units which are kept separate by hostility, cannibalism, head hunting, and divergences of language and religion. Each village is integrated by its own language, religion, and interests. A group of villages is sometimes united into a limited unity by connubium. A wife taken inside of this group unit has full status; one taken outside of it has not. The petty group units are peace groups within and are hostile to all outsiders. The Mbayas of South America believed that their deity had bidden them live by making war on others, taking their wives and property, and killing their men.

17. When Caribs were asked whence they came, they answered, "We alone are people." The meaning of the name Kiowa is "real or principal people." The Lapps call themselves "men," or "human beings." The Greenland Eskimo think that Europeans have been sent to Greenland to learn virtue and good manners from the Greenlanders. Their

highest form of praise for a European is that he is, or soon will be, as good as a Greenlander. The Tunguses call themselves "men." As a rule it is found that nature peoples call themselves "men." Others are something else — perhaps not defined — but not real men. In myths the origin of their own tribe is that of the real human race. They do not account for the others. The Ainos derive their name from that of the first man, whom they worship as a god. Evidently the name of the god is derived from the tribe name. When the tribal name has another sense, it is always boastful or proud. The Ovambo name is a corruption of the name of the tribe for themselves, which means "the wealthy." Amongst the most remarkable people in the world for ethnocentrism are the Seri of Lower California. They observe an attitude of suspicion and hostility to all outsiders, and strictly forbid marriage with outsiders.

18. The Jews divided all mankind into themselves and Gentiles. They were the "chosen people." The Greeks and Romans called all outsiders "barbarians." In Euripides' tragedy of *Iphigenia in Aulis* Iphigenia says that it is fitting the Greeks should rule over barbarians, but not contrariwise, because Greeks are free, and barbarians are slaves. The Arabs regarded themselves as the noblest nation and all others are more or less barbarous. In 1896, the Chinese minister of education and his counselors edited a manual in which this statement occurs: "How grand and glorious is the Empire of China, the middle kingdom! She is the largest and richest in the world. The grandest men in the world have all come from the middle empire." In all the literature of all the states equivalent statements occur, although they are not so naïvely expressed. In Russian books and newspapers the civilizing mission of Russia is talked about, just as, in the books and journals of France, Germany, and the United States, the civilizing mission of those countries is assumed and referred to as well understood. Each state now regards itself as the leader of civilization, the best, the freest, and the wisest, and all others as inferior. Within a few years our own man-on-the-curbstone has learned to class all foreigners of the Latin peoples as "dagos," and "dago" has become an epithet of contempt. These are all cases of ethnocentrism.

34. *Definition of the mores.* When the elements of truth and right are developed into doctrines of welfare, the folkways are raised to another plane.

They then become capable of producing inferences, developing into new forms, and extending their constructive influence over men and society. Then we call them the mores. The mores are the folkways, including the philosophical and ethical generalizations as to societal welfare which are suggested by them, and inherent in them, as they grow.

42. *Purpose of the present work.* "Ethology" would be a convenient term for the study of manners, customs, usages, and mores, including the study of the way in which they are formed, how they grow or decay, and how they affect the interests which it is their purpose to serve. The Greeks applied the term "ethos" to the sum of the characteristic usages, ideas, standards, and codes by which a group was differentiated and individualized in character from other groups. "Ethics" were things which pertained to the ethos and therefore the things which were the standard of right. The Romans used "mores" for customs in the broadest and richest sense of the word, including the notion that customs served welfare, and had traditional and mystic sanction, so that they were properly authoritative and sacred. It is a very surprising fact that modern nations should have lost these words and the significant suggestions which inhere in them. The English language has no derivative noun from "mores," and no equivalent for it. The French *moeurs* is trivial compared with "mores." The German *Sitte* renders "mores" but very imperfectly. The modern peoples have made morals and morality a separate domain, by the side of religion, philosophy, and politics. In that sense, morality is an impossible and unreal category. It has no existence, and can have none. The word "moral" means what belongs or appertains to the mores. Therefore the category of morals can never be defined without reference to something outside of itself. Ethics, having lost connection with the ethos of a people, is an attempt to systematize the current notions of right and wrong upon some basic principle, generally with the purpose of establishing moral on an absolute doctrine, so that it shall be universal, absolute, and everlasting. In a general way also, whenever a thing can be called moral, or connected with some ethical generality, it is thought to be "raised," and disputants whose method is to employ ethical generalities assume especial authority for themselves and their views. These methods of discussion are most employed in treating of social topics, and they are disastrous to sound study of facts. They help to hold the social sciences under the dominion of metaphysics. The abuse has been most developed in connection with political economy, which has been almost robbed of the character of a serious discipline by converting its discussions into ethical disquisitions.

43. *Why use the word mores.* "Ethica," in the Greek sense, or "ethology," as above defined, would be good names for our present work. We aim to study the ethos of groups, in order to see how it arises, its power and influence, the modes of its operation on members of the group, and the various attributes of it (ethica). "Ethology" is a very unfamiliar word. It has been used for the mode of setting forth manners, customs, and mores in satirical comedy. The Latin word "mores" seems to be, on the whole, more practically convenient and available than any other for our purpose, as a name for the folkways with the connotations of right and truth in respect to welfare, embodied in them. The analysis and definition above given show that in the mores we must recognize a dominating force in history, constituting a condition as to what can be done, and as to the methods which can be employed.

44. *Mores are a directive force.* Of course the view which has been stated is antagonistic to the view that philosophy and ethics furnish creative and determining forces in society and history. That view comes down to us from the Greek philosophy and it has now prevailed so long that all current discussion conforms to it. Philosophy and ethics are pursued as independent disciplines, and the results are brought to the science of society and to statesmanship and legislation as authoritative dicta. . . . It can be seen also that philosophy and ethics are products of the folkways. They are taken out of the mores, but are never original and creative; they are secondary and derived. They often interfere in the second stage of the sequence — act, thought, act. Then they produce harm, but some ground is furnished for the claim that they are creative or at least regulative. In fact, the real process in great bodies of men is not one of deduction from any great principle of philosophy or ethics. It is one of minute efforts to live well under existing conditions, which efforts are repeated indefinitely by great numbers, getting strength from habit and from the fellowship of united action. The resultant folkways become coercive. All are forced to conform, and the folkways dominate the societal life. Then they seem true and right, and arise into mores as the norm of welfare. Thence are produced faiths, ideas, doctrines, religions, and philosophies, according to the stage of civilization and the fashions of reflection and generalization.

61. *The mores and institutions.* Institutions and laws are produced out of mores. An institution consists of a concept (idea, notion, doctrine, interest) and a structure. The structure is a framework, or apparatus, or perhaps only a number of functionaries set to coöperate in prescribed ways at a certain conjuncture. The structure holds the concept and furnishes instrumentalities for bringing it into the world of facts and action in a way to serve the interests of men in society. Institutions are either crescive or enacted. They are crescive when they take shape in the mores, growing by the instinctive efforts by which the mores are produced. Then the efforts, through long use, become definite and specific. Property, marriage, and religion are the most primary institutions. They began in folkways. They became customs. They developed into mores by the addition of some philosophy of welfare, however crude. Then they were made more definite and specific as regards the rules, the prescribed acts, and the apparatus to be employed. This produced a structure and the institution was complete. Enacted institutions are products of rational invention and intention. They belong to high civilization. Banks are institutions of credit founded on usages which can be traced back to barbarism. There came a time when, guided by rational reflection on experience, men systematized and regulated the usages which had become current, and thus created positive institutions of credit, defined by law and sanctioned by the force of the state. Pure enacted institutions which are strong and prosperous are hard to find. It is too difficult to invent and create an institution, for a purpose, out of nothing. The electoral college in the Constitution of the United States is an example. In that case the democratic mores of the people have seized upon the device and made of it something quite different from what the inventors planned. All institutions have come out of mores, although the rational element in them is sometimes so large that their origin in the mores is not to be ascertained

except by an historical investigation (legislatures, courts, juries, joint stock companies, the stock exchange). Property, marriage, and religion are still almost entirely in the mores. Amongst nature men any man might capture and hold a woman at any time, if he could. He did it by superior force which was its own supreme justification. But his act brought his group and her group into war, and produced harm to his comrades. They forbade capture, or set conditions for it. Beyond the limits, the individual might still use force, but his comrades were no longer responsible. The glory to him, if he succeeded, might be all the greater. His control over his captive was absolute. Within the prescribed conditions, "capture" became technical and institutional, and rights grew out of it. The woman had a status which was defined by custom, and was very different from the status of a real captive. Marriage was the institutional relation, in the society and under its sanction, of a woman to a man, where the woman had been obtained in a prescribed way. She was then a "wife." What her rights and duties were was defined by the mores, as they are to-day in all civilized society.

62. *Laws.* Acts of legislation come out of the mores. In low civilization all societal regulations are customs and taboos, the origin of which is unknown. Positive laws are impossible until the stage of verification, reflection, and criticism is reached. Until that point is reached there is only customary law, or common law. The customary law may be codified and systematized with respect to some philosophical principles, and yet remain customary. The codes of Manu and Justinian are examples. Enactment is not possible until reverence for ancestors has been so much weakened that it is no longer thought wrong to interfere with traditional customs by positive enactment. Even then there is reluctance to make enactments, and there is a stage of transition during which traditional customs are extended by interpretation to cover new cases and to prevent evils. Legislation, however, has to seek standing ground on the existing mores, and it soon becomes apparent that legislation, to be strong, must be consistent with the mores. Things which have been in the mores are put under police regulation and later under positive law. It is sometimes said that "public opinion" must ratify and approve police regulations, but this statement rests on an imperfect analysis. The regulations must conform to the mores, so that the public will not think them too lax or too strict. The mores of our urban and rural populations are not the same; consequently legislation about intoxicants which is made by one of these sections of the population does not succeed when applied to the other. The regulation of drinking places, gambling places, and disorderly houses has passed through the above-mentioned stages. It is always a question of expediency whether to leave a subject under the mores, or to make a police regulation for it, or to put it into criminal law. Betting, horse racing, dangerous sports, electric cars, and vehicles are cases now of things which seem to be passing under positive enactment and out of the unformulated control of the mores. When an enactment is made there is a sacrifice of the elasticity and automatic self-adaptation of custom, but an enactment is specific and is provided with sanctions. Enactments come into use when conscious purposes are formed, and it is believed that specific devices can be framed by which to realize such purposes in the society. Then also prohibitions take the place of taboos, and punishments are planned to be deterrent rather than revengeful. The mores of different societies, or of different ages, are characterized by greater or less readiness and confidence in regard to the use of positive enactments for the realization of societal purposes.

63. *How laws and institutions differ from mores.* When folkways have become institutions or laws they have changed their character and are to be distinguished from the mores. The element of sentiment and faith inheres in the mores. Laws and institutions have a rational and practical character, and are more mechanical and utilitarian. The great difference is that institutions and laws have a positive character, while mores are unformulated and undefined. There is a philosophy implicit in the folkways; when it is made explicit it becomes technical philosophy. Objectively regarded, the mores are customs which actually conduce to welfare under existing life conditions. Acts under the laws and institutions are conscious and voluntary; under the folkways they are always unconscious and involuntary, so that they have the character of natural necessity. Educated reflection and skepticism can disturb this spontaneous relation. The laws, being positive prescriptions, supersede the mores so far as they are adopted. It fol-

lows that the mores come into operation where laws and tribunals fail. The mores cover the great field of common life where there are no laws or police regulations. They cover an immense and undefined domain, and they break the way in new domains, not yet controlled at all. The mores, therefore, build up new laws and police regulations in time.

80. We learn the mores as unconsciously as we learn to walk and hear and breathe, and we never know any reason why the mores are what they are. The justification of them is that when we wake to consciousness of life we find them facts which already hold us in the bonds of tradition, custom, and habit.

83. *Inertia and rigidity of the mores.* We see that we must conceive of the mores as a vast system of usages, covering the whole of life, and serving all its interests; also containing in themselves their own justification by tradition and use and wont, and approved by mystic sanctions until, by rational reflection, they develop their own philosophical and ethical generalizations, which are elevated into "principles" of truth and right. They coerce and restrict the newborn generation. They do not stimulate to thought, but the contrary. The thinking is already done and is embodied in the mores. They never contain any provision for their own amendment. They are not questions, but answers, to the problem of life. They present themselves as final and unchangeable, because they present answers which are offered as "the truth." No world philosophy, until the modern scientific world philosophy, and that only within a generation or two, has ever presented itself as perhaps transitory, certainly incomplete, and liable to be set aside to-morrow by more knowledge. No popular world philosophy or life policy can ever present itself in that light. It would cost too great a mental strain. All the groups whose mores we consider far inferior to our own are quite as well satisfied with theirs as we are with ours. The goodness or badness of mores consists entirely in their adjustment to the life conditions and the interests of the time and place. . . . Therefore it is a sign of ease and welfare when no thought is given to the mores, but all coöperate in them instinctively. The nations of southeastern Asia show us the persistency of the mores, when the element of stability and rigidity in them becomes predominant. Ghost fear and ancestor worship tend to establish the persistency of the mores by dogmatic authority, strict taboo, and weighty sanctions. The mores then lose their naturalness and vitality. They are stereotypes. They lose all relation to expediency. They become an end in themselves. They are imposed by imperative authority without regard to interests or conditions (caste, child marriage, widows). When any society falls under the dominion of this disease in the mores it must disintegrate before it can live again. In that diseased state of the mores all learning consists in committing to memory the words of the sages of the past who established the formulae of the mores. Such words are "sacred writings," a sentence of which a rule of conduct to be obeyed quite independently of present interests, or of any rational considerations.

232. *Mores and morals; social code.* For every one the mores give the notion of what ought to be. This includes the notion of what ought to be done, for all should coöperate to bring to pass, in the order of life, what ought to be. All notions of propriety, decency, chastity, politeness, order, duty, right, rights, discipline, respect, reverence, coöperation, and fellowship, especially all things in regard to which good and ill depend entirely on the point at which the line is drawn, are in the mores. The mores can make things seem right and good to one group or one age which to another seem antagonistic to every instinct of human nature. The thirteenth century bred in every heart such a sentiment in regard to heretics that inquisitors had no more misgivings in their proceedings than men would have now if they should attempt to exterminate rattlesnakes. The sixteenth century gave to all such notions about witches that witch persecutors thought they were waging war on enemies of God and man. Of course the inquisitors and witch persecutors constantly developed the notions of heretics and witches. They exaggerated the notions and then gave them back again to the mores, in this expanded form, to inflame the hearts of men with terror and hate and to become, in the next stage, so much more fantastic and ferocious motives. Such is the reaction between the mores and the acts of the living generation. The world philosophy of the age is never anything but the reflection on the mental horizon, which is formed out of the mores, of the ruling ideas which are in the mores themselves. It is from a failure to recognize the to and fro in this reaction that the current notion arises that mores are produced by doctrines.

The "morals" of an age are never anything but the consonance between what is done and what the mores of the age require. The whole revolves on itself, in the relation of the specific to the general, within the horizon formed by the mores. Every attempt to win an outside standpoint from which to reduce the whole to an absolute philosophy of truth and right, based on an unalterable principle, is a delusion. New elements are brought in only by new conquests of nature through science and art. The new conquests change the conditions of life and the interests of the members of the society. Then the mores change by adaptation to new conditions and interests. The philosophy and ethics then follow to account for and justify the changes in the mores; often, also, to claim that they have caused the changes. They never do anything but draw new lines of bearing between the parts of the mores and the horizon of thought within which they are inclosed, and which is a deduction from the mores. The horizon is widened by more knowledge, but for one age it is just as much a generalization from the mores as for another. It is always unreal. It is only a product of thought. The ethical philosophers select points on this horizon from which to take their bearings, and they think, that they have won some authority for their systems when they travel back again from the generalization to the specific custom out of which it was deduced. The cases of the inquisitors and witch persecutors who toiled arduously and continually for their chosen ends, for little or new reward, show us the relation between mores on the one side and philosophy, ethics, and religion on the other.

494. *Honor, seemliness, common sense, conscience.* Honor, common sense, seemliness, and conscience seem to belong to the individual domain. They are reactions produced in the individual by the societal environment. Honor is the sentiment of what one owes to one's self. It is an individual prerogative, and an ultimate individual standard. Seemliness is conduct which befits one's character and standards. Common sense, in the current view, is a natural gift and universal outfit. As to honor and seemliness, the popular view seems to be that each one has a fountain of inspiration in himself to furnish him with guidance. Conscience might be added as another natural or supernatural "voice," intuition, and part of the original outfit of all human beings as such. If these notions could be verified, and if they proved true, no discussion of them would be in place here, but as to honor it is a well-known and undisputed fact that societies have set codes and standards of it which were arbitrary, irrational, and both individually and socially inexpedient, as ample experiment has proved. These codes have been and are imperative, and they have been accepted and obeyed by great groups of men who, in their own judgment, did not believe them sound. These codes came out of the folkways of the time and place. Then comes the question whether it is not always so. Is honor, in any case, anything but the code of one's duty to himself which he has accepted from the group in which he was educated? Family, class, religious sect, school, occupation, enter into the social environment. In every environment there is a standard of honor. When a man thinks that he is acting most independently, on his personal prerogative, he is at best only balancing against each other the different codes in which he has been educated, e.g., that of the trades union against that of the Sunday school, or of the school against that of the family. What we think "natural" and universal, and to which we attribute an objective reality, is the sum of traits whose origin is so remote, and which we share with so many, that we do not know when or how we took them up, and we can remember no rational selection by which we adopted them. The same is true of common sense. It is the stock of ways of looking at things which we acquired unconsciously by suggestion from the environment in which we grew up. Some have more common sense than others, because they are more docile to suggestion, or have been taught to make judgments by people who were strong and wise. Conscience also seems best explained as a sum of principles of action which have in one's character the most original, remote, undisputed, and authoritative position, and to which questions of doubt are habitually referred. If these views are accepted, we have in honor, common sense, and conscience other phenomena of the folkways, and the notions of eternal truths of philosophy or ethics, derived from somewhere outside of men and their struggles to live well under the conditions of earth, must be abandoned as myths.

439. *Meaning of "immoral."* When, therefore, the ethnographers apply condemnatory or depreciatory adjectives to the people whom they study, they beg the most important question which we want to investigate; that is, What are standards, codes, and ideas of chastity, decency, propriety, modesty, etc., and whence do they arise? The ethnographical facts contain the answer to this question. . . . "Immoral" never means anything but contrary to the mores of the time and place. Therefore the mores and the morality may move together, and there is no permanent or universal standard by which right and truth in these matters can be established and different folkways compared and criticized.

II.3 A Critique of Ethical Relativism

Louis Pojman

In this article I first analyze the structure of ethical relativism as constituted by two theses: the diversity thesis and the dependency thesis. Then I examine two types of ethical relativism: subjectivism and conventionalism. I argue that both types have serious problems. Next I indicate a way of taking into account the insights of relativism while maintaining an objectivist position, and I conclude by suggesting some reasons why people have been misled by relativist arguments.

"Who's to Judge What's Right or Wrong?"

Like many people, I have always been instinctively a moral relativist. As far back as I can remember . . . it has always seemed to be obvious that the dictates of morality arise from some sort of convention or understanding among people, that different people arrive at different understandings, and that there are no basic moral demands that apply to everyone. This seemed so obvious to me I assumed it was everyone's instinctive view, or at least everyone who gave the matter any thought in this day and age (Gilbert Harman, "Is There a Single True Morality," in *Morality Reason, and Truth,* ed. David Copp and David Zimmerman).

Ethical relativism is the doctrine that the moral rightness and wrongness of actions vary from society to society and that there are no absolute universal moral standards on all men at all times. Accordingly, it holds that whether or not it is right for an individual to act in a certain way depends on or is relative to the society to which he belongs (John Ladd, *Ethical Relativism*).

Gilbert Harman's intuitions about the self-evidence of relativism contrast strikingly with

Plato's or Kant's equal certainty about a form of objectivism. On the basis of polls taken in my ethics and introduction to philosophy classes over the past several years, Harman's views may signal a shift in contemporary society's moral understanding. The polls showed a two-to-one ratio in favor of moral relativism over moral absolutism, with hardly 2 percent of the respondents recognizing that there might be a third position between these two polar opposites. Of course, I'm not suggesting that all of these students had a clear understanding of what relativism entails, for many who said that they were conventional relativists also contended in the same polls that abortion except to save the mother's life is always wrong, that capital punishment is always morally wrong, or that suicide is never morally permissible.

Among my university colleagues, a growing number seem to embrace moral relativism. Recently one of my nonphilosopher colleagues objected to a dissertation proposal because the student assumed an objectivist position in ethics. (Ironically, I found in this same colleague's works rhetorical treatment of individual liberty that raised it to the level of a non-negotiable absolute.) But irony and inconsistency aside, many relativists are aware of the tension between their own subjective positions and their metatheory that entails relativism. I confess that I too am tempted by the allurement of this view and that I find it, in some forms, plausible and worthy of serious examination. However, I am also deeply troubled by it.

In this essay I will examine the central notions of ethical relativism and look at the implications

Written for this anthology, © Louis P. Pojman, 1988.

that seem to follow from it. Then I will present the outline of a very modest objectivism, one that takes into account many of the insights of relativism and yet stands as a viable option to it.

1. An Analysis of Relativism

Let us examine the theses contained in John Ladd's succinct statement on ethical (conventional) relativism that appears at the beginning of this essay. If we analyze it, we derive the following argument:

1. Moral rightness and wrongness of actions vary from society to society, so there are no universal moral standards held by all societies.

2. Whether or not it is right for individuals to act in a certain way depends on (or is relative to) the society to which they belong.

3. Therefore, there are no absolute or objective moral standards that apply to all people everywhere and at all times.

1. The first thesis, which may be called the *diversity thesis,* is simply a description that acknowledges the fact that moral rules differ from society to society. Eskimos allow their elderly to die by starvation, whereas we believe that this is morally wrong. The Spartans of ancient Greece and the Dobu of New Guinea believe that stealing is morally right, but we believe it is wrong. A tribe in East Africa throws deformed infants to the hippopotamuses, but we abhor infanticide. Ruth Benedict described a tribe in Melanesia that views cooperation and kindness as vices. Sexual practices vary over time and with climate. Some cultures permit, while others condemn, homosexual behavior. Some cultures practice polygamy, while others view it as immoral. Some cultures accept cannibalism, while we detest it. Cultural relativism is well documented, and custom seems king over all. There may or may not be moral principles held in common by every society, but if there are any, they seem to be few, at best. Certainly, it would be very difficult to derive any single "true" morality by observing various societies' moral standards.

2. The second thesis, the *dependency thesis,* asserts that individual acts are right or wrong depending on the nature of the society from which they emanate. Morality does not occur in a vacuum, and what is considered morally right or wrong must be seen in a context that depends on the goals, wants, beliefs, history, and environment of the society in question. We could, of course, distinguish between a weak and a strong thesis of dependency, for the nonrelativist can accept a certain degree of relativity in the way moral principles are *applied* in various cultures.

But the ethical relativist must maintain a stronger thesis, one that insists that the moral principles themselves are products of the culture and may vary from society to society. The ethical relativist contends that even beyond environmental factors and differences in beliefs, a fundamental disagreement exists among societies. The best way for the relativist to support this thesis is by appealing to an indeterminacy of translation thesis, which maintains that there is a conceptual relativity among language groups so that we cannot even translate into our language the worldviews of a culture with a radically different language.

In a sense, we all live in radically different worlds. But the relativist wants to go further and maintain that there is something conventional about *any* morality, so that every morality really depends on a level of social acceptance. Not only do various societies adhere to different moral systems, but the very same society could (and often does) change its moral views over place and time. For example, the majority of people in the southern United States now view slavery as immoral, whereas just over one hundred years ago, they did not. Our society's views on divorce and sexuality have changed somewhat as well.

3. The conclusion that there are no absolute or objective moral standards binding on all people follows from the first two propositions. Combining cultural relativism (the diversity thesis) with the dependency thesis yields ethical relativism in its classic form. If there are different moral principles from culture to culture and if all morality is rooted in culture, then it follows that there are no universal moral principles that are valid for all cultures and peoples at all times.

2. *Subjectivism*

Some people think that this conclusion is still too tame, and they maintain that morality is not dependent on the society but rather on the individual. As my students sometimes maintain, "Morality is in the eye of the beholder." This form of moral subjectivism has the sorry consequence that it makes morality a very useless concept, for, on its premises, little or no interpersonal criticism or judgment is logically possible. The only basis for judging John wrong would be if he failed to live up to his own principles, but, of course, one of his principles could be that hypocrisy is morally permissible (for him at least), so that it would be impossible for him to do wrong. For John hypocrisy and nonhyprocrisy are both morally permissible.

On the basis of subjectivism it could very easily turn out that Adolf Hitler was as moral as Gandhi, so long as each believed he was living by his chosen principles. Notions of moral good and bad, or right or wrong, cease to have interpersonal evaluative meaning. A student might not like it when her teacher gives her an F on a test paper, while he gives another student an A for a similar paper, but there is no way to criticize him for injustice, because justice is not one of his chosen principles.

Absurd consequences follow from subjectivism. If it is correct, then morality reduces to aesthetic tastes about which there can be neither argument nor interpersonal judgment. Although many students say that they espouse subjectivism, there is evidence that it conflicts with others of their moral views (for example, that Hitler truly was morally bad). A contradiction seems to exist between subjectivism and the very concept of morality, which it is supposed to characterize, for morality has to do with *proper* resolution of interpersonal conflict and the amelioration of the human predicament (both deontological and teleological systems do this, but in different ways — see Parts V and VI of this book). Whatever else it does, it has a minimal aim of preventing a Hobbesian state of nature. But if so, subjectivism is no help at all in doing this, for it rests neither on social *agreement* of principle (as the conventionalist maintains) nor on an objectively independent set of norms that bind all people for the common good. If there were only one person on earth, there would be no occasion for morality because there wouldn't be any interpersonal conflicts to resolve or others whose suffering he or she would have a duty to ameliorate. Subjectivism implicitly assumes something of this atomism, a state of affairs in which only isolated individuals make up separate universes. In sum, subjectivism is solipsistic — philosophically unaware of human interaction and morality's social function.

3. *Conventionalism*

Conventional ethical relativism, the view that there are no objective moral principles but that all valid moral principles are justified by virtue of their cultural acceptance, recognizes the social nature of morality.[1] That is precisely its power and virtue. It does not seem subject to the same absurd consequences of subjectivism. Recognition of this contextual element has led many people to suppose that ethical relativism is the correct metaethical theory. Furthermore, they are drawn to it for its liberal philosophical stance. It seems to entail or strongly imply an attitude of tolerance toward other cultures. The most famous proponent of this position is the anthropologist Melville Herskovits, who argued that (1) since morality is relative to its culture and (2) we have no independent basis for criticizing any morality of any other culture, therefore (3) we ought to be tolerant of the moralities of other cultures.[2]

Tolerance is certainly a virtue, but is this a good argument for it? I think not. If morality simply is relative to each culture, then if the culture does not have a principle of tolerance, its members have no obligation to be tolerant. Herskovits seems to be treating the principle of tolerance as the one exception to his relativism. But from a relativistic point of view there is no more reason to be tolerant than to be intolerant, and neither stance is objectively morally better than the other.

Not only does the relativist fail to offer a basis for criticizing those who are intolerant, but he cannot also rationally criticize anyone who espouses what he might regard as a heinous principle. If criticism supposes an objective standard, he cannot morally criticize anyone outside his culture. Hitler's actions (so long as they are culturally tolerated) are as legitimate as Mother Teresa's. Genocide of unpopular minorities, oppression of the poor, slavery, and even advocacy of war for its own sake are as equally moral as their opposites. And if a subculture decided that starting a nuclear war was somehow morally acceptable, we could not morally criticize these people.

There are other disturbing consequences of ethical relativism. It seems to entail that reformers are always (morally) wrong because they go against the tide of cultural standards. William Wilberforce was wrong in the early nineteenth century to oppose slavery, and the British were immoral in opposing suttee in India (the burning of widows, which is now illegal there). Gandhi was wrong in trying to bring peace between Moslems and Hindus because the majority of each religious community felt hatred for the other. Jesus was immoral in advocating the beatitudes and principles of the Sermon on the Mount because it is clear that few in his time (or in ours) accepted them. Yet normally we feel just the opposite, that the reformer is the courageous innovator who is right, who has the truth, who is at odds with the mindless majority. We intuitively feel that Kierkegaard was right, that moral truth is often with the insightful individual and error with the crowd. Yet if relativism is correct, the opposite is necessarily the case: truth is with the crowd and error with the individual.

Similarly, moral relativism entails disturbing judgments about the law. Our normal view is that we have a prima facie duty to obey laws, because the law, in general, promotes the human good. According to most objective systems this obligation is not absolute, but rather is relative to the particular law's relationship to a higher moral order. Civil disobedience is warranted in some cases in which the law seems to be seriously in conflict with morality. However, if moral relativism is true, then neither law nor civil disobedience has a firm foundation. Civil disobedience will be morally wrong so long as the culture agrees with the law in question; but to those who belong to the subculture that doesn't recognize the law in question, disobedience will be morally permissible. Both a prima facie duty to obey the law and justification for breaking the law at certain times are dependent on a nonrelativist notion of morality.

A fundamental problem with the dependency thesis, the relativists' assumption that morality is dependent on culture or society, is that it is notoriously difficult to define a culture or society, especially in a pluralistic society like our own. One person may belong to several societies (subcultures) with different values and arrangements of principles. Persons may belong to the society-at-large and hold certain values of patriotism, honor, courage, and respect for the law (including some that are controversial but have majority acceptance, such as the law on abortion). But they may also belong to a church that opposes some secular laws, or they may be integral members of a socially mixed community in which different principles hold sway, or they may belong to clubs and families that adhere to still other rules.

Relativism would seem to contend that when people are members of societies with conflicting moralities they must be judged both wrong and not wrong (either right or permissible) whatever they do. For example, if Mary is a U.S. citizen and a member of the Roman Catholic church, she is wrong (qua Catholic) if she chooses to have an abortion and not wrong (qua citizens of the United States) if she chooses to have an abortion. Likewise, if Sam and Alice are Jehovah's Witnesses, then they are morally wrong (qua Jehovah's Witnesses) in allowing their child, who might otherwise die, to have a blood transfusion, but they are not wrong (qua U.S. citizens) in allowing him to have a transfusion. And conversely, as U.S. citizens they are wrong in prohibiting the transfusion, but as Jehovah's Witnesses they are not wrong if they prohibit it.

Perhaps the relativist would adhere to a metaprinciple that says that in such cases the individual may designate one group as primary. If Mary chooses to have an abortion, she is choosing to belong to the general society relative to that principle. The trouble with this feat is that it seems to lead back to counter-intuitive results. If Gangster Gus feels like killing bank president Ortcutt and wants to feel good about it, he identifies with the underworld society rather than the general public morality. Does this justify the killing? In fact, couldn't one justify anything simply by forming a small subculture that approved of it? Charles Manson would be morally pure in killing innocent people simply by forming a little coterie. How large must the group be in order to be a legitimate subculture or society? Does it need ten or fifteen people? How about just three? Come to think of it, why can't my burglary partner and I form our own society with a morality of its own? Of course, if my partner died, I could still claim that because I was acting from a set of norms that had an interpersonal origin, my act was morally correct. But why can't I dispense with the interpersonal agreements altogether and invent my own morality, since morality, in this view, is only an invention anyway? Conventionalist relativism seems to reduce to subjectivism. And subjectivism leads, as we have seen, to the demise of morality altogether.

If anyone objects that this argument is an instance of the slippery slope fallacy, let that person give an alternative analysis of what constitutes a viable social basis for generating valid moral principles. Perhaps we might agree (for the sake of argument, at least) that the very nature of morality entails two or more people making an agreement. This strategy saves the conventionalist from moral solipsism, but it still permits most any principle to count as moral, and what's more, those principles can be thrown out and their contraries substituted for them as the need arises. If two or three people decide that they will make cheating morally acceptable for them at their university (qua "Cheaters Anonymous"), then cheating is moral. Why not?

However, whereas we may fear the demise of morality as we have known it, this in itself may not be a good reason for rejecting relativism, that is, for judging it false. Alas, truth may not always be edifying. But the consequences of this position are sufficiently alarming to prompt us to look carefully for some weakness in the relativist's argument. So let us reexamine the premises and conclusion listed as the three theses of relativism at the beginning of this essay.

1. Moral rightness and wrongness of actions vary from society to society, so there are no universal moral standards held by all societies.

2. Whether or not it is right for individuals to act in a certain way depends on (or is relative to) the society to which they belong.

3. Therefore, there are no absolute or objective moral standards that apply to all people everywhere and at all times.

Does any one of these seem problematic? The first thesis, the diversity thesis, seems unexceptional. Cultural relativism is a fact, but it is a neutral fact. On the one hand, it does not establish the truth of ethical relativism, for it could be the case that some cultures simply lack correct moral principles. On the other hand, a denial of complete cultural relativism (that is, an admission of some universal principles) does not disprove ethical relativism. For even if we did find one or two universal principles, this would not prove that they had any objective status. We could still *imagine* a culture that was an exception to the rule and be unable to criticize it. So the first premise doesn't by itself imply ethical relativism, and its denial doesn't disprove ethical relativism.

Next we consider the crucial second thesis, the dependency thesis. Morality does not occur in a vacuum, but rather what is considered morally right or wrong must be seen in a context that depends on the goals, wants, beliefs, history, and environment of the society in question. Previously we mentioned weak and strong theses of dependency. The weak thesis says that the application of principles depends on the particular cultural predicament, whereas the strong thesis contends that the principles themselves depend on that predicament. The nonrelativist can accept a certain degree of relativity in the way moral principles are *applied* in various cultures.

For example, a raw environment with scarce natural resources may justify the Eskimos' practice of euthanasia to the objectivist, who would consistently reject that practice in another environment. A tribe in East Africa throws its deformed children into the river because of its belief that such infants *belong* to the hippopotamus, the god of the river. We believe that they have a false belief about this, but the point is that the same principles of respect for property and respect for human life are operative in these contrary practices. They differ from us only in belief, not in substantive moral principle. This example is an illustration of how nonmoral beliefs (for example, deformed children belong to the hippopotamus) cause moral principles (for example, give to each his due) to generate different actions. In our own culture the difference in the nonmoral belief about the status of a fetus generates opposite moral prescriptions.

So the fact that moral principles are weakly dependent doesn't show that ethical relativism is valid.

In spite of this weak dependency on nonmoral factors, a set of general moral norms that are applicable to all cultures (and even recognized in most) and that are disregarded at a culture's own expense could still exist.

What the relativist needs is a strong thesis of dependency that claims that somehow all principles are essentially cultural decisions. But why should we choose to view morality this way? Are there grounds to recommend the strong thesis of dependency over the weak one? One is the simple point that we don't have an obvious impartial standard from which to judge. Who's to say which culture is right and which is wrong? But we can reason and perform thought experiments in order to make a case for one system over another. We may not be able to know with certainty that we are right or relatively more right than the other culture, but we may be justified in believing that we are. If we can be closer to the truth regarding factual or scientific matters, why can't we be closer to the truth on moral matters? Why can't a culture simply be confused or wrong about its moral perceptions? Why can't we say that the society that sees nothing wrong with torturing children is less moral in that regard than the culture that cherishes children and grants them equal rights?

The only plausible argument that I know in favor of the strong dependency thesis is the indeterminacy of translation thesis, which holds that languages are often so fundamentally different from each other that we cannot accurately translate concepts or principles from one to another. But this thesis, while relatively true even within a language community, seems falsified by experience. We do learn foreign languages and learn to translate across linguistic frameworks. For example, people from a myriad of language groups come to the United States and learn to speak English and communicate perfectly well. Rather than a complete hiatus, the interplay between these other cultures eventually enriches the English language with new concepts (for example, forte/foible, taboo, coup de grace), even as English has enriched (or "corrupted," as the purist might say) French and other languages as well. Even if it turns out that there is some indeterminacy of translation between language users, we should not infer from this that no translation is possible. It seems reasonable to believe that general moral principles are precisely those things that can be communicated transculturally. A sufficiently common human nature and human predicament seem to make it possible to speak cross-culturally of a common set of underlying moral principles.

If this is true, then the indeterminacy of translation thesis upon which relativism depends must itself be relativized to the point where it is no objection to objective morality.

4. The Case for Objectivism

If nonrelativists are to make their case, they will have to offer a better explanation of cultural diversity and give reasons for adhering to moral objectivism. One way of doing this is to appeal to a divine law and cite human sin that causes deviation from that law. Although I think that human greed, selfishness, pride, self-deception, and other maladies have a great deal to do with moral differences and that religion may lend great support to morality, I don't think that a religious justification is necessary for validation of moral principles. I shall not build a case for objectivism by an appeal to religion, but I shall instead outline a modest nonreligious objectivism by first appealing to our intuitions and then by giving a naturalist account of morality that transcends individual cultures.

First, I must make it clear that I am distinguishing moral absolutism from moral objectivism. The absolutist believes that there are moral principles that ought never be overridden or violated. Kant's system is a good example of this. One ought never break a promise, no matter what. Act utilitarianism also seems absolutist, for the principle — do that act that has the most promise of yielding the most utility — cannot be overridden. An objectivist need not posit any principles that cannot be overridden, at least not in unqualified general forms. Moral principles are similar to Ross's prima facie principles, which may or may not be arranged hierarchically. But even if they are, the principles may be overridden by another prima facie principle (for example, whereas a principle of justice may generally outweigh a principle of benevolence, there are times when enormous good could be done by sacrificing a small amount of justice, so that an objectivist would be inclined to so act). An unqualified general principle would be of the form "Always do X" or "In general do X," but a qualified general principle would be of the form "In general do X except under condition C" or "Except under condition C, always do X." Suitably conditioned objective principles might turn out to be qualified absolutes.[3]

If we can establish or show that it is reasonable to believe that there is at least one objective moral principle that is binding on all people everywhere in some ideal sense, we shall have shown that relativism is probably false and that a limited objectivism is true. Actually, I believe that there are many qualified general ethical principles that are binding on all rational beings, but one will suffice to refute relativism. The principle I'll choose is the following:

A. It is morally wrong to torture people for the fun of it.

I claim that this principle is binding on all rational agents, so that if some agent, S, rejects A, we should not let that affect our intuition that A is a true principle, but rather try to explain S's behavior as perverse, ignorant, or irrational instead. For example, suppose Hitler didn't accept A. Should that affect our confidence in the truth of A? Is it not more reasonable to infer that Hitler was morally deficient, morally blind, ignorant, or irrational than to suppose that his noncompliance is evidence against the truth of A?

Suppose further that there is a tribe of people somewhere who enjoy torturing people. The whole culture accepts torturing others for the fun of it. Suppose that Mother Teresa or Gandhi tries unsuccessfully to convince them that they should stop torturing people altogether, and they respond by torturing them. Should this affect our confidence in A? Would it not be more reasonable to look for some explanation of the tribe's behavior? For example, we might hypothesize that this tribe lacked a developed sense of sympathetic imagination that is necessary for the moral life. Or we might theorize that this tribe was on a lower evolutionary level than most Homo sapiens. Or we might simply conclude that the tribe was closer to a Hobbesian state of nature than most societies, and as such probably would not survive. But we need not know why the tribe was in such bad shape in order to maintain our confidence in A as a moral principle. If A is a basic or core belief for us, then we will be more likely to doubt the tribe's sanity or ability to think morally than to doubt the validity of A.

Fortunately, it isn't as though A were an ad hoc belief, for we can give reasons for beliefs like A being central to any moral system that we deem adequate. Principles like the Golden Rule (suitably qualified), not killing innocent people, treating equals equally, truth-telling, promise-keeping, and the like are central to the fluid progression of social interaction and to the resolution of conflicts, which is what ethics is about (at least in the case of minimal morality, even though there may be more to morality than simply these kinds of concerns). For example, language itself depends on a general commitment to the principle of truth-telling. Every time we use words correctly we are telling the truth, and without this behavior, language wouldn't be possible. Likewise, without the recognition of a rule of promise-keeping, contracts are of no avail and cooperation is less likely to occur.

A morality would be adequate if it contained a requisite set of these objective principles (call them the stable core of morality), but there could be more than one adequate morality that contained different rankings of these and other principles that are consistent with the core. That is, there may be a certain relativity to secondary principles (whether to opt for monogamy rather than polygamy, whether to include a principle of high altruism in the set of moral duties, whether to allow for limited euthanasia, and so forth), but in every morality a certain core will remain, though it may be applied somewhat differently because of differences in environment, belief, tradition, and the like.

Stated more positively, objectivists who base their moral systems on a common human nature with common needs and desires might construct the following argument for objectivism:

1. Human nature is relatively similar in essential respects, having a common set of needs and interests.

2. Moral principles are functions of human needs and interests and are instituted by reason in order to promote the most significant interests and needs of rational beings (and perhaps of others).

3. Some moral principles promote human interests and meet human needs better than others.

4. Those principles that meet essential needs and promote the most significant interests of

humans in optimal ways can be said to be objectively valid moral principles.

5. Therefore, since there is a common human nature, there is an objectively valid set of moral principles that is applicable to all humanity.

If we leave out any reference to a common human nature, the argument would be even simpler:

1. Objectively valid moral principles are those adherence to which meets the needs and promotes the most significant interests of persons.

2. Some principles are such that adherence to them meets the needs and promotes the most significant interests of persons.

3. Therefore, some objectively valid moral principles exist.

Either argument would satisfy objectivism, but the former makes it clearer that is our common human nature that generates the common principles.[4]

If either argument succeeds, there are ideal moralities (and not simply adequate ones). Of course, there could still be more than one ideal morality, which presumably an ideal observer would choose under optimal conditions. This ideal observer might conclude that out of an infinite set of moralities, three or more combinations would tie for first place. One would expect that these would be similar, but there is every reason to believe that all of these would contain the set of core principles.

Of course, we don't know what an ideal observer would choose, but we can imagine that the conditions which such an observer would choose would be conditions of maximal knowledge and impartiality, second-order qualities that ensure that agents have the best chance of making the best decisions. If this is so, then the more we learn to judge impartially and the more we know about possible forms of life, the better chance we have to approximate an ideal moral system. And if there is the possibility of approximating ideal moral systems with an objective core and other objective components, then ethical relativism is certainly false. We can confidently dismiss it as an aberration and get on with the job of working out better moral systems.

I have been arguing that morality has a point, so that not just anything can count as a valid moral principle. Let me illustrate: Imagine that you have been miraculously transported to the dark kingdom

of hell, and there you get a glimpse of the sufferings of the damned. Their punishment is that they have eternal back itches that ebb and flow constantly. But they cannot scratch their backs, for their arms are paralyzed in a frontal position, so they writhe with itchiness through eternity. And just as you are beginning to feel the itch on your own back, you are suddenly transported to heaven. What do you see in the kingdom of the blessed? You see people who have eternal back itches and cannot scratch their own backs. But they are all smiling instead of writhing. Why? Because everyone has his or her arms stretched out to scratch someone else's back, and so, with their arrangement in one big circle, a hell of agony is turned into a heaven of ecstasy.

If we can imagine some states of affairs or cultures that are better than others in a way that depends on human action, we can ask what are those character traits that make them so. In our story, people in heaven, but not in hell, cooperate for the amelioration of suffering and the production of pleasure. These are very primitive goods, insufficient for a full-blown morality, but they give us a hint concerning the objectivity of morality. Moral goodness has something to do with the ameliorating of suffering, the resolution of conflict, and the promotion of human flourishing. If our heaven of scratching is really better than the eternal itchiness of hell, then whatever makes it so is constitutively related to moral rightness.

Why, then, is there such a strong inclination toward ethical relativism? I think that there are three reasons that haven't been emphasized. The first is the fact that options are usually presented as though absolutism and relativism were the only alternatives, so conventionalism wins out against an implausible competitor. We have seen that this dichotomy is unnecessary. One can have an objective morality without being absolutist.

The second reason is that our recent sensitivity to cultural relativism has made us conscious of the frailty of many aspects of our moral repertoire, so that there is a tendency to wonder who's to judge what's really right or wrong. However, the move from a reasonable cultural relativism, which rightly causes us to rethink our moral systems, to an ethical relativism, which causes us to give up the heart of morality altogether, is an instance of the fallacy of confusing factual or descriptive statements with normative ones. Cultural relativism doesn't entail ethical relativism.

We may well agree that cultures differ and that we ought to be cautious in condemning what we don't understand, but this in no way need imply that there are not better and worse ways of living. We can understand and excuse, to some degree at least, those who differ from our best notions of morality, and we can do this without abdicating the judgment that cultures that lack principles of justice or promise-keeping or protection of the innocent are morally poorer for these omissions.

The third reason, which is influential with philosophers who are overly impressed with metaethics, is that many philosophers believe that it is important to begin to do ethics with a morally neutral definition. As the *Webster's Ninth New Collegiate Dictionary* defines it, ethics is simply "the principles of conduct governing an individual or a group." No judgment is made from the outset about the content of those principles, and since the diversity thesis is plausible, one can be led to think that a certain relativism follows from this definition.

While this definition may be a fair one for sociology or anthropology, it is inadequate for philosophy. There is a narrower definition of the term that has to do with the Good, with human flourishing (and probably nonhuman sentient creatures' flourishing as well). And this flourishing involves the amelioration of suffering, the promotion of happiness, and the resolution of conflicts of interest. Given this content-laden conception of morality, we can explain why we are loathe to call Hitler's actions or torturing little children morally right regardless of whether a majority approves of them.

So, who's to judge what's right or wrong? We are. We are to do so on the basis of the best reasoning we can bring forth, and with sympathy and understanding.

Endnotes

1 Part of this section has been influenced by Fred Feldman's treatment of the same topic in *Introductory Ethics* (Prentice-Hall, 1978).

2 Melville Herskovits, *Cultural Relativism* (Random House, 1972).

3 See Marcus Singer, "The Idea of a Rational Morality," *Proceedings of the American Philosophical Association* (September 1986: 28), in which he argues that such principles as "It is always wrong to lie for lying's sake" are absolutely wrong. "Given any moral rule to the effect that some kind of action is generally wrong, it follows that it is always wrong to do any act of that kind just for the sake of doing it."

4 I owe the reformulation of the argument to Bruce Russell, who, along with Morton Winston, offered valuable criticisms of an earlier version of this article. An anonymous reader also aided in the revision of this article.

II.4 *Moral Relativism Defended*

GILBERT HARMAN

Gilbert Harman is a professor of philosophy at Princeton University and has
done important work in epistemology, action theory, and ethics. A selection
from his book, *The Nature of Morality,* is found in Part IX.3 of this work. In
this essay Harman attempts to reconstruct ethical relativism. It is contractual,
internalist, and relativistic. It is contractual, for according to this position
morality arises from agreements between people about their relations to each
other. It is a form of politics in that it originates in an implicitly bargaining
situation in which various parties decide what are the basic wants that they
have in common. Ethical relativism proceeds from this notion of agreement.
All moral judgments about someone's actions make sense only in relation to
some agreement that the agent has explicitly or implicitly made, so the
defining feature is relative to the agreement and not in any independent norm.
Harman's position is internalist, for it claims that moral judgments do not
apply to agents unless they have motivating reasons for their actions. These
motivating reasons arise in the social agreements they make. Finally, Harman
argues that his theory fits in better with our moral intuitions than objectivist
theories and has greater explanatory power.

My thesis is that morality arises when a group of
people reach an implicit agreement or come to a
tacit understanding about their relations with one
another. Part of what I mean by this is that moral
judgments — or, rather, an important class of
them — make sense only in relation to and with reference to one or another such agreement or understanding. This is vague, and I shall try to make it
more precise in what follows. But it should be clear
that I intend to argue for a version of what has been
called moral relativism.

In doing so, I am taking sides in an ancient controversy. Many people have supposed that the sort
of view which I am going to defend is obviously
correct — indeed, that it is the only sort of account
that could make sense of the phenomenon of morality. At the same time there have also been many who
have supposed that moral relativism is confused, incoherent, and even immoral, at the very least obviously wrong.

Most arguments against relativism make use of
a strategy of dissuasive definition; they define moral
relativism as an inconsistent thesis. For example,
they define it as the assertion that *(a)* there are no
universal moral principles and *(b)* one ought to act
in accordance with the principles of one's own
group, where this latter principle, *(b)* is supposed to
be a universal moral principle.[1] It is easy enough to
show that this version of moral relativism will not
do, but that is no reason to think that a defender of
moral relativism cannot find a better definition.

My moral relativism is a soberly logical thesis —
a thesis about logical form, if you like. Just as the
judgment that something is large makes sense only
in relation to one or another comparison class, so
too, I will argue, the judgment that it is wrong of
someone to do something makes sense only in relation to an agreement or understanding. A dog may
be large in relation to chihuahuas but not large in
relation to dogs in general. Similarly, I will argue, an
action may be wrong in relation to one agreement
but not in relation to another. Just as it makes no
sense to ask whether a dog is large, period, apart
from any relation to a comparison class, so too, I
will argue, it makes no sense to ask whether an ac-

Reprinted with permission from *Philosophical Review* 84
(1975): 3–22.

tion is wrong, period, apart from any relation to an agreement.

There is an agreement, in the relevant sense, if each of a number of people intends to adhere to some schedule, plan, or set of principles, intending to do this on the understanding that the others similarly intend. The agreement or understanding need not be conscious or explicit; and I will not here try to say what distinguishes moral agreements from, for example, conventions of the road or conventions of etiquette, since these distinctions will not be important as regards the purely logical thesis that I will be defending.

Although I want to say that certain moral judgments are made in relation to an agreement, I do not want to say this about all moral judgments. Perhaps it is true that all moral judgments are made in relation to an agreement; nevertheless, that is not what I will be arguing. For I want to say that there is a way in which certain moral judgments are relative to an agreement but other moral judgments are not. My relativism is a thesis only about what I will call "inner judgments," such as the judgment that someone ought not to have acted in a certain way or the judgment that it was right or wrong of him to have done so. My relativism is not meant to apply, for example, to the judgment that someone is evil or the judgment that a given institution is unjust.

In particular, I am not denying (nor am I asserting) that some moralities are "objectively" better than others or that there are objective standards for assessing moralities. My thesis is a soberly logical thesis about logical form.

I. Inner Judgments

We make inner judgments about a person only if we suppose that he is capable of being motivated by the relevant moral considerations. We make other sorts of judgments about those who we suppose are not susceptible of such motivation. Inner judgments include judgments in which we say that someone should or ought to have done something or that someone was right or wrong to have done something. Inner judgments do not include judgments in which we call someone (literally) a savage or say that someone is (literally) inhuman, evil, a betrayer, a traitor, or an enemy.

Consider this example. Intelligent beings from outer space land on Earth, beings without the slightest concern for human life and happiness. That a certain course of action on their part might injure one of us means nothing to them; that fact by itself gives them no reason to avoid the action. In such a case it would be odd to say that nevertheless the beings ought to avoid injuring us or that it would be wrong for them to attack us. Of course we will want to resist them if they do such things and we will make negative judgments about them; but we will judge that they are dreadful enemies to be repelled and even destroyed, not that they should not act as they do.

Similarly, if we learn that a band of cannibals has captured and eaten the sole survivor of a shipwreck, we will speak of the primitive morality of the cannibals and may call them savages, but we will not say that they ought not to have eaten their captive.

Again, suppose that a contented employee of Murder, Incorporated was raised as a child to honor and respect members of the "family" but to have nothing but contempt for the rest of society. His current assignment, let us suppose, is to kill a certain bank manager, Bernard J. Ortcutt. Since Ortcutt is not a member of the "family," the employee in question has no compunction about carrying out his assignment. In particular, if we were to try to convince him that he should not kill Ortcutt, our argument would merely amuse him. We would not provide him with the slightest reason to desist unless we were to point to practical difficulties, such as the likelihood of his getting caught. Now, in this case it would be a misuse of language to say of him that he ought not to kill Ortcutt or that it would be wrong of him to do so, since that would imply that our own moral considerations carry some weight with him, which they do not. Instead we can only judge that he is a criminal, someone to be hunted down by the police, an enemy of peace-loving citizens, and so forth.

It is true that we can make certain judgments about him using the word "ought." For example, investigators who have been tipped off by an informer and who are waiting for the assassin to appear at the bank can use the "ought" of expectation to say, "He ought to arrive soon," meaning that on the basis of their information one would expect him to arrive soon. And, in thinking over how the assassin might carry out his assignment, we can use the "ought" of rationality to say that he ought to go in by the rear door, meaning that it would be more rational for him to do that than to go in by the front door. In neither of these cases is the moral "ought" in question.

There is another use of "ought" which is normative and in a sense moral but which is distinct from what I am calling the moral "ought." This is the use which occurs when we say that something ought or ought not to be the case. It ought not to be the case that members of Murder, Incorporated go around killing people; in other words, it is a terrible thing that they do so.[2] The same thought can perhaps be expressed as "They ought not to go around killing people," meaning that it ought not to be the case that they do, not that they are wrong to do what they do. The normative "ought to be" is used to assess a situation; the moral "ought to do" is used to describe a relation between an agent and a type of act that he might perform or has performed.

The sentence "They ought not to go around killing people" is therefore multiply ambiguous. It can mean that one would not expect them to do so (the "ought" of expectation), that it is not in their interest to do so (the "ought" of rationality), that it is a bad thing that they do so (the normative "ought to be"), or that they are wrong to do so (the moral "ought to do"). For the most part I am here concerned only with the last of these interpretations.

The word "should" behaves very much like "ought to." There is a "should" of expectation ("They should be here soon"), a "should" of rationality ("He should go in by the back door"), a normative "should be" ("They shouldn't go around killing people like that"), and the moral "should do" ("You should keep that promise"). I am of course concerned mainly with the last sense of "should."

"Right" and "wrong" also have multiple uses; I will not try to say what all of them are. But I do want to distinguish using the word "wrong" to say that a particular situation or action is wrong from using the word to say that it is wrong *of someone* to do something. In the former case, the word "wrong" is used to assess an act or situation. In the latter case it is used to describe a relation between an agent and an act. Only the latter sort of judgment is an inner judgment. Although we would not say concerning the contented employee of Murder, Incorporated mentioned earlier that it was wrong *of him* to kill Ortcutt, we could say that *his action* was wrong and

we could say that it is wrong that there is so much killing.

To take another example, it sounds odd to say that Hitler should not have ordered the extermination of the Jews, that it was wrong of him to have done so. That sounds somehow "too weak" a thing to say. Instead we want to say that Hitler was an evil man. Yet we can properly say, "Hitler ought not to have ordered the extermination of the Jews," if what we mean is that it ought never to have happened; and we can say without oddity that what Hitler did was wrong. Oddity attends only the inner judgment that Hitler was wrong to have acted in that way. That is what sounds "too weak."

It is worth noting that the inner judgments sound too weak not because of the enormity of what Hitler did but because we suppose that in acting as he did he shows that he could not have been susceptible to the moral considerations on the basis of which we make our judgment. He is in the relevant sense beyond the pale and we therefore cannot make inner judgments about him. To see that this is so, consider, say, Stalin, another mass-murderer. We can perhaps imagine someone taking a sympathetic view of Stalin. In such a view, Stalin realized that the course he was going to pursue would mean the murder of millions of people and he dreaded such a prospect; however, the alternative seemed to offer an even greater disaster — so, reluctantly and with great anguish, he went ahead. In relation to such a view of Stalin, inner judgments about Stalin are not as odd as similar judgments about Hitler. For we might easily continue the story by saying that, despite what he hoped to gain, Stalin should not have done so. What makes inner judgments about Hitler odd, "too weak," is not that the acts judged seem too terrible for the words used but rather that the agent judged seems beyond the pale — in other words beyond the motivational reach of the relevant moral considerations.

Of course, I do not want to deny that for various reasons a speaker might pretend that an agent is or is not susceptible to certain moral considerations. For example, a speaker may for rhetorical or political reasons wish to suggest that someone is beyond the pale, that he should not be listened to, that he can be treated as an enemy. On the other hand, a speaker may pretend that someone is susceptible to certain moral considerations in an effort to make that person or others susceptible to those considerations. Inner judgments about one's children sometimes have this function. So do inner judgments made in political speeches that aim at restoring a lapsed sense of morality in government.

II. *The Logical Form of Inner Judgments*

Inner judgments have two important characteristics. First, they imply that the agent has reasons to do something. Second, the speaker in some sense endorses these reasons and supposes that the audience also endorses them. Other moral judgments about an agent, on the other hand, do not have such implications; they do not imply that the agent has reasons for acting that are endorsed by the speaker.

If someone S says that A (morally) ought to do D, S implies that A has reasons to do D and S endorses those reasons — whereas if S says that B was evil in what B did, S does not imply that the reasons S would endorse for not doing what B did were reasons for B not to do that thing; in fact, S implies that they were not reasons for B.

Let us examine this more closely. If S says that (morally) A ought to do D, S implies that A has reasons to do D which S endorses. I shall assume that such reasons would have to have their source in goals, desires, or intentions that S takes A to have and that S approves of A's having because S shares those goals, desires, or intentions. So, if S says that (morally) A ought to do D, there are certain motivational attitudes M which S assumes are shared by S, A, and S's audience.

Now, in supposing that reasons for action must have their source in goals, desires, or intentions, I am assuming something like an Aristotelian or Humean account of these matters, as opposed, for example, to a Kantian approach which sees a possible source of motivation in reason itself.[3] I must defer a full-scale discussion of the issue to another occasion. Here I simply assume that the Kantian approach is wrong. In particular, I assume that there might be no reasons at all for a being from outer space to avoid harm to us; that, for Hitler, there might have been no reason at all not to order the extermination of the Jews; that the contented employee of Murder, Incorporated might have no reason at all not to kill Ortcutt; that the cannibals might have no reason not to eat their captive. In other words, I assume that the possession of rationality is not sufficient to provide a source for relevant reasons, that certain desires, goals, or intentions are also necessary. Those who accept this assumption will, I think, find that they distinguish inner moral judgments from other moral judgments in the way that I have indicated.

Ultimately, I want to argue that the shared motivational attitudes M are intentions to keep an agreement (supposing that others similarly intend). For I want to argue that inner moral judgments are made relative to such an agreement. That is, I want to argue that, when S makes the inner judgment that A ought to do D, S assumes that A intends to act in accordance with an agreement which S and S's audience also intend to observe. In other words, I want to argue that the source of the reasons for doing D which S ascribes to A is A's sincere intention to observe a certain agreement. I have not yet argued for the stronger thesis, however. I have argued only that S makes his judgment relative to *some* motivational attitudes M which S assumes are shared by S, A, and S's audience.

Formulating this as a logical thesis, I want to treat the moral "ought" as a four-place predicate (or "operator"), "Ought (A, D, C, M)," which relates an agent A, a type of act D, considerations C, and motivating attitudes M. The relativity to considerations C can be brought out by considering what are sometimes called statements of prima-facie obligation, "Considering that you promised, you ought to go to the board meeting, but considering that you are the sole surviving relative, you ought to go to the funeral; all things considered, it is not clear what you ought to do."[4] The claim that there is *this* relativity, to considerations, is not, of course, what makes my thesis a version of moral relativism, since any theory must acknowledge relativity to considerations. The relativity to considerations does, however, provide a model for a coherent interpretation of moral relativism as a similar kind of relativity.

It is not as easy to exhibit the relativity to motivating attitudes as it is to exhibit the relativity to considerations, since normally a speaker who makes a moral "ought" judgment intends the relevant motivating attitudes to be ones that the speaker shares with the agent and the audience, and normally it will be obvious what attitudes these are. But sometimes a speaker does invoke different attitudes by invoking a morality the speaker does not share. Someone may say, for example, "As a Christian, you ought to turn the other cheek; I, however, propose to strike back." A spy who has been found out by a friend might say, "As a citizen, you ought to turn me in, but I hope that you will not." In these and similar cases a speaker makes a moral "ought" judgment that is explicitly relative to motivating attitudes that the speaker does not share.

In order to be somewhat more precise, then, my thesis is this. "Ought *(A, D, C, M)*" means roughly that, given that *A* has motivating attitudes *M* and given *C*, *D* is the course of action for *A* that is supported by the best reasons. In judgments using this sense of "ought," *C* and *M* are often not explicitly mentioned but are indicated by the context of utterance. Normally, when that happens, *C* will be "all things considered" and *M* will be attitudes that are shared by the speaker and audience.

I mentioned that inner judgments have two characteristics. First, they imply that the agent has reasons to do something that are capable of motivating the agent. Second, the speaker endorses those reasons and supposes that the audience does too. Now, any "Ought *(A, D, C, M)*" judgment has the first of these characteristics, but as we have just seen a judgment of this sort will not necessarily have the second characteristic if made with explicit reference to motivating attitudes not shared by the speaker. If reference is made either implicitly or explicitly (for example, through the use of the adverb "morally") to attitudes that are shared by the speaker and audience, the resulting judgment has both characteristics and is an inner judgment. If reference is made to attitudes that are not shared by the speaker, the resulting judgment is not an inner judgment and does not represent a full-fledged moral judgment on the part of the speaker. In such a case we have an example of what has been called an inverted-commas use of "ought."[5]

III. *Moral Bargaining*

I have argued that moral "ought" judgments are relational, "Ought *(A, D, C, M)*," where *M* represents

certain motivating attitudes. I now want to argue that the attitudes *M* derive from an agreement. That is, they are intentions to adhere to a particular agreement on the understanding that others also intend to do so. Really, it might be better for me to say that I put this forward as a hypothesis, since I cannot pretend to be able to prove that it is true. I will argue, however, that this hypothesis accounts for an otherwise puzzling aspect of our moral views that, as far as I know, there is no other way to account for.

I will use the word "intention" in a somewhat extended sense to cover certain dispositions or habits. Someone may habitually act in accordance with the relevant understanding and therefore may be disposed to act in that way without having any more or less conscious intention. In such a case it may sound odd to say that he *intends* to act in accordance with the moral understanding. Nevertheless, for present purposes I will count that as his having the relevant intention in a dispositional sense.

I now want to consider the following puzzle about our moral views, a puzzle that has figured in recent philosophical discussion of issues such as abortion. It has been observed that most of us assign greater weight to the duty not to harm others than to the duty to help others. For example, most of us believe that a doctor ought not to save five of his patients who would otherwise die by cutting up a sixth patient and distributing his health organs where needed to the others, even though we do think that the doctor has a duty to try to help as many of his patients as he can. For we also think that he has a stronger duty to try not to harm any of his patients (or anyone else) even if by so doing he could help five others.[6]

This aspect of our moral views can seem very puzzling, especially if one supposes that moral feelings derive from sympathy and concern for others. But the hypothesis that morality derives from an agreement among people of varying powers and resources provides a plausible explanation. The rich, the poor, the strong, and the weak would all benefit if all were to try to avoid harming one another. So everyone could agree to that arrangement. But the rich and the strong would not benefit from an arrangement whereby everyone would try to do as much as possible to help those in need. The poor and weak would get all of the benefit of this latter arrangement. Since the rich and the strong could foresee that they would be required to do most of the helping and that they would receive little in return, they would be reluctant to agree to a strong principle of mutual aid. A compromise would be likely and a weaker principle would probably be accepted. In other words, although everyone could agree to a strong principle concerning the avoidance of harm, it would not be true that everyone would favor an equally strong principle of mutual aid. It is likely that only a weaker principle of the latter sort would gain general acceptance. So the hypothesis that morality derives from an understanding among people of different powers and resources can explain (and, according to me, does explain) why in our morality avoiding harm to others is taken to be more important than helping those who need help.

By the way, I am here only trying to *explain* an aspect of our moral views. I am not therefore *endorsing* that aspect. And I defer until later a relativistic account of the way in which aspects of our moral view can be criticized "from within."

Now we need not suppose that the agreement or understanding in question is explicit. It is enough if various members of society knowingly reach an agreement in intentions—each intending to act in certain ways on the understanding that the others have similar intentions. Such an implicit agreement is reached through a process of mutual adjustment and implicit bargaining.

Indeed, it is essential to the proposed explanation of this aspect of our moral views to suppose that the relevant moral understanding is thus the result of *bargaining*. It is necessary to suppose that, in order to further our interests, we form certain conditional intentions, hoping that others will do the same. The others, who have different interests, will form somewhat different conditional intentions. After implicit bargaining, some sort of compromise is reached.

Seeing morality in this way as a compromise based on implicit bargaining helps to explain why our morality takes it to be worse to harm someone than to refuse to help someone. The explanation requires that we view our morality as an implicit agreement about what to do. This sort of explanation could not be given if we were to suppose, say, that our morality represented an agreement only about the facts (naturalism). Nor is it enough simply to suppose that our morality represents an agreement in attitude, if we forget that such agree-

ment can be reached not only by way of such principles as are mentioned, for example, in Hare's "logic of imperatives,"[7] but also through bargaining. According to Hare, to accept a general moral principle is to intend to do something.[8] If we add to his theory that the relevant intentions can be reached through implicit bargaining, the resulting theory begins to look like the one that I am defending.

Many aspects of our moral views can be given a utilitarian explanation. We could account for these aspects, using the logical analysis I presented in the previous section of this paper, by supposing that the relevant "ought" judgments presuppose shared attitudes of sympathy and benevolence. We can equally well explain them by supposing that considerations of utility have influenced our implicit agreements, so that the appeal is to a shared intention to adhere to those agreements. Any aspect of morality that is susceptible of a utilitarian explanation can also be explained by an implicit agreement, but not conversely. There are aspects of our moral views that seem to be explicable only in the second way, on the assumption that morality derives from an agreement. One example, already cited, is the distinction we make between harming and not helping. Another is our feeling that each person has an inalienable right of self-defense and self-preservation. Philosophers have not been able to come up with a really satisfactory utilitarian justification of such a right, but it is easily intelligible on our present hypothesis, as Hobbes observed many years ago. You cannot, except in very special circumstances, rationally form the intention not to try to preserve your life if it should ever be threatened, say, by society or the state, since you know that you cannot now control what you would do in such a situation. No matter what you now decided to do, when the time came, you would ignore your prior decision and try to save your life. Since you cannot now intend to do something later which you now know that you would not do, you cannot now intend to keep an agreement not to preserve your life if it is threatened by others in your society.[9]

This concludes the positive side of my argument that what I have called inner moral judgments are made in relation to an implicit agreement. I now want to argue that this theory avoids difficulties traditionally associated with implicit agreement theories of morality.

IV. Objections and Replies

One traditional difficulty for implicit agreement theories concerns what motivates us to do what we have agreed to do. It will, obviously, not be enough to say that we have implicitly agreed to keep agreements, since the issue would then be why we keep *that* agreement. And this suggests an objection to implicit agreement theories. But the apparent force of the objection derives entirely from taking an agreement to be a kind of ritual. To agree in the relevant sense is not just to say something, it is to intend to do something — namely, to intend to carry out one's part of the agreement on the condition that others do their parts. If we agree in this sense to do something, we intend to do it and intending to do it is already to be motivated to do it. So there is no problem as to why we are motivated to keep our agreements in this sense.

We do believe that in general you ought not to pretend to agree in this sense in order to trick someone else into agreeing. But that suggests no objection to the present view. All that it indicates is that *our* moral understanding contains or implies an agreement to be open and honest with others. If it is supposed that this leaves a problem about someone who has not accepted our agreement — "What reason does *he* have not to pretend to accept our agreement so that he can then trick others into agreeing to various things?" — the answer is that such a person may or may not have such a reason. If someone does not already accept something of our morality it may or may not be possible to find reasons why he should.

A second traditional objection to implicit agreement theories is that there is not a perfect correlation between what is generally believed to be morally right and what actually is morally right. Not everything generally agreed on is right and sometimes courses of action are right that would not be generally agreed to be right. But this is no objection to my thesis. My thesis is not that the implicit agreement from which a morality derives is an agreement in moral judgment; the thesis is rather that moral judgments make reference to and are made in relation to an agreement in intentions. Given that a group of people have agreed in this sense, there can still be disputes as to what the agreement implies for various situations. In my view, many moral disputes are of this sort; they presuppose a basic agreement and they concern what implications that agreement has for particular cases.

There can also be various things wrong with the agreement that a group of people reach, even from the point of view of that agreement, just as there can be defects in an individual's plan of action even from the point of view of that plan. Given what is known about the situation, a plan or agreement can in various ways be inconsistent, incoherent, or self-defeating. In my view, certain moral disputes are concerned with internal defects of the basic moral understanding of a group, and what changes should be made from the perspective of that understanding itself. This is another way in which moral disputes make sense with reference to and in relation to an underlying agreement.

Another objection to implicit agreement theories is that not all agreements are morally binding — for example, those made under compulsion or from a position of unfair disadvantage, which may seem to indicate that there are moral principles prior to those that derive from an implicit agreement. But, again, the force of the objection derives from an equivocation concerning what an agreement is. The principle that compelled agreements do not obligate concerns agreement in the sense of a certain sort of ritual indicating that one agrees. My thesis concerns a kind of agreement in intentions. The principle about compelled agreements is part of, or is implied by, our agreement in intentions. According to me it is only with reference to some such agreement in intentions that a principle of this sort makes sense.

Now it may be true our moral agreement in intentions also implies that it is wrong to compel people who are in a greatly inferior position to accept an agreement in intentions that they would not otherwise accept, and it may even be true that there is in our society at least one class of people in an inferior position who have been compelled thus to settle for accepting a basic moral understanding, aspects of which they would not have accepted had they not been in such an inferior position. In that case there would be an incoherence in our basic moral understanding and various suggestions might be made concerning the ways in which this understanding should be modified. But this moral critique of the understanding can proceed from that understanding itself rather than from "prior" moral principles.

In order to fix ideas, let us consider a society in which there is a well-established and long-standing tradition of hereditary slavery. Let us suppose that everyone accepts this institution, including the slaves. Everyone treats it as in the nature of things that there should be such slavery. Furthermore, let us suppose that there are also aspects of the basic moral agreement which speak against slavery. That is, these aspects together with certain facts about the situation imply that people should not own slaves and that slaves have no obligation to acquiesce in their condition. In such a case, the moral understanding would be defective, although its defectiveness would presumably be hidden in one or another manner, perhaps by means of a myth that slaves are physically and mentally subhuman in a way that makes appropriate the sort of treatment elsewhere reserved for beasts of burden. If this myth were to be exposed, the members of the society would then be faced with an obvious incoherence in their basic moral agreement and might come eventually to modify their agreement so as to eliminate its acceptance of slavery.

In such a case, even relative to the old agreement it might be true that slave owners ought to free their slaves, that slaves need not obey their masters, and that people ought to work to eliminate slavery. For the course supported by the best reasons, given that one starts out with the intention of adhering to a particular agreement, may be that one should stop intending to adhere to certain aspects of that agreement and should try to get others to do the same.

We can also (perhaps — but see below) envision a second society with hereditary slavery whose agreement has no aspects that speak against slavery. In that case, even if the facts of the situation were fully appreciated, no incoherence would appear in the basic moral understanding of the society and it would not be true in relation to that understanding that slave owners ought to free their slaves, that slaves need not obey their master, and so forth. There might nevertheless come a time when there were reasons of a different sort to modify the basic understanding, either because of an external threat from societies opposed to slavery or because of an internal threat of rebellion by the slaves.

Now it is easier for us to make what I have called inner moral judgments about slave owners in the first society than in the second. For we can with reference to members of the first society invoke principles that they share with us and, with reference to those principles, we can say of them that they ought not to have kept slaves and that they were immoral to have done so. This sort of inner judgment becomes increasingly inappropriate, however, the more distant they are from us and the less easy it is for us to think of our moral understanding as continuous with and perhaps a later development of theirs. Furthermore, it seems appropriate to make only non-inner judgments of the slave owners in the second society. We can say that the second society is unfair and unjust, that the slavery that exists is wrong, that it ought not to exist. But it would be inappropriate in this case to say that it was morally wrong of the slave owners to own slaves. The relevant aspects of our moral understanding, which we would invoke in moral judgments about them, are not aspects of the moral understanding that exists in the second society. (I will come back to the question of slavery below.)

Let me turn now to another objection to implicit agreement theories, an objection which challenges the idea that there is an agreement of the relevant sort. For, if we have agreed, when did we do it? Does anyone really remember having agreed? How did we indicate our agreement? What about those who do not want to agree? How do they indicate that they do not agree and what are the consequences of their not agreeing? Reflection on these and similar questions can make the hypothesis of implicit agreement seem too weak a basis on which to found morality.

But once again there is equivocation about agreements. The objection treats the thesis as the claim that morality is based on some sort of ritual rather than on an agreement in intentions. But, as I have said, there is an agreement in the relevant sense when each of a number of people has an intention on the assumption that others have the same intention. In this sense of "agreement," there is no given moment at which one agrees, since one continues to agree in this sense as long as one continues to have the relevant intentions. Someone refuses to agree to the extent that he or she does not share these intentions. Those who do not agree are outside the agreement; in extreme cases they are outlaws or enemies. It does not follow, however, that there are no constraints on how those who agree may act toward those who do not, since for various reasons the agreement itself may contain provisions for dealing with outlaws and enemies.

This brings me to one last objection, which derives from the difficulty people have in trying to give an explicit and systematic account of their moral views. If one actually agrees to something, why is it so hard to say what one has agreed? In response I can say only that many understandings appear to be of this sort. It is often possible to recognize what is in accordance with the understanding and what would violate it without being able to specify the understanding in any general way. Consider, for example, the understanding that exists among the members of a team of acrobats or a symphony orchestra.

Another reason why it is so difficult to give a precise and systematic specification of any actual moral understanding is that such an understanding will not in general be constituted by absolute rules but will take a vaguer form, specifying goals and areas of responsibility. For example, the agreement may indicate that one is to show respect for others by trying where possible to avoid actions that will harm them or interfere with what they are doing; it may indicate the duties and responsibilities of various members of the family—who is to be responsible for bringing up the children, and so forth. Often what will be important will be not so much exactly what actions are done as how willing participants are to do their parts and what attitudes they have—for example, whether they give sufficient weight to the interests of others.

The vague nature of moral understandings is to some extent alleviated in practice. One learns what can and cannot be done in various situations. Expectations are adjusted to other expectations. But moral disputes arise nonetheless. Such disputes may concern what the basic moral agreement implies for particular situations; and, if so, that can happen either because of disputes over the facts or because of a difference in basic understanding. Moral disputes may also arise concerning whether or not changes should be made in the basic agreement. Racial and sexual issues seem often to be of this second sort; but there is no clear line between the two kinds of dispute. When the implications of an agreement for a particular situation are considered, one possible outcome is that it becomes clear that the agreement should be modified.

Moral reasoning is a form of practical reasoning. One begins with certain beliefs and intentions, including intentions that are part of one's acceptance of the moral understanding in a given group. In reasoning, one modifies one's intentions, often by forming new intentions, sometimes by giving up old ones, so that one's plans become more rational and coherent—or, rather, one seeks to make all of one's attitudes coherent with each other.

The relevant sort of coherence is not simply consistency. It is something very like the explanatory coherence which is so important in theoretical reasoning. Coherence involves generality and lack of arbitrariness. Consider our feelings about cruelty to animals. Obviously these do not derive from an agreement that has been reached with animals. Instead it is a matter of coherence. There is a prima-facie arbitrariness and lack of generality in a plan that involves avoiding cruelty to people but not to animals.

On the other hand, coherence in this sense is not the only relevant factor in practical reasoning. Another is conservatism or inertia. A third is an interest in satisfying basic desires or needs. One tries to make the least change that will best satisfy one's desires while maximizing the overall coherence of one's attitudes. Coherence by itself is not an overwhelming force. That is why our attitudes toward animals are weak and wavering, allowing us to use them in ways we would not use people.

Consider again the second hereditary slave society mentioned above. This society was to be one in which no aspects of the moral understanding shared by the masters spoke against slavery. In fact that is unlikely, since there is *some* arbitrariness in the idea that people are to be treated in different ways depending on whether they are born slave or free. Coherence of attitude will no doubt speak at least a little against the system of slavery. The point is that the factors of conservatism and desire might speak more strongly in favor of the status quo, so that, all things considered, the slave owners might have no reason to change their understanding.

One thing that distinguishes slaves from animals is that slaves can organize and threaten revolt, whereas animals cannot. Slaves can see to it that both coherence and desire oppose conservatism, so that it becomes rational for the slave owners to arrive at a new, broader, more coherent understanding, one which includes the slaves.

It should be noted that coherence of attitude provides a constant pressure to widen the consensus and eliminate arbitrary distinctions. In this connection it is useful to recall ancient attitudes toward foreigners, and the ways people used to think about "savages," "natives," and "Indians." Also, recall that infanticide used to be considered as acceptable as we consider abortion to be. There has been a change here in our moral attitudes, prompted, I suggest, largely by considerations of coherence of attitude.

Finally, I would like to say a few brief words about the limiting case of group morality, when the group has only one member; then, as it were, a person comes to an understanding with himself. In my view, a person can make inner judgments in relation to such an individual morality only about himself. A familiar form of pacifism is of this sort. Certain pacifists judge that it would be wrong of them to participate in killing, although they are not willing to make a similar judgment about others. Observe that such a pacifist is unwilling only to make *inner* moral judgments about others. Although he is unwilling to judge that those who do participate are wrong to do so, he is perfectly willing to say that it is a bad thing that they participate. There are of course many other examples of individual morality in this sense, when a person imposes standards on himself that he does not apply to others. The existence of such examples is further confirmation of the relativist thesis that I have presented.

My conclusion is that relativism can be formulated as an intelligible thesis, the thesis that morality derives from an implicit agreement and that moral judgments are in a logical sense made in relation to such an agreement. Such a theory helps to explain otherwise puzzling aspects of our own moral views,

in particular why we think that it is more important to avoid harm to others than to help others. The theory is also partially confirmed by what is, as far as I can tell, a previously unnoticed distinction between inner and non-inner moral judgments. Furthermore, traditional objections to implicit agreement theories can be met.[10]

Endnotes

[1] Bernard Williams, *Morality: An Introduction to Ethics* (New York, 1972), pp. 20–21.

[2] Thomas Nagel has observed that often, when we use the evaluative "ought to be" to say that something ought to be the case, we imply that someone ought to do something or ought to have done something about it. To take his example, we would not say that a certain hurricane ought not to have killed fifty people just on the ground that it was a terrible thing that the hurricane did so but we might say this if we had in mind that the deaths from the hurricane would not have occurred except for the absence of safety or evacuation procedures which the authorities ought to have provided.

[3] For the latter approach, see Thomas Nagel, *The Possibility of Altruism* (Oxford, 1970).

[4] See Donald Davidson, "Weakness of Will," in Joel Feinberg, ed. *Moral Concepts* (Oxford, 1969).

[5] R. M. Hare, *The Language of Morals* (Oxford, 1952): 164–68.

[6] Philippa Foot, "Abortion and the Doctrine of Double Effect," in James Rachels, ed. *Moral Problems* (New York, 1971).

[7] R. M. Hare, *The Language of Morals* and *Freedom and Reason* (Oxford, 1963).

[8] *The Language of Morals*, pp. 18–20, 168–69.

[9] Cf. Thomas Hobbes, *Leviathan* (Oxford, 1957, *inter alia*), pt. 1, chap. 14. "Of the First and Second Natural Laws, And of Contracts."

[10] Many people have given me good advice about the subjects discussed in this paper, which derives from a larger study of practical reasoning and morality. I am particularly indebted to Donald Davidson, Stephen Schiffer, William Alston, Fredrick Schick, Thomas Nagel, Walter Kaufmann, Peter Singer, Robert Audi, and the editors of the *Philosophical Review*.

Suggestions for Further Reading

Fishkin, James. *Beyond Subjective Morality.* Yale University, 1984.

Ladd, John, ed. *Ethical Relativism.* Wadsworth, 1973. A good collection of basic readings.

Mackie, J. L. *Ethics: Inventing Right and Wrong.* Penguin, 1976. A defense of relativism.

Stace, W. T. *The Concept of Morals.* Macmillan, 1937.

Sumner, William Graham. *Folkways.* Ginn & Company, 1906. A classic treatise in defense of ethical relativism.

Taylor, Paul. *Principles of Ethics.* Dickenson, 1975, Chapter 2.

Wellman, Carl. "The Ethical Implications of Cultural Relativity," *Journal of Philosophy,* LX, 1963.

Westermarck, Edward. *Ethical Relativity.* Humanities Press, 1960.

Williams, Bernard. *Morality.* Harper Torchbooks, 1972. Contains a good discussion of ethical relativism.

Williams, Bernard. *Ethics and the Limits of Philosophy.* Harvard University Press, 1985.

Wong, David. *Moral Relativity.* University of California Press, 1985. Defends a sophisticated version of ethical relativism, which has some objectivist elements.

Part III

Ethical Egoism, Altruism, and Evolution

Evaluate this statement: "Everyone is an egoist, for everyone always does what he or she wants to do, that is, that which will bring him or her the greatest amount of satisfaction." Is it true or false?

(FROM A STUDENT QUESTIONNAIRE)

Is egoism a consistent moral theory? Does it make sense? If so, is it an adequate ethical theory? Before we can answer these questions we need to make some careful distinctions and define our terms. First of all, there are at least four different types of egoism: psychological egoism, personal egoism, individual ethical egoism, and universal ethical egoism. These concepts may be roughly defined as follows:

1. Psychological egoism is the doctrine that everyone always does those acts that they per-ceive to be in their own best self-interest. That is, we always seek to maximize our own good and cannot be motivated by anything other than what we believe will promote our interests.

2. Personal egoism is the view that I *will* always serve my own best interest, regardless of what happens to anyone else.

3. Individual ethical egoism is the view that everyone *ought* to serve *my* best interest.

4. Universal ethical egoism is the view that everyone *ought* to do those acts that will serve their own best self-interest, even when it conflicts with the interests of others.

Note that psychological egoism is a *description* of human nature. It claims that we cannot do other than act from self-interested motivation, so that altruism, the theory that we can sometimes act in ways that put others' interests ahead of our own, is simply false. Since, following Kant, 'ought' implies 'can,' (that is, we are under no obligation to do what is impossible), it follows that we cannot be anything but ethical egoists of one sort or another. So ethical egoism seems to be implied by psychological egoism. Is it made inevitable by it?

In our first reading, a selection from his masterpiece in political theory, *Leviathan,* Thomas Hobbes treats people as psychological egoists who cannot obtain any of the basic goods because of their inherent fear and insecurity in an unregulated "state of nature" in which life is "solitary, poor, nasty, brutish, and short." We cannot relax our guard, for everyone constantly fears everyone else. Thus, the prudent person concludes that it really is in each of our self-interests to make a contract — to keep to a minimal morality of respecting human life, to keep covenants made, and to obey the laws of the society. This minimal morality, which Hobbes refers to as "The Laws of Nature," is nothing more than a set of maxims of prudence. In order to ensure that we all obey this covenant, Hobbes proposes a strong sovereign, or Leviathan, to impose severe penalties on those who disobey the laws, for "covenants, without the sword, are but words."

Hobbes's theory presupposes psychological egoism, but in our second reading Joel Feinberg examines four arguments in favor of psychological egoism and contends that none of them is successful. The four arguments are (a) the personal ownership argument, that "every action of mine is prompted by motives or desires or impulses which are *my* motives and not somebody else's,"

which leads to the conclusion that everyone always acts selfishly; (b) the hedonist argument, that we always feel satisfaction when we achieve our desires; (c) the self-deception argument, that the more we know of ourselves, the more we realize how selfish we are, even when we believe that we are acting disinterestedly; and (d) the moral education argument, that hedonistic motivation theory — namely, that we are essentially motivated by pain and pleasure or the anticipation of them — is the proper theory for making sense of education of the young. Feinberg argues that each of these arguments rests at best on minimal empirical evidence, and at worst on conceptual confusion. If Feinberg is correct, psychological egoism is either highly implausible or absurd.

We turn next to personal egoism. Unlike psychological egoism, personal egoism is not a description of human nature, but merely a statement of intention. It does not imply any of the other theories and is neutral between egoist and nonegoist ethical theories. Personal egoism may be most closely equated with selfishness, and it comes closest to *egotism,* the behavioral pattern in which one constantly draws attention to oneself. Egoists need not be egotists, but may be more subtle about their self-interestedness.

Individual ethical egoism is the view that everyone ought to serve *my* self-interest. That is, moral rightness is defined solely in terms of what is good for me, whether or not it is good for anyone else. Of course, each of us may make this claim for ourselves. Say, for example, that Aunt Ruth is an individual ethical egoist. So all moral rightness is defined in terms of what is good for Aunt Ruth. It would follow that whether or not a mother in India loves her child is morally irrelevant, for it has no effect on Aunt Ruth. Now that Aunt Ruth is dead, morality is dead, for it has no object. Interestingly enough, while individual ethical egoism seems implausible, it may be the central position of many people who define ethics as that which serves God's interests and pleases God. Be that as it may, as far as mere mortals are concerned, individual ethical egoism seems a partial and absurd theory. What makes anyone so special that all of us have an obligation to grant that person's interests sole or primary concern?

Universal ethical egoism is the theory that everyone ought always and only to serve his or her own self-interest. That is, everyone ought to do what will maximize one's own expected utility or bring about one's own happiness, even when it means harming others. This view has all the earmarks of a legitimate ethical theory. It is a universal theory, whereas individual egoism is not. It need not be egotistical (that is, self-consciously preoccupied with oneself), but is prudential and favors long-term interests over short-term ones. In its most sophisticated form it urges everyone to *try* to win in the game of life, and it recognizes that in order to do this, some compromises are necessary. Indeed, the universal egoist will admit that to some extent we must all give up a certain amount of freedom and cooperate with others to achieve our ends.

In our third reading, "Ultimate Principles and Ethical Egoism," Brian Medlin distinguishes between categorical and hypothetical egoism, and he argues that the latter is only an apparent egoism. That is, if the egoist claims that when individuals maximize their own utility we are all better off, then he is no longer an egoist, but instead a closet utilitarian who is citing a utilitarian reason for emphasizing self-interested reasons in acting. Medlin argues that ethical egoism is conceptually confused, for it enjoins mutually exclusive desires and advice (for example, both to help Tom and not to help Tom in the same situation). Given the soundness of this argument, which we may call the opposing advice argument, egoism is not even a coherent theory.

In his "In Defense of Egoism," Jesse Kalin argues against Medlin that ethical egoism is coherent, that it should not be equated with selfishness, and that it may be enlightened so that it includes friendship and civic-mindedness. He meets Medlin's objection to the opposing advice argument by using a sports model wherein both sides are supposed to try to win the game. He shows that we can believe that others have obligations without us wanting them to meet those obligations. For example, we may believe that a policeman has an obligation to give us a ticket for speeding but hope that he won't; or my opponent may have a three-move checkmate on me that the nature of the game "obligates" him to make, but I may hope that he won't see it and mate me. Kalin meets several other objections against ethical egoism and concludes that it is indeed a plausible theory. However, at the end of his article he notes several weaknesses of the theory. Ethical egoism cannot easily be made public, nor is the egoist able to engage in interpersonal reasoning. It seems to entail a private morality. Whereas it is in the egoist's interest that there be a public morality, it is not always in his or her interest to act according to that morality.

One question that arises in reading Kalin's article is how is it possible for the egoist to have deep or true friendships? How "enlightened" must the egoist be to maintain this sort of relationship? For deep friendship demands the kind of dispositions that proscribe harming the other, even when it is in one's interest to do so. But can egoism allow such altruism or interest in another? How significant are these problems? Is altruism necessarily immoral in an egoist theory? Or do values like friendship point to a certain paradox of egoism? Is it in my interest to have something that causes me to give up seeking solely (or primarily) my own interest?

A problem that Kalin does not mention, but that the reader will want to consider, is how one is to reconcile egoism with the idea of justice. For example, suppose bank manager Ortcutt can embezzle a million dollars and make off to another country, where he will enjoy himself for the rest of his life. However, taking this money means that hundreds of poor and elderly people will not have enough to support themselves and will suffer greatly. How would an ethical egoist justify this deed? Would he or she be successful?

Suppose the egoist admits that these acts would not be moral; thus, egoism is not a morally acceptable theory, and what follows then? The egoist may simply choose to be immoral, and ask why he or she should be moral all of the time. This issue will be taken up in Part X.

We complete this part of our study with two commissioned essays on the relation of ethics to evolution. In the second half of the nineteenth century, after the publication of Darwin's *Origin of the Species* (1859), philosophers like Herbert Spencer (1820–1903) adapted evolutionary ideas to ethics, arguing for an egoism based on the survival of the fittest. Views like this were labeled "social Darwinism." According to such views, life is a struggle in which natural forces produce progress. While individuals may exercise private charity, the State ought to stay out of the welfare business, for in intervening in these natural processes, it stands in the way of evolutionary progress.

Social Darwinism has come under severe attack as a harsh and inhumane ethical system that is not entailed by evolutionary thought. In our fifth reading, "Evolution and Ethics: The Sociobiological Approach," Michael Ruse argues that Spencer's evolutionism was misguided by both its Lamarckism and its idea of "progress." Ruse argues that evolution does not result in a progression of objective values, for objective values do not exist—there are only valuers. All values are subjective. As an evolutionary ethicist, Ruse argues that evolution has caused us to become altruistic and to have a tendency to adhere to basic moral principles in order to enhance our survival capacity.

Ruse argues that there are no foundations for ethics. We can't provide justifications for our moral beliefs (here he follows J. L. Mackie's account given in reading IX.1). Moral values don't exist—except in our minds. Nevertheless, Ruse rejects relativism. It is not up to us or to our culture to choose our moral principles. Evolution does that for us, and it serves us well.

In our final reading, "Prospects for an Evolutionary Ethics," Elliott Sober argues that while evolutionary theory can contribute to an explanation of ethics, it has limited value in justifying our ethical principles. Ethics has an autonomy of its own that evolutionary ethicists like E. O. Wilson and Michael Ruse fail to take adequately into consideration.

Let us turn now to our readings.

III.1 *The Leviathan*

Thomas Hobbes

Thomas Hobbes (1588–1679), a famous English philosopher, is known primarily for his masterpiece in political theory, *Leviathan,* from which this selection is taken. He developed a moral and political theory based on psychological egoism. In this reading, Hobbes argues that people are all egoists who cannot obtain any of the basic goods because of their inherent fear and insecurity in an unregulated "state of nature" in which life is "solitary, poor, nasty, brutish, and short." We cannot relax our guard, for everyone constantly fears everyone else. Thus the prudent person concludes that it really is in each of our self-interests to make a contract—to keep to a minimal morality of respecting human life, to keep covenants made, and to obey the laws of the society. This minimal morality, which Hobbes refers to as "The Laws of Nature," is nothing more than a set of maxims of prudence. In order to ensure that we all obey this covenant, Hobbes proposes a strong sovereign, or Leviathan, to impose several penalties on those who disobey the laws, for "covenants, without the sword, are but words."

Of the Natural Condition of Mankind as Concerning Their Felicity, and Misery

Nature hath made men so equal, in the faculties of the body, and mind; as that though there be found one man sometimes manifestly stronger in body, or of quicker mind than another; yet when all is reckoned together, the difference between man, and man, is not so considerable, as that one man can thereupon claim to himself any benefit, to which another may not pretend, as well as he. For as to the strength of body, the weakest has strength enough to kill the strongest, either by secret machination, or by confederacy with others, that are in the same danger with himself.

And as to the faculties of the mind, setting aside the arts grounded upon words, and especially that skill of proceeding upon general, and infallible rules, called science; which very few have, and but in few things; as being not a native faculty, born with us; nor attained, as prudence, while we look after somewhat else, I find yet a greater equality amongst men, than that of strength. For prudence, is but experience; which equal time, equally bestows on all men, in those things they equally apply themselves unto. That which may perhaps make such equality incredible, is but a vain conceit of one's own wisdom, which almost all men think they have in a greater degree, than the vulgar; that is, than all men but themselves, and a few others, whom by fame, or for concurring with themselves, they approve. For such is the nature of men, that howsoever they may acknowledge many others to be more witty, or more eloquent, or more learned; yet they will hardly believe there be many so wise as themselves; for they see their own wit at hand, and other men's at a distance. But this proveth rather that men are in that point equal, than unequal. For there is not ordinarily a greater sign of the equal distribution of any thing, than that every man is contented with his share.

From this equality of ability, ariseth equality of hope in the attaining of our ends. And therefore if any two men desire the same thing, which nevertheless they cannot both enjoy, they become enemies; and in the way to their end, which is principally

From *Leviathan,* 1651.

their own conservation, and sometimes their delectation only, endeavour to destroy, or subdue one another. And from hence it comes to pass, that where an invader hath no more to fear, than another man's single power; if one plant, sow, build, or possess a convenient seat, others may probably be expected to come prepared with forces united, to dispossess, and deprive him, not only of the fruit of his labour, but also of his life, or liberty. And the invader again is in the like danger of another.

And from this diffidence of one another, there is no way for any man to secure himself, so reasonable, as anticipation; that is, by force, or wiles, to master the persons of all men he can, so long, till he see no other power great enough to endanger him: and this is no more than his own conservation requireth, and is generally allowed. Also because there be some, that taking pleasure in contemplating their own power in the acts of conquest, which they pursue farther than their security requires; if others, that otherwise would be glad to be at ease within modest bounds, should not by invasion increase their power, they would not be able, long time, by standing only on their defence, to subsist. And by consequence, such augmentation of dominion over men being necessary to a man's conservation, it ought to be allowed him.

Again, men have no pleasure, but on the contrary a great deal of grief, in keeping company, where there is no power able to over-awe them all. For every man looketh that his companion should value him, at the same rate he sets upon himself: and upon all signs of contempt, or undervaluing, naturally endeavours, as far as he dares, (which amongst them that have no common power to keep them in quiet, is far enough to make them destroy each other), to extort a greater value from his condemners, by damage; and from others, by the example.

So that in the nature of man, we find three principal causes of quarrel. First, competition; secondly, diffidence; thirdly, glory.

The first, maketh men invade for gain; the second, for safety; and the third, for reputation. The first use violence, to make themselves masters of other men's persons, wives, children, and cattle; the second, to defend them; the third, for trifles, as a word, a smile, a different opinion, and any other sign of undervalue, either direct in their persons, or by reflection in their kindred, their friends, their nation, their profession, or their name.

Hereby it is manifest, that during the time men live without a common power to keep them all in awe, they are in that condition which is called war; and such a war, as is of every man, against every man. For WAR, consisteth not in battle only, or the act of fighting; but in a tract of time, wherein the will to contend by battle is sufficiently known: and therefore the notion of *time,* is to be considered in the nature of war; as it is in the nature of weather. For as the nature of foul weather, lieth not in the shower or two of rain; but in an inclination thereto of many days together: so the nature of war, consisteth not in actual fighting; but in the known disposition thereto, during all the time there is no assurance to the contrary. All other time is PEACE.

Whatsoever therefore is consequent to a time of war, where every man is enemy to every man; the same is consequent to the time, wherein men live without other security, than what their own strength, and their own invention shall furnish them withal. In such condition, there is no place for industry; because the fruit thereof is uncertain: and consequently no culture of the earth; no navigation, nor use of the commodities that may be imported by sea; no commodious building; no instruments of moving, and removing, such things as require much force; no knowledge of the face of the earth; no account of time; no arts; no letters; no society; and which is worst of all, continual fear, and danger of violent death; and the life of man, solitary, poor, nasty, brutish, and short.

It may seem strange to some man, that has not well weighed these things; that nature should thus dissociate, and render men apt to invade, and destroy one another: and he may therefore, not trusting to this inference, made from the passions, desire perhaps to have the same confirmed by experience. Let him therefore consider with himself, when taking a journey, he arms himself, and seeks to go well accompanied; when going to sleep, he locks his doors; when even in his house he locks his chests; and this when he knows there be laws, and public officers, armed, to revenge all injuries shall be done him; what opinion he has of his fellow-subjects, when he rides armed; of his fellow citizens, when he locks his doors; and of his children, and servants, when he locks his chests. Does he not there as much accuse mankind by his actions, as I do by my words? But neither of us accuse man's nature in it. The desires, and other passions of man, are in themselves no sin. No more are the actions, that proceed from those passions, till they know a law that forbids them: which till laws be made they cannot know: nor can any law be made, till they have agreed upon the person that shall make it.

It may peradventure be thought, there was never such a time, nor condition of war as this; and I believe it was never generally so, over all the world: but there are many places, where they live so now. For the savage people in many places of America, except the government of small families, the concord whereof dependeth on natural lust, have no government at all; and live at this day in that brutish manner, as I said before. Howsoever, it may be perceived what manner of life there would be, where there were no common power to fear, by the manner of life, which men that have formerly lived under a peaceful government, use to degenerate into, in a civil war.

But though there had never been any time, wherein particular men were in a condition of war one against another; yet in all times, kings, and persons of sovereign authority, because of their independency, are in continual jealousies, and in the state and posture of gladiators; having their weapons pointing, and their eyes fixed on one another; that is, their forts, garrisons, and guns upon the frontiers of their kingdoms; and continual spies upon their neighbours; which is a posture of war. But because they uphold thereby, the industry of their subjects; there does not follow from it, that misery, which accompanies the liberty of particular men.

To this war of every man, against every man, this also is consequent; that nothing can be unjust. The notions of right and wrong, justice and injustice have there no place. Where there is no common power, there is no law: where no law, no injustice. Force, and fraud, are in war the two cardinal virtues. Justice, and injustice are none of the faculties neither of the body, nor mind. If they were, they might be in a man that were alone in the world, as well as his senses, and passions. They are qualities, that relate to men in society, not in solitude. It is consequent also to the same condition, that there be no propriety, no dominion, no *mine* and *thine* distinct; but only that to be every man's, that he can get; and for so long, as he can keep it. And thus much for the ill condition, which man by mere nature is actually placed in; though with a possibility to come out of it, consisting partly in the passions, partly in his reason.

The passions that incline men to peace, are fear of death; desire of such things as are necessary to commodious living; and a hope by their industry to obtain them. And reason suggesteth convenient articles of peace, upon which men may be drawn to agreement. These articles, are they, which otherwise are called the Laws of Nature: whereof I shall speak more particularly, in the two following chapters.

Of the First and Second Natural Laws, and of Contracts

The right of nature, which writers commonly call *jus naturale,* is the liberty each man hath, to use his own power, as he will himself, for the preservation of his own nature; that is to say, of his own life; and consequently, of doing any thing, which in his own judgment, and reason, he shall conceive to be the aptest means thereunto.

By LIBERTY, is understood, according to the proper signification of the word, the absence of external impediments: which impediments, may oft take away part of a man's power to do what he would; but cannot hinder him from using the power left him, according as his judgment, and reason shall dictate to him.

A LAW OF NATURE, *les naturalis,* is a precept or general rule, found out by reason, by which a man is forbidden to do that, which is destructive of his life, or taketh away the means of preserving the same; and to omit that, by which he thinketh it may be best preserved. For though they that speak of this subject, use to confound *jus,* and *lex, right* and *law:* yet they ought to be distinguished; because RIGHT, consisteth in liberty to do, or to forbear; whereas LAW, determineth, and bindeth to one of them: so that law, and right, differ as much, as obligation, and liberty; which in one and the same matter are inconsistent.

And because the condition of man, as hath been declared in the precedent chapter, is a condition of war of every one against every one; in which case every one is governed by his own reason; and there is nothing he can make use of, that may not be a help unto him, in preserving his life against his enemies; it followeth, that in such a condition, every man has a right to every thing; even to one another's body. And therefore, as long as this natural right of every man to every thing endureth, there can be no security to any man, how strong or wise soever he be, of living out the time, which nature ordinarily alloweth men to live. And consequently it is a precept, or general rule of reason, *that every man, ought to endeavour peace, as far as he has hope of obtaining it; and when he cannot obtain it, that he may seek, and use, all helps, and advantages of war.* The first branch of which rule, containeth the first, and fundamental law of nature; which is, *to seek peace, and follow it.* The second, the sum of the right of nature; which is, *by all means we can, to defend ourselves.*

From this fundamental law of nature, by which men are commanded to endeavour peace, is derived this second law; *that a man be willing, when others are so too, as far-forth, as for peace, and defence of himself he shall think it necessary, to lay down this right to all things; and be contented with so much liberty against other men, as he would allow other men against himself.* For as long as every man holdeth this right, of doing any thing he liketh; so long are all men in the condition of war. But if other men will not lay down their right, as well as he; then there is no reason for any one, to divest himself of his: for that were to expose himself to prey, which no man is bound to, rather than to dispose himself to peace. This is that law of the Gospel; *whatsoever you require that others should do to you, that do ye to them.* And that law of all men, *quod tibi fieri non vis, alteri ne feceris.* [1]

To *lay down* a man's *right* to any thing, is to *divest* himself of the *liberty,* of hindering another of the benefit of his own right to the same. For he that renounceth, or passeth away his right, giveth not to any other man a right which he had not before; because there is nothing to which every man had not right by nature: but only standeth out of his way, that he may enjoy his own original right, without hindrance from him; not without hindrance from another. So that the effect which redoundeth to one man, by another man's defect of right, is but so much diminution of impediments to the use of his own right original.

Right is laid aside, either by simply renouncing it; or by transferring it to another. By *simply* RENOUNCING; when he cares not to whom the benefit thereof redoundeth. By TRANSFERRING; when he intendeth the benefit thereof to some certain person, or persons. And when a man hath in either manner abandoned, or granted away his right; then is he said to be OBLIGED, or BOUND, not to hinder those, to whom such right is granted, or abandoned, from the benefit of it: and that he *ought,* and it is his DUTY, not to make void that voluntary act of his own: and that such hindrance is INJUSTICE, and INJURY, as being *sine jure.* [2] The right being before renounced, or transferred. So that *injury,* or *injustice,* in the controversies of the world, is somewhat like to that, which in the disputations of scholars is called *absurdity.* For as it is there called an absurdity, to contradict what one maintained in the beginning: so in the world, it is called injustice, and injury, voluntarily to undo that, which from the beginning he had voluntarily done. The way by which a man either simply renounceth, or transferreth his right, is a declaration, or signification, by some voluntary and sufficient sign, or signs, that he doth so renounce, or transfer; or hath so renounced, or transferred the same, to him that accepteth it. And these signs are either words only, or actions only; or, as it happeneth most often, both words, and actions. And the same are the BONDS, by which men are bound, and obliged: bonds, that have their strength, not from their own nature, for nothing is more easily broken than a man's word, but from fear of some evil consequence upon the rupture.

Whensoever a man transferreth his right, or renounceth it; it is either in consideration of some right reciprocally transferred to himself; or for some other good he hopeth for thereby. For it is a voluntary act: and of the voluntary acts of every man, the object is some *good to himself.* And therefore there be some rights, which no man can be understood by any words, or other signs, to have abandoned, or transferred. At first a man cannot lay down the right of resisting them, that assault him by force, to take away his life; because he cannot be understood to aim thereby, at any good to himself. The same may be said of wounds, and chains, and imprisonment; both because there is no benefit consequent to such patience; as there is to the patience of suffering another to be wounded, or imprisoned: as also because a man cannot tell, when he seeth men proceed against him by violence, whether they intend his death or not. And lastly the motive, and end for which this renouncing, and transferring of right is introduced, is nothing else but the security of a man's person, in his life, and in the means of so preserving life, as not to be weary of it. And therefore if a man by words, or other signs, seem to despoil himself of the end, for which those signs were intended; he is not to be understood as if he meant it, or that it was his will; but that he was ignorant of how such words and actions were to be interpreted.

The mutual transferring of right, is that which men call CONTRACT.

There is difference between transferring of right to the thing; and transferring, or tradition, that is delivery of the thing itself. For the thing may be delivered together with the translation of the right; as in buying and selling with ready-money; or exchange of goods, or lands: and it may be delivered some time after.

Again, one of the contractors, may deliver the thing contracted for on his part, and leave the other to perform his part at some determinate time after, and in the mean time be trusted; and then the contract on his part is called PACT, or COVENANT: or both parts may contract now, to perform hereafter: in which cases, he that is to perform in time to come, being trusted, his performance is called *keeping of promise,* or faith; and the failing of performance, if it be voluntary, *violation of faith.*

When the transferring of right, is not mutual: but one of the parties transferreth in hope to gain thereby friendship, or service from another, or from his friends; or in hope to gain the reputation of charity, or magnanimity; or to deliver his mind from the pain of compassion; or in hope of reward in heaven, this is not contract, but GIFT, FREE-GIFT, GRACE: which words signify one and the same thing.

Signs of contract, are either *express,* or *by inference.* Express, are words spoken with understanding of what they signify: and such words are either of the time *present,* or *past;* as, *I give, I grant, I have given, I have granted, I will that this be yours:* or of the future; as, *I will give, I will grant:* which words of the future are called PROMISE.

If a covenant be made, wherein neither of the parties perform presently, but trust one another; in the condition of mere nature, which is a condition of war of every man against every man, upon any reasonable suspicion, it is void: but if there be a common power set over them both, with right and force sufficient to compel performance, it is not void. For he that performeth first, has no assurance the other will perform after; because the bonds of words are too weak to bridle men's ambition, avarice, anger, and other passions, without the fear of some coercive power; which in the condition of mere nature, where all men are equal, and judges of the justness of their own fears, cannot possibly be supposed. And therefore he which performeth first, does but betray himself to his enemy; contrary to the right, he can never abandon, of defending his life, and means of living.

But in a civil estate, where there is a power set up to constrain those that would otherwise violate their faith, that fear is no more reasonable: and for that cause, he which by the covenant is to perform first, is obliged so to do.

The cause of fear, which maketh such a covenant invalid, must be always something arising after the covenant made; as some new fact, or other sign of the will not to perform: else it cannot make the covenant void. For that which could not hinder a man from promising, ought not to be admitted as a hindrance of performing.

Of Other Laws of Nature

From that law of nature, by which we are obliged to transfer to another, such rights, as being retained, hinder the peace of mankind, there followeth a third; which is this, *that men perform their covenants made:* without which, covenants are in vain, and but empty words; and the right of all men to all things remaining, we are still in the condition of war.

And in this law of nature, consisteth the fountain and original of JUSTICE. For where no covenant hath preceded, there hath no right been transferred, and every man has right to every thing; and consequently, no action can be unjust. But when a covenant is made, then to break it is *unjust:* and the definition of INJUSTICE, is no other than *the nonperformance of covenant.* And whatsoever is not unjust, is *just.*

But because covenants of mutual trust, where there is a fear of nonperformance on either part, as hath been said in the former chapter, are invalid; though the original of justice be the making of covenants; yet injustice actually there can be none, till the cause of such fear be taken away; which while men are in the natural condition of war, cannot be done. Therefore before the names of just, and unjust can have place, there must be some coercive power, to compel men equally to the performance of their covenants, by the terror of some punishment, greater than the benefit they expect by the breach of their covenant; and to make good that propriety, which by mutual contract men acquire, in recompense of the universal right they abandon: and such power there is none before the erection of a commonwealth. And this is also to be gathered out of the ordinary definition of justice in the Schools: for they say, that *justice is the constant will of giving to every man his own.* And therefore where there is no *own,* that is, no propriety, there is no injustice; and where there is no coercive power erected, that is, where there is no commonwealth, there is no propriety; all men having right to all things: therefore where there is no commonwealth, there nothing is unjust. So that the nature of justice, consisteth in keeping of valid covenants: but the validity of covenants begins not but with the constitution of a civil power, sufficient to compel men to keep them: and then it is also that propriety begins.

Whatsoever is done to a man, conformable to his own will signified to the doer, is no injury to him. For if he that doeth it, hath not passed away his original right to do what he please, by some antecedent covenant, there is no breach of covenant; and therefore no injury done him. And if he have; then his will to have it done being signified, is a release of that covenant: and so again there is no injury done him.

Justice of actions, is by writers divided into *commutative,* and *distributive:* and the former they say consisteth in proportion arithmetical; the latter in proportion geometrical. Commutative therefore, they place in the equality of value of the things contracted for; and distributive, in the distribution of equal benefit, to men of equal merit. As if it were injustice to sell dearer than we buy; or to give more to a man than he merits. The value of all things contracted for, is measured by the appetite of the contractors: and therefore the just value, is that which they be contented to give. And merit, besides that which is by covenant, where the performance on one part, meriteth the performance of the other part, and falls under justice commutative, not distributive, is not due by justice; but is rewarded of grace only. And therefore this distinction, in the sense wherein it useth to be expounded, is not right. To speak properly, commutative justice is the justice

of a contractor: that is, a performance of covenant, in buying, and selling; hiring, and letting to hire; lending, and borrowing; exchanging, bartering, and other acts of contract.

And distributive justice, the justice of an arbitrator; that is to say, the act of defining what is just. Wherein, being trusted by them that make him arbitrator, if he perform his trust, he is said to distribute to every man his own: and this is indeed just distribution, and may be called, though improperly, distributive justice; but more properly equity; which also is a law of nature, as shall be shown in due place.

As justice dependeth on antecedent covenant; so does GRATITUDE depend on antecedent grace; that is to say, antecedent free gift: and is the fourth law of nature; which may be conceived in this form, *that a man which receiveth benefit from another of mere grace, endeavour that he which giveth it, have no reasonable cause to repent him of his good will.* For no man giveth, but with intention of good to himself; because gift is voluntary; and of all voluntary acts, the object is to every man his own good; of which if men see they shall be frustrated, there will be no beginning of benevolence, or trust; nor consequently of mutual help; nor of reconciliation of one man to another; and therefore they are to remain still in the condition of *war;* which is contrary to the first and fundamental law of nature, which commandeth men to *seek peace.* The breach of this law, is called *ingratitude;* and hath the same relation to grace, that injustice hath to obligation by covenant.

And because, though men be never so willing to observe these laws, there may nevertheless arise questions concerning a man's action; first, whether it were done, or not done; secondly, if done, whether against the law, or not against the law; the former whereof, is called a question *of fact;* the latter a question *of right,* therefore unless the parties to the question, covenant mutually to stand to the sentence of another, they are as far from peace as ever. This other to whose sentence they submit is called an ARBITRATOR. And therefore it is of the law of nature, *that they that are at controversy, submit their right to the judgment of an arbitrator.*

And seeing every man is presumed to do all things in order to his own benefit, no man is a fit arbitrator in his own cause; and if he were never so fit; yet equity allowing to each party equal benefit, if one be admitted to the judge, the other is to be admitted also; and so the controversy, that is, the cause of war, remains, against the law of nature.

For the same reason no man in any cause ought to be received for arbitrator, to whom greater profit, or honour, or pleasure apparently ariseth out of the victory of one party, than of the other: for he hath taken, though an unavoidable bribe, yet a bribe; and no man can be obliged to trust him. And thus also the controversy, and the condition of war remaineth, contrary to the law of nature.

And in a controversy of *fact*, the judge being to give no more credit to one, than to the other, if there be no other arguments, must give credit to a third; or to a third and fourth; or more: for else the question is undecided, and left to force, contrary to the law of nature.

These are the laws of nature, dictating peace, for a means of the conservation of men in multitudes; and which only concern the doctrine of civil society. There be other things tending to the destruction of particular men; as drunkenness, and all other parts of intemperance; which may therefore also be reckoned amongst those things which the law of nature hath forbidden; but are not necessary to be mentioned, nor are pertinent enough to this place.

And though this may seem too subtle a deduction of the laws of nature, to be taken notice of by all men; whereof the most part are too busy in getting food, and the rest too negligent to understand; yet to leave all men inexcusable, they have been contracted into one easy sum, intelligible even to the meanest capacity; and that is, *Do not that to another, which thou wouldest not have done to thyself;* which sheweth him, that he has no more to do in learning the laws of nature, but, when weighing the actions of other men with his own, they seem too heavy, to put them into the other part of the balance, and his own into their place, that his own passions, and self-love, may add nothing to the weight; and then there is none of these laws of nature that will not appear unto him very reasonable.

The laws of nature oblige *in foro interno*,[3] that is to say, they bind to a desire they should take place: but *in foro externo*,[4] that is, to the putting them in act, not always. For he that should be modest, and tractable, and perform all he promises, in such time, and place, where no man else should do so, should

but make himself a prey to others, and procure his own certain ruin, contrary to the ground of all laws of nature, which tend to nature's preservation. And again, he that having sufficient security, that others shall observe the same laws towards him, observes them not himself, seeketh not peace, but war; and consequently the destruction of his nature by violence.

And whatsoever laws bind *in foro interno,* may be broken, not only by a fact contrary to the law, but also by a fact according to it, in case a man think it contrary. For though his action in this case, be according to the law; yet his purpose was against the law; which, where the obligation is *in foro interno,* is a breach.

The laws of nature are immutable and eternal; for injustice, ingratitude, arrogance, pride, inequity, acceptance of persons, and the rest, can never be made lawful. For it can never be that war shall preserve life, and peace destroy it.

The same laws, because they oblige only to a desire, and endeavour, I mean an unfeigned and constant endeavour, are easy to be observed. For in that they require nothing but endeavour, he that endeavoureth their performance, fulfilleth them; and he that fulfilleth the law, is just.

And the science of them, is the true and only moral philosophy. For moral philosophy is nothing else but the science of what is *good*, and *evil,* in the conversation, and society of mankind. *Good,* and *evil,* are names that signify our appetites, and aversions; which in different tempers, customs, and doctrines of men, are different: and divers men, differ not only in their judgment, on the senses of what is pleasant, and unpleasant to the taste, smell, hearing, touch, and sight; but also of what is conformable, or disagreeable to reason, in the actions of common life. Nay, the same man, in divers times, differs from himself; and one time praiseth, that is, calleth good, what another time he dispraiseth, and calleth evil: from whence arise disputes, controversies, and at last war. And therefore so long as a man is in the condition of mere nature, which is a condition of war, as private appetite is the measure of good, and evil: and consequently all men agree on this, that peace is good, and therefore also the way, or means of peace, which, as I have shewed before, are *justice, gratitude, modesty, equity, mercy,* and the rest of the laws of nature, are good; that is to say;

moral virtues; and their contrary *vices,* evil. Now the science of virtue and vice, is moral philosophy; and therefore the true doctrine of the laws of nature, is the true moral philosophy. But the writers of moral philosophy, though they acknowledge the same virtues and vices; yet not seeing wherein consisted their goodness; nor that they come to be praised, as the means of peaceable, sociable, and comfortable living, place them in a mediocrity of passions: as if not the cause, but the degree of daring, made fortitude; or not the cause, but the quantity of a gift, made liberality.

These dictates of reason, men used to call by the name of laws, but improperly: for they are but conclusions, of theorems concerning that conduceth to the conservation and defence of themselves; whereas law, properly, is the word of him, that by right hath command over others. But yet if we consider the same theorems, as delivered in the word of God, that by right commandeth all things; then are they properly called laws.

Of the Causes, Generation, and Definition of a Commonwealth

The final cause, end, or design of men, who naturally love liberty, and dominion over others, in the introduction of that restraint upon themselves, in which we see them live in commonwealths, is the foresight of their own preservation, and of a more contented life thereby; that is to say, of getting themselves out from that miserable condition of war, which is necessarily consequent . . . to the natural passions of men, when there is no visible power to keep them in awe, and tie them by fear of punishment to the performance of their covenants, and observation of those laws of nature set down in the fourteenth and fifteenth chapters.

For the laws of nature, as *justice, equity, modesty, mercy,* and, in sum, *doing to others, as we would be done to,* of themselves, without the terror of some power, to cause them to be observed, are contrary to our natural passions, that carry us to partiality, pride, revenge, and the like. And covenants, without the sword, are but words, and of no strength to secure a man at all. Therefore notwithstanding the laws of

nature, which every one hath then kept, when he has the will to keep them, when he can do it safely, if there be no power erected, or not great enough for our security; every man will, and may lawfully rely on his own strength and art, for caution against all other men. And in all places, where men have lived by small families, to rob and spoil one another, has been a trade, and so far from being reputed against the law of nature, that the greater spoils they gained, the greater was their honour; and men observed no other laws therein, but the laws of honour; that is, to abstain from cruelty, leaving to men their lives, and instruments of husbandry. And as small families did then; so now do cities and kingdoms which are but greater families, for their own security, enlarge their dominions, upon all pretences of danger, and fear of invasion, or assistance that may be given to invaders, and endeavour as much as they can, to subdue, or weaken their neighbours, by open force, and secret arts, for want of other caution, justly; and are remembered for it in after ages with honour.

It is true, that certain living creatures, as bees, and ants, live sociably one with another, which are therefore by Aristotle numbered amongst political creatures; and yet have no other direction, than their particular judgments and appetites; nor speech, whereby one of them can signify to another, what he thinks expedient for the common benefit: and therefore some man may perhaps desire to know, why mankind cannot do the same. To which I answer,

First, that men are continually in competition for honour and dignity, which these creatures are not; and consequently amongst men there ariseth on that ground, envy and hated, and finally war; but amongst these not so.

Secondly, that amongst these creatures, the common good differeth not from the private; and being by nature inclined to their private, they procure thereby the common benefit. But man, whose joy consisteth in comparing himself with other men, can relish nothing but what is eminent.

Thirdly, that these creatures, having not, as man, the use of reason, do not see, nor think they see any fault, in the administration of their common business; whereas amongst men, there are very many, that think themselves wiser, and abler to govern the public, better than the rest; and these strive to reform and innovate, one this way, another that way; and thereby bring it into distraction and civil war.

Fourthly, that these creatures, though they have some use of voice, in making known to one another their desires, and other affections; yet they want that art of words, by which some men can represent to others, that which is good, in the likeness of evil; and evil, in the likeness of good; and augment, or diminish the apparent greatness of good and evil; discontenting men, and troubling their peace at their pleasure.

Fifthly, irrational creatures cannot distinguish between *injury,* and *damage;* and therefore as long as they be at ease, they are not offended with their fellows: whereas man is then most troublesome, when he is most at ease: for then it is that he loves to shew his wisdom, and control the actions of them that govern the commonwealth.

Lastly, the agreement of these creatures is natural; that of men, is by covenant only, which is artificial: and therefore it is no wonder if there be somewhat else required, besides covenant, to make their agreement constant and lasting; which is a common power, to keep them in awe, and to direct their actions to the common benefit.

The only way to erect such a common power, as may be able to defend them from the invasion of foreigners, and the injuries of one another, and thereby to secure them in such sort, as that by their own industry, and by the fruits of the earth, they may nourish themselves and live contentedly; is, to confer all their power and strength upon one man, or upon one assembly of men, that may reduce all their wills, by plurality of voices, unto one will: which is as much as to say, to appoint one man, or assembly of men, to bear their person; and every one to own, and acknowledge himself to be author of whatsoever he that so beareth their person, shall act, or cause to be acted, in those things which concern the common peace and safety; and therein to submit their wills, every one to his will, and their judgments, to his judgment. This is more than consent, or concord; it is a real unity of them all, in one and the same person, made by covenant of every man with every man, in such manner, as if every man should say to every man, *I authorize and give up my right of governing myself, to this man, or to this assembly of men, on this condition, that thou give up thy right to him, and authorize all his actions in like manner.* This done, the multitude so united in one person, is called a COMMONWEALTH, in Latin CIVITAS. This is the generation of the great LEVIATHAN, or rather, to speak more reverently, of that *mortal god,* to which we owe under the *immortal God,* our peace and defence. For by this authority, given him by every particular man in the commonwealth, he hath the use of so much power and strength conferred on him, that by terror thereof, he is enabled to perform the wills of them all, to peace at home, and mutual aid against their enemies abroad. And in him consisteth the essence of the commonwealth; which, to define it, *is one person, of whose acts a great multitude, by mutual covenants one with another, have made themselves every one the author, to the end he may use the strength and means of them all, as he shall think expedient, for their peace and common defence.*

And he that carrieth this person, is called SOVEREIGN, and said to have *sovereign power;* and every one besides, his SUBJECT.

Endnotes

[1] ["What you do not want done to you, do not do to others." — Ed. note.]

[2] [that is, without right. — Ed. note.]

[3] [literally, "in the internal forum" — that is, in a person's mind or conscience. — Ed. note.]

[4] [literally, "in the external forum" — that is, in the public world of action. — Ed. note.]

III.2 *Psychological Egoism*

JOEL FEINBERG

Joel Feinberg is professor of philosophy at the University of Arizona and the author of several works in moral and legal theory. Hobbes's theory presupposes psychological egoism, but in this article Feinberg examines four arguments in favor of psychological egoism and contends that none of them is successful. The four arguments are (1) the personal ownership argument: every action of mine is prompted by motives or desires or impulses that are my motives and not somebody else's, which leads to the conclusion that everyone always acts selfishly; (2) the hedonist argument: we always feel satisfaction when we achieve our desires; (3) the self-deception argument: the more we know of ourselves, the more we realize how selfish we are, even when we believe that we are acting disinterestedly; and (4) hedonistic motivation theory: proclaimed by its proponents as the proper theory for making sense of education of the young. Feinberg argues that each of these arguments rests at best on minimal empirical evidence, and at worst on conceptual confusion.

A. *The Theory*

1. "Psychological egoism" is the name given to a theory widely held by ordinary people, and at one time almost universally accepted by political economists, philosophers, and psychologists, according to which all human actions when properly understood can be seen to be motivated by selfish desires. More precisely, psychological egoism is the doctrine that the only thing anyone is capable of desiring or pursuing ultimately (as an end in itself) is his *own* self-interest. No psychological egoist denies that people sometimes do desire things other than their own welfare — the happiness of other people, for example; but all psychological egoists insist that people are capable of desiring the happiness of others only when they take it to be a *means* to their own happiness. In short, purely altruistic and benevolent actions and desires do not exist; but people sometimes appear to be acting unselfishly and disin-

terestedly when they take the interests of others to be means to the promotion of their own self-interest.

2. This theory is called *psychological* egoism to indicate that it is not a theory about what *ought* to be the case, but rather about what, as a matter of fact, *is* the case. That is, the theory claims to be a description of psychological facts, not a prescription of ethical ideals. It asserts, however, not merely that all men do as a contingent matter of fact "put their own interests first," but also that they are capable of nothing else, human nature being what it is. Universal selfishness is not just an accident or a coincidence on this view; rather, it is an unavoidable consequence of psychological laws.

The theory is to be distinguished from another doctrine, so-called "ethical egoism," according to which all people *ought* to pursue their own well-being. This doctrine, being a prescription of what *ought* to be the case, makes no claim to be a psychological theory of human motives; hence the word "ethical" appears in its name to distinguish it from *psychological* egoism.

3. There are a number of types of motives and desires which might reasonably be called "egoistic" or "selfish," and corresponding to each of them is a

possible version of psychological egoism. Perhaps the most common version of the theory is that apparently held by Jeremy Bentham.[1] According to this version, all persons have only one ultimate motive in all their voluntary behavior and that motive is a selfish one; more specifically, it is one particular kind of selfish motive — namely, a desire for one's own *pleasure*. According to this version of the theory, "the only kind of ultimate desire is the desire to get or to prolong pleasant experiences, and to avoid or to cut short unpleasant experiences for oneself."[2] This form of psychological egoism is often given the cumbersome name — *psychological egoistic hedonism*.

B. *Prima Facie Reasons in Support of the Theory*

4. Psychological egoism has seemed plausible to many people for a variety of reasons, of which the following are typical:

a. "Every action of mine is prompted by motives or desires or impulses which are *my* motives and not somebody else's. This fact might be expressed by saying that whenever I act I am always pursuing my own ends or trying to satisfy my own desires. And from this we might pass on to — 'I am always pursuing something for myself or seeking my own satisfaction.' Here is what seems like a proper description of a man acting selfishly, and if the description applies to all actions of all men, then it follows that all men in all their actions are selfish."[3]

b. It is a truism that when a person gets what he wants he characteristically feels pleasure. This has suggested to many people that what we really want in every case is our own pleasure, and that we pursue other things only as a means.

c. *Self-Deception.* Often we deceive ourselves into thinking that we desire something fine or noble when what we really want is to be thought well of by others or to be able to congratulate ourselves, or to be able to enjoy the pleasures of a good conscience. It is a well-known fact that people tend to conceal their true motives from themselves by camouflaging them with words like "virtue," "duty," etc. Since we are so often misled concerning both our own real motives and the real motives of others, is it not reasonable to suspect that we might *always* be deceived

when we think motives disinterested and altruistic? Indeed, it is a simple matter to explain away all allegedly unselfish motives: "Once the conviction that selfishness is universal finds root in a person's mind, it is very likely to burgeon out in a thousand corroborating generalizations. It will be discovered that a friendly smile is really only an attempt to win an approving nod from a more or less gullible recording angel; that a charitable deed is, for its performer, only an opportunity to congratulate himself on the good fortune or the cleverness that enables him to be charitable; that a public benefaction is just plain good business advertising. It will emerge that gods are worshipped only because they indulge men's selfish fears, or tastes, or hopes; that the 'golden rule' is no more than an eminently sound success formula; that social and political codes are created and subscribed to only because they serve to restrain other men's egoism as much as one's own, morality being only a "special sort of 'racket' or intrigue using weapons of persuasion in place of bombs and machine guns. Under this interpretation of human nature, the categories of commercialism replace those of disinterested service and the spirit of the horse trader broods over the face of the earth."[4]

d. *Moral Education.* Morality, good manners, decency, and other virtues must be teachable. Psychological egoists often notice that moral education and the inculcation of manners usually utilize what Bentham calls the "sanctions of pleasure and pain."[5] Children are made to acquire the civilizing virtues only by the method of enticing rewards and painful punishments. Much the same is true of the history of the race. People in general have been inclined to behave well only when it is made plain to them that there is "something in it for them." Is it not then highly probable that just such a mechanism of human motivation as Bentham describes must be presupposed by our methods of moral education?

C. *Critique of Psychological Egoism: Confusions in the Arguments*

5. *Nonempirical Character of the Arguments.* If the arguments of the psychological egoist consisted for the most part of carefully acquired empirical evidence (well-documented reports of controlled

experiments, surveys, interviews, laboratory data, and so on), then the critical philosopher would have no business carping at them. After all, since psychological egoism purports to be a scientific theory of human motives, it is the concern of the experimental psychologist, not the philosopher, to accept or reject it. But as a matter of fact, empirical evidence of the required sort is seldom presented in support of psychological egoism. Psychologists, on the whole, shy away from generalizations about human motives which are so sweeping and so vaguely formulated that they are virtually incapable of scientific testing. It is usually the "armchair scientist" who holds the theory of universal selfishness, and his usual arguments are either based simply on his "impressions" or else are largely of a nonempirical sort. The latter are often shot full of a very subtle kind of logical confusion, and this makes their criticism a matter of special interest to the analytic philosopher.

6. The psychological egoist's first argument (4a, above) is a good example of logical confusion. It begins with a truism — namely, that all of my motives and desires are *my* motives and desires and not someone else's. (Who would deny this?) But from this simple tautology nothing whatever concerning the nature of my motives or the objective of my desires can possibly follow. The fallacy of this argument consists in its violation of the general logical rule that analytic statements (tautologies) cannot entail synthetic (factual) ones.[6] That every voluntary act is prompted by the agent's own motives is a tautology; hence, it cannot be equivalent to "A person is always seeking something for himself" or "All of a person's motives are selfish," which are synthetic. What the egoist must prove is not merely

(i) Every voluntary action is prompted by a motive of the agent's own.

but rather

(ii) Every voluntary action is prompted by a motive of a quite particular kind, viz. a selfish one.

Statement (i) is obviously true, but it cannot all by itself give any logical support to statement (ii).

The source of the confusion in this argument is readily apparent. It is not the genesis of an action or the *origin* or its motives which makes it a "selfish" one, but rather the "purpose" of the act or the *objective* of its motives; *not where the motive comes from* (in voluntary actions it always come from the agent) but *what it aims at* determines whether or not it is selfish. There is surely a valid distinction between voluntary behavior, in which the agent's action is motivated by purposes of his own, and *selfish* behavior in which the agent's motives are of one exclusive sort. The egoist's argument assimilates all voluntary action into the class of selfish action, by requiring, in effect, that an unselfish action be one which is not really motivated at all. In the words of Lucius Garvin, "to say that an act proceeds from our own . . . desire is only to say that the act is our own. To demand that we should act on motives that are not our own is to ask us to make ourselves living contradictions in terms."[7]

7. But if argument 4a fails to prove its point, argument 4b does no better. From the fact that all our successful actions (those in which we get what we were after) are accompanied or followed by pleasure it does not follow, as the egoist claims, that the *objective* of every action is to get pleasure for oneself. To begin with, the premise of the argument is not, strictly speaking, even true. Fulfillment of desire (simply getting what one was after) is no guarantee of satisfaction (pleasant feelings of gratification in the mind of the agent). Sometimes when we get what we want we *also* get, as a kind of extra dividend, a warm, glowing feeling of contentment; but often, far too often, we get no dividend at all, or, even worse, the bitter taste of ashes. Indeed, it has been said that the characteristic psychological problem of our time is the *dissatisfaction* that attends the fulfillment of our very most powerful desires.

Even if we grant, however, for the sake of argument, that getting what one wants *usually* yields satisfaction, the egoist's conclusion does not follow. We can concede that we normally get pleasure (in the sense of satisfaction) when our desires are satisfied, *no matter what our desires are for;* but it does not follow from this roughly accurate generalization that the only thing we ever desire is our own satisfaction. Pleasure may well be the usual accompaniment of all actions in which the agent gets what he wants; but to infer from this that what the agent always wants is his own pleasure is like arguing, in William James's example,[8] that because an ocean liner constantly consumes coal on its trans-Atlantic passage that therefore the *purpose* of its voyage is to consume coal. The immediate inference from even constant accompaniment to purpose (or motive) is always a *non sequitur.*

Perhaps there is a sense of "satisfaction" (desire fulfillment) such that it is certainly and universally true that we get satisfaction whenever we get what we want. But satisfaction in this sense is simply the "coming into existence of that which is desired." Hence, to say that desire fulfillment always yields "satisfaction" in this sense is to say no more than that we always get what we want when we get what we want, which is to utter a tautology like "a rose is a rose." It can no more entail a synthetic truth in psychology (like the egoist thesis) than "a rose is a rose" can entail significant information in botany.

8. *Disinterested Benevolence*. The fallacy in argument 4b then consists, as Garvin puts it, "in the supposition that the apparently unselfish desire to benefit others is transformed into a selfish one by the fact that we derive pleasure from carrying it out."[9] Not only is this argument fallacious; it also provides us with a suggestion of a counter-argument to show that its conclusion (psychological egoist hedonism) is false. Not only is the presence of pleasure (satisfaction) as a by-product of an action no proof that the action was selfish; in some special cases it provides rather conclusive proof that the action was *unselfish*. For in those special cases the fact that we get pleasure from a particular action *presupposes that we desired something else* — something other than our own pleasure — as an end in itself and not merely as a means to our own pleasant state of mind.

This way of turning the egoistic hedonist's argument back on him can be illustrated by taking a typical egoist argument, one attributed (perhaps apocryphally) to Abraham Lincoln, and then examining it closely:

Mr. Lincoln once remarked to a fellow-passenger on an old-time mud-coach that all men were prompted by selfishness in doing good. His fellow-passenger was antagonizing this position when they were passing over a corduroy bridge that spanned a slough. As they crossed this bridge they espied an old razor-backed sow on the bank making a terrible noise because her pigs had got into the slough and were in danger of drowning. As the old coach began to climb the hill, Mr. Lincoln called out, "Driver, can't you stop just a moment?" Then Mr. Lincoln jumped out, ran back and lifted the little pigs out of the mud and water and placed them on the bank. When he returned, his companion re-marked: "Now Abe, where does selfishness come in on this little episode?" "Why, bless your soul Ed, that was the very essence of selfishness. I should have had no peace of mind all day had I gone on and left that suffering old sow worrying over those pigs. I did it to get peace of mind, don't you see?"[10]

If Lincoln had cared not a whit for the welfare of the little pigs and their "suffering" mother, but only for his own "peace of mind," it would be difficult to explain how he could have derived pleasure from helping them. The very fact that he did feel satisfaction as a result of helping the pigs presupposes that he had a preexisting desire for something other than his own happiness. Then when *that* desire was satisfied, Lincoln of course derived pleasure. The *object* of Lincoln's desire was not pleasure; rather pleasure was the *consequence* of his preexisting desire for something else. If Lincoln had been wholly indifferent to the plight of the little pigs as he claimed, how could he possibly have derived any pleasure from helping them? He could not have achieved peace of mind from rescuing the pigs, had he not a prior concern — on which his peace of mind depended — for the welfare of the pigs for its own sake.

In general, the psychological hedonist analyzes apparent benevolence into a desire for "benevolent pleasure." No doubt the benevolent person does get pleasure from his benevolence, but in most cases, this is only because he has previously desired the good of some person, or animal, or mankind at large. Where there is no such desire, benevolent conduct is not generally found to give pleasure to the agent.

9. *Malevolence*. Difficult cases for the psychological egoist include not only instances of disinterested benevolence, but also cases of "disinterested malevolence." Indeed, malice and hatred are generally no more "selfish" than benevolence. Both are motives likely to cause an agent to sacrifice his own interests — in the case of benevolence, in order to help someone else, in the case of malevolence in order to harm someone else. The selfish person is concerned ultimately only with his own pleasure, happiness, or power; the benevolent person is often equally concerned with the happiness of others; to the malevolent person, the *injury* of another is often an end in itself — an end to be pursued sometimes with no thought for his own interests. There is

reason to think that people have as often sacrificed themselves to injure or kill others as to help or to save others, and with as much "heroism" in the one case as in the other. The unselfish nature of malevolence was first noticed by the Anglican Bishop and moral philosopher Joseph Butler (1692–1752), who regretted that people are no more selfish than they are.[11]

10. *Lack of Evidence for Universal Self-Deception.* The more cynical sort of psychological egoist who is impressed by the widespread phenomenon of self-deception (see 4c above) cannot be so quickly disposed of, for he has committed no *logical* mistakes. We can only argue that the acknowledged frequency of self-deception is insufficient evidence for his universal generalization. His argument is not fallacious, but inconclusive.

No one but the agent himself can ever be certain what conscious motives really prompted his action, and where motives are disreputable, even the agent may not admit to himself the true nature of his desires. Thus, for every apparent case of altruistic behavior, the psychological egoist can argue, with some plausibility, that the true motivation *might* be selfish, appearance to the contrary. Philanthropic acts are really motivated by the desire to receive gratitude; acts of self-sacrifice, when truly understood, are seen to be motivated by the desire to feel self-esteem; and so on. We must concede to the egoist that all apparent altruism might be deceptive in this way; but such a sweeping generalization requires considerable empirical evidence, and such evidence is not presently available.

11. *The "Paradox of Hedonism" and Its Consequences for Education.* The psychological egoistic Hedonist (e.g., Jeremy Bentham) has the simplest possible theory of human motivation. According to this variety of egoistic theory, all human motives without exception can be reduced to one—namely, the desire for one's own pleasure. But this theory, despite its attractive simplicity, or perhaps because of it, involves one immediately in a paradox. Astute observers of human affairs from the time of the ancient Greeks have often noticed that pleasure, happiness, and satisfaction are states of mind which stand in a very peculiar relation to desire. An exclusive desire for happiness is the surest way to prevent happiness from coming into being. Happiness has a way of "sneaking up" on persons when they are preoccupied with other things; but when persons deliberately and single-mindedly set off in pursuit of happiness, it vanishes utterly from sight and cannot be captured. This is the famous "paradox of hedonism": the single-minded pursuit of happiness is necessarily self-defeating, for *the way to get happiness is to forget it;* then perhaps it will come to you. If you aim exclusively at pleasure itself, with no concern for the things that bring pleasure, then pleasure will never come. To derive satisfaction, one must ordinarily first desire something other than satisfaction, and then find the means to get what one desires.

To feel the full force of the paradox of hedonism the reader should conduct an experiment in his imagination. Imagine a person (let's call him "Jones") who is, first of all, devoid of intellectual curiosity. He has no desire to acquire any kind of knowledge for its own sake, and thus is utterly indifferent to questions of science, mathematics, and philosophy. Imagine further that the beauties of nature leave Jones cold: he is unimpressed by the autumn foliage, the snow-capped mountains, and the rolling oceans. Long walks in the country on spring mornings and skiing forays in the winter are to him equally a bore. Moreover, let us suppose that Jones can find no appeal in art. Novels are dull, poetry a pain, paintings nonsense and music just noise. Suppose further that Jones has neither the participant's nor the spectator's passion for baseball, football, tennis, or any other sport. Swimming to him is a cruel aquatic form of calisthenics, the sun only a cause of sunburn. Dancing is coeducational idiocy, conversation a waste of time, the other sex an unappealing mystery. Politics is a fraud; religion mere superstition; and the misery of millions of underprivileged human beings is nothing to be concerned with or excited about. Suppose finally that Jones has no talent for any kind of handicraft, industry, or commerce, and that he does not regret that fact.

What then is Jones interested in? He must desire something. To be sure, he does. Jones has an overwhelming passion for, a complete preoccupation with, his own happiness. The one exclusive desire of his life is *to be happy.* It takes little imagination at this point to see that Jones's one desire is bound to be frustrated. People who—like Jones—most hotly pursue their own happiness are the least likely to find it. Happy people are those who successfully pursue such things as aesthetic or religious experience, self-expression, service to others, victory in competitions, knowledge, power, and so on. If none of these things in themselves and for their own sakes mean anything to a person, if they are valued at all then only as a means to one's own pleasant states of mind — then that pleasure can never come. The way to achieve happiness is to pursue something else.

Almost all people at one time or another in their lives feel pleasure. Some people (though perhaps not many) really do live lives which are on the whole happy. But if pleasure and happiness presuppose desires for something other than pleasure and happiness, then the existence of pleasure and happiness in the experience of some people proves that those people have strong desires for something other than their own happiness — egoistic hedonism to the contrary.

The implications of the "paradox of hedonism" for educational theory should be obvious. The parents least likely to raise a happy child are those who, even with the best intentions, train their children to seek happiness directly. How often have you heard parents say:

> I don't care if my child does not become an intellectual, or a sports star, or a great artist. I just want her to be a plain average sort of person. Happiness does not require great ambitions and great frustrations; it's not worth it to suffer and become neurotic for the sake of science, art, or do-goodism. I just want my child to be happy.

This can be a dangerous mistake, for it is the child (and the adult for that matter) without "outer-directed" interests who is the most likely to be unhappy. The pure egoist would be the most wretched of persons.

The educator might well beware of "life adjustment" as the conscious goal of the educational process for similar reasons. "Life adjustment" can be achieved only as a by-product of other pursuits. A whole curriculum of "life adjustment courses" unsupplemented by courses designed to incite an interest in things other than life adjustment would be tragically self-defeating.

As for moral education, it is probably true that punishment and reward are indispensable means of inculcation. But if the child comes to believe that the *sole* reasons for being moral are that he will escape the pain of punishment thereby and/or that he will gain the pleasure of a good reputation, then what is to prevent him from doing the immoral thing whenever he is sure that he will not be found out? While punishment and reward then are important tools for the moral educator, they obviously have their limitations. Beware of the man who does the moral thing only out of fear of pain or love of pleasure. He is not likely to be wholly trustworthy. Moral education is truly successful when it produces persons who are willing to do the right thing *simply because it is right,* and not merely because it is popular or safe.

12. *Pleasure as Sensation.* One final argument against psychological hedonism should suffice to put that form of the egoistic psychology to rest once and for all. The egoistic hedonist claims that all desires can be reduced to the single desire for one's own *pleasure.* Now the word "pleasure" is ambiguous. On the one hand, it can stand for a certain indefinable, but very familiar and specific kind of sensation, or more accurately, a property of sensations; and it is generally, if not exclusively, associated with the senses. For example, certain taste sensations such as sweetness, thermal sensations of the sort derived from a hot bath or the feel of the August sun while one lies on a sandy beach, erotic sensations, olfactory sensations (say) of the fragrance of flowers or perfume, and tactual and kinesthetic sensations from a good massage, are all pleasant in this sense. Let us call this sense of "pleasure," which is the converse of "physical pain," pleasure$_1$.

On the other hand, the word "pleasure" is often used simply as a synonym for "satisfaction" (in the sense of gratification, not mere desire fulfillment). In this sense, the existence of pleasure presupposes the prior existence of desire. Knowledge, religious experience, aesthetic expression, and other so-called "spiritual activities" often give pleasure in this sense. In fact, as we have seen, we tend to get pleasure in this sense whenever we get what we desire, no matter what we desire. The masochist even derives pleasure (in the sense of "satisfaction") from his own physically painful sensations. Let us call the sense of "pleasure" which means "satisfaction" — pleasure$_2$.

Now we can evaluate the psychological hedonist's claim that the sole human motive is a desire for one's own pleasure, bearing in mind (as he often does not) the ambiguity of the word "pleasure." First let us take the hedonist to be saying that it is the desire for pleasure$_1$ (pleasant sensation) which is the sole ultimate desire of all people and the sole desire capable of providing a motive for action.

Now I have little doubt that all (or most) people desire their own pleasure, *sometimes*. But even this familiar kind of desire occurs, I think, rather rarely. When I am very hungry, I often desire to eat, or, more specifically, to eat this piece of steak and these potatoes. Much less often do I desire to eat certain morsels simply for the sake of the pleasant gustatory sensation they might cause. I have, on the other hand, been motivated in the latter way when I have gone to especially exotic (and expensive) French or Chinese restaurants; but normally, pleasant gastronomic sensations are simply a happy consequence or by-product of my eating, not the antecedently desired objective of my eating. There are, of course, others who take gustatory sensations far more seriously: the *gourmet* who eats only to savor the textures and flavors of fine foods, and the wine fancier who "collects" the exquisitely subtle and very pleasant tastes of rare old wines. Such people are truly absorbed in their taste sensations when they eat and drink, and there may even be some (rich) persons whose desire for such sensations is the sole motive for eating and drinking. It should take little argument, however, to convince the reader that such persons are extremely rare.

Similarly, I usually derive pleasure from taking a hot bath, and on occasion (though not very often) I even decide to bathe simply for the sake of such sensations. Even if this is equally true of everyone, however, it hardly provides grounds for inferring that *no one ever* bathes from *any* other motive. It should be empirically obvious that we sometimes bathe simply in order to get clean, or to please others, or simply from habit.

The view then that we are never after anything in our actions but our own pleasure — that all people are complete "gourmets" of one sort or another — is not only morally cynical; it is also contrary to common sense and everyday experience. In fact, the view that pleasant sensations play such an enormous role in human affairs is so patently false, on the available evidence, that we must conclude that the psychological hedonist has the other sense of "pleasure" — satisfaction — in mind when he states his thesis. If, on the other hand, he really does try to reduce the apparent multitude of human motives to the one desire for pleasant sensations, then the abundance of historical counter-examples justifies our rejection out of hand of his thesis. It surely seems incredible that the Christian martyrs were ardently pursuing their own pleasure when they marched off to face the lions, or that what the Russian soldiers at Stalingrad "really" wanted when they doused themselves with gasoline, ignited themselves, and then threw the flaming torches of their own bodies on German tanks, was simply the experience of pleasant physical sensations.

13. *Pleasure as Satisfaction.* Let us consider now the other interpretation of the hedonist's thesis, that according to which it is one's own pleasure$_2$ (satisfaction) and not merely pleasure$_1$ (pleasant sensation) which is the sole ultimate objective of all voluntary behavior. In one respect, the "satisfaction thesis" is even less plausible than the "physical sensation thesis"; for the latter at least is a genuine empirical hypothesis, testable in experience, though contrary to the facts which experience discloses. The former, however, is so confused that it cannot even be completely stated without paradox. It is, so to speak, defeated in its own formulation. Any attempted explication of the theory that all men at all times desire only their own satisfaction leads to an *infinite regress* in the following way:

"All men desire only satisfaction."
"Satisfaction of what?"
"Satisfaction of their desires."
"Their desires for what?"
"Their desires for satisfaction."
"Satisfaction of what?"
"Their desires."
"For what?"
"For satisfaction" — etc., *ad infinitum.*

In short, psychological hedonism interpreted in this way attributes to all people as their sole motive a wholly vacuous and infinitely self-defeating desire. The source of this absurdity is in the notion that satisfaction can, so to speak, feed on itself, and perform the miracle of perpetual self-regeneration in the absence of desires for anything other than itself.

To summarize the argument of sections 11 and 12: The word "pleasure" is ambiguous. Pleasure$_1$ means a certain indefinable characteristic of physical sensation. Pleasure$_2$ refers to the feeling of satisfaction that often comes when one gets what one desires whatever be the nature of that which one desires. Now, if the hedonist means pleasure$_1$ when he says that one's own pleasure is the ultimate objective of all of one's behavior, then his view is not supported by the facts. On the other hand, if he means pleasure$_2$, then this theory cannot even be clearly formulated, since it leads to the following infinite regress: "I desire only satisfaction of my desire for satisfaction of my desire for satisfaction . . . etc., *ad infinitum.*" I conclude then that psychological hedonism (the most common form of psychological egoism), however interpreted, is untenable.

D. *Critique of Psychological Egoism: Unclear Logical Status of the Theory*

14. There remain, however, other possible forms of the egoistic psychology. The egoist might admit that not all human motives can be reduced to the one ultimate desire for one's own pleasure, or happiness, and yet still maintain that our ultimate motives, whether they be desire for happiness (J. S. Mill), self-fulfillment (Aristotle), power (Hobbes), or whatever, are always *self-regarding* motives. He might still maintain that, given our common human nature, wholly disinterested action impelled by exclusively other-regarding motives is psychologically impossible, and that therefore there is a profoundly important sense in which it is true that, whether they be hedonists or not, *all people are selfish.*

Now it seems to me that this highly paradoxical claim cannot be fully evaluated until it is properly understood, and that it cannot be properly understood until one knows what the psychological egoist is willing to accept as evidence either for or against it. In short, there are two things that must be decided: (a) whether the theory is true or false and (b) whether its truth or falsity (its truth value) depends entirely on the *meanings* of the words in which it is expressed or whether it is made true or false by certain *facts,* in this case the facts of psychology.

15. *Analytic Statements.* Statements whose truth is determined solely by the meanings of the words in which they are expressed, and thus can be held immune from empirical evidence, are often called analytic statements or tautologies. The following are examples of tautologies:

(1) All bachelors are unmarried.

(2) All effects have causes.

(3) Either Providence is the capital of Rhode Island or it is not.

The truth of (1) is derived solely from the meaning of the word "bachelor," which is defined (in part) as "unmarried man." To find out whether (1) is true or false we need not conduct interviews, compile statistics, or perform experiments. All empirical evidence is superfluous and irrelevant; for if we know the meanings of "bachelor" and "unmarried," then we know not only that (1) is true, but that it is *necessarily* true — i.e., that it cannot possibly be false, that no future experiences or observations could possibly upset it, that to deny it would be to assert a logical contradiction. But notice that what a tautology gains in certainty ("necessary truth") it loses in descriptive content. Statement (1) imparts no information whatever about any matter of fact; it simply records our determination to use certain words in a certain way. As we say, "It is true by definition."

Similarly, (2) is (necessarily) true solely in virtue of the meanings of the words "cause" and "effect" and thus requires no further observations to confirm it. And of course, no possible observations could falsify it, since it asserts no matter of fact. And finally, statement (3) is (necessarily) true solely in virtue of the meaning of the English expression "either . . . or." Such terms as "either . . . or," "if . . . then," "and," and "not" are called by logicians "logical constants." The *definitions* of logical constants are made explicit in the so-called "laws of thought" — the law of contradiction, the law of the excluded middle, and the law of identity. These "laws" are not laws in the same sense as are (say) the laws of physics. Rather, they are merely consequences of the *definitions* of logical constants, and as such, though they are necessarily true, they impart no information about the world. "Either Providence is the capital of Rhode Island or it is not" tells us nothing about geography; and "Either it is now raining or else it is not" tells us nothing about the weather. You don't have to look at a map or look out the window to know that they are true. Rather, they are known to be true *a priori* (independently of experience); and, like all (or many)[12] *a priori* statements, they are *vacuous,* i.e., devoid of informative content.

The denial of an analytic statement is called a contradiction. The following are typical examples of contradictions: "Some bachelors are married," "Some causes have no effects," "Providence both is and is not the capital of Rhode Island." As in the case of tautologies, the truth value of contradictions (their falsehood) is logically necessary, not contingent on any facts of experience, and uninformative. Their falsity is derived from the meanings (definitions) of the words in which they are expressed.

16. *Synthetic Statements*. On the other hand, statements whose truth or falsity is derived not from the meanings of words but rather from the facts of experience (observations) are called *synthetic*.[13] Prior to experience, there can be no good reason to think either that they are true or that they are false. That is to say, their truth value is *contingent;* and they can be confirmed or disconfirmed only by empirical evidence,[14] i.e., controlled observations of the world. Unlike analytic statements, they do impart information about matters of fact. Obviously, "It is raining in Newport now," if true, is more informative than "Either it is raining in Newport now or it is not," even though the former *could* be false, while the latter is necessarily true. I take the following to be examples of synthetic (contingent) statements:

(1') All bachelors are neurotic.

(2') All events have causes.

(3') Providence is the capital of Rhode Island.

(3") Newport is the capital of Rhode Island.

Statement (3') is true; (3") is false; and (1') is a matter for a psychologist (not for a philosopher) to decide; and the psychologist himself can only decide *empirically,* i.e., by making many observations. The status of (2') is very difficult and its truth value is a matter of great controversy. That is because its truth or falsity depends on *all* the facts ("all events"); and, needless to say, not all of the evidence is in.

17. *Empirical Hypotheses*. Perhaps the most interesting subclass of synthetic statements are those generalizations of experience of the sort characteristically made by scientists; e.g., "All released objects heavier than air fall," "All swans are white," "All men have Oedipus complexes." I shall call such statements "empirical hypotheses" to indicate that their function is to sum up past experience and enable us successfully to predict or anticipate future experience.[15] They are never logically certain, since it is always at least conceivable that future experience will disconfirm them. For example, zoologists once believed that all swans are white, until black swans were discovered in Australia. The most important characteristic of empirical hypotheses for our pres-

ent purposes is their relation to evidence. A person can be said to understand an empirical hypothesis only if he knows how to recognize evidence against it. *If a person asserts or believes a general statement in such a way that he cannot conceive of any possible experience which he would count as evidence against it, then he cannot be said to be asserting or believing an empirical hypothesis.* We can refer to this important characteristic of empirical hypotheses as *falsifiability in principle.*

Some statements only appear to be empirical hypotheses but are in fact disguised tautologies reflecting the speaker's determination to use words in certain (often eccentric) ways. For example, a zoologist might refuse to allow the existence of "Australian swans" to count as evidence against the generalization that all swans are white, on the grounds that the black Australian swans are not "really" swans at all. This would indicate that he is holding *whiteness* to be part of the definition of "swan," and that therefore, the statement "All swans are white" is, for him, "true by definition" — and thus just as immune from counterevidence as the statement "All spinsters are unmarried." Similarly, most of us would refuse to allow any possible experience to count as evidence against "2 + 2 = 4" or "Either unicorns exist or they do not," indicating that the propositions of arithmetic and logic are not empirical hypotheses.

18. *Ordinary Language and Equivocation*. Philosophers, even more than ordinary people, are prone to make startling and paradoxical claims that take the form of universal generalizations and hence resemble empirical hypotheses. For example, "All things are mental (there are no physical objects)," "All things are good (there is no evil)," "All voluntary behavior is selfish," etc. Let us confine our attention for the moment to the latter which is a rough statement of psychological egoism. At first sight, the statement "All voluntary behavior is selfish" seems obviously false. One might reply to the psychological egoist in some such manner as this:

> I *know* some behavior, at least, is unselfish, because I saw my Aunt Emma yesterday give her last cent to a beggar. Now she will have to go a whole week with nothing to eat. Surely, *that* was not selfish of her.

Nevertheless, the psychological egoist is likely not to be convinced, and insist that, in this case, if we knew enough about Aunt Emma, we would learn that her primary motive in helping the beggar was to promote her own happiness or assuage her own conscience, or increase her own self-esteem, etc. We might then present the egoist with even more difficult cases for his theory—saints, martyrs, military heroes, patriots, and others who have sacrificed themselves for a cause. If psychological egoists nevertheless refuse to accept any of these as examples of unselfish behavior, then we have a right to be puzzled about what they are saying. Until we know what they would count as *unselfish* behavior, we can't very well know what they mean when they say that all voluntary behavior is *selfish*. And at this point we may suspect that they are holding their theory in a "privileged position"—that of immunity to evidence, that they would allow no *conceivable* behavior to count as evidence against it. What they say then, if true, must be true in virtue of the way he defines—or redefines—the word "selfish." And in that case, it cannot be an empirical hypothesis.

If what the psychological egoist says is "true by redefinition," then I can "agree" with him and say "It is true that in *your* sense of the word 'selfish' my Aunt Emma's behavior was selfish; but in the ordinary sense of 'selfish,' which implies blameworthiness, she surely was not selfish." There is no point of course in arguing about a mere word. The important thing is not what particular words a man uses, but rather whether what he wishes to say in those words is true. Departures from ordinary language can often be justified by their utility for certain purposes; but they are dangerous when they invite equivocation. The psychological egoist may be saying something which is true when he says that Emma is selfish in *his* sense, but if he doesn't realize that his sense of "selfish" differs from the ordinary one, he may be tempted to infer that Emma is selfish in the ordinary sense which implies blameworthiness; and this of course would be unfair and illegitimate. It is indeed an extraordinary extension of the meaning of the word "self-indulgent" (as C. G. Chesterton remarks somewhere) which allows a philosopher to say that a man is self-indulgent when he wants to be burned at the stake.

19. *The Fallacy of the Suppressed Correlative.* Certain words in the English language operate in pairs—e.g., "selfish-unselfish," "good-bad," "large-small," "mental-physical." To assert that a thing has one of the above characteristics is to *contrast* it with the opposite in the pair. To know the meaning of one term in the pair, we must know the meaning of the correlative term with which it is contrasted. If we could not conceive of what it would be like for a thing to be bad, for example, then we could not possibly understand what is being said of a thing when it is called "good." Similarly, unless we had a notion of what it would be like for action to be *unselfish,* we could hardly understand the sentence "So-and-so acted selfishly"; for we would have nothing to contrast "selfishly" with. The so-called "fallacy of the suppressed correlative"[16] is committed by a person who consciously or unconsciously redefines one of the terms in a contrasting pair in such a way that its new meaning incorporates the sense of its correlative.

Webster's Collegiate Dictionary defines "selfish" (in part) as "regarding one's own comfort, advantage, etc. in disregard of, or at the expense of that of others." In this ordinary and proper sense of "selfish," Aunt Emma's action in giving her last cent to the beggar certainly was *not* selfish. Emma *disregarded* her *own* comfort (it is not "comfortable" to go a week without eating) and advantage (there is no "advantage" in malnutrition) *for the sake of* (not "at the expense of") another. Similarly, the martyr marching off to the stake is foregoing (not indulging) his "comfort" and indeed his very life for the sake of (not at the expense of) a cause. If Emma and the martyr then are "selfish," they must be so in a strange new sense of the word.

A careful examination of the egoist's arguments (see especially 4b above) reveals what new sense he gives to the word "selfish." He redefines the word so that it means (roughly) "motivated," or perhaps "intentional." "After all," says the egoist, "Aunt Emma had some *purpose* in giving the beggar all her money, and this purpose (desire, intention, motive, aim) was *her* purpose and no one else's. She was out to further some aim of her own, wasn't she? Therefore, she was pursuing her own ends (acting from her own motives); she was after something *for herself* in so acting, and that's what I mean by calling her action selfish. Moreover, all intentional action—action done 'on purpose,' deliberately from the agent's own motives—is selfish in the same sense." We can see now, from this reply, that since the egoist apparently means by "selfish" simply "motivated," when he says that all motivated action is selfish *he is not asserting a synthetic empirical hypothesis about human motives; rather, his statement is a tautology roughly equivalent to "all motivated actions are motivated."* And if that is the case, then what he says is true enough; but, like all tautologies, it is empty, uninteresting, and trivial.

Moreover, in redefining "selfish" in this way, the psychological egoist has committed the fallacy of the suppressed correlative. For what can we now contrast "selfish voluntary action" with? Not only are there no *actual* cases of unselfish voluntary actions on the new definition; there are not even any *theoretically possible* or *conceivable* cases of unselfish voluntary actions. And if we cannot even conceive of what an unselfish voluntary action would be like, how can we give any sense to the expression "selfish voluntary action"? The egoist, so to speak, has so blown up the sense of "selfish" that, like inflated currency, it will no longer buy anything.

20. *Psychological Egoism as a Linguistic Proposal.* There is still no way out for the egoist. He might admit that his theory is not really a psychological hypothesis about human nature designed to account for the facts and enable us to predict or anticipate future events. He may even willingly concede that his theory is really a disguised redefinition of a word. Still, he might argue, he has made no claim to be giving an accurate description of actual linguistic usage. Rather, he is making a proposal to *revise* our usage in the interest of economy and convenience, just as the biologists once proposed that we change the ordinary meaning of "insect" in such a way that spiders are no longer called insects, and the ordinary meaning of "fish" so that whales and seals are no longer called fish.

What are we to say to this suggestion? First of all, stipulative definitions (proposals to revise usage) are never true or false. They are simply useful or not useful. Would it be useful to redefine "selfish" in the way the egoist recommends? It is difficult to see what would be gained thereby. The egoist has noticed some respects in which actions normally called "selfish" and actions normally called "unselfish" are alike, namely they are both motivated and they both can give satisfaction — either in prospect or in retrospect — to the agent. Because of these likenesses, the egoist feels justified in attaching the label "selfish" to *all* actions. Thus one word — "selfish" — must for him do the work of two words ("selfish" and "unselfish" in their old meanings); and as a result, a very real distinction, that between actions for the sake of others and actions at the expense of others, can no

longer be expressed in the language. Because the egoist has noticed some respects in which two types of actions are alike, he wishes to make it impossible to describe the respects in which they differ. It is difficult to see any utility in this state of affairs.

But suppose we adopt the egoist's "proposal" nevertheless. Now we would have to say that all actions are selfish; but, in addition, we would want to say that there are two different kinds of selfish actions, those which regard the interests of others and those which disregard the interests of others, and, furthermore, that only the latter are blameworthy. After a time our ear would adjust to the new uses of the word "selfish," and we would find nothing at all strange in such statements as "Some selfish actions are morally praiseworthy." After a while, we might even invent two new words, perhaps "selfitic" and "unselfitic," to distinguish the two important classes of "selfish" actions. Then we would be right back where we started, with new linguistic tools ("selfish" for "motivated," "selfitic" for "selfish," and "unselfitic" for "unselfish") to do the same old necessary jobs. That is, until some new [egoist philosopher] arose to announce with an air of discovery that "All selfish behavior is really selfitic — there are no truly unselfitic selfish actions." Then, God help us!

Endnotes

1 See Jeremy Bentham, *Introduction to the Principles of Morals and Legislation* (1789), Chap. I, first paragraph: "Nature has placed mankind under the governance of two sovereign masters, *pain* and *pleasure*. It is for them alone to point out what we ought to do, as well as to determine what we shall do. . . . They govern us in all we do, in all we say, in all we think: every effort we can make to throw off our subjection will serve but to demonstrate and confirm it."

2 C. D. Broad, *Ethics and the History of Philosophy* (New York: The Humanities Press, 1952), Essay 10 — "Egoism as a Theory of Human Motives," p. 218. This essay is highly recommended.

3 Austin Duncan-Jones, *Butler's Moral Philosophy* (London: Penguin Books, 1952), p. 96. Duncan-Jones goes on to reject this argument. See p. 512f.

4 Lucius Garvin, *A Modern Introduction to Ethics* (Boston: Houghton Mifflin, 1953), p. 37. Quoted here by permission of the author and publisher.

5 Bentham, *op. cit.,* Chap. III.

6 See Part D, 15 and 16.

7 Garvin, *op. cit.,* p. 39.

8 William James, *The Principles of Psychology* (New York: Henry Holt, 1890), Vol. II, p. 558.

9 Garvin, *op. cit.,* p. 39.

10 Quoted from the *Springfield* (Illinois) *Monitor,* by F. C. Sharp in his *Ethics* (New York: Appleton-Century, 1928), p. 75.

11 See Joseph Butler, *Fifteen Sermons on Human Nature Preached at the Rolls Chapel* (1726), especially the first and eleventh.

12 Whether or not there are some *a priori* statements that are not merely analytic, and hence *not* vacuous, is still a highly controversial question among philosophers.

13 Some philosophers (those called "rationalists") believe that there are some synthetic statements whose truth can be known *a priori* (see note 12). If they are right, then the statement above is not entirely accurate.

14 Again, subject to the qualification in notes 12 and 13.

15 The three examples given above all have the generic character there indicated, but they also differ from one another in various other ways, some of which are quite important. For our present purposes, however, we can ignore the ways in which they differ from one another and concentrate on their common character as generalizations of experience ("inductive generalizations"). As such they are sharply contrasted with such a generalization as "All puppies are young dogs," which is analytic.

16 The phrase was coined by J. Lowenberg. See his article "What Is Empirical?" in the *Journal of Philosophy,* May 1940.

III.3 *Ultimate Principles and Ethical Egoism*

Brian Medlin

Brian Medlin teaches philosophy in Australia. In this article he argues that ethical egoism is not rational, for self-interest cannot provide a proper foundation for rational action. First he distinguishes between two kinds of egoism, categorical and hypothetical egoism, and argues that the latter is only an apparent egoism. Hypothetical egoism is the view that by maximizing one's own utility, we will all be better off. This is not really egoism but a version of closet utilitarianism that cites a utilitarian reason for emphasizing self-interested reasons in acting. Medlin argues that categorical egoism, which simply states that universal egoism is the correct moral theory, is conceptually confused, for it enjoins mutually exclusive desires and advice (for example, both to help Tom and not to help Tom in the same situation). Given the soundness of this argument, which we may call the opposing advice argument, egoism is not even a coherent theory.

I believe that it is now pretty generally accepted by professional philosophers that ultimate ethical principles must be arbitrary. One cannot derive conclusions about what should be merely from accounts of what is the case; one cannot decide how people ought to behave merely from one's knowledge of how they do behave. To arrive at a conclusion in ethics one must have at least one ethical premise. This premise, if it be in turn a conclusion, must be the conclusion of an argument containing at least one ethical premise. And so we can go back, indefinitely but not forever. Sooner or later, we must come to at least one ethical premise which is not deduced but baldly asserted. Here we must be a-rational; neither rational nor irrational, for here there is no room for reason even to go wrong.

But the triumph of Hume in ethics has been a limited one. What appears quite natural to a handful of specialists appears quite monstrous to the majority of decent intelligent men. At any rate, it has been my experience that people who are normally rational resist the above account of the logic of moral language, not by argument—for that can't be done—but by tooth and nail. And they resist from

Reprinted with permission from *Australasian Journal of Philosophy* XXXV (1957): 111–118.

the best motives. They see the philosopher wantonly unraveling the whole fabric of morality. If our ultimate principles are arbitrary, they say, if those principles came out of thin air, then anyone can hold any principle he pleases. Unless moral assertions are statements of fact about the world and either true or false, we can't claim that any man is wrong, whatever his principles may be, whatever his behaviour. We have to surrender the luxury of calling one another scoundrels. That this anxiety flourishes because its roots are in confusion is evident when we consider that we don't call people scoundrels, anyhow, for being mistaken about their facts. Fools, perhaps, but that's another matter. Nevertheless, it doesn't become us to be high-up. The layman's uneasiness, however irrational it may be, is very natural and he must be reassured.

People cling to objectivist theories of morality from moral motives. It's a very queer thing that by doing so they often thwart their own purposes. There are evil opinions abroad, as anyone who walks abroad knows. The one we meet with most often, whether in pub or parlour, is the doctrine that everyone should look after himself. However refreshing he may find it after the high-minded pomposities of this morning's editorial, the good fellow knows this doctrine is wrong and he wants to knock it down. But while he believes that moral language is used to make statements either true or false, the best he can do is to claim that what the egoist says is false. Unfortunately, the egoist can claim that it's true. And since the supposed fact in question between them is not a publicly ascertainable one, their disagreement can never be resolved. And it is here that even good fellows waver, when they find they have no refutation available. The egoist's word seems as reliable as their own. Some begin half to believe that perhaps it is possible to supply an egoistic basis for conventional morality, some that it may be impossible to supply any other basis. I'm not going to try to prop up our conventional morality, which I fear to be a task beyond my strength, but in what follows I do want to refute the doctrine of ethical egoism. I want to resolve this disagreement by showing that what the egoist says is inconsistent. It is true that there are moral disagreements which can never be resolved, but this isn't one of them. The proper objection to the man who says "Everyone should look after his own interests regardless of the interests of others" is not that he isn't speaking the truth, but simply that he isn't speaking.

We should first make two distinctions. This done, ethical egoism will lose much of its plausibility.

1. Universal and Individual Egoism

Universal egoism maintains that everyone (including the speaker) ought to look after his own interests and to disregard those of other people except insofar as their interests contribute towards his own.

Individual egoism is the attitude that the egoist is going to look after himself and no one else. The egoist cannot promulgate that he is going to look after himself. He can't even preach that he *should* look after himself and preach this alone. When he tries to convince me that he should look after himself, he is attempting so to dispose me that I shall approve when he drinks my beer and steals Tom's wife. I cannot approve of his looking after himself and himself alone without so far approving of his achieving his happiness, regardless of the happiness of myself and others. So that when he sets out to persuade me that he should look after himself regardless of others, he must also set out to persuade me that I should look after him regardless of myself and others. Very small chance he has! And if the individual egoist cannot promulgate his doctrine without enlarging it, what he has is no doctrine at all.

A person enjoying such an attitude may believe that other people are fools not to look after themselves. Yet he himself would be a fool to tell them so. If he did tell them, though, he wouldn't consider that he was giving them *moral* advice. Persuasion to the effect that one should ignore the claims of morality because morality doesn't pay, to the effect that one has insufficient selfish motive and, therefore, insufficient motive for moral behaviour is not moral persuasion. For this reason I doubt that we should call the individual egoist's attitude an ethical one. And I don't doubt this in the way someone may doubt whether to call the ethical standards of Satan "ethical" standards. A malign morality is none the less a morality for being malign. But the attitude we're considering is one of mere contempt for all moral considerations whatsoever. An indifference to morals may be wicked, but it is not a perverse morality. So far as I am aware, most egoists imagine that they are putting forward a doctrine in ethics, though there may be a few who are prepared to proclaim themselves individual egoists. If the good fellow wants to know how he should justify conventional morality to an individual egoist, the answer is that he shouldn't and can't. Buy your car elsewhere, blackguard him whenever you meet, and let it go at that.

2. Categorical and Hypothetical Egoism

Categorical egoism is the doctrine that we all ought to observe our own interests, *because that is what we ought to do.* For the categorical egoist the egoistic dogma is the ultimate principle in ethics.

The hypothetical egoist, on the other hand, maintains that we all ought to observe our own interests, because. . . . If we want such and such an end, we must do so and so (look after ourselves). The hypothetical egoist is not a real egoist at all. He is very likely an unwitting utilitarian who believes mistakenly that the general happiness will be increased if each man looks wisely to his own. Of course, a man may believe that egoism is enjoined on us by God and he may therefore promulgate the doctrine and observe it in his conduct, not in the hope of achieving thereby a remote end, but simply in order to obey God. But neither is *he* a real egoist. He believes, ultimately, that we should obey God, even should God command us to altruism.

An ethical egoist will have to maintain the doctrine in both its universal and categorical forms. Should he retreat to hypothetical egoism he is no longer an egoist. Should he retreat to individual egoism his doctrine, while logically impregnable, is no longer ethical, no longer even a doctrine. He may wish to quarrel with this and if so, I submit peacefully. Let him call himself what he will, it makes no difference. I'm a philosopher, not a rat-catcher, and I don't see it as my job to dig vermin out of such burrows as individual egoism.

Obviously something strange goes on as soon as the ethical egoist tries to promulgate his doctrine. What is he doing when he urges upon his audience that they should each observe his own interests and those interests alone? Is he not acting contrary to the egoist principle? It cannot be to his advantage to convince them, for seizing always their own advantage they will impair his. Surely if he does believe

what he says, he should try to persuade them otherwise. Not perhaps that they should devote themselves to his interests, for they'd hardly swallow that; but that everyone should devote himself to the service of others. But is not to believe that someone should act in a certain way to try to persuade him to do so? Of course, we don't always try to persuade people to act as we think they should act. We may be lazy, for instance. But insofar as we believe that Tom should do so and so, we have a tendency to induce him to do so and so. Does it make sense to say: "Of course you should do this, but for goodness' sake don't"? Only where we mean: "You should do this for certain reasons, but here are even more persuasive reasons for not doing it." If the egoist believes ultimately that others should mind themselves alone, then, he must persuade them accordingly. If he doesn't persuade them, he is no universal egoist. It certainly makes sense to say: "I know very well that Tom should act in such and such a way. But I know also that it's not to my advantage that he should so act. So I'd better dissuade him from it." And this is just what the egoist must say, if he is to consider his own advantage and disregard everyone else's. That is, he must behave as an individual egoist, if he is to be an egoist at all.

He may want to make two kinds of objection here:

1. That it will not be to his disadvantage to promulgate the doctrine, provided that his audience fully understand what is to their ultimate advantage. This objection can be developed in a number of ways, but I think that it will always be possible to push the egoist into either individual or hypothetical egoism.

2. That it is to the egoist's advantage to preach the doctrine if the pleasure he gets out of doing this more than pays for the injuries he must endure at the hands of his converts. It is hard to believe that many people would be satisfied with a doctrine which they could only consistently promulgate in very special circumstances. Besides, this looks suspiciously like individual egoism in disguise.

I shall say no more on these two points because I want to advance a further criticism which seems to me at once fatal and irrefutable.

Now it is time to show the anxious layman that we have means of dealing with ethical egoism which are denied him; and denied him by just that objectivism which he thinks essential to morality. For the very fact that our ultimate principles must be arbitrary means they can't be anything we please. Just because they come out of thin air they can't come out of hot air. Because these principles are not propositions about matters of fact and cannot be deduced from propositions about matters of fact, they must be the fruit of our own attitudes. We assert them largely to modify the attitudes of our fellows but by asserting them we express our own desires and purposes. This means that we cannot use moral language cavalierly. Evidently, we cannot say something like "All human desires and purposes are bad." This would be to express our own desires and purposes, thereby committing a kind of absurdity. Nor, I shall argue, can we say "Everyone should observe his own interests regardless of the interests of others."

Remembering that the principle is meant to be both universal and categorical, let us ask what kind of attitude the egoist is expressing. Wouldn't that attitude be equally well expressed by the conjunction of an infinite number of avowals thus?

I want myself to come out on top	and	I don't care about Tom, Dick, Harry
and		and
I want Tom to come out on top	and	I don't care about myself, Dick, Harry . . .
and		and
I want Dick to come out on top	and	I don't care about myself, Tom, Harry . . .
and		and
I want Harry to come out on top	and	I don't care about myself, Dick, Tom . . .
etc.		etc.

From this analysis it is obvious that the principle expressing such an attitude must be inconsistent.

But now the egoist may claim that he hasn't been properly understood. When he says "Everyone should look after himself and himself alone," he means "Let each man do what he wants regardless of what anyone else wants." The egoist may claim that what he values is merely that he and Tom and Dick and Harry should each do what he wants and not care about what anyone else may want and that this doesn't involve his principle in any inconsistency. Nor need it. But even if it doesn't, he's no better off. Just what does he value? Is it the well-being of himself, Tom, Dick and Harry or merely their going on in a certain way regardless of whether or not this is going to promote their well-being? When he urges Tom, say, to do what he wants, is he appealing to Tom's self-interest? If so, his attitude can be expressed thus:

| I want myself to be happy | and | I want myself not to care about Tom, Dick, Harry . . . |

and
I want Tom to be happy

We need go no further to see that the principle expressing such an attitude must be inconsistent. I have made this kind of move already. What concerns me now is the alternative position the egoist must take up to be safe from it. If the egoist values merely that people should go in a certain way, regardless of whether or not this is going to promote their well-being, then he is not appealing to the self-interest of his audience when he urges them to regard their own interests. If Tom has any regard for himself at all, the egoist's blandishments will leave him cold. Further, the egoist doesn't have his own interest in mind when he says that, like everyone else, he should look after himself. A funny kind of egoism this turns out to be.

Perhaps now, claiming that he is indeed appealing to the self-interest of his audience, the egoist may attempt to counter the objection of the previous paragraph. He may move into "Let each man do what he wants and let each man disregard what others want when their desires clash with his own." Now his attitude may be expressed thus:

| I want everyone to be happy | and | I want everyone to disregard the happiness of others when their happiness clashes with his own |

The egoist may claim justly that a man can have such an attitude and also that in a certain kind of world such a man could get what he wanted. Our objection to the egoist has been that his desires are incompatible. And this is still so. If he and Tom and Dick and Harry did go on as he recommends by saying "Let each man disregard the happiness of others, when their happiness conflicts with his own," then assuredly they'd all be completely miserable. Yet he wants them to be happy. He is attempting to counter this by saying that it is merely a fact about the world that they'd make one another miserable by going on as he recommends. The world could conceivably have been different. For this reason, he says, this principle is not inconsistent. This argument may not seem very compelling, but I advance it on the egoist's behalf because I'm interested in the reply to it. For now we don't even need to tell him that the world isn't in fact like that. (What it's like makes no difference.) Now we can point out to him that he is arguing not as an egoist but as a utilitarian. He has slipped into hypothetical egoism to save his principle from inconsistency. If the world were such that we always made ourselves and others happy by doing one another down, then we could find good utilitarian reasons for urging that we should do one another down.

If, then, he is to save his principle, the egoist must do one of two things. He must give up the claim that he is appealing to the self-interest of his audience, that he has even his own interest in mind. Or he must admit that, in the conjunction above, although "I want everyone to be happy" refers to ends, nevertheless "I want everyone to disregard the happiness of others when their happiness conflicts with his own" can refer only to means. That is, his so-called ultimate principle is really compounded of a principle and a moral rule subordinate to that principle. That is, he is really a utilitarian who is urging everyone to go on in a certain way so that everyone may be happy. A utilitarian, what's more, who is ludicrously mistaken about the nature of the world. Things being as they are, his moral rule is a very bad one. Things being as they are, it can only be deduced from his principle by means of an empirical premise which is manifestly false. Good fellows don't need to fear him. They may rest easy that the world is and must be on their side and the best thing they can do is be good.

It may be worth pointing out that objections similar to those I have brought against the egoist can be made to the altruist. The man who holds that the principle "Let everyone observe the interests of others" is both universal and categorical can be compelled to choose between two alternatives, equally repugnant. He must give up the claim that he is concerned for the well-being of himself and others. Or he must admit that, though "I want everyone to be happy" refers to ends, nevertheless "I want everyone to disregard his own happiness when it conflicts with the happiness of others" can refer only to means.

I have said from time to time that the egoistic principle is inconsistent. I have not said it is contradictory. This for the reason that we can, without contradiction, express inconsistent desires and purposes. To do so is not to say anything like "Goliath was ten feet tall and not ten feet tall." Don't we all want to eat our cake and have it too? And when we say we do we aren't asserting a contradiction. We are not asserting a contradiction whether we be making an avowal of our attitudes or stating a fact about them. We all have conflicting motives. As a utilitarian exuding benevolence I want the man who mows my landlord's grass to be happy, but as a slug-abed I should like to see him scourged. None of this, however, can do the egoist any good. For we assert our ultimate principles not only to express our own attitudes but also to induce similar attitudes in others, to dispose them to conduct themselves as we wish. In so far as their desires conflict, people don't know what to do. And, therefore, no expression of incompatible desires can ever serve for an ultimate principle of human conduct.

III.4 *In Defense of Egoism*

JESSE KALIN

Jesse Kalin is professor of philosophy at Vassar College. In this article he argues against Medlin that ethical egoism is coherent, that it should not be equated with selfishness, and that it may be enlightened so that it includes friendship and civic-mindedness. He meets Medlin's objection to the opposing advice argument by using a sports model wherein both sides are supposed to try to win the game. He shows that we can believe that others have obligations without us wanting them to meet those obligations. For example, we may believe that a policeman has an obligation to give us a ticket for speeding, but hope that he won't; or my opponent may have a three-move checkmate on me that the nature of the game "obligates" him to make, but I may hope that he won't see it and mate me. Kalin meets several other objections against ethical egoism and concludes that it is indeed a plausible theory. However, at the end of his article he notes several weaknesses of the theory. Ethical egoism cannot easily be made public or promulgated, nor is the egoist able to engage in interpersonal reasoning. It seems to entail a private morality. Whereas it is in the egoist's interest that there be a public morality, it is not always in his or her interest to act according to that morality.

I

Ethical egoism is the view that it is morally right — that is, morally permissible, indeed, morally obligatory — for a person to act in his own self-interest, even when his self-interest conflicts or is irreconcilable with the self-interest of another. The point people normally have in mind in accepting and advocating this ethical principle is that of justifying or excusing their own self-interested actions by giving them a moral sanction.

This position is sometimes construed as saying that selfishness is moral, but such an interpretation is not quite correct. "Self-interest" is a general term usually used as a synonym for "personal happiness" and "personal welfare," and what would pass as selfish behavior frequently would not pass as self-interested behavior in this sense. Indeed, we have the suspicion that selfish people are characteristically, if not always, unhappy. Thus, in cases where selfishness tends to a person's unhappiness it is not in his self-interest, and as an egoist he ought not to be selfish. As a consequence, ethical egoism does not preclude other-interested, nonselfish, or altruistic behavior, as long as such behavior also leads to the individual's own welfare.

That the egoist may reasonably find himself taking an interest in others and promoting their welfare perhaps sounds nonegoistic, but it is not. Ethical egoism's justification of such behavior differs from other accounts in the following way: The ethical egoist acknowledges no general obligation to help people in need. Benevolence is never justified unconditionally or "categorically." The egoist has an obligation to promote the welfare only of those whom he likes, loves, needs, or can use. The source of this obligation is his interest in them. No interest, no obligation. And when his interest conflicts or is irreconcilable with theirs, he will reasonably pursue his own well-being at their expense, even when this other person is his wife, child, mother, or friend, as well as when it is a stranger or enemy.

Such a pursuit of one's own self-interest is considered *enlightened*. The name Butler provides for ethical egoism so interpreted is "cool self-love."[1] On this view, a person is to harmonize his natural interests, perhaps cultivate some new interests, and optimize their satisfaction. Usually among these interests will be such things as friendships and families (or perhaps one gets his greatest kicks from working for UNICEF). And, of course, it is a part of such enlightenment to consider the "long run" rather than just the present and immediate future.

Given this account of ethical egoism plus the proper circumstances, a person could be morally justified in cheating on tests, padding expense accounts, swindling a business partner, being a slum landlord, draft-dodging, lying, and breaking promises, as well as in contributing to charity, helping friends, being generous or civic minded, and even undergoing hardship to put his children through college. Judged from inside "standard morality," the first actions would clearly be immoral, while the preceding paragraphs suggest the latter actions would be immoral as well, being done from a vicious or improper motive.

With this informal account as background, I shall now introduce a formal definition of ethical egoism, whose coherence will be the topic of the subsequent discussion:

(i) (x) (y) (x ought to do y if and only if y is in x's overall self-interest)

In this formalization, "x" ranges over persons and "y" over particular actions, no kinds of action; "ought" has the sense "ought, all things considered." (i) may be translated as: "A person ought to do a specific action, all things considered, if and only if that action is in that person's overall (enlightened) self-interest."

(i) represents what Medlin calls "universal egoism."[2] The majority of philosophers have considered universalization to be necessary for a sound moral theory, though few have considered it sufficient. This requirement may be expressed as follows: If it is reasonable for A to do *s* in C, it is also reasonable for any similar person to do similar things in similar circumstances. Since everyone has a self-interest and since the egoist is arguing that his actions are right simply because they are self-interested, it is intuitively plausible to hold that he is committed to regarding everyone as morally similar

and as morally entitled (or even morally obligated) to be egoists. His claim that his own self-interested actions are right thus entails the claim that all self-interested actions are right. If the egoist is to reject this universalization, he must show that there are considerations in addition to self-interest justifying his action, considerations making him relevantly different from all others such that his self-interested behavior is justified while theirs is not. I can't imagine what such considerations would be. In any case, egoism has usually been advanced and defended in its universalized form, and it is in this form that it will most repay careful examination. Thus, for the purposes of this paper, I shall assume without further defense the correctness of the universalization requirement.

It has also been the case that the major objections to ethical egoism have been derived from this requirement. Opponents have argued that once egoism is universalized, it can readily be seen to be incoherent. Frankena[3] and Medlin each advance an argument of this sort. In discussing their positions, I shall argue that the universalization of egoism given by (i) is coherent, that there is more than one type of "universalization," and that egoism can, in fact, be universalized in both senses. More importantly, I shall argue that the form of universalization presenting the most problems for the egoist is a form based upon a certain conception of value which the egoist can coherently reject. The result will be that egoism can with some plausibility be defended as an ultimate practical principle. At the least, if egoism is incorrect, this is not due to any incoherence arising from the universalization requirement.

II

One purpose of a moral theory is to provide criteria for first-person moral judgments (such as "I ought to do *s* in C"); another purpose is to provide criteria for second- and third-person moral judgments (such as "Jones ought to do *s* in C"). Any theory which cannot coherently provide such criteria must be rejected as a moral theory. Can ethical egoism do this? Frankena argues that it cannot.

Frankena formulates egoism as consisting of two principles:

(a) If A is judging about himself, then A is to use this criterion: A ought to do *y* if and only if *y* is in A's overall self-interest.

(b) If A is a spectator judging about anyone else, B, then A is to use this criterion: B ought to do *y* if and only if *y* is in A's overall self-interest.

Frankena thinks that [(a) & (b)] is the only interpretation of (i) "consistent with the spirit of ethical egoism."

But isn't it the case that (a) and (b) taken together produce contradictory moral judgments about an important subset of cases, namely, those where people's self-interest conflict or are irreconcilable? If this is so, egoism as formulated by Frankena is incoherent and must be rejected.

To illustrate, let us suppose that B does *s,* and that *s* is in B's overall self-interest, but not in A's. Is *s* right or wrong? Ought, or ought not B do *s?* The answer depends on who is making the judgment. If A is making the judgment, then "B ought not to do *s*" is correct. If B is making the judgment, then "B ought to do *s*" is correct. And, of course, when both make judgments, both "B ought to do *s*" and "B ought not to do *s*" are correct. Surely any principle which has this result as a possibility is incoherent.

This objection may be put another way. The ethical egoist claims that there is one ultimate moral principle applicable to everyone. This is to claim that (i) is adequate for all moral issues, and that all applications of it can fit into a logically coherent system. Given the above illustration, "B ought to do *s*" does follow from (a), and "B ought not to do *s*" does follow from (b), but the fact that they cannot coherently be included in a set of judgments shows that (a) and (b) are not parts of the same ultimate moral principle. Indeed, these respective judgments can be said to follow from a moral principle at all only if they follow from *different* moral principles. Apparently, the ethical egoist must choose between (i)'s parts if he is to have a coherent ethical system, but he can make no satisfactory choice. If (a) is chosen, second- and third-person judgments become impossible. If (b) is chosen, first-person judgments become impossible. His moral theory, however, must provide for both kinds of judgments. Ethical egoism needs what it logically cannot have. Therefore, it can only be rejected.

The incompatibility between (a) and (b) and the consequent incoherence of (i) manifests itself in still a third way. Interpreted as a system of judgments, [(a) & (b)] is equivalent to: Everyone ought to pursue A's self-interest, and everyone ought to pursue B's self-interest, and everyone ought to pursue C's self-interest, and. . . .[4] When the interests of A and B are incompatible, one must pursue both of these incompatible goals, which, of course, is impossible. On this interpretation, ethical egoism must fail in its function of guiding conduct (one of the most important uses of moral judgments). In particular, it must fail with respect to just those cases in which the guidance is most wanted — conflicts of interests. In such situations, the theory implies that one must both do and not do a certain thing. Therefore, since ethical egoism cannot guide conduct in these crucial cases, it is inadequate as a moral theory and must be rejected.

Ethical egoism suffers from three serious defects if it is interpreted as [(a) & (b)]. These defects are closely related. The first is that the theory implies a contradiction, namely, that some actions are both right *and* wrong. The second defect is that the theory, if altered and made coherent by rejecting one of its parts, cannot fulfill one of its essential tasks: Altered, it can provide for first-person moral judgments *or* for second- and third-person moral judgments, but not for both. The third defect is that the theory cannot guide conduct and must fail in its advice-giving function because it advises (remember: advises, all things considered) a person to do what it advises him not to do.

Any one of these defects would be sufficient to refute the theory, and indeed they do refute ethical egoism when it is defined as [(a) & (b)]. The only plausible way to escape these arguments is to abandon Frankena's definition and reformulate egoism so that they are no longer applicable. Clearly, (a) must remain, for it seems central to any egoistic position. However, we can replace (b) with the following:

(c) If A is a spectator judging about anyone else, B, then A is to use this criterion: B ought to do *y* if and only if *y* is in B's overall self-interest.

The objections to [(a) & (b)] given above do not apply to [(a) & (c)]. [(a) & (c)] yields no contradictions, even in cases where self-interests conflict or are irreconcilable. When we suppose that B is the agent, that *s* is in B's overall self-interest, and that *s* is against A's overall self-interest, both B and A will agree in their moral judgments about this case, that is, both will agree that B ought to do *s*. And, of course, the theory provides for all moral judgments, whether first-, second-, or third-person; since it yields no contradictions, there is no need to make it coherent by choosing between its parts and thereby making it inadequate.

Finally, this interpretation avoids the charge that ethical egoism cannot adequately fulfill its conduct guiding function. Given [(a) & (c)], it will never truly be the case that an agent ought to pursue anyone's self-interest except his own. Any judgment of the form "A ought to pursue B's self-interest" will be false, unless it is understood to mean that pursuit of B's self-interest is a part of the pursuit of A's self-interest (and this, of course, would not contribute to any incoherence in the theory). Thus, the theory will have no difficulty in being an effective practical theory; it will not give contradictory advice, even in situations where interests conflict. True, it will not remove such conflicts — indeed, in practice it might well encourage them; but a conflict is not a contradiction. The theory tells A to pursue a certain goal, and it tells B to pursue another goal, and it does this unequivocally. That both cannot succeed in their pursuits is irrelevant to the coherence of the theory and its capacity to guide conduct, since both *can* do what they are advised to do, all things considered — pursue their own self-interests.

(i), when interpreted as [(a) & (c)], is a fully objective moral theory. Therefore, in defending ethical egoism, one need not be driven into the kind of subjectivism which holds that "right," "wrong," "morally justified," and even "true" when used in a moral argument or judgment always mean "right for A," or "right for B," or "wrong for A," or "true for B," or perhaps "right from A's point of view," "wrong from B's point of view," etc.[5] Such usage would be exceedingly peculiar, for in what sense can a judgment or action be said to be justified, all things considered, if it is justified for me and unjustified for you? Thus, interpreting ethical egoism as [(a) & (c)] rather than as [(a) & (b)] has the great merit of making it possible to avoid the temptation to subjectivism.

There remains the question whether [(a) & (c)] is a plausible interpretation of (i), that is, whether it is "consistent with the spirit of ethical egoism." It is

certainly consistent with the "spirit" behind the "ethical" part of egoism in its willingness to universalize the doctrine. It is also consistent with the "egoistic" part of the theory in that if a person does faithfully follow (a) he will behave as an egoist. Adding the fact that [(a) & (c)] is a coherent theory adequate to the special ethical chores so far discussed, do we have any reason for rejecting it as an interpretation of (i) and ethical egoism? So far, I think not. Therefore, I conclude that Frankena has failed to refute egoism. It has thus far survived the test of universalization and still remains as a candidate for "the one true moral theory."

III

In his article, "Ultimate Principles and Ethical Egoism," Brian Medlin maintains that ethical egoism cannot be an ultimate moral principle because it fails to guide our actions, tell us what to do, or determine our choice between alternatives. He bases this charge on his view that because ethical egoism is the expression of inconsistent desires, it will always tell people to do incompatible things. Thus:

> I have said from time to time that the egoistic principle is inconsistent. I have not said it is contradictory. This for the reason that we can, without contradiction, express inconsistent desires and purposes. To do so is not to say anything like "Goliath was ten feet tall and not ten feet tall." Don't we all want to have our cake and eat it too? And when we say we do we aren't asserting a contradiction whether we be making an avowal of our attitudes or stating a fact about them. We all have conflicting motives. None of this, however, can do the egoist any good. For we assert our ultimate principles not only to express our own attitudes but also to induce similar attitudes in others, to dispose them to conduct themselves as we wish. Insofar as their desires conflict, people don't know what to do. And, therefore, no expression of incompatible desires can ever serve for an ultimate principle of human conduct.

That egoism could not successfully guide one's conduct was a criticism discussed and rebutted in section II. There, it rested upon Frankena's formulation of egoism as equal to [(a) & (b)] and was easily circumvented by replacing principle (b) with principle (c). Medlin's charge is significant, however, because it appears to be applicable to [(a) & (c)] as well[6] and therefore must be directly refuted if egoism is to be maintained.

The heart of Medlin's argument is his position that to affirm a moral principle is to express approval of any and all actions following from that principle. This means for Medlin not only that the egoist is committed to approving all egoistic actions but also that such approval will involve wanting those actions to occur and trying to bring them about, even when they would be to one's own detriment.

> But is not to believe that someone should act in a certain way to try to persuade him to do so? Of course, we don't always try to persuade people to act as we think they should act. We may be lazy, for instance. But insofar as we believe that Tom should do so and so, we have a tendency to induce him to do so and so. Does it make sense to say: "Of course you should do this, but for goodness' sake don't"? Only where we mean: "You should do this for certain reasons, but here are even more persuasive reasons for not doing it." If the egoist believes ultimately that others should mind themselves alone, then, he must persuade them accordingly. If he doesn't persuade them, he is no universal egoist.

According to Medlin, if I adopt ethical egoism and am thereby led to approve of A's egoistic actions (as would follow from (c)), I must also *want* A to behave in that way and must want him to be happy, to come out on top, and so forth where wanting is interpreted as setting an end for my own actions and where it tends (according to the intensity of the want, presumably) to issue in my "looking after him."

Of course, I will also approve of my pursuing my own welfare (as would follow from (a)) and will want myself to be happy, to come out on top, and so forth. Since I want my own success, I will want A's noninterference. Indeed, what I will want A to do, and will therefore approve of A's doing, is to pursue my welfare, rather than his own.

It is thus the case that whenever my interest conflicts with A's interest, I will approve of inconsistent ends and will want incompatible things ("I want myself to come out on top and I want Tom to come out on top"). Since I approve of incompatible ends, I will be motivated in contrary directions—both away from and toward my own welfare, for instance. However, this incompatibility of desires is not sufficient to produce inaction and does not itself prove Medlin's point, for one desire may be stronger than the other. If the egoist's approval of his own well-being were always greater than his approval of anyone else's well-being, the inconsistent desires constituting egoism would not prevent (i) from decisively guiding conduct. Unfortunately for the egoist, his principle will in fact lead him to inaction, for in being universal (i) expresses equal approval of each person's pursuing his own self-interest, and therefore, insofar as his desires follow from this principle, none will be stronger than another.

We can now explain Medlin's conclusion that "the proper objection to the man who says 'Everyone should look after his own interests regardless of the interests of others' is not that he isn't speaking the truth, but simply that he isn't speaking." Upon analysis, it is clear that the egoist is "saying" that others should act so that he himself comes out on top and should not care about Tom, Dick, et al., but they should also act so that Tom comes out on top and should not care about himself, Dick, the others, and so forth. This person *appears* to be saying how people should act, and that they should act in a definite way. But his "directions" can guide no one. They give one nothing to do. Therefore, such a man has in fact said nothing.

I think Medlin's argument can be shown to be unsuccessful without a discussion of the emotivism in which it is framed. The egoist can grant that there is a correct sense in which affirmation of a moral principle is the expression of approval. The crux of the issue is Medlin's particular analysis of approbation, and this can be shown to be incorrect.

We may grant that the egoist is committed to approving of anyone's egoistic behavior at least to the extent of believing that the person ought so to behave. Such approval will hold of all egoistic actions, even those that endanger his own welfare. But does believing that A ought to do *y* commit one to wanting A to do *y*? Surely not. This is made clear by the analogy with competitive games. Team A has no difficulty in believing that team B ought to make or try to make a field goal while not wanting team B to succeed, while hoping that team B fails, and, indeed, while trying to prevent team B's success. Or consider this example: I may see how my chess opponent can put my king in check. That is how he ought to move. But believing that he ought to move his bishop and check my king does not commit me to wanting him to do that, nor to persuading him to do so. What *I* ought to do is sit there quietly, hoping he does not move as he ought.

Medlin's mistake is to think that believing that A ought to do *y* commits one to *wanting* A to do *y* and hence to encouraging or otherwise helping A to do *y*. The examples from competitive games show that this needn't be so. The egoist's reply to Medlin is that just as team A's belief that team B ought to do so and so is compatible with their not wanting team B to do so and so, so the egoist's belief that A ought to do *y* is compatible with the egoist's not wanting A to do *y*. Once this is understood, egoism has no difficulty in decisively guiding conduct, for insofar as (i) commits the egoist to wanting anything, it only commits him to wanting his own welfare. Since he does not want incompatible goals, he has no trouble in deciding what to do according to (a) and in judging what others ought to do according to (c).

IV

There is in Medlin's paper confusion concerning what the egoist wants or values and why he believes in ethical egoism. The egoist does not believe that everyone ought to pursue their own self-interest merely because *he* wants to get *his* goodies out of life. If this were all there were to his position, the egoist would not bother with (i) or with moral concepts at all. He would simply go about doing what he wants. What reason, then, does he have to go beyond wanting his own welfare to ethical egoism? On Medlin's emotivist account, his reason must be that he also wants B to have B's goodies, and wants D to have his, and so forth, even when it is impossible that everybody be satisfied. But I argued in the preceding section that the egoist is not committed to wanting such states, and that it is not nonsense for him to affirm (i) and desire his own welfare yet not desire the welfare of others. Therefore, the question remains — why affirm egoism at all?

The egoist's affirmation of (i) rests upon both teleological and deontological elements. What *he*

finds to be of ultimate value is his own welfare. He needn't be selfish or egocentric in the ordinary sense (as Medlin sometimes suggests by such paraphrases as "Let each man do what he wants regardless of what anyone else wants"), but he will value his own interest above that of others. Such an egoist would share Sidgwick's view that when "the painful necessity comes for another man to choose between his own happiness and the general happiness, he must as a reasonable being prefer his own."[7] When this occasion does arise, the egoist will want the other's welfare less than he wants his own, and this will have the practical effect of not wanting the other's welfare at all. It is in terms of this personal value that he guides his actions, judging that he ought to do *y* if and only if *y* is in his overall self-interest. This is the teleological element in his position.

However, there is no reason that others should find his well-being to be of value to them, less more to be of ultimate value; and it is much more likely that each will find his own welfare to be his own ultimate value. But if it is reasonable for the egoist to justify his behavior in terms of what he finds to be of ultimate value, then it is also reasonable for others to justify their behavior in terms of what they find to be of ultimate value. This follows from the requirement of universalization and provides the deontological element. Interpreted as "Similar things are right for similar people in similar circumstances," the universalization principle seems undeniable. Failing to find any relevant difference between himself and others, the egoist must admit that it can be morally permissible for him to pursue his self-interest only if it is morally permissible for each person to pursue his self-interest. He therefore finds himself committed to (i), even though he does not *want* others to compete with him for life's goods.

Medlin and others have not construed egoism in this way. While they have acknowledged the role of deontological considerations in the production of (i) by noting the universalization requirement, they have given more emphasis to its teleological aspects. In particular, they have thought that at the least (i) states that a certain state of affairs is intrinsically valuable and *therefore* ought to be brought about. If this is so, to affirm the principle is to accept this set of values. Medlin then argues that an egoist cannot accept these values and remain a consistent egoist. He asks of the ethical egoist: "Just what does he value? Is it the well-being of himself, Tom, Dick, and Harry or merely their going on in a certain way regardless of whether or not this is going to promote their well-being?"

Consider this latter alternative and the result if everyone were to follow (i) and behave as the egoist claims it is most reasonable for them to do. We would have a state wherein everyone disregarded the happiness of others when their happiness clashed with one's own. Given the normal condition of the world in which the major goods requisite for well-being (food, clothing, sex, glory, etc.) are not in overabundance, we would have a state of competition, struggle, and probably much avoidable misery. Hobbes's overstatement is that it would be a "war of everyman against everyman" in which life is "solitary, poor, nasty, brutish, and short."

Since Medlin holds that acceptance of a moral principle such as (i) rests on valuing that state of affairs which compliance to the principle would bring about, and that acceptance of this principle as ultimate rests on placing ultimate value on that state of affairs (on wanting that state more than any other), it is understandable that ethical egoism should appear to him to be "a funny kind of egoism."

Medlin's point is that a person valuing such a state of affairs is no longer an egoist in any natural sense of that term. An egoist values his own welfare, but the Hobbesian conditions described above include this value only incidentally, if at all. To make his position consistent, therefore, he must choose between the following alternatives. He can accept the actual values promoted by his theory. Since these are not egoistic values (confirmed by the fact that he could not convince others to value and promote such a state of affairs by appealing solely to their self-interest), this is to abandon egoism. Or he can accept self-interest as the ultimate value which, because of the universalization requirement, will involve accepting each person's self-interest as of equal value. This will be to abandon egoism and (i) for a form of utilitarianism.

Medlin's crucial charge against ethical egoism is not that it is incoherent or unable to fulfill the necessary functions of a moral theory such as decisively guiding conduct in cases where interests conflict, but that principle (i) is simply not an expression of egoism. Egoism is an unformulable moral theory, and hence *no* moral theory.[8] This charge rests, however, on what I shall call the material conception of value. Medlin's criticism rests on the assumption that ethical egoism (i.e., principle (i)) is saying that there is something of intrinsic value which everyone ought to pursue—that there is one specific state of affairs everyone ought to pursue. This is false, and is the result of not distinguishing *material* valuations from what I shall call *formal* valuations.

In analyzing the teleological basis of (i), Medlin and others have been misled by imposing on the egoist a conception of intrinsic or ultimate value which he does not hold. They suppose that there is *one* value or set of values which is or ought to be *common* to everyone (or they suppose that principles like (i) express the desire that such a set of values be common to everyone).It is characteristic of this position that these values are of such a nature that everyone ought to promote them; they are objective and binding upon everyone. It is in terms of this common goal that each person's actions are to be guided and justified. Furthermore, these values demand and establish a harmony and concert among men's actions. There is some end, some state of affairs, perhaps quite complex, the establishment of which is the goal of all moral actions. The task of a moral theory, and particularly of any ultimate moral principle, is to direct one to such a goal. I call this view the *material conception of value.*

In utilitarianism, the single, though hardly simple, material value is the state of maximum social welfare—"the greatest happiness of the greatest number," "people being as happy as it is possible to make them," or some such variant. For Moore, it is a state in which there is a maximum of intrinsic goods—that is, of pleasure, knowledge, love, the enjoyment of beauty, moral qualities, and so forth.[9] On his view, Jones's pleasure is as valuable as my pleasure, and I have the same obligation to bring about that pleasure as Jones does. Supremacy of the state views are further instances of this conception, as is the view that each man is an end in himself and as such entitled to one's respect, where one sign of this respect is acting always so that any other being could share the ends of one's actions.

The egoist would replace this standard view with the *formal conception of value.* On this account, that which is to have ultimate value for different people will usually be the same only in the sense that it is the same *kind* of good but not the same particular instance of it. What is valued will be similar but normally not identical. In the statement, "Self-interest is the ultimate good," "self-interest" is used in a generic sense. What is specifically valued — the various contents of these self-interests — is quite different from person to person and sometimes mutually incompatible. What the egoist is saying, of course, is that his welfare has ultimate (or intrinsic) value to himself, though not to anyone else, and that Tom's welfare has ultimate (or intrinsic) value to Tom, but not to himself or others, and that Harry's welfare has ultimate value to Harry, but not . . . , and so forth. He is saying that his interests give him a reason for acting but give Tom and Harry none, and that Tom's interests give Tom a reason for acting but give him and Harry none, and that . . . , and so forth. Here, there is no common value shared by the egoist, Tom, Harry, et al., unless by accident.

According to a teleological moral theory, what a person ought to do is maximize the good or ultimate value, whatever that might be. If ultimate value is understood in the material sense, one will naturally believe that everyone has an obligation to bring about the same particular state of affairs. And since the egoist says everyone ought to act in a certain way, one will assume that this is because there is something ultimately valuable about everyone acting in that way. This would be a mistake. A moral theory may be teleological in terms of merely formal values. Nothing stronger is necessary. One can agree that people ought to maximize the good, but maintain that there is nothing which is good to everyone. Thus, people will be justified in pursuing somewhat different states, and possibly come into conflict. Moral principles will not have the objective of establishing a concert and harmony among men's actions nor of expressing a common goal. (i), in particular, will not have as its purpose the promotion of material values. If everyone does follow (i), states highly disvaluable to some will result, and there is no assurance that the egoist will succeed in maximizing value for himself.

In the previous section, I argued that the egoist's belief that other egoists ought to act in a way harmful to himself could be understood by noting similar beliefs in competitive games. We can likewise understand how the egoist can construct a coherent moral system not essentially dependent on material values by noting that practical systems such as professional football can be explained and justified without assuming a set of ultimate values common to all the parties encompassed by them. Thus, the player's ultimate values are, let us say, winning and being superior, money (for themselves), the satisfaction of playing the game, and glory; the owner's values are money (for *themselves*), promotion of civic or business enterprises, and winning and being superior; the spectator's values are the pleasures of watching the game and being a fan, both aesthetic and more visceral; the official's values are money (for themselves), and perhaps other goods such as superiority or "love of the game." These values are virtually all only formally the same; but their pursuit by the respective parties is sufficient to produce the game. The players' interests, for instance, do not have to be shared or even mutually compatible — only one team can win, glory is a scarce good requiring the defeat of others, and so forth. One player need not care about the others, or the spectators, except insofar as they figure *as means* necessary to his ends. Since he cannot win, or make a fortune, or even play football without others playing too, he must get together with them to form a league with all its paraphernalia. But even with such cooperation, the ultimate values Tom the football player is pursuing are quite different materially from those pursued by Harry the football player, though probably of the same kind. Similarly, acceptance of the egoist principle requires no more of a commitment to common material values than acceptance of the competitive game does, that is, none.

We began this section with a question suggested by Medlin: Why does the egoist believe that everyone ought to pursue his own self-interest rather than believe that everyone ought to pursue *his* self-interest or simply going off to get his own? Medlin thought that the egoist could not coherently maintain (i) and remain an egoist — that he must in fact simply go off to get his own. I have argued that he can, and have tried to answer Medlin's question as follows: The egoist finds that his own self-interest gives him a reason to act in certain ways, but he does not think that this self-interest per se gives any other person a reason to act. Self-interest is an ultimate good in the formal but not the material sense. He therefore holds that what *he* ought to do, all things considered (what it would be most reasonable for him to do), is to pursue his own self-interest, even to the harming of others when necessary. But he further acknowledges that if this form of reasoning is sufficient to justify his egoistic behavior, it is sufficient to justify anyone's, or everyone's egoistic behavior. Consequently, he will accept the universalization of his position to "For each person, it is most reasonable for him to pursue his own self-interest, even to the harming of others if necessary," or to "$(x)(y)(x$ ought to do y if and only if y is in x's overall self-interest)." While this is a teleological moral principle because it states that a person ought to maximize value, it is a mistake to think that it points to one particular state of affairs which is valuable and which *therefore* ought to be promoted by everyone. Such a mistake is based on the failure to distinguish between material and formal valuations. Because (i) establishes others' welfare as valuable only in the formal sense, the egoist can affirm (i) without being committed to accepting either their welfare or Hobbesian-like conditions of competition as valuable, thus avoiding Medlin's dilemma.

V

Medlin remarks that the egoist would be a fool to tell other people they should "look after themselves and no one else." He goes on to say:

> Obviously something strange goes on as soon as the ethical egoist tries to promulgate his doctrine. What is he doing when he urges upon his audience that they should each observe his own interests and those interests alone? Is he not acting contrary to the egoistic principle? It cannot be to his advantage to convince them, for seizing always their own advantage they will impair his.

So far as Medlin is concerned, I discussed this "strange" aspect of egoism when I argued that it was not necessary either to want or to urge another to do what he ought to do in order to believe that he ought to do it. Behind Medlin's requirement of promulgation was seen to be a commitment to the material conception of value. The difficulties such a commitment entail for the egoist can be avoided if he uses only formal valuations. Thus, Medlin has failed to show that the egoist must violate his principle in the very holding of it because he has failed to show that the egoist *must* promulgate that principle *if* he holds it.

At this point, many philosophers would argue that ethical egoism is an even stranger doctrine than Medlin supposes if it can be consistently held only when it is silently held. In this section, I shall examine their argument. We shall first look at what the egoist must abandon along with the requirement of promulgation. It appears as though this must include most of the activities and emotions characterizing morality as such. According to its critics, this would mean that ethical egoism was not a moral theory. We shall then consider the egoist's reply to this criticism.

Taking the long run fully into account, the egoist must hold his position silently if he is to remain prudent. This restriction is more serious than might be suspected, for it means the egoist must refrain not only from advocating his doctrine, but also from a wide range of behavior typical of any morality. For instance, he will not be able to enter into moral discussions, at least not sincerely or as an egoist, for to debate a moral issue will ultimately require him to argue for (i). This will not be to his interest for at least the reason that others will become suspicious of him and cease to trust him. They will learn he is an egoist and treat him accordingly. It would be even worse if he should win the debate and convince them.

Nor will he be able to give or receive moral advice. If it is objected that he can advise others as long as interests do not conflict, it will do to note that it is not to his interest to have his egoistic views known. Giving of advice involves giving reasons for certain actions; inquiries about the moral principle upon which that advice is based are therefore appropriate. Of course, the egoist can lie. When Harry comes to Tom about his affair with Dick's wife, Tom can approve, professing enlightened views about marriage, noting that there are no children, that both are adults, and so forth, although he knows Harry's behavior will soon lead to a scandal ruining Harry's career — all to Tom's advantage. Tom has advised Harry, but not sincerely; he has not told Harry *what he thinks Harry really ought to do* — what would be most in Harry's overall self-interest. And Tom ought not, since he himself is following (i). This all goes to make the point; the egoist is not sincerely advising Harry, but rather pretending to sincerely advise him while really deceiving and manipulating him.

This use of advice — to manipulate others — is limited, and perhaps bought at a price too great for the egoist to pay. Since advising is a public activity, urging others to be benevolent (in order to benefit from their actions) gives them grounds to require one to be benevolent toward them, and thus to create sanctions restricting the scope of his self-interested behavior.

Worst of all, it will do the egoist himself no good to *ask* for moral advice for he is bound not to get what he wants. If he asks nonegoists, he will be told to do things which might be in his self-interest, but usually won't be. What sort of help could he get from a Kantian or a utilitarian? Their advice will follow from the wrong moral principle. If he asks another egoist, he is no better off, since he cannot be trusted. Knowing that he is an egoist, he knows that he is following (a), acting in his own self-interest, and lying if he can benefit from it. The egoist is truly isolated from any moral community, and must always decide and act alone, without the help of others.

It will not be to the egoist's self-interest to support his moral principle with sanctions. He will be unable to praise those who do what they ought, unable to blame those who flagrantly shirk their moral tasks. Nor will he be able to establish institutions of rewards and punishments founded on his principle. The egoist cannot sincerely engage in any of these activities. He will punish or blame people for doing what they ought not to do (for doing what is not in their self-interests) only by coincidence and then under some other rubric than violation of (i). To punish people for not being egoists is to encourage them to be egoists, and this is not to his interest. Similarly, the egoist, if he engages in such an activity at all, will praise people for doing what they ought to do only by chance, and always under a different, nonegoistic label.

A corollary to this is the egoist's inability to teach (i) to his children (while himself following it). It is imprudent to raise egoistic children, since among other things, the probability of being abandoned in old age is greatly increased. Therefore, the egoist can give his children no sincere moral instruction, and most likely will be advised to teach them to disapprove of his actions and his character, should they become aware of their true nature.

Finally, one of the points of appealing to a moral principle is to justify one's behavior *to others*—to convince them that their (sometimes forcible) opposition to this behavior is unwarranted and ought to be withdrawn. When we do convince someone of the rightness of our actions, he normally comes onto our side, even if reluctantly. Thus, the teenage daughter tries to convince her father that it is right and proper for sixteen year old girls to stay out until 12:30 (rather than 11:00) because if she is successful and he agrees with her, he then has *no excuse* (other things being equal) for still withholding his permission. For an ethical egoist, this point is doomed to frustration for two reasons: first, because justifying one's behavior in terms of (i) gives an opponent no reason to cease his opposition if maintaining it would be in his own interest; and second, because it will not be to the egoist's interest to publicly justify his behavior to others on egoistic grounds, thereby running the risk of converting them to egoism. Therefore, the egoist is unable to engage in *interpersonal reasoning* with his moral principle as its basis—he can neither justify nor excuse his egoistic actions as such in the interpersonal sense of "justify" and "excuse."

Adherence to the egoistic principle makes it impossible, because imprudent, for one to sincerely engage in any of these moral activities. There are also typical moral attitudes and emotions which, while perhaps not impossible for an egoist to sincerely have, it is impossible for him to sincerely express. I have in mind remorse, regret, resentment, repentance, forgiveness, revenge, outrage and indignation, and the form of sympathy known as moral support. Let us take forgiveness. When can the egoist forgive another, and for what? One forgives the other's wrongs, wrongs which are normally done against oneself. First, it is hard to see how someone could wrong someone else given ethical egoism, for (i) gives one no obligations to others, and hence no way of shirking those obligations. At least, one has no such obligations directly. Second, what is the nature of the wrong action which is to be forgiven? It must be a failure to properly pursue self-interest. Suppose Harry makes this lapse. Can Tom forgive him? Insofar as such forgiveness involves nonexpressed beliefs and attitudes, yes. But Tom would be unwise to express this attitude or to forgive Harry in the fuller, public sense. Partly because if their interests conflict, Tom's good will involve Harry's harm; Tom does not want Harry to do what he ought, and Tom ought not to encourage him to do so, which would be involved in overtly forgiving him. And partly because of the general imprudence of making it known that one is an egoist, which would be involved in expressing forgiveness of nonegoistic behavior. If the egoist is to forgive people where this involves the expression of forgiveness, his doing so must be basically insincere.

Similar considerations hold for the expression of the other emotions and attitudes mentioned. As for those which are not so clearly dependent upon some manner of public expression, such as resentment and remorse, it is perhaps not impossible for the egoist to have them (or to be capable of having them), but it is clear that their objects and occasion will be quite different from what they are in the standard morality. Resentment as a moral attitude involves taking offense at someone's failure to do what they ought. But why should the egoist be offended if other people don't look after their interests, at least when their interests are not connected with his own? And when their interests are connected, the offense does not arise from the fact that the other did something wrong—failed to properly pursue his own interests—but because of the further and undesirable consequences of this failure, but consequences for which that person was not liable. Resentment here is very strange, all the more so because of the formal rather than material commitment of the egoist to the obligation to pursue one's own self-interest. Since he doesn't value others' doing what they ought, any resentment he feels must be slight and rather abstract, amounting to little more than the belief that they ought not to behave that way.

Granting that it would not be in his overall self-interest for others to be egoists too, the ethical egoist has compelling reasons not to engage sincerely in any of the activities mentioned above, as well as not to give expression to various typical moral attitudes and emotions. This is strange not because the egoist is in some sense required to promulgate his doctrine while at the same time faithfully follow it, for we saw above that he can coherently reject this demand, but strange because his position seems to have lost most of the features characterizing a morality. When put into practice, ethical egoism discards the moral activities of advocacy, moral discussion, giving and asking of advice, using sanctions to reward and punish, praising and blaming, moral instruction and training, and interpersonal excusing and justification, as well as the expressing of many moral attitudes and emotions. With these features gone, what remains that constitutes a morality? The egoist may, indeed, have a coherent practical system, but

since it lacks certain major structural features of a morality, it is not a *moral theory*. Consider a legal theory which, when put into practice, turns out to have neither trials, nor judges, nor juries, nor sentencing, nor penal institutions, nor legislating bodies. Could it still be a legal theory and lack all of these? Isn't the case similar with ethical egoism?

If the above account is correct, its conclusion would be that egoism is a coherent practical theory, able to guide behavior and provide for the critical assessment of the actions of others without contradiction, but simply not a moral theory of conduct. Many philosophers would agree to the basis of this conclusion—that a theory lacking the wide range of typical moral activities and expressions that egoism lacks is not a moral theory—among them Frankena and Medlin. On their views, a morality must be interpersonal in character if it is not interpersonal through a commitment to material values, at least interpersonal through a commitment to the various public activities mentioned, and perhaps to methods of carrying them out which will tend toward producing harmonious, if not common, values. Since the egoist is committed to a noninterpersonal morality, a private not public morality, and to only formal values, his position is in their view a nonmoral position, many of whose conclusions will be judged immoral by any legitimate moral theory.

Frankena and Medlin agree that a silent theory is not a moral theory. A moral theory requires publicity, and cannot be private. Thus, Frankena says:

> Here we must understand that the ethical egoist is not just taking the egoistic principle of acting and judging as his own private maxim. One could do this, and at the same time keep silent about it or even advocate altruism to everyone else, which might well be to one's advantage. But if one does this, one is not adopting a moral principle, for as we shall see, if one takes a maxim as a moral principle, one must be ready to universalize it.

Here, Frankena connects nonuniversalization with silence, and thereby universalization with promulgation. This is a very strong sense of "universalize" which goes well beyond the principle "What's right for one person is right for similar people in similar circumstances." One can satisfy the universalization requirement in this latter sense by acknowledging that everyone would be justified in behaving as you are. As we have seen, this can be done without either wanting or urging others to do what they ought. But Frankena takes universalization to be much more, as is made clear by this earlier passage:

> Now morality in the sense indicated is, in one aspect, a social enterprise, not just a discovery or invention of the individual for his own guidance . . . it is not social merely in the sense of being a system governing the relations of one individual to others . . . it is also social in its origins, sanctions, and functions. It is an instrument of society as a whole for the guidance of individuals and smaller groups. It makes demands on individuals which are, initially at least, external to them. . . . As a social institution, morality must be contrasted with prudence.

What it is important to note about this conception of universalization and morality is that it can coherently be rejected.[10] Universalization in this strong sense is not a rational requirement (not analytic) as it appears to be in the weak sense. Our extended analogy between ethical egoism and competitive games shows just how coherently these strong conditions can be abandoned. At the most, this strong sense (in part explicated in terms of the various moral activities discussed above) may be part of the notion of "morality"; if so, egoism could not correctly label itself "ethical" or claim to be a moral theory. But this fact does not show that egoism as defined by (i) is mistaken, unreasonable, or inferior to any moral theory.

I personally think that it makes sense to speak of egoism as a morality, since I think it makes sense to speak of a "private morality" and of its being superior to "public moralities." The egoist's basic question is "What ought I to do; what is most reasonable for me to do?" This question seems to be a moral question through and through, and any coherent answer to it thereby deserves to be regarded as a moral theory. What is central here is the rational justification of a certain course of behavior. Such behavior will be justified in the sense that its reasonableness follows from a coherent and plausible set of premises. This kind of justification and moral reasoning can be carried out on the desert island and is not necessarily interpersonal — it does not have as one of its goals the minimal cooperation of some second party. Whether one *calls* the result a "moral-

ity" or not is of no matter, for its opponents must show it to be a poor competitor to the other alternatives. With respect to egoism, they cannot do this by arguing that (i) is logically incoherent or is incapable of being a practical system or violates any "principles of reason," such as universalization. I have tried to show how all these attempts would fail. I have even suggested in sections III and IV the way the egoist can argue for the reasonableness of his position (and it has, of course, seemed eminently reasonable to innumerable men, the "common man" not being the least among these). I therefore conclude that ethical egoism is a possible moral theory, not to be lightly dismissed. Its challenge to standard moralities is great, and not easily overcome.

If one insists that egoism is without the pall of morality, the obvious question one must face is: "Why be moral?" It is not at all easy to convincingly show that the egoist should (that it would be most reasonable for him to) abandon his position for one which could require him to sacrifice his self-interest, even to the point of death. What must be shown is not simply that it is to the egoist's interests to *be in* a society structured by various social, moral, and legal institutions, all of which limit categorically certain expressions of self-interest (as do the penalty rules in football), which is Hobbes's point, but that the egoist also has compelling reasons (always) to abide by its rules, to continue to be moral, social, or legal when "the painful necessity comes for a man to choose between his own happiness and the general happiness."

The egoist can acknowledge that it is in his long-range self-interest to be in a moral system and thus that there should be categorical public rules restricting his egoistic behavior. Publicly, these rules will be superior to self-interest, and will be enforced as such. But according to his private morality, they will not be superior. Rather, they will be interpreted as hypotheticals setting prices (sometimes very dear) upon certain forms of conduct. Thus, the egoist will believe that, while it is always reasonable to be in a moral system, it is not always reasonable to act morally while within that system (just as it is not always reasonable to obey the rules of football). The opponent of egoism, in order to soundly discredit it, must show that moral behavior is always reasonable.[11] If the conception of "formal value" is admitted as sound, and if the egoist is correct in his claim that there are no material values, I do not see how such attempts could be successful.

Endnotes

[1] Joseph Butler, *Fifteen Sermons Preached at the Rolls Chapel* (1726). Standard anthologies of moral philosophy include the most important of these sermons; or see the Library of Liberal Arts Selection, *Five Sermons* (New York: The Bobbs-Merrill Company, Inc., 1950). See particularly Sermons I and XI. In XI, Butler says of rational self-love that "the object the former pursues is something internal — our own happiness, enjoyment, satisfaction. . . . The principle we call 'self-love' never seeks anything external for the sake of the thing, but only as a means of happiness or good." Butler is not, however, an egoist for there is also in man conscience and "a natural principle of benevolence" (see Sermon I).

[2] Brian Medlin, "Ultimate Principles and Ethical Egoism," *Australasian Journal of Philosophy,* XXXV (1957):111 — 18.

[3] William Frankena, *Ethics* (Englewood Cliffs, N.J.: Prentice-Hall, Inc., 1963): pp. 16 – 18. References to Frankena in sections II and V are to this book.

[4] This can be shown as follows:
  i. Suppose A is the evaluator, then
   What ought A to do? A ought to do what's in A's interest. (by (a))
   What ought B to do? B ought to do ” (by (b))
   What ought C to do? C ought to do ” (by (b))
   etc.
   Therefore, everyone ought to do what's in A's interest. (by (a) & (b))
  ii. Suppose B is the evaluator, then
   What ought A to do? A ought to do what's in B's interest. (by (b))
   What ought B to do? B ought to do ” (by (a))
   What ought C to do? C ought to do ” (by (b))
   etc.
   Therefore, everyone ought to do what's in B's interest. (by (a) & (b))
  iii. Suppose C is the evaluator, then
      "
      "
    etc.
Conclusion: Everyone ought to do what's in A's interest, and everyone ought to do what's in B's interest, and . . . *etc.*

[5] As is Gardner Williams, *Humanistic Ethics* (New York: Philosophical Library, 1951); see Chapter III, particularly pp. 29–31.

[6] Medlin himself does not distinguish between (b) and (c). Some of his remarks suggest (c). Thus, at one point he says:

> When he [the egoist] tries to convince me that he should look after himself, he is attempting so to dispose me that I shall approve when he drinks my beer and steals Tom's wife. I cannot approve of his looking after himself and himself alone without so far approving of his achieving his happiness, regardless of the happiness of myself and others.

This passage implies that as a spectator assessing another's conduct, I should employ principle (c) and approve of A's

doing *y* whenever *y* promotes A's interest, even if this is at the expense of my welfare.

But other of his remarks suggest (b). Thus, the above passage continues:

> So that when he sets out to persuade me that he should look after himself regardless of others, he must also set out to persuade me that I should look after him regardless of myself and others. Very small chance he has!

Here, the implication is that the egoist as a spectator and judge of another should assess the other's behavior according to his own interests, not the other's, which would be in accordance with (b).

Perhaps Medlin is arguing that the egoist is committed to accepting both (b) and (c), as well as (a). This interpretation is consistent with his analysis of "approval."

[7] Henry Sidgwick, *The Methods of Ethics,* 7th ed. (London: Macmillan and Co., 1907), preface to the 6th edition, p. xvii.

[8] The egoist "must behave as an individual egoist, if he is to be an egoist at all," but since "the individual egoist cannot promulgate his doctrine without enlarging it, what he has is no doctrine at all."

[9] G. E. Moore, *Ethics* (London: Oxford University Press, 1912), Chapter VII, "Intrinsic Value," pp. 140, 146–47, 152–53.

[10] This sense of universalization needn't be rejected. One can coherently promulgate (i), but as we saw in section IV, doing so would make one something other than an egoist in the fullest sense. At the least, such a person would appear to value the state wherein everyone pursues their own welfare, wherein everyone tries to come out on top; this is a material, not formal value. ("But perhaps neither gain nor loss. For us, there is only the trying. The rest is not our business." T. S. Eliot.) The more one stresses the "moral" aspects of adopting (i) which seem to require sincere participation in the various public activities mentioned above, the more the "egoist" will be committed to the other than egoistic values which will result if everyone heeds him, such as: conflict, struggle, and competition, strength, craft, and strategic ability, excitement, danger, and insecurity. While it is true that strictly speaking these values are not egoistic, even so (i) retains its egoistic "flavor." This is evident when it is applied to situations of irreconcilable conflict. The issue is to be settled by force or craft, or whatever, just in the way that it would be settled under the full-fledged, nonpromulgated egoism. It is perhaps difficult to imagine someone having the outlook needed in order to publicly promulgate (i) in such inhospitable conditions; nonetheless, it seems a possibility, and perhaps the professional soldier or gambler, or Zorba the Greek are approximations. Certainly, he would not be Medlin's misguided utilitarian.

[11] This brief discussion of the question "Why be moral?" has Baier's attempt to show that egoism is ultimately unreasonable as its specific background, and is formulated in terms most appropriate to his treatment of the problem. See Kurt Baier, *The Moral Point of View* (New York: Random House, 1965), Chapter 7, especially sections 3 and 4.

III.5 *Evolution and Ethics: The Sociobiological Approach*

Michael Ruse

Michael Ruse is a professor of philosophy at Guelph University in Canada and a leading advocate of sociobiological ethics. Ruse offers the following abstract of his essay:

Traditional evolutionary ethics "social Darwinism," has long been an object of philosophical scorn. In this essay, I suggest that much of the criticism is misdirected, but agree that ultimately the attempt to use biology to justify moral claims is doomed. However, recent exciting advances in the theory of social evolution — "sociobiology" — invite one to try again to relate morality to biology. It is this which I try to do, suggesting that this can indeed be done, in a very fruitful manner. The trick is to take a neo-Humean approach, denying ultimate foundations and trying rather to show how it is that ethics, "a collective illusion of the genes," is a function of the human evolutionary move to sociality. Thus one avoids mistaken attempts to bridge the is/ought barrier but is able nevertheless to answer all of those traditional questions about morality that have a genuine solution.

Evolutionary ethics is one of those subjects with a bad philosophical smell. Everybody knows (or "knows") that it has been the excuse for some of the worst kinds of fallacious arguments in the philosophical workbook and that in addition it has been used as support for socioeconomic policies of the most grotesque and hateful nature, all the way from cruel nineteenth-century capitalism to twentieth-century concentration camps (Jones 1980; Richards 1987; Russett 1976; Ruse 1986). It has been enough for the student to murmur the magical phrase "naturalistic fallacy," in order to be able to move on to the next question, confident of having gained full marks thus far on the exam (Flew 1967; Singer 1981).

Having once felt precisely this way myself, I now see that I was wrong — wrong about science, wrong about history, and wrong about philosophy. It is true that my newfound enthusiasm is connected with exciting developments in modern evolutionary biology, especially that part which deals with social behavior (sociobiology), and it is true also that much that has been written in the past does not bear full critical philosophical scrutiny, but evolutionary ethics has rarely if ever had the awful nature of legend. The simple fact of the matter is that, like everyone else, philosophers have been only too happy to have had a convenient "Aunt Sally" against which they can hurl their critical coconuts and demonstrate their own intellectual purity, before going on to develop an alternative position of their own (Ruse 1979a, 1986, 1994).

In this essay, I shall put the case for an adequate, up-to-date evolutionary ethics. I shall do this partly historically, starting with the roots of the philosophy in the middle of the nineteenth century when it first began to attract attention and support, and working up to the most recent and still-enthusiastic proponents. I shall do this partly analytically, by arguing that modern advances in science enable one to appreciate the convictions of those that have gone before — that it really has to matter that we humans are the product of a long, slow, natural process of evolution rather than the miraculous products of a good God on the sixth day — and yet arguing that we can produce a moral philosophy that is

This article was commissioned for this work and appears in print for the first time here.

no less sensitive to important issues than it is to crucial insights grasped by past students of ethics.

As I set out on my task, however, let me remind you of a distinction that it is always useful to make when talking theoretically of moral matters, and that will certainly prove its worth to us. This is the distinction between prescriptions or exhortations about what one ought to do, and the justification that might be offered for such norms of conduct. The former level of discussion is generally known as *normative* or *prescriptive* ethics and the latter level as *metaethics* (Taylor 1978).

Simply to illustrate this distinction, let me take Christianity, which is nothing if not a religion with a strong moral basis. At the normative level, we find the Believer instructed to obey the Love Commandment: "Love your neighbor as yourself." At the metaethical level, we frequently find invocation of some version of the Divine Command theory: "That which is good is that which is the will of God." As it happens, there are sincere Christians who would challenge both of these ideas—some think faith more important than works, and, long before Christ, Plato was showing the problems with an appeal to God's Will (Could He really will us to do something that we now consider to be truly bad?). But I am not going to argue these matters here. For me, it is enough that you can now surely see how, when you are thinking about moral matters, there are these two levels of inquiry.

Social Darwinism

In 1859, the English scientist Charles Robert Darwin published his great book, *On the Origin of Species*. Before this, evolution had at best been a half-idea, at the realm of pseudo-science. After this, educated people the world over accepted that all organisms, including ourselves, have natural, developmental origins (Ruse 1979b; Bowler 1984). It is therefore not surprising that, from about this time, many people began turning from traditional sources of wisdom, especially religion, to science (evolution in particular) for help and guidance in what we should do and what we should think (Moore 1979).

It would be a mistake to think that Darwin himself was the chief spokesperson for the new

evolutionary ethics, even though it was his work that inspired and gave confidence. For all that the position was labeled "social Darwinism"—scholars debate to this day whether Darwin was really a genuine social Darwinian—the chief enthusiast ("proselytzer" is not too strong a word) was Darwin's fellow Englishman, Herbert Spencer (Jones 1980; Russett 1976). It was he who spent his life promoting evolution, not just as a science but as a whole way of life, including a way of moral life (Spencer 1904; Duncan 1908).

Thinking first at the normative level, we find what seems to be a fairly straightforward connection between Spencer's evolutionary beliefs and his prescriptions for moral conduct (Ruse 1986). Consider for a moment the theory or mechanism for evolution that Darwin proposed in the *Origin*. He argued that more organisms are always being born than can possibly survive and reproduce. There will thus be a "struggle for existence"; only some will survive and reproduce; and because success in the struggle will (on average) be a function of superior qualities, there will be an ongoing process of "natural selection" or (to use a phrase that Spencer invented and Darwin adopted) the "survival of the fittest." Given enough time, this will all add up to evolution, with the development of "adaptations," that is to say, features that help in life's battles.

It was Spencer's contention that, generally speaking, evolution is a good thing, a very good thing. Therefore, he argued simply and directly, what we humans ought to do is promote the forces of evolution or, at least, not stand in the way of their natural execution and consequences (Spencer 1892). How does this cash out as a social or moral philosophy? We have to face the fact that for humans, like for the rest of the living world, life is a struggle, and it always will and must be. In the world of business, as well as every other dimension of human existence, there will be those who succeed and those who fail. We therefore should do nothing to impede this natural process, and indeed we should do all that we can to promote it.

Simply put, in the words of the economists, we should promote a *laissez-faire* philosophy of life, where there is an absolute minimum of state interference in the running of daily affairs. Private charity may come to the aid of widows and children who stand in danger of going to the wall, but government has no right to interfere; let the chips fall where they may. Spencer (1851) even went so far as to argue that the state ought not provide light-houses to guide ships at sea. If the owners want them badly enough, they will provide them!

As it happens, recent scholarship has started to suggest that the connection between Spencer's evolutionism and his ethicizing is more complex than appears at first sight (Peel 1971; Wiltshire 1978; Richards 1987). But, whatever the true connections in Spencer's mind, there is little doubt that his philosophy was widely popular, especially when it was transported to the New World. Spencer's books far outsold those of Darwin. But the fate of his philosophy in that land illustrates a point we should keep always in mind when looking at sweeping moral philosophies. As with Christianity, very different normative consequences can supposedly be drawn from the same premises.

Some barons of industry and their supporters went whole hog on a philosophy of individualism and minimal state interference. Supposedly, John D. Rockefeller, Sr. told a Sunday school class (no less!) that the law of big business is the law of God and that it was right and proper that Standard Oil (which he founded and from which he made his wealth) should have crushed its competitors, whatever the economic and social consequences. Others, however, no less ardent in their Spencerianism, felt quite differently. One was the Scottish immigrant Andrew Carnegie, as successful as Rockefeller; it was he who founded U.S. Steel in Pittsburgh. In midlife, he took to the founding of public libraries, explicitly using the evolutionary justification that through such institutions the poor but gifted child would be able to practice self-improvement: survival of the fittest, as opposed to nonsurvival of the nonfittest!

Spencerianism went east also. At the turn of this century, the Chinese were his followers to the man(darin) (Pusey 1983). It was Germany, however, that saw the greatest flowering of evolutionary ethics, partly in consequence of and partly in parallel with the thinking of Spencer himself. The greatest proponent (of what came to be known as "Darwinismus") was the biologist Ernst Haeckel (1866). Yet, once again showing how ideas can change and be molded, we find that far from promoting individualism, Haeckel argued that one ought to endorse strong state controls, particularly as enforced through a trained and powerful civil service

(Haeckel 1868). This was a philosophy admirably suited to his society, for it was just at this time that Bismarck was extending Prussian rule, which did incorporate tight state control, to the rest of Germany.

To Haeckel, however, there was nothing artificial or forced about his moral thinking for, unlike Spencer (and Darwin), Haeckel located the center of life's struggles as occurring not between individuals but between groups or societies. To him, therefore — remember, this was just the time when Prussian virtues apparently triumphed through a massive defeat of France — evolutionary success demanded that one promote harmony and control within the group, for the betterment of all within against those without.

Many people think that, as we came into this century, traditional evolutionary ethics declined and vanished, or should have done, since it was transformed into an apology for some of the most vile social systems that humankind has ever known. In fact, as with perceptions of this philosophy in the nineteenth century, these claims are likewise somewhat mythical. Indeed, whether social Darwinism had any real connection (as many believe) with the worst movement of all, National Socialism (Nazism), is by no means a proven point (Gasman 1971; Kelley 1981). It is true that *something* had to be responsible for the movement, and apart from the nationalism in Haeckel's writings, his anti-Semitism would have struck a concordant note. But, against this, one would not have expected the Nazis to welcome a world philosophy that stressed the interrelated nature of all living things — monkeys and humans, Jews and Aryans. And they did not!

More to the point is the fact that there were still many evolutionary ethicists, even if drawn mainly from the ranks of biologists themselves. The most voluble and effective was probably Julian Huxley (1947), brother of the novelist Aldous, and grandson of Darwin's famous supporter, Thomas Henry Huxley. He thought the way to promote evolution lay in the spread of knowledge, especially scientific knowledge. In this fashion would humankind be able to conquer life's problems, like disease and poverty and war, and ensure a happier future. He was able to further his ends when, after the Second World War, with the founding of the United Nations, he was appointed first director general of UNESCO (Huxley 1948). Others who endorsed an evolutionary ethics included the great modern evolutionists Theodosius Dobzhansky (1967) and Ernst Mayr (1988).

And today the philosophy is far from moribund. Most widely published in recent years has been the Harvard entomologist and sociobiologist Edward O. Wilson (1978). A great admirer of Spencer, Wilson believes that humans live in symbiotic relationship with the rest of the living world, and that, by our very natures, we would literally wither and die without a diverse range of flora and fauna surrounding us (Wilson 1984). Life in an all-plastic world would be impossible. Hence, Wilson would have us promote biodiversity, and as a student of tropical ants, he himself is much concerned with movements to save the rain forests of South America. And all in the name of evolution!

Evolution and Progress

But now, guided by our distinction, let us turn to the question of metaethics. Even if you agree with me that evolutionary ethics has not been nearly as crude and offensive as legend would tell, there is still the matter of justification. Why should we promote laissez-faire and free enterprise? Why should we found public libraries? Why should we favor an efficient civil service, a world body for science and culture, the preservation of the rain forests?

It is at this point that, traditionally, philosophers swing into critical action. Inspired by a devastating critique of Spencer by G. E. Moore, in his *Principia Ethica* published in 1903, it is argued that admirable though any (or at least most) of these various directives may be, their supposed derivation stands in flat violation of the supposed "naturalistic fallacy" (Flew 1967; Waddington 1960). In Moore's language, goodness is a non-natural property, and one simply cannot define or explicate it in terms of natural properties like happiness or the course of evolution.

Another way of putting the point, reaching back to an older and more venerable philosophy, that of David Hume (1978), is to say that there is a logical difference between claims about matters of fact ("is" statements) and claims about morality

("ought" statements), and that traditional evolutionary ethics violates this distinction (Hudson 1983; Ruse 1979a). One derives claims about the way one ought to behave ("Found public libraries," "Preserve the rain forests") from claims about the way that things are ("Evolution works to preserve the fittest, to make humans dependent upon nature").

As it happens, I have considerable sympathy for these criticisms, and not simply because I am a professional philosopher. Indeed, as you will learn, I think David Hume was absolutely right to draw a distinction of kind between claims about matters of fact and claims about matters of obligation. This will be a key element in the evolutionary ethics that I myself will propose. But my experience is that those who endorse a traditional form of evolutionary ethics tend to find these arguments profoundly unconvincing — and not simply because they are not trained philosophers. Why should one claim that goodness is a non-natural property? Surely that is to presuppose the very point at issue?

And why should one declare a priori that there is ever a gap between "is" and "ought"? Perhaps there is usually, but what makes evolution exceptional — or so claim the enthusiasts — is that here uniquely one can bridge the gap. If it is all a question of personal intuition, then the traditional evolutionary ethicists beg to differ with respect to their intuitions. One cannot simply point to the difference in language. Deductions from talk of one kind to talk of another kind are meat and drink to scientists (Nagel 1961). There is surely at least as much a gap between talk of molecules and talk of pendulums as there is between talk of fact and talk of morality.

If we are to offer an adequate critique of social Darwinism, we must dig more deeply, turning back to the evolutionary ethicists themselves and seeing precisely what they thought were the metaethical (although they probably never used this term) foundations of their moral theorizing. And in truth this is no difficult task. To a person, the traditional evolutionary ethicist makes justificatory appeal to one thing, and one thing only. This is quite irrespective of the norm being prescribed. It is claimed simply that the process and pattern of evolution makes sense. Change may be slow and seemingly meaningless, but when looked at as a whole, one sees that evolution is essentially *progressive*. It is not a meandering path going nowhere. Rather, for all the undoubted backsliding, it is an upward climb, from simplicity to complexity, from the single-celled organism to the multi-celled organism, from that which is a jack-of-all-trades to that which incorporates an efficient division of labor, from the diffuse to the organized, from the homogeneous to the heterogeneous, from — to use a phrase much liked by Darwin — the monad to the man.

For Spencer, for Rockefeller, for Carnegie, for Haeckel, for Huxley, for Wilson, it is this progressiveness, this upward thrust that is the defining mark of evolution. "Whether it be in the development of the Earth, in the development of Life upon its surface, in the development of Society, of Government, of Manufactures, of Commerce, Language, Literature, Science, Art, this same evolution of the simple into the complex, through successive differentiations, holds throughout" (Spencer 1857, reprinted in Spencer 1868, p. 3). And since this pattern is that which generates us humans as its unique, triumphant endpoint, we see that evolution is a process which, in itself, generates value (Ruse 1988, 1993).

At once we have our metaethical justification. No one likes the fact that widows and children go to the wall — Spencer himself would have been horrified were any actions of his to lead directly to such a result — but he believed unless we let the forces of nature have full reign, progress will stop, and (even worse) degeneration will set in. Short-term kindness may well lead to long-term disaster. Likewise thought Haeckel. Unless we promote an efficient state, run by a trained bureaucracy, we could all decline to the flabby level of the French. And Wilson. For him, sociality is everything, and thus judged he sees humans as the very pinnacle of the evolutionary process (Wilson 1975). His oft-expressed fear is that, if biodiversity be lost, then so also will go humankind. At best we will survive as stunted halfbeings, if at all (Wilson 1984).

I will not labor this firmly established point about people's interpretation of evolution. What is fascinating historically is how much more powerful was Spencer's message of progress than his immediate prescriptions for social action. At the end of the last century in America we find that, along with Rockefeller and Carnegie, the socialists and Marxists were putting themselves under the banner of Spencer in the name of progress! (See Pittenger 1993.)

But, history notwithstanding, will that message do? Let me say flatly at this point that I side with Julian Huxley's grandfather, Thomas Henry (Paradis and Williams 1989). He felt the attractions of progressiveness — so do we all, for we are human and come out at the top — but, for the life of him, he could not see any justification for the belief. He valued humans more than others — his life was dedicated to the improvement of their lot — but he could not see that this was something to be read from the fact and processes of evolution.

The contrary, if anything, seems to be the case. To use examples in tune with our own time, why should we say that humans are the great success story of evolution? However you classify us, we humans have had a pathetically short life span compared with the 150 million years that the dinosaurs ruled the globe; and, given our weapons of mass destruction, who would dare say that we will last into the future to outstrip the success of those extinct brutes? Or, if you insist on taking organisms still alive and well, can one honestly say that, from an evolutionary perspective, humans are that much more successful than, say, the AIDS virus? Of course, we humans are more intelligent and more social and more many other things that we humans value. But that is not quite the point. Anyone can set up their own criteria and then declare us the winners, especially if the criteria are "humanlike" by another name. The point is whether in looking at evolution and its record, as is, we see progress and an increase in value. And this is another matter. Bluntly, the answer is: "No, we are not the success story of evolution!" (See Gould 1989.)

What I conclude therefore is that, although traditional evolutionary ethics has far more variety and interest than one would suppose from the usual caricature, and although the usual dismissals of its metaethical foundations are (at the very least) more satisfying than convincing, ultimately it is deeply flawed. Indeed, to return once again to religion, my suspicion is that the progressionist reading of evolution is more a function of submerged Christian thoughts of redemption and ultimate salvation than it is of anything to be found in the fossil record (Spadefora 1990). This is not necessarily to say that Christianity is wrong, but it is to say that it is not a true foundation for an adequate evolutionary ethics.

Sociobiology

Having refuted my case before I have begun, what can I possibly hope to do for an encore? Is this all there is to be said on the subject of evolution and ethics? I rather think not. There has always been an as-yet-undiscussed kind of subtheme to writings on evolution and ethics, a subtheme that I shall suggest leads to a far more satisfactory melding of the insights of the evolutionist with the demands of the ethicist.

It is possible that this subtheme was that which inspired Darwin himself when he turned to discuss morality in our own species in his *Descent of Man* (1871). But history aside, it is certainly the case that with recent advances in evolutionary biology, advances that I would also say were certainly implicit in Darwin although not developed by him, the proper way to develop this subtheme is now a great deal more obvious. Not that I want to take credit from those who have gone before me in traveling this path, most notably the Australian philosopher, the late John Mackie (1978, 1979). (Also Murphy 1982.)

First, let me talk about the science. When I have done that, I will turn to the concerns of moral philosophers, and as I have done for others, I will structure my discussion around the distinction between normative ethics and metaethics. I should say that, as I begin — and here I speak as critically of my former self as I do of others — I intend what I have to say now to be taken a lot more literally than one usually takes discussions of fact in philosophical writings. It is our stock-in-trade to think up fanciful examples to illustrate philosophical points, and no one really thinks the worse if it be pointed out that the example could never really obtain. What I have to say now is at the cutting edge of science, and requires a certain amount of projection and faith. But if the science is not essentially true, then my philosophy fails. I mean my evolutionary ethics to be genuinely evolutionary.

The advances to which I am referring come under the heading of sociobiology. If life really is a struggle, and the race goes to the swift — less metaphorically, if only some survive and (more importantly) reproduce — then as Darwin (1859) pointed out, behavior is just as important as physique. Adaptation is required in the world of action as well as in that of form. It is no use having the build of Tarzan (or Jane), if your only interest in life is philosophy. If you are not prepared to make the effort and act on it, then your chances for reproduction and adding to the evolutionary line are minimal.

Of course, no one who takes natural selection seriously would ever want to deny this. The antelope fleeing the lion, the battle of the male walruses for mates, the mosquito in search of its feast of blood, these are the commonplaces of evolution. What is not quite so commonplace, or rather what is apparently just as commonplace but not quite so obvious, is the fact that behavior is not exclusively a question of combat, hand raised against hand. As Darwin always stressed, the "struggle" for existence must not be interpreted too literally. Often in this life, you can get far more by cooperating than by going into attack mode. *Social* behavior can be a good biological strategy, as much as or even more than blind antagonism.

Darwin thought much on these matters and discussed them extensively in the *Origin*. I have noted how he always favored an interpretation of natural selection that focused on the individual, and this led to an intense interest in the social insects, especially the hymenoptera — ants, bees, wasps — where one seemingly has individuals (sterile "workers") devoting their whole lives to the reproductive benefits of others. Primarily because he possessed no adequate theory of heredity, he was unable adequately to resolve what seemed to him to be in flat contradiction to his basic premises. (See Ruse 1980.)

However, some thirty years ago the breakthrough occurred when the then-graduate student William Hamilton (1964a, b) saw that social cooperation is possible — can indeed be a direct result of natural selection — so long as the individual giving aid benefits biologically, *even if this benefit comes about vicariously.* Close relatives share the same units of heredity (genes), and so inasmuch as one's relatives succeed in life's struggles and reproduce, one is oneself reproducing, by proxy as it were. Hamilton pointed out that the social insects are just an extreme case of such cooperation, and that even they are no exception to selection's rule.

This theory of "kin selection," and related models, spurred massive interest in the evolution of social behavior, at both the theoretical and observational levels (Dawkins 1976, 1986; Cronin 1991). And with such interest came one overwhelming conclusion. Although the social insects may be an extreme, cooperation is virtually the norm rather than the exception, in the animal world. As soon as one gets into detailed study of just about any species — reptile, mammal, bird, invertebrate — one finds individuals working together. Most often this is between mates and relatives — parents and children for instance — but it can occur even between strangers and possibly across species. Nonrelative cooperation is usually thought to be a form of enlightened self-interest, and is revealingly ascribed to "reciprocal altruism" (Trivers 1971).

Now, without wanting to seem tendentious, let me pause for a moment, and, putting on my philosophical hat, make a terminological point. Famously, notoriously, the theory about which I am talking, a theory that shows how even the most giving of actions can be related back to self-interest, has been labeled the "selfish-gene" view of evolution (Dawkins 1976). As it happens, I think this is a terrific term — it is a brilliant use of language to hammer home a basic point — but note that it is a metaphor. Genes are not selfish, nor are their possessors as such. Selfishness is a human attribute, something that results of thinking only of yourself and not of others. I have no reason to believe that ants or bees or wasps ever think, so literally speaking neither they nor their genes are selfish. The point of using the term "selfish" is to draw attention to the fact that the units of inheritance work in such a way as to benefit their possessor's biological ends, whatever the behavior.

Some philosophers have objected that one should never use such a metaphor as selfish gene (Midgley 1979, 1985). But this is just plain silly. I doubt you could even open your mouth without using a metaphor, much less express a coherent thought. (Where do you think the word "express" comes from?!) Scientists use them all of the time — "work," "force," "attraction," and all the rest. The

point, however, is that you should be careful with your metaphors and not kid yourself that they prove more than they do. As I have just said, genes may be selfish. That is no warrant for thinking the same may be true of ants.

This brings me to the nub of what I want to say, speaking philosophically. The flip side to the selfish gene is the cooperating organism. The term that biologists use here is "altruism," and they thus speak happily of the widespread altruism that they have discovered through the animal world (Trivers 1971; West Eberhard 1975). But I want to stress that this is no less metaphorical a usage. "Altruism," like "selfishness," is a human term. It means not thinking of yourself but thinking of others. Mother Teresa is an altruist as she bathes the brows of the dying poor of Calcutta. Just as I have no reason to think that ants are selfish, so in this sense I have no reason to think that ants are altruists.

My point then is simply that we should remember that the biologists' term "altruist" is a technical term, with only a metaphorical connection to the literal human term. It speaks not of intentions or thinking or anything like that. Rather it is used simply to designate social behavior that one has reason to think occurs because ultimately it benefits the biological ends of the performer. A bird that helps to raise its siblings is (most probably) this kind of "altruist." Hence, although it would be somewhat precious of biologists to insist on putting their word in quotations, for this discussion I shall show its metaphorical nature by always so doing.

Homo Sapiens: From "Altruism" to Altruism

Animal altruism is a fact of nature, and we now have a good theoretical understanding of its existence. Let me therefore move straight to the organism that interests me, namely Homo sapiens. In the technical biological sense I have just been discussing, we human are "altruists" par excellence. People often say that our defining characteristic is our use of language. I prefer to say that it is our "altruism," although I am cheating a bit because I would count language as one of our chief means for effecting such "altruism." The point is that we cooperate flat out and because we do cooperate we succeed mightily in surviving and reproducing.

Of course I am not saying that we humans never quarrel and fight, even unto the death. I am hardly that insensitive to the horrific events of this century. But even if you take into the account the carnage of the two world wars, not forgetting the deaths of six million Jews and twenty million Russians, the human species still comes low on the scale of mammalian intraspecific carnage. The murder rate in a pride of lions is far higher than that in the slums of Detroit. And without forgetting the counterevidence, all of that popular talk about humans being the killer apes, with the mark of Cain forever on their foreheads, is just plain nonsense (Wilson 1975; Betzig, Borgerhoff Mulder, and Turke 1987).

Humans did not simply wake up one morning and decide to be "altruists." Their evolution has clearly been one of feedback, with social success promoting the evolution of ever more efficient tools of cooperation, be these positive like speech or negative like our low excitability levels. Obviously the evolution of the brain has been important, but so also have other things, like the hand with its opposable thumb. At the same time, we have failed to acquire or lost other features possessed by many mammals, for instance the large teeth which can be used to attack or to tear apart large chunks of raw meat.

I will not spend time here giving a detailed discussion of the ways in which paleoanthropologists (students of human evolution) think we have actually evolved (Isaac 1983; Pilbeam 1984). Probably at some crucial point, dating back to our ape ancestors, we were scavengers, stealing the kills of fiercer animals. This would obviously put a major premium on "altruism," as would another suggested factor, the threat that roving bands of humans would pose toward their fellow bands. At the risk of sounding desperately politically incorrect, male strife for mates may well have been significant here (especially if contemporary anthropological evidence is any judge) combined, if my own experience is any measure, with great doses of female choice. (In *The Descent of Man,* Darwin argued that a sexual selection of partners is very important. See also Ruse 1989, especially Chapter 7.)

We humans are "altruists," meaning that we cooperate for the biological ends of survival and reproduction (Ruse and Wilson 1986). The next question is how exactly our "altruism" gets put into action. To use an Aristotelian term, what are the proximate causes of our "altruism"? How do we set about being "altruists"? I can think of at least three possible ways, and in some respects I suspect that we humans have taken all three.

The first way is that of the ants (Holldobler and Wilson 1990). They are, to make heavy use of metaphor, hard-wired to work together. They do not have to learn to cooperate. The instructions are burned into their brains by their genes. Their "altruism" is innate, in the strongest possible sense. And clearly, this kind of "altruism" is to be found among humans in many forms. Anybody who has seen the care and affection shown by a mother toward her young child has to be moved by this basic animal nature. It is not something one strives for or has to learn. It is there. This is not to deny that there are freaks who do not have this instinct any more than that there are people born without two legs.

Of course, I am not saying that this kind of innate "altruism" is everything to humans. We are not ants. Much that we do socially required learning, and, in a point to which I shall return, we seem to have a dimension of freedom, of flexibility, not possessed by the ants. Which is just as well, biologically speaking. Genetic hard-wiring is fine and dandy, so long as nothing goes wrong. But when there are new challenges, it is powerless to pull back and reconsider. Ants, for instance, do much of their traveling outside the nest guided by chemical (pheromone) trails. Generally this is incredibly efficient. There is no need for them to buy a map or a guide to find their way. But a major disturbance like a thunderstorm can spell disaster, with the loss of literally hundreds of insects.

Ants can afford this loss. (I speak now in universal terms, but you can put the point in terms of individual selection.) Mother ant has millions of offspring. What is the loss of a few hundred? Humans, to the contrary, in major part because of the kind of social strategy we have taken, cannot afford such a loss. Rather than having many offspring to whom we give relatively little care, we have but a few offspring to whom we give much care. One simply cannot risk losing a child in a rain shower every time it goes to McDonald's. Hence, ubiquitous genetic innateness is not for us. We needed an "altruism" that allows for problem-solving.

The need for problem-solving ability points very clearly to the second way of effecting "altruism." Why not simply have efficient on-board computers (call them "brains," if you will) that allow us to negotiate with our fellows so that if a certain course of social action is in our biological self-interests we will decide to act positively on it and not otherwise? Cooperation will come about, simply because it is the rational thing to do. Note that there is no morality involved here, but neither is there immorality. Beings with superbrains are often portrayed in fiction as being like Darth Vader — evil and wanting to conquer the world. However, if everyone were similarly endowed, I see no reason why there should be constant strife. To me, intelligent moves would seem to end in the opposite direction.

Again, I think we humans have taken this strategy to some extent (Axelrod 1984; Sober 1993; Gibbard 1982, 1990). We do spend much of our lives in negotiation and bargaining without much more than self-interest being involved. I buy a loaf of bread from the baker: He gives me the bread, I give him the money. Neither is doing the other a favor, but neither is doing the other down. We have a happy division of labor where I do my thing and he does his, and everybody else does theirs, and then (through the monetary system) we get together to swap the fruits of our efforts. From an overall evolutionary perspective, taking home one loaf of bread may seem a bit removed from having larger families; but, ultimately, this is what it all adds up to.

However, again this is not all that there is to human "altruism" and again there are good biological reasons why it is not. There may be biological constraints on producing humans with megabrains — how wide a pelvis did you want your mother to have? — but negotiating toward a perfect solution has its costs too. Most obviously, it can take a great deal of time, and time in evolutionary terms is money. Often what one wants in biology is a quick and dirty solution — something that works pretty well, pretty cheaply, most of the time — rather than perfection with its attendant price. It is not much use working out if it is in your biological interest to save your chum from the tiger if, by the time you have finished your sums, you are both in the tiger's belly.

This points us toward the third strategy for achieving human "altruism," something that can be more readily illustrated by means of an analogy. The second way, just discussed, highlights a problem much akin to that faced by the people who built the first generation of chess-playing computers. They programmed in all of the right moves and then discovered that the computers were virtually useless because, after a couple of moves, they were paralyzed. Time stood still as they ran through all of the possible options, seeking the best. But, unfortunately, in this real world, we do not have the luxury of infinite time.

Now, however, we have chess-playing computers that are very good indeed. They do not always win against the top competition, but even the best human players are firmly in their sights. How is this possible? Simply because the computers are programmed to recognize (or "recognize," if you dislike the anthropomorphism) certain situations and then to act according to predetermined strategies. Sometimes the strategies fail the computers, and they lose. But generally the strategies, which are built on past experience, prove reliable, and the computers can win within specified times.

I would argue we humans are much like the new breed of chess machines. We have certain built-in strategies, hard-wired into our brains if you like, which we bring into play and which guide our actions when we are faced with certain social situations. Sometimes things do not work out — I will talk more about this in a moment — but generally these strategies provide just the kind of quick and dirty solution that we super-"altruists" require.

One more step is needed to complete my argument, and you can probably guess what it is going to be. How do these strategies present themselves to us in our consciousness? In a word, they are the rules of moral conduct! We think that we ought to do certain things and that we ought not to do other things because this is our biology's way of making us break from our usual selfish or self-interested attitudes and get on with the job of cooperating with others. In short, what I am arguing is that in order to make us "altruists" in the metaphorical biological sense, biology has made us altruists in the literal moral sense.

In the language of the evolutionist, therefore, morality is no more — although certainly no less — than an adaptation, and as such has the same status as things like teeth and eyes and noses. And, as I come to the end of this part of my discussion, let me stress, as I stressed earlier, that I mean this claim to be a literal matter of biological fact. I am pushing off somewhat from firmly established truth. But although I simply do not have room to go into empirical details (I must nevertheless mention that we now have knowledge of what can be described at the very least, as quasi-morality from the ape world [de Waal 1982; Goodall 1986]), if I am wrong, then I am afraid that you are wasting your time as you read on. (In my *Taking Darwin Seriously* [1986] I do talk more about the empirical evidence.)

Substantive Questions

Let us return to the philosophical questions, and being guided (as promised) by our two-fold distinction, let us ask first about the substantive ethics that I am proposing. In truth, and this may rather disappoint you, I do not have anything very surprising to say at this point. In fact, I am rather pleased because I am always very wary of sweeping claims to originality; they are usually wrong or have been made by somebody before. More seriously, it seems to me to be profoundly implausible that no one before Darwin ever grasped the essence of substantive ethics properly understood. Further, it would seem profoundly depressing to me as a professional philosopher if no philosopher before Darwin had ever had things of importance to say on such matters.

Indeed, let me speak more strongly on this. As one who is trying to bring ethics into tune with modern science in the sense of wanting to show how ethics can be grounded (I use this word without prejudice to what I shall be arguing shortly about justification) in evolutionary thought, I am clearly what is known as a philosophical "naturalist" (Ruse 1994). And this being so, my crucial intent is to do justice to the way things are — how people feel about morality and how it has evolved — rather than how some idealist would like them to be. I would be deeply worried if what I wanted to say was not, at some level, general knowledge. The astronomer tries to explain why the sun rises above the horizon; he or she does not deny that this is what we see.

(Is this to admit that I shall fail to tackle the real problem of the moral philosopher — prescription of the true nature of morality? I think not, for this is to confuse the preacher with the teacher. The job of the moral philosopher is not to prescribe some new morality but to explain and justify the nature of morality as we know it. This, of course, may involve showing that our present beliefs are inconsistent, and on the basis of such a conclusion, the philosopher may urge us to rethink some of our beliefs. The point is that, from the pre-Socratics on, no philosopher qua philosopher has tried to spin substantive ethics out of thin air. Think of how Plato, a master at telling us what we should do, was forever getting his circle to reflect on their experiences and feelings.)

What I want to say, therefore, is that the kind of beings on whose evolution I was speculating in the last section, that is to say ourselves, is one whose prescriptive morality is going to be fairly commonplace — commonplace in the sense of familiar and not at all in the sense of trivial or unimportant (Mackie 1977). One is going to feel an obligation to help people, especially those in need, like children, the old, the sick. One will feel that one ought to give up one's seat to a mother with a young child, or to an old man bent over with arthritis, without being asked. One will feel that one ought to try to be fair and not to be influenced by favoritism. Therefore, for example, a male professor should not give a higher mark to a pretty young woman because she is pretty nor, if she has earned it, should he withhold one because she is a woman. One will feel that one should not be thoughtless or wantonly cruel. Leaving one's children at home to go on holiday might make a good movie, but in real life it is wrong because it is unkind and irresponsible.

If you complain to me that moral prescriptions ought to be about sterner things, such as murder and stealing and the like, I shall agree that morality should cover these. Let me assure you that, as an evolutionary ethicist, I am personally against them. But I would also point out that most moral decisions, for most of us most of the time, are much more low key. I have never felt the urge to rob a bank and if I did I would not know how to set about it. But I have had lots of pretty young women in my classes. This is part of what I mean by saying that morality (in the sense of normative ethics) is commonplace.

If you complain to me that this all starts to sound like warmed-over Christianity, I shall agree again. "Love your neighbor as yourself" sounds like a pretty good guide to life to me, and I gather it also does to many other people in non-Christian cultures. I take it that a major reason why Christianity was such a raging success was that it did speak to fairly basic feelings that humans had about themselves and their fellow humans. But I do not want to give all the glory to religion. Secular thinkers have grasped the major insights of morality (prescriptively speaking) also. Immanuel Kant (1959), for instance, put tremendous emphasis on respecting people for their own sake, as persons. Is this not a major basis of cooperation?

Actually, speaking of Kantians, you will have noticed that I claim that one major part of morality is the urge toward fairness. In fact, I would say that this is a very major part, although perhaps I am prejudiced as one who is the father of five children and has spent his whole adult life as a teacher. Humans spend incredible amounts of time worrying about getting their fair share. I am convinced that we would all happily pay another dime on the dollar in taxes if we knew at last that the filthy rich would pay their dues.

Today's most eminent neo-Kantian moral philosopher has made a whole system out of fairness, and it is just the sort of system favored and expected by the evolutionist. In particular, John Rawls (1971) invites us to put ourselves in a "position of ignorance." If we knew beforehand what kind of place and talents we were to have in society, then we would (out of self-interest) rationally argue for a system that rewarded most highly such persons as us. Knowing that you were going to be female, intelligent, and healthy would make you argue for the benefits properly accruing to the female, intelligent, and healthy. But what if you ended up male, dumb, and sick?

Rawls suggests that, given our ignorance about our ticket in life's lottery, we should aim for a just society, where this is to be interpreted as a fair society, where everyone gets the best out of society that could possibly be arranged. This does not mean total equality. If the only way you can get the most qualified people to be doctors is by paying them twice as much as anyone else, then we all benefit by such an uneven distribution. But this and all such inequalities need to be justified.

It seems to me that this is just the kind of set-up that our genes would favor. If we are going to have to get along and everybody wants a share of the pie, then let us have some way of sharing it out as evenly

as possible. In fact, as Rawls himself notes, the evolutionist nicely closes a gap that has always faced the social contract theorist, which is what Rawls (and Kant before him) exemplifies. It is all very well talking about positions of ignorance, but this is surely hypothetical. Hence, while it may do to give an analysis of morality, it hardly does to explain its origin. But if we put on the genes (as selected in life's struggles) the burden of explaining how morality actually came into play, there is no longer need to suppose some surely fictional bunch of protohumans sitting around talking of "positions of ignorance" and planning moral strategies.

Indeed, I would make the case even more strongly than this. One of the major weaknesses of any system of morality like Rawls's (or Kant's before him), which tries to derive moral rules from rational principles of self-interest, is that it really cannot get at the true nature of morality. To pick up again on Hume's is/ought distinction, a defining mark of moral claims is that they really do seem to be different — there is a sense of obligation about them that is missing from a simple factual statement. Even if you think that the gap can be bridged, then it is surely up to you to show how it is to be done. And simply translating morality in terms of self-interest is not enough. The whole point is that Mother Teresa is not helping the sick and dying out of self-interest; she is doing it because it is right.

Here is a point of real strength in the evolutionist's approach. He or she argues that there is indeed something logically distinct about the nature of moral claims. The is/ought barrier is not to be jumped or ignored. The key point, never to be forgotten, is that we are in many respects self-centered. Nature has made us that way and it is just as well or we would never survive and reproduce. Imagine if every time you got a piece of bread you gave it away! Imagine if every time you fell in love you denied your feelings so someone else could take your place! But because we have taken the route of sociality, we need a mechanism to make us break through that self-centered nature on many, many occasions. Evolution has given us this logically odd sense of oughtness to do precisely that.

Two more points, and then I am done with the normative side to my case. You may be wondering if I am not a little bit too ecumenical in my attitude to other moral systems, religious and secular. Christianity, Kantianism, probably utilitarianism, and more. Should one not plumb for one system and have done with it? After all, as moral philosophers delight in showing, there are certain crucial cases where one system succeeds and others fail. (Paradigm example: You are held prisoner by a vile regime. If you escape, you have the knowledge and means to end this rule and save the lives and happiness of millions. But to do so, you must bribe the guard with your chocolate ration. Should you do so? Most systems cry out Yes! The Kantian, however, regrets that you are not treating the guard as a person in his own right.)

Again, I would claim a strength not a weakness for the evolutionist. The simple fact of the matter is that it is the philosopher's stock-in-trade to look for counterexamples to established moral systems. But most of the time, the well-known and tried systems agree on what one should do. Kantians, Christians, and everyone else agree that you should not hurt small children for fun and that if you are blessed with plenty then you should help the poor person at your door. Standard moral systems do not urge you to do crazy moral things.

And where there are points of conflict, perhaps this tells us something about morality itself. Moral philosophers tend to think that their own favored moral system can solve all of the problems, so long as you push it long enough and hard enough, and perhaps this is a reasonable belief if you think that morality is backed by a good God or a Platonic form or some such thing. But, if you deny such a foundation, it could just be that there are some problems to which there are no proper moral solutions. We may have to make a decision, because life must go on, but there is no uniquely compelling right answer. We are going to feel bad, whatever we do.

This, it seems to me, is precisely what the evolutionist would expect. Adaptations are rarely perfect. Big brains are a bright idea and so is bipedalism. Put them together and you have the agony of human childbirth. Biological life is a matter of compromise, building the best that you can with the materials that nature has dealt you. Ethics is a good adaptation, but sometimes it simply breaks down, and cannot function. The oddity is to be surprised by this rather than to expect it.

Yet is there nothing that my kind of evolutionary ethicist would say that would give us pause to think? I believe there is one such thing, familiar and yet somewhat disturbing. This concerns the scope of (normative) ethics. "Love your neighbor as yourself." Yes, but who is my neighbor? And what should I do about those who are not my neighbors?

The Arabs have the answer: "My brother and I against our cousin. My cousin and I against the stranger." This was surely first spoken by a sociobiologist. Biologically, one is more closely related to one's siblings than to one's cousins, and to one's cousins than to strangers. One would certainly expect the emotions to grow more faint as the blood ties loosen. The obligations would loosen. This is not to say that they would vanish, nor is it to say that without blood ties there can be no morality. Where kin selection fails, reciprocal altruism provides a back-up. But again, as one grows more distant in one's social relationship, one would expect the feelings to decline.

I want to emphasize that I am not just talking about warm feelings of love here, but of morality. I believe that my kind of evolutionary ethicist expects the very call of morality to decline as one moves away from one's immediate circle. Of course we love our children more than we do those of others; but, also, we have a stronger sense of morality toward them. And the same is true of our immediate neighbors and friends, as opposed to those more distant. I stress that, even toward strangers, the sociobiologist can see reason for some moral feelings — we are all here together on planet earth — but it is silly to pretend that our dealings across countries are going to be intimate or driven by much beyond self-interest.

As it happens, although this may seem a somewhat stern consequence, it is not really so much out of line with traditional thought. Historically, ethicists of all stripes have divided somewhat on this question, and how they have divided seems to have had little to do per se with whether they were religious or secular. There are some who have said flatly that one has an equal obligation to everyone, whether it is your favorite child or a stranger in an unknown land. Everyone is my neighbor. That is precisely the moral to be drawn from the parable of the Good Samaritan. Others have argued for a more restricted morality, maintaining that there is a falling-away of the moral imperatives as one moves further from oneself, one's family, one's friends, one's society, and one's country. The whole point of the parable is that the Good Samaritan saw the man injured by the road and at that point they did become neighbors. Jesus did not suggest that the samaritan was in the general business of charity to strangers (Wallwork 1982).

For myself—a person with rather mushy left-wing sentiments who was initially somewhat shocked by the implications of my philosophy—I have found that, as I think about these things, my intuitions start to fall in line with the evolutionary implications. Suppose you learned that your philosophy professor, known to have a family dependent on her, was giving virtually all of her salary to some charity for African relief and that as a result the family was living on hand-outs from the Salvation Army and the local soup kitchen. Would you think of such a person as a saint or a moral monster? And what about yourself? Are you on a par with a child-killer because you do not give every last penny to relief, even though you know full well that the money you could give probably would make a life-and-death difference to more than one person? (I am not implying that you should not give more than you do.)

I think it interesting that charities have come to realize that their advertising is much more effective when they show pictures of people in actual need. These ads, and in like fashion television reports of people in dire straits bring the needy into our neighborhood, just as effectively as if they had moved in.

"Charity begins at home" is the motto of the evolutionary ethicist.

Foundations?

With good reason you may be wondering now about the metaethics of the position I am explaining and promoting. I have explained the problems of progress and the distinction between "is" statements and "ought" statements, carefully arguing that the distinction is a crucial piece of my overall picture. How then can I go on to talk about justification? Have I not undercut my own position? Even if you agree with me, more or less, about the normative claims I would make, and in fact I think there are many moral philosophers roughly sympathetic to something along the lines I have sketched, is not the metaethical position impossible? Or at least, does one not have to go outside the bounds of evolutionary biology for help and support?

I rather think not, although I am not sure that you will much like the answer I am now about to give—helpfully, I will give you biological reasons why you will not like the answer I am about to give!

What I want to argue is that there are no foundations to normative ethics. If you think that to be true a claim has to refer to some particular thing or things, my claim is that in an important sense normative ethics is false. Although, to be frank, I prefer not to use the word "false" here, for I have no intention of denying that a claim like "rape is wrong" is true.

What I believe is that the claims of normative ethics are like the rules of a game. In baseball, it is true that after three strikes the batter is out; but this claim does not have any reference or correspondence in absolute reality. Indeed, one can imagine a game where it would take four strikes to get the batter out. Whether ethics has this kind of flexibility—could one imagine a case where rape is not always wrong?—is a matter I will raise in a moment. The point now is that normative ethics is indeed not justified by progress or anything else of a natural kind, for it is not justified in this way by anything!

The position I am endorsing is known technically as ethical skepticism, and I must stress that the skepticism is about the metaethical foundations, not the prescriptions of ethics (Mackie 1977). Alternatively it is known as noncognitivism, although I shall be at pains shortly to explain where I differ from other noncognitivist positions like emotivism. A major attraction to my position in my eyes is that one simply cannot be guilty of committing the naturalistic fallacy or violating the is/ought barrier, because one is simply not in the justification business at all. To use a sporting metaphor, instead of trying to drive through these things, one does an end run around them.

This is all very well, but am I not just stating my preferred position rather than arguing for it? What right have I to say, *as an evolutionist,* that normative ethics has no foundation? I may not offer justification for normative ethics, but, surely, I must offer justification for the claim that normative ethics has no justification! In fact, this I think I can do, for (to use the language of causes and reasons) I believe that sometimes when one has given a causal analysis of why someone believes something, one has shown that the call for reasoned justification is inappropriate—there is none (Murphy 1982). I would argue that we have just such a case here. I have argued that normative ethics is a biological adaptation, and I would argue that as such it can be seen to have no being or reality beyond this. We believe normative ethics for our own (biological) good, and that is that. The causal account of why we believe makes inappropriate the inquiry into the justification of what we believe.

An analogy may help. During the First World War, on the death of their loved ones, many of the survivors back home turned to spiritualism for solace. And sure enough, through the Ouija board or whatever would come the comforting messages: "It's all right, Mum! Don't worry about me! I've gone to a better place. I'm just waiting for you and Dad." Now, how do we explain these messages, other than through outright fraud, which may have happened sometimes but, I am sure, did not happen universally? The answer is surely not to offer the justification that the late Private Higgins, sitting on a cloud, dressed in a bedsheet, and holding a number four sized harp, was speaking to his mum and dad. Rather, one would say (truly) that the strain of the loss, combined with known facts about human nature, yielded a causal explanation that made any further inquiry redundant.

The same is the case for normative ethics, except that, rather than an individual illusion, here we have a collective illusion of the genes, bringing us all in (except for the morally blind). We need to believe in morality, and so, thanks to our biology, we do believe in morality. There is no foundation for this "out there," beyond human nature.

But can this truly be so? Is my analogy well taken? Consider another analogy. Our eyes are no less an adaptation than is our normative ethics. They have a more secure status in the opinion of some. They too help in the business of living, for instance in the avoidance of danger as exemplified by the speeding train heading toward us. But would anyone seriously suggest that this means that the train does not have an objective existence, independent of us? Why then should we assume that our normative ethics fails to have an objective existence, independent of us? Why should our moral sense, if we can so call it, be a trickster in a way that is not true of our more conventional five senses? (See Nozick 1981.)

Actually, I am not that sure that our physical senses never do deceive us for our own good. Sight is a pretty complex matter, with a fair amount of input by the looker. But leave this, for I fully agree that the train does have an independent existence. My counter is that I am not sure that the analogy between external objects like the train and substantive ethics holds true.

Think for the moment about the train. Why do we, as evolutionists, think that it has an external existence and is not just a figment of our senses? First, there is no obvious reason why our senses would deceive us on this point. Why think there is an approaching train if there is none? Second, there are good reasons why we would think there is a train and why our senses would not deceive us. Trains kill. More than this, even if there were no need to think there was a train, we would think there was a train. Do I really need to think there is, say, a moon? Third, although we humans may have our distinctive ways of finding out about trains, it seems that (if necessary) other organisms likewise can find out about trains in their ways, through sounds or pheromones and so forth.

I am not sure that any of these points hold in the case of normative ethics. There are very good reasons why we would believe in normative ethics whether it had independent existence or not. We need it for "altruism." Perhaps if such ethics did exist, we would believe in it — let me be fair, I am sure we would — but if we did not need it, I cannot imagine it would be in evolution's interest to make us aware of it. And I simply cannot see how one would get at such ethics without the moral sense or something akin, which, I am happy to agree, may not be exclusively human.

Let me put my collective point another way. Do we really need an objectively existing normative ethics to believe in it? I can see nothing in the argument I have given for the existence of normative ethics that supposes that it exists "out there," whatever that might mean. In fact, let me put things more strongly. An objective ethics strikes me as being redundant, which is a pretty funny state of affairs for an objective ethics ("You should do this because God wants you to; but, anyway, no matter what God wants, you will believe that you should do it.")

If there is no objective ethics, and if you do not believe in progress (as I do not), then you might think that nature could have had other ways of getting you to cooperate — after all, to get from A to B, humans walk, horses run, fish swim, birds fly, snakes slither, monkeys swing. But, far from taking this as an objection, my response is that this might well have been the case. In the 1950s, at the height of the Cold War, American Secretary of State John Foster Dulles thought he had a moral obligation to hate (rather than to love) the Russians. But he realized that they felt the same way about him. Therefore, we had a very successful system of reciprocation. Why should not nature have provided a Dulles morality rather than a Christian/Kantian/etc. morality?

We now seem to have the position that objective morality could exist but that it is quite other than anything we believe. "God wants us to hate our neighbors, but because of our biology we think we should love them." "God is indifferent to rape, but because of our biology we think it is wrong." This is even more of a paradox than before and yet one more reason why I want to drop the whole talk of objective foundations. I admit of course that my Dulles morality shares with our morality some kind of structuring according to formal rules of reciprocation; but as I have pointed out earlier, this in itself is simply not morality. "I will help you if you will help me" is simply not normative ethics. Hence, I feel confident in arguing that ethical skepticism is not only the answer to the evolutionist's needs but also the way pointed by evolution.

Objections and Consequences

My position raises all sorts of implications and questions. Let me conclude my discussion by mentioning three of the most common.

First, there is the question of determinism. The most common charge against human sociobiology is that it is an exercise in biological or genetic "determinism" (Allen and others 1976; Burian 1981). It is not always made crystal clear exactly what this means, but whatever it is, it is not a good thing. Most obviously, in the present connection, if the charge be well taken, it throws serious doubt on the whole enterprise of articulating an evolutionary ethics. The most crucial presupposition of ethics, speaking now at the normative level, is that we have a dimension of freedom. You must be able to choose between right and wrong, otherwise there is no credit for good actions and, equally, no credit for bad ones.

However, drawing now as much on standard philosophical results as on biology, although one can see that this charge does point to some important aspects of my evolutionary ethics, it certainly does not point to unique or unanswerable problems. Perhaps, indeed, the contrary is the case. And

to see this, consider for a moment the level at which my science does suppose that there is a direct genetic causal input: the structuring of our thinking in such a way that we believe in moral norms. (I am not denying that a mad psychologist could probably rear a child to be morally blind. Hence, even here I am allowing — demanding — an environmental causal input. But I do want to argue for a strong sense of genetic determinism at this point.)

However, did any moral thinker, except perhaps the French existentialists at their most bizarre and unconvincing, ever truly think that we chose the rules of moral action? This is what makes traditional social-contract thinking so implausible. Moral choice comes into whether we obey the rules of morality, not whether we chose the rules themselves. We are not free to decide whether killing is wrong or not. It is wrong! The freedom comes in deciding if we are going to kill nevertheless.

My morality certainly allows for freedom at this level. Indeed, the whole point is that we humans are (not exclusively) like the ants, in being determined in all of our actions. We have a dimension of flexibility. Although (and because) morality is an adaptation, I am not saying that we will always be moral — for biological or nonbiological reasons we may break from morality. The point is that we can break from it. To use an analogy, whereas ants are rather like simple (and cheap) rockets shot off at a target, we humans are like the more complex (and expensive) missiles that possess homing devices able to correct and change direction in midflight.

(This analogy highlights the fact that I am committed to some sort of general causal determinism. But in line with other philosophers, notably David Hume (1978), I would argue that such determinism is a condition of moral choice rather than a barrier to it. Technically, I am a "soft determinist" or "compatibilist." See Hudson 1983.)

Second, what about the question of relativism? Since I am a subjectivist — or at least not an objectivist in believing in some sort of external foundation for morals — does not this mean that at some level "anything goes"? Am I not reduced to the therapist's, "If it feels good to you, then it's O.K."? Even worse, am I not committed to the consequence that for some societies at some times, grossly awful things like rape may be morally permissible?

Such a conclusion would indeed be the very refutation of my philosophy. I would immediately set about denying my premises! But, fortunately, I am able to argue that the very opposite is the case, for I am a subjectivist of a very distinctive kind. For a start, the whole point about having morality as an adaptation is that it has to be a *shared* adaptation. If only I am moral and you are not, then you will win, and I and my bloodline will soon be eliminated. Morality (in the sense of normative ethics) is a social phenomenon, and unless we all have it, it fails.

In this respect, morality is like speech, where without shared comprehension it is pointless. Of course, language does vary across cultures and so does morality, somewhat. But, just as Noam Chomsky (1957) has shown that language may yet share a (biologically based) "deep structure," so I would argue that the same may well be true of morality. In line with conventional philosophical thought about ethical norms, it would seem to me that particular manifestations of the norms may vary according to circumstance while the underlying structure remains constant.

Perhaps I must concede intergalactic relativism (Ruse 1985), but for humans here on earth, given their shared evolutionary history, I am not much of a relativist. I condemn as strongly as anyone the rapes in Yugoslavia, the atrocities of Hitler, the ongoing practice of female circumcision. Yet there is another point about my subjectivism that is worth making. Although I am a noncognitivist, in crucial respects I differ from other noncognitivists. For someone like the emotivist, normative ethics has to be translated but as a report on feelings, perhaps combined with a bit of exhortation. "I don't like killing! Boo hoo! Don't you do it either!" (See Ayer 1946; Hudson 1983.) For me, this is simply not strong enough. I believe that, if emotivism were the complete answer, genes for cheating would soon make a spectacular appearance in the human species, or rather, those genes already existing would make an immediate gain.

The way in which biology avoids this happening is by making moral claims seem *as if they were objective*! To use a useful if ugly word of Mackie (1979), we "objectify" morality. We think that killing is wrong because it seems to us that killing *is* wrong. Somehow, whatever the truth may be, the foundation of morality does seem to be something "out there," binding on us.

In other words, what I want to suggest is that—contrary to the emotivists' belief—the *meaning* of morality is that it is objective. Because it is not objective (in the sense of having an independent existence), it is in a sense an illusion; although, because it is thrust upon us by evolution (it is not arbitrary), it is not relative; this is why you may find my argument implausible! This is also a reason why I do not fear that my telling you all of this will let you go away and sin with impunity. Your genes are a lot stronger than my words. The truth does not always set you free.

Third, what about predecessors? My rather gloomy experience, when I have made a successful argument, is that somebody claims that it has all been made before. Although, actually, as with the science and with normative ethics, I am fairly happy to seek and acknowledge that others have been there before me. The most obvious pre-evolutionary predecessor is Immanuel Kant (1949, 1959), for not only did he have a form of social-contract ethics but he (like me) argued that one should not seek the foundation of ethics in some sort of external reality, "out there." Rather, Kant argued that we find the basis for ethics in the interrelation of rational beings as they attempt to live and work together. Without ethics, in the normative sense, we run into "contradictions," where these are to be understood as failures of social living rather than anything in a formal sort of way. (This is also the position of Rawls 1980.)

Yet, although I am quite sympathetic to the Kantian perspective—after all, I have spoken in a positive way of Rawls's system of moral philosophy—I believe that, in one crucial way, my system of evolutionary ethics can never be that of the Kantian. For Kant, the ethics we have is uniquely that possessed by rational beings, here on earth and anywhere else. This, to the Darwinian evolutionist, smacks altogether too much of a kind of progressionist upward drive to the one unique way of doing things. As I have argued, why should not the John Foster Dulles way of doing ethics have become the biologically fixed norm? (Perhaps it has, as a kind of minor subvariety.) The Kantian wants to bar intergalactic relativism, and this I am not prepared to do. (Although he finds Darwinism useful for explaining the origins of morality, Rawls [1971] explicitly denies that Darwinism can throw light on the foundations of morality.)

Rather, I would recommend to my readers the ethical system of David Hume (1978). As an eighteenth-century Scot, he was certainly not insensitive to the significance of reciprocation in human relationships. This meant that he was unwilling to see everything collapse into some kind of whimsical relativism, even though, at the same time, he felt that ethics could be no more than a subjective phenomenon. Resolving this dilemma, he saw the psychological phenomenon of objectification as being a major element in the ethical experience (Mackie 1979). This is the position that I endorse.

There are other reasons why I think of my position as being essentially that of David Hume brought up to date by Charles Darwin. One is that Hume is the authority for the compatibilist approach that I have taken to the problem of free will and determinism. Another is that Hume, like me, sees morality as being a differential phenomenon, weakening as one moves away from one's relatives and friends. But most crucially, Hume is my mentor because he went before me in trying to provide a completely naturalistic theory of ethics. He was no evolutionist but he wanted to base his philosophy in tune with the best science of his day. And this is enough for me. (On philosophical antecedents, see also Ruse 1990.)

Conclusion

There are as many questions raised as answered. This is no fault, but the mark of a vital ongoing inquiry. A scientific "paradigm" is something that gives you things to think about, and this is precisely what sells my position to me. I want to ask, for instance, about the relationship of my evolutionary ethics to conventional religion, especially Christianity (which is the one in my background). Can one be an evolutionist of my kind and yet still accept the central elements of Christian faith? One certainly cannot do so if one is a fundamentalist, taking the Bible absolutely literally, but more sophisticated Christians have always prided themselves on being able to resolve the demands of faith with the findings of science. (See Ruse 1989 for some thoughts on this question.)

I want to know also if one can use the knowledge of evolution to work with one's ethical commitments, recognizing them for what they are and not necessarily as the ideal strategy for long-term survival and reproduction in an era of high technology. Could we possibly owe it to our children to be immoral—in the short term, at least, for the long-term benefits? Even if we could see that this would make sense, would it be possible, or am I right in fearing that our biology will always be too strong for us to break from or around it?

These and many other questions come to mind. If you are spurred to answer them, then my defense of an updated evolutionary ethics has not been in vain.

Bibliography

Allen, E., and others. "Sociobiology: A new biological determinism," *BioScience* 26 (1976): 182–186.

Axelrod, R. *The Evolution of Cooperation.* New York: Basic Books, 1984.

Ayer, A. J. *Language, Truth, and Logic,* 2d ed. London: Gollancz, 1946.

Betzig, C. C., M. Borgerhoff Muldur, and Turke P. W. *Human Reproductive Behavior.* Cambridge: Cambridge University Press, 1987.

Bowler, P. *Evolution: The History of an Idea.* Berkeley: University of California Press, 1984.

Burian, R. M. "Human sociobiology and genetic determinism," *Philosophical Forum* 13(2–3) (1981): 43–66.

Chomsky, N. *Syntactic Structures.* The Hague: Mouton, 1957.

Cronin, H. *The Ant and the Peacock.* Cambridge: Cambridge University Press, 1991.

Darwin, C. *On the Origin of Species.* London: John Murray, 1859.

———. *The Descent of Man.* London: John Murray, 1871.

Dawkins, R. *The Selfish Gene*. Oxford: Oxford University Press, 1976.

_____. *The Blind Watchmaker*. New York: Norton, 1986.

De Waal, F. *Chimpanzee Politics: Power and Sex Among Apes*. New York: HarperCollins Publishers, Inc., 1982.

Dobzhansky, T. *The Biology of Ultimate Concern*. New York: New American Library, 1967.

Duncan, D., ed. *Life and Letters of Herbert Spencer*. London: Williams and Norgate, 1908.

Flew, A. *Evolution and Ethics*. London: Macmillan, 1967.

Gasman, D. *The Scientific Origins of National Socialism: Social Darwinism in Ernst Haeckel and the Monist League*. New York: Elsevier, 1971.

Gibbard, A. 1982. "Human evolution and the sense of justice." *Midwest Studies in Philosophy*, ed. P. French. Minneapolis: University of Minnesota Press, 1982, 31–46.

_____. *Wise Choices, Apt Feelings: A Theory of Normative Judgment*. Cambridge, Mass.: Harvard University Press, 1990.

Goodall, J. *The Chimpanzees of Gombe: Patterns of Behavior*. Cambridge, Mass.: Belknap, 1986.

Gould, S. J. *Wonderful Life*. New York: Norton, 1989.

Haeckel, E. *Generelle Morphologie der Organismen*. Berlin: Reimer, 1866.

_____. *The History of Creation*. London: Kegan Paul, Trench, 1868.

Hamilton, W. D. "The genetical evolution of social behaviour I," *Journal of Theoretical Biology 7* (1964a) 1–16.

_____. "The genetical evolution of social behaviour II," *Journal of Theoretical Biology 7* (1964b) 17–32.

Holldobler, B., and E. O. Wilson. *The Ants*. Cambridge, Mass.: Harvard University Press, 1990.

Hudson, W. D. *Modern Moral Philosophy*, 2d ed. London: Macmillan, 1983.

Hume, D. *A Treatise of Human Nature*. Oxford: Oxford University Press, 1978.

Huxley, J. S. *Evolution and Ethics*. London: Pilot, 1947.

_____. *UNESCO: Its Purpose and Its Philosophy*. Washington, D.C.: Public Affairs Press, 1948.

Isaac, G. "Aspects of human evolution." *Evolution from Molecules to Men*, ed. D. S. Bendall. Cambridge: Cambridge University Press, 1983, 509–543.

Jones, G. *Social Darwinsim and English Thought*. Brighton: Harvester, 1980.

Kant, I. *Critique of Practical Reason*, tr. L. W. Beck. Chicago: University of Chicago Press, 1949.

_____. *Foundations of the Metaphysics of Morals*, tr. L. W. Beck. Indianapolis: Bobbs-Merrill, 1959.

Kelley, A. *The Descent of Darwin: The Popularization of Darwinism in Germany, 1860–1914*. Chapel Hill: University of North Carolina Press, 1981.

Mackie, J. L. *Ethics*. Harmondsworth, Middlesex: Penguin, 1977.

_____. "The law of the jungle," *Philosophy* 53 (1978): 553–573.

_____. *Hume's Moral Theory*. London: Routledge and Kegan Paul, 1979.

Mayr, E. *Towards a New Philosophy of Biology: Observations of an Evolutionist*. Cambridge, Mass.: Belknap, 1988.

Midgley, M. "Gene-juggling," *Philosophy* 54 (1979): 439–458.

_____. *Evolution as Religion: Strange Hopes and Stranger Fears*. London: Methuen, 1985.

Moore, G. E. *Principia Ethica*. Cambridge: Cambridge University Press, 1903.

Moore, J. The Post-Darwinian Controversies. Cambridge: Cambridge University Press, 1979.

Murphy, J. *Evolution, Morality, and the Meaning of Life*. Totowa, N.J.: Rowman and Littlefield, 1982.

Nagel, E. *The Structure of Science*. London: Routledge and Kegan Paul, 1961.

Nozick, R. *Philosophical Explanations*. Cambridge, Mass.: Harvard University Press, 1981.

Paradis, J., and G. C. Williams, eds. *Evolution and Ethics: T. H. Huxley's "Evolution and Ethics" with New Essays on Its Victorian and Sociobiological Context*. Princeton, N.J. Princeton University Press, 1989.

Peel, J. D. Y. *Herbert Spencer: The Evolution of a Sociologist*. London: Heinemann, 1971.

Pilbeam, D. "The descent of hominoids and hominids," *Scientific American* 250 (3) (1984): 84–97.

Pittenger, M. *American Socialists and Evolutionary Thought, 1870–1920*. Madison, Wis.: University of Wisconsin Press, 1993.

Pusey, J. R. *China and Charles Darwin*. Cambridge, Mass.: Harvard University Press, 1983.

Rawls, J. *A Theory of Justice*. Cambridge, Mass.: Harvard University Press, 1971.

——. "Kantian constructivism in moral theory," *Journal of Philosophy* 77 (1980): 515–572.

Richards, R. J. *Darwin and the Emergence of Evolutionary Theories of Mind and Behavior*. Chicago: University of Chicago Press, 1987.

Ruse, M. *Sociobiology: Sense or Nonsense?* Dordrecht, Holland: Reidel, 1979a.

——. *The Darwinian Revolution: Science Red in Tooth and Claw*. Chicago: University of Chicago Press, 1979b.

——. "Charles Darwin and group selection," *Annals of Science 37* (1980): 615–630.

——. "Is rape wrong on Andromeda? An introduction to extraterrestrial evolution, science, and morality." *Extraterrestrials: Science and Alien Intelligence*. ed. E. Regis. Cambridge: Cambridge University Press, 1985, 43–78.

——. *Taking Darwin Seriously*. Oxford: Blackwell, 1986.

——. "Molecules to men: the concept of progress in evolutionary biology." *Evolutionary Progress,* ed. M. Nitecki. Chicago: University of Chicago Press, 1988, 97–128.

——. *The Darwinian Paradigm: Essays on Its History, Philosophy, and Religious Implications*. London: Routledge, 1989.

——. "Evolutionary ethics and the search for predecessors: Kant, Hume, and all the way back to Aristotle?" *Social Philosophy and Policy* 8 (1) (1990): 59–87.

——. "Evolution and progress," *Trends in Ecology and Evolution* 8 (2) (1993): 55–59.

——. *Evolutionary Naturalism*. London: Routledge, 1994.

Ruse, M., and E. O. Wilson. "Moral philosophy as applied science," *Philosophy* 61 (1986): 173–192.

Russett, C. E. *Darwin in America: The Intellectual Response. 1865–1912*. San Francisco: Freeman, 1976.

Singer, P. *The Expanding Circle: Ethics and Sociobiology*. New York: Farrar, Straus & Giroux, 1981.

Sober, E. "Did evolution make us psychological egoists?" in *Pittsburgh Studies in the Philosophy of Science*, ed. J. Earman. Pittsburgh: University of Pittsburgh Press, 1993.

Spadefora, D. *The Concept of Progress in Eighteenth Century Britain*. New Haven, Conn.: Yale University Press, 1990.

Spencer, H. *Social Statics: Or, the Conditions Essential to Human Happiness Specified, and the First of Them Developed*. London: Chapman, 1851.

——. Progress: Its law and cause. *Westminster Review,* 1857.

——. *Essays: Scientific, Political, and Speculative*. London: Williams and Norgate, 1868.

——. *The Principles of Ethics*. London: Williams and Norgate, 1892.

——. *Autobiography*. London: Williams and Norgate, 1904.

Taylor, P. W., ed. *Problems of Moral Philosophy*. Belmont, Calif.: Wadsworth, 1978.

Trivers, R. "The evolution of reciprocal altruism," *Quarterly Review of Biology* 46 (1971): 35–57.

Waddington, C. H. *The Ethical Animal*. London: Allen and Unwin, 1960.

Wallwork, E. "Thou shalt love thy neighbour as thyself: the Freudian critique," *Journal of Religious Ethics* 10 (1982): 264–319.

West Eberhard, M. J. "The evolution of social behavior by kin selection," *Quarterly Review of Biology* 50 (1975): 1–33.

Wilson, E. O. *Sociobiology: The New Synthesis*. Cambridge, Mass.: Harvard University Press, 1975.

——. *On Human Nature*. Cambridge, Mass.: Cambridge University Press, 1978.

——. *Biophilia*. Cambridge, Mass.: Harvard University Press, 1984.

Wiltshire, D. *The Social and Political Thought of Herbert Spencer*. Oxford: Oxford University Press, 1978.

III.6 *Prospects for an Evolutionary Ethics*

Elliott Sober

Elliott Sober is professor of philosophy at the University of Wisconsin and the author of several works in philosophy of science, including *Reconstructing the Past: Parsimony, Evolution and Inference* (1988) and *Philosophy of Biology* (1993). Sober maintains that there are two avenues by which evolutionary theory might be relevant to ethics. Biology might help explain why we have the ethical thoughts and feelings that we do, or it might help justify or undermine various normative propositions. This essay explores each of these possibilities.

1. *Two Kinds of Questions*

Human beings are a product of evolution. This means that the *existence* of our species is explained by the process of descent with modification. But, in addition, it also means that various *phenotypic characteristics* of our species — features of morphology, physiology, and behavior — have evolutionary explanations.

Some see in this simple idea the promise of a new understanding of the problems of ethics. Others grant its truth but reject its relevance. The first group insists that if evolutionary biology can provide insights into the workings of the human mind, these insights cannot fail to transform our understanding of right and wrong. But for the doubters, the fact that human beings have an evolutionary past has no more significance than the fact that the human body must obey the laws of physics. It is true that our bodies are subject to the law of gravity, but apparently that is of little help in understanding why we think and act as we do.

To assess the relevance of evolutionary ideas to the problems of ethics, we must distinguish two quite different projects. The first is the task of ac-

counting for why people have the ethical thoughts and feelings they do. The second concerns the problem of deciding what the status of those thoughts and feelings is. The difference between these two projects is illustrated by the following pair of questions:

(1) Why do people have the views they do concerning when it is morally permissible to kill?

(2) When is killing morally permissible?

Problem (1) poses a problem of *explanation*, while (2) engages the task of *justification*. One of the main issues I want to consider is how these questions are related to each other. This is a matter of some intricacy. But at the simplest level, it is important to recognize that there is no automatic connection between the two types of problems.

It is quite obvious that a person can believe the right thing for the wrong reason. Consider my friend Alf, who thinks the earth is round but does so because he thinks that the earth is perfect and that roundness is the perfect shape. Alf also happens to know various facts that the rest of us recognize as evidence for the earth's being round. But Alf's predicament is that he does not see these facts as having any particular evidential significance. Alf believes *E* and also believes *R*, but he does not believe *R because* he believes *E*. *E* is evidence for *R*; *E* is *a* reason to believe *R*, but it is not *Alf's* reason for believing *R*.

This example encapsulates two lessons. First, it is possible to show whether a proposition is justified without saying anything, one way or the other, by way of explaining why someone happens to believe

This article was commissioned for this work and appears in print here for the first time. Some passages from this article are excerpted from Sober (1993). I am grateful to James Anderson and Louis Pojman for useful discussion.

that proposition. *E* justifies *R*, but that says nothing about why Alf believes *R*. Second, and conversely, an explanation of why someone believes a proposition may leave open whether the proposition is in fact well supported by evidence. Alf's strange ideas about perfection explain why he believes *R*. But this quirk of Alf's psychology does not tell us whether *R*, in fact, is a proposition that is well supported by evidence.

So the following two questions are quite different from each other:

(3) Why does Alf believe that the earth is round?

(4) Is the proposition that the earth is round strongly supported by evidence?

I hope the parallel between problems (1) and (2) on the one hand and problems (3) and (4) on the other is suggestive. In each pair, it is possible to answer one question without thereby answering the other. In summary, we have the following slogan: *An explanation for why someone believes a proposition may fail to show whether the proposition is justified, and a justification of a proposition may fail to explain why someone believes the proposition.* This simple conclusion is the beginning, not the end, of our discussion of the relationship between such questions as (1) and (2).

2. Patterns of Evolutionary Explanation

Before we can address the question of how the problem of explanation and the problem of justification are related, it is well to get clear on how evolution can contribute to getting clear on the problem of explanation. How might evolutionary theory help explain why we have the ethical thoughts and feelings that we possess?

Although natural selection is just one of the processes that can produce evolutionary change, it is the one of greatest interest to sociobiologists. When natural selection is cited by way of explaining why a trait is currently found in some population, an ancestral population is postulated in which the trait was one of several variants that were represented. These traits are claimed to have differed in their *fitness* — their capacity to help the individuals

possessing them to survive and reproduce. Through a process of differential survival and reproduction, the population moved from a mixed condition to the homogeneous condition we now observe. Why do zebras now run fast when a predator approaches? Because, ancestrally, zebras differed in running speed, and the fast zebras survived and reproduced more successfully than the slow ones.

Within this basic outline, it is important to distinguish two quite different patterns of explanation that may be used to elaborate the idea that natural selection explains what we observe. In both instances, the goal is to explain why a certain *pattern of variation* exists.

Why do polar bears have thicker fur than brown bears? The reason is that polar bears live in colder climates than brown bears. In particular, natural selection favored one trait for the organisms in the one habitat and a different trait for the organisms in the other. More specifically still, there are genetic differences between the two species that account for the difference in the thickness of their coats. These genetic differences arose because of selective differences in the bears' environments.

Why do the polar bears who live near the North Pole have thicker fur than the polar bears who live farther south? The reason is that the bears in the first group live in a colder climate than do the bears in the second. In particular, natural selection favored polar bears who possessed *phenotypic plasticity*. The bears evolved a set of genes that permitted them to respond to changes in the ambient temperature. The bears in the two groups differ in coat thickness, but this is not because they are genetically different. Rather, the difference in phenotype is to be explained by appeal to an environmental difference.

There is a truism that neither of these patterns of explanation contradicts. Every trait a bear has is a product of the genes it possesses interacting with the environment in which it lives. This remark is a truism because "environment" is defined as a garbage-can category; it includes all factors that are not considered "genetic."

If genetic and environmental causes both play a role in the development of a trait, we still may wish to say which was more "important." This question quickly leads to nonsense if we apply it to the trait exhibited by a single organism. It is meaningless to say that three inches of Smokey's fur were provided by his genes and two inches by his environment. If we wish to assess the relative importance of causes, we must examine a population of bears in which there is variation. And, as we have seen, some patterns of variation will mainly be due to genetic differences, while others will mainly be due to differences in environment.

When sociobiologists attempt to provide evolutionary explanations of human behavioral and psychological characteristics, they are often accused of endorsing the doctrine of "genetic determinism." However, I hope these two examples show that evolutionary explanations are not automatically committed to the primacy of genetic over environmental explanation. Natural selection can have the result that phenotypic differences are due to genetic differences. But natural selection also can have the consequence that phenotypic differences are explained by differences in environment.

Let us now apply this lesson to problems like (1). Just as coat thickness can vary among bears, so views about killing can vary within and among human societies. Once again, it is useful to think about the pattern of variation that needs to be explained. Contemporary societies differ from each other, and individual societies have changed their views over time. In addition, we must remember that societies are not monolithic entities; if we look carefully *within* a society, we often will discern variation in opinion about when killing is permissible.

It is important not to confuse the code followed in a society with the simple slogans that the society endorses. First, there is the gap between ideals and reality. But, in addition, the slogans often do not begin to capture what the ideals really are. The sixth commandment says "Thou shalt not kill," but very few believers have thought that killing is *always* impermissible.

The ethical code endorsed by a society, or by an individual, is a complex object, one that is often difficult to articulate precisely. Ethical codes are in this respect like languages. You and I know how to speak English, but which of us is able to describe precisely the rules that define grammatical English? If we wish to explain why people have the views they do about the permissibility of killing, we first must obtain an accurate description of what those views actually are. "Why do people think that killing is wrong?" is a poorly formulated question.

Social scientists and evolutionary biologists have different contributions to make to our understanding of problem (1). In many parts of the world, capital punishment is now much less popular than it was a hundred years ago. Why did this transition occur? In contrast, consider the fact that all (or virtually all) human societies have regarded the killing of one's children as a much more serious matter than the killing of a chicken. Why is this so? Perhaps historians have more to tell us than evolutionists about the first question, but the reverse is true with respect to the second. There need be no battle among these disciplines concerning which holds the key. Ethical beliefs about killing are complex and multifaceted; different beliefs in this complex may fall within the domains of different disciplines.

If recent changes in view as to the permissibility of capital punishment don't have an evolutionary explanation, what does this mean? Of course, it is not to be denied that having ethical opinions requires a reasonably big brain, and our big brain is the product of evolution. What I mean is that the *difference* between people a hundred years ago who favored capital punishment and people now who oppose capital punishment is not to be explained by appeal to evolutionary factors. Again, the problem that matters concerns how one should explain a pattern of variation.

My example about the chicken may suggest that evolutionary considerations can be brought to bear only on characteristics that are invariant across cultures. Many sociobiologists reject this limitation. For example, Alexander (1987) and Wilson (1978) grant that human beings have enormous behavioral plasticity. We have an astonishing ability to modify our behavior in the light of environmental circumstances. Nonetheless, these sociobiologists also maintain that evolution has caused us to produce behaviors that, in the environment at hand, maximize fitness. For them, human behavioral variation is to be explained by the same kind of account I described above for geographical variation in polar bear coat thickness.

An example of this sort is provided by Alexander's (1987) explanation of the kinship system known as the avunculate. In this arrangement, a husband takes care of his sister's children far more than he takes care of his wife's. Alexander's hypothesis was that the avunculate occurs when and where it does as an adaptive response to high levels of female promiscuity. If a husband is more likely to be genetically related to his sister's children than to his wife's, he maximizes his inclusive fitness by directing care to his nephews and nieces.

I am not interested here in exploring whether this suggested explanation of the avunculate is empirically plausible. My point has to do with the form of the explanation proposed. Alexander is trying to explain a behavior that is *not* a cultural universal. And his preferred explanation is *not* to say that societies with the avunculate are genetically different from societies with other kinship systems. Rather, Alexander's hypothesis is that there is a universal tendency to behave in fitness-maximizing ways; this universal tendency leads people in different environments to behave differently.

My pair of examples about coat thickness in bears was intended to demonstrate that we should not equate "evolutionary explanation" with "genetic explanation." The evolutionary process can have the result that phenotypic differences are explained by genetic differences, but it also can have the result that phenotypic differences are explained by environmental differences. This flexibility in evolutionary explanation raises a question, however. If evolutionary explanations can encompass both genetic and environmental factors, what would a *non-evolutionary* explanation look like?

A useful example is provided by the rapid decline in birth rates that occurred in Europe in the second half of the nineteenth century. In some areas of Italy, for instance, average family size declined from more than five children to a little more than two (Cavalli-Sforza and Feldman 1981). Why did this demographic transition occur?

Reducing family size did not enhance a parent's biological fitness. In fact, exactly the reverse was true. It is important to remember that fitness concerns survival *and* reproductive success. In this instance, forces of cultural change worked in opposition to the direction of natural selection. Cultural change overwhelmed the weaker opposing force of biological evolution. It is the historian, not the evolutionist, who will explain the demographic transition.

In discussing the fur thickness of bears, I mentioned a truism: Every trait a bear has is due to the genes it possesses interacting with the environment in which it lives. This truism applies with equal force to human beings. When a woman in nineteenth-century Italy has only two children, this behavior is the product of a developmental process in which her genes and her environment both participate. However, I hope it is clear that this truism does not tell us what sort of explanation will be relevant to the explanation of patterns of variation. The demographic transition may have a quite different type of explanation from the account that Alexander recommends for understanding the distribution of the avunculate.

The question "Can evolution explain ethics?" has usually elicited two simple responses. The first is "*Yes*, since ethics is a facet of human behavior and human behavior is a product of evolution." The second is "*No*, since ethics is a facet of human behavior and human behavior is a product of a culture." Both of these sweeping pronouncements neglect the fact that "ethics" is not the name of a single simple trait but rather of something complex and multifaceted. *Ethics* is a "supertrait," which has many "subtrait" components. The whole must be broken into its parts if we are to make headway on problems of explanation. It is reasonable to expect that some subtraits will have an evolutionary explanation while others will be explained culturally. For each subtrait that we wish to study, we must determine which form of explanation is more plausible.

3. *Three Metaethical Positions*

In my opinion, it is obvious that biology and the social sciences can collectively claim problem (1) as their own. The alternative is to think that human behavior is not susceptible to scientific explanation at all. No argument for this negative thesis has ever been remotely plausible. And progress in biology and the social sciences lends empirical support to the idea that science does not stop where human behavior begins.

Even if the status of the explanatory problem (1) is reasonably clear, the question of justification (2) is not nearly so straightforward. Question (2) concerns a *normative* matter. Does it have an answer, and if it does, how is that answer related to nonnormative matters of fact?

First, some terminology. Let us say that a statement describes something *subjective* if its truth or falsity is settled by what some subject believes; a statement describes something *objective*, in contrast, if its truth or falsity is independent of what anyone believes. "People believe that the Rockies are in North America" describes something subjective. "The Rockies are in North America," in contrast, describes something objective. When people study geography, there is both a subjective and an objective side to this activity; there are the opinions that people have about geography, but in addition, there are objective geographical facts.

Many people now believe that slavery is wrong. This claim about present-day opinion describes a subjective matter. Is there, in addition to this widespread belief, a fact of the matter as to whether slavery really is wrong? *Ethical subjectivism,* as I will use the term, maintains that there are no objective facts in ethics. In ethics, there is opinion and nothing else.

According to subjectivism, neither of the following statements is true:

Killing is always wrong.
Killing is sometimes permissible.

Naively, it might seem that one or the other of these statements must be true. Subjectivists disagree. According to them, no normative ethical statement is true.

Ethical realism is a position that conflicts with ethical subjectivism. Realism says that in ethics there are facts as well as opinions. Besides the way a murder makes people feel, there is, in addition, the question of whether the action really is wrong. Realism does not maintain that it is always obvious which actions are right and which are wrong; realists realize that uncertainty and disagreement surround many ethical issues. However, for the realist, there are truths in ethics that are independent of anyone's opinion.[1]

There is a third position that bears mentioning. The position I'll call *ethical conventionalism* asserts that some ethical statements are true but maintains that they are made true by some person's or persons' belief that they are true. For example, so-called *ethical relativists* say that murder is right or wrong only because various people in a society have come to believe that it is. And advocates of the *divine command theory* say that murder is wrong only because God believes (or says) that it is. And some versions of *existentialism* maintain that what is right or wrong for a person to do is settled by a decision the person makes about what sort of person he or she wishes to be.

This triplet of positions is summarized in the following diagram. They constitute the three possible answers to two sequential yes/no questions:

Are ethical statements ever true?

Yes
If an ethical statement
is true, is it true
independently of whether various
people believe or say it is
true?

Yes   No   No
REALISM   CONVENTIONALISM   SUBJECTIVISM

Although it may not be clear which of these three positions is most plausible, it should be clear that they are incompatible. Exactly one of them is correct.[2]

The distinction between subjectivism and its alternatives is important to bear in mind when one considers what evolution can tell us about the status of problems like that posed by (2). Are facts about human biology going to tell us when and why murder is wrong? Or are biological facts going to show that all normative beliefs are untrue? Here we are forced to choose; evolution cannot simultaneously tell us which ethical norms are correct *and* that all ethical statements are illusions.

Unfortunately, some evolutionary ethicists have wanted to have it both ways. For example, Ruse and Wilson (1986) have argued that an evolutionary understanding of why we have the ethical beliefs we do shows that those ethical beliefs cannot be objectively correct. Here is a characteristic passage:

Human beings function better if they are deceived by their genes into thinking that there is a disinterested objective morality binding upon them, which all should obey. We help others because it is "right" to help them and because we know that they are inwardly compelled to reciprocate in equal measure. What Darwinian evolutionary theory shows is that this sense of "right" and the corresponding sense of "wrong," feelings we take to be above individual desire and in some fusion outside biology, are in fact brought about by ultimately biological processes. (p. 179)

Ruse and Wilson seem to favor an emotivist account of ethical statements, according to which those statements merely express the feelings of speakers but never say anything true. Their emotivism is a form of ethical subjectivism as defined above.

At the same time, Ruse and Wilson sometimes suggest that biology provides guidance about which norms we should adopt. Consider the following:

> Human mental development has proved to be far richer and more structured and idiosyncratic than previously suspected. The constraints on this development are the sources of our strongest feelings of right and wrong, and they are powerful enough to serve as a foundation for ethical codes. But the articulation of enduring codes will depend upon a more detailed knowledge of the mind and human evolution than we now possess. We suggest that it will prove possible to proceed with a knowledge of the material basis of moral feeling to generally accepted rules of conduct. To do so will be to escape—not a minute too soon—from the debilitating absolute distinction between *is* and *ought*. (p. 174)

Here biology seems to be in the business of telling us which ethical codes are correct. Biology grounds ethics rather than unmasking it.

Ruse and Wilson sometimes draw a contrast between "internal" and "external" sources of norms. Internal norms are said to be "rooted" in our biology, whereas external ones are divinely given, or hold true independently of details about human biology. Ruse and Wilson clearly believe that ethics is "internal" and that evolutionary biology shows that this is so.

It is important to see that the distinction between subjectivism and realism differs from the internal/external distinction. Realists can easily maintain that an action has the ethical properties it does because of facts about our biology. When you ask your dinner companion to pass the salt and he doesn't immediately comply, why would it be wrong to stab his hand with your fork? Realists are entitled to answer this question by pointing out that stabbing someone *causes pain*. They are allowed to admit that if stabbing didn't cause pain, then the action might have quite different ethical properties.

Ruse and Wilson maintain that ethics cannot be objective if it is "internal." No such consequence follows.

4. The Is/Ought Gap

The goal of this paper is not to reach some general assessment of the three metaethical positions just described. Rather, the question is whether evolutionary considerations can tell us which is most plausible.

In this section I want to formulate and criticize one argument for subjectivism that I believe has had a great deal of influence. This argument makes no specific reference to evolutionary considerations, but it is in the background of many discussions about evolutionary ethics.

The argument I'll formulate has its provenance in Hume's distinction between *is* and *ought,* a distinction to which Ruse and Wilson alluded in the passage quoted before. I will say that an *is*-statement describes what is the case without making any moral judgment about whether this situation is good or bad. An *ought*-statement, in contrast, makes a moral judgment about the moral characteristics (rightness, wrongness, etc.) that some action or class of actions has. For example, "Thousands of people are killed by handguns every year in the United States" is an *is*-statement; "it is wrong that handguns are unregulated" is an *ought*-statement.

Hume defended the thesis that *ought*-statements cannot be deduced from exclusively *is*-statements. For example, he would regard the following argument as deductively invalid:

Torturing people for fun causes great suffering.

Torturing people for fun is wrong.

The conclusion does not follow deductively from the premises. However, if we supply an additional premise, the argument can be made deductively valid:

Torturing people for fun causes great suffering.
It is wrong to cause great suffering.

Torturing people for fun is wrong.

Notice that this second argument, unlike the first, has an *ought*-statement as one of its premises. Hume's thesis says that *a deductively valid argument for an ought-conclusion must have at least one ought-premise.*

The term "naturalistic fallacy" is sometimes applied to any attempt to deduce *ought*-statements from exclusively *is*-premises. The terminology is a bit misleading, since it was G. E. Moore in *Principia Ethica* (1903) who invented the idea of a "naturalistic fallacy," and Moore's idea differs in some respects from the one just described. Unfortunately, most people discussing evolutionary ethics tend to use Moore's label to name Hume's insight. I want to keep them separate. The proposition I'll call *Hume's thesis* says you can't deduce an *ought* from an *is.* Hume's thesis, I believe, is correct.[3]

Hume's thesis, by itself, does not entail subjectivism. However, it plays a role in the following argument for subjectivism:

> *Ought*-statements cannot be deduced validly from exclusively *is*-premises.
> If *ought*-statements cannot be deduced validly from exclusively *is*-premises, then no *ought*-statements are true.

> No *ought*-statements are true.

The first premise is Hume's thesis. The second premise, which is needed to reach the subjectivist conclusion, is a *reductionist assumption.* It says that for an *ought*-statement to be true, it must reduce to (be deducible from) exclusively *is*-premises.

My doubts about this argument center on the second premise. Why should the fact that ethics cannot be deduced from purely *is*-propositions show that no ethical statements are true? Why can't ethical statements be true, though irreducible? It is important to remember that Hume's thesis concerns deductive arguments. Consider an analogy: Scientific theories about unobservable entities cannot be deduced from premises that are strictly about observables, but this provides no reason to think that theories about unobservables are always untrue.

My remarks on this argument provide no positive defense of ethical realism. However, I hope they do show that one influential argument behind ethical subjectivism is not as decisive as it might seem.

5. Genetic Arguments

I now want to consider a second argument for ethical subjectivism. It asserts that ethical beliefs cannot be true because the beliefs we have about right and wrong are merely the products of evolution. An alternative formulation of this idea would be that subjectivism must be true because our ethical views result from the socialization we experience in early life. These two ideas may be combined as follows:

> (G) We believe the ethical statements we do because of our evolution and because of facts about our socialization.

> No ethical statement is true.

Philosophers are often quick to dismiss arguments like (G) on the grounds that these arguments are guilty of what has come to be called *the genetic fallacy.* A genetic argument describes the genesis (origin) of a belief and attempts to extract some conclusion about the belief's truth or plausibility.

The dim view that many philosophers take of genetic arguments reflects a standard philosophical distinction between the *context of discovery* and the *context of justification.* This distinction, emphasized by the logician Gottlob Frege, was widely embraced by the positivists.

Hempel (1965) tells the story of the chemist Kekulé, who worked on the problem of determining the structure of benzene. After a long day at the lab, Kekulé found himself gazing wearily at a fire. He hallucinated a pair of whirling snakes, which grabbed each other's tails and formed a circle. Kekulé, in a flash of creative insight, came up with the idea of the benzene ring.

The fact that Kekulé arrived at the idea of the benzene ring while hallucinating does not settle the question of whether benzene really has that structure. It is for psychologists to describe the context of discovery—the (possibly) idiosyncratic psychological processes that led Kekulé to his insight. After Kekulé came up with his idea, he was able to do experiments and muster evidence. This latter set of considerations concerns the logic of justification.

I agree that one can't *deduce* whether Kekulé's hypothesis was true just from the fact that the idea first occurred to him in a dream. The same holds true of my friend Alf; one can't *deduce* that his belief about the shape of the earth is mistaken just from the fact that he reached this belief because of his weird ideas about perfection. However, it is a mistake to overinterpret this point. I want to suggest that there can be perfectly reasonable genetic arguments. These will be nondeductive in form.

Consider my colleague Ben, who walks into his Introduction to Philosophy class one day with the idea that he will decide how many people are in the room by drawing a slip of paper from an urn. In the urn are a hundred such slips, each with a different number written on it. Ben reaches into the urn, draws a slip on which seventy-eight is written, and announces that he believes that exactly seventy-eight people are present.

Surely it is reasonable to conclude that Ben's belief is probably incorrect. This conclusion is justified because of the process that led Ben to his belief. If so, the following is a perfectly sensible genetic argument:

> Ben decided that there were seventy-eight people in the room by drawing the number seventy-eight at random from an urn.
>
> p ===================
>
> It isn't true that there were seventy-eight people in the room.

I have drawn a double line between premise and conclusion to indicate that the argument is not supposed to be deductively valid. The "p" next to the double line represents the probability that the premise confers on the conclusion. I claim that p is high in this argument.

It is quite true that one cannot *deduce* that a proposition is untrue just from a description of how someone came to believe it. After all, the fact that Ben drew the number seventy-eight from the urn doesn't absolutely rule out the possibility that there are exactly seventy-eight people in the room. Still, given the process by which he formed his belief, it would be something of a miracle if his belief just happened to be correct. In this case, the context of discovery *does* provide evidence as to whether a belief is true. If so, we must be careful not to conflate two quite different formulations of what the genetic fallacy is supposed to involve:

(5) Conclusions about the truth of a proposition cannot be *deduced validly* from premises that describe why someone came to believe the proposition.

(6) Conclusions about the truth of a proposition cannot be *inferred* from premises that describe why someone came to believe the proposition.

I think that (5) is true but (6) is false. Inference encompasses more than deductive inference. I conclude that argument (*G*) for ethical subjectivism cannot be dismissed simply with the remark that it commits "the genetic fallacy."

The genetic argument concerning Ben's belief is convincing. Why? the reason is that *what caused him to reach the belief had nothing to do with how many students were in the room.* When this *independence relation* obtains, the genetic argument shows that the belief is implausible. In contrast, when a *dependence relation* obtains, the description of the belief's genesis can lead to the conclusion that the belief is probably correct.

As an example of how a genetic argument can show that someone's belief is probably true, consider my colleague Cathy, who decided that there are thirty-four people in her philosophy class by carefully counting the people present. I suggest that the premise in the following argument confers a high probability on the conclusion:

> Cathy carefully counted the people in her class and consequently believed that thirty-four people were present.
>
> p ===================
>
> Thirty-four people were present in Cathy's class.

When Cathy did her methodical counting, the thing that caused her to believe that there were thirty-four people present was *not* independent of how many people actually were there. Because the process of belief formation was influenced in the right way by how many people were actually in the room, we are prepared to grant that a description of the context of *discovery* provides a *justification* of the resulting belief.

Let us turn now to the argument (*G*) for ethical subjectivism stated before. As the comparison of Ben and Cathy shows, the argument for subjectivism is incomplete. We need to add some premise about how the process by which we arrive at our moral beliefs is related to which moral beliefs (if any) are true. The argument requires something like the following thesis:

(A)   The processes that determine what moral beliefs people have are entirely independent of which moral statements (if any) are true.

This proposition, if correct, would support the following conclusion: *The moral beliefs we currently have are probably untrue.*

The first thing to notice about this conclusion is that it does *not* say that ethical subjectivism is correct. It says that our *current* moral beliefs are probably untrue, not that *all* ethical statements are untrue. Here we have an important difference between (G) and the quite legitimate genetic arguments about Ben and Cathy. It is clear that a genetic argument might support the thesis that the ethical statements we happen to believe are untrue. I do not see how it can show that no ethical statements are true.

The next thing to notice about argument (G) concerns assumption (A). To decide whether (A) is correct, we would need to describe

(i) the processes that lead people to arrive at their ethical beliefs,

and

(ii) the facts about the world, if any, that make ethical beliefs true or false.

We then would have to show that (i) and (ii) are entirely independent of each other, as (A) asserts.

Argument (G) provides a very brief answer to (i) — it cites "evolution" and "socialization." However, with respect to problem (ii), the argument says nothing at all. Of course, if subjectivism were correct, there would be no such thing as ethical facts. But to *assume* that subjectivism is true in the context of this argument would be question-begging.

Because (G) says only a little about (i) and nothing at all about (ii), I suggest that it is impossible to tell from this argument whether (A) is correct. A large number of our beliefs stem either from evolution or from socialization. Mathematical beliefs are of this sort, but that doesn't show that no mathematical statements are true (Kitcher 1993). I conclude that (G) is a weak argument for ethical subjectivism.[4]

Perhaps many of our current ethical beliefs *are* confused. I am inclined to think that morality is one of the last frontiers that human knowledge can aspire to cross. Even harder than the problems of natural science is the question of how we ought to lead our lives. This question is harder for us to come to grips with because it is clouded with self-deception. Powerful impulses disincline us to stare moral issues squarely in the face. No wonder it has taken humanity so long to traverse so modest a distance. Moral beliefs generated by superstition and prejudice probably *are* untrue. Moral beliefs with this sort of pedigree deserve to be undermined by genetic arguments. However, from this critique of some elements of existing morality, one cannot conclude that subjectivism about ethics is correct.

There is a somewhat different formulation of the genetic argument for ethical subjectivism that is worth considering. Harman (1977) suggests that we do not need to postulate the existence of ethical facts to explain why we have the ethical thoughts and feelings that we do. Psychological and evolutionary considerations suffice to do the explaining. Harman draws the conclusion that it is reasonable to deny the existence of ethical facts. His argument implicitly appeals to *Ockham's razor* (the *principle of parsimony*), which says that we should deny the existence of entities and processes that are not needed to explain anything.[5] We may schematize this argument as follows:

We do not need to postulate the existence of ethical facts to explain why people have the ethical beliefs they do.

It is reasonable to postulate the existence of ethical facts only if that postulate is needed to explain why people have the ethical beliefs they do.

There are no ethical facts.

As before, I draw a double line between premises and conclusion to indicate that the argument is supposed to be nondeductive in character. Ethical subjectivism is here recommended on the ground that it is more *parsimonious* than alternative theories.[6]

I think the first premise of this argument is correct. Psychological and biological facts about the human mind suffice to explain why we have the ethical beliefs we do. For example, we can explain why someone believes that capital punishment is wrong without committing ourselves, one way or the other, on the question of whether capital punishment really is wrong.[7]

Nonetheless, I think that the second premise is radically implausible. For consider an analogy. Imagine that you are attending a class in statistics in which the professor repeatedly advances claims concerning how people should reason when they face inference problems of various sorts. After several weeks, a student stands up and claims that the professor's normative remarks cannot be correct, on the grounds that they do not describe or explain how people actually think and behave. The professor, I take it, would be right to reply that statistics is not the same as psychology. Maybe human beings reason in normatively *incorrect* ways. The goal of statistics is not to describe or explain behavior, but to change it.

Precisely the same remarks apply to ethics. Ethics is not psychology. The point of normative ethical statements is not to *describe* why we believe and act as we do but to *guide* our thought and behavior. We should not endorse ethical subjectivism simply because psychological explanations don't require ethical premises.

6. A *Nondeductive Analog of Hume's Thesis*

Hume said you can't deduce an *ought*-conclusion from purely *is*-premises. This thesis, I have emphasized, leaves open whether purely *is*-premises provide *non*deductive evidence for the truth of *ought*-conclusions.

On the face of it, the nondeductive connection of *ought* and *is* may seem obvious. Surely the first of the following two statements provides some evidence that the second is true:

(7) Action *X* will produce more pleasure and less pain than will action *Y*.

(8) You should perform action *X* rather than action *Y*.

I agree that (7) is evidence for (8), but I suggest that the two are connected in this way only because of a background assumption that we find so obvious that it perhaps escapes our notice — that pleasure is usually good and pain is usually bad. Without some such assumption, the evidential connection of (7) to (8) is severed.

In the light of examples like (7) and (8), I propose a generalization of Hume's thesis: *Purely is-premises cannot, by themselves, provide nondeductive support for an ought-conclusion.* In my opinion, Hume's thesis about deduction also applies to nondeductive relations.[8]

My discussion of genetic arguments may seem to undermine this general thesis. After all, I claimed that facts about how people form their ethical beliefs can provide evidence concerning whether those beliefs are true. If the relevant facts about the process of belief formation were describable by purely *is*-propositions, then we could see genetic arguments as forging a nondeductive connection between *is* and *ought*. Just as Ben's belief about the attendance at his lecture is probably *false* and Cathy's belief about the size of her class is probably *true,* given the procedures that each followed in forming their beliefs, so we can examine how people form their ethical convictions and draw conclusions concerning whether those ethical beliefs are probably *true.*

But there is a hitch. Descriptions of the process of belief formation cannot provide information about whether the beliefs are true unless we make assumptions about the nature of those propositions and the connections they bear to the process of belief formation.

The nature of these assumptions becomes clearer if we compare the story about Alf with the one about Ben. When I pointed out that Alf thinks that the earth is round because he believes that the earth is perfect and that roundness is the perfect shape, this did nothing to undermine our confidence that the earth is round. We simply concluded that Alf believes the right thing for the wrong reason. In contrast, the fact that Ben formed his belief about the number of students in his classroom by drawing a slip of paper from an urn did lead us to conclude that his belief was probably untrue. Why did we react differently to these two examples?

The reason is that we have independent reason to think that the earth is round, but none of us has independent knowledge of the number of students in Ben's class. In the former case, we begin by thinking that the earth is round, and what we learn about Alf's peculiar thought processes does nothing to undermine our confidence. In the latter case, we begin by thinking that various enrollment figures are about equally probable, and the information about Ben's draw from the urn does nothing to modify that picture. So we end as we began, by thinking that an enrollment of exactly seventy-eight has a low probability.

A genetic argument draws a conclusion about whether the members of some class of statements S are true. It draws this conclusion by describing the procedures that people follow in forming their opinions concerning the propositions in S. My suggestion is that you can't get something from nothing: An argument concerning the status of S must include some premises about the status of the members of S. In particular, if you make no assumptions at all about the status of *ought*-statements, no conclusion can be drawn by a genetic argument concerning the status of those *ought*-statements. This was the point of emphasizing the role of consideration (ii) in genetic arguments. I conclude that genetic arguments, if they are to provide evidence that an *ought*-statement is untrue, must make assumptions about normative matters.

My generalization of Hume's thesis, if correct, has interesting implications concerning what evolutionary biology, and science in general, can teach us about normative issues. Let us begin with one clear format in which scientific matters can help us decide what is right and what is wrong.

Consider the relationship between statements (7) and (8). According to the thesis we are considering, (7) provides evidence for the truth of (8) only if further normative assumptions are provided. Hedonistic utilitarianism is one way to bridge the gap. This theory says that one action is morally preferable to another if the first produces more pleasure

and less pain than the second. Hedonistic utilitarianism provides the sort of ethical principle that allows (7) to furnish evidence that (8) is correct.

Proposition (7) is the sort of claim that the sciences (in particular, psychology) may be in a position to establish. So, if hedonistic utilitarianism were true, the sciences would provide evidence concerning whether *ought*-statements like (8) are correct. The thing to notice about this dialectic is that the sciences do not provide evidence about (8) *on their own*. Science, on its own, does not generate ethical conclusions; rather, a more accurate formulation would be that science, *when conjoined with ethical assumptions,* generates ethical conclusions. Hedonistic utilitarianism entails that psychological facts like (7) have ethical implications. But hedonistic utilitarianism is not something that science shows us is correct.[9]

My suspicion is that evolutionary ethics will always find itself in this situation. It may turn out that evolutionary findings do sometimes help us answer normative questions, although the proof of this pudding will be entirely in the eating. Just as hedonistic utilitarianism makes it possible for psychologists to provide information that helps decide what is right and what is wrong, this and other ethical theories may provide a similar opening for evolutionary biologists. This cannot be ruled out in advance. However, evolutionary findings will be able to achieve this result only when they are informed by ethical ideas that are not themselves supplied by evolutionary theory. Evolutionary theory cannot, all by itself, tell us whether there are any ethical facts. Nor, if ethical facts exist, can evolutionary theory tell us, all by itself, what some of those facts are. For better or worse, ethics will retain a certain degree of autonomy from the natural sciences. This doesn't mean that they are mutually irrelevant, of course. But it does mean that evolutionary ethicists who try to do too much will end up doing too little.

References

Alexander, R. *The Biology of Moral Systems.* Aldine DeGruyter, 1987.

Cavalli-Sforza, L., and Feldman, M. *Cultural Transmission and Evolution.* Princeton University Press, 1981.

Harman, G. *The Nature of Morality.* Oxford University Press, 1977.

Hempel, C. *Aspects of Scientific Explanation.* Free Press, 1965.

Kitcher, P. "Four Ways to 'Biologicize' Ethics," in *Evolution und Ethik,* ed. K. Bayertz. Reclam, 1993. Reprinted in *Conceptual Issues in Evolutionary Biology,* 2d ed., ed. E. Sober. MIT Press, 1993.

Moore, G. E. *Principia Ethica.* Cambridge University Press, 1903.

Ruse, M., and Wilson, E. "Moral Philosophy as Applied Science," *Philosophy* 61 (1986): 173–192. Reprinted in *Conceptual Issues in Evolutionary Biology,* 2d ed., ed. E. Sober. MIT Press, 1993.

Sober, E. *Reconstructing the Past: Parsimony, Evolution, and Inference.* MIT Press, 1988.

Sober, E. "Let's Razor Ockham's Razor." *Explanation and Its Limits,* in ed. D. Knowles. Cambridge University Press, 1990.

Sober, E. *Philosophy of Biology.* Westview Press, 1993.

Wilson, E. *On Human Nature.* Harvard University Press, 1978.

Endnotes

[1] Some philosophers whom I would want to call ethical realists refuse to apply the terms "true" and "false" to normative statements but prefer terms like "valid" or "correct." I happen to think that use of the term "true" in this context is fairly unproblematic; if murder is sometimes permissible, then it is true that murder is sometimes permissible. In any event, my use of the term "true" is something of an expository convenience. Realists maintain, for example, that murder is either sometimes permissible, or never permissible, and that the permissibility of murder is not settled by anyone's ethical opinion or say-so. This remark describes an *instance* of the realist position. To state it in full generality, some term such as true or correct is useful, if not outright necessary.

[2] I've omitted skepticism as an option in this classification of positions. "Don't know" is not an answer that is incompatible with "yes" or "no."

[3] Hume's thesis, as I understand it, does not deny that there are terms in natural languages that have both normative and descriptive content. Arguably, to say that someone is *rude* or *cruel* is to advance both a descriptive and a normative claim. It is enough for my purposes if such claims can be construed as conjunctions, one conjunct of which is purely descriptive while the other is normative.

[4] It is useful to represent genetic arguments in a Bayesian format. Consider the case of Cathy. Let C be the proposition that there are 34 students in her classroom. Let B be the proposition that Cathy believes C. The process by which Cathy formed her belief will have implications about the values of $\Pr(B/C)$ and $\Pr(B/-C)$. Bayes's theorem tells us what must be true in order for facts about the genesis of the belief to have implications about whether the belief is probably correct:

$$\Pr(C/B) = \Pr(B/C)\Pr(C)/[\Pr(B/C)\Pr(C) + \Pr(B/-C)\Pr(-C)].$$

If $\Pr(B/C)$ is high and $\Pr(B/-C)$ is low, then further information about the value of $\Pr(C)$ will settle whether $\Pr(C/B)$ is high or low. Notice that the process *alone* (as described by the conditional probabilities $\Pr[B/C]$ and $\Pr[B/-C]$ does not fix a value for $\Pr(C/B)$; additional information about $\Pr(C)$ is needed.

[5] For discussion of the status of Ockham's razor in scientific inference, see Sober (1988, 1990).

[6] Ruse and Wilson (1986, pp. 186–187) advance something very much like this parsimony argument when they say that "the evolutionary explanation makes the objective morality redundant, for even if external ethical premises did not exist, we would go on thinking about right and wrong in the way that we do. And surely, redundancy is the last predicate that an objective morality can possess."

[7] In this respect, I am in agreement with Harman when he points out that there is a disanalogy between ethical beliefs and many perceptual beliefs. Part of the explanation of why you now believe that there is a book in front of you is that there is a book in front of you.

[8] The proposed generalization of Hume's thesis parallels a familiar point about confirmation in a purely nonnormative

context: An observation confirms or disconfirms a theory only in the light of background assumptions. See Sober (1988) for discussion.

[9] Kitcher (1993) is careful to distinguish the following two projects:

(B) Sociobiology can teach us facts about human beings that, in conjunction with moral principles that we already accept, can be used to derive normative principles that we have not yet appreciated.

(D) Sociobiology can lead us to revise our system of ethical principles, not simply by leading us to accept new derivative statements — as in (B) — but by teaching us new fundamental normative principles.

I agree with Kitcher that (B) is far more plausible than (D).

Suggestions for Further Reading On Egoism

Falk, W. D. "Morality, Self, and Others," in *Ethics,* eds. J. J. Thomson and G. Dworkin. Harper and Row, 1968.

Gauthier, David, ed. *Morality and Rational Self-Interest.* Prentice-Hall, 1970.

Gauthier, David. *Morality by Agreement.* Clarendon Press, 1986.

MacIntyre, Aladair. "Egoism and Altruism," in *The Encyclopedia of Philosophy,* ed. Paul Edwards. Macmillan, 1967.

Nagel, Thomas. *The Possibility of Altruism.* Clarendon Press, 1970.

Rachels, James. *The Elements of Moral Philosophy.* Random House, 1986.

Sidgwick, Henry. *The Methods of Ethics,* 7th edition. Hackett Publishing Company, 1981.

Slote, Michael. "An Empirical Basis for Psychological Egoism," *Journal of Philosophy,* 61, 1967.

On Evolution and Ethics

Darwin, Charles. *The Descent of Man.* John Murray, 1871.

Dawkins, Richard. *The Selfish Gene.* Oxford University Press, 1976.

Kitcher, Phillip. "Four Ways to 'Biologize' Ethics," in *Conceptual Issues in Evolutionary Biology,* 2d ed., ed. E. Sober. MIT Press, 1993.

Murphy, Jeffrie. *Evolution, Morality, and the Meaning of Life.* Rowman and Littlefield, 1982.

Ruse, Michael. *Taking Darwin Seriously.* Blackwells, 1986.

Ruse, Michael. *The Darwinian Paradigm: Essays on Its History, Philosophy, and Religious Implications.* Routledge, 1989.

Singer, Peter. *The Expanding Circle: Ethics and Sociobiology.* Farrar, Straus & Giroux.

Sober, Elliott. *Philosophy of Biology.* Westview Press, 1993.

Sober, Elliott, ed. *Conceptual Issues in Evolutionary Biology.* MIT Press, 1993.

Wilson, E. O. *On Human Nature.* Harvard University Press, 1978.

Wilson, E. O. *Biophilia.* Harvard University Press, 1984.

Part IV

Value

SOCRATES: Tell me, do you think there is a kind of good which we welcome not because we desire its consequences but for its own sake: joy, for example, and all the harmless pleasures which have no further consequences beyond the joy which one finds in them?

GLAUCON: Certainly, I think there is such a good.

SOCRATES: Further, there is the good which we welcome for its own sake and also for its consequences, knowledge, for example, and sight and health. Such things we somehow welcome on both accounts.

GLAUCON: Yes.

SOCRATES: Are you also aware of a third kind such as physical training, being treated when ill, the practice of medicine, and other ways of making money? We should say that these are wearisome but beneficial to us; we should not want them for their own sake, but because of the rewards and other benefits which result from them.

Plato's *Republic,* Book II, translated by G. M. A. Grube
Hackett Publishing Company, 1974

The term 'value' (from the Latin *valere,* meaning to be of worth) is highly ambiguous. Sometimes it is used narrowly as a synonym for 'good' or 'valuable,' and sometimes it is used broadly for the whole scope of evaluative terms, ranging from the highest good through the indifferent to the worst evil. In the narrow sense the opposite of 'value' is 'evil' or 'disvalue,' but in the broader sense its opposite is 'fact,' which suggests that values are not recognized in the same way that empirical facts are. In a comprehensive value theory the broader meaning of the word is used. In this introduction we shall generally refer to negative value as 'disvalue' and use 'value' to signify that which is good or valuable, and we shall use the term 'value theory' to refer to the whole range of positive and negative values. The range may be illustrated by the following diagram:

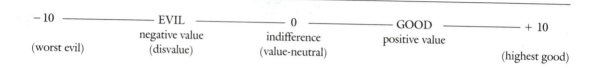

The central questions in value theory are these:

1. What things or activities are valuable or good?

2. What are the different types of values and how are they related to each other?

3. Are values objective or subjective? That is, do we desire the good because it is good, or is the good good because we desire it?

4. What is the relationship of value to morality?

5. What is the good life?

Let us briefly examine each of these questions.

1. What things are good? Philosophers divide into two broad camps with regard to this question: hedonists and nonhedonists (or pluralists). Hedonists (a term derived from the Greek word for pleasure) assert that pleasure is the only experience that is good in itself and that all other goodness is derived from this value. Hedonists further subdivide into sensualists and satisfactionists; the former equate all pleasure with sensual titillation, the latter with satisfaction or enjoyment, which may not involve sensuality. Nonhedonists almost universally admit pleasure (in at least one of the above senses) as a value, but they contend that there are other values as well, such as knowledge, beauty, freedom, friendship, moral obligation, good character, and so on.

A hedonist such as Jeremy Bentham argues in Part IV.1 that while these qualities are good, their goodness is *derived* from the fact that they bring pleasure or satisfaction. But the nonhedonist argues that this is counterintuitive. For example, imagine two lives, those of Suzy and Izzy. Suzy possesses 100 hedons (units of pleasure) but is severely retarded and physically handicapped, and Izzy enjoys great mental acumen and physical prowess but only possesses 99 hedons. Isn't it obvious that Izzy has the better life? But hedonists are committed to saying that Suzy's life is better, a position that seems implausible.

It was this sort of situation that led John Stuart Mill in his classic work *Utilitarianism* to modify the hedonic doctrine, admitting that "it is better to be a human dissatisfied than a pig satisfied; better to be Socrates dissatisfied than a fool satisfied" and suggesting that there were different qualities of pleasures that could be distinguished by those who had experienced them. Whether the notion of 'quality of pleasure' can be made to save hedonism is a question we will want to consider when we read Mill (see Part V.1). Meanwhile, Robert Nozick addresses the issue of hedonism in this part's second reading, "The Experience Machine."

2. We next turn to our second question: What types of values are there? At the outset of this part we quoted from the second book of the *Republic*, in which Plato distinguishes three kinds of good: purely intrinsic good (of which simple joys are an example), purely instrumental good (of which medicine and making money are examples), and combination goods (such as knowledge, sight, and health), which are both good in themselves and as a means to further goods. A foundational model of value would posit some intrinsic good(s) from which all other goods are derived, whereas a coherence model of value would assert that goodness is in the organic unity of the values. Foundationalists, whether they be hedonists or pluralists, assert that all values are either intrinsic or derived from intrinsic values. A coherentist asserts that all intrinsic value emerges

in the relationship of the (extrinsic) parts to each other, the end being a happy life.

Paul Taylor divides values somewhat differently, into extrinsic and intrinsic ones, and makes the following further subdivisions in terms of value judgments that we make:

- **A.** Judgments of extrinsic value.
  - **1.** Judgments of instrumental value.
  - **2.** Judgments of contributory value.
  - **3.** Judgments of inherent value.
- **B.** Judgments of intrinsic value.

Instrumental values are those that have instrumental functions only, such as a house key or paper currency. Contributory value involves being part of a larger whole that contributes to the worth of the whole, such as spark plugs in the motor of a car or a dark shade of color in an artist's landscape. Inherent value refers to the inherent potential in something to produce intrinsic value, such as the music of Handel, which has the power to produce deep delight in music lovers.

3. Our third question is: Are values objective or subjective? That is, do we desire the good because it is good, or is the good good because we desire it?

The classic objectivist view on values (the absolutist version) is given by Plato, who taught that the Good was the highest form — ineffable, godlike, independent, and knowable only after a protracted education in philosophy. We desire the Good because it is good. Philosophers in the Platonic tradition, such as G. E. Moore (see Part VIII.2), hold to the independent existence of values apart form human or rational interest. Moore claims that the Good is a simple, unanalyzable quality like the color yellow, but one that must be known through the intuitions. Moore believes that a world with beauty is more valuable than one that is a garbage dump, regardless of whether there are conscious beings in those worlds.

Other weaker objectivist versions treat values as supervenient qualities that emerge in the nature of things. That is, just as smoothness is not in the table I am touching, but in the relationship between the electrical charges of the subatomic particles of which the table is made and my nervous system, so values (or good qualities) emerge in the relationship between conscious beings and the physical and social existence. For example, if we were not conative beings, we would not be in a position to appreciate values, but once there are such beings, certain things (for example, pleasure, knowledge, health) will be valuable and others not so, depending on objective factors. Perhaps this weaker objectivist version should be called a mixed view, for it recognizes both a subjective and an objective aspect to value.

In our readings Thomas Nagel (Part IV.6) argues for the plausibility of this sort of objectivism, and Richard Kraut (Part IV.5) suggests a version of this so-called mixed view of values.

Subjectivism considers values as mere products of conscious desire. In his interest theory of values, R. B. Perry (1876–1957) states that a value is simply the object of interest. Values are created by desires and they are valuable just to that degree to which they are desired — the stronger the desire, the greater the value. The difference between the subjectivist's and the weak objectivist's positions is simply that the subjectivist makes no normative claims about "proper desiring," but instead deems all desires equal.

4. Our fourth question is: What is the relationship of value to morality? Typically, value theory is at the heart of moral theory. The question, however, is whether moral right and wrong are themselves intrinsic values (as Kant states, the moral law is a jewel that shines in its own light), or whether rightness and wrongness are defined by their ability to further nonmoral values (such as pleasure, happiness, health, and political harmony). Richard Taylor (Part IV.3) defends this latter view. Ethical principles are based on what we value, defined in terms of desire. Morality, as a set of principles and practices, is an outcome of a long history of attempting to harmonize

interpersonal interests. In the next reading (Part IV.4), Friedrich Nietzsche maintains a similar position with regard to the dependence of morality on values. The special feature of Nietzsche's ethics is that he posits the will to power as the dominant value that humans, like all creatures caught in the evolutionary struggle for survival, desire most. Genuine morality is based on this will to power, but there is a constant tendency on the part of the mediocre ("the herd") to invert morality and promulgate a morality that promotes the passive virtues of self-denial, tolerance, humility, and resignation. This "slave morality" is opposed to the higher life of the excellent and noble, who will eventually win out in the struggle.

In the next two parts of this book we shall take up this issue. Part V examines the teleologists or utilitarians, who define right and wrong according to how actions promote these nonmoral goals, and Part VI examines the deontologists, who treat moral right and wrong as having value in themselves.

5. In our final question we ask, What is the good life? We want to ask what kind of life is most worth living. What is happiness? Again, the field is divided among objectivists, subjectivists, and combination theorists. The objectivists, following Plato and Aristotle, speak of a single ideal for human nature. If we do not reach it, we have failed. Just as knives have functions, so do species, even the human species. Our function (sometimes called our essence) is to live according to reason and thereby become a certain sort of highly rational, disciplined being.

The subjectivist version of happiness states that happiness is in the eyes of the beholder. We are just as happy as we think we are; no more, no less. The concept is not a descriptive one, but a first-person evaluation. If I feel very happy, I am that, even though everyone else despises my lifestyle.

The combination view tries to incorporate aspects of both of these views. One version of this combination view is the "plan-of-life" conception of happiness, which states that there are a plurality of life plans open to a person and that what is important is that the plan be an integrated whole and the person be successful in realizing his or her goals. This view is subjective in that it recognizes the person as the autonomous chooser of goals and a plan, but it is also objective in that it affirms happiness to be an intrinsic good "by virtue of the fact that it is the authentic manifestation of an individual's autonomous choice of his own selfhood," to quote Paul Taylor.

IV.1 *Classical Hedonism*

JEREMY BENTHAM

Jeremy Bentham (1748–1832) was a British utilitarian and legal reformer. In this essay from *An Introduction to the Principles of Morals and Legislation,* he argues that pleasure is the only intrinsic value and pain the only intrinsic evil. All other goods and evils are derived from these two qualities. Moral rightness and wrongness are defined in his hedonistic utilitarian approach according to their consequences in producing pleasure and pain.

Of the Principle of Utility

I. Nature has placed mankind under the governance of two sovereign masters, *pain* and *pleasure*. It is for them alone to point out what we ought to do, as well as to determine what we shall do. On the one hand the standard of right and wrong, on the other the chain of causes and effects, are fastened to their throne. They govern us in all we do, in all we say, in all we think: every effort we can make to throw off our subjection, will serve but to demonstrate and confirm it. In words a man may pretend to abjure their empire: but in reality he will remain subject to it all the while. The *principle of utility* recognizes this subjection, and assumes it for the foundation of that system, the object of which is to rear the fabric of felicity by the hands of reason and of law. Systems which attempt to question it, deal in sounds instead of sense, in caprice instead of reason, in darkness instead of light.

But enough of metaphor and declamation: it is not by such means that moral science is to be improved.

II. The principle of utility is the foundation of the present work: it will be proper therefore at the outset to give an explicit and determinate account of what is meant by it. By the principle of utility is meant that principle which approves or disapproves of every action whatsoever, according to the tendency which it appears to have to augment or diminish the happiness of the party whose interest is in question: or, what is the same thing in other words, to promote or to oppose that happiness. I say of every action whatsoever; and therefore not only of every action of a private individual, but of every measure of government.

III. By utility is meant that property in any object, whereby it tends to produce benefit, advantage, pleasure, good, or happiness, (all this in the present case comes to the same thing) or (what comes again to the same thing) to prevent the happening of mischief, pain, evil, or unhappiness to the party whose interest is considered: if that party be the community in general, then the happiness of the community: if a particular individual, then the happiness of that individual.

Value of a Lot of Pleasure or Pain, How to Be Measured

I. Pleasures then, and the avoidance of pains, are the *ends* which the legislator has in view: it behoves him therefore to understand their *value*. Pleasures and pains are the *instruments* he has to work with: it behoves him therefore to understand their force, which is again, in other words, their value.

II. To a person considered *by himself,* the value of a pleasure or pain considered *by itself,* will be

Excerpted from *An Introduction to the Principles of Morals and Legislation* (1789).

greater or less, according to the four following circumstances:

1. Its *intensity.*

2. Its *duration.*

3. Its *certainty* or *uncertainty.*

4. Its *propinquity* or *remoteness.*

III. These are the circumstances which are to be considered in estimating a pleasure or a pain considered each of them by itself. But when the value of any pleasure or pain is considered for the purpose of estimating the tendency of any *act* by which it is produced, there are two other circumstances to be taken into the account; these are,

5. Its *fecundity,* or the chance it has of being followed by sensations of the *same* kind: that is, pleasures, if it be a pleasure: pains, if it be a pain.

6. Its *purity,* or the chance it has of *not* being followed by sensations of the *opposite* kind: that is, pains, if it be a pleasure: pleasures, if it be a pain.

These two last, however, are in strictness scarcely to be deemed properties of the pleasure or the pain itself; they are not, therefore, in strictness to be taken into the account of the value of that pleasure or that pain. They are in strictness to be deemed properties only of the act, or other event, by which such pleasure or pain has been produced; and accordingly are only to be taken into the account of the tendency of such act or such event.

IV. To a *number* of persons, with reference of each of whom the value of a pleasure or a pain is considered, it will be greater or less, according to seven circumstances: to wit, the six preceding ones; *viz.*

1. Its *intensity.*

2. Its *duration.*

3. Its *certainty* or *uncertainty.*

4. Its *propinquity* or *remoteness.*

5. Its *fecundity.*

6. Its *purity.*

And one other; to wit:

7. Its *extent;* that is, the number of persons to whom it *extends;* or (in other words) who are affected by it.

V. To take an exact account then of the general tendency of any act, by which the interests of a community are affected, proceed as follows. Begin with any one person of those whose interests seem most immediately to be affected by it: and take an account,

1. Of the value of each distinguishable *pleasure* which appears to be produced by it in the *first* instance.

2. Of the value of each *pain* which appears to be produced by it in the *first* instance.

3. Of the value of each pleasure which appears to be produced by it *after* the first. This constitutes the *fecundity* of the first *pleasure* and the *impurity* of the first *pain.*

4. Of the value of each *pain* which appears to be produced by it after the first. This constitutes the *fecundity* of the first *pain,* and the *impurity* of the first pleasure.

5. Sum up all the values of all the *pleasures* on the one side, and those of all the pains on the other. The balance, if it be on the side of pleasure, will give the *good* tendency of the act upon the whole, with respect to the interests of that *individual* person; if on the side of pain, the *bad* tendency of it upon the whole.

6. Take an account of the *number* of persons whose interests appear to be concerned; and repeat the above process with respect to each. *Sum up* the numbers expressive of the degrees of *good* tendency, which the act has, with respect to each individual, in regard to whom the tendency of it is *good* upon the whole: do this again with respect to each individual, in regard to whom the tendency of it is *good* upon the whole: do this again with respect to each individual, in regard to whom the tendency of it is *bad* upon the whole. Take the *balance;* which, if on the side of *pleasure,* will give the general *good tendency* of the act, with respect to the total number or community of individuals concerned; if on the side of pain, the general *evil tendency,* with respect to the same community.

VI. It is not to be expected that this process should be strictly pursued previously to every moral judgment, or to every legislative or judicial operation. It may, however, be always kept in view: and as near as the process actually pursued on these occasions approaches to it, so near will such process approach to the character of an exact one.

VII. The same process is alike applicable to pleasure and pain, in whatever shape they appear: and by whatever denomination they are distinguished: to pleasure, whether it be called *good* (which is properly the cause or instrument of pleasure) or *profit* (which is distant pleasure, or the cause or instrument of distant pleasure), or *convenience*, or *advantage, benefit, emolument, happiness,* and so forth: to pain, whether it be called *evil,* (which corresponds to *good*) or *mischief,* or *inconvenience,* or *disadvantage,* or *loss,* or *unhappiness,* and so forth.

VIII. Nor is this a novel and unwarranted, any more than it is a useless theory. In all this there is nothing but what the practice of mankind, wheresoever they have a clear view of their own interest, is perfectly conformable to. An article of property, an estate in land, for instance, is valuable, on what account? On account of the pleasures of all kinds which it enables a man to produce, and what comes to the same thing the pains of all kinds which it enables him to avert. But the value of such an article of property is universally understood to rise or fall according to the length or shortness of the time which a man had in it: the certainty or uncertainty of its coming into possession: and the nearness or remoteness of the time at which, if at all, it is to come into possession. As to the *intensity* of the pleasures which a man may derive from it, this is never thought of, because it depends upon the use which each particular person may come to make of it; which cannot be estimated till the particular pleasures he may come to derive from it, or the particular pains he may come to exclude by means of it, are brought to view. For the same reason, neither does he think of the *fecundity* or *purity* of those pleasures.

Thus much for pleasure and pain, happiness and unhappiness, in *general.*

XVII. Under the Gentoo and Mahometan religions, the interests of the rest of the animal creation seem to have met with some attention. Why have they not, universally, with as much as those of human creatures, allowance made for the difference in point of sensibility? Because the laws that are have

been the work of mutual fear; a sentiment which the less rational animals have not had the same means as man has of turning to account. Why **ought** they not? No reason can be given. If the being eaten were all, there is very good reason why we should be suffered to eat such of them as we like to eat: we are the better for it, and they are never the worse. They have none of those long-protracted anticipations of future misery which we have. The death they suffer in our hands commonly is, and always may be, a speedier, and by that means a less painful one, than that which would await them in the inevitable course of nature. If the being killed were all, there is very good reason why we should be suffered to kill such as molest us: we should be the worse for their living, and they are never the worse for being dead. But is there any reason why we should be suffered to torment them? Not any that I can see. Are there any why we should **not** be suffered to torment them? Yes, several. The day has been, I grieve to say in many places it is not yet past, in which the greater part of the species, under the denomination of slaves, have been treated by the law exactly upon the same footing, as, in England for example, the inferior races of animals are still. The day may come, when the rest of the animal creation may acquire those rights which never could have been withholden from them but by the hand of tyranny. The French have already discovered that the blackness of the skin is no reason why a human being should be abandoned without redress to the caprice of a tormentor. It may come one day to be recognized, that the number of the legs, the villosity of the skin, or the termination of the **os sacrum,** are reasons equally insufficient for abandoning a sensitive being to the same fate. What else is it that should trace the insuperable line? Is it the faculty of reason, or, perhaps, the faculty of discourse? But a full-grown horse or dog is beyond comparison a more rational, as well as a more conversable animal, than an infant of a day, or a week, or even a month, old. But suppose the case were otherwise, what would it avail? The question is not, Can they **reason**? nor, Can they **talk**? but, Can they **suffer**?

IV.2 The Experience Machine

Robert Nozick

Robert Nozick is professor of philosophy at Harvard University. In this
selection from his *Anarchy, State, and Utopia*, he argues against the hedonism
of Bentham, for if pleasure were our sole value, we would have a conclusive
reason to plug into an experience machine. The fact that most of us are
revolted by this idea is good evidence against the claims of hedonism, as well
as for a wider view of what is good.

There are also substantial puzzles when we ask what
matters other than how *people's* experiences feel
"from the inside." Suppose there were an experience
machine that would give you any experience you desired. Superduper neuropsychologists could stimulate your brain so that you would think and feel you
were writing a great novel, or making a friend, or
reading an interesting book. All the time you would
be floating in a tank, with electrodes attached to
your brain. Should you plug into this machine for
life, preprogramming your life's experiences? If you
are worried about missing out on desirable experiences, we can suppose that business enterprises have
researched thoroughly the lives of many others. You
can pick and choose from their large library or
smorgasbord of such experiences, selecting your
life's experiences for, say, the next two years. After
two years have passed, you will have ten minutes or
ten hours out of the tank, to select the experiences of
your *next* two years. Of course, while in the tank you
won't know that you're there; you'll think it's all actually happening. Others can also plug in to have
the experiences they want, so there's no need to stay
unplugged to serve them. (Ignore problems such as
who will service the machines if everyone plugs in.)
Would you plug in? *What else can matter to us, other
than how our lives feel from the inside?* Nor should you
refrain because of the few moments of distress between the moment you've decided and the moment
you're plugged. What's a few moments of distress
compared to a lifetime of bliss (if that's what you
choose), and why feel any distress at all if your decision *is* the best one?

What does matter to us in addition to our experiences? First, we want to *do* certain things, and not
just have the experience of doing them. In the case
of certain experiences, it is only because first we
want to do the actions that we want the experiences
of doing them or thinking we've done them. (But
why do we want to do the activities rather than
merely to experience them?) A second reason for
not plugging in is that we want to *be* a certain way,
to be a certain sort of person. Someone floating in a
tank is an indeterminate blob. There is no answer to
the question of what a person is like who has long
been in the tank. Is he courageous, kind, intelligent,
witty, loving? It's not merely that it's difficult to tell;
there's no way he is. Plugging into the machine is a
kind of suicide. It will seem to some, trapped by a
picture, that nothing about what we are like can
matter except as it gets reflected in our experiences.
But should it be surprising that what *we are* is important to us? Why should we be concerned only
with how our time is filled, but not with what we
are?

Thirdly, plugging into an experience machine
limits us to a man-made reality, to a world no deeper
or more important than that which people can construct. There is no *actual* contact with any deeper
reality, though the experience of it can be simulated.
Many persons desire to leave themselves open to
such contact and to a plumbing of deeper signifi-

cance.[1] This clarifies the intensity of the conflict over psychoactive drugs, which some view as mere local experience machines, and others view as avenues to a deeper reality; what some view as equivalent to surrender to the experience machine, others view as following one of the reasons *not* to surrender!

We learn that something matters to us in addition to experience by imagining an experience machine and then realizing that we would not use it. We can continue to imagine a sequence of machines each designed to fill lacks suggested for the earlier machines. For example, since the experience machine doesn't meet our desire to *be* a certain way, imagine a transformation machine which transforms us into whatever sort of person we'd like to be (compatible with our staying us). Surely one would not use the transformation machine to become as one would wish, and thereupon plug into the experience machine![2] So something matters in addition to one's experiences *and* what one is like. Nor is the reason merely that one's experiences are unconnected with what one is like. For the experience machine might be limited to provide only experiences possible to the sort of person plugged in. Is it that we want to make a difference in the world? Consider then the result machine, which produces in the world any result you would produce and injects your vector input into any joint activity. We shall not pursue here the fascinating details of these or other machines. What is most disturbing about them is their living of our lives for us. Is it misguided to search for *particular* additional functions beyond the competence of machines to do for us? Perhaps what we desire is to live (an active verb)

ourselves, in contact with reality. (And this, machines cannot do *for* us.) Without elaborating on the implications of this, which I believe connect surprisingly with issues about free will and causal accounts of knowledge, we need merely note the intricacy of the question of what matters *for people* other than their experiences. Until one finds a satisfactory answer, and determines that this answer does not *also* apply to animals, one cannot reasonably claim that only the felt experiences of animals limit what we may do to them.

Endnotes

[1] Traditional religious views differ on the *point* of contact with a transcendent reality. Some say that contact yields eternal bliss or Nirvana, but they have not distinguished this sufficiently from merely a *very* long run on the experience machine. Others think it is intrinsically desirable to do the will of a higher being which created us all, though presumably no one would think this if we discovered we had been created as an object of amusement by some superpowerful child from another galaxy or dimension. Still others imagine an eventual merging with a higher reality, leaving unclear its desirability, or where that merging leaves *us*.

[2] Some wouldn't use the transformation machine at all; it seems like *cheating*. But the one-time use of the transformation machine would not remove all challenges; there would still be obstacles for the new us to overcome, a new plateau from which to strive even higher. And is this plateau any the less earned or deserved than that provided by genetic endowment and early childhood environment? But if the transformation machine could be used indefinitely often, so that we could accomplish anything by pushing a button to transform ourselves into someone who could do it easily, there would remain no limits we *need* to strain against or try to transcend. Would there be anything left to *do*? Do some theological views place God outside of time because an omniscient omnipotent being couldn't fill up his days?

IV.3 *Value and the Origin of Right and Wrong*

Richard Taylor

Until his recent retirement, Richard Taylor was professor of philosophy at Rochester University. In this essay he argues for an interest theory of values. Values arise because people are *conative* beings (that is, we have interests in terms of desires, needs, and purposes). If we had no desires, there would be no values—no good or evil. Reason, rather than being the defining feature of humanity and morality, is merely the servant of the passions and aids us in reaching our goals. Right and wrong emerge in social situations and are relative to interpersonal value systems. Those rules that either promote cooperation toward meeting our desires or resolve interpersonal conflict are the right rules to follow, and those rules or practices that hinder cooperation and conflict resolution are wrong ones.

It has, as we have seen, been fairly characteristic of moral philosophers to begin with an assumed dichotomy between what *is* and what *ought* to be. Having turned their backs on the former as having little relevance to philosophical ethics, they have proclaimed the content of the latter as the unique realm of ethics. Some, in fact, have declared it a fallacy even to attempt to derive any philosophy of what ought to be from what in fact is, which pretty much amounts to declaring that facts can have little bearing upon ethics. One result of this is that moral philosophy has all too often resembled declamation. The advocates for the various and conflicting programs have had little to appeal to other than their own intuitions of things, these being sometimes baptized as the deliverances of "practical reason" and the like.

I am now going to remove this distinction between *is* and *ought*. More precisely, I shall show that all moral distinctions, beginning with the basic distinction between good and evil, are based entirely on certain facts and, in particular, on facts concerning human nature. It is because men are the kind of beings they are—namely, what I have called conative beings—that the distinction between good and evil arises in the first place. Once this has been seen,

we can see what good and evil in fact are. This basic distinction then having been made clear—and having been based not on intuitions and sentiments or abstract reasoning but on a certain conception of human nature—we can derive the further distinctions between moral right and wrong and give a fairly clear content to the idea of the common good.

Men as Conative Beings

Men are rational or cognitive beings, but to say this is very far from stating the whole truth about them. So far as ethics is concerned, it leaves entirely out of account the most important fact about men, that they are desiderative or conative beings as well. I have already explained what this means, but it needs to be briefly reiterated here, as it is crucial to establishing the distinction between good and evil.

To describe men as conative is not to say anything at all abstruse or metaphysical, as this bit of terminology might suggest. It is only to call attention to a fact of human nature with which everyone is perfectly familiar: men have needs, desires, and goals; they pursue ends; they have certain wants and generally go about trying to satisfy them in various ways. Psychologists, metaphysicians, and others might have conflicting theories concerning how this

From *Good and Evil* by Richard Taylor (Prometheus Books, 1986). Reprinted by permission of Prometheus Books.

fact is to be understood and explained, but the fact itself is hardly open to any question. It is more obvious that men are, in the sense just explained, conative beings, than that they are rational ones. There are men whom one might genuinely doubt to be rational, but it is doubtful whether anyone has ever seen a living man whom he suspected had no needs, desires, or wants. Such a man would be totally inactive and resemble a statue more than a man.

Thus, when a man is seen doing anything, it can generally be asked why he is doing it, what he is doing it for, or what he is trying to accomplish. This need not suggest that his behavior is not caused in the usual way, although some might want to maintain this. What it does mean is that there is some point to what he is doing, some outcome that he intends. It implies nothing more.

For example, a man is seen operating a typewriter. Why is he doing that? Perhaps he is writing a letter, or an editorial, or something of that sort. In short, he has some purpose, and his typewriting activity is his means to fulfilling it. Or a man is seen running. What for? Perhaps to get to a store before it closes, or to catch a bus. Again, he has some purpose and is trying to fulfill it by running. Or once more, a man is seen walking toward a pump with an empty bucket. What for? Presumably, to fill the bucket (a goal) to enable himself to drink, wash, and so on (further purposes or goals).

I have used these exceedingly commonplace examples of human activity to illustrate three points. The first is that voluntary or deliberate human activity is generally interpreted as goal-directed. When we ask why a man is doing whatever it is that he is doing, we are usually seeking some explanation in terms of what he is trying to accomplish by that activity. This presupposes something abut men that is universally taken for granted: men have goals and purposes and wants and desires, and they generally act in ways they consider appropriate to fulfilling them. It presupposes, in fact, that they are conative beings or, as I shall sometimes express it, that they are beings having desires and wants.

The second point is that, in speaking of a man's goals or purposes, one need not be referring to some *ultimate* goal, or even to any that is very important. The goal of one's activity might be exceedingly trivial and of only momentary significance, as in the foregoing examples. It could hardly be one's ultimate goal, or the goal of one's lifetime, to fill a bucket with water or to catch a bus. Yet, that might be precisely what his goal is then and there. Of course most men do have larger, more long-range goals. A man will spend years struggling, for example, in pursuit of some objective important to him, such as a degree in medicine, or perhaps fame as an author. Some men do devote the better part of their lives to ends having that kind of personal importance. In speaking of human behavior as goal-directed, however, I do not have this sort of thing primarily in mind, even though I include it. What I am calling attention to is much simpler and more commonplace. The conative aspect of human nature is as well exhibited by a man munching an apple or swatting a fly as it is by someone devoting his lifetime to a great ambition.

And the third point is that reason appears to enter into men's purposeful activity primarily to devise the means to attain the ends and has little to do with ends themselves. Thus, if a man wants to fill a bucket with water, it is in the clearest sense rational that he should carry it to the pump, as the most elementary reason or intelligence indicates that this is the appropriate means to that end. Merely wishing that pail might become filled, or trying to find some way to bring the pump to the pail, would be unreasonable, precisely in the sense that these are not means that give much promise of working. There is not, however, any reason for filling the pail in the first place. There is, to be sure, some further purpose that can thus be fulfilled — the purpose of drinking, for example, or of washing — but this only indicates that filling the pail, which is his immediate purpose, is in turn a means to still some further purpose. It is, for example, neither rational nor irrational that one should want to drink; it is merely an expression of fact that he is thirsty. In the same sense, it is neither rational nor irrational that a man should want to swat a fly, or catch a bus, or become a physician, or attain fame as an author. These are simply statements of this or that man's aims or goals, both trivial and great, and they have nothing to do with reason. How they are to be reached, on the other hand, has a great deal to do with reason, for in general, one can set about trying to accomplish whatever it is he wants to accomplish in either an intelligent and rational way or otherwise. To say he is pursuing his goals in an intelligent way is only to say, as an inference from experience, that the means he adopts has some promise of succeeding.

Conation as the Precondition of Good and Evil

With these rather commonplace observations in mind, let us now ask what conditions are necessary in order that any distinction between good and evil and between right and wrong can be made. That is, what must be presupposed in saying of something that it is good, or that it is bad, or in saying of an action that it is morally right or morally wrong?

Unthinking men have a tendency to assume that some things are just naturally good and others bad, and some actions right and some wrong, and that we need only to discover which are which. Even some of the most thoughtful philosophers, as we have seen, have started out with the same assumption. Thus, it is supposed that men are born into a world in which these distinctions already hold. Many have insisted that these distinctions cannot either have been contrived by men, or have awaited man's invention of laws, conventions, and customs. Ever so many things are man-made, including laws and moral customs; however, it is often thought that we cannot suppose the ultimate distinctions between good and evil or right and wrong to be such, for this would render all ethics, all justice, and all morality entirely relative. Indeed, most philosophers have thought that the problem of the moralist is simply to discover the true nature of goodness and rightness; they have disagreed not on whether such things exist independently of men, but on what *is* truly good, and what is truly right.

But now let us note that the basic distinction between good and evil could not even theoretically be drawn in a world that we imagined to be devoid of all life. That is, if we suppose the world to be exactly as it is, except that it contains not one living thing, it seems clear that nothing in it would be good and nothing bad. It would just be a dead world, turning through space with a lifeless atmosphere. Having deprived our imagined world of all life, we can modify it in numberless ways, but by no such modification can we ever produce the slightest hint of good or evil in it until we introduce at least one living being capable of reacting in one way or another to the world as that being finds it. Thus, we can imagine on the one hand that it is filled with things satisfying, lovely, and beautiful—with sun-

rises and sunsets, pleasing sights and sounds and fragrant odors, and with all things that beings like ourselves would find necessary and agreeable to life. Or we can imagine the opposite—a world that is dark and cold, filled with nauseous smells and barren of anything that would redeem such bleak aspects. But so long as we suppose that neither of these worlds does contain any being like ourselves, or any sentient being whatever, then neither world is *better* or *worse* than the other. Each is simply a world of facts, neutral with respect to good or evil, and destined to remain so until we suppose at least one onlooker capable of some sort of reaction to such facts.

Next we note that, if we begin to add inhabitants to this world who are, like ourselves, more or less rational, intelligent, and capable of perception but who, unlike ourselves, have no needs, purposes, or desires, the distinction between good and evil still does not arise. Imagine, for example, a whole colony of machinelike beings, living together and interacting in various ways. These beings, we can suppose, can perceive what is going on around them, distinguish between true and false, and make various inferences; but they are machinelike in that nothing matters to them, nothing makes any difference so far as their needs and purposes are concerned, because they have no needs or purposes, they do not care about anything. If it is raining, they observe that it is raining, but they seek no shelter, for they have no interest in being dry. If it is bitterly cold, then again they note this fact, but make no attempt to warm themselves because they care not whether they are warm or cold. If one of these beings observes another moving with great speed and force toward itself, it infers that a collision is impending, but makes no attempt to step aside, because it has no purpose that would be frustrated by such a collision. It has not even the desire to perpetuate its own existence, because it has no desires whatever. Having then been run down and broken by the onrushing being, losing a few limbs perhaps, it simply notes that this has happened, but it does not retaliate, because it had no interest in preserving any of its limbs or other parts anyway; and so on.

Such beings are, to be sure, difficult to imagine, for if we suppose them to be capable of perceiving, then we seem to imagine them to be living things, and it is difficult to imagine *any* living thing having no interests or purposes whatever, not even an interest in self-preservation. But of course we need not imagine that they are living things; we can instead suppose that they are enormously complicated machines, if that makes it easier. And then we need only suppose that they share with certain living things, such as ourselves, the capacity to perceive what is going on and to draw certain conclusions from what they perceive, but that they do *not* share with other living things, such as ourselves, any interest in what is going on. They are, in short, possessed of some degree of intelligence, but of no will whatever.

Now I think it is clear that a world inhabited by such beings would still be a world devoid of any good or evil. Like the first world we imagined, which did not even contain any beings of the most elementary intelligence, this one might contain anything we care to put into it without there arising the least semblance of good or of evil — until we imagine it to contain at least one being having some need, interest, or purpose. It would not matter to the beings just described whether their world was one filled with sunlight, warmth, and beauty, or dark and cold and filled with nauseous smells, because nothing would matter to them. They could tell the difference between sunlight and darkness, between warmth and cold, but they could in no way tell the difference between good and bad. Such a distinction would in fact have no meaning to them, and if they found their world dark, smelly, and cold they would have no basis for pronouncing it bad, simply because they would have no preference for any other kind of world.

The Emergence of Good and Evil

Thus far, then, there is no good and no evil; there is nothing but bare facts of this kind or that.

But now let us suppose a world, much like our own, except that it contains throughout its vastness just one sentient being, a being who, like ourselves, cannot only perceive what is contained in the world around him and make certain inferences, but one to whom what he finds makes a difference. Suddenly, with the introduction of just one such being, certain things in the world do acquire the aspect of good and evil. Those things are good that this one being

finds satisfying to his needs and desires, and those bad to which he reacts in the opposite way. Things in the world are not merely perceived by this being, but perceived as holding promise or threat to whatever interests him. Thus, the things that nourish and give warmth and enhance life are deemed good, and those that frustrate and threaten are deemed bad. The distinction between good and evil in a world containing only one living being possessed of needs and wants arises, then, only in relation to those needs and wants, and in no way existed in their absence. In the most general terms, those things are good that satisfy this being's actual wants, those that frustrate them are bad.

Now, with this picture still before us, let us note two things that are highly significant for the problems before us. The first is that the judgments of this solitary being concerning good and evil are as *absolute* as any judgment can be. Such a being is, indeed, the measure of all things: of good things as good and of bad things as bad. Whatever this being finds and declares to be good *is* good, and what he similarly finds to be evil, *is* evil. No distinction can be made, in terms of this being, between what is merely good *for him* and what is good *absolutely.* Whatever is good for him *is* good absolutely; there is no higher standard of goodness. For what could it be? If good and evil in this world arise only in relation to this being's wants and needs, then what could it possibly mean to say that something satisfies these but is nevertheless bad, or that something frustrates them but is nevertheless good? There simply is nothing else, apart from these wants and needs, in terms of which good and evil can possibly be measured, or even exist.

The second thing to note is that, even though good and evil have emerged with the appearance in this world of a single living being having wants and needs, no more obligation has similarly arisen. The distinction between moral *right* and *wrong* has not yet come into the picture at all. That such a being should find something useful and agreeable and subsequently seize it, or find something threatening and shun it, is neither right nor wrong. Whatever he finds and wants is his for the taking, by a kind of natural right that is nothing but the absence of any natural wrong, and he cannot possibly have an obligation to undertake what would injure him, or even so much as make him the least uncomfortable. Although he can in this moral solitude create good and evil for himself, merely by his own declaration of what he finds things to be, he can in no way inflict them. For who could be his beneficiary or victim, besides himself? To whom could he owe any obligation to do anything? And by what standard, other than good and evil themselves, over which he is the sole judge, could any action of his be deemed right or wrong? He could, to be sure, fail to act in his own best interest, or even injure himself through neglect or stupidity, for which he would be accountable to no one. It would be as inappropriate to ascribe any moral responsibility to this solitary being as to the merest insect crawling through the grass.

Our next step, then, is to add another being like ourselves, another conative being with his own feelings, wants, and interests, and to suppose that the two who now inhabit our world have some interaction with each other. No new distinction between good and evil is introduced with the introduction of this new inhabitant, for that distinction emerged, complete and perfect, a soon as we assumed the existence of but one such inhabitant. With this small plurality of beings, it remains just what it was before. The first inhabitant deemed those things good that he found agreeable to his needs and purposes, and those things bad that threatened the opposite, and in this judgment he was absolutely correct. For him, the good and evil of things consisted of precisely such promise and threat to his interests. Such, accordingly, will it also be for our second sentient and goal-directed inhabitant. Those things will be good for him that promise fulfillment of his aims, whether grand or trifling, and those that threaten the opposite will be bad. In this judgment he, too, cannot err. For this will be precisely what the distinction between good and evil will mean to him, as it is what it means to the first; it will be the condition, and the only condition, of such a distinction being drawn by either of them. And we are not, it should be noted, here supposing any power of reasoning in either of our two beings. We do not suppose them to be appraising the various features of their common environment in terms of what they promise or threaten, and then *inferring* from such features that they have the moral qualities of good or evil. We do not even assume these two beings to be rational, though the picture is not altered in case they are. We only assume them to be sentient beings with needs, or in other words, beings who desire and shun, and can feel it when their needs are fulfilled, and when they are not.

The Emergence of Right and Wrong

There was, we noted, no place for such ethical notions as right and wrong or for moral obligation, so long as we imagined a world containing only one purposeful and sentient being, although the presence of such a being was enough to produce good and evil. With the introduction of a multiplicity of such beings, however, we have supplied the foundation for these additional notions, for they are based on the fact that the aims or purposes of such beings can conflict. Thus, two or more such beings can covet the same thing. In that case each will deem it a good, but it can easily arise that not both can possess it, that its possession by one will mean deprivation for the other. The result is a conflict of wills, which can lead to a mutual aggression in which each stands to lose more than the thing for which they are contending is worth to either of them. Such a situation can produce a threat to life itself, for example, and without life all good and evil are reduced to zero.

There is, moreover, another side to the coin. For just as the wills of two purposeful beings can conflict, in the manner just suggested, so also can they coincide in a very significant way. That is, situations can arise in which each of two such beings needs the help of the other in order to attain what it wants, or to ward off some evil. They may, for example, be threatened by some force, animate or inanimate, that the strength of neither is sufficient to overcome, but from which their combined strength offers some hope of safety. Or again, each may find that he possesses in excess of his own needs something that the other requires. One, for example, may possess an excess of food, of which the other has none, while the latter one possesses an excess of the requirements for shelter, entirely lacking to the former. The possibility of mutual giving and taking thus presents itself, wherein each can benefit greatly at small cost to himself. Or again, two such beings may have some common end, such as the begetting of children, for which some sort of cooperation is needed by the very nature of things, and so on.

The supposition of a multiplicity of beings, each with its own needs and purposes, presents, in short, numberless possibilities for (1) conflict, and (2) cooperation. Possibilities of the first kind are loaded with the threat of evil, and those of the second kind with the promise of good, still thinking of good and evil in the sense already adduced — namely, as that which satisfies or fulfills, and that which frustrates felt needs and goals.

Right and Wrong as Relative to Rules

If needs are to be satisfied and goals fulfilled, however, then situations of conflict and, particularly, situations of cooperation must be resolved in the context of *rules,* using the notion of rules in an extremely broad sense that encompasses any regular and predictable behavior. Thus, it becomes a "rule" that two or more such beings, faced with a common threat, shall abstain from attacking each other until that threat is overcome. It becomes another rule that they shall meet the threat together by combining their resources, inasmuch as acting in accordance with such rules will enable each to avoid what appears as an evil. When two such beings each covet the same thing, and not both can possess it, it may become a rule that it remains with him who first possessed it. The underlying basis for such a rule is that, if it is disregarded, the coveted thing may end up in the hands of neither, and that evils even greater than this, such as mutual injury or even death, may follow instead. When each of two such beings possesses an excess of what is sought by the other, a rule of trading becomes obviously advantageous to both. Through such behavior, the good of each is enhanced at no significant cost. The alternative is combat, in which each would be faced with the possibility of total loss.

Now it should be clear from this that by rules I do not mean rational principles of conduct, in the sense that it would require any powers of reason to discover them, much less do I mean principles that are set forth in any coherent writing or speech. They need not be things that are formulated at all. Rules, in the sense that I am now considering them, are nothing but practices or ways of behaving that are more or less regular and that can, therefore, be expected. They are, on the other hand, rational in this sense: such behavior offers promise, to those who behave in the manner in question, of avoiding evil and attaining good. Mutual aggression, for example, always presents the threat of great and unpredictable evil to each aggressor, and the possibility of such evil is almost certain to outweigh any

possibility of good. To the extent, therefore, that some good can be ensured by a certain mode of behavior or, as I am using the term, by action in accordance with a rule, and that such behavior will remove the threat of evil contained in any situation of combat, then action in accordance with the rule is better than combat. In that sense, but only in that sense, it is more rational.

Suppose, for example, that among a certain people the practice arises that men, on approaching one another, extend a forearm with the palm of the hand open and exposed to view, each thus indicating that he is unarmed. The gesture is recognized and acknowledged by each then grasping the other's open hand, that is, by shaking hands. Now here, clearly, is a rule, as I am using the term, even though it does not need to be formulated or embodied in any code. It is simply a regular mode of behavior. It has as its obvious purpose the avoidance of evil and the advancement of good and is in that sense, but that sense only, rational. It would be most treacherously violated by one who, extending his open hand of friendship, assaulted his greeter with a weapon concealed in his other hand. The treachery of this would consist in using the rule to promote the very evil the rule was meant to avoid.

The World as It Is

We have been imagining, then, a world, at first lifeless and barren, that gradually becomes occupied with beings having needs, feelings, and purposes. Until the appearance of the first such being, that world contains no hint of good or evil, but both arise the moment he comes into the picture. With the multiplication of such beings, the possibilities of further goods and evils arise with the appearance of situations of cooperation and conflict. Good is increased and enhanced by the former and evil by the latter. Cooperation, however, and the safe resolution of conflict obviously require certain regular modes of behavior, or what I have called rules. These notions having been made tolerably clear, we can now refine and elaborate on the imaginary picture with which we began until it begins to resemble the world of men in which we actually live.

Thus, we can suppose that the multiplicity of sentient and purposeful beings by which our imaginary world is inhabited are men like ourselves, for we, too, are sentient and purposeful beings. We can suppose that those modes of behavior required for cooperation and the resolution of conflict situations become actual precepts, conveyed by one generation to the next, and that the most important of them come to be rules embodied in traditional literature for which men have a certain awe. They are, thus, passed from generation to generation, like the Ten Commandments of scripture. Others come to assume the form of written laws, and various practical means are hit on for securing, as nearly as possible, the adherence to them on the part of all. Groupings of men are formed for the attainment of the maximum of good for some or all and the minimization of evil. Thus do societies arise, by their common adherence to rules that become more elaborate as the societies themselves become larger and more complex. The behavior required by such rules rises, by some degree or other, to that level we call civilized conduct; but the basic principle of those rules remains exactly what it was from the outset: the minimization of conflict and its consequent evil, and the maximization of cooperation and its consequent good.

All this is, of course, but a sketch, and a very superficial one, but no more is really needed for our present purpose, which is to explain good and evil and moral right and wrong.

How, then, do moral right and wrong arise? The answer is fairly obvious in the light of what has been said. Right is simply the adherence to rule, and wrong is violation of it. The notions of right and wrong absolutely presuppose the existence of rules, at least in the broad sense of rule with which we began. That two beings should fight and injure each other in their contest for something that each covets, and thereby, perhaps, each lose the good he wanted to seize, is clearly an evil to both. But in the absence of a rule of behavior—that is, some anticipated behavior to the contrary—no wrong has been done; only an evil has been produced. Given such a rule, however—for example, given the simple and rudimentary expectation that the thing in question shall be his who first took it—then a wrong is committed by the one who attempts to divest the holder of that good. The wrong comes into being with the violation of the rule, and in no way existed ahead of the rule. The same is, of course, true of right. If, for example, we presuppose no expectation that a good may be enjoyed in peace by whoever first seizes it, then, if another nevertheless, in the absence of any such rule, abstains from seizing that good from its first possessor, this potential aggressor has clearly fostered a good, simply by eschewing an evil. But he has in no way done "the right thing," for the notion of *right* conduct can have no meaning in the absence of some sort of rule. If one is tempted to say that this would-be aggressor has done something morally right, then one will find that all he means is that he has produced an effect that was good. That is something entirely different. One also may be reading into a situation, in which, by hypothesis, there is no rule to which to adhere, certain rules of right and wrong that one has learned to respect.

IV.4 *The Transvaluation of Values*

FRIEDRICH NIETZSCHE

Friedrich Nietzsche (1844–1900) was a German existentialist who has played a major role in contemporary intellectual development. Descended through both of his parents from Christian ministers, Nietzsche was brought up in a pious German Lutheran home and was known as "the little Jesus" by his schoolmates. He studied theology at the University of Bonn and philology at Leipzig, becoming an atheist in the process. At the age of twenty-four he was appointed professor of classical philology at the University of Basel in Switzerland, where he taught for ten years until forced by ill health to retire. Eventually he became mentally ill. He died on August 25, 1900.

Nietzsche believes that the fundamental creative force that motivates all creation is the will to power. We all seek to affirm ourselves, to flourish and dominate. Since we are essentially unequal in ability, it follows that the fittest will survive and be victorious in the contest with the weaker and the baser. There is great aesthetic beauty in the noble spirit coming to fruition, but this process is hampered by Judeo-Christian morality, which Nietzsche labels "slave morality." Slave morality, which is the invention of jealous priests, envious and resentful of the power of the noble, prescribes that we give up the will to power and excellence and become meek and mild, that we believe the lie of all humans having equal worth. In our reading, Nietzsche also refers to this as the ethics of resentment.

Nietzsche's ideas of inegalitarian ethics are based on his notion of the death of God. God plays no vital role in our culture — except as a protector of the slave morality, including the idea of equal worth of all persons. If we recognize that there is no rational basis for believing in God, we will see that the whole edifice of slave morality must crumble and with it the notion of equal worth. In its place will arise the morality of the noble person based on the virtues of high courage, discipline, and intelligence, in the pursuit of self-affirmation and excellence.

We begin this section with Nietzsche's famous description of the madman who announces the death of God; we then turn to selections from *Beyond Good and Evil, The Genealogy of Morals,* and *The Twilight of the Idols.*

The Madman and the Death of God

Have you ever heard of the madman who on a bright morning lighted a lantern and ran to the market-place calling out unceasingly: "I seek God! I seek God!" — As there were many people standing about who did not believe in God, he caused a great deal of amusement. Why! is he lost? said one. Has he strayed away like a child? said another. Or does he keep himself hidden? Is he afraid of us? Has he taken a sea-voyage? Has he emigrated? — the people cried out laughingly, all in a hubbub. The insane man jumped into their midst and transfixed them with his glances. "Where is God gone?" he called out. "I mean to tell you! *We have killed him,* — you and I! We are all his murderers! But how have we done it? How were we able to drink up the sea?

Reprinted from *The Complete Works of Nietzsche,* ed. Oscar Levy, vols. 10 and 11 (T. N. Foulis, 1910).

Who gave us the sponge to wipe away the whole horizon? What did we do when we loosened this earth from its sun? Whither does it now move? Whither do we move? Away from all suns? Do we not dash on unceasingly? Backwards, sideways, forwards, in all directions? Is there still an above and below? Do we not stray, as through infinite nothingness? Does not empty space breathe upon us? Has it not become colder? Does not night come on continually, darker and darker? Shall we not have to light lanterns in the morning? Do we not hear the noise of the grave-diggers who are burying God? Do we not smell the divine putrefaction? — for even Gods putrefy! God is dead! God remains dead! And we have killed him! How shall we console ourselves, the most murderous of all murderers? The holiest and the mightiest that the world has hitherto possessed, has bled to death under our knife, — who will wipe the blood from us? With what water could we cleanse ourselves? What lustrums, what sacred games shall we have to devise? Is not the magnitude of this deed too great for us? Shall we not ourselves have to become Gods, merely to seem worthy of it? There never was a greater event, — and on account of it, all who are born after us belong to a higher history than any history hitherto!" — Here the madman was silent and looked again at his hearers; they also were silent and looked at him in surprise. At last he threw his lantern on the ground, so that it broke in pieces and was extinguished. "I come too early," he then said, "I am not yet at the right time. This prodigious event is still on its way, and is travelling, — it has not yet reached men's ears. Lightning and thunder need time, the light of the stars needs time, deeds need time, even after they are done, to be seen and heard. This deed is as yet further from them than the furthest star, — *and yet they have done it!*" — It is further stated that the madman made his way into different churches on the same day, and there intoned his *Requiem aeternam deo.* When led out and called to account, he always gave the reply: "What are these churches now, if they are not the tombs and monuments of God?" — . . .

What Is Noble?

Every elevation of the type "man," has hitherto been the work of an aristocratic society and so it will always be — a society believing in a long scale of gradations of rank and differences of worth among human beings, and requiring slavery in some form or other. Without the *pathos of distance,* such as grows out of the incarnated difference of classes, out of the constant outlooking and downlooking of the ruling caste on subordinates and instruments, and out of their equally constant practice of obeying and commanding, of keeping down and keeping at a distance — that other more mysterious pathos could never have arisen, the longing for an ever new widening of distance within the soul itself, the formation of ever higher, rarer, further, more extended, more comprehensive states, in short, just the elevation of the type "man," the continued "self-surmounting of man," to use a moral formula in a supermoral sense. To be sure, one must not resign oneself to any humanitarian illusions about the history of the origin of an aristocratic society (that is to say, of the preliminary condition for the elevation of the type "man"): the truth is hard. Let us acknowledge unprejudicedly how ever higher civilisation hitherto has *originated!* Men with a still natural nature, barbarians in every terrible sense of the word, men of prey, still in possession of unbroken strength of will and desire for power, threw themselves upon weaker, more moral, more peaceful races (perhaps trading or cattle-rearing communities), or upon old mellow civilisations in which the final vital force was flickering out in brilliant fireworks of wit and depravity. At the commencement, the noble caste was always the barbarian caste: their superiority did not consist first of all in their physical, but in their psychical power — they were more *complete* men (which at every point also implies the same as "more complete beasts").

Corruption — as the indication that anarchy threatens to break out among the instincts, and that the foundation of the emotions, called "life," is convulsed — is something radically different according to the organisation in which it manifests itself. When, for instance, an aristocracy like that of France at the beginning of the Revolution, flung away its privileges with sublime disgust and sacrificed itself to an excess of its moral sentiments, it was corruption: — it was really only the closing act of the corruption which had existed for centuries, by virtue of which that aristocracy had abdicated step by step its lordly prerogatives and lowered itself to a *function* of royalty (in the end even to its decoration and parade-dress). The essential thing, however, in a good and healthy aristocracy is that it should *not* regard itself as a function either of the kingship or the commonwealth, but as the *significance* and highest justification thereof — that it should therefore accept with a good conscience the sacrifice of a legion of individuals, who, *for its sake,* must be suppressed and reduced to imperfect men, to slaves and instruments. Its fundamental belief must be precisely that society is *not* allowed to exist for its own sake, but only as a foundation and scaffolding, by means of which a select class of beings may be able to elevate themselves to their higher duties, and in general to a higher *existence*: like those sun-seeking climbing plants in Java — they are called *Sipo Matador,* — which encircle an oak so long and so often with their arms, until at last, high above it, but supported by it, they can unfold their tops in the open light, and exhibit their happiness.

To refrain mutually from injury, from violence, from exploitation, and put one's will on a par with that of others: this may result in a certain rough sense in good conduct among individuals when the necessary conditions are given (namely, the actual similarity of the individuals in amount of force and degree of worth, and their co-relation within one organisation). As soon, however, as one wished to take this principle more generally, and if possible even as *the fundamental principle of society,* it would immediately disclose what it really is — namely, a Will to the *denial* of life, a principle of dissolution and decay. Here one must think profoundly to the very basis and resist all sentimental weakness: life itself is *essentially* appropriation, injury, conquest of the strange and weak, suppression, severity, obtrusion of peculiar forms, incorporation, and at the least, putting it mildest, exploitation; — but why should one for ever use precisely these words on which for ages a disparaging purpose has been stamped? Even the organisation within which, as was previously supposed, the individuals treat each other as equal — it takes place in every healthy aristocracy — must itself, if it be a living and not a dying organisation, do all that towards other bodies, which the individuals within it refrain from doing to each other: it will have to be the incarnated Will to Power, it will endeavour to grow, to gain ground, attract to itself and acquire ascendancy — not owing to any morality or immorality, but because it *lives,* and because life *is* precisely Will to Power. On no point, however, is the ordinary consciousness of Europeans more unwilling to be corrected than on this matter; people now rave everywhere, even under the guise of science, about coming conditions of society in which "the exploiting character" is to be absent: — that sounds to my ears as if they promised to invent a mode of life which should refrain from all organic functions. "Exploitation" does not belong to a depraved, or imperfect and primitive society: it belongs to the *nature* of the living being as a primary organic function; it is a consequence of the intrinsic Will to Power, which is precisely the Will to Life. — Granting that as a theory this is a novelty — as a reality it is the *fundamental fact* of all history: let us be so far honest towards ourselves!

Master and Slave Morality

In a tour through the many finer and coarser moralities which have hitherto prevailed or still prevail on the earth, I found certain traits recurring regularly together, and connected with one another, until finally two primary types revealed themselves to me, and a radical distinction was brought to light. There is *master-morality* and *slave-morality*; — I would at once add, however, that in all higher and mixed civilisations, there are also attempts at the reconciliation of the two moralities; but one finds still oftener the confusion and mutual misunderstanding of them, indeed, sometimes their close juxtaposition — even in the same man, within one soul. The distinctions of moral values have either originated in a ruling caste, pleasantly conscious of being different from the ruled — or among the ruled class, the slaves and dependents of all sorts. In the first case, when it is the rulers who determine the conception "good," it is the exalted, proud disposition which is regarded as the distinguishing feature, and that which determines the order of rank. The noble type of man separates from himself the beings in whom the opposite of this exalted, proud disposition displays itself: he despises them. Let it at once be noted that in this first kind of morality the antithesis "good" and "bad" means practically the same as "noble" and "despicable"; — the antithesis "good" and "*evil*" is of a different origin. The cowardly, the timid, the insignificant, and those thinking merely of narrow utility are despised; moreover, also, the distrustful, with their constrained glances, the self-abasing, the doglike kind of men who let themselves be abused, the mendicant flatterers, and above all the liars: — it is a fundamental belief of all aristocrats that the common people are untruthful. "We truthful ones"—the nobility in ancient Greece called themselves. It is obvious that everywhere the designations of moral value were at first applied to *men,* and were only derivatively and at a later period applied to *actions*; it is a gross mistake, therefore, when historians of morals start with questions like, "Why have sympathetic actions been praised?" The noble type of man regards *himself* as a determiner of values; he does not require to be approved of; he passes the judgment: "What is injurious to me is injurious in itself"; he knows that it is he himself only who confers honour on things; he is a *creator of values.* He honours whatever he recognises in himself: such morality is self-glorification. In the foreground there is the feeling of plenitude, of power, which seeks to overflow, the happiness of high tension, the consciousness of a wealth which would fain give and bestow:—the noble man also helps the unfortunate, but not—or scarcely—out of pity, but rather from an impulse generated by the superabundance of power. The noble man honours in himself the powerful one, him also who has power over himself, who knows how to speak and how to keep silence, who takes pleasure in subjecting himself to severity and hardness, and has reverence for all that is severe and hard. "Wotan placed a hard heart in my breast," says an old Scandinavian Saga: it is thus rightly expressed from the soul of a proud Viking. Such a type of man is even proud of *not* being made for sympathy; the hero of the Saga therefore adds warningly: "He who has not a hard heart when young, will never have one." The noble and brave who think thus are the furthest removed from the morality which sees precisely in sympathy, or in acting for the good of others, or in *désintéressement,* the characteristic of the moral; faith in oneself, pride in oneself, a radical enmity and irony towards "selflessness," belong as definitely to noble morality, as do a careless scorn and precaution in presence of sympathy and the "warm heart."—It is the powerful who *know* how to honour, it is their art, their domain for invention. The profound reverence for age and for tradition—all law rests on this double reverence,—the belief and prejudice in favour of ancestors and unfavourable to newcomers, is typical in the morality of the powerful; and if, reversely, men of "modern ideas" believe almost instinctively in "progress" and the "future," and are more and more lacking in respect for old age, the ignoble origin of these "ideas" has complacently betrayed itself thereby. A morality of the ruling class, however, is more especially foreign and irritating to present-day taste in the sternness of its principle that one has duties only to one's equals; that one may act towards beings of a lower rank, towards all that is foreign, just as seems good to one, or "as the heart desires," and in any case "beyond good and evil": it is here that sympathy and similar sentiments can have a place. The ability and obligation to exercise prolonged gratitude and prolonged revenge—both only within the circle of equals,—artfulness in retaliation, *raffinement* of the idea in friendship, a certain necessity to have enemies (as outlets for the emotions of envy, quarrelsomeness, arrogance—in fact, in order to be a good *friend*): all these are typical characteristics of the noble morality, which, as has been pointed out, is not the morality of "modern ideas," and is therefore at present difficult to realise and also to unearth and disclose.—It is otherwise with the second type of morality, *slave-morality.* Supposing that the abused, the oppressed, the suffering, the unemancipated, the weary, and those uncertain of themselves, should moralise, what will be the common element in their moral estimates? Probably a pessimistic suspicion with regard to the entire situation of man will find expression, perhaps a condemnation of man, together with his situation. The slave has an unfavourable eye for the virtues of the powerful; he has a skepticism and distrust, a *refinement* of distrust of everything "good" that is there honoured—he would fain persuade himself that the very happiness there is not genuine. On the other hand, *those* qualities which serve to alleviate the existence of sufferers are brought into prominence and flooded with light; it is here that sympathy, the kind, helping hand, the warm heart, patience, diligence, humility, and friendliness attain to honour; for here these are the most useful qualities, and almost the only means of supporting the burden of existence. Slave-morality is essentially the morality of utility. Here is the seat of the origin of the famous antithesis "good" and "evil":—power and dangerousness are assumed to reside in the evil, a certain dreadfulness, subtlety, and strength, which do not admit of being despised. According to slave-morality, therefore, the "evil" man arouses fear; according to master-morality, it is precisely the "good" man who arouses fear and seeks to arouse it, while the bad man is regarded as the despicable being. The contrast attains its maximum when, in accordance with the logical consequences of slave-morality, a shade of depreciation — it may be slight and well-intentioned — at last attaches itself to the "good" man of this morality; because, according to the servile mode of thought, the good man must in any case be the *safe* man: he is good-natured, easily deceived, perhaps a little stupid, *un bonhomme*. Everywhere that slave-morality gains the ascendancy, language shows a tendency to approximate the significations of the words "good" and "stupid." — A last fundamental difference: the desire for *freedom*, the instinct for happiness and the refinements of the feeling of liberty belong as necessarily to slave-morals and morality, as artifice and enthusiasm in reverence and devotion are the regular symptoms of an aristocratic mode of thinking and estimating. — Hence we can understand without further detail why love *as a passion* — it is our European specialty — must absolutely be of noble origin; as is well known, its invention is due to the Provençal poet-cavaliers, those brilliant, ingenious men of the *"gai saber,"* to whom Europe owes so much, and almost owes itself. . . .

There is an *instinct for rank,* which more than anything else is already the sign of a *high* rank; there is a *delight* in the *nuances* of reverence which leads one to infer noble origin and habits. The refinement, goodness, and loftiness of a soul are put to a perilous test when something passes by that is of the highest rank, but is not yet protected by the awe of authority from obtrusive touches and incivilities: something that goes its way like a living touchstone, undistinguished, undiscovered, and tentative, perhaps voluntarily veiled and disguised. He whose task and practice it is to investigate souls, will avail himself of many varieties of this very art to determine the ultimate value of a soul, the unalterable, innate order of rank to which it belongs: he will test it by its *instinct for reverence. Différence engendre haine* [Difference engenders hate. — ED.]: the vulgarity of many a nature spurts up suddenly like dirty water, when any holy vessel, any jewel from closed shrines, any book bearing the marks of great destiny, is brought before it; while on the other hand, there is an involuntary silence, a hesitation of the eye, a cessation of all gestures, by which it is indicated that a soul *feels* the nearness of what is worthiest of respect. . . .

The revolt of the slaves in morals begins in the very principle of *resentment* becoming creative and giving birth to values — a resentment experienced by creatures who, deprived as they are of the proper outlet of action, are forced to find their compensation in an imaginary revenge. While every aristocratic morality springs from a triumphant affirmation of its own demands, the slave morality says "no" from the very outset to what is "outside itself," "different from itself," and "not itself": and this "no" is its creative deed. This reversal of the valuing standpoint — this *inevitable* gravitation to the objective instead of back to the subjective — is typical of "resentment": the slave-morality requires as the condition of its existence an external and objective world, to employ physiological terminology, it requires objective stimuli to be capable of action at all — its action is fundamentally a reaction. The contrary is the case when we come to the aristocrat's system of values: it acts and grows spontaneously, it merely seeks its antithesis in order to pronounce a more grateful and exultant "yes" to its own self; — its negative conception, "low," "vulgar," "bad," is merely a pale late-born foil in comparison with its positive and fundamental conception (saturated as it is with life and passion), of "we aristocrats, we good ones, we beautiful ones, we happy ones."

When the aristocratic morality goes astray and commits sacrilege on reality, this is limited to that particular sphere with which it is *not* sufficiently acquainted — a sphere, in fact, from the real knowledge of which it disdainfully defends itself. It misjudges, in some cases, the sphere which it despises, the sphere of the common vulgar man and the low people: on the other hand, due weight should be given to the consideration that in any case the mood of contempt, of disdain, of superciliousness, even on the supposition that it *falsely* portrays the object of its contempt, will always be far removed from that degree of falsity which will always characterise the attacks — in effigy, of course — of the vindictive hatred and revengefulness of the weak in onslaughts on their enemies. In point of fact, there is in contempt too strong an admixture of nonchalance, of casualness, of boredom, of impatience, even of personal exultation, for it to be capable of distorting its victim into a real caricature or a real monstrosity. Attention again should be paid to the almost benevolent *nuances* which, for instance, the Greek nobility imports into all the words by which it distinguishes the common people from itself; note how continuously a kind of pity, care, and consideration imparts its honeyed *flavour,* until at last almost all the words which are applied to the vulgar man survive finally as expressions for "unhappy," "worthy of pity" . . . —and how, conversely, "bad," "low," "unhappy" have never ceased to ring in the Greek ear with a tone in which "unhappy" is the predominant note: this is a heritage of the old noble aristocratic morality, which remains true to itself even in contempt. . . . The "well-born" simply *felt* themselves the "happy"; they did not have to manufacture their happiness artificially through looking at their enemies, or in cases to talk and lie themselves into happiness (as is the custom with all resentful men); and similarly, complete men as they were, exuberant with strength, and consequently *necessarily* energetic, they were too wise to dissociate happiness from action—activity becomes in their minds necessarily counted as happiness (that is the etymology of ευ πράττειν)—all in sharp contrast to the "happiness" of the weak and the oppressed, with their festering venom and malignity, among whom happiness appears essentially as a narcotic, a deadening, a quietude, a peace, a "Sabbath," an enervation of the mind and relaxation of the limbs,—in short, a purely *passive* phenomenon. While the aristocratic man lived in confidence and openness with himself (γεν-ναῖος, "noble-born," emphasises the nuance "sincere," and perhaps also "naïf"), the resentful man, on the other hand, is neither sincere nor naïf, nor honest and candid with himself. His soul *squints*; his mind loves hidden crannies, tortuous paths and back doors, everything secret appeals to him as *his* world, *his* safety, *his* balm; he is past master in silence, in not forgetting, in waiting, in provisional self-depreciation and self-abasement. A race of such *resentful* men will of necessity eventually prove more *prudent* than any aristocratic race, it will honour prudence on quite a distinct scale, as, in fact, a paramount condition of existence, while prudence among aristocratic men is apt to be tinged with a delicate flavour of luxury and refinement; so among them it plays nothing like so integral a part as that complete certainty of function of the governing *unconscious* instincts, or as indeed a certain lack of prudence, such as a vehement and valiant charge, whether against danger or the enemy, or as those ecstatic bursts of rage, love, reverence, gratitude, by which at all times noble souls have recognised each other. When the resentment of the aristocratic man

manifests itself, it fulfils and exhausts itself in an immediate reaction, and consequently instills no *venom*: on the other hand, it never manifests itself at all in countless instances, when in the case of the feeble and weak it would be inevitable. An inability to take seriously for any length of time their enemies, their disasters, their *misdeeds*—that is the sign of the full strong natures who possess a superfluity of moulding plastic force, that heals completely and produces forgetfulness: a good example of this in the modern world is Mirabeau, who had no memory for any insults and meannesses which were practised on him, and who was only incapable of forgiving because he forgot. Such a man indeed shakes off with a shrug many a worm which would have buried itself in another; it is only in characters like these that we see the possibility (supposing, of course, that there is such a possibility in the world) of the real "*love* of one's enemies." What respect for his enemies is found, forsooth, in an aristocratic man—and such a reverence is already a bridge to love! He insists on having his enemy to himself as his distinction. He tolerates no other enemy but a man in whose character there is nothing to despise and *much* to honour! On the other hand, imagine the "enemy" as the resentful man conceives him— and it is here exactly that we see his work, his creativeness; he has conceived "the evil enemy," the "evil one," and indeed that is the root idea from which he now evolves as a contrasting and corresponding figure a "good one," himself—his very self!

The method of this man is quite contrary to that of the aristocratic man, who conceives the root idea "good" spontaneously and straight away, that is to say, out of himself, and from that material then creates for himself a concept of "bad"! This "bad" of aristocratic origin and that "evil" out of the cauldron of unsatisfied hatred—the former an imitation, an "extra," and additional nuance; the latter, on the other hand, the original, the beginning, the essential act in the conception of a slave-morality— these two words "bad" and "evil," how great a difference do they mark, in spite of the fact that they have an identical contrary in the idea "good." But the idea "good" is *not* the same: much rather let the question be asked, "Who is really evil according to the meaning of the morality of resentment?" In all sternness let it be answered thus:—*just* the good man of the other morality, just the aristocrat, the powerful one, the one who rules, but who is distorted by the venomous eye of resentfulness, into a new colour, a new signification, a new appearance. This particular point we would be the last to deny: the man who learnt to know those "good" ones only as enemies, learnt at the same time not to know them only as *"evil enemies,"* and the same men who . . . were kept so rigorously in bounds through convention, respect, custom, and gratitude, though much more through mutual vigilance and jealousy, . . . these men who in their relations with each other find so many new ways of manifesting consideration, self-control, delicacy, loyalty, pride, and friendship, these men are in reference to what is outside their circle (where the foreign element, a *foreign* country, begins), not much better than beasts of prey, which have been let loose. They enjoy there freedom from all social control, they feel that in the wilderness they can give vent with impunity to that tension which is produced by enclosure and imprisonment in the peace of society, they *revert* to the innocence of the beast-of-prey conscience, like jubilant monsters, who perhaps come from a ghostly bout of murder, arson, rape, and torture, with bravado and a moral equanimity, as though merely some wild student's prank had been played, perfectly convinced that the poets have now an ample theme to sing and celebrate. It is impossible not to recognise at the core of all these aristocratic races the beast of prey; the magnificent *blonde brute,* avidly rampant for spoil and victory; this hidden core needed an outlet from time to time, the beast must get loose again, must return into the wilderness — the Roman, Arabic, German, and Japanese nobility, the Homeric heroes, the Scandinavian Vikings, are all alike in this need. It is the aristocratic races who have left the idea "Barbarian" on all the tracks in which they have marched; nay, a consciousness of this very barbarianism, and even a pride in it, manifests itself even in their highest civilisation (for example, when Pericles says to his Athenians in that celebrated funeral oration, "Our audacity has forced a way over every land and sea, rearing everywhere imperishable memorials of itself for *good* and for *evil*"). This audacity of aristocratic races, mad, absurd, and spasmodic as may be its expression; the incalculable and fantastic nature of their enterprises, . . . their nonchalance and contempt for safety, body,

life, and comfort, their awful joy and intense delight in all destruction, in all the ecstasies of victory and cruelty, — all these features become crystallised, for those who suffered thereby in the picture of the "barbarian," of the "evil enemy," perhaps of the "Goth" and of the "Vandal." The profound, icy mistrust which the German provokes, as soon as he arrives at power, — even at the present time, — is always still an aftermath of that inextinguishable horror with which for whole centuries Europe has regarded the wrath of the blonde Teuton beast. . . .

. . . One may be perfectly justified in being always afraid of the blonde beast that lies at the core of all aristocratic races, and in being on one's guard: but who would not a hundred times prefer to be afraid, when one at the same time admires, than to be immune from fear, at the cost of being perpetually obsessed with the loathsome spectacle of the distorted, the dwarfed, the stunted, the envenomed? And is that not our fate? What produces today our repulsion towards "man"? — for we *suffer* from "man," there is no doubt about it. It is not fear; it is rather that we have nothing more to fear from men; it is that the worm "man" is in the foreground and pullulates; it is that the "tame man," the wretched mediocre and unedifying creature, has learnt to consider himself a goal and a pinnacle, an inner meaning, an historic principle, a "higher man"; yes, it is that he has a certain right so to consider himself, in so far as he feels that in contrast to that excess of deformity, disease, exhaustion, and effeteness whose odour is beginning to pollute present-day Europe, he at any rate has achieved a relative success, he at any rate still says "yes" to life.

Goodness and the *Will to Power*

What is good? — All that enhances the feeling of power, the Will to Power, and the power itself in man. What is bad? — All that proceeds from weakness. What is happiness? — The feeling that power is increasing — that resistance has been overcome.

Not contentment, but more power; not peace at any price but war; not virtue, but competence (virtue in the Renaissance sense, *virtu,* free from all moralistic acid). The first principle of our humanism: The weak and the failures shall perish. They ought even to be helped to perish.

What is more harmful than any vice? — Practical sympathy and pity for all the failures and all the weak: Christianity.

Christianity is the religion of pity. Pity opposes the noble passions which heighten our vitality. It has a depressing effect, depriving us of strength. As we multiply the instances of pity we gradually lose our strength of nobility. Pity makes suffering contagious and under certain conditions it may cause a total loss of life and vitality out of all proportion to the magnitude of the cause. . . . Pity is the practice of nihilism.

IV.5 Two Conceptions of Happiness

RICHARD KRAUT

Richard Kraut is professor of philosophy at the University of Illinois, Chicago. In this essay he subtly contrasts Aristotle's view of happiness with our own. Whereas Aristotle views happiness in terms of an objective and stringent standard, we tend to be more subjective and flexible in describing a life as happy. Kraut argues that our conception includes subjective and objective factors, so that while not just any and every subjective evaluation of happiness is valid, people can reduce their standards and be described as happy relative to those standards.

I

In this paper, I want to contrast two ways of judging whether people are leading happy lives: Aristotle's and our own. I will argue that there are some striking similarities between these two conceptions of happiness. To live happily, for both Aristotle and for us, is to have certain attitudes toward one's life, and to measure up to certain standards. Where we and Aristotle sharply disagree is over the standards to be used in evaluating lives. Roughly, he insists on an objective and stringent standard, whereas our test is more subjective and flexible. I will also argue that we have good reason to reject his conception of happiness, for his standards can be employed only by those who know things we do not. If we ever acquired such knowledge, we might make judgments about happiness that are like the ones Aristotle makes in the *Nicomachean Ethics*. We would, in other words, drop our present conception of happiness and adopt something like his.

The approach I am taking to this subject differs from the usual one. Scholars and philosophers who study the *Ethics* often claim that Aristotle has no conception of happiness at all, in our sense of the word. They notice that when his term *eudaimonia* receives the traditional translation, "happiness," a number of his points sound dubious and even silly. For example, he is made to say that everything should be sought for the sake of happiness, and that children and evil adults are never happy because they have not developed such traits as justice, courage, and self-control. Furthermore, *eudaimonia* does not name a feeling or emotion, whereas we think that happiness is, or at least involves, a certain state of mind. And so we are warned, for example, by Henry Sidgwick, that the word "happiness" that

Reprinted with permission from *Philosophical Review* 88 (1979): 167–197 and the author.

we find in translations of Aristotle does not have its contemporary meaning in English.[1] Occasionally a different translation is proposed: W. D. Ross suggests "well-being"[2] (despite the fact that he sticks to "happiness" in the Oxford edition of the *Ethics*); John Cooper proposes "flourishing."[3] The idea is that we should assign a meaning to *eudaimonia* that makes Aristotle disagree with us as little as possible. Since we believe that some children definitely are happy, and that some evil people might very well be, Aristotle's *eudaimonia* cannot mean "happiness" in its usual sense.

I think this approach rests on an oversimplified view both of happiness and of *eudaimonia*. Sidgwick makes the dubious claim that our term is "commonly used in Bentham's way as convertible with Pleasure." Ross tells us that " 'happiness' means a state of feeling, differing from 'pleasure' only by its suggestion of permanence, depth, and serenity." And Cooper says that it "tends to be taken as referring exclusively to a subjective psychological state." The common error here is the belief that the only thing we mean when we judge a person happy is that he is in a certain state of mind. As I will argue, we often mean something more than this: we are saying that the individual is happy because his life meets a certain standard (a subjective one). Furthermore, when Aristotle calls someone *eudaimon,* he means not only that the individual meets a certain standard (an objective one), but that he is in a certain state of mind — the very same state we say people are in when we call them happy. To think that happiness just involves a psychological condition and that *eudaimonia* does not is to get both concepts wrong.

It is an illusion, at any rate, to think that we foster a better understanding of Aristotle if we use "well-being" or "flourishing" as translations of *eudaimonia,* rather than "happiness." If we use these words, Aristotle will be made to say that children and evil men do not attain well-being, or do not flourish. Are these claims any more plausible than the ones they are supposed to replace? If a young tree can flourish in the right conditions, why not a young person?[4] Why say that well-being is beyond the reach of children and evil people? Certainly we do things for their well-being — don't we ever succeed?

We could of course leave *eudaimonia* untranslated and let its meaning be gathered from the statements Aristotle makes about it. But that would leave unanswered a question I think we should ask: When we say that a person is leading a happy life, and Aristotle says that the same person is not *eudaimon,* do we have anything to argue about? I think we do. As I will try to show, the conception of *eudaimonia* in the *Nicomachean Ethics* is best interpreted as a challenge to the way we go about judging people to be happy. If we were convinced that what Aristotle says about *eudaimonia* is true, we would no longer believe that children or evil people can be happy. And if we began to make judgments of happiness in the way he makes judgments of *eudaimonia,* we would not be changing the meaning of "happiness."

II

Aristotle thinks that the most *eudaimon* individual is someone who has fully developed and regularly exercises the various virtues of the soul, both intellectual and moral. Such a person engages in philosophical activity (since this is the full flowering of his capacity to reason theoretically) and also in moral activities, which display his justice, generosity, temperance, etc. Though he may experience minor mishaps, he cannot have recently suffered any severe misfortunes, such as the death of close friends or dearly loved children. Aristotle thinks that a virtuous person will make the best of any situation, but that in extreme circumstances *eudaimonia* is lost. It may be regained, but only after a long period of time during which many fine things have been achieved.

Consider such a person — a philosopher and a good man — at a time of life that is not marred by misfortunes. Aristotle thinks he would in these conditions be as *eudaimon* as any human being can be. I want to ask: is he a happy person? Is he in the same psychological state as any individual who is leading a happy life? When we say that someone is living happily, we imply that he has certain attitudes toward his life: he is very glad to be alive; he judges that on balance his deepest desires are being satisfied and that the circumstances of his life are turning out well. Does Aristotle's paradigm of *eudaimonia* have these same attitudes? I think so. For such a person loves the activities he regularly and successfully engages in. He thinks that exercising one's intellectual and moral capacities is the greatest good available to human beings, and he knows he possesses this good. Furthermore, he has all the other major goods he wants. His desire for such external goals as honor, wealth, and physical pleasure is moderate, and should be easy enough to satisfy in a normal life. If, however, some great misfortune does occur — if, for example, he is totally deprived of honor — then Aristotle insists that he is no longer *eudaimon*. So, the individual who is most *eudaimon* on Aristotle's theory passes our tests for happiness with flying colors. All his major goals are being achieved, to a degree that satisfies him. Knowing this, he greatly enjoys his life and has nothing serious to complain of.

Furthermore, there is a passage in which Aristotle explicitly tells us how a *eudaimon* individual will look upon his life. It occurs in the midst of an involved proof that whoever is *eudaimon* needs friends: "All men desire (life), and particularly those who are good and supremely happy (*makarios*), for to such men life is most desirable, and their existence is the most supremely happy (*makariōtatē*)" (1170a26–29). To put it somewhat differently: one who is good and highly *eudaimon* has an especially strong desire for life, and this psychological condition is based on the perception of how very desirable his life is. Now, when Aristotle says that one who is virtuous and *eudaimon* particularly desires life, he cannot mean that he will struggle to stay alive at any cost. Rather, he must mean that such individuals are more glad to be alive than others; the kind of existence they enjoy gives them a heightened love of life. As Aristotle says elsewhere (1117b9–13), these are the people who have the most reason to live, and therefore the thought of death — even death in battle — is especially painful to them. In their attitude towards themselves and their lives, they are the very opposite of the sort of individual who is so miserable and filled with self-hatred that he contemplates suicide (1166b11–28). It is undeniable, then, that the *eudaimon* individual, as Aristotle depicts him, is fully satisfied with his life. He is, in other words, a happy person.

There is another way of arriving at this same conclusion. Let us for the moment ignore Aristotle's belief that *eudaimonia* consists in virtuous activity. He has many other convictions about the *eudaimon* life besides this one, and from these alone we can infer that whoever is *eudaimon* must be happy with

his life. Consider the following points, all of which Aristotle affirms or presupposes: We human beings are different from plants, in that we would never be able to attain our good with any regularity, unless we had effective desires for what we think is worthwhile. Since we are creatures with strong desires for the good, as we variously conceive it, it is natural and inevitable for us to develop a deep interest in whether or not such desires are being satisfied. An animal with first-order desires, but no strong second-order interest in whether those first-order desires are being fulfilled, would not be fully human. Put otherwise: no person would choose a life in which he remains continually unaware of whether or not he possesses the good; that would be a life befitting plants, not human beings. Now, any deep desire which develops naturally and universally is a desire which must be satisfied, if we are to attain our good. So a major human good is the second-order good which consists in the perception that our major first-order desires are being satisfied. And this second-order good is one we must have in order to be *eudaimon*, since a *eudaimon* life can have no serious deficiency (1097b14–15). Even if someone correctly understood his good and attained it, he still would not be *eudaimon*, if he mistakenly thought that he lacked a major part of that good. For example, suppose someone whose family is living abroad is told that they have recently been killed. Let us assume that he is deeply affected, and views his loss as a great tragedy. Even if he should discover, after a year's time, that he was misinformed, that his family has all this time been alive and well, it remains true that he lacked *eudaimonia* during that year. His life may in fact have possessed every first-order good that a well-lived life requires; still, it undeniably contained a serious second-order evil. To think, over a long period of time, that dear friends or family members have recently died, is by itself a major misfortune. For it involves the perception — or, in the case imagined, the misperception — that one lacks a great good, and this in itself is a great evil. *Eudaimonia* involves the recognition that one's desire for the good is being fulfilled, and therefore one who attains *eudaimonia* is necessarily happy with his life. His deepest desires are being satisfied, and realizing this, he has an especially affirmative attitude towards himself and his life.

Notice that in reaching this conclusion, no appeal was made to Aristotle's theory that the best life is devoted to virtuous activity. So, if the argument I have just reconstructed is correct, then all of the various and conflicting theories of the good life ought to recognize that a *eudaimon* individual, whatever else may be true of him, has a certain attitude toward his life. Even if one disagrees with Aristotle about the importance of virtue, that is no reason for denying the connection between *eudaimonia* and the perceived satisfaction of major desires. For that connection depends solely on some highly general features of human nature, and the point that a *eudaimon* life is without major defects. Therefore, any adequate theory of the best human life — whether it identifies the good with honor or pleasure or virtue — ought to characterize a *eudaimon* individual as someone who knowingly satisfies his deepest desires. Furthermore, if *eudaimonia* and desire-satisfaction are connected in the way described, then there is a fair empirical test by which competing theories of *eudaimonia* can be partially evaluated. If the individuals who are pronounced *eudaimones* by a certain theory of *eudaimonia* believe there is little reason to be alive, and are given to thoughts of suicide, then that theory cannot be right. Contrariwise, if those who are pronounced *eudaimones* have a highly positive attitude toward their lives, and those who are alleged to be quite distant from *eudaimonia* are deeply dissatisfied with themselves, then that is some confirmation for the theory which reaches this result. A theory of *eudaimonia,* in other words, ought to harmonize, at least partly, with the way people feel about their lives: that is the upshot of our argument linking *eudaimonia* and the perception that one's major desires are being fulfilled. And Aristotle can claim that his own particular theory, which connects *eudaimonia* with virtuous activity, satisfies this requirement. For, as we have seen, he thinks that the virtuous and *eudaimon* individual is especially glad to be alive, whereas the individual who most sorely lacks *eudaimonia* — the evil man, hated for his misdeeds — is given to thoughts of suicide.

Let me emphasize two points about my interpretation. First, I have not said that the word *eudaimon,* by virtue of its everyday meaning, could only have been applied to satisfied individuals. Perhaps, as K. J. Dover claims, a Greek could have applied that term, without irony or contradiction, to a person who was deeply dissatisfied with his life.[5] What I want to emphasize is that Dover's thesis about ordinary Greek usage does not conflict with

my own thesis about Aristotle. The *Nicomachean Ethics* does not merely record linguistic conventions about the term *eudaimon,* and in many ways Aristotle's treatment of this subject is controversial. His idea that *eudaimonia* consists in contemplation, for example, is no part of the meaning of the word *eudaimonia,* but is instead a product of philosophical argument. Similarly, the psychological condition presupposed by Aristotle — that *eudaimonia* requires full and conscious satisfaction of desire — is a product of his own reflections, and need not have been a linguistic convention or a matter of universal agreement. So if we ever find among Greek authors genuine cases in which a deeply dissatisfied individual is called *eudaimon,* we merely will have discovered an application of that term against which Aristotle would protest, just as he protests against those who call only the wealthy *eudaimones.*

Second, I am not saying that, according to Aristotle, whoever perceives that his major desires are being satisfied is *eudaimon.* Complete fulfillment of desire is a necessary condition of *eudaimonia,* but not a sufficient one. For on Aristotle's theory, those desires must be directed at worthwhile goals, and they must be proportionate in strength to the value of those goals; otherwise, one is not *eudaimon,* however satisfied one feels. Now, it might be claimed that this is a striking difference between *eudaimonia* and happiness. If a person's desires are fully satisfied — so the claim goes — then he is happy; but, as I have just said, this condition is not sufficient, in Aristotle's eyes, for *eudaimonia.* And it might be said that this difference is enough to show that "happiness" is not a good translation of Aristotle's *eudaimonia.* In the remaining sections of this paper, I will be presenting my reply to this line of argument. For now, I would like to stress the point that, however one wants to translate Aristotle's term *eudaimonia,* one ought to have a clear understanding of the similarities and differences between that notion and our notion of a happy life. And one remarkable similarity, which scholars have not recognized, is this: A *eudaimon* individual, as Aristotle conceives him, is in the very same psychological state as a person who is living happily. Such individuals have a highly affirmative attitude toward their lives, since they perceive that their major desires are being fulfilled. In spite of the fact that "happiness" is the traditional translation of *eudaimonia,* one of the most important connections between the two concepts has curiously been ignored.

III

Let us take a closer look now at how we judge whether someone is happy. The following example will help focus our ideas: Suppose a man is asked what his idea of happiness is, and he replies, "Being loved, admired, or at least respected by my friends. But I would hate to have friends who only pretend to have these attitudes toward me. If they didn't like me, I would want to know about it. Better to have no friends at all, and realize it, than to have false friends one cannot see through." Suppose that what this man hates actually comes to pass. His so-called friends orchestrate an elaborate deception, giving him every reason to believe that they love and admire him, though in fact they don't. And he is taken in by the illusion.

Is this a happy life? Is he a happy man? Some people will say yes, without a moment's thought. On their view (which I will call "extreme subjectivism"), happiness is a psychological state and nothing more; it involves, among other things, the belief that one is getting the important things one wants, as well as certain pleasant affects that normally go along with this belief. So the deceived man is living just as happily as he would be if he were not deceived. Just as unfounded fear is still fear, so unfounded happiness is still happiness. For consider what we would say if the deceived man became suspicious of his friends, and came upon an opportunity to discover what they really think of him. Would we say that he is finding out whether he is really happy? Wouldn't it be more natural to say that he is finding out whether his happiness has been based on an illusion?

I think extreme subjectivism is a half-truth. Our reaction to the case of the deceived man is really more complicated than this doctrine admits. We do have some tendency to say that the deceived man is happy, but at the same time we have a definite reluctance to say this. The basis for our reluctance seems to be this: When a person is asked what his idea of happiness is, he quite naturally answers by describing the kind of life he would like to lead. It would therefore be misleading for the man in the above example to reply that he will be happy whether his friends deceive him or not. That would imply that he attaches some significant value to the situation in which he is deceived. Evidently, when we ask someone, "What will make you happy? What is your idea of happiness?", we are not requesting that he specify the conditions under which he will be in a certain psychological state. It is not like asking, "What will make you angry?" Rather, it is inquiring about the standards he imposes on himself, and the goals he is seeking. And this makes us hesitant to say that the deceived man is happy or has a happy life. Judged by his own standards of happiness, he has not attained it, though he is in the same psychological condition he would be in if he had attained it. Merely being in that psychological state is not something to which he attaches any value, and so it is odd to say that he has attained a happy life merely by being in that psychological state.

I think we can improve on the way extreme subjectivism describes our use of "happiness." We are not at all reluctant to say that the deceived man *feels happy* about his life. But we are quite reluctant to say that *the life he is leading is a happy life*. And we are at sea when we have to decide whether he is *happy*; the word "happiness" seems to lean in two directions, sometimes referring to the *feeling* of happiness, sometimes to the kind of *life* that is happy. For a person to be living happily, or to have a happy life, he must attain all the important things he values, or he must come reasonably close to this standard. But one can feel happy with one's life even if one comes nowhere near this goal; one need only believe that one is meeting one's standard. The deceived man, then, has a feeling of happiness, but when he is asked what he thinks happiness is, he is not being asked for the conditions under which he will have this feeling. Rather, he is being asked for his view about what a happy life is. If he discovers that his friends were deceiving him, he should say that although his feeling of happiness was based on an illusion, it really did exist. At no time, however, was he really leading a happy life.

In what follows, I will, for the sake of convenience, use the terms "happiness" and "a happy life" interchangeably. I am not denying that it is sometimes correct to call a person happy merely because he feels that way about his life. Aristotle never uses *eudaimonia* in this way, and in this respect his term differs markedly from our own. But once this point is made, an important question remains: What is the difference between being *eudaimon* and leading a happy life?

IV

On our view, a person is living happily only if he realizes that he is attaining the important things he values, or if he comes reasonably close to this high standard. Of course, this is not the only condition one must meet. One must also find that the things one values are genuinely rewarding, and not merely the best of a bad range of alternatives. And perhaps further conditions are necessary as well. What I want to focus on is a certain subjectivism in our conception of happiness. On our view, a person is happy only if he meets the standards *he* imposes on his life. Even if many others consider his standards too low, and would never switch places with him, he can still have a happy life. Consider, for example, a person who is severely retarded and thus quite limited in his aims and abilities. Though we would never wish for such a fate, we still think that under favorable conditions such a person can lead a happy life. For he can achieve the things he values, given the right circumstances. It is irrelevant that more fortunate individuals have more ambitious goals and would not be satisfied if their achievements were so very limited.

Contrast this with a more objective way of determining whether people are leading happy lives. We can define "objectivism" as the view that people should not be considered happy unless they are coming reasonably close to living the best life they are capable of. According to the objectivist, each person has certain capacities and talents which can be fully developed under ideal conditions. And if someone is very distant from his full development, he is not and should not be considered happy, even if he meets the standards he imposes on his life. For he could have been leading a much better life, as determined by some ideal standard. The objectivist thinks that it is not up to you to determine where your happiness lies; it is fixed by your nature, and your job is to discover it.

The objective conception of happiness is in some important ways modeled on Aristotle's conception of *eudaimonia*. He thinks that to be *eudaimon* one must completely fulfill the function of a human being, or come reasonably close to doing so. And in his opinion, most people don't know what their function is; they may not even believe that they

have one. Therefore they never attain *eudaimonia*, whether they realize it or not. Now, even though the objective view of happiness is patterned after Aristotle's approach to *eudaimonia*, a modern-day objectivist need not be as narrow. The *Nicomachean Ethics* argues that there is just one life that is best for everyone — the philosophical life — but objectivists can disagree. They might believe that for each of us there is a large class of ideal lives, and that to be happy we have to come reasonably close to one of those lives. And an objectivist can also say that different types of individuals have different capacities, so that what is ideal for one person may not be ideal for another. We can think of the objectivist as a reformed Aristotelian: he wants us to make judgments of happiness in somewhat the way the *Ethics* makes judgments of *eudaimonia*, but he is free to modify Aristotle's doctrine here and there, so that his own proposal will be more reasonable.

It is important not to overestimate the differences between the subjective and objective ways of judging a person to be living happily. The objectivist, like us, recognizes that a happy person must have certain attitudes toward himself; he must be satisfied with the way his life is going, and he must find his projects fulfilling. Furthermore, we are like the objectivist in that we believe that living happily does not merely consist in having a highly positive attitude toward one's life. We agree that to lead a happy life a person must actually meet a certain standard; seeming to meet it is not enough. Finally, we resemble the objectivist in this further respect: in our assessment of how happy a person is, we take into account the extent to which he has realized his capacities. We think that if someone falls far short of developing himself, then although he may be happy, he is not as happy as he might have been. For example, even if a retarded person manages to achieve a happy life, he might have been happier had he realized to a greater degree the normal capacities of a human being. In better circumstances, he could have chosen his interests from a wider range of alternatives, and he would have found more rewarding activities for himself. Much the same can be said of normal individuals who grow up in environments that do not elicit their talents and abilities. They too might have led happier lives, though they can be successful in pursuing the things they value, and therefore be happy.

But the objectivist says that a person is not happy if he is very distant from leading the best life he is capable of. We say instead that such a person is happy, though he might have been happier. What sort of disagreement is this, and how important is it?

V

Is the difference between subjectivism and objectivism merely verbal? Does the objectivist assign a different meaning to the word "happiness"? Should we say that he is only adopting a misleading way of talking, and that he would make his point more clearly and effectively if he used a different word instead of "happiness"? We might recommend, for example, that he express himself in this way: "A person can be happy if his life meets his own standards, but *to flourish* he must realize his capacities and come reasonably close to the best life he is capable of. So one can be happy but not flourish."

I think the objectivist has good reason to reject this proposal. He is someone who sees, in a number of cases, a huge gap between the lives people are leading and the lives that would be best for them. He may want to shock them into the realization that they are doing a terrible job with their lives. In this way perhaps they will change for the better, and at any rate others will not be tempted to imitate them. Furthermore, the objectivist may succeed in changing people's minds about whether their lives have been happy. He may convince them that their lives have been sorely lacking in qualities whose importance they suddenly recognize. After reevaluating themselves in the light of newly acquired standards, they may thank the objectivist for making them see that they have unknowingly been leading unhappy lives. Since such reevaluations do take place, it is hardly appropriate to tell the objectivist that he is misusing the word "happiness." Notice too that it is not very disturbing to be told that although one is happy one could be even happier. Quite naturally, people will reply that they are satisfied just to be happy: why should they keep striving for more and more? Why should we make radical changes in our lives, as the objectivist urges, merely to exchange a happy life for a happier one? Similarly, no one is

going to be upset if he is told that he is not flourishing (most people will wonder what flourishing amounts to) or fully realizing his talents. Happiness is what people want for themselves, and the objectivist is right in his conviction that people are unlikely to change drastically for their own sake unless they believe that they are not presently leading happy lives. So if we take the word "happiness" away from the objectivist, we take away a strategic tool, which he rightly insists on using.

Furthermore, the objectivist may challenge us in the following way: "As you saw earlier, a person is not leading a happy life if he falsely believes that he is achieving his most valued goals. But can't people suffer from an illusion that is equally bad for them, if not worse? They can have radically false beliefs about what goals they should pursue. If a person wants to lead the best life he is capable of, but is deeply mistaken about what this life consists in or how it is to be accomplished, then he is in as sorry a state as the man who is deceived into believing that he is loved by his friends. Both think they are leading a certain sort of life, but they are far from it, and so neither is living a happy life—though they may *feel* happy."

We can reply to this challenge by showing what the difficulties of objectivism are, and I will be doing that in a later section. But enough has been said to show that the objectivist is not simply adopting an arbitrary and misleading way of talking. He thinks that the way we talk about happiness deceives people into leading what is, from their own point of view, the wrong kind of life. So we would be missing his point if we were to look upon his way of judging people happy to be nothing but a misuse of the word.

Nor would it be correct to say that the objectivist is proposing a new meaning for the word "happiness." To see this, consider the following analogy: Suppose that a certain society takes tallness to be an invaluable property, though the greatest height attained is five feet. A group of scientists discovers that under optimal conditions human beings can reach a height of between five and seven feet, and they propose that steps be taken to achieve these conditions, so that young people and future generations will achieve their ideal height. To make people sense the urgent need for change, they stop calling anyone—even five-footers—tall, and they recommend that everyone else adopt this new standard. It would be a strategic mistake for them to introduce a new word to mean "attaining one's ideal height." Since "tallness" is already a familiar term for an esteemed property, they should simply deny what their society has affirmed: that a five-foot person is tall.

It would be wrong to say that these scientists are proposing a new meaning for the word "tall." To be tall is to meet or exceed a specified standard of height, and the scientists are not trying to change this definition. Rather, they are proposing a different standard. They think that tallness should no longer be a matter of exceeding the norm, but of coming close to an ideal, and there is no more a change of meaning here than in any other case in which standards for the application of a term are revised. What once passed for a good recording, for example, would no longer do so, but that hardly shows that the meaning of "good recording" has changed.

The objective conception of happiness should be treated in the same way. It proposes that we drop our current subjective standard of happiness,[6] and judge each person instead by a more severe and objective test. And the objectivist can reasonably argue that when he talks about a happy life, "happy" means just what it does for the subjectivist: a happy person has a highly affirmative attitude toward his life, and comes reasonably close to attaining the important things he values; a happy life, furthermore, is one that is highly desirable from the standpoint of the person leading it. But how should we characterize that standpoint? The objectivist says that a life is desirable from your own standpoint only if it comes fairly close to your ideal life, whereas the subjectivist thinks your current goals fix the standpoint from which your life should be evaluated. This difference hardly amounts to a difference in the meaning of the term "happiness."

I think this bears on the question of how to translate Aristotle. For the objectivist wants us to use the expression "living happily" in very much the way the *Ethics* uses *eudaimonia*. As we have seen, Aristotle thinks that if someone is *eudaimon*, then he has a highly affirmative attitude toward his life, and his deepest desires are being satisfied. Aristotle differs from us only in that he thinks a *eudaimon* life must come very close to the ideal, whereas our judgments of happiness rely on a subjective standard. And as I have just argued, this sort of difference is not plausibly viewed as a difference in meaning.

VI

We can get a clearer picture of the objectivist's proposal if we ask what it is to wish someone future happiness. More specifically, what are we wishing for when we say of a newborn baby, "I hope he has a happy life"? The subjectivist might be tempted to reply: "We are wishing the child success in attaining the things he will come to value, whatever these things are; and we are hoping he will find these goals, whatever they are, fulfilling." But I do not think this is the right account. For think of all the terrible things that would not be excluded by the wish for happiness, if this were all it amounted to. A newborn child might become retarded—yet still live happily; he might be enslaved, or blinded, or severely incapacitated in other ways—yet still live happily. Even though these are awful misfortunes, they do not so restrict us that a happy life becomes impossible, given the subjective account of happiness. Yet when we wish a happy life to a newborn baby, we are wishing for something better than such lives as these. The child's parents, upon hearing our wishes, do not respond: "But why are you being so ungenerous? Why don't you wish our baby all the best, rather than merely a happy life? You've said nothing so far to exclude the major misfortunes— things one should not wish even upon one's enemies!"

Why don't parents make this accusation of ungenerosity? To answer this question, it will be useful to remind ourselves that there is a close linguistic connection between happiness and good fortune. "Hap" means chance; a hapless person is luckless; a happy turn of events is always good news; the first dictionary definition of "happy" is: "characterized by luck or good fortune." I suggest that when we wish a child a life of happiness, we are tacitly relying on this connection between hap and happiness. We hope that the child will achieve the things he values, and find these things rewarding; but we also hope that the child's range of choices will not be restricted by unfortunate—that is, unhappy—circumstances. This explains why we do not react in different ways to the wish that a baby have all the best and the wish that he lead a life of happiness.

As children grow up and their lives take on a definite shape, their parents and others will employ our usual subjective test for determining whether they are happy. A parent might judge that his children are very distant from the best life that was available to them, but that they are nonetheless happy. We are objective in our early hopes and subjective in our later judgments. That is, when we wish someone a happy life, we hope he comes as close as possible to one of the best lives available to him; yet later our assessments of happiness abandon any reference to an ideal. The objectivist's proposal is that we bring our judgments of happiness into line with our early wishes. He says that we should only judge a person happy if he is leading the kind of life we should have wished for him when he was a newborn baby. Some explanation is needed of why we do not adopt this practice.

Notice, by the way, how silly it would be to say that "happiness" has two different meanings: one when we wish children a happy life, and another when we assess the happiness of adults. Quite clearly what is happening is not a change in meaning but a change in standards. We include more in a happy life, when we wish it to the newborn, than we require of such a life, when we judge that someone has achieved it. All the more reason, then, to think that objectivists and subjectivists mean the same by "happiness," and that Aristotle's *eudaimon* is properly rendered, "leading a happy life."

VII

The objectivist wants us to change our linguistic habits and use his test for determining whether people are happy. To convince us, he must give us a definite idea of how to use that test. That is, he must tell us how to determine what the ideal life (or set of ideals) is for each person. We must have a fairly complete picture of what must be included in such lives and of what can safely be left out. Further, the objectivist must convince us that the lives he calls ideal really deserve that name. When people engage in the activities he calls ideal, and refrain from the ones he thinks unimportant, they must find their lives more rewarding than they were before. Conversely, when people move away from lives the objectivist considers ideal, and try different alternatives, they must come to regret their decisions. And the objectivist ought to have some explanation of

why people prefer the kind of life which he says is best for them. He must point to certain deep-seated facts of human nature and social organization which incline people to find a certain way of life best from their own point of view. Without such an explanation we may suspect that the objectivist merely has acquired a powerful hold over people who cannot consider themselves happy unless they do what he tells them. Furthermore, the objectivist must say something about what it is for a person to come *reasonably* close to leading his ideal life. Obviously, he cannot require that a happy life be absolutely perfect—there are no such lives. But unless we have some idea of what deviations from the ideal are compatible with happiness, it would be pointless to try to judge whether anyone is living happily. It would be like trying to decide whether London is reasonably close to Bristol.

The trouble with objectivism is that no one has worked out a detailed and plausible theory that satisfies these demands. And so even if we are attracted by the objectivist's proposal, we have very little idea of how to put it into practice. For example, suppose we read Aristotle's discussion of *eudaimonia* as a recommendation about how to determine whether people are living happily. (This is how he should be read, if *eudaimonia* means "leading a happy life.") The idea that the best life is philosophical seems much too narrow, so let us leave this aside and consider Aristotle's claim that the best life must make an excellent use of reason. Two questions arise: First, might someone make a poor use of his reasoning abilities, but make such excellent use of other capacities and talents that he comes reasonably close to leading one of the lives that could be ideal for him? Aristotle does not give any convincing reason for believing that this cannot happen. Second, there is the question of what constitutes an excellent use of reason. Here Aristotle has a lot to say. Using reason in an excellent way about practical matters requires exercising the virtues as he interprets them: one must be temperate in matters of physical pleasure, rather than a sensualist or an ascetic; one must be courageous, chiefly on the battlefield; and so on. Here too, Aristotle has worked out his theory too narrowly. There is no reason to believe that a person fully realizes his capacities only if he adopts Aristotle's attitudes toward physical pleasure and the use of force. Any objective theory of happiness which tries to do better than Aristotle's conception of *eu-*

daimonia will have to avoid his narrowness, without becoming so vague and general as to be useless.

I want to emphasize that I am making a limited point against objectivism. I do not claim that in principle such a theory cannot be found. Great figures have claimed to see what the ideal life is for each individual, and the only rational response to these philosophies is to examine them case by case. Perhaps with more work we can provide objectivism with the philosophical foundations it requires. My point is that at present we have no defensible method for discovering each person's distance from his ideal lives. And so if we drop our subjective judgments of happiness, we have no workable and systematic alternative to put in their place. Unless some incoherence can be found in our subjective conception of happiness — and so far none has — we have good reason to continue our present practice. Even so, our interest in the alternative provided by objectivism is bound to continue. For subjectivism says so little about how we should lead our lives: it tells us that if we want to be happy we should make up our minds about what we value most, and this is of little help to those who are uncertain about what kind of life to lead. Subjectivism requires less of a philosophical foundation than objectivism, but as a result it is, from a practical standpoint, the less informative theory.

VIII

One final complaint must be lodged against Aristotle's particular brand of objectivism: the standard by which he evaluates lives is too rigid. To see this, consider his doctrine of natural slavery. He thinks there are individuals who are constitutionally incapable of rational deliberation (1260a12, 1280a32–34), and for whom the best life is one of docile subordination to a wise master (1254b16–20, 1278b34–35). These natural slaves are not wholly devoid of reason (1254b22–23). Like all human beings, and unlike other animals, they are capable of emotions and desires which are persuaded and therefore altered by rational argument. But since they cannot rationally plan their lives on their own, they need to attach themselves to a benevolent superior who will regularly do this for them. If natural slaves discipline

themselves so that their emotions and desires conform with their masters' correct conception of the good, they will achieve a low-grade form of virtue (1260a34–36). But even so — and this is the point I want to emphasize — Aristotle says that they can never attain *eudaimonia*, no matter how well they do within their limits (1280a33–34). Evidently, his test for *eudaimonia* is not how well one is doing, given one's limitations, but how close one comes to a perfect human life. Since the best a slave can do still falls far short of the ideal available to some, he can never be *eudaimon*. An objective theory of happiness that follows Aristotle on this point will say that a mentally retarded person can never live happily, even in the best of circumstances. Is there something wrong with this uncompromising form of objectivism?

Aristotle's inflexibility might be defended in this way: even if a slave cannot achieve *eudaimonia*, he nonetheless has every reason to try to come as near as he possibly can to that ultimate end. Certain ways of life will move him closer to this ideal and others will move him farther away, so his conception of *eudaimonia* will influence him as much as it influences those who can actually achieve it. What harm is done, then, if Aristotle's rigid standard makes the slave incapable of *eudaimonia*?

The answer is that Aristotle's inflexibility makes it difficult, if not impossible, for seriously handicapped individuals to maintain their self-esteem and vitality. On his view, only a *eudaimon* life is well lived (1095a18–20), and so slaves cannot justifiably believe that they are doing a good job of living their lives. The most favorable point they can make about their existence is that among the bad lives theirs are not the worst: quite a negative judgment about the worth of being alive. Similarly, a slave is never justified in congratulating himself on the way he is living, nor can others justifiably congratulate him. For to congratulate someone on his life is to call him *eudaimon* — and the slave is utterly distant from that end. Now, just as a dedicated singer would find it hard to live with the public recognition that he sings poorly, so a person who wants to see some good in his being alive will find it hard to do so if he and others judge that his life can never be well lived. The singer, at least, can try to change his role, but one cannot turn to some other activity besides living one's life. The slave is kept going by the biological urge for survival and can develop no justified confidence that his existence is preferable to death. Aristotle himself suggests that when we ask what *eudaimonia* is, we are asking what makes life worth living, that is, what reasons there are to choose to stay alive (*Eudemian Ethics* I 5). Since the slave has such a small sampling of those goods that make life worthwhile, he can never be *eudaimon*, and can find little reason to be glad that he is alive. Aristotle's conception of self-love (*Nicomachean Ethics* IX 4) yields the same dismal conclusion: the less virtuous one is, the less one can justifiably love oneself, and so, since the slave can at best achieve a reduced form of virtue, he is entitled to little self-regard.

I suggest that there is something inhumane about Aristotle's doctrine, and that an objective theory of happiness should depart from his lead in some way. Objectivism, as I have described it, takes happiness to be a highly valuable goal, and it urges us to be dissatisfied with our lives if they are not objectively happy. But if a person is permanently handicapped, there is no reason why we should persuade him to be unhappy with his life, distant though it may be from the ideal he might have achieved. Rather, objectivism will be a more humane doctrine if it evaluates each person's life by a standard which reflects his unalterable capacities and circumstances. What an objectivist should say is this: Happy individuals can fall far short of the ideal they might have achieved, but they must do reasonably well with whatever restrictions currently surround their lives. A person is happy only if (1) he meets the standards he has set for himself, and finds his life highly desirable; and (2) nothing he can now do would make his life significantly better.

Notice that the objectivist who takes this line must give up a claim made earlier, in Section VI. He said that we ought to call someone happy only if he is leading the kind of life we should have wished for him when he was a newborn baby. But what happens when a normal baby later receives severe physical injuries which cause some retardation? Humane objectivists would not have wished such a life upon this unfortunate person, but they will nonetheless judge him happy if he is doing his best under the circumstances. So flexible objectivists, no less than subjectivists, allow for a discrepancy between early wishes and later judgments. When they wish a baby a happy life, they mean to exclude certain events which, if they occur at a later time, do not prevent them from calling that life happy.

By tailoring each person's ideal to fit his current limitations, and thus departing from Aristotle's conception of *eudaimonia,* objectivism can be a humane outlook. But its main difficulty still remains. It requires us to judge someone happy only if his life cannot be significantly better; but we do not know how to determine this, in so many cases. Of course, all of our lives, or nearly all, could be somewhat better — but could they be significantly better? To answer this question, the objectivist will have to say what the best attainable life is for each of us, and he must provide some reasonable way of measuring our distance from this reachable ideal.

To summarize, let me turn back once more to Aristotle: his differences with us stem from the fact that he calls someone *eudaimon* only if that person comes fairly close to the ideal life for all human beings, whereas our standard of happiness is more subjective and flexible. We do not have a defensible theory about which lives are ideal, and even if we did, we would not want to judge people happy only if they come close to the best life a human being can lead. So, when Aristotle says that a slave cannot be *eudaimon,* and we say that in certain conditions he can be happy, we are not, strictly speaking, contradicting each other. He is measuring the slave's distance from the ideal for all human beings, while we are saying that the slave's life can meet his own reduced standards. But even though we are not contradicting Aristotle on this point, we still have something to argue about. He would accuse us, and we should accuse him, of measuring people's lives by an inappropriate standard.[7]

Endnotes

[1] Henry Sidgwick, *The Methods of Ethics,* 7th ed. (London, 1907), pp. 92–93.

[2] W. D. Ross, *Aristotle: A Complete Exposition of His Works and Thought,* Meridian ed. (Cleveland, 1959), p. 186. Unless otherwise noted, quotations are from the Ross translation.

[3] John Cooper, *Reason and Human Good in Aristotle* (Cambridge, MA, 1975), pp. 89–90, n. 1. Cooper says that "happiness" is not a good translation since "much that Aristotle says about *eudaimonia* manifestly fails to hold true of happiness as ordinarily understood." (Ibid.) To support this point, he calls attention to Aristotle's claim that a child can be called *eudaimon* only in the expectation that he will achieve *eudaimonia* as an adult.

[4] It would be desirable, in translating Aristotle's *eudaimonia,* to find an English expression that plays pretty much the

same role in our language that *eudaimonia* played in his. On this score, "flourishing" is quite inadequate:

A. *Eudaimon* and its cognates were everyday words that occurred frequently not only in philosophical works but also in Greek drama, oratory, and poetry. Our term "flourishing" is less common. If a student in a philosophy course were asked, "What is human flourishing?" his first reaction would be that this is a philosopher's question that has no obvious connection with ordinary life. But when Aristotle asked in his classroom what *eudaimonia* is, his audience immediately recognized this as a common and urgent practical question. (In this respect, asking "What is happiness?" is very much like asking what *eudaimonia* is.)

B. When "flourishing" is used in common speech, it is most often attached to nonhuman subjects: ant colonies, flowers, towns, businesses, etc., are much more likely to be called flourishing than human beings. *Eudaimonia*, on the other hand, is attributed only to human and divine persons. (Notice how odd it would be to say that an animal or plant is leading a happy life. Though dogs and cats can be happy, they still do not lead happy lives; the latter expression has pretty much the same range of application as *eudaimonia*.)

C. When human beings are said to flourish, it is often meant that they flourish in a certain role or activity. For ex-

ample: artists do not flourish in military dictatorships, pornographers flourish in democracies, and evil men flourish when moral standards are too lax or too strict. Roughly what is meant is that they succeed in these roles under the conditions specified. This common use of the term "flourish" is far from Aristotle's use of *eudaimonia*. When he says that an evil man cannot be *eudaimon* under any conditions, he is hardly denying that evil can flourish.

5 K. J. Dover, *Greek Popular Morality in the Time of Plato and Aristotle* (Oxford, 1974), p. 174, and n. 5.

6 This is a crucial feature of objectivism, as I conceive it. It is not the mild view that on occasion we are justified in using an objective standard, and that for the most part a subjective test of happiness is legitimate. Rather, the objectivist holds that our subjective test for happiness should never be employed.

7 I am grateful to D. Blumenfeld, C. Chastain, G. Dworkin, R. Meerbote, G. Watson, and two anonymous referees, for their comments on earlier drafts. I also profited from reading this paper to the philosophy departments at Northwestern University and the University of Wisconsin at Milwaukee.

IV.6 *Value: The View from Nowhere*

Thomas Nagel

Thomas Nagel is professor of philosophy at New York University and is the author of several works in ethics. In this essay he argues that although values are neither physical nor mental, they have an objective status in that they provide reasons for acting that are independent of anyone's personal situation. Values presume an impartial perspective — a view from nowhere. For example, the evil of pain is a reason for us to want it eliminated, even if we are not ourselves suffering. We do not need *additional* reasons for wanting it removed from the sufferer. Nagel concedes that there are no conclusive arguments in favor of his thesis that values are objective, but he contends that there are reasons to accept this thesis as the best explanation of our moral sentiments. This thesis increases in cogency indirectly as we defeat objections to it, which is what Nagel does in the latter portion of his essay.

1. Whether values can be objective depends on whether an interpretation of objectivity can be found that allows us to advance our knowledge of what to do, what to want, and what things provide reasons for and against action. Last week I argued that the physical conception of objectivity was not able to provide an understanding of the mind, but that another conception was available which allowed external understanding of at least some *aspects* of mental phenomena. A still different conception is

Reprinted with permission from *The Tanner Lectures in Human Values* (University of Utah Press, 1980).

required to make sense of the objectivity of values, for values are neither physical nor mental. And even if we find a conception, it must be applied with care. Not all values are likely to prove to be objective in any sense.

Let me say in advance that my discussion of values and reasons in this lecture will be quite general. I shall be talking largely about what determines whether something has value, or whether someone has a reason to do or want something. I shall say nothing about how we pass from the identification of values and reasons to a conclusion as to what should be *done*. That is of course what makes reasons important; but I shall just assume that values do often provide the basis for such conclusions, without trying to describe even in outline how the full process of practical reasoning works. I am concerned here only with the general question, whether values have an objective foundation at all.

In general, as I said last time, objectivity is advanced when we step back, detach from our earlier point of view toward something, and arrive at a new view of the whole that is formed by including ourselves and our earlier viewpoint in what is to be understood.

In theoretical reasoning this is done by forming a new conception of reality that includes ourselves as components. This involves an alteration, or at least an extension, of our beliefs. Whether the effort to detach will actually result in an increase of understanding depends on the creative capacity to form objective ideas which is called into action when we add ourselves to the world and start over.

In the sphere of values or practical reasoning, the problem is somewhat different. As in the theoretical case, in order to pursue objectivity we must take up a new, comprehensive viewpoint after stepping back and including our former perspective in what is to be understood. But in this case the new viewpoint will be *not* a new set of *beliefs*, but a new, or extended, set of *values*. If objectivity means anything here, it will mean that when we detach from our individual perspective and the values and reasons that seem acceptable from within it, we can sometimes arrive at a new conception which may endorse some of the original reasons but will reject some as subjective appearances and add others. This is what is usually meant by an objective, disinterested view of a practical question.

The basic step of placing ourselves and our attitudes within the world to be considered is familiar, but the form of the result — a new set of values, reasons, and motives — is different. In order to discover whether there are any objective values or reasons we must try to arrive at *normative* judgments, with *motivational content,* from an impersonal standpoint: a standpoint outside of our lives. We cannot use a *non-normative* criterion of objectivity: for *if* any values are objective, they are objective *values,* not objective anything else.

2. There are many opinions about whether what we have reason to do or want can be determined from a detached standpoint toward ourselves and the world. They range all the way from the view that objectivity has *no* place in this domain except what is inherited from the objectivity of those theoretical and factual elements that play a role in practical reasoning, to the view that objectivity applies here, but with a nihilistic result: i.e., that nothing is objectively right or wrong because objectively nothing matters. In between are many positive objectifying views which claim to get some definite results from a detached standpoint. Each of them is criticized by adherents of opposing views either for trying to force too much into a single objective framework or for according too much or too little respect to divergent subjective points of view.

Here as elsewhere there is a direct connection between the goal of objectivity and the belief in *realism.* The most basic idea of practical objectivity is arrived at by a practical analogue of the rejection of solipsism or idealism in the theoretical domain. Just as realism about the facts leads us to seek a detached point of view from which reality can be discerned and appearance corrected, so realism about values leads us to seek a detached point of view from which it will be possible to correct inclination and to discern what we really should do, or want. Practical objectivity means that practical reason can be understood and even engaged in by the objective self.

This assumption, though powerful, is not yet an ethical position. It merely marks the place which an ethical position will occupy if we can make any sense of the subject. It says that the world of reasons, including my reasons, does not exist only from my point of view. I am in a world whose properties are to a certain extent independent of what I think, and if I have reasons to act it is because the person who I am has those reasons, in virtue of his condition and circumstances. One would expect those reasons to be understandable from outside. Here as elsewhere objectivity is a form of understanding not necessarily available for all of reality. But it is reasonable at least to look for such understanding over as wide an area as possible.

3. It is important not to lose sight of the dangers of *false* objectification, which too easily elevate personal tastes and prejudices into cosmic values. But initially, at least, it is natural to look for some objective account of those reasons that appear from one's own point of view.

In fact those reasons usually present themselves with some pretensions of objectivity to begin with, just as perceptual appearances do. When two things look the same size to me, they look at least initially as if they *are* the same size. And when I want to take aspirin because it will cure my headache, I believe at least initially that this *is* a reason for me to take aspirin, that it can be recognized as a reason from outside, and that if I failed to take it into account, that would be a mistake, and others could recognize this.

The ordinary process of deliberation, aimed at finding out what I have reason to do, assumes that the question has an answer. And in difficult cases especially, deliberation is often accompanied by the belief that I may not *arrive* at that answer. I do not assume that the correct answer is just whatever will result or has resulted from consistent application of deliberative methods — even assuming perfect information about the facts. In deliberation we are trying to arrive at conclusions that are correct in virtue of something *independent* of our arriving at them. If we arrive at a conclusion, we believe that it would have been correct even if we *hadn't* arrived at it. And we can also acknowledge that we might be *wrong,* since the process of reasoning doesn't guarantee the correctness of the result. So the pursuit of an objective account of practical reasons has its basis in the realist claims of ordinary practical reasoning. In accordance with pretheoretical judgment we adopt the working hypothesis that there are reasons which may diverge from actual motivation even under conditions of perfect information — as reality can diverge from appearance — and then consider what form these reasons take. I shall say more about the general issue of realism later on. But first I want to concentrate on the process of thought by which, against a realist background, one might try to arrive at objective conclusions about reasons for action. In other words, if there really are values, how is objective knowledge of them possible?

In this inquiry no particular hypothesis occupies a privileged position, and it is certain that some of our starting points will be abandoned as we proceed. However, one condition on reasons obviously presents itself for consideration: a condition of generality. This is the condition that if something provides a reason for a particular individual to do something, then there is a general form of that reason which applies to anyone else in comparable circumstances. What counts as comparable circumstances depends on the general form of the reason. This condition is not tautological. It is a rather strong condition which may be false, or true only for some kinds of reasons. But the search for generality is a natural beginning.

4. There is more than one type of generality, and no reason to assume that a single form will apply to every kind of reason or value. In fact I think that the choice among types of generality defines some of the central issues of contemporary moral theory.

One respect in which reasons may vary is in their *breadth.* A general principle may apply to everyone but be quite specific in content, and it is an open question to what extent narrower principles of practical reasons (don't lie; develop your talents) can be subsumed under broader ones (don't hurt others; consider your long-term interests), or even at the limit under a single widest principle from which all the rest derive. Reasons may be general, in other words, without forming a unified system that always provides a method for arriving at determinate conclusions about what one should do.

A second respect in which reasons vary is in their *relativity to the agent,* the person for whom they are reasons. The distinction between reasons that are relative to the agent and reasons that are not is an extremely important one. I shall follow Derek Parfit in using the terms 'agent-relative' and 'agent-neutral' to mark this distinction. (Formerly I used the terms 'subjective' and 'objective,' but those terms are here reserved for other purposes.)

If a reason can be given a general form which does *not* include an essential reference to the person to whom it applies, it is an *agent-neutral* reason. For example, if it is a reason for *anyone* to do or want something that it would reduce the amount of wretchedness in the world, then that is an agent-neutral reason.

If on the other hand the general form of a reason *does* include an essential reference to the person to whom it applies, it is an *agent-relative* reason. For example, if it is a reason for anyone to do or want something that it would be in *his* interest, then that is an agent-relative reason. In such a case, if something were in Jones's interest but contrary to Smith's, Jones would have reason to want it to happen and Smith would have the *same* reason to want it *not* to happen. (Both agent-relative and agent-neutral reasons are objective, since both can be understood from outside the viewpoint of the individual who has them.)

A third way in which reasons may vary is in their degree of externality, or independence of the interests of sentient beings. Most of the apparent reasons that initially present themselves to us are intimately connected with interests and desires, our own or those of others, and often with experiential satisfaction. But it is conceivable that some of these interests give evidence that their objects have intrinsic value independent of the satisfaction that anyone may derive from them or of the fact that anyone wants them—independent even of the existence of beings who can take an interest in them. I shall call a reason *internal* if it depends on the existence of an interest or desire in someone, and *external* if it does not. External reasons were believed to exist by Plato, and more recently by G. E. Moore, who believed that aesthetic value provided candidates for this kind of externality.

These three types of variation cut across one another. Formally, a reason may be narrow, external, and agent-relative (don't eat pork, keep your promises), or broad, internal, and agent-relative (promote your own happiness). There may be other significant dimensions of variation. I want to concentrate on these because they locate the main controversies about what ethics is. Reasons and values that can be described in these terms provide the materials for objective judgments. If one looks at human action and its conditions from outside and considers whether some normative principles are plausible, these are the forms they will take.

The actual *acceptance* of a general normative judgment will have motivational implications, for it will commit you under some circumstances to the acceptance of reasons to want and do things *yourself*.

This is most clear when the objective judgment is that something has *agent-neutral* value. That means *anyone* has reason to want it to happen—*and that includes someone considering the world in detachment from the perspective of any particular person within it*. Such a judgment has motivational content

even before it is brought back down to the particular perspective of the individual who has accepted it objectively.

Agent-relative reasons are different. An objective judgment that some kind of thing has *agent-relative* value commits us only to believing that someone has reason to want and pursue it if it is related to him in the right way (being in *his* interest, for example). Someone who accepts this judgment is not committed to wanting it to *be the case* that people in general are influenced by such reasons. The judgment commits him to wanting something only when its implications are drawn *for the individual person he happens to be*. With regard to others, the content of the objective judgment concerns only what *they* should do or want.

I believe that judgments of both these kinds, as well as others, are evoked from us when we take up an objective standpoint. And I believe such judgments can be just as true and compelling as objective factual judgments about the real world that contains us.

5. When we take the step to objectivity in practical reasoning by detaching from our own point of view, the question we must ask ourselves is this: What reasons for action can be said to apply to people when we regard them from a standpoint detached from the values of any particular person?

The simplest answer, and one that some people would give, is "None." But that is not the only option. The suggested classification of types of generality provides a range of alternative hypotheses. It also provides some flexibility of response, for which regard to any reason that may appear to a particular individual to exist subjectively, the corresponding objective judgment may be that it does not exist at all, or that it corresponds to an agent-neutral, external value, or anything in between.

The choice among these hypotheses, plus others not yet imagined, is difficult, and there is no general method of making it any more than there is a general method of selecting the most plausible objective account of the facts on the basis of the appearances. The only 'method,' here or elsewhere, is to try to generate hypotheses and then to consider which of them seems most reasonable, in light of everything else one is fairly confident of.

This is not quite empty, for it means at least that logic alone can settle nothing. We do *not* have to be shown that the denial of some kind of objective values is *self-contradictory* in order to be reasonably led to accept their existence. There is no constraint to pick the weakest or narrowest or most economical principle consistent with the initial data that arise from individual perspectives. Our admission of reasons beyond these is determined *not* by logical entailment, but by what we cannot help believing, or at least finding most plausible among the alternatives.

In this respect it is no different from anything else: theoretical knowledge does not arise by deductive inference from the appearances either. The main difference is that our objective thinking about practical reasons is very primitive, and has difficulty taking even the first step. Philosophical skepticism and idealism about values are much more popular than their metaphysical counterparts. Nevertheless I believe they are no more correct. I shall argue that although no *single* objective principle of practical reason like egoism or utilitarianism covers everything, the acceptance of some objective values is unavoidable — not because the alternative is inconsistent but because it is not *credible*. Someone who, as in Hume's example, prefers the destruction of the whole world to the scratching of his finger, may not be involved in a *contradiction* or in any false *expectations,* but he is unreasonable nonetheless (to put it mildly), and anyone else not in the grip of an overly narrow conception of what reasoning is would regard his preference as objectively wrong.

6. But even if it is unreasonable to deny that anyone ever objectively has a reason to do anything, it is not easy to find positive objective principles that *are* reasonable. I am going to attempt to defend a few in the rest of this lecture. But I want to acknowledge in advance that it is not easy to follow the objectifying impulse without distorting individual life and personal relations. We want to be able to understand and accept the way we live from outside, but it may not always follow that we should control our lives from inside by the terms of that external understanding. Often the objective viewpoint will not be suitable as a replacement for the subjective, but will coexist with it, setting a standard with which the subjective is constrained not to clash. In deciding what to do, for example, we should not reach a result different from what we could decide objectively that that *person* should do — but we need not arrive at the result in the same way from the two standpoints.

Sometimes, also, the objective standpoint will allow us to judge how people should *be* or should live, without permitting us to translate this into a judgment about what they have *reasons* to do. For in some respects it is better to live and act not for reasons, but because we cannot help it. This is especially true of close personal relations. Here the objective standpoint cannot be brought into the perspective of *action* without destroying precisely what it affirms the value of. Nevertheless the possibility of this objective affirmation is important. We should be *able* to view our lives from outside without extreme dissociation or distaste, and the extent to which we should live without *considering* the objective point of view or even any reasons *at all* is itself *determined* largely from that point of view.

It is also possible that some idiosyncratic individual grounds of action, or the values of strange communities, will prove objectively inaccessible. To take an example in our midst: I don't think that people who want to be able to run twenty-six miles without stopping are irrational, but their reasons can be understood only from the perspective of a value system that is completely alien to me, and will I hope remain so. A correct objective view will have to allow for such pockets of unassimilable subjectivity, which need not clash with objective principles but won't be affirmed by them either. Many aspects of personal taste will come in this category, if, as I think, they cannot all be brought under a general hedonistic principle.

But the most difficult and interesting problems of accommodation appear where objectivity *can* be employed as a standard, but we have to decide *how.* Some of the problems are these: To what extent should an objective view admit *external* values? To what extent should it admit *internal* but *agent-neutral* values? To what extent should the reasons to respect the interests of *others* take an *agent-relative* form? To what extent is it legitimate for each person to give priority to his own interests? These are all questions about the proper form of generality for different kinds of practical reasoning, and the proper relation between objective principles and the deliberation of individual agents. I shall return to some of them later, but there is a great deal that I shall not get to.

I shall not, for example, discuss the question of external values, i.e., values which may be *revealed* to us by the attractiveness of certain things, but whose existence is independent of the existence of any interests or desires. I am not sure whether there are any such values, though the objectifying tendency produces a strong impulse to believe that there are, especially in aesthetics where the object of interest is external and the interest seems perpetually capable of criticism in light of further attention to the object.

What I shall discuss is the proper form of *internal* values or reasons—those which depend on interests or desires. They can be objectified in more than one way, and I believe different forms of objectification are appropriate for different cases.

7. Let me begin with a case for which I think the solution is simple: that of pleasure and pain. I am not an ethical hedonist, but I think pleasure and pain are very important, and they have a kind of neutrality that makes them fit easily into ethical thinking—unlike preferences or desires, for example, which I shall discuss later on.

I mean the kinds of pleasure and pain that do not depend on activities or desires which *themselves* raise questions of justification and value. Many pleasures and pains are just sensory experiences in relation to which we are fairly passive, but toward which we feel involuntary desire or aversion. Almost everyone takes the avoidance of his own pain and the promotion of his own pleasure as subjective reasons for action in a fairly simple way; they are not backed up by any further reasons. On the other hand if someone pursues pain or avoids pleasure, these idiosyncrasies usually *are* backed up by further reasons, like guilt or sexual masochism. The question is, what sort of general value, if any, ought to be assigned to pleasure and pain when we consider these facts from an objective standpoint?

It seems to me that the least plausible hypothesis is the zero position, that pleasure and pain have no value of any kind that can be objectively recognized. That would mean that looking at it from outside, you couldn't even say that someone had a reason not to put his hand on a hot stove. Try looking at it from the outside and see whether you can manage to withhold that judgment.

But I want to leave this position aside, because what really interests me is the choice between two other hypotheses, both of which admit that people have reason to avoid their own pain and pursue their own pleasure. They are the fairly obvious general hypotheses formed by assigning (a) agent-relative or (b) agent-neutral value to those experiences.

If the avoidance of pain has only agent-relative value, then people have reason to avoid their own pain, but not to avoid the pain of others (unless other kinds of reasons come into play). If the avoidance of pain has agent-neutral value as well, then *anyone* has a reason to want *any* pain to stop, whether or not it is his. From an objective standpoint, which of these hypotheses is more plausible? Is the value of sensory pleasure and pain agent-relative or agent-neutral?

I believe it is agent-neutral, at least in part. That is, I believe pleasure is a good thing and pain is a bad thing, and that the most reasonable objective principle which admits that each of us has reason to pursue his own pleasure and avoid his own pain will acknowledge that these are not the only reasons present. This is a normative claim. Unreasonable, as I have said, does not mean inconsistent.

In arguing for this claim, I am somewhat handicapped by the fact that I find it self-evident. It is therefore difficult for me to find something still more certain with which to back it up. But I shall try to say what is wrong with rejecting it, and with the reasons that may lie behind its rejection. What would it be to really *accept* the alternative hypothesis that pleasure and pain are not impersonally good or bad? If I accept this hypothesis, assuming at the same time that each person has reason to seek pleasure and avoid pain for *himself,* then when I regard the matter objectively the result is very peculiar. I will have to believe that I have a reason to take aspirin for a headache, but that there *is no reason* for me to *have* an aspirin. And I will have to believe the same about anyone else. From an objective standpoint I must judge that everyone has reason to pursue a type of result that is *impersonally valueless,* that has value only to *him.*

This needs to be explained. If agent-neutral reasons are not ruled out of consideration from the start (and one would need reasons for that), why do we not have evidence of them here? The avoidance of pain is not an individual project, expressing the agent's personal values. The desire to make pain stop is simply *evoked* in the person who feels it. He may decide for various reasons not to stop it, but in the first instance he doesn't have to *decide* to want it to stop: he just does. He wants it to go away because it's *bad*: it is not *made* bad by his deciding that he wants it to go away. And I believe that when we think about it objectively, concentrating on what pain is *like*, and ask ourselves whether it is (a) not bad at all, (b) bad only for its possessor, or (c) bad *period*, the third answer is the one that needs to be argued *against,* not the one that needs to be argued *for.* The philosophical problem here is to get rid of the obstacles to the admission of the obvious. But first they have to be identified.

Consider how *strange* is the question posed by someone who wants a justification for altruism about such a basic matter as this. Suppose he and some other people have been admitted to a hospital with severe burns after being rescued from a fire. "I understand how *my* pain provides *me* with a reason to take an analgesic," he says, "and I understand how my groaning neighbor's pain gives *him* a reason to take an analgesic; but how does *his* pain give *me* any reason to want him to be given an analgesic? How can *his* pain give *me* or anyone else looking at it from outside a reason?"

This question is *crazy.* As an expression of puzzlement, it has that characteristic philosophical craziness which indicates that something very fundamental has gone wrong. This shows up in the fact that the *answer* to the question is *obvious,* so obvious that to ask the question is obviously a philosophical act. The answer is that pain is *awful.* The pain of the man groaning in the next bed is just as awful as yours. That's your reason to want him to have an analgesic.

Yet to many philosophers, when they think about the matter theoretically, this answer seems not to be available. The pain of the person in the next bed is thought to need major external help before it can provide me with a reason for wanting or doing anything: otherwise it can't get its hooks into me. Since most of these people are perfectly aware of the force such considerations actually have for them, justifications of some kind are usually found. But they take the form of working *outward* from the desires and interests in the individual for whom reasons are being sought. The burden of proof is thought always to be on the claim that he has reason to care about anything that is not *already* an object of his interest.

These justifications are unnecessary. They plainly falsify the real nature of the case. My reason for wanting my neighbor's pain to cease is just that it's awful, and I know it.

8. What is responsible for this demand for justification with its special flavor of philosophical madness? I believe it is something rather deep, which doesn't surface in the ordinary course of life: an inappropriate sense of the burden of proof. Basically, we are being asked for a demonstration of the *possibility* of real impersonal values, on the assumption that they are *not* possible unless such a general proof can be given.

But I think this is wrong. We can already *conceive* of such a possibility, and once we take the step of thinking about what reality, if any, there is in the domain of practical reason, it becomes a possibility we are bound to consider, that we cannot help considering. If there really are *reasons,* not just motivational pushes and pulls, and if agent-neutral reasons are among the kinds we can conceive of, then it becomes an obvious possibility that physical pain is simply bad: that even from an impersonal standpoint there is reason to want it to stop. When we view the matter objectively, this is one of the general positions that naturally suggests itself.

And once this is seen as a *possibility,* it becomes difficult *not* to accept it. It becomes a hypothesis that has to be *dislodged* by anyone who wishes to claim, for example, that all reasons are agent-relative. The question is, what are the alternatives, once we take up the objective standpoint? We must think *something.* If there is room in the realistic conception of reasons for agent-neutral values, then it is unnatural *not* to ascribe agent-neutral badness to burn pains. That is the natural conclusion from the fact that anyone who has a burn pain and is therefore closest to it wants acutely to be rid of it, and requires no indoctrination or training to want this. This evidence does not *entail* that burn pains are impersonally bad. It is logically conceivable that there is nothing bad about them at all, or that they provide only agent-relative reasons to their possessors to want them to go away. But to take such hypotheses seriously we would need justifications of a kind that seem totally unavailable in this case.

What could possibly show us that acute physical pain, which everyone finds horrible, is in reality not impersonally bad at all, so that except from the point of view of the sufferer it doesn't in itself matter? Only a very remarkable and farfetched picture of the value of a cosmic order beyond our immediate grasp, in which pain played an essential part which made it good or at least neutral — or else a demonstration that there can *be* no agent-neutral values. But I take it that neither of these is available: the first because the Problem of Evil has not been solved, the second because the absence of a logical demonstration that there *are* agent-neutral values is not a demonstration that there are *not* agent-neutral values.

My position is this. No demonstration is necessary in order to allow us to *consider* the possibility of agent-neutral reasons: the possibility simply *occurs* to us once we take up an objective stance. And there is no mystery about how an individual could have a reason to want something independently of its relation to his particular interests or point of view, because beings like ourselves are not *limited* to the particular point of view that goes with their personal position inside the world. They are also, as I have put it earlier, *objective selves*; they cannot *help* forming an objective conception of the world with themselves in it; they cannot help trying to arrive at judgments of *value* from that standpoint; they cannot help asking whether, from that standpoint, in abstraction from who in the world they are, they have any reason to want anything to be the case or not — any reason to want anything to happen or not.

Agent-neutral reasons do not have to find a miraculous source in our personal lives, because we are not *merely* personal beings: we are also importantly and essentially viewers of the world *from nowhere within it* — and in this capacity we remain open to judgments of value, both general and particular. The possibility of agent-neutral values is evident as soon as we begin to think from this standpoint about the reality of any reasons whatever. If we acknowledge the possibility of realism, then we cannot rule out agent-neutral values in advance.

Realism is therefore the fundamental issue. If there really are values and reasons, then it should be possible to expand our understanding of them by objective investigation, and there is no reason to rule out the natural and compelling objective judgment that pain is impersonally bad and pleasure impersonally good. So let me turn now to the abstract issue of realism about values.

9. Like the presumption that things exist in an external world, the presumption that there are real values and reasons can be defeated in individual cases, if a purely subjective account of the appearances is more plausible. And like the presumption of an external world, its complete falsity is not self-contradictory. The reality of values, agent-neutral or otherwise, is not *entailed* by the totality of appearances any more than the reality of a physical universe is. But if either of them is recognized as a possibility, then its reality in detail can be confirmed by appearances, at least to the extent of being rendered more plausible than the alternatives. So a lot depends on whether the possibility of realism is admitted in the first place.

It is very difficult to argue for such a possibility. Sometimes there will be arguments against it, which one can try to refute. Berkeley's argument against the conceivability of a world independent of experience is an example. But what is the result when such an argument is refuted? Is the possibility in a stronger position? I believe so: in general, there is no way to prove the possibility of realism; one can only refute impossibility arguments, and the more often one does this the more confidence one may have in the realist alternative. So to consider the merits of an admission of realism about value, we have to consider the reasons against it. I shall discuss three. They have been picked for their apparent capacity to convince people.

The first argument depends on the question-begging assumption that if values are real, they must be real objects of some other kind. John Mackie, for example, in his recent book *Ethics,* denies the objectivity of values by saying that they are not part of the fabric of the world, and that if they were, they would have to be "entities or qualities or relations of a very strange sort, utterly different from anything else in the universe."[1] Apparently he has a very definite picture of what the universe is like, and assumes that realism about value would require crowding it with extra entities, qualities, or relations — things like Platonic Forms or Moore's non-natural qualities. But this assumption is not correct. The impersonal badness of pain is not some mysterious further property that all pains have, but just the fact that there is reason for anyone capable of viewing the world objectively to want it to *stop,* whether it is his or someone else's. The view that values are real is not the view that they are real occult entities or properties, but that they are real *values*: that our claims about value and about what people have reason to do may be *true* or *false* independently of our beliefs and inclinations. No *other* kinds of truths are involved. Indeed, no other kinds of truths *could* imply the reality of values.[2]

The second argument I want to consider is not, like the first, based on a misinterpretation of moral objectivity. Instead, it tries to represent the unreality of values as an objective *discovery*. The argument is that if claims of value have to be objectively correct or incorrect, and if they are not reducible to any *other* kind of objective claim, then we can just *see* that all positive value claims must be false. Nothing has any objective value, because objectively nothing matters at all. If we push the claims of objective detachment to their logical conclusion, and survey the world from a standpoint completely detached from all interests, we discover that there is *nothing* — no values left of any kind: things can be said to matter at all only to individuals within the world. The result is objective nihilism.

I don't deny that the objective standpoint tempts one in this direction. But I believe this can seem like the required conclusion only if one makes the mistake of assuming that objective judgments of value must emerge from the detached standpoint *alone*. It is true that with nothing to go on but a conception of the world from nowhere, one would have no way of telling whether anything had value. But an objective view has more to go on, for its data include the appearance of value to individuals with particular perspectives, including oneself. In this respect practical reason is no different from anything else. Starting from a pure idea of a possible reality and a very impure set of appearances, we try to fill in the idea of reality so as to make some partial sense of the appearances, using objectivity as a method. To find out what the world is like from outside we have to approach it from within: it is no wonder that the same is true for ethics. And indeed, when we take up the objective standpoint, the problem is not that values seem to disappear but that there seem to be too many of them, coming from every life and drowning out those that arise from our own. It is just as easy to form desires from an objective standpoint as it is to form beliefs. Probably easier. Like beliefs, these desires and evaluations must be criticized and justified partly in *terms* of the appearances. But they are not just further appearances, any more than the beliefs about the world which arise

from an impersonal standpoint are just further appearances.

The third type of argument against the objective reality of values is an empirical argument. It is also perhaps the most common. It is intended not to rule out the possibility of real values from the start, but rather to demonstrate that even if their *possibility* is admitted, we have no reason to believe that there are any. The claim is that if we consider the wide cultural variation in normative beliefs, the importance of social pressure and other psychological influences to their formation, and the difficulty of settling moral disagreements, it becomes highly implausible that they are anything but pure appearances.

Anyone offering this argument must admit that not every psychological factor in the explanation of an appearance shows that the appearance corresponds to nothing real. Visual capacities and elaborate training play a part in explaining the physicist's perception of a cloud-chamber track, or a student's coming to believe a proposition of geometry, but the path of the particle and the truth of the proposition also play an essential part in these explanations. So far as I know, no one has produced a general account of the kinds of psychological explanation that discredit an appearance. But some skeptics about ethics feel that because of the way we acquire moral beliefs and other impressions of value, there are grounds for confidence that no real, objective values play a part in the explanation.

I find the popularity of this argument surprising. The fact that morality is socially inculcated and that there is radical disagreement about it across cultures, over time, and even within cultures at a time is a poor reason to conclude that values have no objective reality. Even where there is truth, it is not always easy to discover. Other areas of knowledge are taught by social pressure, many truths as well as falsehoods are believed without rational grounds, and there is wide disagreement about scientific and social facts, especially where strong interests are involved which will be affected by different answers to a disputed question. This last factor is present throughout ethics to a uniquely high degree: it is an area in which one would expect extreme variation of belief and radical disagreement however objectively real the subject actually was. For comparably motivated disagreements about matters of fact, one has to go to the heliocentric theory, the theory of evolution, the Dreyfus case, the Hiss case, and the genetic contribution to racial differences in I.Q.

Although the methods of ethical reasoning are rather primitive, the degree to which agreement can be achieved and social prejudices transcended in the face of strong pressures suggests that something real is being investigated, and that part of the explanation of the appearances, both at simple and at complex levels, is that we perceive, often inaccurately, that certain reasons for action exist, and go on to infer, often erroneously, the general form of the principles that best accounts for those reasons.

The controlling conception that supports these efforts at understanding, in ethics as in science, is realism, or the possibility of realism. Without being sure that we will find one, we look for an account of what reasons there really are, an account that can be objectively understood.

I have not discussed all the possible arguments against realism about values, but I have tried to give general reasons for skepticism about such argu-ments. It seems to me that they tend to be supported by a narrow preconception of what there *is*, and that this is essentially question-begging.

Endnotes

[1] J. L. Mackie, *Ethics* (Harmondsworth, Middlesex: Penguin Books, 1977), p. 38.

[2] In discussion, Mackie claimed that I had misrepresented him, and that his disbelief in the reality of values and reasons does not depend on the assumption that to be real they must be strange *entities* or *properties*. As he says in his book, it applies directly to reasons themselves. For whatever they are they are not needed to explain anything that happens, and there is consequently no reason to believe in their existence. But I would reply that this raises the same issue. It begs the question to assume that *explanatory* necessity is the test of reality in this area. The claim that certain reasons exist is a normative claim, not a claim about the best explanation of anything. To assume that only what has to be included in the best explanatory picture of the world is real, is to assume that there are no irreducibly normative truths.

There is much more to be said on both sides of this issue, and I hope I have not misrepresented Mackie in this short note.

Suggestions for Further Reading

Baier, Kurt, and Nicholas Rescher, eds. *Values and the Future.* Macmillan, 1969.

Bond, E. J. *Reason and Value.* Cambridge University Press, 1983.

Brandt, Richard B. *A Theory of the Good and the Right.* Oxford University Press, 1979.

Nagel, Thomas. *The View from Nowhere.* Oxford University Press, 1986.

Nietzsche, Friedrich. *Beyond Good and Evil,* tr. Walter Kaufmann. Random House, 1966.

Perry, Ralph B. *Realms of Value.* Harvard University Press, 1954.

Rescher, Nicholas. *Introduction to Value Theory.* Prentice-Hall, 1982.

Ross, W. D. *The Right and the Good.* Oxford University Press, 1930.

Taylor, Paul. *Principles of Ethics.* Wadsworth, 1975.

Taylor, Richard. *Good and Evil.* Macmillan, 1970.

Wiggens, David. "Truth, Invention and the Meaning of Life," *Proceedings of the British Academy,* 62, 1976.

Part V

Utilitarianism

"The Greatest Happiness for the Greatest Number"

FRANCIS HUTCHESON
Inquiry Concerning Moral Good and Evil

"If we possess our *why* of life we can put up with almost any *how* — man
does not strive after happiness; only the Englishman does that."

FRIEDRICH NIETZSCHE
Twilight of the Idols

Traditionally, two major types of ethical systems have dominated the field: one in which the locus of value is the act or kind of act, the other in which the locus of value is the outcome or consequence of the act. The former type of theory is called *deontological* (from the Greek *deon,* which means 'duty'), and the latter is called *teleological* (from the Greek *telos,* which means 'end' or 'goal'). Whereas in teleological systems the ultimate criterion of morality lies in some nonmoral value that results from acts, in deontological systems certain features in the act itself have intrinsic value. For example, a teleologist would judge whether lying was morally right or wrong by the consequences it produced, but a deontologist would see something intrinsically wrong in the very act of lying. In this section we shall consider teleological ethical theories, and in Part VI we shall study deontological theories.

In order to get to the heart of these types of theories, let us begin with a frequently used example. Suppose there is a raft floating in the Pacific Ocean. On the raft are two men who are starving to death. One day they discover some food in an inner compartment of a box on the raft. They have reason to believe that the food will be sufficient to keep one of them alive until the raft reaches a certain island where help is available but that if they share the food both will most likely die. Now one of these men is a brilliant scientist who has in his mind the cure for cancer. The other man is undistinguished. Otherwise there is no relevant difference between the two men. What is the morally right thing to do? Share the food and hope against the odds for a miracle? Flip a coin in order to see which man gets the food? Give the food to the scientist?

If you voted to flip a coin or share the food, your perspective is deontological; but if you voted to give the food to the scientist, then your perspective is teleological, or utilitarian, for you calculated that there would be greater good accomplished if the scientist got the food and survived than in any of the other likely outcomes.

The standard for right or wrong action for the teleologist involves the comparative consequences of the available actions: That act is right which produces the best consequences. Whereas the deontologist is concerned only with the rightness of the act itself, the teleologist asserts that there is no such thing as an act that has intrinsic worth. The deontologist contends that there is something intrinsically bad about lying, but for the teleologist the only thing wrong with lying is the bad consequences it produces. Under a teleological point of view, if one can reasonably calculate that a lie will do even slightly more good than telling the truth, one has an obligation to lie.

We have already examined one type of teleological ethics: ethical egoism, the view that the act that produces the greatest amount of good for the agent is the right act. Egoism is teleological ethics narrowed to the viewpoint of the agent. Utilitarianism, on the other hand, is a universal teleological system that calls for the maximization of goodness in society, or, put another way, the greatest goodness for the greatest number.

There are two main features of utilitarianism: the consequentialist principle (its teleological aspect) and the utility principle (its hedonic aspect). The consequentialist principle states that the rightness or wrongness of an act is determined by the results that flow from it. The utility principle states that the only thing that is good in itself is some specific type of state (for example, pleasure, happiness, welfare, fulfillment). Hedonistic utilitarianism views pleasure as the sole good and pain as the only evil. To quote the English philosopher Jeremy Bentham (1748–1832), the first to systematize classical utilitarianism, "Nature has placed mankind under the governance of two sovereign masters, pain and pleasure. It is for them alone to point out what we ought to do, as well as what we shall do."

Bentham's philosophy has often been criticized for being too simplistic. Pleasure seems either too sensuous or too ambiguous a notion. In fact, in his own day Bentham's version was referred to as the pig philosophy because a pig enjoying its life would constitute a higher moral state than a slightly dissatisfied person. For this reason John Stuart Mill (1806–1873) sought to distinguish happiness from mere sensual pleasure: "A being of higher faculties requires more to make him happy, is capable probably of more acute suffering, and is certainly accessible to it at more points, than one of an inferior type," but still he is qualitatively better off than the person without these higher faculties. Mill contended, "It is better to be a human being dissatisfied than a pig satisfied; better to be Socrates dissatisfied than a fool satisfied." Mill's version of utilitarianism has been called *eudaimonistic utilitarianism* (from the Greek *eudaimonia,* which means 'happiness') in order to distinguish it from Bentham's hedonistic utilitarianism.

A third version of utilitarianism, known as *agathistic* (from the Greek *agathos,* meaning 'good') or *ideal utilitarianism,* was set forth by G. E. Moore and is discussed in Part VI.2 by

W. D. Ross. Ideal utilitarianism says that it is not simply pleasure or happiness that constitutes the proper end state, but a plurality of values, such as knowledge, freedom, justice, and others.

Utilitarians can be divided into two types: act utilitarians and rule utilitarians. In applying the principle of utility, act utilitarians say that we ought ideally to apply the principle to all of the alternatives open to us at any given moment. Of course, we cannot do this for each possible act, for often we must act spontaneously and quickly. So rules of thumb (for example, in general don't lie, generally keep your promises) are of practical importance. However, the right act is still that alternative that will result in the most utility.

Rule utilitarians, on the other hand, state that an act is right if it conforms to a valid rule within a system of rules that, if followed, will result in the best possible state of affairs (or the least bad state of affairs, if it is a question of all the alternatives being bad). The rule utilitarian resembles the rule deontologist (a deontologist who holds that we ought always to act according to principle rather than according to our intuition at the moment; to be discussed in Part VI) in that both emphasize the importance of following specific principles that are public and universal. The difference between them is that the deontologist sees the principles as having intrinsic value, whereas the utilitarian sees the principles as having only instrumental value. Nonetheless, it is arguable that they could have identical principles for different reasons.

An oft-debated question in ethics is whether or not rule utilitarianism is a consistent version of utilitarianism. Briefly summarized, the argument that rule utilitarianism is an inconsistent version, which must either become a deontological system or transform itself into act utilitarianism, goes like this. Imagine that the set of general rules of a rule utilitarian system yields 100 hedons (positive utility units). We could always find a case in which breaking the general rule would result in additional hedons without decreasing

the sum of the whole. So we could imagine breaking the general rule "Never lie" in order to spare someone's feelings and so create more utility (for example, 102 hedons) than would have otherwise existed. Do you think that this is a good argument?

Whether John Stuart Mill was a rule utilitarian or an act utilitarian is a subject of keen debate. He doesn't seem to have noticed the difference, and aspects of both theories seem present in his work. Our second reading, Kai Nielsen's "Against Moral Conservatism," is a clearer example of act utilitarianism. Nielsen defines moral conservatism as "a normative ethical theory which maintains that there is a privileged moral principle or cluster of moral principles, prescribing determinate actions, with which it would always be wrong not to act in accordance no matter what the consequences." For Nielsen, no rules are sacrosanct, but different situations call forth different actions, and potentially any rule could be overridden (though in fact we may need to treat some as absolutes for the good of society).

Nielsen's argument in favor of utilitarianism makes strong use of the notion of negative responsibility. That is, we are not only responsible for the consequences of our actions but we are also responsible for the consequences of our nonactions. Suppose that you are the driver of a streetcar and suddenly you discover that your brakes have failed. You are just about to run over five workmen on the track ahead of you. However, if you quickly turn the steering wheel you will cause the trolley to turn onto a sidetrack where only one man is working. What should you do?

One who makes a strong distinction between active and passive evil (allowing versus doing evil) would argue that you should do nothing and merely allow the trolley to kill the five men, but one who denies that this is an absolute distinction would prescribe that you do something positive in order to minimize evil. Negative responsibility means that you are going to be responsible for someone's death in either case. Doing the right thing, the utilitarian urges us, means minimizing the amount of evil. So we should actively cause the one to die in order to save the five.

Many would agree that in this case we ought to kill one in order to save five, but sometimes our intuitions work the other way. Suppose you are a doctor and have five needy patients, all of whom are in danger of dying unless you obtain suitable organs within the day. One patient needs a heart transplant, two need kidneys, another needs a lung, and still another needs a liver. A hermit who has no family walks into the hospital for a routine checkup. By killing him and using his organs for the five you could save five persons and restore them to health. If you don't kill the hermit, are you negatively responsible for the death of the five patients? What is the difference, if any, between these two cases?

In our third reading, "Against Utilitarianism," Bernard Williams argues that utilitarianism violates personal integrity by commanding that we violate those principles that are central and deepest in our lives: "How can a man, as a utilitarian agent, come to regard as one satisfaction among others, and a dispensable one, a project or attitude round which he has built his life, just because someone else's projects have so structured the causal scene that that is how the utilitarian sum comes out?" His conclusion is that utilitarianism leads to personal alienation, and so is deeply flawed.

In our fourth reading, "Alienation, Consequentialism, and the Demands of Morality," Peter Railton addresses Williams's conclusion and argues that some alienation may be necessary for the moral life, but the utilitarian (even the act utilitarian whom he is defending here) can take this into account in devising strategies of action. Railton's article is a fine example of sophisticated utilitarianism, wherein such items as character and motivation are woven into a utilitarian account of ethics.

In our fifth reading, "Moral Side Constraints," Robert Nozick argues from the perspective of a Kantian and one supporting libertarian rights. Under no circumstances may we violate another person's rights for the "social" good. "There is no *social entity* with a good that undergoes some sacrifice for its own sake. There are only individual people," he says, with individual goods. In our sixth article, "Utilitarianism and the Virtues," Philippa Foot asks why utilitarianism haunts even those of us who do not believe in it. We feel there is something right about it, although we also feel there is something radically wrong with it. She identifies our attraction with the idea that it can never be right to prefer a worse state to a better one. But what is wrong with utilitarianism? It is its *consequentialism,* which focuses on a total outcome from an impersonal perspective, aiming to maximize happiness or some good state of affairs. Utilitarianism is the most prominent form of consequentialism. Other forms of consequentialism might be perfectionism or aestheticism (the maximization of some aesthetic good). Foot argues that there are no better and worse states of affairs, as the consequentialist contends. We can speak of "good states of affairs" in an agent-relative sense but not with regard to an overall moral perspective, when, for example, they are outcomes of unjust acts.

In our final essay, Samuel Scheffler takes issue with Nozick and Foot on the issue of consequentialism. The puzzle: How can it be rational to prohibit an action "that would have the effect of minimizing the total number of comparably objectionable actions that were performed and would have no other morally relevant consequences?" Scheffler examines Foot's argument and offers several objections to it, contending that she has failed to remove the fundamental paradox from deontological ethical systems.

Let us turn to our readings.

V.1 *Utilitarianism*

JOHN STUART MILL

John Stuart Mill (1806–1873), one of the most important British philosophers of the nineteenth century, made significant contributions to logic, philosophy of science, political theory, and ethics. His essay here contains most of Chapters I, II, IV, and V of his book *Utilitarianism,* which is generally considered the authoritative essay on classical utilitarianism. It was written against the background of keen debate over Jeremy Bentham's hedonistic utilitarianism and represents an attempt to rebut critics who dismissed utilitarianism as a pig philosophy (because of Bentham's emphasis on pleasure). In response to these critics, in Chapter II Mill modifies Bentham's theory by substituting happiness for pleasure. More precisely, Mill argues that there are different qualities of pleasure and that the cultural and the intellectual are superior to the sensual. This version is called *eudaimonistic utilitarianism.* In Chapter IV Mill attempts to prove that utilitarianism is the correct moral theory, and in Chapter V he answers objections that utilitarianism is at odds with the principle of justice.

Chapter I
General Remarks

There are few circumstances among those which make up the present condition of human knowledge, more unlike what might have been expected, or more significant of the backward state in which speculation on the most important subjects still lingers, than the little progress which has been made in the decision of the controversy respecting the criterion of right and wrong. From the dawn of philosophy, the question concerning the *summum bonum,* or, what is the same thing, concerning the foundation of morality, has been accounted the main problem in speculative thought, has occupied the most gifted intellects, and divided them into sects and schools, carrying on a vigorous warfare against one another. And after more than two thousand years the same discussions continue, philosophers are still ranged under the same contending banners, and neither thinkers nor mankind at large seem nearer to being unanimous on the subject, than when the youth Socrates listened to the old Protagoras, and asserted (if Plato's dialogue be grounded on a real conversation) the theory of utilitarianism against the popular morality of the so-called sophist.

It is true that similar confusion and uncertainty, and in some cases similar discordance, exist respecting the first principles of all the sciences, not excepting that which is deemed the most certain of them, mathematics; without much impairing, generally indeed without impairing at all, the trustworthiness of the conclusions of those sciences. An apparent anomaly, the explanation of which is, that the detailed doctrines of a science are not usually deduced from, nor depend for their evidence upon, what are called its first principles. Were it not so, there would be no science more precarious, or whose conclusions were more insufficiently made out, than algebra; which derives none of its certainty from what are commonly taught to learners as its elements, since these, as laid down by some of its most eminent teachers, are as full of fictions as English law, and of mysteries as theology. The truths which are ultimately accepted as the first principles of a science, are really the last results of metaphysical analysis, practised on the elementary notions with which

Reprinted from *Utilitarianism* (1863).

the science is conversant; and their relation to the science is not that of foundations to an edifice, but of roots to a tree, which may perform their office equally well though they be never dug down to and exposed to light. But though in science the particular truths precede the general theory, the contrary might be expected to be the case with a practical art, such as morals or legislation. All action is for the sake of some end, and rules of action, it seems natural to suppose, must take their whole character and colour from the end to which they are subservient. When we engage in a pursuit, a clear and precise conception of what we are pursuing would seem to be the first thing we need, instead of the last we are to look forward to. A test of right and wrong must be the means, one would think, of ascertaining what is right or wrong, and not a consequence of having already ascertained it.

The difficulty is not avoided by having recourse to the popular theory of a natural faculty, a sense or instinct, informing us of right and wrong. For — besides that the existence of such a moral instinct is itself one of the matters in dispute — those believers in it who have any pretensions to philosophy, have been obliged to abandon the idea that it discerns what is right or wrong in the particular case in hand, as our other senses discern the sight or sound actually present. Our moral faculty, according to all those of its interpreters who are entitled to the name of thinkers, supplies us only with the general principles of moral judgments; it is a branch of our reason, not of our sensitive faculty; and must be looked to for the abstract doctrines of morality, not for perception of it in the concrete. The intuitive, no less than what may be termed the inductive, school of ethics, insists on the necessity of general laws. They both agree that the morality of an individual action is not a question of direct perception, but of the application of a law to an individual case. They recognise also, to a great extent, the same moral laws; but differ as to their evidence, and the source from which they derive their authority. According to the one opinion, the principles of morals are evident *à priori,* requiring nothing to command assent, except that the meaning of the terms be understood. According to the other doctrine, right and wrong, as well as truth and falsehood, are questions of observation and experience. But both hold equally that morality must be deduced from principles; and the intuitive school affirm as strongly as the inductive,

that there is a science of morals. Yet they seldom attempt to make out a list of the *à priori* principles which are to serve as the premises of the science; still more rarely do they make any effort to reduce those various principles to one first principle, or common ground of obligation. They either assume the ordinary precepts of morals as of *à priori* authority, or they lay down as the common groundwork of those maxims, some generality much less obviously authoritative than the maxims themselves, and which has never succeeded in gaining popular acceptance. Yet to support their pretensions there ought either to be some one fundamental principle or law, at the root of all morality, or if there be several, there should be a determinate order of precedence among them; and the one principle, or the rule for deciding between the various principles when they conflict, ought to be self-evident.

To inquire how far the bad effects of this deficiency have been mitigated in practice, or to what extent the moral beliefs of mankind have been vitiated or made uncertain by the absence of any distinct recognition of an ultimate standard, would imply a complete survey and criticism of past and present ethical doctrine. It would, however, be easy to show that whatever steadiness or consistency these moral beliefs have attained, has been mainly due to the tacit influence of a standard not recognised. Although the non-existence of an acknowledged first principle has made ethics not so much a guide as a consecration of men's actual sentiments, still, as men's sentiments, both of favour and of aversion, are greatly influenced by what they suppose to be the effects of things upon their happiness, the principle of utility, or as Bentham latterly called it, the greatest happiness principle, has had a large share in forming the moral doctrines even of those who most scornfully reject its authority. Nor is there any school of thought which refuses to admit that the influence of actions on happiness is a most material and even predominant consideration in many of the details of morals, however unwilling to acknowledge it as the fundamental principle of morality, and the source of moral obligation. I might go much further, and say that to all those *à priori* moralists who deem it necessary to argue at all, utilitarian arguments are indispensable. It is not my present purpose to criticize these thinkers; but I cannot help referring, for illustration, to a systematic treatise by one of the most illustrious of them, the *Metaphysics of Ethics,* by Kant. This remarkable man, whose system of thought will long remain one of the landmarks in the history of philosophical speculation, does, in the treatise in question, lay down an universal first principle as the origin and ground of moral obligation; it is this: — 'So act, that the rule on which thou actest would admit of being adopted as a law by all rational beings.' But when he begins to deduce from this precept any of the actual duties of morality, he fails, almost grotesquely, to show that there would be any contradiction, any logical (not to say physical) impossibility, in the adoption by all rational beings of the most outrageously immoral rules of conduct. All he shows is that the *consequences* of their universal adoption would be such as no one would choose to incur.

On the present occasion, I shall, without further discussion of the other theories, attempt to contribute something towards the understanding and appreciation of the Utilitarian or Happiness theory, and towards such proof as it is susceptible of. It is evident that this cannot be proof in the ordinary and popular meaning of the term. Questions of ultimate ends are not amenable to direct proof. Whatever can be proved to be good, must be so by being shown to be a means to something admitted to be good without proof. The medical art is proved to be good, by its conducing to health; but how is it possible to prove that health is good? The art of music is good, for the reason, among others, that it produces pleasure; but what proof is it possible to give that pleasure is good? If, then, it is asserted that there is a comprehensive formula, including all things which are in themselves good, and that whatever else is good, is not so as an end, but as a mean, the formula may be accepted or rejected, but it is not a subject of what is commonly understood by proof. We are not, however, to infer that its acceptance or rejection must depend on blind impulse, or arbitrary choice. There is a larger meaning of the word proof, in which this question is as amenable to it as any other of the disputed questions of philosophy. The subject is within the cognizance of the rational faculty; and neither does that faculty deal with it solely in the way of intuition. Considerations may be presented capable of determining the intellect either to give or withhold its assent to the doctrine; and this is equivalent to proof.

We shall examine presently of what nature are these considerations; in what manner they apply to the case, and what rational grounds, therefore, can be given for accepting or rejecting the utilitarian formula. But it is a preliminary condition of rational acceptance or rejection, that the formula should be correctly understood. I believe that the very imperfect notion ordinarily formed of its meaning, is the chief obstacle which impedes its reception; and that could it be cleared, even from only the grosser misconceptions, the question would be greatly simplified, and a large proportion of its difficulties removed. Before, therefore, I attempt to enter into the philosophical grounds which can be given for assenting to the utilitarian standard, I shall offer some illustrations of the doctrine itself, with the view of showing more clearly what it is, distinguishing it from what it is not, and disposing of such of the practical objections to it as either originate in, or as closely connected with, mistaken interpretations of its meaning. Having thus prepared the ground, I shall afterwards endeavour to throw such light as I can upon the question, considered as one of philosophical theory.

Chapter II
What Utilitarianism Is

A passing remark is all that needs be given to the ignorant blunder of supposing that those who stand up for utility as the test of right and wrong, used the term in that restricted and merely colloquial sense in which utility is opposed to pleasure. An apology is due to the philosophical opponents of utilitarianism, for even the momentary appearance of confounding them with any one capable of so absurd a misconception; which is the more extraordinary, inasmuch as the contrary accusation, of referring everything to pleasure, and that too in its grossest form, is another of the common charges against utilitarianism: and, as has been pointedly remarked by an able writer, the same sort of persons, and often the very same persons, denounce the theory 'as impracticably dry when the word utility precedes the word pleasure, and as too practically voluptuous when the word pleasure precedes the word utility.' Those who know anything about the matter are aware that every writer, from Epicurus to Bentham, who maintained the theory of utility, meant by it, not something to be contra-distinguished from pleasure, but pleasure itself, together with exemption from pain; and instead of opposing the useful to the agreeable or the ornamental, have always declared that the useful means these, among other things. Yet the common herd, including the herd of writers, not only in newspapers and periodicals, but in books of weight and pretension, are perpetually falling into this shallow mistake. Having caught up the word utilitarian, while knowing nothing whatever about it but its sound, they habitually express by it the rejection, or the neglect, of pleasure in some of its forms; of beauty, of ornament, or of amusement. Nor is the term thus ignorantly misapplied solely in disparagement, but occasionally in compliment; as though it implied superiority to frivolity and the mere pleasures of the moment. And this perverted use is the only one in which the word is popularly known, and the one from which the new generation are acquiring their sole notion of its meaning. Those who introduced the word, but who had for many years discontinued it as a distinctive appellation, may well feel themselves called upon to resume it, if by doing so they can hope to contribute anything towards rescuing it from this utter degradation.

The creed which accepts as the foundation of morals, Utility, or the Greatest Happiness Principle, holds that actions are right in proportion as they tend to promote happiness, wrong as they tend to produce the reverse of happiness. By happiness is intended pleasure, and the absence of pain; by unhappiness, pain, and the privation of pleasure. To give a clear view of the moral standard set up by the theory, much more requires to be said; in particular, what things it includes in the ideas of pain and pleasure; and to what extent this is left an open question. But these supplementary explanations do not affect the theory of life on which this theory of morality is grounded—namely, that pleasure, and freedom from pain, are the only things desirable as ends; and that all desirable things (which are as numerous in the utilitarian as in any other scheme) are desirable either for the pleasure inherent in themselves, or as means to the promotion of pleasure and the prevention of pain.

Now, such a theory of life excites in many minds, and among them in some of the most estimable in feeling and purpose, inveterate dislike. To suppose that life has (as they express it) no higher end than pleasure—no better and nobler object of desire and pursuit—they designate as utterly mean and grovelling; as a doctrine worthy only of swine, to whom the followers of Epicurus were, at a very early period, contemptuously likened; and modern holders of the doctrine are occasionally made the subject of equally polite comparisons by its German, French, and English assailants.

When thus attacked, the Epicureans have always answered, that it is not they, but their accusers, who represent human nature in a degrading light; since the accusation supposes human beings to be capable of no pleasures except those of which swine are capable. If this supposition were true, the charge could not be gainsaid, but would then be no longer an imputation; for if the sources of pleasure were precisely the same to human beings and to swine, the rule of life which is good enough for the one would be good enough for the other. The comparison of the Epicurean life to that of beasts is felt as degrading, precisely because a beast's pleasures do not satisfy a human being's conceptions of happiness. Human beings have faculties more elevated than the animal appetites, and when once made conscious of them, do not regard anything as happiness which does not include their gratification. I do not, indeed, consider the Epicureans to have been by any means faultless in drawing out their scheme of consequences from the utilitarian principle. To do this in any sufficient manner, many Stoic, as well as Christian elements require to be included. But there is no known Epicurean theory of life which does not assign to the pleasures of the intellect, of the feelings and imagination, and of the moral sentiments, a much higher value as pleasures than to those of mere sensation. It must be admitted, however, that utilitarian writers in general have placed the superiority of mental over bodily pleasures chiefly in the greater permanency, safety, uncostliness, &c., of the former—that is, in their circumstantial advantages rather than in their intrinsic nature. And on all these points utilitarians have fully proved their case; but they might have taken the other, and, as it may be called, higher ground, with entire consistency. It is quite compatible with the principle of utility to recognise the fact, that some *kinds* of pleasure are more desirable and more valuable than others. It would be absurd that while, in estimating all other things, quality is considered as well as quantity, the estimation of pleasures should be supposed to depend on quantity alone.

If I am asked, what I mean by difference of quality in pleasures, or what makes one pleasure more valuable than another, merely as a pleasure, except its being greater in amount, there is but one possible answer. Of two pleasures, if there be one to which all or almost all who have experience of both give a decided preference, irrespective of any feeling of moral obligation to prefer it, that is the more desirable pleasure. If one of the two is, by those who are competently acquainted with both, placed so far above the other that they prefer it, even though knowing it to be attended with a greater amount of discontent, and would not resign it for any quantity of the other pleasure which their nature is capable of, we are justified in ascribing to the preferred enjoyment a superiority in quality, so far outweighing quantity as to render it, in comparison, of small account.

Now it is an unquestionable fact that those who are equally acquainted with, and equally capable of appreciating and enjoying, both, do give a most marked preference to the manner of existence which employs their higher faculties. Few human creatures would consent to be changed into any of the lower animals, for a promise of the fullest allowance of a beast's pleasures; no intelligent human being would consent to be a fool, no instructed person would be an ignoramus, no person of feeling and conscience would be selfish and base, even though they should be persuaded that the fool, the dunce, or the rascal is better satisfied with his lot than they are with theirs. They would not resign what they possess more than he, for the most complete satisfaction of all the desires which they have in common with him. If they ever fancy they would, it is only in cases of unhappiness so extreme, that to escape from it they would exchange their lot for almost any other, however undesirable in their own eyes. A being of higher faculties requires more to make him happy, is capable probably of more acute suffering, and is certainly accessible to it at more points, than one of an inferior type; but in spite of these liabilities, he can never really wish to sink into what he feels to be a lower grade of existence. We may give what explanation we please of this unwillingness; we may attribute it to pride, a name which is given indiscriminately to some of the most and to some of the least estimable feelings for which mankind are capa-

ble; we may refer it to the love of liberty and personal independence, an appeal to which was with the Stoics one of the most effective means for the inculcation of it; to the love of power, or to the love of excitement, both of which do really enter into and contribute to it; but its most appropriate appellation is a sense of dignity, which all human beings possess in one form or other, and in some, though by no means in exact, proportion to their higher faculties, and which is so essential a part of the happiness of those in whom it is strong, that nothing which conflicts with it could be, otherwise than momentarily, an object of desire to them. Whoever supposes that this preference takes place at a sacrifice of happiness — that the superior being, in anything like the equal circumstances, is not happier than the inferior — confounds the two very different ideas, of happiness, and content. It is indisputable that the being whose capacities of enjoyment are low, has the greatest chance of having them fully satisfied; and a highly-endowed being will always feel that any happiness which he can look for, as the world is constituted, is imperfect. But he can learn to bear its imperfections, if they are at all bearable; and they will not make him envy the being who is indeed unconscious of the imperfections, but only because he feels not at all the good which those imperfections qualify. It is better to be a human being dissatisfied than a pig satisfied; better to be Socrates dissatisfied than a fool satisfied. And if the fool, or the pig, is of a different opinion, it is because they only know their own side of the question. The other party to the comparison knows both sides.

It may be objected, that many who are capable of the higher pleasures, occasionally, under the influence of temptation, postpone them to the lower. But this is quite compatible with a full appreciation of the intrinsic superiority of the higher. Men often, from infirmity of character, make their election for the nearer good, though they know it to be the less valuable; and this no less when the choice is between two bodily pleasures, than when it is between bodily and mental. They pursue sensual indulgences to the injury of health, though perfectly aware that health is the greater good. It may be further objected, that many who begin with youthful enthusiasm for everything noble, as they advance in years sink into indolence and selfishness. But I do not believe that those who undergo this very common change, voluntarily choose the lower description of pleasures in preference to the higher. I believe that before they devote themselves exclusively to the one, they have already become incapable of the other. Capacity for the nobler feelings is in most natures a very tender plant, easily killed, not only by hostile influences, but by mere want of sustenance; and in the majority of young persons it speedily dies away if the occupations to which their position in life has devoted them, and the society into which it has thrown them, are not favourable to keeping that higher capacity in exercise. Men lose their high aspirations as they lose their intellectual tastes, because they have not time or opportunity for indulging them; and they addict themselves to inferior pleasures, not because they deliberately prefer them, but because they are either the only ones to which they have access, or the only ones which they are any longer capable of enjoying. It may be questioned whether any one who has remained equally susceptible to both classes of pleasures, ever knowingly and calmly preferred the lower; though many, in all ages, have broken down in an ineffectual attempt to combine both.

From this verdict of the only competent judges, I apprehend there can be no appeal. On a question which is the best worth having of two pleasures, or which of two modes of existence is the most grateful to the feelings, apart from its moral attributes and from its consequences, the judgment of those who are qualified by knowledge of both, or, if they differ, that of the majority among them, must be admitted as final. And there needs be the less hesitation to accept this judgment respecting the quality of pleasures, since there is no other tribunal to be referred to even on the question of quantity. What means are there of determining which is the acutest of two pains, or the intensest of two pleasurable sensations, except the general suffrage of those who are familiar with both? Neither pains nor pleasures are homogeneous, and pain is always heterogeneous with pleasure. What is there to decide whether a particular pleasure is worth purchasing at the cost of a particular pain, except the feelings and judgment of the experienced? When, therefore, those feelings and judgment declare the pleasures derived from the higher faculties to be preferable *in kind,* apart from the question of intensity, to those of which the animal nature, disjoined from the higher faculties, is susceptible, they are entitled on this subject to the same regard.

I have dwelt on this point, as being a necessary part of a perfectly just conception of Utility or Happiness, considered as the directive rule of human conduct. But it is by no means an indispensable condition to the acceptance of the utilitarian standard; for that standard is not the agent's own greatest happiness, but the greatest amount of happiness altogether; and if it may possibly be doubted whether a noble character is always the happier for its nobleness, there can be no doubt that it makes other people happier, and that the world in general is immensely a gainer by it. Utilitarianism, therefore, could only attain its end by the general cultivation of nobleness of character, even if each individual were only benefited by the nobleness of others, and his own, so far as happiness is concerned, were a sheer deduction from the benefit. But the bare enunciation of such an absurdity as this last, renders refutation superfluous.

According to the Greatest Happiness Principle, as above explained, the ultimate end, with reference to and for the sake of which all other things are desirable (whether we are considering our own good or that of other people), is an existence exempt as far as possible from pain, and as rich as possible in enjoyments, both in point of quantity and quality; the test of quality, and the rule for measuring it against quantity, being the preference felt by those who, in their opportunities of experience, to which must be added their habits of self-consciousness and self-observation, are best furnished with the means of comparison. This, being, according to the utilitarian opinion, the end of human action, is necessarily also the standard of morality; which may accordingly be defined, the rules and precepts for human conduct, by the observance of which an existence such as has been described might be, to the greatest extent possible, secured to all mankind; and not to them only, but, so far as the nature of things admits, to the whole sentient creation.

Against this doctrine, however, arises another class of objectors, who say that happiness, in any form, cannot be the rational purpose of human life and action; because, in the first place, it is unattainable: and they contemptuously ask, What right hast thou to be happy? a question which Mr. Carlyle clenches by the addition, What right, a short time ago, hadst thou even *to be?* Next, they say, that men can do *without* happiness; that all noble human beings have felt this, and could not have become noble but by learning the lesson of Entsagen, or renunciation; which lesson, thoroughly learnt and submitted to, they affirm to be the beginning and necessary condition of all virtue.

The first of these objections would go to the root of the matter were it well founded; for if no happiness is to be had at all by human beings, the attainment of it cannot be the end of morality, or of any rational conduct. Though, even in that case, something might still be said for the utilitarian theory; since utility includes not solely the pursuit of happiness, but the prevention of mitigation of unhappiness; and if the former aim be chimerical, there will be all the greater scope and more imperative need for the latter, so long at least as mankind think fit to live, and do not take refuge in the simultaneous act of suicide recommended under certain conditions by Novalis. When, however, it is thus positively asserted to be impossible that human life should be happy, the assertion, if not something like a verbal quibble, is at least an exaggeration. If by happiness be meant a continuity of highly pleasurable excitement, it is evident enough that this is impossible. A state of exalted pleasure lasts only moments, or in some cases, and with some intermissions, hours or days, and is the occasional brilliant flash of enjoyment, not its permanent and steady flame. Of this the philosophers who have taught that happiness is the end of life were as fully aware as those who taunt them. The happiness which they meant was not a life of rapture; but moments of such, in an existence made up of few and transitory pains, many and various pleasures, with a decided predominance of the active over the passive, and having as the foundation of the whole, not to expect more from life than it is capable of bestowing. A life thus composed, to those who have been fortunate enough to obtain it, has always appeared worthy of the name of happiness. And such an existence is even now the lot of many, during some considerable portion of their lives. The present wretched education, and wretched social arrangements, are the only real hindrance to its being attainable by almost all.

. . . All the grand sources, in short, of human suffering are in a great degree, many of them almost entirely, conquerable by human care and effort; and though their removal is grievously slow — though a long succession of generations will perish in the breach before the conquest is completed, and this

world becomes all that if will and knowledge were not wanting, it might easily be made — yet every mind sufficiently intelligent and generous to bear a part, however small and unconspicuous, in the endeavour, will draw a noble enjoyment from the contest itself, which he would not for any bribe in the form of selfish indulgence consent to be without.

And this leads to the true estimation of what is said by the objectors concerning the possibility, and the obligation, of learning to do without happiness. Unquestionably it is possible to do without happiness; it is done involuntarily by nineteen-twentieths of mankind, even in those parts of our present world which are least deep in barbarism; and it often has to be done voluntarily by the hero or the martyr, for the sake of something which he prizes more than his individual happiness. But this something, what is it, unless the happiness of others, or some of the requisites of happiness? It is noble to be capable of resigning entirely one's own portion of happiness, or chances of it: but, after all, this self-sacrifice must be for some end; it is not its own end; and if we are told that its end is not happiness, but virtue, which is better than happiness, I ask, would the sacrifice be made if the hero or martyr did not believe that it would earn for others immunity from similar sacrifices? Would it be made, if he thought that his renunciation of happiness for himself would produce no fruit for any of his fellow creatures, but to make their lot like his, and place them also in the condition of persons who have renounced happiness? All honour to those who can abnegate for themselves the personal enjoyment of life, when by such renunciation they contribute worthily to increase the amount of happiness in the world; but he who does it, or professes to do it, for any other purpose, is no more deserving of admiration than the ascetic mounted on his pillar. He may be an inspiriting proof of what men *can* do, but assuredly not an example of what they *should*.

Though it is only in a very imperfect state of the world's arrangements that any one can best serve the happiness of others by the absolute sacrifice of his own, yet so long as the world is in that imperfect state, I fully acknowledge that the readiness to make such a sacrifice is the highest virtue which can be found in man. I will add, that in this condition of the world, paradoxical as the assertion may be, the conscious ability to do without happiness gives the best prospect of realizing such happiness as is attainable. For nothing except that consciousness can raise a person above the chances of life, by making him feel that, let fate and fortune do their worst, they have not power to subdue him: which, once felt, frees him from excess of anxiety concerning the evils of life, and enables him, like many a Stoic in the worst times of the Roman Empire, to cultivate in tranquillity the sources of satisfaction accessible to him, without concerning himself about the uncertainty of their duration, any more than about their inevitable end.

Meanwhile, let utilitarians never cease to claim the morality of self-devotion as a possession which belongs by as good a right to them, as either to the Stoic or to the Transcendentalist. The utilitarian morality does recognise in human beings the power of sacrificing their own greatest good for the good of others. It only refuses to admit that the sacrifice is itself a good. A sacrifice which does not increase, or tend to increase, the sum total of happiness, it considers as wasted. The only self-renunciation which it applauds, is devotion to the happiness, or to some of the means of happiness, of others; either of mankind collectively, or of individuals within the limits imposed by the collective interests of mankind.

I must again repeat, what the assailants of utilitarianism seldom have the justice to acknowledge, that the happiness which forms the utilitarian standard of what is right in conduct, is not the agent's own happiness, but that of all concerned. As between his own happiness and that of others, utilitarianism requires him to be as strictly impartial as a disinterested and benevolent spectator. In the golden rule of Jesus of Nazareth, we read the complete spirit of the ethics of utility. To do as one would be done by, and to love one's neighbour as oneself, constitute the ideal perfection of utilitarian morality. As the means of making the nearest approach to this ideal, utility would enjoin, first, that laws and social arrangements should place the happiness, or (as speaking practically it may be called) the interest, of every individual, as nearly as possible in harmony with the interest of the whole; and secondly, that education and opinion, which have so vast a power over human character, should so use that power as to establish in the mind of every individual an indissoluble association between his own happiness and the good of the whole; especially between his own happiness and the practice of such modes of conduct, negative and positive, as regard

for the universal happiness prescribes: so that not only he may be unable to conceive the possibility of happiness to himself, consistently with conduct opposed to the general good, but also that a direct impulse to promote the general good may be in every individual one of the habitual motives of action, and the sentiments connected therewith may fill a large and prominent place in every human being's sentient existence. If the impugners of the utilitarian morality represented it to their own minds in this its true character, I know not what recommendation possessed by any other morality they could possibly affirm to be wanting to it: what more beautiful or more exalted developments of human nature any other ethical system can be supposed to foster, or what springs of action, not accessible to the utilitarian, such systems rely on for giving effect to their mandates.

The objectors to utilitarianism cannot always be charged with representing it in a discreditable light. On the contrary, those among them who entertain anything like a just idea of its disinterested character, sometimes find fault with its standard as being too high for humanity. They say it is exacting too much to require that people shall always act from the inducement of promoting the general interests of society. But this is to mistake the very meaning of a standard of morals, and to confound the rule of action with the motive of it. It is the business of ethics to tell us what are our duties, or by what test we may know them; but no system of ethics requires that the sole motive of all we do shall be a feeling of duty; on the contrary, ninety-nine hundredths of all our actions are done from other motives, and rightly so done, if the rule of duty does not condemn them. It is the more unjust to utilitarianism that this particular misapprehension should be made a ground of objection to it, inasmuch as utilitarian moralists have gone beyond almost all others in affirming that the motive has nothing to do with the morality of the action, though much with the worth of the agent. He who saves a fellow creature from drowning does what is morally right, whether his motive be duty, or the hope of being paid for his trouble: he who betrays the friend that trusts him, is guilty of a crime, even if his object be to serve another friend to whom he is under greater obligations.[1] But to speak only of actions done from the motive of duty, and in direct obedience to principle: it is a misapprehension of the utilitarian mode of thought, to conceive it as implying that people should fix their minds upon so wide a generality as the world, or society at large. The great majority of good actions are intended, not for the benefit of the world, but for that of individuals, of which the good of the world is made up; and the thoughts of the most virtuous man need not on these occasions travel beyond the particular persons concerned, except so far as is necessary to assure himself that in benefiting them he is not violating the rights — that is, the legitimate and authorized expectations — of any one else. The multiplication of happiness is, according to the utilitarian ethics, the object of virtue: the occasions on which any person (except one in a thousand) has it in his power to do this on an extended scale, in other words, to be a public benefactor, are but exceptional; and on these occasions alone is he called on to consider public utility; in every other case, private utility, the interest or happiness of some few persons, is all he has to attend to. Those alone the influence of whose actions extends to society in general, need concern themselves habitually about so large an object. In the case of abstinences indeed — of things which people forbear to do, from moral considerations, though the consequences in the particular case might be beneficial — it would be unworthy of an intelligent agent not to be consciously aware that the action is of a class which, if practised generally, would be generally injurious, and that this is the ground of the obligation to abstain from it. The amount of regard for the public interest implied in this recognition, is no greater than is demanded by every system of morals; for they all enjoin to abstain from whatever is manifestly pernicious to society.

Again, Utility is often summarily stigmatized as an immoral doctrine by giving it the name of Expediency, and taking advantage of the popular use of that term to contrast it with Principle. But the Expedient, in the sense in which it is opposed to the Right, generally means that which is expedient for the particular interest of the agent himself; as when a minister sacrifices the interest of his country to keep himself in place. When it means anything better than this, it means that which is expedient for some immediate object, some temporary purpose, but which violates a rule whose observance is expedient in a much higher degree. The Expedient, in this sense, instead of being the same thing with the

useful, is a branch of the hurtful. Thus, it would often be expedient for the purpose of getting over some momentary embarrassment, or attaining some object immediately useful to ourselves or others, to tell a lie. But inasmuch as the cultivation in ourselves of a sensitive feeling on the subject of veracity, is one of the most useful, and the enfeeblement of that feeling one of the most hurtful, things to which our conduct can be instrumental; and inasmuch as any, even unintentional, deviation from truth, does that much towards weakening the trustworthiness of human assertion, which is not only the principal support of all present social well-being, but the insufficiency of which does more than any one thing that can be named to keep back civilization, virtue, everything on which human happiness on the largest scale depends; we feel that the violation, for a present advantage, of a rule of such transcendant expediency, is not expedient, and that he who, for the sake of a convenience to himself or to some other individual, does what depends on him to deprive mankind of the good, and inflict upon them the evil, involved in the greater or less reliance which they can place in each other's word, acts the part of one of their worst enemies. Yet that even this rule, sacred as it is, admits of possible exceptions, is acknowledged by all moralists; the chief of which is when the withholding of some fact (as of information from a malefactor, or of bad news from a person dangerously ill) would preserve some one (especially a person other than one-self) from great and unmerited evil, and when the withholding can only be effected by denial. But in order that the exception may not extend itself beyond the need, and may have the least possible effect in weakening reliance on veracity, it ought to be recognised, and, if possible, its limits defined; and if the principle of utility is good for anything, it must be good for weighing these conflicting utilities against one another, and marking out the region within which one or the other preponderates.

Again, defenders of utility often find themselves called upon to reply to such objections as this — that there is not time, previous to action, for calculating and weighing the effects of any line of conduct on the general happiness. This is exactly as if any one were to say that it is impossible to guide our conduct by Christianity, because there is not time, on every occasion on which anything has to be done, to read through the Old and New Testaments. The answer to the objection is, that there has been ample time, namely, the whole past duration of the human species. During all that time mankind have been learning by experience the tendencies of actions; on which experience all the prudence, as well as all the morality of life, is dependent. People talk as if the commencement of this course of experience had hitherto been put off, and as if, at the moment when some man feels tempted to meddle with the property or life of another, he had to begin considering for the first time whether murder and theft are injurious to human happiness. Even then I do not think that he would find the question very puzzling; but, at all events, the matter is now done to his hand. It is truly a whimsical supposition that if mankind were agreed in considering utility to be the test of morality, they would remain without any agreement as to what *is* useful, and would take no measures for having their notions on the subject taught to the young, and enforced by law and opinion. There is no difficulty in proving any ethical standard whatever to work ill, if we suppose universal idiocy to be conjoined with it, but on any hypothesis short of that, mankind must by this time have acquired positive beliefs as to the effects of some actions on their happiness; and the beliefs which have thus come down are the rules of morality for the multitude, and for the philosopher until he has succeeded in finding better. That philosophers might easily do this, even now, on many subjects; that the received code of ethics is by no means of divine right; and that mankind have still much to learn as to the effects of actions on the general happiness, I admit, or rather, earnestly maintain. The corollaries from the principle of utility, like the precepts of every practical art, admit of indefinite improvement, and, in a progressive state of the human mind, their improvement is perpetually going on. But to consider the rules of morality as improvable, is one thing; to pass over the intermediate generalizations entirely, and endeavour to test each individual action directly by the first principle, is another. It is a strange notion that the acknowledgment of a first principle is inconsistent with the admission of secondary ones. To inform a traveller respecting the place of his ultimate destination, is not to forbid the use of landmarks and direction-posts on the way. The proposition that happiness is the end and aim of morality, does not mean that no road ought to be laid down to that goal, or that persons going thither should not be advised to take one direction rather than another. Men really ought to leave off talking a kind of nonsense on this subject, which they would neither talk nor listen to in other matters of practical concernment. Nobody argues that the art of navigation is not founded on astronomy, because sailors cannot wait to calculate the Nautical Almanack. Being rational creatures, they go to sea with it ready calculated; and all rational creatures go out upon the sea of life with their minds made up on the common questions of right and wrong, as well as on many of the far more difficult questions of wise and foolish. And this, as long as foresight is a human quality, it is to be presumed they will continue to do. Whatever we adopt as the fundamental principle of morality, we require subordinate principles to apply it by: the impossibility of doing without them, being common to all systems, can afford no argument against any one in particular: but gravely to argue as if no such secondary principles could be had, and as if mankind had remained till now, and always must remain, without drawing any general conclusions from the experience of human life, is as high a pitch, I think, as absurdity has ever reached in philosophical controversy.

The remainder of the stock arguments against utilitarianism mostly consist in laying to its charge the common infirmities of human nature, and the general difficulties which embarrass conscientious persons in shaping their course through life. We are told that an utilitarian will be apt to make his own particular case an exception to moral rules, and, when under temptation, will see an utility in the breach of a rule, greater than he will see in its observance. But is utility the only creed which is able to furnish us with excuses for evil doing, and means of cheating our own conscience? They are afforded in abundance by all doctrines which recognise as a fact in morals the existence of conflicting considerations; which all doctrines do, that have been believed by sane persons. It is not the fault of any creed, but of the complicated nature of human affairs, that rules of conduct cannot be so framed as to require no exceptions, and that hardly any kind of action can safely be laid down as either always obligatory or always condemnable. There is no ethical creed which does not temper the rigidity of its laws, by giving a certain latitude, under the moral responsibility of the agent, for accommodation to peculiarities of circumstances; and under every creed, at the opening thus made, self-deception and dishonest casuistry get in. There exists no moral system under which there do not arise unequivocal cases of conflicting obligation. These are the real difficulties, the knotty points both in the theory of ethics, and in the conscientious guidance of personal conduct. They are overcome practically with greater or with less success according to the intellect and virtue of the individual; but it can hardly be pretended that any one will be the less qualified for dealing with them, from possessing an ultimate standard to which conflicting rights and duties can be referred. If utility is the ultimate source of moral obligations, utility may be invoked to decide between them when their demands are incompatible. Though the application of the standard may be difficult, it is better than none at all: while in other systems, the moral laws all claiming independent authority, there is no common umpire entitled to interfere between them; their claims to precedence one over another rest on little better than sophistry, and unless determined, as they generally are, by the unacknowledged influence of considerations of utility, afford a free scope for the action of personal desires and partialities. We must remember that only in these cases of conflict between secondary principles is it requisite that first principles should be appealed to. There is no case of moral obligation in which some secondary principle is not involved; and if only one, there can seldom be any real doubt which one it is, in the mind of any person by whom the principle itself is recognised.

Chapter IV
Of What Sort of Proof the Principle of Utility Is Susceptible

It has already been remarked, that questions of ultimate ends do not admit of proof, in the ordinary acceptation of the term. To be incapable of proof by reasoning is common to all first principles; to the first premises of our knowledge, as well as to those of our conduct. But the former, being matters of fact, may be the subject of a direct appeal to the faculties which judge of fact—namely, our senses, and our internal consciousness. Can an appeal be made to the same faculties on questions of practical ends? Or by what other faculty is cognizance taken of them?

Questions about ends are, in other words, questions what things are desirable. The utilitarian doctrine is, that happiness is desirable, and the only thing desirable, as an end; all other things being only desirable as means to that end. What ought to be required of this doctrine—what conditions is it requisite that the doctrine should fulfil—to make good its claim to be believed?

The only proof capable of being given that an object is visible, is that people actually see it. The only proof that a sound is audible, is that people hear it: and so of the other sources of our experience. In like manner, I apprehend, the sole evidence it is possible to produce that anything is desirable, is that people do actually desire it. If the end which the utilitarian doctrine proposes to itself were not, in theory and in practice, acknowledged to be an end, nothing could ever convince any person that it was so. No reason can be given why the general happiness is desirable, except that each person, so far as he believes it to be attainable, desires his own happiness. This, however, being a fact, we have not only all the proof which the case admits of, but all which it is possible to require, that happiness is a good: that each person's happiness is a good to that person, and the general happiness, therefore, a good to the aggregate of all persons. Happiness has made out its title as *one* of the ends of conduct, and consequently one of the criteria of morality.

But it has not, by this alone, proved itself to be the sole criterion. To do that, it would seem, by the same rule, necessary to show, not only that people desire happiness, but that they never desire anything else. Now it is palpable that they do desire things which, in common language, are decidedly distinguished from happiness. They desire, for example, virtue, and the absence of vice, no less really than pleasure and the absence of pain. The desire of virtue is not as universal, but it is as authentic a fact, as the desire of happiness. And hence the opponents of the utilitarian standard deem that they have a right to infer that there are other ends of human action besides happiness, and that happiness is not the standard of approbation and disapprobation.

But does the utilitarian doctrine deny that people desire virtue, or maintain that virtue is not a thing to be desired? The very reverse. It maintains not only that virtue is to be desired, but that it is to be desired disinterestedly, for itself. Whatever may be the opinion of utilitarian moralists as to the original conditions by which virtue is made virtue; however they may believe (as they do) that actions and dispositions are only virtuous because they promote another end than virtue; yet this being granted, and it having been decided, from considerations of this description, what *is* virtuous, they not only place virtue at the very head of the things which are good as means to the ultimate end, but they also recognise as a psychological fact the possibility of its being, to the individual, a good in itself, without looking to any end beyond it; and hold, that the mind is not in a right state, not in a state conformable to Utility, not in the state most conducive to the general happiness, unless it does love virtue in this manner — as a thing desirable in itself, even although, in the individual instance, it should not produce those other desirable consequences which it tends to produce, and on account of which it is held to be virtue. This opinion is not, in the smallest degree, a departure from the Happiness principle. The ingredients of happiness are very various, and each of them is desirable in itself, and not merely when considered as swelling an aggregate. The principle of utility does not mean that any given pleasure, as music, for instance, or any given exemption from pain, as for example health, are to be looked upon as a means to a collective something termed happiness, and to be desired on that account. They are desired and desirable in and for themselves; besides being means, they are a part of the end. Virtue, according to the utilitarian doctrine, is not naturally and originally part of the end, but it is capable of becoming so; and in those who love it disinterestedly it has become so, and is desired and cherished, not as a means to happiness, but as a part of their happiness.

To illustrate this farther, we may remember that virtue is not the only thing, originally a means, and which if it were not a means to anything else, would be and remain indifferent, but which by association with what it is a means to, comes to be desired for itself, and that too with the utmost intensity. What, for example, shall we say of the love of money? There is nothing originally more desirable about money than about any heap of glittering pebbles. Its worth is solely that of the things which it will buy; the desires for other things than itself, which it is a means of gratifying. Yet the love of money is not only one of the strongest moving forces of human life, but money is, in many cases, desired in and for itself; the desire to possess it is often stronger than the desire to use it, and goes on increasing when all the desires which point to ends beyond it, to be encompassed by it, are falling off. It may be then said truly, that money is desired not for the sake of an end, but as part of the end. From being a means to happiness, it has come to be itself a principal ingredient of the individual's conception of happiness. The same may be said of the majority of the great objects of human life — power, for example, or fame; except that to each of these there is a certain amount of immediate pleasure annexed, which has at least the semblance of being naturally inherent in them; a thing which cannot be said of money. Still, however, the strongest natural attraction, both of power and of fame, is the immense aid they give to the attainment of our other wishes; and it is the strong association thus generated between them and all our objects of desire, which gives to the direct desire of them the intensity it often assumes, so as in some characters to surpass in strength all other desires. In these cases the means have become a part of the end, and a more important part of it than any of the things which they are means to. What was once desired as an instrument for the attainment of happiness, has come to be desired for its own sake. In being desired for its own sake it is, however, desired as *part* of happiness. The person is made, or thinks he would be made, happy by its mere possession; and is made unhappy by failure to obtain it. The desire of it is not a different thing from the desire of happiness, any more than the love of music, or the desire of health. They are included in happiness. They are some of the elements of which the desire of happiness is made up. Happiness is not an abstract idea, but a concrete whole; and these are some of its parts. And the utilitarian standard sanctions and approves their being so. Life would be a poor thing, very ill provided with sources of happiness, if there were not this provision of nature, by which things originally indifferent, but conducive to, or otherwise associated with, the satisfaction of our primitive desires, become in themselves sources of pleasure more valuable than the primitive pleasures, both in permanency, in the space of human existence than they are capable of covering, and even in intensity.

Virtue, according to the utilitarian conception, is a good of this description. There was no original desire of it, or motive to it, save its conduciveness to pleasure, and especially to protection from pain. But through the association thus formed, it may be felt a good in itself, and desired as such with as great intensity as any other good; and with this difference between it and the love of money, of power, or of fame, that all of these may, and often do, render the individual noxious to the other members of the society to which he belongs, whereas there is nothing which makes him so much a blessing to them as the cultivation of the disinterested love of virtue. And consequently, the utilitarian standard, which it tolerates and approves those other acquired desires, up to the point beyond which they would be more injurious to the general happiness than promotive of it, enjoins and requires the cultivation of the love of virtue up to the greatest strength possible, as being above all things important to the general happiness.

It results from the preceding considerations, that there is in reality nothing desired except happiness. Whatever is desired otherwise than as a means to some end beyond itself, and ultimately to happiness, is desired as itself a part of happiness, and is not desired for itself until it has become so. Those who desire virtue for its own sake, desire it either because the consciousness of it is a pleasure, or because the consciousness of being without it is a pain, or for both reasons united; as in truth the pleasure and pain seldom exist separately, but almost always together, the same person feeling pleasure in the degree of virtue attained, and pain in not having attained more. If one of these gave him no pleasure, and the other no pain, he would not love or desire virtue, or would desire it only for the other benefits which it might produce to himself or to persons whom he cared for.

We have now, then, an answer to the question, of what sort of proof the principle of utility is susceptible. If the opinion which I have now stated is psychologically true — if human nature is so constituted as to desire nothing which is not either a part of happiness or a means of happiness, we can have no other proof, and we require no other, that these are the only things desirable. If so, happiness is the sole end of human action, and the promotion of it the test by which to judge of all human conduct; from whence it necessarily follows that it must be the criterion of morality, since a part is included in the whole.

And now to decide whether this is really so; whether mankind do desire nothing for itself but that which is a pleasure to them, or of which the absence is a pain; we have evidently arrived at a question of fact and experience, dependent, like all similar questions, upon evidence. It can only be determined by practised self-consciousness and self-observation, assisted by observation of others. I believe that these sources of evidence, impartially consulted, will declare that desiring a thing and finding it pleasant, aversion to it and thinking of it as painful, are phenomena entirely inseparable, or rather two parts of the same phenomenon; in strictness of language, two different modes of naming the same psychological fact: that to think of an object as desirable (unless for the sake of its consequences), and to think of it as pleasant, are one and the same thing; and that to desire anything, except in proportion as the idea of it is pleasant, is a physical and metaphysical impossibility.

So obvious does this appear to me, that I expect it will hardly be disputed: and the objection made will be, not that desire can possibly be directed to anything ultimately except pleasure and exemption from pain, but that the will is a different thing from desire; that a person of confirmed virtue, or any other person whose purposes are fixed, carries out his purposes without any thought of the pleasure he has in contemplating them, or expects to derive from their fulfilment; and persists in acting on them, even though these pleasures are much diminished, by changes in his character or decay of his passive sensibilities, or are outweighed by the pains which the pursuit of the purposes may bring upon him. All this I fully admit, and have stated it elsewhere, as positively and emphatically as any one. Will, the active phenomenon, is a different thing from desire, the state of passive sensibility, and though originally an offshoot from it, may in time take root and detach itself from the parent stock; so much so, that in the case of an habitual purpose, instead of willing the thing because we desire it, we often desire it only because we will it. This, however, is but an instance of that familiar fact, the power of habit, and is nowise confined to the case of virtuous actions. Many indifferent things, which men originally did from a motive of some sort, they continue to do from habit. Sometimes this is done unconsciously, the consciousness coming only after the action: at other times with conscious volition, but volition which has become habitual, and is put into operation by the force of habit, in opposition perhaps to the deliberate preference, as often happens with those who have contracted habits of vicious or hurtful indulgence. Third and last comes the case in which the habitual act of will in the individual instance is not in contradiction to the general intention prevailing at other times, but in fulfilment of it; as in the case of the person of confirmed virtue, and of all who pursue deliberately and consistently any determinate end. The distinction between will and desire thus understood, is an authentic and highly important psychological fact; but the fact consists solely in this — that will, like all other parts of our constitution, is amenable to habit, and that we may will from habit what we no longer desire for itself, or desire only because we will it. It is not the less true that will, in the beginning, is entirely produced by desire; including in that term the repelling influence of pain as well as the attractive one of pleasure. Let us take into consideration, no longer the person who has a confirmed will to do right, but him in whom that virtuous will is still feeble, conquerable by temptation, and not to be fully relied on; by what means can it be strengthened? How can the will to be virtuous, where it does not exist in sufficient force, be implanted or awakened? Only by making the person *desire* virtue — by making him think of it in a pleasurable light, or of its absence in a painful one. It is by associating the doing right with pleasure, or the doing wrong with pain, or by eliciting and impressing and bringing home to the person's experience the pleasure naturally involved in the one or the pain in the other, that it is possible to call forth that will to be virtuous, which, when confirmed, acts without any thought of either pleasure or pain. Will is the child of desire, and passes out of the dominion of its parent only to come under that of habit. That which is the result of habit affords no presumption of being intrinsically good; and there would be no reason for wishing that the purpose of virtue should become independent of pleasure and pain, were it not that the influence of the pleasurable and painful associations which prompt to virtue is not sufficiently to be depended on for unerring constancy of action until it has acquired the support of habit. Both in feeling and in conduct, habit is the only thing which imparts certainty; and it is because of the importance to others of being able to rely absolutely on one's feelings and conduct,

and to oneself of being able to rely on one's own, that the will to do right ought to be cultivated into this habitual independence. In other words, this state of the will is a means to good, not intrinsically a good; and does not contradict the doctrine that nothing is a good to human beings but in so far as it is either itself pleasurable, or a means of attaining pleasure or averting pain.

But if this doctrine be true, the principle of utility is proved. Whether it is so or not, must now be left to the consideration of the thoughtful reader.

Chapter V
On the Connexion Between Justice and Utility

In all ages of speculation, one of the strongest obstacles to the reception of the doctrine that Utility or Happiness is the criterion of right and wrong, has been drawn from the idea of Justice. The powerful sentiment, and apparently clear perception, which that word recalls with a rapidity and certainty resembling an instinct, have seemed to the majority of thinkers to point to an inherent quality in things; to show that the Just must have an existence in Nature as something absolute — generically distinct from every variety of the Expedient, and, in idea, opposed to it, though (as is commonly acknowledged) never, in the long run, disjoined from it in fact.

In the case of this, as of our other moral sentiments, there is no necessary connexion between the question of its origin, and that of its binding force. That a feeling is bestowed on us by Nature, does not necessarily legitimate all its promptings. The feeling of justice might be a peculiar instinct, and might yet require, like our other instincts, to be controlled and enlightened by a higher reason. It we have intellectual instincts, leading us to judge in a particular way, as well as animal instincts that prompt us to act in a particular way, there is no necessity that the former should be more infallible in their sphere than the latter in theirs: it may as well happen that wrong judgments are occasionally suggested by those, as wrong actions by these. But though it is one thing to believe that we have natural feelings of justice, and another to acknowledge them as an ultimate criterion of conduct, these two opinions are very closely connected in point of fact. Mankind are always predisposed to believe that any subjective feeling, not otherwise accounted for, is a revelation of some objective reality. Our present object is to determine whether the reality, to which the feeling of justice corresponds, is one which needs any such special revelation; whether the justice or injustice of an action is a thing intrinsically peculiar, and distinct from all its other qualities, or only a combination of certain of those qualities, presented under a peculiar aspect. For the purpose of this inquiry, it is practically important to consider whether the feeling itself, of justice and injustice, is *sui generis* like our sensations of colour and taste, or a derivative feeling, formed by a combination of others. And this it is the more essential to examine, as people are in general willing enough to allow, that objectively the dictates of justice coincide with a part of the field of General Expediency; but inasmuch as the subjective mental feeling of Justice is different from that which commonly attaches to simple expediency, and, except in extreme cases of the latter, is far more imperative in its demands, people find it difficult to see, in Justice, only a particular kind or branch of general utility, and think that its superior binding force requires a totally different origin.

To throw light upon this question, it is necessary to attempt to ascertain what is the distinguishing character of justice, or of injustice: what is the quality, or whether there is any quality, attributed in common to modes of conduct designated as unjust (for justice, like many other moral attributes, is best defined by its opposite), and distinguishing them from such modes of conduct as are disapproved, but without having that particular epithet of disapprobation applied to them. If, in everything which men are accustomed to characterize as just or unjust, some one common attribute or collection of attributes is always present, we may judge whether this particular attribute or combination of attributes would be capable of gathering round it a sentiment of that peculiar character and intensity by virtue of the general laws of our emotional constitution, or whether the sentiment is inexplicable, and requires to be regarded as a special provision of Nature. If we find the former to be the case, we shall, in resolving this question, have resolved also the main problem: if the latter, we shall have to seek for some other mode of investigating it.

To find the common attributes of a variety of objects, it is necessary to begin by surveying the objects themselves in the concrete. Let us therefore advert successively to the various modes of action, and arrangements of human affairs, which are classed, by universal or widely spread opinion, as Just or as Unjust. The things well known to excite the sentiments associated with those names, are of a very multifarious character. I shall pass them rapidly in review, without studying any particular arrangement.

In the first place, it is mostly considered unjust to deprive any one of his personal liberty, his property, or any other thing which belongs to him by law. Here, therefore, is one instance of the application of the terms just and unjust in a perfectly definite sense, namely, that it is just to respect, unjust to violate, the *legal rights* of any one. But this judgment admits of several exceptions, arising from the other forms in which the notions of justice and injustice present themselves. For example, the person who suffers the deprivation may (as the phrase is) have *forfeited* the rights which he is so deprived of: a case to which we shall return presently. But also,

Secondly; the legal rights of which he is deprived, may be rights which *ought* not to have belonged to him; in other words, the law which confers on him these rights, may be a bad law. When it is so, or when (which is the same thing for our purpose) it is supposed to be so, opinions will differ as to the justice or injustice of infringing it. Some maintain that no law, however bad, ought to be disobeyed by an individual citizen; that his opposition to it, if shown at all, should only be shown in endeavouring to get it altered by competent authority. This opinion (which condemns many of the most illustrious benefactors of mankind, and would often protect pernicious institutions against the only weapons which, in the state of things existing at the time, have any chance of succeeding against them) is defended, by those who hold it, on grounds of expediency; principally on that of the importance, to the common interest of mankind, of maintaining inviolate the sentiment of submission to law. Other persons, again, hold the directly contrary opinion, that any law, judged to be bad, may blamelessly be disobeyed, even though it be not judged to be unjust, but only inexpedient; while others would confine the licence of disobedience to the case of unjust laws: but again, some say, that all laws which are inexpedient are unjust; since every law imposes some restriction on the natural liberty of mankind, which restriction is an injustice, unless legitimated by tending to their good. Among these diversities of opinion, it seems to be universally admitted that there may be unjust laws, and that law, consequently, is not the ultimate criterion of justice, but may give to one person a benefit, or impose on another an evil, which justice condemns. When, however, a law is thought to be unjust, it seems always to be regarded as being so in the same way in which a breach of law is unjust, namely, by infringing somebody's right; which, as it cannot in this case be a legal right, receives a different appellation, and is called a moral right. We may say, therefore, that a second case of injustice consists in taking or withholding from any person that to which he has a *moral right.*

Thirdly, it is universally considered just that each person should obtain that (whether good or evil) which he *deserves;* and unjust that he should obtain a good, or be made to undergo an evil, which he does not deserve. This is, perhaps, the clearest and most emphatic form in which the idea of justice is conceived by the general mind. As it involves the notion of desert, the question arises what constitutes desert? Speaking in a general way, a person is understood to deserve good if he does right, evil if he does wrong; and in a more particular sense, to deserve good from those to whom he does or has done good, and evil from those to whom he does or has done evil. The precept of returning good for evil has never been regarded as a case of the fulfilment of justice, but as one in which the claims of justice are waived, in obedience to other considerations.

Fourthly, it is confessedly unjust to *break faith* with any one: to violate an engagement, either express or implied, or disappoint expectations raised by our own conduct, at least if we have raised those expectations knowingly and voluntarily. Like the other obligations of justice already spoken of, this one is not regarded as absolute, but as capable of being overruled by a stronger obligation of justice on the other side; or by such conduct on the part of the person concerned as is deemed to absolve us from our obligation to him, and to constitute a *forfeiture* of the benefit which he has been led to expect.

Fifthly, it is, by universal admission, inconsistent with justice to be *partial;* to show favour and preference to one person over another, in matters to which favour and preference do not properly apply.

Impartiality, however, does not seem to be regarded as a duty in itself, but rather as instrumental to some other duty; for it is admitted that favour and preference are not always censurable, and indeed the cases in which they are condemned are rather the exception than the rule. A person would be more likely to be blamed than applauded for giving his family or friends no superiority in good offices over strangers, when he could do so without violating any other duty; and no one thinks it unjust to seek one person in preference to another as a friend, connexion, or companion. Impartiality where rights are concerned is of course obligatory, but this is involved in the more general obligation of giving to every one his right. A tribunal, for example, must be impartial, because it is bound to award, without regard to any other consideration, a disputed object to the one of two parties who has the right to it. There are other cases in which impartiality means, being solely influenced by desert; as with those who, in the capacity of judges, preceptors, or parents, administer reward and punishment as such. There are cases, again, in which it means, being solely influenced by consideration for the public interest; as in making a selection among candidates for a government employment. Impartiality, in short, as an obligation of justice, may be said to mean, being exclusively influenced by the considerations which it is supposed ought to influence the particular case in hand; and resisting the solicitation of any motives which prompt to conduct different from what those considerations would dictate.

Nearly allied to the idea of impartiality, is that of *equality;* which often enters as a component part both into the conception of justice and into the practice of it, and, in the eyes of many persons, constitutes its essence. But in this, still more than in any other case, the notion of justice varies in different persons, and always conforms in its variations to their notion of utility. Each person maintains that equality is the dictate of justice, except where he thinks that expediency requires inequality. The justice of giving equal protection to the rights of all, is maintained by those who support the most outrageous inequality in the rights themselves. Even in slave countries it is theoretically admitted that the rights of the slave, such as they are, ought to be as sacred as those of the master; and that a tribunal which fails to enforce them with equal strictness is wanting in justice; while, at the same time, institutions which leave to the slave scarcely any rights to enforce, are not deemed unjust, because they are not deemed inexpedient. Those who think that utility requires distinctions of rank, do not consider it unjust that riches and social privileges should be unequally dispensed; but those who think this inequality inexpedient, think it unjust also. Whoever thinks that government is necessary, sees no injustice in as much inequality as is constituted by giving to the magistrate powers not granted to other people. Even among those who hold levelling doctrines, there are as many questions of justice as there are differences of opinion about expediency. Some Communists consider it unjust that the produce of the labour of the community should be shared on any other principle than that of exact equality; others think it just that those should receive most whose needs are greatest; while others hold that those who work harder, or who produce more, or whose services are more valuable to the community, may justly claim a larger quota in the division of the produce. And the sense of natural justice may be plausibly appealed to in behalf of every one of these opinions.

Among so many diverse applications of the term Justice, which yet is not regarded as ambiguous, it is a matter of some difficulty to seize the mental link which holds them together, and on which the moral sentiment adhering to the term essentially depends.

. . . We do not call anything wrong, unless we mean to imply that a person ought to be punished in some way or other for doing it; if not by law, by the opinion of his fellow creatures; if not by opinion, by the reproaches of his own conscience. This seems the real turning point of the distinction between morality and simple expediency. It is a part of the notion of Duty in every one of its forms, that a person may rightfully be compelled to fulfil it. Duty is a thing which may be *exacted* from a person, as one exacts a debt. Unless we think that it might be exacted from him, we do not call it his duty. Reasons of prudence, or the interest of other people, may militate against actually exacting it; but the person himself, it is clearly understood, would not be entitled to complain. There are other things, on the contrary, which we wish that people should do, which we like or admire them for doing, perhaps dislike or despise them for not doing, but yet admit that they are

not bound to do; it is not a case of moral obligation; we do not blame them, that is, we do not think that they are proper objects of punishment. How we come by these ideas of deserving and not deserving punishment, will appear, perhaps, in the sequel; but I think there is no doubt that this distinction lies at the bottom of the notions of right and wrong; that we call any conduct wrong, or employ instead, some other term of dislike or disparagement, according as we think that the person ought, or ought not, to be punished for it; and we say that it would be right to do so and so, or merely that it would be desirable or laudable, according as we would wish to see the person whom it concerns, compelled or only persuaded and exhorted, to act in that manner.

This, therefore, being the characteristic difference which marks off, not justice, but morality in general, from the remaining provinces of Expediency and Worthiness; the character is still to be sought which distinguishes justice from other branches of morality. Now it is known that ethical writers divide moral duties into two classes, denoted by the ill-chosen expressions, duties of perfect and of imperfect obligation; the latter being those in which, though the act is obligatory, the particular occasions of performing it are left to our choice; as in the case of charity or beneficence, which we are indeed bound to practise, but not towards any definite person, nor at any prescribed time. In the more precise language of philosophic jurists, duties of perfect obligation are those duties in virtue of which a correlative *right* resides in some person or persons; duties of imperfect obligation are those moral obligations which do not give birth to any right. I think it will be found that this distinction exactly coincides with that which exists between justice and the other obligations of morality. In our survey of the various popular acceptations of justice, the term appeared generally to involve the idea of a personal right — a claim on the part of one or more individuals, like that which the law gives when it confers a proprietary or other legal right. Whether the injustice consists in depriving a person of a possession, or in breaking faith with him, or in treating him worse than he deserves, or worse than other people who have no greater claims, in each case the supposition implies two things — a wrong done, and some assignable person who is wronged. Injustice may also be done by treating a person better than others; but the wrong in this case is to his competitors, who are also assignable persons. It seems to me that this feature in the case—a right in some person, correlative to the moral obligation—constitutes the specific difference between justice, and generosity or beneficence. Justice implies something which it is not only right to do, and wrong not to do, but which some individual person can claim from us as his moral right. No one has a moral right to our generosity or beneficence, because we are not morally bound to practise those virtues towards any given individual. And it will be found with respect to this as with respect to every correct definition, that the instances which seem to conflict with it are those which most confirm it. For if a moralist attempts, as some have done, to make out that mankind generally, though not any given individual, have a right to all the good we can do them, he at once, by that thesis, includes generosity and beneficence within the category of justice. He is obliged to say, that our utmost exertions are *due* to our fellow creatures, thus assimilating them to a debt; or that nothing less can be a sufficient *return* for what society does for us, thus classing the case as one of gratitude; both of which are acknowledged cases of justice. Wherever there is a right, the case is one of justice, and not of the virtue of beneficence: and whoever does not place the distinction between justice and morality in general where we have now placed it, will be found to make no distinction between them at all, but to merge all morality in justice.

The sentiment of justice, in that one of its elements which consist of the desire to punish, is . . . , I conceive, the natural feeling of retaliation or vengeance, rendered by intellect and sympathy applicable to those injuries, that is, to those hurts, which wound us through, or in common with, society at large. This sentiment, in itself, has nothing moral in it; what is moral is, the exclusive subordination of it to the social sympathies, so as to wait on and obey their call. For the natural feeling tends to make us resent indiscriminately whatever any one does that is disagreeable to us; but when moralized by the social feeling, it only acts in the directions conformable to the general good: just persons resenting a hurt to society, though not otherwise a hurt to themselves, and not resenting a hurt to themselves, however painful, unless it be of the kind which society has a common interest with them in the repression of.

It is no objection against this doctrine to say, that when we feel our sentiment of justice outraged, we are not thinking of society at large, or of any collective interest, but only of the individual case. It is common enough certainly, though the reverse of commendable, to feel resentment merely because we have suffered pain; but a person whose resentment is really a moral feeling, that is, who considers whether an act is blameable before he allows himself to resent it—such a person, though he may not say expressly to himself that he is standing up for the interest of society, certainly does feel that he is asserting a rule which is for the benefit of others as well as for his own. If he is not feeling this—if he is regarding the act solely as it affects him individually—he is not consciously just; he is not concerning himself about the justice of his actions. This is admitted even by anti-utilitarian moralists. When Kant (as before remarked) propounds as the fundamental principle of morals, 'So act, that thy rule of conduct might be adopted as a law by all rational beings,' he virtually acknowledges that the interest of mankind collectively, or at least of mankind indiscriminately, must be in the mind of the agent when conscientiously deciding on the morality of the act. Otherwise he uses words without a meaning: for, that a rule even of utter selfishness could not *possibly* be adopted by all rational beings—that there is any insuperable obstacle in the nature of things to its adoption—cannot be even plausibly maintained. To give any meaning to Kant's principle, the sense put upon it must be, that we ought to shape our conduct by a rule which all rational beings might adopt *with benefit to their collective interest.*

To recapitulate: the idea of justice supposes two things; a rule of conduct, and a sentiment which sanctions the rule. The first must be supposed common to all mankind, and intended for their good. The other (the sentiment) is a desire that punishment may be suffered by those who infringe the rule. There is involved, in addition, the conception of some definite person who suffers by the infringement; whose rights (to use the expression appropriated to the case) are violated by it. And the sentiment of justice appears to me to be, the animal desire to repel or retaliate a hurt or damage to oneself, or to those with whom one sympathizes, widened so as to include all persons, by the human capacity of enlarged sympathy, and the human conception of intelligent self-interest. From the latter elements, the feeling derives its morality; from the former, its peculiar impressiveness, and energy of self-assertion.

I have, throughout, treated the idea of a *right* residing in the injured person, and violated by the injury, not as a separate element in the composition of the idea and sentiment, but as one of the forms in which the other two elements clothe themselves. These elements are, a hurt to some assignable person or persons on the one hand, and a demand for punishment on the other. An examination of our own minds, I think, will show, that these two things include all that we mean when we speak of violation of a right. When we call anything a person's right, we mean that he has a valid claim on society to protect him in the possession of it, either by the force of law, or by that of education and opinion. If he has what we consider a sufficient claim, on whatever account, to have something guaranteed to him by society, we say that he has a right to it. If we desire to prove that anything does not belong to him by right, we think this done as soon as it is admitted that society ought not to take measures for securing it to him, but should leave it to chance, or to his own exertions. Thus, a person is said to have a right to what he can earn in fair professional competition; because society ought not to allow any other person to hinder him from endeavouring to earn in that manner as much as he can. But he has not a right to three hundred a year, though he may happen to be earning it; because society is not called on to provide that he shall earn that sum. On the contrary, if he owns ten thousand pounds three per cent. stock he *has* a right to three hundred a year; because society has come under an obligation to provide him with an income of that amount.

To have a right, then, is, I conceive, to have something which society ought to defend me in the possession of. If the objector goes on to ask why it ought, I can give him no other reason than general utility. If that expression does not seem to convey a sufficient feeling of the strength of the obligation, nor to account for the peculiar energy of the feeling, it is because there goes to the composition of the sentiment, not a rational only but also an animal element, the thirst for retaliation; and this thirst derives its intensity, as well as its moral justification, from the extraordinarily important and impressive kind of utility which is concerned. The interest involved is that of security, to every one's feelings the

most vital of all interests. Nearly all other earthly benefits are needed by one person, not needed by another; and many of them can, if necessary, be cheerfully foregone, or replaced by something else; but security no human being can possibly do without; on it we depend for all our immunity from evil, and for the whole value of all and every good, beyond the passing moment; since nothing but the gratification of the instant could be of any worth to us, if we could be deprived of everything the next instant by whoever was momentarily stronger than ourselves. Now this most indispensable of all necessaries, after physical nutriment, cannot be had, unless the machinery for providing it is kept unintermittedly in active play. Our notion, therefore, of the claim we have on our fellow creatures to join in making safe for us the very groundwork of our existence, gathers feelings round it so much more intense than those concerned in any of the more common cases of utility, that the difference in degree (as is often the case in psychology) becomes a real difference in kind. The claim assumes that character of absoluteness, that apparent infinity, and incommensurability with all other considerations, which constitute the distinction between the feeling of right and wrong and that of ordinary expediency and inexpediency. The feelings concerned are so powerful, and we count so positively on finding a responsive feeling in others (all being alike interested), that *ought* and *should* grow into *must,* and recognised indispensability becomes a moral necessity, analogous to physical, and often not inferior to it in binding force.

. . . Justice is a name for certain classes of moral rules, which concern the essentials of human well-being more nearly, and are therefore of more absolute obligation, than any other rules for the guidance of life; and the notion which we have found to be of the essence of the idea of justice, that of a right residing in an individual, implies and testifies to this more binding obligation.

The moral rules which forbid mankind to hurt one another (in which we must never forget to include wrongful interference with each other's freedom) are more vital to human well-being than any maxims, however important, which only point out the best mode of managing some department of human affairs. They have also the peculiarity, that they are the main element in determining the whole of the social feelings of mankind. It is their observance which alone preserves peace among human beings: if obedience to them were not the rule, and disobedience the exception, every one would see in every one else a probable enemy, against whom he must be perpetually guarding himself. What is hardly less important, these are the precepts which mankind have the strongest and the most direct inducements for impressing upon one another. By merely giving to each other prudential instruction or exhortation, they may gain, or think they gain, nothing: in inculcating on each other the duty of positive beneficence they have an unmistakeable interest, but far less in degree: a person may possibly not need the benefits of others; but he always needs that they should not do him hurt. Thus the moralities which protect every individual from being harmed by others, either directly or by being hindered in his freedom of pursuing his own good, are at once those which he himself has most at heart, and those which he has the strongest interest in publishing and enforcing by word and deed. It is by a person's observance of these, that his fitness to exist as one of the fellowship of human beings, is tested and decided; for on that depends his being a nuisance or not to those with whom he is in contact. Now it is these moralities primarily, which compose the obligations of justice. The most marked cases of injustice, and those which give the tone to the feeling of repugnance which characterizes the sentiment, are acts of wrongful aggression, or wrongful exercise of power over some one; the next are those which consist in wrongfully withholding from him something which is his due; in both cases, inflicting on him a positive hurt, either in the form of direct suffering, or of the privation of some good which he had reasonable ground either of a physical or of a social kind, for counting upon.

The same powerful motives which command the observance of these primary moralities, enjoin the punishment of those who violate them; and as the impulses of self-defence, of defence of others, and of vengeance, are all called forth against such persons, retribution, or evil for evil, becomes closely connected with the sentiment of justice, and is universally included in the idea. Good for good is also one of the dictates of justice; and this, though its social utility is evident, and though it carries with it a natural human feeling, has not at first sight that obvious connexion with hurt or injury, which, existing in the most elementary cases of just and unjust, is the source of the characteristic intensity of the sentiment. But the connexion, though less obvious, is not less real. He who accepts benefits, and denies a return of them when needed, inflicts a real hurt, by disappointing one of the most natural and reasonable of expectations, and one which he must at least tacitly have encouraged, otherwise the benefits would seldom have been conferred. The important rank, among human evils and wrongs, of the disappointment of expectation, is shown in the fact that it constitutes the principal criminality of two such highly immoral acts as a breach of friendship and a breach of promise. Few hurts which human beings can sustain are greater, and none wound more, than when that on which they habitually and with full assurance relied, fails them in the hour of need; and few wrongs are greater than this mere withholding of good; none excite more resentment, either in the person suffering, or in a sympathizing spectator. The principle, therefore, of giving to each what they deserve, that is, good for good as well as evil for evil, is not only included within the idea of Justice as we have defined it, but is a proper object of that intensity of sentiment, which places the Just, in human estimation, above the simply Expedient.

Most of the maxims of justice current in the world, and commonly appealed to in its transactions, are simply instrumental to carrying into effect the principles of justice which we have now spoken of. That a person is only responsible for what he has done voluntarily, or could voluntarily have avoided; that it is unjust to condemn any person unheard; that the punishment ought to be proportioned to the offence, and the like, are maxims intended to prevent the just principle of evil for evil from being perverted to the infliction of evil without justification. The greater part of these common maxims have come into use from the practice of courts of justice, which have been naturally led to a more complete recognition and elaboration than was likely to suggest itself to others, of the rules necessary to enable them to fulfil their double function, of inflicting punishment when due, and of awarding to each person his right.

That first of judicial virtues, impartiality, is an obligation of justice, partly for the reason last mentioned; as being a necessary condition of the fulfilment of the other obligations of justice. But this is not the only source of the exalted rank, among human obligations, of those maxims of equality and impartiality, which, both in popular estimation and in that of the most enlightened, are included among the precepts of justice. In one point of view, they may be considered as corollaries from the principles already laid down. If it is a duty to do to each according to his deserts, returning good for good as well as repressing evil by evil, it necessarily follows that we should treat all equally well (when no higher duty forbids) who have deserved equally well of us, and that society should treat all equally well who have deserved equally well of it, that is, who have deserved equally well absolutely. This is the highest abstract standard of social and distributive justice; towards which all institutions, and the efforts of all virtuous citizens, should be made in the utmost possible degree to converge. But this great moral duty rests upon a still deeper foundation, being a direct emanation from the first principle of morals, and not a mere logical corollary from secondary or derivative doctrines. It is involved in the very meaning of Utility, or the Greatest-Happiness Principle. That principle is a mere form of words without rational signification, unless one person's happiness, supposed equal in degree (with the proper allowance made for kind), is counted for exactly as much as another's. Those conditions being supplied, Bentham's dictum, 'everybody to count for one, nobody for more than one,' might be written under the principle of utility as an explanatory commentary. The equal claim of everybody to happiness in the estimation of the moralist and the legislator, involves an equal claim to all the means of happiness, except in so far as the inevitable conditions of human life, and the general interest, in which that of every individual is included, set limits to the maxim; and those limits ought to be strictly construed. As every other maxim of justice, so this, is by no means applied or held applicable universally; on the contrary, as I have already remarked, it bends to every person's ideas of social expediency. But in whatever case it is deemed applicable at all, it is held to be the dictate of justice. All persons are deemed to have a *right* to equality of treatment, except when some recognised social expediency requires the reverse. And hence all social inequalities which have ceased to be considered expedient, assume the character not of simple inexpediency, but of injustice, and appear so tyrannical, that people are apt to wonder how they ever could have been tolerated; forgetful

that they themselves perhaps tolerate other inequalities under an equally mistaken notion of expediency, the correction of which would make that which they approve seem quite as monstrous as what they have at last learnt to condemn. The entire history of social improvement has been a series of transitions, by which one custom or institution after another, from being a supposed primary necessity of social existence, has passed into the rank of an universally stigmatized injustice and tyranny. So it has been with the distinctions of slaves and freemen, nobles and serfs, patricians and plebians; and so it will be, and in part already is, with the aristocracies of colour, race, and sex. . . .

Endnote

[1] An opponent, whose intellectual and moral fairness it is a pleasure to acknowledge (the Rev. J. Llewellyn Davies), has objected to this passage, saying, "Surely the rightness or wrongness of saving a man from drowning does depend very much upon the motive with which it is done. Suppose that a tyrant, when his enemy jumped into the sea to escape from him, saved him from drowning simply in order that he might inflict upon him more exquisite tortures, would it tend to clearness to speak of that rescue as 'a morally right action?' Or suppose again, according to one of the stock illustrations of ethical inquiries, that a man betrayed a trust received from a friend, because the discharge of it would fatally injure that friend himself or some one belonging to him, would utilitarianism compel one to call the betrayal 'a crime' as much as if it had been done from the meanest motive?"

I submit, that he who saves another from drowning in order to kill him by torture afterwards, does not differ only in motive from him who does the same thing from duty or benevolence; the act itself is different. The rescue of the man is, in the case supposed, only the necessary first step of an act far more atrocious than leaving him to drown would have been. Had Mr. Davies said, "The rightness or wrongness of saving a man from drowning does depend very much" — not upon the motive, but — "upon the *intention*," no utilitarian would have differed from him. Mr. Davies, by an oversight too common not to be quite venial, has in this case confounded the very different ideas of Motive and Intention. There is no point which utilitarian thinkers (and Bentham pre-eminently) have taken more pains to illustrate than this. The morality of the action depends entirely upon the intention — that is, upon what the agent *wills to do*. But the motive, that is, the feeling which makes him will so to do, when it makes no difference in the act, makes none in the morality: though it makes a great difference in our moral estimation of the agent, especially if it indicates a good or bad habitual *disposition* — a bent of character from which useful, or from which hurtful actions are likely to arise.

V.2 *Against Moral Conservatism*

KAI NIELSEN

Kai Nielsen is professor of philosophy at Calgary University who has written
important works in philosophy of religion and political theory, as well as in
ethics. This essay is a clear example of act utilitarianism. Nielsen sets forth his
theory as a credible alternative to moral conservatism or deontological ethics,
which maintain that there are "moral principles, prescribing determinate
actions, with which it would always be wrong not to act in accordance no
matter what the consequences." He argues, to the contrary, that it is the
consequences that determine the moral worth of an action.

Nielsen's argument in favor of utilitarianism in part depends on the
notion of negative responsibility. That is, we are not only responsible for the
consequences of our actions but we are also responsible for the consequences
of our nonactions.

I

It is sometimes claimed that any consequentialist
view of ethics has monstrous implications which
make such a conception of morality untenable.
What we must do — so the claim goes — is reject all
forms of consequentialism and accept what has been
labeled 'conservatism' or 'moral absolutism.' By
'conservatism' is meant, here, a normative ethical
theory which maintains that there is a privileged
moral principle or cluster of moral principles, prescribing determinate actions, with which it would
always be wrong not to act in accordance no matter
what the consequences. A key example of such a
principle is the claim that it is always wrong to kill
an innocent human, whatever the consequences of
not doing so.

I will argue that such moral conservatism is itself unjustified and, indeed, has morally unacceptable consequences, while consequentialism does not
have implications which are morally monstrous and
does not contain evident moral mistakes.

A consequentialist maintains that actions,
rules, policies, practices, and moral principles are ultimately to be judged by certain consequences: to
wit (for a very influential kind of consequentialism),
by whether doing them more than, or at least as
much as doing anything else, or acting in accordance with them more than or at least as much as
acting in accordance with alternative policies, practices, rules or principles, tends, on the whole, and
for *everyone* involved, to maximize satisfaction and
minimize dissatisfaction. The states of affairs to be
sought are those which maximize these things to the
greatest extent possible for all mankind. But while
this all sounds very humane and humanitarian,
when its implications are thought through, it has
been forcefully argued, it will be seen actually to
have inhumane and morally intolerable implications. Circumstances could arise in which one holding such a view would have to assert that one was
justified in punishing, killing, torturing, or deliberately harming the innocent, and such a consequence
is, morally speaking, unacceptable.[1] As Anscombe
has put it, anyone who "really thinks, *in advance,*
that it is open to question whether such an action as
procuring the judicial execution of the innocent
should be quite excluded from consideration — I do
not want to argue with him; he shows a corrupt
mind."[2]

From *Ethics* 82 (1972): 113–124. Reprinted with permission of The University of Chicago Press and the author.

At the risk of being thought to exhibit a corrupt mind and a shallow consequentialist morality, I should like to argue that things are not as simple and straightforward as Anscombe seems to believe.

Surely, every moral man must be appalled at the judicial execution of the innocent or at the punishment, torture, and killing of the innocent. Indeed, being appalled by such behavior partially defines what it is to be a moral agent. And a consequentialist has very good utilitarian grounds for being so appalled, namely, that it is always wrong to inflict pain for its own sake. But this does not get to the core considerations which divide a conservative position such as Anscombe's from a consequentialist view. There are a series of tough cases that need to be taken to heart and their implications thought through by any reflective person, be he a conservative or a consequentialist. By doing this, we can get to the heart of the issue between conservatism and consequentialism. Consider this clash between conservatism and consequentialism arising over the problem of a 'just war.'

> If we deliberately bomb civilian targets, we do not pretend that civilians are combatants in any simple fashion, but argue that this bombing will terminate hostilities more quickly, and will minimize all around suffering. It is hard to see how any brand of utilitarian will escape Miss Anscombe's objections. We are certainly killing the innocent . . . we are not killing them for the sake of killing them, but to save the lives of other innocent persons. Utilitarians, I think, grit their teeth and put up with this as part of the logic of total war; Miss Anscombe and anyone who thinks like her surely has to either redescribe the situation to ascribe guilt to the civilians or else she has to refuse to accept this sort of military tactics as simply wrong.[3]

It is indeed true that we cannot but feel the force of Anscombe's objections here. But is it the case that anyone shows a corrupt mind if he defends such bombing when, horrible as it is, it will quite definitely lessen appreciably the total amount of suffering and death in the long run, and if he is sufficiently nonevasive not to rationalize such a bombing of civilians into a situation in which all the putatively innocent people—children and all—are somehow in some measure judged guilty? Must such a man exhibit a corrupt moral sense if he refuses to hold that such military tactics are never morally justified? Must this be the monstrous view of a fanatical man devoid of any proper moral awareness? It is difficult for me to believe that this must be so.

Consider the quite parallel actions of guerrilla fighters and terrorists in wars of national liberation. In certain almost unavoidable circumstances, they must deliberately kill the innocent. We need to see some cases in detail here to get the necessary contextual background, and for this reason the motion picture *The Battle of Algiers* can be taken as a convenient point of reference. There we saw Algerian women—gentle, kindly women with children of their own and plainly people of moral sensitivity—with evident heaviness of heart, plant bombs which they had every good reason to believe would kill innocent people, including children; and we also saw a French general, also a human being of moral fiber and integrity, order the torture of Arab terrorists and threaten the bombing of houses in which terrorists were concealed but which also contained innocent people, including children. There are indeed many people involved in such activities who are cruel, sadistic beasts, or simply morally indifferent or, in important ways, morally uncomprehending. But the characters I have referred to from *The Battle of Algiers* were not of that stamp. They were plainly moral agents of a high degree of sensitivity, and yet they deliberately killed or were prepared to kill the innocent. And, with inessential variations, this is a recurrent phenomenon of human living in extreme situations. Such cases are by no means desert-island or esoteric cases.

It is indeed arguable whether such actions are always morally wrong—whether anyone should ever act as the Arab women or French general acted. But what could not be reasonably maintained, *pace* Anscombe, by any stretch of the imagination, is that the characters I described from *The Battle of Algiers* exhibited corrupt minds. Possibly morally mistaken, yes; guilty of moral corruption, no.

Dropping the charge of moral corruption but sticking with the moral issue about what actions are right, is it not the case that my consequentialist position logically forces me to conclude that under some circumstances—where the good to be achieved is great enough—I must not only countenance but actually advocate such violence toward the innocent? But is it not always, no matter what the circumstances or consequences, wrong to countenance, advocate, or engage in such violence? To answer such a question affirmatively is to commit oneself to the kind of moral absolutism or conservatism which Anscombe advocates. But, given the alternatives, should not one be such a conservative or at least hold that certain deontological principles must never be overridden?

I will take, so to speak, the papal bull by the horns and answer that there are circumstances when such violence must be reluctantly assented to or even taken to be something that one, morally speaking, must do. But, *pace* Anscombe, this very much needs arguing, and I shall argue it; but first I would like to set out some further but simpler cases which have a similar bearing. They are, by contrast, artificial cases. I use them because, in their greater simplicity, by contrast with my above examples, there are fewer variables to control and I can more conveniently make the essential conceptual and moral points. But, if my argument is correct for these simpler cases, the line of reasoning employed is intended to be applicable to those more complex cases as well.

━━

II

Consider the following cases embedded in their exemplary tales:

1. The Case of the Innocent Fat Man

Consider the story (well known to philosophers) of the fat man stuck in the mouth of a cave on a coast. He was leading a group of people out of the cave when he got stuck in the mouth of the cave and in a very short time high tide will be upon them, and unless he is promptly unstuck, they all will be drowned except the fat man, whose head is out of the cave. But, fortunately or unfortunately, someone has with him a stick of dynamite. The short of the matter is, either they use the dynamite and blast the poor innocent fat man out of the mouth of the cave or everyone else drowns. Either one life or many lives. Our conservative presumably would take the attitude that it is all in God's hands and say that he ought never to blast the fat man out, for it is always

wrong to kill the innocent. Must or should a moral man come to that conclusion? I shall argue that he should not.

My first exemplary tale was designed to show that our normal, immediate, rather absolutistic, moral reactions need to be questioned along with such principles as 'The direct intention of the death of an innocent person is never justifiable.' I have hinted (and later shall argue) that we should *beware* of our moral outrage here — our naturally conservative and unreflective moral reactions — for here the consequentialist has a strong case for what I shall call 'moral radicalism.' But, before turning to a defense of that, I want to tell another story taken from Phillipa Foot but used for my own purposes.[4] This tale, I shall argue, has a different import than our previous tale. Here our unrehearsed, commonsense moral reactions will stand up under moral scrutiny. But, I shall also argue when I consider them in Section III, that our commonsense moral reactions here, initial expectations to the contrary not withstanding, can be shown to be justified on consequentialist grounds. The thrust of my argument for this case is that we are not justified in opting for a theistic and/or deontological absolutism or in rejecting consequentialism.

2. The Magistrate and the Threatening Mob

A magistrate or judge is faced with a very real threat from a large and uncontrollable mob of rioters demanding a culprit for a crime. Unless the criminal is produced, promptly tried, and executed, they will take their own bloody revenge on a much smaller and quite vulnerable section of the community (a kind of frenzied pogrom). The judge knows that the real culprit is unknown and that the authorities do not even have a good clue as to who he may be. But he also knows that there is within easy reach a disreputable, thoroughly disliked, and useless man, who, though innocent, could easily be framed so that the mob would be quite convinced that he was guilty and would be pacified if he were promptly executed. Recognizing that he can prevent the occurrence of extensive carnage only by framing some innocent person, the magistrate has him framed, goes through the mockery of a trial, and has him executed. Most of us regard such a framing and execution of such a man in such circumstances as totally unacceptable.[5] There are some who would say that it is categorically wrong — morally inexcusable — *whatever the circumstances*. Indeed, such a case remains a problem for the consequentialist, but here again, I shall argue, one can consistently remain a consequentialist and continue to accept commonsense moral convictions about such matters.

My storytelling is at an end. The job is to see what the stories imply. We must try to determine whether thinking through their implications should lead a clear-headed and morally sensitive man to abandon consequentialism and to adopt some form of theistic absolutism and/or deontological absolutism. I shall argue that it does not.

III

I shall consider the last case first because there are good reasons why the consequentialist should stick with commonsense moral convictions for such cases. I shall start by giving my rationale for that claim. If the magistrate were a tough-minded but morally conscientious consequentialist, he could still, on straightforward consequentialist grounds, refuse to frame and execute the innocent man, even knowing that this would unleash the mob and cause much suffering and many deaths. The rationale for his particular moral stand would be that, by so framing and then executing such an innocent man, he would, in the long run, cause still more suffering through the resultant corrupting effect on the institution of justice. That is, in a case involving such extensive general interest in the issue — without that, there would be no problem about preventing the carnage or call for such extreme measures — knowledge that the man was framed, that the law had prostituted itself, would, surely, eventually leak out. This would encourage mob action in other circumstances, would lead to an increased skepticism about the incorruptibility or even the reliability of the judicial process, and would set a dangerous precedent for less clearheaded or less scrupulously humane magistrates. Given such a potential for the corruption of justice, a utilitarian or consequentialist judge or magistrate could, on good utilitarian or consequentialist grounds, argue that it was morally wrong to frame an innocent man. If the mob must rampage if such a sacrificial lamb is not provided, then the mob must rampage.

Must a utilitarian or consequentialist come to such a conclusion? The answer is no. It is the conclusion which is, as things stand, the most reasonable conclusion, but that he *must* come to it is far too strong a claim. A consequentialist could *consistently* — I did not say successfully — argue that, in taking the above tough-minded utilitarian position, we have overestimated the corrupting effects of such judicial railroading. His circumstance was an extreme one: a situation not often to be repeated even if, instead of acting as he did, he had set a precedent by such an act of judicial murder. A utilitarian rather more skeptical than most utilitarians about the claims of commonsense morality might reason that the lesser evil here is the judicial murder of an innocent man, vile as it is. He would persist in his moral iconoclasm by standing on the consequentialist rock that the lesser evil is always to be preferred to the greater evil.

The short of it is that utilitarians could disagree, as other consequentialists could disagree, about what is morally required of us in that case. The disagreement here between utilitarians or consequentialists of the same type is not one concerning fundamental moral principles but a disagreement about the empirical facts, about what course of action would in the long run produce the least suffering and the most happiness for *everyone* involved.[6]

However, considering the effect advocating the deliberate judicial killing of an innocent man would have on the reliance people put on commonsense moral beliefs of such a ubiquitous sort as the belief that the innocent must not be harmed, a utilitarian who defended the centrality of commonsense moral beliefs would indeed have a strong utilitarian case here. But the most crucial thing to recognize is that, to regard such judicial bowing to such a threatening mob as unqualifiedly wrong, as morally intolerable, one need not reject utilitarianism and accept some form of theistic or deontological absolutism.

It has been argued, however, that, in taking such a stance, I still have not squarely faced the moral conservative's central objection to the judicial railroading of the innocent. I allow, as a consequentialist, that there could be circumstances, at least as far as logical possibilities are concerned, in which such a railroading would be justified but that, as things actually go, it is not and probably never in fact will be justified. But the conservative's point is that in *no circumstances, either actual or conceivable, would it be justified*. No matter what the consequences, it is unqualifiedly unjustified. To say, as I do, that the situations in which it might be justified are desert-island, esoteric cases which do not occur in life, is not to the point, for, as Alan Donagan argues, "Moral theory is *a priori,* as clear-headed utilitarians like Henry Sidgwick recognized. It is, as Leibniz would say, 'true of all possible worlds.'"[7] Thus, to argue as I have and as others have that the counterexamples directed against the consequentialist's appeal to conditions which are never in fact fulfilled or are unlikely to be fulfilled is beside the point.[8] Whether "a moral theory is true or false depends on whether its implications for all possible worlds are true. Hence, whether utilitarianism (or consequentialism) is true or false cannot depend on how the actual world is."[9] It is possible to specify logically conceivable situations in which consequentialism would have implications which are monstrous—for example, certain beneficial judicial murders of the innocent (whether they are even remotely likely to obtain is irrelevant)—hence consequentialism must be false.

We should not take such a short way with consequentialists, for what is true in Donagan's claim about moral theory's being a priori will not refute or even render implausible consequentialism, and what would undermine it in such a claim about the a priori nature of moral theory and presumably moral claims is not true.

To say that moral theory is a priori is probably correct if that means that categorical moral claims—fundamental moral statements—cannot be deduced from empirical statements or nonmoral theological statements, such that it is a contradiction to assert the empirical and/or nonmoral theological statements and deny the categorical moral claims or vice versa.[10] In that fundamental sense, it is reasonable and, I believe, justifiable to maintain that moral theory is autonomous and a priori. It is also a priori in the sense that moral statements are not themselves a kind of empirical statement. That is, if I assert 'One ought never to torture any sentient creature' or 'One ought never to kill an innocent man,' I am not trying to predict or describe what people do or are likely to do but am asserting what they are *to do.* It is also true that, if a moral statement is true, it holds for all possible worlds *in which situations are exactly the sort characterized in the statement obtain.* If it is true for one, it is true for all. You cannot consistently say that A ought to do B in situation Y and deny that

someone exactly like A in a situation exactly like Y ought to do B.

In these ways, moral claims and indeed moral theory are a priori. But it is also evident that none of these ways will touch the consequentialist or utilitarian arguments. After all, the consequentialist need not be, and typically has not been, an ethical naturalist—he need not think moral claims are derivable from factual claims or that moral claims are a subspecies of empirical statement and he could accept—indeed, he must accept—what is an important truism anyway, that you cannot consistently say that A ought to do B in situation Y and deny that someone exactly like A in a situation exactly like Y ought to do B. But he could and should deny that moral claims are a priori in the sense that rational men must or even will make them without regard for the context, the situation, in which they are made. We say people ought not to drive way over the speed limit, or speed on icy roads, or throw knives at each other. But, if human beings had a kind of metallic exoskeleton and would not be hurt, disfigured, or seriously inconvenienced by knives sticking in them or by automobile crashes, we would not—so evidently at least—have good grounds for saying such speeding or knife throwing is wrong. It would not be so obvious that it was unreasonable and immoral to do these things if these conditions obtained.

In the very way we choose to describe the situation when we make ethical remarks, it is important in making this choice that we know what the world is like and what human beings are like. Our understanding of the situation, our understanding of human nature and motivation cannot but affect our structuring of the moral case. The consequentialist is saying that, as the world goes, there are good grounds for holding that judicial killings are morally intolerable, though he would have to admit that if the world (including human beings) were very different, such killings could be something that ought to be done. But, in holding this, he is not committed to denying the universalizability of moral judgments, for, where he would reverse or qualify the moral judgment, the situation must be different. He is only committed to claiming that, where the situation is the same or relevantly similar and the persons are relevantly similar, they must, if they are to act morally, do the same thing. However, he is claiming both (1) that, as things stand, judicial killing of the innocent is always wrong and (2) that it is an irrational moral judgment to assert of reasonably determinate actions (e.g., killing an innocent man) that they are unjustifiable and morally unacceptable in all *possible* worlds, whatever the situation and whatever the consequences.

Donagan's claims about the a priori nature of moral theories do not show such a consequentialist claim to be mistaken or even give us the slightest reason for thinking that it is mistaken. What is brutal and vile, for example, throwing a knife at a human being just for the fun of it, would not be so, if human beings were invulnerable to harm from such a direction because they had a metallic exoskeleton. Similarly, what is, as things are, morally intolerable, for example, the judicial killing of the innocent, need not be morally intolerable in all conceivable circumstances.

Such considerations support the utilitarian or consequentialist skeptical of simply taking the claims of our commonsense morality as a rock-bottom ground of appeal for moral theorizing. Yet it may also well be the case — given our extensive cruelty anyway — that, if we ever start sanctioning such behavior, an even greater callousness toward life than the very extensive callousness extant now will, as a matter of fact, develop. Given a normative ethical theory which sanctions, *under certain circumstances,* such judicial murders, there may occur an undermining of our moral disapproval of killing and our absolutely essential moral principle that all human beings, great and small, are deserving of respect. This is surely enough, together with the not unimportant weight of even our unrehearsed moral feelings, to give strong utilitarian weight *here* to the dictates of our commonsense morality. Yet, I think I have also said enough to show that someone who questions their 'unquestionableness' in such a context does not thereby exhibit a 'corrupt mind' and that it is an open question whether he must be conceptually confused or morally mistaken over this matter.

IV

So far, I have tried to show with reference to the case of the magistrate and the threatening mob how consequentialists can reasonably square their normative ethical theories with an important range of commonsense moral convictions. Now, I wish by reference to the case of the innocent fat man to establish that there is at least a serious question concerning whether such fundamental commonsense moral convictions should always function as 'moral facts' or a kind of moral ground to test the adequacy of normative ethical theories or positions. I want to establish that careful attention to such cases shows that we are not justified in taking the principles embodied in our commonsense moral reasoning about such cases as normative for all moral decisions. That a normative ethical theory is incompatible with some of our 'moral intuitions' (moral feelings or convictions) does not refute the normative ethical theory. What I will try to do here is to establish that this case, no more than the case examined in Section III, gives us adequate grounds for abandoning consequentialism and for adopting moral conservativism.

Forget the levity of the example and consider the case of the innocent fat man. If there really is no other way of unsticking our fat man and if plainly, without blasting him out, everyone in the cave will drown, then, innocent or not, he should be blasted out. This indeed overrides the principle that the innocent should never be deliberately killed, but it does not reveal a callousness toward life, for the people involved are caught in a desperate situation in which, if such extreme action is not taken, many lives will be lost and far greater misery will obtain. Moreover, the people who do such a horrible thing or acquiesce in the doing of it are not likely to be rendered more callous about human life and human suffering as a result. Its occurrence will haunt them for the rest of their lives and is as likely as not to make them more rather than less morally sensitive. It is not even correct to say that such a desperate act shows a lack of respect for persons. We are not treating the fat man merely as a means. The fat man's person — his interests and rights — are not ignored. Killing him is something which is undertaken with the greatest reluctance. It is only when it is quite certain that there is no other way to save the lives of the others that such a violent course of action is justifiably undertaken.

Alan Donagan, arguing rather as Anscombe argues, maintains that "to use any innocent man ill for the sake of some public good is directly to degrade him to being a mere means" and to do this is of course to violate a principle essential to morality, that is, that human beings should never merely be treated as means but should be treated as ends in themselves (as persons worthy of respect.)[11] But, as in my above remarks show, it need not be the case, and in the above situation it is not the case, that in killing such an innocent man we are treating him *merely* as a means. The action is universalizable, all alternative actions which would save his life are duly considered, the blasting out is done only as a last and desperate resort with the minimum of harshness and indifference to his suffering and the like. It indeed sounds ironical to talk this way, given what is done to him. But if such a terrible situation were to arise, there would always be more or less humane ways of going about one's grim task. And in acting in the more humane ways toward the fat man, as we do what we must do and would have done to ourselves were the roles reversed, we show a respect for his person.[12]

In so treating the fat man — not just to further the public good but to prevent the certain death of a whole group of people (that is, to prevent an even greater evil than his being killed in this way) — the claims of justice are not overridden either, for each individual involved, if he is reasoning correctly, should realize that if he were so stuck rather than the fat man, he should in such situations be blasted out. Thus, there is no question of being unfair. Surely we must choose between evils here, but is there anything more reasonable, more morally appropriate, than choosing the lesser evil when doing or allowing some evil cannot be avoided? That is, where there is no avoiding both and where our actions can determine whether a greater or lesser evil obtains, should we not plainly always opt for the lesser evil? And is it not obviously a greater evil that all those other innocent people should suffer and die than that the fat man should suffer and die? Blowing up the fat man is indeed monstrous. But letting him remain stuck while the whole group drowns is still more monstrous.

The consequentialist is on strong moral ground here, and, if his reflective moral convictions do not square either with certain unrehearsed or with certain reflective particular moral convictions of human beings, so much the worse for such commonsense moral convictions. One could even usefully and relevantly adapt here — though for a quite different purpose — an argument of Donagan's. Consequentialism of the kind I have been arguing for

provides so persuasive "a theoretical basis for common morality that when it contradicts some moral intuition, it is natural to suspect that intuition, not theory, is corrupt."[13] Given the comprehensiveness, plausibility, and overall rationality of consequentialism, it is not unreasonable to override even a deeply felt moral conviction if it does not square with such a theory, though, if it made no sense or overrode the bulk of or even a great many of our considered moral convictions, that would be another matter indeed.

Anticonsequentialists often point to the inhumanity of people who will sanction such killing of the innocent, but cannot the compliment be returned by speaking of the even greater inhumanity, conjoined with evasiveness, of those who will allow even more death and far greater misery and then excuse themselves on the ground that they did not intend the death and misery but merely forbore to prevent it? In such a context, such reasoning and such forbearing to prevent seems to me to constitute a moral evasion. I say it is evasive because rather than steeling himself to do what in normal circumstances would be a horrible and vile act but in this circumstance is a harsh moral necessity, he allows, when he has the power to prevent it, a situation which is still many times worse. He tries to keep his 'moral purity' and avoid 'dirty hands' at the price of utter moral failure and what Kierkegaard called 'doublemindedness.' It is understandable that people should act in this morally evasive way but this does not make it right.

My consequentialist reasoning about such cases as the case of the innocent fat man is very often resisted on the grounds that it starts a very dangerous precedent. People rationalize wildly and irrationally in their own favor in such situations. To avoid such rationalization, we must stubbornly stick to our deontological principles and recognize as well that very frequently, if people will put their wits to work or just endure, such admittedly monstrous actions done to prevent still greater evils will turn out to be unnecessary.

The general moral principles surrounding bans on killing the innocent are strong and play such a crucial role in the ever-floundering effort to humanize the savage mind — savage as a primitive and savage again as a contemporary in industrial society — that it is of the utmost social utility, it can be argued, that such bans against killing the innocent not be called into question in any practical manner by consequentialist reasoning.

However, in arguing in this way, the moral conservative has plainly shifted his ground, and he is himself arguing on consequentialist grounds that we must treat certain nonconsequentialist moral principles as absolute (as principles which can never *in fact,* from a reasonable moral point of view, be overridden, for it would be just too disastrous to do so).[14] But now he is on my home court, and my reply is that there is no good evidence at all that in the circumstances I characterized, overriding these deontological principles would have this disastrous effect. I am aware that a bad precedent could be set. Such judgments must not be made for more doubtful cases. But my telling my two stories in some detail, and my contrasting them, was done in order to make evident the type of situation, with its attendant rationale, in which the overriding of those deontological principles can be seen clearly to be justified and the situations in which this does obtain and why. My point was to specify the situations in which we ought to override our commonsense moral convictions about those matters, and the contexts in which we are not so justified or at least in which it is not clear which course of action is justified.[15]

If people are able to be sufficiently clearheaded about these matters, they can see that there are relevant differences between the two sorts of cases. But I was also carefully guarding against extending such 'moral radicalism' — if such it should be called — to other and more doubtful cases. Unless solid empirical evidence can be given that such a 'moral radicalism' would — if it were to gain a toehold in the community — overflow destructively and inhumanely into the other doubtful and positively unjustifiable situations, nothing has been said to undermine the correctness of my consequentialist defense of 'moral radicalism' in the contexts in which I defended it.[16]

Endnotes

[1] Alan Donagan, "Is There a Credible Form of Utilitarianism?" and H. J. McCloskey, "A Non-Utilitarian Approach to Punishment," both in Michael D. Bayles, ed. *Contemporary Utilitarianism* (Garden City, N.Y.: Doubleday, 1968).

[2] Elizabeth Anscombe, "Modern Moral Philosophy," *Philosophy* 23 (January 1957): 16–17.

[3] Alan Ryan, "Review of Jan Narveson's *Morality and Utility,*" *Philosophical Books* 9, no. 3(October 1958): 14.

[4] Phillipa Foot, "The Problem of Abortion and the Doctrine of the Double Effect," *Oxford Review*, no. 5(1967): 5–15.

[5] Later, I shall show that there are desert-island circumstances — i.e., highly improbable situations — in which such judicial railroading might be a moral necessity. But I also show what little force desert-island cases have in the articulation and defense of a normative ethical theory.

[6] 'Everyone' here is used distributively; i.e., I am talking about the interests of each and every one. In that sense, everyone's interests need to be considered.

[7] Donagan, *op. cit.,* p. 189.

[8] T. L. S. Sprigge argues in such a manner in his "A Utilitarian Reply to Dr. McCloskey," in Michael D. Bayles, ed. *Contemporary Utilitarianism* (Garden City, N.Y.: Doubleday, 1968).

[9] Donagan, *op. cit.,* p. 194.

[10] There is considerable recent literature about whether it is possible to derive moral claims from nonmoral claims. See W. D. Hudson, ed., *The Is-Ought Question: A Collection of Papers on the Central Problem in Moral Philosophy* (New York: St. Martin's Press, 1969).

[11] Donagan, *op. cit.,* pp. 199–200.

[12] Again, I am not asserting that we would have enough fortitude to assent to it were the roles actually reversed. I am making a conceptual remark about what as moral beings we must try to do and not a psychological observation about what we can do.

[13] Donagan, *op. cit.,* p. 198.

[14] Jonathan Bennett, "Whatever the Consequences," *Analysis* 26 (1966), has shown that this is a very common equivocation for the conservative and makes, when unnoticed, his position seem more plausible than it actually is.

[15] I have spoken, conceding this to the Christian absolutist for the sake of the discussion, as if (1) it is fairly evident what our commonsense moral convictions are here and (2) that they are deontological principles taken to hold no matter what the consequences. But that either (1) or (2) is clearly so seems to me very much open to question.

[16] I do not mean to suggest that I am giving a blanket defense to our commonsense morality; that is one of the last things I would want to do. Much of what we or any other tribe take to be commonsense morality is little better than a set of magical charms to deal with our social environment. But I was defending the importance of such cross-culturally ubiquitous moral principles as that one ought not to harm the innocent or that promises ought to be kept. However, against Christian absolutists of the type I have been discussing, I take them to be prima facie obligations. This means that they always hold *ceteris paribus;* but the *ceteris paribus* qualification implies that they can be overridden on occasion. On my account, appeal to consequences and considerations about justice and respect for persons determines when they should on a given occasion be overridden.

V.3 Against Utilitarianism

Bernard Williams

Bernard Williams is provost of King's College, Cambridge. He has made
important contributions to philosophy of the mind, as well as to moral theory.
In this essay he argues that utilitarianism violates personal integrity by
commanding that we violate those principles that are central and deepest in
our lives. That is, utilitarianism often calls on us to reject conscience and
compunction and do the "lesser of evils"—even when it is loathsome to do so.
He illustrates this by two examples. In one, an unemployed scientist, George,
is offered a job doing research in biological warfare, to which he is opposed.
Yet it turns out that on utilitarian grounds he would be obligated to take this
job, for it would be even worse if an unscrupulous scientist were involved in
the research. In the second example, a soldier will shoot twenty innocent
Indians unless Jim, an unlucky tourist, shoots one of them. If Jim kills one,
the rest of the Indians will be freed. Jim finds killing anyone abhorrent.
Williams examines these cases carefully and argues that because the precepts of
utilitarianism cause deep alienation, utilitarianism is deeply flawed.

Negative Responsibility: And Two Examples

Consequentialism is basically indifferent to whether
a state of affairs consists in what I do, or is produced
by what I do, where that notion is itself wide
enough to include, for instance, situations in which
other people do things which I have made them do,
or allowed them to do, or encouraged them to do,
or given them a chance to do. All that consequentialism is interested in is the idea of these doings
being *consequences* of what I do, and that is a relation
broad enough to include the relations just mentioned, and many others.

Just what the relation is, is a different question,
and at least as obscure as the nature of its relative,
cause and effect. It is not a question I shall try to
pursue; I will rely on cases where I suppose that any

Reprinted with permission from *Utilitarianism: For and
Against,* by Bernard Williams and J. J. C. Smart (Cambridge University Press, 1973), pp. 97–99; 101–103; 108–
109; 112–116.

consequentialist would be bound to regard the situations in question as consequences of what the
agent does. There are cases where the supposed
consequences stand in a rather remote relation to
the action, which are sometimes difficult to assess
from a practical point of view, but which raise no
very interesting question for the present enquiry.
The more interesting points about consequentialism lie rather elsewhere. There are certain situations
in which the causation of the situation, the relation
it has to what I do, is in no way remote or problematic in itself, and entirely justifies the claim that the
situation is a consequence of what I do: for instance,
it is quite clear, or reasonably clear, that if I do a
certain thing, this situation will come about, and if I
do not, it will not. So from a consequentialist point
of view it goes into the calculation of consequences
along with any other state of affairs accessible to me.
Yet from some, at least, non-consequentialist points
of view, there is a vital difference between some such
situations and others: namely, that in some a vital
link in the production of the eventual outcome is
provided by *someone else's* doing something. But for
consequentialism, all causal connexions are on the
same level, and it makes no difference, so far as that

goes, whether the causation of a given state of affairs lies through another agent, or not.

Correspondingly, there is no relevant difference which consists *just* in one state of affairs being brought about by me, without intervention of other agents, and another being brought about through the intervention of other agents; although some genuinely causal differences involving a difference of value may correspond to that (as when, for instance, the other agents derive pleasure or pain from the transaction), that kind of difference will already be included in the specification of the state of affairs to be produced. Granted that the states of affairs have been adequately described in causally and evaluatively relevant terms, it makes no further comprehensible difference who produces them. It is because consequentialism attaches value ultimately to states of affairs, and its concern is with what states of affairs the world contains, that it essentially involves the notion of *negative responsibility:* that if I am ever responsible for anything, then I must be just as much responsible for things that I allow or fail to prevent, as I am for things that I myself, in the more everyday restricted sense, bring about.[1] Those things also must enter my deliberations, as a responsible moral agent, on the same footing. What matters is what states of affairs the world contains, and so what matters with respect to a given action is what comes about if it is done, and what comes about if it is not done, and those are questions not intrinsically affected by the nature of the causal linkage, in particular by whether the outcome is partly produced by other agents.

The strong doctrine of negative responsibility flows directly from consequentialism's assignment of ultimate value to states of affairs. Looked at from another point of view, it can be seen also as a special application of something that is favoured in many moral outlooks not themselves consequentialist — something which, indeed, some thinkers have been disposed to regard as the essence of morality itself: a principle of impartiality. Such a principle will claim that there can be no relevant difference from a moral point of view which consists just in the fact, not further explicable in general terms, that benefits or harms accrue to one person rather than to another — 'it's me' can never in itself be a morally comprehensible reason.[2] [By] this principle, familiar with regard to the reception of harms and benefits, we can see consequentialism as extending to their

production: from the moral point of view, there is no comprehensible difference which consists just in my bringing about a certain outcome rather than someone else's producing it. That the doctrine of negative responsibility represents in this way the extreme of impartiality, and abstracts from the identity of the agent, leaving just a locus of causal intervention in the world — that fact is not merely a surface paradox. It helps to explain why consequentialism can seem to some to express a more serious attitude than nonconsequentialist views, why part of its appeal is to a certain kind of high-mindedness. Indeed, that is part of what is wrong with it.

For a lot of the time so far we have been operating at an exceedingly abstract level. This has been necessary in order to get clearer in general terms about the differences between consequentialist and other outlooks, an aim which is important if we want to know what features of them lead to what results for our thought. Now, however, let us look more concretely at two examples, to see what utilitarianism might say about them, what we might say about utilitarianism and, most importantly of all, what would be implied by certain ways of thinking about the situations. The examples are inevitably schematized, and they are open to the objection that they beg as many questions as they illuminate. There are two ways in particular in which examples in moral philosophy tend to beg important questions. One is that, as presented, they arbitrarily cut off and restrict the range of alternative courses of action — this objection might particularly be made against the first of my two examples. The second is that they inevitably present one with the situation as a going concern, and cut off questions about how the agent got into it, and correspondingly about moral considerations which might flow from that: this objection might perhaps specially arise with regard to the second of my two situations. These difficulties, however, just have to be accepted, and if anyone finds these examples cripplingly defective in this sort of respect, then he must in his own thought rework them in richer and less question-begging form. If he feels that no presentation of any imagined situation can ever be other than misleading in morality, and that there can never be any substitute for the concrete experienced complexity of actual moral situations, then this discussion, with him, must certainly grind to a halt: but then one may legitimately wonder whether every discussion with him about conduct will not grind to a half, including any discussion about the actual situations, since discussion about how one would think and feel about situations somewhat different from the actual (that is to say, situations to that extent imaginary) plays an important role in discussion of the actual.

(1) George, who has just taken his Ph.D. in chemistry, finds it extremely difficult to get a job. He is not very robust in health, which cuts down the number of jobs he might be able to do satisfactorily. His wife has to go out to work to keep them, which itself causes a great deal of strain, since they have small children and there are severe problems about looking after them. The results of all this, especially on the children, are damaging. An older chemist, who knows about this situation, says that he can get George a decently paid job in a certain laboratory, which pursues research into chemical and biological warfare. George says that he cannot accept this, since he is opposed to chemical and biological warfare. The older man replies that he is not too keen on it himself, come to that, but after all George's refusal is not going to make the job or the laboratory go away; what is more, he happens to know that if George refuses the job, it will certainly go to a contemporary of George's who is not inhibited by any such scruples and is likely if appointed to push along the research with greater zeal than George would. Indeed, it is not merely concern for George and his family, but (to speak frankly and in confidence) some alarm about this other man's excess of zeal, which has led the older man to offer to use his influence to get George the job. . . . George's wife, to whom he is deeply attached, has views (the details of which need not concern us) from which it follows that at least there is nothing particularly wrong with research into CBW. What should he do?

(2) Jim finds himself in the central square of a small South American town. Tied up against the wall are a row of twenty Indians, most terrified, a few defiant, in front of them several armed men in uniform. A heavy man in a sweat-stained khaki shirt turns out to be the captain in charge and, after a good deal of questioning of Jim which establishes that he got there by accident while on a botanical expedition, explains that the Indians are a random group of the inhabitants who, after recent acts of protest against the government, are just about to be killed to remind other possible protestors of the advantages of not protesting. However, since Jim is an honoured visitor from another land, the captain is happy to offer him a guest's privilege of killing one of the Indians himself. If Jim accepts, then as a special mark of the occasion, the other Indians will be let off. Of course, if Jim refuses, then there is no special occasion, and Pedro here will do what he was about to do when Jim arrived, and kill them all. Jim, with some desperate recollection of schoolboy fiction, wonders whether if he got hold of a gun, he could hold the captain, Pedro and the rest of the soldiers to threat, but it is quite clear from the set-up that nothing of that kind is going to work: any attempt at that sort of thing will mean that all the Indians will be killed, and himself. The men against the wall, and the other villagers, understand the situation, and are obviously begging him to accept. What should he do?

To these dilemmas, it seems to me that utilitarianism replies, in the first case, that George should accept the job, and in the second, that Jim should kill the Indian. Not only does utilitarianism give these answers but, if the situations are essentially as described and there are no further special factors, it regards them, it seems to me, as *obviously* the right answers. But many of us would certainly wonder whether, in (1), that could possibly be the right answer at all; and in the case of (2), even one who came to think that perhaps that was the answer, might well wonder whether it was obviously the answer. Nor is it just a question of the rightness or obviousness of these answers. It is also a question of what sort of considerations come into finding the answer. A feature of utilitarianism is that it cuts out a kind of consideration which for some others makes a difference to what they feel about such cases: a consideration involving the idea, as we might first and very simply put it, that each of us is specially responsible for what *he* does, rather than for what other people do. This is an idea closely connected with the value of integrity. It is often suspected that utilitarianism, at least in its direct forms, makes integrity as a value more or less unintelligible. I shall try to show that this suspicion is correct. Of course, even if that is correct, it would not necessarily follow that we should reject utilitarianism; perhaps, as utilitarians sometimes suggest, we should just forget about integrity, in favour of such things as a concern for the general good. However, if I am right, we cannot merely do that, since the reason why utilitarianism cannot understand integrity is that it cannot coherently describe the relations between a man's projects and his actions.

Two Kinds of Remoter Effect

A lot of what we have to say about this question will be about the relations between my projects and other people's projects. But before we get on to that, we should first ask whether we are assuming too hastily what the utilitarian answers to the dilemmas will be. In terms of more direct effects of the possible decisions, there does not indeed seem much doubt about the answer in either case; but it might be said that in terms of more remote or less evident effects counterweights might be found to enter the utilitarian scales. Thus the effect on George of a decision to take the job might be invoked, or its effect on others who might know of his decision. The possibility of there being more beneficent labours in the future from which he might be barred or disqualified, might be mentioned; and so forth. Such effects — in particular, possible effects on the agent's character, and effects on the public at large — are often invoked by utilitarian writers dealing with problems about lying or promise-breaking, and some similar considerations might be invoked here.

There is one very general remark that is worth making about arguments of this sort. The certainty that attaches to these hypotheses about possible effects is usually pretty low; in some cases, indeed, the hypothesis invoked is so implausible that it would scarcely pass if it were not being used to deliver the respectable moral answer, as in the standard fantasy that one of the effects of one's telling a particular lie is to weaken the disposition of the world at large to tell the truth. The demands on the certainty or probability of these beliefs as beliefs about particular actions are much milder than they would be on beliefs favouring the unconventional course. It may be said that this is as it should be, since the presumption must be in favour of the conventional course: but that scarcely seems a *utilitarian* answer, unless utilitarianism has already taken off in the direction of not applying the consequences to the particular act at all.

Leaving aside that very general point, I want to consider now two types of effect that are often invoked by utilitarians, and which might be invoked in connexion with these imaginary cases. The attitude or tone involved in invoking these effects may sometimes seem peculiar; but that sort of peculiarity soon becomes familiar in utilitarian discussions, and indeed it can be something of an achievement to retain a sense of it.

First, there is the psychological effect on the agent. Our descriptions of these situations have not so far taken account of how George or Jim will be after they have taken the one course or the other; and it might be said that if they take the course which seemed at first the utilitarian one, the effects on them will be in fact bad enough and extensive enough to cancel out the initial utilitarian advantages of that course. Now there is one version of this effect in which, for a utilitarian, some confusion must be involved, namely that in which the agent feels bad, his subsequent conduct and relations are crippled and so on, *because he thinks that he has done the wrong thing* — for if the balance of outcomes was as it appeared to be *before* invoking this effect, then he has not (from the utilitarian point of view) done the wrong thing. So that version of the effect, for a rational and utilitarian agent, could not possibly make any difference to the assessment of right and wrong. However, perhaps he is not a thoroughly rational agent, and is disposed to have bad feelings, whichever he decided to do. Now such feelings, which are from a strictly utilitarian point of view irrational — nothing, a utilitarian can point out, is advanced by having them — cannot, consistently, have any great weight in a utilitarian calculation. I shall consider in a moment an argument to suggest that they should have no weight at all in it. But short of that, the utilitarian could reasonably say that such feelings should not be encouraged, even if we accept their existence, and that to give them a lot of weight is to encourage them. Or, at the very best, even if they are straightforwardly and without any discount to be put into the calculation, their weight must be small: they are after all (and at best) one man's feelings.

That consideration might seem to have particular force in Jim's case. In George's case, his feelings represent a larger proportion of what is to be weighed, and are more commensurate in character with other items in the calculation. In Jim's case, however, his feelings might seem to be of very little weight compared with other things that are at stake. There is a powerful and recognizable appeal that can be made on this point: as that a refusal by Jim to do what he has been invited to do would be a kind of self-indulgent squeamishness. That is an appeal which can be made by other than utilitarians — indeed, there are some uses of it which cannot be consistently made by utilitarians, as when it essentially involves the idea that there is something dishonourable about such self-indulgence. But in some versions it is a familiar, and it must be said a powerful, weapon of utilitarianism. One must be clear, though, about what it can and cannot accomplish. The most it can do, so far as I can see, is to invite one to consider how seriously, and for what reasons, one feels that what one is invited to do is (in these circumstances) wrong, and in particular, to consider that question from the utilitarian point of view. When the agent is not seeing the situation from a utilitarian point of view, the appeal cannot force him to do so; and if he does come round to seeing it from a utilitarian point of view, there is virtually nothing left for the appeal to do. If he does not see it from a utilitarian point of view, he will not see his resistance to the invitation, and the unpleasant feelings he associates with accepting it, *just* as disagreeable experiences of his; they figure rather as emotional expressions of a thought that to accept would be wrong. He may be asked, as by the appeal, to consider whether he is right, and indeed whether he is fully serious, in thinking that. But the assertion of the appeal, that he is being self-indulgently squeamish, will not itself answer that question, or even help to answer it, since it essentially tells him to regard his feelings just as unpleasant experiences of his, and he cannot, by doing that, answer the question they pose when they are precisely not so regarded, but are regarded as indications[3] of what he thinks is right and wrong. If he does come round fully to the utilitarian point of view then of course he will regard these feelings just as unpleasant experiences of his. And once Jim — at least — has come to see them in that light, there is nothing left for the appeal to do, since *of course* his feelings, so regarded, are of virtually no weight at all in relation to the other things at stake. The 'squeamishness' appeal is not an argument which adds in a hitherto neglected consideration. Rather, it is an invitation to consider the situation, and one's own feelings, from a utilitarian point of view.

The reason why the squeamishness appeal can be very unsettling, and one can be unnerved by the suggestion of self-indulgence in going against utilitarian considerations, is not that we are utilitarians who are uncertain what utilitarian value to attach to our moral feelings, but that we are partially at least not utilitarians, and cannot regard our moral feelings merely as objects of utilitarian value. Because our moral relation to the world is partly given by such feelings, and by a sense of what we can or cannot 'live with,' to come to regard those feelings from a purely utilitarian point of view, that is to say, as happenings outside one's moral self, is to lose a sense of one's moral identity; to lose, in the most literal way, one's integrity. At this point utilitarianism alienates one from one's moral feelings; we shall see a little later how, more basically, it alienates one from one's actions as well.

If, then, one is really going to regard one's feelings from a strictly utilitarian point of view, Jim should give very little weight at all to his; it seems almost indecent, in fact, once one has taken that point of view, to suppose that he should give any at all. In George's case one might feel that things were slightly different. It is interesting, though, that one reason why one might think that — namely that one person principally affected is his wife — is very dubiously available to a utilitarian. George's wife has some reason to be interested in George's integrity and his sense of it; the Indians, quite properly, have no interest in Jim's. But it is not at all clear how utilitarianism would describe that difference.

There is an argument, and a strong one, that a strict utilitarian should give not merely small extra weight, in calculations of right and wrong, to feelings of this kind, but that he should give absolutely no weight to them at all. This is based on the point, which we have already seen, that if a course of action is, before taking these sorts of feelings into account, utilitarianly preferable, then bad feelings about that kind of action will be from a utilitarian point of view irrational. Now it might be thought that even if that is so, it would not mean that in a utilitarian calculation such feelings should not be taken into account; it is after all a well-known boast of utilitarianism that it is a realistic outlook which seeks the best in the world as it is, and takes any form of happiness or unhappiness into account. While a utilitarian will no doubt seek to diminish the incidence of feelings which are utilitarianly irrational — or at least of disagreeable feelings which are so — he might be expected to take them into account while they exist. This is without doubt classical utilitarian doctrine, but there is good reason to think that utilitarianism cannot stick to it without embracing results which are startlingly unacceptable and perhaps self-defeating.

Suppose that there is in a certain society a racial minority. Considering merely the ordinary interests of the other citizens, as opposed to their sentiments, this minority does no particular harm; we may suppose that it does not confer any very great benefits either. Its presence is in those terms neutral or mildly beneficial. However, the other citizens have such prejudices that they find the sight of this group, even the knowledge of its presence, very disagreeable. Proposals are made for removing in some way this minority. If we assume various quite plausible things (as that programmes to change the majority sentiment are likely to be protracted and ineffective) then even if the removal would be unpleasant for the minority, a utilitarian calculation might well end up favouring this step, especially if the minority were a rather small minority and the majority were very severely prejudiced, that is to say, were made very severely uncomfortable by the presence of the minority.

A utilitarian might find that conclusion embarrassing; and not merely because of its nature, but because of the grounds on which it is reached. While a utilitarian might be expected to take into account certain other sorts of consequences of the prejudice, as that a majority prejudice is likely to be displayed in conduct disagreeable to the minority, and so forth, he might be made to wonder whether the unpleasant experiences of the prejudiced people should be allowed, *merely as such,* to count. If he does count them, merely as such, then he has once more separated himself from a body of ordinary moral thought which he might have hoped to accommodate; he may also have started on the path of defeating his own view of things. For one feature of these sentiments is that they are from the utilitarian point of view itself irrational, and a thoroughly utilitarian person would either not have them, or if he found that he did tend to have them, would himself seek to discount them. Since the sentiments in question are such that a rational utilitarian would discount them in himself, it is reasonable to suppose that he should discount them in his calculations about society; it does seem quite unreasonable for

him to give just as much weight to feelings — considered just in themselves, one must recall, as experiences of those that have them — which are essentially based on views which are from a utilitarian point of view irrational, as to those which accord with utilitarian principles. Granted this idea, it seems reasonable for him to rejoin a body of moral thought in other respects congenial to him, and discount those sentiments, just considered in themselves, totally, on the principle that no pains or discomforts are to count in the utilitarian sum which their subjects have just because they hold views which are by utilitarian standards irrational. But if he accepts that, then in the cases we are at present considering no extra weight at all can be put in for bad feelings of George or Jim about their choices, if those choices are, leaving out those feelings, on the first round utilitarianly rational.

Integrity

The [two] situations have in common that if the agent does not do a certain disagreeable thing, someone else will, and in Jim's situation at least the result, the state of affairs after the other man has acted, if he does, will be worse than after Jim has acted, if Jim does. The same, on a smaller scale, is true of George's case. I have already suggested that it is inherent in consequentialism that it offers a strong doctrine of negative responsibility: if I know that if I do X, O_1 will eventuate, and if I refrain from doing X, O_2 will, and that O_2 is worse than O_1, then I am responsible for O_2 if I refrain voluntarily from doing X. 'You could have prevented it,' as will be said, and truly, to Jim, if he refuses, by the relatives of the other Indians.

In the present cases, the situation of O_2 includes another agent bringing about results worse than O_1. So far as O_2 has been identified up to this point — merely as the worse outcome which will eventuate if I refrain from doing X — we might equally have said that what that other brings about is O_2; but that would be to underdescribe the situation. For what occurs if Jim refrains from action is not solely twenty Indians dead, but *Pedro's killing twenty Indians,* and that is not a result which Pedro brings about, though the death of the Indians is. We can say: what one does is not included in the outcome of what one does, while what another does can be included in the outcome of what one does. For that to be so, as the terms are now being used, only a very weak condition has to be satisfied: for Pedro's killing the Indians to be the outcome of Jim's refusal, it only has to be causally true that if Jim had not refused, Pedro would not have done it.

That may be enough for us to speak, in some sense, of Jim's responsibility for that outcome, if it occurs; but it is certainly not enough, it is worth noticing, for us to speak of Jim's *making* those things happen. For granted this way of their coming about, he could have made them happen only by making Pedro shoot, and there is no acceptable sense in which his refusal makes Pedro shoot. If the captain had said on Jim's refusal, 'you leave me with no alternative,' he would have been lying, like most who use that phrase. While the deaths, and the killing, may be the outcome of Jim's refusal, it is misleading to think, in such a case, of Jim having an *effect* on the world through the medium (as it happens) of Pedro's acts; for this is to leave Pedro out of the picture in his essential role of one who has intentions and projects, projects for realizing which Jim's refusal would leave an opportunity. Instead of thinking in terms of supposed effects of Jim's projects on Pedro, it is more revealing to think in terms of the effects of Pedro's projects on Jim's decision.

Utilitarianism would do well then to acknowledge the evident fact that among the things that make people happy is not only making other people happy, but being taken up or involved in any of a vast range of projects, or — if we waive the evangelical and moralizing associations of the word — commitments. One can be committed to such things as a person, a cause, an institution, a career, one's own genius, or the pursuit of danger.

Now none of these is itself the *pursuit of happiness:* by an exceedingly ancient platitude, it is not at all clear that there could be anything which was just that, or at least anything that had the slightest chance of being successful. Happiness, rather, requires being involved in, or at least content with, something else. It is not impossible for utilitarianism to accept that point: it does not have to be saddled with a naïve and absurd philosophy of mind about the relation between desire and happiness. What it does have to say is that if such commitments are worthwhile, then pursuing the projects that flow

from them, and realizing some of those projects, will make the person for whom they are worthwhile, happy. It may be that to claim that is still wrong: it may well be that a commitment can make sense to a man (can make sense of his life) without his supposing that it will make him *happy.* But that is not the present point; let us grant to utilitarianism that all worthwhile human projects must conduce, one way or another, to happiness. The point is that even if that is true, it does not follow, nor could it possibly be true, that those projects are themselves projects of pursuing happiness. One has to believe in, or at least want, or quite minimally, be content with, other things, for there to be anywhere that happiness can come from.

Utilitarianism, then, should be willing to agree that its general aim of maximizing happiness does not imply that what everyone is doing is just pursuing happiness. On the contrary, people have to be pursuing other things. What those other things may be, utilitarianism, sticking to its professed empirical stance, should be prepared just to find out. No doubt some possible projects it will want to discourage, on the grounds that their being pursued involves a negative balance of happiness to others: though even there, the unblinking accountant's eye of the strict utilitarian will have something to put in the positive column, the satisfactions of the destructive agent. Beyond that, there will be a vast variety of generally beneficent or at least harmless projects; and some no doubt, will take the form not just of tastes or fancies, but of what I have called 'commitments.' It may even be that the utilitarian researcher will find that many of those with commitments, who have really identified themselves with objects outside themselves, who are thoroughly involved with other persons, or institutions, or activities or causes, are actually happier than those whose projects and wants are not like that. If so, that is an important piece of utilitarian empirical love.

When I say 'happier' here, I have in mind the sort of consideration which any utilitarian would be committed to accepting: as for instance that such people are less likely to have a breakdown or commit suicide. Of course that is not all that is actually involved, but the point in this argument is to use to the maximum degree utilitarian notions, in order to locate a breaking point in utilitarian thought. In appealing to this strictly utilitarian notion, I am being more consistent with utilitarianism than Smart is.

In his struggles with the problem of the brain-electrode man, Smart commends the idea that 'happy' is a partly evaluative term, in the sense that we call 'happiness' those kinds of satisfaction which, as things are, we approve of. But *by what standard* is this surplus element of approval supposed, from a utilitarian point of view, to be allocated? There is no source for it, on a strictly utilitarian view, except further degrees of satisfaction, but there are none of those available, or the problem would not arise. Nor does it help to appeal to the fact that we dislike in prospect things which we like when we get there, for from a utilitarian point of view it would seem that the original dislike was merely irrational or based on an error. Smart's argument at this point seems to be embarrassed by a well-known utilitarian uneasiness, which comes from a feeling that it is not respectable to ignore the 'deep,' while not having anywhere left in human life to locate it.

Let us now go back to the agent as utilitarian, and his higher-order project of maximizing desirable outcomes. At this level, he is committed only to that: what the outcome will actually consist of will depend entirely on the facts, on what persons with what projects and what potential satisfactions there are within calculable reach of the causal levers near which he finds himself. His own substantial projects and commitments come into it, but only as one lot among others — they potentially provide one set of satisfactions among those which he may be able to assist from where he happens to be. He is the agent of the satisfaction system who happens to be at a particular point at a particular time: in Jim's case, our man in South America. His own decisions as a utilitarian agent are a function of all the satisfactions which he can effect from where he is: and this means that the projects of others, to an indeterminately great extent, determine his decision.

This may be so either positively or negatively. It will be so positively if agents within the causal field of his decision have projects which are at any rate harmless, and so should be assisted. It will equally be so, but negatively, if there is an agent within the causal field whose projects are harmful, and have to be frustrated to maximize desirable outcomes. So it is with Jim and the soldier Pedro. On the utilitarian view, the undesirable projects of other people as much determine, in this negative way, one's decisions as the desirable ones do positively: if those people were not there, or had different projects, the causal nexus would be different, and it is the actual state of the causal nexus which determines the decision. The determination to an indefinite degree of my decisions by other people's projects is just another aspect of my unlimited responsibility to act for the best in a causal framework formed to a considerable extent by their projects.

The decision so determined is, for utilitarianism, the right decision. But what if it conflicts with some project of mine? This, the utilitarian will say, has already been dealt with: the satisfaction to you of fulfilling your project, and any satisfactions to others of your so doing, have already been through the calculating device and have been found inadequate. Now in the case of many sorts of projects, that is a perfectly reasonable sort of answer. But in the case of projects of the sort I have called 'commitments,' those with which one is more deeply and extensively involved and identified, this cannot just by itself be an adequate answer, and there may be no adequate answer at all. For, to take the extreme sort of case, how can a man, as a utilitarian agent, come to regard as one satisfaction among others, and a dispensable one, a project or attitude round which he has built his life, just because someone else's projects have so structured the causal scene that that is how the utilitarian sum comes out?

The point here is not, as utilitarians may hasten to say, that if the project or attitude is that central to his life, then to abandon it will be very disagreeable to him and great loss of utility will be involved. I have already argued in section 4 that it is not like that; on the contrary, once he is prepared to look at it like that, the argument in any serious case is over anyway. The point is that he is identified with his actions as flowing from projects and attitudes which in some cases he takes seriously at the deepest level, as what his life is about (or, in some cases, this section of his life — seriousness is not necessarily the same as persistence). It is absurd to demand of such a man, when the sums come in from the utility network which the projects of others have in part determined, that he should just step aside from his own project and decision and acknowledge the decision which utilitarian calculation requires. It is to alienate him in a real sense from his actions and the source of his action in his own convictions. It is to make him into a channel between the input of everyone's projects, including his own, and an output of optimistic decision; but this is to neglect the extent to which *his* actions and *his* decisions have to be seen as the actions and decisions which flow from the projects and attitudes with which he is most closely identified. It is thus, in the most literal sense, an attack on his integrity.

These sorts of considerations do not in themselves give solutions to practical dilemmas such as those provided by our examples; but I hope they help to provide other ways of thinking about them. In fact, it is not hard to see that in George's case, viewed from this perspective, the utilitarian solution would be wrong. Jim's case is different, and harder. But if (as I suppose) the utilitarian is probably right in this case, that is not to be found out just by asking the utilitarian's questions. Discussions of it—and I am not going to try to carry it further here—will have to take seriously the distinction between my killing someone, and its coming about because of what I do that someone else kills them: a distinction based, not so much on the distinction between action and inaction, as on the distinction between my projects and someone else's projects. At least it will have to start by taking that seriously, as utilitarianism does not; but then it will have to build out from there by asking why that distinction seems to have less, or a different, force in this case than it has in George's. One question here would be how far one's powerful objection to killing people just is, in fact, an application of a powerful objection to their being killed. Another dimension of that is the issue of how much it matters that the people at risk are actual, and there, as opposed to hypothetical, or future, or merely elsewhere.

There are many other considerations that could come into such a question, but the immediate point of all this is to draw one particular contrast with utilitarianism: that to reach a grounded decision in such a case should not be regarded as a matter of just discounting one's reactions, impulses and deeply held projects in the face of the pattern of utilities, nor yet merely adding them in—but in the first instance of trying to understand them.

Of course, time and circumstances are unlikely to make a grounded decision, in Jim's case at least, possible. It might not even be decent. Instead of thinking in a rational and systematic way either about utilities or about the value of human life, the relevance of the people at risk being present, and so forth, the presence of the people at risk may just have its effect. The significance of the immediate

should not be underestimated. Philosophers, not only utilitarian ones, repeatedly urge one to view the world *sub specie aeternitatis,* but for most human purposes that is not a good *species* to view it under. If we are not agents of the universal satisfaction system, we are not primarily janitors of any system of values, even our own: very often, we just act, as a possibly confused result of the situation in which we are engaged. That, I suspect, is very often an exceedingly good thing.

Utilitarianism is in more than one way an important subject; at least I hope it is, or these words, and this book, will have been wasted. One important feature of it, which I have tried to bring out, is the number of dimensions in which it runs against the complexities of moral thought: in some part because of its consequentialism, in some part because of its view of happiness, and so forth. A common element in utilitarianism's showing in all these respects, I think, is its great simple-mindedness. This is not at all the same thing as lack of intellectual sophistication: utilitarianism, both in theory and practice, is alarmingly good at combining technical complexity with simple-mindedness. Nor is it the same as simple-heartedness, which it is at least possible (with something of an effort and in private connexions) to regard as a virtue. Simple-mindedness consists in having too few thoughts and feelings to match the world as it really is. In private life and the field of personal morality it is often possible to survive in that state—indeed, the very statement of the problem for that case is over-simple, since the question of what moral demands life makes is not independent of what one's morality demands of it. But the demands of political reality and the complexities of political thought are obstinately what they are, and in face of them the simple-mindedness of utilitarianism disqualifies it totally.

The important issues that utilitarianism raises should be discussed in contexts more rewarding than that of utilitarianism itself. The day cannot be too far off in which we hear no more of it.

Endnotes

[1] This is a fairly modest sense of 'responsibility,' introduced merely by one's ability to reflect on, and decide, what one ought to do. This presumably escapes J. J. C. Smart's ban

on the notion of 'the responsibility' as 'a piece of metaphysical nonsense'—his remark seems to be concerned solely with situations of interpersonal blame.

2 There is a tendency in some writers to suggest that it is not a comprehensible reason at all. But this, I suspect, is

due to the overwhelming importance those writers ascribe to the moral point of view.

3 On the noncognitivist metaethic in terms of which Smart presents his utilitarianism, the term 'indications' here would represent an understatement.

V.4 *Alienation, Consequentialism, and the Demands of Morality*

Peter Railton

Peter Railton is a professor of philosophy at the University of Michigan. In this essay he addresses Williams's critique of utilitarianism on the basis of its tendency to produce alienation (see the previous reading in this book). Railton defends utilitarianism by defending two theses: (1) some alienation may be necessary for the moral life, but (2) the utilitarian (even the act utilitarian whom he is defending here) can take this into account in devising strategies of action. Railton's article is an example of sophisticated utilitarianism, wherein such items as character and motivation are woven into a utilitarian account of ethics.

Introduction

Living up to the demands of morality may bring with it alienation—from one's personal commitments, from one's feelings or sentiments, from other people, or even from morality itself. In this article I will discuss several apparent instances of such alienation, and attempt a preliminary assessment of their bearing on questions about the acceptability of certain moral theories. Of special concern will be the question whether problems about alienation show consequentialist moral theories to be self-defeating.

I will not attempt a full or general characterization of alienation. Indeed, at a perfectly general level alienation can be characterized only very roughly as a kind of estrangement, distancing, or separateness (not necessarily consciously attended to) resulting in some sort of loss (not necessarily consciously

noticed).[1] Rather than seek a general analysis I will rely upon examples to convey a sense of what is involved in the sorts of alienation with which I am concerned. There is nothing in a word, and the phenomena to be discussed below could all be considered while avoiding the controversial term 'alienation.' My sense, however, is that there is some point in using this formidable term, if only to draw attention to commonalities among problems not always noticed. For example, in the final section of this article I will suggest that one important form of alienation in moral practice, the sense that morality confronts us as an alien set of demands, distant and disconnected from our actual concerns, can be mitigated by dealing with other sorts of alienation morality may induce. Finally, there are historical reasons, which will not be entered into here, for bringing these phenomena under a single label; part of the explanation of their existence lies in the conditions of modern "civil society," and in the philosophical traditions of empiricism and rationalism—which include a certain picture of the self's relation to the world—that have flourished in it.

Let us begin with two examples.

From *Philosophy and Public Affairs* 13(1984): 134–171. Copyright © 1984 by Princeton University Press. Reprinted by permission of the author and publisher.

I. *John and Anne and Lisa and Helen*

To many, John has always seemed a model husband. He almost invariably shows great sensitivity to his wife's needs, and he willingly goes out of his way to meet them. He plainly feels great affection for her. When a friend remarks upon the extraordinary quality of John's concern for his wife, John responds without any self-indulgence or self-congratulation. "I've always thought that people should help each other when they're in a specially good position to do so. I know Anne better than anyone else does, so I know better what she wants and needs. Besides, I have such affection for her that it's no great burden — instead, I get a lot of satisfaction out of it. Just think how awful marriage would be, or life itself, if people didn't take special care of the ones they love." His friend accuses John of being unduly modest, but John's manner convinces him that he is telling the truth: this is really how he feels.

Lisa has gone through a series of disappointments over a short period, and has been profoundly depressed. In the end, however, with the help of others she has emerged from the long night of anxiety and melancholy. Only now is she able to talk openly with friends about her state of mind, and she turns to her oldest friend, Helen, who was a mainstay throughout. She'd like to find a way to thank Helen, since she's only too aware of how much of a burden she's been over these months, how much of a drag and a bore, as she puts it. "You don't have to thank me, Lisa," Helen replies, "you deserved it. It was the least I could do after all you've done for me. We're friends, remember? And we said a long time ago that we'd stick together no matter what. Some day I'll probably ask the same thing of you, and I know you'll come through. What else are friends for?" Lisa wonders whether Helen is saying this simply to avoid creating feelings of guilt, but Helen replies that she means every word — she couldn't bring herself to lie to Lisa if she tried.

II. *What's Missing?*

What is troubling about the words of John and Helen? Both show stout character and moral awareness. John's remarks have a benevolent, consequentialist cast, while Helen reasons in a deontological language of duties, reciprocity, and respect. They are not self-centered or without feeling. Yet something seems wrong.

The place to look is not so much at what they say as what they don't say. Think, for example, of how John's remarks might sound to his wife. Anne might have hoped that it was, in some ultimate sense, in part for *her* sake and the sake of their love as such that John pays such special attention to her. That he devotes himself to her because of the characteristically good consequences of doing so seems to leave her, and their relationship as such, too far out of the picture — this despite the fact that these characteristically good consequences depend in important ways on his special relation to her. She is being taken into account by John, but it might seem she is justified in being hurt by the way she is being taken into account. It is as if John viewed her, their relationship, and even his own affection for her from a distant, objective point of view — a moral point of view where reasons must be reasons for any rational agent and so must have an impersonal character even when they deal with personal matters. His wife might think a more personal point of view would also be appropriate, a point of view from which "It's my wife" or "It's Anne" would have direct and special relevance, and play an unmediated role in his answer to the question "*Why* do you attend to her so?"

Something similar is missing from Helen's account of why she stood by Lisa. While we understand that the specific duties she feels toward Lisa depend upon particular features of their relationship, still we would not be surprised if Lisa finds Helen's response to her expression of gratitude quite distant, even chilling. We need not question whether she has strong feeling for Lisa, but we may wonder at how that feeling finds expression in Helen's thinking.[2]

John and Helen both show alienation: there would seem to be an estrangement between their affections and their rational, deliberative selves; an abstract and universalizing point of view mediates their responses to others and to their own sentiments. We should not assume that they have been caught in an uncharacteristic moment of moral reflection or after-the-fact rationalization; it is a settled part of their characters to think and act from a moral point of view. It is as if the world were for them a fabric of obligations and permissions in which personal considerations deserve recognition only to the extent that, and in the way that, such considerations find a place in this fabric.

To call John and Helen alienated from their affections or their intimates is not of itself to condemn them, nor is it to say that they are experiencing any sort of distress. One may be alienated from something without recognizing this as such or suffering in any conscious way from it, much as one may simply be uninterested in something without awareness or conscious suffering. But alienation is not mere lack of interest: John and Helen are not *uninterested* in their affections or in their intimates; rather, their interest takes a certain alienated form. While this alienation may not itself be a psychological affliction, it may be the basis of such afflictions — such as a sense of loneliness or emptiness — or of the loss of certain things of value — such as a sense of belonging or the pleasures of spontaneity. Moreover, their alienation may cause psychological distress in others, and make certain valuable sorts of relationships impossible.

However, we must be on guard lest oversimple categories distort our diagnosis. It seems to me wrong to picture the self as ordinarily divided into cognitive and affective halves, with deliberation and rationality belonging to the first, and sentiments belonging to the second. John's alienation is not a problem on the boundary of naturally given cognitive and affective selves, but a problem partially constituted by the bifurcation of his psyche into these separate spheres. *John's* deliberative self seems remarkably divorced from his affections, but not all psyches need be so divided. That there is a cognitive element in affection — that affection is not a mere "feeling" that is a given for the deliberative self but rather involves as well certain characteristic modes of thought and perception — is suggested by the difficulty some may have in believing that John really does love Anne if he persistently thinks about her in the way suggested by his remarks. Indeed, his affection for Anne does seem to have been demoted to a mere "feeling." For this reason among others, we should not think of John's alienation from his affections and his alienation from Anne as wholly independent phenomena, the one the cause of the other. Of course, similar remarks apply to Helen.

III. *The Moral Point of View*

Perhaps the lives of John and Anne or Helen and Lisa would be happier or fuller if none of the alienation mentioned were present. But is this a problem for *morality*? If, as some have contended, to have a morality is to make normative judgments from a moral point of view and be guided by them, and if by its nature a moral point of view must exclude considerations that lack universality, then any genuinely moral way of going about life would seem liable to produce the sorts of alienation mentioned above. Thus it would be a conceptual confusion to ask that we never be required by morality to go beyond a personal point of view, since to fail ever to look at things from an impersonal (or nonpersonal) point of view would be to fail ever to *be* distinctively moral — not immoralism, perhaps, but amoralism. This would not be to say that there are not other points of view on life worthy of our attention, or that taking a moral point of view is always appropriate — one could say that John and Helen show no moral defect in thinking so impersonally, although they do moralize to excess. But the fact that a particular morality requires us to take an impersonal point of view could not sensibly be held against it, for that would be what makes it a morality at all.

This sort of position strikes me as entirely too complacent. First, we must somehow give an account of practical reasoning that does not merely multiply points of view and divide the self — a more unified account is needed. Second, we must recognize that loving relationships, friendships, group loyalties, and spontaneous actions are among the most important contributors to whatever it is that makes life worthwhile; any moral theory deserving serious consideration must itself give them serious consideration. As William K. Frankena has written, "Morality is made for man, not man for morality." Moral considerations are often supposed to be overriding in practical reasoning. If we were to find that adopting a particular morality led to irreconcilable conflict with central types of human well-being — as cases akin to John's and Helen's have led some to suspect — then this surely would give us good reason to doubt its claims.

For example, in the closing sentences of *A Theory of Justice* John Rawls considers the "perspective of eternity," which is impartial across all individuals and times, and writes that this is a "form of *thought and feeling* that rational persons can adopt in the world." "Purity of heart," he concludes, "would be to see clearly and act with grace and self-command from this point of view." This may or may not be purity of heart, but it could not be the standpoint of actual life without radically detaching the individual from a range of personal concerns and commitments. Presumably we should not read Rawls as recommending that we adopt this point of view in the bulk of our actions in daily life, but the fact that so purely abstracted a perspective is portrayed as a kind of moral ideal should at least start us wondering. If to be more perfectly moral is to ascend ever higher toward *sub specie aeternitatis* abstraction, perhaps we made a mistake in boarding the moral escalator in the first place. Some of the very "weaknesses" that prevent us from achieving this moral ideal — strong attachments to persons or projects — seem to be part of a considerably more compelling human ideal.

Should we say at this point that the lesson is that we should give a more prominent role to the value of nonalienation in our moral reasoning? That would be too little too late: the problem seems to be the way in which morality asks us to look at things, not just the things it asks us to look at.

IV. *The "Paradox of Hedonism"*

Rather than enter directly into the question whether being moral is a matter of taking a moral point of view and whether there is thus some sort of necessary connection between being moral and being alienated in a way detrimental to human flourishing, I will consider a related problem the solution to which may suggest a way of steering around obstacles to a more direct approach.

One version of the so-called "paradox of hedonism" is that adopting as one's exclusive ultimate end in life the pursuit of maximum happiness may well prevent one from having certain experiences or engaging in certain sorts of relationships or commitments that are among the greatest sources of happiness. The hedonist, looking around him, may discover that some of those who are less concerned with their own happiness than he is, and who view people and projects less instrumentally than he does, actually manage to live happier lives than he despite his dogged pursuit of happiness. The "paradox" is pragmatic, not logical, but it looks deep nonetheless: the hedonist, it would appear, ought not to be a hedonist. It seems, then, as if we have come across a second case in which mediating one's relations to people or projects by a particular point of view — in this case, a hedonistic point of view — may prevent one from attaining the fullest possible realization of sought-after values.

However, it is important to notice that even though adopting a hedonistic life project may tend to interfere with realizing that very project, there is no such natural exclusion between acting for the sake of another or a cause as such and recognizing how important this is to one's happiness. A spouse who acts for the sake of his mate may know full well that this is a source of deep satisfaction for him — in addition to providing him with reasons for acting internal to it, the relationship may also promote the external goal of achieving happiness. Moreover, while the pursuit of happiness may not be the reason he entered or sustains the relationship, he may also recognize that if it had not seemed likely to make him happy he would not have entered it, and that if it proved over time to be inconsistent with his happiness he would consider ending it.

It might be objected that one cannot really regard a person or a project as an end as such if one's commitment is in this way contingent or overridable. But were this so, we would be able to have very few commitments to ends as such. For example, one could not be committed to both one's spouse and one's child as ends as such, since at most one of these commitments could be overriding in cases of conflict. It is easy to confuse the notion of a commitment to an end *as such* (or *for its own sake*) with that of an *overriding* commitment, but strength is not the same as structure. To be committed to an end as such is a matter of (among other things) whether it furnishes one with reasons for acting that are not mediated by other concerns. It does not follow that these reasons must always outweigh whatever opposing reasons one may have, or that one may not at the same time have other, mediating reasons that also incline one to act on behalf of that end.

Actual commitments to ends as such, even when very strong, are subject to various qualifications and contingencies. If a friend grows too predictable or moves off to a different part of the world, or if a planned life project proves less engaging or practical than one had imagined, commitments and affections naturally change. If a relationship were highly vulnerable to the least change, it would be strained to speak of genuine affection rather than, say, infatuation. But if members of a relationship came to believe that they would be better off without it, this ordinarily would be a nontrivial change, and it is not difficult to imagine that their commitment to the relationship might be contingent in this way but nonetheless real. Of course, a relationship involves a shared history and shared expectations as well as momentary experiences, and it is unusual that affection or concern can be changed overnight, or relationships begun or ended at will. Moreover, the sorts of affections and commitments that can play a decisive role in shaping one's life and in making possible the deeper sorts of satisfactions are not those that are easily overridden or subject to constant reassessment or second-guessing. Thus a sensible hedonist would not forever be subjecting his affections or commitments to egoistic calculation, nor would he attempt to break off a relationship or commitment merely because it might seem to him at a given moment that some other arrangement would make him happier. Commitments to others or to causes as such may be very closely linked to the self, and a hedonist who knows what he's about will not be one who turns on his self at the slightest provocation. Contingency is not expendability, and while some commitments are remarkably noncontingency — such as those of parent to child or patriot to country — it cannot be said that commitments of a more contingent sort are never genuine, or never conduce to the profounder sorts of happiness.

Following these observations, we may reduce the force of the "paradox of hedonism" if we distinguish two forms of hedonism. *Subjective hedonism* is the view that one should adopt the hedonistic point of view in action, that is, that one should whenever possible attempt to determine which act seems most likely to contribute optimally to one's happiness, and behave accordingly. *Objective hedonism* is the view that one should follow that course of action which would in fact most contribute to one's happiness, even when this would involve *not* adopting the hedonistic point of view in action. An act will be

called *subjectively hedonistic* if it is done from a hedonistic point of view; an act is *objectively hedonistic* if it is that act, of those available to the agent, which would most contribute to his happiness.[3] Let us call someone a *sophisticated hedonist* if he aims to lead an objectively hedonistic life (that is, the happiest life available to him in the circumstances) and yet is not committed to subjective hedonism. Thus, within the limits of what is psychologically possible, a sophisticated hedonist is prepared to eschew the hedonistic point of view whenever taking this point of view conflicts with following an objectively hedonistic course of action. The so-called paradox of hedonism shows that there will be such conflicts: certain acts or courses of action may be objectively hedonistic only if not subjectively hedonistic. When things are put this way, it seems that the sophisticated hedonist faces a problem rather than a paradox: how to act in order to achieve maximum possible happiness if this is at times — or even often — *not* a matter of carrying out hedonistic deliberations.

The answer in any particular case will be complex and contextual — it seems unlikely that any one method of decision-making would always promote thought and action most conducive to one's happiness. A sophisticated hedonist might proceed precisely by looking at the complex and contextual: observing the actual modes of thought and action of those people who are in some ways like himself and who seem most happy. If our assumptions are right, he will find that few such individuals are subjective hedonists; instead, they act for the sake of a variety of ends as such. He may then set out to develop in himself the traits of character, ways of thought, types of commitment, and so on, that seem common in happy lives. For example, if he notes that the happiest people often have strong loyalties to friends, he must ask how he can become a more loyal friend — not merely how he can seem to be a loyal friend (since those he has observed are not happy because they merely seem loyal) — but how he can in fact be one.

Could one really make such changes if one had as a goal leading an optimally happy life? The answer seems to me a qualified *yes,* but let us first look at a simpler case. A highly competitive tennis player comes to realize that his obsession with winning is keeping him from playing his best. A pro tells him that if he wants to win he must devote himself more to the game and its play as such and think less about his performance. In the commitment and concentration made possible by this devotion, he is told, lies the secret of successful tennis. So he spends a good deal of time developing an enduring devotion to many aspects of the activity, and finds it peculiarly satisfying to become so absorbed in it. He plays better, and would have given up the program of change if he did not, but he now finds that he plays tennis more for its own sake, enjoying greater internal as well as external rewards from the sport. Such a person would not keep thinking—on or off the court—"No matter how I play, the only thing I really care about is whether I win!" He would recognize such thoughts as self-defeating, as evidence that his old, unhelpful way of looking at things was returning. Nor would such a person be self-deceiving. He need not hide from himself his goal of winning, for this goal is consistent with his increased devotion to the game. His commitment to the activity is not eclipsed by, but made more vivid by, his desire to succeed at it.

The same sort of story might be told about a sophisticated hedonist and friendship. An individual could realize that his instrumental attitude toward his friends prevents him from achieving the fullest happiness friendship affords. He could then attempt to focus more on his friends as such, doing this somewhat deliberately, perhaps, until it comes more naturally. He might then find his friendships improved and himself happier. If he found instead that his relationships were deteriorating or his happiness declining, he would reconsider the idea. None of this need be hidden from himself: the external goal of happiness reinforces the internal goals of his relationships. The sophisticated hedonist's motivational structure should therefore meet a *counterfactual condition:* he need not always act for the sake of happiness, since he may do various things for their own sake or for the sake of others, but he would not act as he does if it were not compatible with his leading an objectively hedonistic life. Of course, a sophisticated hedonist cannot guarantee that he will meet this counterfactual condition, but only attempt to meet it as fully as possible.

Success at tennis is a relatively circumscribed goal, leaving much else about one's life undefined. Maximizing one's happiness, by contrast, seems all-consuming. Could commitments to other ends survive alongside it? Consider an analogy. Ned needs to make a living. More than that, he needs to make as much money as he can—he has expensive tastes, a second marriage, and children reaching college age, and he does not have extensive means. He sets out to invest his money and his labor in ways he thinks will maximize return. Yet it does not follow that he acts as he does solely for the sake of earning as much as possible. Although it is obviously true that he does what he does because he believes that it will maximize return, this does not preclude his doing it for other reasons as well, for example, for the sake of living well or taking care of his children. This may continue to be the case even if Ned comes to want money for its own sake, that is, if he comes to see the accumulation of wealth as intrinsically as well as extrinsically attractive. Similarly, the stricture that one seek the objectively hedonistic life certainly provides one with considerable guidance, but it does not supply the whole of one's motives and goals in action.

My claim that the sophisticated hedonist can escape the paradox of hedonism was, however, qualified. It still seems possible that the happiest sorts of lives ordinarily attainable are those led by people who would reject even sophisticated hedonism, people whose character is such that if they were presented with a choice between two entire lives, one of which contains less total happiness but nonetheless realizes some other values more fully, they might well knowingly choose against maximal happiness. If this were so, it would show that a sophisticated hedonist might have reason for changing his beliefs so that he no longer accepts hedonism in any form. This still would not refute objective hedonism as an account of the (rational, prudential, or moral) *criterion* one's acts should meet, for it would be precisely in order to meet this criterion that the sophisticated hedonist would change his beliefs.

V. The Place of Non-Alienation Among Human Values

Before discussing the applicability of what has been said about hedonism to morality, we should notice that alienation is not always a bad thing, that we may not want to overcome all forms of alienation, and that other values, which may conflict with non-alienation in particular cases, may at times have a greater claim on us. Let us look at a few such cases.

It has often been argued that a morality of duties and obligations may appropriately come into play in familial or friendly relationships when the relevant sentiments have given out, for instance, when one is exasperated with a friend, when love is tried, and so on. 'Ought' implies 'can' (or, at least, 'could'), and while it may be better in human terms when we do what we ought to do at least in part out of feelings of love, friendship, or sympathy, there are times when we simply cannot muster these sentiments, and the right thing to do is to act as love or friendship or sympathy would have directed rather than refuse to perform any act done merely from a sense of duty.

But we should add a further role for unspontaneous, morally motivated action: even when love or concern is strong, it is often desirable that people achieve some distance from their sentiments or one another. A spouse may act toward his mate in a grossly overprotective way; a friend may indulge another's ultimately destructive tendencies; a parent may favor one child inordinately. Strong and immediate affection may overwhelm one's ability to see what another person actually needs or deserves. In such cases a certain distance between people or between an individual and his sentiments, and an intrusion of moral considerations into the gap thus created, may be a good thing, and part of genuine affection or commitment. The opposite view, that no such mediation is desirable as long as affection is strong, seems to me a piece of romanticism. Concern over alienation therefore ought not to take the form of a cult of "authenticity at any price."

Moreover, there will occur regular conflicts between avoiding alienation and achieving other important individual goals. One such goal is autonomy. Bernard Williams has emphasized that many of us have developed certain "ground projects" that give shape and meaning to our lives, and has drawn attention to the damage an individual may suffer if he is alienated from his ground projects by being forced to look at them as potentially overridable by moral considerations. But against this it may be urged that it is crucial for autonomy that one hold one's commitments up for inspection — even one's

ground projects. Our ground projects are often formed in our youth, in a particular family, class, or cultural background. It may be alienating and even disorienting to call these into question, but to fail to do so is to lose autonomy. Of course, autonomy could not sensibly require that we question all of our values and commitments at once, nor need it require us to be forever detached from what we are doing. It is quite possible to submit basic aspects of one's life to scrutiny and arrive at a set of autonomously chosen commitments that form the basis of an integrated life. Indeed, psychological conflicts and practical obstacles give us occasion for reexamining our basic commitments rather more often than we'd like.

At the same time, the tension between autonomy and non-alienation should not be exaggerated. Part of avoiding exaggeration is giving up the Kantian notion that autonomy is a matter of escaping determination by any contingency whatsoever. Part, too, is refusing to conflate autonomy with sheer independence from others. Both Rousseau and Marx emphasized that achieving control over one's own life requires participation in certain sorts of social relations — in fact, relations in which various kinds of alienation have been minimized.

Autonomy is but one value that may enter into complex trade-offs with non-alienation. Alienation and inauthenticity do have their uses. The alienation of some individuals or groups from their milieu may at times be necessary for fundamental social criticism or cultural innovation. And without some degree of inauthenticity, it is doubtful whether civil relations among people could long be maintained. It would take little ingenuity, but too much of the reader's patience, to construct here examples involving troubling conflicts between non-alienation and virtually any other worthy goal.

VI. *Reducing Alienation in Morality*

Let us now move to morality proper. To do this with any definiteness, we must have a particular morality in mind. For various reasons, I think that the most plausible sort of morality is consequentialist in form, assessing rightness in terms of contribution to the good. In attempting to sketch how we might reduce alienation in moral theory and practice, therefore, I will work within a consequentialist framework (although a number of the arguments I will make could be made, *mutatis mutandis,* by a deontologist).

Of course, one has adopted no morality in particular even in adopting consequentialism unless one says what the good is. Let us, then, dwell briefly on axiology. One mistake of dominant consequentialist theories, I believe, is their failure to see that things other than subjective states can have intrinsic value. Allied to this is a tendency to reduce all intrinsic values to one — happiness. Both of these features of classical utilitarianism reflect forms of alienation. First, in divorcing subjective states from their objective counterparts, and claiming that we seek the latter exclusively for the sake of the former, utilitarianism cuts us off from the world in a way made graphic by examples such as that of the experience machine, a hypothetical device that can be programmed to provide one with whatever subjective states he may desire. The experience machine affords us decisive subjective advantages over actual life: few, if any, in actual life think they have achieved all that they could want, but the machine makes possible for each an existence that he cannot distinguish from such a happy state of affairs. Despite this striking advantage, most rebel at the notion of the experience machine. As Robert Nozick and others have pointed out, it seems to matter to us what we actually *do* and *are* as well as how life *appears* to us. We see the point of our lives as bound up with the world and other people in ways not captured by subjectivism, and our sense of loss in contemplating a life tied to an experience machine, quite literally alienated from the surrounding world, suggests where subjectivism has gone astray. Second, the reduction of all goals to the purely abstract goal of happiness or pleasure, as in hedonistic utilitarianism, treats all other goals instrumentally. Knowledge or friendship may promote happiness, but is it a fair characterization of our commitment to these goals to say that this is the only sense in which they are ultimately valuable? Doesn't the insistence that there is an abstract and uniform goal lying behind all of our ends bespeak an alienation from these particular ends?

Rather than pursue these questions further here, let me suggest an approach to the good that seems to me less hopeless as a way of capturing human value: a pluralistic approach in which several goods are viewed as intrinsically, non-morally valuable — such as happiness, knowledge, purposeful activity, autonomy, solidarity, respect, and beauty.[4] These goods need not be ranked lexically, but may be attributed weights, and the criterion of rightness for an act would be that it most contribute to the weighted sum of these values in the long run. This creates the possibility of trade-offs among values of the kinds discussed in the previous section. However, I will not stop here to develop or defend such an account of the good and the right, since our task is to show how certain problems of alienation that arise in moral contexts might be dealt with if morality is assumed to have such a basis.

Consider, then, Juan, who, like John, has always seemed a model husband. When a friend remarks on the extraordinary concern he shows for his wife, Juan characteristically responds: "I love Linda. I even *like* her. So it means a lot to me to do things for her. After all we've been through, it's almost a part of me to do it." But his friend knows that Juan is a principled individual, and asks Juan how his marriage fits into that larger scheme. After all, he asks, it's fine for Juan and his wife to have such a close relationship, but what about all the other, needier people Juan could help if he broadened his horizon still further? Juan replies, "Look, it's a better world when people can have a relationship like ours — and nobody could if everyone were always asking themselves who's got the most need. It's not easy to make things work in this world, and one of the best things that happens to people is to have a close relationship like ours. You'd make things worse in a hurry if you broke up those close relationships for the sake of some higher goal. Anyhow, I know that you can't always put family first. The world isn't such a wonderful place that it's OK just to retreat into your own little circle. But still, you need that little circle. People get burned out, or lose touch, if they try to save the world by themselves. The ones who can stick with it and do a good job of making things better are usually the ones who can make that fit into a life that does not make them miserable. I haven't met any real saints lately, and I don't trust people who think they *are* saints."

If we contrast Juan with John, we do not find that the one allows moral considerations to enter his personal life while the other does not. Nor do we find that one is less serious in his moral concern. Rather, what Juan recognizes to be morally required is not by its nature incompatible with acting directly for the sake of another. It is important to Juan to subject his life to moral scrutiny — he is not merely stumped when asked for a defense of his acts above a personal level, he does not *just* say "Of course I take care of her, she's my wife!" or "It's Linda" and refuse to listen to the more impersonal considerations raised by his friend. It is consistent with what he says to imagine that his motivational structure has a form akin to that of the sophisticated hedonist, that is, his motivational structure meets a counterfactual condition: while he ordinarily does not do what he does simply for the sake of doing what's right, he would seek to lead a different sort of life if he did not think his were morally defensible. His love is not a romantic submersion in the other to the exclusion of worldly responsibilities, and to that extent it may be said to involve a degree of alienation from Linda. But this does not seem to drain human value from their relationship. Nor need one imagine that Linda would be saddened to hear Juan's words the way Anne might have been saddened to overhear the remarks of John.

Moreover, because of his very willingness to question his life morally, Juan avoids a sort of alienation not sufficiently discussed — alienation from others, beyond one's intimate ties. Individuals who will not or cannot allow questions to arise about what they are doing from a broader perspective are in an important way cut off from their society and the larger world. They may not be troubled by this in any very direct way, but even so they may fail to experience that powerful sense of purpose and meaning that comes from seeing oneself as part of something larger and more enduring than oneself or one's intimate circle. The search for such a sense of purpose and meaning seems to be ubiquitous — surely much of the impulse to religion, to ethnic or regional identification (most strikingly, in the "rediscovery" of such identities), or to institutional loyalty stems from this desire to see ourselves as part of a more general, lasting, and worthwhile scheme of things. This presumably is part of what is meant by saying that secularization has led to a sense of meaninglessness, or that the decline of traditional communities and societies has meant an increase in anomie. (The sophisticated hedonist, too, should take note: one way to gain a firmer sense that one's life is worthwhile, a sense that may be important to realizing various values in one's own life, is it overcome alienation from others.)

Drawing upon our earlier discussion of two kinds of hedonism, let us now distinguish two kinds of consequentialism. *Subjective consequentialism* is the view that whenever one faces a choice of actions, one should attempt to determine which act of those available would most promote the good, and should then try to act accordingly. One is behaving as subjective consequentialism requires — that is, leading a *subjectively consequentialist life* — to the extent that one uses and follows a distinctively consequentialist mode of decision making, consciously aiming at the overall good and conscientiously using the best available information with the greatest possible rigor. *Objective consequentialism* is the view that the criterion of the rightness of an act or course of action is whether it in fact would most promote the good of those acts available to the agent. Subjective consequentialism, like subjective hedonism, is a view that prescribes following a particular mode of deliberation in action; objective consequentialism, like objective hedonism, concerns the outcomes actually brought about, and thus deals with the question of deliberation only in terms of the tendencies of certain forms of decision making to promote appropriate outcomes. Let us reserve the expression *objectively consequentialist act (or life)* for those acts (or that life) of those available to the agent that would bring about the best outcomes. To complete the parallel, let us say that a *sophisticated consequentialist* is someone who has a standing commitment to leading an objectively consequentialist life, but who need not set special stock in any particular form of decision making and therefore does not necessarily seek to lead a subjectively consequentialist life. Juan, it might be argued (if the details were filled in), is a sophisticated consequentialist, since he seems to believe he should act for the best but does not seem to feel it appropriate to bring a consequentialist calculus to bear on his every act.

Is it bizarre, or contradictory, that being a sophisticated consequentialist may involve rejecting subjective consequentialism? After all, doesn't an adherent of subjective consequentialism also seek to lead an objectively consequentialist life? He may, but then he is mistaken in thinking that this means he should always undertake a distinctively consequentialist deliberation when faced with a choice. To see his mistake, we need only consider some examples.

It is well known that in certain emergencies, the best outcome requires action so swift as to preclude consequentialist deliberation. Thus a sophisticated consequentialist has reason to inculcate in himself certain dispositions to act rapidly in obvious emergencies. The disposition is not a mere reflex, but a developed pattern of action deliberately acquired. A simple example, but it should dispel the air of paradox.

Many decisions are too insignificant to warrant consequentialist deliberation ("Which shoelace should I do up first?") or too predictable in outcome ("Should I meet my morning class today as scheduled or should I linger over the newspaper?"). A famous old conundrum for consequentialism falls into a similar category: before I deliberate about an act, it seems I must decide how much time would be optimal to allocate for this deliberation; but then I must first decide how much time would be optimal to allocate for this time-allocation decision; but before that I must decide how much time would be optimal to allocate for *that* decision; and so on. The sophisticated consequentialist can block this paralyzing regress by noting that often the best thing to do is not to ask questions about time allocation at all; instead, he may develop standing dispositions to give more or less time to decisions depending upon their perceived importance, the amount of information available, the predictability of his choice, and so on. I think we all have dispositions of this sort, which account for our patience with some prolonged deliberations but not others.

There are somewhat more intriguing examples that have more to do with psychological interference than mere time efficiency: the timid, put-upon employee who knows that if he deliberates about whether to ask for a raise he will succumb to his timidity and fail to demand what he actually deserves; the self-conscious man who knows that if, at social gatherings, he is forever wondering how he should act, his behavior will be awkward and unnatural, contrary to his goal of acting naturally and ap-

propriately; the tightrope walker who knows he must not reflect on the value of keeping his concentration; and so on. People can learn to avoid certain characteristically self-defeating lines of thought—just as the tennis player in an earlier example learned to avoid thinking constantly about winning—and the sophisticated consequentialist may learn that consequentialist deliberation is in a variety of cases self-defeating, so that other habits of thought should be cultivated.

The sophisticated consequentialist need not be deceiving himself or acting in bad faith when he avoids consequentialist reasoning. He can fully recognize that he is developing the dispositions he does because they are necessary for promoting the good. Of course, he cannot be preoccupied with this fact all the while, but then one cannot be *preoccupied* with anything without this interfering with normal or appropriate patterns of thought and action.

To the list of cases of interference we may add John, whose all-purpose willingness to look at things by subjective consequentialist lights prevents the realization in him and in his relationships with others of values that he would recognize to be crucially important.

Bernard Williams has said that it shows consequentialism to be in grave trouble that it may have to usher itself from the scene as a mode of decision making in a number of important areas of life. Though I think he has exaggerated the extent to which we would have to exclude consequentialist considerations from our lives in order to avoid disastrous results, it is fair to ask: If maximizing the good were in fact to require that consequentialist reasoning be *wholly* excluded, would this refute consequentialism? Imagine an all-knowing demon who controls the fate of the world and who visits unspeakable punishment upon man to the extent that he does not employ a Kantian morality. (Obviously, the demon is not himself a Kantian.) If such a demon existed, sophisticated consequentialists would have reason to convert to Kantianism, perhaps even to make whatever provisions could be made to erase consequentialism from the human memory and prevent any resurgence of it.

Does this possibility show that objective consequentialism is self-defeating? On the contrary, it shows that objective consequentialism has the virtue of not blurring the distinction between the *truth-conditions* of an ethical theory and its *acceptance-conditions* in particular contexts, a distinction philosophers have generally recognized for theories concerning other subject matters. It might be objected that, unlike other theories, ethical theories must meet a condition of publicity, roughly to the effect that it must be possible under all circumstances for us to recognize a true ethical theory as such and to promulgate it publicly without thereby violating that theory itself. Such a condition might be thought to follow from the social nature of morality. But any such condition would be question-begging against consequentialist theories, since it would require that one class of actions—acts of adopting or promulgating an ethical theory—*not* be assessed in terms of their consequences. Moreover, I fail to see how such a condition could emanate from the social character of morality. To prescribe the adoption and promulgation of a mode of decision making regardless of its consequences seems to me radically detached from human concerns, social or otherwise. If it is argued that an ethical theory that fails to meet the publicity requirement could under certain conditions endorse a course of action leading to the abuse and manipulation of man by man, we need only reflect that no psychologically possible decision procedure can guarantee that its widespread adoption could never have such a result. A "consequentialist demon" might increase the amount of abuse and manipulation in the world in direct proportion to the extent that people act according to the categorical imperative. Objective consequentialism (unlike certain deontological theories) has valuable flexibility in permitting us to take consequences into account in assessing the appropriateness of certain modes of decision making, thereby avoiding any sort of self-defeating decision procedure worship.

A further objection is that the lack of any direct link between objective consequentialism and a particular mode of decision making leaves the view too vague to provide adequate guidance in practice. On the contrary, objective consequentialism sets a definite and distinctive criterion of right action, and it becomes an empirical question (though not an easy one) which modes of decision making should be employed and when. It would be a mistake for an objective consequentialist to attempt to tighten the connection between his criterion of rightness and any particular mode of decision making: someone who recommended a particular mode of decision making regardless of consequences would not be a hard-nosed, non-evasive objective consequentialist, but a self-contradicting one.

VII. *Contrasting Approaches*

The seeming "indirectness" of objective consequentialism may invite its confusion with familiar indirect consequentialist theories, such as rule-consequentialism. In fact, the subjective/objective distinction cuts across the rule/act distinction, and there are subjective and objective forms of both rule- and act-based theories. Thus far, we have dealt only with subjective and objective forms of act-consequentialism. By contrast, a *subjective rule*-consequentialist holds (roughly) that in deliberation we should always attempt to determine which act, of those available, conforms to that set of rules general acceptance of which would most promote the good; we then should attempt to perform this act. An *objective rule*-consequentialist sets actual conformity to the rules with the highest acceptance value as his criterion of right action, recognizing the possibility that the best set of rules might in some cases—or even always—recommend that one not perform rule-consequentialist deliberation.

Because I believe this last possibility must be taken seriously, I find the objective form of rule-consequentialism more plausible. Ultimately, however, I suspect that rule-consequentialism is untenable in either form, for it could recommend acts that (subjectively or objectively) accord with the best set of rules even when these rules are *not* in fact generally accepted, and when as a result these acts would have devastatingly bad consequences. "Let the rules with greatest acceptance utility be followed, though the heavens fall!" is no more plausible than *"Fiat justitia, ruat coelum!"*—and a good bit less ringing. Hence, the arguments in this article are based entirely upon act-consequentialism.

Indeed, once the subjective/objective distinction has been drawn, an act-consequentialist can capture some of the intuitions that have made rule- or trait-consequentialism appealing. Surely part of the attraction of these indirect consequentialisms is the idea that one should have certain traits of character, or commitments to persons or principles, that are sturdy enough that one would at least sometimes refuse to forsake them even when this refusal is known to conflict with making some gain—perhaps small—in total utility. Unlike his subjective counterpart, the objective act-consequentialist is able to endorse characters and commitments that are sturdy in just this sense.

To see why, let us first return briefly to one of the simple examples of Section VI. A sophisticated act-consequentialist may recognize that if he were to develop a standing disposition to render prompt assistance in emergencies without going through elaborate act-consequentialist deliberation, there would almost certainly be cases in which he would perform acts worse than those he would have performed had he stopped to deliberate, for example, when his prompt action is misguided in a way he would have noticed had he thought the matter through. It may still be right for him to develop this disposition, for without it he would act rightly in emergencies still less often—a quick response is appropriate much more often than not, and it is not practically possible to develop a disposition that would lead one to respond promptly in exactly those cases where this would have the best results. While one can attempt to cultivate dispositions that are responsive to various factors which might indicate whether promptness is of greater importance than further thought, such refinements have their own costs and, given the limits of human resources, even the best cultivated dispositions will sometimes lead one astray. The objective act-consequentialist would thus recommend cultivating dispositions that will sometimes lead him to violate his own criterion of right action. Still, he will not, as a trait-consequentialist would, shift his criterion and say that an act is right if it stems from the traits it would be bet overall to have (given the limits of what is humanly achievable, the balance of costs and benefits, and so on). Instead, he continues to believe that an act may stem from the dispositions it would be best to have, and yet be wrong (because it would produce worse consequences than other acts available to the agent in the circumstances).

This line of argument can be extended to patterns of motivation, traits of character, and rules. A sophisticated act-consequentialist should realize that certain goods are reliably attainable—or attainable at all—only if people have well-developed characters; that the human psyche is capable of only so much self-regulation and refinement; and that human perception and reasoning are liable to a host of biases and errors. Therefore, individuals may be more likely to act rightly if they possess certain enduring motivational patterns, character traits, or *prima facie* commitments to rules in addition to whatever commitment they have to act for the best. Because such individuals would not consider consequences in all cases, they would miss a number of opportunities to maximize the good; but if they were instead always to attempt to assess outcomes, the overall result would be worse, for they would act correctly less often.

We may now strengthen the argument to show that the objective act-consequentialist can approve of dispositions, characters, or commitments to rules that are sturdy in the sense mentioned above, that is, that do not merely supplement a commitment to act for the best, but sometimes override it, so that one knowingly does what is contrary to maximizing the good. Consider again Juan and Linda, whom we imagine to have a commuting marriage. They normally get together only every other week, but one week she seems a bit depressed and harried, and so he decides to take an extra trip in order to be with her. If he did not travel, he would save a fairly large sum that he could send OXFAM to dig a well in a drought-stricken village. Even reckoning in Linda's uninterrupted malaise, Juan's guilt, and any ill effects on their relationship, it may be that for Juan to contribute the fare to OXFAM would produce better consequences overall than the unscheduled trip. Let us suppose that Juan knows this, and that he could stay home and write the check if he tried. Still, given Juan's character, he in fact will not try to perform this more beneficial act but will travel to see Linda instead. The objective act-consequentialist will say that Juan performed the wrong act on this occasion. Yet he may also say that if Juan had had a character that would have led him to perform the better act (or made him more inclined to do so), he would have had to have been less devoted to Linda. Given the ways Juan can affect the world, it may be that if he were less devoted to Linda his overall contribution to human well-being would be less in the end, perhaps because he would become more cynical and self-centered. Thus it may be that Juan should have (should develop, encourage, and so on) a character such that he sometimes knowingly and deliberately acts contrary to his objective consequentialist duty. Any other character, of those actually available to him, would lead him to depart still further from an objectively consequentialist life. The issue is not whether staying home would *change* Juan's character—for we may suppose that it would not—but whether he would in fact decide to stay home if he had that character, of those available, that would lead him to perform the most beneficial overall sequence of acts. In some cases, then, there will exist an objective act-consequentialist argument for developing and sustaining characters of a kind Sidgwick and others have thought an act-consequentialist must condemn.

VIII. *Demands and Disruptions*

Before ending this discussion of consequentialism, let me mention one other large problem involving alienation that has seemed uniquely troubling for consequentialist theories and that shows how coming to terms with problems of alienation may be a social matter as well as a matter of individual psychology. Because consequentialist criteria of rightness are linked to maximal contribution to the good, whenever one does not perform the very best act one can, one is "negatively responsible" for any shortfall in total well-being that results. Bernard Williams has argued that to accept such a burden of responsibility would force most of us to abandon or be prepared to abandon many of our most basic individual commitments, alienating ourselves from the very things that mean the most to us.

To be sure, objective act-consequentialism of the sort considered here is a demanding and potentially disruptive morality, even after allowances have been made for the psychological phenomena thus far discussed and for the difference between saying an act is wrong and saying that the agent ought to be blamed for it. But just *how* demanding or disruptive it would be for an individual is a function—as it arguably should be—of how bad the state of the world is, how others typically act, what institutions

exist, and how much that individual is capable of doing. If wealth were more equitably distributed, if political systems were less repressive and more responsive to the needs of their citizens, and if people were more generally prepared to accept certain responsibilities, then individuals' everyday lives would not have to be constantly disrupted for the sake of the good.

For example, in a society where there are no organized forms of disaster relief, it may be the case that if disaster were to strike a particular region, people all over the country would be obliged to make a special effort to provide aid. If, on the other hand, an adequate system of publicly financed disaster relief existed, then it probably would be a very poor idea for people to interrupt their normal lives and attempt to help—their efforts would probably be uncoordinated, ill-informed, an interference with skilled relief work, and economically disruptive (perhaps even damaging to the society's ability to pay for the relief effort).

By altering social and political arrangements we can lessen the disruptiveness of moral demands on our lives, and in the long run achieve better results than free-lance good-doing. A consequentialist theory is therefore likely to recommend that accepting negative responsibility is more a matter of supporting certain social and political arrangements (or rearrangements) than of setting out individually to save the world. Moreover, it is clear that such social and political changes cannot be made unless the lives of individuals are psychologically supportable in the meanwhile, and this provides substantial reason for rejecting the notion that we should abandon all that matters to us as individuals and devote ourselves solely to net social welfare. Finally, in many cases what matters most is *perceived* rather than actual demandingness or disruptiveness, and this will be a relative matter, depending upon normal expectations. If certain social or political arrangements encourage higher contribution as a matter of course, individuals may not sense these moral demands as excessively intrusive.

To speak of social and political changes is, of course, to suggest eliminating the social and political preconditions for a number of existing projects and relationships, and such changes are likely to produce some degree of alienation in those whose lives have been disrupted. To an extent such people may be able to find new projects and relationships as well as maintain a number of old projects and relationships, and thereby avoid intolerable alienation. But not all will escape serious alienation. We thus have a case in which alienation will exist whichever course of action we follow — either the alienation of those who find the loss of the old order disorienting, or the continuing alienation of those who under the present order cannot lead lives expressive of their individuality or goals. It would seem that to follow the logic of Williams's position would have the unduly conservative result of favoring those less alienated in the present state of affairs over those who might lead more satisfactory lives if certain changes were to occur. Such conservatism could hardly be warranted by a concern about alienation if the changes in question would bring about social and political preconditions for a more widespread enjoyment of meaningful lives. For example, it is disruptive of the ground projects of many men that women have begun to demand and receive greater equality in social and personal spheres, but such disruption may be offset by the opening of more avenues of self-development to a greater number of people.

In responding to Williams's objection regarding negative responsibility, I have focused more on the problem of disruptiveness than the problem of demandingness, and more on the social than the personal level. More would need to be said than I am able to say here to come fully to terms with his objection, although some very general remarks may be in order. The consequentialist starts out from the relatively simple idea that certain things seem to matter to people above all else. His root conception of moral rightness is therefore that it should matter above all else whether people, insofar as possible, actually realize these ends.[5] Consequentialist moralities of the sort considered here undeniably set a demanding standard, calling upon us to do more for one another than is now the practice. But this standard plainly does not require that most people lead intolerable lives for the sake of some greater good: the greater good is empirically equivalent to the best possible lives for the largest possible number of people. Objective consequentialism gives full expression to this root intuition by setting as the criterion of rightness actual contribution to the realization of human value, allowing practices and forms of reasoning to take whatever shape this requires. It is thus not equivalent to requiring a certain, alienated

way of thinking about ourselves, our commitments, or how to act.

Samuel Scheffler has recently suggested that one response to the problems Williams raises about the impersonality and demandingness of consequentialism could be to depart from consequentialism at least far enough to recognize as a fundamental moral principle an agent-centered prerogative, roughly to the effect that one is not always obliged to maximize the good, although one is always permitted to do so if one wishes. This prerogative would make room for agents to give special attention to personal projects and commitments. However, the argument of this article, if successful, shows there to be a firm place in moral practice for prerogatives that afford such room even if one accepts a fully consequentialist fundamental moral theory.

IX. *Alienation from Morality*

By way of conclusion, I would like to turn to alienation from morality itself, the experience (conscious or unconscious) of morality as an external set of demands not rooted in our lives or accommodating to our perspectives. Giving a convincing answer to the question "Why should I be moral?" must involve diminishing the extent that morality appears alien.

Part of constructing such an answer is a matter of showing that abiding by morality need not alienate us from the particular commitments that make life worthwhile, and in the previous sections we have begun to see how this might be possible within an objective act-consequentialist account of what morality requires. We saw how in general various sorts of projects or relationships can continue to be a source of intrinsic value even though one recognizes that they might have to undergo changes if they could not be defended in their present form on moral grounds. And again, knowing that a commitment is morally defensible may well deepen its value for us, and may also make it possible for us to feel part of a larger world in a way that is itself of great value. If our commitments are regarded by others as responsible and valuable (or if we have reason to think that others should so regard them), this may enhance the meaning or value they have for our-selves, while if they are regarded by others as irre-sponsible or worthless (especially, if we suspect that others regard them so justly), this may make it more difficult for us to identify with them or find purpose or value in them. Our almost universal urge to ratio-nalize our acts and lives attests our wish to see what we do as defensible from a more general point of view. I do not deny that bringing a more general perspective to bear on one's life may be costly to the self—it may cause reevaluations that lower self-esteem, produce guilt, alienation, and even prob-lems of identity. But I do want to challenge the simple story often told in which there is a per-sonal point of view from which we glimpse mean-ings which then vanish into insignificance when we adopt a more general perspective. In thought and action we shuttle back and forth from more personal to less personal standpoints, and both play an important role in the process whereby purpose, meaning, and identity are generated and sustained. Moreover, it may be part of mature com-mitments, even of the most intimate sort, that a measure of perspective beyond the personal be maintained.

These remarks about the role of general per-spectives in individual lives lead us to what I think is an equally important part of answering the question "Why should I be moral?": reconceptualization of the terms of the discussion to avoid starting off in an alienated fashion and ending up with the result that morality still seems alien. Before pursuing this idea, let us quickly glance at two existing approaches to the question.

Morality may be conceived of as in essence self-less, impartial, impersonal. To act morally is to sub-ordinate the self and all contingencies concerning the self's relations with others or the world to a set of imperatives binding on us solely as rational be-ings. We should be moral, in this view, because it is ideally rational. However, morality thus conceived seems bound to appear as alien in daily life. "Purity of heart" in Rawls's sense would be essential to act-ing morally, and the moral way of life would appear well removed from our actual existence, enmeshed as we are in a web of "particularistic" commit-ments—which happen to supply our *raisons d'être*.

A common alternative conception of morality is not as an elevated purity of heart but as a good strategy for the self. Hobbesian atomic individuals are posited and appeal is made to game theory to show that pay-offs to such individuals may be greater in certain conflict situations—such as reite-rated prisoners' dilemmas—if they abide by certain constraints of a moral kind (at least, with regard to those who may reciprocate) rather than act merely prudentially. Behaving morally, then, may be an ad-vantageous policy in certain social settings. How-ever, it is not likely to be the *most* advantageous pol-icy in general, when compared to a strategy that cunningly mixes some compliance with norms and some non-compliance; and presumably the Hobbes-ian individual is interested only in maximal self-advantage. Yet even if we leave aside worries about how far such arguments might be pushed, it needs to be said that morality as such would confront such an entrepreneurial self as an alien set of demands, for central to morality is the idea that others' inter-ests must sometimes be given weight for reasons un-related to one's own advantage.

Whatever their differences, these two appar-ently antithetical approaches to the question "Why should I be moral?" have remarkably similar under-lying pictures of the problem. In these pictures, a presocial, rational, abstract individual is the starting point, and the task is to construct proper interper-sonal relations out of such individuals. Of course, this conceit inverts reality: the rational individual of these approaches is a social and historical *product*. But that is old hat. We are not supposed to see this as any sort of history, we are told, but rather as a way of conceptualizing the questions of morality. Yet why when conceptualizing are we drawn to such asocial and ahistorical images? My modest proposal is that we should keep our attention fixed on society and history at least long enough to try recasting the problem in more naturalistic terms.

As a start, let us begin with individuals situated in society, complete with identities, commitments, and social relations. What are the ingredients of such identities, commitments, and relations? When one studies relationships of deep commitment—of parent to child, or wife to husband—at close range, it becomes artificial to impose a dichotomy between what is done for the self and what is done for the other. We cannot decompose such relationships into a vector of self-concern and a vector of other-concern, even though concern for the self and the other are both present. The other has come to figure in the self in a fundamental way—or, perhaps a better way of putting it, the other has become a reference point of the self. If it is part of one's identity to be the parent of Jill or the husband of Linda, then the self has reference points beyond the ego, and that which affects these reference points may affect the self in an unmediated way. These reference points do not all fall within the circle of intimate relationships, either. Among the most important constituents of identities are social, cultural, or religious ties—one is a Jew, a Southerner, a farmer, or an alumnus of Old Ivy. Our identities exist in relational, not absolute space, and except as they are fixed by reference points in others, in society, in culture, or in some larger constellation still, they are not fixed at all.

There is a worthwhile analogy between meaning in lives and meaning in language. It has been a while since philosophers have thought it helpful to imagine that language is the arrangement resulting when we hook our private meanings up to a system of shared symbols. Meaning, we are told, resides to a crucial degree in use, in public contexts, in referential systems—it is possible for the self to use a language with meanings because the self is embedded in a set of social and historical practices. But ethical philosophers have continued to speak of the meaning of life in surprisingly private terms. Among recent attempts to give a foundation for morality, Nozick's perhaps places greatest weight on the idea of the meaning of life, which he sees as a matter of an individual's "ability to regulate and guide [his] life in accordance with some overall conception [he] chooses to accept," emphasizing the idea that an individual creates meaning through choice of a life plan; clearly, however, in order for choice to play a self-defining role, the options among which one chooses must already have some meaning independent of one's decisions.

It is not only "the meaning of life" that carries such presuppositions. Consider, for example, another notion that has played a central role in moral discourse: respect. If the esteem of others is to matter to an individual those others must themselves have some significance to the individual; in order for their esteem to constitute the sought-after respect, the individual must himself have some degree of respect for them and their judgment. If the self loses significance for others, this threatens its significance even for itself; if others lose significance for the self, this threatens to remove the basis for self-significance. It is a commonplace of psychology and sociology that bereaved or deracinated individuals

suffer not only a sense of loss owing to broken connections with others, but also a loss in the solidity of the self, and may therefore come to lose interest in the self or even a clear sense of identity. Reconstructing the self and self-interest in such cases is as much a matter of constructing new relations to others and the world as it is a feat of self-supporting self-reconstruction. Distracted by the picture of a hypothetical, presocial individual, philosophers have found it very easy to assume, wrongly, that in the actual world concern for oneself and one's goals is quite automatic, needing no outside support, while a direct concern for others is inevitably problematic, needing some further rationale.

It does not follow that there is any sort of categorical imperative to care about others or the world beyond the self as such. It is quite possible to have few external reference points and go through life in an alienated way. Life need not have much meaning in order to go on, and one does not even have to care whether life goes on. We cannot show that moral skepticism is necessarily irrational by pointing to facts about meaning, but a naturalistic approach to morality need no more refute radical skepticism than does a naturalistic approach to epistemology. For actual people, there may be surprisingly little distance between asking in earnest "Why should I take any interest in anyone else?" and asking "Why should I take any interest in myself?" The proper response to the former is not merely to point out the indirect benefits of caring about things beyond the self, although this surely should be done, but to show how denying the significance of anything beyond the self may undercut the basis of significance for the self. There is again a close, but not exact parallel in language: people can get along without a language, although certainly not as well as they can with it; if someone were to ask "Why should I use my words the same way as others?" the proper response would be not only to point out the obvious benefits of using his words in this way but also to point out that by refusing to use words the way others do he is undermining the basis of meaning in his own use of language.

These remarks need not lead us to a conservative traditionalism. We must share and preserve meanings in order to have a language at all, but we may use a common language to disagree and innovate. Contemporary philosophy of language makes us distrust any strict dichotomy between meaning, on the other hand, and belief and value, on the other; but there is obviously room within a system of meanings for divergence and change on empirical and normative matters. Language itself has undergone considerable change over the course of history, coevolving with beliefs and norms without in general violating the essential conditions of meaningfulness. Similarly, moral values and social practices may undergo change without obliterating the basis of meaningful lives, so long as certain essential conditions are fulfilled. (History does record some changes, such as the uprooting of tribal peoples, where these conditions were not met, with devastating results.)

A system of available, shared meanings would seem to be a precondition for sustaining the meaningfulness of individual lives in familiar sorts of social arrangements. Moreover, in such arrangements identity and self-significance seem to depend in part upon the significance of others to the self. If we are prepared to say that a sense of meaningfulness is a precondition for much else in life, then we may be on the way to answering the question "Why should I be moral?" for we have gone beyond pure egocentrism precisely by appealing to facts about the self. Our earlier discussions have yielded two considerations that make the rest of the task of answering this question more tractable. First, we noted in discussing hedonism that individual lives seem most enjoyable when they involve commitments to causes beyond the self or to others as such. Further, we remarked that it is plausible that the happiest sorts of lives do not involve a commitment to hedonism even of a sophisticated sort. If a firm sense of meaningfulness is a precondition of the fullest happiness, this speculation becomes still more plausible. Second, we sketched a morality that began by taking seriously the various forms of human nonmoral value, and then made room for morality in our lives by showing that we can raise moral questions without thereby destroying the possibility of realizing various intrinsic values from particular relationships and activities. That is, we saw how being moral might be compatible (at least in these respects) with living a desirable life. It would take another article, and a long one, to show how these various pieces of the answer to "Why should I be moral?" might be made less rough and fitted together into a more solid structure. But by adopting a nonalienated starting point—that of situated rather than presocial individuals—and by showing how some of the alienation associated with bringing morality to bear

on our lives might be avoided, perhaps we have reduced the extent to which morality seems alien to us by its nature.[6]

Endnotes

[1] The loss in question need not be a loss of something of value, and *a fortiori* need not be a bad thing overall: there are some people, institutions, or cultures alienation from which would be a boon. Alienation is a more or less troubling phenomenon depending upon what is lost; and in the cases to be considered, what is lost is for the most part of substantial value. It does not follow, as we will see in Section V, that in all such cases alienation is a bad thing on balance. Moreover, I do not assume that the loss in question represents an actual *decline* in some value as the result of a separation coming into being where once there was none. It seems reasonable to say that an individual can experience a loss in being alienated from nature, for example, without assuming that he was ever in communion with it, much as we say it is a loss for someone never to receive an education or never to appreciate music. Regrettably, various relevant kinds and sources of alienation cannot be discussed here. A general, historical discussion of alienation may be found in Richard Schacht, *Alienation* (Garden City, N.Y.: Doubleday, 1971).

[2] This is not to say that no questions arise about whether Helen's (or John's) feelings and attitudes constitute the fullest sort of affection, as will become shortly.

[3] A few remarks are needed. First, I will say that an act is available to an agent if he would succeed in performing it if he tried. Second, here and elsewhere in this article I mean to include quite "thick" descriptions of actions, so that it may be part of an action that one perform it with a certain intention or goal. In the short run (but not so much the long run) intentions, goals, motives, and the like are usually less subject to our deliberate control than overt behavior—it is easier to say "I'm sorry" than to say it and mean it. This, however, is a fact about the relative availability of acts to the agent at a given time, and should not dictate what is to count as an act. Third, here and elsewhere I ignore for simplicity's sake the possibility that more than one course of action may be maximally valuable. And fourth, for reasons I will not enter into here, I have formulated objective hedonism in terms of actual outcomes rather than expected values (relative to the information available to the agent). One could make virtually the same argument using an expected value formulation.

[4] To my knowledge, the best-developed method for justifying claims about intrinsic value involves thought-experiments of a familiar sort, in which, for example, we imagine two lives, or two worlds, alike in all but one respect, and then attempt to determine whether rational, well-informed, widely-experienced individuals would (when vividly aware of both alternatives) be indifferent between the two or have a settled preference for one over the other. Since no one is ideally rational, fully informed, or infinitely experienced, the best we can do is to take more seriously the judgments of those who come nearer to approximating these conditions. Worse yet: the best we can do is to take more seriously the judgments of those we *think* better approximate these

conditions. (I am not supposing that facts or experience somehow entail values, but that in rational agents, beliefs and values show a marked mutual influence and coherence.) We may overcome some narrowness if we look at behavior and preferences in other societies and other epochs, but even here we must rely upon interpretations colored by our own beliefs and values. Within the confines of this article I must leave unanswered a host of deep and troubling questions about the nature of values and value judgments. Suffice it to say that there is no reason to think that we are in a position to give anything but a tentative list of intrinsic goods.

It becomes a complex matter to describe the psychology of intrinsic value. For example, should we say that one values a relationship of solidarity, say, a friendship, *because it is* a friendship? That makes it sound as if it were somehow instrumental to the realization of some abstract value, friendship. Surely this is a misdescription. We may be able to get a clearer idea of what is involved by considering the case of happiness. We certainly do not value a particular bit of experienced happiness because it is instrumental in the realization of the abstract goal, happiness—we value the experience for its own sake because it is a happy experience. Similarly, a friendship is itself the valued thing, the thing of a valued kind. Of course, one can say that one values friendship and therefore seeks friends, just as one can say one values happiness and therefore seeks happy experiences. But this locution must be contrasted with what is being said when, for example, one talks of seeking *things that make one happy.* Friends are not "things that make one achieve friendship"—they partially constitute friendships, just as particular happy experiences partially constitute happiness for an individual. Thus taking friendship as an intrinsic value does not entail viewing particular friendships instrumentally.

5 I appealed to this "root conception" in rejecting rule-consequentialism in Section VII. Although consequentialism is often condemned for failing to provide an account of morality consistent with respect for persons, this root conception provides the basis for a highly plausible notion of such respect. I doubt, however, that any fundamental ethical dispute between consequentialists and deontologists can be resolved by appeal to the idea of respect for persons. The deontologist has his notion of respect—e.g., that we not use people in certain ways—and the consequentialist has *his*—e.g., that the good of every person has an equal claim upon us, a claim unmediated by any notion of right or contract, so that we should do the most possible to bring about outcomes that actually advance the good of persons. For every consequentially justified act of manipulation to which the deontologist can point with alarm there is a deontologically justified act that fails to promote the well-being of some person(s) as fully as possible to which the consequentialist can point, appalled. Which notion takes "respect for persons" more seriously? There may be no non-question-begging answer, especially once the consequentialist has recognized such things as autonomy or respect as intrinsically valuable.

6 I am grateful to a number of people for criticisms of earlier drafts of this paper and helpful suggestions for improving it. I would especially like to thank Marcia Baron, Stephen Darwall, William K. Frankena, Allan Gibbard, Samuel Scheffler, Rebecca Scott, Michael Stocker, Nicholas Sturgeon, Gregory Trianoski-Stillwell, and Susan Wolf.

V.5 *Side Constraints*

ROBERT NOZICK

Robert Nozick is professor of philosophy at Harvard University. In this selection from *Anarchy, State, and Utopia* he argues that from a libertarian point of view (supporting the ultraminimal state, in which the state's only obligations are to defend citizens from violence and ensure just transferences of property), we have no right to be aided when we are in need, but we have the right not to be used as means to social ends. Therefore, utilitarianism violates our rights by using us as a means to some end state.

I. *The Minimal State and the Ultraminimal State*

The night-watchman state of classical liberal theory, limited to the functions of protecting all its citizens against violence, theft, and fraud, and to the enforcement of contracts, and so on, appears to be redistributive.[1] We can imagine at least one social arrangement intermediate between the scheme of private protective associations and the night-watchman state. Since the night-watchman state is often called a minimal state, we shall call this other arrangement the *ultraminimal state*. An ultraminimal state maintains a monopoly over all use of force except that necessary in immediate self-defence, and so excludes private (or agency) retaliation for wrong and exaction of compensation; but it provides protection and enforcement services *only* to those who purchase its protection and enforcement policies. People who don't buy a protection contract from the monopoly don't get protected. The minimal (night-watchman) state is equivalent to the ultraminimal state conjoined with a (clearly redistributive) Friedmanesque voucher plan, financed from tax revenues.[2] Under this plan all people, or some (for example, those in need), are given tax-funded vouchers that can be used only for their purchase of a protection policy from the ultraminimal state.

Since the night-watchman state appears redistributive to the extent that it compels some people to pay for the protection of others, its proponents must explain why this redistributive function of the state is unique. If some redistribution is legitimate in order to protect everyone, why is redistribution not legitimate for other attractive and desirable purposes as well? What rationale specifically selects protective services as the sole subject of legitimate redistributive activities? A rationale, once found, may show that this provision of protective services is *not* redistributive. More precisely, the term 'redistributive' applies to types of *reasons* for an arrangement, rather than to an arrangement itself. We might elliptically call an arrangement 'redistributive' if its major (only possible) supporting reasons are themselves redistributive. ('Paternalistic' functions similarly.) Finding compelling nonredistributive reasons would cause us to drop this label. Whether we say an institution that takes money from some and gives it to others is redistributive will depend upon *why* we think it does so. Returning stolen money or compensating for violations of rights are *not* redistributive reasons. I have spoken until now of the night-watchman state's *appearing* to be redistributive, to leave open the possibility that nonredistributive types of reasons might be found to justify the provisions of protective services for some by others. . . .

A proponent of the ultraminimal state may seem to occupy an inconsistent position, even though he avoids the question of what makes protection uniquely suitable for redistributive provision. Greatly concerned to protect rights against violation, he makes this the sole legitimate function of the state; and he protests that all other functions are illegitimate because they themselves involve the violation of rights. Since he accords paramount place to the protection and non-violation of rights, how can he support the ultraminimal state, which would seem to leave some persons' rights unprotected or ill protected? How can he support this *in the name of* the non-violation of rights?

2. *Moral Constraints and Moral Goals*

This question assumes that a moral concern can function only as a moral *goal,* as an end state for some activities to achieve as their result. It may, indeed, seem to be a necessary truth that 'right,' 'ought,' 'should,' and so on, are to be explained in terms of what is, or is intended to be, productive of the greatest good, with all goals built into the good.[3] Thus it is often thought that what is wrong with utilitarianism (which *is* of this form) is its too narrow conception of good. Utilitarianism doesn't, it is said, properly take rights and their non-violation into account; it instead leaves them a derivative status. Many of the counter-example cases to utilitarianism fit under this objection, for example, punishing an innocent man to save a neighbourhood from a vengeful rampage. But a theory may include in a primary way the nonviolation of rights, yet include it in the wrong place and the wrong manner. For suppose some condition about minimizing the total (weighted) amount of violations of rights is built into the desirable end state to be achieved. We then would have something like a 'utilitarianism of rights'; violations of rights (to be *minimized*) merely would replace the total happiness as the relevant end state in the utilitarian structure. (Note that we do not hold the non-violation of our rights as our sole greatest good or even rank it first lexicographically to exclude trade-offs, if there is some desirable society we would choose to inhabit even though in it some rights of ours sometimes are violated, rather than move to a desert island where we could survive alone.) This still would require us to violate some-

one's rights when doing so minimizes the total (weighted) amount of the violation of rights in the society. For example, violating someone's rights might deflect others from *their* intended action of gravely violating rights, or might remove their motive for doing so, or might divert their attention, and so on. A mob rampaging through a part of town killing and burning *will* violate the rights of those living there. Therefore, someone might try to justify his punishing another *he* knows to be innocent of a crime that enraged a mob, on the grounds that punishing this innocent person would help to avoid even greater violations of rights by others, and so would lead to a minimum weighted score for rights violations in the society.

In contrast to incorporating rights into the end state to be achieved, one might place them as side constraints upon the actions to be done: don't violate constraints C. The rights of others determine the constraints upon your actions. (A *goal-directed* view with constraints added would be: among those acts available to you that don't violate constraints C, act so as to maximize goal G. Here, the rights of others would constrain your goal-directed behaviour. I do not mean to imply that the correct moral view includes mandatory goals that must be pursued, even within the constraints.) This view differs from one that tries to build the side constraints C *into* the goal G. The side-constraint view forbids you to violate these moral constraints in the pursuit of your goals; whereas the view whose objective is to minimize the violation of these rights allows you to violate the rights (the constraints) in order to lessen their total violation in the society.[4]

The claim that the proponent of the ultraminimal state is inconsistent, we now can see, assumes that he is a 'utilitarian of rights.' It assumes that his goal is, for example, to minimize the weighted amount of the violation of rights in the society, and that he should pursue this goal even through means that themselves violate people's rights. Instead, he may place the non-violation of rights as a constraint upon action, rather than (or in addition to) building it into the end state to be realized. The position held by this proponent of the ultraminimal state will be a consistent one if his conception of rights holds that your being *forced* to contribute to another's welfare violates your rights, whereas someone else's not providing you with things you need greatly, including things essential to the protection of your rights, does not *itself* violate your rights, even though it avoids making it more difficult for someone else to violate them. (That conception will be consistent provided it does not construe the monopoly element of the ultraminimal state as itself a violation of rights.) That it is a consistent position does not, of course, show that it is an acceptable one.

3. *Why Side Constraints?*

Isn't it *irrational* to accept a side constraint *C*, rather than a view that directs minimizing the violations of *C*? (The latter view treats *C* as a condition rather than a constraint.) If non-violation of *C* is so important, shouldn't that be the goal? How can a concern for the non-violation of *C* lead to the refusal to violate *C* even when this would prevent other more extensive violations of *C*? What is the rationale for placing the non-violation of rights as a side constraint upon action instead of including it solely as a goal of one's actions?

Side constraints upon action reflect the underlying Kantian principle that individuals are ends and not merely means; they may not be sacrificed or used for the achieving of other ends without their consent. Individuals are inviolable. More should be said to illuminate this talk of ends and means. Consider a prime example of a means, a tool. There is no side constraint on how we may use a tool, other than the moral constraints on how we may use it upon others. There are procedures to be followed to preserve it for future use ('don't leave it out in the rain'), and there are more and less efficient ways of using it. But there is no limit on what we may do to it to best achieve our goals. Now imagine that there was an overridable constraint *C* on some tool's use. For example, the tool might have been lent to you only on the condition that *C* not be violated unless the gain from doing so was above a certain specified amount, or unless it was necessary to achieve a certain specified tool. Here the object is not *completely* your tool, for use according to your wish or whim. But it is a tool nevertheless, even with regard to the overridable constraint. If we add constraints on its use that may not be overridden, then the object may not be used as a tool *in those ways. In those respects,* it is not a tool at all. Can one add enough constraints so that an object cannot be used as a tool at all, in *any* respect?

Can behaviour toward a person be constrained so that he is not to be used for any end except as he chooses? This is an impossibly stringent condition if it requires everyone who provides us with a good to approve positively of every use to which we wish to put it. Even the requirement that he merely should not object to any use we plan would seriously curtail bilateral exchange, not to mention sequences of such exchanges. It is sufficient that the other party stands to gain enough from the exchange so that he is willing to go through with it, even though he objects to one or more of the uses to which you shall put the good. Under such conditions, the other party is not being used solely as a means, in that respect. Another party, however, who would not choose to interact with you if he knew of the uses to which you *intend* to put his actions or good, *is* being used as a means, even if he receives enough to choose (in his ignorance) to interact with you. ('All along, you were just *using* me' can be said by someone who chose to interact only because he was ignorant of another's goals and of the uses to which he himself would be put.) Is it morally incumbent upon someone to reveal his intended uses of an interaction if he has good reason to believe the other would refuse to interact if he knew? Is he *using* the other person, if he does not reveal this? And what of the cases where the other does not choose to be of use at all? In getting pleasure from seeing an attractive person go by, does one use the other solely as a means? Does someone so use an object of sexual fantasies? These and related questions raise very interesting issues for moral philosophy; but not, I think, for political philosophy.

Political philosophy is concerned only with *certain* ways that persons may not use others; primarily, physically aggressing against them. A specific side constraint upon action toward others expresses the fact that others may not be used in the specific ways the side constraint excludes. Side constraints express the inviolability of others, in the ways they specify. These modes of inviolability are expressed by the following injunction: 'Don't use people in specified ways.' An end-state view, on the other hand, would express the view that people are ends and not merely means (if it chooses to express this view at all), by a different injunction: 'Minimize the use in specified ways of persons as means.' Following this precept itself may involve using someone as a means in one of the ways specified. Had Kant held this view, he would have given the second formula of the categorical imperative as, 'So act as to minimize the use of humanity simply as a means,' rather than the one he actually used: 'Act in such a way that you always treat humanity, whether in your own person or in the person of any other, never simply as a means, but always at the same time as an end.'

Side constraints express the inviolability of other persons. But why may not one violate persons for the greater social good? Individually, we each sometimes choose to undergo some pain or sacrifice for a greater benefit or to avoid a greater harm: we go to the dentist to avoid worse suffering later; we do some unpleasant work for its results; some persons diet to improve their health or looks; some save money to support themselves when they are older. In each case, some cost is borne for the sake of the greater overall good. Why not, *similarly,* hold that some persons have to bear some costs that benefit other persons more, for the sake of the overall social good? But there is no *social entity* with a good that undergoes some sacrifice for its own good. There are only individual people, different individual people, with their own individual lives. Using one of these people for the benefit of others, uses him and benefits the others. Nothing more. What happens is that something is done to him for the sake of others. Talk of an overall social good covers this up. (Intentionally?) To use a person in this way does not sufficiently respect and take account of the fact that he is a separate person,[5] that his is the only life he has. *He* does not get some overbalancing good from his sacrifice, and no one is entitled to force this upon him — least of all a state or government that claims his allegiance (as other individuals do not) and that therefore scrupulously must be *neutral* between its citizens.

Endnotes

[1] Here and in the next section I draw upon and amplify my discussion of these issues in footnote 4 of 'On the Randian Argument,' *The Personalist* (Spring 1971).

[2] M. Friedman, *Capitalism and Freedom* (Chicago: University of Chicago Press, 1962), ch. 6. Friedman's school vouchers, of course, allow a choice about who is to supply the product, and so differ from the protection vouchers imagined here.

[3] For a clear statement that this view is mistaken, see J. Rawls, *A Theory of Justice,* pp. 30, 565–6.

[4] Unfortunately, too few models of the structure of moral views have been specified heretofore, though there are surely other interesting structures. Hence an argument for a side-constraint structure that consists largely in arguing against an end-state maximization structure is inconclusive, for these alternatives are not exhaustive. An array of structures must be precisely formulated and investigated; perhaps some novel structure then will seem most appropriate.

The issue of whether a side-constraint view can be put in the form of the goal-without-side-constraint view is a tricky one. One might think, for example, that each person could distinguish in his goal between *his* violating rights and someone else's doing it. Give the former infinite (negative) weight in his goal, and no amount of stopping others from violating rights can outweigh his violating someone's rights. In addition to a component of a goal receiving infinite weight, indexical expressions also appear, for example, '*my* doing something.' A careful statement delimiting 'constraint views' would exclude these gimmicky ways of transforming side constraints into the form of an end-state view as sufficient to constitute a view as end state. Mathematical methods of transforming a constrained minimization problem into a sequence of unconstrained minimizations of an auxiliary function are presented in A. Fiacco and G. McCormick, *Nonlinear Programming: Sequential Unconstrained Minimization Techniques* (New York: Wiley, 1968). The book is interesting both for its methods and for their limitations in illuminating our area of concern; note the way in which the penalty functions include the constraints, the variation in weights of penalty functions (sec. 7.1), and so on.

The question of whether these side constraints are absolute, or whether they may be violated in order to avoid catastrophic moral horror, and, if the latter, what the resulting structure might look like, is one I hope largely to avoid.

[5] See J. Rawls, *A Theory of Justice,* secs. 5, 6, 30.

V.6 *Utilitarianism and the Virtues*

PHILIPPA FOOT

Philippa Foot is professor of philosophy at the University of California at Los Angeles and a fellow at Sommerville College, Oxford University. She has written important articles in moral theory, many of which are contained in her book, *Virtues and Vices* (1978).

Foot argues that although utilitarianism has a deep attraction, it is based on the idea that it can never be rational to prefer the lesser good to the greater. But, the argument continues, the consequentialism it seeks conflicts with our moral intuitions that the good is always agent-relative, always someone's specific good. It is within the framework of virtue ethics, and not utilitarianism, that the agent-relative evaluation makes sense.

It is remarkable how utilitarianism tends to haunt even those of us who will not believe in it. It is as if we for ever feel that it must be right, although we insist that it is wrong. T. M. Scanlon hits the nail on the head when he observes, in his article 'Contractualism and Utilitarianism,' that the theory occupies a central place in the moral philosophy of our time in spite of the fact that, as he puts it, 'the implications of act utilitarianism are wildly at variance with firmly held moral convictions, while rule utilitarianism . . . strikes most people as an unstable compromise.'[1] He suggests that what we need to break this spell is to find a better alternative to utilitarian theories, and I am sure that that is right. But what I want to do is to approach the business of exorcism more directly. Obviously something drives us towards utilitarianism, and must it not be an assumption or thought which is in some way mistaken? For otherwise why is the theory unacceptable? We must be going wrong somewhere and should find out where it is.

I want to argue that what is most radically wrong with utilitarianism is its consequentialism, but I also want to suggest that its consequentialist element is one of the main reasons why utilitarianism seems so compelling. I need therefore to say

something about the relation between the two theory descriptions 'utilitarian' and 'consequentialist.' Consequentialism in its most general form simply says that it is by 'total outcome,' that is, by the whole formed by an action and its consequences, that what is done is judged right or wrong. A consequentialist theory of ethics is one which identifies certain states of affairs as *good* states of affairs and says that the rightness or goodness of actions (or of other subjects of moral judgement) consists in their positive productive relationship to these states of affairs. Utilitarianism as it is usually defined consists of consequentialism together with the identification of the best state of affairs with the state of affairs in which there is most happiness, most pleasure, or the maximum satisfaction of desire. Strictly speaking utilitarianism — taken here as welfare utilitarianism — is left behind when the distribution of welfare is said in itself to affect the goodness of states of affairs; or when anything other than welfare is allowed as part of the good. But it is of course possible also to count a theory as utilitarian if right action is taken to be that which produces 'good states of affairs,' whatever these are supposed to be; and then 'utilitarianism' becomes synonymous with 'consequentialism.' By 'utilitarianism' I shall here mean 'welfare utilitarianism,' though it is with consequentialism in one form or another that I shall be most concerned.

Although I believe that what is radically wrong with utilitarianism is its consequentialism, what has

Reprinted from "Utilitarianism and the Virtues," *Mind* 94 (1985), copyright © Philippa Foot, by permission of Oxford University Press.

often seemed to be most wrong with it has been either welfarism or the sum ranking of welfare. So it has been suggested that 'the good' is not automatically increased by an increase in pleasure, but by nonmalicious pleasure, or first-order pleasure, or something of the kind; in order to get over difficulties about the pleasures of watching a public execution or the pleasures and pains of the bigot or the prude.[2] Furthermore distribution principles have been introduced so that actions benefiting the rich more than they harm the poor no longer have to be judged morally worthy. Thus the criteria for the goodness of states of affairs have continually been modified to meet one objection after another; but it seems that the modifications have never been able to catch up with the objections. For the distribution principles and the discounting of certain pleasures and pains did nothing to help with problems about, e.g., the wrongness of inducing cancer in a few experimental subjects to make a substantial advance in finding a cure for the disease. If the theory was to give results at all in line with common moral opinion *rights* had to be looked after in a way that was so far impossible within even the modified versions of utilitarianism.

It was therefore suggested, by Amartya Sen, that 'goal rights' systems should be considered; the idea being that the respecting or violating of rights should be counted as itself a good or an evil in the evaluation of states of affairs.[3] This would help to solve some problems because if the respecting of the rights of the subject were weighted heavily enough the cancer experiment could not turn out to be 'optimific' after all. Yet this seems rather a strange suggestion, because as Samuel Scheffler has remarked, it is not clear why, in the measurement of the goodness of states of affairs or total outcomes, killings for instance should count so much more heavily than deaths.[4] But what is more important is that this 'goal rights' system fails to deal with certain other examples of actions that most of us would want to call wrong. Suppose, for instance, that some evil person threatens to kill or torture a number of victims unless we kill or torture one, and suppose that we have every reason to believe that he will do as he says. Then in terms of their total outcomes (again consisting of the states of affairs made up of an action and its consequences) we have the choice between more killings or torturings and less, and a consequentialist will have to say that we are justified

in killing or torturing the one person, and indeed that we are morally obliged to do it, always supposing that no indirect consequences have tipped the balance of good and evil. There will in fact be nothing that it will not be right to do to a perfectly innocent individual if that is the only way of preventing another agent from doing more things of the same kind.

Now I find this a totally unacceptable conclusion and note that it is a conclusion not of utilitarianism in particular but rather of consequentialism in any form. So it is the spellbinding force of consequentialism that we have to think about. Welfarism has its own peculiar attraction, which has to do with the fact that pleasure, happiness, and the satisfaction of desire are things seen as in some way good. But this attraction becomes less powerful as distribution principles are added and pleasures discounted on an *ad hoc* basis to destroy the case for such things as public executions.

If having left welfarist utilitarianism behind we still find ourselves unable, in spite of its difficulties, to get away from consequentialism, there must be a reason for this. What is it, let us now ask, that is so compelling about consequentialism? It is, I think, the rather simple thought that it can never be right to prefer a worse state of affairs to a better.[5] It is this thought that haunts us and, incidentally, this thought that makes the move to rule utilitarianism an unsatisfactory answer to the problem of reconciling utilitarianism with common moral opinion. For surely it will be irrational, we feel, to obey even the most useful rule if in a particular instance we clearly see that such obedience will not *have the best results*. Again following Scheffler we ask if it is not paradoxical that it should ever be morally objectionable to act in such a way as to minimize morally objectionable acts of just the same type.[6] If it is a bad state of affairs in which one of these actions is done it will presumably be a worse state of affairs in which several are. And must it not be irrational to prefer the worse to the better state of affairs?

This thought does indeed seem compelling. And yet it leads to an apparently unacceptable conclusion about what it is right to do. So we ought, as I said, to wonder whether we have not gone wrong somewhere. And I think that indeed we have. I believe (and this is the main thesis of the paper) that we go wrong in accepting the idea that there *are* better and worse states of affairs in the sense that consequentialism requires. As Wittgenstein says in a different context, 'The decisive movement in the conjuring trick has been made, and it was the very one that we thought quite innocent.'[7]

Let us therefore look into the idea of a good state of affairs, as this appears in the thought that we can judge certain states of affairs to be better than others and then go on to give moral descriptions to actions related productively to these states of affairs.

We should begin by asking why we are so sure that we even understand expressions such as 'a good state of affairs' or 'a good outcome'; for as Peter Geach pointed out years ago there are phrases with the word 'good' in them, as, e.g., 'a good event,' that do *not* at least as they stand have a sense.[8] Following this line one might suggest that philosophers are a bit hasty in using expressions such as 'a better world.' One may *perhaps* understand this when it is taken to mean a 'deontically better world' defined as one in which fewer duties are left unfulfilled; but obviously this will not help to give a sense to 'better state of affairs' as the consequentialist needs to use this expression, since he is wanting to fix our obligations not to refer to their fulfilment.

Nevertheless it may seem that combinations of words such as 'a good state of affairs' are beyond reproach or question, for such expressions are extremely familiar. Do we not use them every day? We say that it is a good thing that something or other happened; what difficulty can there be in constructing from such elements anything we want in the way of aggregates such as total outcomes which (in principle) take into account all the elements of a possible world and so constitute good states of affairs? Surely no one can seriously suggest that 'good state of affairs' is an expression that we do not understand?

It would, of course, be ridiculous to query the sense of the ordinary things that we say about its being 'a good thing' that something or other happened, or about a certain state of affairs being good or bad. The doubt is not about whether there is some way of using the words, but rather about the way they appear in the exposition of utilitarian and other consequentialist moral theories. It is important readily to accept the fact that we talk in a natural and familiar way about good states of affairs, and that there is nothing problematic about such usage. But it is also important to see how such expressions actually work in the contexts in which they are at home, and in particular to ask about the status of a good state of affairs. Is it something impersonal to be recognized (we hope) by all reasonable men? It seems, surprisingly, that this is not the case at least in many contexts of utterance of the relevant expressions. Suppose, for instance, that the supporters of different teams have gathered in the stadium and that the members of each group are discussing the game; or that two racegoers have backed different horses in a race. Remarking on the course of events one or the other may say that things are going well or badly, and when a certain situation has developed may say that it is a good or a bad state of affairs. More commonly they will welcome some developments and deplore others, saying 'Oh good!' or 'That's bad!', calling some news good news and some news bad, sometimes describing what has happened as 'a good thing' and sometimes not. We could develop plenty of other examples of this kind, thinking for instance of the conversations about the invention of a new burglar alarm that might take place in the police headquarters and in the robbers' den.

At least two types of utterance are here discernible. For 'good' and its cognates may be used to signal the speaker's attitude to a result judged as an end result, and then he says 'Good!' or 'I'm glad' or 'That's good' where what he is glad about is something welcomed in itself and not for any good it will bring. But a state of affairs may rather be judged by its connection with other things called good. And even what is counted as in itself good may be said to be bad when it brings enough evil in its train.

Now what shall we say about the truth or falsity of these utterances? It certainly seems that they can be straightforwardly true or false. For perhaps what appears to be going to turn out well is really going to turn out badly: what seemed to be a good thing was really a bad thing, and an apparently good state of affairs was the prelude to disaster. 'You are quite wrong' one person may say to another and events may show that he *was* wrong. Nevertheless we can see that this quasi-objectivity, which is not to be questioned when people with similar aims, interests, or desires are speaking together, flies out of the window if we try to set the utterances of those in one group against the utterances of those in another. One will say 'a good thing' where another says 'a bad thing,' and it is the same for states of affairs. It would be bizarre to suggest that at the races it really *is* a good thing that one horse or the other is gaining (perhaps because of the pleasure it will bring to the majority, or the good effect on the future of racing) and so that the utterance of one particular punter, intent only on making a packet, will be the one that is true.

This is not to say, however, that what a given person says to be a good thing or a good state of affairs must relate to his own advantage. For anyone may be *interested in* the future of racing, and people commonly are *interested in,* e.g., the success of their friends, saying 'that's a good thing' if one of them looks like winning a prize or getting a job; incidentally without worrying much about whether he is the very best candidate for it.

Now it may be thought that these must be rather special uses of expressions such as 'good state of affairs,' because we surely must speak quite differently when we are talking about public matters, as when for instance we react to news of some far-away disaster. We say that the news is bad because a lot of people have lost their lives in an earthquake. Later we may say that things are not as bad as we feared and someone may remark 'that's a good thing.' 'A bad state of affairs,' we might remark on hearing the original news about people dead or homeless, and this will usually have nothing to do with harm to us or to our friends.

In this way the case is different from that of the racegoers or the cops and robbers, but this is not of course to imply that what we say on such occasions has a different status from the utterances we have considered so far. For why should its truth not be 'speaker-relative' too, also depending on what the speakers and their group are *interested in* though not now on the good or harm that will come to them themselves? Is it not more plausible to think this than to try to distinguish two kinds of uses of these expressions, one speaker-relative and the other not? For are there really two ways in which the police for instance might speak? And two ways in which the robbers could speak as well? Are we really to say that although when they are both speaking in the speaker-relative way they do not contradict each other, and may both speak truly, when speaking in the 'objective' way one group will speak truly and the other not? What shows that the second way of speaking exists?

What thoughts, one may ask, can we really be supposed to have which must be expressed in the disputed mode? Considering examples such as that of the far-away earthquake we may think that we believe the best state of affairs to be the one in which there is most happiness and least misery, or something of the sort. But considering other examples we may come to wonder whether any such thought can really be attributed to us.

Suppose for instance that when walking in a poor district one of us should lose a fairly considerable sum of money which we had intended to spend on something rather nice. Arriving home we discover the loss and telephone the police on the off chance that our wad of notes has been found and turned in. To our delight we find that it was picked up by a passing honest policeman, and that we shall get it back. 'What a good thing' we say 'that an officer happened to be there.' What seemed to be a bad state of affairs has turned out not to be bad after all: things are much better than we thought they were. And all's well that ends well. But how, it may now be asked, *can* we say that things have turned out better than we thought? Were we not supposed to believe that the best state of affairs was the one in which there was most happiness and least misery? So surely it would have been *better* if the money had not been returned to us but rather found and kept as treasure trove by some poor inhabitant of the region? We simply had not considered that because most of us do not actually *have* the thought that the best state of affairs is the one in which we lose and they gain. Perhaps we should have had this thought if it had been a small amount of money, but this was rather a lot.

No doubt it will seem to many that there must be nonspeaker-relative uses of words evaluating states of affairs because moral judgements cannot have speaker-relative status. But if one is inclined, as I am, to doubt whether propositions of this form play any part in the fundamentals of ethical theory there is no objection on this score. It is important however that the preceding discussion has been about propositions of a particular form and nothing has been said to suggest that all judgements about what is good and bad have speaker-relative status. I have not for instance made this suggestion for what Geach called 'attributive' judgements concerning things good or bad of a kind—good knives and houses and essays, or even good actions, motives, or men. If there is some reason for calling these 'speaker-relative' the reason has not been given here.

Nor has anything been said about the status of propositions about what is *good for* anyone or anything, or about that in which their good consists.

What has I hope now been shown is that we should not take it for granted that we even know what we are talking about if we enter into a discussion with the consequentialist about whether it can ever be right to produce something other than 'the best state of affairs.'

It might be suggested by way of reply that what is in question in these debates is not just the best state of affairs without qualification but rather *the best state of affairs from an impersonal point of view.* But what does this mean? A good state of affairs from an impersonal point of view is presumably opposed to a good state of affairs from *my* point of view or from *your* point of view, and as a good state of affairs from my point of view is a state of affairs which is advantageous to me, and a good state of affairs from your point of view is a state of affairs that is advantageous to you, a good state of affairs from an impersonal point of view presumably means a state of affairs which is generally advantageous, or advantageous to most people, or something like that. About the idea of maximum welfare we are not (or so we are supposing for the sake of the argument) in any difficulty.[9] But an account of the idea of a good state of affairs which simply defines it in terms of maximum welfare is no help to us here. For our problem is that something is supposed to be being said *about* maximum welfare and we cannot figure out what this is.

In a second reply, more to the point, the consequentialist might say that what we should really be dealing with in this discussion is states of affairs which are good or bad, not simply, but *from the moral point of view.* The qualification is, it will be suggested, tacitly understood in moral contexts, where no individual speaker gives his own private interests or allegiances a special place in any debate, the speaker-relativity found in other contexts thus being left behind. This seems to be a pattern familiar from other cases, as, e.g., from discussions in meetings of the governors of public institutions. Why should it not be in a similar way that we talk of a good and a bad thing to happen 'from a moral point of view'? And is it not hard to reject the conclusion that right action is action producing *this* 'best state of affairs'?

That special contexts can create special uses of the expressions we are discussing is indeed true. But before we proceed to draw conclusions about moral judgements we should ask why we think that it makes sense to talk about morally good and bad states of affairs, or to say that it is a good thing (or is good that) something happened 'from a moral point of view.' For after all we cannot concoct a meaningful sentence by adding just any qualification of this verbal form to expressions such as these. What would it mean, for instance, to say that a state of affairs was good or bad 'from a legal point of view' or 'from the point of view of etiquette?' Or that it was a good thing that a certain thing happened from these same 'points of view?' Certain interpretations that suggest themselves are obviously irrelevant, as, for instance, that it is a good state of affairs from a legal point of view when the laws are clearly stated, or a good state of affairs from the point of view of etiquette when everyone follows the rules.

It seems, therefore, that we do not solve the problem of the meaning of 'best state of affairs' when supposed to be used in a nonspeaker-relative way simply by tacking on 'from a moral point of view'; since it cannot be assumed that the resulting expression has any sense. Nevertheless it would be wrong to suggest that 'good state of affairs from a moral point of view' is a concatenation of words which in fact has no meaning in *any* of the contexts in which it appears, and to see this we have only to look at utilitarian theories of the type put forward by John C. Harsanyi and R. M. Hare, in which a certain interpretation is implicitly provided for such expressions.[10]

Harsanyi for instance argues that the only *rational* morality is one in which the rightness or wrongness of an action is judged by its relation to a certain outcome, i.e., the maximization of social utility. The details of this theory, which defines social utility in terms of individual preferences, do not concern us here. The relevant point is that within it there appears the idea of an end which is the goal of moral action, and therefore the idea of a best state of affairs from a moral point of view. (It does not of course matter whether Harsanyi uses these words.)

Similarly Hare, by a more elaborate argument from the universalizability and prescriptivity of moral judgements, tries to establish the proposition that one who takes the moral point of view must have as his aim the maximization of utility, reflecting this in one way in his day-to-day prescriptions and in another in 'critical' moral judgements. So here too a clear sense can be given to the idea of a best state of affairs from a moral point of view: it is the state of affairs which a man aims at when he takes the moral point of view and which in one way or another determines the truth of moral judgements.

Within these theories there is, then, no problem about the meaning of expressions such as 'the best state of affairs from the moral point of view.' It does not follow, however, that those who reject the theories should be ready to discuss the pros and cons of consequentialism in these terms. For unless the arguments given by Hare and Harsanyi are acceptable it will not have been shown that there is any reference for expressions such as 'the aim which each man has in so far as he takes up the moral point of view' or *a fortiori* 'the best state of affairs from the moral point of view.'

If my main thesis is correct this is a point of the first importance. For I am arguing that where non-consequentialists commonly go wrong is in accepting from their opponents questions such as 'Is it ever right to act in such a way as to produce something less than the best state of affairs that is within one's reach?'[11] Summing up the results reached so far we may say that if taken in one way, with no special reference to morality, talk about good states of affairs seems to be speaker-relative. But if the qualification 'from a moral point of view' is added the resulting expression may mean nothing; and it may lack a reference when a special consequentialist theory has given it a sense.

In the light of this discussion we should find it significant that many people who do not find any particular consequentialist theory compelling nevertheless feel themselves driven towards consequentialism by a thought which turns on the idea that there are states of affairs which are better or worse from a moral point of view. What is it that seems to make this an inescapable idea?

Tracing the assumption back in my own mind I find that what seems preposterous is to deny that there are some things that a moral person must want and aim at in so far as he is a moral person and that he will count it 'a good thing' when these things happen and 'a good state of affairs' either when they are happening or when things are disposed in their favour. For surely he must want others to be happy. To deny this would be to deny that benevolence is a virtue — and who wants to deny that?

Let us see where this line of thought will take us, accepting without any reservation that benevolence is a virtue and that a benevolent person must often aim at the good of others and call it 'a good thing' when for instance a far-away disaster turns out to have been less serious than was feared. Here we do indeed have the words 'a good thing' (and just as obviously a 'good state of affairs') necessarily appearing in moral contexts. And the use is explained not by a piece of utilitarian theory but by a simple observation about benevolence.

This, then, seems to be the way in which seeing states of affairs in which people are happy as good states of affairs really is an essential part of morality. But it is very important that we have found this end *within* morality, and forming part of it, not standing outside it as the 'good state of affairs' by which moral action in general is to be judged. For benevolence is only one of the virtues, and we shall have to look at the others before we can pronounce on any question about good or bad action in particular circumstances. Off-hand we have no reason to think that whatever is done with the aim of improving the lot of other people will be morally required or even morally permissible. For firstly there are virtues such as friendship which play their part in determining the requirements of benevolence, e.g., by making it consistent with benevolence to give service to friends rather than to strangers or acquaintances. And secondly there is the virtue of justice, taken in the old wide sense in which it had to do with everything *owed*. In our common moral code we find numerous examples of limitations which justice places on the pursuit of welfare. In the first place there are principles of distributive justice which forbid, on grounds of fairness, the kind of 'doing good' which increases the wealth of rich people at the cost of misery to the poor. Secondly, rules such as truth telling are not to be broken wherever and whenever welfare would thereby be increased. Thirdly, considerations about rights, both positive and negative, limit the action which can be taken for the sake of welfare. Justice is primarily concerned with the following of certain rules of fairness and honest dealing and with respecting prohibitions on interference with others rather than with attachment to any end. It is true that the just man must also fight injustice, and here justice like benevolence is a matter of ends, but of course the end is not the same end as the one that benevolence seeks and need not be coincident with it.

I do not mean to go into these matters in detail here, but simply to point out that we find in our ordinary moral code many requirements and prohibitions inconsistent with the idea that benevolence is the whole of morality. From the point of view of the present discussion it would be acceptable to describe the situation in terms of a tension between, for instance, justice and benevolence. But it is not strictly accurate to think of it like this, because that would suggest that someone who does an unjust act for the sake of increasing total happiness has a higher degree of benevolence than one who refuses to do it. Since someone who refuses to sacrifice an innocent life for the sake of increasing happiness is not to be counted as less benevolent than someone who is ready to do it, this cannot be right. We might be tempted to think that the latter would be acting 'out of benevolence' because his aim is the happiness of others, but this seems a bad way of talking. Certainly benevolence does not require unjust action, and we should not call an act which violated rights an act of benevolence. It would not, for instance, be an act of benevolence to induce cancer in one person (or deliberately to let it run its course) even for the sake of alleviating much suffering.

What we should say therefore is that even perfection in benevolence does not imply a readiness to do anything and everything of which it can be said that it is highly probable that it will increase the sum of human happiness. And this, incidentally, throws some light on a certain type of utilitarian theory which identifies the moral assessment of a situation with that of a sympathetic impartial observer whose benevolence extends equally to all mankind.[12] For what, we may ask, are we to suppose about this person's *other* characteristics? Is he to be guided simply and solely by a desire to relieve suffering and increase happiness; or is he also just? If it is said that for him the telling of truth, keeping of promises, and respecting of individual autonomy are to be recommended only in so far as these serve to maximize welfare then we see that the 'impartial sympathetic observer' is by definition one with a utilitarian point of view. So the utilitarians are defining moral assessment in their own terms.

Returning to the main line of our argument we now find ourselves in a better position to see that there indeed is a place *within* morality for the idea of better and worse states of affairs. That there is such a place is true if only because the proper end of benevolence is the good of others, and because in many situations the person who has this virtue will be able to think of good and bad states of affairs, in terms of the general good. It does not, however, follow that he will always be able to do so. For sometimes justice will forbid a certain action, as it forbids the harmful experiment designed to further cancer research; and then it will not be possible to ask whether 'the state of affairs' containing the action and its results will be better or worse than one in which the action is not done. The action is one that *cannot* be done, because justice forbids it, and nothing that has this moral character comes within the scope of the kind of comparison of total outcomes that benevolence may sometimes require. Picking up at this point the example discussed earlier about the morality of killing or torturing to prevent more killings or torturings we see the same principle operating here. If it were a question of riding out to rescue a small number or a large number then benevolence would, we may suppose, urge that the larger number be saved. But if it is a matter of preventing the killing *by* killing (or conniving at a killing) the case will be quite different. One does not have to believe that all rights to non-interference are absolute to believe that *this* is an unjust action, and if it is unjust the moral man says to himself that he cannot do it and does not include it in an assessment he may be making about the good and bad states of affairs that he can bring about.

What has been said in the last few paragraphs is, I suggest, a sketch of what can truly be said about the important place that the idea of maximum welfare has in morality. It is not that in the guise of 'the best outcome' it stands *outside* morality as its foundation and arbiter, but rather that it appears *within* morality as the end of one of the virtues.

When we see it like this, and give expressions such as 'best outcome' and 'good state of affairs' no special meaning in moral contexts other than the one that the virtues give them, we shall no longer think the paradoxical thought that it is sometimes right to act in such a way that the total outcome, consisting of one's action and its results, is less good than some other accessible at the time. In the abstract a benevolent person must wish that loss and harm should be minimized. He does not, however, wish that the whole consisting of a killing to minimize killings should be actualized either by his agency or that of anyone else. So there is no reason on this score to think that he must regard it as 'the best state of affairs.'[13] And therefore there is no reason for the non-consequentialist, whose thought of good and bad states of affairs in moral contexts comes only from the virtues themselves, to describe the refusal as a choice of a worse total outcome. If he does so describe it he will be giving the words the sense they have in his opponents' theories, and it is not surprising that he should find himself in their hands.

We may also remind ourselves at this point that benevolence is not the only virtue which has to do, at least in part, with ends rather than with the observance of rules. As mentioned earlier there belongs to the virtue of justice the readiness to fight for justice as well as to observe its laws; and there belongs to truthfulness not only the avoidance of lying but also that other kind of attachment to truth which has to do with its preservation and pursuit. A man of virtue must be a lover of justice and a lover of truth. Furthermore he will seek the special good of his family and friends. Thus there will be many things which he will want and will welcome, sometimes sharing these aims with others and sometimes opposing them, as when working differentially for his own children or his own friends.[14] Similarly someone who is judging a competition and is a fair judge must try to see to it that the best man wins. The existence of these 'moral aims' will of course give opportunity for the use, in moral contexts, of such expressions as 'a good thing' or 'the best state of affairs.' But nothing of a consequentialist nature follows from such pieces of usage, found here and there within morality.

An analogy will perhaps help to make my point. Thinking about good manners we might decide that someone who has good manners tries to avoid embarrassing others in social situations. This must, let us suppose, be one of his aims; and we might even decide that so far as manners is concerned this, or something like it, is the only prescribed *end*. But of course this does not mean that what good manners require of anyone is universally determined by this end. A consequentialist theory of good manners would presumably be mistaken; because good manners, not being solely a matter of purposes, also require that certain things be done or not done: e.g., that hospitality not be abused by frank discussion of the deficiencies of one's host as soon as he leaves the room.[15] So if invited to take part in such discussions a well-mannered person will, if necessary, maintain a silence embarrassing to

an interlocutor, because the rule here takes precedence over the aim prescribed. Assuming that this is a correct account of good manners — and it does not of course matter whether it is or not — we can now see the difficulty that arises if we try to say which choice open to the agent results in the best state of affairs from the point of view of manners. In certain contexts the state of affairs containing no embarrassment will be referred to as a good state of affairs, because avoiding embarrassment is by our hypothesis the one *end* prescribed by good manners. But we should not be surprised if the right action from the point of view of good manners is sometimes the one that produces something *other* than this good state of affairs. We have no right to take an end from within the whole that makes up good manners and turn it, just because it is an *end*, into the single guide to action to be used by the well-mannered man.

This analogy serves to illustrate my point about the illegitimacy of moving what is found within morality to a criterial position outside it. But it may also bring to the surface a reason many will be ready to give for being dissatisfied with my thesis. For surely a morality is unlike a code of manners in claiming rational justification for its ordinances? It cannot be enough to say that we *do* have such things as rules of justice in our present system of virtues: the question is whether we should have them, and if so why we should. And the reason this is crucial in the present context is that the justification of a moral code may seem inevitably to involve the very idea that has been called in question in this paper.

This is a very important objection. In its most persuasive form it involves a picture of morality as a rational device developed to serve certain purposes, and therefore answerable to these purposes. Morality, it will be suggested, is a device with a certain object, having to do with the harmonizing of ends or the securing of the greatest possible general good, or perhaps one of these things plus the safeguarding of rights. And the content of morality — what really is right and wrong — will be thought to be determined by what it is rational to require in the way of conduct given that these are our aims. Thus morality is thought of as a kind of tacit legislation by the community, and it is, of course, significant that the early utilitarians, who were much interested in the rationalizing of actual Parliamentary legislation, were ready to talk in these terms.[16] In moral legislation our aim is, they thought, the general good.

With this way of looking at morality there reappears the idea of better and worse states of affairs from the moral point of view. Moreover consequentialism *in some form* is necessarily reinstated. For while there is room on such a model for rational moral codes which enjoin something other than the pursuit of 'the best state of affairs for the moral point of view' this will be only in so far as it is by means of such ordinances that the object of a moral code is best achieved.[17]

Thus it may seem that we must after all allow that the idea of a good state of affairs appears at the most basic level in the critical appraisal of any moral code. This would, however, be too hasty a conclusion. Consequentialism in some form follows from the premise that morality is a device for achieving a certain shared end. But why should we accept this view of what morality is and how it is to be judged? Why should we not rather see that as itself a consequentialist assumption, which has come to seem neutral and inevitable only in so far as utilitarianism and other forms of consequentialism now dominate moral philosophy?

To counter this bewitchment let us ask awkward questions about who is supposed to *have* the end which morality is supposed to be in aid of. J. S. Mill notoriously found it hard to pass from the premise that the end of each is the good of each to the proposition that the end of all is the good of all.[18] Perhaps no such *shared end* appears in the foundations of ethics, where we may rather find individual ends and rational compromises between those who have them. Or perhaps at the most basic level lie facts about the way individual human beings can find the greatest goods which they are capable of possessing. The truth is, I think, that we simply do not have a satisfactory theory of morality, and need to look for it. Scanlon was indeed right in saying that the real answer to utilitarianism depends on progress in the development of alternatives. Meanwhile, however, we have no reason to think that we must accept consequentialism in any form. If the thesis of this paper is correct we should be more alert than we usually are to the possibility that we may unwittingly, and unnecessarily, surrender to consequentialism by uncritically accepting its key idea. Let us remind ourselves that the idea of the goodness of total states of affairs played no part in Aristotle's moral philosophy, and that in modern times it plays no part either in Rawls's account of

justice or in the theories of more thoroughgoing contractualists such as Scanlon.[19] If we accustom ourselves to the thought that there is simply a blank where consequentialists see 'the best state of affairs' we may be better able to give other theories the hearing they deserve.

Endnotes

[1] T. M. Scanlon, 'Contractualism and Utilitarianism', pp. 103–28.

[2] See, e.g., A. Sen, 'Utilitarianism and Welfarism', pp. 463–89.

[3] A. Sen, 'Rights and Agency' [reprinted in this collection as Chapter 9—Ed.].

[4] S. Scheffler, *The Rejection of Consequentialism*, pp. 108–12.

[5] The original version continued 'How could it ever be right, we think, to produce less good rather than more good?' I have excised this sentence because in the context the use of the expression 'doing more good' suggested an identification which I was at pains to deny. At all times I have allowed *doing good* as an unproblematic notion, because although it does raise many problems, e.g. about different distributions of benefits, it does not raise the particular problems with which I am concerned. I want to insist that however well we might understand what it was to 'do as much good as possible' in the sense of producing maximum benefit, it would not follow that we knew what we meant by expressions such as 'the best outcome' or 'the best state of affairs' as these are used by moral philosophers. . . .

[6] Scheffler, *The Rejection of Consequentialism*, p. 121.

[7] L. Wittgenstein, *Philosophical Investigations* (Macmillan 1953 and Blackwell 1958), § 308.

[8] P. Geach, 'Good and Evil', *Analysis* 17 (1956), pp. 33–42.

[9] Cf. endnote 5.

[10] See, e.g., J. C. Harsanyi, 'Morality and the Theory of Rational Behavior', *Social Research* 44 (1977), reprinted in Sen and Williams, *Utilitarianism and Beyond*, pp. 39–62; and R. M. Hare, *Moral Thinking*.

[11] See, e.g., T. Nagel, 'The Limits of Objectivity', p. 131, where he says that '. . . things would be better, what *happened* would be better' if I twisted a child's arm in circumstances where (by Nagel's hypothesis) this was the only way to get medical help for the victims of an accident. He supposes that I might have done something worse if I hurt the child than if I did not do it, but that the total outcome would have been better. It does not, I think, occur to him to question the idea of *things* being better—or *things* being worse.

[12] See Harsanyi, 'Morality and the Theory of Rational Behavior', Sen and Williams, *Utilitarianism and Beyond*, p. 39.

[13] I have discussed examples of this kind in more detail in 'Morality, Action, and Outcome', in T. Honderich, ed., *Morality and Objectivity: A Tribute to J. L. Mackie*.

14 See D. Parfit, 'Prudence, Morality, and the Prisoner's Dilemma,' and A. Sen, 'Rights and Agency.'

15 It is customary to wait until later.

16 See, e.g., J. Bentham, *An Introduction to the Principles of Legislation* (1789), ch. 3, Section 1.

17 For discussions of this possibility see, e.g., R. Adams,

'Motive Utilitarianism,' and D. Parfit, *Reasons and Persons,* pp. 24–8.

18 J. S. Mill, *Utilitarianism,* ch. 4.

19 J. Rawls, *A Theory of Justice;* T. M. Scanlon, 'Contractualism and Utilitarianism.'

V.7 *Agent-Centered Restrictions, Rationality, and the Virtues*

SAMUEL SCHEFFLER

Samuel Scheffler is professor of philosophy at the University of California at Berkeley and the author of *The Rejection of Consequentialism* (1982) and *Human Morality* (1992).

Recognizing that our commonsense morality, as well as the type adhered to by most ethicists, is deontological, Scheffler focuses on the paradox contained in deontological ethical systems. They are characterized by "agent-centered restrictions," restrictions that "it is at least sometimes impermissible to violate in circumstances where a violation would serve to minimize total overall violations of the very same restriction, and would have no other morally relevant consequence." The paradoxicality of this position is brought out by the following questions: How can it be wrong to violate a rule if doing so would have the consequence of minimizing overall violations of that very rule? How can the minimization of morally objectionable conduct be morally unacceptable?

Scheffler examines Foot's position (see previous reading) and others, and argues that their attempts in dissolving the paradox are unsuccessful.

Since the term has been used differently by different philosophers, it should be pointed out that Scheffler uses "consequentialism" to signify the idea that the right act is the one that produces the best overall state of affairs. Utilitarianism is one type of consequentialism. Perfectionism, the maximizing of moral values, is another. Egoism is not a type of consequentialism, since it aims at maximizing not the overall good but only individual goods.

There is no substantive moral theory that is obviously correct. All such theories stand in need of some defence. However, in my book *The Rejection of Consequentialism*,[1] I argued that the need is particularly acute in the case of typical deontological theories. For although the common-sense morality of

our culture is substantially deontological in content, and although many moral philosophers find themselves drawn toward some version of deontology, I maintained that there is a distinct air of paradox surrounding such views. And this mixture of real appeal and apparent paradox — always a potent combination in philosophy — lends a special urgency to the defence of deontology.

That typical deontological views are apparently paradoxical, I argued, is to be explained by their inclusion of what I call 'agent-centred restrictions.' An

Reprinted from *Mind* 94 (1985) by permission of the author and Oxford University Press.

agent-centred restriction is, roughly, a restriction which it is at least sometimes impermissible to violate in circumstances where a violation would serve to minimize total overall violations of the very same restriction, and would have no other morally relevant consequences. Thus, for example, a prohibition against killing one innocent person even in order to minimize the total number of innocent people killed would ordinarily count as an agent-centred restriction. The inclusion of agent-centred restrictions gives traditional deontological views considerable anti-consequentialist force, and also considerable intuitive appeal. Despite their congeniality to moral common sense, however, agent-centred restrictions are puzzling. For how can it be rational to forbid the performance of a morally objectionable action that would have the effect of minimizing the total number of comparably objectionable actions that were performed and would have no other morally relevant consequences? How can the minimization of morally objectionable conduct be morally unacceptable?

In the two published versions of her Presidential Address to the Pacific Division of the American Philosophical Association,[2] Philippa Foot attempts 'to show that there is no paradox at the heart of non-consequentialist morality.'[3] Foot agrees that agent-centred restrictions *appear* paradoxical. And she believes that consequentialism, which first gives some principle for ranking overall states of affairs from best to worst from an impersonal or agent-neutral standpoint, and then says that the right act in a given situation is the one that will produce the best overall outcome of any act available, has a 'spell-binding force.'[4] But she also believes that a certain kind of non-consequentialist moral view can in the end be shown to be free of paradox despite the fact that it includes agent-centred restrictions, and that the spell of consequentialism can thus be broken. The kind of moral view she has in mind is one in which a conception of the virtues plays a central role. Now many of what I have been calling traditional deontological views do not assign this kind of role to the virtues. Indeed, so-called 'virtue theories' are often thought to represent an alternative to both consequentialist and deontological moral conceptions. For the purposes of this discussion, therefore, it is important to remember that Foot's claim is, in effect, that agent-centred restrictions are not paradoxical when they are set in the context of a non-consequentialist view of a certain kind. There will

be occasion later in this paper to consider the extent to which assignment of a central role to the virtues really is essential to the sort of defence of agent-centred restrictions that Foot wants to give.

Foot says that what seems compelling about consequentialism is 'the rather simple thought that it can never be right to prefer a worse state of affairs to a better.'[5] And what seems paradoxical about those non-consequentialist views that include agent-centred restrictions is that they appear to claim that it is sometimes morally impermissible to produce the best state of affairs that one is in a position to produce. Sometimes, they seem to say, we must do less good, or prevent less evil, than we could. Perhaps, for example, we must refrain from harming one innocent person even if harming that person would result in the minimization of the total number of innocent people comparably harmed. That consequentialism should seem compelling, and that agent-centred restrictions should seem paradoxical, Foot believes, is inevitable once we grant the apparently innocent idea 'that there *are* better or worse states of affairs in the sense that consequentialism requires.'[6] But, she maintains, this idea is really not so innocent; it can be challenged, and it is through such a challenge that she hopes to break the spell of consequentialism and dissolve the air of paradox surrounding agent-centred restrictions.

Foot does not claim, as some others have, that evaluations of states of affairs never make sense in moral contexts. On the contrary, she thinks it is important 'to see the place that there indeed is *within* morality for the idea of better and worse states of affairs.'[7] 'That there is such a place,' she adds, 'follows from the fact that the proper end of benevolence is the good of others, and that in many situations the person who has this virtue will be able to think of good and bad states of affairs in terms of the general good.'[8] Thus, for example, if there is 'a question of riding out to rescue a small number or a large number then benevolence would urge that the larger number be saved.'[9] What Foot wants to argue, however, is the following. Although someone who possesses the virtue of benevolence will indeed be disposed to promote good states of affairs in certain circumstances, benevolence is not the only virtue. Justice, for example, is also a virtue. And there are various rules and requirements that the person who possesses the virtue of justice must observe: rules of distributive justice, truth telling, respect for rights, and so on. Rules and requirements such as these restrict the area 'in which benevolence is free to pursue its ends';[10] for 'sometimes justice will forbid a certain action, . . . and then it will not be possible to ask whether "the state of affairs" containing the action and its result will be better or worse than the one in which the action is not done. The action is one that *cannot* be done because justice forbids it, and nothing that has this moral character comes within the scope of the kind of comparison of total outcomes that benevolence may sometimes require.[11]

Now by itself the claim that an unjust action falls outside 'the scope of the kind of comparison of total outcomes that benevolence may sometimes require' is not entirely unambiguous. One might wonder whether it means that no meaningful comparison of outcomes is *possible* in cases where one of the outcomes would result from an unjust action, or whether it means instead that since one must not perform the unjust action in any case, it is inappropriate actually to *carry out* the relevant comparison of overall outcomes. However, the following passage from the earlier version of Foot's paper suggests that it is the first interpretation that more nearly reflects her thinking:

> When we . . . give expressions such as 'best outcome' and 'good state of affairs' no special meaning in moral contexts other than the one that the virtues give them, we shall no longer think the paradoxical thought that it is sometimes right to act in such a way that the total outcome, consisting of one's action and its results, is less good than some other accessible at the time. What the non-consequentialist should say is that 'good state of affairs' is an expression which has a very limited use in these contexts. It belongs in cases in which benevolence is free to pursue its ends, and chooses among possibilities . . . But the expression has no meaning when we try to use it to say something about a whole consisting of what we would illicitly do, allow, or wish for, together with its consequences. In the abstract a benevolent person must wish that loss and harm should be minimized. He does not, however, wish that the whole consisting of a killing to minimize killings should be actualized either by his own agency or that of anyone else. So there is no reason on this

score to say that he must regard it as the 'better state of affairs.' And therefore there is no reason for the non-consequentialist, whose thought of good and bad states of affairs in moral contexts comes only from the virtues themselves, to describe the refusal as a choice of a worse state of affairs. If he does so describe it he will be giving the words the sense they have in his opponents' theories, and it is not surprising that he should find himself in their hands.[12]

The view expressed in this passage seems to be that comparisons of overall states of affairs in moral contexts can only be meaningfully made when action aimed at promoting the good of others is called for, that such action is forbidden in cases where it would transgress some rule of justice, and that in cases of this kind it is not possible meaningfully to say that the prohibited action would produce a better overall state of affairs than the alternative. Now in the later version of her paper, Foot has eliminated that portion of the passage just quoted which begins with the words 'What the non-consequentialist should say' and ends with the words 'together with its consequences,' thus withdrawing the explicit claim that the expression 'good state of affairs' has no meaning when the outcome of an unjust act is in question. Nevertheless, the broad outlines of her position remain unchanged. She continues to maintain that while comparisons of states of affairs in moral contexts can meaningfully be made when benevolent action is called for, the claim that some unjust act would result in a better overall state of affairs than any of the available alternatives lacks any clear sense in ordinary non-consequentialist moral thought. And, she argues, while consequentialist theories may *give* it a sense, someone who has not already accepted one of those theories has no reason to believe that there *are* better and worse states of affairs in the consequentialist's sense.[13] Thus, Foot believes, the air of paradox surrounding non-consequentialist views that include agent-centred restrictions can be dispelled. For what seems paradoxical about those views, according to Foot, is that they appear to claim that we must sometimes produce a worse overall outcome instead of a better one. And if she is right, this appearance can be shown to be illusory. There will of course be situations in which the *consequentialist will describe the non-consequentialist as* insisting that we must produce a worse overall outcome rather than a better one. But the non-consequentialist can, if Foot is right, deny that that description has any ordinary meaning in such situations. The non-consequentialist can thus maintain that either the consequentialist is talking nonsense, or else he is supplying his words with some special meaning derived from his own theory, in which case he is begging the question against the non-consequentialist.

There seem to me, however, to be three reasons for doubting whether Foot has really succeeded in dispelling the air of paradox surrounding agent-centred restrictions. First, I am sceptical of the idea that, in ordinary non-consequentialist moral discourse, evaluations of overall states of affairs are meaningful when benevolent action is called for, but meaningless when the outcome of an unjust action is in question. People who deny that such evaluations *ever* make sense typically do so because they do not believe that the benefits and harms of different human beings can be meaningfully summed. But this worry about aggregation does not seem to be what concerns Foot, since she is happy to speak, for example, of 'the important place that the idea of maximum welfare has in morality'.[14] And, as we have seen, she wants to claim, not that evaluations of states of affairs never make sense in moral contexts, but only that they may lose their sense whenever the candidate for assessment is the outcome of an unjust act. But do we really cease to understand what is meant by 'a better state of affairs' if the question is raised whether infringing a right or telling a lie or treating a particular individual unfairly might perhaps produce a better state of affairs than failing to do so? I do not think so. Many moral dilemmas take the form of conflicts between considerations of justice, rights, or fairness on the one hand, and considerations of aggregate well-being on the other. And it seems to me quite natural to characterize the dilemmatic feature of a situation of this kind by saying, for example, that one is faced with a problem because violating someone's rights would in this case produce better results on the whole than would respecting them. I do not think that it is only consequentialists who think of matters in these terms, and unless it can be shown that there is something incoherent about *any* interpersonal aggregation of benefits and burdens, I see no reason to deny us this way of speaking and conceiving of the matter.

Second, in order for Foot's attempt to dissolve the apparent paradox surrounding agent-centred restrictions to be successful, it must be the case that the alleged paradox cannot be formulated without using the idea of one overall state of affairs being better than another. But, as my initial characterization of the paradox at the beginning of this paper was meant to suggest, it can in fact be formulated without using the notion of an 'overall state of affairs' at all. How, I asked, can it be rational to forbid the performance of a morally objectionable action that will have the effect of minimizing the total number of comparably objectionable actions that are performed and will have no other morally relevant consequences? How can the minimization of morally objectionable conduct itself be morally unacceptable? Even if, for the sake of argument, we grant Foot's claim that the idea of one overall state of affairs being better than another lacks any clear non-consequentialist sense in cases of injustice, *these* questions can still be formulated and understood, and the answers to them still do not seem obvious. Even if Foot's claim is granted, the defender of agent-centred restrictions can hardly say that it is meaningless to assert that circumstances can arise in which a certain moral rule will be violated several times unless I violate it once. And while he can, if Foot's claim is granted, deny that it is meaningful to say that the state of affairs containing several violations is worse than the state of affairs containing just one violation, I do not believe that we need the latter claim in order to see the agent-centred prohibition as puzzling. All we need is the recognition that fewer violations will occur if I act one way rather than another, together with the idea that such violations are morally objectionable, in the rather unambitious sense that it is morally preferable that no such violations should occur than that any should. And while Foot may in fact want to reject even this weaker idea, I believe, as I shall argue in a few pages, that the costs of doing so are prohibitive.

Third, although Foot begins her paper by acknowledging that 'utilitarianism tends to haunt even those of us who will not believe in it,'[15] and although her paper is meant as an 'exorcism,'[16] an attempt to rid consequentialism of its 'spellbinding force,' the way in which she ultimately tries to do this is such as to make it seem mysterious how consequentialism was ever taken seriously in the first place, let alone viewed as spellbinding. For if, in asking how it can ever be right 'to prefer a worse state of affairs to a better,'[17] the consequentialist is either talking nonsense or else using the language of his own theory instead of the language that the rest of us speak, how is it that we find his question troubling, haunting? After all, if Foot is right, it is not clear that we even understand the question. So wherein lies its power to haunt us? I do not believe that Foot's view allows any adequate answer to this question, and for this reason if for no other her position seems to me worrisome.

Although I do not agree with the idea that attempts to make agent-centred restrictions seem paradoxical are question-begging, or with the idea that we will find views that include such restrictions paradoxical only if we have already conceded the truth of consequentialism in accepting the description of those views that is supposed to generate the difficulty, I think I understand one reason why these ideas seem tempting. Moreover, although I do not agree with them, I think that there is *something* right about them, and that in an appreciation of what is right about them lies the key to any adequate defence of agent-centred restrictions. These ideas seem tempting partly, I believe, because we have the sense that in finding the restrictions paradoxical, we are relying on a conception of rationality that seems to lie at the heart of consequentialism, and that if accepted seems inevitably to make the restrictions look problematic. And there is a way in which this is right. The reason that it is nevertheless not question-begging to say that the restrictions seem paradoxical is that although the conception of rationality that generates the appearance of paradox lies at the heart of consequentialism, it is not peculiar to consequentialism. On the contrary, it is a fundamental and familiar conception of rationality that we accept and operate with in a very wide and varied range of contexts. The fact that this powerful conception of rationality seems both to lie at the heart of consequentialism and to generate the sense that agent-centred restrictions are paradoxical does not show that the restrictions will only seem paradoxical to us if we have already, wittingly or unwittingly, accepted consequentialism. It shows rather that the 'spellbinding force' of consequentialism, its capacity to haunt even those who do not accept it, derives from the fact that it appears to embody a notion of rationality which we recognize from myriad diverse contexts, and whose power we have good independent reason to respect. It also shows that the seeming paradox of agent-centred restrictions goes deep; no questions need be begged to find the apparent clash between the morality of common sense and the rationality of common sense troubling, haunting, difficult to ignore or dismiss. At the same time it suggests that a fully satisfying defence of agent-centred restrictions could take one of two forms. It might, first, consist in showing that the conflict between such restrictions and the kind of rationality they seem to defy is only apparent: that, appearances to the contrary notwithstanding, the restrictions can be reconciled with that familiar form of rationality. Or it might, alternatively, consist in showing that the restrictions embody a limitation on the scope of that form of rationality, and give expression to a different form of rationality which we also recognize and which also has its place in our lives.

The kind of rationality that consequentialism seems so clearly to embody, and which makes so much trouble for views that incorporate agent-centred restrictions, is what we may call *maximizing* rationality. The core of this conception of rationality is the idea that if one accepts the desirability of a certain goal being achieved, and if one has a choice between two options, one of which is certain to accomplish the goal better than the other, then it is, *ceteris paribus,* rational to choose the former over the latter. Consequentialism seems to embody this kind of rationality because it starts from a conception of what is desirable (the overall good) and then tells us always to promote as much of it as we can. Views that incorporate agent-centred restrictions, by contrast, seem troubling, relative to this notion of rationality. For they appear to identify certain kinds of actions as morally objectionable or undesirable, in the sense that it is morally preferable that no such actions should occur than that any should, but then tell us that there are situations in which we must act in such a way that a greater rather than a lesser number of these actions are actually performed.

There is, of course, nothing within maximizing rationality itself that requires us to accept the consequentialist's choice of goals, and so although consequentialism embodies that form of rationality, it is not the only normative theory of action that does so. For example egoism, construed here as the view that one ought always to pursue one's *own* greatest advantage, also embodies maximizing rationality.

Indeed common-sense deontological morality, standing between egoism and consequentialism, sometimes seems to be caught in a kind of normative squeeze, with its rationality challenged in parallel ways by (as it were) the maximizers of the right and of the left: those who think that one ought always to pursue one's own good, and those who are convinced that one should promote the good of all.

I said a moment ago that a satisfying defence of agent-centred restrictions could take one of two forms. The first would be to show that, appearances to the contrary notwithstanding, there really is no conflict between such restrictions and maximizing rationality. Thus it might be denied, to start with, that views incorporating agent-centred restrictions actually do present as desirable any goal whose maximum accomplishment they then prohibit. They assign each person the agent-relative goal of not violating any restrictions himself, it might be said, but they do not present the overall non-occurrence of such violations as desirable. Thus in forbidding the minimization of overall violations, they are not in fact thwarting the achievement of any goal whose desirability they recognize.

Now I do not believe that defenders of standard *deontological* views are really in a position to make these claims. The difficulty is that such views do, as I have suggested, seem committed to the idea that violations of the restrictions are morally objectionable or undesirable, in the sense that there is a moral point of view from which it is preferable that no violations should occur than that any should. Defenders of deontological views are typically happy to say things like this, and with good reason. For on standard deontological views, morality evaluates actions from a vantage-point which is concerned with more than just the interests of the individual agent. In other words, an action will be right or wrong, on such a view, relative to a standard of assessment that takes into account a number of factors quite independent of the interests of the agent. And defenders of such views are unlikely to claim that the relevant standard of assessment includes agent-centred restrictions, but that it is a matter of indifference, from the vantage-point represented by that standard, whether or not those restrictions are violated. For if it is not the case that it is preferable, from *that* vantage-point, that no violations should occur than that any should, it is hard to see how individual agents could possibly be thought to have

reason to observe the restrictions when doing so did not happen to coincide with their own interests or the interests of those they cared about. In other words, deontological views need the idea that violations of the restrictions are morally objectionable or undesirable if the claim that people ought not to commit such violations when doing so would be in their own interests is to be plausible. Yet if such views do regard violations as morally objectionable or undesirable, in the sense that it is morally preferable that none should occur than that any should, it does then seem paradoxical that they tell us there are times when we must act in such a way that a larger rather than a smaller number of violations actually takes place. Notice that egoism, by contrast, *does* seem committed exclusively to agent-relative goals. It assigns each person the agent-relative goal of maximizing his own advantage. And since it does not purport to assess actions from a point of view which is concerned with more than just the interests of the individual agent, it is not committed in the way deontology is to presenting as desirable any non-relative goal whose maximum accomplishment it then prohibits. That is why *it does not for a moment seem paradoxical for the egoist to say that one ought to maximize one's own advantage even if that means that fewer people overall will be able to maximize theirs.*

Thus defenders of standard deontological views do not appear to be in a position to make the claim that, in forbidding us to minimize the violation of those restrictions they insist on, they are not thwarting the achievement of any goal whose desirability they recognize. The situation may be different, however, with other kinds of non-consequentialist views. In particular, someone who accepts a view like Foot's may be in a position to make this claim more plausibly. For if agent-centred restrictions are seen as restrictions that those who possess certain virtues will be disposed to observe, and if these virtues are thought of as traits of character whose possession enables a person to live the kind of life that is good for him,[18] then it may perhaps be denied that the commitment to agent-centred restrictions involves any commitment to assessing actions from a 'moral point of view' which is concerned with something more than just the interests of the individual agent.[19] Such a denial would reveal a significant difference between this kind of view and standard deontological views, and it would make the assignment of a central role to the virtues essential to the defence of agent-centred restrictions; but it would also carry with it a commitment to the idea that actions are right or wrong—if at all—relative to a standard of assessment that does not ultimately take anything but the well-being of the agent into account. Thus, perhaps, what would be wrong with injustice, lying, and the like would be, roughly, that the disposition to engage in such activities does not contribute to a good life for the agent, and that the disposition not to does. But this, it seems to me, rather glaringly fails to capture our actual sense of what is ordinarily wrong with these things. Even if we agree that the disposition to behave unjustly does not in fact contribute to the agent's ability to live a life that is good for him, we are unlikely to agree that that is the only reason injustice is wrong. It may be objected that the kind of view under discussion is best understood as claiming, not that certain kinds of actions are wrong because the disposition to perform them does not contribute to the living of a good life by the agent, but rather that the disposition to perform them does not contribute to the living of a good life by the agent because they are wrong (by some independent standard).[20] Understood in this way, however, the view loses its ability to avoid the deontologist's predicament. For it no longer claims that the standard relative to which actions are right or wrong is one that takes nothing but the well-being of those who perform them into account. It thus loses its ability to disclaim any commitment to the idea of assessing actions from a point of view which is concerned with more than just the interests of the individual agent, and hence to the idea that there is a moral point of view from which it is preferable that no violations of the restrictions should occur than that any should. And so it loses its ability to make the claim that, in forbidding the minimization of overall violations, it is not thwarting the achievement of any goal whose desirability it recognizes.

As an alternative to trying to make that claim, someone who wanted to show that there was no conflict between agent-centred restrictions and maximizing rationality might point out that, if the *ceteris paribus* clause in the formulation of maximizing rationality were fully cashed out, one of its main features would be a provision to the effect that it can sometimes be rational to act in such a way as to worse achieve one goal if that will make it possible to better achieve another. Since that is so, it might be said, views that include agent-centred restrictions need not come into conflict with maximizing rationality when they tell us to further the agent-relative goal of not violating the restrictions ourselves at the expense of the non-relative goal of minimizing violations of the restrictions. By itself, however, this claim is not fully persuasive. The problem is that the agent-relative goal and the non-relative goal appear to be related to each other in such a way as to make the insistence on giving priority to the relative goal puzzling, from the standpoint of maximizing rationality. Since, as our earlier discussion suggested, the fact that violations of the restrictions are objectionable from a moral point of view constitutes at least part of the basis for claiming that individual agents ought not ordinarily to commit such violations, the agent-relative goal looks as if it is derivative from, and given life by, the non-relative objection, and does not appear to represent something independently desirable. Rather, the desirability of achieving the agent-relative goal seems contingent on its serving to advance the non-relative goal of minimizing the morally objectionable. And if that is so, then the insistence that one must satisfy the agent-relative goal even when doing so will inhibit achievement of the non-relative goal is incompatible with considerations of maximizations.

The project of reconciling agent-centred restrictions with maximizing rationality thus faces the following difficulty. On the one hand, as I have already argued, the compatibility of such restrictions with that form of rationality cannot be satisfactorily established by dispensing altogether with the idea of a moral point of view. For if one dispenses with that idea, one cannot do justice to our sense of what is ordinarily wrong with the conduct that the restrictions prohibit. Nor, as I have also argued, can the compatibility of the restrictions with maximizing rationality be established accepting the notion that morality evaluates actions from a point of view that is concerned with more than just the interests of the individual agent, but denying that violations of the restrictions are objectionable or undesirable from that point of view. For if one accepts the former notion, then one needs the claim that violations are morally objectionable or undesirable in order to explain why individuals ought not to commit such violations when doing so would be in their own interests. On the other hand, however, the argument of the preceding paragraph suggests that, if the compatibility of agent-centred restrictions and maximizing rationality is to be established, neither can it be conceded that the *entire basis* for the restrictions is the objectionableness from the moral point of view of the behaviour they prohibit. For if one makes that concession, then the requirement that the agent-relative goal be given priority over the non-relative goal cannot be reconciled with considerations of maximization. To show that agent-centred restrictions are compatible with maximizing rationality, therefore, one must agree that the behaviour they rule out is morally objectionable or undesirable, but deny that that very objectionableness constitutes the entire rationale for the restrictions. And then, of course, one must supply the remainder of the rationale.

One idea, along these lines, would be to argue that agent-centred restrictions serve some independent maximizing purpose. Thus it might be said, for example, that the inclusion of such restrictions enables a moral conception to give more weight than consequentialism does to some important fact or consideration: some natural feature of persons, perhaps. In *The Rejection of Consequentialism* I tried to use a strategy of roughly this kind to motivate an 'agent-centred prerogative,' a prerogative allowing each agent to devote energy and attention to his own projects and commitments out of proportion of the weight in any impersonal calculus of his doing so. If my argument there was correct, such a strategy can thus be used to explain why one is not always *required* to give the non-relative goal of minimizing overall violations priority over the agent-relative goal of avoiding violations oneself. At the same time, I indicated that I myself do not see how, specifically, to deploy such a strategy in defence of agent-centred restrictions: in defence of the view that one is not always *permitted* to give the non-relative goal priority over the relative one. I do not, in other words, see how to make a convincing case that there is some particular important fact or consideration to which a moral theory gives sufficient weight only if it includes agent-centred restrictions. Obviously, however, that is hardly conclusive, and this strategy continues to represent a means by which it might be possible to reconcile agent-centred restrictions and maximizing rationality, thereby dispelling the apparent paradox attached to the restrictions.

Of course, even if no reconciliation were possible, that would not show that agent-centred restrictions are indefensible. As I said earlier, a satisfying defence of the restrictions could take either of two forms. Reconciliation with maximizing rationality would be one sort of defence. But it is, after all, not obvious that maximizing rationality constitutes the whole of rationality. And if in fact there were no way to defend agent-centred restrictions while remaining within the framework of maximizing rationality, then the alternative for a defender of the restrictions would be to try to show that they embody a departure from maximization which is licensed by the more comprehensive tapestry of full human rationality. In other words, the task would be to try to set the restrictions convincingly within the broad contours of practical rationality as we understand it.

Now it might be thought that this task could be easily dispatched. After all, if it really is true that, as I said earlier, agent-centred restrictions are congenial to the common-sense morality of our culture, and if the restrictions thus embody constraints on practical reasoning that seem to us natural and intuitively appealing, then that might be thought sufficient to show that they do in fact have their place within what we are prepared to recognize as human practical rationality, even if they represent a departure from maximization. This idea may not in fact be so very different from what Foot wishes to maintain. The difficulty with this quick solution is that the appearance that the restrictions are *irrational* is generated by an apparently appropriate application of a very powerful form of thought which itself occupies a central place within what we recognize as human practical rationality. The seeming paradox arises out of a process of reasoning that itself seems natural and intuitively compelling, and not through the introduction of some theoretically attractive but humanly unrecognizable model of rationality. Thus to dispel the paradox and give a satisfying account of the place of the restrictions within full human rationality, more must be done than simply to call attention to their naturalness and appeal. For to do no more than that is to leave in place all of those elements which combine to create the impression that, in so far as it is drawn to agent-centred restrictions, human practical reason may be at war with itself.

Viewed from one perspective, it may seem odd that agent-centred restrictions should be thought to have a specially insecure relationship to considerations of practical rationality. For such restrictions are often thought of as broadly Kantian in spirit, and it is Kant, along with Aristotle, who is most closely associated with the idea that moral norms are rooted in the structure of practical reason. The oddity may be lessened somewhat if we remember that the normative view whose rationality is in question, although standardly referred to as Kantian, represents at most one aspect of Kant's own view. Roughly speaking, we can distinguish the following elements, among others, in Kant's moral thought: a view about the nature of moral motivation (an act done purely from inclination lacks any genuine moral worth), a view about the constraints imposed by reason on the maxim of an action (the categorical imperative procedure), and a view about the substantive moral norms derivable from the categorical imperative. If there is a genuinely Kantian view being challenged here, it is this: that it is possible to interpret the categorical imperative in such a way that it is plausibly thought of both as a requirement of practical reason and as supporting agent-centred restrictions in particular. This leaves much of what Kant thought about the relation of morality and rationality untouched. At the same time, the question it does raise is one to which the answer, I think, is not at all clear.

Endnotes

1 Oxford, Clarendon Press, 1982.

2 The reference for the first version is 'Utilitarianism and the Virtues,' *Proceedings and Addresses of the American Philosophical Association* (abbreviated hereafter as *PAAPA*) 57 (1983). 273–83. The second version appeared, with the same title, in *Mind* 94 (1985), pp. 196–209. [The *Mind* version is reprinted in this collection as reading V.6.] Foot described it as 'an expanded version.' She added: 'Much of the text is unaltered and all the ideas are the same, but I hope to have explained myself more clearly this time around.' See *Mind*, p. 196. When quoting, I will always indicate whether or not the passage as quoted appears in both versions of Foot's paper. Where it does, I will give both page references. Where it does not, I will give the page reference for the version in which it does appear, and I will also compare the quoted passage with the corresponding passage in the other version, if there is one. If there is no corresponding passage, I will so indicate.

3 *PAAPA*, p. 282. These words have been eliminated from the second version, but the description they provide of the aim of the paper fits both versions equally well.

4 *PAAPA*, p. 274; *Mind*, p. 198.

5 *PAAPA*, p. 275; *Mind*, p. 198.

6 *PAAPA*, p. 275; *Mind*, p. 199.

7 *PAAPA*, p. 281. In the *Mind* version, the quoted material has been slightly altered: 'to see that there indeed is a place *within* morality for the idea of better and worse states of affairs' (*Mind*, p. 206).

8 *PAAPA*, pp. 281–2. In *Mind*, the corresponding passage reads: 'That there is such a place is true if only because the proper end of benevolence is the good of others, and because in many situations the person who has this virtue will be able to think of good and bad states of affairs, in terms of the general good' (*Mind*, p. 206).

9 *PAAPA*, p. 282. In the *Mind* version, the phrase 'we may suppose' has been inserted between 'would' and 'urge.' See *Mind*, p. 206.

10 *PAAPA*, p. 282. This phrase does not appear in the *Mind* version, but the view I am describing surely does.

11 *PAAPA*, p. 282. In *Mind*, the corresponding passage reads: 'sometimes justice will forbid a certain action, . . . and then it will not be possible to ask whether "the state of affairs" containing the action and its result will be better or worse than one in which the action is not done. The action is one that *cannot* be done, because justice forbids it, and nothing that has this moral character comes within the scope of the kind of comparison of total outcomes that benevolence may sometimes require' (*Mind*, p. 206).

12 *PAAPA*, p. 282.

13 The expression 'good state of affairs from a moral point of view,' she writes in the second version of her paper, 'may mean nothing; and it may lack a reference when a special consequentialist theory has given it a sense' (*Mind*, p. 204).

14 *PAAPA*, p. 282; *Mind*, p. 206.

15 *PAAPA*, p. 273; *Mind*, p. 196.

16 *PAAPA*, p. 273; *Mind*, p. 196.

17 *PAAPA*, p. 275; *Mind*, p. 198.

18 I am not in fact sure that Foot herself would be prepared to say this. (See endnote 20.) But the argument I am imagining in defence of agent-centred restrictions depends on a willingness to say it. And as indicated in endnote 19, that argument seems in obvious respects to be rather in the spirit of Foot's overall position.

19 Such a denial would of course be entirely consistent with Foot's general scepticism, expressed in both versions of her paper, about the phrase 'the moral point of view.' It would, I think, also be in keeping with the spirit of the following passage from the second version: 'Perhaps no . . . *shared end* appears in the foundations of ethics, where we may rather find individual ends and rational compromises between those who have them. Or perhaps at the most basic level lie facts about the way individual human beings can find the greatest goods which they are capable of possessing' (*Mind*, p. 209).

20 Judging from various of Foot's other published works, it is not clear that *she* would want to make *either* of these claims. For in some of her more recent writings she has expressed increasing doubts about the closeness of the connection between one's possession of the virtues and one's good. (See, for example, her introduction to *Virtues and Vices*, her paper 'Morality as a System of Hypothetical Imperatives' [reprinted in *Virtues and Vices*], and the final footnote in the version of 'Moral Beliefs' that appears in the same volume.) Without something like the first claim, however, the defence of agent-centred restrictions that I have been sketching does not get off the ground. And as I indicated in the preceding note, Foot does seem to have more than a little sympathy for at least some elements of that defence.

Suggestions for Further Reading

Bentham, Jeremy. *Introduction to the Principles of Morals and Legislation,* ed. W. Harrison. Oxford University Press, 1948.

Brandt, Richard. "In Search of a Credible Form of Rule-Utilitarianism," in *Morality and the Language of Conduct,* eds. H. N. Castaneda and George Nakhnikian. Wayne State University, 1953. This oft-anthologized article is one of the most sophisticated defenses of utilitarianism.

Brandt, Richard. *A Theory of the Good and the Right.* Clarendon Press, 1979.

Brink, David. *Moral Realism and the Foundation of Ethics.* Cambridge University Press, 1989. Chapter 8 is an excellent discussion of utilitarianism.

Brock, Dan. "Recent Work in Utilitarianism," *American Philosophical Quarterly* 10(October 1973).

Hardin, Russell. *Morality Within the Limits of Reason.* University of Chicago, 1988. A cogent contemporary defense of utilitarianism.

Hare, R. M. *Moral Thinking.* Oxford University Press, 1981.

Lyons, David. *Forms and Limits of Utilitarianism.* Oxford University Press, 1965.

Mill, John Stuart. *Utilitarianism.* Bobbs-Merrill, 1957.

Miller, Harlan B., and William Williams, eds. *The Limits of Utilitarianism.* University of Minnesota Press, 1982. Contains important but advanced articles.

Parfit, Derik. *Reasons and Persons.* Oxford University Press, 1984.

Quinton, Anthony. *Utilitarian Ethics.* Macmillan, 1973. A clear exposition of classical utilitarianism.

Scheffler, Samuel. *The Rejection of Consequentialism.* Clarendon Press, 1982. A careful discussion, including an outline of a hybrid system between deontological and utilitarian theories.

Scheffler, Samuel, ed. *Consequentialism and Its Critics.* Oxford University Press, 1988. Contains important selections, many of which refocus the debate between consequentialists and deontologists.

Sen, Amartya, and Bernard Williams, eds. *Utilitarianism and Beyond.* Cambridge University Press, 1982. Contains important readings.

Smart, J. J. C., and Williams, Bernard. *Utilitarianism: For & Against.* Cambridge University Press, 1973. A classic debate on the subject.

Taylor, Paul. *Principles of Ethics.* Dickenson, 1975.

Part VI

Kantian and Deontological Systems

Even if it should happen that, owing to special disfavour of fortune, or the niggardly provision of a step-motherly nature, this [Good] will should wholly lack power to accomplish its purpose, if with its greatest efforts it should yet achieve nothing, and there should remain only the good will. . ., then, like a jewel, it would still shine by its own light, as a thing which has its whole value in itself. Its usefulness or fruitfulness can neither add to nor take away anything from this value.

IMMANUEL KANT
The Foundations of the Metaphysic of Morals, Section I

If I were ever to find, as I luckily never have, a man who assured me that he really *believed* Kant's metaphysical morals, and that he modeled his own conduct and his relations with others after those principles, then my incredulity and distrust of him as a human being could not be greater than if he told me he regularly drowned children just to see them squirm.

RICHARD TAYLOR
Good and Evil, p. xii

Whereas teleological systems (discussed in Part V) place the ultimate criterion of morality in some nonmoral value (for example, happiness) that results from acts, deontological systems assert that certain features in the act itself have intrinsic value. Accordingly, there is something right about truth-telling and promise-keeping even when so acting may bring about some harm, and there is something wrong about lying even if it may produce some good consequences. Acting unjustly is wrong even if it will maximize expected utility.

Deontological theories break down into two kinds: act and rule deontological systems.

Act deontologists see each act as a separate ethical occasion and believe that we may decide on what is right or wrong in each situation by consulting our consciences or intuitions apart from any rules. An instance of this view is found in one of Bishop Joseph Butler's sermons:

[If] any plain honest man, before he engages in any course of action, ask himself, Is this I am going about right, or is it wrong? . . . I do not in the least doubt that this question would be answered agreeably to truth and virtue, by almost any fair man in almost any circumstance. (*Five Sermons,* New York: Liberal Arts Press, 1949, p. 45)

Contemporary examples of act deontological ethics include many versions of existentialism, as well as so-called situation ethics, which calls on us to see each situation as a unique one that demands a separate moral judgment. Those who advocate "let your conscience be your guide" may be advocating this type of ethical program. What most of these systems have in common is an appeal to intuition. The decision lies in a moral perception and not in some abstract, general rule.

Act deontological systems have some serious disadvantages. First, it is difficult to see how any argument could take place with an intuitionist. Either you both have the same intuition about lying or you don't, and that's all there is to it. Second, there seem to be similarities between different cases that allow us to discover general rules of action. For instance, we intuit that it is wrong to lie in situation S_1, but find that situation S_2 is similar to S_1. It would be inconsistent to believe that it is wrong to lie in S_1 but not in S_2 without some morally relevant difference between the two cases.

It seems that rules are necessary to all reasoning, let alone moral reasoning. According to R. M. Hare, "To learn to do anything is never to learn to do an individual act; it is always to learn to do acts of a certain kind in a certain kind of situation; and this is to learn a principle. . . . Without principles we could not learn anything whatever from our elders. . . . Every generation would have to start from scratch and teach itself. But . . . self-teaching, like all other teaching, is the teaching of principles" (*Language of Morals,* Oxford University Press, 1952, p. 60f). You may test this by thinking about learning to drive a car, to do long division, or to type. Even though the

initial principles may eventually be internalized as habits so that we are no longer conscious of them, nevertheless a rule could be cited that covers our actions. For example, a driver may no longer remember the rule for accelerating an automobile (for example, put the car into first gear, then gently let out the clutch pedal with the left foot while pressing the accelerator with the right foot), but there was an original experience of learning the rule, an experience the driver continues unwittingly to follow.

Many ethicists believe that there are common features that different situations share, so that it would be inconsistent for us to prescribe different moral actions. Suppose you believe that it is morally wrong for John to cheat on his math exam. If you also believe that it is morally permissible for you to cheat on the same exam, don't you need to explain what it is that makes your situation different from John's? If I say that it is wrong for John to cheat on exams, am I not implying that it is wrong for anyone relevantly similar to John (for example, any student at all) to cheat on exams? That is, morality seems to involve a universal aspect. If one judges that act A is right (or wrong), then one is committed to judging that any act relevantly similar to A is right (or wrong). This principle is sometimes referred to as the principle of universalizability. If it is sound, act deontological ethics are misguided.

Most deontologists have been rule deontologists, who believe that there are universal rules that provide standards of right and wrong behavior. Such rules as "We ought never lie," "We ought always to keep our promises," and "We ought never to execute an innocent person" constitute a set of valid prescriptions regardless of the outcomes.

Rule deontological systems (RDS) accept the principle of universalizability, as well as the notion that in making moral judgments we are appealing to universal principles. Examples of such principles found in most RDSs are promise-keeping, truth-telling, nonmalevolence, and justice.

There are different types of rule deontological systems. Some RDSs hold that moral rules are absolute and cannot be overridden. An adequate moral system can never produce moral conflict, nor can a basic moral principle be overridden by another moral principle. Other RDSs allow principles to be overridden. Let us illustrate this difference. Suppose that you have promised your friend to help her with her ethics homework at 3 P.M. As you are going to meet her, you encounter a lost, crying child. There is no one else around to help the little boy, so you help him find his way home, but in doing so you miss your appointment. Have you done the morally right thing? Have you broken your promise? We can construe this situation so that it constitutes a conflict between moral principles:

1. We ought always to keep our promises.

2. We ought always to help people in need when it is not unreasonably inconvenient to do so.

In helping the child find his way home you decided that principle (2) overrides (1). This does not mean that (1) is not a valid principle, only that the word "ought" in it is not an absolute ought. In our second reading the Oxford University philosopher W. D. Ross (1877–1971) calls this sort of duty a "prima facie duty," one having presumptive force but one that nevertheless can be overridden by another principle. That is, the principle has objective validity, but it is not always decisive, depending on which other principles may be applicable to the situation.

We said above that act deontologists were intuitionists, but rule deontologists may also be intuitionists. Ross, for example, believes that there are several prima facie principles that can be discovered by intuition and that intuition instructs us in how to judge between them.

However, some rule deontologists are not intuitionists. Some, like Immanuel Kant, the author of our first reading, are rationalists. Kant, perhaps the most well-known deontologist, was both an absolutist and a rationalist. He believed that we could use reason to work out a consistent set of moral principles that cannot be overridden.

Kant constructed an outline of his ethical system, most of which is included in our first reading, in his book *The Foundations of the Metaphysic of Morals*. In this work he presents a series of arguments that culminates in his famous categorical imperative, the main form of which reads, "Act only on that maxim whereby thou canst at the same time will that it would become a universal law." This imperative is given as the criterion (or second-order principle) by which to judge all other principles. If we could consistently will that everyone would do some type of action, then there is an application of the categorical imperative enjoining that type of action. If we cannot consistently will that everyone would do some type of action, then that type of action is morally wrong. Kant argues, for example, that we cannot consistently will that everyone make "lying promises," for the very institution of promising entails or depends on general adherence to keeping the promise or an intention to do so.

Kant offered three formulations of the categorical imperative; the first is cited above. The second formulation is: "So act as to treat humanity, whether in your own person or in that of any other, in every case as an end and never as merely a means only." Each rational person has dignity and profound worth, which implies that he or she must never be exploited or manipulated or merely used as a means to our notion of what is for the general good. Kant thought that this formulation was substantively identical with the first, but most scholars disagree with him.

In our third reading Fred Feldman gives an excellent analysis of the central argument surrounding Kant's first formulation of the categorical imperative and offers an important critique of it.

In our fourth reading Philippa Foot argues that Kant is wrong in viewing morality as categorical rather than hypothetical. Kant has been credited by the vast majority of ethicists, even those who disagree with him on other issues, with establishing the necessity of grounding moral judgments in categorical imperatives, rather than in hypothetical ones. Moral judgments are objectively necessary—not a mere means to achieving something one desires, as prudential judgments are. Foot argues that Kant seems to be wrong here, and that the categorical aspect of morality may stem more from the way it is taught than the way it really is. Nonetheless, while eliminating the categorical aspect from moral prescriptions takes morality down from its pedestal, morality retains its importance. It is simply that it is not always the most important thing.

Finally, in our last reading, "Moral Luck," Thomas Nagel challenges the whole Kantian view of morality, which presumes that we are all, qua rational, equal participants in the moral enterprise who have equal opportunity to be moral. The locus of the moral enterprise is the good will, the will to do our duty according to reason's dictates, the only purely good thing in the world. Although we all have different nonmoral abilities, even different characters inclining us to virtue, only the resolved intention to do one's duty matters.

A useful model to illustrate this view is Jesus's parable of the talents (Matt. 25:14–30). Before he embarks on a journey a man gives his servants various amounts of money to invest while he is away. To one he gives ten talents, to a second five, and to a third only one talent. The word 'talent' here means a unit of money, but it might as well mean 'ability,' which is what we mean by 'talent' today. When the man returns he asks for an accounting of how the three servants

have used their talents. The first gained ten more talents, the second five more, but the third hid his talent, fearing to lose it. The first two were rewarded accordingly, but the third servant was punished for not using the little that was given to him. The idea is that we are all given different amounts of ability and we must be faithful to what we have. Only God (or a mythical Ideal Observer) knows the burdens under which each of us has to labor, so only God can tell where we stand morally, but each of us is to be judged in accordance with how dedicated we were to the moral law.

Nagel argues that this view is too simple and doesn't take into account the way external factors impinge upon us. External factors introduce the notion of moral luck, which Nagel defines thusly: "Where a significant aspect of what someone does depends on factors beyond his control, yet we continue to treat him in that respect as an object of moral judgment, it can be called moral luck."

Nagel discusses four types of moral luck: constitutional luck, circumstantial luck, consequential luck in which consequences retrospectively justify an otherwise immoral act (or fail to justify an otherwise moral act), and consequential luck in which the consequences affect the type or quality of blame or remorse (or moral praise).

An example of constitutional luck is being born into a morally sensitive family that bring you up to have good character and principles. An example of circumstantial luck is people who lived in, say, Canada during the Second World War who, had they lived in Nazi Germany, would have behaved badly toward the Jews. An example of retrospective consequential luck is the painter Gauguin, who abandoned his family for his art, and whose only hope for justification lay in his success. An example of consequential luck that affects the quality of remorse is the comparison of a drunk driver who runs over a child with the drunk driver who gets home without mishap.

Both did the same thing (namely, got drunk and drove) and are equally culpable, but one has a case of involuntary manslaughter on his hands. The former simply had bad moral luck and the latter good moral luck.

Nagel's article challenges our traditional way of viewing ethics as being beyond accident and luck. The challenge before us is to assess the validity of Nagel's arguments and examples.

VI.1 *The Foundations of the Metaphysic of Morals*

IMMANUAL KANT

Immanuel Kant (1724–1804), who taught at the University of Königsberg in Germany, is one of the premier philosophers in the Western tradition. In this classic work, *The Foundations of the Metaphysic of Morals,* written in 1785, he outlines his ethical system. Kant's concern is to reject those ethical theories, such as the theory of moral sentiments, set forth by the Scottish moralists Francis Hutcheson (1694–1746) and David Hume (1711–1776), in which morality is contingent and hypothetical. It is contingent in that it is based on human nature and, in particular, on our feelings or sentiments. Had we been created differently, we would have a different nature and, hence, different moral duties. Moral duties or imperatives are hypothetical in that they depend on our desires for their realization. For example, we should obey the law because we want a peaceful, orderly society.

Kant rejects this naturalistic account of ethics. Ethics is not contingent but absolute, and its duties or imperatives are not hypothetical but categorical. Ethics is based not on feelings but on reason. It is because we are rational beings that we are valuable and capable of discovering moral laws that are binding on all persons at all times. As such, our moral duties are dependent not on feelings but on reason. They are unconditional, universally valid, and necessary, regardless of the possible consequences or opposition to our inclinations.

Kant's first formulation of his *categorical imperative* is, "Act only on that maxim whereby thou canst at the same time will that it would become a universal law." This imperative is given as the criterion by which to judge all other principles. If we could consistently will that everyone would do some type of action, then there is an application of the categorical imperative enjoining that type of action. If we cannot consistently will that everyone would do some type of action, then that type of action is morally wrong. Kant argues, for example, that we cannot consistently will that everyone make lying promises, for the very institution of promising entails or depends on general adherence to keeping the promise or an intention to do so.

Kant offers a second formulation of the categorical imperative: "So act as to treat humanity, whether in your own person or in that of any other, in every case as an end and never as merely a means only." Each person by virtue of his or her reason has dignity and profound worth, which entails that he or she must never be exploited or manipulated or merely used as a means to our idea of what is for the general good.

Preface

As my concern here is with moral philosophy, I limit the question suggested to this: Whether it is not of the utmost necessity to construct a pure moral philosophy, perfectly cleared of everything which is only empirical, and which belongs to anthropology? for that such a philosophy must be possible is evident from the common idea of duty and of the moral laws. Everyone must admit that if a law is to have moral force, *i.e.* to be the basis of an obligation, it must carry with it absolute necessity; that, for example, the precept, "Thou shalt not lie," is not valid for men alone, as if other rational beings had no need to observe it; and so with all the other moral laws properly so called; that, therefore, the basis of obligation must not be sought in the nature of man, or in the circumstances in the world in which he is placed, but *à priori* simply in the conceptions of pure reason; and although any other precept which is founded on principles of mere experience may be in certain respects universal, yet in as far as it rests even in the least degree on an empirical basis, perhaps only as to a motive, such a precept, while it may be a practical rule, can never be called a moral law.

Thus not only are moral laws with their principles essentially distinguished from every other kind of practical knowledge in which there is anything empirical, but all moral philosophy rests wholly on its pure part. When applied to man, it does not borrow the least thing from the knowledge of man himself (anthropology), but gives laws *à priori* to him as a rational being. No doubt these laws require a judgment sharpened by experience, in order on the one hand to distinguish in what cases they are applicable, and on the other to procure for them access to the will of the man, and effectual influence on conduct; since man is acted on by so many inclinations that, though capable of the idea of a practical pure reason, he is not so easily able to make it effective *in concreto* in his life.

A metaphysic of morals is therefore indispensably necessary, not merely for speculative reasons, in order to investigate the sources of the practical principles which are to be found *à priori* in our reason, but also because morals themselves are liable to all sorts of corruption, as long as we are without that clue and supreme canon by which to estimate them correctly. For in order that an action should be morally good, it is not enough that it *conform* to the moral law, but it must also be done *for the sake of the law,* otherwise that conformity is only very contingent and uncertain; since a principle which is not moral, although it may now and then produce actions conformable to the law, will also often produce actions which contradict it. Now it is only in a pure philosophy that we can look for the moral law in its purity and genuineness (and, in a practical matter, this is of the utmost consequence): we must, therefore, begin with pure philosophy (metaphysic), and without it there cannot be any moral philosophy at all. That which mingles these pure principles with the empirical does not deserve the name of philosophy (for what distinguishes philosophy from common rational knowledge is, that it treats in separate sciences what the latter only comprehends confusedly); much less does it deserve that of moral philosophy, since by this confusion it even spoils the purity of morals themselves, and counteracts its own end.

First Section: Transition from the Common Rational Knowledge of Morality to the Philosophical

The Good Will

Nothing can possibly be conceived in the world, or even out of it, which can be called good, without qualification, except a Good Will. Intelligence, wit, judgment, and the other *talents* of the mind, however they may be named, or courage, resolution, perseverance, as qualities of temperament, are undoubtedly good and desirable in many respects; but these gifts of nature may also become extremely bad and mischievous if the will which is to make use of them, and which, therefore, constitutes what is called *character,* is not good. It is the same with the *gifts of fortune.* Power, riches, honour, even health,

Reprinted from *The Foundations of the Metaphysic of Morals,* translated by T. K. Abbott (this translation first published in 1873).

and the general well-being and contentment with one's condition which is called *happiness,* inspire pride, and often presumption, if there is not a good will to correct the influence of these on the mind, and with this also to rectify the whole principle of acting, and adapt it to its end. The sight of a being who is not adorned with a single feature of a pure and good will, enjoying unbroken prosperity, can never give pleasure to an impartial rational spectator. Thus a good will appears to constitute the indispensable condition even of being worthy of happiness.

There are even some qualities which are of service to this good will itself, and may facilitate its action, yet which have no intrinsic unconditional value, but always presuppose a good will, and this qualifies the esteem that we justly have for them, and does not permit us to regard them as absolutely good. Moderation in the affections and passions, self-control, and calm deliberation are not only good in many respects, but even seem to constitute part of the intrinsic worth of the person; but they are far from deserving to be called good without qualification, although they have been so unconditionally praised by the ancients. For without the principles of a good will, they may become extremely bad; and the coolness of a villain not only makes him far more dangerous, but also directly makes him more abominable in our eyes than he would have been without it.

A good will is good not because of what it performs or effects, not by its aptness for the attainment of some proposed end, but simply by virtue of the volition, that is, it is good in itself, and considered by itself is to be esteemed much higher than all that can be brought about by it in favour of any inclination, nay, even of the sum-total of all inclinations. Even if it should happen that, owing to special disfavour of fortune, or the niggardly provision of a step-motherly nature, this will should wholly lack power to accomplish its purpose, if with its greatest efforts it should yet achieve nothing, and there should remain only the good will (not, to be sure, a mere wish, but the summoning of all means in our power), then, like a jewel, it would still shine by its own light, as a thing which has its whole value in itself. Its usefulness or fruitlessness can neither add to nor take away anything from this value. It would be, as it were, only the setting to enable us to handle it the more conveniently in common commerce, or to attract to it the attention of those who are not yet connoisseurs, but not to recommend it to true connoisseurs, or to determine its value.

Why Reason Was Made to Guide the Will

There is, however, something so strange in this idea of the absolute value of the mere will, in which no account is taken of its utility, that notwithstanding the thorough assent of even common reason to the idea, yet a suspicion must arise that it may perhaps really be the product of mere high-blown fancy, and that we may have misunderstood the purpose of nature in assigning reason as the governor of our will. Therefore we will examine this idea from this point of view.

In the physical constitution of an organized being, that is, a being adapted suitably to the purposes of life, we assume it as a fundamental principle that no organ for any purpose will be found but what is also the fittest and best adapted for that purpose. Now in a being which has reason and a will, if the proper object of nature were its *conservatism,* its *welfare,* in a word, its *happiness,* then nature would have hit upon a very bad arrangement in selecting the reason of the creature to carry out this purpose. For all the actions which the creature has to perform with a view to this purpose, and the whole rule of its conduct, would be far more surely prescribed to it by instinct, and that end would have been attained thereby much more certainly than it ever can be by reason. Should reason have been communicated to this favoured creature over and above, it must only have served it to contemplate the happy constitution of its nature, to admire it, to congratulate itself thereon, and to feel thankful for it to the beneficent cause, but not that it should subject its desires to that weak and delusive guidance, and meddle bunglingly with the purpose of nature. In a word, nature would have taken care that reason should not break forth into *practical exercise,* nor have the presumption, with its weak insight, to think out for itself the plan of happiness, and of the means of attaining it. Nature would not only have taken on herself the choice of the ends, but also of the means, and with wise foresight would have entrusted both to instinct.

And, in fact, we find that the more a cultivated reason applies itself with deliberate purpose to the enjoyment of life and happiness, so much the more does the man fail of true satisfaction. And from this circumstance there arises in many, if they are candid enough to confess it, a certain degree of *misology,* that is, hatred of reason, especially in the case of those who are most experienced in the use of it, because after calculating all the advantages they derive, I do not say from the invention of all the arts of common luxury, but even from the sciences (which seem to them to be after all only a luxury of the understanding), they find that they have, in fact, only brought more trouble on their shoulders, rather than gained in happiness; and they end by envying, rather than despising, the more common stamp of men who keep closer to the guidance of mere instinct, and do not allow their reason much influence on their conduct. And this we must admit, that the judgment of those who would very much lower the lofty eulogies of the advantages which reason gives us in regard to the happiness and satisfaction of life, or who would even reduce them below zero, is by no means morose or ungrateful to the goodness with which the world is governed, but that there lies at the root of these judgments the idea that our existence has a different and far nobler end, for which, and not for happiness, reason is properly intended, and which must, therefore, be regarded as the supreme condition to which the private ends of man must, for the most part, be postponed.

For as reason is not competent to guide the will with certainty in regard to its objects and the satisfaction of all our wants (which it to some extent even multiplies), this being an end to which an implanted instinct would have led with much greater certainty; and since, nevertheless, reason is imparted to us as a practical faculty, *i.e.* as one which is to have influence on the *will,* therefore, admitting that nature generally in the distribution of her capacities has adapted the means to the end, its true destination must be to produce a *will,* not merely good as a *means* to something else, but *good in itself,* for which reason was absolutely necessary. This will then, though not indeed the sole and complete good, must be the supreme good and the condition of every other, even of the desire of happiness. Under these circumstances, there is nothing inconsistent with the wisdom of nature in the fact that the cultivation of the reason, which is requisite for the first and unconditional purpose, does in many ways interfere, at least in this life, with the attainment of

the second, which is always conditional, namely, happiness. Nay, it may even reduce it to nothing, without nature thereby failing in her purpose. For reason recognizes the establishment of a good will as its highest practical destination, and in attaining this purpose is capable only of a satisfaction of its own proper kind, namely, that from the attainment of an end, which end again is determined by reason only, notwithstanding that this may involve many a disappointment to the ends of inclination.

The First Proposition of Morality

We have then to develop the notion of a will which deserves to be highly esteemed for itself, and is good without a view to anything further, a notion which exists already in the sound natural understanding, requiring rather to be cleared up than to be taught, and which in estimating the value of our actions always takes the first place, and constitutes the condition of all the rest. In order to do this, we will take the notion of duty, which includes that of a good will, although implying certain subjective restrictions and hindrances. These, however, far from concealing it, or rendering it unrecognizable, rather bring it out by contrast, and make it shine forth so much the brighter.

I omit here all actions which are already recognized as inconsistent with duty although they may be useful for this or that purpose, for with these the question whether they are done *from duty* cannot arise at all, since they even conflict with it. I also set aside those actions which really conform to duty, but to which men have *no* direct *inclination,* performing them because they are impelled thereto by some other inclination. For in this case we can readily distinguish whether the action which agrees with duty is done *from duty,* or from a selfish view. It is much harder to make this distinction when the action accords with duty, and the subject has besides a *direct* inclination to it. For example, it is always a matter of duty that a dealer should not overcharge an inexperienced purchaser; and wherever there is much commerce the prudent tradesman does not overcharge, but keeps a fixed price for everyone, so that a child buys of him as well as any other. Men are thus *honestly* served; but this is not enough to make us believe that the tradesman has so acted from duty and from principles of honesty: his own advantage required it; it is out of the question in this case to suppose that he might besides have a direct inclination in favour of the buyers, so that, as it were, from love he should give no advantage to one over another. Accordingly the action was done neither from duty nor from direct inclination, but merely with a selfish view.

On the other hand, it is a duty to maintain one's life; and, in addition, everyone has also a direct inclination to do so. But on this account the often anxious care which most men take for it has no intrinsic worth, and their maxim has no moral import. They preserve their life *as duty requires,* no doubt, but not *because duty requires.* On the other hand, if adversity and hopeless sorrow have completely taken away the relish for life; if the unfortunate one, strong in mind, indignant at his fate rather than desponding or dejected, wishes for death, and yet preserves his life without loving it — not from inclination or fear, but from duty — then his maxim has a moral worth.

To be beneficent when we can is a duty; and besides this, there are many minds so sympathetically constituted that, without any other motive of vanity or self-interest, they find a pleasure in spreading joy around them, and can take delight in the satisfaction of others so far as it is their own work. But I maintain that in such a case an action of this kind, however proper, however amiable it may be, has nevertheless no true moral worth, but is on a level with other inclinations, *e.g.* the inclination to honour, which, if it is happily directed to that which is in fact of public utility and accordant with duty, and consequently honourable, deserves praise and encouragement, but not esteem. For the maxim lacks the moral import, namely, that such actions be done *from duty,* not from inclination. Put the case that the mind of that philanthropist was clouded by sorrow of his own, extinguishing all sympathy with the lot of others, and that while he still has the power to benefit others in distress, he is not touched by their trouble because he is absorbed with his own; and now suppose that he tears himself out of this dead insensibility, and performs the action without any inclination to it, but simply from duty, then first has his action its genuine moral worth. Further still; if nature has put little sympathy in the heart of this or that man; if he, supposed to be an upright man, is by temperament cold and indifferent to the sufferings of others, perhaps because in respect of his own he is provided with the special

gift of patience and fortitude, and supposes, or even requires, that others should have the same — and such a man would certainly not be the meanest product of nature — but if nature had not specially framed him for a philanthropist, would he not still find in himself a source from whence to give himself a far higher worth than that of a good-natured temperament could be? Unquestionably. It is just in this that the moral worth of the character is brought out which is incomparably the highest of all, namely, that he is beneficent, not from inclination, but from duty.

To secure one's own happiness is a duty, at least indirectly; for discontent with one's condition, under a pressure of many anxieties and amidst unsatisfied wants, might easily become a great *temptation to transgression of duty.* But here again, without looking to duty, all men have already the strongest and most intimate inclination to happiness, because it is just in this idea that all inclinations are combined in one total. But the precept of happiness is often of such a sort that it greatly interferes with some inclinations, and yet a man cannot form any definite and certain conception of the sum of satisfaction of all of them which is called happiness. It is not then to be wondered at that a single inclination, definite both as to what it promises and as to the time within which it can be gratified, is often able to overcome such a fluctuating idea, and that a gouty patient, for instance, can choose to enjoy what he likes, and to suffer what he may, since, according to his calculation, on this occasion at least, he has [only] not sacrificed the enjoyment of the present moment to a possibly mistaken expectation of a happiness which is supposed to be found in health. But even in this case, if the general desire for happiness did not influence his will, and supposing that in his particular case health was not a necessary element in this calculation, there yet remains in this, as in all other cases, this law, namely, that he should promote his happiness not from inclination but from duty, and by this would his conduct first acquire true moral worth.

It is in this manner, undoubtedly, that we are to understand those passages of Scripture also in which we are commanded to love our neighbour, even our enemy. For love, as an affection, cannot be commanded, but beneficence for duty's sake may; even though we are not impelled to it by any inclination — nay, are even repelled by a natural and unconquerable aversion. This is *practical* love, and not *pathological* — a love which is seated in the will, and not in the . . . sense — in principles of action and not of tender sympathy; and it is this love alone which can be commanded.

The Second Proposition of Morality

The second proposition is: That an action done from duty derives its moral worth, *not from the purpose* which is to be attained by it, but from the maxim by which it is determined, and therefore does not depend on the realization of the object of the action, but merely on the *principle of volition* by which the action has taken place, without regard to any object of desire. It is clear from what precedes that the purposes which we may have in view in our actions, or their effects regarded as ends and springs of the will, cannot give to actions any unconditional or moral worth. In what, then, can their worth lie, if it is not to consist in the will and in reference to its expected effect? It cannot lie anywhere but in the *principle of the will* without regard to the ends which can be attained by the action. For the will stands between its *à priori principle,* which is formal, and its *à posteriori* spring, which is material, as between two roads, and as it must be determined by something, it follows that it must be determined by the formal principle of volition when an action is done from duty, in which case every material principle has been withdrawn from it.

The Third Proposition of Morality

The third proposition, which is a consequence of the two preceding, I would express thus: *Duty is the necessity of acting from respect for the law.* I may have *inclination* for an object as the effect of my proposed action, but I cannot have *respect* for it, just for this reason, that it is an effect and not an energy of will. Similarly, I cannot have respect for inclination, whether my own or another's; I can at most, if my own, approve it; if another's, sometimes even love it; *i.e.* look on it as favourable to my own interest. It is only what is connected with my will as a principle, by no means as an effect — what does not subserve my inclination, but overpowers it, or at least in case of choice excludes it from its calculation — in other words, simply the law of itself, which can be an ob-

ject of respect, and hence a command. Now an action done from duty must wholly exclude the influence of inclination, and with it every object of the will, so that nothing remains which can determine the will except objectively the *law,* and subjectively *pure respect* for this practical law, and consequently the maxim[1] that I should follow this law even to the thwarting of all my inclinations.

Thus the moral worth of an action does not lie in the effect expected from it, nor in any principle of action which requires to borrow its motive from this expected effect. For all these effects — agreeableness of one's condition, and even the promotion of the happiness of others — could have been also brought about by other causes, so that for this there would have been no need of the will of a rational being; whereas it is in this alone that the supreme and unconditional good can be found. The pre-eminent good which we call moral can therefore consist in nothing else than *the conception of law* in itself, *which certainly is only possible in a rational being,* in so far as this conception, and not the expected effect, determines the will. This is a good which is already present in the person who acts accordingly, and we have not to wait for it to appear first in the result.

The Supreme Principle of Morality: The Categorical Imperative

But what sort of law can that be, the conception of which must determine the will, even without paying any regard to the effect expected from it, in order that this will may be called good absolutely and without qualification? As I have deprived the will of every impulse which could arise to it from obedience to any law, there remains nothing but the universal conformity of its actions to law in general, which alone is to serve the will as a principle, *i.e.* I am never to act otherwise than so *that I could also will that my maxim should become a universal law.* Here, now, it is the simple conformity to law in general, without assuming any particular law applicable to certain actions, that serves the will as its principle, and must so serve it, if duty is not to be a vain delusion and a chimerical notion. The common reason of men in its practical judgments perfectly coincides with this, and always has in view the principle here suggested. Let the question be, for example: May I when in distress make a promise with the intention not to keep it? I readily distinguish here between the two significations which the question may have: Whether it is prudent, or whether it is right, to make a false promise? The former may undoubtedly often be the case. I see clearly indeed that it is not enough to extricate myself from a present difficulty by means of this subterfuge, but it must be well considered whether there may not hereafter spring from this lie much greater inconvenience than that from which I now free myself, and as, with all my supposed *cunning,* the consequences cannot be so easily foreseen but that credit once lost may be much more injurious to me than any mischief which I seek to avoid at present, it should be considered whether it would not be more *prudent* to act herein according to a universal maxim, and to make it a habit to promise nothing except with the intention of keeping it. But it is soon clear to me that such a maxim will still only be based on the fear of consequences. Now it is a wholly different thing to be truthful from duty, and to be so from apprehension of injurious consequences. In the first case, the very notion of the action already implies a law for me; in the second case, I must first look about elsewhere to see what results may be combined with it which would affect myself. For to deviate from the principle of duty is beyond all doubt wicked; but to be unfaithful to my maxim of prudence may often be very advantageous to me, although to abide by it is certainly safer. The shortest way, however, and an unerring one, to discover the answer to this question whether a lying promise is consistent with duty, is to ask myself, Should I be content that my maxim (to extricate myself from difficulty by a false promise) should hold good as a universal law, for myself as well as for others? and should I be able to say to myself, "Every one may make a deceitful promise when he finds himself in a difficulty from which he cannot otherwise extricate himself"? Then I presently become aware that while I can will the lie, I can by no means will that lying should be a universal law. For with such a law there would be no promises at all, since it would be in vain to allege my intention in regard to my future actions to those who would not believe this allegation, or if they over-hastily did so, would pay me back in my own coin. Hence my maxim, as soon as it should be made a universal law, would necessarily destroy itself.

I do not, therefore, need any far-reaching penetration to discern what I have to do in order that my will may be morally good. Inexperienced in the course of the world, incapable of being prepared for all its contingencies, I only ask myself: Canst thou also will that thy maxim should be a universal law? If not, then it must be rejected, and that not because of a disadvantage accruing from myself or even to others, but because it cannot enter as a principle into a possible universal legislation, and reason extorts from me immediate respect for such legislation. I do not indeed as yet *discern* on what this respect is based (this the philosopher may inquire), but at least I understand this, that it is an estimation of the worth which far outweighs all worth of what is recommended by inclination, and that the necessity of acting from *pure* respect for the practical law is what constitutes duty, to which every other motive must give place, because it is the condition of a will being good *in itself,* and the worth of such a will is above everything.

Thus, then, without quitting the moral knowledge of common human reason, we have arrived at its principle. And although, no doubt, common men do not conceive it in such an abstract and universal form, yet they always have it really before their eyes, and use it as the standard of their decision.

Second Section: Transition from Popular Moral Philosophy to the Metaphysic of Morals

The Impossibility of an Empirical Moral Philosophy

If we have hitherto drawn our notion of duty from the common use of our practical reason, it is by no means to be inferred that we have treated it as an empirical notion. On the contrary, if we attend to the experience of men's conduct, we meet frequent and, as we ourselves allow, just complaints that one cannot find a single certain example of the disposition to act from pure duty. Although many things are done in *conformity* with what *duty* prescribes, it is nevertheless always doubtful whether they are done strictly *from duty,* so as to have a moral worth. Hence there have at all times been philosophers who have altogether denied that this disposition actually exists at all in human actions, and have ascribed everything to a more or less refined self-love. Not that they have on that account questioned the soundness of the conception of morality; on the contrary, they spoke with sincere regret of the frailty and corruption of human nature, which though noble enough to take as its rule an idea so worthy of respect, is yet too weak to follow it, and employs reason, which ought to give it the law, only for the purpose of providing for the interest of the inclinations, whether singly or at the best in the greatest possible harmony with one another.

In fact, it is absolutely impossible to make out by experience with complete certainty a single case in which the maxim of an action, however right in itself, rested simply on moral grounds and on the conception of duty. Sometimes it happens that with the sharpest self-examination we can find nothing beside the moral principle of duty which could have been powerful enough to move us to this or that action and to so great a sacrifice; yet we cannot from this infer with certainty that it was not really some secret impulse of self-love, under the false appearance of duty, that was the actual determining cause of the will. We like then to flatter ourselves by falsely taking credit for a more noble motive; whereas in fact we can never, even by the strictest examination, get completely behind the secret springs of action; since, when the question is of moral worth, it is not with the actions which we see that we are concerned, but with those inward principles of them which we do not see.

Moreover, we cannot better serve the wishes of those who ridicule all morality as a mere chimera of human imagination overstepping itself from vanity, than by conceding to them that notions of duty must be drawn only from experience (as from indolence, people are ready to think is also the case with all other notions); for this is to prepare for them a certain triumph. I am willing to admit out of love of humanity that even most of our actions are correct, but if we look closer at them we everywhere come upon the dear self which is always prominent, and it is this they have in view, and not the strict command of duty which would often require self-denial. Without being an enemy of virtue, a cool observer, one that does not mistake the wish for good, however lively, for its reality, may sometimes doubt whether true virtue is actually found anywhere in the world, and this especially as years increase and the judgment is partly made wiser by experience, and partly also more acute in observation. This being so, nothing can secure us from falling away altogether from our ideas of duty, or maintain in the soul a well-grounded respect for its law, but the clear conviction that although there should never have been actions which really sprang from such pure sources, yet whether this or that takes place is not at all the question; but that reason of itself, independent on all experience, ordains what ought to take place, that accordingly actions of which perhaps the world has hitherto never given an example, the feasibility even of which might be very much doubted by one who founds everything on experience, are nevertheless inflexibly commanded by reason; that, [for example], even though there might never yet have been a sincere friend, yet not a whit the less is pure sincerity in friendship required of every man, because, prior to all experience, this duty is involved as duty in the idea of a reason determining the will by *à priori* principles.

When we add further that, unless we deny that the notion of morality has any truth or reference to any possible object, we must admit that its law must be valid, not merely for men, but for all *rational creatures generally,* not merely under certain contingent conditions or with exceptions, but *with absolute necessity,* then it is clear that no experience could enable us to infer even the possibility of such apodictic laws. For with what right could we bring into unbounded respect as a universal precept for every rational nature that which perhaps holds only under the contingent conditions of humanity? Or how could laws of the determination of *our* will be regarded as laws of the determination of the will of rational beings generally, and for us only as such, if they were merely empirical, and did not take their origin wholly *à priori* from pure but practical reason?

Nor could anything be more fatal to morality than that we should wish to derive it from examples. For every example of it that is set before me must be first itself tested by principles of morality, whether it is worthy to serve as an original example, *i.e.* as a pattern, but by no means can it authoritatively furnish the conception of morality. Even the Holy One of the Gospels must first be compared with our ideal of moral perfection before we can recognize Him as such; and so He says of Himself, "Why call ye Me [whom you see] good; none is good [the model of good] but God only [whom ye do not see]." But whence have we the conception of God as the supreme good? Simply from the *idea* of moral perfection, which reason frames *à priori,* and connects inseparably with the notion of a free will. Imitation finds no place at all in morality, and examples serve only for encouragement, *i.e.* they put beyond doubt the feasibility of what the law commands, they make visible that which the practical rule expresses more generally, but they can never authorize us to set aside the true original which lies in reason, and to guide ourselves by examples.

From what has been said, it is clear that all moral conceptions have their seat and origin completely *à priori* in the reason, and that, moreover, in the commonest reason just as truly as in that which is in the highest degree speculative; that they cannot be obtained by abstraction from any empirical, and therefore merely contingent knowledge; that it is just this purity of their origin that makes them worthy to serve as our supreme practical principle, and that just in proportion as we add anything empirical, we detract from their genuine influence, and from the absolute value of actions; that it is not only of the greatest necessity, in a purely speculative point of view, but is also of the greatest practical importance, to derive these notions and laws from pure reason, to present them pure and unmixed, and even to determine the compass of this practical or pure rational knowledge, *i.e.* to determine the whole faculty of pure practical reason; and, in doing so, we must not make its principles dependent on the particular nature of human reason, though in speculative philosophy this may be permitted, or may even at times be necessary; but since moral laws ought to hold good for every rational creature, we must derive them from the general concept of a rational being. In this way, although for its *application* to man morality has need of anthropology, yet, in the first instance, we must treat it independently as pure philosophy, *i.e.* as metaphysic, complete in itself (a thing which in such distinct branches of science is easily done); knowing well that unless we are in possession of this, it would not only be vain to determine the moral element of duty in right actions for purposes of speculative criticism, but it would be impossible to base morals on their genuine principles, even for common practical purposes, especially of moral instruction, so as to produce pure moral dispositions, and to engraft them on men's minds to the promotion of the greatest possible good in the world.

But in order that in this study we may not merely advance by the natural steps from the common moral judgment (in this case very worthy of respect) to the philosophical, as has been already done, but also from a popular philosophy, which goes no further than it can reach by groping with the help of examples, to metaphysic (which does not allow itself to be checked by anything empirical, and as it must measure the whole extent of this kind of rational knowledge, goes as far as ideal conceptions, where even examples fail us), we must follow and clearly describe the practical faculty of reason, from the general rules of its determination to the point where the notion of duty springs from it.

Imperatives: Hypothetical and Categorical

Everything in nature works according to laws. Rational beings alone have the faculty of acting according *to the conception* of laws, that is according to principles, *i.e.* have a *will.* Since the deduction of actions from principles requires *reason,* the will is nothing but practical reason. If reason infallibly determines the will, then the actions of such a being which are recognized as objectively necessary are subjectively necessary also, *i.e.* the will is a faculty to choose *that only* which reason independent on inclination recognizes as practically necessary, *i.e.* as good. But if reason of itself does not sufficiently determine the will, if the latter is subject also to subjective conditions (particular impulses) which do not always coincide with the objective conditions; in a word, if the will does not *in itself* completely accord with reason (which is actually the case with men), then the actions which objectively are recognized as necessary are subjectively contingent, and the determination of such a will according to objective laws is *obligation,* that is to say, the relation of the objective laws to a will that is not thoroughly good is conceived as the determination of the will of a rational being by principles of reason, but which the will from its nature does not of necessity follow.

The conception of an objective principle, in so far as it is obligatory for a will, is called a command (of reason), and the formula of the command is called an Imperative.

All imperatives are expressed by the word *ought* [or *shall*], and thereby indicate the relation of an objective law of reason to a will, which from its subjective constitution is not necessarily determined by it (an obligation). They say that something would be good to do or to forbear, but they say it to a will which does not always do a thing because it is conceived to be good to do it. That is practically *good,* however, which determines the will by means of the conceptions of reason, and consequently not from subjective causes, but objectively, that is on principles which are valid for every rational being as such. It is distinguished from the *pleasant,* as that which influences the will only by means of sensation from merely subjective causes, valid only for the sense of this or that one, and not as a principle of reason, which holds for every one.

A perfectly good will would therefore be equally subject to objective laws (viz. laws of good), but could not be conceived as *obliged* thereby to act lawfully, because of itself from its subjective constitution it can only be determined by the conception of good. Therefore no imperatives hold for the Divine will, or in general for a *holy* will; *ought* is here out of place, because the volition is already of itself necessarily in unison with the law. Therefore imperatives are only formulae to express the relation of objective laws of all volition to the subjective imperfection of the will of this or that rational being, *e.g.* the human will.

Now all *imperatives* command either *hypothetically* or *categorically.* The former represent the practical necessity of a possible action as means to something else that is willed (or at least which one might possibly will). The categorical imperative would be that which represented an action as necessary of itself without reference to another end, *i.e.,* as objectively necessary.

Since every practical law represents a possible action as good, and on this account, for a subject who is practically determinable by reason, necessary, all imperatives are formulae determining an action which is necessary according to the principle of a will good in some respects. If now the action is good only as a means *to something else,* then the imperative is *hypothetical;* if it is conceived as good *in itself* and consequently as being necessarily the principle of a will which of itself conforms to reason, then it is *categorical.*

Thus the imperative declares what action possible by me would be good, and presents the practical rule in relation to a will which does not forthwith perform an action simply because it is good, whether because the subject does not always know that it is good, or because, even if it know this, yet its maxims might be opposed to the objective principles of practical reason.

Accordingly the hypothetical imperative only says that the action is good for some purpose, *possible* or *actual.* In the first case it is a Problematical, in the second an Assertorial practical principle. The categorical imperative which declares an action to be objectively necessary in itself without reference to any purpose, *i.e.* without any other end, is valid as an Apodictic (practical) principle.

Whatever is possible only by the power of some rational being may also be conceived as a possible purpose of some will; and therefore the principles of action as regards the means necessary to attain some possible purpose are in fact infinitely numerous. All sciences have a practical part, consisting of problems expressing that some end is possible for us, and of imperatives directing how it may be attained. These may, therefore, be called in general imperatives of Skill. Here there is no question whether the end is rational and good, but only what one must do in order to attain it. The precepts for the physician to make his patient thoroughly healthy, and for a poisoner to ensure certain death, are of equal value in this respect, that each serves to effect its purpose perfectly. Since in early youth it cannot be known what ends are likely to occur to us in the course of life, parents seek to have their children taught a *great many things,* and provide for their *skill* in the use of means for all sorts of arbitrary ends, of none of which can they determine whether it may not perhaps hereafter be an object to their pupil, but which it is at all events *possible* that he might aim at; and this anxiety is so great that they commonly neglect to form and correct their judgment on the value of the things which may be chosen as ends.

There is *one* end, however, which may be assumed to be actually such to all rational beings (so far as imperatives apply to them, viz. as dependent beings), and, therefore, one purpose which they not merely *may* have, but which we may with certainty assume that they all actually *have* by a natural necessity, and this is *happiness.* The hypothetical imperative which expresses the practical necessity of an action as means to the advancement of happiness is Assertorial. We are not to present it as necessary for an uncertain and merely possible purpose, but for a purpose which we may presuppose with certainty and *à priori* in every man, because it belongs to his being. Now skill in the choice of means to his own greatest well-being may be called *prudence,* in the narrowest sense. And thus the imperative which refers to the choice of means to one's own happiness, *i.e.* the precept of prudence, is still always *hypothetical;* the action is not commanded absolutely, but only as means to another purpose.

Finally, there is an imperative which commands a certain conduct immediately, without having as its condition any other purpose to be attained by it. This imperative is Categorical. It concerns not the matter of the action, or its intended result, but its form and the principle of which it is itself a result; and what is essentially good in it consists in the mental disposition, let the consequence be what it may. This imperative may be called that of Morality.

There is a marked distinction also between the volitions on these three sorts of principles in the *dissimilarity* of the obligation of the will. In order to mark this difference more clearly, I think they would be most suitably named in their order if we said they are either *rules* of skill, or *counsels* of prudence, or *commands (laws)* of morality. For it is *law* only that involves the conception of an *unconditional* and objective necessity, which is consequently universally valid; and commands are laws which must be obeyed, that is, must be followed, even in opposition to inclination. *Counsels,* indeed, involve necessity, but one which can only hold under a contingent subjective condition, viz. they depend on whether this or that man reckons this or that as part of his happiness; the categorical imperative, on the contrary, is not limited by any condition, and as being absolutely, although practically, necessary, may be quite properly called a command. We might also call the first kind of imperative *technical* (belonging to art), the second *pragmatic* (to welfare), the third *moral* (belonging to free conduct generally, that is, to morals).

The Rational Ground of Hypothetical Imperatives

Now arises the question, how are all these imperatives possible? This question does not seek to know how we can conceive the accomplishment of the action which the imperative ordains, but merely how we can conceive the obligation of the will which the imperative expresses. No special explanation is needed to show how an imperative of skill is possible. Whoever wills the end, wills also (so far as reason decides his conduct) the means in his power which are indispensably necessary thereto. This proposition is, as regards the volition, analytical; for, in willing an object as my effect, there is already thought the causality of myself as an acting cause, that is to say, the use of the means; and the imperative educes from the conception of volition of an end the conception of actions necessary to this end. Synthetical propositions must no doubt be employed in defining the means to a proposed end; but they do not concern the principle, the act of the will, but the object and its realization. [For example], that in order to bisect a line on an unerring principle I must draw from its extremities two intersecting arcs; this no doubt is taught by mathematics only in synthetical propositions; but if I know that it is only by this process that the intended operation can be performed, then to say that if I fully will the operation, I also will the action required for it, is an analytical proposition; for it is one and the same thing to conceive something as an effect which I can produce in a certain way, and to conceive myself as acting in this way.

If it were only equally easy to give a definite conception of happiness, the imperatives of prudence would correspond exactly with those of skill, and would likewise be analytical. For in this case as in that, it could be said, whoever wills the end, wills also (according to the dictate of reason necessarily) the indispensable means thereto which are in his power. But, unfortunately, the notion of happiness is so indefinite that although every man wishes to attain it, yet he never can say definitely and consistently what it is that he really wishes and wills. The reason of this is that all the elements which belong to the notion of happiness are altogether empirical, *i.e.* they must be borrowed from experience, and nevertheless the idea of happiness requires an absolute whole, a maximum of welfare in my present and all future circumstances. Now it is impossible that the most clear-sighted and at the same time most powerful being (supposed finite) should frame to himself a definite conception of what he really wills in this. Does he will riches, how much anxiety, envy, and snares might he not thereby draw upon his shoulders? Does he will knowledge and discernment, perhaps it might prove to be only an eye so much the sharper to show him so much the more fearfully the evils that are now concealed from him, and that cannot be avoided, or to impose more wants or desires, which already give him concern enough. Would he have long life? who guarantees to him that it would not be a long misery? would he at least have health? how often has uneasiness of the body restrained from excesses into which perfect health would have allowed one to fall? and so on. In short, he is unable, on any principle, to determine with certainty what would make him truly happy; because to do so he would need to be omniscient. We cannot therefore act on any definite principles to secure happiness, but only on empirical counsels, [for example] of regimen, frugality, courtesy, reserve, &c., which experience teaches do, on the average, most promote well-being. Hence it follows that the imperatives of prudence do not, strictly speaking, command at all, that is, they cannot present actions objectively as practically *necessary;* that they are rather to be regarded as counsels (*consilia*) than precepts (*praecepta*) of reason, that the problem to determine certainly and universally what action would promote the happiness of a rational being is completely insoluble, and consequently no imperative respecting it is possible which should, in the strict sense, command to do what makes [for happiness]; because happiness is not an ideal of reason but of imagination, resting solely on empirical grounds, and it is vain to expect that these should define an action by which one could attain the totality of a series of consequences which is really endless. This imperative of prudence would, however, be an analytical proposition if we assume that the means to happiness could be certainly assigned; for it is distinguished from the imperative of skill only by this, that in the latter the end is merely possible, in the former it is given; as, however, both only ordain the means to that which we suppose to be willed as an end, it follows that the imperative which ordains the willing of the means to him who wills the end is in both cases analytical. Thus there is no difficulty in regard to the possibility of an imperative of this kind either.

The Rational Ground of the Categorical Imperative

On the other hand, the question, how the imperative of *morality* is possible, is undoubtedly one, the only one, demanding a solution, as this is not at all hypothetical, and the objective necessity which it presents cannot rest on any hypothesis, as is the case with the hypothetical imperatives. Only here we must never leave out of consideration that we *cannot* make out *by any example,* in other words empirically, whether there is such an imperative at all; but it is rather to be feared that all those which seem to be categorical may yet be at bottom hypothetical. For instance, when the precept is: Thou shalt not promise deceitfully; and it is assumed that the necessity of this is not a mere counsel to avoid some other evil, so that it should mean: Thou shalt not make a lying promise, lest if it become known thou shouldst destroy thy credit, but that an action of this kind must be regarded as evil in itself, so that the imperative of the prohibition is categorical; then we cannot show with certainty in any example that the will was determined merely by the law, without any other spring of action, although it may appear to be so. For it is always possible that fear of disgrace, perhaps also obscure dread of other dangers, may have a secret influence on the will. Who can prove by experience the nonexistence of a cause when all that experience tells us is that we do not perceive it? But in such a case the so-called moral imperative, which as such appears to be categorical and unconditional, would in reality be only a pragmatic precept, drawing our attention to our own interests, and merely teaching us to take these into consideration.

We shall therefore have to investigate *à priori* the possibility of a categorical imperative, as we have not in this case the advantage of its reality being given in experience, so that [the elucidation of] its possibility should be requisite only for its explanation, not for its establishment. In the meantime it may be discerned beforehand that the categorical imperative alone has the purport of a practical law: all the rest may indeed be called *principles* of the will but not laws, since whatever is only necessary for the attainment of some arbitrary purpose may be considered as in itself contingent, and we can at any time be free from the precept if we give up the purpose: on the contrary, the unconditional command leaves the will no liberty to choose the opposite; consequently it alone carries with it that necessity which we require in a law.

Secondly, in the case of this categorical imperative or law of morality, the difficulty (of discerning its possibility) is a very profound one. It is an *à priori* synthetical practical proposition[2]; and as there is so much difficulty in discerning the possibility of speculative propositions of this kind, it may readily be supposed that the difficulty will be no less with the practical.

First Formulation of the Categorical Imperative: Universal Law

In this problem we will first inquire whether the mere conception of a categorical imperative may not perhaps supply us also with the formula of it, containing the proposition which alone can be a categorical imperative; for even if we know the tenor of such an absolute command, yet how it is possible will require further special and laborious study, which we postpone to the last section.

When I conceive a hypothetical imperative, in general I do not know beforehand what it will contain until I am given the condition. But when I conceive a categorical imperative, I know at once what it contains. For as the imperative contains besides the law only the necessity that the maxims[3] shall conform to this law, while the law contain no conditions restricting it, there remains nothing but the general statement that the maxim of the action should conform to a universal law, and it is this conformity alone that the imperative properly represents as necessary.

There is therefore but one categorical imperative, namely, this: *Act only on that maxim whereby thou canst at the same time will that it should become a universal law.*

Now if all imperatives of duty can be deduced from this one imperative as from their principle, then, although it should remain undecided whether what is called duty is not merely a vain notion, yet at least we shall be able to show what we understand by it and what this notion means.

Since the universality of the law according to which effects are produced constitutes what is properly called *nature* in the most general sense (as to form), that is the existence of things so far as it is determined by general laws, the imperative of duty may be expressed thus: *Act as if the maxim of thy action were to become by thy will a universal law of nature.*

Four Illustrations

We will now enumerate a few duties, adopting the usual division of them into duties to ourselves and to others, and into perfect and imperfect duties.

1. A man reduced to despair by a series of misfortunes feels wearied by life, but is still so far in possession of his reason that he can ask himself whether it would not be contrary to his duty to himself to take his own life. Now he inquires whether the maxim of his action could become a universal law of nature. His maxim is: From self-love I adopt it as a principle to shorten my life when its longer duration is likely to bring more evil than satisfaction. It is asked then simply whether this principle founded on self-love can become a universal law of nature. Now we see at once that a system of nature of which it should be a law to destroy life by means of the very feeling whose special nature it is to impel to the improvement of life would contradict itself, and therefore could not exist as a system of nature; hence that maxim cannot possibly exist as a universal law of nature, and consequently would be wholly inconsistent with the supreme principle of all duty.

2. Another finds himself forced by necessity to borrow money. He knows that he will not be able to repay it, but sees also that nothing will be lent to him, unless he promises stoutly to repay it in a definite time. He desires to make this promise, but he has still so much conscience as to ask himself: Is it not unlawful and inconsistent with duty to get out of a difficulty in this way? Suppose, however, that he resolves to do so, then the maxim of his action would be expressed thus: When I think myself in want of money, I will borrow money and promise to repay it, although I know that I never can do so. Now this principle of self-love or of one's own advantage may perhaps be consistent with my whole future welfare; but the question now is, Is it right? I change then the suggestion of self-love into a universal law, and state the question thus: How would it be if my maxim were a universal law? Then I see at once that it could never hold as a universal law of nature, but would necessarily contradict itself. For supposing it to be a universal law that everyone when he thinks himself in a difficulty should be able to promise whatever he pleases, with the purpose of not keeping his promise, the promise itself would become impossible, as well as the end that one might have in view in it, since no one would consider that anything was promised to him, but would ridicule all such statements as vain pretenses.

3. A third finds in himself a talent which with the help of some culture might make him a useful man in many respects. But he finds himself in comfortable circumstances, and prefers to indulge in

pleasure rather than to take pains in enlarging and improving his happy natural capacities. He asks, however, whether his maxim of neglect of his natural gifts, besides agreeing with his inclination to indulgence, agrees also with what is called duty. He sees then that a system of nature could indeed subsist with such a universal law although men (like the South Sea islanders) should let their talents rest, and resolve to devote their lives merely to idleness, amusement, and propagation of their species — in a word, to enjoyment; but he cannot possibly *will* that this should be a universal law of nature, or be implanted in us as such by a natural instinct. For, as a rational being, he necessarily wills that his faculties be developed, since they serve him, and have been given him, for all sorts of possible purposes.

4. A fourth, who is in prosperity, while he sees that others have to contend with great wretchedness and that he could help them, thinks: What concern is it of mine? Let everyone be as happy as Heaven pleases, or as he can make himself; I will take nothing from him nor even envy him, only I do not wish to contribute anything to his welfare or to his assistance in distress! Now no doubt if such a mode of thinking were a universal law, the human race might very well subsist, and doubtless even better than in a state in which everyone talks of sympathy and goodwill, or even takes care occasionally to put it into practice, but, on the other side, also cheats when he can, betrays the rights of men, or otherwise violates them. But although it is possible that a universal law of nature might exist in accordance with that maxim, it is impossible to *will* that such a principle should have the universal validity of a law of nature. For a will which resolved this would contradict itself, inasmuch as many cases might occur in which one would have need of the love and sympathy of others, and in which, by such a law of nature, sprung from his own will, he would deprive himself of all hope of the aid he desires.

These are a few of the many actual duties, or at least what we regard as such, which obviously fall into two classes on the one principle that we have laid down. We must be *able to will* that a maxim of our action should be a universal law. This is the canon of the moral appreciation of the action generally. Some actions are of such a character that their maxim cannot without contradiction be even *conceived* as a universal law of nature, far from it being possible that we should *will* that it *should* be so. In others this intrinsic impossibility is not found, but still it is impossible to *will* that their maxim should be raised to the universality of a law of nature, since such a will would contradict itself. It is easily seen that the former violate strict or rigorous (inflexible) duty; the latter only laxer (meritorious) duty. Thus it has been completely shown by these examples how all duties depend as regards the nature of the obligation (not the object of the action) on the same principle.

Transgressions of the Moral Law

If now we attend to ourselves on occasion of any transgression of duty, we shall find that we in fact do not will that our maxim should be a universal law, for that is impossible for us; on the contrary, we will that the opposite should remain a universal law, only we assume the liberty of making an *exception* in our own favour or (just for this time only) in favour of our inclination. Consequently if we considered all cases from one and the same point of view, namely, that of reason, we should find a contradiction in our own will, namely, that a certain principle should be objectively necessary as a universal law, and yet subjectively should not be universal, but admit of exceptions. As, however, we at one moment regard our action from the point of view of a will wholly conformed to reason, and then again look at the same action from the point of view of a will affected by inclination, there is not really any contradiction, but an antagonism of inclination to the precept of reason, whereby the universality of the principle is changed into a mere generality, so that the practical principle of reason shall meet the maxim half way. Now, although this cannot be justified in our own impartial judgment, yet it proves that we do really recognize the validity of the categorical imperative and (with all respect for it) only allow ourselves a few exceptions, which we think unimportant and forced from us.

The Need for an A Priori Proof of the Categorical Imperative

We have thus established at least this much, that if duty is a conception which is to have any import and real legislative authority for our actions, it can only be expressed in categorical, and not at all in hypothetical imperatives. We have also, which is of great importance, exhibited clearly and definitely for every practical application the content of the categorical imperative, which must contain the principle of all duty if there is such a thing at all. We have not yet, however, advanced so far as to prove *à priori* that there actually is such an imperative, that there is a practical law which commands absolutely of itself, and without any other impulse, and that the following of this law is duty.

With the view of attaining to this it is of extreme importance to remember that we must not allow ourselves to think of deducing the reality of this principle from the *particular attributes of human nature*. For duty is to be a practical, unconditional necessity of action; it must therefore hold for all rational beings (to whom an imperative can apply at all), and *for this reason only* be also a law for all human wills. On the contrary, whatever is deduced from the particular natural characteristics of humanity, from certain feelings and propensities, nay, even, if possible, from any particular tendency proper to human reason, and which need not necessarily hold for the will of every rational being; this may indeed supply us with a maxim, but not with a law; with a subjective principle on which we may have a propensity and inclination to act, but not with an objective principle on which we should be *enjoined* to act, even though all our propensities, inclinations, and natural dispositions were opposed to it. In fact, the sublimity and intrinsic dignity of the command in duty are so much the more evident, the less subjective impulses favour it and the more they oppose it, without being able in the slightest degree to weaken the obligation of the law or to diminish its validity.

Here then we see philosophy brought to a critical position, since it has to be firmly fixed, notwithstanding that it has nothing to support it in heaven or earth. Here it must show its purity as absolute director of its own laws, not the herald of those which are whispered to it by an implanted sense or who knows what tutelary nature. Although these may be better than nothing, yet they can never afford principles dictated by reason, which must have their source wholly *à priori* and thence their commanding authority, expecting everything from the supremacy of the law the due respect for it, nothing from inclination, or else condemning the man to self-contempt and inward abhorrence.

Thus every empirical element is not only quite incapable of being an aid to the principle of morality, but is even highly prejudicial to the purity of morals; for the proper and inestimable worth of an absolutely good will consists just in this, that the principle of action is free from all influence of contingent grounds, which alone experience can furnish. We cannot too much or too often repeat our warning against this lax and even mean habit of thought which seeks for its principle amongst empirical motives and laws; for human reason in its weariness is glad to rest on this pillow, and in a dream of sweet illusions (in which, instead of Juno, it embraces a cloud) it substitutes for morality a bastard patched up from limbs of various derivation, which looks like anything one chooses to see in it; only not like virtue to one who has once beheld her in her true form.[4]

The question then is this: Is it a necessary law *for all rational beings* that they should always judge of their actions by maxims of which they can themselves will that they should serve as universal laws? If it is so, then it must be connected (altogether *à priori*) with the very conception of the will of a rational being generally. But in order to discover this connexion we must, however reluctantly, take a step into metaphysic, although into a domain of it which is distinct from speculative philosophy, namely, the metaphysic of morals. In a practical philosophy, where it is not the reasons of what *happens* that we have to ascertain, but the laws of what *ought to happen,* even although it never does, *i.e.* objective practical laws, there it is not necessary to inquire into the reason why anything pleases or displeases, how the pleasure of mere sensation differs from taste, and whether the latter is distinct from a general satisfaction of reason; on what the feeling of pleasure or pain rests, and how from its desires and inclinations arise, and from these again maxims by the co-operation of reason: for all this belongs to an empirical psychology, which would constitute the second part of physics, if we regard physics as the *philosophy* of nature, so far as it is based on *empirical laws*. But here we are concerned with objective practical laws, and consequently with the relation of the will to itself so far as it is determined by reason alone, in which case whatever has reference to anything empirical is necessarily excluded; since if *reason of itself alone* determines the conduct (and it is the possibility of this that we are now investigating), it must necessarily do so *a priori*.

Second Formulation of the Categorical Imperative: Humanity as an End in Itself

The will is conceived as a faculty of determining oneself to action *in accordance with the conception of certain laws*. And such a faculty can be found only in rational beings. Now that which serves the will as the objective ground of its self-determination is the *end,* and if this is assigned by reason alone, it must hold for all rational beings. On the other hand, that which merely contains the ground of possibility of the action of which the effect is the end, this is called the *means*. The subjective ground of the desire is the *spring,* the objective ground of the volition is the *motive;* hence the distinction between subjective ends which rest on springs, and objective ends which depend on motives valid for every rational being. Practical principles are *formal* when they abstract from all subjective ends; they are *material* when they assume these, and therefore particular springs of action. The ends which a rational being proposes to himself at pleasure as *effects* of his actions (material ends) are all only relative, for it is only their relation to the particular desires of the subject that gives them their worth, which therefore cannot furnish principles universal and necessary for all rational beings and for every volition, that is to say practical laws. Hence all these relative ends can give rise only to hypothetical imperatives.

Supposing, however, that there were something *whose existence* has *in itself* an absolute worth, something which, being *an end in itself,* could be a source of definite laws, then in this and this alone would lie the source of a possible categorical imperative, *i.e.* a practical law.

Now I say: man and generally any rational being *exists* as an end in himself, *not merely as a means* to be arbitrarily used by this or that will, but in all his actions, whether they concern himself or other rational beings, must be always regarded at the same time as an end. All objects of the inclinations have only a conditional worth; for if the inclinations and the wants founded on them did not exist, then their object would be without value. But the inclinations themselves being sources of want are so far from having an absolute worth for which they should be desired, that, on the contrary, it must be the universal wish of every rational being to be wholly free from them. Thus the worth of any object which is *to be acquired* by our action is always conditional. Be-

ings whose existence depends not on our will but on nature's, have nevertheless, if they are nonrational beings, only a relative value as means, and are therefore called *things;* rational beings, on the contrary, are called *persons,* because their very nature points them out as ends in themselves, that is as something which must not be used merely as means, and so far therefore restricts freedom of action (and is an object of respect). These, therefore, are not merely subjective ends whose existence has a worth *for us* as an effect of our action, but *objective ends,* that is things whose existence is an end in itself: an end moreover for which no other can be substituted, which they should subserve *merely* as means, for otherwise nothing whatever would possess *absolute worth;* but if all worth were conditioned and therefore contingent, then there would be no supreme practical principle of reason whatever.

If then there is a supreme practical principle or, in respect of the human will, a categorical imperative, it must be one which, being drawn from the conception of that which is necessarily an end for everyone because it is *an end in itself*, constitutes an *objective* principle of will, and can therefore serve as a universal practical law. The foundation of this principle is: *rational nature exists as an end in itself.* Man necessarily conceives his own existence as being so: so far then this is a *subjective* principle of human actions. But every other rational being regards its existence similarly, just on the same rational principle that holds for me[5]: so that it is at the same time an objective principle, from which as a supreme practical law all laws of the will must be capable of being deduced. Accordingly the practical imperative will be as follows: *So act as to treat humanity, whether in thine own person or in that of any other, in every case as an end withal, never as means only.* We will now inquire whether this can be practically carried out.

Four Illustrations

To abide by the previous examples:

Firstly, under the head of necessary duty to oneself: He who contemplates suicide should ask himself whether his actions can be consistent with the idea of humanity *as an end in itself*. If he destroys himself in order to escape from painful circumstances, he uses a person merely as *a means* to maintain a tolerable condition up to the end of life. But a man is not a thing, that is to say, something which can be used merely as means, but must in all his actions be always considered as an end in himself. I cannot, therefore, dispose in any way of a man in my own person so as to mutilate him, to damage or kill him. (It belongs to ethics proper to define this principle more precisely, so as to avoid all misunderstanding, *e.g.* as to the amputation of the limbs in order to preserve myself; as to exposing my life to danger with a view to preserve it, &c. This question is therefore omitted here.)

Secondly, as regards necessary duties, or those of strict obligation, towards others; he who is thinking of making a lying promise to others will see at once that he would be using another man *merely as a mean,* without the latter containing at the same time the end in himself. For he whom I propose by such a promise to use for my own purposes cannot possibly assent to my mode of acting towards him, and therefore cannot himself contain the end of this action. This violation of the principle of humanity in other men is more obvious if we take in examples of attacks on the freedom and property of others. For then it is clear that he who transgresses the rights of men intends to use the person of others merely as means, without considering that as rational beings they ought always to be esteemed also as ends, that is, as beings who must be capable of containing in themselves the end of the very same action.[6]

Thirdly, as regards contingent (meritorious) duties to oneself; it is not enough that the action does not violate humanity in our own person as an end in itself, it must also *harmonize with* it. Now there are in humanity capacities of greater perfection which belong to the end that nature has in view in regard to humanity in ourselves as the subject: to neglect these might perhaps be consistent with the *maintenance* of humanity as an end in itself, but not with the *advancement* of this end.

Fourthly, as regards meritorious duties towards others: the natural end which all men have is their own happiness. Now humanity might indeed subsist, although no one should contribute anything to the happiness of others, provided he did not intentionally withdraw anything from it; but after all, this would only harmonize negatively, not positively, with *humanity as an end in itself,* if everyone does not also endeavour, as far as in him lies, to forward the ends of others. For the ends of any subject which is an end in himself, ought as far as possible to be *my* ends also, if that conception is to have its *full* effect with me.

Third Formulation of the Categorical Imperative: The Autonomy of the Will as Universal Legislator

This principle, that humanity and generally every rational nature is *an end in itself* (which is the supreme limiting condition of every man's freedom of action), is not borrowed from experience, *firstly*, because it is universal, applying as it does to all rational beings whatever, and experience is not capable of determining anything about them; *secondly*, because it does not present humanity as an end to men (subjectively), that is as an object which men do of themselves actually adopt as an end; but as an objective end, which must as a law constitute the supreme limiting condition of all our subjective ends, let them be what we will; it must therefore spring from pure reason. In fact the objective principle of all practical legislation lies (according to the first principle) in *the rule* and its form of universality which makes it capable of being a law (say, *e.g.*, a law of nature); but the *subjective* principle is in the *end*; now by the second principle the subject of all ends is each rational being inasmuch as it is an end in itself. Hence follows the third practical principle of the will, which is the ultimate condition of its harmony with the universal practical reason, viz.: the idea of *the will of every rational being as a universally legislative will.*

On this principle all maxims are rejected which are inconsistent with the will being itself universal legislator. Thus the will is not subject simply to the law, but so subject that it must be regarded *as itself giving the law,* and on this ground only, subject to the law (of which it can regard itself as the author).

In the previous imperatives, namely, that based on the conception of the conformity of actions to general laws, as in a *physical system of nature,* and that based on the universal *prerogative* of rational beings as *ends* in themselves—these imperatives just because they were conceived as categorical, excluded from any share in their authority all admixture of any interest as a spring of action; they were, however, only *assumed* to be categorical, because such an assumption was necessary to explain the conception of duty. But we could not prove independently that there are practical propositions which command categorically, nor can it be proved in this section; one thing, however, could be done, namely, to indicate in the imperative itself by some determinate expression, that in the case of volition from duty all interest is renounced, which is the specific criterion of categorical as distinguished from hypothetical imperatives. This is done in the present (third) formula of the principle, namely, in the idea of the will of every rational being as a *universally legislating will.*

For although a will *which is subject to laws* may be attached to this law by means of an interest, yet a will which is itself a supreme lawgiver so far as it is such cannot possibly depend on any interest, since a will so dependent would itself still need another law restricting the interest of its self-love by the condition that it should be valid as universal law.

Thus the *principle* that every human will is *a will which in all its maxims gives universal laws,*[7] provided it be otherwise justified, would be very *well adapted* to be the categorical imperative, in this respect, namely, that just because of the idea of universal legislation it is *not based on any interest,* and therefore it alone among all possible imperatives can be *unconditional.* Or still better, converting the proposition, if there is a categorical imperative (*i.e.,* a law for the will of every rational being), it can only command that everything be done from maxims of one's will regarded as a will which could at the same time will that it should itself give universal laws, for in that case only the practical principle and the imperative which it obeys are unconditional, since they cannot be based on any interest.

Looking back now on all previous attempts to discover the principle of morality, we need not wonder why they all failed. It was seen that man was bound to laws by duty, but it was not observed that the laws to which he is subject are *only those of his own giving,* though at the same time they are *universal,* and that he is only bound to act in conformity with his own will; a will, however, which is designed by nature to give universal laws. For when one has conceived man only as subject to a law (no matter what), then this law required some interest, either by way of attraction or constraint, since it did not originate as a law from *his own* will, but this will was according to a law obliged by *something else* to act in a certain manner. Now by this necessary conse-

quence all the labour spent in finding a supreme principle of *duty* was irrevocably lost. For men never elicited duty, but only a necessity of acting from a certain interest. Whether this interest was private or otherwise, in any case the imperative must be conditional, and could not by any means be capable of being a moral command. I will therefore call this the principle of *Autonomy* of the will, in contrast with every other which I accordingly reckon as *Heteronomy.*

The Kingdom of Ends

The conception of every rational being as one which must consider itself as giving in all the maxims of its will universal laws, so as to judge itself and its actions from this point of view — this conception leads to another which depends on it and is very fruitful, namely, that of a *kingdom of ends.*

By a *kingdom* I understand the union of different rational beings in a system by common laws. Now since it is by laws that ends are determined as regards their universal validity, hence, if we abstract from the personal differences of rational beings, and likewise from all the content of their private ends, we shall be able to conceive all ends combined in a systematic whole (including both rational beings as ends in themselves, and also the special ends which each may propose to himself), that is to say, we can conceive a kingdom of ends, which on the preceding principles is possible.

For all rational beings come under the *law* that each of them must treat itself and all others *never merely as means,* but in every case *at the same time as ends in themselves.* Hence results a systematic union of rational beings by common objective laws, *i.e.,* a kingdom which may be called a kingdom of ends, since what these laws have in view is just the relation of these beings to one another as ends and means. It is certainly only an ideal.

A rational being belongs as a *member* to the kingdom of ends when, although giving universal laws in it, he is also himself subject to these laws. He belongs to it *as sovereign* when, while giving laws, he is not subject to the will of any other.

A rational being must always regard himself as giving laws either as member or as sovereign in a kingdom of ends which is rendered possible by the freedom of will. He cannot, however, maintain the latter position merely by the maxims of his will, but only in case he is a completely independent being without wants and with unrestricted power adequate to his will.

Morality consists then in the reference of all action to the legislation which alone can render a kingdom of ends possible. This legislation must be capable of existing in every rational being, and of emanating from his will, so that the principle of this will is, never to act on any maxim which could not without contradiction be also a universal law, and accordingly always so to act *that the will could at the same time regard itself as giving in its maxims universal laws.* If now the maxims of rational beings are not by their own nature coincident with this objective principle, then the necessity of acting on it is called practical necessitation, i.e. *duty*. Duty does not apply to the sovereign in the kingdom of ends, but it does to every member of it and to all in the same degree.

The practical necessity of acting on this principle, *i.e.* duty, does not rest at all on feelings, impulses, or inclinations, but solely on the relation of rational beings to one another, a relation in which the will of a rational being must always be regarded as *legislative,* since otherwise it could not be conceived as *an end in itself.* Reason then refers every maxim of the will, regarding it as legislating universally, to every other will and also to every action towards oneself; and this not on account of any other practical motive or any future advantage, but from the idea of the *dignity* of a rational being, obeying no law but that which he himself also gives.

In the kingdom of ends everything has either Value or Dignity. Whatever has a value can be replaced by something else which is *equivalent;* whatever, on the other hand, is above all value, and therefore admits of no equivalent, has a dignity.

Whatever has reference to the general inclinations and wants of mankind has a *market value;* whatever, without presupposing a want, corresponds to a certain taste, that is to a satisfaction in the mere purposeless play of our faculties, has a *fancy value;* but that which constitutes the condition under which alone anything can be an end in itself, this has not merely a relative worth, *i.e.* value, but an intrinsic worth, that is *dignity.*

Now morality is the condition under which alone a rational being can be an end in himself, since by this alone it is possible that he should be a legislating member in the kingdom of ends. Thus morality, and humanity as capable of it, is that which alone has dignity. Skill and diligence in labour have a market value; wit, lively imagination, and humour, have fancy value; on the other hand, fidelity to promises, benevolence from principle (not from instinct), have an intrinsic worth. Neither nature nor art contains anything which in default of these it could put in their place, for their worth consists not in the effects which spring from them, not in the use and advantage which they secure, but in the disposition of mind, that is, the maxims of the will which are ready to manifest themselves in such actions, even though they should not have the desired effect. These actions also need no recommendation from any subjective taste or sentiment, that they may be looked on with immediate favour and satisfaction: they need no immediate propension or feeling for them; they exhibit the will that performs them as an object of an immediate respect, and nothing but reason is required to *impose* them on the will; not to *flatter* it into them, which, in the case of duties, would be a contradiction. This estimation therefore shows that the worth of such a disposition is dignity, and places it infinitely above all value, with which it cannot for a moment be brought into comparison or competition without as it were violating its sanctity.

What then is it which justifies virtue or the morally good disposition, in making such lofty claims? It is nothing less than the privilege it secures to the rational being of participating in the giving of universal laws, by which it qualifies him to be a member of a possible kingdom of ends, a privilege to which he was already destined by his own nature as being an end in himself, and on that account legislating in the kingdom of ends; free as regards all laws of physical nature, and obeying those only which he himself gives, and by which his maxims can belong to a system of universal law, to which at the same time he submits himself. For nothing has any worth except what the law assigns it. Now the legislation itself which assigns the worth of everything must for that very reason possess dignity, that is an unconditional incomparable worth; and the word *respect* alone supplies a becoming expression for the esteem which a rational being must have for it. *Autonomy* then is the basis of the dignity of human and of every rational nature.

The Autonomy of the Will as the Supreme Principle of Morality Autonomy of the will is that property of it by which it is a law to itself (independently on any property of the objects of volition). The principle of autonomy then is: Always so to choose that the same volition shall comprehend the maxims of our choice as a universal law. We cannot prove that this practical rule is an imperative, *i.e.,* that the will of every rational being is necessarily bound to it as a condition, by a mere analysis of the conceptions which occur in it, since it is a synthetical proposition; we must advance beyond the cognition of the objects to a critical examination of the subject, that is of the pure practical reason, for this synthetic proposition which commands apodictically must be capable of being cognized wholly *à priori*. This matter, however, does not belong to the present section. But that the principle of autonomy in question is the sole principle of morals can be readily shown by mere analysis of the conceptions of morality. For by this analysis we find that its principle must be a categorical imperative, and that what this commands is neither more nor less than this very autonomy.

Heteronomy of the Will as the Source of All Spurious Principles of Morality If the will seeks the law which is to determine it *anywhere else* than in the fitness of its maxims to be universal laws of its own dictation, consequently if it goes out of itself and seeks this law in the character of any of its objects, there always results *heteronomy.* The will in that case does not give itself the law, but it is given by the object through its relation to the will. This relation, whether it rests on inclination or on conceptions of reason, only admits of hypothetical imperatives: I ought to do something *because I wish for something else.* On the contrary, the moral, and therefore categorical, imperative says: I ought to do so and so, even though I should not wish for anything else. [For example], the former says: I ought not to lie if I would retain my reputation; the latter says: I ought not to lie although it should not bring me the least discredit. The latter therefore must so far abstract from all objects that they shall have no *influence* on the will, in order that practical reason (will) may not be restricted to administering an interest not be-

longing to it, but may simply show its own commanding authority as the supreme legislation. Thus, [for example], I ought to endeavour to promote the happiness of others, not as if its realization involved any concern of mine (whether by immediate inclination or by any satisfaction indirectly gained through reason), but simply because a maxim which excludes it cannot be comprehended as a universal law in one and the same volition.

Third Section: Transition from the Metaphysic of Morals to the Critique of Pure Practical Reason

The Concept of Freedom Is the Key That Explains the Autonomy of the Will The will is a kind of causality belonging to living beings in so far as they are rational, and *freedom* would be this property of such causality that it can be efficient, independently on foreign causes *determining* it; just as *physical necessity* is the property that the causality of all irrational beings has of being determined to activity by the influence of foreign causes.

The preceding definition of freedom is *negative,* and therefore unfruitful for the discovery of its essence; but it leads to a *positive* conception which is so much the more full and fruitful. Since the conception of causality involves that of laws, according to which, by something that we call cause, something else, namely, the effect, must be produced [laid down]; hence, although freedom is not a property of the will depending on physical laws, yet it is not for that reason lawless; on the contrary, it must be a causality acting according to immutable laws, but a peculiar kind; otherwise a free will would be an absurdity. Physical necessity is a heteronomy of the efficient causes, for every effect is possible only according to this law, that something else determines the efficient cause to exert its causality. What else then can freedom of the will be but autonomy, that is the property of the will to be a law to itself? But the proposition: The will is in every action a law to itself, only expresses the principle, to act on no other maxim than that which can also have as an object itself as a universal law. Now this is precisely the formula of the categorical imperative and is the principle of morality, so that a free will and a will subject to moral laws are one and the same.

On the hypothesis, then, of freedom of the will, morality together with its principle follows from it by mere analysis of the conception. However, the latter is a synthetic proposition; viz., an absolutely good will is that whose maxim can always include itself regarded as a universal law; for this property of its maxim can never be discovered by analysing the conception of an absolutely good will. Now such synthetic propositions are only possible in this way: that the two cognitions are connected together by their union with a third in which they are both to be found. The *positive* concept of freedom furnishes this third cognition, which cannot, as with physical causes, be the nature of the sensible world (in the concept of which we find conjoined the concept of something in relation as cause to *something else* as effect). We cannot now at once show what this third is to which freedom points us, and of which we have an idea *à priori*, nor can we make intelligible how the concept of freedom is shown to be legitimate from principles of pure practical reason, and with it the possibility of a categorical imperative; but some further preparation is required.

Freedom Must be Presupposed as a Property of the Will of All Rational Beings It is not enough to predicate freedom of our own will, from whatever reason, if we have not sufficient grounds for predicating the same of all rational beings. For as morality serves as a law for us only because we are *rational beings,* it must also hold for all rational beings; and as it must be deduced simply from the property of freedom, it must be shown that freedom also is a property of all rational beings. It is not enough, then, to prove it from certain supposed experiences of human nature (which indeed is quite impossible, and it can only be shown *à priori*), but we must show that it belongs to the activity of all rational beings endowed with a will. Now I say every being that cannot act except *under the idea of freedom* is just for that reason in a practical point of view really free, that is to say, all laws which are inseparably connected with freedom have the same force for him as if his will had been shown to be free in itself by a proof theoretically conclusive.[8] Now I affirm that we must attribute to every rational being which has a will that it has also the idea of freedom and acts entirely under this idea. For in such a being we conceive a reason that is prac-

tical, that is, has causality in reference to its objects. Now we cannot possibly conceive a reason consciously receiving a bias from any other quarter with respect to its judgments, for then the subject would ascribe the determination of its judgment not to its own reason, but to an impulse. It must regard itself as the author of its principles independent on foreign influences. Consequently as practical reason or as the will of a rational being it must regard itself as free, that is to say, the will of such a being cannot be a will of its own except under the idea of freedom. This idea must therefore in a practical point of view be ascribed to every rational being.

Of the Interest Attaching to the Ideas of Morality We have finally reduced the definite conception of morality to the idea of freedom. This latter, however, we could not prove to be actually a property of ourselves or of human nature; only we saw that it must be presupposed if we would conceive a being as rational and conscious of its causality in respect of its actions, *i.e.,* as endowed with a will; and so we find that on just the same grounds we must ascribe to every being endowed with reason and will this attribute of determining itself to action under the idea of its freedom.

Now it resulted also from the presupposition of this idea that we became aware of a law that the subjective principles of action, *i.e.* maxims, must also be so assumed that they can also hold as objective, that is, universal principles, and so serve as universal laws of our own dictation. But why, then, should I subject myself to this principle and that simply as a rational being, thus also subjecting to it all other beings endowed with reason? I will allow that no interest *urges* me to this, for that would not give a categorical imperative, but I must *take* an interest in it and discern how this comes to pass; for this "I ought" is properly an "I would," valid for every rational being, provided only that reason determined his actions without any hindrance. But for beings that are in addition affected as we are by springs of a different kind, namely sensibility, and in whose case that is not always done which reason alone would do, for these that necessity is expressed only as an "ought," and the subjective necessity is different from the objective.

It seems, then, as if the moral law, that is, the principle of autonomy of the will, were properly speaking only presupposed in the idea of freedom, and as if we could not prove its reality and objective necessity independently. In that case we should still have gained something considerable by at least determining the true principle more exactly than had previously been done; but as regards its validity and the practical necessity of subjecting oneself to it, we should not have advanced a step. For if we were asked why the universal validity of our maxim as a law must be the condition restricting our actions, and on what we ground the worth which we assign to this matter of acting — a worth so great that there cannot be any higher interest; and if we were asked further how it happens that it is by this alone a man believes he feels his own personal worth, in comparison with which that of an agreeable or disagreeable condition is to be regarded as nothing, to these questions we could give no satisfactory answer.

We find indeed sometimes that we can take an interest in a personal quality which does not involve any interest of external condition, provided this quality makes us capable of participating in the condition in case reason were to effect the allotment; that is to say, the mere being worthy of happiness can interest of itself even without the motive of participating in this happiness. This judgment, however, is in fact only the effect of the importance of the moral law which we before presupposed (when by the idea of freedom we detach ourselves from every empirical interest); but that we ought to detach ourselves from these interests, *i.e.,* to consider ourselves as free in action and yet as subject to certain laws, so as to find a worth simply in our own person which can compensate us for the loss of everything that gives worth to our condition; this we are not yet able to discern in this way, nor do we see how it is possible so to act — in other words, *whence the moral law derives its obligation.*

It must be freely admitted that there is a sort of circle here from which it seems impossible to escape. In the order of efficient causes we assume ourselves free, in order that in the order of ends we may conceive ourselves as subject to moral laws: and we afterwards conceive ourselves as subject to these laws, because we have attributed to ourselves freedom of will: for freedom and self-legislation of will are both autonomy, and therefore are reciprocal conceptions, and for this very reason one must not be used to explain the other or give the reason of it, but at most only for logical purposes to reduce ap-

parently different notions of the same object to one single concept (as we reduce different fractions of the same value to the lowest terms).

The Two Points of View

One resource remains to us, namely, to inquire whether we do not occupy different points of view when by means of freedom we think ourselves as causes efficient *à priori,* and when we form our conception of ourselves from our actions as effects which we see before our eyes.

It is a remark which needs no subtle reflection to make, but which we may assume that even the commonest understanding can make, although it be after its fashion by an obscure discernment of judgment which it calls feeling, that all the "ideas" that come to us involuntarily (as those of the senses) do not enable us to know objects otherwise than as they affect us; so that what they may be in themselves remains unknown to us, and consequently that as regards "ideas" of this kind even with the closest attention and clearness that the understanding can apply to them, we can by them only attain to the knowledge of *appearances,* never to that of *things in themselves.* As soon as this distinction has once been made (perhaps merely in consequence of the difference observed between the ideas given us from without, and in which we are passive, and those that we produce simply from ourselves, and in which we show our own activity), then it follows of itself that we must admit and assume behind the appearance something else that is not an appearance, namely, the things in themselves; although we must admit that as they can never be known to us except as they affect us, we can come no nearer to them, nor can we ever know what they are in themselves. This must furnish a distinction, however crude, between a *world of sense* and the *world of understanding,* of which the former may be different according to the difference of the sensuous impressions in various observers, while the second which is its basis always remains the same. Even as to himself, a man cannot pretend to know what he is in himself from the knowledge he has by internal sensation. For as he does not as it were create himself, and does not come by the conception of himself *à priori* but empirically, it naturally follows that he can obtain his knowledge even of himself only by the inner sense, and consequently only through the appearances of his nature and the way in which his consciousness is affected. At the same time beyond these characteristics of his own subject, made up of mere appearances, he must necessarily suppose something else as their basis, namely, his *ego,* whatever its characteristics in itself may be. Thus in respect to mere perception and receptivity of sensations he must reckon himself as belonging to the *world of sense;* but in respect of whatever there may be of pure activity in him (that which reaches consciousness immediately and not through affecting the senses) he must reckon himself as belonging to the *intellectual world,* of which, however, he has no further knowledge. To such a conclusion the reflecting man must come with respect to all the things which can be presented to him: it is probably to be met with even in persons of the commonest understanding, who, as is well known, are very much inclined to suppose behind the objects of the sense something else invisible and acting of itself. They spoil it, however, by presently sensualizing this invisible again; that is to say, wanting to make it an object of intuition, so that they do not become a whit the wiser.

Now man really finds in himself a faculty by which he distinguishes himself from everything else, even from himself as affected by objects, and that is *Reason.* This being pure spontaneity is even elevated above the *understanding.* For although the latter is a spontaneity and does not, like sense, merely contain intuitions that arise when we are affected by things (and are therefore passive), yet it cannot produce from its activity any other conceptions than those which merely serve *to bring the intuitions of sense under rules,* and thereby to unite them in one consciousness, and without this use of the sensibility it could not think at all; whereas, on the contrary, Reason shows so pure a spontaneity in the case of what I call Ideas [Ideal Conceptions] that it thereby far transcends everything that the sensibility can give it, and exhibits its most important function in distinguishing the world of sense from that of understanding, and thereby prescribing the limits of the understanding itself.

For this reason a rational being must regard himself *qua* intelligence (not from the side of his lower faculties) as belonging not to the world of sense, but to that of understanding; hence he has two points of view from which he can regard himself, and recognize laws of the exercise of his faculties, and consequently of all his actions: *first,* so far as he belongs to the world of sense, he finds himself subject to laws of nature (heteronomy); *secondly,* as belonging to the intelligible world, under laws which, being independent on nature, have their foundation not in experience but in reason alone.

As a reasonable being, and consequently belonging to the intelligible world, man can never conceive the causality of his own will otherwise than on condition of the idea of freedom, for independence on the determining causes of the sensible world (an independence which Reason must always ascribe to itself) is freedom. Now the idea of freedom is inseparably connected with the conception of *autonomy,* and this again with the universal principle of morality which is ideally the foundation of all actions of *rational* beings, just as the law of nature is of all phenomena.

Now the suspicion is removed which we raised above, that there was a latent circle involved in our reasoning from freedom to autonomy, and from this to the moral law, [namely]: that we laid down the idea of freedom because of the moral law only that we might afterwards in turn infer the latter from freedom, and that consequently we could assign no reason at all for this law, but could only [present] it as a *petitio principii*[9] which well-disposed minds would gladly concede to us, but which we could never put forward as a provable proposition. For now we see that when we conceive ourselves as free we transfer ourselves into the world of understanding as members of it, and recognize the autonomy of the will with its consequence, morality; whereas, if we conceive ourselves as under obligation, we consider ourselves as belonging to the world of sense, and at the same time to the world of understanding.

How Is a Categorical Imperative Possible? Every rational being reckons himself *qua* intelligence as belonging to the world of understanding, and it is simply as an efficient cause belonging to that world that he calls his causality a *will.* On the other side he is also conscious of himself as a part of the world of sense in which his actions, which are mere appearances [phenomena] of that causality, are displayed; we cannot, however, discern how they are possible from this causality which we do not know; but instead of that, these actions as belonging to the sensible world must be viewed as determined by other phenomena, namely, desires and inclinations. If therefore I were only a member of the world of understanding, then all my actions would perfectly conform to the principle of autonomy of the pure will; if I were only a part of the world of sense, they would necessarily be assumed to conform wholly to the natural laws of desires and inclinations, in other words, to the heteronomy of nature. (The former would rest on morality as the supreme principle, the latter on happiness.) Since, however, *the world of understanding contains the foundation of the world of sense, and consequently of its laws also,* and accordingly gives the law to my will (which belongs wholly to the world of understanding) directly, and must be conceived as doing so, it follows that, although on the one side I must regard myself as a being belonging to the world of sense, yet on the other side I must recognize myself as subject as an intelligence to the law of the world of understanding, *i.e.* to reason, which contains this law in the idea of freedom, and therefore as subject to the autonomy of the will: consequently I must regard the laws of the world of understanding as imperatives for me, and the actions which conform to them as duties.

And thus what makes categorical imperatives possible is this, that the idea of freedom makes me a member of an intelligible world, in consequence of which, if I were nothing else, all my actions *would* always conform to the autonomy of the will; but as I at the same time intuit myself as a member of the world of sense, they *ought* so to conform, and this *categorical* "ought" implies a synthetic *à priori* proposition, inasmuch as besides my will as affected by sensible desires there is added further the idea of the same will, but as belonging to the world of the understanding, pure and practical of itself, which contains the supreme condition according to Reason of the former will; precisely as to the intuitions of sense there are added concepts of the understanding which of themselves signify nothing but regular form in general, and in this way synthetic *à priori* propositions become possible, on which all knowledge of physical nature rests.

The practical use of common human reason confirms this reasoning. There is no one, not even the most consummate villain, provided only that he is otherwise accustomed to the use of reason, who, when we set before him examples of honesty of purpose, of steadfastness in following good maxims, of sympathy and general benevolence (even combined with great sacrifices of advantages and comfort), does not wish that he might also possess these qualities. Only on account of his inclinations and impulses he cannot attain this in himself, but at the same time he wishes to be free from such inclinations which are burdensome to himself. He proves by this that he transfers himself in thought with a will free from the impulses of the sensibility into an order of things wholly different from that of his desires in the field of the sensibility; since he cannot expect to obtain by that wish any gratification of his desires nor any position which would satisfy any of his actual or supposable inclinations (for this would destroy the pre-eminence of the very idea which wrests that wish from him): he can only expect a greater intrinsic worth of his own person. This better person, however, he imagines himself to be when he transfers himself to the point of view of a member of the world of the understanding, to which he is involuntarily forced by the idea of freedom, *i.e.,* of independence on *determining* causes of the world of sense; and from this point of view he is conscious of a good will, which by his own confession constitutes the law for the bad will that he possesses as a member of the world of sense—a law whose authority he recognizes while transgressing it. What he morally "ought" is then what he necessarily "would" as a member of the world of the understanding, and is conceived by him as an "ought" only inasmuch as he likewise considers himself as a member of the world of sense.

The question then: How a categorical imperative is possible can be answered to this extent that we can assign the only hypothesis on which it is possible, namely, the idea of freedom; and we can also discern the necessity of this hypothesis, and this is sufficient for the *practical exercise* of reason, that is, for the conviction of the *validity of this imperative,* and hence of the moral law; but how this hypothesis itself is possible can never be discerned by any human reason. On the hypothesis, however, that the will of an intelligence is free, its *autonomy,* as the essential formal condition of its determination, is a necessary consequence.

Endnotes

[1] A *maxim* is the subjective principle of volition. The objective principle (*i.e.* that which would also serve subjectively as a practical principle to all rational beings if reason had full power over the faculty of desire) is the practical *law*.

[2] I connect the act with the will without presupposing any condition resulting from any inclination, but *à priori*, and therefore necessarily (though only objectively, *i.e.* assuming the idea of a reason possessing full power over all subjective motives). This is accordingly a practical proposition which does not deduce the willing of an action by mere analysis from another already presupposed (for we have not such a perfect will), but connects it immediately with the conception of the will of a rational being, as something not contained in it.

[3] A maxim is a subjective principle of action, and must be distinguished from the *objective principle,* namely, practical law. The former contains the practical rule set by reason according to the conditions of the subject (often its ignorance or its inclinations), so that it is the principle on which the subject *acts;* but the law is the objective principle valid for every rational being, and is the principle on which it *ought to act* that is an imperative.

[4] To behold virtue in her proper form is nothing else but to contemplate morality stripped of all admixture of sensible things and of every spurious ornament of reward or self-love. How much she then eclipses everything else that appears charming to the affections, every one may readily perceive with the least exertion of his reason, if it be not wholly spoiled for abstraction.

[5] This proposition is here stated as a postulate. The ground of it will be found in the concluding section.

[6] Let it not be thought that the common: *quod tibi non vis fieri, &c.,* [that which you do not wish to be done to you, do not do to others] could serve here as the rule or principle. For it is only a deduction from the former, though with several limitations; it cannot be a universal law, for it does not contain the principle of duties to oneself, nor of the duties of benevolence to others (for many a one would gladly consent that others should not benefit him, provided only that he might be excused from showing benevolence to them), nor finally that of duties of strict obligation to one another, for on this principle the criminal might argue against the judge who punishes him, and so on.

[7] I may be excused from adducing examples to elucidate this principle, as those which have already been used to elucidate the categorical imperative and its formula would all serve for the like purpose here.

[8] I adopt this method of assuming freedom merely *as an idea* which rational beings suppose in their actions, in order to avoid the necessity of proving it in its theoretical aspect also. The former is sufficient for my purpose; for even though the speculative proof should not be made out, yet a being that cannot act except with the idea of freedom is bound by the same laws that would oblige a being who was actually free. Thus we can escape here from the onus which presses on the theory.

[9] [a begging of the question — Ed. note.]

VI.2 *What Makes Right Acts Right?*

W. D. ROSS

Sir William David Ross (1877–1971) was provost of Oriel College, Oxford University. His book, *The Right and the Good* (1930), is a classic treatise in defense of the theory of ethical intuitionism. In this selection from that work, Ross argues against utilitarianism, that optimal consequences have nothing to do with moral rightness or wrongness. We have intuitive knowledge of rightness and wrongness in terms of action-guiding principles, such as to keep promises made, to promote justice, to show gratitude for benefits rendered, and to refrain from harming others. Unlike Kant, however, these principles are not absolutes, that is, duties that must never be overridden. On the contrary, putative moral duties may be overridden by more binding moral duties. Moral principles are prima facie duties. That is, while their intrinsic value is not dependent on circumstances, their application is. They can be overridden by other prima facie duties. So, for example, our prima facie duty to tell the truth will be overridden by another prima facie duty to save innocent life in a situation in which a gangster asks us where his intended victim is hiding. Essentially, these principles are the outcome of generations of reflection, and their holistic schema has been internalized within us, so that ultimately the "decision lies in the perception."

...A... theory has been put forward by Professor Moore: that what makes actions right is that they are productive of more *good* than could have been produced by any other action open to the agent.

This theory is in fact the culmination of all the attempts to base rightness on productivity of some sort of result. The first form this attempt takes is the attempt to base rightness on conduciveness to the advantage or pleasure of the agent. This theory comes to grief over the fact, which stares us in the face, that a great part of duty consists in an observance of the rights and a furtherance of the interests of others, whatever the cost to ourselves may be. Plato and others may be right in holding that a regard for the rights of others never in the long run involves a loss of happiness for the agent, that 'the just life profits a man.' But this, even if true, is irrelevant to the rightness of the act. As soon as a man

From *The Right and the Good* (Oxford University Press, 1930). Reprinted by permission of Oxford University Press.

does an action *because* he thinks he will promote his own interests thereby, he is acting not from a sense of its rightness but from self-interest.

To the egoistic theory hedonistic utilitarianism supplies a much-needed amendment. It points out correctly that the fact that a certain pleasure will be enjoyed by the agent is no reason why he *ought* to bring it into being, rather than an equal or greater pleasure to be enjoyed by another, though, human nature being what it is, it makes it not unlikely that he *will* try to bring it into being. But hedonistic utilitarianism in its turn needs a correction. On reflection it seems clear that pleasure is not the only thing in life that we think good in itself, that for instance we think the possession of a good character, or an intelligent understanding of the world, as good or better. A great advance is made by the substitution of 'productive of the greatest good' for 'productive of the greatest pleasure.'

Not only is this theory more attractive than hedonistic utilitarianism, but its logical relation to that theory is such that the latter could not be true unless *it* were true, while it might be true though hedonistic utilitarianism were not. It is in fact one of the logical bases of hedonistic utilitarianism. For the view that what produces the maximum pleasure is right has for its bases the views (1) that what produces the maximum good is right, and (2) that pleasure is the only thing good in itself. If they were not assuming that what produces the maximum *good* is right, the utilitarians' attempt to show that pleasure is the only thing good in itself, which is in fact the point they take most pains to establish, would have been quite irrelevant to their attempt to prove that only what produces the maximum *pleasure* is right. If, therefore, it can be shown that productivity of the maximum good is not what makes all right actions right, we shall *a fortiori* have refuted hedonistic utilitarianism.

When a plain man fulfils a promise because he thinks he ought to do so, it seems clear that he does so with no thought of its total consequences, still less with any opinion that these are likely to be the best possible. He thinks in fact much more of the past than of the future. What makes him think it right to act in a certain way is the fact that he has promised to do so — that and, usually, nothing more. That his act will produce the best possible consequences is not his reason for calling it right. What lends colour to the theory we are examining, then, is not the actions (which form probably a great majority of our actions) in which some such reflection as 'I have promised' is the only reason we give ourselves for thinking a certain action right, but the exceptional cases in which the consequences of fulfilling a promise (for instance) would be so disastrous to others that we judge it right not to do so. It must of course be admitted that such cases exist. If I have promised to meet a friend at a particular time for some trivial purpose, I should certainly think myself justified in breaking my engagement if by doing so I could prevent a serious accident or bring relief to the victims of one. And the supporters of the view we are examining hold that my thinking so is due to my thinking that I shall bring more good into existence by the one action than by the other. A different account may, however, be given of the matter, an account which will, I believe, show itself to be the true one. It may be said that besides the duty of fulfilling promises I have and recognize a duty of relieving distress,[1] and that when I think it

right to do the latter at the cost of not doing the former, it is not because I think I shall produce more good thereby but because I think it the duty which is in the circumstances more of a duty. This account surely corresponds much more closely with what we really think in such a situation. If, so far as I can see, I could bring equal amounts of good into being by fulfilling my promise and by helping some one to whom I had made no promise, I should not hesitate to regard the former as my duty. Yet on the view that what is right is right because it is productive of the most good I should not so regard it.

There are two theories, each in its way simple, that offer a solution of such cases of conscience. One is the view of Kant, that there are certain duties of perfect obligation, such as those of fulfilling promises, of paying debts, of telling the truth, which admit of no exception whatever in favour of duties of imperfect obligation, such as that of relieving distress. The other is the view of, for instance, Professor Moore and Dr. Rashdall, that there is only the duty of producing good, and that all 'conflicts of duties' should be resolved by asking 'by which action will most good be produced?' But it is more important that our theory fit the facts than that it be simple, and the account we have given above corresponds (it seems to me) better than either of the simpler theories with what we really think, viz. that normally promise-keeping, for example, should come before benevolence, but that when and only when the good to be produced by the benevolent act is very great and the promise comparatively trivial, the act of benevolence becomes our duty.

In fact the theory of 'ideal utilitarianism,' if I may for brevity refer so to the theory of Professor Moore, seems to simplify unduly our relations to our fellows. It says, in effect, that the only morally significant relation in which my neighbours stand to me is that of being possible beneficiaries by my action.[2] They do stand in this relation to me, and this relation is morally significant. But they may also stand to me in the relation of promisee to promiser, of creditor to debtor, of wife to husband, of child to parent, of friend to friend, of fellow countryman to fellow countryman, and the like; and each of these relations is the foundation of a *prima facie* duty, which is more or less incumbent on me according to the circumstances of the case. When I am in a situation, as perhaps I always am, in which more than one of these *prima facie* duties is incumbent on me, what I have to do is to study the situation as fully as I can until I form the considered opinion (it is never more) that in the circumstances one of them is more incumbent than any other; then I am bound to think that to do this *prima facie* duty is my duty *sans phrase* in the situation.

I suggest '*prima facie* duty' or 'conditional duty' as a brief way of referring to the characteristic (quite distinct from that of being a duty proper) which an act has, in virtue of being of a certain kind (e.g. the keeping of a promise), of being an act which would be a duty proper if it were not at the same time of another kind which is morally significant. Whether an act is a duty proper or actual duty depends on *all* the morally significant kinds it is an instance of. The phrase '*prima facie* duty' must be apologized for, since (1) it suggests that what we are speaking of is a certain kind of duty, whereas it is in fact not a duty, but something related in a special way to duty. Strictly speaking, we want not a phrase in which duty is qualified by an adjective, but a separate noun. (2) '*Prima*' facie suggests that one is speaking only of an appearance which a moral situation presents at first sight, and which may turn out to be illusory; whereas what I am speaking of is an objective fact involved in the nature of the situation, or more strictly in an element of its nature, though not, as duty proper does, arising from its *whole* nature. I can, however, think of no term which fully meets the case. 'Claim' has been suggested by Professor Prichard. The word 'claim' has the advantage of being quite a familiar one in this connexion, and it seems to cover much of the ground. It would be quite natural to say, 'a person to whom I have made a promise has a claim on me,' and also, 'a person whose distress I could relieve (at the cost of breaking the promise) has a claim on me.' But (1) while 'claim' is appropriate from *their* point of view, we want a word to express the corresponding fact from the agent's point of view—the fact of his being subject to claims that can be made against him; and ordinary language provides us with no such correlative to 'claim.' And (2) (what is more important) 'claim' seems inevitably to suggest two persons, one of whom might make a claim on the other; and while this covers the ground of social duty, it is inappropriate in the case of that important part of duty which is the duty of cultivating a certain kind of character in oneself. It would be artificial, I think,

and at any rate metaphorical, to say that one's character has a claim on oneself.

There is nothing arbitrary about these *prima facie* duties. Each rests on a definite circumstance which cannot seriously be held to be without moral significance. Of *prima facie* duties I suggest, without claiming completeness or finality for it, the following division.[3]

(1) Some duties rest on previous acts of my own. These duties seem to include two kinds, (*a*) those resting on a promise or what may fairly be called an implicit promise, such as the implicit undertaking not to tell lies which seems to be implied in the act of entering into conversation (at any rate by civilized men), or of writing books that purport to be history and not fiction. These may be called the duties of fidelity. (*b*) Those resting on a previous wrongful act. These may be called the duties of reparation. (2) Some rest on previous acts of other men, i.e. services done by them to me. These may be loosely described as the duties of gratitude. (3) Some rest on the fact or possibility of a distribution of pleasure or happiness (or of the means thereto) which is not in accordance with the merit of the persons concerned; in such cases there arises a duty to upset or prevent such a distribution. These are the duties of justice. (4) Some rest on the mere fact that there are other beings in the world whose condition we can make better in respect of virtue, or of intelligence, or of pleasure. These are the duties of beneficence. (5) Some rest on the fact that we can improve our own condition in respect of virtue or of intelligence. These are the duties of self-improvement. (6) I think that we should distinguish from (4) the duties that may be summed up under the title of 'not injuring others.' No doubt to injure others is incidentally to fail to do them good; but it seems to me clear that non-maleficence is apprehended as a duty distinct from that of beneficence, and as a duty of a more stringent character. It will be noticed that this alone among the types of duty has been stated in a negative way. An attempt might no doubt be made to state this duty, like the others, in a positive way. It might be said that it is really the duty to prevent ourselves from acting either from an inclination to harm others or from an inclination to seek our own pleasure, in doing which we should incidentally harm them. But on reflection it seems clear that the primary duty here is the duty not to harm others, this being a duty whether or not we

have an inclination that if followed would lead to our harming them; and that when we have such an inclination the primary duty not to harm others gives rise to a consequential duty to resist the inclination. The recognition of this duty of non-maleficence is the first step on the way to the recognition of the duty of beneficence; and that accounts for the prominence of the commands 'thou shalt not kill,' 'thou shalt not commit adultery,' 'thou shalt not steal,' 'thou shalt not bear false witness,' in so early a code as the Decalogue. But even when we have come to recognize the duty of beneficence, it appears to me that the duty of non-maleficence is recognized as a distinct one, and as *prima facie* more binding. We should not in general consider it justifiable to kill one person in order to keep another alive, or to steal from one in order to give alms to another.

The essential defect of the 'ideal utilitarian' theory is that it ignores, or at least does not do full justice to, the highly personal character of duty. If the only duty is to produce the maximum of good, the question who is to have the good — whether it is myself, or my benefactor, or a person to whom I have made a promise to confer that good on him, or a mere fellow man to whom I stand in no such special relation — should make no difference to my having a duty to produce that good. But we are all in fact sure that it makes a vast difference.

One or two other comments must be made on this provisional list of the divisions of duty. (1) The nomenclature is not strictly correct. For by 'fidelity' or 'gratitude' we mean, strictly, certain states of motivation; and, as I have urged, it is not our duty to have certain motives, but to do certain acts. By 'fidelity,' for instance, is meant, strictly, the disposition to fulfil promises and implicit promises *because we have made them.* We have no general word to cover the actual fulfilment of promises and implicit promises *irrespective of motive;* and I use 'fidelity,' loosely but perhaps conveniently, to fill this gap. So too I use 'gratitude' for the returning of services, irrespective of motive. The term 'justice' is not so much confined, in ordinary usage, to a certain state of motivation, for we should often talk of a man as acting justly even when we did not think his motive was the wish to do what was just simply for the sake of doing so. Less apology is therefore needed for our use of 'justice' in this sense. And I have used the word 'beneficence' rather than 'benevolence,' in order to emphasize the fact that it is our duty to do

certain things, and not to do them from certain motives.

(2) If the objection be made, that this catalogue of the main types of duty is an unsystematic one resting on no logical principle, it may be replied, first, that it makes no claim to being ultimate. It is a *prima facie* classification of the duties which reflection on our moral convictions seems actually to reveal. And if these convictions are, as I would claim that they are, of the nature of knowledge, and if I have not misstated them, the list will be a list of authentic conditional duties, correct as far as it goes though not necessarily complete. The list of *goods* put forward by the rival theory is reached by exactly the same method — the only sound one in the circumstances — viz. that of direct reflection on what we really think. Loyalty to the facts is worth more than a symmetrical architectonic or a hastily reached simplicity. If further reflection discovers a perfect logical basis for this or for a better classification, so much the better.

(3) It may, again, be objected that our theory that there are these various and often conflicting types of *prima facie* duty leaves us with no principle upon which to discern what is our actual duty in particular circumstances. But this objection is not one which the rival theory is in a position to bring forward. For when we have to choose between the production of two heterogeneous goods, say knowledge and pleasure, the 'ideal utilitarian' theory can only fall back on an opinion, for which no logical basis can be offered, that one of the goods is the greater; and this is no better than a similar opinion that one of two duties is the more urgent. And again, when we consider the infinite variety of the effects of our actions in a way of pleasure, it must surely be admitted that the claim which *hedonism* sometimes makes, that it offers a readily applicable criterion of right conduct, is quite illusory.

I am unwilling, however, to content myself with an *argumentum ad hominem,* and I would contend that in principle there is no reason to anticipate that every act that is our duty is so for one and the same reason. Why should two sets of circumstances, or one set of circumstances, *not* possess different characteristics, any one of which makes a certain act our *prima facie* duty? When I ask what it is that makes me in certain cases sure that I have a *prima facie* duty to do so and so, I find that it lies in the fact that I have made a promise; when I ask the same question in another case, I find the answer lies in the fact that I have done a wrong. And if on reflection I find (as I think I do) that neither of these reasons is reducible to the other, I must not on any *a priori* ground assume that such a reduction is possible.

It is necessary to say something by way of clearing up the relation between *prima facie* duties and the actual or absolute duty to do one particular act in particular circumstances. If, as almost all moralists except Kant are agreed, and as most plain men think, it is sometimes right to tell a lie or to break a promise, it must be maintained that there is a difference between *prima facie* duty and actual or absolute duty. When we think ourselves justified in breaking, and indeed morally obliged to break, a promise in order to relieve some one's distress, we do not for a moment cease to recognize a *prima facie* duty to keep our promise, and this leads us to feel, not indeed shame or repentance, but certainly compunction, for behaving as we do; we recognize, further, that it is our duty to make up somehow to the promisee for the breaking of the promise. We have to distinguish from the characteristic of being our duty that of tending to be our duty. Any act that we do contains various elements in virtue of which it falls under various categories. In virtue of being the breaking of a promise, for instance, it tends to be wrong; in virtue of being an instance of relieving distress it tends to be right. Tendency to be one's duty may be called a parti-resultant attribute, i.e. one which belongs to an act in virtue of some one component in its nature. *Being* one's duty is a toti-resultant attribute, one which belongs to an act in virtue of its whole nature and of nothing less than this.

Something should be said of the relation between our apprehension of the *prima facie* rightness of certain types of acts and our mental attitude towards particular acts. It is proper to use the word 'apprehension' in the former case and not in the latter. That an act, *qua* fulfilling a promise, or *qua* effecting a just distribution of good, or *qua* returning services rendered, or *qua* promoting the good of others, or *qua* promoting the virtue or insight of the agent, is *prima facie* right, is self-evident; not in the sense that it is evident from the beginning of our lives, or as soon as we attend to the proposition for the first time, but in the sense that when we have reached sufficient mental maturity and have given

sufficient attention to the proposition it is evident without any need of proof, or of evidence beyond itself. It is self-evident just as a mathematical axiom, or the validity of a form of inference, is evident. The moral order expressed in these propositions is just as much part of the fundamental nature of the universe (and, we may add, of any possible universe in which there were moral agents at all) as is the spatial or numerical structure expressed in the axioms of geometry or arithmetic. In our confidence that these propositions are true there is involved the same trust in our reason that is involved in our confidence in mathematics; and we should have no justification for trusting it in the latter sphere and distrusting it in the former. In both cases we are dealing with propositions that cannot be proved, but that just as certainly need no proof.

Supposing it to be agreed, as I think on reflection it must, that no one *means* by 'right' just 'productive of the best possible consequences,' or 'optimific,' the attributes 'right' and 'optimific' might stand in either of two kinds of relation to each other. (1) They might be so related that we could apprehend *a priori*, either immediately or deductively, that any act that is optimific is right and any act that is right is optimific, as we can apprehend that any triangle that is equilateral is equiangular and *vice versa*. Professor Moore's view is, I think, that the coextensiveness of 'right' and 'optimific' is apprehended immediately.[4] He rejects the possibility of any proof of it. Or (2) the two attributes might be such that the question whether they are invariably connected had to be answered by means of an inductive inquiry. Now at first sight it might seem as if the constant connexion of the two attributes could be immediately apprehended. It might seem absurd to suggest that it could be right for any one to do an act which would produce consequences less good than those which would be produced by some other act in his power. Yet a little thought will convince us that this is not absurd. The type of case in which it is easiest to see that this is so is, perhaps, that in which one has made a promise. In such a case we all think that *prima facie* it is our duty to fulfil the promise irrespective of the precise goodness of the total consequences. And though we do not think it is necessarily our actual or absolute duty to do so, we are far from thinking that any, even the slightest, gain in the value of the total consequences will necessarily justify us in doing something else instead. Suppose, to simplify the case by abstraction, that the fulfilment of a promise to A would produce 1,000 units of good[5] for him, but that by doing some other act I could produce 1,001 units of good for B, to whom I have made no promise, the other consequences of the two acts being of equal value; should we really think it self-evident that it was our duty to do the second act and not the first? I think not. We should, I fancy, hold that only a much greater disparity of value between the total consequences would justify us in failing to discharge our *prima facie* duty to A. After all, a promise is a promise, and is not to be treated so lightly as the theory we are examining would imply. What, exactly, a promise is, is not so easy to determine, but we are surely agreed that it constitutes a serious moral limitation to our freedom of action. To produce the 1,001 units of good for B rather than fulfil our promise to A would be to take, not perhaps our duty as philanthropists too seriously, but certainly our duty as makers of promises too lightly.

Or consider another phase of the same problem. If I have promised to confer on A a particular benefit containing 1,000 units of good, is it self-evident that if by doing some different act I could produce 1,001 units of good for A himself (the other consequences of the two acts being supposed equal in value), it would be right for me to do so? Again, I think not. Apart from my general *prima facie* duty to do A what goal I can, I have another *prima facie* duty to do him the particular service I have promised to do him, and this is not to be set aside in consequence of a disparity of good of the order of 1,001 to 1,000, though a much greater disparity might justify me in so doing.

Or again, suppose that A is a very good and B a very bad man, should I then, even when I have made no promise, think it self-evidently right to produce 1,001 units of good for B rather than 1,000 for A? Surely not. I should be sensible of a *prima facie* duty of justice, i.e. of producing a distribution of goods in proportion to merit, which is not outweighed by such a slight disparity in the total goods to be produced.

Such instances — and they might easily be added to — make it clear that there is no self-evident connexion between the attributes 'right' and 'optimific'. The theory we are examining has a certain attractiveness when applied to our decision that a particular act is our duty (though I have tried to show that it does not agree with our actual moral judgments even here). But it is not even plausible when applied to our recognition of *prima facie* duty. For if it were self-evident that the right coincides with the optimific, it should be self-evident that what is *prima facie* right is *prima facie* optimific. But whereas we are certain that keeping a promise is *prima facie* right, we are not certain that it is *prima facie* optimific (though we are perhaps certain that it is *prima facie* bonific). Our certainty that it is *prima facie* right depends not on its consequences but on its being the fulfilment of a promise. The theory we are examining involves too much difference between the evident ground of our conviction about *prima facie* duty and the alleged ground of our conviction about actual duty.

The coextensiveness of the right and the optimific is, then, not self-evident. And I can see no way of proving it deductively; nor, so far as I know, has any one tried to do so. There remains the question whether it can be established inductively. Such an inquiry, to be conclusive, would have to be very thorough and extensive. We should have to take a large variety of the acts which we, to the best of our ability, judge to be right. We should have to trace as far as possible their consequences, not only for the persons directly affected but also for those indirectly affected, and to these no limit can be set. To make our inquiry thoroughly conclusive, we should have to do what we cannot do, viz. trace these consequences into an unending future. And even to make it reasonably conclusive, we should have to trace them far into the future. It is clear that the most we could possibly say is that a large variety of typical acts that are judged right appear, so far as we can trace their consequences, to produce more good than any other acts possible to the agents in the circumstances. And such a result falls far short of proving the constant connexion of the two attributes. But it is surely clear that no inductive inquiry justifying even this result has ever been carried through. The advocates of utilitarian systems have been so much persuaded either of the identity or of the self-evident connexion of the attributes 'right' and 'optimific' (or 'felicific') that they have not attempted even such an inductive inquiry as is possible. And in view of the enormous complexity of the task and the inevitable inconclusiveness of the result, it is worth no one's while to make the attempt. What, after all, would be gained by it? If, as I have tried to show, for an act to be right and to be optimific are not the same thing, and an act's being optimific is not even the ground of its being right, then if we could ask ourselves (though the question is really unmeaning) which we ought to do, right acts because they are right or optimific acts because they are optimific, our answer must be 'the former.' If they are optimific as well as right, that is interesting but not morally important; if not, we still ought to do them (which is only another way of saying that they *are* the right acts), and the question whether they are optimific has no importance for moral theory.

There is one direction in which a fairly serious attempt has been made to show the connexion of the attributes 'right' and 'optimific.' One of the most evident facts of our moral consciousness is the sense which we have of the sanctity of promises, a sense which does not, on the face of it, involve the thought that one will be bringing more good into existence by fulfilling the promise than by breaking it. It is plain, I think, that in our normal thought we consider that the fact that we have made a promise is in itself sufficient to create a duty of keeping it, the sense of duty resting on remembrance of the past promise and not on thoughts of the future consequences of its fulfilment. Utilitarianism tries to show that this is not so, that the sanctity of promises rests on the good consequences of the fulfilment of them and the bad consequences of their nonfulfilment. It does so in this way: it points out that when you break a promise you not only fail to confer a certain advantage on your promisee but you diminish his confidence, and indirectly the confidence of others, in the fulfilment of promises. You thus strike a blow at one of the devices that have been found most useful in the relations between man and man — the device on which, for example, the whole system of commercial credit rests — and you tend to bring about a state of things wherein each man, being entirely unable to rely on the keeping of promises by others, will have to do everything for himself, to the enormous impoverishment of human well-being.

To put the matter otherwise, utilitarians say that when a promise ought to be kept it is because the total good to be produced by keeping it is greater than the total good to be produced by breaking it, the former including as its main element the maintenance and strengthening of general mutual confidence, and the latter being greatly diminished by a weakening of this confidence. They say, in fact, that the case I put some pages back never arises — the case in which by fulfilling a promise I shall bring into being 1,000 units of good for my promisee, and by breaking it 1,001 units of good for some one else, the other effects of the two acts being of equal value. The other effects, they say, never are of equal value. By keeping my promise I am helping to strengthen the system of mutual confidence; by breaking it I am helping to weaken this; so that really the first act produces $1,000 + x$ units of good, and the second $1,001 - y$ units, and the difference between $+x$ and $-y$ is enough to outweigh the slight superiority in the *immediate* effects of the second act. In answer to this it may be pointed out that there must be *some* amount of good that exceeds the difference between $+x$ and $-y$ (i.e. exceeds $x + y$); say, $x + y + z$. Let us suppose the *immediate* good effects of the second act to be assessed not at 1,001 but at $1,000 + x + y + z$. Then its *net* good effects are $1,000 + x + z$, i.e. greater than those of the fulfilment of the promise; and the utilitarian is bound to say forthwith that the promise should be broken. Now, we may ask whether that is really the way we think about promises? Do we really think that the production of the slightest balance of good, no matter who will enjoy it, by the breach of a promise frees us from the obligation to keep our promise? We need not doubt that a system by which promises are made and kept is one that has great advantages for the general well-being. But that is not the whole truth. To make a promise is not merely to adapt an ingenious device for promoting the general well-being; it is to put oneself in a new relation to one person in particular, a relation which creates a specifically new *prima facie* duty to him, not reducible to the duty of promoting the general well-being of society. By all means let us try to foresee the net good effects of keeping one's promise and the net good effects of breaking it, but even if we assess the first at $1,000 + x$ and the second at $1,000 + x + z$, the question still remains whether it is not our duty to fulfil the promise. It may be suspected, too, that the effect of a single keeping or breaking of a promise in strengthening or weakening the fabric of mutual confidence is greatly exaggerated by the theory we are examining. And if we suppose two men dying together alone, do we think that the duty of one to fulfil before he dies a promise he has made to the other would be extinguished by the fact that neither act would have any effect on the general confidence? Any one who holds this may be suspected of not having reflected on what a promise is.

I conclude that the attributes 'right' and 'optimific' are not identical, and that we do not know either by intuition, by deduction, or by induction that they coincide in their application, still less that the latter is the foundation of the former. It must be added, however, that if we are ever under no special obligation such as that of fidelity to a promisee or of gratitude to a benefactor, we ought to do what will produce most good; and that even when we are under a special obligation the tendency of acts to promote general good is one of the main factors in determining whether they are right.

In what has preceded, a good deal of use has been made of 'what we really think' about moral questions; a certain theory has been rejected because it does not agree with what we really think. It might be said that this is in principle wrong; that we should not be content to expound what our present moral consciousness tells us but should aim at a criticism of our existing moral consciousness in the light of theory. Now I do not doubt that the moral consciousness of men has in detail undergone a good deal of modification as regards the things we think right, at the hands of moral theory. But if we are told, for instance, that we should give up our view that there is a special obligatoriness attaching to the keeping of promises because it is self-evident that the only duty is to produce as much good as possible, we have to ask ourselves whether we really, when we reflect, *are* convinced that this is self-evident, and whether we really *can* get rid of our view that promise-keeping has a bindingness independent of productiveness of maximum good. In my own experience I find that I cannot, in spite of a very genuine attempt to do so; and I venture to think that most people will find the same, and that just because they cannot lose the sense of special obligation, they cannot accept as self-evident, or even as true, the theory which would require them to do so. In fact it seems, on reflection, self-evident that a promise, simply as such, is something that *prima facie* ought to be kept, and it does *not,* on reflection, seem self-evident that production of maximum good is the only thing that makes an act obligatory. And to ask us to give up at the bidding of a theory

our actual apprehension of what is right and what is wrong seems like asking people to repudiate their actual experience of beauty, at the bidding of a theory which says 'only that which satisfies such and such conditions can be beautiful.' If what I have called our actual apprehension is (as I would maintain that it is) truly an apprehension, i.e. an instance of knowledge, the request is nothing less than absurd.

I would maintain, in fact, that what we are apt to describe as 'what we think' about moral questions contains a considerable amount that we do not think but know, and that this forms the standard by reference to which the truth of any moral theory has to be tested, instead of having itself to be tested by reference to any theory. I hope that I have in what precedes indicated what in my view these elements of knowledge are that are involved in our ordinary moral consciousness.

It would be a mistake to found a natural science on 'what we really think,' i.e. on what reasonably thoughtful and well-educated people think about the subjects of the science before they have studied them scientifically. For such opinions are interpretations, and often misinterpretations, of sense-experience; and the man of science must appeal from these to sense-experience itself, which furnishes his real data. In ethics no such appeal is possible. We have no more direct way of access to the facts about rightness and goodness and about what things are right or good, than by thinking about them; the moral convictions of thoughtful and well-educated people are the data of ethics just as sense-perceptions are the data of a natural science. Just as some of the latter have to be rejected as illusory, so have some of the former; but as the latter are rejected only when they are in conflict with other more accurate sense-perceptions, the former are rejected only when they are in conflict with other convictions which stand better the test of reflection. The existing body of moral convictions of the best people is the cumulative product of the moral reflection of many generations, which has developed an extremely delicate power of appreciation of moral distinctions; and this the theorist cannot afford to treat with anything other than the greatest respect. The verdicts of the moral consciousness of the best people are the foundation on which he must build; though he must first compare them with one another and eliminate any contradictions they may contain.

Endnotes

[1] These are not strictly speaking duties, but things that tend to be our duty, or *prima facie* duties. Cf. below.

[2] Some will think it, apart from other considerations, a sufficient refutation of this view to point out that I also stand in that relation to myself, so that for this view the distinction of oneself from others is morally insignificant.

[3] I should make it plain at this stage that I am *assuming* the correctness of some of our main convictions as to *prima facie* duties, or, more strictly, am claiming that we *know* them to be true. To me it seems as self-evident as anything could be, that to make a promise, for instance, is to create a moral claim on us in someone else. Many readers will perhaps say that they do *not* know this to be true. If so, I certainly cannot prove it to them; I can only ask them to reflect again, in the hope that they will ultimately agree that they also know it to be true. The main moral convictions of the plain man seem to me to be, not opinions which it is for philosophy to prove or disprove, but knowledge from the start; and in my own case I seem to find little difficulty in distinguishing these essential convictions from other moral convictions which I also have, which are merely fallible opinions based on an imperfect study of the working for good or evil of certain institutions or types of action.

[4] G. E. Moore, *Ethics*. Cambridge University Press, 1903, p. 181.

[5] I am assuming that good is objectively quantitative, but not that we can accurately assign an exact quantitative measure to it. Since it is of a definite amount, we can make the *supposition* that its amount is so-and-so, though we cannot with any confidence *assert* that it is.

VI.3 *Kantian Ethics*

FRED FELDMAN

Fred Feldman is professor of philosophy at the University of Massachusetts and the author of *Introductory Ethics,* from which this essay is taken. Feldman analyzes the central concepts and argument surrounding Kant's first formulation of the categorical imperative and offers an important critique of plausible interpretations of it.

Sometimes our moral thinking takes a decidedly nonutilitarian turn. That is, we often seem to appeal to a principle that is inconsistent with the whole utilitarian standpoint. One case in which this occurs clearly enough is the familiar tax-cheat case. A person decides to cheat on his income tax, rationalizing his misbehavior as follows: "The government will not be injured by the absence of my tax money. After all, compared with the enormous total they take in, my share is really a negligible sum. On the other hand, I will be happier if I have the use of the money. Hence, no one will be injured by my cheating, and one person will be better off. Thus, it is better for me to cheat than it is for me to pay."

In response to this sort of reasoning, we may be included to say something like this: "Perhaps you are right in thinking that you will be better off if you cheat. And perhaps you are right in thinking that the government won't even know the difference. Nevertheless, your act would be wrong. For if everyone were to cheat on his income taxes, the government would soon go broke. Surely you can see that you wouldn't want others to act in the way you propose to act. So you shouldn't act in that way." While it may not be clear that this sort of response would be decisive, it should be clear that this is an example of a sort of response that is often given.

There are several things to notice about this response. For one, it is not based on the view that the example of the tax cheat will provoke everyone else to cheat too. If that were the point of the response, then the response might be explained on the basis of

From *Introductory Ethics* (Prentice-Hall, 1978) © 1978, pp. 97–99, 101–117. Reprinted by permission of the author and Prentice-Hall, Inc., Englewood Cliffs, New Jersey.

utilitarian considerations. We could understand the responder to be saying that the tax cheater has miscalculated his utilities. Whereas he thinks his act of cheating has high utility, in fact it has low utility because it will eventually result in the collapse of the government. It is important to recognize that the response presented above is not based upon any such utilitarian considerations. This can be seen by reflecting on the fact that the point could just as easily have been made in this way: "Of course, very few other people will know about your cheating, and so your behavior will not constitute an example to others. Thus, it will not provoke others to cheat. Nevertheless, your act is wrong. For if everyone were to cheat as you propose to do, then the government would collapse. Since you wouldn't want others to behave in the way you propose to behave, you should not behave in that way. It would be wrong to cheat."

Another thing to notice about the response in this case is that the responder has not simply said, "What you propose to do would be cheating; hence, it is wrong." The principle in question is not simply the principle that cheating is wrong. Rather, the responder has appealed to a much more general principle, which seems to be something like this: If you wouldn't want everyone else to act in a certain way, then you shouldn't act in that way yourself.

This sort of general principle is in fact used quite widely in our moral reasoning. If someone proposes to remove the pollution-control devices from his automobile, his friends are sure to say "What if everyone did that?" They would have in mind some dire consequences for the quality of the air, but their point would not be that the removal of the pollution-control device by one person will in fact cause others to remove theirs, and will thus eventually lead to the destruction of the environment. Their point, rather, is that if their friend would not want others to act in the way he proposes to act, then it would be wrong for him to act in that way. This principle is also used against the person who refrains from giving to charity; the person who evades the draft in time of national emergency; the person who tells a lie in order to get out of a bad spot; and even the person who walks across a patch of newly seeded grass. In all such cases, we feel that the person acts wrongly not because his actions will have bad results, but because he wouldn't want others to behave in the way he behaves.

A highly refined version of this nonutilitarian principle is the heart of the moral theory of Immanuel Kant.[1] In his *Groundwork of the Metaphysic of Morals,*[2] Kant presents, develops, and defends the thesis that something like this principle is the "supreme principle of morality." Kant's presentation is rather complex; in parts, it is very hard to follow. Part of the trouble arises from his use of a rather unfamiliar technical vocabulary. Another source of trouble is that Kant is concerned with establishing a variety of other points in this little book, and some of these involve fairly complex issues in metaphysics and epistemology. Since our aim here is simply to present a clear, concise account of Kant's basic moral doctrine, we will have to ignore quite a bit of what he says in the book.

Kant formulates his main principle in a variety of different ways. All of the members of the following set of formulations seem to have a lot in common:

I ought never to act except in such a way that my maxim should become a universal law.[3]

Act only on that maxim through which you can at the same time will that it should become a universal law.[4]

Act as if the maxim of your action were to become through your will a universal law of nature.[5]

We must be able to will that a maxim of our action should become a universal law — this is the general canon for all moral judgment of action.[6]

Before we can evaluate this principle, which Kant calls the *categorical imperative,* we have to devote some attention to figuring out what it is supposed to mean. To do this, we must answer a variety of questions. What is a maxim? What is meant by "universal law"? What does Kant mean by "will"? Let us consider these questions in turn.

Maxims

In a footnote, Kant defines *maxim* as "a subjective principle of volition."[7] This definition is hardly helpful. Perhaps we can do better. First, however, a little background.

Kant apparently believes that when a person engages in genuine action, he always acts on some sort of general principle. The general principle will explain what the person takes himself to be doing and the circumstances in which he takes himself to be doing it. For example, if I need money, and can get some only by borrowing it, even though I know I won't be able to repay it, I might proceed to borrow some from a friend. My maxim in performing this act might be, "Whenever I need money and can get it by borrowing it, then I will borrow it, even if I know I won't be able to repay it."

Notice that this maxim is *general*. If I adopt it, I commit myself to behaving in the described way *whenever* I need money and the other conditions are satisfied. In this respect, the maxim serves to formulate a general principle of action rather than just some narrow reason applicable in just one case.[8] So a maxim must describe some general sort of situation, and then propose some form of action for the situation. To adopt a maxim is to commit yourself to acting in the described way whenever the situation in question arises.

It seems clear that Kant holds that every action has a maxim, although he does not explicitly state this view. When we speak of an action here, we mean a concrete, particular action, or *act-token*, rather than an *act-type*. Furthermore, we must distinguish between genuine actions and what we may call "mere bodily movements." It would be absurd to maintain that a man who scratches himself in his sleep is acting on the maxim "When I itch, I shall scratch." His scratching is a mere bodily movement, and has no maxim. A man who deliberately sets out to borrow some money from a friend, on the other hand, does perform an action. And according to our interpretation of Kant, his action must have a maxim.

It would be implausible to maintain that before we act, we always consciously formulate the maxim of our action. Most of the time we simply go ahead and perform the action without giving any conscious thought to what we're doing, or what our situation is. We're usually too intent on getting the job done. Nevertheless, if we are asked after the fact, we often recognize that we actually were acting on a general policy, or maxim. For example, if you are taking a test, and you set about to answer each question correctly, you probably won't give any conscious thought to your maxim. You will be too busy thinking about the test. But if someone were to ask you to explain what you are doing and to explain the policy upon which you are doing it, you might then realize that in fact you have been acting a maxim. Your maxim my be, "Whenever I am taking an academic test, and I believe I know the correct answers, I shall give what I take to be the correct answers." So a person may act on a maxim even though she hasn't consciously entertained it.

In one respect, the maxim of an action may be inaccurate: it does not so much represent the actual situation of the action as it does the situation the agent takes himself to be in. Suppose, for example, that I have a lot of money in my savings account but I have forgotten all abut it. I take myself to be broke. When I go out to borrow some money from a friend, my maxim might be, "When I am broke and can get money in no other way, I shall borrow some from a friend." In this case, my maxim does not apply to my actual situation. For my actual situation is not one in which I am broke. Yet the maxim does apply to the situation I take myself to be in. For I believe that I am broke, and I believe that I can get money in no other way. So it is important to recognize that a maxim is a general policy statement that describes the sort of situation the agent takes himself to be in when he performs an action, and the sort of action he takes himself to be performing. In fact, both the situation and the action may be different from what the agent takes them to be.

Another point about maxims that should be recognized is this. Externally similar actions may in fact have radically different maxims. Here is an elaborated version of an example given by Kant that illustrates this point.[9] Suppose there are two grocers, Mr. Grimbley and Mr. Hughes. Mr. Grimbley's main goal in life is to get rich. After careful consideration, he has decided that in the long run he'll make more money if he gains a reputation for treating his customers fairly. In other words, he believes that "honesty is the best policy—because it pays." Hence, Mr. Grimbley scrupulously sees to it that every customer gets the correct change. When Mr. Grimbley gives correct change to a customer, he acts on this maxim:

M_1: When I can gain a good business reputation by giving correct change, I shall give correct change.

Mr. Hughes, on the other hand, has decided that it would be morally wrong to cheat his customers. This decision has moved him to adopt the policy of always giving the correct change. He doesn't care whether his honest dealings will in the long run contribute to an increase in sales. Even if he were to discover that honesty in business dealings does *not* pay, he would still treat his customers honestly. So Mr. Hughes apparently acts on some maxim such as this:

M_2: When I can perform a morally right act by giving correct change, I shall give correct change.

Mr. Grimbley's overt act of giving correct change to a customer looks just like Mr. Hughes's overt act of giving correct change to a customer. Their customers cannot tell, no matter how closely they observe the behavior of Mr. Grimbley and Mr. Hughes, what their maxims are. However, as we have seen, the actions of Mr. Grimbley are associated with a maxim radically different from that associated with the actions of Mr. Hughes.

For our purposes, it will be useful to introduce a concept that Kant does not employ. This is the concept of the *generalized form* of a maxim. Suppose I decide to go to sleep one night and my maxim in performing this act is this:

M_3: Whenever I am tired, I shall sleep.

My maxim is stated in such a way as to contain explicit references to me. It contains two occurrences of the word "I." The generalized form of my maxim is the principle we would get if we were to revise my maxim so as to make it applicable to everyone. Thus, the generalized form of my maxim is this:

GM_3: Whenever anyone is tired, he will sleep.

In general, then, we can represent the form of a maxim in this way:

M: Whenever I am _____, I shall _____.

Actual maxims have descriptions of situations in the first blank and descriptions of actions in the second blank. The generalized form of a maxim can be represented in this way:

GM: Whenever anyone is _____, she will _____.

So much, then, for maxims. Let us turn to our second question, "What is meant by universal law?"

Universal Law

When, in the formulation of the categorical imperative, Kant speaks of "universal law," he seems to have one or the other of two things in mind. Sometimes he seems to be thinking of a *universal law of nature,* and sometimes he seems to be thinking of a *universal law of freedom.*

A *law of nature* is a fully general statement that describes not only how things are, but how things always *must* be. Consider this example: If the temperature of a gas in an enclosed container is increased, then the pressure will increase too. This statement accurately describes the behavior of gases in enclosed containers. Beyond this, however, it describes behavior that is, in a certain sense, necessary. The pressure not only *does* increase, but it *must* increase if the volume remains the same and the temperature is increased. This "must" expresses not logical or moral necessity, but "physical necessity." Thus, a law of nature is a fully general statement that expresses a physical necessity.

A *universal law of freedom* is a universal principle describing how all people ought to act in a certain circumstance. It does not have to be a legal enactment—it needn't be passed by Congress or signed by the president. Furthermore, some universal laws of freedom are not always followed—although they should be. If in fact it is true that all promises ought to be kept, then this principle is a universal law of freedom: If anyone has made a promise, he keeps it. The "must" in a statement such as "If you have made a promise, then you must keep it" does not express logical or physical necessity. It may be said to express moral necessity. Using this concept of moral necessity, we can say that a universal law of freedom is a fully general statement that expresses a moral necessity.

Sometimes Kant's categorical imperative is stated in terms of universal laws of nature, and sometimes in terms of universal laws of freedom. We will consider the "law of nature" version, since Kant appeals to it in discussing some fairly important examples.

Willing

To will that something be the case is more than to merely wish for it to be the case. A person might wish that there would be peace everywhere in the world. Yet knowing that it is not within his power to bring about this wished-for state of affairs, he might refrain from willing that there be peace everywhere in the world. It is not easy to say just what a person does when he wills that something be the case. According to one view, willing that something be the case is something like commanding yourself to make it be the case. So if I will my arm to go up, that would be something like commanding myself to raise my arm. The Kantian concept of willing is a bit more complicated, however. According to Kant, it makes sense to speak of willing something to happen, even if that something is not an action. For example, we can speak of someone willing that everyone keep their promises.

Some states of affairs are impossible. They simply cannot occur. For example, consider the state of affairs of your jumping up and down while remaining perfectly motionless. It simply cannot be done. Yet a sufficiently foolish or irrational person might will that such a state of affairs occur. That would be as absurd as commanding someone else to jump up and down while remaining motionless. Kant would say of a person who has willed in this way that his will has "contradicted itself." We can also put the point by saying that the person has willed inconsistently.

Inconsistency in willing can arise in another, somewhat less obvious way. Suppose a person has already willed that he remain motionless. He does not change this volition, but persists in willing that he remain motionless. At the same time, however, he begins to will that he jump up and down. Although each volition is self-consistent, it is inconsistent to will both of them at the same time. This is a second way in which inconsistency in willing can arise.

It may be the case that there are certain things that everyone must always will. For example, we may have to will that we avoid intense pain. Anyone who wills something that is inconsistent with something everyone must will, thereby wills inconsistently.

Some of Kant's examples suggest that he held that inconsistency in willing can arise in a third way.

This form of inconsistency is a bit more complex to describe. Suppose a person wills to be in Boston on Monday and also wills to be in San Francisco on Tuesday. Suppose, furthermore, that because of certain foul-ups at the airport it will be impossible for her to get from Boston to San Francisco on Tuesday. In this case, Kant would perhaps say that the person has willed inconsistently.

In general, we can say that a person wills inconsistently if he wills that p be the case and he wills that q be the case and it is impossible for p and q to be the case together.

The Categorical Imperative

With all this as background, we may be in a position to interpret the first version of Kant's categorical imperative. Our interpretation is this:

CI_1: An act is morally right if and only if the agent of the act can consistently will that the generalized form of the maxim of the act be a law of nature.

We can simplify our formulation slightly by introducing a widely used technical term. We can say that a maxim is *universalizable* if and only if the agent who acts upon it can consistently will that its generalized form be a law of nature. Making use of this new term, we can restate our first version of the categorical imperative as follows:

CI_1': An act is morally right if and only if its maxim is universalizable.

As formulated here, the categorical imperative is a statement of necessary and sufficient conditions for the moral rightness of actions. Some commentators have claimed that Kant did not intend his principle to be understood in this way. They have suggested that Kant meant it to be understood merely as a necessary but not sufficient condition for morally right action. Thus, they would prefer to formulate the imperative in some way such as this:

CI_1'': An act is morally right only if its maxim is universalizable.

Understood in this way, the categorical imperative points out one thing to avoid in action. That is, it tells us to avoid actions whose maxims cannot be universalized. But it does not tell us the distinguishing feature of the actions we should perform. Thus, it does not provide us with a criterion of morally right action. Since Kant explicitly affirms that his principle is "the supreme principle of morality," it is reasonable to suppose that he intended it to be taken as a statement of necessary and sufficient conditions for morally right action. In any case, we will take the first version of the categorical imperative to be CI_1, rather than CI_1''.

It is interesting to note that other commentators have claimed that the categorical imperative isn't a criterion of right action at all. They have claimed that it was intended to be understood as a criterion of correctness for *maxims*.[10] These commentators might formulate the principle in this way:

CI_1''': A maxim is normally acceptable if and only if it is universalizable.

This interpretation is open to a variety of objections. In the first place, it is not supported by the text. Kant repeatedly states that the categorical imperative is the basic principle by which we are to evaluate actions.[11] Furthermore, when he presents his formulations of the categorical imperative, he generally states it as a principle about the moral rightness of action. Finally, it is somewhat hard to see why we should be interested in a principle such as CI_1'''. For it does not constitute a theory about right action, or good persons, or anything else that has traditionally been a subject of moral enquiry. CI_1, on the other hand, competes directly with act utilitarianism, rule utilitarianism, and other classical moral theories.

In order to gain a better insight into the workings of the categorical imperative, it may be worthwhile to compare it with a doctrine with which it is sometimes confused — the golden rule. The golden rule has been formulated in a wide variety of ways.[12] Generally, however, it looks something like this:

GR: An act is morally right if and only if, in performing it, the agent refrains from treating others in ways in which he would not want the others to treat him.

According to GR, then, if you wouldn't want others to lie to you, it is wrong to lie to them. If you would want others to treat you with respect, then it is right to treat others with respect.

Kant explicitly rejects the view that his categorical imperative is equivalent to the golden rule.[13] He points out a number of respects in which the two doctrines differ. For one, GR is not applicable to cases in which only one person is involved. Consider suicide. When a person commits suicide, he does not "treat others" in any way; he only "treats himself." Hence, when a person commits suicide, he does not treat others in ways in which he would not want the others to treat him. Therefore, under GR, anyone who commits suicide performs a morally right act. CI_1, on the other hand, may not yield this result. For if a person commits suicide, he does so on a maxim, whether other people are involved or not. Either his maxim is universalizable, or it is not. If it is not, CI_1 entails that his action is not right. If it is, CI_1 entails that his action is right. In this respect, CI_1 is clearly distinct from GR.

Kant also hints at another aspect in which the two doctrines differ. Suppose a person considers herself to be utterly self-sufficient. She feels that she has no need of aid from others. GR then has nothing to say against her refraining from extending any kindness to others. After all, she has no objection to being treated in this unkind way by them. So GR entails that her behavior is morally right. CI_1, on the other hand, has no such consequence. Whether this person is willing to be mistreated by others or not, it may still be irrational of her to will that it be a law of nature that no one help anyone else. If so, CI_1 rules out uncharitableness, whether the agent likes it or not.

Similar considerations apply to masochists, whose behavior is not adequately guided by GR. After all, we surely don't want to allow the masochist to torture others simply on the grounds that he wouldn't object to being tortured by them! The unusual desires of masochists do not pose any special threat to CI_1.

So the main difference between GR and CI_1 seems to be this: According to GR, what makes an act right is the fact that the agent would not object to "having it done to himself." This opens the door to incorrect results in cases in which the agent, for some unexpected reason, would not object to being mistreated. According to CI₁, what makes an act right is the fact that the agent's maxim in performing it can be universalized. Thus, even if he would not object to being mistreated by others, his mistreatment of them may be wrong simply because it would be *irrational* to will that everyone should mistreat others in the same way.

Kant's Four Examples

In a very famous passage in Chapter II of the *Groundwork,* Kant presents four illustrations of the application of the categorical imperative.[14] In each case, in Kant's opinion, the act is morally wrong and the maxim is not universalizable. Thus, Kant holds that his theory implies that each of these acts is wrong. If Kant is right about this, then he has given us four positive instances of his theory. That is, he has given us four cases in which his theory yields correct results. Unfortunately, the illustrations are not entirely persuasive.

Kant distinguishes between "duties to self" and "duties to others." He also distinguishes between "perfect" and "imperfect" duties. This gives him four categories of duty: "perfect to self," "perfect to others," "imperfect to self," and "imperfect to others." Kant gives one example of each type of duty. By "perfect duty," Kant says he means a duty "which admits of no exception in the interests of inclination."[15] Kant seems to have in mind something like this: If a person has a perfect duty to perform a certain kind of action, then he must *always* do that kind of action when the opportunity arises. For example, Kant apparently holds that we must always perform the (negative) action of refraining from committing suicide. This would be a perfect duty. On the other hand, if a person has an imperfect duty to do a kind of action, then he must at least *sometimes* perform an action of that kind when the opportunity arises. For example, Kant maintains that we have an imperfect duty to help others in distress. We should devote at least some of our time to charitable activities, but we are under no obligation to give all of our time to such work.

The perfect/imperfect distinction has been drawn in a variety of ways—none of them entirely clear. Some commentators have said that if a person has a perfect duty to do a certain action, *a,* then there must be someone else who has a corresponding right to demand that *a* be done. This seems to be the case in Kant's second example, but not in his first example. Thus, it isn't clear that we should understand the concept of perfect duty in this way. Although the perfect/imperfect distinction is fairly interesting in itself, it does not play a major role in Kant's theory. Kant introduces the distinction primarily to ensure that his examples will illustrate different kinds of duty.

Kant's first example illustrates the application of CI₁ to a case of perfect duty to oneself—the alleged duty to refrain from committing suicide. Kant describes the miserable state of the person contemplating suicide, and tries to show that his categorical imperative entails that the person should not take his own life. In order to simplify our discussion, let us use the abbreviation "a₁" to refer to the act of suicide the man would commit, if he were to commit suicide. According to Kant, every act must have a maxim. Kant tells us the maxim of a₁: "From self-love I make it my principle to shorten my life if its continuance threatens more evil than it promises pleasure."[16] Let us simplify and clarify this maxim, understanding it as follows:

M(a₁): When continuing to live will bring me more pain than pleasure, I shall commit suicide out of self-love.

The generalized form of this maxim is as follows:

GM(a₁): Whenever continuing to live will bring anyone more pain than pleasure, he will commit suicide out of self-love.

Since Kant believes that suicide is wrong, he attempts to show that his moral principle, the categorical imperative, entails that a₁ is wrong. To do this, of course, he needs to show that the agent of a₁ cannot consistently will that GM(a₁) be a law of nature. Kant tries to show this in the following passage:

> . . . a system of nature by whose law the very same feeling whose function is to stimulate the furtherance of life should actually destroy

life would contradict itself and consequently could not subsist as a system of nature. Hence this maxim cannot possibly hold as a universal law of nature and is therefore entirely opposed to the supreme principle of all duty.[17]

The general outline of Kant's argument is clear enough:

Suicide Example

1. $GM(a_1)$ cannot be a law of nature.
2. If $GM(a_1)$ cannot be a law of nature, then the agent of a_1 cannot consistently will that $GM(a_1)$ be a law of nature.
3. a_1 is morally right if and only if the agent of a_1 can consistently will that $GM(a_1)$ be a law of nature.
4. Therefore, a_1 is not morally right.

In order to determine whether Kant really has shown that his theory entails that a_1 is not right, let us look at this argument more closely. First of all, for our purposes we can agree that the argument is valid. If all the premises are true, then the argument shows that the imagined act of suicide would not be right. CI_1, here being used as premise (3), would thus be shown to imply that a_1 is not right.

Since we are now interested primarily in seeing how Kant makes use of CI_1, we can withhold judgment on the merits of it for the time being.

The second premise seems fairly plausible. For although an irrational person could probably will almost anything, it surely would be difficult for a perfectly rational person to will that something be a law of nature if that thing could not be a law of nature. Let us grant, then, that it would not be possible for the agent to consistently will that $GM(a_1)$ be a law of nature if in fact $GM(a_1)$ could not be a law of nature.

The first premise is the most troublesome. Kant apparently assumes that "self-love" has as its function, the stimulation of the furtherance of life. Given this, he seems to reason that self-love cannot also contribute sometimes to the destruction of life. Perhaps Kant assumes that a given feeling cannot have two "opposite" functions. However, if $GM(a_1)$ were a law of nature, self-love would have to contribute toward self-destruction in some cases.

Hence, Kant seems to conclude, $GM(a_1)$ cannot be a law of nature. And so we have our first premise.

If this is Kant's reasoning, it is not very impressive. In the first place, it is not clear why we should suppose that self-love has the function of stimulating the furtherance of life. Indeed, it is not clear why we should suppose that self-love has any function at all! Second, it is hard to see why self-love can't serve two "opposite" functions. Perhaps self-love motivates us to stay alive when continued life would be pleasant, but motivates us to stop living when continued life would be unpleasant. Why should we hold this to be impossible?

So it appears that Kant's first illustration is not entirely successful. Before we turn to the second illustration, however, a few further comments may be in order. First, some philosophers would say that it is better that Kant's argument failed here. Many moralists would take the following position: Kant's view about suicide is wrong. The act of suicide out of self-love, a_1, is morally blameless. In certain circumstances suicide is each person's "own business." Thus, these moralists would say that if the categorical imperative did imply that a_1 is morally wrong, as Kant tries to show, then Kant's theory would be defective. But since Kant was not entirely successful in showing that his theory had this implication, the theory has not been shown to have any incorrect results.

A second point to notice about the suicide example is its scope. It is important to recognize that in this passage Kant has not attempted to show that suicide is always wrong. Perhaps Kant's personal view is that it is never right to commit suicide. However, in the passage in question he attempts to show only that a certain act of suicide, one based on a certain maxim, would be wrong. For all Kant has said here, other acts of suicide, done according to other maxims, might be permitted by the categorical imperative.

Let us turn now to the second illustration. Suppose I find myself hard pressed financially and I decide that the only way in which I can get some money is by borrowing it from a friend. I realize that I will have to promise to repay the money, even though I won't in fact be able to do so. For I foresee that my financial situation will be even worse later on than it is at present. If I perform this action, a_2, of borrowing money on a false promise, I will perform it on this maxim:

M(a$_2$): When I need money and can get some by borrowing it on a false promise, then I shall borrow the money and promise to repay, even though I know that I won't be able to repay.

The generalized form of my maxim is this:

GM(a$_2$): Whenever anyone needs money and can get some by borrowing it on a false promise, then he will borrow the money and promise to repay, even though he knows that he won't be able to repay.

Kant's view is that I cannot consistently will that GM(a$_2$) be a law of nature. This view emerges clearly in the following passage:

> . . . I can by no means will a universal law of lying; for by such a law there could properly be no promises at all, since it would be futile to profess will for future action to others who would not believe my profession or who, if they did so over-hastily, would pay me back in like coin; and consequently my maxim, as soon as it was made a universal law, would be bound to annul itself.[18]

It is important to be clear about what Kant is saying here. He is not arguing against lying on the grounds that if I lie, others will soon lose confidence in me and eventually won't believe my promises. Nor is he arguing against lying on the grounds that my lie will contribute to a general practice of lying, which in turn will lead to a breakdown of trust and the destruction of the practice of promising. These considerations are basically utilitarian. Kant's point is more subtle. He is saying that there is something covertly self-contradictory about the state of affairs in which, as a law of nature, everyone makes a false promise when in need of a loan. Perhaps Kant's point is this: Such a state of affairs is self-contradictory because, on the one hand, in such a state of affairs everyone in need would borrow money on a false promise, and yet, on the other hand, in that state of affairs no one could borrow money on a false promise — for if promises were always violated, who would be silly enough to loan any money?

Since the state of affairs in which everyone in need borrows money on a false promise is covertly self-contradictory, it is irrational to will it to occur. No one can consistently will that this state of affairs should occur. But for me to will that GM(a$_2$) be a law of nature is just for me to will that this impossi- ble state of affairs occur. Hence, I cannot consis- tently will that the generalized form of my maxim be a law of nature. According to CI$_1$, my act is not right unless I can consistently will that the gener- alized form of its maxim be a law of nature. Hence, according to CI$_1$, my act of borrowing the money on the false promise is not morally right.

We can restate the essentials of this argument much more succinctly:

Lying-Promise Example

1. GM(a$_2$) cannot be a law of nature.

2. If GM(a$_2$) cannot be a law of nature, then I cannot consistently will that GM(a$_2$) be a law of nature.

3. a$_2$ is morally right if and only if I can consis- tently will that GM(a$_2$) be a law of nature.

4. Therefore, a$_2$ is not morally right.

The first premise is based upon the view that it would somehow be self-contradictory for it to be a law of nature that everyone in need makes a lying promise. For in that (allegedly impossible) state of affairs there would be promises, since those in need would make them, and there would also not be promises, since no one would believe that anyone was really committing himself to future payment by the use of the words "I promise." So, as Kant says, the generalized form of the maxim "annuls itself." It cannot be a law of nature.

The second premise is just like the second premise in the previous example. It is based on the idea that it is somehow irrational to will that some- thing be the case if in fact it is impossible for it to be the case. So if it really is impossible for GM(a$_2$) to be a law of nature, then it would be irrational of me to will that it be so. Hence, I cannot consistently will that the generalized form of my maxim be a law of nature. In other words, I cannot consistently will that it be a law of nature that whenever anyone needs money and can get some on a false promise, then he will borrow some and promise to repay, even though he knows that he won't be able to repay.

The third premise of the argument is the cate- gorical imperative. If the rest of the argument is ac- ceptable, then the argument as a whole shows that the categorical imperative, together with these other facts, implies that my lying promise would not be morally right. This would seem to be a reasonable result.

Some readers have apparently taken this example to show that according to Kantianism, it is always wrong to make a false promise. Indeed, Kant himself may have come to this conclusion. Yet if we reflect on the argument for a moment, we will see that the view of these readers is surely not the case. At best, the argument shows only that one specific act of making a false promise would be wrong. That one act is judged to be wrong because its maxim allegedly cannot be universalized. Other acts of making false promises would have to be evaluated independently. Perhaps it will turn out that every act of making a false promise has a maxim that cannot be universalized. If so, CI_1 would imply that they are all wrong. So far, however, we have been given no reason to suppose that this is the case.

Other critics would insist that Kant hasn't even succeeded in showing that a_2 is morally wrong. They would claim that the first premise of the argument is false. Surely it could be a law of nature that everyone will make a false promise when in need of money, they would say. If people borrowed money on false promises rarely enough, and kept their word on other promises, then no contradiction would arise. There would then be no reason to support that "no one would believe he was being promised anything, but would laugh at utterances of this kind as empty shams."[19]

Let us turn, then, to the third example. Kant now illustrates the application of the categorical imperative to a case of imperfect duty to oneself. The action in question is the "neglect of natural talents." Kant apparently holds that it is wrong for a person to let all of his natural talents go to waste. Of course, if a person has several natural talents, he is not required to develop all of them. Perhaps Kant considers this to be an imperfect duty partly because a person has the freedom to select which talents he will develop and which he will allow to rust.

Kant imagines the case of someone who is comfortable as he is and who, out of laziness, contemplates performing the act, a_3, of letting all his talents rust. His maxim in doing this would be

$M(a_3)$: When I am comfortable as I am, I shall let my talents rust.

When generalized, the maxim becomes

$GM(a_3)$: Whenever anyone is comfortable as he is, he will let his talents rust.

Kant admits that $GM(a_3)$ could be a law of nature. Thus, his argument in this case differs from the arguments he produced in the first two cases. Kant proceeds to outline the reasoning by which the agent would come to see that it would be wrong to perform a_3:

> He then sees that a system of nature could indeed always subsist under such a universal law, although (like the South Sea Islanders) every man should let his talents rust and should be bent on devoting his life solely to idleness, indulgence, procreation, and, in a word, to enjoyment. Only he cannot possibly *will* that this should become a universal law of nature or should be implanted in us as such a law by a natural instinct. For as a rational being he necessarily wills that all his powers should be developed, since they serve him, and are given him, for all sorts of possible ends.[20]

Once again, Kant's argument seems to be based on a rather dubious appeal to natural purposes. Allegedly, nature implanted our talents in us for all sorts of purposes. Hence, we necessarily will to develop them. If we also will to let them rust, we are willing both to develop them (as we must) and to refrain from developing them. Anyone who wills both of these things obviously wills inconsistently. Hence, the agent cannot consistently will that his talents rust. This, together with the categorical imperative, implies that it would be wrong to perform the act, a_3, of letting one's talents rust.

The argument can be put as follows:

Rusting-Talents Example

1. Everyone necessarily wills that all his talents be developed.

2. If everyone necessarily wills that all his talents be developed, then the agent of a_3 cannot consistently will that $GM(a_3)$ be a law of nature.

3. a_3 is morally right if and only if the agent of a_3 can consistently will that $GM(a_3)$ be a law of nature.

4. Therefore a_3 is not morally right.

This argument seems even less persuasive than the others. In the quoted passage Kant himself presents a counterexample to the first premise. The South Sea Islanders, according to Kant, do not will to develop their talents. This fact, if it is one, is surely inconsistent with the claim that we all necessarily will that all our talents be developed. Even if Kant is wrong about the South Sea Islanders, his first premise is still extremely implausible. Couldn't there be a rational person who, out of idleness, simply does not will to develop his talents? If there could not be such a person, then what is the point of trying to show that we are under some specifically moral obligation to develop all our talents?

Once again, however, some philosophers may feel that Kant would have been worse off if his example had succeeded. These philosophers would hold that we in fact have no moral obligation to develop our talents. If Kant's theory had entailed that we have such an obligation, they would insist, then that would have shown that Kant's theory is defective.

In Kant's fourth illustration the categorical imperative is applied to an imperfect duty to others — the duty to help others who are in distress. Kant describes a man who is flourishing and who contemplates performing the act, a_4, of giving nothing to charity. His maxim is not stated by Kant in this passage, but it can probably be formulated as follows:

$M(a_4)$: When I'm flourishing and others are in distress, I shall give nothing to charity.

When generalized, this maxim becomes

$GM(a_4)$: Whenever anyone is flourishing and others are in distress, he will give nothing to charity.

As in the other example of imperfect duty, Kant acknowledges that $GM(a_4)$ could be a law of nature. Yet he claims once again that the agent cannot consistently will that it be a law of nature. He explains this by arguing as follows:

> For a will which decided in this way would be in conflict with itself, since many a situation might arise in which the man needed love and sympathy from others, and in which, by such a law of nature sprung from his own will, he would rob himself of all hope of the help he wants for himself.[21]

Kant's point here seems to be this: The day may come when the agent is no longer flourishing. He may need charity from others. If that day does come, then he will find that he wills that others give him such aid. However, in willing that $GM(a_4)$ be a law of nature, he has already willed that no one should give charitable aid to anyone. Hence, on that dark day, his will will contradict itself. Thus, he cannot consistently will that $GM(a_4)$ be a law of nature. This being so, the categorical imperative entails that a_4 is not right.

If this is Kant's reasoning, then his reasoning is defective. For we cannot infer from the fact that the person *may* someday want aid from others, that he in fact already is willing inconsistently when he wills today that no one should give aid to anyone. The main reason for this is that that dark day may not come, in which case no conflict will arise. Furthermore, as is pretty obvious upon reflection, even if that dark day does arrive, the agent may steadfastly stick to his general policy. He may say, "I didn't help others when they were in need, and now that I'm in need I don't want any help from them." In this way, he would avoid having inconsistent policies. Unless this attitude is irrational, which it does not seem to be, Kant's fourth example is unsuccessful.

More Examples

It should be clear, then, that Kant has not provided us with a clear, persuasive example of the application of the categorical imperative. In light of this, some may feel that the categorical imperative is a worthless doctrine. Such a harsh judgment would probably be premature. For in the first place, Kant surely would have been worse off if he had succeeded in showing that suicide, or letting your talents rust, are invariably wrong. The normative status of these acts is hardly as obvious as Kant suggests. In the second place, the failure of Kant's illustrations may be due in part to his choice of some rather strange maxims, and to the fact that he presupposed some questionable views about the purposes of nature. Let us attempt to develop a more plausible illustration of the application of the categorical imperative.

In attempting to develop such an example, we should turn to the sort of case in which the categorical imperative stands the greatest chance of working correctly. This would be a case in which an agent proposes to take unfair advantage of his neighbors. It would be a case in which others, out of regard for the common good, have generously refrained from performing a certain kind of act, even though many of them might like to do such an act. Our agent, however, finds that he can get away with the act. The crucial feature of this case is that the agent cannot consistently will that the others act in the way he proposes to act. For if they all were to try to act in this way, that would destroy his opportunity for so acting.

Here is a good example of this sort of case. Primarily out of laziness, Miss Perkins, a college student, buys a term paper for her ethics course and submits it as her own work. Miss Perkins deals with a skillful term paper manufacturer, so she is assured of getting a very high grade. There is no chance that she will be found out. Most of us would say that regardless of its utility, Miss Perkins's act is morally wrong. She should not deceive her instructor and take advantage of her fellow students in this way. What does the categorical imperative say?

Let us call Miss Perkins's act of submitting the phony term paper "a_5," and let us suppose that her maxim in performing a_5 is

M(a_5): When I need a term paper for a course and don't feel like writing one, I shall buy a term paper and submit it as my own work.

The generalized form of her maxim is

GM(a_5): Whenever anyone needs a term paper for a course and doesn't feel like writing one, she will buy one and submit it as her own work.

According to Kant's doctrine, a_5 is morally right only if Miss Perkins can consistently will that GM(a_5) be a law of nature. So to see if a_5 is right, we must determine whether Miss Perkins can consistently will that everyone needing a term paper but not feeling like writing one should submit a store-bought one.

It is reasonable to suppose that Miss Perkins cannot will that GM(a_5) be a law of nature. For consider what would happen if GM(a_5) were a law of nature, and everyone needing a term paper but not feeling like writing one were therefore to submit a store-bought one. Clearly, college instructors

would soon realize that they were reading work not produced by their students. The instructors would have to deal with the problem — perhaps by resorting to a system under which each student would be required to take a final oral exam instead of submitting a term paper. If some such alteration in the course requirements were instituted, Miss Perkins would lose her opportunity to get a good grade by cheating. Thus, she surely does not will that any such change in the system should occur. She prefers to have the system remain as it is. Since it is clear that some such change would occur if GM(a_5) were a law of nature, Miss Perkins cannot consistently will that GM(a_5) be a law of nature. Thus, according to CI_1, her act is not right.

The essentials of this example are simple. Miss Perkins wills that the system remain as it is — thus providing her with the opportunity to take advantage of her instructor and her fellow students. She recognizes that if everyone were to submit a store-bought term paper, the system would be changed. Hence, she cannot consistently will that everyone should submit a store-bought term paper. In other words, she cannot consistently will that GM(a_5) be a law of nature. CI_1, together with this fact, entails that a_5 is morally wrong.

One of the most troubling aspects of this example is that it is pretty easy to see how the categorical imperative can be short-circuited. That is, it is pretty easy to see how Miss Perkins can make Kant's doctrine yield the result that her act is morally right. She needs only to change her maxim in a fairly trivial way:

M(a_6): When I need a term paper for a course, and I don't feel like writing one, and no change in the system will occur if I submit a store-bought one, then I shall buy a term paper and submit it as my own work.

M(a_6) differs from M(a_5) in only one respect. M(a_6) contains the extra phrase "and no change in the system will occur if I submit a store-bought one." But this little addition makes a big difference to the argument. We found that Miss Perkins could not consistently will that GM(a_5) be a law of nature. For if she willed that GM(a_5) be a law of nature, she would, indirectly, will that the system be changed. But she already willed that the system remain as it is. However, no such argument applies to GM(a_6). For it appears that if GM(a_6) were a law of nature, the system would not be changed. Apparently, then, Miss Perkins can consistently will that $GM(a_6)$ be a law of nature. Hence, according to CI_1, her act of submitting a store-bought term paper, if performed under $M(a_6)$ rather than under $M(a_5)$, would be morally acceptable. This seems wrong.

The categorical imperative, interpreted as CI_1, yields incorrect results in another sort of case too. Consider a man who has a large amount of money in a savings account. He decides that he will wait until the stock market index reaches 1000 and then take all of his money out of the bank. This act seems quite acceptable from the moral point of view. However, it seems that CI_1 yields the odd result that the act is morally wrong. Let us consider why this is so.

We can call the man's act of removing his money from the bank "a_7." The maxim of a_7 is

$M(a_7)$: When the stock market index reaches 1000, I shall withdraw all my money from the bank.

The generalized form of $M(a_7)$ is

$GM(a_7)$: Whenever the stock market index reaches 1000, everyone shall withdraw all of their money from the bank.

It should be clear that the man cannot consistently will that $GM(a_7)$ be a law of nature. For banks have loaned out most of the money deposited in them. If everyone came to withdraw their savings from their bank, banks would soon run out of money. Not everyone can withdraw simultaneously. Hence, $GM(a_7)$ cannot be a law of nature. Thus, the agent cannot consistently will that it be so. CI_1 entails, together with this fact, that it would not be right for the man to withdraw his own money under this maxim. Surely, there is something wrong with a moral theory that has this result.

This same problem arises in any number of cases. Whenever, for some irrelevant reason, an otherwise innocent maxim cannot be universalized, CI_1 yields the result that the act is wrong. So if a person acts on the maxim, for example, of not becoming a doctor, he acts wrongly. For he surely could not will that *everyone* should refrain from becoming a doctor. As a rational being, he recognizes that there must be some doctors. Similarly, if a person acts on the maxim of always using adequate contraceptive de-

vices when engaging in sexual intercourse, she acts wrongly, according to this interpretation of CI_1. For if everyone were to do what she does, there would soon be no human race at all. This, Kant would think, is something no rational agent can consistently will.

These absurd results show that there is a very deep problem with CI_1. The problem, in general, is that there are many different reasons why a maxim may fail to be universalizable. Some of these reasons have nothing whatever to do with morality. Yet, as far as can be discerned from the text of the *Groundwork*, Kant nowhere attempts to distinguish between innocent-but-nonuniversalizable maxims, on the one hand, and evil-and-nonuniversalizable ones, on the other. Without such a distinction, CI_1 yields obviously incorrect results in innumerable cases.

So we can conclude that there are very serious problems with CI_1. Perhaps CI_1 is not an adequate interpretation of Kant's categorical imperative. Perhaps a more adequate version of that doctrine would not have these unsatisfactory results. However, if CI_1 is not Kant's theory, then it is very hard to see what Kant's theory might be.

Endnotes

1 Immanuel Kant (1724–1804) is one of the greatest Continental philosophers. He produced quite a few philosophical works of major importance. The *Critique of Pure Reason* (1781) is perhaps his most famous work.

2 Kant's *Grundlegung zur Metaphysik der Sitten* (1785) has been translated into English many times. All references here are to Immanuel Kant, *Groundwork of the Metaphysic of Morals*, translated and analysed by H. J. Paton (New York: Harper & Row, 1964).

3 Kant, *Groundwork*, p. 70.

4 *Ibid.*, p. 88.

5 *Ibid.*, p. 89.

6 *Ibid.*, p. 91.

7 *Ibid.*, p. 69n.

8 In some unusual cases, it may accidentally happen that the situation to which the maxim applies can occur only once, as, for example, in the case of successful suicide. Nevertheless, the maxim is general in form.

9 Kant, *Groundwork*, p. 65.

10 See, for example, Robert Paul Wolff, *The Autonomy of Reason* (New York: Harper & Row, 1973), p. 163.

11 This is stated especially clearly on p. 107 of the *Groundwork*.

12 For an interesting discussion of various formulations of the golden rule, see Marcus Singer, "The Golden Rule," in Paul Edwards, ed. *The Encyclopedia of Philosophy* (New York: Macmillan, Free Press, 1967), Vol. 3, pp. 365–67.

13 Kant, *Groundwork*, p. 97n.

14 *Ibid.*, pp. 89–91.

15 *Ibid.*, p. 89n.

16 *Ibid.*, p. 89.

17 *Ibid.*

18 *Ibid.*, p. 71.

19 *Ibid.*

20 *Ibid.*

21 *Ibid.*, p. 91.

VI.4 *Morality as a System of Hypothetical Imperatives*

PHILIPPA FOOT

Philippa Foot is professor of philosophy at the University of California at Los Angeles and a fellow at Sommerville College, Oxford University. She has written important articles in moral theory, including this selection. Here she argues that Kant is wrong in viewing morality as categorical rather than hypothetical. Kant has been credited by the vast majority of ethicists, even those who disagree with him on other issues, with establishing the necessity of grounding moral judgements in categorical imperatives, rather than in hypothetical ones. Moral judgments are objectively necessary—not a mere means to achieving something one desires, as prudential judgments are. Foot argues that Kant seems to be wrong here, and that the categorical aspect of morality may stem more from the way it is taught than the way it really is. Nonetheless, while taking a certain transcendence away from morality, a morality based on hypothetical considerations may still be adequate and important and true.

There are many difficulties and obscurities in Kant's moral philosophy, and few contemporary moralists will try to defend it all. Many, for instance, agree in rejecting Kant's derivation of duties from the mere form of the law expressed in terms of a universally legislative will. Nevertheless, it is generally supposed, even by those who would not dream of calling themselves his followers, that Kant established one thing beyond doubt—namely, the necessity of distinguishing moral judgments from hypothetical imperatives. That moral judgments cannot be hypothetical imperatives has come to seem an unquestionable truth. It will be argued here that it is not.

In discussing so thoroughly Kantian a notion as that of the hypothetical imperative, one naturally begins by asking what Kant himself meant by a hypothetical imperative, and it may be useful to say a little about the idea of an imperative as this appears in Kant's works. In writing about imperatives Kant seems to be thinking at least as much of statements about what ought to be or should be done, as of injunctions expressed in the imperative mood. He even describes as an imperative the assertion that it would be 'good to do or refrain from doing something'[1] and explains that for a will that 'does not

Reprinted with permission from *Philosophical Review* 84(1972): 305–316. Philippa Foot added the following footnote in 1987: "I now think that this paper shows a mistaken bias in favor of a Humean theory of reasons for action. But its question, 'Why is it rational to follow moral rules but not those of etiquette?' still seems to need an answer."

always do something simply because it is presented to it as a good thing to do' this has the force of a command of reason. We may therefore think of Kant's imperatives as statements to the effect that something ought to be done or that it would be good to do it.

The distinction between hypothetical imperatives and categorical imperatives, which plays so important a part in Kant's ethics, appears in characteristic form in the following passages from the *Foundations of the Metaphysics of Morals:*

> All imperatives command either hypothetically or categorically. The former present the practical necessity of a possible action as a means to achieving something else which one desires (or which one may possibly desire). The categorical imperative would be one which presented an action as of itself objectively necessary, without regard to any other end.[2]
>
> If the action is good only as a means to something else, the imperative is hypothetical; but if it is thought of as good in itself, and hence as necessary in a will which of itself conforms to reason as the principle of this will, the imperative is categorical.[3]

The hypothetical imperative, as Kant defines it, 'says only that the action is good to some purpose' and the purpose, he explains, may be possible or actual. Among imperatives related to actual purposes Kant mentions rules of prudence, since he believes that all men necessarily desire their own happiness. Without committing ourselves to this view it will be useful to follow Kant in classing together as 'hypothetical imperatives' those telling a man what he ought to do because (or if) he wants something and those telling him what he ought to do on grounds of self-interest. Common opinion agrees with Kant in insisting that a moral man must accept a rule of duty whatever his interests or desires.

Having given a rough description of the class of Kantian hypothetical imperatives it may be useful to point to the heterogeneity within it. Sometimes what a man should do depends on his passing inclination, as when he wants his coffee hot and should warm the jug. Sometimes it depends on some long-term project, when the feelings and inclinations of the moment are irrelevant. If one wants to be a respectable philosopher one should get up in the mornings and do some work, though just at that

moment when one should do it the thought of being a respectable philosopher leaves one cold. It is true nevertheless to say of one, at that moment, that one wants to be a respectable philosopher, and this can be the foundation of a desire-dependent hypothetical imperative. The term 'desire' as used in the original account of the hypothetical imperative was meant as a grammatically convenient substitute for 'want,' and was not meant to carry any implication of inclination rather than long-term aim or project. Even the word 'project,' taken strictly, introduces undesirable restrictions. If someone is devoted to his family or his country or to any cause, there are certain things he wants, which may then be the basis of hypothetical imperatives, without either inclinations or projects being quite what is in question. Hypothetical imperatives should already be appearing as extremely diverse; a further important distinction is between those that concern an individual and those that concern a group. The desires on which a hypothetical imperative is dependent may be those of one man, or may be taken for granted as belonging to a number of people engaged in some common project or sharing common aims.

Is Kant right to say that moral judgements are categorical, not hypothetical, imperatives? It may seem that he is, for we find in our language two different uses of words such as 'should' and 'ought,' apparently corresponding to Kant's hypothetical and categorical imperatives, and we find moral judgements on the 'categorical' side. Suppose, for instance, we have advised a traveller that he should take a certain train, believing him to be journeying to his home. If we find that he has decided to go elsewhere, we will most likely have to take back what we said: the 'should' will now be unsupported and in need of support. Similarly, we must be prepared to withdraw our statement about what he should do if we find that the right relation does not hold between the action and the end—that it is either no way of getting what he wants (or doing what he wants to do) or not the most eligible among possible means. The use of 'should' and 'ought' in moral contexts is, however, quite different. When we say that a man should do something and intend a moral judgement we do not have to back up what we say by considerations about his interests or his desires; if no such connexion can be found the 'should' need not be withdrawn. It follows that the agent cannot rebut an assertion about what, morally speaking, he should do by showing that the action is not ancillary to his interests or desires. Without such a connexion the 'should' does not stand unsupported and in need of support; the support that *it* requires is of another kind.

There is, then, one clear difference between moral judgements and the class of 'hypothetical imperatives' so far discussed. In the latter 'should' is 'used hypothetically,' in the sense defined, and if Kant were merely drawing attention to this piece of linguistic usage his point would easily be proved. But obviously Kant meant more than this; in describing moral judgements as non-hypothetical— that is, categorical imperatives—he is ascribing to them a special dignity and necessity which this usage cannot give. Modern philosophers follow Kant in talking, for example, about the 'unconditional requirement' expressed in moral judgements. These, they say, tell us what we have to do whatever our interests or desires, and by their inescapability they are distinguished from hypothetical imperatives.

The problem is to find proof for this further feature of moral judgements. If anyone fails to see the gap that has to be filled it will be useful to point out to him that we find 'should' used non-hypothetically in some non-moral statements to which no one attributes the special dignity and necessity conveyed by the description 'categorical imperative.' For instance, we find this non-hypothetical use of 'should' in sentences enunciating rules of etiquette, as, for example, that an invitation in the third person should be answered in the third person, where the rule does not *fail to apply* to someone who has his own good reasons for ignoring this piece of nonsense, or who simply does not care about what, from the point of view of etiquette, he should do. Similarly, there is a non-hypothetical use of 'should' in contexts where something like a club rule is in question. The club secretary who has told a member that he should not bring ladies into the smoking-room does not say, 'Sorry, I was mistaken' when informed that this member is resigning tomorrow and cares nothing about his reputation in the club. Lacking a connexion with the agent's desires or interests, this 'should' does not stand 'unsupported and in need of support'; it requires only the backing of the rule. This use of 'should' is therefore 'non-hypothetical' in the sense defined.

It follows that if a hypothetical use of 'should' gave a hypothetical imperative, and a non-hypothetical use of 'should' a categorical imperative, then 'should' statements based on rules of etiquette, or rules of a club would be categorical imperatives. Since this would not be accepted by defenders of the categorical imperative in ethics, who would insist that these other 'should' statements give hypothetical imperatives, they must be using this expression in some other sense. We must therefore ask what they mean when they say that 'You should answer . . . in the third person' is a hypothetical imperative. Very roughly the idea seems to be that one may reasonably ask why anyone should bother about what should (from the point of view of etiquette) be done, and that such considerations deserve no notice unless reason is shown. So although people give as their reason for doing something the fact that it is required by etiquette, we do not take this consideration as *in itself giving us reason to act*. Considerations of etiquette do not have any automatic reason-giving force, and a man might be right if he denied that he had reason to do 'what's done.'

This seems to take us to the heart of the matter, for, by contrast, it is supposed that moral considerations necessarily give reasons for acting to any man. The difficulty is, of course, to defend this proposition which is more often repeated than explained. Unless it is said, implausibly, that all 'should' or 'ought' statements give reasons for acting, which leaves the old problem of assigning a special categorical status to moral judgement, we must be told what it is that makes the moral 'should' relevantly different from the 'shoulds' appearing in normative statements of other kinds.[4] Attempts have sometimes been made to show that some kind of irrationality is involved in ignoring the 'should' of morality: in saying "Immoral—so what?" as one says "Not *comme il faut*—so what?" But as far as I can see these have all rested on some illegitimate assumption, as, for instance, of thinking that the amoral man, who agrees that some piece of conduct is immoral but takes no notice of that, is inconsistently disregarding a rule of conduct that he has accepted; or again of thinking it inconsistent to desire that others will not do to one what one proposes to do to them. The fact is that the man who rejects morality because he sees no reason to obey its rules can be convicted of villainy but not of inconsistency. Nor will his action necessarily be irrational. Irrational actions are those in which a man in some way defeats his own purposes, doing what is calculated to be disadvantageous or to frustrate his ends. Immorality does not *necessarily* involve any such thing.

It is obvious that the normative character of moral judgement does not guarantee its reason-giving force. Moral judgements are normative, but so are judgements of manners, statements of club rules, and many others. Why should the first provide reasons for acting as the others do not? In every case it is because there is a background of teaching that the non-hypothetical 'should' can be used. The behaviour is required, not simply recommended, but the question remains as to why we should do what we are required to do. It is true that moral rules are often enforced much more strictly than the rules of etiquette, and our reluctance to press the non-hypothetical 'should' of etiquette may be one reason why we think of the rules of etiquette as hypothetical imperatives. But are we then to say that there is nothing behind the idea that moral judgements are categorical imperatives but the relative stringency of our moral teaching? I believe that this may have more to do with the matter than the defenders of the categorical imperatives would like to admit. For if we look at the kind of thing that is said in its defence we may find ourselves puzzled about what the words can even mean unless we connect them with the feelings that this stringent teaching implants. People talk, for instance, about the 'binding force' of morality, but it is not clear what this means if not that we *feel* ourselves unable to escape. Indeed the 'inescapability' of moral requirements is often cited when they are being contrasted with hypothetical imperatives. No one, it is said, escapes the requirements of ethics by having or not having particular interests or desires. Taken in one way this only reiterates the contrast between the 'should' of morality and the hypothetical 'should,' and once more places morality alongside of etiquette. Both are inescapable in that behaviour does not cease to offend against either morality or etiquette because the agent is indifferent to their purposes and to the disapproval he will incur by flouting them. But morality is supposed to be inescapable in some special way and this may turn out to be merely the reflection of the way morality is taught. Of course, we must try other ways of expressing the fugitive thought. It may be said, for instance, that moral judgements have a kind of necessity since they tell us what we 'must do' or 'have to do' whatever our interests and desires. The sense of this is, again, obscure. Sometimes when we use such expressions we are referring to physical or mental compulsion. (A

man has to go along if he is pulled by strong men and he has to give in if tortured beyond endurance.) But it is only in the absence of such conditions that moral judgements apply. Another and more common sense of the words is found in sentences such as 'I caught a bad cold and had to stay in bed' where a penalty for acting otherwise is in the offing. The necessity of acting morally is not, however, supposed to depend on such penalties. Another range of examples, not necessarily having to do with penalties, is found where there is an unquestioned acceptance of some project or role, as when a nurse tells us that she has to make her rounds at a certain time, or we say that we have to run for a certain train. But these too are irrelevant in the present context, since the acceptance condition can always be revoked.

No doubt it will be suggested that it is in some other sense of the words 'have to' or 'must' that one has to or must do what morality demands. But why should one insist that there must be such a sense when it proves so difficult to say what it is? Suppose that what we take for a puzzling thought were really no thought at all but only the reflection of our *feelings* about morality? Perhaps it makes no sense to say that we 'have to' submit to the moral law, or that morality is 'inescapable' in some special way. For just as one may feel as if one is falling without believing that one is moving downward, so one may feel as if one has to do what is morally required without believing oneself to be under physical or psychological compulsion, or about to incur a penalty if one does not comply. No one thinks that if the word 'falling' is used in a statement reporting one's sensations it must be used in a special sense. But this kind of mistake may be involved in looking for the special sense in which one 'has to' do what morality demands. There is no difficulty about the idea that we feel we *have to* behave morally, and given the psychological conditions of the learning of moral behaviour it is natural that we should have such feelings. What we cannot do is quote them in support of the doctrine of the categorical imperative. It seems, then, that in so far as it is backed up by statements to the effect that the moral law *is* inescapable, or that we *do* have to do what is morally required of us, it is uncertain whether the doctrine of the categorical imperative even makes sense.

The conclusion we should draw is that moral judgements have no better claim to be categorical imperatives than do statements about matters of etiquette. People may indeed follow either morality or etiquette without asking why they should do so, but equally well they may not. They may ask for reasons and may reasonably refuse to follow either if reasons are not to be found.

It will be said that this way of viewing moral considerations must be totally destructive of morality, because no one could ever act morally unless he accepted such considerations as in themselves sufficient reason for action. Actions that are truly moral must be done 'for their own sake,' 'because they are right,' and not for some ulterior purpose. This argument we must examine with care, for the doctrine of the categorical imperative has owed much to its persuasion.

Is there anything to be said for the thesis that a truly moral man acts 'out of respect for the moral law' or that he does what is morally right because it is morally right? That such propositions are not prima facie absurd depends on the fact that moral judgement concerns itself with a man's reasons for acting as well as with what he does. Law and etiquette require only that certain things are done or left undone, but no one is counted as charitable if he gives alms 'for the praise of men,' and one who is honest only because it pays him to be honest does not have the virtue of honesty. This kind of consideration was crucial in shaping Kant's moral philosophy. He many times contrasts acting out of respect for the moral law with acting from an ulterior motive, and what is more from one that is self-interested. In the early *Lectures on Ethics* he gave the principle of truth-telling under a system of hypothetical imperatives as that of not lying *if it harms one to lie*. In the *Metaphysic of Morals* he says that ethics cannot start from the ends which a man may propose to himself, since these are all 'selfish.'[5] In the *Critique of Practical Reason* he argues explicitly that when acting not out of respect for moral law but 'on a material maxim' men do what they do for the sake of pleasure or happiness.

> All material practical principles are, as such, of one and the same kind and belong under the general principle of self-love or one's own happiness.[6]

Kant, in fact, was a psychological hedonist[7] in respect of all actions except those done for the sake of the moral law, and this faulty theory of human nature was one of the things preventing him from see-ing that moral virtue might be compatible with the rejection of the categorical imperative.

If we put this theory of human action aside, and allow as ends the things that seem to be ends, the picture changes. It will surely be allowed that quite apart from thoughts of duty a man may care about the suffering of others, having a sense of identification with them, and wanting to help if he can. Of course he must want not the reputation of charity, nor even a gratifying rôle helping others, but, quite simply, their good. If this is what he does care about, then he will be attached to the end proper to the virtue of charity and a comparison with someone acting from an ulterior motive (even a respectable ulterior motive) is out of place. Nor will the conformity of his action to the rule of charity be merely contingent. Honest action may happen to further a man's career; charitable actions do not *happen* to further the good of others.[8]

Can a man accepting only hypothetical imperatives possess other virtues besides that of charity? Could he be just or honest? This problem is more complex because there is no end related to such virtues as the good of others is related to charity. But what reason could there be for refusing to call a man a just man if he acted justly because he loved truth and liberty, and wanted every man to be treated with a certain respect? And why should the truly honest man not follow honesty for the sake of the good that honest dealing brings to men? Of course, the usual difficulties can be raised about the rare case in which no good is foreseen from an individual act of honesty. But it is not evident that a man's desires could not give him reason to act honestly even here. He wants to live openly and in good faith with his neighbours; it is not all the same to him to lie and conceal.

If one wants to know whether there could be a truly moral man who accepted moral principles as hypothetical rules of conduct, as many people accept rules of etiquette as hypothetical rules of conduct, one must consider the right kind of example. A man who demanded that morality should be brought under the heading of self-interest would not be a good candidate, nor would anyone who was ready to be charitable or honest only so long as he felt inclined. A cause such as justice makes strenuous demands, but this is not peculiar to morality, and men are prepared to toil to achieve many ends not endorsed by morality. That they are prepared to fight so hard for moral ends—for example, for liberty and justice—depends on the fact that these are the kinds of ends that arouse devotion. To sacrifice a great deal for the sake of etiquette one would need to be under the spell of the emphatic 'ought.' One could hardly be devoted to behaving *comme il faut*.

In spite of all that has been urged in favour of the hypothetical imperative in ethics, I am sure that many people will be unconvinced and will argue that one element essential to moral virtue is still missing. This missing feature is the recognition of a *duty* to adopt those ends which we have attributed to the moral man. We have said that he *does* care about others, and about causes such as liberty and justice; that it is on this account that he will accept a system of morality. But what if he never cared about such things, or what if he ceased to care? Is it not the case that he *ought* to care? This is exactly what Kant would say, for though at times he sounds as if he thought that morality is not concerned with ends, at others he insists that the adoption of ends such as the happiness of others is itself dictated by morality.[9] How is this proposition to be regarded by one who rejects all talk about the binding force of the moral law? He will agree that a moral man has moral ends and cannot be indifferent to matters such as suffering and injustice. Further, he will recognise in the statement that one *ought* to care about these things a correct application of the non-hypothetical moral 'ought' by which society is apt to voice its demands. He will not, however, take the fact that he ought to have certain ends as in itself reason to adopt them. If he himself is a moral man then he cares about such things, but not 'because he ought.' If he is an amoral man he may deny that he has any reason to trouble his head over this or any other moral demand. Of course he may be mistaken, and his life as well as others' lives may be most sadly spoiled by his selfishness. But this is not what is urged by those who think they can close the matter by an emphatic use of 'ought.' My argument is that they are relying on an illusion, as if trying to give the moral 'ought' a magic force.[10]

This conclusion may, as I said, appear dangerous and subversive of morality. We are apt to panic at the thought that we ourselves, or other people, might stop caring about the things we do care about, and we feel that the categorical imperative gives us some control over the situation. But it is interesting that the people of Leningrad were not struck by the thought that only the *contingent* fact that other citizens shared their loyalty and devotion to the city stood between them and the Germans during the terrible years of the siege. Perhaps we should be less troubled than we are by fear of defection from the moral cause; perhaps we should even have less reason to fear it if people thought of themselves as volunteers banded together to fight for liberty and justice and against inhumanity and oppression. It is often felt, even if obscurely, that there is an element of deception in the official line about morality. And while some have been persuaded by talk about the authority of the moral law, others have turned away with a sense of distrust.

Endnotes

[1] Immanuel Kant, *Foundations of the Metaphysic of Morals*, L. W. Beck, trans. (Bobbs-Merrill, 1959), sec. II.

[2] Ibid.

[3] Ibid.

[4] To say that moral considerations are *called* reasons is blatantly to ignore the problem.

In the case of etiquette or club rules it is obvious that the non-hypothetical use of 'should' has resulted in the loss of the usual connexion between what one should do and what one has reason to do. Someone who objects that in the moral case a man cannot be justified in restricting his practical reasoning in this way, since every moral 'should' gives reasons for acting, must face the following dilemma. Either it is possible to create reasons for acting simply by putting together any silly rules and introducing a non-hypothetical 'should,' or else the non-hypothetical 'should' does not necessarily imply reasons for acting. If it does not necessarily imply reasons for acting we may ask why it is supposed to do so in the case of morality. Why cannot the indifferent amoral man say that for him 'should$_m$' gives no reason for acting, treating 'should$_m$' as most of us treat 'should$_e$'? Those who insist that 'should$_m$' is categorical in this second 'reason-giving' sense do not seem to realise that they never prove this to be so. They sometimes say that moral considerations 'just do' give reasons for acting, without explaining why some devotee of etiquette could not say the same about the rules of etiquette.

[5] Immanuel Kant, *Metaphysic of Morals*, Pt. II, Introduction, sec. II.

[6] Immanuel Kant, *Critique of Practical Reason*, trans. L. W. Beck, p. 133.

[7] One who believes that actions are performed to gain pleasure or avoid pain. [See Joel Feinberg, "Psychological Egoism," Part III.2 of this anthology.]

[8] It is not, of course, necessary that charitable actions should *succeed* in helping others; but when they do so they

do not *happen* to do so, since that is necessarily their aim. (Footnote added, 1977.)

[9] Kant, *The Metaphysic of Morals*, Pt. II, sec. XXX.

[10] See G. E. M. Anscombe, 'Modern Moral Philosophy,' *Philosophy* (1958). My view is different from Miss Anscombe's, but I have learned from her.

VI.5 *Moral Luck*

Thomas Nagel

Thomas Nagel is professor of philosophy at New York University and the author of several important works in philosophy of the mind and moral theory. In this essay Nagel questions the whole Kantian way of looking at morality, which presumes that we are all, qua rational, equal participants in the moral enterprise who have equal opportunity to be moral. The locus of the moral enterprise is the good will, the will to do our duty according to reason's dictates, the only purely good thing in the world. Although we all have different nonmoral abilities, even different characters inclining us to virtue, only the resolved intention to do one's duty matters.

Nagel argues that this view is too simple and doesn't take into account the way external factors impinge upon us. External factors introduce the notion of moral luck, which Nagel defines thusly: "Where a significant aspect of what someone does depends on factors beyond his control, yet we continue to treat him in that respect as an object of moral judgment, it can be called moral luck."

Nagel discusses four types of moral luck: constitutional luck, circumstantial luck, consequential luck in which consequences retrospectively justify an otherwise immoral act (or fail to justify an otherwise moral act), and consequential luck in which the consequences affect the type or quality of blame or remorse (or moral praise). Nagel's article challenges our traditional way of viewing ethics as being beyond accident and luck.

Kant believed that good or bad luck should influence neither our moral judgment of a person and his actions, nor his moral assessment of himself.

The good will is not good because of what it effects or accomplishes or because of its adequacy to achieve some proposed end; it is good only because of its willing, i.e., it is good of itself. And, regarded for itself, it is to be esteemed incomparably higher than any-thing which could be brought about by it in favor of any inclination or even of the sum total of all inclinations. Even if it should happen that, by a particular unfortunate fate or by the niggardly provision of a stepmotherly nature, this will should be wholly lacking in power to accomplish its purpose, and if even the greatest effort should not avail it to achieve anything of its end, and if there remained only the good will (not as a mere wish but as the summoning of all the means in our power), it would sparkle like a jewel in its own right, as something that had its full worth in itself.

Reprinted with permission from *Mortal Questions* (Cambridge University Press, 1979).

Usefulness or fruitlessness can neither diminish nor augment this worth.[1]

He would presumably have said the same thing about a bad will: whether it accomplishes its evil purposes is morally irrelevant. And a course of action that would be condemned if it had a bad outcome cannot be vindicated if by luck it turns out well. There cannot be moral risk. This view seems to be wrong, but it arises in response to a fundamental problem about moral responsibility to which we possess no satisfactory solution.

The problem develops out of the ordinary conditions of moral judgment. Prior to reflection it is intuitively plausible that people cannot be morally assessed for what is not their fault, or for what is due to factors beyond their control. Such judgment is different from the evaluation of something as a good or bad thing, or state of affairs. The latter may be present in addition to moral judgment, but when we blame someone for his actions we are not merely saying it is bad that they happened, or bad that he exists: we are judging *him,* saying he is bad, which is different from his being a bad thing. This kind of judgment takes only a certain kind of object. Without being able to explain exactly why, we feel that the appropriateness of moral assessment is easily undermined by the discovery that the act or attribute, no matter how good or bad, is not under the person's control. While other evaluations remain, this one seems to lose its footing. So a clear absence of control, produced by involuntary movement, physical force, or ignorance of the circumstances, excuses what is done from moral judgment. But what we do depends in many more ways than these on what is not under our control — what is not produced by a good or a bad will in Kant's phrase. And external influences in this broader range are not usually thought to excuse what is done from moral judgment, positive or negative.

Let me give a few examples, beginning with the type of case Kant has in mind. Whether we succeed or fail in what we try to do nearly always depends to some extent on factors beyond our control. This is true of murder, altruism, revolution, the sacrifice of certain interests for the sake of others — almost any morally important act. What has been done, and what is morally judged, is partly determined by external factors. However jewel-like the good will may be in its own right, there is a morally significant difference between rescuing someone from a burning building and dropping him from a twelfth-story window while trying to rescue him. Similarly, there is a morally significant difference between reckless driving and manslaughter. But whether a reckless driver hits a pedestrian depends on the presence of the pedestrian at the point where he recklessly passes a red light. What we do is also limited by the opportunities and choices with which we are faced, and these are largely determined by factors beyond our control. Someone who was an officer in a concentration camp might have led a quiet and harmless life if the Nazis had never come to power in Germany. And someone who led a quiet and harmless life in Argentina might have become an officer in a concentration camp if he had not left Germany for business reasons in 1930.

I shall say more later about these and other examples. I introduce them here to illustrate a general point. Where a significant aspect of what someone does depends on factors beyond his control, yet we continue to treat him in that respect as an object of moral judgment, it can be called moral luck. Such luck can be good or bad. And the problem posed by this phenomenon, which led Kant to deny its possibility, is that the broad range of external influences here identified seems on close examination to undermine moral assessment as surely as does the narrower range of familiar excusing conditions. If the condition of control is consistently applied, it threatens to erode most of the moral assessments we find it natural to make. The things for which people are morally judged are determined in more ways than we at first realize by what is beyond their control. And when the seemingly natural requirement of fault or responsibility is applied in light of these facts, it leaves few pre-reflective moral judgments intact. Ultimately, nothing or almost nothing about what a person does seems to be under his control.

Why not conclude, then, that the condition of control is false — that it is an initially plausible hypothesis refuted by clear counter-examples? One could in that case look instead for a more refined condition which picked out the *kinds* of lack of control that really undermine certain moral judgments, without yielding the unacceptable conclusion derived from the broader condition, that most or all ordinary moral judgments are illegitimate.

What rules out this escape is that we are dealing not with a theoretical conjecture but with a philosophical problem. The condition of control does not suggest itself merely as a generalization from certain clear cases. It seems *correct* in the further cases to which it is extended beyond the original set. When we undermine moral assessment by considering new ways in which control is absent, we are not just discovering what *would* follow given the general hypothesis, but are actually being persuaded that in itself the absence of control is relevant in these cases too. The erosion of moral judgment emerges not as the absurd consequence of an over-simple theory, but as a natural consequence of the ordinary idea of moral assessment, when it is applied in view of a more complete and precise account of the facts. It would therefore be a mistake to argue from the unacceptability of the conclusions to the need for a different account of the conditions of moral responsibility. The view that moral luck is paradoxical is not a *mistake,* ethical or logical, but a perception of one of the ways in which the intuitively acceptable conditions of moral judgment threaten to undermine it all.

It resembles the situation in another area of philosophy, the theory of knowledge. There too conditions which seem perfectly natural, and which grow out of the ordinary procedures for challenging and defending claims to knowledge, threaten to undermine all such claims if consistently applied. Most skeptical arguments have this quality: they do not depend on the imposition of arbitrarily stringent standards of knowledge, arrived at by misunderstanding, but appear to grow inevitably from the consistent application of ordinary standards.[2] There is a substantive parallel as well, for epistemological skepticism arises from consideration of the respects in which our beliefs and their relation to reality depend on factors beyond our control. External and internal causes produce our beliefs. We may subject these processes to scrutiny in an effort to avoid error, but our conclusions at this next level also result, in part, from influences which we do not control directly. The same will be true no matter how far we carry the investigation. Our beliefs are always, ultimately, due to factors outside our control, and the impossibility of encompassing those factors without being at the mercy of others leads us to doubt whether we know anything. It looks as though, if any of our beliefs are true, it is pure biological luck rather than knowledge.

Moral luck is like this because while there are various respects in which the natural objects of moral assessment are out of our control or influenced by what is out of our control, we cannot reflect on these facts without losing our grip on the judgments.

There are roughly four ways in which the natural objects of moral assessment are disturbingly subject to luck. One is the phenomenon of constitutive luck—the kind of person you are, where this is not just a question of what you deliberately do, but of your inclinations, capacities, and temperament. Another category is luck in one's circumstances—the kind of problems and situations one faces. The other two have to do with the causes and effects of action: luck in how one is determined by antecedent circumstances, and luck in the way one's actions and projects turn out. All of them present a common problem. They are all opposed by the idea that one cannot be more culpable or estimable for anything than one is for that fraction of it which is under one's control. It seems irrational to take or dispense credit or blame for matters over which a person has no control, or for their influence on results over which he has partial control. Such things may create the conditions for action, but action can be judged only to the extent that it goes beyond these conditions and does not just result from them.

Let us first consider luck, good and bad, in the way things turn out. Kant, in the above-quoted passage, has one example of this in mind, but the category covers a wide range. It includes the truck driver who accidentally runs over a child, the artist who abandons his wife and five children to devote himself to painting,[3] and other cases in which the possibilities of success and failure are even greater. The driver, if he is entirely without fault, will feel terrible about his role in the event, but will not have to reproach himself. Therefore this example of agent-regret[4] is not yet a case of *moral* bad luck. However, if the driver was guilty of even a minor degree of negligence—failing to have his brakes checked recently, for example—then if that negligence contributes to the death of the child, he will not merely feel terrible. He will blame himself for the death. And what makes this an example of moral luck is that he would have to blame himself only slightly for the negligence itself if no situation arose which required him to brake suddenly and violently to avoid hitting a child. Yet the *negligence* is the same in both cases, and the driver has no control over whether a child will run into his path.

The same is true at higher levels of negligence. If someone has had too much to drink and his car swerves onto the sidewalk, he can count himself morally lucky if there are no pedestrians in his path. If there were, he would be to blame for their deaths, and would probably be prosecuted for manslaughter. But if he hurts no one, although his recklessness is exactly the same, he is guilty of a far less serious legal offense and will certainly reproach himself and be reproached by others much less severely. To take another legal example, the penalty for attempted murder is less than that for successful murder — however similar the intentions and motives of the assailant may be in the two cases. His degree of culpability can depend, it would seem, on whether the victim happened to be wearing a bullet-proof vest, or whether a bird flew into the path of the bullet — matters beyond his control.

Finally, there are cases of decision under uncertainty — common in public and in private life. Anna Karenina goes off with Vronsky, Gauguin leaves his family, Chamberlain signs the Munich Agreement, the Decembrists persuade the troops under their command to revolt against the czar, the American colonies declare their independence from Britain, you introduce two people in an attempt at matchmaking. It is tempting in all such cases to feel that some decision must be possible, in the light of what is known at the time, which will make reproach unsuitable no matter how things turn out. But this is not true; when someone acts in such ways he takes his life, or his moral position, into his hands, because how things turn out determines what he has done. It is possible *also* to assess the decision from the point of view of what could be known at the time, but this is not the end of the story. If the Decembrists had succeeded in overthrowing Nicholas I in 1825 and establishing a constitutional regime, they would be heroes. As it is, not only did they fail and pay for it, but they bore some responsibility for the terrible punishments meted out to the troops who had been persuaded to follow them. If the American Revolution had been a bloody failure resulting in greater repression, then Jefferson, Frank-

lin, and Washington would still have made a noble attempt, and might not even have regretted it on their way to the scaffold, but they would also have had to blame themselves for what they had helped to bring on their compatriots. (Perhaps peaceful efforts at reform would eventually have succeeded.) If Hitler had not overrun Europe and exterminated millions, but instead had died of a heart attack after occupying the Sudetenland, Chamberlain's action at Munich would still have utterly betrayed the Czechs, but it would not be the great moral disaster that has made his name a household word.[5]

In many cases of difficult choice the outcome cannot be foreseen with certainty. One kind of assessment of the choice is possible in advance, but another kind must await the outcome, because the outcome determines what has been done. The same degree of culpability or estimability in intention, motive, or concern is compatible with a wide range of judgments, positive or negative, depending on what happened beyond the point of decision. The *mens rea* which could have existed in the absence of any consequences does not exhaust the grounds of moral judgment. Actual results influence culpability or esteem in a large class of unquestionably ethical cases ranging from negligence through political choice.

That these are genuine moral judgments rather than expressions of temporary attitude is evident from the fact that one can say *in advance* how the moral verdict will depend on the results. If one negligently leaves the bath running with the baby in it, one will realize, as one bounds up the stairs toward the bathroom, that if the baby has drowned one has done something awful, whereas if it has not one has merely been careless. Someone who launches a violent revolution against an authoritarian regime knows that if he fails he will be responsible for much suffering that is in vain, but if he succeeds he will be justified by the outcome. I do not mean that *any* action can be retroactively justified by history. Certain things are so bad in themselves, or so risky, that no results can make them all right. Nevertheless, when moral judgment does depend on the outcome, it is objective and timeless and not dependent on a change of standpoint produced by success or failure. The judgment after the fact follows from an hypothetical judgment that can be made beforehand, and it can be made as easily by someone else as by the agent.

From the point of view which makes responsibility dependent on control, all this seems absurd. How is it possible to be more or less culpable depending on whether a child gets into the path of one's car, or a bird into the path of one's bullet? Perhaps it is true that what is done depends on more than the agent's state of mind or intention. The problem then is, why is it not irrational to base moral assessment on what people do, in this broad sense? It amounts to holding them responsible for the contributions of fate as well as for their own — provided they have made some contribution to begin with. If we look at cases of negligence or attempt, the pattern seems to be that overall culpability corresponds to the product of mental or intentional fault and the seriousness of the outcome. Cases of decision under uncertainty are less easily explained in this way, for it seems that the overall judgment can even shift from positive to negative depending on the outcome. But here too it seems rational to subtract the effects of occurrences subsequent to the choice, that were merely possible at the time, and concentrate moral assessment on the actual decision in light of the probabilities. If the object of moral judgment is the *person,* then to hold him accountable for what he has done in the broader sense is akin to strict liability, which may have its legal uses but seems irrational as a moral position.

The result of such a line of thought is to pare down each act to its morally essential core, an inner act of pure will assessed by motive and intention. Adam Smith advocates such a position in *The Theory of Moral Sentiments,* but notes that it runs contrary to our actual judgments.

> But how well soever we may seem to be persuaded of the truth of this equitable maxim, when we consider it after this manner, in abstract, yet when we come to particular cases, the actual consequences which happen to proceed from any action, have a very great effect upon our sentiments concerning its merit or demerit, and almost always either enhance or diminish our sense of both. Scarce, in any one instance, perhaps, will our sentiments be found, after examination, to be entirely regulated by this rule, which we all acknowledge ought entirely to regulate them.[6]

Joel Feinberg points out further that restricting the domain of moral responsibility to the inner world will not immunize it to luck. Factors beyond the agent's control, like a coughing fit, can interfere with his decisions as surely as they can with the path of a bullet from his gun.[7] Nevertheless the tendency to cut down the scope of moral assessment is pervasive, and does not limit itself to the influence of effects. It attempts to isolate the will from the other direction, so to speak, by separating out constitutive luck. Let us consider that next.

Kant was particularly insistent on the moral irrelevance of qualities of temperament and personality that are not under the control of the will. Such qualities as sympathy or coldness might provide the background against which obedience to moral requirements is more or less difficult, but they could not be objects of moral assessment themselves, and might well interfere with confident assessment of its proper object — the determination of the will by the motive of duty. This rules out moral judgment of many of the virtues and vices, which are states of character that influence choice but are certainly not exhausted by dispositions to act deliberately in certain ways. A person may be greedy, envious, cowardly, cold, ungenerous, unkind, vain, or conceited, but *behave* perfectly by a monumental effort of will. To possess these vices is to be unable to help having certain feelings under certain circumstances, and to have strong spontaneous impulses to act badly. Even if one controls the impulses, one still has the vice. An envious person hates the greater success of others. He can be morally condemned as envious even if he congratulates them cordially and does nothing to denigrate or spoil their success. Conceit, likewise, need not be displayed. It is fully present in someone who cannot help dwelling with secret satisfaction on the superiority of his own achievements, talents, beauty, intelligence, or virtue. To some extent such a quality may be the product of earlier choices; to some extent it may be amenable to change by current actions. But it is largely a matter of constitutive bad fortune. Yet people are morally condemned for such qualities, and esteemed for others equally beyond control of the will: they are assessed for what they are *like.*

To Kant this seems incoherent because virtue is enjoined on everyone and therefore must in principle be possible for everyone. It may be easier for some than for others, but it must be possible to achieve it by making the right choices, against whatever temperamental background.[8] One may want to have a generous spirit, or regret not having one, but it makes no sense to condemn oneself or anyone else for a quality which is not within the control of the will. Condemnation implies that you should not be like that, not that it is unfortunate that you are.

Nevertheless, Kant's conclusion remains intuitively unacceptable. We may be persuaded that these moral judgments are irrational, but they reappear involuntarily as soon as the argument is over. This is the pattern throughout the subject.

The third category to consider is luck in one's circumstances, and I shall mention it briefly. The things we are called upon to do, the moral tests we face, are importantly determined by factors beyond our control. It may be true of someone that in a dangerous situation he would behave in a cowardly or heroic fashion, but if the situation never arises, he will never have the chance to distinguish or disgrace himself in this way, and his moral record will be different.[9]

A conspicuous example of this is political. Ordinary citizens of Nazi Germany had an opportunity to behave heroically by opposing the regime. They also had an opportunity to behave badly, and most of them are culpable for having failed this test. But it is a test to which the citizens of other countries were not subjected, with the result that even if they, or some of them, would have behaved as badly as the Germans in like circumstances, they simply did not and therefore are not similarly culpable. Here again one is morally at the mercy of fate, and it may seem irrational upon reflection, but our ordinary moral attitudes would be unrecognizable without it. We judge people for what they actually do or fail to do, not just for what they would have done if circumstances had been different.

This form of moral determination by the actual is also paradoxical, but we can begin to see how deep in the concept of responsibility the paradox is embedded. A person can be morally responsible only for what he does; but what he does results from a great deal that he does not do; therefore he is not morally responsible for what he is and is not responsible for. (This is not a contradiction, but it is a paradox.)

It should be obvious that there is a connection between these problems about responsibility and control and an even more familiar problem, that of freedom of the will. That is the last type of moral luck I want to take up, though I can do no more within the scope of this essay than indicate its connection with the other types.

If one cannot be responsible for consequences of one's acts due to factors beyond one's control, or for antecedents of one's acts that are properties of temperament not subject to one's will, or for the circumstances that pose one's moral choices, then how can one be responsible even for the stripped-down acts of the will itself, if *they* are the product of antecedent circumstances outside of the will's control?

The area of genuine agency, and therefore of legitimate moral judgment, seems to shrink under this scrutiny to an extensionless point. Everything seems to result from the combined influence of factors, antecedent and posterior to action, that are not within the agent's control. Since he cannot be responsible for them, he cannot be responsible for their results — though it may remain possible to take up the aesthetic or other evaluative analogues of the moral attitudes that are thus displaced.

It is also possible, of course, to brazen it out and refuse to accept the results, which indeed seem unacceptable as soon as we stop thinking about the arguments. Admittedly, if certain surrounding circumstances had been different, then no unfortunate consequences would have followed from a wicked intention, and no seriously culpable act would have been performed; but since the circumstances were *not* different, and the agent *in fact* succeeded in perpetrating a particularly cruel murder, *that* is what he did, and that is what he is responsible for. Similarly, we may admit that if certain antecedent circumstances had been different, the agent would never have developed into the sort of person who would do such a thing; but since he *did* develop (as the inevitable result of those antecedent circumstances) into the sort of swine he is, and into the person who committed such a murder, *that* is what he is blamable for. In both cases one is responsible for what one actually does — even if what one actually does depends in important ways on what is not within one's control. This [compatibilist] account of our moral judgments would leave room for the ordinary conditions of responsibility—the absence of coercion, ignorance, or involuntary movement—as part of the determination of what someone has done—but it is understood not to exclude the influence of a great deal that he has not done.

The only thing wrong with this solution is its failure to explain how skeptical problems arise. For they arise not from the imposition of an arbitrary external requirement, but from the nature of moral judgment itself. Something in the ordinary idea of what someone does must explain how it can seem necessary to subtract from it anything that merely happens—even though the ultimate consequence of such subtraction is that nothing remains. And something in the ordinary idea of knowledge must explain why it seems to be undermined by any influences on belief not within the control of the subject—so that knowledge seems impossible without an impossible foundation in autonomous reason. But let us leave epistemology aside and concentrate on action, character, and moral assessment.

The problem arises, I believe, because the self which acts and is the object of moral judgment is threatened with dissolution by the absorption of its acts and impulses into the class of events. Moral judgment of a person is judgment not of what happens to him, but of him. It does not say merely that a certain event or state of affairs is fortunate or unfortunate or even terrible. It is not an evaluation of a state of the world, or of an individual as part of the world. We are not thinking just that it would be better if he were different, or did not exist, or had not done some of the things he has done. We are judging *him*, rather than his existence or characteristics. The effect of concentrating on the influence of what is not under his control is to make this responsible self seem to disappear, swallowed up by the order of mere events.

What, however, do we have in mind that a person must *be* to be the object of these moral attitudes? While the concept of agency is easily undermined, it is very difficult to give it a positive characterization. That is familiar from the literature on Free Will.

I believe that in a sense the problem has no solution, because something in the idea of agency is incompatible with actions being events, or people being things. But as the external determinants of what someone has done are gradually exposed, in their effect on consequences, character, and choice itself, it becomes gradually clear that actions are events and people things. Eventually nothing remains which can be ascribed to the responsible self, and we are left with nothing but a portion of the larger sequences of events, which can be deplored or celebrated, but not blamed or praised.

Though I cannot define the idea of the active self that is thus undermined, it is possible to say something about its sources. There is a close connection between our feelings about ourselves and our feelings about others. Guilt and indignation, shame and contempt, pride and admiration are internal and external sides of the same moral attitudes. We are unable to view ourselves simply as portions of the world, and from inside we have a rough idea of the boundary between what is us and what is not, what we do and what happens to us, what is our personality and what is an accidental handicap. We apply the same essentially internal conception of the self to others. About ourselves we feel pride, shame, guilt, remorse—and agent-regret. We do not regard our actions and our characters merely as fortunate or unfortunate episodes—though they may also be that. We cannot *simply* take an external evaluative view of ourselves—of what we most essentially are and what we do. And this remains true even when we have seen that we are not responsible for our own existence, or our nature, or the choices we have to make, or the circumstances that give our acts the consequences they have. Those acts remain ours and we remain ourselves, despite the persuasiveness of the reasons that seem to argue us out of existence.

It is this internal view that we extend to others in moral judgment—when we judge *them* rather than their desirability or utility. We extend to others the refusal to limit ourselves to external evaluation, and we accord to them selves like our own. But in both cases this comes up against the brutal inclusion of humans and everything about them in a world from which they cannot be separated and of which they are nothing but contents. The external view forces itself on us at the same time that we resist it. One way this occurs is through the gradual erosion of what we do by the subtraction of what happens.

The inclusion of consequences in the conception of what we have done is an acknowledgment that we are parts of the world, but the paradoxical character of moral luck which emerges from this acknowledgment shows that we are unable to operate with such a view, for it leaves us with no one to be. The same thing is revealed in the appearance that determinism obliterates responsibility. Once we see an aspect of what we or someone else does as something that happens, we lose our grip on the idea that it has been done and that we can judge the doer and not just the happening. This explains why the absence of determinism is no more hospitable to the concept of agency than is its presence—a point that has been noticed often. Either way the act is viewed externally, as part of the course of events.

The problem of moral luck cannot be understood without an account of the internal conception of agency and its special connection with the moral attitudes as opposed to other types of value. I do not have such an account. The degree to which the problem has a solution can be determined only by seeing whether in some degree the incompatibility between this conception and the various ways in which we do not control what we do is only apparent. I have nothing to offer on that topic either. But it is not enough to say merely that our basic moral attitudes toward ourselves and others are determined by what is actual; for they are also threatened by the sources of that actuality, and by the external view of action which forces itself on us when we see how everything we do belongs to a world that we have not created.

Endnotes

[1] Immanuel Kant, *Foundations of the Metaphysics of Morals,* L. W. Beck, trans. (Bobbs-Merrill, 1959), sec. I, paragraph 3.

[2] See Thompson Clark, "The Legacy of Skepticism," *Journal of Philosophy,* LXIX, no. 20 (November 9, 1972): 754–69.

[3] Such a case, modelled on the life of Gauguin, is discussed by Bernard Williams in "Moral Luck," *Proceedings of the Aristotelian Society,* supplementary vol. L (1976): 115–35 (to which the original version of this essay was a reply). He points out that though success or failure cannot be predicted in advance, Gauguin's most basic retrospective feelings about the decision will be determined by the development of his talent. My disagreement with Williams is that his account fails to explain why such retrospective attitudes can be called moral. If success does not permit Gauguin to justify himself to others, but still determines his most basic feelings, that shows only that his most basic feelings need not be moral. It does not show that morality is subject to luck. If the retrospective judgment were moral, it would imply the truth of a hypothetical judgment made in advance, of the form 'If I leave my family and become a great painter, I will be justified by success; if I don't become a great painter, the act will be unforgivable.'

[4] Williams's term (*ibid.*).

[5] For a fascinating but morally repellent discussion of the topic of justification by history, see Maurice Merleau-Ponty, *Humanisme et Terreur* (Paris: Gallimard, 1947), translated as *Humanism and Terror* (Boston: Beacon Press, 1969).

[6] Adam Smith, *The Theory of Moral Sentiments,* 1759, Pt. II, sec. 3, Introduction, para. 5.

[7] "Problematic Responsibility in Law and Morals," in Joel Feinberg, *Doing and Deserving* (Princeton: Princeton University Press, 1970).

[8] 'If nature has put little sympathy in the heart of a man, and if he, though an honest man, is by temperament cold and indifferent to the sufferings of others, perhaps because he is provided with special gifts of patience and fortitude and expects or even requires that others should have the same—and such a man would certainly not be the meanest product of nature—would not he find in himself a source from which to give himself a far higher worth than he could have got by having a good-natured temperament?' (Kant, *Foundations of the Metaphysics of Morals,* first section, eleventh paragraph).

[9] Cf. Thomas Gray, 'Elegy Written in a Country Churchyard':
    Some mute inglorious Milton here may rest,
    Some Cromwell, guiltless of his country's blood.
An unusual example of circumstantial moral luck is provided by the kind of moral dilemma with which someone can be faced through no fault of his own, but which leaves him with nothing to do which is not wrong.

Suggestions for Further Reading

Acton, Harry. *Kant's Moral Philosophy*. Macmillan, 1970.

Baier, Kurt. *The Moral Point of View*. Cornell University Press, 1958.

Broad, C. D. *Five Types of Ethical Theory*. Routledge and Kegan Paul, 1930.

Donagan, Alan. *The Theory of Morality*. University of Chicago Press, 1977. A comprehensive deontological account of ethical theory.

Feldman, Fred. *Introductory Ethics*. Prentice-Hall, 1978, Chapters 7 and 8. A clear and critical exposition.

Gewirth, Alan. *Reason and Morality*. University of Chicago, 1978. Important but advanced.

Harris, C. E. *Applying Moral Theories*. Wadsworth, 1986, Chapter VII. An excellent exposition of contemporary deontological theories, especially of Gewirth's work.

Kant, Immanuel. *Critique of Practical Reason*, tr. Lewis White Beck. Bobbs-Merrill, 1956.

Kant, Immanuel. *Foundations of the Metaphysics of Morals*, tr. Lewis White Beck. Bobbs-Merrill, 1959.

Louden, Robert. *Morality and Moral Theory* (Oxford: Oxford University Press, 1991). A sophisticated contemporary account combining Kantian and Virtue ethics.

O'Neill, Onora. *Acting on Principle: An Essay on Kantian Ethics*. Columbia University, 1975.

————. *Constructions of Reason*. Cambridge University Press, 1989.

Raphael, D. D. *Moral Philosophy*. Oxford University Press, 1981, Chapter 6.

Ross, W. D. *Kant's Ethical Theory*. Clarendon Press, 1954.

Ward, Kieth. *The Development of Kant's Views of Ethics*. Blackwell's, 1972.

Wolff, Robert P. *The Autonomy of Reason: A Commentary on Kant's "Groundwork of the Metaphysics of Morals."* HarperCollins, 1973.

Part VII

Virtue-Based Ethical Systems

Morality is internal. The moral law . . . has to be expressed in the form, "be this," not in the form "do this." . . . [T]he true moral law says "hate not," instead of "kill not." . . . [T]he only mode of stating the moral law must be as a rule of character.

LESLIE STEPHENS
The Science of Ethics, G. P. Putnam's Sons, 1882, pp. 155, 158

Whereas most ethical theories, whether deontological or teleological, have been duty- or action-oriented, there is a third tradition that goes back to Aristotle and Plato and that received support from the Epicureans, Stoics, and some sections of the early Christian church. I refer to the virtue-based systems, sometimes called *aretaic* (from the Greek *arete,* which we translate as 'excellence' or 'virtue'). Rather than viewing the heart of ethics to be in actions or duties, virtue-based ethical systems center in the heart of the agent — in the character and dispositions of persons. Whereas action-oriented ethics emphasizes *doing,* virtue- or agent-based ethics emphasizes *being* — being a certain type of person who will no doubt manifest his or her being in actions or nonactions.

For traditional duty-based ethics, the question is, What should I do? For aretaic ethics, the question is, What sort of person should I become? Aretaic ethics seeks to produce excellent persons who both act well (out of spontaneous goodness) and serve as examples to inspire others. It seeks to create people who, like Socrates, Jesus,

St. Francis of Assisi, Gandhi, and Mother Teresa, stand out as "jewels who shine in their own light" (to paraphrase Kant's characterization of the morally good will). There is a teleological aspect to aretaic ethics, but it is not of the kind, usually found in utilitarianism, that asks what sort of action will maximize happiness or utility. The aretaic concept of teleology focuses instead on the *goal* of life—living well and achieving excellence.

Our first reading is from the first two books of Aristotle's *Nicomachean Ethics,* the classic work on the virtues written in the fourth century B.C. Virtues are simply those characteristics that enable individuals to live well in communities. In order to achieve a state of well-being (*eudaimonia,* often translated as 'happiness'), proper social institutions are necessary. Thus the moral person cannot really exist apart from a flourishing political setting that enables the individual to develop the requisite virtues for the good life. For this reason, Aristotle considers ethics to be a branch of politics.

After locating ethics as a part of politics, Aristotle explains that moral virtues are different from intellectual ones. While the intellectual virtues may be taught directly, the moral ones must be lived in order to be learned. By living well we acquire the right habits. These habits are in fact the virtues. The virtues are to be sought as the best guarantee to the happy life. But, again, happiness requires that one be lucky enough to live in a flourishing state. The morally virtuous life consists in living in moderation according to the "golden mean."

In our second reading, "Virtue and the Moral Life," Bernard Mayo provides a contemporary expression of the Aristotelian perspective. Mayo contrasts the deontologists' and teleologists' ethics of "doing" with the ethics of "being" or character demonstrated by the saints and heroes. He contends that the saints and heroes show us that a living example, not rigid rules, is

important in ethics. We learn more about ethics by looking at the lives of such people than by learning a set of principles.

Virtue ethicists are more likely than ethicists of other persuasions to bring ethics closer to political theory, as Aristotle himself did, and ask what kinds of upbringing and social institutions are most likely to give rise to the good life and produce good people. They tend to despair of arguing about objective moral principles or right and wrong action, which is putting the cart before the horse. Many modern aretaics (for example, Alasdair MacIntyre in our fifth reading) urge us to go back to the Greeks and center our ethics on the quest for virtue that is connected with happiness, rather than on questions of right and wrong, which really have their place in custom and law, not in humanistic ethics. They believe that duty-based ethics has its origin and justification in religious authority, as divinely given laws that are enforced by the gods or God. Removal of that authority leaves only a relativistic morass. The only way to escape chaotic relativism, in which everyone does what is right in his or her own eyes, is to return to a virtue-based ethics.

Action- or duty-based ethical theorists do not deny the importance of character. But they claim that the nature of the virtues can only be derived from right actions or good consequences. As William Frankena puts it in our third reading, "Traits without principles are blind. . . ." Where there is a virtue, there must be some possible action to which the virtue corresponds and from which it derives its virtuosity. For example, the character trait of truthfulness is a virtue because telling the truth, in general, is a moral duty. Likewise, conscientiousness is a virtue because we have a general duty to be morally sensitive. There is a correspondence between virtues and principles—the virtues are derived from the principles—as the following diagram suggests:

The Correspondence Theory of Virtues

THE VIRTUE	that is derived from	THE PRINCIPLE
Truthfulness		Telling the truth
Conscientiousness		Being sensitive to one's duty
Benevolence		Being beneficent
Faithfulness		Being loyal or faithful

The fact that the virtues are not originative but derived from principles does not seriously diminish their importance for the moral life. They provide the dispositions that generate right action. In a sense, they are motivationally indispensable. To complete Frankena's passage quoted above, "Traits without principles are blind, but principles without traits are impotent." Frankena further modifies the above position, distinguishing between two types of virtues: the standard moral virtues that correspond to specific kinds of moral principles, and nonmoral virtues, such as natural kindliness or gratefulness (I would suggest that courage also fits in here), that support morality.

The relationship looks something like this:

specific principle 'Always come to the aid of drowning people,' and gives rise to a tendency to try to save the drowning child (4), but whether or not you actually dive into the lake may depend on (5), the enabling (nonmoral) virtue of courage. Courage itself is not a moral virtue like benevolence or justice, for it is the kind of virtue that enhances and augments both virtues and vices (for example, think of the courageous murderer). If the process is completed without a hitch, the agent does the moral act (6). He or she attempts to save the drowning child.

Views like Frankena's are criticized by Walter Schaller in our fourth selection, "Are Virtues No More Than Dispositions to Obey Moral Rules?" Labeling positions like Frankena's "the Standard

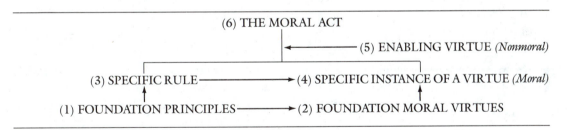

(6) THE MORAL ACT

(5) ENABLING VIRTUE *(Nonmoral)*

(3) SPECIFIC RULE ──────────► (4) SPECIFIC INSTANCE OF A VIRTUE *(Moral)*

(1) FOUNDATION PRINCIPLES ──────────► (2) FOUNDATION MORAL VIRTUES

For example, take a situation in which you have an obligation to save a drowning child, in spite of some risk to your life. The specific rule (3) is grounded in a foundation principle of general beneficence (1), which in turn generates the foundation virtue of benevolence (2). In this instance, the foundation virtue applies to (3), the

View," Schaller argues that morality is more than rule-following and that the virtues have intrinsic, as well as instrumental, value. He argues that the duty of beneficence and the virtues of gratitude and self-respect all defy the logic of the Standard View. The duty of beneficence cannot be clearly stated without including the virtue of benevolence in the description of the duty. The virtues of gratitude and self-respect need not result in actions in order to be morally significant.

Schaller rejects both an exclusively duty-based morality and an exclusively virtue-based morality. The two types of morality should complement rather than compete with each other.

In his "Some Vices of Virtue Ethics," Robert Louden raises one of the perennial criticisms of virtue-based ethical systems, namely, that such theories provide no guidance in resolving moral dilemmas. Virtue ethicists like Aristotle say precious little about what we are supposed to *do*. One would think that ethics should be, at least to some extent, action-guiding. Aristotle's answer seems to be, Do what a good person would do. But, the question arises: Who is the good person and how shall I recognize him or her? Furthermore, even if we could answer that question without reference to kinds of actions or principles addressed by the nonvirtue-oriented ethicists, it is not always clear what ideal persons would do in our situations. Sometimes Aristotle writes as though the right action is that intermediate or "golden" mean between two extremes, but it is not always easy to understand what this means in concrete situations. As J. L. Mackie says:

> As guidance about what is the good life, what precisely one ought to do, or even by what standard one should try to decide what one ought to do, this is too circular to be very helpful. And though Aristotle's account is filled out with detailed descriptions of many of the virtues, moral as well as intellectual, the air of indeterminacy persists. We learn the names of the pairs of contrary vices that contrast with each of the virtues, but very little about where or how to draw the dividing lines, where or how to fix the mean. As Sidgwick says, he "only indicates the whereabouts of virtue." (*Ethics: Inventing Right and Wrong,* Penguin Books, 1977, p. 186)

Our sixth reading, Alasdair MacIntyre's "The Nature of the Virtues," carries on the Aristotelian project of grounding morality in the virtues. In this essay MacIntyre asks whether there is some core conception of the virtues, some vital components that are necessary to any social endeavor or practice. He compares five different conceptions of the virtues as they appear in the works of Homer, Aristotle, Jane Austen, and Benjamin Franklin, and in the New Testament. Five different theories seem to emerge, although MacIntyre finds elements of commonality among them.

MacIntyre argues that in every society there must be practices in which virtues are exhibited and become defined. Even though practices may vary from society to society, so that different virtues will be highlighted differently in different societies, nevertheless a core set of virtues is necessary for the successful functioning of any practice. This set includes such virtues as justice, courage, and honesty, without which the practice is in danger of decay. And without some practice, and more broadly, a moral tradition, we are in danger of falling into a Hobbesian state of nature. MacIntyre ends his essay by comparing his theory of the virtues with Aristotle's project and by arguing that his work is within the Aristotelian tradition.

In our seventh reading, "Moral Saints," Susan Wolf challenges the idea that moral perfection is a desirable goal. She contends that seeking saintliness would deprive us of other valuable traits, such as intellectual and cultural excellence, and produce boring and uninteresting people. Morality should be seen as one value among many, and not always the highest. Simply because morality is a good thing does not mean that we should have as much of it as possible regardless of the cost to other values. That is, we can have too much of a good thing—even moral goodness. In the final essay I take issue with Wolf and defend the ideal of moral, secular saintliness. I argue that what is and what is not boring is largely a subjective matter, that we may have a duty to forgo certain interesting things in life that may entail activities that bore others or ourselves, and that utilitarians and Kantians have arguments available to them to defeat the criticisms of Wolf.

VII.1 *The Ethics of Virtue*

ARISTOTLE

Aristotle (384–322 B.C.), Greek physician, tutor to Alexander the Great, and one of the most important philosophers who ever lived, wrote important treatises on every major subject in philosophy. This selection is from the first two books of the *Nicomachean Ethics*. After a general discussion of the nature of ethics and human existence, Aristotle turns to the nature of virtue. Virtues are simply those characteristics that enable individuals to live well in communities. In order to achieve a state of well-being (*eudaimonia*, often translated as 'happiness'), proper social institutions are necessary. Thus the moral person cannot really exist apart from a flourishing political setting that enables the individual to develop the requisite virtues for the good life. Ethics is thus a species of politics.

Next, Aristotle distinguishes moral virtues from intellectual ones. Whereas the intellectual virtues may be taught directly, the moral ones must be lived in order to be learned. By living well we acquire the right habits. These habits are in fact the virtues. The virtues are to be sought as the best guarantee to the happy life. But, again, happiness requires that one be lucky enough to live in a flourishing state. The morally virtuous life consists in living in moderation, according to the "golden mean."

Book I

Chapter 1. Every art and every scientific inquiry, and similarly every action and purpose, may be said to aim at some good. Hence the good has been well defined as that at which all things aim. But it is clear that there is a difference in ends; for the ends are sometimes activities, and sometimes results beyond the mere activities. Where there are ends beyond the action, the results are naturally superior to the action.

As there are various actions, arts, and sciences, it follows that the ends are also various. Thus health is the end of the medical art, a ship of shipbuilding, victory of strategy, and wealth of economics. It often happens that a number of such arts or sciences combine for a single enterprise, as the art of making bridles and all such other arts as furnish the implements of horsemanship combine for horsemanship, and horsemanship and every military action for strategy; and in the same way, other arts or sciences combine for others. In all these cases, the ends of the master arts or sciences, whatever they may be, are more desirable than those of the subordinate

Reprinted from *Aristotle's Nicomachean Ethics*, translated by James E. C. Weldon (Macmillan, 1897).

arts or sciences, as it is for the sake of the former that the latter are pursued. It makes no difference to the argument whether the activities themselves are the ends of the action, or something beyond the activities, as in the above-mentioned sciences.

If it is true that in the sphere of action there is some end which we wish for its own sake, and for the sake of which we wish everything else, and if we do not desire everything for the sake of something else (for, if that is so, the process will go on *ad infinitum,* and our desire will be idle and futile), clearly this end will be good and the supreme good. Does it not follow then that the knowledge of this good is of great importance for the conduct of life? Like archers who have a mark at which to aim, shall we not have a better chance of attaining what we want? If this is so, we must endeavor to comprehend, at least in outline, what this good is, and what science or faculty makes it its object.

It would seem that this is the most authoritative science. Such a kind is evidently the political, for it is that which determines what sciences are necessary in states, and what kinds should be studied, and how far they should be studied by each class of inhabitant. We see too that even the faculties held in highest esteem, such as strategy, economics, and rhetoric, are subordinate to it. Then since politics makes use of the other sciences and also rules what people may do and what they may not do, it follows that its end will comprehend the ends of the other sciences, and will therefore be the good of mankind. For even if the good of an individual is identical with the good of a state, yet the good of the state is evidently greater and more perfect to attain or to preserve. For though the good of an individual by himself is something worth working for, to ensure the good of a nation or a state is nobler and more divine.

These then are the objects at which the present inquiry aims, and it is in a sense a political inquiry. . . .

Chapter 2. As every science and undertaking aims at some good, what is in our view the good at which political science aims, and what is the highest of all practical goods? As to its name there is, I may say, a general agreement. The masses and the cultured classes agree in calling it happiness, and conceive that "to live well" or "to do well" is the same thing as "to be happy." But as to what happiness is they do not agree, nor do the masses give the same account of it as the philosophers. The former take it to be something visible and palpable, such as pleasure, wealth, or honor; different people, however, give different definitions of it, and often even the same man gives different definitions at different times. When he is ill, it is health, when he is poor, it is wealth; if he is conscious of his own ignorance, he envies people who use grand language above his own comprehension. Some philosophers, on the other hand, have held that, besides these various goods, there is an absolute good which is the cause of goodness in them all.[1] It would perhaps be a waste of time to examine all these opinions; it will be enough to examine such as are most popular or as seem to be more or less reasonable.

Chapter 3. Men's conception of the good or of happiness may be read in the lives they lead. Ordinary or vulgar people conceive it to be a pleasure, and accordingly choose a life of enjoyment. For there are, we may say, three conspicuous types of life, the sensual, the political, and, thirdly, the life of thought. Now the mass of men present an absolutely slavish appearance, choosing the life of brute beasts, but they have ground for so doing because so many persons in authority share the tastes of Sardanapalus.[2] Cultivated and energetic people, on the other hand, identify happiness with honor, as honor is the general end of political life. But this seems too superficial an idea for our present purpose; for honor depends more upon the people who pay it than upon the person to whom it is paid, and the good we feel is something which is proper to a man himself and cannot be easily taken away from him. Men too appear to seek honor in order to be assured of their own goodness. Accordingly, they seek it at the hands of the sage and of those who know them well, and they seek it on the ground of their virtue; clearly then, in their judgment at any rate, virtue is better than honor. Perhaps then we might look on virtue rather than honor as the end of political life. Yet even this idea appears not quite complete; for a man may possess virtue and yet be asleep or inactive throughout life, and not only so, but he may experience the greatest calamities and misfortunes. Yet no one would call such a life a life of happiness, unless he were maintaining a paradox. But we need not dwell further on this subject, since it is sufficiently discussed in popular philosophical treatises. The third life is the life of thought, which we will discuss later.

The life of money making is a life of constraint; and wealth is obviously not the good of which we are in quest; for it is useful merely as a means to something else. It would be more reasonable to take the things mentioned before — sensual pleasure, honor, and virtue — as ends than wealth, since they are things desired on their own account. Yet these too are evidently not ends, although much argument has been employed to show that they are. . . .

Chapter 5. But leaving this subject for the present, let us revert to the good of which we are in quest and consider what it may be. For it seems different in different activities or arts; it is one thing in medicine, another in strategy, and so on. What is the good in each of these instances? It is presumably that for the sake of which all else is done. In medicine this is health, in strategy victory, in architecture a house, and so on. In every activity and undertaking it is the end, since it is for the sake of the end that all people do whatever else they do. If then there is an end for all our activity, this will be the good to be accomplished; and if there are several such ends, it will be these.

Our argument has arrived by a different path at the same point as before; but we must endeavor to make it still plainer. Since there are more ends than one, and some of these ends — for example, wealth, flutes, and instruments generally — we desire as means to something else, it is evident that not all are final ends. But the highest good is clearly something final. Hence if there is only one final end, this will be the object of which we are in search; and if there are more than one, it will be the most final. We call that which is sought after for its own sake more final than that which is sought after as a means to something else; we call that which is never desired as a means to something else more final than things that are desired both for themselves and as means to something else. Therefore, we call absolutely final that which is always desired for itself and never as a means to something else. Now happiness more than anything else answers to this description. For happiness we always desire for its own sake and never as a means to something else, whereas honor, pleasure, intelligence, and every virtue we desire partly for their own sakes (for we should desire them independently of what might result from them), but partly also as means to happiness, because we suppose they will prove instruments of happiness. Happiness, on the other hand, nobody desires for the sake of these things, nor indeed as a means to anything else at all.

If we start from the point of view of self-sufficiency, we reach the same conclusion; for we assume that the final good is self-sufficient. By self-sufficiency we do not mean that a person leads a solitary life all by himself, but that he has parents, children, wife and friends and fellow citizens in general, as man is naturally a social being. Yet here it is necessary to set some limit; for if the circle must be extended to include ancestors, descendants, and friends' friends, it will go on indefinitely. Leaving this point, however, for future investigation, we call the self-sufficient that which, taken even by itself, makes life desirable and wanting nothing at all; and this is what we mean by happiness.

Again, we think happiness the most desirable of all things, and that not merely as one good thing among others. If it were only that, the addition of the smallest more good would increase its desirableness; for the addition would make an increase of goods, and the greater of two goods is always the more desirable. Happiness is something final and self-sufficient and the end of all action.

Chapter 6. Perhaps, however, it seems a commonplace to say that happiness is the supreme good; what is wanted is to define its nature a little more clearly. The best way of arriving at such a definition will probably be to ascertain the function of man. For, as with a flute player, a sculptor, or any artist, or in fact anybody who has a special function or activity, his goodness and excellence seem to lie in his function, so it would seem to be with man, if indeed he has a special function. Can it be said that, while a carpenter and a cobbler have special functions and activities, man, unlike them, is naturally functionless? Or, as the eye, the hand, the foot, and similarly each part of the body has a special function, so may man be regarded as having a special function apart from all these? What, then, can this function be? It is not life; for life is apparently something that man shares with plants; and we are looking for something peculiar to him. We must exclude therefore the life of nutrition and growth. There is next what may be called the life of sensation. But this too, apparently, is shared by man with horses, cattle, and all other animals. There remains what I may call the active life of the rational part of man's being. Now this rational part is twofold; one part is rational in the sense of being obedient to reason, and the other in the sense of possessing and exercising reason and intelligence. The active life too may be conceived of in two ways, either as a state of character, or as an activity; but we mean by it the life of activity, as this seems to be the truer form of the conception.

The function of man then is activity of soul in accordance with reason, or not apart from reason. Now, the function of a man of a certain kind, and of a man who is good of that kind—for example, of a harpist and a good harpist—are in our view the same in kind. This is true of all people of all kinds without exception, the superior excellence being only an addition to the function; for it is the function of a harpist to play the harp, and of a good harpist to play the harp well. This being so, if we define the function of man as a kind of life, and this life as an activity of the soul or a course of action in accordance with reason, and if the function of a good man is such activity of a good and noble kind, and if everything is well done when it is done in accordance with its proper excellence, it follows that the good of man is activity of soul in accordance with virtue, or, if there are more virtues than one, in accordance with the best and most complete virtue. But we must add the words "in a complete life." For as one swallow or one day does not make a spring, so one day or a short time does not make a man blessed or happy. . . .

Chapter 8. Goods have been divided into three classes: external goods as they are called, goods of the soul, and goods of the body. Of these three classes goods of the soul are considered goods in the strictest and truest sense. To the soul are ascribed spiritual actions and activities. Thus our definition must be a good one, at least according to this theory, which is both ancient and accepted by philosophers at the present time. It is correct too, inasmuch as we call certain actions and activities the end; for we put the end in some good of the soul and not in an external good. By a similar theory the happy man lives well and does well, and happiness, we have said, is in fact a kind of living and doing well. . . .

Chapter 10. The question is consequently raised whether happiness is something that can be learned or acquired by habit or training of some kind, or whether it comes by some divine dispensation, or even by chance.

Now if there is anything in the world that is a gift of the gods to men, it is reasonable to take happiness as a divine gift, and especially divine as it is the best of human things. This point, however, is perhaps more appropriate to another investigation than the present. But even if happiness is not sent by the gods but is the result of goodness and of learning or training of some kind, it is apparently one of the most divine things in the world; for that which is the prize and end of goodness would seem the best good and in its nature godlike and blessed. It may also be widely extended; for all persons who are not morally deformed may share in it by a process of study and care. And if it is better that happiness should come in this way than by chance, we may reasonably suppose that it does so come, since the order of things in Nature is the best possible, as it is in art and in causation generally, and most of all in the highest kind of causation. And to leave what is greatest and noblest to chance would be altogether unworthy. The definition of happiness itself helps to clear up the question; for happiness we have defined as a kind of virtuous activity of the soul. . . .

It is reasonable then not to call an ox or a horse or any other animal happy; for none of them is capable of sharing in this activity. For the same reason no child can be happy, since the youth of a child keeps him for the time being from such activity; if a child is ever called happy, the ground of felicitation is his promise, rather than his actual performance. For happiness demands, as we said, a complete virtue and a complete life. And there are all sorts of changes and chances in life, and the most prosperous of men may in his old age fall into extreme calamities, as Priam did in the heroic legends.[3] And a person who has experienced such chances and died a miserable death, nobody calls happy.

Chapter 13. Inasmuch as happiness is an activity of soul in accordance with perfect virtue, we must now consider virtue, as this will perhaps be the best way of studying happiness. . . . Clearly it is human virtue we have to consider; for the good of which we are in search is, as we said, human good, and the happiness, human happiness. By human virtue or excellence we mean not that of the body, but that of the soul, and by happiness we mean an activity of the soul.

There are some facts concerning the soul which are adequately stated in popular discourses, and these we may rightly accept. It is said, for example, that the soul has two parts, one irrational and the other rational. Whether these parts are separate like the parts of the body or like anything divisible, or whether they are theoretically distinct but in fact inseparable, like the convex and concave in the circumference of a circle, is of no importance to the present inquiry.

Of the irrational part of the soul one part is shared by man with all living things, and vegetative; I mean the part which is the cause of nutrition and growth. For we may assume such a faculty of the soul to exist in all young things that take food, even in embryos, and the same faculty to exist in things full grown, since it is more reasonable to suppose it is the same faculty than something different. Manifestly the virtue or excellence of this faculty is not peculiarly human but is shared by man with all living things; this part or faculty seems especially active in sleep, whereas goodness and badness never show so little as in sleep. Hence the saying that during half their lives there is no difference between the happy and the unhappy. And this is only natural; for sleep is an inactivity of the soul as regards its goodness or badness, except in so far as certain impulses affect it slightly and make the dreams of good men better than those of ordinary people. Enough, however, on this point; we shall now leave the faculty of nutrition, as it has by its nature no part in human goodness.

There is, we think, another natural element of the soul which is irrational and yet in a sense partakes of reason. For in continent and incontinent persons we praise their reason, and that part of their soul which possesses reason, because it counsels them aright and directs them to the best conduct. But we know there is in them also another element naturally opposed to reason that fights and contends against reason. Just as paralyzed parts of the body, when we try to move them to the right, pull in a contrary direction to the left, so it is with the soul; the impulses of incontinent people run counter to reason. But while in the body we see the part which pulls awry, in the soul we do not see it. We may, however, suppose with equal certainty that in the soul too there is something alien to reason, which opposes and thwarts it. The sense in which it is distinct from other things is unimportant. But it too partakes of reason, as we said; at all events, in a continent person it obeys reason, and in a temperate and brave man it is probably still more obedient, for in him it is absolutely harmonious with reason.

It appears then that the irrational part of the soul is twofold; for the vegetative faculty does not participate at all in reason, but the element of appetite and desire in general shares in it, in so far as it is submissive and obedient to reason. It is so in the sense in which we speak of "paying attention" to a father or to friends, but not in the sense in which we speak of "paying attention" to mathematics. All advice, reproof, and exhortation are witness that this irrational part of the soul is in a sense subject to influence by reason. And if we say that this part participates in reason, then as a part possessing reason, it will be twofold, one element possessing reason absolutely and in itself, the other listening to it as a child listens to its father.

Virtue too may be divided to correspond to this difference. For we call some virtues intellectual and others moral. Wisdom, intelligence, and prudence are intellectual; liberality and temperance moral. In describing a person's moral character we do not say that he is wise or intelligent but that he is gentle or temperate. A wise man, however, we praise for his mentality, and such mentality as deserves praise we call virtuous.

Book II

Moral virtues can best be acquired by practice and habit. They imply a right attitude toward pleasures and pains. A good man deliberately chooses to do what is noble and right for its own sake. What is right in matters of moral conduct is usually a mean between two extremes.

Chapter 1. Virtue then is twofold, partly intellectual and partly moral, and intellectual virtue is originated and fostered mainly by teaching; it demands therefore experience and time. Moral virtue on the other hand is the outcome of habit, and accordingly its name, *ethike*, is derived by a slight variation from *ethos*, habit. From this fact it is clear that moral virtue is not implanted in us by nature; for nothing that exists by nature can be transformed by habit. Thus a stone, that naturally tends to fall downwards, cannot be habituated or trained to rise upwards, even if we tried to train it by throwing it up ten thousand times. Nor again can fire be trained to sink downwards, nor anything else that follows one natural law be habituated or trained to follow another. It is neither by nature then nor in defiance of nature that virtues grow in us. Nature gives us the capacity to receive them, and that capacity is perfected by habit.

Again, if we take the various natural powers which belong to us, we first possess the proper faculties and afterwards display the activities. It is obviously so with the senses. Not by seeing frequently or hearing frequently do we acquire the sense of seeing or hearing; on the contrary, because we have the senses we make use of them; we do not get them by making use of them. But the virtues we get by first practicing them, as we do in the arts. For it is by doing what we ought to do when we study the arts that we learn the arts themselves; we become builders by building and harpists by playing the harp. Similarly, it is by doing just acts that we become just, by doing temperate acts that we become temperate, by doing brave acts that we become brave. The experience of states confirms this statement, for it is by training in good habits that lawmakers make the citizens good. This is the object all lawmakers have at heart; if they do not succeed in it, they fail of their purpose; and it makes the distinction between a good constitution and a bad one.

Again, the causes and means by which any virtue is produced and destroyed are the same; and equally so in any part. For it is by playing the harp that both good and bad harpists are produced; and the case of builders and others is similar, for it is by building well that they become good builders and by building badly that they become bad builders. If it were not so, there would be no need of anybody to teach them; they would all be born good or bad in their several crafts. The case of the virtues is the same. It is by our actions in dealings between man and man that we become either just or unjust. It is by our actions in the face of danger and by our training ourselves to fear or to courage that we become either cowardly or courageous. It is much the same with our appetites and angry passions. People be-

come temperate and gentle, others licentious and passionate, by behaving in one or the other way in particular circumstances. In a word, moral states are the results of activities like the states themselves. It is our duty therefore to keep a certain character in our activities, since our moral states depend on the differences in our activities. So the difference between one and another training in habits in our childhood is not a light matter, but important, or rather, all-important.

Chapter 2. Our present study is not, like other studies, purely theoretical in intention; for the object of our inquiry is not to know what virtue is but how to become good, and that is the sole benefit of it. We must, therefore, consider the right way of performing actions, for it is acts, as we have said, that determine the character of the resulting moral states.

That we should act in accordance with right reason is a common general principle, which may here be taken for granted. The nature of right reason, and its relation to the virtues generally, will be discussed later. But first of all it must be admitted that all reasoning on matters of conduct must be like a sketch in outline; it cannot be scientifically exact. We began by laying down the principle that the kind of reasoning demanded in any subject must be such as the subject matter itself allows; and questions of conduct and expediency no more admit of hard and fast rules than questions of health.

If this is true of general reasoning on ethics, still more true is it that scientific exactitude is impossible in treating of particular ethical cases. They do not fall under any art or law, but the actors themselves have always to take account of circumstances, as much as in medicine or navigation. Still, although such is the nature of our present argument, we must try to make the best of it.

The first point to be observed is that in the matters we are now considering deficiency and excess are both fatal. It is so, we see, in questions of health and strength. (We must judge of what we cannot see by the evidence of what we do see.) Too much or too little gymnastic exercise is fatal to strength. Similarly, too much or too little meat and drink is fatal to health, whereas a suitable amount produces, increases, and sustains it. It is the same with temperance, courage, and other moral virtues. A person who avoids and is afraid of everything and faces nothing becomes a coward; a person who is not afraid of anything but is ready to face everything becomes foolhardy. Similarly, he who enjoys every pleasure and abstains from none is licentious; he who refuses all pleasures, like a boor, is an insensible sort of person. For temperance and courage are destroyed by excess and deficiency but preserved by the mean.

Again, not only are the causes and agencies of production, increase, and destruction in moral states the same, but the field of their activity is the same also. It is so in other more obvious instances, as, for example, strength; for strength is produced by taking a great deal of food and undergoing a great deal of exertion, and it is the strong man who is able to take most food and undergo most exertion. So too with the virtues. By abstaining from pleasures we become temperate, and, when we have become temperate, we are best able to abstain from them. So again with courage; it is by training ourselves to despise and face terrifying things that we become brave, and when we have become brave, we shall be best able to face them.

The pleasure or pain which accompanies actions may be regarded as a test of a person's moral state. He who abstains from physical pleasures and feels pleasure in so doing is temperate; but he who feels pain at so doing is licentious. He who faces dangers with pleasure, or at least without pain, is brave; but he who feels pain at facing them is a coward. For moral virtue is concerned with pleasures and pains. It is pleasure which makes us do what is base, and pain which makes us abstain from doing what is noble. Hence the importance of having a certain training from very early days, as Plato says, so that we may feel pleasure and pain at the right objects; for this is true education. . . .

Chapter 3. But we may be asked what we mean by saying that people must become just by doing what is just and temperate by doing what is temperate. For, it will be said, if they do what is just and temperate they are already just and temperate themselves, in the same way as, if they practice grammar and music, they are grammarians and musicians.

But is this true even in the case of the arts? For a person may speak grammatically either by chance or at the suggestion of somebody else; hence he will not be a grammarian unless he not only speaks grammatically but does so in a grammatical manner, that is, because of the grammatical knowledge which he possesses.

There is a point of difference too between the arts and the virtues. The productions of art have their excellence in themselves. It is enough then that, when they are produced, they themselves should possess a certain character. But acts in accordance with virtue are not justly or temperately performed simply because they are in themselves just or temperate. The doer at the time of performing them must satisfy certain conditions; in the first place, he must know what he is doing; secondly, he must deliberately choose to do it and do it for his own sake; and thirdly, he must do it as part of his own firm and immutable character. If it be a question of art, these conditions, except only the condition of knowledge, are not raised; but if it be a question of virtue, mere knowledge is of little or no avail; it is the other conditions, which are the results of frequently performing just and temperate acts, that are not slightly but all-important. Accordingly, deeds are called just and temperate when they are such as a just and temperate person would do; and a just and temperate person is not merely one who does these deeds but one who does them in the spirit of the just and the temperate.

It may fairly be said that a just man becomes just by doing what is just, and a temperate man becomes temperate by doing what is temperate, and if a man did not so act, he would not have much chance of becoming good. But most people, instead of acting, take refuge in theorizing; they imagine that they are philosophers and that philosophy will make them virtuous; in fact, they behave like people who listen attentively to their doctors but never do anything that their doctors tell them. But a healthy state of the soul will no more be produced by this kind of philosophizing than a healthy state of the body by this kind of medical treatment.

Chapter 4. We have next to consider the nature of virtue. Now, as the properties of the soul are three, namely, emotions, faculties, and moral states, it follows that virtue must be one of the three. By emotions I mean desire, anger, fear, pride, envy, joy, love, hatred, regret, ambition, pity — in a word, whatever feeling is attended by pleasure or pain. I call those faculties through which we are said to be capable of experiencing these emotions, for instance, capable of getting angry or being pained or feeling pity. And I call those moral states through which we are well or ill disposed in our emotions, ill disposed, for instance, in anger, if our anger be too violent or too feeble, and well disposed, if it be rightly moderate; and similarly in our other emotions.

Now neither the virtues nor the vices are emotions; for we are not called good or bad for our emotions but for our virtues or vices. We are not praised or blamed simply for being angry, but only for being angry in a certain way; but we are praised or blamed for our virtues or vices. Again, whereas we are angry or afraid without deliberate purpose, the virtues are matters of deliberate purpose, or require deliberate purpose. Moreover, we are said to be moved by our emotions, but by our virtues or vices we are not said to be moved but to have a certain disposition.

For these reasons the virtues are not faculties. For we are not called either good or bad, nor are we praised or blamed for having simple capacity for emotion. Also while Nature gives us our faculties, it is not Nature that makes us good or bad; but this point we have already discussed. If then the virtues are neither emotions nor faculties, all that remains is that they must be moral states.

Chapter 5. The nature of virtue has been now described in kind. But it is not enough to say merely that virtue is a moral state; we must also describe the character of that moral state.

We may assert then that every virtue or excellence puts into good condition that of which it is a virtue or excellence, and enables it to perform its work well. Thus excellence in the eye makes the eye good and its function good, for by excellence in the eye we see well. Similarly, excellence of the horse makes a horse excellent himself and good at racing, at carrying its rider and at facing the enemy. If then this rule is universally true, the virtue or excellence of a man will be such a moral state as makes a man good and able to perform his proper function well. How this will be the case we have already explained, but another way of making it clear will be to study the nature or character of virtue.

Now of everything, whether it be continuous or divisible, it is possible to take a greater, a smaller, or an equal amount, and this either in terms of the thing itself or in relation to ourselves, the equal being a mean between too much and too little. By the mean in terms of the thing itself, I understand that which is equally distinct from both its extremes, which is one and the same for every man. By the mean relatively to ourselves, I understand that which is neither too much nor too little for us; but this is not one nor the same for everybody. Thus if 10 be too much and 2 too little, we take 6 as a mean in terms of the thing itself; for 6 is as much greater than 2 as it is less than 10, and this is a mean in arithmetical proportion. But the mean considered relatively to ourselves may not be ascertained in that way. It does not follow that if 10 pounds of meat is too much and 2 too little for a man to eat, the trainer will order him 6 pounds, since this also may be too much or too little for him who is to take it; it will be too little, for example, for Milo but too much for a beginner in gymnastics. The same with running and wrestling; the right amount will vary with the individual. This being so, the skillful in any art avoids alike excess and deficiency; he seeks and chooses the mean, not the absolute mean, but the mean considered relatively to himself.

Every art then does its work well, if it regards the mean and judges the works it produces by the mean. For this reason we often say of successful works of art that it is impossible to take anything from them or to add anything to them, which implies that excess or deficiency is fatal to excellence but that the mean state ensures it. Good artists too, as we say, have an eye to the mean in their works. Now virtue, like Nature herself, is more accurate and better than any art; virtue, therefore, will aim at the mean. I speak of moral virtue, since it is moral virtue which is concerned with emotions and actions, and it is in these we have excess and deficiency and the mean. Thus it is possible to go too far, or not far enough in fear, pride, desire, anger, pity, and pleasure and pain generally, and the excess and the deficiency are alike wrong; but to feel these emotions at the right times, for the right objects, towards the right persons, for the right motives, and in the right manner, is the mean or the best good, which signifies virtue. Similarly, there may be excess, deficiency, or the mean, in acts. Virtue is concerned with both emotions and actions, wherein excess is an error and deficiency a fault, while the mean is successful and praised, and success and praise are both characteristics of virtue.

It appears then that virtue is a kind of mean because it aims at the mean.

On the other hand, there are many different ways of going wrong; for evil is in its nature infinite, to use the Pythagorean phrase, but good is finite and there is only one possible way of going right. So the former is easy and the latter is difficult; it is easy to miss the mark but difficult to hit it. And so by our reasoning excess and deficiency are characteristics of vice and the mean is a characteristic of virtue.

"For good is simple, evil manifold."

Chapter 6. Virtue then is a state of deliberate moral purpose, consisting in a mean relative to ourselves, the mean being determined by reason, or as a prudent man would determine it. It is a mean, firstly, as lying between two vices, the vice of excess on the one hand, the vice of deficiency on the other, and, secondly, because, whereas the vices either fall short of or go beyond what is right in emotion and action, virtue discovers and chooses the mean. Accordingly, virtue, if regarded in its essence or theoretical definition, is a mean, though, if regarded from the point of view of what is best and most excellent, it is an extreme.

But not every action or every emotion admits of a mean. There are some whose very name implies wickedness, as, for example, malice, shamelessness, and envy among the emotions, and adultery, theft, and murder among the actions. All these and others like them are marked as intrinsically wicked, not merely the excesses or deficiencies of them. It is never possible then to be right in them; they are always sinful. Right or wrong in such acts as adultery does not depend on our committing it with the right woman, at the right time, or in the right manner; on the contrary, it is wrong to do it at all. It would be equally false to suppose that there can be a mean or an excess or deficiency in unjust, cowardly or licentious conduct; for, if that were so, it would be a mean of excess and deficiency, an excess of excess and a deficiency of deficiency. But as in temperance and courage there can be no excess or deficiency, because the mean there is in a sense an extreme, so too in these other cases there cannot be a mean or an excess or a deficiency, but however the acts are done, they are wrong. For in general an excess or deficiency does not have a mean, nor a mean an excess or deficiency. . . .

Chapter 8. There are then three dispositions, two being vices, namely, excess and deficiency, and one virtue, which is the mean between them; and they are all in a sense mutually opposed. The extremes are opposed both to the mean and to each other, and the mean is opposed to the extremes. For as the equal if compared with the less is greater, but if compared with the greater is less, so the mean state, whether in emotion or action, if compared with deficiency is excessive, but if compared with excess is deficient. Thus the brave man appears foolhardy compared with the coward, but cowardly compared with the foolhardy. Similarly, the temperate man appears licentious compared with the insensible man but insensible compared with the licentious; and the liberal man appears extravagant compared with the stingy man but stingy compared with the spendthrift. The result is that the extremes each denounce the mean as belonging to the other extreme; the coward calls the brave man foolhardy, and the foolhardy man calls him cowardly; and so on in other cases.

But while there is mutual opposition between the extremes and the mean, there is greater opposition between the two extremes than between extreme and the mean; for they are further removed from each other than from the mean, as the great is further from the small and the small from the great than either from the equal. Again, while some extremes show some likeness to the mean, as foolhardiness to courage and extravagance to liberality, there is the greatest possible dissimilarity between extremes. But things furthest removed from each other are called opposites; hence the further things are removed, the greater is the opposition between them.

In some cases it is deficiency and in others excess which is more opposed to the mean. Thus it is not foolhardiness, an excess, but cowardice, a deficiency, which is more opposed to courage, nor is it insensibility, a deficiency, but licentiousness, an excess, which is more opposed to temperance. There are two reasons why this should be so. One lies in the nature of the matter itself; for when one of two extremes is nearer and more like the mean, it is not this extreme but its opposite that we chiefly contrast with the mean. For instance, as foolhardiness seems more like and nearer to courage than cowardice, it is cowardice that we chiefly contrast with courage; for things further removed from the mean seem to be more opposite to it. This reason lies in the nature of the matter itself; there is a second which lies in our own nature. The things to which we ourselves are naturally more inclined we think more opposed to the mean. Thus we are ourselves naturally more inclined to pleasures than to their opposites, and are more prone therefore to self-indulgence than to moderation. Accordingly we speak of those things in which we are more likely to run to great lengths as more opposed to the mean. Hence licentiousness, which is an excess, seems more opposed to temperance than insensibility.

Chapter 9. We have now sufficiently shown that moral virtue is a mean, and in what sense it is so; that it is a mean as lying between two vices, a vice of excess on the one side and a vice of deficiency on the other, and as aiming at the mean in emotion and action.

That is why it is so hard to be good; for it is always hard to find the mean in anything; it is not everyone but only a man of science who can find the mean or center of a circle. So too anybody can get angry—that is easy—and anybody can give or spend money, but to give it to the right person, to give the right amount of it, at the right time, for the right cause and in the right way, this is not what anybody can do, nor is it easy. That is why goodness is rare and praiseworthy and noble. One then who aims at a mean must begin by departing from the extreme that is more contrary to the mean; he must act in the spirit of Calypso's advice,

"Far from this spray and swell hold thou thy ship,"

for of the two extremes one is more wrong than the other. As it is difficult to hit the mean exactly, we should take the second best course, as the saying is, and choose the lesser of two evils. This we shall best do in the way described, that is, steering clear of the evil which is further from the mean. We must also note the weaknesses to which we are ourselves particularly prone, since different natures tend in different ways; and we may ascertain what our tendency is by observing our feelings of pleasure and pain. Then we must drag ourselves away towards the opposite extreme; for by pulling ourselves as far as possible from what is wrong we shall arrive at the mean, as we do when we pull a crooked stick straight.

In all cases we must especially be on our guard against the pleasant, or pleasure, for we are not impartial judges of pleasure. Hence our attitude towards pleasure must be like that of the elders of the people in the *Iliad* towards Helen, and we must constantly apply the words they use; for if we dismiss pleasure as they dismissed Helen, we shall be less likely to go wrong. By action of this kind, to put it summarily, we shall best succeed in hitting the mean.

Undoubtedly this is a difficult task, especially in individual cases. It is not easy to determine the right manner, objects, occasion and duration of anger. Sometimes we praise people who are deficient in anger, and call them gentle, and at other times we praise people who exhibit a fierce temper as high spirited. It is not however a man who deviates a little from goodness, but one who deviates a great deal, whether on the side of excess or of deficiency, that is blamed; for he is sure to call attention to himself. It is not easy to decide in theory how far and to what extent a man may go before he becomes blameworthy, but neither is it easy to define in theory anything else in the region of the senses; such things depend on circumstances, and our judgment of them depends on our perception.

So much then is plain, that the mean is everywhere praiseworthy, but that we ought to aim at one time towards an excess and at another towards a deficiency; for thus we shall most easily hit the mean, or in other words reach excellence.

Endnotes

1 These were members of Plato's school of thought.

2 A half-legendary ruler of ancient Assyria, whose name to the Greeks stood for the extreme of Oriental luxury and extravagance.

3 The disastrous fate of Priam, king of Troy, was part of the well-known Homeric tales.

VII.2 *Virtue and the Moral Life*

Bernard Mayo

Bernard Mayo is a British philosopher and the author of *Ethics and the Moral Life,* from which this selection is taken. Mayo contrasts the deontologists' and teleologists' ethics of "doing" with the ethics of "being" or character demonstrated by the saints and heroes. He contends that the saints and heroes show us that a living example, not rigid rules, is important in ethics. We learn more about ethics by looking at the lives of such people than by learning a set of principles.

The philosophy of moral principles, which is characteristic of Kant and the post-Kantian era, is something of which hardly a trace exists in Plato. . . . Plato says nothing about rules or principles or laws, except when he is talking politics. Instead he talks about virtues and vices, and about certain types of human character. The key word in Platonic ethics is Virtue; the key word in Kantian ethics is Duty. And modern ethics is a set of footnotes, not to Plato, but to Kant. . . .

Attention to the novelists can be a welcome correction to a tendency of philosophical ethics of the last generation or two to lose contact with the ordinary life of man which is just what the novelists, in their own way, are concerned with. Of course there are writers who can be called in to illustrate problems about Duty (Graham Greene is a good example). But there are more who perhaps never mention the words duty, obligation, or principle. Yet they are all concerned — Jane Austen, for instance, entirely and absolutely — with the moral qualities or defects of their heroes and heroines and other characters. This points to a radical one-sidedness in the philosophers' account of morality in terms of principles: it takes little or no account of qualities, of what people *are*. It is just here that the old-fashioned word Virtue used to have a place; and it is just here that the work of Plato and Aristotle can

be instructive. Justice, for Plato, though it is closely connected with acting according to law, does not *mean* acting according to law: it is a quality of character, and a just action is one such as a just man would do. Telling the truth, for Aristotle, is not, as it was for Kant, fulfilling an obligation; again it is a quality of character, or, rather, a whole range of qualities of character, some of which may actually be defects, such as tactlessness, boastfulness, and so on — a point which can be brought out, in terms of principles, only with the greatest complexity and artificiality, but quite simply and naturally in terms of character.

If we wish to enquire about Aristotle's moral views, it is no use looking for a set of principles. Of course we can find *some* principles to which he must have subscribed — for instance, that one ought not to commit adultery. But what we find much more prominently is a set of character-traits, a list of certain types of person — the courageous man, the niggardly man, the boaster, the lavish spender, and so on. The basic moral question, for Aristotle, is not, What shall I do? but, What shall I be?

These contrasts between doing and being, negative and positive, and modern as against Greek morality were noted by John Stuart Mill; I quote from the *Essay on Liberty*:

> Christian morality (so-called) has all the characters of a reaction; it is, in great part, a protest against Paganism. Its ideal is negative rather than positive, passive rather than active; Innocence rather than Nobleness; Abstinence from Evil, rather than energetic Pursuit

From *Ethics and the Moral Life* (Macmillan, 1958). Reprinted by permission of Macmillan, London and Basingstoke.

of the Good; in its precepts (as has been well said) "Thou shalt not" predominates unduly over "Thou shalt . . ." Whatever exists of magnanimity, highmindedness, personal dignity, even the sense of honour, is derived from the purely human, not the religious part of our education, and never could have grown out of a standard of ethics in which the only worth, professedly recognized, is that of obedience.

Of course, there are connections between being and doing. It is obvious that a man cannot just *be;* he can only be what he is by doing what he does; his moral qualities are ascribed to him because of his actions, which are said to manifest those qualities. But the point is that an ethics of Being must include this obvious fact, that Being involves Doing; whereas an ethics of Doing, such as I have been examining, may easily overlook it. As I have suggested, a morality of principles is concerned only with what people do or fail to do, since that is what rules are for. And as far as this sort of ethics goes, people might well have no moral qualities at all except the possession of principles and the will (and capacity) to act accordingly.

When we speak of a moral quality such as courage, and say that a certain action was courageous, we are not merely saying something about the action. We are referring, not so much to what is done, as to the kind of person by whom we take it to have been done. We connect, by means of imputed motives and intentions, with the character of the agent as courageous. This explains, incidentally, why both Kantians and Utilitarians encounter, in their different ways, such difficulties in dealing with motives, which their principles, on the face of it, have no room for. A Utilitarian, for example, can only praise a courageous action in some such way as this: the action is of a sort such as a person of courage is likely to perform, and courage is a quality of character the cultivation of which is likely to increase rather than diminish the sum total of human happiness. But Aristotelians have no need of such circumlocution. For them a courageous action just is one which proceeds from and manifests a certain type of character, and is praised because such a character trait is good, or better than others, or is a virtue. An evaluative criterion is sufficient: there is no need to look for an imperative criterion as well, or rather instead, according to which it is not the character which is

good, but the cultivation of the character which is right. . . .

No doubt the fundamental moral question is just "What ought I to do?" And according to the philosophy of moral principles, the answer (which must be an imperative "Do this") must be derived from a conjunction of premises consisting (in the simplest case) firstly of a rule, or universal imperative, enjoining (or forbidding) all actions of a certain type in situations of a certain type, and, secondly, a statement to the effect that this is a situation of that type, falling under that rule. In practice the emphasis may be on supplying only one of these premises, the other being assumed or taken for granted: one may answer the question "What ought I to do?" either by quoting a rule which I am to adopt, or by showing that my case is legislated for by a rule which I do adopt. . . . [I]f I am in doubt whether to tell the truth about his condition to a dying man, my doubt may be resolved by showing that the case comes under a rule about the avoidance of unnecessary suffering, which I am assumed to accept. But if the case is without precedent in my moral career, my problem may be soluble only by adopting a new principle about what I am to do now and in the future about cases of this kind.

This second possibility offers a connection with moral ideas. Suppose my perplexity is not merely an unprecedented situation which I could cope with by adopting a new rule. Suppose the new rule is thoroughly inconsistent with my existing moral code. This may happen, for instance, if the moral code is one to which I only pay lip-service, if . . . its authority is not yet internalised, or if it has ceased to be so; it is ready for rejection, but its final rejection awaits a moral crisis such as we are assuming to occur. What I now need is not a rule for deciding how to act in this situation and others of its kind. I need a whole set of rules, a complete morality, new principles to live by.

Now, according to the philosophy of moral character, there is another way of answering the fundamental question "What ought I to do?" Instead of quoting a rule, we quote a quality of character, a virtue: we say "Be brave," or "Be patient" or "Be lenient." We may even say "Be a man": if I am in doubt, say, whether to take a risk, and someone says "Be a man," meaning a morally sound man, in this case a man of sufficient courage. (Compare the very different ideal invoked in "Be a gentleman." I shall not discuss whether this is a *moral* ideal.) Here, too, we have the extreme cases, where a man's moral perplexity extends not merely to a particular situation but to his whole way of living. And now the question "What ought I to do?" turns into the question "What ought I to be?" — as, indeed, it was treated in the first place. ("Be brave.") It is answered, not by quoting a rule or a set of rules, but by describing a quality of character or a type of person. And here the ethics of character gains a practical simplicity which offsets the greater logical simplicity of the ethics of principles. We do not have to give a list of characteristics or virtues, as we might list a set of principles. We can give a unity to our answer.

Of course we can in theory give a unity to our principles: this is implied by speaking of a *set* of principles. But if such a set is to be a system and not merely aggregate, the unity we are looking for is a logical one, namely the possibility that some principles are deductible from others, and ultimately from one. But the attempt to construct a deductive moral system is notoriously difficult, and in any case ill-founded. Why should we expect that all rules of conduct should be ultimately reducible to a few?

Saints and Heroes

But when we are asked "What shall I be?" we can readily give a unity to our answer, though not a logical unity. It is the unity of character. A person's character is not merely a list of dispositions; it has the organic unity of something that is more than the sum of its parts. And we can say, in answer to our morally perplexed questioner, not only "Be this" and "Be that," but also "Be like So-and-So" — where So-and-So is either an ideal type of character, or else an actual person taken as representative of the ideal, as exemplar. Examples of the first are Plato's "just man" in the Republic; Aristotle's man of practical wisdom, in the *Nicomachean Ethics;* Augustine's citizen of the City of God; the good Communist; the American way of life (which is a collective expression for a type of character). Examples of the second

kind, the exemplar, are Socrates, Christ, Buddha, St. Francis, the heroes of epic writers and of novelists. Indeed the idea of the Hero, as well as the idea of the Saint, are very much the expression of this attitude to morality. Heroes and saints are not merely people who did things. They are people whom we are expected, and expect ourselves, to imitate. And imitating them means not merely doing what they did; it means being like them. Their status is not in the least like that of legislators whose laws we admire; for the character of a legislator is irrelevant to our judgment about his legislation. The heroes and saints did not merely give us principles to live by (though some of them did that as well): they gave us examples to follow.

Kant, as we should expect, emphatically rejects this attitude as "fatal to morality." According to him, examples serve only to render *visible* an instance of the moral principle, and thereby to demonstrate its practical feasibility. But every exemplar, such as Christ himself, must be judged by the independent criterion of the moral law, before we are entitled to recognize him as worthy of imitation. I am not suggesting that the subordination of exemplars to principles is incorrect, but that it is one-sided and fails to do justice to a large area of moral experience.

Imitation can be more or less successful. And this suggests another defect of the ethics of principles. It has no room for ideals, except the ideal of a perfect set of principles (which, as a matter of fact, is intelligible only in terms of an ideal character or way of life), and the ideal of perfect conscientiousness (which is itself a character-trait). This results, of course, from the "black-or-white" nature of moral verdicts based on rules. There are no degrees by which we approach or recede from the attainment of a certain quality or virtue; if there were not, the word "ideal" would have no meaning. Heroes and saints are not people whom we try to be *just* like, since we know that is impossible. It is precisely because it is impossible for ordinary human beings to achieve the same qualities as the saints, and in the same degree, that we do set them apart from the rest of humanity. It is enough if we try to be a little like them. . . .

VII.3 A *Critique of Virtue-Based Ethical Systems*

William Frankena

Until his recent retirement, William Frankena was professor of philosophy at
the University of Michigan. He is the author of several works in ethical
theory. Frankena disagrees with the virtue ethicist that moral virtues are a
proper basis for an ethical system. Whereas virtues are vital to the moral life,
they need to be grounded in principles of right actions or good consequences:
"Traits without principles are blind. . . ." Where there is a virtue, there must be
some possible action to which the virtue corresponds and from which it
derives its virtuosity. For example, the character trait of truthfulness is a virtue
because telling the truth, in general, is a moral duty. Likewise, conscientiousness is a virtue because we have a general duty to be morally sensitive. There is
a correspondence between principles and virtues.

Although the virtues are best seen as depending on moral principles for
their validity, they play an important role in the moral life. They provide the
dispositions that generate right action. In a sense, they are motivationally
indispensable. To complete the passage quoted above, "Traits without
principles are blind, but principles without traits are impotent." Frankena
modifies the above position, distinguishing two types of virtues: the standard
moral virtues that correspond to specific kinds of moral principles, and
nonmoral virtues (such as natural kindliness, gratefulness, and courage) that
enhance our ability to perform moral acts.

Morality and Cultivation of Traits

Our present interest, then, is not in moral principles
nor in nonmoral values, but in moral values, in what
is morally good or bad. Throughout its history morality has been concerned about the cultivation of
certain dispositions, or traits, among which are
"character" and such "virtues" (an old-fashioned
but still useful term) as honesty, kindness, and conscientiousness. Virtues are dispositions or traits that
are not wholly innate; they must all be acquired, at
least in part, by teaching and practice, or, perhaps,
by grace. They are also traits of "character," rather
than traits of "personality" like charm or shyness,

and they all involve a tendency to do certain kinds of
action in certain kinds of situations, not just to think
or feel in certain ways. They are not just abilities or
skills, like intelligence or carpentry, which one may
have without using.

In fact, it has been suggested that morality is or
should be conceived as primarily concerned, not
with rules or principles as we have been supposing
so far, but with the cultivation of such dispositions
or traits of character. Plato and Aristotle seem to
conceive of morality in this way, for they talk mainly
in terms of virtues and the virtuous, rather than in
terms of what is right or obligatory. Hume uses similar terms, although he mixes in some nonmoral
traits like cheerfulness and wit along with moral
ones like benevolence and justice. More recently,
Leslie Stephen stated the view in these words:

> . . . morality is internal. The moral law . . .
> has to be expressed in the form, "be this," not
> in the form, "do this." . . . the true moral law

From *Ethics,* Second Edition (Prentice-Hall, 1973), pp. 63–
71, © 1973. Reprinted by permission of Prentice-Hall, Inc.,
Englewood Cliffs, New Jersey.

says "hate not," instead of "kill not." . . . the only mode of stating the moral law must be as a rule of character.[1]

Ethics of Virtue

Those who hold this view are advocating an *ethics of virtue* or being, in opposition to an ethics of duty, principle, or doing, and we should note here that, although the ethical theories criticized or defended . . . were all stated as kinds of ethics of duty, they could also be recast as kinds of ethics of virtue. The notion of an ethics of virtue is worth looking at here, not only because it has a long history but also because some spokesmen of "the new morality" seem to espouse it. What would an ethics of virtue be like? It would, of course, not take deontic judgments or principles as basic in morality, as we have been doing; instead, it would take as basic aretaic judgments like "That was a courageous deed," "His action was virtuous," or "Courage is a virtue," and it would insist that deontic judgments are either derivative from such aretaic ones or can be dispensed with entirely. Moreover, it would regard aretaic judgments about actions as secondary and as based on aretaic judgments about agents and their motives or traits, as Hume does when he writes:

> . . . when we praise any actions, we regard only the motives that produced them. . . . The external performance has no merit. . . . all virtuous actions derive their merit only from virtuous motives.[2]

For an ethics of virtue, then, what is basic in morality is judgments like "Benevolence is a good motive," "Courage is a virtue," "The morally good man is kind to everyone" or, more simply and less accurately, "Be loving!"—not judgments or principles about what our duty is or what we ought to do. But, of course, it thinks that its basic instructions will guide us, not only about what to be, but also about what to do.

It looks as if there would be three kinds of ethics of virtue, corresponding to the three kinds of ethics of duty covered earlier. The question to be answered is, What dispositions or traits are moral virtues? *Trait egoism* replies that the virtues are the

dispositions that are most conducive to one's own good or welfare, or, alternatively, that prudence or a careful concern for one's own good is the cardinal or basic moral virtue, other virtues being derivative from it. *Trait utilitarianism* asserts that the virtues are those traits that most promote the general good, or, alternatively, that benevolence is the basic or cardinal moral virtue. These views may be called *trait-teleological,* but, of course, there are also *trait-deontological theories,* which will hold that certain traits are morally good or virtuous simply as such, and not just because of the non-moral value they may have or promote, or, alternatively, that there are other cardinal or basic virtues besides prudence or benevolence, for example, obedience to God, honesty, or justice. If they add that there is only one such cardinal virtue, they are monistic, otherwise pluralistic.

To avoid confusion, it is necessary to notice here that we must distinguish between *virtues* and *principles of duty* like "We ought to promote the good" and "We ought to treat people equally." A virtue is not a principle of this kind; it is a disposition, habit, quality, or trait of the person or soul, which an individual either has or seeks to have. Hence, I speak of the principle of *beneficence* and the virtue of *benevolence,* since we have two words with which to mark the difference. In the case of justice, we do not have different words, but still we must not confuse the principle of equal treatment with the disposition to treat people equally.

On the basis of our earlier discussions, we may assume at this point that views of the first two kinds are unsatisfactory, and that the most adequate ethics of virtue would be one of the third sort, one that would posit two cardinal virtues, namely, benevolence and justice, considered now as dispositions or traits of character rather than as principles of duty. By a set of cardinal virtues is meant a set of virtues that (1) they cannot be derived from one another and (2) all other moral virtues can be derived from or shown to be forms of them. Plato and other Greeks thought there were four cardinal virtues in this sense: wisdom, courage, temperance, and justice. Christianity is traditionally regarded as having seven cardinal virtues: three "theological" virtues—faith, hope, and love; and four "human" virtues—prudence, fortitude, temperance, and justice. This was essentially St. Thomas Aquinas's view; since St. Augustine regarded the last four as forms of love, only the first three were really cardinal for him.

However, many moralists, among them Schopenhauer, have taken benevolence and justice to be the cardinal moral virtues, as I would. It seems to me that all of the usual virtues (such as love, courage, temperance, honesty, gratitude, and considerateness), at least insofar as they are *moral* virtues, can be derived from these two. Insofar as a disposition cannot be derived from benevolence and justice, I should try to argue either that it is not a *moral* virtue (e.g., I take faith, hope, and wisdom to be religious or intellectual, not moral, virtues) or that it is not a virtue at all.

On Being and Doing: Morality of Traits vs. Morality of Principles

We may now return to the issue posed by the quotation from Stephen, though we cannot debate it as fully as we should. To be or to do, that is the question. Should we construe morality as primarily a following of certain principles or as primarily a cultivation of certain dispositions and traits? Must we choose? It is hard to see how a morality of principles can get off the ground except through the development of dispositions to act in accordance with its principles, else all motivation to act on them must be of an *ad hoc* kind, either prudential or impulsively altruistic. Moreover, morality can hardly be content with a mere conformity to rules, however willing and self-conscious it may be, unless it has no interest in the spirit of its law but only in the letter. On the other hand, one cannot conceive of traits of character except as including dispositions and tendencies to act in certain ways in certain circumstances. Hating involves being disposed to kill or harm, being just involves tending to do just acts (acts that conform to the principle of justice) when the occasion calls. Again, it is hard to see how we could know what traits to encourage or inculcate if we did not subscribe to principles, for example, to the principle of utility, or to those of benevolence and justice.

I propose therefore that we regard the morality of duty and principles and the morality of virtues or traits of character not as rival kinds of morality between which we must choose, but as two complementary aspects of the same morality. Then, for every principle there will be a morally good trait, often going by the same name, consisting of a disposition or tendency to act according to it; and for every morally good trait there will be a principle defining the kind of action in which it is to express itself. To parody a famous dictum of Kant's, I am inclined to think that principles without traits are impotent and traits without principles are blind.

Even if we adopt this double-aspect conception of morality, in which principles are basic, we may still agree that morality does and must put a premium on *being* honest, conscientious, and so forth. If its sanctions or sources of motivation are not to be entirely external (for example, the prospect of being praised, blamed, rewarded, or punished by others) or adventitious (for example, a purely instinctive love of others), if it is to have adequate "internal sanctions," as Mill called them, then morality must foster the development of such dispositions and habits as have been mentioned. It could hardly be satisfied with a mere conformity to its principles even if it could provide us with fixed principles of actual duty. For such a conformity might be motivated entirely by extrinsic or nonmoral considerations, and would then be at the mercy of these other considerations. It could not be counted on in a moment of trial. Besides, since morality cannot provide us with fixed principles of actual duty but only with principles of prima facie duty, it cannot be content with the letter of its law, but must foster in us the dispositions that will sustain us in the hour of decision when we are choosing between conflicting principles of prima facie duty or trying to revise our working rules of right and wrong.

There is another reason why we must cultivate certain traits of character in ourselves and others, or why we must be certain sorts of persons. Although morality is concerned that we act in certain ways, it cannot take the hard line of insisting that we act in precisely those ways, even if those ways could be more clearly defined. We cannot praise and blame or apply other sanctions to an agent simply on the ground that he has or has not acted on conformity with certain principles. It would not be right. Through no fault of his own, the agent may not have known all the relevant facts. What action the principles of morality called for in the situation may not have been clear to him, again through no fault of his own, and he may have been honestly mistaken about his duty. Or his doing what he ought to have done might have carried with it an intolerable sacrifice on his part. He may even have been simply incapable of doing it. Morality must therefore recognize various sorts of excuses and extenuating circumstances. All it can really insist on, then, except in certain critical cases, is that we develop and manifest fixed dispositions to find out what the right thing is and to do it if possible. In this sense a person must "be this" rather than "do this." But it must be remembered that "being" involves at least *trying* to "do." Being without doing, like faith without works, is dead.

At least it will be clear from this discussion that an ethics of duty or principles also has an important place for the virtues and must put a premium on their cultivation as a part of moral education and development. The place it has for virtue and/or the virtues is, however, different from that accorded them by an ethics of virtue. Talking in terms of the theory defended . . . , which was an ethics of duty, we may say that, if we ask for *guidance* about what to do or not do, then the answer is contained, at least primarily, in two deontic principles and their corollaries, namely, the principles of beneficence and equal treatment. Given these two deontic principles, plus the necessary clarity of thought and factual knowledge, we can know what we morally ought to do or not do, except perhaps in cases of conflict between them. We also know that we should cultivate two virtues, a disposition to be beneficial (i.e., benevolence) and a disposition to treat people equally (justice as a trait). But the point of acquiring these virtues is not further guidance or instruction; the function of the virtues in an ethics of duty is not to tell us what to do but to ensure that we will do it willingly in whatever situations we may face. In an ethics of virtue, on the other hand, the virtues play a dual role — they must not only move us to do what we do, they must also tell us what to do. To parody Alfred Lord Tennyson:

Theirs not (only) to do or die,
Theirs (also) to reason why.

Moral Ideals

This is the place to mention ideals again, which are among what we called the ingredients of morality. One may, perhaps, identify moral ideals with moral principles, but, more properly speaking, moral ideals are ways of being rather than of doing. Having a moral ideal is wanting to be a person of a certain sort, wanting to have a certain trait of character rather than others, for example, moral courage or perfect integrity. That is why the use of exemplary persons like Socrates, Jesus, or Martin Luther King has been such an important part of moral education and self-development, and it is one of the reasons for the writing and reading of biographies or of novels and epics in which types of moral personality are portrayed, even if they are not all heroes or saints. Often such moral ideals of personality go beyond what can be demanded or regraded as obligatory, belonging among the things to be praised rather than required, except as one may require them of oneself. It should be remembered, however, that not all personal ideals are moral ones. Achilles, Hercules, Napoleon, and Prince Charming may all be taken as ideals, but the ideals they represent are not moral ones, even though they may not be immoral ones either. Some ideals, e.g., those of chivalry, may be partly moral and partly nonmoral. There is every reason why one should pursue nonmoral as well as moral ideals, but there is no good reason for confusing them.

When one has a moral ideal, wanting to be a certain sort of moral person, one has at least some motivation to live in a certain way, but one also has something to guide him in living. Here the idea of an ethics of virtue may have a point. One may, of course, take as one's ideal that of being a good man who always does his duty from a sense of duty, perhaps gladly, and perhaps even going a second mile on occasion. Then one's guidance clearly comes entirely from one's rules and principles of duty. However, one may also have an ideal that goes beyond anything that can be regarded by others or even oneself as strict duty or obligation, a form or style of personal being that may be morally good or virtuous, but is not morally required of one. An ethics of virtue seems to provide for such an aspiration more naturally than an ethics of duty or principle, and perhaps an adequate morality should at least contain a region in which we can follow such an idea, over and beyond the region in which we are to listen to the call of duty. There certainly should be moral heroes and saints who go beyond the merely good man, if only to serve as an inspiration to others to be better and do more than they would otherwise be or do. Granted all this, however, it still seems to me that, if one's ideal is truly a moral one, there will be nothing in it that is not covered by the principles of beneficence and justice conceived as principles of what we ought to do in the wider sense referred to earlier.

Dispositions to Be Cultivated

Are there any other moral virtues to be cultivated besides benevolence and justice? No cardinal ones, of course. In this sense our answer to Socrates' question whether virtue is one or many is that it is two. We saw, however, that the principles of beneficence and equality have corollaries like telling the truth, keeping promises, etc. It follows that character traits like honesty and fidelity are virtues, though subordinate ones, and should be acquired and fostered. There will then be other such virtues corresponding to other corollaries of our main principles. Let us call all of these virtues, cardinal and non-cardinal, first-order moral virtues. Besides first-order virtues like these, there are certain other moral virtues that ought also to be cultivated, which are in a way more abstract and general and may be called second-order virtues. Conscientiousness is one such virtue; it is not limited to a certain sector of the moral life, as gratitude and honesty are, but is a virtue covering the whole of the moral life. Moral courage, or courage when moral issues are at stake, is another such second-order virtue; it belongs to all sectors of the moral life. Others that overlap with these are integrity and good-will, understanding good-will in Kant's sense of respect for the moral law.

In view of what was said . . . , we must list two other second-order traits: a disposition to find out and respect the relevant facts and a disposition to think clearly. These are not just abilities but character traits; one might have the ability to think intelligently without having a disposition to use it. They are therefore virtues, though they are intellectual virtues, not moral ones. Still, though their role is not limited to the moral life, they are necessary to it. More generally speaking, we should cultivate the virtue Plato called wisdom and Aristotle practical wisdom, which they thought of as including all of the intellectual abilities and virtues essential to the moral life.

Still other second-order qualities, which may be abilities rather than virtues, but which must be cultivated for moral living, and so may, perhaps, best be mentioned here, are moral autonomy, the ability to make moral decisions and to revise one's principles if necessary, and the ability to realize vividly, in imagination and feeling, the "inner lives" of others. Of these second-order qualities, the first two have been referred to on occasion and will be again, but something should be said about the last.

If our morality is to be more than a conformity to internalized rules and principles, if it is to include and rest on an understanding of the point of these rules and principles, and certainly if it is to involve *being* a certain kind of person and not merely *doing* certain kinds of things, then we must somehow attain and develop an ability to be aware of others as persons, as important to themselves as we are to ourselves, and to have a lively and sympathetic representation in imagination of their interests and of the effects of our actions on their lives. The need for this is particularly stressed by Josiah Royce and William James. Both men point out how we usually go our own busy and self-concerned ways, with only an external awareness of the presence of others, much as if they were things, and without any realization of their inner and peculiar worlds of personal experience; and both emphasize the need and the possibility of a "higher vision of an inner significance" which pierces this "certain blindness in human beings" and enables us to realize the existence of others in a wholly different way, as we do our own.

> What then is thy neighbor? He too is a mass of states, of experiences, thoughts and desires, just as concrete, as thou art. . . . Dost thou believe this? Art thou sure what it means? This is for thee the turning-point of thy whole conduct towards him.

These are Royce's quaint old-fashioned words. Here are James's more modern ones.

> This higher vision of an inner significance in what, until then, we had realized only in the dead external way, often comes over a person suddenly; and, when it does so, it makes an epoch in his history.

Royce calls this more perfect recognition of our neighbors "the moral insight" and James says that its practical consequence is "the well-known democratic respect for the sacredness of individuality." It is hard to see how either a benevolent (loving) or a just (equalitarian) disposition could come to fruition without it. To quote James again,

We ought, all of us, to realize each other in this intense, pathetic, and important way.

Doing this is part of what is involved in fully taking the moral point of view.

Two Questions

We can now deal with the question, sometimes raised, whether an action is to be judged right or wrong because of its results, because of the principle it exemplifies, or because the motive, intention, or trait of character involved is morally good or bad. The answer, implied in what was said [earlier], is that an action is to be judged *right* or *wrong* by reference to a principle or set of principles. Even if we say it is right or wrong because of its effects, this means that it is right or wrong by the principle of utility or some other teleological principle. But an act may also be said to be *good* or *bad,* praiseworthy or blameworthy, noble or despicable, and so on, and then the moral quality ascribed to it will depend on the agent's motive, intention, or disposition in doing it.

Another important question here is: What is moral goodness? When is a person morally good and when are his actions, dispositions, motives, or intentions morally good? Not just when he does what is actually right, for he may do what is right from bad motives, in which case he is not morally good, or he may fail to do what is right though sincerely trying to do it, in which case he is not morally bad. Whether he and his actions are morally good or not depends, not on the rightness of what he does or on its consequences, but on his character or motives; so far the statement quoted from Hume is certainly correct. But when are his motives and dispositions morally good? Some answer that a person and his actions are morally good if and only if they are motivated wholly by a sense of duty or a desire to do what is right; the Stoics and Kant sometimes seem to take this extreme view. Others hold that a man and his actions are morally good if and only if they are motivated primarily by a sense of duty or desire to do what is right, though other motives may be present too; still others contend, with Aristotle, that they are at any rate not morally good unless they are motivated at least in part by such a sense or desire. A more reasonable view, to my mind, is that a man and his actions are morally good if it is at least true that, whatever his actual motives in acting are, his sense of duty or desire to do the right is so strong in him that it would keep him trying to do his duty anyway.

Actually, I find it hard to believe that no dispositions or motivations are good or virtuous from the moral point of view except those that include a will to do the right as such. It is more plausible to distinguish two kinds of morally good dispositions or traits of character, first, those that are usually called moral virtues and do include a will to do the right, and second, others like purely natural kindliness or gratefulness, which, while they are nonmoral, are still morality-supporting, since they dispose us to do such actions as morality requires and even to perform deeds, for example, in the case of motherly love, which are well beyond the call of duty.

It has even been alleged that conscientiousness or moral goodness in the sense of a disposition to act from a sense of duty alone is not a good thing or not a virtue—that it is more desirable to have people acting from motives like friendship, gratitude, honor, love, and the like, than from a dry or driven sense of obligation. There is something to be said for this view, though it ignores the nobility of great moral courage and of the higher reaches of moral idealism. But even if conscientiousness or good will is not the only thing that is unconditionally good, as Kant believed, or the greatest of intrinsically good things, as Ross thought, it is surely a good thing from the moral point of view. For an ethics of duty, at any rate, it must be desirable that people do what is right for its own sake, especially if they do it gladly, as a gymnast may gladly make the right move just because it is right.

Endnotes

1 Leslie Stephen, *The Science of Ethics* (New York: G. P. Putnam's Sons, 1882), pp. 155, 158.

2 David Hume, *Treatise of Human Nature* (1739), Book III, Part II, opening of Sec. I.

VII.4 Are Virtues No More Than Dispositions to Obey Moral Rules?

WALTER SCHALLER

Walter Schaller is associate professor of philosophy at Texas Tech University and the author of several articles in moral philosophy. In this essay he challenges "the Standard View," which makes rules the essence of moral theory, and argues that the virtues play a complementary role, not a subordinate one, in a complete theory. Here is an abstract submitted by Schaller:

The [Standard View] concerning the relationship between virtues and vices holds that (1) moral duties can be stated in terms of rules for actions; (2) the virtues are dispositions to obey moral rules; and (3) the virtues have only instrumental value (as motives for obeying those rules).

I argue that the virtues of benevolence, gratitude, and self-respect do not conform to this view. Analysis of these recalcitrant virtues offers support for the following conclusions: (1) the duties of beneficence, gratitude, and self-respect are best understood as requiring persons to cultivate the corresponding virtue; (2) persons lacking the virtue of gratitude, for example, cannot perform acts of gratitude, for the latter just are actions motivated by gratitude (and the same is true of self-respect); and (3) the motive of duty is not always an adequate substitute for these virtues. Acts of gratitude and sympathy, for example, cannot be motivated by duty but only by those virtues.

Recent interest in the virtues has prompted reconsideration of certain questions concerning their place and function within ethical theory. On the one side of the debate are philosophers (Alasdair MacIntyre prominent among them) who argue that the virtues properly occupy center stage in morality and that the "function and authority of rules" can only be understood by reference to the virtues. On the other side are proponents of the prevailing wisdom: the moral rules are "the primary concept of the moral life" and the virtues are derived from them, for morality is concerned, first and foremost, with right and wrong conduct, with how persons ought to act.[1]

In addition to the general question of the relative importance of duties and virtue within ethical theory, there are more specific ones about the relationship between duties and virtues: Do aretaic judgments (about the goodness or virtuousness of persons) presuppose prior deontic judgments (about the rightness of actions)? Is it possible, in other words, to judge that an action is selfish, or unkind, or disrespectful, but not wrong; or does the fact that an action manifests a vice imply that it also violates some moral rule?

I shall argue that the prevailing or Standard View of the connection between virtues and duties is false; it purports to represent the nature of all moral virtues vis-à-vis the moral rules, but there are some virtues which are recalcitrant: they do not conform to its analysis. After summarizing the central tenets of the Standard View, I shall argue that the virtues of benevolence, gratitude, and self-respect cannot be conceived as the Standard View requires; they do not stand in the prescribed relation to the moral rules, nor is their moral significance or value limited in the way the Standard View supposes.

Reprinted with permission from *Philosopha* 20 (July 1990):1–2 and the author.

The Standard View

What I have been calling the Standard View consists of the following three theses:

(1) Moral rules require persons to perform or omit certain actions (act-types), and these actions can be performed by persons who lack no less than by those who possess the various virtues. On this analysis, the rule against lying, for example, can be obeyed perfectly well even by persons who lack the virtue of honesty or veracity. One's motives in obeying the rule are irrelevant to whether one has fulfilled its requirements;

(2) The moral virtues are, fundamentally and essentially, dispositions to obey the moral rules, i.e., to perform or omit certain actions.[2] Thus the heart of the virtue of honesty is a disposition to obey the moral rule which forbids telling lies, and at the core of the virtue of honesty is a disposition to obey the moral rule which forbids telling lies, and at the core of the virtue of benevolence is a disposition to perform those actions that fulfill the duty of beneficence; and

(3) The moral virtues have only instrumental or derivative value: individuals who possess the virtues are more likely to do what is right — i.e., to obey the moral rules — than are people who lack such dispositions. Certain dispositions or character traits are *virtues,* therefore, just because they motivate right conduct, and others are *vices,* because they motivate wrong actions.

Contemporary statements and defenses of the Standard View abound.[3] In *The Moral Rules* Bernard Gert defends the first two theses: moral rules are, he says, "primarily concerned with actions" and a moral virtue is "any character trait that involves unjustifiably obeying the moral rules or following moral ideals." Thus, "the degree to which one has a particular moral virtue or vice is determined by the extent to which one unjustifiably breaks the corresponding moral rule."[4]

In his response to MacIntyre's own controversial critique of the Standard View in *After Virtue,* Alan Gewirth explicitly argues for all three theses, contending that

(1) The moral rules concern only actions and not dispositions;

(2) "To have a moral virtue is to be disposed to act as moral rules direct," on the ground that "moral virtues derive their contents from the requirements set by moral rules"; and

(3) "These virtues are good to have precisely because persons who have them are more likely to do what the Principle of Generic Consistency requires," i.e., to act in accordance with the fundamental principle of morality.[5]

And finally, even though the nature of the virtues is far from the central concerns of *A Theory of Justice,* John Rawls too accepts the Standard View: "The virtues are . . . related families of dispositions and propensities regulated by a higher-order desire . . . to act from the corresponding moral principle." They are "habitual attitudes leading us to act on certain principles of right."[6]

How accurate is the Standard View? Does it withstand scrutiny when applied to three particular virtues?

The Duty of Beneficence

What I shall argue in this section is that the duty of beneficence cannot be satisfactorily formulated in accordance with the first thesis of the Standard View — that the moral rules command only certain act-types — and, consequently, the virtue of benevolence is inaccurately characterized by the second and third theses.

The claim that beneficence is a duty — and not merely supererogatory — should elicit little dissent: we *ought* to help people in need. But when we try to formulate this duty as a "moral rule for conduct" (to borrow Alan Gewirth's phrase), well-known difficulties surface. Some formulations — "Help everyone who needs help" — are clearly too strong, too demanding. Others are more plausible but otherwise flawed. The rule "Help other people as much as possible" raises the question: how much is "possible"? It is possible to give all of one's money to the poor and homeless, but doing so would surely go beyond the requirements of this duty.

Other formulations of the duty in terms of obligatory actions are inadequate because they allow persons too much latitude or discretion. The rule "One ought to help other people sometimes, to some extent"[7] is flawed for just this reason: it fails to capture the fact that on some occasions the refusal to help another person is wrong (e.g., when a drowning child can be rescued with no danger to the rescuer). And even if it is true that people who fulfill the duty of beneficence have acted beneficently "sometimes, to some extent," that way of stating the duty is inadequate as a general moral rule, as a normative guide to conduct (for an individual who helps one other person once a year has acted in conformity with that rule but is most unlikely to have satisfied the duty).

Notice, furthermore, that if the duty of beneficence cannot be stated successfully as a rule for action,[8] then the *virtue* of benevolence cannot be defined in accordance with the second thesis of the Standard View, namely, as a disposition to obey such a rule.

Given the problems that confront the attempt to conceive of the duty of beneficence in accordance with the Standard View, let us consider a different approach. Instead of defining the virtue in terms of the duty and trying to formulate the duty as an action-guiding rule sufficiently fine-grained to tell us when, how much, how often, and toward whom we ought to act beneficently, suppose the duty is conceived as requiring persons to cultivate — to seek to acquire — the virtue of benevolence, to become benevolent persons, in other words.[9]

Understanding the duty of beneficence in this way does not solve all the problems that have plagued attempts to define it along the lines of the Standard View. In particular, there is still no rule or decision-procedure for determining when, or how much, or whom one must help. But that is simply because, as Kant and Mill (among others) have pointed out, beneficence is an imperfect duty, which allows persons a certain latitude (though not in every case) in deciding how to *act* in fulfilling it. The very nature of the duty precludes a precise general statement of how persons are required to act. Nevertheless, formulating the duty in terms of the virtue does solve some of the problems — both theoretical and practical — that have undermined alternative, more traditional formulations.

First, the objections to requiring persons to *act* beneficently "as much as possible" do not extend to the obligation to develop the virtue of benevolence as much as possible. What the latter duty requires is that people become ever more willing to help those who are in need, to become less and less indifferent to human suffering. (Whether one actually does —

and ought to — act beneficently in a particular case will depend upon the total circumstances, e.g., whether there are overriding reasons for not helping, whether one is capable of providing the requisite assistance, etc.).

Second, consider the case of the infant drowning in a shallow pool who could be easily rescued. Someone who had a policy of acting beneficently "sometimes, to some extent" could callously walk past this child without violating that policy; but letting that child drown is clearly inconsistent with possessing the virtue of benevolence. Not trying to save that infant would thus be prima facie evidence (of a very compelling sort) that one lacks the virtue of benevolence. In short, since there should be no doubt that one has a duty to rescue a child in such straits, formulating the general duty of beneficence in terms of the virtue yields a conclusion more in conformity with our intuitions about what ought to be done than do formulations of the duty in terms of obligatory actions.

Third, if the duty of beneficence is explicated in terms of actions some of which are optional, then an individual's refusal to perform a particular helping act which (unlike saving the drowning baby) is not obligatory provides no reason by itself for concluding that that person is not fulfilling the duty satisfactorily. If Alex, for example, obstinately refuses to perform a simple helping action which would cost him little in terms of time, money, or effort, yet which he is not duty-bound to perform, his selfish refusal may indicate a shortcoming[10] in his character (in the sense that he has not acted as the perfectly virtuous person would act), but, according to the Standard View, he has not acted wrongly. A negative aretaic judgment might be in order, but not a negative deontic judgment.

But if Alex has a duty to cultivate a benevolent disposition, then his selfish refusal to perform this particular action is at least prima facie evidence of a failure to fulfill that duty (for selfishness is incompatible with benevolence). On this interpretation of the duty of beneficence, there is not a sharp division between virtue and duty: The aretaic judgments that are properly made about a person bear on the question whether he has fulfilled his duties.

Furthermore, on the present interpretation of this duty, a later generous action does not excuse or "make up for" an earlier selfish one. A person can at best only partially overcome the prima facie implication of selfishness arising from a selfish action by subsequently carrying out a benevolent one. Thus, Alex's refusal to help Jack at t_1 does not cease to be a selfish action—and a sign of his lack of benevolence—just because he helps Jill at t_2. To be sure, the fact that Alex does help Jill after having failed to lend a hand to Jack indicates that he is less selfish than if he ignored Jill's needs too. But even if the good of the latter action outweighs the harm resulting from the former, this does not justify or excuse the earlier action. (Compare this to the way that a baseball player can compensate for a costly fielding error or strikeout by hitting a game-winning home run later; the latter action erases the negative effects of the former.)

Fourth, for the person who has cultivated the virtue of benevolence, the question whether she *ought* to help a needy individual on a given occasion will often be subordinated to, or even displaced by, the question whether this is a person whom she is *able* to help. Nonbenevolent persons will tend to ask whether they "have to" perform a given beneficent action and may often seek reasons or excuses not to. But the more one possesses the virtue of benevolence, the less will the fact that a particular action is not, strictly speaking, obligatory count as a reason not to perform it. The benevolent person will *want* to help people in need and will look for ways to overcome whatever obstacles might stand in the way of providing the needed aid or assistance.

Formulating the duty of beneficence in terms of the character trait of benevolence thus has the virtue of providing a middle path between the two extremes rejected above (that one ought to help other people "sometimes, to some extent," and that individuals must help others as much as possible).

The argument to this point has been that the duty of beneficence cannot be adequately formulated consistent with the first two theses of the Standard View. Next I want to show that the third thesis must also be rejected (or at least revised). It holds that the virtues have only instrumental value: people who possess them are more likely to obey the moral rules for the simple reason that the virtues just are dispositions to obey those rules. Moreover (and this is the point I want to stress), a person who lacks a particular virtue is not thereby disabled from fulfilling completely and satisfactorily the correlative duty. Good character is not required for right conduct.

In treating the virtues as having only instrumental value, the Standard View overlooks the fact that on some occasions a person who lacks the virtues of benevolence or sympathy is thereby unable to provide the kind of assistance that another person needs.[11] For what is required in such circumstances is not some external good or service—which could be supplied by persons acting from duty, or even from self-interest—but sympathy itself (or love, compassion, or some other altruistic emotion). In these cases the needy individual will not be benefited except by the action of someone who *is* sympathetic and who *feels* compassion, i.e., someone who possesses these virtues. Possessing the virtue is thus not good or necessary simply as a motive for an independently specified act of beneficence; on the contrary, the beneficent action itself is not possible except for one who is motivated by benevolence, sympathy, or some other altruistic emotion.[12]

The Virtue of Gratitude[13]

The Standard View also fails to describe accurately either the virtue or the duty of gratitude. On that view it should be possible (1) to formulate a "rule for conduct" obedience to which will fully satisfy the duty, and (2) for persons who lack the virtue to satisfy the duty (by obeying the rule from, say, the motive of duty).

Let us consider the second claim first. Recall that with respect to beneficence, it is possible for a nonbenevolent (even a selfish) person to perform beneficent actions. There is nothing problematic about acting beneficently from the motive of duty. But gratitude is different, for what constitutes an act of gratitude is the motive from which it is done (along with the beliefs and attitudes of the agent). In order to perform an act of gratitude, one must *be* grateful (at least on that occasion, though not necessarily in the sense of having the virtue as an enduring character trait). Duty cannot serve as a substitute or back-up motive without altering the nature of the action being performed.

Now it is of course possible to perform what *appear* to be acts of gratitude even if one lacks the virtue, even if one is not grateful for the favor or benefit one has received. Moreover, we should agree that if someone has done you a favor, or voluntarily benefited you in some way, then you generally ought to act *as if* you are grateful even if you are not.

The only thing worse than an insincere show of gratitude is no show of gratitude (even if the former is pure show and the latter is genuine). There is something to be said for keeping up appearances in morality no less than in etiquette.

So let us grant that it is possible to formulate a "rule for action" concerning gratitude to the effect that whenever one is the beneficiary of another's benevolence, one has a duty to express gratitude, to act as if one is grateful, even at the cost of insincerity. This is a rule which persons who are ungrateful (who lack the virtue) can fulfill as well as those who are grateful — just as the Standard View's first thesis requires.

But the fact that such a rule for behavior can be formulated does not imply that the duty of gratitude is fulfilled simply by obeying it. On the contrary, in acting "gratefully" from some other motive, one does not so much fulfill that duty as avoid the greater wrong of acting as if one is ungrateful, of appearing to have the vice of ingratitude.

In short, the duty of gratitude cannot be stated satisfactorily as a moral rule for action; on the contrary, in order to fulfill it, one must possess the virtue of gratitude. And from this requirement it follows that the second thesis of the Standard View is also false as regards gratitude: This virtue is not simply a disposition to obey a moral rule for action. It consists rather in having certain beliefs, feelings, and attitudes toward, and about, one's benefactors (and, of course, in acting in the appropriate ways).

Finally, gratitude's value as a virtue is not merely instrumental. For although it will typically serve as a motive for acts of gratitude,[14] its value does not lie solely in its utility as a motive. Insofar as the duty of gratitude can be understood in Kantian terms as following from the more general duty to regard or value — to respect — persons as ends in themselves, it follows that what this duty requires first and foremost is that persons *appreciate* the favor that has been done them and that they do not regard their benefactor as existing solely to provide such favors (i.e., merely as an instrument for promoting their happiness). The value of acts of gratitude thus lies less in the benefits they confer upon the original benefactor than in the fact that they are evidence of certain beliefs and attitudes (e.g., of respect) on the part of the agent. The value of grateful acts is derived from the value of the virtue of gratitude, and not conversely (as the Standard View suggests).

The Virtue of Self-Respect

The Kantian idea that self-respect is a moral virtue, even a duty, does not command widespread acceptance these days. Yet, despite the various objections that can be — and have been — raised against it (that there are no duties to oneself, for example), it is not such an unreasonable idea. For just as other people ought to be respected because of their autonomy and rationality, so individuals ought to respect themselves for the same reasons. Following Kant's analysis of the Principle of Humanity, it is clear that persons are capable of acting in ways which are inconsistent with their own capacity for autonomy: they can fail to value and treat themselves as ends just as they can fail to treat others as ends.

In the interests of brevity I shall not attempt a full defense of the Kantian doctrine of respect and self-respect. Instead, drawing upon Thomas E. Hill, Jr.'s well-known account of servility and self-respect,[15] I shall argue that *if* self-respect is a virtue (and a duty), it provides a third counterexample to the Standard View.

If the Standard View were true with respect to self-respect, then it should be possible (in accordance with the first thesis) to formulate a moral rule for action which could be obeyed even by persons who lack this virtue, indeed, even by persons who have the opposite trait of servility. But no such rule is possible, for servility and self-respect are fundamentally matters of attitude and belief, not merely of conduct. Whether an action counts as servile, for example, depends less upon *what* the agent does than upon his or her beliefs, attitudes, and reasons for performing the action. The Deferential Wife — to take the best-known of Hill's three examples of servility — is not servile merely because of what she does (namely, defer to her husband's preferences), for deference is not the same as servility, but rather because of her reasons for deferring, because of the beliefs and attitudes she has about her own moral rights, worth, and status. Like the Uncle Tom and the Self-Deprecator (Hill's other two examples of servile character types), the Deferential Wife has a tendency "to deny or disavow" her moral rights; she fails to "understand or acknowledge" her rights and place as an equal within the moral community.

In short, the virtue of self-respect does not conform to the Standard View's first thesis for the same reason the virtue of gratitude did not: In neither case can a sharp distinction be drawn between motive and action. Just as a grateful action is one motivated by the virtue of gratitude, so a self-respecting action (or, more accurately, an action exhibiting self-respect) is one which is done from that virtue. Consequently, no rule for action concerning self-respect can be formulated which could be obeyed by persons who lack self-respect. If there is a *duty* of self-respect, it must be understood not in terms of a rule for action but rather on the model of gratitude, as a duty to seek to cultivate the virtue of self-respect.

Furthermore, in the absence of such a rule for action, the virtue of self-respect cannot be merely a disposition to obey such a rule (as the second thesis requires). Instead, the virtue must consist in having the appropriate beliefs and attitudes about one's moral worth, dignity, and rights (as well as in acting in accordance with them). And from this it follows, just as it did for gratitude, that the virtue of self-respect cannot be of merely instrumental value.

Conclusions

1. Not all virtues are alike. Some conform to the Standard View, but others do not. With respect to the latter group, the Standard View gets the relationship between duties and virtues backwards: in each of these cases, since the kind of action in question cannot (always) be carried out by persons who lack the virtue — by persons acting from the motive of duty, for example — possessing the virtue is of central, not of secondary or derivative, importance. Persons lacking the virtue of sympathy cannot respond helpfully to people who need sympathy, and individuals who lack the virtues of gratitude and self-respect can at best only imitate the actions called for by those duties. For these reasons the duties of beneficence, gratitude, and self-respect are best interpreted, not simply as duties to perform certain actions, but as duties to cultivate a virtue, to develop certain character traits. (This is not to deny that one cannot fulfill these duties without also acting.)

2. Neither the moral rules nor the virtues stand alone at the heart of moral theory. On the one hand, not all virtues can be analyzed as dispositions to fulfill duties which are *prior* to and more *basic* than

those virtues; on the other hand, I do not wish to defend a full-fledged ethics of virtue which expels the moral rules and the concept of duty from ethical theory altogether.

3. Without denying that ethics is fundamentally practical, that it is essentially concerned with conduct, I would argue that it is not concerned *just* with (external) conduct. More specifically, the moral importance of the virtues is not exhausted by their relation to conduct (even if that relation is more complex and multidimensional than the Standard View allows). Consider the virtue of gratitude again. Typically, one who is the recipient of another's generosity is under an obligation to *do* something, if at all possible, in return (if only to say "Thank you"). And of course, one should also *be* grateful: the point of the action is to demonstrate the fact of one's gratitude.

But with a little imagination we could sketch a case in which one person (let's call her Pat) does a small but nevertheless not insignificant favor for another person (call her Chris), and the debt of gratitude which Chris incurs by accepting the favor is completely discharged if Chris simply *is* grateful and does not do or say anything to manifest her gratitude. The "moral order" is restored if (1) Chris *acknowledges* (to herself) that Pat's action shows that she values Chris and Chris's happiness, and (2) Chris *appreciates* Pat's favor, or at least appreciates the fact that another person values her enough to do such a favor.

Such a conclusion is possible because the duty of gratitude is essentially a duty to respect other persons. The fact that one is grateful for a favor shows that one does not regard one's benefactor merely as an instrument of one's own happiness. And the duty of respect is not limited to conduct: besides being obligated to *treat* persons with respect, we ought also to *regard* or *value* them as ends and not merely as means. It is for this reason that Chris is able to satisfy the duty of gratitude simply by *being* grateful. The duty of respect, and thus the duty of gratitude, do not always require any further action.

Endnotes

[1] Quoted phrases in this paragraph are from Alasdair MacIntyre, *After Virtue* (Notre Dame: University of Notre Dame Press, 1981), pp. 112, 239.

[2] I am grateful to Robert C. Roberts for the observation (addressed to an earlier version of this paper read at the Central Division meetings of the APA) that it is unexceptional to say (as I had) that virtues are (among other things) dispositions to obey moral rules, but that saying they are *nothing but* such dispositions (which is what I clearly intended to imply) is obviously false. The virtue of honesty incorporates a number of dispositions (e.g., dispositions to feel guilt if one lies, or to feel revulsion at the lies told by others), and not simply a disposition to honest behavior.

While Roberts is right to point out the internal complexity of the virtues, the point I was making is unaffected. For what is the value of a disposition to feel guilt except that such guilt is instrumental in preventing further acts of lying, or that it shows that the person who lied still respects the rule he has broken. These other dispositions are part of the virtue only because they support the central and more fundamental disposition to act as the rule requires. Their value, in other words, must be cashed out in terms of the value of the rule for action, as the third thesis states.

[3] In addition to the statements of the Standard View cited in notes 4–7, see also John Kilcullen, "Utilitarianism and Virtue," *Ethics* 93 (1983). The leading exponent is, of course, Kant (at least as he has traditionally been interpreted); I have argued elsewhere (see note 9 below), however, that Kant is best interpreted as a critic of the Standard View.

[4] Bernard Gert, *The Moral Rules* (New York: Harper and Row, 1966), pp. 153, 155, 156. For Gert, it should be noted, one does not possess a virtue just because (as a sufficient condition) one obeys the corresponding moral rule. Being honest or benevolent or kind (to name three virtues) also requires acting for the right reasons or having the right motives. But this is still consistent with the first thesis of the Standard View.

[5] Alan Gewirth, *Reason and Morality* (Chicago: University of Chicago Press, 1978), p. 339, and "Rights and Virtues," *Review of Metaphysics* 38 (1985), pp. 739–762.

[6] John Rawls, *A Theory of Justice* (Cambridge: Harvard University Press, 1971), pp. 192, 437.

[7] For this formulation see Thomas E. Hill, Jr., "Kant on Imperfect Duty and Supererogation," *Kant–Studien* 62 (1971), p. 56.

[8] Admittedly, I have not surveyed all attempts to formulate the duty of beneficence in terms of obligatory actions. A more complete argument would need to cover a wider range of alternative formulations.

[9] I have argued for this interpretation of Kant's duties of virtue in "Sympathy and Moral Worth in Kant's Ethics," *Southern Journal of Philosophy* (Winter 1987) and in "Kant's Architectonic of Duty," *Philosophy and Phenomenological Research* (December 1987).

[10] I adopt the notion of a shortcoming from an insightful article by Gregory W. Trianosky, "Supererogation, Wrongdoing, and Vice: On the Autonomy of the Ethics of Virtue," *Journal of Philosophy* 83 (1986), pp. 26–40. Trianosky writes that "the deliberate omission of a supererogatory act on a given occasion entails that the agent's motivational structure on that occasion falls short of what the ideal, fully virtuous person would display" and thus reveals a shortcoming (31).

[11] This has been argued by a number of critics of Kant's doctrine of moral worth. See, for example, Lawrence Blum, *Friendship, Altruism, and Morality* (London: Routledge and Kegan Paul, 1980), pp. 37–38, 142–143.

A word of caution against a possible misunderstanding. The argument is not merely that sympathy or benevolence is sometimes necessary as a motive for beneficent action (although that is true), for that implies that the action can be conceived independently of the motive. Rather, the argument here is that on occasion a person lacking the virtue is unable to perform the needed action, for what is needed is an action done from a certain motive. To speak of the motive as distinct from the action is in these cases misleading, for the action confers a good only because it is done from that motive. If carried out from, say, the motive of duty, the good to the recipient would be far less.

[12] Tolstoy's short story, "The Death of Ivan Ilych," illustrates how people who lack sympathy and compassion are handicapped when confronted with certain kinds of human need. Toward the end of the story, when Ivan is near death, Tolstoy writes:

> He saw that no one felt for him, because no one even wished to grasp his position. Only Gerasim recognized it and pitied him. . . . And so Ivan Ilych felt at ease only with him. . . . Gerasim alone did not lie; everything showed that he alone understood the facts of the case and did not consider it necessary to disguise them, but simply felt sorry for his emaciated and enfeebled master. . . . And in Gerasim's attitude toward him there was something akin to what he wished for, and so that attitude comforted him.

(*The Death of Ivan Ilych and Other Stories* (New York: New American Library, 1960), p. 138). Gerasim cannot save Ivan from death; all he can do is sympathize with (in this translation, pity) him; nonetheless, Ivan finds this beneficial. It is, one might say, just what the doctor ordered (or should have ordered) but could not himself provide.

This scene illustrates that in addition to his "impersonal" or external needs (which could be provided equally well by his family, his doctor, or even by a competent stranger), Ivan felt the need for someone else — for another human being — to understand that he was dying and to have sympathy or pity for him. Far from having instrumental value (as a means to, or motive for, providing something else which Ivan wanted), Gerasim's capacity for sympathy was essential to his ability to comfort Ivan. For what Ivan needed was sympathy itself, not those things which result from actions that happen to be motivated by sympathy.

[13] The following account of gratitude draws on Fred Berger, "Gratitude," *Ethics* 85 (1985), pp. 298–305, and A. D. M. Walter, "Gratefulness and Gratitude," *Proceedings of The Aristotelian Society* 81 (1980–81), pp. 39–55.

Berger argues that "expressions of gratitude are demonstrations of a complex of belief, feelings, and attitudes"; in particular, that (1) we believe that our benefactor *intended* to benefit us ("gratitude is a response to the benevolence of others"); (2) we recognize the value of the benefactor's act; (3) we do not regard our benefactor "as having the value only of an instrument of [our] welfare," i.e., we respect him or her; and (4) we appreciate the favor, gift, or benefit.

Walker, while taking issue with Berger's account at several points, is in agreement on the fundamental point that "the distinctive feature of the grateful return is its motivation, that the grateful return must be made from a desire to favour one's benefactor because he has favoured oneself and be accompanied by good will" (51).

[14] In fact, to speak of the virtue as a motive for action is redundant: an act of gratitude just is an action motivated by gratitude. The motive is not something distinct from the ac-

tion such that one could perform that kind of action from a different motive.

[15] "Servility and Self-Respect," *The Monist* 57 (1973), pp. 87–104. See also Marcia Baron, "Servility, Critical Deference, and the Deferential Wife," *Philosophical Studies* 48 (1985), pp. 393–400, and Hill, "Self-Respect Revisited," *Tulane Studies in Philosophy,* Vol. 31 (New Orleans: Tulane University, 1982), pp. 129–137.

VII.5 *Some Vices of Virtue Ethics*

Robert Louden

Robert Louden is professor of philosophy at the University of Southern Maine. In this essay he raises one of the perennial criticisms of virtue-based ethical systems, namely, that such theories provide no guidance in ways to resolve an ethical dilemma. In Aristotle's *Nicomachean Ethics,* precious little is said about what we are supposed to *do.* One would think that ethics should be, at least to some extent, action-guiding. Aristotle's answer seems to be: Do what a good person would do. But, the question arises: Who is the good person and how shall I recognize him or her? Furthermore, even if we could answer that question without reference to kinds of actions or principles addressed by the nonvirtue-oriented ethicists, it is not always clear what ideal persons would do in our situations. Sometimes Aristotle writes as though the right action is that intermediate or "golden" mean between two extremes, but it is often difficult, if not impossible, to determine how to apply this concept in actual situations.

Louden raises a number of other important questions and presents other criticisms, aimed for the most part at complete virtue-based ethical systems accounts, such as those of G. E. M. Anscombe, Philippa Foot, and Richard Taylor, wherein no principle is valid apart from a virtue. Louden suggests that other principles are needed. Whether his criticisms can be met or whether there is a modified ethics of virtue to replace the pure virtue-based theories is a matter left for readers to decide for themselves.

It is common knowledge by now that recent philosophical and theological writing about ethics reveals a marked revival of interest in the virtues. But what exactly are the distinctive features of a so-called virtue ethics? Does it have a special contribution to make to our understanding of moral experience? Is

there a price to be paid for its different perspective, and if so, is the price worth paying?

Contemporary textbook typologies of ethics still tend to divide the terrain of normative ethical theory into the teleological and deontological. Both types of theory, despite their well-defined differences, have a common focus on acts as opposed to qualities of agents. The fundamental question that both types of theory are designed to answer is: What ought I to do? What is the correct analysis and

Reprinted with permission from *American Philosophical Quarterly* 21 (1984):227–236.

resolution of morally problematic situations? A second feature shared by teleological and deontological theories is conceptual reductionism. Both types of theory start with a primary irreducible element and then proceed to introduce secondary derivative concepts which are defined in terms of their relations to the beginning element. Modern teleologists (the majority of whom are utilitarians) begin with a concept of the good—here defined with reference to states of affairs rather than persons. After this criterion of the good is established, the remaining ethical categories are defined in terms of this starting point. Thus, according to the classic maxim, one ought always to promote the greatest good for the greatest number. Duty, in other words, is defined in terms of the element of ends—one ought always to maximize utility. The concepts of virtue and rights are also treated as derivative categories of secondary importance, definable in terms of utility. For the classic utilitarian, a right is upheld "so long as it is upon the whole advantageous to the society that it should be maintained," while virtue is construed as a "tendency to give a net increase to the aggregate quantity of happiness in all its shapes taken together."[1]

For the deontologist, on the other hand, the concept of duty is the irreducible starting point, and any attempt to define this root notion of being morally bound to do something in terms of the good to be achieved is rejected from the start. The deontologist is committed to the notion that certain acts are simply inherently right. Here the notion of the good is only a derivative category, definable in terms of the right. The good that we are to promote is right action for its own sake—duty for duty's sake. Similarly, the virtues tend to be defined in terms of pro-attitudes toward one's duties. Virtue is important, but only because it helps us do our duty.

But what about virtue ethics? What are the hallmarks of this approach to normative ethics? One problem confronting anyone who sets out to analyze the new virtue ethics in any detail is that we presently lack fully developed examples of it in the contemporary literature. Most of the work done in this genre has a negative rather than positive thrust—its primary aim is more to criticize the traditions and research programs to which it is opposed rather than to state positively and precisely what its own alternative is. A second hindrance is that the literature often has a somewhat misty antiquarian air. It is frequently said, for instance, that the Greeks advocated a virtue ethics, though what precisely it is that they were advocating is not always spelled out. In describing contemporary virtue ethics, it is therefore necessary, in my opinion, to do some detective work concerning its conceptual shape, making inferences based on the unfortunately small number of remarks that are available.

For purposes of illustration, I propose to briefly examine and expand on some key remarks made by two contemporary philosophers—Elizabeth Anscombe and Philippa Foot—whose names have often been associated with the revival of the virtue movement. Anscombe, in her frequently cited article, "Modern Moral Philosophy," writes: "you can do ethics without it [viz., the notion of 'obligation' or 'morally ought'], as is shown by the example of Aristotle. It would be a great improvement if, instead of 'morally wrong,' one always named a genus such as 'untruthful,' 'unchaste,' 'unjust.'"[2] Here we find an early rallying cry for an ethics of virtue program, to be based on contemporary efforts in philosophical psychology and action theory. On the Anscombe model, strong, irreducible duty and obligation notions drop out of the picture, and are to be replaced by vices such as unchasteness and untruthfulness. But are we to take the assertion literally, and actually attempt to do moral theory without any concept of duty whatsoever? On my reading, Anscombe is not really proposing that we entirely dispose of moral oughts. Suppose one follows her advice, and replaces "morally wrong" with "untruthful," "unchaste," etc. Isn't this merely shorthand for saying that agents *ought* to be truthful and chaste, and that untruthful and unchaste acts are *morally wrong* because good agents don't perform such acts? The concept of the moral ought, in other words, seems now to be explicated in terms of what the good person would do.[3]

A similar strategy is at work in some of Foot's articles. In the Introduction to her recent collection of essays, *Virtues and Vices and Other Essays in Moral Philosophy,* she announces that one of the two major themes running throughout her work is "the thought that a sound moral philosophy should start from a theory of virtues and vices."[4] When this thought is considered in conjunction with the central argument in her article, "Morality as a System of Hypothetical Imperatives," the indication is that another virtue-based moral theory is in the making. For in this essay Foot envisions a moral community composed of an "army of volunteers," composed, that is, of agents who voluntarily commit themselves to such moral ideals as truth, justice, generosity, and kindness.[5] In a moral community of this sort, all moral imperatives become hypothetical rather than categorical: there are things an agent morally ought to do if he or she wants truth, justice, generosity, or kindness, but no things an agent morally ought to do if he or she isn't first committed to these (or other) moral ideals. On the Foot model (as presented in "Morality as a System"), what distinguishes an ethics of virtue from its competitors is that it construes the ideal moral agent as acting from a direct desire, without first believing that he or she morally ought to perform that action or have that desire. However, in a more recent paper, Foot has expressed doubts about her earlier attempts to articulate the relationship between oughts and desires. In "William Frankena's Carus Lectures" (1981), she states that "*thoughts* [my emphasis] about what is despicable or contemptible, or low, or again admirable, glorious or honourable may give us the key to the problem of rational moral action."[6] But regardless of whether she begins with desires or with thoughts, it seems clear her strategy too is not to dispense with oughts entirely, but rather to employ softer, derivative oughts.

In other words, conceptual reductionism is at work in virtue ethics too. Just as its utilitarian and deontological competitors begin with primitive concepts of the good state of affairs and the intrinsically right action respectively and then drive secondary concepts out of their starting points, so virtue ethics, beginning with a root conception of the morally good person, proceeds to introduce a different set of secondary concepts which are defined in terms of their relationship to the primitive element. Though the ordering of primitive and derivatives differs in each case, the overall strategy remains the same. Viewed from this perspective, virtue ethics is not unique at all. It has adopted the traditional mononomic strategy of normative ethics. What sets it apart from other approaches, again, is its strong agent orientation.

So for virtue ethics, the primary object of moral evaluation is not the act or its consequences, but rather the agent. And the respective conceptual starting points of agent and act-centered ethics result in other basic differences as well, which may be briefly summarized as follows. First of all, the two camps are likely to employ different models of practical reasoning. Act theorists, because they focus on discrete acts and moral quandaries, are naturally very interested in formulating decision procedures for making practical choices. The agent, in their conceptual scheme, needs a guide — hopefully a determinate decision procedure — for finding a way out of the quandary. Agent-centered ethics, on the other hand, focuses on long-term characteristic patterns of action, intentionally downplaying atomic acts and particular choice situations in the process. They are not as concerned with portraying practical reason as a rule-governed enterprise which can be applied on a case-by-case basis.

Secondly, their views on moral motivation differ. For the deontological act theorist, the preferred motive for moral action is the concept of duty itself; for the utilitarian act theorist, it is the disposition to seek the happiness of all sentient creatures. But for the virtue theorist, the preferred motivation factor is the virtues themselves (here understood non-reductionistically). The agent who correctly acts from the disposition of charity does so (according to the virtue theorist) not because it maximizes utility or because it is one's duty to do so, but rather out of a commitment to the value of charity for its own sake.

While I am sympathetic to recent efforts to recover virtue from its long-standing neglect, my purpose in this essay is not to contribute further to the campaign for virtue. Instead, I wish to take a more critical look at the phenomenon, and to ask whether there are certain important features of morality which a virtue-based ethics either handles poorly or ignores entirely. In the remainder of this essay, I shall sketch some objections which (I believe) point to genuine shortcomings of the virtue approach to ethics. My object here is not to offer an exhaustive or even thoroughly systematic critique of virtue ethics, but rather to look at certain mundane regions of the moral field and to ask first what an ethics of virtue might say about them, and second whether what it says about them seems satisfactory.

Agents vs. Acts

As noted earlier, it is a commonplace that virtue theorists focus on good and bad agents rather than on right and wrong acts. In focusing on good and bad agents, virtue theorists are thus forced to deemphasize discrete acts in favor of long-term, characteristic patterns of behavior. Several related problems arise for virtue ethics as a result of this particular conceptual commitment.

a. *Casuistry and Applied Ethics.* It has often been said that for virtue ethics the central question is not "What ought I to *do?*" but rather "What sort of person ought I to *be?*"[7] However, people have always expected ethical theory to tell them something about what they ought to do, and it seems to me that virtue ethics is structurally unable to say much of anything about this issue. If I'm right, one consequence of this is that a virtue-based ethics will be particularly weak in the areas of casuistry and applied ethics. A recent reviewer of Foot's *Virtues and Vices,* for instance, notes that "one must do some shifting to gather her view on the virtues." "Surprisingly," he adds, "the studies of abortion and euthanasia are not of much use."[8] And this is odd, when one considers Foot's demonstrated interest in applied ethics in conjunction with her earlier cited prefatory remark that a "sound moral theory should start from a theory of virtues and vices." But what can a virtues and vices approach say about specific moral dilemmas? As virtue theorists from Aristotle onward have rightly emphasized, virtues are not simply dispositions to behave in specified ways, for which rules and principles can always be cited. In addition, they involve skills of perception and articulation, situation-specific "know-how," all of which are developed only through recognizing and acting on what is relevant in concrete moral contexts as they arise. These skills of moral perception and practical reason are not completely routinizable, and so cannot be transferred from agent to agent as any sort of decision procedure "package deal." Due to the very nature of the moral virtues, there is thus a very limited amount of advice on moral quandaries that one can reasonably expect from the virtue-oriented approach. We ought, of course, to do what the virtuous person would do, but it is not always easy to fathom what the hypothetical moral exemplar would do were he in our shoes, and sometimes even he will act out of character. Furthermore, if one asks him why he did what he did, or how he knew what to do, the answer — if one is offered — might not be very enlightening. One would not necessarily expect him to appeal to any rules or principles which might be of use to others.

We can say, à la Aristotle, that the virtuous agent acts for the sake of the noble *(tou kalou heneka),* that he will not do what is base or depraved, etc. But it seems to me that we cannot intelligently say things like: "The virtuous person (who acts for the sake of the noble) is also one who recognizes that all mentally deficient eight-month-old fetuses should (or should not) be aborted, that the doctor/patient principle of confidentiality must always (or not always) be respected, etc." The latter simply sound too strange, and their strangeness stems from the fact that motives of virtue and honor cannot be fully routinized.

Virtue theory is not a problem-oriented or quandary approach to ethics: it speaks of rules and principles of action only in a derivative manner. And its derivative oughts are frequently too vague and unhelpful for persons who have not yet acquired the requisite moral insight and sensitivity. Consequently, we cannot expect it to be of great use in applied ethics and casuistry. The increasing importance of these two subfields of ethics in contemporary society is thus a strike against the move to revive virtue ethics.

b. *Tragic Humans.* Another reason for making sure that our ethical theory allows us to talk about features of acts and their results in abstraction from the agent and his conception of what he is doing is that sometimes even the best person can make the wrong choices. There are cases in which a man's choice is grounded in the best possible information, his motives honorable and his action not at all out of character. And yet his best laid plans may go sour. Aristotle, in his *Poetics,* suggests that here lies the source of tragedy: we are confronted with an eminent and respected man, "whose misfortune, however, is brought upon him not by vice *(kakia)* and depravity *(moktheira)* but by some error of judgment *(amartia)*" . . . . But every human being is morally fallible, for there is a little Oedipus in each of us. So Aristotle's point is that *regardless of character,* anyone can fall into the sort of mistake of which tragedies are made. Virtue ethics, however, since its conceptual scheme is rooted in the notion of the good person, is unable to assess correctly the occasional (inevitable) tragic outcomes of human action.

Lawrence Becker, in his article, "The Neglect of Virtue," seems at first to draw an opposite conclusion from similar reflections about virtue theory and tragedy, for it is his view that virtue ethics makes an indispensable contribution to our understanding of tragedy. According to him, "there are times when the issue is not how much harm has been done, or the value to excusing the wrongdoer, or the voluntary nature of the offending behavior, but rather whether the sort of character indicated by the behavior is 'acceptable' or not — perhaps even ideal — so that the 'wrongful' conduct must be seen simply as an unavoidable defect of it."[9] As Becker sees it, Oedipus merely comes off as a fool who asked too many questions when viewed from the perspective of act theories. Only a virtue ethics, with its agent perspective, allows us to differentiate tragic heroes from fools, and to view the acts that flow from each character type in their proper light. And the proper light in the case of tragic heroes is that there are unavoidable defects in this character type, even though it represents a human ideal. Becker's point is well taken, but its truth does not cancel out my criticism. My point is that virtue ethics is in danger of blinding itself to the wrongful conduct in Oedipal acts, simply because it views the Oedipuses of the world as honorable persons *and* because its focus is on long-term character manifestations rather than discrete acts. To recognize the wrong in Oedipal behavior, a theory with the conceptual tools enabling one to focus on discrete acts is needed. (Notice, incidentally, that Becker's own description does just this.)

c. *Intolerable Actions.* A third reason for insisting that our moral theory enable us to assess acts in abstraction from agents is that we need to be able to identify certain types of action which produce harms of such magnitude that they destroy the bonds of community and render (at least temporarily) the achievement of moral goods impossible. In every traditional moral community one encounters prohibitions or "barriers to action" which mark off clear boundaries in such areas as the taking of innocent life, sexual relations, and the administration of justice according to local laws and customs.[10] Such rules are needed to teach citizens what kinds of actions are to be regarded not simply as bad (a table of vices can handle this) but as intolerable.[11] Theorists must resort to specific lists of offenses to emphasize the fact that there are some acts which are absolutely prohibited. We cannot articulate this sense of absolute prohibition by referring merely to characteristic patterns of behavior.

In rebuttal here, the virtue theorist may reply by saying: "Virtue ethics does not need to articulate these prohibitions — let the law do it, with its list of do's and don'ts." But the sense of requirement and prohibition referred to above seems to me to be at bottom inescapably moral rather than legal. Morality can (and frequently does) invoke the aid of law in such cases, but when we ask *why* there is a law against e.g., rape or murder, the proper answer is that it is morally intolerable. To point merely to a legal convention when asked why an act is prohibited or intolerable raises more questions than it answers.

d. *Character Change.* A fourth reason for insisting that a moral theory be able to assess acts in abstraction from agents and their conception of what they're doing is that people's moral characters may sometimes change. Xenophon, toward the beginning of his *Memorabilia* (I.II.21), cites an unknown poet who says: "Ah, but a good man is at one time noble (*esthlos*), at another wicked (*kakos*)." Xenophon himself agrees with the poet: ". . . many alleged (*phaskonton*) philosophers may say: A just (*dikaios*) man can never become unjust; a self-controlled (*sophron*) man can never become wanton (*hubristes*); in fact no one having learned any kind of knowledge (*mathesis*) can become ignorant of it. I do not hold this view. . . . For I see that, just as poetry is forgotten unless it is often repeated, so instruction, when no longer heeded, fades from the mind."[12]

Xenophon was a practical man who was not often given to speculation, but he arrived at his position on character change in the course of his defense of Socrates. One of the reasons Socrates got into trouble, Xenophon believed, was due to his contact with Critias and Alcibiades during their youth. For of all Athenians, "none wrought so many evils to the *polis*." However, Xenophon reached the conclusion that Socrates should not be blamed for the disappearance of his good influence once these two had ceased their close contact with him.

If skills can become rusty, it seems to me that virtues can too. Unless we stay in practice we run the risk of losing relative proficiency. We probably can't forget them completely (in part because the opportunities for exercising virtues are so pervasive in everyday life), but we can lose a certain sensitivity. People do become morally insensitive, relatively speaking — missing opportunities they once would have noticed, although perhaps when confronted with a failure they might recognize that they had failed, showing at least that they hadn't literally "forgotten the difference between right and wrong." If the moral virtues are acquired habits rather than innate gifts, it is always possible that one can lose relative proficiency in these habits. Also, just as one's interests and skills sometimes change over the course of a life as new perceptions and influences take hold, it seems too that aspects of our moral characters can likewise alter. (Consider religious conversion experiences.) Once we grant the possibility of such changes in moral character, the need for a more "character free" way of assessing action becomes evident. Character is not a permanent fixture, but rather plastic. A more reliable yardstick is sometimes needed.[13]

e. *Moral Backsliding.* Finally, the focus on good and bad agents rather than on right and wrong actions may lead to a peculiar sort of moral backsliding. Because the emphasis in agent ethics is on long-term, characteristic patterns of behavior, its advocates run the risk of overlooking occasional lies or acts of selfishness on the ground that such performances are mere temporary aberrations—acts out of character. Even the just man may on occasion act unjustly, so why haggle over specifics? It is unbecoming to a virtue theorist to engage in such pharisaic calculations. But once he commits himself to the view that assessments of moral worth are not simply a matter of whether we have done the right thing, backsliding may result. . . .

I have argued that there is a common source behind each of these vices. The virtue theorist is committed to the claim that the primary object of moral evaluation is not the act or its consequences but rather the agent—specifically, those character traits of the agent which are judged morally relevant. This is not to say that virtue ethics does not ever address the issue of right and wrong actions, but rather that it can only do so in a derivative manner. Sometimes, however, it is clearly acts rather than agents which ought to be the primary focus of moral evaluation.

Who Is Virtuous?

There is also an epistemological issue which becomes troublesome when one focuses on qualities of persons rather than on qualities of acts. Baldly put, the difficulty is that we do not seem to be able to know with any degree of certainty who really is virtuous and who vicious. For how is one to go about establishing an agent's true moral character? The standard strategy is what might be called the "externalist" one: we try to infer character by observing conduct. While not denying the existence of some connection between character and conduct, I believe that the connection between the two is not nearly as tight as externalists have assumed. The relationship is not a necessary one, but merely contingent. Virtue theorists themselves are committed to this claim, though they have not always realized it. For one central issue behind the "Being vs. Doing" debate is the virtue theorist's contention that the moral value of Being is not reducible to or dependent on Doing; that the measure of an agent's character is not exhausted by or even dependent on the values of the actions which he may perform. On this view, the most important moral traits are what may be called "spiritual" rather than "actional."[14]

Perhaps the most famous example of a spiritual virtue would be Plato's definition of justice (*dikaiosunē*). Plato, it will be remembered, argued that attempts to characterize *dikaiosunē* in terms of an agent's conduct are misguided and place the emphasis in the wrong place. *Dikaiosunē* for Plato is rather a matter of the correct harmonious relationship between the three parts of the soul: "It does not lie in a man's external actions, but in the way he acts within himself (*tēn entos*), really concerned with himself and his inner parts (*peri eauton kai ta eautou*)" (*Rep.* 443d.) Other spiritual virtues would include such attitudes as self-respect and integrity. These are traits which do have a significant impact on what we do, but whose moral value is not wholly derivable from the actions to which they may give rise.

If there are such spiritual virtues, and if they rank among the most important of moral virtues, then the externalist strategy is in trouble. For those who accept spiritual virtues, the Inner is not reducible to or dependent on the Outer. We cannot always know the moral value of a person's character by assessing his or her actions.

But suppose we reject the externalist approach and take instead the allegedly direct internalist route. Suppose, that is, that we could literally "see inside" agents and somehow observe their character traits first-hand. (The easiest way to envision this is to assume that some sort of identity thesis with respect to moral psychology and neurophysiology is in principle correct. Lest the reader object that this is only a modern materialist's silly pipe dream, I might add that at least one commentator has argued that Aristotle's considered view was that the presence of the virtues and vices depends on modifications of the brain and nervous system; and that the relevant mental processes in ethics have accompanying bodily states.)[15] Here the goal will be to match specific virtues with specific chemicals, much in the manner that identity theorists have sought to match other types of mental events with other specific neurophysiological events. However, even on this materialistic reading of the internalist strategy, nothing could be settled about virtues by analyzing chemicals without first deciding who has what virtue. For we would first need to know who possessed and exhibited which virtue, and then look for specific physical traces in him that were missing in other agents. But as indicated earlier in my discussion of the externalist strategy, this is precisely what we don't know. An analogy might be the attempt to determine which objects have which colors. Regardless of how much we know about the physical make-up of the objects in question, we must first make color judgments. However, at this point the analogy breaks down, for the epistemological problems involved in making color judgments are not nearly as troublesome as are those involved in making virtue judgments.[16]

To raise doubts about our ability to know who is virtuous is to bring skepticism into the center of virtue ethics, for it is to call into question our ability to identify the very object of our inquiry. This is not the same skepticism which has concerned recent writers such as Bernard Williams and Thomas Nagel when they reflect on the fact that "the natural objects of moral assessment are disturbingly subject to luck."[17] Theirs is more a skepticism *about* morality, while mine is a skepticism *within* morality. The sort of skepticism to which I am drawing attention occurs after one has convinced oneself that there are genuine moral agents who really do things rather than have things happen to them. As such, my skepticism is narrower but also more morality-specific: it concerns not so much queries about causality and free will as doubts about our ability to know the motives of our own behavior. As Kant wrote, "the real morality of actions, their merit or guilt, even that of our own conduct, . . . remains entirely hidden from us."[18] Aquinas too subscribed to a similar

skepticism: "Man is not competent to judge of interior movements, that are hidden, but only of exterior acts which are observable; and yet for the perfection of virtue it is necessary for man to conduct himself rightly in both kinds of acts."[19]

Now it may be objected here that I am making too much of this epistemological error, that no one actually "lives it" or contests the fact that it is an error. But I think not. To advocate an ethics of virtue is, among other things, to presuppose that we can clearly differentiate the virtuous from the vicious. Otherwise, the project lacks applicability.

Consider for a moment the Aristotelian notion of the *spoudaios* (good man) or *phronimos* (man of practical wisdom) — two essentially synonymous terms which together have often been called the touchstone of Aristotle's ethics. Again and again in the *Nicomachean Ethics* the *spoudaios/phronimos* is pointed to as the solution to a number of unanswered problems in Aristotle's ethical theory. For instance, we are told to turn to the *spoudaios* in order to learn what really is pleasurable (1113a26–28). And we must turn to an actual *phronimos* in order to find out what the abstract and mysterious *orthos logos* really is (right reason or rational principle — a notion which plays a key role in the definition of virtue) (1107a2, 1144b24). Even in discussing the intellectual virtue of *phronēsis* or practical wisdom, Aristotle begins by announcing that "we shall get at the truth by considering who are the persons we credit with it" (1140a24). But who are the *phronimoi*, and how do we know one when we see one? Aristotle does say that Pericles "and men like him" are *phronimoi*, "because they can see what is good for themselves and what is good for men in general" (1140b8–10). However, beyond this rather casual remark he does not give the reader any hints on how to track down a *phronimos*. Indeed, he does not even see it as a problem worth discussing.

The reasons for this strange lacuna, I suggest, are two. First, Aristotle is dealing with a small face to face community, where the pool of potential *phronimoi* generally come from certain well established families who are well known throughout the *polis*. Within a small face to face community of this sort, one would naturally expect to find wide agreement about judgments of character. Second, Aristotle's own methodology is itself designed to fit this sort of moral community. He is not advocating a Platonic ethics of universal categories.

Within the context of a *polis* and an ethical theory intended to accompany it, the strategy of pointing to a *phronimos* makes a certain sense. However, to divorce this strategy from its social and economic roots and to then apply it to a very different sort of community — one where people really do not know each other all that well, and where there is wide disagreement on values — does not. And this, I fear, is what contemporary virtue ethicists have tried to do.[20]

Style Over *Substance*

In emphasizing Being over Doing, the Inner over the Outer, virtue theorists also lay themselves open to the charge that they are more concerned with style than with substance. For as I argued earlier, virtue theorists are committed to the view that the moral value of certain key character traits is not exhausted by or even dependent on the value of the actions to which they may give rise. When this gulf between character and conduct is asserted, and joined with the claim that it is agents rather than actions which count morally, the conclusion is that it is not the substance of an agent's action which is the focus of moral appraisal. The implication here seems to be that if you have style, i.e., the style of the virtuous person, as defined in the context of a concrete moral tradition, it doesn't so much matter what the results are. ("It's not whether you win or lose, but how you play the game that counts.") As Frankena remarks, in a passage which underscores an alleged basic difference between ancient and contemporary virtue ethics:

> The Greeks held . . . that being virtuous entails not just having good motives or intentions but also doing the right thing. Modern views typically differ from Greek views here; perhaps because of the changed ways of thinking introduced by the Judeo-Christian tradition, we tend to believe that being morally good does not entail doing what is actually right . . . even if we believe (as I do) that doing what is actually right involves more than only having a good motive or intention. Today many people go so far as to think that in morality it does not matter much

what you do; all that matters, they say, is *how* you do it. To parody a late cigarette advertisement: It's not how wrong you make it, it's how you make it wrong.[21]

But it is sophistry to claim that the consequences of the lies of gentlemen or Aristotelian *kaloikagathoi* aren't very important, or that the implications of their rudeness are somehow tempered by the fact that they are who they are. This line of thought flies in the face of our basic conviction that moral assessment must strive toward impartiality and the bracketing of morally irrelevant social and economic data.

It seems to me that this particular vice of virtue ethics is analogous to the Hegelian "duty for duty's sake" critique of formalist deontologies. Virtue-based and duty-based theories are both subject to the "style over substance" charge because their notion of ends is too weak. Both types of theory speak of ends only in a derivative sense. For the duty-based theorist, the good is an inherent feature of dutiful action, so that the only proclaimed end is right action itself. For the virtue-based theorist, the good is defined in terms of the virtuous agent. ("Virtue is its own reward.") Aristotle, as noted earlier, in distinguishing the true from the apparent good, remarks that "that which is in truth an object of wish is an object of wish to the good man *(spoudaios)*, while any chance thing may be so the bad man" (*EN* 1113a26–28).

While no one (except the most obstinate utilitarian) would deny these two respective ends their place in a list of moral goods, it appears that there is another important type of end which is left completely unaccounted for. This second type of end is what may be called a *product-end,* a result or outcome of action which is distinct from the activity that produces it. (An example would be a catastrophe or its opposite.) Virtue-based and duty-based theories, on the other hand, can account only for *activity-ends,* ends which are inherent features of (virtuous or dutiful) action. Virtue-based theories then, like their duty-based competitors, reveal a structural defect in their lack of attention to product-ends.[22]

Now it might be said that the "style over substance" charge is more appropriately directed at those who emphasize Doing over Being, since one can do the right things just to conform or for praise. One can cultivate the externalities, but be inwardly wretched or shallow. I grant that this is a problem for act theorists, but it is a slightly different criticism than mine, using different senses of the words "style" and "substance." "Style," as used in my criticism, means roughly "morally irrelevant mannerisms and behavior," while "substance," as I used it, means something like "morally relevant results of action." The "substance" in this new criticism refers to good moral character and the acts which flow from it, while "style" here means more "doing the right thing, but without the proper fixed trait behind it." However, granted that both "style over substance" criticisms have some validity, I would also argue that mine points to a greater vice. It is one thing to do what is right without the best disposition, it is another not to do what is right at all.

Utopianism

The last vice I shall mention has a more socio-historical character. It seems to me that there is a bit of utopianism behind the virtue theorist's complaints about the ethics of rules. Surely, one reason there is more emphasis on rules and regulations in modern society is that things have gotten more complex. Our moral community (insofar as it makes sense to speak of "community" in these narcissistic times) contains more ethnic, religious, and class groups than did the moral community which Aristotle theorized about. Unfortunately, each segment of society has not only its own interests but its own set of virtues as well. There is no general agreed upon and significant expression of desirable moral character in such a world. Indeed, our pluralist culture prides itself on and defines itself in terms of its alleged value neutrality and its lack of allegiance to any one moral tradition. This absence of agreement regarding human purposes and moral ideals seems to drive us (partly out of lack of alternatives) to a more legalistic form of morality. To suppose that academic theorists can alter the situation simply by reemphasizing certain concepts is illusory. Our world lacks the sort of moral cohesiveness and value unity which traditional virtue theorists saw as prerequisites of a viable moral community.[23]

The table of vices sketched above is not intended to be exhaustive, but even in its incomplete state I believe it spells trouble for virtue-based moral theories. For the shortcomings described are not esoteric — they concern mundane features of moral experience which any minimally adequate moral theory should be expected to account for. While I do think that contemporary virtue theorists are correct in asserting that any adequate moral theory must account for the fact of character, and that no ethics of rules, pure and unsupplemented, is up to this job, the above analysis also suggests that no ethics of virtue, pure and unsupplemented, can be satisfactory.

My own view (which can only be stated summarily here) is that we need to begin efforts to coordinate irreducible or strong notions of virtue along with irreducible or strong conceptions of the various act notions into our conceptual scheme of morality. This appeal for coordination will not satisfy those theorists who continue to think in the single-element or mononomic tradition (a tradition which contemporary virtue-based theorists have inherited from their duty-based and goal-based ancestors), but I do believe that it will result in a more realistic account of our moral experience. The moral field is not unitary, and the values we employ in making moral judgments sometimes have fundamentally different sources. No single reductive method can offer a realistic means of prioritizing these different values. There exists no single scale by means of which disparate moral considerations can always be measured, added, and balanced.[24] The theoretician's quest for conceptual economy and elegance has been won at too great a price, for the resulting reductionist definitions of the moral concepts are not true to the facts of moral experience. It is important now to see the ethics of virtue and the ethics of rules as adding up, rather than as canceling each other out.[25]

Endnotes

[1] The rights definition is from Bentham's "Anarchical Fallacies," reprinted in A. I. Melden, ed. *Human Rights* (Belmont: Wadsworth, 1970), p. 32. The virtue definition is from Bentham's "The Nature of Virtue," reprinted in Bhiku Parekh, ed. *Bentham's Political Thought* (New York: Barnes and Noble, 1973), p. 89.

[2] G. E. M. Anscombe, "Modern Moral Philosophy," *Philosophy* 33 (1958):1–19; reprinted in J. J. Thomson and G. Dworkin, eds. *Ethics* (New York: Harper & Row, 1968), p. 196.

[3] Anscombe appears to believe also that moral oughts and obligations only make sense in a divine law context, which would mean that only divine command theories of ethics employ valid concepts of obligation. I see no reason to accept such a narrow definition of duty. See pp. 192, 202 of "Modern Moral Philosophy." For one argument against her restrictive divine law approach to moral obligation, see Alan Donagan, *The Theory of Morality* (Chicago: University of Chicago Press, 1977), p. 3.

[4] Philippa Foot, *Virtues and Vices and Other Essays in Moral Philosophy* (Berkeley and Los Angeles: University of California Press, 1978), p. xi.

[5] Foot, "Morality as a System of Hypothetical Imperatives," *Philosophical Review* 81 (1972):305–16; reprinted in *Virtues and Vices,* pp. 157–73. See especially the long concluding footnote, added in 1977.

[6] Foot, "William Frankena's Carus Lectures," *The Monist* 64(1981):311.

[7] For background on this "Being vs. Doing" debate, see Bernard Mayo, *Ethics and the Moral Life* (London: Macmillan & Co., Ltd., 1958), pp. 211–14, and William K. Frankena, *Ethics,* 2nd ed. (Englewood Cliffs, N.J.: Prentice-Hall, 1973), pp. 65–66.

[8] Arthur Flemming, "Reviving the Virtues." Review of Foot's *Virtues and Vices* and James Wallace's *Virtues and Vices, Ethics* 90 (1980):588.

[9] Lawrence Becker, "The Neglect of Virtue," *Ethics* 85 (1975):111.

[10] Stuart Hampshire, ed. *Private and Public Morality* (New York: Cambridge University Press, 1978), p. 7.

[11] Alasdair MacIntyre, *After Virtue* (Notre Dame: University of Notre Dame Press, 1981), p. 142.

[12] It is curious to note that contemporary philosophers as different as Gilbert Ryle and H. G. Gadamer have argued, against Xenophon and myself, that character cannot change. See H. G. Gadamer, "The Problem of Historical Consciousness," p. 140, in P. Rabinow and W. M. Sullivan, eds. *Interpretive Social Science* (Berkeley and Los Angeles: University of California Press, 1979), and Gilbert Ryle, "On Forgetting the Difference Between Right and Wrong," in A. I. Melden, ed. *Essays in Moral Philosophy* (Seattle: University of Washington Press, 1958).

[13] One possibility here might be to isolate specific traits and then add that the virtuous agent ought to *retain* such traits throughout any character changes (e.g.: "The good man will not do what is base, regardless of whether he be Christian, Jew, or atheist"). However, it is my view that very few if any moral traits have such a "transcharacter" status. The very notion of what counts as a virtue or vice itself changes radically when one looks at different traditions. (Compare Aristotle's praise for *megalopsuchia* or pride as the "crown of

the virtues" with the New Testament emphasis on humility.) Also, one would expect basic notions about what is base or noble to themselves undergo shifts of meaning as they move across traditions.

[14] I have borrowed this terminology from G. W. Trianosky-Stillwell, *Should We Be Good? The Place of Virtue in Our Morality* (doctoral dissertation, University of Michigan, 1980).

[15] W. F. R. Hardie, *Aristotle's Ethical Theory,* 2nd ed. (Oxford: Clarendon Press, 1980), Ch. VI, esp. pp. 111–13.

[16] I am indebted to Bill Robinson for help on this criticism of the internalist strategy.

[17] Thomas Nagel, "Moral Luck," in *Mortal Questions* (New York: Cambridge University Press, 1979), p. 28. See also Bernard Williams, "Moral Luck," in *Moral Luck: Philosophical Papers 1973–1980* (New York: Cambridge University Press, 1981).

[18] Kant, *Critique of Pure Reason,* A552 = B580, n. 1.

[19] Thomas Aquinas, Saint. *Summa Theologica,* I-II Q.91, a. 4.

[20] I would like to thank Arthur Adkins for discussion on these points.

[21] William K. Frankena, *Thinking About Morality* (Ann Arbor: University of Michigan Press, 1980), pp. 52–53.

[22] My own position on this topic is contra that of utilitarianism. I believe that activity-ends are clearly the more important of the two, and that most product-ends ultimately derive their moral value from more fundamental activity-ends. (The importance of saving lives, for instance, borrows its value from the quality of life it makes possible. "Life at any price" is nonsense.) But I also believe, contra deontology and virtue ethics, that any adequate moral theory must find room for both types of ends.

[23] For similar criticism, see Mayo, *Ethics and the Moral Life,* p. 217; and MacIntyre, *After Virtue.*

[24] See Thomas Nagel, "The Fragmentation of Value," pp. 131–32, 135, in *Mortal Questions* (New York: Cambridge University Press, 1979). A similar position is defended by Charles Taylor in his recent essay, "The Diversity of Goods," in A. Sen and B. Williams, eds. *Utilitarianism and Beyond* (New York: Cambridge University Press, 1982).

[25] Earlier versions of this essay were read at the 1982 American Philosophical Association Pacific Division Meetings, and at the 1981 Iowa Philosophical Society Meeting at Grinnell College. I am very grateful for useful criticisms and suggestions offered on these occasions. I would also like to thank Marcia Baron, Lawrence Becker, James Gustafson, W. D. Hamlyn, Bob Hollinger, Joe Kupfer, and Warner Wick for criticisms of earlier drafts. Portions of the present version are taken from my doctoral dissertation, *The Elements of Ethics: Toward a Topography of the Moral Field* (University of Chicago, 1981).

VII.6 *The Nature of the Virtues*

ALASDAIR MACINTYRE

Alasdair MacIntyre is professor of philosophy at the University of Notre Dame and the author of several works in philosophy of religion, social theory, and ethics. In this selection from his influential work *After Virtue,* MacIntyre carries on the Aristotelian project of grounding morality in the virtues. He asks whether there is a core conception of the virtues, some vital components that are necessary to any social endeavor or practice. He compares five different conceptions of the virtues as they appear in the works of Homer, Aristotle, Jane Austen, and Benjamin Franklin, and in the New Testament. Five different theories seem to emerge, although MacIntyre finds elements of commonality among them.

 MacIntyre argues that in every society there must be practices in which virtues are exhibited and become defined. Even though practices may vary from society to society, so that different virtues will be highlighted differently in different societies, nevertheless a core set of virtues is necessary for the successful functioning of any practice. This set includes such virtues as justice, courage, and honesty, without which the practice is in danger of decay. And without some practice, and more broadly, a moral tradition, we are in danger of falling into a Hobbesian state of nature. MacIntyre ends his essay by comparing his theory of the virtues with Aristotle's project and by arguing that his work is within the Aristotelian tradition.

One response to the history [of Greek and medieval thought about the virtues] might well be to suggest that even within the relatively coherent tradition of thought which I have sketched there are just too many different and incompatible conceptions of a virtue for there to be any real unity to the concept or indeed to the history. Homer, Sophocles, Aristotle, the New Testament and medieval thinkers differ from each other in too many ways. They offer us different and incompatible lists of the virtues; they give a different rank order of importance to different virtues; and they have different and incompatible theories of the virtues. If we were to consider later Western writers on the virtues, the list of differences and incompatibilities would be enlarged still further; and if we extended our enquiry to Japanese,

say, or American Indian cultures, the differences would become greater still. It would be all too easy to conclude that there are a number of rival and alternative conceptions of the virtues, but, even within the tradition which I have been delineating, no single core conception.

 The case for such a conclusion could not be better constructed than by beginning from a consideration of the very different lists of items which different authors in different times and places have included in their catalogues of virtues. Some of these catalogues — Homer's, Aristotle's and the New Testament's — I have already noticed at greater or lesser length. Let me at the risk of some repetition recall some of their key features and then introduce for further comparison the catalogues of two later Western writers, Benjamin Franklin and Jane Austen.

 The first example is that of Homer. At least some of the items in a Homeric list of the *aretai*

Reprinted by permission of University of Notre Dame Press and the author.

would clearly not be counted by most of us nowadays as virtues at all, physical strength being the most obvious example. To this it might be replied that perhaps we ought not to translate the word *areté* in Homer by our word 'virtue,' but instead by our word 'excellence'; and perhaps, if we were so to translate it, the apparently surprising difference between Homer and ourselves would at first sight have been removed. For we could allow without any kind of oddity that the possession of physical strength is the possession of an excellence. But in fact we would not have removed, but instead would merely have relocated, the difference between Homer and ourselves. For we would now seem to be saying that Homer's concept of an *areté,* an excellence, is one thing and that our concept of a virtue is quite another since a particular quality can be an excellence in Homer's eyes, but not a virtue in ours and *vice versa.*

But of course it is not that Homer's list of virtues differs only from our own; it also notably differs from Aristotle's. And Aristotle's of course also differs from our own. For one thing, as I noticed earlier, some Greek virtue-words are not easily translatable into English or rather out of Greek. Moreover consider the importance of friendship as a virtue in Aristotle's list — how different from us! Or the place of *phronêsis* — how different from Homer and from us! The mind receives from Aristotle the kind of tribute which the body receives from Homer. But it is not just the case that the difference between Aristotle and Homer lies in the inclusion of some items and the omission of others in their respective catalogues. It turns out also in the way in which those catalogues are ordered, in which items are ranked as relatively central to human excellence and which marginal.

Moreover the relationship of virtues to the social order has changed. For Homer the paradigm of human excellence is the warrior; for Aristotle it is the Athenian gentleman. Indeed according to Aristotle certain virtues are only available to those of great riches and of high social status; there are virtues which are unavailable to the poor man, even if he is a free man. And those virtues are on Aristotle's view ones central to human life; magnanimity — and once again, any translation of *megalopsuchia* is unsatisfactory — and munificence are not just virtues, but important virtues within the Aristotelian scheme.

At once it is impossible to delay the remark that the most striking contrast with Aristotle's catalogue is to be found neither in Homer's nor in our own, but in the New Testament's. For the New Testament not only praises virtues of which Aristotle knows nothing — faith, hope and love — and says nothing about virtues such as *phronêsis* which are crucial for Aristotle, but it praises at least one quality as a virtue which Aristotle seems to count as one of the vices relative to magnanimity, namely humility. Moreover since the New Testament quite clearly sees the rich as destined for the pains of Hell, it is clear that the key virtues cannot be available to them; yet they *are* available to slaves. And the New Testament of course differs from both Homer and Aristotle not only in the items included in its catalogue, but once again in its rank ordering of the virtues.

Turn now to compare all three lists of virtues considered so far — the Homeric, the Aristotelian, and the New Testament's — with two much later lists, one which can be compiled from Jane Austen's novels and the other which Benjamin Franklin constructed for himself. Two features stand out in Jane Austen's list. The first is the importance that she allots to the virtue which she calls 'constancy,' a virtue about which I shall say more in a later chapter. In some ways constancy plays a role in Jane Austen analogous to that of *phronêsis* in Aristotle; it is a virtue the possession of which is a prerequisite for the possession of other virtues. The second is the fact that what Aristotle treats as the virtue of agreeableness (a virtue for which he says there is no name) she treats as only the simulacrum of a genuine virtue — the genuine virtue in question is the one she calls amiability. For the man who practices agreeableness does so from considerations of honour and expediency, according to Aristotle; whereas Jane Austen thought it possible and necessary for the possessor of that virtue to have a certain real affection for people as such. (It matters here that Jane Austen is a Christian.) Remember that Aristotle himself had treated military courage as a simulacrum of true courage. Thus we find here yet another type of disagreement over the virtues; namely, one as to which human qualities are genuine virtues and which mere simulacra.

In Benjamin Franklin's list we find almost all the types of differences from at least one of the other catalogues we have considered and one more. Franklin includes virtues which are new to our consideration such as cleanliness, silence and industry; he clearly considers the drive to acquire itself a part of virtue, whereas for most ancient Greeks this is the vice of *pleonexia;* he treats some virtues which earlier ages had considered minor as major; but he also redefines some familiar virtues. In the list of thirteen virtues which Franklin compiled as part of his system of private moral accounting, he elucidates each virtue by citing a maxim obedience to which *is* the virtue in question. In the case of chastity the maxim is 'Rarely use venery but for health or offspring — never to dullness, weakness or the injury of your own or another's peace or reputation.' This is clearly not what earlier writers had meant by 'chastity.'

We have therefore accumulated a startling number of differences and incompatibilities in the five stated and implied accounts of the virtues. So the question which I raised at the outset becomes more urgent. If different writers in different times and places, but all within the history of Western culture, include such different sets and types of items in their lists, what grounds have we for supposing that they do indeed aspire to list items of one and the same kind, that there is any shared concept at all? A second kind of consideration reinforces the presumption of a negative answer to this question. It is not just that each of these five writers lists different and differing kinds of items; it is also that each of these lists embodies, is the expression of a different theory about what a virtue is.

In the Homeric poems a virtue is a quality the manifestation of which enables someone to do exactly what their well-defined social role requires. The primary role is that of the warrior king and that Homer lists those virtues which he does becomes intelligible at once when we recognise that the key virtues therefore must be those which enable a man to excel in combat and in the games. It follows that we cannot identify the Homeric virtues until we have first identified the key social roles in Homeric society and the requirements of each of them. The concept of *what anyone filling such-and-such a role ought to do* is prior to the concept of a virtue; the latter concept has application only via the former.

On Aristotle's account matters are very different. Even though some virtues are available only to certain types of people, none the less virtues attach not to men as inhabiting social roles, but to man as such. It is the *telos* of man as a species which determines what human qualities are virtues. We need to

remember however that although Aristotle treats the acquisition and exercise of the virtues as means to an end, the relationship of means to end is internal and not external. I call a means internal to a given end when the end cannot be adequately characterised independently of a characterisation of the means. So it is with the virtues and the *telos* which is the good life for man on Aristotle's account. The exercise of the virtues is itself a crucial component of the good life for man. This distinction between internal and external means to an end is not drawn by Aristotle himself in the *Nicomachean Ethics*, as I noticed earlier, but it is an essential distinction to be drawn if we are to understand what Aristotle intended. The distinction *is* drawn explicitly by Aquinas in the course of his defence of St. Augustine's definition of a virtue, and it is clear that Aquinas understood that in drawing it he was maintaining an Aristotelian point of view.

The New Testament's account of the virtues, even if it differs as much as it does in content from Aristotle's — Aristotle would certainly not have admired Jesus Christ and he would have been horrified by St. Paul — does have the same logical and conceptual structure as Aristotle's account. A virtue is, as with Aristotle, a quality the exercise of which leads to the achievement of the human telos. *The* good for man is of course a supernatural and not only a natural good, but supernature redeems and completes nature. Moreover the relationship of virtues as means to the end which is human incorporation in the divine kingdom of the age to come is internal and not external, just as it is in Aristotle. It is of course this parallelism which allows Aquinas to synthesise Aristotle and the New Testament. A key feature of this parallelism is the way in which the concept of *the good life for man* is prior to the concept of a virtue in just the way in which on the Homeric account the concept of a social role was prior. Once again it is the way in which the former concept is applied which determines how the latter is to be applied. In both cases the concept of a virtue is a secondary concept.

The intent of Jane Austen's theory of the virtues is of another kind. C. S. Lewis has rightly emphasised how profoundly Christian her moral vision is and Gilbert Ryle has equally rightly emphasised her inheritance from Shaftesbury and from Aristotle. In fact her views combine elements from Homer as well, since she is concerned with social roles in a way that neither the New Testament nor Aristotle are. She is therefore important for the way in which she finds it possible to combine what are at first sight disparate theoretical accounts of the virtues. But for the moment any attempt to assess the significance of Jane Austen's synthesis must be delayed. Instead we must notice the quite different style of theory articulated in Benjamin Franklin's account of the virtues.

Franklin's account, like Aristotle's, is teleological; but unlike Aristotle's, it is utilitarian. According to Franklin in his *Autobiography* the virtues are means to an end, but he envisages the means-ends relationship as external rather than internal. The end to which the cultivation of the virtues ministers is happiness, but happiness understood as success, prosperity in Philadelphia and ultimately in heaven. The virtues are to be useful and Franklin's account continuously stresses utility as a criterion in individual cases: 'Make no expence but to do good to others or yourself; i.e. waste nothing,' 'Speak not but what may benefit others or yourself. Avoid trifling conversation' and, as we have already seen, 'Rarely use venery but for health or offspring. . . ?' 'When Franklin was in Paris he was horrified by Parisian architecture: 'Marble, porcelain and gilt are squandered without utility.'

We thus have at least three very different conceptions of a virtue to confront: a virtue is a quality which enables an individual to discharge his or her social role (Homer); a virtue is a quality which enables an individual to move towards the achievement of the specifically human *telos,* whether natural or supernatural (Aristotle, the New Testament and Aquinas); a virtue is a quality which has utility in achieving earthly and heavenly success (Franklin). Are we to take these as three rival accounts of the same thing? Or are they instead accounts of three different things? Perhaps the moral structures in archaic Greece, in fourth-century Greece, and in eighteenth-century Pennsylvania were so different from each other that we should treat them as embodying quite different concepts, whose difference is initially disguised from us by the historical accident of an inherited vocabulary which misleads us by linguistic resemblance long after conceptual identity and similarity have failed. Our initial question has come back to us with redoubled force.

Yet although I have dwelt upon the *prima facie* case for holding that the differences and incompatibilities between different accounts at least suggest that there is no single, central, core conception of the virtues which might make a claim for universal allegiance, I ought also to point out that each of the five moral accounts which I have sketched so summarily does embody just such a claim. It is indeed just this feature of those accounts that makes them of more than sociological or antiquarian interest. Every one of these accounts claims not only theoretical, but also an institutional hegemony. For Odysseus the Cyclopes stand condemned because they lack agriculture, on *agora* and *themis.* For Aristotle the barbarians stand condemned because they lack the *polis* and are therefore incapable of politics. For New Testament Christians there is no salvation outside the apostolic church. And we know that Benjamin Franklin found the virtues more at home in Philadelphia than in Paris and that for Jane Austen the touchstone of the virtues is a certain kind of marriage and indeed a certain kind of naval officer (that is, a certain kind of *English* naval officer).

The question can therefore now be posed directly: are we or are we not able to disentangle from these rival and various claims a unitary core concept of the virtues of which we can give a more compelling account than any of the other accounts so far? I am going to argue that we can in fact discover such a core concept and that it turns out to provide the tradition of which I have written the history with its conceptual unity. It will indeed enable us to distinguish in a clear way those beliefs about the virtues which genuinely belong to the tradition from those which do not. Unsurprisingly perhaps it is a complex concept, different parts of which derive from different stages in the development of the tradition. Thus the concept itself in some sense embodies the history of which it is the outcome.

One of the features of the concept of a virtue which has emerged with some clarity from the argument so far is that it always requires for its application the acceptance of some prior account of certain features of social and moral life in terms of which it has to be defined and explained. So in the Homeric account the concept of a virtue is secondary to that of *a social role,* in Aristotle's account it is secondary to that of *the good life for man* conceived as the *telos* of human action and in Franklin's much later account it is secondary to that of utility. What is it in the account which I am about to give which provides in a similar way the necessary background against which the concept of a virtue has to be made intelligible? It is in answering this question that the complex, historical, multi-layered character of the core concept of virtue becomes clear. For there are no less than three stages in the logical development of the concept which have to be identified in order, if the core conception of a virtue is to be understood, and each of these stages has its own conceptual background. The first stage requires a background account of what I shall call a practice, the second an account of what I have already characterised as the narrative order of a single human life and the third an account a good deal fuller than I have given up to now of what constitutes a moral tradition. Each later stage presupposes the earlier, but not *vice versa*. Each earlier stage is both modified by and reinterpreted in the light of, but also provides an essential constituent of each later stage. The progress in the development of the concept is closely related to, although it does not recapitulate in any straightforward way, the history of the tradition of which it forms the core.

In the Homeric account of the virtues — and in heroic societies more generally — the exercise of a virtue exhibits qualities which are required for sustaining a social role and for exhibiting excellence in some well-marked area of social practice: to excel is to excel at war or in the games, as Achilles does, in sustaining a household, as Penelope does, in giving counsel in the assembly, as Nestor does, in the telling of a tale, as Homer himself does. When Aristotle speaks of excellence in human activity, he sometimes though not always, refers to some well-defined type of human practice: flute-playing, or war, or geometry. I am going to suggest that this notion of a particular type of practice as providing the arena in which the virtues are exhibited and in terms of which they are to receive their primary, if incomplete, definition is crucial to the whole enterprise of identifying a core concept of the virtues. I hasten to add two *caveats* however.

The first is to point out that my argument will not in any way imply that virtues are *only* exercised in the course of what I am calling practices. The second is to warn that I shall be using the word 'practice' in a specially defined way which does not completely agree with current ordinary usage, including my own previous use of that word. What am I going to mean by it?

By a 'practice' I am going to mean any coherent and complex form of socially established coopera-tive human activity through which goods internal to that form of activity are realised in the course of trying to achieve those standards of excellence which are appropriate to, and partially definitive of, that form of activity, with the result that human powers to achieve excellence, and human conceptions of the ends and goods involved, are systematically extended. Tic-tac-toe is not an example of a practice in this sense, nor is throwing a football with skill; but the game of football is, and so is chess. Bricklaying is not a practice; architecture is. Planting turnips is not a practice; farming is. So are the enquiries of physics, chemistry and biology, and so is the work of the historian, and so are painting and music. In the ancient and medieval worlds the creation and sustaining of human communities — of households, cities, nations — is generally taken to be a practice in the sense in which I have defined it. Thus the range of practices is wide: arts, sciences, games, politics in the Aristotelian sense, the making and sustaining of family life, all fall under the concept. But the question of the precise range of practices is not at this stage of the first importance. Instead let me explain some of the key terms involved in my definition, beginning with the notion of goods internal to a practice.

Consider the example of a highly intelligent seven-year-old child whom I wish to teach to play chess, although the child has no particular desire to learn the game. The child does however have a very strong desire for candy and little chance of obtaining it. I therefore tell the child that if the child will play chess with me once a week I will give the child 50¢ worth of candy; moreover I tell the child that I will always play in such a way that it will be difficult, but not impossible, for the child to win and that, if the child wins, the child will receive an extra 50¢ worth of candy. Thus motivated the child plays and plays to win. Notice however that, so long as it is the candy alone which provides the child with a good reason for playing chess, the child has no reason not to cheat and every reason to cheat, provided he or she can do so successfully. But, so we may hope, there will come a time when the child will find in those goods specific to chess, in the achievement of a certain highly particular kind of analytical skill, strategic imagination and competitive intensity, a new set of reasons, reasons now not just for winning on a particular occasion, but for trying to excel in whatever way the game of chess demands. Now if the child cheats, he or she will be defeating not me, but himself or herself.

There are thus two kinds of goods possibly to be gained by playing chess. On the one hand there are those goods externally and contingently attached to chess-playing and to other practices by the accidents of social circumstance — in the case of the imaginary child candy, in the case of real adults such goods as prestige, status, and money. There are always alternative ways for achieving such goods, and their achievement is never to be had *only* by engaging in some particular kind of practice. On the other hand there are the goods internal to the practice of chess which cannot be had in any way but by playing chess or some other game of that specific kind. We call them internal for two reasons: first, as I have already suggested, because we can only specify them in terms of chess or some other game of that specific kind and by means of examples from such games (otherwise the meagerness of our vocabulary for speaking of such goods forces us into such devices as my own resort to writing of 'a certain highly particular kind of'); and secondly because they can only be identified and recognised by the experience of participating in the practice in question. Those who lack the relevant experience are incompetent thereby as judges of internal goods.

This is clearly the case with all the major examples of practices: consider for example — even if briefly and inadequately — the practice of portrait painting as developed in Western Europe from the late middle ages to the eighteenth century. The successful portrait painter is able to achieve many goods which are in the sense just defined external to the practice of portrait painting — fame, wealth, social status, even a measure of power and influence at courts upon occasion. But those external goods are not to be confused with the goods which are internal to the practice. The internal goods are those which result from an extended attempt to show how Wittgenstein's dictum 'The human body is the best picture of the human soul' (*Investigations*, p. 178e) might be made to become true by teaching us 'to regard . . . the picture on our wall as the object itself (the men, landscape, and so on) depicted there' (p. 205e) in a quite new way. What is misleading about Wittgenstein's dictum as it stands is its neglect of the truth in George Orwell's thesis 'At 50 everyone has the face he deserves.' What painters

from Giotto to Rembrandt learnt to show was how the face at any age may be revealed as the face that the subject of a portrait deserves.

Originally in medieval paintings of the saints the face was an icon; the question of a resemblance between the depicted face of Christ or St. Peter and the face that Jesus or Peter actually possessed at some particular age did not even arise. The antithesis to this iconography was the relative naturalism of certain fifteenth-century Flemish and German painting. The heavy eyelids, the coifed hair, the lines around the mouth undeniably represent some particular woman, either actual or envisaged. Resemblance has usurped the iconic relationship. But with Rembrandt there is, so to speak, synthesis: the naturalistic portrait is now rendered as an icon, but an icon of a new and hitherto inconceivable kind. Similarly in a very different kind of sequence mythological faces in a certain kind of seventeenth-century French painting become aristocratic faces in the eighteenth century. Within each of these sequences at least two different kinds of good internal to the painting of human faces and bodies are achieved.

There is first of all the excellence of the products, both the excellence in performance by the painters and that of each portrait itself. This excellence — the very verb 'excel' suggests it — has to be understood historically. The sequences of development find their point and purpose in a progress towards and beyond a variety of types and modes of excellence. There are of course sequences of decline as well as of progress, and progress is rarely to be understood as straightforwardly linear. But it is in participation in the attempts to sustain progress and to respond creatively to moments that the second kind of good internal to the practices of portrait painting is to be found. For what the artist discovers within the pursuit of excellence in portrait painting — and what is true of portrait painting is true of the practice of the fine arts in general — is the good of a certain kind of life. That life may not constitute the whole of life for someone who is a painter by a very long way or it may at least for a period, Gauguin-like, absorb him or her at the expense of almost everything else. But it is the painter's living out of a greater or lesser part of his or her life *as a painter* that is the second kind of good internal to painting. And judgment upon these goods requires at the very least the kind of competence that is only to be acquired either as a painter or as someone willing to learn systematically what the portrait painter has to teach.

A practice involves standards of excellence and obedience to rules as well as the achievement of goods. To enter into a practice is to accept the authority of those standards and the inadequacy of my own performance as judged by them. It is to subject my own attitudes, choices, preferences and tastes to the standards which currently and partially define the practice. Practices of course, as I have just noticed, have a history: games, sciences and arts all have histories. Thus the standards are not themselves immune from criticism, but none the less we cannot be initiated into a practice without accepting the authority of the best standards realised so far. If, on starting to listen to music, I do not accept my own incapacity to judge correctly, I will never learn to hear, let alone to appreciate, Bartok's last quartets. If, on starting to play baseball, I do not accept that others know better than I when to throw a fastball and when not, I will never learn to appreciate good pitching let alone to pitch. In the realm of practices the authority of both goods and standards operates in such a way as to rule out all subjectivist and emotivist analyses of judgment. De gustibus *est* disputandum.

We are now in a position to notice an important difference between what I have called internal and what I have called external goods. It is characteristic of what I have called external goods that when achieved they are always some individual's property and possession. Moreover characteristically they are such that the more someone has of them, the less there is for other people. This is sometimes necessarily the case, as with power and fame, and sometimes the case by reason of contingent circumstance as with money. External goods are therefore characteristically objects of competition in which there must be losers as well as winners. Internal goods are indeed the outcome of competition to excel, but it is characteristic of them that their achievement is a good for the whole community who participate in the practice. So when Turner transformed the seascape in painting or W. G. Grace advanced the art of batting in cricket in a quite new way their achievement enriched the whole relevant community.

But what does all or any of this have to do with the concept of the virtues? It turns out that we are now in a position to formulate a first, even if partial and tentative definition of a virtue: *A virtue is an acquired human quality the possession and exercise of which tends to enable us to achieve those goods which are internal to practices and the lack of which effectively prevents us from achieving any such goods.* Later this definition will need amplification and amendment. But as a first approximation to an adequate definition it already illuminates the place of the virtues in human life. For it is not difficult to show for a whole range of key virtues that without them the goods internal to practices are barred to us, but not just barred to us generally, barred in a very particular way.

It belongs to the concept of a practice as I have outlined it — and as we are all familiar with it already in our actual lives, whether we are painters or physicists or quarterbacks or indeed just lovers of good painting or first-rate experiments or a well-thrown pass — that its goods can only be achieved by subordinating ourselves to the best standard so far achieved, and that entails subordinating ourselves within the practice in our relationship to other practitioners. We have to learn to recognise what is due to whom; we have to be prepared to take whatever self-endangering risks are demanded along the way; and we have to listen carefully to what we are told about our own inadequacies and to reply with the same carefulness for the facts. In other words we have to accept as necessary components of any practice with internal goods and standards of excellence the virtues of justice, courage and honesty. For not to accept these, to be willing to cheat as our imagined child was willing to cheat in his or her early days at chess, so far bars us from achieving the standards of excellence or the goods internal to the practice that it renders the practice pointless except as a device for achieving external goods.

We can put the same point in another way. Every practice requires a certain kind of relationship between those who participate in it. Now the virtues are those goods by reference to which, whether we like it or not, we define our relationships to those other people with whom we share the kind of purposes and standards which inform practices. Consider an example of how reference to the virtues has to be made in certain kinds of human relationship.

A, B, C, and D are friends in that sense of friendship which Aristotle takes to be primary: they share in the pursuit of certain goods. In my terms they share in a practice. D dies in obscure circumstances, A discovers how D died and tells the truth about it to B while lying to C. C discovers the lie. What A cannot then intelligibly claim is that he stands in the same relationship of friendship to both B and C. By telling the truth to one and lying to the other he has partially defined a difference in the relationship. Of course it is open to A to explain this difference in a number of ways; perhaps he was trying to spare C pain or perhaps he is simply cheating C. But some difference in the relationship now exists as a result of the lie. For their allegiance to each other in the pursuit of common goods has been put in question.

Just as, so long as we share the standards and purposes characteristic of practices, we define our relationships to each other, whether we acknowledge it or not, by reference to standards of truthfulness and trust, as we define them too by reference to standards of justice and of courage. If A, a professor, gives B and C the grades that their papers deserve, but grades D because he is attracted by D's blue eyes or is repelled by D's dandruff, he has defined his relationship to D differently from his relationship to the other members of the class, whether he wishes it or not. Justice requires that we treat others in respect of merit or desert according to uniform and impersonal standards; to depart from the standards of justice in some particular instance defines our relationship with the relevant person as in some way special or distinctive.

The case with courage is a little different. We hold courage to be a virtue because the care and concern for individuals, communities and causes which is so crucial to so much in practices requires the existence of such a virtue. If someone says that he cares for some individual, community or cause, but is unwilling to risk harm or danger on his, her or its own behalf, he puts in question the genuineness of his care and concern. Courage, the capacity to risk harm or danger to oneself, has its role in human life because of this connection with care and concern. This is not to say that a man cannot genuinely care and also be a coward. It is in part to say that a man who genuinely cares and has not the capacity for risking harm or danger has to define himself, both to himself and to others, as a coward.

I take it then that from the standpoint of those types of relationship without which practices cannot be sustained truthfulness, justice and courage — and perhaps some others — are genuine excellences, are virtues in the light of which we have to characterise ourselves and others, whatever our private moral standpoint or our society's particular codes may be. For this recognition that we cannot escape the definition of our relationships in terms of such goods is perfectly compatible with the acknowledgment that different societies have and have had different codes of truthfulness, justice and courage. Lutheran pietists brought up their children to believe that one ought to tell the truth to everybody at all times, whatever the circumstances or consequences, and Kant was one of their children. Traditional Bantu parents brought up their children not to tell the truth to unknown strangers, since they believed that this could render the family vulnerable to witchcraft. In our culture many of us have been brought up not to tell the truth to elderly great-aunts who invite us to admire their new hats. But each of these codes embodies an acknowledgment of the virtue of truthfulness. So it is also with varying codes of justice and of courage.

Practices then might flourish in societies with very different codes; what they could not do is flourish in societies in which the virtues were not valued, although institutions and technical skills serving unified purposes might well continue to flourish. (I shall have more to say about the contrast between institutions and technical skills mobilised for a unified end, on the one hand, and practices on the other, in a moment.) For the kind of cooperation, the kind of recognition of authority and of achievement, the kind of respect for standards and the kind of risk-taking which are characteristically involved in practices demand for example fairness in judging oneself and others — the kind of fairness absent in my example of the professor, a ruthless truthfulness without which fairness cannot find application — the kind of truthfulness absent in my example of A, B, C and D — and willingness to trust the judgments of those whose achievement in the practice give them an authority to judge which presupposes fairness and truthfulness in those judgments, and from time to time the taking of self-endangering, reputation-endangering and even achievement-endangering risks. It is no part of my thesis that great violinists cannot be vicious or great chess-players mean-spirited. Where the virtues are required, the vices also may flourish. It is just that the vicious and mean-spirited necessarily rely on the virtues of others for the practices in which they engage to flourish and also deny themselves the experience of achieving those internal goods which may reward even not very good chess-players and violinists.

To situate the virtues any further within practices it is necessary now to clarify a little further the nature of a practice by drawing two important contrasts. The discussion so far I hope makes it clear that a practice, in the sense intended, is never just a set of technical skills, even when directed towards some unified purpose and even if the exercise of those skills can on occasion be valued or enjoyed for its own sake. What is distinctive of a practice is in part the way in which conceptions of the relevant goods and ends which the technical skills serve — and every practice does require the exercise of technical skills — are transformed and enriched by these extensions of human powers and by that regard for its own internal goods which are partially definitive of each particular practice or type of practice. Practices never have a goal or goals fixed for all time — painting has no such goal nor has physics — but the goals themselves are transmuted by the history of the activity. It therefore turns out not to be accidental that every practice has its own history and a history which is more and other than that of the improvement of the relevant technical skills. This historical dimension is crucial in relation to the virtues.

To enter into a practice is to enter into a relationship not only with its contemporary practitioners, but also with those who have preceded us in the practice, particularly those whose achievements extended the reach of the practice to its present point. It is thus the achievement, and *a fortiori* the authority, of a tradition which I then confront and from which I have to learn. And for this learning and the relationship to the past which it embodies, the virtues of justice, courage and truthfulness are prerequisite in precisely the same way and for precisely the same reasons as they are in sustaining present relationships within practices.

It is not only of course with sets of technical skills that practices ought to be contrasted. Practices must not be confused with institutions. Chess, physics and medicine are practices; chess clubs, laboratories, universities and hospitals are institutions.

Institutions are characteristically and necessarily concerned with what I have called external goods. They are involved in acquiring money and other material goods; they are structured in terms of power and status, and they distribute money, power and status as rewards. Nor could they do otherwise if they are to sustain not only themselves, but also the practices of which they are the bearers. For no practices can survive for any length of time unsustained by institutions. Indeed so intimate is the relationship of practices to institutions — and consequently of the goods external to the goods internal to the practices in question — that institutions and practices characteristically form a single causal order in which the ideals and the creativity of the practice are always vulnerable to the acquisitiveness of the institution, in which the cooperative care for common goods of the practice is always vulnerable to the competitiveness of the institution. In this context the essential function of the virtues is clear. Without them, without justice, courage and truthfulness, practices could not resist the corrupting power of institutions.

Yet if institutions do have corrupting power, the making and sustaining of forms of human community — and therefore of institutions — itself has all the characteristics of a practice, and moreover of a practice which stands in a peculiarly close relationship to the exercise of the virtues in two important ways. The exercise of the virtues is itself apt to require a highly determinate attitude to social and political issues; and it is always within some particular community with its own specific institutional forms that we learn or fail to learn to exercise the virtues. There is of course a crucial difference between the way in which the relationship between moral character and political community is envisaged from the standpoint of liberal individualist modernity and the way in which that relationship was envisaged from the standpoint of the type of ancient and medieval tradition of the virtues which I have sketched. For liberal individualism a community is simply an arena in which individuals each pursue their own self-chosen conception of the good life, and political institutions exist to provide that degree of order which makes such self-determined activity possible. Government and law are, or ought to be, neutral between rival conceptions of the good life for man, and hence, although it is the task of government to promote law-abidingness, it is on the liberal view no part of the legitimate function of government to inculcate any one moral outlook.

By contrast, on the particular ancient and medieval view which I have sketched political community not only requires the exercise of the virtues for its own sustenance, but is one of the tasks of government to make its citizens virtuous, just as it is one of the tasks of parental authority to make children grow up so as to be virtuous adults. The classical statement of this analogy is by Socrates in the *Crito*. It does not of course follow from an acceptance of the Socratic view of political community and political authority that we ought to assign to the modern state the moral function which Socrates assigned to the city and its laws. Indeed the power of the liberal individualist standpoint partly derives from the evident fact that the modern state is indeed totally unfitted to act as moral educator of any community. But the history of how the modern state emerged is of course itself a moral history. If my account of the complex relationship of virtues to practices and to institutions is correct, it follows that we shall be unable to write a true history of practices and institutions unless that history is also one of the virtues and vices. For the ability of a practice to retain its integrity will depend on the way in which the virtues can be and are exercised in sustaining the institutional forms which are the social bearers of the practice. The integrity of a practice causally requires the exercise of the virtues by at least some of the individuals who embody it in their activities; and conversely the corruption of institutions is always in part at least an effect of the vices.

The virtues are of course themselves in turn fostered by certain types of social institution an endangered by others. Thomas Jefferson thought that only in a society of small farmers could the virtues flourish; and Adam Ferguson with a good deal more sophistication saw the institutions of modern commercial society as endangering at least some traditional virtues. It is Ferguson's type of sociology which is the empirical counterpart of the conceptual account of the virtues which I have given, a sociology which aspires to lay bare the empirical, causal connection between virtues, practices and institutions. For this kind of conceptual account has strong empirical implications; it provides an explanatory scheme which can be tested in particular cases. Moreover my thesis has empirical content in an-

other way; it does entail that without the virtues there could be a recognition only of what I have called external goods and not at all of internal goods in the context of practices. And in any society which recognised only external goods competitiveness would be the dominant and even exclusive feature. We have a brilliant portrait of such a society in Hobbes's account of the state of nature; and Professor Turnbull's report of the fate of the Ik suggests that social reality does in the most horrifying way confirm both my thesis and Hobbes's.

Virtues then stand in a different relationship to external and to internal goods. The possession of the virtues—and not only of their semblance and simulacra—is necessary to achieve the latter; yet the possession of the virtues may perfectly well hinder us in achieving external goods. I need to emphasise at this point that external goods genuinely are goods. Not only are they characteristic objects of human desire, whose allocation is what gives point to the virtues of justice and of generosity, but no one can despise them altogether without a certain hypocrisy. Yet notoriously the cultivation of truthfulness, justice and courage will often, the world being what it contingently is, bar us from being rich or famous or powerful. Thus although we may hope that we can not only achieve the standards of excellence and the internal goods of certain practices by possessing the virtues *and* become rich, famous and powerful, the virtues are always a potential stumbling block to this comfortable ambition. We should therefore expect that, if in a particular society the pursuit of external goods were to become dominant, the concept of the virtues might suffer first attrition and then perhaps something near total effacement, although simulacra might abound.

The time has come to ask the question of how far this partial account of a core conception of the virtues—and I need to emphasise that all that I have offered so far is the first stage of such an account—is faithful to the tradition which I delineated. How far, for example, and in what ways is it Aristotelian? It is—happily—not Aristotelian in two ways in which a good deal of the rest of the tradition also dissents from Aristotle. First, although this account of the virtues is teleological, it does not require the identification of any teleology in nature, and hence it does not require any allegiance to Aristotle's metaphysical biology. And secondly, just because of the multiplicity of human practices and the consequent multiplicity of goods in the pursuit of which the virtues may be exercised — goods which will often be contingently incompatible and which will therefore make rival claims upon our allegiance — conflict will not spring solely from flaws in individual character. But it was just on these two matters that Aristotle's account of the virtues seemed most vulnerable; hence if it turns out to be the case that this socially teleological account can support Aristotle's general account of the virtues as well as does his own biologically teleological account, these differences from Aristotle himself may well be regarded as strengthening rather than weakening the case for a generally Aristotelian standpoint.

There are at least three ways in which the account that I have given *is* clearly Aristotelian. First it requires for its completion a cogent elaboration of just those distinctions and concepts which Aristotle's account requires: voluntariness, the distinction between the intellectual virtues and the virtues of character, the relationship of both to natural abilities and to the passions and the structure of practical reasoning. On every one of these topics something very like Aristotle's view has to be defended, if my own account is to be plausible.

Secondly my account can accommodate an Aristotelian view of pleasure and enjoyment, whereas it is interestingly irreconcilable with any utilitarian view and more particularly with Franklin's account of the virtues. We can approach these questions by considering how to reply to someone who, having considered my account of the differences between goods internal to and goods external to a practice required into which class, if either, does pleasure or enjoyment fall? The answer is, 'Some types of pleasure into one, some into the other.'

Someone who achieves excellence in a practice, who plays chess or football well, or who carries through an enquiry in physics or an experimental mode in painting with success, characteristically enjoys his achievement and his activity in achieving. So does someone who, although not breaking the limit of achievement, plays or thinks or acts in a way that leads towards such a breaking of limit. As Aristotle says, the enjoyment of the activity and the enjoyment of achievement are not the ends at which the agent aims, but the enjoyment supervenes upon the successful activity in such a way that the activity achieved and the activity enjoyed are one and the same state. Hence to aim at the one is to aim at the

other; and hence also it is easy to confuse the pursuit of excellence with the pursuit of enjoyment *in this specific sense*. This particular confusion is harmless enough; what is not harmless is the confusion of enjoyment *in this specific sense* with other forms of pleasure.

For certain kinds of pleasure are of course external goods along with prestige, status, power and money. Not all pleasure is the enjoyment supervening upon achieved activity; some is the pleasure of psychological or physical states independent of all activity. Such states — for example that produced on a normal palate by the closely successive and thereby blended sensations of Colchester oyster, cayenne pepper and Veuve Cliquot — may be sought as external goods, as external rewards which may be purchased by money or received in virtue of prestige. Hence the pleasures are categorised neatly and appropriately by the classification into internal and external goods.

It is just this classification which can find no place within Franklin's account of the virtues which is formed entirely in terms of external relationships and external goods. Thus although by this stage of the argument it is possible to claim that my account does capture a conception of the virtues which is at the core of the particular ancient and medieval tradition which I have delineated, it is equally clear that there is more than one possible conception of the virtues and that Franklin's standpoint and indeed any utilitarian standpoint is such that to accept it will entail rejecting the tradition and *vice versa*.

One crucial point of incompatibility was noted long ago by D. H. Lawrence. When Franklin asserts, 'Rarely use venery but for health or offspring ...,' Lawrence replies, 'Never *use* venery.' It is of the character of a virtue that in order that it be effective in producing the internal goods which are the rewards of the virtues it should be exercised without regard to consequences. For it turns out to be the case that — and this is in part at least one more empirical factual claim — although the virtues are just those qualities which tend to lead to the achievement of a certain class of goods, none the less unless we practice them irrespective of whether in any particular set of contingent circumstances they will produce those goods or not, we cannot possess them at all. We cannot be genuinely courageous or truthful and be so only on occasion. Moreover, as we have seen, cultivation of the virtues always may and often does hinder the achievement of those external goods which are the mark of worldly success. The road to success in Philadelphia and the road to heaven may not coincide after all.

Furthermore we are now able to specify one crucial difficulty for *any* version of utilitarianism — in addition to those which I noticed earlier. Utilitarianism cannot accommodate the distinction between goods internal to and goods external to a practice. Not only is that distinction marked by none of the classical utilitarians — it cannot be found in Bentham's writings nor in those of either of the Mills or of Sidgwick — but internal goods and external goods are not commensurable with each other. Hence the notion of summing goods — and *a fortiori* in the light of what I have said about kinds of pleasure and enjoyment the notion of summing happiness — in terms of one single formula or conception of utility, whether it is Franklin's or Bentham's or Mill's, makes no sense. None the less we ought to note that although *this* distinction is alien to J. S. Mill's thought, it is plausible and in no way patronising to suppose that something like this is the distinction which he was trying to make in *Utilitarianism* when he distinguished between 'higher' and 'lower' pleasures. At the most we can say 'something like this'; for J. S. Mill's upbringing had given him a limited view of human life and powers, had unfitted him, for example, for appreciating games just because of the way it had fitted him for appreciating philosophy. None the less the notion that the pursuit of excellence in a way that extends human powers is at the heart of human life is instantly recognisable as at home in not only J. S. Mill's political and social thought but also in his and Mrs. Taylor's life. Were I to choose human exemplars of certain of the virtues as I understand them, there would of course be many names to name, those of St. Benedict and St. Francis of Assisi and St. Theresa *and* those of Frederick Engels and Eleanor Marx and Leon Trotsky among them. But that of John Stuart Mill would have to be there as certainly as any other.

Thirdly my account is Aristotelian in that it links evaluation and explanation in a characteristically Aristotelian way. From an Aristotelian standpoint to identify certain actions as manifesting or failing to manifest a virtue or virtues is never only to evaluate; it is also to take the first step towards explaining why those actions rather than some others were performed. Hence for an Aristotelian quite as much as for a Platonist the fate of a city or an individual can be explained by citing the injustice of a tyrant or the courage of its defenders. Indeed without allusion to the place that justice and injustice, courage and cowardice play in human life very little will be genuinely explicable. It follows that many of the explanatory projects of the modern social sciences, a methodological canon of which is the separation of 'the facts' . . . from all evaluation, are bound to fail. For the fact that someone was or failed to be courageous or just cannot be recognised as 'a fact' by those who accept that methodological canon. The account of the virtues which I have given is completely at one with Aristotle's on this point. But now the question may be raised: your account may be in many respects Aristotelian, but is it not in some respects false? Consider the following important objection.

I have defined the virtues partly in terms of their place in practices. But surely, it may be suggested, some practices — that is, some coherent human activities which answer to the description of what I have called a practice — are evil. So in discussions by some moral philosophers of this type of account of the virtues it has been suggested that torture and sado-masochistic sexual activities might be examples of practices. But how can a disposition be a virtue if it is the kind of disposition which sustains practices and some practices issue in evil? My answer to this objection falls into two parts.

First I want to allow that there *may* be practices — in the sense in which I understand the concept — which simply *are* evil. I am far from convinced that there are, and I do not in fact believe that either torture or sado-masochistic sexuality answer to the description of a practice which my account of the virtues employs. But I do not want to rest my case on this lack of conviction, especially since it is plain that as a matter of contingent fact many types of practice may on particular occasions be productive of evil. For the range of practices includes the arts, the sciences and certain types of intellectual and athletic game. And it is at once obvious that any of these may under certain conditions be a source of evil: the desire to excel and to win can corrupt, a man may be so engrossed by his painting that he neglects his family, what was initially an honourable resort to war can issue in savage cruelty. But what follows from this?

It certainly is not the case that my account entails *either* that we ought to excuse or condone such evils *or* that whatever flows from a virtue is right. I do have to allow that courage sometimes sustains injustice, that loyalty has been known to strengthen a murderous aggressor and that generosity has sometimes weakened the capacity to do good. But to deny this would be to fly in the face of just those empirical facts which I invoked in criticising Aquinas's account of the unity of the virtues. That the virtues need initially to be defined and explained with reference to the notion of a practice thus in no way entails approval of all practices in all circumstances. That the virtues—as the objection itself presupposed—*are* defined not in terms of good and right practices, but of practices, does not entail or imply that practices as actually carried through at particular times and places do not stand in need of moral criticism. And the resources for such criticism are not lacking. There is in the first place no inconsistency in appealing to the requirements of a virtue to criticise a practice. Justice may be initially defined as a disposition which in its particular way is necessary to sustain practices; it does not follow that in pursuing the requirements of a practice violations of justice are not to be condemned. Moreover I already pointed out . . . that a morality of virtues requires as its counterpart a conception of moral law. Its requirements too have to be met by practices. But, it may be asked, does not all this imply that more needs to be said about the place of practices in some larger moral context? Does not this at least suggest that there is more to the core concept of a virtue than can be spelled out in terms of practices? I have after all emphasised that the scope of any virtue in human life extends beyond the practices in terms of which it is initially defined. What then is the place of the virtues in the larger arenas of human life?

I stressed earlier that any account of the virtues in terms of practices could only be a partial and first account. What is required to complement it? The most notable difference so far between my account and any account that could be called Aristotelian is that although I have in no way restricted the exercise of the virtues to the context of practices, it is in terms of practices that I have located their point and function. Whereas Aristotle locates that point and function in terms of the notion of a type of whole human life which can be called good. And it does seem that the question 'What would a human being lack who lacked the virtues?' must be given a kind of answer which goes beyond anything which I have said so far. For such an individual would not merely fail *in a variety of particular ways* in respect of the kind of excellence which can be achieved through participation in practices and in respect of the kind of human relationship required to sustain such excellence. His own life *viewed as a whole* would perhaps be defective; it would not be the kind of life which someone would describe in trying to answer the question 'What is the best kind of life for this kind of man or woman to live?' And that question cannot be answered without at least raising Aristotle's own question, 'What is the good life for man?' Consider three ways in which a human life informed only by the conception of the virtues sketched so far would be defective.

It would be pervaded, first of all, by *too many* conflicts and *too much* arbitrariness. I argued earlier that it is a merit of an account of the virtues in terms of a multiplicity of goods that it allows for the possibility of tragic conflict in a way in which Aristotle's does not. But it may also produce even in the life of someone who is virtuous and disciplined too many occasions when one allegiance points in one direction, another in another. The claims of one practice may be incompatible with another in such a way that one may find oneself oscillating in an arbitrary way, rather than making rational choices. So it seems to have been with T. E. Lawrence. Commitment to sustaining the kind of community in which the virtues can flourish may be incompatible with the devotion which a particular practice—of the arts, for example—requires. So there may be tensions between the claims of family life and those of the arts—the problem that Gauguin solved or failed to solve by fleeing to Polynesia, or between the claims of politics and those of the arts—the problem that Lenin solved or failed to solve by refusing to listen to Beethoven.

If the life of the virtues is continuously fractured by choices in which one allegiance entails the apparently arbitrary renunciation of another, it may seem that the goods internal to practices do after all derive their authority from our individual choices; for when different goods summon in different and in incompatible directions, 'I' have to choose between their rival claims. The modern self with its criterionless choices apparently reappears in the alien context of what was claimed to be an Aristotelian world. This accusation might be rebutted in part by returning to the question of why both goods and virtues do have authority in our lives and repeating what was said earlier in this chapter. But this reply would only be partly successful; the distinctively modern notion of choice would indeed have reappeared, even if with a more limited scope for its exercise than it has usually claimed.

Secondly without an overriding conception of the *telos* of a whole human life, conceived as a unity, our conception of certain individual virtues has to remain partial and incomplete. Consider two examples. Justice, on an Aristotelian view, is defined in terms of giving each person his or her due or desert. To deserve well is to have contributed in some substantial way to the achievement of those goods, the sharing of which and the common pursuit of which provide foundations for human community. But the goods internal to practices, including the goods internal to the practice of making and sustaining forms of community, need to be ordered and evaluated in some way if we are to assess relative desert. Thus only substantive application of an Aristotelian concept of justice requires an understanding of goods and of the good that goes beyond the multiplicity of goods which inform practices. As with justice, so also with patience. Patience is the virtue of waiting attentively without complaint, but not of waiting thus for anything at all. To treat patience as a virtue presupposes some adequate answer to the question: waiting for what? Within the context of practices a partial, although for many purposes adequate, answer can be given: the patience of a craftsman with refractory material, of a teacher with a slow pupil, of a politician in negotiations, are all species of patience. But what if the material is just too refractory, the pupil too slow, the negotiations too frustrating? Ought we always at a certain point just to give up in the interests of the practice itself? The medieval exponents of the virtue of patience claimed that there are certain types of situation in which the virtue of patience requires that I do not ever give up on some person or task, situations in which, as they would have put it, I am required to embody in my attitude to that person or task something of the patient attitude of God towards his creation. But this could only be so if patience served some overriding good, some *telos* which warranted putting other goods in a subordinate place. Thus it turns out that the content of the virtue of patience depends upon how we order various goods in a hierarchy and *a fortiori* on whether we are able rationally so to order these particular goods.

I have suggested so far that unless there is a *telos* which transcends the limited goods of practices by constituting the good of a whole human life, the good of a human life conceived as a unity, it will *both* be the case that a certain subversive arbitrariness will invade the moral life *and* that we shall be unable to specify the context of certain virtues adequately. These two considerations are reinforced by a third: that there is at least one virtue recognised by the tradition which cannot be specified at all except with reference to the wholeness of a human life — the virtue of integrity or constancy. 'Purity of heart,' said Kierkegaard, 'is to will one thing.' This notion of singleness of purpose in a whole life can have no application unless that of a whole life does.

VII.7 *Moral Saints*

SUSAN WOLF

Susan Wolf is professor of philosophy at Johns Hopkins University. She has
published a number of essays in ethics. In this article she challenges the notion
that moral saintliness is a worthy goal. She argues that being preoccupied with
moral perfection could rob us of other virtues — intellectual, social, and
cultural — and produce bland and boring people.

I don't know whether there are any moral saints.
But if there are, I am glad that neither I nor those
about whom I care most are among them. By *moral
saint* I mean a person whose every action is as morally good as possible, a person, that is, who is as
morally worthy as can be. Though I shall in a moment acknowledge the variety of types of person
that might be thought to satisfy this description, it
seems to me that none of these types serve as unequivocally compelling personal ideals. In other
words, I believe that moral perfection, in the sense
of moral saintliness, does not constitute a model of
personal well-being toward which it would be particularly rational or good or desirable for a human
being to strive.

Outside the context of moral discussion, this
will strike many as an obvious point. But, within
that context, the point, if it be granted, will be
granted with some discomfort. For within that context it is generally assumed that one ought to be as
morally good as possible and that what limits there
are to morality's hold on us are set by features of
human nature of which we ought not to be proud.
If, as I believe, the ideals that are derivable from
common sense and philosophically popular moral
theories do not support these assumptions, then
something has to change. Either we must change
our moral theories in ways that will make them yield
more palatable ideals, or, as I shall argue, we must
change our conception of what is involved in affirming a moral theory.

Reprinted with permission from *Journal of Philosophy*
79(1982):419–439.

In this paper, I wish to examine the notion of a
moral saint, first, to understand what a moral saint
would be like and why such a being would be unattractive, and second, to raise some questions about
the significance of this paradoxical figure for moral
philosophy. I shall look first at the model(s) of
moral sainthood that might be extrapolated from
the morality or moralities of common sense. Then I
shall consider what relations these have to conclusions that can be drawn from utilitarian and Kantian
moral theories. Finally, I shall speculate on the implications of these considerations for moral
philosophy.

Moral Saints and Common Sense

Consider first what, pretheoretically, would count
for us — contemporary members of Western culture — as a moral saint. A necessary condition of
moral sainthood would be that one's life be dominated by a commitment to improving the welfare of
others or of society as a whole. As to what role this
commitment must play in the individual's motivational system, two contrasting accounts suggest
themselves to me which might equally be thought
to qualify a person for moral sainthood.

First, a moral saint might be someone whose
concern for others plays the role that is played in
most of our lives by more selfish, or, at any rate, less
morally worthy concerns. For the moral saint, the
promotion of the welfare of others might play the
role that is played for most of us by the enjoyment of
material comforts, the opportunity to engage in the

intellectual and physical activities of our choice, and the love, respect, and companionship of people whom we love, respect, and enjoy. The happiness of the moral saint, then, would truly lie in the happiness of others, and so he would devote himself to others gladly, and with a whole and open heart.

On the other hand, a moral saint might be someone for whom the basic ingredients of happiness are not unlike those of most of the rest of us. What makes him a moral saint is rather that he pays little or no attention to his own happiness in light of the overriding importance he gives to the wider concerns of morality. In others words, this person sacrifices his own interests to the interests of others, and feels the sacrifice as such.

Roughly, these two models may be distinguished according to whether one thinks of the moral saint as being a saint out of love or one thinks of the moral saint as being a saint out of duty (or some other intellectual appreciation and recognition of moral principles). We may refer to the first model as the model of the Loving Saint; to the second, as the model of the Rational Saint.

The two models differ considerably with respect to the qualities of the motives of the individuals who conform to them. But this difference would have limited effect on the saints' respective public personalities. The shared content of what these individuals are motivated to be—namely, as morally good as possible—would play the dominant role in the determination of their characters. Of course, just as a variety of large-scale projects, from tending the sick to political campaigning, may be equally and maximally morally worthy, so a variety of characters are compatible with the ideal of moral sainthood. One moral saint may be more or less jovial, more or less garrulous, more or less athletic than another. But above all, a moral saint must have and cultivate those qualities which are apt to allow him to treat others as justly and kindly as possible. He will have the standard moral virtues to a nonstandard degree. He will be patient, considerate, even-tempered, hospitable, charitable in thought as well as in deed. He will be very reluctant to make negative judgments of other people. He will be careful not to favor some people over others on the basis of properties they could not help but have.

Perhaps what I have already said is enough to make some people begin to regard the absence of moral saints in their lives as a blessing. For there comes a point in the listing of virtues that a moral saint is likely to have where one might naturally begin to wonder whether the moral saint isn't after all, too good—if not too good for his own good, at least too good for his own well-being. For the moral virtues, given that they are, by hypothesis, *all* present in the same individual, and to an extreme degree, are apt to crowd out the nonmoral virtues, as well as many of the interests and personal characteristics that we generally think contribute to a healthy, well-rounded, richly developed character.

In other words, if the moral saint is devoting all his time to feeding the hungry or healing the sick or raising money for Oxfam, then necessarily he is not reading Victorian novels, playing the oboe, or improving his backhand. Although no one of the interests or tastes in the category containing these latter activities could be claimed to be a necessary element in a life well lived, a life in which *none* of these possible aspects of character are developed may seem to be a life strangely barren.

The reasons why a moral saint cannot, in general, encourage the discovery and development of significant nonmoral interests and skills are not logical but practical reasons. There are, in addition, a class of nonmoral characteristics that a moral saint cannot encourage in himself for reasons that are not just practical. There is a more substantial tension between having any of these qualities unashamedly and being a moral saint. These qualities might be described as going against the moral grain. For example, a cynical or sarcastic wit, or a sense of humor that appreciates this kind of wit in others, requires that one take an attitude of resignation and pessimism toward the flaws and vices to be found in the world. A moral saint, on the other hand, has reason to take an attitude in opposition to this—he should try to look for the best in people, give them the benefit of the doubt as long as possible, try to improve regrettable situations as long as there is any hope of success. This suggests that, although a moral saint might well enjoy a good episode of *Father Knows Best,* he may not in good conscience be able to laugh at a Marx Brothers movie or enjoy a play by George Bernard Shaw.

An interest in something like gourmet cooking will be, for different reasons, difficult for a moral saint to rest easy with. For it seems to me that no plausible argument can justify the use of human resources involved in producing a *pâté de canard en croûte* against possible alternative beneficent ends to which these resources might be put. If there is a justification for the institution of haute cuisine, it is one which rests on the decision *not* to justify every activity against morally beneficial alternatives, and this is a decision a moral saint will never make. Presumably, an interest in high fashion or interior design will fare much the same, as will, very possibly, a cultivation of the finer arts as well.

A moral saint will have to be very, very nice. It is important that he not be offensive. The worry is that, as a result, he will have to be dull-witted or humorless or bland.

This worry is confirmed when we consider what sorts of characters, taken and refined both from life and from fiction, typically form our ideals. One would hope they would be figures who are morally good—and by this I mean more than just not morally bad—but one would hope, too, that they are not *just* morally good, but talented or accomplished or attractive in nonmoral ways as well. We may make ideals out of athletes, scholars, artists—more frivolously, out of cowboys, private eyes, and rock stars. We may strive for Katherine Hepburn's grace, Paul Newman's "cool"; we are attracted to the high-spirited passionate nature of Natasha Rostov; we admire the keen perceptiveness of Lambert Strether. Though there is certainly nothing immoral about the ideal characters or traits I have in mind, they cannot be superimposed upon the ideal of a moral saint. For although it is a part of many of these ideals that the characters set high, and not merely acceptable, moral standards for themselves, it is also essential to their power and attractiveness that the moral strengths go, so to speak, alongside of specific, independently admirable, nonmoral ground projects and dominant personal traits.

When one does finally turn one's eyes toward lives that are dominated by explicitly moral commitments, moreover, one finds oneself relieved at the discovery of idiosyncrasies or eccentricities not quite in line with the picture of moral perfection. One prefers the blunt, tactless, and opinionated Betsy Trotwood to the unfailingly kind and patient Agnes Copperfield; one prefers the mischievousness and the sense of irony in Chesterton's Father Brown to the innocence and undiscriminating love of St. Francis.

It seems that, as we look in our ideals for people who achieve nonmoral varieties of personal excellence in conjunction with or colored by some version of high moral tone, we look in our paragons of moral excellence for people whose moral achievements occur in conjunction with or colored by some interests or traits that have low moral tone. In other words, there seems to be a limit to how much morality we can stand.

One might suspect that the essence of the problem is simply that there is a limit to how much of *any* single value, or any single type of value, we can stand. Our objection then would not be specific to a life in which one's dominant concern is morality, but would apply to any life that can be so completely characterized by an extraordinarily dominant concern. The objection in that case would reduce to the recognition that such a life is incompatible with well-roundedness. If that were the objection, one could fairly reply that well-roundedness is no more supreme a virtue than the totality of moral virtues embodied by the ideal it is being used to criticize. But I think this misidentifies the objection. For the way in which a concern for morality may dominate a life, or, more to the point, the way in which it may dominate an ideal of life, is not easily imagined by analogy to the dominance an aspiration to become an Olympic swimmer or a concert pianist might have.

A person who is passionately committed to one of these latter concerns might decide that her attachment to it is strong enough to be worth the sacrifice of her ability to maintain and pursue a significant portion of what else life might offer which a proper devotion to her dominant passion would require. But a desire to be as morally good as possible is not likely to take the form of one desire among others which, because of its peculiar psychological strength, requires one to forego the pursuit of other weaker and separately less demanding desires. Rather, the desire to be as morally good as possible is apt to have the character not just of a stronger, but of a higher desire, which does not merely successfully compete with one's other desires but which rather subsumes or demotes them. The sacrifice of other interests for the interest in morality, then, will have the character, not of a choice, but of an imperative.

Moreover, there is something odd about the idea of morality itself, or moral goodness, serving as the object of a dominant passion in the way that a more concrete and specific vision of a goal (even a concrete *moral* goal) might be imagined to serve. Morality itself does not seem to be a suitable object of passion. Thus, when one reflects, for example, on the Loving Saint easily and gladly giving up his fishing trip or his stereo or his hot fudge sundae at the drop of the moral hat, one is apt to wonder not at how much he loves morality, but at how little he loves these other things. One thinks that, if he can give these up so easily, he does not know what it *is* to truly love them. There seems, in other words, to be a kind of joy which the Loving Saint, either by nature or by practice, is incapable of experiencing. The Rational Saint, on the other hand, might retain strong nonmoral and concrete desires — he simply denies himself the opportunity to act on them. But this is no less troubling. The Loving Saint one might suspect of missing a piece of perceptual machinery, of being blind to some of what the world has to offer. The Rational Saint, who sees it but foregoes it, one suspects of having a different problem — a pathological fear of damnation, perhaps, or an extreme form of self-hatred that interferes with his ability to enjoy the enjoyable in life.

In other words, the ideal of a life of moral sainthood disturbs not simply because it is an ideal of a life in which morality unduly dominates. The normal person's direct and specific desires for objects, activities, and events that conflict with the attainment of moral perfection are not simply sacrificed but removed, suppressed, or subsumed. The way in which morality, unlike other possible goals, is apt to dominate is particularly disturbing, for it seems to require either the lack or the denial of the existence of an identifiable, personal self.

This distinctively troubling feature is not, I think, absolutely unique to the ideal of the moral saint, as I have been using that phrase. It is shared by the conception of the pure aesthete, by a certain kind of religious ideal, and, somewhat paradoxically, by the model of the thorough-going, self-conscious egoist. It is not a coincidence that the ways of comprehending the world of which these ideals are the extreme embodiments are sometimes described as "moralities" themselves. At any rate, they compete with what we ordinarily mean by 'morality.' Nor is it a coincidence that these ideals are naturally described as fanatical. But it is easy to see that these other types of perfection cannot serve as

satisfactory personal ideals; for the realization of these ideals would be straightforwardly immoral. It may come as a surprise to some that there may in addition be such a thing as a *moral* fanatic.

Some will object that I am being unfair to "common-sense morality" — that it does not really require a moral saint to be either a disgusting goody-goody or an obsessive ascetic. Admittedly, there is no logical inconsistency between having any of the personal characteristics I have mentioned and being a moral saint. It is not morally wrong to notice the faults and shortcomings of others or to recognize and appreciate nonmoral talents and skills. Nor is it immoral to be an avid Celtics fan or to have a passion for caviar to be an excellent cellist. With enough imagination, we can always contrive a suitable history and set of circumstances that will embrace such characteristics in one or another specific fictional story of a perfect moral saint.

If one turned onto the path of moral sainthood relatively late in life, one may have already developed interests that can be turned to moral purposes. It may be that a good golf game is just what is needed to secure that big donation to Oxfam. Perhaps the cultivation of one's exceptional artistic talent will turn out to be the way one can make one's greatest contribution to society. Furthermore, one might stumble upon joys and skills in the very service of morality. If, because the children are short a ninth player for the team, one's generous offer to serve reveals a natural fielding arm or if one's part in the campaign against nuclear power requires accepting a lobbyist's invitation to lunch at Le Lion d'Or, there is no moral gain in denying the satisfaction one gets from these activities. The moral saint, then, may, by happy accident, find himself with nonmoral virtues on which he can capitalize morally or which make psychological demands to which he has no choice but to attend. The point is that, for a moral saint, the existence of these interests and skills can be given at best the status of happy accidents — they cannot be encouraged for their own sakes as distinct, independent aspects of the realization of human good.

It must be remembered that from the fact that there is a tension between having any of these qualities and being a moral saint it does not follow that having any of these qualities is immoral. For it is not part of common-sense morality that one ought to be a moral saint. Still, if someone just happened to want to be a moral saint, he or she would not have or encourage these qualities, and, on the basis of our common-sense values, this counts as a reason *not* to want to be a moral saint.

One might still wonder what kind of reason this is, and what kind of conclusion this properly allows us to draw. For the fact that the models of moral saints are unattractive does not necessarily mean that they are unsuitable ideals. Perhaps they are unattractive because they make us feel uncomfortable — they highlight our own weaknesses, vices, and flaws. If so, the fault lies not in the characters of the saints, but in those of our unsaintly selves.

To be sure, some of the reasons behind the disaffection we feel for the model of moral sainthood have to do with a reluctance to criticize ourselves and a reluctance to committing ourselves to trying to give up activities and interests that we heartily enjoy. These considerations might provide an *excuse* for the fact that we are not moral saints, but they do not provide a basis for criticizing sainthood as a possible ideal. Since these considerations rely on an appeal to the egoistic, hedonistic side of our natures, to use them as a basis for criticizing the ideal of the moral saint would be at best to beg the question and at worst to glorify features of ourselves that ought to be condemned.

The fact that the moral saint would be without qualities which we have and which, indeed, we like to have, does not in itself provide reason to condemn the ideal of the moral saint. The fact that some of these qualities are good qualities, however, and that they are qualities we *ought* to like, does provide reason to discourage this ideal and to offer other ideals in its place. In other words, some of the qualities the moral saint necessarily lacks are virtues, albeit nonmoral virtues, in the unsaintly characters who have them. The feats of Groucho Marx, Reggie Jackson, and the head chef at Lutèce are impressive accomplishments that it is not only permissible but positively appropriate to recognize as such. In general, the admiration of and striving toward achieving any of a great variety of forms of personal excellence are character traits it is valuable and desirable for people to have. In advocating the development of these varieties of excellence, we advocate nonmoral reasons for acting, and in thinking that it is good for a person to strive for an ideal that gives a substantial role to the interests and values that correspond to these virtues, we implicitly acknowledge the goodness of ideals incompatible with that of the moral saint. Finally, if we think that it is *as* good, or even better for a person to strive for one of these ideals than it is for him or her to strive for and realize the ideal of the moral saint, we express a conviction that it is good not to be a moral saint.

Moral Saints and Moral Theories

I have tried so far to paint a picture — or rather, two pictures — of what a moral saint might be like, drawing on what I take to be the attitudes and beliefs about morality prevalent in contemporary, common-sense thought. To my suggestion that common-sense morality generates conceptions of moral saints that are unattractive or otherwise unacceptable, it is open to someone to reply, "so much the worse for common-sense morality." After all, it is often claimed that the goal of moral philosophy is to correct and improve upon common-sense morality, and I have as yet given no attention to the question of what conceptions of moral sainthood, if any, are generated from the leading moral theories of our time.

A quick, breezy reading of utilitarian and Kantian writings will suggest the images, respectively, of the Loving Saint and the Rational Saint. A utilitarian, with his emphasis on happiness, will certainly prefer the Loving Saint to the Rational one, since the Loving Saint will himself be a happier person than the Rational Saint. A Kantian, with his emphasis on reason, on the other hand, will find at least as much to praise in the latter as in the former. Still, both models, drawn as they are from common sense, appeal to an impure mixture of utilitarian and Kantian intuitions. A more careful examination of these moral theories raises questions about whether either model of moral sainthood would really be advocated by a believer in the explicit doctrines associated with either of these views.

Certainly, the utilitarian in no way denies the value of self-realization. He in no way disparages the development of interests, talents, and other personally attractive traits that I have claimed the moral saint would be without. Indeed, since just these features enhance the happiness both of the individuals who possess them and of those with whom they associate, the ability to promote these features both in oneself and in others will have considerable positive weight in utilitarian calculations.

This implies that the utilitarian would not support moral sainthood as a universal ideal. A world in which everyone, or even a large number of people, achieved moral sainthood—even a world in which they *strove* to achieve it—would probably contain less happiness than a world in which people realized a diversity of ideals involving a variety of personal and perfectionist values. More pragmatic considerations also suggest that, if the utilitarian wants to influence more people to achieve more good, then he would do better to encourage them to pursue happiness-producing goals that are more attractive and more within a normal person's reach.

These considerations still leave open, however, the question of what kind of an ideal the committed utilitarian should privately aspire to himself. Utilitarianism requires him to want to achieve the greatest general happiness, and this would seem to commit him to the ideal of the moral saint.

One might try to use the claims I made earlier as a basis for an argument that a utilitarian should choose to give up utilitarianism. If, as I have said, a moral saint would be a less happy person both to be and to be around than many other possible ideals, perhaps one could create more total happiness by not trying too hard to promote the total happiness. But this argument is simply unconvincing in light of the empirical circumstances of our world. The gain in happiness that would accrue to oneself and one's neighbors by a more well-rounded, richer life than that of the moral saint would be pathetically small in comparison to the amount by which one could increase the general happiness if one devoted oneself explicitly to the care of the sick, the downtrodden, the starving, and the homeless. Of course, there may be psychological limits to the extent to which a person can devote himself to such things without going crazy. But the utilitarian's individual limitations would not thereby become a positive feature of his personal ideals.

The unattractiveness of the moral saint, then, ought not rationally convince the utilitarian to abandon his utilitarianism. It may, however, convince him to take efforts not to wear his saintly moral aspirations on his sleeve. If it is not too difficult, the utilitarian will try not to make those

around him uncomfortable. He will not want to appear "holier than thou"; he will not want to inhibit others' ability to enjoy themselves. In practice, this might make the perfect utilitarian a less nauseating companion than the moral saint I earlier portrayed. But insofar as this kind of reasoning produces a more bearable public personality, it is at the cost of giving him a personality that must be evaluated as hypocritical and condescending when his private thoughts and attitudes are taken into account.

Still, the criticisms I have raised against the saint of common-sense morality should make some difference to the utilitarian's conception of an ideal which neither requires him to abandon his utilitarian principles nor forces him to fake an interest he does not have or a judgment he does not make. For it may be that a limited and carefully monitored allotment of time and energy to be devoted to the pursuit of some nonmoral interests or to the development of some nonmoral talents would make a person a better contributor to the general welfare than he would be if he allowed himself no indulgences of this sort. The enjoyment of such activities in no way compromises a commitment to utilitarian principles as long as the involvement with these activities is conditioned by a willingness to give them up whenever it is recognized that they cease to be in the general interest.

This will go some way in mitigating the picture of the loving saint that an understanding of utilitarianism will on first impression suggest. But I think it will not go very far. For the limitations on time and energy will have to be rather severe, and the need to monitor will restrict not only the extent but also the quality of one's attachment to these interests and traits. They are only weak and somewhat peculiar sorts of passions to which one can consciously remain so conditionally committed. Moreover, the way in which the utilitarian can enjoy these "extra-curricular" aspects of his life is simply not the way in which these aspects are to be enjoyed insofar as they figure into our less saintly ideals.

The problem is not exactly that the utilitarian values these aspects of his life only as a means to an end, for the enjoyment he and others get from these aspects are not a means to, but a part of, the general happiness. Nonetheless, he values these things only because of and insofar as they *are* a part of the general happiness. He values them, as it were, under the description 'a contribution to the general happiness? This is to be contrasted with the various ways in which these aspects of life may be valued by non-utilitarians. A person might love literature because of the insights into human nature literature affords. Another might love the cultivation of roses because roses are things of great beauty and delicacy. It may be true that these features of the respective activities also explain why these activities are happiness-producing. But, to the nonutilitarian, this may not be to the point. For if one values these activities in these more direct ways, one may not be willing to exchange them for others that produce an equal, or even a greater amount of happiness. From that point of view, it is not because they produce happiness that these activities are valuable; it is because these activities are valuable in more direct and specific ways that they produce happiness.

To adopt a phrase of Bernard Williams', the utilitarian's manner of valuing the not explicitly moral aspects of his life "provides (him) with one thought too many."[1] The requirement that the utilitarian have this thought — periodically, at least — is indicative of not only a weakness but a shallowness in his appreciation of the aspects in question. Thus, the ideals toward which a utilitarian could acceptably strive would remain too close to the model of the common-sense moral saint to escape the criticisms of that model which I earlier suggested. Whether a Kantian would be similarly committed to so restrictive and unattractive a range of possible ideals is a somewhat more difficult question.

The Kantian believes that being morally worthy consists in always acting from maxims that one could will to be universal law, and doing this not out of any pathological desire but out of reverence for the moral law as such. Or, to take a different formulation of the categorical imperative, the Kantian believes that moral action consists in treating other persons always as ends and never as means only. Presumably, and according to Kant himself, the Kantian thereby commits himself to some degree of benevolence as well as to the rules of fair play. But we surely would not will that *every* person become a moral saint, and treating others as ends hardly requires bending over backwards to protect and promote their interests. On one interpretation of Kantian doctrine, then, moral perfection would be achieved simply by unerring obedience to a limited set of side-constraints. On this interpretation, Kantian theory simply does not yield an ideal conception of a person of any fullness comparable to that of the moral saints I have so far been portraying.

On the other hand, Kant does say explicitly that we have a duty of benevolence, a duty not only to allow others to pursue their ends, but to take up their ends as our own. In addition, we have positive duties to ourselves, duties to increase our natural as well as our moral perfection. These duties are unlimited in the degree to which they *may* dominate a life. If action in accordance with and motivated by the thought of these duties is considered virtuous, it is natural to assume that the more one performs such actions, the more virtuous one is. Moreover, of virtue in general Kant says, "it is an ideal which is unattainable while yet our duty is constantly to approximate to it."[2] On this interpretation, then, the Kantian moral saint, like the other moral saints I have been considering, is dominated by the motivation to be moral.

Which of these interpretations of Kant one prefers will depend on the interpretation and the importance one gives to the role of the imperfect duties in Kant's over-all system. Rather than choose between them here, I shall consider each briefly in turn.

On the second interpretation of Kant, the Kantian moral saint is, not surprisingly, subject to many of the same objections I have been raising against other versions of moral sainthood. Though the Kantian saint may differ from the utilitarian saint as to *which* actions he is bound to perform and which he is bound to refrain from performing, I suspect that the range of activities acceptable to the Kantian saint will remain objectionably restrictive. Moreover, the manner in which the Kantian saint must think about and justify the activities he pursues and the character traits he develops will strike us, as it did with the utilitarian saint, as containing "one thought too many." As the utilitarian could value his activities and character traits only insofar as they fell under the description of 'contributions to the general happiness,' the Kantian would have to value his activities and character traits insofar as they were manifestations of respect for the moral law. If the development of our power to achieve physical, intellectual, or artistic excellence, or the activities directed toward making others happy are to have any moral worth, they must arise from a reverence for the dignity that members of our species have as a result of being endowed with pure practical reason.

This is a good and noble motivation, to be sure. But it is hardly what one expects to be dominantly behind a person's aspirations to dance as well as Fred Astaire, to paint as well as Picasso, or to solve some outstanding problem in abstract algebra, and it is hardly what one hopes to find lying dominantly behind a father's action on behalf of his son or a lover's on behalf of her beloved.

Since the basic problem with any of the models of moral sainthood we have been considering is that they are dominated by a single, all-important value under which all other possible values must be subsumed, it may seem that the alternative interpretation of Kant, as providing a stringent but finite set of obligations and constraints, might provide a more acceptable morality. According to this interpretation of Kant, one is as morally good as can be so long as one devotes some limited portion of one's energies toward altruism and the maintenance of one's physical and spiritual health, and otherwise pursues one's independently motivated interests and values in such a way as to avoid overstepping certain bounds. Certainly, if it be a requirement of an acceptable moral theory that perfect obedience to its laws and maximal devotion to its interests and concerns be something we can wholeheartedly strive for in ourselves and wish for in those around us, it will count in favor of this brand of Kantianism that its commands can be fulfilled without swallowing up the perfect moral agent's entire personality.

Even this more limited understanding of morality, if its connection to Kant's views is to be taken at all seriously, is not likely to give an unqualified seal of approval to the nonmorally directed ideals I have been advocating. For Kant is explicit about what he calls "duties of apathy and self-mastery" . . . —duties to ensure that our passions are never so strong as to interfere with calm, practical deliberation, or so deep as to wrest control from the more disinterested, rational part of ourselves. The tight and self-conscious rein we are thus obliged to keep on our commitments to specific individuals and causes will doubtless restrict our value in these things, assigning them a necessarily attenuated place.

A more interesting objection to this brand of Kantianism, however, comes when we consider the implications of placing the kind of upper bound on moral worthiness which seemed to count in favor of this conception of morality. For to put such a limit

on one's capacity to be moral is effectively to deny, not just the moral necessity, but the moral goodness of a devotion to benevolence and the maintenance of justice that passes beyond a certain, required point. It is to deny the possibility of going morally above and beyond the call of a restricted set of duties. Despite my claim that all-consuming moral saintliness is not a particularly healthy and desirable ideal, it seems perverse to insist that, were moral saints to exist, they would not, in their way, be remarkably noble and admirable figures. Despite my conviction that it is as rational and as good for a person to take Katherine Hepburn or Jane Austen as her role model instead of Mother Teresa, it would be absurd to deny that Mother Teresa is a morally better person.

I can think of two ways of viewing morality as having an upper bound. First, we can think that altruism and impartiality are indeed positive moral interests, but that they are moral only if the degree to which these interests are actively pursued remains within certain fixed limits. Second, we can think that these positive interests are only incidentally related to morality and that the essence of morality lies elsewhere, in, say, an implicit social contract or in the recognition of our own dignified rationality. According to the first conception of morality, there is a cut-off line to the amount of altruism or to the extent of devotion to justice and fairness that is worthy of moral praise. But to draw this line earlier than the line that brings the altruist in question to a worse-off position than all those to whom he devotes himself seems unacceptably artificial and gratuitous. According to the second conception, these positive interests are not essentially related to morality at all. But then we are unable to regard a more affectionate and generous expression of good will toward others as a natural and reasonable extension of morality, and we encourage a cold and unduly self-centered approach to the development and evaluation of our motivations and concerns.

A moral theory that does not contain the seeds of an all-consuming ideal of moral sainthood thus seems to place false and unnatural limits on our opportunity to do moral good and our potential to deserve moral praise. Yet the main thrust of the arguments of this paper has been leading to the conclusion that, when such ideals are present, they are not ideals to which it is particularly reasonable or healthy or desirable for human beings to aspire. These claims, taken together, have the appearance of a dilemma from which there is no obvious escape. In a moment, I shall argue that, despite appearances, these claims should not be understood as constituting a dilemma. But, before I do, let me briefly describe another path which those who are convinced by my above remarks may feel inclined to take.

If the above remarks are understood to be implicitly critical of the views on the content of morality which seem most popular today, an alternative that naturally suggests itself is that we revise our views about the content of morality. More specifically, my remarks may be taken to support a more Aristotelian, or even a more Nietzschean, approach to moral philosophy. Such a change in approach involves substantially broadening or replacing our contemporary intuitions about which character traits constitute moral virtues and vices and which interests constitute moral interests. If, for example, we include personal bearing, or creativity, or sense of style, as features that contribute to one's *moral* personality, then we can create moral ideals which are incompatible with and probably more attractive than the Kantian and utilitarian ideals I have discussed. Given such an alteration of our conception of morality, the figures with which I have been concerned above might, far from being considered to be moral saints, be seen as morally inferior to other more appealing or more interesting models of individuals.

This approach seems unlikely to succeed, if for no other reason, because it is doubtful that any single, or even any reasonably small number of substantial personal ideals could capture the full range of possible ways of realizing human potential or achieving human good which deserve encouragement and praise. Even if we could provide a sufficiently broad characterization of the range of positive ways for human beings to live, however, I think there are strong reasons not to want to incorporate such a characterization more centrally into the framework of morality itself. For, in claiming that a character trait or activity is morally good, one claims that there is a certain kind of reason for developing that trait or engaging in that activity. Yet, lying behind our criticism of more conventional conceptions of moral sainthood, there seems to be a recognition that among the immensely valuable traits and activities that a human life might positively embrace are some of which we hope that, if a person does embrace them, he does so *not* for moral reasons. In other words, no matter how flexible we make the guide to conduct which we choose to label "morality," no matter how rich we make the life in which perfect obedience to this guide would result, we will have reason to hope that a person does not wholly rule and direct his life by the abstract and impersonal consideration that such a life would be morally good.

Once it is recognized that morality itself should not serve as a comprehensive guide to conduct, moreover, we can see reasons to retain the admittedly vague contemporary intuitions about what the classification of moral and nonmoral virtues, interests, and the like should be. That is, there seem to be important differences between the aspects of a person's life which are currently considered appropriate objects of moral evaluation and the aspects that might be included under the altered conception of morality we are now considering, which the latter approach would tend wrongly to blur or to neglect. Moral evaluation now is focused primarily on features of a person's life over which that person has control; it is largely restricted to aspects of his life which are likely to have considerable effect on other people. These restrictions seem as they should be. Even if responsible people could reach agreement as to what constituted good taste or a healthy degree of well-roundedness, for example, it seems wrong to insist that everyone try to achieve these things or to blame someone who fails or refuses to conform.

If we are not to respond to the unattractiveness of the moral ideals that contemporary theories yield either by offering alternative theories with more palatable ideals or by understanding these theories in such a way as to prevent them from yielding ideals at all, how, then, are we to respond? Simply, I think, by admitting that moral ideals do not, and need not, make the best personal ideals. Earlier, I mentioned one of the consequences of regarding as a test of an adequate moral theory that perfect obedience to its laws and maximal devotion to its interests be something we can wholeheartedly strive for in ourselves and wish for in those around us. Drawing out the consequences somewhat further should, I think, make us more doubtful of the proposed test than of the theories which, on this test, would fail. Given the empirical circumstances of our world, it seems to be an ethical fact that we have unlimited potential to be morally good, and endless opportunity to promote moral interests. But this is not incompatible with the not-so-ethical fact that we have sound, compelling, and not particularly selfish reasons to choose not to devote ourselves univocally to realizing this potential or to taking up this opportunity.

Thus, in one sense at least, I am not really criticizing either Kantianism or utilitarianism. Insofar as the point of view I am offering bears directly on recent work in moral philosophy, in fact, it bears on critics of these theories who, in a spirit not unlike the spirit of most of this paper, point out that the perfect utilitarian would be flawed in this way or the perfect Kantian flawed in that.[3] The assumption lying behind these claims, implicitly or explicitly, has been that the recognition of these flaws shows us something wrong with utilitarianism, as opposed to Kantianism, or something wrong with Kantianism as opposed to utilitarianism, or something wrong with both of these theories as opposed to some nameless third alternative. The claims of this paper suggest, however, that the assumption is unwarranted. The flaws of a perfect master of a moral theory need not reflect flaws in the intramoral content of the theory itself.

Moral Saints and Moral Philosophy

In pointing out the regrettable features and the necessary absence of some desirable features in a moral saint, I have not meant to condemn the moral saint or the person who aspires to become one. Rather, I have meant to insist that the ideal of moral sainthood should not be held as a standard against which any other ideal must be judged or justified, and that the posture we take in response to the recognition that our lives are not as morally good as they might be need not be defensive.[4] It is misleading to insist that one is *permitted* to live a life in which the goals, relationships, activities, and interests that one pursues are not maximally morally good. For our lives are not so comprehensively subject to the requirement that we apply for permission, and our nonmoral reasons for the goals we set ourselves are not

excuses, but may rather be positive, good reasons which do not exist *despite* any reasons that might threaten to outweigh them. In other words, a person may be *perfectly wonderful* without being *perfectly moral*.

Recognizing this requires a perspective which contemporary moral philosophy has generally ignored. This perspective yields judgments of a type that is neither moral nor egoistic. Like moral judgments, judgments about what it would be good for a person to be are made from a point of view outside the limits set by the values, interests, and desires that the person might actually have. And, like moral judgments, these judgments claim for themselves a kind of objectivity or a grounding in a perspective which any rational and perceptive being can take up. Unlike moral judgments, however, the good with which these judgments are concerned is not the good of anyone or any group other than the individual himself.

Nonetheless, it would be equally misleading to say that these judgments are made for the sake of the individual himself. For these judgments are not concerned with what kind of life it is in a person's interest to lead, but with what kind of interests it would be good for a person to have, and it need not be in a person's interest that he acquire or maintain objectively good interests. Indeed, the model of the Loving Saint, whose interests are identified with the interests of morality, is a model of a person for whom the dictates of rational self-interest and the dictates of morality coincide. Yet, I have urged that we have reason not to aspire to this ideal and that some of us would have reason to be sorry if our children aspired to and achieved it.

The moral point of view, we might say, is the point of view one takes up insofar as one takes the recognition of the fact that one is just one person among others equally real and deserving of the good things of life as a fact with practical consequences, a fact the recognition of which demands expression in one's actions and in the form of one's practical deliberations. Competing moral theories offer alternative answers to the question of what the most correct or the best way to express this fact is. In doing so, they offer alternative ways to evaluate and to compare the variety of actions, states of affairs, and so on that appear good and bad to agents from other, nonmoral points of view. But it seems that alternative interpretations of the moral point of view do not exhaust the ways in which our actions, characters, and their consequences can be comprehensively and objectively evaluated. Let us call the point of view from which we consider what kinds of lives are good lives, and what kinds of persons it would be good for ourselves and others to be, the *point of view of individual perfection*.

Since either point of view provides a way of comprehensively evaluating a person's life, each point of view takes account of, and, in a sense, subsumes the other. From the moral point of view, the perfection of an individual life will have some, but limited, value—for each individual remains, after all, just one person among others. From the perfectionist point of view, the moral worth of an individual's relation to his world will likewise have some, but limited, value—for, as I have argued, the (perfectionist) goodness of an individual's life does not vary proportionally with the degree to which it exemplifies moral goodness.

It may not be the case that the perfectionist point of view is like the moral point of view in being a point of view we are ever *obliged* to take up and express in our actions. Nonetheless, it provides us with reasons that are independent of moral reasons for wanting ourselves and others to develop our characters and live our lives in certain ways. When we take up this point of view and ask how much it would be good for an individual to act from the moral point of view, we do not find an obvious answer.[5]

The considerations of this paper suggest, at any rate, that the answer is not "as much as possible." This has implications both for the continued development of moral theories and for the development of metamoral views and for our conception of moral philosophy more generally. From the moral point of view, we have reasons to want people to live lives that seem good from outside that point of view. If, as I have argued, this means that we have reason to want people to live lives that are not morally perfect, then any plausible moral theory must make use of some conception of supererogation.[6]

If moral philosophers are to address themselves at the most basic level to the question of how people should live, however, they must do more than adjust the content of their moral theories in ways that leave room for the affirmation of nonmoral values. They must examine explicitly the range and nature of these nonmoral values, and, in light of this examina-

tion, they must ask how the acceptance of a moral theory is to be understood and acted upon. For the claims of this paper do not so much conflict with the content of any particular currently popular moral theory as they call into question a metamoral assumption that implicitly surrounds discussions of moral theory more generally. Specifically, they call into question the assumption that it is always better to be morally better.

The role morality plays in the development of our characters and the shape of our practical deliberations need be neither that of a universal medium into which all other values must be translated nor that of an everpresent filter through which all other values must pass. This is not to say that moral value should not be an important, even the most important, kind of value we attend to in evaluating and improving ourselves and our world. It is to say that our values cannot be fully comprehended on the model of a hierarchical system with morality at the top.

The philosophical temperament will naturally incline, at this point, toward asking, "What, then, *is* at the top—or, if there is no top, how *are* we to decide when and how much to be moral?" In other words, there is a temptation to seek a metamoral—though not, in the standard sense, metaethical—theory that will give us principles, or, at least, informal directives on the basis of which we can develop and evaluate more comprehensive personal ideals. Perhaps a theory that distinguishes among the various roles a person is expected to play within a life—as professional, as citizen, as friend, and so on—might give us some rules that would offer us, if nothing else, a better framework in which to think about and discuss these questions. I am pessimistic, however, about the changes of such a theory to yield substantial and satisfying results. For I do not see how a metamoral theory could be constructed which would not be subject to considerations parallel to those which seem inherently to limit the appropriateness of regarding moral theories as ultimate comprehensive guides for action.

This suggests that, at some point, both in our philosophizing and in our lives, we must be willing to raise normative questions from a perspective that is unattached to a commitment to any particular well-ordered system of values. It must be admitted that, in doing so, we run the risk of finding normative answers that diverge from the answers given by whatever moral theory one accepts. This, I take it, is the grain of truth in G. E. Moore's "open question" argument. In the background of this paper, then, there lurks a commitment to what seems to me to be a healthy form of intuitionism. It is a form of intuitionism which is not intended to take the place of more rigorous, systematically developed, moral theories — rather, it is intended to put these more rigorous and systematic moral theories in their place.[7]

Endnotes

[1] Bernard Williams, "Persons, Character and Morality," in Amelie Rorty, ed. *The Identities of Persons* (Berkeley: University of California Press, 1976), p. 214.

[2] Immanuel Kant, *The Doctrine of Virtue,* Mary J. Gregor, trans. (New York: Harper & Row, 1964), p. 71.

[3] See Williams, *op. cit.* and J. J. C. Smart and Bernard Williams, *Utilitarianism: For and Against* (New York: Cambridge, 1973). Also, Michael Stocker, "The Schizophrenia of Modern Ethical Theories," *Journal of Philosophy* 63(1976):453–66.

[4] George Orwell makes a similar point in "Reflections on Gandhi," in *A Collection of Essays by George Orwell* (New York: Harcourt Brace Jovanovich, 1945), p. 176: "sainthood is . . . a thing that human beings must avoid . . . It is too readily assumed that . . . the ordinary man only rejects it because it is too difficult; in other words, that the average human being is a failed saint. It is doubtful whether this is true. Many people genuinely do not wish to be saints, and it is probable that some who achieve or aspire to sainthood have never felt much temptation to be human beings."

[5] A similar view, which has strongly influenced mine, is expressed by Thomas Nagel in "The Fragmentation of Value," in *Mortal Questions* (New York: Cambridge, 1979), pp. 128–141. Nagel focuses on the difficulties such apparently incommensurable points of view create for specific, isolable practical decisions that must be made both by individuals and by societies. In focusing on the way in which these points of view figure into the development of individual personal ideals, the questions with which I am concerned are more likely to lurk in the background of any individual's life.

[6] The variety of forms that a conception of supererogation might take, however, has not generally been noticed. Moral theories that make use of this notion typically do so by identifying some specific set of principles as universal moral requirements and supplement this list with a further set of directives which it is morally praiseworthy but not required for an agent to follow. [See, e.g., Charles Fried, *Right and Wrong* (Cambridge, Mass.: Harvard, 1979).] But it is possible that the ability to live a morally blameless life cannot be so easily or definitely secured as this type of theory would suggest. The fact that there are some situations in which an agent is morally required to do something and other situations in which it would be good but not required for an agent to do something does not imply that there are specific principles such that, in any situation, an agent is required to act in accordance with these principles and other specific principles such that, in any situation, it would be good but not required for an agent to act in accordance with those principles.

[7] I have benefited from the comments of many people who have heard or read an earlier draft of this paper. I wish particularly to thank Douglas MacLean, Robert Nozick, Martha Nussbaum, and the Society for Ethics and Legal Philosophy.

VII.8 *In Defense of Moral Saints*

Louis P. Pojman

In this essay, I respond to Susan Wolf's thesis that moral saints, if they exist, have serious character flaws. She claims that they are boring and unattractive, for they must almost inevitably lack the nonmoral virtues that make life interesting. Many philosophers, including the Christian philosopher Robert M. Adams, have endorsed Wolf's assessment. Adams argues that the notion of saint is only suitable for religious people.

I argue against both Wolf and Adams. As opposed to Adams, I hold that he fails to make his case for the uniqueness of religious saints. As opposed to Wolf, I argue three points: (1) whether morality is or is not attractive is largely a subjective matter, and the fact that we find the saint unattractive says more about us than about the saint; (2) we may have a duty to forgo certain interesting things in life, and this denial of the interesting may cause us to be bored and even boring; and (3) both utilitarians and Kantians have arguments available to them to offset Wolf's criticisms. At the end of the essay I give an account of two different visions of morality that are at the heart of my disagreement with Wolf.

In her brilliantly provocative article "Moral Saints,"[1] Susan Wolf argues that moral saints, if they exist, are unattractive (419, 426F) because they lack the "ability to enjoy the enjoyable in life" (424) and are so "very, very nice" that they have to be "dull-witted or humorless or bland" (422). They have no time for literature, music, or sports and so live a life that seems "strangely barren" (421). Wolf argues that what is missing in the saint's life are the nonmoral virtues: a robust sense of humor, a refined musical or artistic ability, culinary acuity, and athletic prowess. It is not that these virtues are logically incompatible with saintliness (a saint could accidentally possess one or more of these virtues if, for example, he became a saint late in life), but saintliness simply provides no time to develop these talents. "The moral virtues, given that they are, by hypothesis, all present in the same individual, and to an extreme degree, are apt to crowd out the non-moral virtues, as well as many of the interests and personal characteristics that we generally think contribute to a healthy, well-rounded, richly developed character" (421).

The moral saint seems to lack a self: "The normal person's direct and specific desires for objects, activities, and events that conflict with the attainment of moral perfection are not simply sacrificed but removed, suppressed, or subsumed. The way in which morality, unlike other possible goals, is apt to dominate is particularly disturbing, for it seems to require either the lack or the denial of the existence of an identifiable, personal self" (424).

Wolf seems to equivocate on exactly what constitutes a moral saint. At various times she defines the concept in terms of actions ("by moral saint I mean a person whose every action is as good as possible" [419]); at other times in terms of character and virtue ("a person who is as morally worthy as can be" [419]; "he will have the standard moral virtues to a nonstandard degree" [421]); and at still other times in terms of motivation ("the shared contents of what these individuals are motivated to be—namely, as morally good as possible" [421]; a life "dominated by a commitment to improving the welfare of others or of society as a whole" [420]). Although she seems to think that these definitions are equivalent, they are not (for example, our motives may be pure but the act that results may not be the best possible; nor need it be the case that someone who is as morally worthy as possible always does the very best act).

Perhaps we could take these conditions as individually necessary and jointly sufficient conditions, but I suggest that we should reject the first condition. Excellent moral character and pure motivation are consistent with doing less than maximally good actions. Gandhi may break his fast rather than protest yet another injustice, or he may get some sleep when there is still suffering in the world to be alleviated. He may even lose his temper on rare occasions without forfeiting the high designation of 'saint.' Mother Teresa may indulge herself a swim once in a while, rather than save as many of the destitute as theoretically possible. The first condition seems suitable only to a perfect being like God, but not to fallible beings, even if they are morally pure. Indeed, most of Wolf's article proceeds on the basis of the second and third conditions, and I suggest that these are the more fruitful ways to analyze the concept of saintliness.

The best response to Wolf's article is that of Robert M. Adams's "Saints,"[2] in which he argues that saints are not boring and that Wolf has misconstrued the nature of saintliness. Essentially, 'saintliness' is a religious concept. A saint need not always be doing the action that is as good as possible, for he or she trusts in God who is ultimately in control of the world and who values other things (for example, beauty) in addition to morality. Wolf's analysis applies only to secular saints, and to that extent she is on target. They are limited and unattractive. We ought not make a religion of morality, but rather see morality as part of a larger religious worldview.

In this paper I will argue against both Wolf's thesis (that we have overriding reasons to reject moral saintliness) and against Adams's thesis (that saintliness ought to be confined to religion). I begin with Adams's article.

Adams gives two arguments in favor of the superiority of religious saints over mere moral saints, arguments that show why the former escape Wolf's net. First, the religious saint is not proscribed from the nonmoral values or virtues because they are valued by God. Because God is interested in them, the saints (who are God-like, holy) are also interested in them. Second, the saints need not be overly concerned about the salvation of the world because they know that God is doing this. They need not bear the burdens of the whole world on their shoulders, but trusting God, they can both have confidence in the final victory of good over evil and rejoice in the good things of life. Their sorrow at suffering and evil can be graced with a tone of lightheartedness and humor, and they can develop their talents and nonmoral virtues with a clear conscience.

My argument against Adams is not based on the unimportance of religion, but on the autonomy of ethics and other values. That is, while being religious may provide added incentive for being moral, whatever is right or good is so whether or not a God exists. Let us examine Adams's two arguments for the validity of religious saintliness.

His first argument is that the saint will not be proscribed from nonmoral values and virtues in the same way that the secular moralist may be. He argues that because God values beauty, the religious moralist will also. But, we may respond, if God values beauty, that must be because beauty is worthy to be desired, either because it has instrumental value or because it has intrinsic value. And if it is worthy of being desired, the perceptive person will also value it for its own sake. So the secular moralist may value beauty and other nonmoral values and virtues just as much as the religious person.

Adams's second argument states that the religious saint knows or believes something that the secular saint does not—that God is working for the redemption of the universe—so she may rejoice in the midst of the battle. This surely makes some difference. Nevertheless, it may not make a decisive difference. The moral saint may be as realistic about his limited powers as the religious saint and may also be grateful for many blessings in life. He may rejoice in these and confine his moral activities to areas in which he is reasonably sure that they will do some good. In light of the enormous amount of evil in the world, he will not be able to become overly ecstatic, but perhaps the religious saint ought to let the presence of evil sober her as well. In sum, in the areas mentioned by Adams there doesn't seem to be a qualitative difference between the values of the religious and the moral saint. Both may value nonmoral values and both may experience joy and celebration in the midst of moral struggle. Both may develop some of their talents with a clear conscience, and both may be required to sacrifice some development for moral reasons.

Adams's claim that there is a danger of making morality an idol, a surrogate for religion, seems misplaced. If saintliness is a condition of having the standard virtues to a nonstandard degree, then as far as the virtues go, the moral saint will be indistinguishable from the religious saint. It is not the case that the moral saint worships some hypostatized concept of morality any more than the religious saint does. It is simply that morality stands for a set of values and processes that are taken to be overriding in regard to virtues and action-guiding procedures.

It may well be the case that for the religious person there is a greater attention to religious motifs than to moral reasons, but, generally, both religious and secular moralists put constraints on what is religiously permissible. Even religious people judge as immoral those who claim to rape or kill the innocent in God's name. Although there is much more that needs to be said on this issue, we may say that the case for a qualitative difference between the religious and the secularly moral saint has not been made.

This brings us directly to the heart of matter: Wolf's charge of a character flaw in moral saints. They are boring and unattractive, for they will almost inevitably lack the nonmoral virtues that make life interesting. I wish to make three points: (1) what is and what is not boring or unattractive is largely a subjective matter, and the fact that we find the saint boring may say more about us than about him or her; (2) we may have a duty to forgo certain interesting things in life, which may cause us to be bored or boring; and (3) both utilitarians and Kantians have arguments available to them to offset Wolf's criticisms.

dents bored to tears. For those deeply interested in morality, subtle moral arguments, as well as exquisite moral action and character, are profoundly interesting. Perhaps we would be overdoing it by always talking about moral dilemmas or admiring the virtuous, but, I submit, these things will be fascinating to people who value them. I, for one, confess to admiring an underweight, ugly, unathletic, wizened old saint like Gandhi far more than the heroes that Wolf says evince our ideals (Katharine Hepburn, Paul Newman, Fred Astaire, Natasha Rostov, and Lambert Strether [422, 431] — these are certainly not my heroes). It is not that we never admire the nonmoral virtues (or those who possess them). It is simply that Wolf underestimates the attractiveness of the moral virtues or those who embody them. Can she have read a biography of Gandhi, or even seen Richard Attenborough's film about him?[3]

Perhaps Wolf simply means that the saint has too much of a single type of virtue (424). It is possible to have too much of a good thing. Carrots are nutritious but people who have eaten too many of them have died of carotene poisoning, and one can get sick of a favorite food, movie, or acquaintance if one has no respite from them. This may mean that normal humans need a certain amount of variety in life. If this is the case, and I think it is, then morality can take variety into account in building the completely happy life or the highest type of society. It can build a prima facie duty to display variety in the scheme of things.

It might be contended that I've missed the point that morality "does not seem to be a suitable object of passion" (424). My response is that becoming a certain kind of person or creating a certain kind of a world are suitable passions, and these are what morality is really about.

(1) *The Subjective Element in Boredom*

My wife finds football exceedingly dull, whereas I find it exhilarating. Albert Einstein might seem boring to a group of basketball fanatics, whereas Bobby Knight might not be the most intriguing guest at a conference for astronomical research. Wolf's article, which excites most philosophers, leaves some stu-

(2) *The Duty to Boredom*

We may have a duty to forgo certain interesting things in life, which may cause us to be bored or boring. It may be the case that a moral saint will be more boring than he or she would have been if he or she had not been a saint. Suppose Gauguin, instead of abandoning his wife and five children for an artistic career in Tahiti, had stayed at home and cared for his family. He would never have painted *Ia Orana Maria* or *Manao Tupapau* but would instead have gone through life as a quiet stockbroker and an un-distinguished father and husband. But suppose that we agree that he had a moral duty to stay home. Suppose that we could reasonably predict that his abandonment of his wife and children would cause them unacceptable suffering. Then the fascination we have with his life in Tahiti and his art are ill-begotten. We may appreciate his paintings' genius while deploring their causal history in much the same way that we appreciate and make use of the results of Nazi experiments on Jews while con-demning the experiments. No doubt there are innu-merable men and women who have stayed at home because they saw it as their moral duty to do so and thus are less interesting than they would otherwise have been.

Gauguin may well have asked himself, Why should I accept a boring life when I can have the delights of Tahiti? But if people do seriously con-sider these sorts of questions, it is an indication that moral education has failed. A society that has a well-ordered set of values will aim at inculcating a deep sense of satisfaction in being moral and a corre-sponding deep sense of guilt in being immoral. Moral virtue will be a prime index of social approba-tion. People should be valued, I am suggesting, not equally, as is currently recommended in an egali-tarian society, but according to their moral merit. In a moral meritocracy the issue of separating self-interested reasons from moral reasons becomes less acute.

Wolf and Adams speak of making morality an idol, but our times, which Wolf's judgments reflect, have made the interesting, the aesthetically and sen-suously gratifying, into an idol. Evil, like a myste-rious plague, is often fascinating, but it invariably turns out to be destructive. Indeed, we need a lot more "boring," dedicated, moral human beings—a lot more saints—who find deep fascination in the "boringness" of life, if we are to make this a better world, or even survive.

(3) *Kantian and Utilitarian Responses*

Both Kantians and utilitarians have responses to Wolf's thesis about reasons to reject saintliness.

Wolf offers two interpretations of Kant, one in which the categorical imperative would seem to prohibit universalizing moral saintliness, and the other that would allow it under the duty to the self to "increase our natural as well as our moral perfec-tion. These duties are unlimited in the degree to which they may dominate life" [430]. Wolf argues that the first interpretation is inadequate for our no-tion of moral saintliness because it puts severe lim-itations on altruism. She rejects the second inter-pretation because it is counterintuitive. People aim at the nonmoral virtues for their own sake, not for the sake of the morality.

It seems to me that Wolf misses the proper Kantian response. The Kantian can argue that we have duties to ourselves that include developing our talents. These are not perfect duties, for they may be fulfilled in optional ways and be overridden by other, more stringent principles, but they are nev-ertheless duties. In Gauguin's case, to be perfectly moral may well include making less money as a stockbroker so that he can spend more time devel-oping his art. Perhaps if people were more morally developed, they would be able to channel their lives and budget their time in ways that would allow them to develop their talents. If Joe Shlunk were more disciplined and liberated from watching TV five hours a night, he might become a first-rate poet. And if his wife, Jane Shlunk, were more virtuous, she might find time to develop her musical ability. Perhaps each of them could develop their talents even further by deserting their family, but develop-ing talents to their highest point is not a duty and may not be worth the moral costs.

Deontological ethics in general has precisely the asset that saves it from losing itself in global salvation schemes. The Kantian saint internalizes the moral law, including the principle of self-development, in a way that provides personal space. Having a holy will and possessing high moral char-acter involves an appreciation of the nonmoral virtues.

The utilitarian uses a different type of argu-ment to establish the duty to develop nonmoral vir-tues. First, there is an argument for virtues that strictly speaking are not moral virtues but enable one to bring about moral goodness. In order to maximize utility, saints must not only be as harmless as doves, but as cunning as foxes. So the moral saint should be highly intelligent and well-educated in order to obtain and process large amounts of information. All things being equal, the more information and the better the understanding of that information, the better the chances of making the right decision. Education, intelligence, courage, and a sense for the ridiculous may be necessary enabling virtues for the utilitarian saint.

Second, the utilitarian saint will see that other virtues, which traditionally have been deemed to be nonmoral, significantly contribute to the moral community. Music, sports, dance, art, literature, good food, and good conversation all make life more enjoyable. So the requisite virtues connected with these activities will be encouraged in the moral community by the utilitarian saint. Different people will contribute differently, and it may well be the case that there is a trade-off between individual moral development and development of nonmoral talents.

It may not be necessary that everyone actually becomes a moral saint in the utilitarian kingdom. In fact it may be very un-utilitarian for everyone to be maximally moral for exactly the reasons that Wolf gives. Developing only the moral virtues or the enabling virtues may preclude other good results. If one community in which all are saints yields 1000 hedons, but another in which half are saints and half are talented, good people who add artistic spice to life yields 2000 hedons, then the latter state is to be preferred. But this is not a judgment against saintliness or morality. Rather, it is a simple recognition that there are other values and virtues that serve morality and which themselves are not necessarily moral virtues or values.

Wolf follows Bernard Williams in dismissing utilitarianism altogether for putting the car before the horse: "It is not because they produce happiness that these activities are valuable; it is because these activities are valuable in more direct and specific ways that they produce happiness" (429). But this argument isn't successful. First of all, we could follow Moore in becoming agathistic or ideal utilitarians and speak of maximizing the ideal values, rather than happiness, and still make our point. Second, we could argue that if, on reflection, the nonmoral virtues didn't promote happiness in some sense, it would be doubtful if they could sustain themselves as high values. This is not the place to argue for the truth of utilitarianism. If utilitarianism is false, then its notion of a moral saint won't make

much sense. However, Wolf hasn't shown that it is a false view of morality.

Essentially, Wolf's thesis does not rest on conclusive arguments against Kantian and utilitarian interpretations of saintliness, but rather on her own (and many other modern moralists') intuitions that when ideals of moral perfection "are present, they are not ideals to which it is particularly reasonable or healthy or desirable for human beings to aspire" (433). Somehow it seems obvious that whatever values a person embraces, "he does so *not* for moral reasons. In other words, no matter how flexible we make the guide to conduct which we choose to label 'morality,' no matter how rich we make the life in which perfect obedience to this guide would result, we will have reason to hope that a person does not wholly rule and direct his life by the abstract and impersonal consideration that such a life would be morally good" (434).

But this seems to miss a level distinction. Just as a self-interested person may paradoxically see it as in his best interest to become an altruist in order to serve his best interest, and just as the rational hedonist may see that in order to reach maximal happiness, she must paradoxically give up the pursuit of her happiness and live for others; so one who would be morally as perfect as possible may paradoxically see that the best way to become so is by not being preoccupied with saintliness in carrying out his duties, but simply by concentrating on the matters at hand and living faithfully according to his lights. One may have a second-order desire to be maximally virtuous, but realize that the way to achieve that end is by thinking about the needs of others instead, rather than becoming maximally virtuous. I may want to be a moral person more strongly than anything else and still realize that becoming better and being moral sometimes involves self-forgetfulness, sometimes involves even forgetting about being moral, and sometimes involves acting spontaneously. The saint need not be self-indulgently moral. The two concepts (saintliness and spontaneous action that is not motivated by the wish to be saintly) are compatible.

Wolf presents us with an alternate vision of moral reasons in the scheme of things. Moral values are simply another type of value on a par with aesthetic, athletic, and prudential values. There are no clear rules for deciding which of these values is to be preferred. Bernard Williams, Michael Slote, and

Philippa Foot have enunciated similar sentiments.[4] The standard view of the place of morality, from Socrates to Kurt Baier, has been that moral reasons are overriding. Moral principles are objectively right, absolute, and decisive. They, not rights, serve as trumps over all other principles in human action. If and only if Gauguin can make a moral case for the abandonment of his family (for example, "Our marriage is on the rocks, the children will be better off without having a frustrated father around," and so on), is his action then permissible, absolutely permissible. If he cannot make that case, his action is wrong. Not just morally wrong, as though there were some other sense of right that could override that judgment, but wrong absolutely.

The motivation of the classical account is that ethics is action-guiding. There must be some set of constraints and ideals that have to do with actions and outcomes. The dominance of ethical reasons is included, implicitly at least, in the definition of ethics as that which strives to promote the flourishing of rational beings, the amelioration of suffering, and the resolution of conflicts of interests. We want to know what is the best way to live, all things considered, and we presume that there is an answer to this question that is universalizable, and we call this way to live ethical. While the application of ethical principles may be relative, ethics, as that which aims at realizable ideals, is absolute and unconditionally binding.

However, although moral reasons are paramount, this does not imply that we ought to be morally perfect. There are other level distinctions to be made. We have moral reasons for allowing (and even prescribing) that people not be overly preoccupied with being moral. Much of morality is imbibed during the socialization process of early childhood. Thus, it may be that moral character is a gift of good upbringing, one that frees us to some extent for other pursuits in adolescence and adulthood. The appropriate strategy, then, would be to enhance moral education in early childhood. Saintliness may be too heavy a burden, as Wolf clearly points out, for ordinary adults to bear—unless they have been predisposed to a virtuous life from childhood. But if they are virtuous by upbringing, there is little worry of saints lacking a self, as Wolf fears. These people, corresponding roughly to Wolf's "Loving Saint," would be to a large degree spontaneously saintly.

Susan Wolf doesn't want to know any moral saints: "I don't know whether there are any moral saints. But if there are, I am glad that neither I nor those about whom I care most are among them" (419). If what I have argued is correct, Wolf is depriving herself of some wonderful experiences. Moreover, her attitude, which seems to mirror today's Nietzschian distrust of the hegemony of morality, may ironically be depriving us of better and more interesting people. It may be the case that only by having a sufficient number of moral saints in key social and political positions can our society and world be saved.

Endnotes

1 Susan Wolf, "Moral Saints," *Journal of Philosophy* 79, 8 (August 1982); 419–439. All page references in text are to this journal. Unfortunately, space prohibits a fuller discussion of the merits of this worthy article.

2 Robert M. Adams, "Saints," *Journal of Philosophy* 81, 7 (July 1984); 392–401. My own analysis has been greatly aided by Adams's article.

3 Adams develops this point at length. The saints are attractive people who lived interesting lives. Where we differ is that I believe that there are secular saints as well as religious ones. We find them in ordinary life. Two of the most saintly persons I know neither believe in God nor in life after death. Rawls speaks of living by an impartial "form of thought and feeling that rational persons can adopt in the world," the "perspective of eternity," and concludes that "purity of heart would be to see clearly and act with grace and self-command from this point of view" (*A Theory of Justice*, Harvard University Press, 1971). I identify this sort of description with being a moral saint.

4 See Bernard Williams, "Persons, Character, and Morality" in his book *Moral Luck* (Cambridge University Press, 1981), and in his *Ethics and the Limits of Philosophy* (Harvard University Press, 1985). Philippa Foot argued this point with me in a personal conversation over the Gauguin case. She accused me of exalting morality to a place that is unreasonable for it to occupy. Michael Slote also sets forth a deflationary view of ethics in his *Goods and Virtues* (Oxford University Press, 1983).

Suggestions for Further Reading

Anscombe, Elizabeth. "Modern Moral Philosophy" *Philosophy* 33 (1958).

Blum, Lawrence A. *Friendship, Altruism, and Morality*. Routledge and Kegan Paul, 1980. A pioneering work in contemporary virtue theory, including a sustained critique of both utilitarian and Kantian ethics.

Foot, Philippa. *Virtues and Vices*. Blackwell, 1978. A collection of articles by one of the foremost virtue ethicists.

Frankena, William. *Ethics*. Prentice-Hall, 1973.

French, Peter, Theodore Uehling, Jr., and Howard K. Wettstein, eds. "Ethical Theory: Character and Virtue," in *Midwest Studies in Philosophy Vol. XIII*. University of Notre Dame Press, 1988.

Gert, Bernard. *The Moral Rules*. 2nd ed. HarperCollins, 1988, Chapter 9.

Gewirth, Alan. "Rights and Virtues," *Review of Metaphysics* 38 (1985), pp. 739–762.

Hardie, W. F. R. *Aristotle's Ethical Theory*. Clarendon Press, 1968.

Hill, Thomas. *Autonomy and Self-Respect* (Cambridge: Cambridge University Press, 1991).

Kruschwitz, Robert, and Robert Roberts, eds. *The Virtues*. Wadsworth, 1987. Contains excellent readings and bibliography.

Louden, Robert. *Morality and Moral Theory: A Reappraisal and Reaffirmation*. Oxford University Press, 1992.

MacIntyre, Alasdair. *After Virtue*. University of Notre Dame, 1981.

Mayo, Bernard. *Ethics and the Moral Life*. Macmillan, 1958.

Murdoch, Iris. *The Sovereignty of Good*. Schocken Books, 1971.

Pence, Gregory. "Recent Work on Virtues." *American Philosophical Quarterly* 21 (1984).

Pincoffs, Edmund. *Quandries and Virtues*. University of Kansas, 1986.

Roberts, Robert. "Willpower and the Virtues." *Philosophical Review* 93 (1984).

Taylor, Richard. *Ethics, Faith, and Reason*. Prentice-Hall, 1985.

Trianosky, Gregory. "Supererogation, Wrongdoing, and Vice: On the Autonomy of the Ethics of Virtue." *Journal of Philosophy* 83 (1986), pp. 26–40.

————. "Virtue, Action, and the Good Life: A Theory of the Virtues." *Pacific Journal of Philosophy*, 1988.

Wallace, James. *Virtues and Vices*. Cornell University Press, 1978.

Warnock, Geoffrey. *The Object of Morality*. Methuen, 1971.

Part VIII

The Fact/Value Problem: Metaethics in the Twentieth Century

In every system of morality which I have hitherto met with, I have always remarked, that the author proceeds for some time in the ordinary way of reasoning, and establishes the being of a God, or makes observations concerning human affairs; when of a sudden I am surprised to find, that instead of the usual copulations of propositions, *is,* and *is not,* I meet with no proposition that is not connected with an *ought,* or an *ought not.* This change is imperceptible; but is, however, of the last consequence. For as this *ought,* or *ought not,* expresses some new relation or affirmation, it is necessary that it should be observed and explained; and at the same time that a reason should be given, for what seems altogether inconceivable, how this new relation can be a deduction from others, which are entirely different from it.

DAVID HUME,
A Treatise on Human Nature, Book III, ii

In this classic quotation from David Hume's work on philosophical anthropology (our first reading in this section) the question of the relationship of "is" to "ought," of facts to values, is raised. How can we get a normative conclusion from an argument containing only factual premises? In Part VIII of our work we consider various responses to Hume's question. We want to know whether values are essentially different from facts or derived from facts, and whether value statements can be true or false like descriptive statements about the world or mathematical equations. In Part IX we shall ask whether and, if so, how we can justify our claims to know that there are moral truths.

To get us started in our inquiry, consider the following situation. Jill is pregnant and wants to have an abortion. Ought she to obtain one? The statement "Jill is pregnant and wants to have an abortion" is a factual one, but is it a fact that she *ought* to obtain one? Where does the value term "ought" come in? What if her husband, Jack, asserts that Jill ought not to have an abortion? How can we decide who is right? Does an action-guiding directive, an obligation either to have or not to have an abortion, follow from some description of Jill—for example, that she is pregnant and wants an abortion? From the premise:

1. Jill is pregnant and wants to have an abortion.

can we infer the conclusion:

2. Jill ought to obtain an abortion;

or from the premise:

1′. Jill promised her husband Jack that she would bear his child.

can we infer the conclusion:

2′. Jill ought not to obtain an abortion?

"Hume's Law," as it is sometimes called, is based on the elementary conservative principle of logic that you can't get something in the conclusion that you haven't already put into the premise. In this part of our study we shall first read the crucial section from Hume's original treatise wherein he argued that moral judgments were based on feelings, not reason, and that, as such, they lacked truth values, so that one can not derive ought judgments from factual premises. Then we shall consider various responses to Hume's Law, positive and negative: naturalism, intuitionism, noncognitivism (emotivism and prescriptivism), and neo-naturalism (descriptivism). These notions will become clearer as we go along.

Naturalism is the theory that certain types of facts entail values, or that value statements can be defined in terms of factual statements. 'Fact' refers to what is signified by empirically verifiable statements, for example, that Jill had an abortion. 'Value' refers to what is signified by an evaluative sentence, for example, "Abortion is wrong." When we claim that something is a fact, we imply that some object or state of affairs exists. When we make a value judgment, we are evaluating or appraising something.

According to naturalism, we can derive a conclusion, either (2) or (2′), from the statement about Jill's situation. The other theories (intuitionism, emotivism, and prescriptivism) deny this, while neo-naturalism seeks an innovative compromise. The history of ethical theory in the twentieth century is largely the history of the development of these theories as responses to the fact/value problem.

In 1903 one of the most influential books in the history of ethics, G. E. Moore's *Principia Ethica,* was published. It inaugurated a sustained inquiry about the meaning of ethical terms and the relationship of facts to values that was to dominate moral philosophy in the twentieth century. This mode of inquiry was later to be known as *metaethics,* that is, philosophizing *about* the very terms and structure of ethics as an object of inquiry. Whereas philosophers before Moore mainly set forth systematic attempts to describe the correct moral theory, philosophers after Moore would be concerned with the functions of ethical terms, the status of moral judgments, and the relationship of ethical judgments to nonethical factual statements (the is/ought problem). Normative concerns (for example, is it possible to fight a just war?) were replaced by logical and epistemological concerns. The central questions became, what, if anything, is the meaning of the terms 'good' or 'right'? How, if at all, can we justify our moral beliefs? While these questions were raised prior to Moore, they became as a result of his work the sum and substance of moral philosophy for over two generations. It will be worth our while to outline Moore's argument.

Moore begins *Principia Ethics* by announcing that philosophers have been muddled about ethical problems largely because they have not first clearly defined the province of ethics and limited the kinds of questions that philosophers were able to ask and answer. Philosophers must first determine the exact domain of ethics before they can deal with the further implications of ethics. "That province may indeed be defined as the whole truth about that which is at the same time common to all such judgments and peculiar to them."

Ultimately, Moore is interested in making ethics a science with clear decision-making procedures. Getting clear on the domain of ethics is but the first step in this direction. Moore thinks that the way to understand 'right,' as in right action (which has often been the subject matter of ethics), is first to discover what is the meaning of the term 'good.' This, at first glance, seems odd, for we generally think of the domain designated by the term 'good' to be the general area of axiology (including aesthetics and prudence, as well as ethics). Moore may be broadening the notion of 'ethics' to be coterminus with axiology, or perhaps he thinks that axiology is the door to ethics. He does not make his position clear.

The philosopher, qua philosopher, is not concerned with morality—right or wrong behavior—but with the meaning of fundamental terms. "There are far too many persons, things, and events in the world, past, present, or to come, for a discussion of their individual merits to be embraced in any science. Ethics, therefore, does not deal at all with facts of this nature, facts that are unique, individual, absolutely particular . . . and, for this reason, it is not the business of the ethical philosopher to give personal advice or exhortation" (G. E. Moore, *Principia Ethica*, p. 3).

Our second reading begins with section 5 of *Principia Ethica*. From there through section 11 Moore explains that the task of ethics proper is to define the term 'good': "That which is meant by 'good' is, in fact, except its converse 'bad,' the *only* simple object of thought which is peculiar to Ethics. . . . Unless this first question be fully understood, and its true answer clearly recognised, the rest of Ethics is as good as useless from the point of view of systematic knowledge."

'Good,' it turns out, must be a simple notion like yellow, and, just as we cannot explain what yellow is to anyone who does not already know it, so we cannot explain what good is. No further analysis is possible, for analysis always involves making the complex simpler, and the good is already a simple, atomic kind of fact that we use to

build up more complex ideas. Here, Moore contrasts the notion of 'good' with that of 'horse,' which is complex and in need of further analysis.

Next, Moore distinguishes 'the good' from 'good' in a way that is problematic. 'Good' is an adjective, and there must be something to which the adjective applies—that is, *the good,* the total set of good things. Pleasure, intelligence, and all other good things together make up the set of 'the good,' and in principle we could itemize every member of the class of 'the good' to which our adjective applies. The difference between these terms is the same as that between denotation and connotation, or reference and meaning, of a term. We can point out the reference of the good, but we cannot give the meaning of 'good,' although presumably we all understand its meaning by intuition. It is simple, has no parts, and so is indefinable—an ultimate term, like 'yellow,' 'pleasure,' and 'consciousness.'

In sections 12 to 13 we approach the heart of Moore's argument against naturalism. Moore's argument may be compared to David Hume's version of the naturalistic fallacy in the passage quoted at the beginning of this introduction. Hume believes that naturalists confuse facts with values. His point is that we cannot go from fact statements ('is' statements) to value statements ('ought' statements) without including a value statement as one of our premises. He criticizes those who argue in the following manner:

A. 1. Jill is pregnant and wants to have an abortion.

2. Therefore, Jill ought to obtain an abortion, or,

2'. Therefore, Jill ought not to obtain an abortion.

or

B. 1. God has commanded us to love our neighbor.

2. Therefore, we ought to love our neighbor.

According to Hume, both of these arguments are invalid because they commit the naturalistic fallacy—they move from a factual statement to a value statement without including a value statement in the premises. Naturalistic fallacies have the following form:

1. Fact
2. Therefore, value

This is an invalid form, because in order to get a value in the conclusion, at least one value must be included in one of the premises.

But Moore means more than simply this. For Hume could still allow ethical terms to be reduced to nonethical ones. He could fill out the above arguments by adding a second premise that includes a value statement, as follows:

A. 1. Jill is pregnant and wants an abortion.

2. Pregnant women who want abortions ought to be allowed to have them.

3. Therefore, Jill ought to be allowed to have an abortion.

and

B. 1. God has commanded us to love our neighbor.

2. We ought to do what God commands.

3. Therefore, we ought to love our neighbor.

A Humean could define 'good' in terms of meeting human need (or desire) or obedience to God. That is, he could define 'good' in terms of natural terms. Put another way, a Humean could be a self-reflective naturalist, one who understands that a justification for his conclusion is needed in terms of an explicit moral theory.

But Moore would not accept this reasoning. He is more radical than Hume, for according to Moore's interpretation of the naturalist fallacy, we cannot reduce ethical (normative) terms to nonethical (natural) terms. Ethical characteristics are different in kind from nonethical ones, and hence we cannot deduce ethical propositions

from nonethical ones in the way that even a Humean would allow; for Hume would, but Moore would not, allow that ethical terms are definable in terms of nonethical terms.

Moore's argument against naturalism is called the open question argument. He asks us to imagine some naturalistic definition of 'good,' such as the complex statement, "Good means that which we desire to desire." But when we analyze that statement carefully, we find a problem. We can still ask, "Is it good to desire to desire A?", which reduces to "Is the desire to desire A one of the things that we desire to desire?" or "Do we desire to desire to desire to desire A?" This seems ridiculous and not at all equivalent to the question, "Is A good?", which seems to be a simple question, not at all complex.

We can use the substitution test, in which we interchange other concepts, in order to determine whether we have arrived at a definition of the good. Suppose you say, "Pleasure is good" and I respond, "Torturing children gives me pleasure, but is it good?" We seem to have a counterexample to our claim. If we say, "Jogging is pleasant, but is it pleasant?", we see that the sentence makes no sense, for we are asking a tautological question (one of the form: X is A, but is it A?). But if we say, "Jogging is pleasurable, but is it good?" we have asked a meaningful question—something nontautological—which this question would be if good meant "that which gives pleasure." We can apply this test to any candidate for a definition of 'good,' and Moore thinks that the result will be the same. We will find that 'good' is indefinable. Moore's conclusion "as to the subject matter of Ethics is, then, that there is a simple, indefinable, unanalyzable object of thought by reference to which it must be defined? (*Principia Ethica*, p. 21).

One may ask whether Moore is right about all this. Does the open question test show that 'good' is entirely an indefinable, non-natural property? According to traditions that date at least as far back as Aristotle, the good was viewed as a natural property either in terms of the object of desire or some psychological state (such as pleasure or, more complexly, happiness). Could this form of empirical theory of values be saved? During the first half of the twentieth century, the prospects looked bleak.

According to Moore, intuitionism was the correct route to go. If 'good' could not be identified with a natural property, it must ostensibly be definable as a non-natural one resembling a Platonic form (for example, the Good), which we all know by intuition. It is by adhering to our intuitions, then, that morality gets off the ground — that we know its nature and become moral people. The influence of Moore on subsequent ethics cannot be overemphasized. On the one hand, it inspired intuitionism to new endeavors. On the other hand, those who were skeptical of non-natural properties, forms of the good, and other ideals, concluded that the whole enterprise was a mistake, that this was no subject matter for ethics. These skeptics contended that ethics was only about emotions, which brings us to the next school to be studied: *emotivism.*

It may be helpful to put matters in the following schema. Moore's intuitionism includes four theses:

1. The Human Thesis: 'Ought' statements cannot be derived from 'is' statements.

2. The Platonic Thesis: Basic value terms, including moral statements, refer to non-natural properties.

3. The Cognitive Thesis: Moral statements are either true or false. That is, they are objective, putative claims about reality, which can be known.

4. The Intuition Theses: Moral truths are discovered by intuition. They are self-evident on reflection.

Moore held only the cognitive thesis in common with the naturalist.

We can best understand emotivism, which was a reaction to intuitionism, as a rigorously empirical analysis of these four theses. Emotivists

accept (1), but deny (3) and (4). (2) is the crucial thesis. Emotivists agree that evaluative statements *claim* to refer to a non-natural world, but because there is no way to find out whether there is a non-natural world, there is no way to know whether they do indeed refer to it. Because meaningful discourse, according to the emotivists, is made up of either tautologies or empirical statements that can be verified, we must reject evaluative language as meaningless or, as C. L. Stevenson does, give it a separate, noncognitive meaning (for example, use the term 'meaning' in a way that does not depend on whether a sentence is true or false). Value sentences are neither true nor false, but are without a clear sense, and there is no reason to think that intuition will help here. Intuitive speculation is unverifiable and, hence, still nonsense.

In our third reading, the Oxford University philosopher A. J. Ayer sets forth the emotivist view of ethical sentences. If the only sentences that are meaningful are either analytic statements (mathematical and logical truths) or synthetic statements that can in principle be verified (for example, there is a dog in the garage; you have a blue book in your library), then value and moral statements are meaningless, for they are neither analytic nor empirically verifiable. They are a type of nonsense, albeit a useful type. Whereas they cannot be said to be true or false, they express our emotions. "Murder is evil" is really only a shorthand way of expressing our dislike for acts of murder. Saying "Murder is morally wrong" is equivalent to saying "Murder — Boo!", and saying "Helping people is morally good" is like saying "Helping people — Hoorah!" The only other function ethical statements have is to persuade others to take our attitude toward the activity in question: "Murder — Boo! Don't you agree?"

In our fourth reading, C. L. Stevenson's "The Emotive Meaning of Ethical Terms," we have a more sophisticated version of emotivism. Stevenson does not deny that moral language has meaning, as Ayer does. It is just that it has a different sort of meaning, emotive meaning, rather than descriptive meaning. Stevenson provides a careful analysis of the term 'good,' arguing that any adequate analysis must meet three criteria: We must be able to disagree about whether something is good; 'goodness' must possess a magnetism, a tendency to act in its favor; and 'goodness' must not be discoverable solely through scientific theory. He then argues that naturalist theories fail for one reason or another to satisfy these criteria, but that emotivism, which applies the difference between descriptive and emotive meaning, does satisfy all the criteria.

Disagreement over whether something is good, Stevenson argues, is simply disagreement in attitude. If you say stealing is bad and I say that it is good, we simply are manifesting different attitudes toward stealing. This attitude theory emphasizes that it is precisely the magnetic aspect of the term 'good' that is important, and that it has laudatory meaning. And finally, emotivism recognizes that fundamental disagreements (ones not rooted in mere disagreement in beliefs about some nonmoral facts) will not be resolved by empirical methods. If I have a pro-stealing attitude and have considered all the facts relevant to that activity, reason and science are impotent to effect a change in me.

Emotivism is a form of noncognitivism, the view that sentences expressing ethical judgment have no cognitive content. We cannot have moral knowledge, for there is nothing to have knowledge of. But emotivism is not the only kind of noncognitivism. Another version, which was first set forth by R. M. Hare in *The Language of Morals* (1952), accepts Moore's naturalistic fallacy argument along with the emotivists' radical separation of facts from values. While he agrees with the emotivists that we cannot ascribe truth or falsity to moral statements and that moral judgments are attitudinal, Hare changes the emphasis regarding moral terms from feelings of approval (or disapproval) to certain types of judgment that include a universalizability feature and a prescriptive element.[1] To say that "You ought not steal from your boss" entails, via the principle of universalizability (or consistency) that the speaker believes that no one should steal in relevantly similar circumstances. Furthermore, for you to say that I should not steal is for you to commit yourself to a principle of forbidding stealing, and it is from that commitment that you are *prescribing* that others live that way also. Not only does ethical language mean that you are prescribing it universally, but being willing to commit yourself to that prescription is a necessary and sufficient condition for the justification of that principle. Hare writes:

> A complete justification of a decision would consist of a complete account of its effects, together with a complete account of the principles which it observed, and the effects of observing those principles. . . . If pressed to justify a decision completely, we have to give a complete specification of the way of life of which it is a part. This complete specification it is impossible in practice to give; the nearest attempts are those given by the great religions. . . . If the inquirer still goes on asking "But why *should* I live like that?" then there is no further answer to give him, because we have already, *ex hypothesi,* said everything that could be included in this further answer. We can only ask him to make up his own mind which way he ought to live; for in the end everything rests upon such a decision of principle.[2]

Hare's system, like Ayer's and Stevenson's, seems relativistic, but, unlike the emotivists, he believes that if all normal people use his approach, they will in fact end up with an objective normative moral theory—some form of utilitarianism. Although this point is not made in Hare's selection in this Part of this anthology (our fifth reading), the reader may want to ask whether such an entailment is legitimate.

At this point it may be useful to present a diagram of the positions we have surveyed:[3]

	Problems of Meaning	Problems of Justification
COGNITIVISM [Ethical claims have truth value and it is possible to know what it is.]		
A. NATURALISM	Ethical terms are defined through factual terms. They refer to natural properties.	Ethical judgments are disguised assertions of some kind of fact, and thus can be justified empirically.
1. *Subjective*	Their truth originates in individual or social decision.	
2. *Objective*	Their truth is independent of individual or social decision.	
B. NON-NATURALISM	Ethical terms cannot be defined with factual terms. They refer to non-natural properties.	Ethical conclusions cannot be derived from empirically confirmed propositions.
1. *Intuitionism*		Intuitionism alone provides confirmation.
2. *Religious Revelation*		Some form of divine revelation provides confirmation.
NONCOGNITIVISM [Ethical claims do not have truth value.]		
A. EMOTIVISM	Ethical terms do not ascribe properties, and their meaning is not factual, but rather, emotive.	Ethical judgments are not justifiable factually, rationally, or by intuition.
B. PRESCRIPTIVISM	Ethical terms do not ascribe properties, and their meaning is not factual, but signifies universal prescriptions.	Ethical judgments are not factually, intuitively, or rationally justifiable, but are existentially justified.

Our sixth reading, Philippa Foot's "Moral Beliefs," which was delivered at the Aristotelian Society in 1958, represents the first clear critique of the whole formalist enterprise of the noncognitivists. She argues that the noncognitivists have separated the evaluative meaning of good from the descriptive meaning in an implausible way. There are limits to what we can reasonably prescribe as a moral judgment, and there are some so-called 'descriptive' concepts that include moral overtones: 'danger,' 'courage,' 'injury,' and 'justice.' Foot is not a naturalist, for she doesn't believe that value terms can be defined by factual statements, but she tries to show that there is not a complete logical gap between facts and values (as all the other ethicists in this part of the book have maintained in their adherence to the naturalistic fallacy). Certain facts logically entail values. Foot's compromise position was labeled *Descriptivism* or *neo-naturalism*.[4]

In our final reading, "The Object of Morality," Geoffrey Warnock goes even further than Foot. Warnock claims that the formalist nature of moral philosophy among the noncognitivists is barren and misses the point of morality. That is, morality has a content that, he claims, has to do with the amelioration of the human predicament, which has a tendency to worsen. Like Foot, he argues that not everything can be a moral principle and that some principles (those central to promoting human betterment) are necessarily moral principles. In Warnock's work we have come full circle from the naturalism of Hume, Bentham, and Mill, to which the non-naturalists reacted in the first place some three-quarters of a century earlier.

The debate between cognitivism and non-cognitivism, and between these various renditions of naturalism and non-naturalism, is still going on. I hope the series of selections in this

Part of our study will help you understand the major aspects of the debate and help you judge where you stand on these issues.

Endnotes

[1] In a later article, "Some Confusion About Subjectivity" (in *Freedom and Morality,* J. Bricke, ed. University of Kansas, 1976), Hare qualifies this by saying that *derivative* moral judgments can be true or false. The reader is left to determine whether the qualification is satisfactory.

[2] R. M. Hare, *The Language of Morals* (Oxford: Oxford University Press, 1952), p. 69.

[3] This figure is modeled on one by Tom L. Beauchamp, *Philosophical Ethics* (New York: McGraw-Hill, 1982), p. 359, and was influenced by suggestions of Bruce Russell, to whom I am indebted for his help in writing this introduction.

[4] If one defines a naturalist as one who holds that factual claims entail (or are entailed by) fundamental ethical claims, then one will call Foot a naturalist. We would need to amend our figure to include a form of naturalism that was not definitional (that is, did not define ethical terms by natural ones), but instead was broadly logical.

VIII.1 *On Reason and the Emotions: The Fact/Value Distinction*

DAVID HUME

David Hume (1711–1776) was born in Edinburgh. A self-educated philosopher, he wrote his *Treatise of Human Nature* while in his early twenties, completing it by the time he was twenty-six. The book, now recognized as a classic in British empiricism, fell "deadborn from the press," selling only a few dozen copies.

The subtitle of the *Treatise* is "An Attempt to Introduce the Experimental Method of Reasoning into Moral Subjects." Hume sought to do with morality what Newton had done with physics: reduce the subject to a few laws from which all other observations would be derived.

Hume's central idea is that the principles of morality are based not on pure reason or intuition but on feeling or sentiment. Reason can never motivate us, since it is confined to relations (Hume's term for relations of ideas, e.g., mathematics and logic) and matters of fact. Neither of these can motivate us to act. What moves us to act is the prospect of pleasure or pain (this includes sympathy at the prospect of someone else suffering). The passions, not reason, are aroused by the anticipation of pleasure and pain. Reason can only inform the subject that it is wrong about its means to achieve pleasure or that a more effective means exists. It cannot criticize the passions, "so that it is not contrary to reason to prefer the destruction of the whole world to the scratching of my finger. . . . Reason is and ought to be the slave of the passions."

It follows that values are of a separate domain from facts, the latter being based on observation and the former being rooted in our passions. Hence, we cannot correctly reason from facts to values, from descriptive statements to value judgments. We cannot derive "ought" from "is."

In the first section of our reading Hume argues for the subordination of reason to the passions. In the second section he argues that moral judgments are derived from our passions, not from reason.

[1. *Reason is Subordinate to the Emotions*]

Nothing is more usual in philosophy, and even in common life, than to talk of the combat of passion and reason, to give the preference to reason, and assert that men are only so far virtuous as they conform themselves to its dictates. Every rational crea-

ture, it is said, is obliged to regulate his actions by reason; and if any other motive or principle challenge the direction of his conduct, he ought to oppose it, till it be entirely subdued, or at least brought to a conformity with that superior principle. On this method of thinking the greatest part of moral philosophy, ancient and modern, seems to be founded; nor is there an ampler field, as well for metaphysical arguments, as popular declamations, than this supposed pre-eminence of reason above passion. The eternity, invariableness, and divine origin of the former have been displayed to the best advantage: the blindness, inconstancy, and deceitfulness of the latter have been as strongly insisted on. In order to

From *A Treatise of Human Nature* (1738), Book II, Part III, and Book III, Part I and II. Footnotes have been deleted.

show the fallacy of all this philosophy, I shall endeavor to prove *first,* that reason alone can never be a motive to any action of the will; and *secondly,* that it can never oppose passion in the direction of the will.

The understanding exerts itself after two different ways, as it judges from demonstration or probability; as it regards the abstract relations of our ideas, or those relations of objects, of which experience only gives us information. I believe it scarce will be asserted, that the first species of reasoning alone is ever the cause of any action. As its proper province is the world of ideas, and as the will always places us in that of realities, demonstration and volition seem, upon that account, to be totally removed from each other. Mathematics, indeed, are useful in all mechanical operations, and arithmetic in almost every art and profession: but it is not of themselves they have any influence. Mechanics are the art of regulating the motions of bodies *to some designed end or purpose;* and the reason why we employ arithmetic in fixing the proportions of numbers, is only that we may discover the proportions of their influence and operation. A merchant is desirous of knowing the sum total of his accounts with any person: why? but that he may learn what sum will have the same *effects* in paying his debt, and going to market, as all the particular articles taken together. Abstract or demonstrative reasoning, therefore, never influences any of our actions, but only as it directs our judgment concerning causes and effects; which leads us to the second operation of the understanding.

It is obvious that when we have the prospect of pain or pleasure from any object, we feel a consequent emotion of aversion or propensity, and are carried to avoid or embrace what will give us this uneasiness or satisfaction. It is also obvious that this emotion rests not here, but making us cast our view on every side, comprehends whatever objects are connected with its original one by the relation of cause and effect. Here then reasoning takes place to discover this relation; and according as our reasoning varies, our actions receive a subsequent variation. But it is evident in this case, that the impulse arises not from reason, but is only directed by it. It is from the prospect of pain or pleasure that the aversion or propensity arises towards any object: and these emotions extend themselves to the causes and effects of that object, as they are pointed out to us by reason and experience. It can never in the least concern us to know that such objects are causes, and such others effects, if both the causes and effects be indifferent to us. Where the objects themselves do not affect us, their connection can never give them any influence; and it is plain, that as reason is nothing but the discovery of this connection, it cannot be by its means that the objects are able to affect us.

Since reason alone can never produce any action, or give rise to volition, I infer, that the same faculty is as incapable of preventing volition, or of disputing the preference with any passion or emotion. This consequence is necessary. It is impossible reason could have the latter effect of preventing volition, but by giving an impulse in a contrary direction to our passion; and that impulse, had it operated alone, would have been able to produce volition. Nothing can oppose or retard the impulse of passion, but a contrary impulse; and if this contrary impulse ever arises from reason, that latter faculty must have an original influence on the will, and must be able to cause, as well as hinder any act of volition. But if reason has no original influence, it is impossible it can withstand any principle, which has such an efficacy, or ever keep the mind in suspense a moment. Thus it appears, that the principle, which opposes our passion, cannot be the same with reason, and is only called so in an improper sense. We speak not strictly and philosophically when we talk of the combat of passion and of reason. Reason is, and ought only to be the slave of the passions, and can never pretend to any other office than to serve and obey them. As this opinion may appear somewhat extraordinary, it may not be improper to confirm it by some other considerations.

A passion is an original existence, or, if you will, modification of existence, and contains not any representative quality, which renders it a copy of any other existence or modification. When I am angry, I am actually possessed with the passion, and in that emotion have no more a reference to any other object, than when I am thirsty, or sick, or more than five foot high. It is impossible, therefore, that this passion can be opposed by, or be contradictory to truth and reason; since this contradiction consists in the disagreement of ideas, considered as copies, with those objects, which they represent.

What may at first occur on this head is that as nothing can be contrary to truth or reason, except what has a reference to it, and as the judgments of our understanding only have this reference, it must follow, that passions can be contrary to reason only so far as they are *accompanied* with some judgment or opinion. According to this principle, which is so obvious and natural, it is only in two senses, that any affection can be called unreasonable. First, when a passion, such as hope or fear, grief or joy, despair or security, is founded on the supposition of the existence of objects, which really do not exist. Secondly, when in exerting any passion in action, we choose means insufficient for the designed end, and deceive ourselves in our judgment of causes and effects. Where a passion is neither founded on false suppositions, nor chooses means insufficient for the end, the understanding can neither justify nor condemn it. It is not contrary to reason to prefer the destruction of the whole world to the scratching of my finger. It is not contrary to reason for me to choose my total ruin to prevent the least uneasiness of an Indian or person wholly unknown to me. It is as little contrary to reason to prefer even my own acknowledged lesser good to my greater, and have a more ardent affection for the former than the latter. A trivial good may, from certain circumstances, produce a desire superior to what arises from the greatest and most valuable enjoyment; nor is there any thing more extraordinary in this, than in mechanics to see one pound weight raise up a hundred by the advantage of its situation. In short, a passion must be accompanied with some false judgment, in order to its being unreasonable; and even then it is not the passion, properly speaking, which is unreasonable, but the judgment.

The consequences are evident. Since a passion can never, in any sense, be called unreasonable, but when founded on a false supposition, or when it chooses means insufficient for the designed end, it is impossible, that reason and passion can ever oppose each other, or dispute for the government of the will and actions. The moment we perceive the falsehood of any supposition, or the insufficiency of any means, our passions yield to our reason without any opposition. I may desire any fruit as of an excellent relish; but whenever you convince me of my mistake, my longing ceases. I may will the performance of certain actions as means of obtaining any desired good; but as my willing of these actions is only secondary, and founded on the supposition, that they

are causes of the proposed effect; as soon as I discover the falsehood of that supposition, they must become indifferent to me. . . .

2. Moral Distinctions [Are] Not Derived from Reason

It has been observed, that nothing is ever present to the mind but its perceptions; and that all the actions of seeing, hearing, judging, loving, hating, and thinking, fall under this denomination. The mind can never exert itself in any action, which we may not comprehend under the term of *perception;* and consequently that term is no less applicable to those judgments, by which we distinguish moral good and evil, than to every other operation of the mind. To approve of one character, to condemn another, are only so many different perceptions.

Now as perceptions resolve themselves into two kinds, viz. *impressions* and *ideas,* this distinction gives rise to a question, with which we shall open up our present inquiry concerning morals, *Whether it is by means of our* ideas *or* impressions *we distinguish betwixt vice and virtue, and pronounce an action blameable or praise-worthy?* This will immediately cut off all loose discourses and declamations, and reduce us to something precise and exact on the present subject.

Those who affirm that virtue is nothing but a conformity to reason; that there are eternal fitnesses and unfitnesses of things, which are the same to every rational being that considers them; that the immutable measures of right and wrong impose an obligation, not only on human creatures, but also on the Deity himself: all these systems concur in the opinion, that morality, like truth, is discerned merely by ideas, and by their juxtaposition and comparison. In order, therefore, to judge of these systems, we need only consider, whether it be possible, from reason alone, to distinguish betwixt moral good and evil, or whether there must concur some other principles to enable us to make that distinction. . . .

Since morals, therefore, have an influence on the actions and affections, it follows, that they cannot be derived from reason; and that because reason alone, as we have already proved, can never have any such influence. Morals excite passions, and produce or prevent actions. Reason of itself is utterly impotent in this particular. The rules of morality, therefore, are not conclusions of our reason.

No one, I believe, will deny the justness of this inference; nor is there any other means of evading it, than by denying that principle, on which it is founded. As long as it is allowed, that reason has no influence on our passions and actions, it is in vain to pretend, that morality is discovered only by a deduction of reason. An active principle can never be founded on an inactive; and if reason be inactive in itself, it must remain so in all its shapes and appearances, whether it exerts itself in natural or moral subjects, whether it considers the powers of external bodies, or the actions of rational beings.

It would be tedious to repeat all the arguments, by which I have proved, that reason is perfectly inert, and can never either prevent or produce any action or affection. It will be easy to recollect what has been said upon that subject. I shall only recall on this occasion one of these arguments, which I shall endeavour to render still more conclusive, and more applicable to the present subject.

Reason is the discovery of truth or falsehood. Truth or falsehood consists in an agreement or disagreement either to the *real* relations of ideas, or to *real* existence and matter of fact. Whatever, therefore, is not susceptible of this agreement or disagreement, is incapable of being true or false, and can never be an object of our reason. Now it is evident our passions, volitions, and actions, are not susceptible of any such agreement or disagreement; being original facts and realities, complete in themselves, and implying no reference to other passions, volitions, and actions. It is impossible, therefore, they can be pronounced either true or false, and be either contrary or conformable to reason.

This argument is of double advantage to our present purpose. For it proves *directly*, that actions do not derive their merit from a conformity to reason, nor their blame from a contrariety to it; and it proves the same truth more *indirectly*, by showing us, that as reason can never immediately prevent or produce any action by contradicting or approving of it, it cannot be the source of moral good and evil, which are found to have that influence. Actions may be laudable or blameable; but they cannot be rea-

sonable or unreasonable: laudable or blameable, therefore, are not the same with reasonable or unreasonable. The merit and demerit of actions frequently contradict, and sometimes control our natural propensities. But reason has no such influence. Moral distinctions, therefore, are not the offspring of reason. Reason is wholly inactive, and can never be the source of so active a principle as conscience, or a sense of morals. . . .

Should it be pretended, that though a mistake of *fact* be not criminal, yet a mistake of *right* often is; and that this may be the source of immorality: I would answer, that it is impossible such a mistake can ever be the original source of immorality, since it supposes a real right and wrong; that is, a real distinction in morals, independent of these judgements. A mistake, therefore, of right may become a species of immorality; but it is only a secondary one, and is founded on some other, antecedent to it.

As to those judgements which are the *effects* of our actions, and which, when false, give occasion to pronounce the actions contrary to truth and reason; we may observe, that our actions never cause any judgement, either true or false, in ourselves, and that it is only on others they have such an influence. It is certain, that an action, on many occasions, may give rise to false conclusions in others; and that a person, who through a window sees any lewd behaviour of mine with my neighbour's wife, may be so simple as to imagine she is certainly my own. In this respect my action resembles somewhat a lie or falsehood; only with this difference, which is material, that I perform not the action with any intention of giving rise to a false judgement in another, but merely to satisfy my lust and passion. It causes, however, a mistake and false judgement by accident; and the falsehood of its effects may be ascribed, by some odd figurative way of speaking, to the action itself. But still I can see no pretext of reason for asserting, that the tendency to cause such an error is the first spring or original source of all immorality.

Thus upon the whole, it is impossible, that the distinction betwixt moral good and evil, can be made by reason; since that distinction has an influence upon our actions, of which reason alone is incapable. Reason and judgement may, indeed, be the mediate cause of an action, by prompting, or by directing a passion: but it is not pretended, that a judgement of this kind, either in its truth or falsehood, is attended with virtue or vice. And as to the judgements, which are caused by our judgements, they can still less bestow those moral qualities on the actions, which are their causes.

But to be more particular, and to show, that those eternal immutable fitnesses and unfitnesses of things cannot be defended by sound philosophy, we may weigh the following considerations.

If the thought and understanding were alone capable of fixing the boundaries of right and wrong, the character of virtuous and vicious either must lie in some relations of objects, or must be a matter of fact, which is discovered by our reasoning. This consequence is evident. As the operations of human understanding divide themselves into two kinds, the comparing of ideas, and the inferring of matter of fact; were virtue discovered by the understanding; it must be an object of one of these operations, nor is there any third operation of the understanding, which can discover it. There has been an opinion very industriously propagated by certain philosophers, that morality is susceptible of demonstration; and though no one has ever been able to advance a single step in those demonstrations; yet it is taken for granted, that this science may be brought to an equal certainty with geometry or algebra. Upon this supposition, vice and virtue must consist in some relations; since it is allowed on all hands, that no matter of fact is capable of being demonstrated. Let us, therefore, begin with examining this hypothesis, and endeavour, if possible, to fix those moral qualities, which have been so long the objects of our fruitless researches. Point out distinctly the relations, which constitute morality or obligation, that we may know wherein they consist, and after what manner we must judge of them.

If you assert, that vice and virtue consist in relations susceptible of certainty and demonstration, you must confine yourself to those *four* relations, which alone admit of that degree of evidence; and in that case you run into absurdities, from which you will never be able to extricate yourself. For as you make the very essence of morality to lie in the relations, and as there is no one of these relations but what is applicable, not only to an irrational, but also to an inanimate object; it follows, that even such objects must be susceptible of merit or demerit. *Resemblance, contrariety, degrees in quality,* and *proportions in quantity and number;* all these relations belong as properly to matter, as to our actions, passions, and volitions. It is unquestionable, therefore, that morality lies not in any of these relations, nor the sense of it in their discovery.

Should it be asserted, that the sense of morality consists in the discovery of some relation, distinct from these, and that our enumeration was not complete, when we comprehended all demonstrable relations under the four general heads: to this I know not what to reply, till some one be so good as to point out to me this new relation. It is impossible to refute a system, which has never yet been explained. In such a manner of fighting in the dark, a man loses his blows in the air, and often places them where the enemy is not present.

I must, therefore, on this occasion, rest contended with requiring the two following conditions of any one that would undertake to clear up this system. *First,* as moral good and evil belong only to the actions of the mind, and are derived from our situation with regard to external objects, the relations, from which these moral distinctions arise, must lie only betwixt internal actions, and external objects, and must not be applicable either to internal actions, compared among themselves, or to external objects, when placed in opposition to other external objects. For as morality is supposed to attend certain relations, if these relations could belong to internal actions considered singly, it would follow, that we might be guilty of crimes in ourselves, and independent of our situation, with respect to the universe: and in like manner, if these moral relations could be applied to external objects, it would follow, that even inanimate beings would be susceptible of moral beauty and deformity. Now it seems difficult to imagine, that any relation can be discovered betwixt our passions, volitions and actions, compared to external objects, which relation might not belong either to these passions and volitions, or to these external objects, compared among *themselves.*

But it will be still more difficult to fulfil the *second* condition, requisite to justify this system. According to the principles of those who maintain an abstract rational difference betwixt moral good and evil, and a natural fitness and unfitness of things, it is not only supposed, that these relations, being eternal and immutable, are the same, when considered by every rational creature, but their *effects* are also supposed to be necessarily the same; and it is concluded they have no less, or rather a greater, influence in directing the will of the Deity, than in governing the rational and virtuous of our own species. These two particulars are evidently distinct. It is one thing to know virtue, and another to conform the will to it. In order, therefore, to prove, that the measures of right and wrong are eternal laws, *obligatory* on every rational mind, it is not sufficient to show the relations upon which they are founded: we must also point out the connection betwixt the relation and the will; and must prove that this connection is so necessary, that in every well-disposed mind, it must take place and have its influence; though the difference betwixt these minds be in other respects immense and infinite. Now besides what I have already proved, that even in human nature no relation can ever alone produce any action; besides this, I say, it has been shown, in treating of the understanding, that there is no connection of cause and effect, such as this is supposed to be, which is discoverable otherwise than by experience, and of which we can pretend to have any security by the simple consideration of the objects. All beings in the universe, considered in themselves, appear entirely loose and independent of each other. It is only by experience we learn their influence and connection; and this influence we ought never to extend beyond experience.

Thus it will be impossible to fulfil the *first* condition required to the system of eternal rational measures of right and wrong; because it is impossible to show those relations, upon which such a distinction may be founded: and it is as impossible to fulfil the *second* condition; because we cannot prove *a priori*, that these relations, if they really existed and were perceived, would be universally forcible and obligatory.

But to make these general reflections more clear and convincing, we may illustrate them by some particular instances, wherein this character of moral good or evil is the most universally acknowledged. Of all crimes that human creatures are capable of committing, the most horrid and unnatural is ingratitude, especially when it is committed against parents, and appears in the more flagrant instances of wounds and death. This is acknowledged by all mankind, philosophers as well as the people; the question only arises among philosophers, whether the guilt or moral deformity of this action be discovered by demonstrative reasoning, or be felt by an internal sense, and by means of some sentiment, which the reflecting on such an action naturally occasions. This question will soon be decided against the former opinion, if we can show the same relations in other objects, without the notion of any guilt or iniquity attending them. Reason or science is nothing but the comparing of ideas, and the discovery of their relations; and if the same relations have different characters, it must evidently follow, that those characters are not discovered merely by reason. To put the affair, therefore, to this trial, let us choose any inanimate object, such as an oak or elm; and let us suppose, that by the dropping of its seed, it produces a sapling below it, which springing up by degrees, at last overtops and destroys the parent tree: I ask, if in this instance there be wanting any relation, which is discoverable in parricide or ingratitude? Is not the one tree the cause of the other's existence; and the latter the cause of the destruction of the former, in the same manner as when a child murders his parent? It is not sufficient to reply, that a choice or will is wanting. For in the case of parricide, a will does not give rise to any *different* relations, but is only the cause from which the action is derived; and consequently produces the *same* relations, that in the oak or elm arise from some other principles. It is a will or choice, that determines a man to kill his parent; and they are the laws of matter and motion, that determine a sapling to destroy the oak, from which it sprung. Here then the same relations have different causes; but still the relations are the same: and as their discovery is not in both cases attended with a notion of immorality, it follows, that that notion does not arise from such a discovery.

But to choose an instance, still more resembling; I would fain ask any one, why incest in the human species is criminal, and why the very same action, and the same relations in animals have not the smallest moral turpitude and deformity? If it be answered, that this action is innocent in animals, because they have not reason sufficient to discover its turpitude; but that man, being endowed with that faculty, which *ought* to restrain him to his duty, the same action instantly becomes criminal to him; should this be said, I would reply, that this is evidently arguing in a circle. For before reason can perceive this turpitude, the turpitude must exist; and consequently is independent of the decisions of our reason, and is their object more properly than their effect. According to this system, then, every animal, that has sense, and appetite, and will; that is, every animal, must be susceptible of all the same virtues and vices, for which we ascribe praise and blame to human creatures. All the difference is, that our superior reason may serve to discover the vice or virtue, and by that means may augment the blame or praise: but still this discovery supposes a separate being in these moral distinctions, and a being, which depends only on the will and appetite, and which, both in thought and reality, may be distinguished from the reason. Animals are susceptible of the same relations, with respect to each other, as the human species, and therefore would also be susceptible of the same morality, if the essence of morality consisted in these relations. Their want of a sufficient degree of reason may hinder them from perceiving the duties and obligations of morality, but can never hinder these duties from existing; since they must antecedently exist, in order to their being perceived. Reason must find them, and can never produce them. This argument deserves to be weighed, as being, in my opinion, entirely decisive.

Nor does this reasoning only prove, that morality consists not in any relations, that are the objects of science; but if examined, will prove with equal certainty, that it consists not in any *matter of fact,* which can be discovered by the understanding. This is the *second* part of our argument; and if it can be made evident, we may conclude, that morality is not an object of reason. But can there be any difficulty in proving, that vice and virtue are not matters of fact, whose existence we can infer by reason? Take any action allowed to be vicious: wilful murder, for instance. Examine it in all lights, and see if you can find that matter of fact, or real existence, which you call *vice*. In whichever way you take it, you find only certain passions, motives, volitions and thoughts. There is no other matter of fact in the case. The vice entirely escapes you, as long as you consider the object. You never can find it, till you turn your reflection into your own breast, and find a sentiment of disapprobation, which arises in you, towards this action. Here is a matter of fact; but it is the object of feeling, not of reason. It lies in yourself, not in the object. So that when you pronounce any action or character to be vicious, you mean nothing, but that from the constitution of your nature you have a feeling or sentiment of blame from the contemplation of it. Vice and virtue, therefore, may be compared to sounds, colours, heat and cold, which, according to modern philosophy, are not qualities in objects, but perceptions in the mind: and this discovery in morals, like that other in physics, is to be regarded as a considerable advancement of the speculative sciences; though, like that too, it has little or no influence on practice. Nothing can be more real, or concern us more, than our own sentiments of pleasure and uneasiness; and if these be favourable to virtue, and unfavourable to vice, no more can be requisite to the regulation of our conduct and behaviour.

I cannot forbear adding to these reasonings an observation, which may, perhaps, be found of some importance. In every system of morality, which I have hitherto met with, I have always remarked, that the author proceeds for some time in the ordinary way of reasoning, and establishes the being of a God, or makes observations concerning human affairs; when of a sudden I am surprised to find, that instead of the usual copulations of propositions, *is,* and *is not,* I meet with no proposition that is not connected with an *ought,* or an *ought not.* This change is imperceptible; but is, however, of the last consequence. For as this *ought,* or *ought not,* expresses some new relation or affirmation, it is necessary that it should be observed and explained; and at the same time that a reason should be given, for what seems altogether inconceivable, how this new relation can be a deduction from others, which are entirely different from it. But as authors do not commonly use this precaution, I shall presume to recommend it to the readers; and am persuaded, that this small attention would subvert all the vulgar systems of morality, and let us see, that the distinction of vice and virtue is not founded merely on the relations of objects, nor is perceived by reason.

VIII.2 *Non-Naturalism and the Indefinability of the Good*

G. E. MOORE

G. E. Moore (1873–1958) taught philosophy at Cambridge University and was editor of the important British philosophy journal *Mind*. He was one of the most influential philosophers of the twentieth century, and a good part of his fame derives from his major work in ethics, *Prinicipia Ethica* (1903), from which this selection is taken. Moore turns his attention to the meaning of moral terms, especially the terms 'good' and 'right.' Unless philosophers can define their terms, philosophy can never become the exact science that it must become if we are to have clear decision-making procedures. Moore thinks that what is right must be defined in terms of the 'good,' and that 'good' is a simple notion, which, like yellow, cannot be verbally defined. However, unlike yellow, goodness is not a natural property that we can perceive with our senses. It is a simple, unanalyzable, non-natural property that must be discovered by intuition. Through his open question argument, Moore attempts to show just why goodness cannot be identified with such natural qualities as pleasure or being the object of desire.

5. How 'good' is to be defined, is the most fundamental question in all Ethics. That which is meant by 'good' is, in fact, except its converse 'bad,' the *only* simple object of thought which is peculiar to Ethics. Its definition is, therefore, the most essential point in the definition of Ethics; and moreover a mistake with regard to it entails a far larger number of erroneous ethical judgments than any other. Unless this first question be fully understood, and its true answer clearly recognised, the rest of Ethics is as good as useless from the point of view of systematic knowledge. True ethical judgments, of the two kinds last dealt with, may indeed be made by those who do not know the answer to this question as well as by those who do; and it goes without saying that the two classes of people may lead equally good lives. But it is extremely unlikely that the *most general* ethical judgments will be equally valid, in the absence of a true answer to this question: I shall presently try to shew that the gravest errors have been largely due to beliefs in a false answer. And, in any case, it is impossible that, till the answer to this question be known, any one should know *what is the evidence* for any ethical judgment whatsoever. But the main object of Ethics, as a systematic science, is to give correct *reasons* for thinking that this or that is good; and, unless this question be answered, such reasons cannot be given. Even, therefore, apart from the fact that a false answer leads to false conclusions, the present enquiry is a most necessary and important part of the science of Ethics.

6. What, then, is good? How is good to be defined? Now, it may be thought that this is a verbal question. A definition does indeed often mean the expressing of one word's meaning in other words. But this is not the sort of definition I am asking for. Such a definition can never be of ultimate importance in any study except lexicography. If I wanted that kind of definition I should have to consider in the first place how people generally used the word 'good'; but my business is not with its proper usage, as established by custom. I should, indeed, be foolish, if I tried to use it for something which it did not usually denote: if, for instance, I were to announce that, whenever I used the word 'good,' I must be understood to be thinking of that object

which is usually denoted by the word 'table.' I shall, therefore, use the word in the sense in which I think it is ordinarily used; but at the same time I am not anxious to discuss whether I am right in thinking that it is so used. My business is solely with that object or idea, which I hold, rightly or wrongly, that the word is generally used to stand for. What I want to discover is the nature of that object or idea, and about this I am extremely anxious to arrive at an agreement.

But, if we understand the question in this sense, my answer to it may seem a very disappointing one. If I am asked 'What is good?' my answer is that good is good, and that is the end of the matter. Or if I am asked 'How is good to be defined?' my answer is that it cannot be defined, and that is all I have to say about it. But disappointing as these answers may appear, they are of the very last importance. To readers who are familiar with philosophic terminology, I can express their importance by saying that they amount to this: That propositions about the good are all of them synthetic and never analytic; and that is plainly no trivial matter. And the same thing may be expressed more popularly, by saying that, if I am right, then nobody can foist upon us such an axiom as that 'Pleasure is the only good' or that 'The good is the desired' on the pretence that this is 'the very meaning of the word.'

7. Let us, then, consider this position. My point is that 'good' is a simple notion, just as 'yellow' is a simple notion; that, just as you cannot, by any manner of means, explain to any one who does not already know it, what yellow is, so you cannot explain what good is. Definitions of the kind that I was asking for, definitions which describe the real nature of the object or notion denoted by a word, and which do not merely tell us what the word is used to mean, are only possible when the object or notion in question is something complex. You can give a definition of a horse, because a horse has many different properties and qualities, all of which you can enumerate. But when you have enumerated them all, when you have reduced a horse to his simplest terms, then you can no longer define those terms. They are simply something which you think of or perceive, and to any one who cannot think of or perceive them, you can never, by any definition, make their nature known. It may perhaps be objected to this that we are able to describe to others, objects which they have never seen or thought of.

We can, for instance, make a man understand what a chimaera is, although he has never heard of one or seen one. You can tell him that it is an animal with a lioness's head and body, with a goat's head growing from the middle of its back, and with a snake in place of a tail. But here the object which you are describing is a complex object; it is entirely composed of parts, with which we are all perfectly familiar—a snake, a goat, a lioness; and we know, too, the manner in which those parts are to be put together, because we know what is meant by the middle of a lioness's back, and where her tail is wont to grow. And so it is with all objects, not previously known, which we are able to define: they are all complex; all composed of parts, which may themselves, in the first instance, be capable of similar definition, but which must in the end be reducible to simplest parts, which can no longer be defined. But yellow and good, we say, are not complex: they are notions of that simple kind, out of which definitions are composed and with which the power of further defining ceases.

8. When we say, as Webster says, 'The definition of horse is "A hoofed quadruped of the genus Equus,"' we may, in fact, mean three different things. (1) We may mean merely: 'When I say "horse," you are to understand that I am talking about a hoofed quadruped of the genus Equus.' This might be called the arbitrary verbal definition: and I do not mean that good is indefinable in that sense. (2) We may mean, as Webster ought to mean: 'When most English people say "horse," they mean a hoofed quadruped of the genus Equus.' This may be called the verbal definition proper, and I do not say that good is indefinable in this sense either; for it is certainly possible to discover how people use a word: otherwise, we could never have known that 'good' may be translated by 'gut' in German and by 'bon' in French. But (3) we may, when we define horse, mean something much more important. We may mean that a certain object, which we all of us know, is composed in a certain manner: that it has four legs, a head, a heart, a liver, etc., etc., all of them arranged in definite relations to one another. It is in this sense that I deny good to be definable. I say that it is not composed of any parts, which we can substitute for it in our minds when we are thinking of it. We might think just as clearly and correctly about a horse, if we thought of all its parts and their arrangements instead of thinking of the whole; we

could, I say, think how a horse differed from a donkey just as well, just as truly, in this way, as now we do, only not so easily; but there is nothing whatsoever which we could so substitute for good; and that is what I mean, when I say that good is indefinable.

9. But I am afraid I have still not removed the chief difficulty which may prevent acceptance of the proposition that good is indefinable. I do not mean to say that *the* good, that which is good, is thus indefinable; if I did think so, I should not be writing on Ethics, for my main object is to help towards discovering that definition. It is just because I think there will be less risk of error in our search for a definition of 'the good,' that I am now insisting that *good* is indefinable. I must try to explain the difference between these two. I suppose it may be granted that 'good' is an adjective. Well 'the good, that which is good,' must therefore be the substantive to which the adjective 'good' will apply: it must be the whole of that to which the adjective will apply, and the adjective must *always* truly apply to it. But if it is that to which the adjective will apply, it must be something different from that adjective itself; and the whole of that something different, whatever it is, will be our definition of *the* good. Now it may be that this something will have other adjectives, beside 'good,' that will apply to it. It may be full of pleasure, for example: it may be intelligent: and if these two adjectives are really part of its definition, then it will certainly be true, that pleasure and intelligence are good. And many people appear to think that, if we say 'Pleasure and intelligence are good,' or if we say 'Only pleasure and intelligence are good,' we are defining 'good.' Well, I cannot deny that propositions of this nature may sometimes be called definitions; I do not know well enough how the word is generally used to decide upon this point. I only wish it to be understood that that is not what I mean when I say there is no possible definition of good, and that I shall not mean this if I use the word again. I do most fully believe that some true proposition of the form 'Intelligence is good and intelligence alone is good' can be found; if none could be found, our definition of *the* good would be impossible. As it is, I believe *the* good to be definable; and yet I still say that good itself is indefinable.

10. 'Good,' then, if we mean by it that quality which we assert to belong to a thing, when we say that the thing is good, is incapable of any definition, in the most important sense of that word. The most important sense of 'definition' is that in which a definition states what are the parts which invariably compose a certain whole; and in this sense 'good' has no definition because it is simple and has no parts. It is one of those innumerable objects of thought which are themselves incapable of definition, because they are the ultimate terms by reference to which whatever *is* capable of definition must be defined. That there must be an indefinite number of such terms is obvious, on reflection; since we cannot define anything except by an analysis, which, when carried as far as it will go, refers us to something, which is simply different from anything else, and which by that ultimate difference explains the peculiarity of the whole which we are defining: for every whole contains some parts which are common to other wholes also. There is, therefore, no intrinsic difficulty in the contention that 'good' denotes a simple and indefinable quality. There are many other instances of such qualities.

Consider yellow, for example. We may try to admire it, by describing its physical equivalent; we may state what kind of light-vibrations must stimulate the normal eye, in order that we may perceive it. But a moment's reflection is sufficient to shew that those light-vibrations are not themselves what we mean by yellow. *They* are not what we perceive. Indeed we should never have been able to discover their existence, unless we had first been struck by the patent difference of quality between the different colours. The most we can be entitled to say of those vibrations is that they are what corresponds in space to the yellow which we actually perceive.

Yet a mistake of this simple kind has commonly been made about 'good.' It may be true that all things which are good are *also* something else, just as it is true that all things which are yellow produce a certain kind of vibration in the light. And it is a fact, that Ethics aims at discovering what are those other properties belonging to all things which are good. But far too many philosophers have thought that when they named those other properties they were actually defining good; that these properties, in fact, were simply not 'other,' but absolutely and entirely the same with goodness. This view I propose to call the 'naturalistic fallacy' and of it I shall now endeavour to dispose.

11. Let us consider what it is such philosophers say. And first it is to be noticed that they do not

agree among themselves. They not only say that they are right as to what good is, but they endeavour to prove that other people who say that it is something else, are wrong. One, for instance, will affirm that good is pleasure, another, perhaps, that good is that which is desired; and each of these will argue eagerly to prove that the other is wrong. But how is that possible? One of them says that good is nothing but the object of desire, and at the same time tries to prove that it is not pleasure. But from his first assertion, that good just means the object of desire, one of two things must follow as regards his proof:

(1) He may be trying to prove that the object of desire is not pleasure. But, if this be all, where is his Ethics? The position he is maintaining is merely a psychological one. Desire is something which occurs in our minds, and pleasure is something else which so occurs; and our would-be ethical philosopher is merely holding that the latter is not the object of the former. But what has that to do with the question in dispute? His opponent held the ethical proposition that pleasure was the good, and although he should prove a million times over the psychological proposition that pleasure is not the object of desire, he is no nearer proving his opponent to be wrong. The position is like this. One man says a triangle is a circle: another replies 'A triangle is a straight line, and I will prove to you that I am right: *for*' (this is the only argument) 'a straight line is not a circle.' 'That is quite true,' the other may reply; 'but nevertheless a triangle is a circle, and you have said nothing whatever to prove the contrary. What is proved is that one of us is wrong, for we agree that a triangle cannot be both a straight line and a circle: but which is wrong, there can be no earthly means of proving, since you define triangle as straight line and I define it as circle.'—Well, that is one alternative which any naturalistic Ethics has to face; if good is *defined* as something else, it is then impossible either to prove that any other definition is wrong or even to deny such definition.

(2) The other alternative will scarcely be more welcome. It is that the discussion is after all a verbal one. When A says 'Good means pleasant' and B says 'Good means desired,' they may merely wish to assert that most people have used the word for what is pleasant and for what is desired respectively. And this is quite an interesting subject for discussion: only it is not a whit more an ethical discussion than the last was. Nor do I think that any exponent of

naturalistic Ethics would be willing to allow that this was all he meant. They are all so anxious to persuade us that what they call the good is what we really ought to do. 'Do, pray, act so, because the word "good" is generally used to denote actions of this nature': such, on this view, would be the substance of their teaching. And in so far as they tell us how we ought to act, their teaching is truly ethical, as they mean it to be. But how perfectly absurd is the reason they would give for it! 'You are to do this, because most people use a certain word to denote conduct such as this.' 'You are to say the thing which is not, because most people call it lying?' That is an argument just as good!—My dear sirs, what we want to know from you as ethical teachers, is not how people use a word; it is not even, what kind of actions they approve, which the use of this word 'good' may certainly imply: what we want to know is simply what *is* good. We may indeed agree that what most people do think good, is actually so; we shall at all events be glad to know their opinions: but when we say their opinions about what *is* good, we do mean what we say; we do not care whether they call that thing which they mean 'horse' or 'table' or 'chair,' 'gut' or 'bon' or 'ἀγαθός'; we want to know what it is that they so call. When they say 'Pleasure is good,' we cannot believe that they merely mean 'Pleasure is pleasure' and nothing more than that.

12. Suppose a man says 'I am pleased'; and suppose that is not a lie or a mistake but the truth. Well, if it is true, what does that mean? It means that his mind, a certain definite mind, distinguished by certain definite marks from all others, has at this moment a certain definite feeling called pleasure. 'Pleased' *means* nothing but having pleasure, and though we may be more pleased or less pleased, and even, we may admit for the present, have one or another kind of pleasure; yet in so far as it is pleasure we have, whether there be more or less of it, and whether it be of one kind or another, what we have is one definite thing, absolutely indefinable, some one thing that is the same in all the various degrees and all the various kinds of it that there may be. We may be able to say how it is related to other things: that, for example, it is in the mind, that it causes desire, that we are conscious of it, etc., etc. We can, I say, describe its relations to other things, but define it we can *not*. And if anybody tried to define pleasure for us as being any other natural object; if anybody were to say, for instance, that pleasure *means* the

sensation of red, and were to proceed to deduce from that that pleasure is a colour, we should be entitled to laugh at him and to distrust his future statements about pleasure. Well, that would be the same fallacy which I have called the naturalistic fallacy. That 'pleased' does not mean 'having the sensation of red,' or anything else whatever, does not prevent us from understanding what it does mean. It is enough for us to know that 'pleased' does mean 'having the sensation of pleasure,' and though pleasure is absolutely indefinable, though pleasure is pleasure and nothing else whatever, yet we feel no difficulty in saying that we are pleased. The reason is, of course, that when I say 'I am pleased,' I do *not* mean that 'I' am the same thing as 'having pleasure.' And similarly no difficulty need be found in my saying that 'pleasure is good' and yet not meaning that 'pleasure' is the same thing as 'good,' that pleasure *means* good, and that good *means* pleasure. If I were to imagine that when I said 'I am pleased,' I meant that I was exactly the same thing as 'pleased,' I should not indeed call that a naturalistic fallacy, although it would be the same fallacy as I have called naturalistic with reference to Ethics. The reason of this is obvious enough. When a man confuses two natural objects with one another, defining the one by the other, if for instance, he confuses himself, who is one natural object, with 'pleased' or with 'pleasure' which are others, then there is no reason to call the fallacy naturalistic. But if he confuses 'good,' which is not in the same sense a natural object, with any natural object whatever, then there is a reason for calling that a naturalistic fallacy; its being made with regard to 'good' marks it as something quite specific, and this specific mistake deserves a name because it is so common. As for the reasons why good is not to be considered a natural object, they may be reserved for discussion in another place. But, for the present, it is sufficient to notice this: Even if it were a natural object, that would not alter the nature of the fallacy nor diminish its importance one whit. All that I have said about it would remain quite equally true: only the name which I have called it would not be so appropriate as I think it is. And I do not care about the name: what I do care about is the fallacy. It does not matter what we call it, provided we recognise it when we meet with it. It is to be met with in almost every book on Ethics; and yet it is not recognised: and that is why it is necessary to multiply illustrations of it, and con-

venient to give it a name. It is a very simple fallacy indeed. When we say that an orange is yellow, we do not think our statement binds us to hold that 'orange' means nothing else than 'yellow,' or that nothing can be yellow but an orange. Supposing the orange is also sweet! Does that bind us to say that 'sweet' is exactly the same thing as 'yellow,' that 'sweet' must be defined as 'yellow'? And supposing it be recognised that 'yellow' just means 'yellow' and nothing else whatever, does that make it any more difficult to hold that oranges are yellow? Most certainly it does not: on the contrary, it would be absolutely meaningless to say that oranges were yellow, unless yellow did in the end mean just 'yellow' and nothing else whatever — unless it was absolutely indefinable. We should not get any very clear notion about things, which are yellow — we should not get very far with our science, if we were bound to hold that everything which was yellow, *meant* exactly the same thing as yellow. We should find we had to hold that an orange was exactly the same thing as a stool, a piece of paper, a lemon, anything you like. We could prove any number of absurdities; but should we be the nearer to the truth? Why, then, should it be different with 'good'? Why, if good is good and indefinable, should I be held to deny that pleasure is good? Is there any difficulty in holding both to be true at once? On the contrary, there is no meaning in saying that pleasure is good, unless good is something different from pleasure. It is absolutely useless, so far as Ethics is concerned, to prove, as Mr. Spencer tries to do, that increase of pleasure coincides with increase of life, unless good *means* something different from either life or pleasure. He might just as well try to prove that an orange is yellow by shewing that it always is wrapped up in paper.

13. In fact, if it is not the case that 'good' denotes something simple and indefinable, only two alternatives are possible: either it is a complex, a given whole, about the correct analysis of which there may be disagreement; or else it means nothing at all, and there is no such subject as Ethics. In general, however, ethical philosophers have attempted to define good, without recognising what such an attempt must mean. They actually use arguments which involve one or both of the absurdities considered in § 11. We are, therefore, justified in concluding that the attempt to define good is chiefly due to want of clearness as to the possible nature of defini-

tion. There are, in fact, only two serious alternatives to be considered, in order to establish the conclusion that 'good' does denote a simple and indefinable notion. It might possibly denote a complex, as 'horse' does; or it might have no meaning at all. Neither of these possibilities has, however, been clearly conceived and seriously maintained, as such, by those who presume to define good; and both may be dismissed by a simple appeal to facts.

(1) The hypothesis that disagreement about the meaning of good is disagreement with regard to the correct analysis of a given whole, may be most plainly seen to be incorrect by consideration of the fact that, whatever definition be offered, it may be always asked, with significance, of the complex so defined, whether it is itself good. To take, for instance, one of the more plausible, because one of the more complicated, of such proposed definitions, it may easily be thought, at first sight, that to be good may mean to be that which we desire to desire. Thus if we apply this definition to a particular instance and say 'When we think that A is good, we are thinking that A is one of the things which we desire to desire,' our proposition may seem quite plausible. But, if we carry the investigation further, and ask ourselves 'Is it good to desire to desire A?' it is apparent, on a little reflection, that this question is itself as intelligible, as the original question 'Is A good?' — that we are in fact, now asking for exactly the same information about the desire to desire A, for which we formerly asked with regard to A itself. But it is also apparent that the meaning of this second question cannot be correctly analysed into 'Is the desire to desire A one of the things which we desire to desire?': we have not before our minds anything so complicated as the question 'Do we desire to desire to desire to desire A?' Moreover any one can easily convince himself by inspection that the predicate of this proposition — 'good' — is positively different from the notion of 'desiring to desire' which enters into its subject: 'That we should desire to desire A is good' is *not* merely equivalent to 'That A should be good is good.' It may indeed be true that what we desire to desire is always also good; perhaps, even the converse may be true: but it is very doubtful whether this is the case, and the mere fact that we understand very well what is meant by doubting it, shews clearly that we have two different notions before our minds.

(2) And the same consideration is sufficient to dismiss the hypothesis that 'good' has no meaning whatsoever. It is very natural to make the mistake of supposing that what is universally true is of such a nature that its negation would be self-contradictory: the importance which has been assigned to analytic propositions in the history of philosophy shews how easy such a mistake is. And thus it is very easy to conclude that what seems to be a universal ethical principle is in fact an identical proposition; that, if, for example, whatever is called 'good' seems to be pleasant, the proposition 'Pleasure is the good' does not assert a connection between two different notions, but involves only one, that of pleasure, which is easily recognised as a distinct entity. But whoever will attentively consider with himself what is actually before his mind when he asks the question 'Is pleasure (or whatever it may be) after all good?' can easily satisfy himself that he is not merely wondering whether pleasure is pleasant. And if he will try this experiment with each suggested definition in succession, he may become expert enough to recognise that in every case he has before his mind a unique object, with regard to the connection of which with any other object, a distinct question may be asked. Every one does in fact understand the question 'Is this good?' When he thinks of it, his state of mind is different from what it would be, were he asked 'Is this pleasant, or desired, or approved?' It has a distinct meaning for him, even though he may not recognise in what respect it is distinct. Whenever he thinks of 'intrinsic value,' or 'intrinsic worth,' or says that a thing 'ought to exist,' he has before his mind the unique object — the unique property of things — which I mean by 'good.' Everybody is constantly aware of this notion, although he may never become aware at all that it is different from other notions of which he is also aware. But, for correct ethical reasoning, it is extremely important that he should become aware of this fact; and, as soon as the nature of the problem is clearly understood, there should be little difficulty in advancing so far in analysis.

VIII.3 *Emotivism*

A. J. AYER

A. J. Ayer (1910–89) was Wykeham Professor of Logic at Oxford University. He is famous for his espousal of logical positivism, set forth pungently in his doctoral dissertation, *Language, Truth and Logic,* from which this selection is taken. The logical positivists believe that the only sentences that are meaningful (that is, that can be true or false) are either tautologies (for example, mathematical formulas, like $2 + 2 = 4$) or empirically verifiable sentences. All else is nonsense, including the theological sentences (for example, "God is love"). Ethical judgements are neither tautologies nor empirically verifiable, so they are meaningless. Unlike theological sentences, however, they are nonsense of a useful sort, for they express emotions and are useful in persuading others to act in ways we desire them to act. This view, for obvious reasons, became known as *emotivism.*

There is still one objection to be met before we can claim to have justified our view that all synthetic propositions are empirical hypotheses. This objection is based on the common supposition that our speculative knowledge is of two distinct kinds — that which relates to questions of empirical fact, and that which relates to questions of value. It will be said that "statements of value" are genuine synthetic propositions, but that they cannot with any show of justice be represented as hypotheses, which are used to predict the course of our sensations; and, accordingly, that the existence of ethics and aesthetics as branches of speculative knowledge presents an insuperable objection to our radical empiricist thesis.

In face of this objection, it is our business to give an account of "judgements of value" which is both satisfactory in itself and consistent with our general empiricist principles. We shall set ourselves to show that in so far as statements of value are significant, they are ordinary "scientific" statements; and that in so far as they are not scientific, they are not in the literal sense significant, but are simply expressions of emotion which can be neither true nor false. In maintaining this view, we may confine ourselves for the present to the case of ethical statements. What is said about them will be found to apply, *mutatis mutandis,* to the case of aesthetic statements also.

The ordinary system of ethics, as elaborated in the works of ethical philosophers, is very far from being a homogeneous whole. Not only is it apt to contain pieces of metaphysics, and analyses of nonethical concepts: its actual ethical contents are themselves of very different kinds. We may divide them, indeed, into four main classes. There are, first of all, propositions which express definitions of ethical terms, or judgements about the legitimacy or possibility of certain definitions. Secondly, there are propositions describing the phenomena of moral experience, and their causes. Thirdly, there are exhortations to moral virtue. And, lastly, there are actual ethical judgements. It is unfortunately the case that the distinction between these four classes, plain as it is, is commonly ignored by ethical philosophers; with the result that it is often very difficult to tell from their works what it is that they are seeking to discover or prove.

In fact, it is easy to see that only the first of our four classes, namely that which comprises the propositions relating to the definitions of ethical terms, can be said to constitute ethical philosophy. The propositions which describe the phenomena of moral experience, and their causes, must be assigned to the science of psychology, or sociology. The ex-

Reprinted with permission from *Language, Truth, and Logic* (Dover Publications, 1946).

hortations to moral virtue are not propositions at all, but ejaculations or commands which are designed to provoke the reader to action of a certain sort. Accordingly, they do not belong to any branch of philosophy or science. As for the expressions of ethical judgements, we have not yet determined how they should be classified. But inasmuch as they are certainly neither definitions nor comments upon definitions, nor quotations, we may say decisively that they do not belong to ethical philosophy. A strictly philosophical treatise on ethics should therefore make no ethical pronouncements. But it should, by giving an analysis of ethical terms, show what is the category to which all such pronouncements belong. And this is what we are now about to do.

A question which is often discussed by ethical philosophers is whether it is possible to find definitions which would reduce all ethical terms to one or two fundamental terms. But this question, though it undeniably belongs to ethical philosophy, is not relevant to our present enquiry. We are not now concerned to discover which term, within the sphere of ethical terms, is to be taken as fundamental; whether, for example, "good" can be defined in terms of "right" or "right" in terms of "good," or both in terms of "value." What we are interested in is the possibility of reducing the whole sphere of ethical terms to non-ethical terms. We are enquiring whether statements of ethical value can be translated into statements of empirical fact.

That they can be so translated is the contention of those ethical philosophers who are commonly called subjectivists, and of those who are known as utilitarians. For the utilitarian defines the rightness of actions, and the goodness of ends, in terms of the pleasure, or happiness, or satisfaction, to which they give rise; the subjectivist, in terms of the feelings of approval which a certain person, or group of people, has towards them. Each of these types of definition makes moral judgements into a sub-class of psychological or sociological judgements; and for this reason they are very attractive to us. For, if either was correct, it would follow that ethical assertions were not generically different from the factual assertions which are ordinarily contrasted with them; and the account which we have already given of empirical hypotheses would apply to them also.

Nevertheless we shall not adopt either a subjectivist or a utilitarian analysis of ethical terms. We reject the subjectivist view that to call an action right, or a thing good, is to say that it is generally approved of, because it is not self-contradictory to assert that some actions which are generally approved of are not right, or that some things which are generally approved of are not good. And we reject the alternative subjectivist view that a man who asserts that a certain action is right, or that a certain thing is good, is saying that he himself approves of it, on the ground that a man who confessed that he sometimes approved of what was bad or wrong would not be contradicting himself. And a similar argument is fatal to utilitarianism. We cannot agree that to call an action right is to say that of all the actions possible in the circumstances it would cause, or be likely to cause, the greatest happiness, or the greatest balance of pleasure over pain, or the greatest balance of satisfied over unsatisfied desire, because we find that it is not self-contradictory to say that it is sometimes wrong to perform the action which would actually or probably cause the greatest happiness, or the greatest balance of pleasure over pain, or of satisfied over unsatisfied desire. And since it is not self-contradictory to say that some pleasant things are not good, or that some bad things are desired, it cannot be the case that the sentence "x is good" is equivalent to "x is pleasant," or to "x is desired." And to every other variant of utilitarianism with which I am acquainted the same objection can be made. And therefore we should, I think, conclude that the validity of ethical judgements is not determined by the felicific tendencies of actions, any more than by the nature of people's feelings; but that it must be regarded as "absolute" or "intrinsic," and not empirically calculable.

If we say this, we are not, of course, denying that it is possible to invent a language in which all ethical symbols are definable in non-ethical terms, or even that it is desirable to invent such a language and adopt it in place of our own; what we are denying is that the suggested reduction of ethical to non-ethical statements is consistent with the conventions of our actual language. That is, we reject utilitarianism and subjectivism, not as proposals to replace our existing ethical notions by new ones, but as analyses of our existing ethical notions. Our contention is simply that, in our language, sentences which contain normative ethical symbols are not equivalent to sentences which express psychological propositions, or indeed empirical propositions of any kind.

It is advisable here to make it plain that it is only normative ethical symbols, and not descriptive ethical symbols, that are held by us to be indefinable in factual terms. There is a danger of confusing these two types of symbols, because they are commonly constituted by signs of the same sensible form. Thus a complex sign of the form "*x* is wrong" may constitute a sentence which expresses a moral judgement concerning a certain type of conduct, or it may constitute a sentence which states that a certain type of conduct is repugnant to the moral sense of a particular society. In the latter case, the symbol "wrong" is a descriptive ethical symbol, and the sentence in which it occurs expresses an ordinary sociological proposition; in the former case, the symbol "wrong" is a normative ethical symbol, and the sentence in which it occurs does not, we maintain, express an empirical proposition at all. It is only with normative ethics that we are at present concerned; so that whenever ethical symbols are used in the course of this argument without qualification, they are always to be interpreted as symbols of the normative type.

In admitting that normative ethical concepts are irreducible to empirical concepts, we seem to be leaving the way clear for the "absolutist" view of ethics — that is, the view that statements of value are not controlled by observation, as ordinary empirical propositions are, but only by a mysterious "intellectual intuition." A feature of this theory, which is seldom recognized by its advocates, is that it makes statements of value unverifiable. For it is notorious that what seems intuitively certain to one person may seem doubtful, or even false, to another. So that unless it is possible to provide some criterion by which one may decide between conflicting intuitions, a mere appeal to intuition is worthless as a test of a proposition's validity. But in the case of moral judgements, no such criterion can be given. Some moralists claim to settle the matter by saying that they "know" that their own moral judgements are correct. But such an assertion is of purely psychological interest, and has not the slightest tendency to prove the validity of any moral judgement. For dissentient moralists may equally well "know" that their ethical views are correct. And, as far as subjective certainty goes, there will be nothing to choose between them. When such differences of opinion arise in connection with an ordinary empirical proposition, one may attempt to resolve them by referring to, or actually carrying out, some relevant empirical test. But with regard to ethical statements, there is, on the "absolutist" or "intuitionist" theory, no relevant empirical test. We are therefore justified in saying that on this theory ethical statements are held to be unverifiable. They are, of course, also held to be genuine synthetic propositions.

Considering the use which we have made of the principle that a synthetic proposition is significant only if it is empirically verifiable, it is clear that the acceptance of an "absolutist" theory of ethics would undermine the whole of our main argument. And as we have already rejected the "naturalistic" theories which are commonly supposed to provide the only alternative to "absolutism" in ethics, we seem to have reached a difficult position. We shall meet the difficulty by showing that the correct treatment of ethical statements is afforded by a third theory, which is wholly compatible with our radical empiricism.

We begin by admitting that the fundamental ethical concepts are unanalysable, inasmuch as there is no criterion by which one can test the validity of the judgements in which they occur. So far we are in agreement with the absolutists. But, unlike the absolutists, we are able to give an explanation of this fact about ethical concepts. We say that the reason why they are unanalysable is that they are mere pseudo-concepts. The presence of an ethical symbol in a proposition adds nothing to its factual content. Thus if I say to someone, "You acted wrongly in stealing that money," I am not stating anything more than if I had simply said, "You stole that money." In adding that this action is wrong I am not making any further statement about it. I am simply evincing my moral disapproval of it. It is as if I had said, "You stole that money," in a peculiar tone of horror, or written it with the addition of some special exclamation marks. The tone, or the exclamation marks, adds nothing to the literal meaning of the sentence. It merely serves to show that the expression of it is attended by certain feelings in the speaker.

If now I generalise my previous statement and say, "Stealing money is wrong," I produce a sentence which has no factual meaning — that is, expresses no proposition which can be either true or false. It is as if I had written "Stealing money!!" — where the shape and thickness of the exclamation marks show, by a suitable convention, that a special sort of moral disapproval is the feeling which is being expressed. It is clear that there is nothing said here which can be true or false. Another man may disagree with me about the wrongness of stealing, in the sense that he may not have the same feelings about stealing as I have, and he may quarrel with me on account of my moral sentiments. But he cannot, strictly speaking, contradict me. For in saying that a certain type of action is right or wrong, I am not making any factual statement, not even a statement about my own state of mind: I am merely expressing certain moral sentiments. And the man who is ostensibly contradicting me is merely expressing his moral sentiments. So that there is plainly no sense in asking which of us is in the right. For neither of us is asserting a genuine proposition.

What we have just been saying about the symbol "wrong" applies to all normative ethical symbols. Sometimes they occur in sentences which record ordinary empirical facts besides expressing ethical feeling about those facts: sometimes they occur in sentences which simply express ethical feeling about a certain type of action, or situation, without making any statement of fact. But in every case in which one would commonly be said to be making an ethical judgement, the function of the relevant ethical word is purely "emotive." It is used to express feeling about certain objects, but not to make any assertion about them.

It is worth mentioning that ethical terms do not serve only to express feeling. They are calculated also to arouse feeling, and so to stimulate action. Indeed some of them are used in such a way as to give the sentences in which they occur the effect of commands. Thus the sentence "It is your duty to tell the truth" may be regarded both as the expression of a certain sort of ethical feeling about truthfulness and as the expression of the command "Tell the truth." The sentence "You ought to tell the truth" also involves the command "Tell the truth," but here the tone of the command is less emphatic. In the sentence "It is good to tell the truth" the command has become little more than a suggestion. And thus the "meaning" of the word "good," in its ethical usage, is differentiated from that of the word "duty" or the word "ought." In fact we may define the meaning of the various ethical words in terms both of the different feelings they are ordinarily taken to express, and also the different responses which they are calculated to provoke.

We can now see why it is impossible to find a criterion for determining the validity of ethical judgements. It is not because they have an "absolute" validity which is mysteriously independent of ordinary sense-experience, but because they have no objective validity whatsoever. If a sentence makes no statement at all, there is obviously no sense in asking whether what it says is true or false. And we have seen that sentences which simply express moral judgements do not say anything. They are pure expressions of feeling and as such do not come under the category of truth and falsehood. They are unverifiable for the same reason as a cry of pain or a word of command is unverifiable — because they do not express genuine propositions.

Thus, although our theory of ethics might fairly be said to be radically subjectivist, it differs in a very important respect from the orthodox subjectivist theory. For the orthodox subjectivist does not deny, as we do, that the sentences of a moralizer express genuine propositions. All he denies is that they express propositions of a unique non-empirical character. His own view is that they express propositions about the speaker's feelings. If this were so, ethical judgements clearly would be capable of being true or false. They would be true if the speaker had the relevant feelings, and false if he had not. And this is a matter which is, in principle, empirically verifiable. Furthermore they could be significantly contradicted. For if I say, "Tolerance is a virtue," and someone answers, "You don't approve of it," he would, on the ordinary subjectivist theory, be contradicting me. On our theory, he would not be contradicting me, because, in saying that tolerance was a virtue, I should not be making any statement about my own feelings or about anything else. I should simply be evincing my feelings, which is not at all the same thing as saying that I have them.

The distinction between the expression of feeling and the assertion of feeling is complicated by the fact that the assertion that one has a certain feeling often accompanies the expression of that feeling, and is then, indeed, a factor in the expression of that feeling. Thus I may simultaneously express boredom and say that I am bored, and in that case my utterance of the words, "I am bored," is one of the circumstances which make it true to say that I am expressing or evincing boredom. But I can express boredom without actually saying that I am bored. I can express it by my tone and gestures, while making a statement about something wholly unconnected with it, or by an ejaculation, or without uttering any words at all. So that even if the assertion that one has a certain feeling always involves the expression of that feeling, the expression of a feeling assuredly does not always involve the assertion that one has it. And this is the important point to grasp in considering the distinction between our theory and the ordinary subjectivist theory. For whereas the subjectivist holds that ethical statements actually assert the existence of certain feelings, we hold that ethical statements are expressions and excitants of feeling which do not necessarily involve any assertions.

We have already remarked that the main objective to the ordinary subjectivist theory is that the validity of ethical judgements is not determined by the nature of their author's feelings. And this is an objection which our theory escapes. For it does not imply that the existence of any feelings is a necessary and sufficient condition of the validity of an ethical judgement. It implies, on the contrary, that ethical judgements have no validity.

There is, however, a celebrated argument against subjectivist theories which our theory does not escape. It has been pointed out by Moore that if ethical statements were simply statements about the speaker's feelings, it would be impossible to argue about questions of value. To take a typical example: if a man said that thrift was a virtue, and another replied that it was a vice, they would not, on this theory, be disputing with one another. One would be saying that he approved of thrift, and the other that *he* didn't; and there is no reason why both these statements should not be true. Now Moore held it to be obvious that we do dispute about questions of value, and accordingly concluded that the particular form of subjectivism which he was discussing was false.

It is plain that the conclusion that it is impossible to dispute about questions of value follows from our theory also. For as we hold that such sentences as "Thrift is a virtue" and "Thrift is a vice" do not express propositions at all, we clearly cannot hold that they express incompatible propositions. We must therefore admit that if Moore's argument really refutes the ordinary subjectivist theory, it also refutes ours. But, in fact, we deny that it does refute even the ordinary subjectivist theory. For we hold that one really never does dispute about questions of value.

This may seem, at first sight, to be a very paradoxical assertion. For we certainly do engage in disputes which are ordinarily regarded as disputes about questions of value. But, in all such cases, we find, if we consider the matter closely, that the dispute is not really about a question of value, but about a question of fact. When someone disagrees with us about the moral value of a certain action or type of action, we do admittedly resort to argument in order to win him over to our way of thinking. But we do not attempt to show by our arguments that he has the "wrong" ethical feeling towards a situation whose nature he has correctly apprehended. What we attempt to show is that he is mistaken about the facts of the case. We argue that he has misconceived the agent's motive; or that he has misjudged the effects of the action, or its probable effects in view of the agent's knowledge; or that he has failed to take into account the special circumstances in which the agent was placed. Or else we employ more general arguments about the effects which actions of a certain type tend to produce, or the qualities which are usually manifested in their performance. We do this in the hope that we have only to get our opponent to agree with us about the nature of the empirical facts for him to adopt the same moral attitude towards them as we do. And as the people with whom we argue have generally received the same moral education as ourselves, and live in the same social order, our expectation is usually justified. But if our opponent happens to have undergone a different process of moral "conditioning" from ourselves, so that, even when he acknowledges all the facts, he still disagrees with us about the moral value of the actions under discussion, then we abandon the attempt to convince him by argument. We say that it is impossible to argue with him because he has a distorted or undeveloped moral sense; which signifies merely that he employs a different set of values from our own. We feel that our own system of values is superior, and therefore speak in such derogatory terms of his. But we cannot bring forward any arguments to show that our system is superior. For our judgement that it is so is itself a judgement of value, and accordingly outside the scope of argument. It is because argument fails us when we come to deal with pure questions of value, as distinct from questions of fact, that we finally resort to mere abuse.

In short, we find that argument is possible on moral questions only if some system of values is presupposed. If our opponent concurs with us in expressing moral disapproval of all actions of a given type *t,* then we may get him to condemn a particular action A, by bringing forward arguments to show that A is of type *t.* For the question whether A does or does not belong to that type is a plain question of fact. Given that a man has certain moral principles, we argue that he must, in order to be consistent, react morally to certain things in a certain way. What we do not and cannot argue about is the validity of these moral principles. We merely praise or condemn them in the light of our own feelings.

If anyone doubts the accuracy of this account of moral disputes, let him try to construct even an imaginary argument on a question of value which does not reduce itself to an argument about a question of logic or about an empirical matter of fact. I am confident that he will not succeed in producing a single example. And if that is the case, he must allow that its involving the impossibility of purely ethical arguments is not, as Moore thought, a ground of objection to our theory, but rather a point in favour of it.

Having upheld our theory against the only criticism which appeared to threaten it, we may now use it to define the nature of all ethical enquiries. We find that ethical philosophy consists simply in saying that ethical concepts are pseudo-concepts and therefore unanalysable. The further task of describing the different feelings that the different ethical terms are used to express, and the different reactions that they customarily provoke, is a task for the psychologist. There cannot be such a thing as ethical science, if by ethical science one means the elaboration of a "true" system of morals. For we have seen that, as ethical judgements are mere expressions of feeling, there can be no way of determining the validity of any ethical system, and, indeed, no sense in asking whether any such system is true. All that one may legitimately enquire in this connection is, What are the moral habits of a given person or group of people, and what causes them to have precisely those habits and feelings? And this enquiry falls wholly within the scope of the existing social sciences.

It appears, then, that ethics, as a branch of knowledge, is nothing more than a department of psychology and sociology. And in case anyone thinks that we are overlooking the existence of casuistry, we may remark that casuistry is not a science, but is a purely analytical investigation of the structure of a given moral system. In other words, it is an exercise in formal logic.

When one comes to pursue the psychological enquiries which constitute ethical science, one is immediately enabled to account for the Kantian and hedonistic theories of morals. For one finds that one of the chief causes of moral behaviour is fear, both conscious and unconscious, of a god's displeasure, and fear of the enmity of society. And this, indeed, is the reason why moral precepts present themselves to some people as "categorical" commands. And one finds, also, that the moral code of a society is partly determined by the beliefs of that society concerning the conditions of its own happiness — or, in other words, that a society tends to encourage or discourage a given type of conduct by the use of moral sanctions according as it appears to promote or detract from the contentment of the society as a whole. And this is the reason why altruism is recommended in most moral codes and egotism condemned. It is from the observation of this connection between morality and happiness that hedonistic or eudaemonistic theories of morals ultimately spring, just as the moral theory of Kant is based on the fact, previously explained, that moral precepts have for some people the force of inexorable commands. As each of these theories ignores the fact which lies at the root of the other, both may be criticized as being one-sided; but this is not the main objection to either of them. Their essential defect is that they treat propositions which refer to the causes and attributes of our ethical feelings as if they were definitions of ethical concepts. And thus they fail to recognise that ethical concepts are pseudo-concepts and consequently indefinable.

VIII.4 *The Emotive Meaning of Ethical Terms*

C. L. STEVENSON

Charles Stevenson (1908–1979) was professor of philosophy at the University of Michigan for many years. His major works were his books, *Ethics and Language* and *Facts and Value*. Stevenson does not deny that moral language has meaning, as Ayer does. It is just that it has a different sort of meaning: emotive meaning, rather than descriptive meaning. In this article he carries out a careful analysis of the term 'good,' arguing that any adequate analysis must meet three criteria: We must be able to disagree about whether something is good; 'goodness' must possess a magnetism, a tendency to act in its favor; and 'good' must not be discoverable solely through scientific theory. He then argues that naturalist theories fail for one reason or another to satisfy these criteria, but that emotivism, which applies the difference between descriptive and emotive meaning, does satisfy all the criteria.

According to Stevenson, disagreement over whether something is good is simply disagreement in attitude. If you say stealing is bad and I say that it is good, we simply are manifesting different attitudes toward stealing. This attitude theory emphasizes that *good* is precisely the magnetic aspect of the term that is important, and that it has laudatory meaning. And finally, emotivism recognizes that fundamental disagreements (ones not rooted in mere disagreement in belief about some nonmoral facts) will not be resolved by empirical methods. If I have a pro-stealing attitude and have considered all the facts relevant to that activity, reason and science are impotent to effect a change in me.

I

Ethical questions first arise in the form "Is so and so good?" or "Is this alternative better than that?" These questions are difficult partly because we don't quite know what we are seeking. We are asking, "Is there a needle in that haystack?" without even knowing just what a needle is. So the first thing to do is to examine the questions themselves. We must try to make them clearer, either by defining the terms in which they are expressed, or by any other method that is available.

The present paper is concerned wholly with this preliminary step of making ethical questions clear. In order to help answer the question "Is X good?" we must *substitute* for it a question which is free from ambiguity and confusion.

It is obvious that in substituting a clearer question we must not introduce some utterly different kind of question. It won't do (to take an extreme instance of a prevalent fallacy) to substitute for "Is X good?" the question "Is X pink with yellow trimmings?" and then point out how easy the question really is. This would beg the original question, not help answer it. On the other hand, we must not expect the substituted question to be strictly "identical" with the original one. The original question may embody hypostatization, anthropomorphism, vagueness, and all the other ills to which our ordinary discourse is subject. If our substituted question is to be clearer, it must remove these ills. The questions will be identical only in the sense that a child is identical with the man he later becomes. Hence we

Reprinted from *Mind* 46(1937):14–31 by permission of Oxford University Press.

must not demand that the substitution strike us, on immediate introspection, as making no change in meaning.

Just how, then, must the substituted question be related to the original? Let us assume (inaccurately) that it must result from replacing "good" by some set of terms which define it. The question then resolves itself to this: How must the defined meaning of "good" be related to its original meaning?

I answer that it must be *relevant*. A defined meaning will be called "relevant" to the original meaning under these circumstances: Those who have understood the definition must be able to say all that they then want to say by using the term in the defined way. They must never have occasion to use the term in the old, unclear sense. (If a person did have to go on using the word in the old sense, then to this extent his meaning would not be clarified, and the philosophical task would not be completed.) It frequently happens that a word is used so confusedly and ambiguously that we must give it *several* defined meanings, rather than one. In this case only the whole set of defined meanings will be called "relevant," and any one of them will be called "partially relevant." This is not a rigorous treatment of *relevance*, by any means, but it will serve for the present purposes.

Let us now turn to our particular task — that of giving a relevant definition of "good." Let us first examine some of the ways in which others have attempted to do this.

The word "good" has often been defined in terms of *approval*, or similar psychological attitudes. We may take as typical examples: "good" means *desired by me* (Hobbes); and "good" means *approved by most people* (Hume, in effect). It will be convenient to refer to definitions of this sort as "interest theories," following Mr. R. B. Perry, although neither "interest" nor "theory" is used in the most usual way.

Are definitions of this sort relevant?

It is idle to deny their *partial* relevance. The most superficial inquiry will reveal that "good" is exceedingly ambiguous. To maintain that "good" is *never* used in Hobbes's sense, and never in Hume's, is only to manifest an insensitivity to the complexities of language. We must recognize, perhaps, not only these senses, but a variety of similar ones, differing both with regard to the kind of interest in question, and with regard to the people who are said to have the interest.

But this is a minor matter. The essential question is not whether interest theories are *partially* relevant, but whether they are *wholly* relevant. This is the only point for intelligent dispute. Briefly: Granted that some senses of "good" may relevantly be defined in terms of interest, is there some *other* sense which is *not* relevantly so defined? We must give this question careful attention. For it is quite possible that when philosophers (and many others) have found the question "Is X good?" so difficult, they have been grasping for this *other* sense of "good," and not any sense relevantly defined in terms of interest. If we insist on defining "good" in terms of interest, and answer the question when thus interpreted, we may be begging *their* question entirely. Of course this *other* sense of "good" may not exist, or it may be a complete confusion, but that is what we must discover.

Now many have maintained that interest theories are *far* from being completely relevant. They have argued that such theories neglect the very sense of "good" which is most vital. And certainly, their arguments are not without plausibility.

Only . . . what *is* this "vital" sense of "good"? The answers have been so vague, and so beset with difficulties, that one can scarcely determine.

There are certain requirements, however, with which this "vital" sense has been expected to comply — requirements which appeal strongly to our common sense. It will be helpful to summarize these, showing how they exclude the interest theories:

In the first place, we must be able sensibly to *disagree* about whether something is "good." This condition rules out Hobbes's definition. For consider the following argument: "This is good." "That isn't so; it's not good." As translated by Hobbes, this becomes: "I desire this." "That isn't so, for *I* don't." The speakers are not contradicting one another, and think they are, only because of an elementary confusion in the use of pronouns. The definition, "good" means *desired by my community,* is also excluded, for how could people from different communities disagree?[1]

In the second place, "goodness" must have, so to speak, a magnetism. A person who recognizes X to be "good" must *ipso facto* acquire a stronger tendency to act in its favour than he otherwise would have had. This rules out the Humian type of definition. For according to Hume, to recognize that something is "good" is simply to recognize that the majority approve of it. Clearly, a man may see that the majority approve of X without having, himself, a stronger tendency to favour it. This requirement excludes any attempt to define "good" in terms of the interest of people *other* than the speaker.[2]

In the third place, the "goodness" of anything must not be verifiable solely by use of the scientific method. "Ethics must not be psychology." This restriction rules out all of the traditional interest theories, without exception. It is so sweeping a restriction that we must examine its plausibility. What are the methodological implications of interest theories which are here rejected?

According to Hobbes's definition, a person can prove his ethical judgments, with finality, by showing that he is not making an introspective error about his desires. According to Hume's definition, one may prove ethical judgments (roughly speaking) by taking a vote. *This* use of the empirical method, at any rate, seems highly remote from what we usually accept as proof, and reflects on the complete relevance of the definitions which imply it.

But aren't there more complicated interest theories which are immune from such methodological implications? No, for the same factors appear; they are only put off for a while. Consider, for example, the definition: "X is good" means *most people would approve of X if they knew its nature and consequences.* How, according to this definition, could we prove that a certain X was good? We should first have to find out, empirically, just what X was like, and what its consequences would be. To this extent the empirical method, as required by the definition, seems beyond intelligent objection. But what remains? We should next have to discover whether most people would approve of the sort of thing we had discovered X to be. This couldn't be determined by popular vote — but only because it would be too difficult to explain to the voters, beforehand, what the nature and consequences of X really were. Apart from this, voting would be a pertinent method. We are again reduced to counting noses, as a *perfectly final* appeal.

Now we need not scorn voting entirely. A man who rejected interest theories as irrelevant might readily make the following statement: "If I believed that X would be approved by the majority, when they knew all about it, I should be strongly *led* to say that X was good." But he would continue: "*Need* I say that X was good, under the circumstances? Wouldn't my acceptance of the alleged 'final proof'

result simply from my being democratic? What about the more aristocratic people? They would simply say that the approval of most people, even when they knew all about the object of their approval, simply had nothing to do with the goodness of anything, and they would probably add a few remarks about the low state of people's interests." It would indeed seem, from these considerations, that the definition we have been considering has presupposed democratic ideals from the start; it has dressed up democratic propaganda in the guise of a definition.

The omnipotence of the empirical method, as implied by interest theories and others, may be shown unacceptable in a somewhat different way. Mr. G. E. Moore's familiar objection about the open question is chiefly pertinent in this regard. No matter what set of scientifically knowable properties a thing may have (says Moore, in effect), you will find, on careful introspection, that it is an open question to ask whether anything having these properties is *good*. It is difficult to believe that this recurrent question is a totally confused one, or that it seems open only because of the ambiguity of "good." Rather, we must be using some sense of "good" which is not definable, relevantly, in terms of anything scientifically knowable. That is, the scientific method is not sufficient for ethics.[3]

These, then, are the requirements with which the "vital" sense of "good" is expected to comply: (1) goodness must be a topic for intelligent disagreement; (2) it must be "magnetic"; and (3) it must not be discoverable solely through the scientific method.

II

I can now turn to my proposed analysis of ethical judgments. First let me present my position dogmatically, showing to what extent I vary from tradition.

I believe that the three requirements, given above, are perfectly sensible; that there is some *one* sense of "good" which satisfies all three requirements; and that no traditional interest theory satisfies them all. But this does not imply that "good" must be explained in terms of a Platonic Idea, or of a categorical imperative, or of an unique, unanalyzable property. On the contrary, the three requirements can be met by a *kind* of interest theory. *But we must give up a presupposition which all the traditional interest theories have made.*

Traditional interest theories hold that ethical statements are *descriptive* of the existing state of interests — that they simply *give information* about interests. (More accurately, ethical judgments are said to describe what the state of interests is, was, or will be, or to indicate what the state of interests *would* be under specified circumstances.) It is this emphasis on description, on information, which leads to their incomplete relevance. Doubtless there is always *some* element of description in ethical judgments, but this is by no means all. Their major use is not to indicate facts, but to *create an influence*. Instead of merely describing people's interests, they *change* or *intensify* them. They *recommend* an interest in an object, rather than state that the interest already exists.

For instance: When you tell a man that he oughtn't to steal, your object isn't merely to let him know that people disapprove of stealing. You are attempting, rather, to get *him* to disapprove of it. Your ethical judgment has a quasi-imperative force which, operating through suggestion, and intensified by your tone of voice, readily permits you to begin to *influence*, to *modify*, his interests. If in the end you do not succeed in getting *him* to disapprove of stealing, you will feel that you've failed to convince him that stealing is wrong. You will continue to feel this, even though he fully acknowledges that you disapprove of it, and that almost everyone else does. When you point out to him the consequences of his actions — consequences which you suspect he already disapproves of — these *reasons* which support your ethical judgment are simply a means of facilitating your influence. If you think you can change his interests by making vivid to him how others will disapprove of him, you will do so; otherwise not. So the consideration about other people's interest is just an additional means you may employ, in order to move him, and is not a part of the ethical judgment itself. Your ethical judgment doesn't merely describe interests to him, it directs his very interests. The difference between the traditional interest theories and my view is like the difference between describing a desert and irrigating it.

Another example: A munition maker declares that war is a good thing. If he merely meant that he approved of it, he would not have to insist so strongly, nor grow so excited in his argument. People would be quite easily convinced that he approved of it. If he merely meant that most people approved of war, or that most people would approve of it if they knew the consequences, he would have to yield his point if it were proved that this wasn't so. But he wouldn't do this, nor does consistency require it. He is not *describing* the state of people's approval; he is trying to *change* it by his influence. If he found that few people approved of war, he might insist all the more strongly that it was good, for there would be more changing to be done.

This example illustrates how "good" may be used for what most of us would call bad purposes. Such cases are as pertinent as any others. I am not indicating the *good* way of using "good." I am not influencing people, but am describing the way this influence sometimes goes on. If the reader wishes to say that the munition maker's influence is bad — that is, if the reader wishes to awaken people's disapproval of the man, and to make him disapprove of his own actions — I should at another time be willing to join in this undertaking. But this is not the present concern. I am not using ethical terms, but am indicating how they *are* used. The munition maker, in his use of "good," illustrates the persuasive character of the word just as well as does the unselfish man who, eager to encourage in each of us a desire for the happiness of all, contends that the supreme good is peace.

Thus ethical terms are *instruments* used in the complicated interplay and readjustment of human interests. This can be seen plainly from more general observations. People from widely separated communities have different moral attitudes. Why? To a great extent because they have been subject to different social influences. Now clearly this influence doesn't operate through sticks and stones alone; words play a great part. People praise one another, to encourage certain inclinations, and blame one another, to discourage others. Those of forceful personalities issue commands which weaker people, for complicated instinctive reasons, find it difficult to disobey, quite apart from fears of consequences. Further influence is brought to bear by writers and orators. Thus social influence is exerted, to an enormous extent, by means that have nothing to do with physical force or material reward. The ethical terms facilitate such influence. Being suited for use in *suggestion*, they are a means by which men's attitudes may be led this way or that. The reason, then, that we find a greater similarity in the moral attitudes of one community than in those of different communities is largely this: ethical judgments propagate themselves. One man says "This is good"; this may influence the approval of another person, who then makes the same ethical judgment, which in turn influences another person, and so on. In the end, by a process of mutual influence, people take up more or less the same attitudes. Between people of widely separated communities, of course, the influence is less strong; hence different communities have different attitudes.

These remarks will serve to give a general idea of my point of view. We must now go into more detail. There are several questions which must be answered: How does an ethical sentence acquire its power of influencing people—why is it suited to suggestion? Again, what has this influence to do with the *meaning* of ethical terms? And finally, do these considerations really lead us to a sense of "good" which meets the requirements mentioned in the preceding section?

Let us deal first with the question about *meaning*. This is far from an easy question, so we must enter into a preliminary inquiry about meaning in general. Although a seeming digression, this will prove indispensable.

III

Broadly speaking, there are two different *purposes* which lead us to use language. On the one hand we use words (as in science) to record, clarify, and communicate *beliefs*. On the other hand we use words to give vent to our feeling (interjections), or to create moods (poetry), or to incite people to actions or attitudes (oratory).

The first use of words I shall call "descriptive"; the second, "dynamic." Note that the distinction depends solely upon the *purpose* of the *speaker*.

When a person says "Hydrogen is the lightest known gas," his purpose *may* be simply to lead the hearer to believe this, or to believe that the speaker believes it. In that case the words are used descriptively. When a person cuts himself and says "Damn," his purpose is not ordinarily to record, clarify, or communicate any belief. The word is used dynam-

ically. The two ways of using words, however, are by no means mutually exclusive. This is obvious from the fact that our purposes are often complex. Thus when one says "I want you to close the door," part of his purpose, ordinarily, is to lead the hearer to believe that he has this want. To that extent the words are used descriptively. But the major part of one's purpose is to lead the hearer to *satisfy* the want. To that extent the words are used dynamically.

It very frequently happens that the same sentence may have a dynamic use on one occasion, and may not have a dynamic use on another; and that it may have different dynamic uses on different occasions. For instance: A man says to a visiting neighbor, "I am loaded down with work." His purpose may be to let the neighbor know how life is going with him. This would *not* be a dynamic use of words. He may make the remark, however, in order to drop a hint. This *would* be dynamic usage (as well as descriptive). Again, he may make the remark to arouse the neighbor's sympathy. This would be a *different* dynamic usage from that of hinting.

Or again, when we say to a man, "Of course you won't make those mistakes any more," we *may* simply be making a prediction. But we are more likely to be using "suggestion," in order to encourage him and hence *keep* him from making mistakes. The first use would be descriptive; the second, mainly dynamic.

From these examples it will be clear that we can't determine whether words are used dynamically or not, merely by reading the dictionary—even assuming that everyone is faithful to dictionary meanings. Indeed, to know whether a person is using a word dynamically we must note his tone of voice, his gestures, the general circumstances under which he is speaking, and so on.

We must now proceed to an important question: What has the dynamic use of words to do with their *meaning*? One thing is clear—we must not define "meaning" in a way that would make meaning vary with dynamic usage. If we did, we should have no use for the term. All that we could say about such "meaning" would be that it is very complicated and subject to constant change. So we must certainly distinguish between the dynamic use of words and their meaning.

It does not follow, however, that we must define "meaning" in some nonpsychological fashion. We must simply restrict the psychological field. Instead of identifying meaning with *all* the psychological causes and effects that attend a word's utterance, we must identify it with those that it has a *tendency* (causal property, dispositional property) to be connected with. The tendency must be of a particular kind, moreover. It must exist for all who speak the language; it must be persistent and must be realizable more or less independently of determinate circumstances attending the word's utterance. There will be further restrictions dealing with the interrelations of words in different contexts. Moreover, we must include, under the psychological responses which the words tend to produce, not only immediately introspectable experiences but *dispositions* to react in a given way with appropriate stimuli. I hope to go into these matters in a subsequent essay. Suffice it now to say that I think "meaning" may be thus defined in a way to include "propositional" meaning as an important kind.

The definition will readily permit a distinction between meaning and dynamic use. For when words are accompanied by dynamic purposes, it does not follow that they *tend* to be accompanied by them in the way mentioned above. E.g. there need be no tendency realizable more or less independently of the determinate circumstances under which the words are uttered.

There will be a kind of meaning, however, in the sense above defined, which has an intimate relation to dynamic usage. I refer to "emotive" meaning (in a sense roughly like that employed by Ogden and Richards). The emotive meaning of a word is a tendency of a word, arising through the history of its usage, to produce (result from) *affective* responses in people. It is the immediate aura of feeling which hovers about a word. Such tendencies to produce affective responses cling to words very tenaciously. It would be difficult, for instance, to express merriment by using the interjection "alas." Because of the persistence of such affective tendencies (among other reasons) it becomes feasible to classify them as "meanings."

Just *what* is the relation between emotive meaning and the dynamic use of words? Let us take an example. Suppose that a man tells his hostess, at the end of a party, that he thoroughly enjoyed himself, and suppose that he was in fact bored. If we consider his remark an innocent one, are we likely to remind him, later, that he "lied" to his hostess? Obviously not, or at least, not without a broad smile;

for although he told her something that he believed to be false, and with the intent of making her believe that it was true — those being the ordinary earmarks of a lie — the expression, "you lied to her," would be emotively too strong for our purposes. It would seem to be a reproach, even if we intended it not to be a reproach. So it will be evident that such words as "lied" (and many parallel examples could be cited) become suited, on account of their emotive meaning, to a certain kind of dynamic use — so well suited, in fact, that the hearer is likely to be misled when we use them in any other way. The more pronounced a word's emotive meaning is, the less likely people are to use it purely descriptively. Some words are suited to encourage people, some to discourage them, some to quiet them, and so on.

Even in these cases, of course, the dynamic purposes are not to be identified with any sort of meaning; for the emotive meaning accompanies a word much more persistently than do the dynamic purposes. But there is an important contingent relation between emotive meaning and dynamic purpose: the former assists the latter. Hence if we define emotively laden terms in a way that neglects their emotive meaning, we become seriously confused. *We lead people to think that the terms defined are used dynamically less often than they are.*

IV

Let us now apply these remarks in defining "good." This word may be used morally or nonmorally. I shall deal with the nonmoral usage almost entirely, but only because it is simpler. The main points of the analysis will apply equally well to either usage.

As a preliminary definition let us take an inaccurate approximation. It may be more misleading than helpful but will do to begin with. Roughly, then, the sentence "X is good" means *we like* X. ("We" includes the hearer or hearers.)

At first glance this definition sounds absurd. If used, we should expect to find the following sort of conversation: A. "This is good." B. "But I *don't* like it. What led you to believe that I did?" The unnaturalness of B's reply, judged by ordinary word usage, would seem to cast doubt on the relevance of my definition.

B's unnaturalness, however, lies simply in this: he is assuming that "we like it" (as would occur implicitly in the use of "good") is being used descriptively. This will not do. When "we like it" is to take the place of "this is good," the former sentence must be used not purely descriptively, but dynamically. More specifically, it must be used to promote a very subtle (and for the nonmoral sense in question, a very easily resisted) kind of *suggestion*. To the extent that "we" refers to the hearer it must have the dynamic use, essential to suggestion, of leading the hearer to *make* true what is said, rather than merely to believe it. And to the extent that "we" refers to the speaker, the sentence must have not only the descriptive use of indicating belief about the speaker's interest, but the quasi-interjectory, dynamic function of giving direct expression to the interest. (This immediate expression of feelings assists in the process of suggestion. It is difficult to disapprove in the face of another's enthusiasm.)

For an example of a case where "we like this" is used in the dynamic way that "this is good" is used, consider the case of a mother who says to her several children, "one thing is certain, *we all like to be neat.*" If she really believed this, she would not bother to say so. But she is not using the words descriptively. She is *encouraging* the children to like neatness. By telling them that they like neatness, she will lead them to *make* her statement true, so to speak. If, instead of saying "we all like to be neat" in this way, she had said "it's a good thing to be neat," the effect would have been approximately the same.

But these remarks are still misleading. Even when "we like it" is used for suggestion, it is not quite like "this is good." The latter is more subtle. With such a sentence as "this is a good book," for example, it would be practically impossible to use instead "we like this book." When the latter is used it must be accompanied by so exaggerated an intonation, to prevent its becoming confused with a descriptive statement, that the force of suggestion becomes stronger and ludicrously more overt than when "good" is used.

The definition is inadequate, further, in that the definiens has been restricted to dynamic usage. Having said that dynamic usage was different from meaning, I should not have to mention it in giving the *meaning* of "good."

It is in connection with this last point that we must return to emotive meaning. The word "good" has a laudatory emotive meaning that fits it for the dynamic use of suggesting favorable interest. But the sentence "we like it" has no such emotive meaning. Hence my definition has neglected emotive meaning entirely. Now to neglect emotive meaning serves to foster serious confusions, as I have previously intimated; so I have sought to make up for the inadequacy of the definition by letting the restriction about dynamic usage take the place of emotive meaning. What I should do, of course, is to find a definiens whose emotive meaning, like that of "good," simply does *lead* to dynamic usage.

Why did I not do this? I answer that it is not possible if the definition is to afford us increased clarity. No two words, in the first place, have quite the same emotive meaning. The most we can hope for is a rough approximation. But if we seek for such an approximation for "good," we shall find nothing more than synonyms, such as "desirable" or "valuable"; and these are profitless because they do not clear up the connection between "good" and favorable interest. If we reject such synonyms, in favor of nonethical terms, we shall be highly misleading. For instance "this is good" has something like the meaning of "I *do* like this; do so as well." But this is certainly not accurate. For the imperative makes an appeal to the conscious efforts of the hearer. Of course he cannot like something just by trying. He must be led to like it through suggestion. Hence an ethical sentence differs from an imperative in that it enables one to make changes in a much more subtle, less fully conscious way. Note that the ethical sentence centers the hearer's attention not on his interests but on the object of interest, and thereby facilitates suggestion. Because of its subtlety, moreover, an ethical sentence readily permits counter-suggestion and leads to the give and take situation that is so characteristic of arguments about values.

Strictly speaking, then, it is impossible to define "good" in terms of favorable interest if emotive meaning is not to be distorted. Yet it is possible to say that "this is good" is *about* the favorable interest of the speaker and the hearer or hearers, and that it has a laudatory emotive meaning which fits the words for use in suggestion. This is a rough description of meaning, not a definition. But it serves the same clarifying function that a definition ordinarily does, and that, after all, is enough.

A word must be added about the moral use of "good." This differs from the above in that it is about a different kind of interest. Instead of being about what the hearer and speaker *like,* it is about a stronger sort of approval. When a person *likes* something, he is pleased when it prospers and disappointed when it does not. When a person *morally approves* of something he experiences a rich feeling of security when it prospers and is indignant or "shocked" when it does not. These are rough and inaccurate examples of the many factors which one would have to mention in distinguishing the two kinds of interest. In the moral usage, as well as in the nonmoral, "good" has an emotive meaning which adapts it to suggestion.

And now, are these considerations of any importance? Why do I stress emotive meanings in this fashion? Does the omission of them really lead people into errors? I think, indeed, that the errors resulting from such omissions are enormous. In order to see this, however, we must return to the restrictions, mentioned in Section I, with which the typical sense of "good" has been expected to comply.

V

The first restriction, it will be remembered, had to do with disagreement. Now there is clearly some sense in which people disagree on ethical points, but we must not rashly assume that all disagreement is modeled after the sort that occurs in the natural sciences. We must distinguish between "disagreement in belief" (typical of the sciences) and "disagreement in interest." Disagreement in belief occurs when A believes *p* and B disbelieves it. Disagreement in interest occurs when A has a favorable interest in X and when B has an unfavorable one in it. (For a full-bodied disagreement, neither party is content with the discrepancy.)

Let me give an example of disagreement in interest. A. "Let's go to a cinema tonight." B. "I don't want to do that. Let's go to the symphony." A continues to insist on the cinema, B on the symphony. This is disagreement in a perfectly conventional sense. They cannot agree on where they want to go, and each is trying to redirect the other's interest. (Note that imperatives are used in the example.)

It is a disagreement in *interest* which takes place in ethics. When C says "this is good," and D says

"no, it's bad," we have a case of suggestion and counter-suggestion. Each man is trying to redirect the other's interest. There obviously need be no domineering, since each may be willing to give ear to the other's influence; but each is trying to move the other none the less. It is in this sense that they disagree. Those who argue that certain interest theories make no provision for disagreement have been misled, I believe, simply because the traditional theories, in leaving out emotive meaning, give the impression that ethical judgments are used descriptively only; and of course when judgments are used purely descriptively, the only disagreement that can arise is disagreement *in belief.* Such disagreement may be disagreement in belief *about* interests, but this is not the same as disagreement *in* interest. My definition does not provide for disagreement in belief about interests any more than does Hobbes's; but that is no matter, for there is no reason to believe, at least on common sense grounds, that this kind of disagreement exists. There is only disagreement *in* interest. (We shall see in a moment that disagreement in interest does not remove ethics from sober argument — that this kind of disagreement may often be resolved through empirical means.)

The second restriction, about "magnetism," or the connection between goodness and actions, requires only a word. This rules out only those interest theories that do *not* include the interest of the speaker in defining "good." My account does include the speaker's interest, hence is immune.

The third restriction, about the empirical method, may be met in a way that springs naturally from the above account of disagreement. Let us put the question in this way: When two people disagree over an ethical matter, can they completely resolve the disagreement through empirical considerations, assuming that each applies the empirical method exhaustively, consistently, and without error?

I answer that sometimes they can and sometimes they cannot, and that at any rate, even when they can, the relation between empirical knowledge and ethical judgments is quite different from the one that traditional interest theories seem to imply.

This can best be seen from an analogy. Let us return to the example where A and B could not agree on a cinema or a symphony. The example differed from an ethical argument in that imperatives were used, rather than ethical judgments, but was analogous to the extent that each person was endeavoring to modify the other's interest. Now how would these people argue the case, assuming that they were too intelligent just to shout at one another?

Clearly, they would give "reasons" to support their imperatives. A might say, "but you know, Garbo is at the Bijou." His hope is that B, who admires Garbo, will acquire a desire to go to the cinema when he knows what film will be there. B may counter, "but Toscanini is guest conductor tonight, in an all-Beethoven program." And so on. Each supports his imperative ("*let's* do so and so") by reasons which may be empirically established.

To generalize from this: disagreement in interest may be rooted in disagreement in belief. That is to say, people who disagree in interest would often cease to do so if they knew the precise nature and consequences of the object of their interest. To this extent disagreement in interest may be resolved by securing agreement in belief, which in turn may be secured empirically.

This generalization holds for ethics. If A and B, instead of using imperatives, had said, respectively, "it would be *better* to go to the cinema," and "it would be *better* to go to the symphony," the reasons which they would advance would be roughly the same. They would each give a more thorough account of the object of interest, with the purpose of completing the redirection of interest which was begun by the suggestive force of the ethical sentence. On the whole, of course, the suggestive force of the ethical statement merely exerts enough pressure to start such trains of reasons, since the reasons are much more essential in resolving disagreement in interest than the persuasive effect of the ethical judgment itself.

Thus the empirical method is relevant to ethics simply because our knowledge of the world is a determining factor to our interests. But note that empirical facts are not inductive grounds from which the ethical judgment problematically follows. (This is what traditional interest theories imply.) If someone said "close the door," and added the reason "we'll catch cold," the latter would scarcely be called an inductive ground of the former. Now imperatives are related to the reasons which support them in the same way that ethical judgments are related to reasons.

Is the empirical method *sufficient* for attaining ethical agreement? Clearly not. For empirical knowledge resolves disagreement in interest only to the extent that such disagreement is rooted in disagreement in belief. Not all disagreement in interest is of this sort. For instance: A is of a sympathetic nature and B is not. They are arguing about whether a public dole would be good. Suppose that they discovered all the consequences of the dole. Is it not possible, even so, that A will say that it is good and B that it is bad? The disagreement in interest may arise not from limited factual knowledge but simply from A's sympathy and B's coldness. Or again, suppose in the above argument that A was poor and unemployed and that B was rich. Here again the disagreement might not be due to different factual knowledge. It would be due to the different social positions of the men, together with their predominant self-interest.

When ethical disagreement is not rooted in disagreement in belief, is there *any* method by which it may be settled? If one means by "method" a *rational* method, then there is no method. But in any case there is a "way." Let us consider the above example again, where disagreement was due to A's sympathy and B's coldness. Must they end by saying, "well, it's just a matter of our having different temperaments"? Not necessarily. A, for instance, may try to *change* the temperament of his opponent. He may pour out his enthusiasms in such a moving way—present the sufferings of the poor with such appeal—that he will lead his opponent to see life through different eyes. He may build up by the contagion of his feelings an influence which will modify B's temperament and create in him a sympathy for the poor which did not previously exist. This is often the only way to obtain ethical agreement, if there is any way at all. It is persuasive, not empirical or rational; but that is no reason for neglecting it. There is no reason to scorn it, either, for it is only by such means that our personalities are able to grow, through our contact with others.

The point I wish to stress, however, is simply that the empirical method is instrumental to the ethical agreement only to the extent that disagreement in interest is rooted in disagreement in belief. There is little reason to believe that all disagreement is of this sort. Hence the empirical method is not sufficient for ethics. In any case, ethics is not psychology, since psychology does not endeavor to *direct* our interests; it discovers facts about the ways in which interests are or can be directed, but that is quite another matter.

To summarize this section: my analysis of ethical judgments meets the three requirements for the typical sense of "good" that were mentioned in Section I. The traditional interest theories fail to meet these requirements simply because they neglect emotive meaning. This neglect leads them to neglect dynamic usage, and the sort of disagreement that results from such usage, together with the method of resolving the disagreement. I may add that my analysis answers Moore's objection about the open question. Whatever scientifically knowable properties a thing may have, it *is* always open to question whether a thing having these (enumerated) qualities is good. For to ask whether it is good is to ask for *influence*. And whatever I may know about an object, I can still ask, quite pertinently, to be influenced with regard to my interest in it.

VI

And now, have I really pointed out the "typical" sense of "good"?

I suppose that many will still say "no," claiming that I have simply failed to set down *enough* requirements that this sense must meet, and that my analysis, like all others given in terms of interest, is a way of begging the issue. They will say: "When we ask 'is X good?' we don't want mere influence, mere advice. We decidedly don't want to be influenced through persuasion, nor are we fully content when the influence is supported by a wide scientific knowledge of X. The answer to our question will, of course, modify our interests. But this is only because a unique sort of truth will be revealed to us — a truth that must be apprehended a priori. We want our interests to be guided by this truth and by nothing else. To substitute for this special truth mere emotive meaning and mere factual truth is to conceal from us the very object of our search."

I can only answer that I do not understand. What is this truth to be *about*? For I recollect no Platonic Idea, nor do I know what to *try* to recollect. I find no indefinable property nor do I know what to look for. And the "self-evident" deliverances of reason, which so many philosophers have mentioned, seem on examination to be deliverances of their respective reasons only (if of anyone's) and not of mine.

I strongly suspect, indeed, that any sense of "good" which is expected both to unite itself in synthetic a priori fashion with other concepts and to influence interest as well, is really a great confusion. I extract from this meaning the power of influence alone, which I find the only intelligible part. If the rest is confusion, however, then it certainly deserves more than the shrug of one's shoulders. What I should like to do is to *account* for the confusion — to examine the psychological needs which have given rise to it and show how these needs may be satisfied in another way. This is *the* problem, if confusion is to be stopped at its source. But it is an enormous problem and my reflections on it, which are at present worked out only roughly, must be reserved until some later time.

I may add that if "X is good" has the meaning that I ascribe to it, then it is not a judgment that professional philosophers and only professional philosophers are qualified to make. To the extent that ethics predicates the ethical terms of anything, rather than explains their meaning, it becomes more than a purely intellectual study. Ethical judgments are social instruments. They are used in a cooperative enterprise that leads to a mutual readjustment of human interests. Philosophers have a part in this; but so too do all men.

Endnotes

[1] See G. E. Moore's *Philosophical Studies*, pp. 332–334.

[2] See G. C. Field's *Moral Theory*, pp. 52, 56–57.

[3] See G. E. Moore's *Principia Ethica*, Chap. i. I am simply trying to preserve the spirit of Moore's objection, and not the exact form of it.

VIII.5 Prescriptivism: The Structure of Ethics and Morals

R. M. HARE

Richard M. Hare (1919–   ) is professor of philosophy at the University of Florida and until recently was White's Professor of Moral Philosophy at Oxford University. His two most significant works in ethics are *The Language of Morals* and *Freedom and Reason*.

Two features of Hare's moral theory stand out: his notion of universalizability and his notion of prescriptivism. Hare accepts Moore's naturalistic fallacy argument, along with the emotivists' radical separation of facts from values. Whereas he agrees with the emotivists that we cannot ascribe truth or falsity to moral statements and that moral judgments are attitudinal, he changes the emphasis regarding moral terms from feelings of approval (or disapproval) to certain types of judgment that include a universalizability feature and a prescriptive element. To say that "You ought not steal from your boss" entails, via the principle of universalizability (or consistency), that the speaker believes that no one should steal in relevantly similar circumstances. Furthermore, for you to say that I should not steal is for you to commit yourself to a principle of forbidding stealing, and it is from that commitment that you are *prescribing* that others live that way also. Ethical language means that you are not only prescribing it universally but also willing to commit yourself to that prescription as a necessary and sufficient condition for the justification of that principle.

I start by saying what I think is the object of the enterprise called moral philosophy. It is to find a way of thinking better—that is, more rationally— about moral questions. The first step towards this is, *Understand the questions you are asking.* That might seem obvious; but hardly anybody tries to do it. We have to understand what we mean by expressions like 'I ought.' And to understand the meaning of a word like this involves understanding its logical properties, or in other words what it implies or what saying it commits us to. Then, if we find that we cannot accept what it commits us to, we shall have to give up saying it. And that is what moral argument essentially is. Ethics, the study of moral argument, is thus a branch of logic. This is one of the levels of thinking that are the concern of the

moral philosopher. The others are about more substantial questions; but this first one, the logical or, as it is sometimes called, metaethical level is the foundation of the others.

Since the kind of ethics we are doing is a kind of logic, it has to use the methods of logic. But what are these? How do we find out what follows from what, what implies what, or what saying, for example, 'I ought to join the Army' or 'I ought to join the Revolution' commits me to? That is partly a general question about logical method, into which I shall not have room to go at all deeply. I can only declare what side I am on as regards some crucial questions. First, I think it is useful and indeed essential, and I hope it will not be thought pedantic, to distinguish between two kinds of questions. I am going to call the first kind *formal* questions, and the second kind *substantial* questions. Formal questions are questions that can be answered solely by appeal to the form—that is, the purely logical properties—of proposed answers to them. That is the sort of question we are concerned with in metaethics. In this part of our work we are not allowed to bring in any substantial assumptions.

I will illustrate the distinction by an example which has nothing to do with ethics, because it is a clearer example and does not beg any ethical questions. It comes from a well-known paper by Professors Strawson and Grice (1956) refuting (in my view successfully) a claim made in an even better-known paper by Professor Quine (1951; some of Quine's claims may be all right, but it is pretty clear that Strawson an Grice have refuted this one). Suppose I say 'My three-year-old child understands Russell's Theory of Types.' Everyone will be sure that what I have said is false. But logically it could be true. On the other hand, suppose I say 'My three-year-old child is an adult.' We know that I cannot consistently say this, if we know what the words mean and nothing else; and this is obviously not the case with the first proposition.

This illustrates the distinction between what I am calling formal questions and what I am calling substantial questions. It applies equally to moral questions, which can also be divided into these two kinds. Suppose I say "There is nothing wrong with flogging people for fun.' People's reasons for disagreeing with me (and I will come later to what these reasons might be) are of a quite different sort from what they would be if I had said 'There is nothing wrong in doing what one ought not to do.' We know that I cannot consistently say the latter if we just know the meanings of the words 'ought' and 'wrong'; whereas I could *consistently* utter the first proposition; we all think it is a dreadful thing to say — only a very wicked person would say it — but in saying it he would not be being *logically* inconsistent.

It is not necessary here to discuss Quine's rejection of the notion of analyticity and of that of synonymy. Strawson and Grice may be right in defending these notions; but even if they are not, the formal claims that I need to make about moral concepts do not have to be stated in terms of them, but only in terms of the notion of logical truth, which Quine in that paper accepts. This is because the moral concepts are formal in an even stricter sense than I have so far claimed. That is, they require for their explanation no material semantic stipulations but only reference to their purely logical properties.

The semantic properties of moral words have to do with their particular descriptive meanings only, which are not part of their meaning in the narrow sense and do not affect their logic, though the fact that they have to have some descriptive meaning does affect it. . . .

It will be noticed that the example I have just given of a moral statement which we should all reject on logical grounds, 'There is nothing wrong in doing what we ought not to do,' is one whose contradictory ('There is something wrong in doing what we ought not to do') is a logical truth. This is because 'ought' and 'wrong' are interdefinable in terms purely of their logical properties without bringing in their descriptive meanings or semantics, just as are 'all' and 'some' in most systems of quantificational logic.

Next, I must mention a point which will turn out to be of fundamental importance for moral argument. When we are settling questions of the second kind in each case (that is, formal questions) we are not allowed to appeal to any other kind of consideration except those which can be established on the basis of our understanding of the words or concepts used. To take our two examples: we know that we cannot say 'There is nothing wrong in doing what one ought not to do' because we know what 'wrong' and 'ought' mean; and we know that we cannot say 'My three-year-old child is an adult' because we know what 'child' and 'adult' mean. If, in order to establish that we could not say these things, we had to appeal to any other considerations than these, the questions of whether we could say them would not be formal questions.

In general, we establish theses in logic (or in the kind of logic I am speaking of, which includes the kind we use in ethics) by appeal to our understanding of the uses of words, and nothing else. It is because this logic is the foundation of moral argument that it is so important to understand the words. We must notice that this is a feature of the method I am advocating which distinguishes it quite radically from almost all the ethical theories which we find being proposed at the present time. All these theories appeal at some point or other, and often very frequently, to the substantial moral convictions which their proponents have, and which they hope their readers will share. Although I recognize that many people do not believe in the distinction that I have been making between formal and substantial moral questions, and therefore feel at liberty to use what I would call substantial convictions of theirs to support their theories, I still think that my way of proceeding provides a firmer basis for ethics.

Let me give very briefly my reasons for this confidence. If we are arguing about some moral question (for example about the question 'Ought I to join the Army?' or 'Ought I to join the Revolution?'), one of the things we have to get clear about at the beginning is what the *question* is. That is to say, if we are not to talk at cross purposes, we have to be meaning the same things by the words in which we are asking our question. But if we *are* meaning the same by the words, we have a solid basis of agreement (albeit formal and not substantial agreement) on which we can found our future arguments. If the distinction between formal and substantial holds, then we can have this formal agreement in spite of our substantial disagreement. We can then, as I hope to show, use the formal agreement to test the arguments either of us uses to support his views. We can ask, 'Can he consistently *say* this?' or 'Can he consistently say *this,* if he also says *that?*'

On the other hand, if people import their own substantial convictions into the very foundations of their moral arguments, they will not be able to argue cogently against anybody who does not share those convictions. This is what the philosophers called *intuitionists* do; and I say with some confidence that my own position is much stronger than theirs, because I do not rely on anything except what everybody has to agree to who is asking the same questions as I am trying to answer. That was why I said that before an argument begins we have to agree on the meaning we attach to our questions. That is *all* I require to start off with.

So much, then, for the question of ethical method. I could say, and in order to plug all the holes would have to say, a great deal more about it, and have done this elsewhere . . . ; but now I wish to go on, and say what I hope to establish by this method and how it helps with real substantial questions. At the formal or metaethical level I need to establish just two theses; and for the sake of simplicity I shall formulate them as theses about the word 'ought' and its logic. I could have spoken instead about other words, such as 'right' and 'good.' But I prefer to talk about 'ought,' because it is the simplest word that we use in our moral questionings.

Here, then, are two logical features of the word 'ought,' as it occurs in the questions 'Ought I to join the Army?' and 'Ought I to join the Revolution?' They are parts of what I commit myself to if I say 'Yes, I ought.' The first is sometimes called the *prescriptivity* of moral judgements. If I say 'Yes, I ought to join the Army,' and mean it sincerely, and in its full sense — if I really think I ought — I shall join the Army. Of course there are plenty of less than full-blooded senses of 'ought,' or of 'think that I ought,' in which I could say 'I think that I ought, but I'm not going to,' or 'I ought, but so what?' But anyone who has been in this situation (as I have — it was one of the things that made me take up philosophy) will know that the whole point of asking 'Ought I?' is to help us decide the question 'Shall I?', and the answer to the first question, when asked in this sense, implies an answer to the second question. If it did not, what would have been the point of asking it?

The second feature of the word 'ought' that I shall be relying on is usually called *universalizability.* When I say that I ought, I commit myself to more than that *I* ought. Prescriptivity demands that the man who says 'I ought' should himself act accordingly, if the judgement applies to him and if he can so act. Universalizability means that, by saying 'I ought,' he commits himself to agreeing that *anybody* ought who is in just those circumstances. If I say 'I ought, but there is someone else in exactly the same circumstances, doing it to someone who is just like the person I should be doing it to, but he ought not to do it,' then logical eyebrows will be raised; it is *logically inconsistent* to say, of two exactly similar people in exactly similar situations, that the first ought to do something and the second ought not. I must explain that the similarity of the situations extends to the personal characteristics, and in particular to the likes and dislikes, of the people in them. If, for example, the person I was flogging actually liked being flogged (some people do) that would mean that the situation was not exactly similar to the normal case, and the difference might be relevant.

So, putting together these two features of prescriptivity and universalizability, we see that if I say 'I ought to do it to him,' I commit myself to say, not just that I should do it to him (and accordingly doing it), but that he should do it to me were our roles precisely reversed. That is, as we shall see, how moral argument gets its grip. I must repeat that it is not an essential part of my argument that *all* uses of 'ought' have these features. All I am maintaining now is that we do sometimes, when asking 'Ought I?', use the word in this way. I am addressing myself to those who are asking such questions, as I am sure many people do. If anybody wished to ask *different* questions, he might have to use a different logic. But I am quite sure that we do sometimes find ourselves asking, and disagreeing about, universal prescriptive questions—that is, about what to prescribe universally for all situations of a given kind, no matter who is the agent or the victim. I shall be content if I can show how we can validly argue about such questions, whose logical character is determined by their being *those* questions, i.e. universal prescriptive ones.

I might add that the whole point of having a moral language with these features—a language whose meaning is determined by its logical characteristics alone, and which can therefore be used in discussion by two people who have very different substantial moral convictions, is that then the words will mean the same to both of them, and they will be bound by the same logical rules in their argument. If their different moral convictions had somehow got written into the very meanings of their moral words (as does happen with *some* moral words, and as some philosophers mistakenly think happens with all of them . . .) then they would be at cross purposes from the start; their moral argument would very quickly break down, and they would just have to fight it out. It is because of this formal character of my theory about the moral words that I think it more helpful than the theories of other philosophers who try to write their own moral convictions into the meanings of the words or the rules of argument. This is especially true when we come to deal with the kinds of moral problems about which people have radically different convictions. If the convictions have infected the words, they will not be able to communicate rationally with one another. That is indeed what we see happening all over the world (think of South Africa, for example, where I gave an earlier version of this paper). In this situation the theories I am criticizing are of no help at all, because people will appeal to their opposing convictions, and serious, fruitful argument cannot even begin.

The next thing that I have to make clear is the place in moral argument of appeal to *facts*. If I ask 'Ought I to join the Army?', the first thing, as I said, is to be clear about what I mean by 'ought.' But that is not enough. I have to be clear what I am asking; but another important part of this is what the words 'join the Army' imply. In other words, what should I be doing if I joined the Army? There are some philosophers who use the word 'consequentialist' as a term of abuse for their opponents. Now I readily agree that there may be a sense in which we ought to do what is right and damn the consequences. But these philosophers are really very confused if they think that in deciding what we ought to do we can ignore what we should be doing if we did one or other of the things we could do. If someone thinks he ought not to join the Army, or that it would be wrong to do it, his reason (what in his view makes it wrong), must have something to do with what he would be doing if he joined the Army. That is the act or series of acts about whose morality we are troubled. Joining the Army means, in his circumstances (if that is the sort of regime he lives in, as in South Africa), committing himself to shooting people in the streets if the Government tells him to. That is what becoming a soldier involves in his present situation. Anyone who thinks that in this sense consequences are irrelevant to moral decisions cannot have understood what morality is about: it is about actions; that is, about what we do; and that is, what we are bringing about—the difference we are making to the course of events. These are the facts we have to know.

There are some ethical theories, known generally as *naturalistic* theories, which make facts relevant to moral decisions in a very direct way. They do it by saying that what moral words *mean* is something factual. To give a very crude example: if 'wrong' *meant* 'such as would endanger the State,' then obviously it would be wrong to do anything that would endanger the State, and we ought not to do it. The trouble with such theories is the same, in effect, as with those I mentioned earlier. It makes a theory useless for the purposes of moral argument if its author writes his own moral convictions into the theory itself; and *one* of the ways of doing this is to write them into the meanings of the moral words. This makes communication and rational argument between people of different moral convictions impossible. . . . If 'wrong' did mean what has just been suggested, somebody who thought that there were some things more important morally than the preservation of the State could not use the word to argue with a supporter of the regime. One of them would just have to join the Army and the other the Revolution; they would just have to fight.

I am not saying what naturalists say, because the account I have given of the meaning of 'ought' in terms of prescriptivity and universalizability does *not* incorporate any substantial moral convictions; it is *neutral* between the two participants in such a dispute, and both of them can therefore use the words, if I am right, in discussing their disagreement. I therefore have to give, and have already partly given, a different account of how facts are relevant to moral decisions. This goes via an account of rationality itself — of the notion of a reason.

It may be helpful if we start with something simpler than moral judgements: with plain imperatives. These two sorts of speech acts must not be confused, because there are important differences; but imperatives like 'Join the Army' do illustrate in a much simpler way the point I am trying to explain. They are the simplest kind of prescriptions (moral judgements are a much more complex kind because of universalizability). To take an even simpler example: suppose I say 'Give me tea' and not 'Give me coffee.' I say this because of *something about* drinking tea or drinking coffee just then. That is my reason for saying it. If drinking tea were of a different character, I might not have said it. I want, or choose, to drink tea not coffee because I believe that that is what drinking tea would be like, i.e. because of a (supposed) fact about it. I hope that, if it is clear that, even in the case of simple imperatives like this, facts can be reasons for uttering them, it will be equally clear that moral judgements too can be uttered for reasons, even though they are not *themselves* (or not just) statements of fact, but are prescriptive. It would be irrational to ask for tea in complete disregard of what, in fact, it would be like to drink tea. . . . Note that what I have just said in no way depends on universalizability; I have deliberately taken the case of plain simple imperatives which are *not* universalizable. We shall later be making a move which depends on universalizability; but it is not necessary at this stage.

Now I wish to introduce another move, which does not depend on universalizability either, and indeed is independent of everything I have said so far. It too is a logical move, which depends on the meanings of words. It concerns the relation between *knowing* what it is to experience something, and ex-

periencing it. The relevance of this to what I have been saying so far is that, if we are to know the facts about what we should be doing if we did something, one of the things we have to know is what we, or others, would experience if we did it. For example, if we are thinking of flogging somebody for fun, it is important that what we should be doing if we flogged him would be giving him *that* extremely unpleasant experience. If he did not mind it, or even liked it, our act would be different in a morally relevant respect. So it is important to consider what are the conditions for being said really to know what an experience (our own or somebody else's) which would be the result of our proposed act would be like.

Suppose that the experience in question is (as in this case) *suffering* of some kind. I wish to claim that we cannot suffer without knowing that we are suffering, nor know that we are suffering without suffering. The relation between having experiences and knowing that we are having them was noticed already by Aristotle (1120^{a}29). There are two distinct reasons for the last half of the thesis I have just put forward. The first is that we cannot know *anything* without its being the case (that is the sort of word that 'know' is). The second reason is a particular one, and more important for our argument: if we did not have the experience of suffering, there would be nothing to know, and no means of knowing it. The knowledge that we are having the experience of suffering is *direct* knowledge, not any kind of knowledge by inference, and so cannot exist without the object of knowledge (that is, the suffering) being present in our experience. That, indeed, is why it is so difficult to know what the sufferings of other people are like. As we shall see, imagination has to fill, in an inadequate way, the place of experience.

Next, we cannot be suffering without having the preference, *pro tanto,* so far as that goes, that we should not be. If we did not prefer, other things being equal, that it should stop, it is not suffering. The preference that it should stop is what would be expressed, if it were expressed in language, by means of a prescription that it should stop. So, putting all this together, if we are suffering, and therefore know that we are, we are bound to assent to the prescription that, other things being equal, it should stop. We must want it to stop, or it is not suffering.

So much for our own present sufferings. We have now to consider what is implied by the knowledge that we *shall,* or *would* under certain conditions, be suffering, or that *somebody else* is suffering. Let us take the last-mentioned case first. What am I committed to if I truly claim that I know how somebody else is suffering, or what it is like for him to suffer like that? The touchstone for this is, it seems to me, the question 'What are my preferences (or in other words, to what prescriptions do I assent) regarding a situation in which *I* was forthwith to be put into *his* exact situation, suffering just like that?' If he is suffering like that, he knows that he is, and has the preference that it should stop (a preference of a determinate strength, depending on how severe the suffering is). He thus assents, with a determinate strength of assent, to the prescription that it should stop. This preference and this assent are part of his situation, and therefore part of what I have to imagine myself experiencing, were I to be transferred forthwith into it.

I asked just now, 'What am I committed to if I truly claim that I know how he is suffering?' My thesis is going to be that I am committed to having myself a preference that, if I were myself to be transferred forthwith into his situation with his preferences, the suffering should stop; and the strength of this preference that I am committed to having is the same as the strength of his preference.

I said that that was going to be my thesis. But I have not yet argued for it, and the argument for it will be, I am sure, controversial. The move I am going to make is this: whether I am really thinking of the person who would be put forthwith into that situation as *myself* depends on whether I associate myself with, or take to myself, the preferences which that person (i.e. I myself) would have. Of course, as before, we have to add 'other things being equal'; there may well be other things which I prefer so strongly that they outweigh my preference that that person's preference (the person who I imagine myself being) should be satisfied. . . . But *other things being equal* I have to be preferring that it be satisfied, with the same strength of preference as I should have were I in that situation with those preferences. If I am not, then either I do not really know what it is like to be in that situation with those preferences (I am not really fully representing it to myself), or I am not really thinking of the person who would be in that situation as myself.

Let me give an example to illustrate all this. . . . Suppose that somebody has been tied up and a tyre put round his neck, and the tyre ignited with petrol. He is suffering to a certain extreme degree, and therefore knows that he is suffering. What is it for *me* to know what it is like for him to suffer like that? Or, to put it in terms of preferences: he prefers very much that he should stop being burnt in that way; what it is for me to know what it is like to have a preference like that for that outcome, or of that strength (to be saying 'Oh, stop! Stop!' with that degree of anguish)? And suppose then that I claim to know just what it is like for him to have such a preference and to be suffering like that; and then suppose that somebody offers to do the same to me without further delay, and I say 'I don't mind; it's all the same to me.' That would surely show that I do not know what it is like for him. This presumes that if I had it done to me, I should have the same experiences and the same preferences as the person to whom it is being done. I think that the same could be shown in less dramatic examples, and that, when we have made due allowance for other things not being equal (that is, for competing preferences), I could show convincingly that the thesis stands up; but I am not going to go on defending it now, because I want to draw conclusions from it for my main argument.

Let me first sum up the theses that I have advanced so far. We have the prescriptivity and the universalizability of moral judgements, which, I claim, can be established by arguments based on the meanings of words — logical arguments. Then we have the necessity, if we are to assent rationally to prescriptions, including prescriptions expressed with 'ought,' of correct factual information. Lastly we have the thesis that we are *not* in possession of correct factual information about someone else's suffering, or in general about his preferences, unless we ourselves have preferences that, were *we* in his situation with his preferences, those preferences should be satisfied. Note, again, that although I claimed to be able to establish universalizability, I have not yet used it in the argument. That is what I am going to do now, in conjunction with the other theses.

Let us suppose that it is I who am causing the victim to suffer. He very much wants me to untie him. That is to say, he assents with a certain very high strength of assent to the prescription that I should untie him. Already, without bringing in universalizability, we can say, on the strength of our previous theses, that I, if I know what it is like, for him, to be in that state (and if I do not know that, my moral judgement is faulted for lack of information) — I must myself have a preference that if I were in that state they should untie me. That is, I must be prescribing that they should, in those hypothetical circumstances, untie me. Now suppose that I ask myself what *universal* prescription I am prepared to assent to with regard to my present conduct which is causing him to suffer; that is, what I am prepared to say that I *ought* now to do to him. The 'ought' here expresses a universal prescription, so that, if I say 'I ought not to untie him,' I am committed to the prescription that they should not untie me in similar circumstances.

I can of course say that I am not prepared to assent to *any* universal prescription. That is the position of the person whom I have elsewhere called the *amoralist,* and indicated how I would deal with him. . . . But suppose I am not an amoralist, and am therefore prepared to assent to some universal prescription for people in precisely the present situation. The question is what this is going to be. If I universalize the prescription to go on making him suffer, then this entails prescribing that, if anybody were making me suffer in a precisely analogous situation, he should carry on doing it. But this runs counter to a prescription which, as we have seen, I already must be assenting to if I know what it is like to be in the situation of my victim: the prescription that if I were in that situation they should *not* carry on doing it, but should untie me. Thus I am in the predicament that Kant called a contradiction in the will. . . .

How is the contradiction to be resolved? The answer becomes obvious if we notice that what is happening (what has to happen if I am trying to universalize my prescriptions) is that I am being constrained to treat other people's preferences as if they were my own. This is just another way of putting the requirement to universalize my prescriptions. But if in this situation the two preferences which have come into contradiction were both my own, what I would do would be to let the stronger of them override the weaker. And that is what I am constrained to do in the present case, where, as a result of the attempt to universalize, I have landed myself with two mutually contradictory preferences

or prescriptions as to what should be done to me in the hypothetical situation in which I was in the other person's shoes. So the answer is that if my victim's preference that I should desist from tormenting him is stronger than my own preference that I should not desist (as it certainly will be), I should desist.

We have thus, in this simple bilateral case involving only two people, arrived at what is essentially a utilitarian answer to our moral problem; and we have arrived at it by a Kantian route. People talk as if Kant and the utilitarians were at opposite poles in moral philosophy; but this just shows how little they have understood either the utilitarians or Kant. . . . We are led to give weight to the preferences of all the affected parties (in this case, two) in proportion to their strengths, and to say that we ought to act on the stronger. I could, if there were room, show how, by generalizing this argument to cover multilateral situations in which the preferences of many parties are affected, we should also adopt utilitarian answers, namely that we ought in each case so to act as to maximize the satisfactions of the preferences of all affected parties, treated impartially. But I am not going to attempt this now; I have done it elsewhere . . . , and I have to go on to explain how this way of thinking is going to work out in the course of our actual moral lives, when we have to decide practical issues. I shall be able to do this only in very general terms.

It might be thought that what we have arrived at is a kind of act-utilitarianism; and this is in fact true. But it is not the kind of act-utilitarianism to which all beginner philosophy students are taught the standard objections. I will now try to explain how the kind of act-utilitarianism that I am advocating differs from the crude kind. The difference is not, strictly speaking, a theoretical one. It derives rather from a consideration of our actual human predicament when we are doing our moral thinking. To see this, let us think what it would be like if we had no human limitations. Suppose, that is to say, that we had infinite knowledge and clarity of thought and no partiality to self or other human weaknesses. Elsewhere I have called a being who has these superhuman powers the *archangel.* . . . He really could think in an act-utilitarian way. But it would often be disastrous if we humans tried to do it, for obvious reasons. First of all, we lack the necessary information nearly always; in particular, we are very bad at putting ourselves in other people's shoes and imagining what it is like to be them. Secondly, we lack the time for acquiring and thinking about this information; and then we lack the ability to think clearly. These three handicaps make it all too easy for us to pretend to ourselves that some act is likely to be for the best (to satisfy preferences maximally and impartially) when in fact what commends it to us is our own self-interest. One sees this kind of special pleading going on all the time.

Suppose that, conscious of these handicaps, we went to an archangel for advice, not about a particular situation (for we shall not always have access to him, and therefore want him to give us advice for the future) but about how in general to minimize their bad effects. People think that they can appeal to God in this way; though what they say he tells them varies from one person to another. But let us suppose that we *had* immediate access to some supreme or at least superior being who could advise us. He would point out that the best we can do is on each occasion to make as great as possible the expectation of preference-satisfaction resulting from our actions. I am sure that this is what God would do, because he loves his creatures, and he wants us to do the best we can for them.

The expectation of preference-satisfaction (of utility, for short) is the sum of the products of the utility and the probability of the outcome for all the alternative possible outcomes of the action. This is what I mean by 'Acting for the best.' The question is, How shall we achieve this? Given our limitations, we shall not achieve it by doing a utilitarian calculation or a cost-benefit analysis on each occasion. The archangel will tell us, rather, to cultivate in ourselves a set of dispositions or principles, together with the attitudes or feelings or, if anybody wishes to use the word, intuitions that go with them: a set such that the cultivation of them is most likely on the whole to lead to the maximization of preference-satisfaction. The archangel, who can get the right answer on every single occasion, can do better than us; but that is the best that we can do.

It will be noticed that this, although in a sense it is a form of rule-utilitarianism, is a form which is not incompatible with act-utilitarianism. For what the archangel is advising us to do is to perform certain acts, namely acts of cultivating dispositions; and his reason for advising this is that these acts are the most likely to be for the best — which is exactly what an act-utilitarian would advise. However, this version of utilitarianism secures the advantages which older forms of rule-utilitarianism claimed, in particular the advantage of making our proposed system immune to objections based on the counter-intuitiveness of its consequences. For the intuitions which the act-utilitarian archangel will bid us cultivate are the *same* intuitions as those to which the objectors are appealing.

The effect of this move is to divide moral thinking into two levels (in addition to the third or meta-ethical level which is concerned, not with substantial moral thinking, but with the form of moral thinking (that is, with the logic of the moral language). I call these two levels the *intuitive* level and the *critical* level. If we follow the archangel's advice, we shall do nearly all our moral thinking at the intuitive level; in fact, for nearly all the time, we shall behave just as the intuitionists say we do and should. The difference, however, will be that because, as everyone realizes, the good dispositions and principles and attitudes that we rightly cultivate are to some degree general and simple and unspecific (if they were not, they would be unmanageable and unhelpful and unteachable), they will come into conflict in particular hard cases; and then, unlike intuitionists, we shall know what we have to try to do, difficult and dangerous as it is. Since we do not in fact have archangels on call, we have to do the best we can to think critically like archangels on those problematic occasions. But when our intuitions give us clear guidance, we shall follow them — at least that is what our utilitarian archangel will advise us during our once-for-all counselling session with him.

But, it will be said, this presumes that our intuitions are the right ones. Indeed it does. This gives us another reason for using critical thinking. It is dangerous to use it in crises; but when they are over, or in anticipation of them, it may be essential. Otherwise how shall we have any confidence that the intuitions we happen to have grown up with are the best ones? Intuitions about how Whites should treat Blacks, for example, or men women? So what the wise archangel will advise, and what wise human educators and self-educators will practise, will be a judicious admixture of intuitive and critical thinking, each employed on appropriate occasions. And this is what wise people do already.

VIII.6 *Moral Beliefs*

PHILIPPA FOOT

Philippa Foot (1920–   ) is professor of philosophy at the University of California at Los Angeles and senior research fellow at Somerville College, Oxford. Many of her significant essays are published in *Virtues and Vices*. The essay reprinted here was delivered at the Aristotelian Society in 1958 and represents the first clear critique of the whole formalist enterprise of the noncognitivists. Foot argues that the noncognitivists have separated the evaluative meaning from the descriptive meaning of 'good' in an implausible way. There are limits to what we can reasonably prescribe as a moral judgment, and there are some so-called 'descriptive' concepts that include moral overtones: 'danger,' 'courage,' 'injury,' and 'justice.' Foot is not a naturalist, for she doesn't believe that value terms can be defined by factual statements, but she tries to show that there is not a complete logical gap between facts and values (as all of the other ethicists in this part of the book have maintained in their adherence to the naturalistic fallacy). Certain facts logically entail values. Foot's compromise position was labeled *descriptivism* or *neo-naturalism*.

I

To many people it seems that the most notable advance in moral philosophy during the past fifty years or so has been the refutation of naturalism; and they are a little shocked that at this late date such an issue should be reopened. It is easy to understand their attitude: given certain apparently unquestionable assumptions, it would be about as sensible to try to reintroduce naturalism as to try to square the circle. Those who see it like this have satisfied themselves that they know in advance that any naturalistic theory must have a catch in it somewhere, and are put out at having to waste more time exposing an old fallacy. This paper is an attempt to persuade them to look critically at the premises on which their arguments are based.

From *Proceedings of the Aristotelian Society* 59(1958–59): 410–425, © the Aristotelian Society. Reprinted by permission of the editor.

It would not be an exaggeration to say that the whole of moral philosophy, as it is now widely taught, rests on a contrast between statements of fact and evaluations, which runs something like this: 'The truth or falsity of statements of fact is shown by means of evidence; and what counts as evidence is laid down in the meaning of the expressions occurring in the statement of fact. (For instance, the meaning of "round" and "flat" made Magellan's voyages evidence for the roundness rather than the flatness of the Earth; someone who went on questioning whether the evidence was evidence could eventually be shown to have made some linguistic mistake.) It follows that no two people can make the same statement and count completely different things as evidence; in the end one at least of them could be convicted of linguistic ignorance. It also follows that if a man is given good evidence for a factual conclusion he cannot just refuse to accept the conclusion on the ground that in his scheme of things this evidence is not evidence at all. With evaluations, however, it is different. An evaluation is not connected logically with the factual statements on which it is based. One man may say that a thing is good because of some fact about it, and another may refuse to take that fact as any evidence at all, for nothing is laid down in the meaning of "good" which connects it with one piece of "evidence" rather than another. It follows that a moral eccentric could argue to moral conclusions from quite idiosyncratic premises; he could say, for instance, that a man was a good man because he clasped and unclasped his hands, and never turned NNE after turning SSW. He could also reject someone else's evaluation simply by denying that his evidence was evidence at all.

The fact about "good" which allows the eccentric still to use this term without falling into a morass of meaninglessness is its "action-guiding" or "practical" function. This it retains; for like everyone else he considers himself bound to choose the things he calls "good" rather than those he calls "bad." Like the rest of the world he uses "good" in connection only with a "pro-attitude"; it is only that he has pro-attitudes to quite different things, and therefore calls them good.

There are here two assumptions about 'evaluations,' which I will call assumption (1) and assumption (2).

Assumption (1) is that some individual may, without logical error, base his beliefs about matters of value entirely on premises which no one else would recognise as giving any evidence at all. Assumption (2) is that, given the kind of statement which other people regard as evidence for an evaluative conclusion, he may refuse to draw the conclusion because *this* does not count as evidence for *him*.

Let us consider assumption (1). We might say that this depends on the possibility of keeping the meaning of 'good' steady through all changes in the facts about anything which are to count in favour of its goodness. (I do not mean, of course, that a man can make changes as fast as he chooses; only that, whatever he has chosen, it will not be possible to rule him out of order.) But there is a better formulation, which cuts out trivial disputes about the meaning which 'good' happens to have in some section of the community. Let us say that the assumption is that the evaluative function of 'good' can remain constant through changes in the evaluative principle; on this ground it could be said that even if no one can call a man *good* because he clasps and un-

clasps his hands, he can commend him or express his *pro-attitude* towards him, and if necessary can invent a new moral vocabulary to express his unusual moral code.

Those who hold such a theory will naturally add several qualifications. In the first place, most people now agree with Hare, against Stevenson, that such words as 'good' only apply to individual cases through the application of general principles, so that even the extreme moral eccentric must accept principles of commendation. In the second place 'commending,' 'having a pro-attitude,' and so on, are supposed to be connected with doing and choosing, so that it would be impossible to say, e.g. that a man was a good man only if he lived for a thousand years. The range of evaluation is supposed to be restricted to the range of possible action and choice. I am not here concerned to question these supposed restrictions on the use of evaluative terms, but only to argue that they are not enough.

The crucial question is this. Is it possible to extract from the meaning of words such as 'good' some element called 'evaluative meaning' which we can think of as externally related to its objects? Such an element would be represented, for instance, in the rule that when any action was 'commended' the speaker must hold himself bound to accept an imperative 'let me do these things.' This is externally related to its object because, within the limitation which we noticed earlier, to possible actions, it would make sense to think of anything as the subject of such 'commendation.' On this hypothesis a moral eccentric could be described as commending the clasping of hands as the action of a good man, and we should not have to look for some background to give the supposition sense. That is to say, on this hypothesis the clasping of hands could be commended without any explanation; it could be what those who hold such theories call 'an ultimate moral principle.'

I wish to say that this hypothesis is untenable, and that there is no describing the evaluative meaning of 'good,' evaluation, commending, or anything of the sort, without fixing the object to which they are supposed to be attached. Without first laying hands on the proper object of such things as evaluation, we shall catch in our net either something quite different, such as accepting an order or making a resolution, or else nothing at all.

Before I consider this question, I shall first discuss some other mental attitudes and beliefs which have this internal relation to their object. By this I hope to clarify the concept of internal relation to an object, and incidentally, if my examples arouse resistance, but are eventually accepted, to show how easy it is to overlook an internal relation where it exists.

Consider, for instance, pride.

People are often surprised at the suggestion that there are limits to the things a man can be proud of, about which indeed he can feel pride. I do not know quite what account they want to give of pride; perhaps something to do with smiling and walking with a jaunty air, and holding an object up where other people can see it; or perhaps they think that pride is a kind of internal sensation, so that one might naturally beat one's breast and say 'pride is something I feel *here*.' The difficulties of the second view are well known; the logically private object cannot be what a name in the public language is the name of.[1] The first view is the more plausible, and it may seem reasonable to say that given certain behaviour a man can be described as showing that he is proud of something, whatever that something may be. In one sense this is true, and in another sense not. Given any description of an object, action, personal characteristic, etc., it is not possible to rule it out as an object of pride. Before we can do so we need to know what would be said about it by the man who is to be proud of it, or feels proud of it; but if he does not hold the right beliefs about it then whatever his attitude is it is not pride. Consider, for instance, the suggestion that someone might be proud of the sky or the sea: he looks at them and what he feels is *pride,* or he puffs out his chest and gestures with *pride* in their direction. This makes sense only if a special assumption is made about his beliefs, for instance, that he is under some crazy delusion and believes that he has saved the sky from falling, or the sea from drying up. The characteristic object of pride is something seen (*a*) as in some way a man's own, and (*b*) as some sort of achievement or advantage; without this object pride cannot be described. To see that the second condition is necessary, one should try supposing that a man happens to feel proud because he has laid one of his hands on the other, three times in an hour. Here again the supposition that it is pride that he feels will make perfectly good sense if a special background is filled in. Perhaps he is ill, and it is an achievement even to

do this; perhaps this gesture has some religious or political significance, and he is a brave man who will so defy the gods or the rulers. But with no special background there can be no pride, not because no one could psychologically speaking feel pride in such a case, but because whatever he did feel could not logically be pride. Of course, people can see strange things as achievements, though not just anything, and they can identify themselves and with remote ancestors, and relations, and neighbours, and even on occasions with Mankind. I do not wish to deny there are many far-fetched and comic examples of pride.

We could have chosen many other examples of mental attitudes which are internally related to their object in a similar way. For instance, fear is not just trembling, and running, and turning pale; without the thought of some menacing evil no amount of this will add up to fear. Nor could anyone be said to feel dismay about something he did not see as bad; if his thoughts about it were that it was altogether a good thing, he could not say that (oddly enough) what he felt about it was dismay. 'How odd, I feel dismayed when I ought to be pleased' is the prelude to a hunt for the adverse aspect of the thing, thought of as lurking behind the pleasant facade. But someone may object that pride and fear and dismay are feelings or emotions and therefore not a proper analogy for 'commendation,' and there will be an advantage in considering a different kind of example. We could discuss, for instance, the belief that a certain thing is dangerous, and ask whether this could logically be held about anything whatsoever. Like 'this is good,' 'this is dangerous' is an assertion, which we should naturally accept or reject by speaking of its truth or falsity; we seem to support such statements with evidence, and moreover there may seem to be a 'warning function' connected with the word 'dangerous' as there is supposed to be a 'commending function' connected with the word 'good.' For suppose that philosophers, puzzled about the property of dangerousness, decided that the word did not stand for a property at all, but was essentially a practical or action-guiding term, used for *warning.* Unless used in an 'inverted comma sense' the word 'dangerous' was used to warn, and this meant that anyone using it in such a sense committed himself to avoiding the things he called dangerous, to preventing other people from going near them, and perhaps to running in the opposite direction. If the conclusion were not obviously ridiculous, it would be easy to infer that a man whose application of the term was different from ours throughout might say that the oddest things were dangerous without fear of disproof; the idea would be that he could still be described as 'thinking them dangerous,' or at least as 'warning,' because by his attitude and actions he would have fulfilled the conditions for these things. This is nonsense because without its proper object *warning,* like *believing dangerous,* will not be there. It is logically impossible to warn about anything not thought of as threatening evil, and for danger we need a particular kind of serious evil such as injury or death.

There are, however, some differences between thinking a thing dangerous and feeling proud, frightened or dismayed. When a man says that something is dangerous he must support his statement with a special kind of evidence; but when he says that he feels proud or frightened or dismayed the description of the object of his pride or fright or dismay does not have quite this relation to his original statement. If he is shown that the thing he was proud of was not his after all, or was not after all anything very grand, he may have to say that his pride was not justified, but he will not have to take back the statement that he was proud. On the other hand, someone who says that a thing is dangerous, and later sees that he made a mistake in thinking that an injury might result from it, has to go back on his original statement and admit that he was wrong. In neither case, however, is the speaker able to go on as before. A man who discovered that it was not his pumpkin but someone else's which had won the prize could only say that he still felt proud, if he could produce some other ground for pride. It is in this way that even feelings are logically vulnerable to facts.

It will probably be objected against these examples that for part of the way at least they beg the question. It will be said that indeed a man can only be proud of something he thinks a good action, or an achievement, or a sign of noble birth; as he can only feel dismay about something which he sees as bad, frightened at some threatened evil; similarly he can only warn if he is also prepared to speak, for instance, of injury. But this will only limit the range of possible objects of those attitudes and beliefs if the range of these terms is limited in its turn. To meet this objection I shall discuss the meaning of 'injury' because this is the simplest case. Anyone who feels inclined to say that anything could be counted as an achievement, or as the evil of which people were afraid, or about which they felt dismayed, should just try this out. I wish to consider the proposition that anything could be thought of as dangerous, because if it causes injury it is dangerous, and anything could be counted as an injury. I shall consider bodily injury because this is the injury connected with danger; it is not correct to put up a notice by the roadside reading 'Danger!' on account of bushes which might scratch a car. Nor can a substance be labelled 'dangerous' on the ground that it can injure delicate fabrics; although we can speak of the danger that it may do so, that is not the use of the word which I am considering here.

When a body is injured it is changed for the worse in a special way, and we want to know which changes count as injuries. First of all, it matters how an injury comes about; e.g. it cannot be caused by natural decay. Then it seems clear that not just any kind of thing will do, for instance, any unusual mark on the body, however much trouble a man might take to have it removed. By far the most important class of injuries are injuries to a part of the body, counting as injuries because there is interference with the function of that part; injury to a leg, an eye, an ear, a hand, a muscle, the heart, the brain, the spinal cord. An injury to an eye is one that affects, or is likely to affect, its sight; an injury to a hand one which makes it less well able to reach out and grasp, and perform other operations of this kind. A leg can be injured because its movements and supporting power can be affected; a lung because it can become too weak to draw in the proper amount of air. We are most ready to speak of an injury where the function of a part of the body is to perform a characteristic operation, as in these examples. We might hesitate to say that a skull can be injured, and might prefer to speak of damage to it, since although there is indeed a function (a protective function) there is no operation. But thinking of the protective function of the skull we may want to speak of injury here. In so far as the concept of *injury* depends on that of *function* it is narrowly limited, since not even every use to which a part of the body is put will count as its function. Why is it that, even if it is the means by which they earn their living, we would never consider the removal of the dwarf's hump or the bearded lady's beard as a bodily injury? It will be tempting to say that these things are disfigurements, but this is not the point; if we suppose that a man who had some invisible extra muscle made his living as a court jester by waggling his ears, the ear would not have been injured if this were made to disappear. If it were natural to men to communicate by movements of the ear, then ears would have the function of signalling (we have no word for this kind of 'speaking') and an impairment of this function would be an injury; but things are not like this. This court jester would use his ears to make people laugh, but this is not the function of ears.

No doubt many people will feel impatient when such facts are mentioned, because they think that it is quite unimportant that this or that *happens* to be the case, and it seems to them arbitrary that the loss of the beard, the hump, or the ear muscle would not be called an injury. Isn't the loss of that by which one makes one's living a pretty catastrophic loss? Yet it seems quite natural that these are not counted as injuries if one thinks about the conditions of human life, and contrasts the loss of a special ability to make people gape or laugh with the ability to see, hear, walk, or pick things up. The first is only needed for one very special way of living; the other in any foreseeable future for any man. This restriction seems all the more natural when we observe what other threats besides that of injury can constitute danger: of death, for instance, or mental derangement. A shock which could cause mental instability or impairment of memory would be called dangerous, because a man needs such things as intelligence, memory, and concentration as he needs sight or hearing or the use of hands. Here we do not speak of injury unless it is possible to connect the impairment with some physical change, but we speak of danger because there is the same loss of a capacity which any man needs.

There can be injury outside the range we have been considering; for a man may sometimes be said to have received injuries where no part of his body has had its function interfered with. In general, I think that any blow which disarranged the body in such a way that there was lasting pain would inflict an injury, even if no other ill resulted, but I do not know of any other important extension of the concept.

It seems therefore that since the range of things which can be called injuries is quite narrowly restricted, the word 'dangerous' is restricted in so far as it is connected with injury. We have the right to say that a man cannot decide to call just anything dangerous, however much he puts up fences and shakes his head.

So far I have been arguing that such things as pride, fear, dismay, and the thought that something is dangerous have an internal relation to their object, and hope that what I mean is becoming clear. Now we must consider whether those attitudes or beliefs which are the moral philosopher's study are similar, or whether such things as 'evaluation' and 'thinking something good' and 'commendation' could logically be found in combination with any object whatsoever. All I can do here is to give an example which may make this suggestion seem implausible, and to knock away a few of its supports. The example will come from the range of trivial and pointless actions such as we were considering in speaking of the man who clasped his hands three times an hour, and we can point to the oddity of the suggestion that this can be called a good action. We are bound by the terms of our question to refrain from adding any special background, and it should be stated once more that the question is about what can count in favour of the goodness or badness of a man or an action, and not what could be, or be thought, good or bad with a special background. I believe that the view I am attacking often seems plausible only because the special background is surreptitiously introduced.

Someone who said that clasping the hands three times in an hour was a good action would first have to answer the question 'How do you mean?' For the sentence 'this is a good action' is not one which has a clear meaning. Presumably, since our subject is moral philosophy, it does not here mean 'that was a good thing to do' as this might be said of a man who had done something sensible in the course of any enterprise whatever; we are to confine our attention to 'the moral use of "good."' I am not clear that it makes sense to speak of a 'moral use of "good,"' but we can pick out a number of cases which raise moral issues. It is because these are so diverse and because 'this is a good action' does not pick out any one of them, that we must ask 'How do you mean?' For instance, some things that are done fulfil a duty, such as the duty of parents to children or children to parents. I suppose that when philosophers speak of good actions they would include these. Some come under the heading of a virtue such as charity, and they will be included too. Others again are actions which require the virtues of courage or temperance, and here the moral aspect is due to the fact that they are done in spite of fear or the temptation of pleasure; they must indeed be done for the sake of some real or fancied good, but not necessarily what philosophers would want to call a moral good. Courage is not *particularly* concerned with saving other people's lives, or temperance with leaving them their share of the food and drink, and the goodness of *what is done* may here be all kinds of usefulness. It is because there are these very diverse cases included (I suppose) under the expression 'a good action' that we should refuse to consider applying it without asking what is meant, and we should now ask what is intended when someone is supposed to say that 'clasping the hands three times in an hour is a good action.' Is it supposed that this action fulfils a duty? Then in virtue of what does a man have this duty, and to whom does he owe it? We have promised not to slip in a special background, but he cannot possibly have a *duty* to clasp his hands unless such a background exists. Nor could it be an act of charity, for it is not thought to do anyone any good, nor again a gesture of humility unless a special assumption turns it into this. The action could be courageous, but only if it were done both in the face of fear and for the sake of a good; and we are not allowed to put in special circumstances which could make this the case.

I am sure that the following objection will now be raised. 'Of course clasping one's hand three times in an hour cannot be brought under one of the virtues which we recognise, but that is only to say that it is not a good action by our current moral code. It is logically possible that in a quite different moral code quite different virtues should be recognised, for which we have not even got a name.' I cannot answer this objection properly, for that would need a satisfactory account of the concept of a virtue. But anyone who thinks it would be easy to describe a new virtue connected with clasping the hands three times in an hour should just try. I think he will find that he has to cheat, and suppose that in the community concerned the clasping of hands has been

given some special significance, or is thought to have some special effect. The difficulty is obviously connected with the fact that without a special background there is no possibility of answering the question 'What's the point?' It is no good saying that here would be a point in doing the action because the action was a morally good action: the question is how it can be given any such description if we cannot first speak about the point. And it is just as crazy to suppose that we can call *anything* the point of doing something without having to say what the point of *that* is. In clasping one's hands one may make a slight sucking noise, but what is the point of that? It is surely clear that moral virtues must be connected with human good and harm, and that it is quite impossible to call anything you like good or harm. Consider, for instance, the suggestion that a man might say he had been harmed because a bucket of water had been taken out of the sea. As usual it would be possible to think up circumstances in which this remark would make sense; for instance, when coupled with a belief in magical influences; but then the harm would consist in what was done by the evil spirits, not in the taking of the water from the sea. It would be just as odd if someone were supposed to say that harm had been done to him because the hairs of his head had been reduced to an even number.[2]

I conclude that assumption (1) is very dubious indeed, and that no one should be allowed to speak as if we can understand 'evaluation,' 'commendation' or 'pro-attitude,' whatever the actions concerned.

II

I propose now to consider what was called assumption (2), which said that a man might always refuse to accept the conclusion of an argument about values, because what counted as evidence for other people did not count for him. Assumption (2) could be true even if assumption (1) were false, for it might be that once a particular question of values — say a moral question — had been accepted, any disputant was bound to accept particular pieces of evidence as relevant, the same pieces as everyone else, but that he could always refuse to draw any moral conclusions whatsoever or to discuss any questions which introduced moral terms. Nor do we mean 'he might refuse to draw the conclusion' in the trivial sense in which anyone can perhaps refuse to draw *any* conclusion; the point is that any statement of value always seems to go beyond any statement of fact, so that he might have a reason for accepting the factual premises but refusing to accept the evaluative conclusion. That this is so seems to those who argue in this way to follow from the practical implications of evaluation. When a man uses a word such as 'good' in an 'evaluative' and not an 'inverted comma' sense, he is supposed to commit his will. From this it has seemed to follow inevitably that there is a logical gap between fact and value; for is it not one thing to say that a thing is so, and another to have a particular attitude towards its being so; one thing to see that certain effects will follow from a given action, and another to care? Whatever account was offered of the essential feature of evaluation—whether in terms of feelings, attitudes, the acceptance of imperatives or what not—the fact remained that with an evaluation there was a committal in a new dimension, and that this was not guaranteed by any acceptance of facts.

I shall argue that this view is mistaken; that the practical implication of the use of moral terms has been put in the wrong place, and that if it is described correctly the logical gap between factual premises and moral conclusion disappears.

In this argument it will be useful to have as a pattern the practical or 'action-guiding' force of the word 'injury,' which is in some, though not all, ways similar to that of moral terms. It is clear I think that any injury is necessarily something bad and therefore something which as such anyone always has a reason to avoid, and philosophers will therefore be tempted to say that anyone who uses 'injury' in its full 'action-guiding' sense commits himself to avoiding the things he calls injuries. They will then be in the usual difficulties about the man who says he knows he ought to do something but does not intend to do it; perhaps also about weakness of the will. Suppose that instead we look again at the kinds of things which count as injuries, to see if the connection with the will does not start here. As has been shown, a man is injured whenever some part of his body, in being damaged, has become less well able to fulfil its ordinary function. It follows that he

suffers a disability, or is liable to do so; with an injured hand he will be less well able to pick things up, hold on to them, tie them together or chop them up, and so on. With defective eyes there will be a thousand other things he is unable to do, and in both cases we should naturally say that he will often be unable to get what he wants to get or avoid what he wants to avoid.

Philosophers will no doubt seize on the word 'want,' and say that if we suppose that a man happens to want the things which an injury to his body prevents him from getting, we have slipped in a supposition about a 'pro-attitude' already; and that anyone who does not happen to have these wants can still refuse to use 'injury' in its prescriptive, or 'action-guiding' sense. And so it may seem that the only way to make a *necessary* connection between 'injury' and the things that are to be avoided, is to say that it is only used in an 'action-guiding sense' when applied to something the speaker intends to avoid. But we should look carefully at the crucial move in that argument, and query the suggestion that someone might happen not to want anything for which he would need the use of hands or eyes. Hands and eyes, like ears and legs, play a part in so many operations that a man could only be said not to need them if he had no wants at all. That such people exist, in asylums, is not to the present purpose at all; the proper use of his limbs is something a man has reason to want if he wants anything.

I do not know just what someone who denies this proposition could have in mind. Perhaps he is thinking of changing the facts of human existence, so that merely wishing, or the sound of the voice, will bring the world to heel? More likely he is proposing to rig the circumstances of some individual's existence within the framework of the ordinary world, by supposing for instance that he is a prince whose servants will sow and reap and fetch and carry for him, and so use their hands and eyes in his service that he will not need the use of his. Let us suppose that such a story could be told about a man's life; it is wildly implausible, but let us pretend that it is not. It is clear that in spite of this we could say that any man had a reason to shun injury; for even if at the end of his life it could be said that by a strange set of circumstances he had never needed the use of his eyes, or his hands, this could not possibly be foreseen. Only by once more changing the facts of human existence, and supposing every vicissitude foreseeable, could such a supposition be made.

This is not to say that an injury might not bring more incidental gain than necessary harm; one has only to think of times when the order has gone out that able-bodied men are to be put to the sword. Such a gain might even, in some peculiar circumstances, be reliably foreseen, so that a man would have even better reason for seeking than for avoiding injury. In this respect the word 'injury' differs from terms such as 'injustice'; the practical force of 'injury' means only that anyone has *a* reason to avoid injuries, not that he has an overriding reason to do so.

It will be noticed that this account of the 'action-guiding' force of 'injury' links it with reasons for acting rather than with actually doing something. I do not think, however, that this makes it a less good pattern for the 'action-guiding' force of moral terms. Philosophers who have supposed that actual action was required if 'good' were to be used in a sincere evaluation have got into difficulties over weakness of will, and they should surely agree that enough has been done if we can show that any man has reason to aim at virtue and avoid vice. But is this impossibly difficult if we consider the kinds of things that count as virtue and vice? Consider, for instance, the cardinal virtues, prudence, temperance, courage and justice. Obviously any man needs prudence, but does he not also need to resist the temptation of pleasure when there is harm involved? And how could it be argued that he would never need to face what was fearful for the sake of some good? It is not obvious what someone would mean if he said that temperance or courage were not good qualities, and this not because of the 'praising' sense of these *words,* but because of the things that courage and temperance are.

I should like to use these examples to show the artificiality of the notions of 'commendation' and of 'pro-attitudes' as these are commonly employed. Philosophers who talk about these things will say that after the facts have been accepted — say that X is the kind of man who will climb a dangerous mountain, beard an irascible employer for a rise in pay, and in general face the fearful for the sake of something he thinks worth while — there remains the question of 'commendation' or 'evaluation.' If the word 'courage' is used they will ask whether or not the man who speaks of another as having courage is

supposed to have commended him. If we say 'yes' they will insist that the judgement about courage *goes beyond the facts,* and might therefore be rejected by someone who refused to do so; if we say 'no' they will argue that 'courage' is being used in a purely descriptive or 'inverted comma sense,' and that we have not got an example of the evaluative use of language which is the moral philosopher's special study. What sense can be made, however, of the question 'does he commend?' What is this extra element which is supposed to be present or absent after the facts have been settled? It is not a matter of liking the man who has courage, or of thinking him altogether good, but of 'commending him for his courage.' How are we supposed to do that? The answer that will be given is that we only commend someone else in speaking of him as courageous if we accept the imperative 'let me be courageous' for ourselves. But this is quite unnecessary. I can speak of someone else as having the virtue of courage, and of course recognise it as a virtue in the proper sense, while knowing that I am a complete coward, and making no resolution to reform. I know that I should be better off if I were courageous, and so have a reason to cultivate courage, but I may also know that I will do nothing of the kind.

If someone were to say that courage was not a virtue he would have to say that it was not a quality by which a man came to act well. Perhaps he would be thinking that someone might be worse off for his courage, which is true, but only because an incidental harm might arise. For instance, the courageous man might have underestimated a risk, and run into some disaster which a cowardly man would have avoided because he was not prepared to take any risk at all. And his courage, like any other virtue, could be the cause of harm to him because possessing it he fell into some disastrous state of pride.[3] Similarly, those who question the virtue of temperance are probably thinking not of the virtue itself but of men whose temperance has consisted in resisting pleasure for the sake of some illusory good, or those who have made this virtue their pride.

But what, it will be asked, of justice? For while prudence, courage and temperance are qualities which benefit the man who has them, justice seems rather to benefit others, and to work to the disadvantage of the just man himself. Justice as it is treated here, as one of the cardinal virtues, covers all those things owed to other people: it is under injustice that murder, theft and lying come, as well as the withholding of what is owed for instance by parents to children and by children to parents, as well as the dealings which would be called unjust in everyday speech. So the man who avoids injustice will find himself in need of things he has returned to their owner, unable to obtain an advantage by cheating and lying; involved in all those difficulties painted by Thrasymachus in the first book of the Republic, in order to show that injustice is more profitable than justice to a man of strength and wit. We will be asked how, on our theory, justice can be a virtue and injustice a vice, since it will surely be difficult to show that any man whatsoever must need to be just as he needs the use of his hands and eyes, or needs prudence, courage and temperance?

Before answering this question I shall argue that if it cannot be answered, then justice can no longer be recommended as a virtue. The point of this is not to show that it must be answerable, since justice is a virtue, but rather to suggest that we should at least consider the possibility that justice is not a virtue. This suggestion was taken seriously by Socrates in the *Republic,* where it was assumed by everyone that if Thrasymachus could establish his premise—that injustice was more profitable than justice—his conclusion would follow: that a man who had the strength to get away with injustice had reason to follow this as the best way of life. It is a striking fact about modern moral philosophy that no one sees any difficulty in accepting Thrasymachus's premise and rejecting his conclusion, and it is because Nietzsche's position is at this point much closer to that of Plato that he is remote from academic moralists of the present day.

In the *Republic* it is assumed that if justice is not a good to the just man, moralists who recommend it as a virtue are perpetrating a fraud. Agreeing with this, I shall be asked where exactly the fraud comes in; where the untruth that justice is profitable to the individual is supposed to be told? As a preliminary answer we might ask how many people are prepared to say frankly that injustice is more profitable than justice? Leaving aside, as elsewhere in this paper, religious beliefs which might complicate the matter, we will suppose that some tough atheistical character has asked 'Why should I be just?' (Those who believe that this question has something wrong with it can employ their favourite device for sieving out 'evaluating meaning,' and suppose that the question is 'Why should I be "just"?') Are we prepared to

reply 'As far as you are concerned you will be better off if you are unjust, but it matters to the rest of us that you should be just, so we are trying to get you to be just?' He would be likely to enquire into our methods, and then take care not to be found out, and I do not think that many of those who think that it is not necessary to show that justice is profitable to the just man would easily accept that there was nothing more they could say.

The crucial question is: 'Can we give anyone, strong or weak, a reason why he should be just?'—and it is no help at all to say that since 'just' and 'unjust' are 'action-guiding words' no one can even ask 'Why should I be just?' Confronted with that argument the man who wants to do unjust things has only to be careful to avoid the *word,* and he has not been given a reason why he should not do the things which other people call 'unjust.' Probably it will be argued that he has been given a reason so far as anyone can ever be given a reason for doing or not doing anything, for the chain of reasons must always come to an end somewhere, and it may seem that one man may always reject the reason which another man accepts. But this is a mistake; some answers to the question 'why should I?' bring the series to a close and some do not. Hume showed how *one* answer closed the series in the following passage:

'Ask a man *why he uses exercise;* he will answer, *because he desires to keep his health.* If you then enquire, *why he desires health,* he will readily reply, *because sickness is painful.* If you push your enquiries further, and desire a reason *why he hates pain,* it is impossible he can ever give any. This is an ultimate end, and is never referred to any other object.' (*Enquiries,* appendix I, para. v.) Hume might just as well have ended this series with boredom: sickness often brings boredom, and no one is required to give a reason why he does not want to be bored, any more than he has to give a reason why he does want to pursue what interests him. In general, anyone is given a reason for acting when he is shown the way to something he wants; but for some wants the question 'Why do you want that?' will make sense, and for others it will not.[4] It seems clear that in this division justice falls on the opposite side from pleasure and interest and such things. 'Why shouldn't I do that?' is not answered by the words 'because it is unjust' as it is answered by showing that the action will bring boredom, loneliness, pain, discomfort or certain kinds of incapacity, and this is why it is not true to say that 'it's unjust' gives a reason in so far as any reasons can ever be given. 'It's unjust' gives a reason only if the nature of justice can be shown to be such that it is necessarily connected with what a man wants.

This shows why a great deal hangs on the question of whether justice is or is not a good to the just man, and why those who accept Thrasymachus's premise and reject his conclusion are in a dubious position. They recommend justice to each man, as something he has a reason to follow, but when challenged to show why he should do so they will not always be able to reply. This last assertion does not depend on any 'selfish theory of human nature' in the philosophical sense. It is often possible to give a man a reason for acting by showing him that someone else will suffer if he does not; someone else's good may really be more to him than his own. But the affection which mothers feel for children, and lovers for each other, and friends for friends, will not take us far when we are asked for reasons why a man should be just; partly because it will not extend far enough, and partly because the actions dictated by benevolence and justice are not always the same. Suppose that I owe someone money; '. . . what if he be my enemy, and has given me just cause to hate him? What if he be a vicious man, and deserves the hatred of all mankind? What if he be a miser, and can make no use of what I would deprive him of? What if he be a profligate debauchee, and would rather receive harm than benefit from large possessions?'[5] Even if the general practice of justice could be brought under the motive of universal benevolence — the desire for the greatest happiness of the greatest number — many people certainly do not have any such desire. So that if injustice is only to be recommended on these grounds a thousand tough characters will be able to say that they have been given no reason for practising justice, and many more would say the same if they were not too timid or too stupid to ask questions about the code of behaviour which they have been taught. Thus, given Thrasymachus's premise Thrasymachus's point of view is reasonable; we have no particular reason to admire those who practise justice through timidity or stupidity.

It seems to me, therefore, that if Thrasymachus's thesis is accepted things cannot go on as before; we shall have to admit that the belief on which the status of justice as a virtue was founded is mistaken, and if we still want to get people to be just we must recommend justice to them in a new way. We shall have to admit that injustice is more profitable than justice, at least for the strong, and then do our best to see that hardly anyone can get away with being unjust. We have, of course, the alternative of keeping quiet, hoping that for the most part people will follow convention into a kind of justice, and not ask awkward questions, but this policy might be overtaken by a vague scepticism even on the part of those who do not know just what is lacking; we should also be at the mercy of anyone who was able and willing to expose our fraud.

Is it true, however, to say that justice is not something a man needs in his dealings with his fellows, supposing only that he be strong? Those who think that he can get on perfectly well without being just should be asked to say exactly how such a man is supposed to live. We know that he is to practise injustice whenever the unjust act would bring him advantage; but what is he to say? Does he admit that he does not recognise the rights of other people, or does he pretend? In the first case even those who combine with him will know that on a change of fortune, or a shift of affection, he may turn to plunder them, and he must be as wary of their treachery as they are of his. Presumably the happy unjust man is supposed, as in Book II of the *Republic*, to be a very cunning liar and actor, combining complete injustice with the appearance of justice: he is prepared to treat others ruthlessly, but pretends that nothing is further from his mind. Philosophers often speak as if a man could thus hide himself even from those around him, but the supposition is doubtful, and in any case the price in vigilance would be colossal. If he lets even a few people see his true attitude he must guard himself against them; if he lets no one into the secret he must always be careful in case the least spontaneity betray him. Such facts are important because the need a man has for justice in dealings with other men depends on the fact that they are men and not inanimate objects or animals. If a man only needed other men as he needs household objects, and if men could be manipulated like household objects, or beaten into a reliable submission like donkeys, the case would be different. As things are, the supposition that injustice is more profitable than justice is very dubious, although like cowardice and intemperance it might turn out incidentally to be profitable.

The reason why it seems to some people so impossibly difficult to show that justice is more profitable than injustice is that they consider in isolation particular just acts. It is perfectly true that if a man is just it follows that he will be prepared, in the event of very evil circumstances, even to face death rather than to act unjustly — for instance, in getting an innocent man convicted of a crime of which he has been accused. For him it turns out that his justice brings disaster on him, and yet like anyone else he had good reason to be a just and not an unjust man. He could not have it both ways and while possessing the virtue of justice hold himself ready to be unjust should any great advantage accrue. The man who has the virtue of justice is not ready to do certain things, and if he is too easily tempted we shall say that he was ready after all.

Endnotes

1 See L. Wittgenstein, *Philosophical Investigations* (1953), especially sections 243–315.

2 In face of this sort of example many philosophers take refuge in the thicket of aesthetics. It would be interesting to know if they are willing to let their whole case rest on the possibility that there might be aesthetic objections to what was done.

3 Cf. Thomas Aquinas, *Summa Theologica*, I-II, q. 55, Art. 4.

4 For an excellent discussion of reasons for action, see G. E. M. Anscombe, *Intention* (Oxford 1957), sections 34–40.

5 David Hume, *Treatise*, III.ii.I.

VIII.7 *The Object of Morality*

Geoffrey Warnock

Geoffrey J. Warnock is principal of Hertford College, Oxford University. In this reading from his book, *The Object of Morality,* Warnock goes even further than Foot, claiming that the formalist nature of moral philosophy among the noncognitivists is barren and misses the point of morality. That is, morality has a content, the purpose of which is to ameliorate the human predicament, which has a tendency to worsen. Like Foot, he argues that not everything can be a moral principle and that some principles (those central to promoting human betterment) are necessarily moral principles. To quote from an earlier work of his: "Not just anything can function as a criterion of *moral* evaluation. . . . That there *are* such limits seems to me perfectly evident. . . . The limits are set somewhere within the general area of concern with the welfare of human beings. . . . The *relevance* of considerations as to the welfare of human beings *cannot*, in the context of moral debate, be denied. (Again, of course, we do not *choose* that this should be so; it *is* so, simply because of what 'moral' means.)" (*Contemporary Moral Philosophy*, St. Martin's Press, 1967, p. 67f.)

Moral concepts come into a certain kind, or perhaps one should say certain kinds, of evaluation. By this I do not mean to say that there is any one thing which we use them in doing, but only that 'evaluation' is a good enough name for what, in one way or another, they have in general to do with. Moral discourse, in which moral concepts are employed, has to do, in one way or another, with issues about what is good or bad, right or wrong, to be commended or condemned. Obviously there is evaluation that is not moral. Good weather is not morally good; the wrong way to sew on a button is not morally wrong; commendation of your style as a golfer, or of you for your style as a golfer, would not be moral

Reprinted with permission from *The Object of Morality* (Methuen and Company, 1971).

commendation. What morality has to do with is a *kind* of evaluation. The question, *what* kind, is, I suppose, just the question to which most of this book is intended to suggest an answer. Let us begin with a simpler question: evaluation of what?

There is perhaps no very useful short answer to this question; but if we had to give one, the best answer, though it immediately calls for some qualification, sees to be: the actions of rational beings. Why 'actions'? Well, it is clearly not *only* actions that are ever the topic of moral thought, or moral discussion or remark. Failures to act perhaps scarcely need separate mention. But also, people may be said to be morally good or bad; so may their characters, or their motives, or their feelings; so may practices and institutions; perhaps even objects sometimes, like books or pictures. But it seems reasonable to say that, even in these other cases, some more or less direct reference to actions is always present, and is fundamental. A person is morally good or bad primarily at least because of what he does or omits to do. A morally bad character is a disposition to act morally badly, or wrongly. Motives typically, and feelings often, tend to issue in actions. A morally objectionable institution, like slavery perhaps or an oppressive system of law or government, is morally objectionable in that it permits, or even requires, things to be done that morally ought not to be done, or prevents things being done that should be done. If a book could sensibly be said to be morally bad, that might be because writing or publishing it was taken to be a morally bad thing to do, or perhaps because reading it was thought liable to prompt people towards acting in morally exceptionable ways. So it seems that, when moral issues come up, there is always involved, more or less directly, some question of the doings or non-doings of rational beings.

Why 'rational beings'? Why not simply say 'people,' or 'human beings'? The distinction is perhaps not a very important one, in practice at any rate; but still, it does seem to be the case that what makes 'people' eligible for consideration, and sometimes for judgement, as moral agents is that they are in a certain sense rational, and not that they constitute a particular biological species, that of humans. For one's doings to be a proper or possible object of moral evaluation whether by others or by oneself, it is a necessary condition that one should have at least some ability to perceive and consider alternative courses of action, to appreciate what is to be said for or against the alternatives, to make a choice or decision, and to act accordingly. But it is, one would think, a purely contingent matter that the only beings we know to exist who clearly satisfy this condition, or at any rate the only ones we commonly come across, are human beings, biped mammalian inhabitants of our particular planet. If there had been other sorts of animals on this planet, or if there were other beings elsewhere, who were rational in this somewhat minimal but essential sense, then they would have been, or would be, potential moral agents, notwithstanding the fact that they happened not to be human. One might even be inclined to regret that we come across no such beings. Our capacity to envisage a diversity of forms of life would surely be expanded by acquaintance with beings, able much as we are to choose within limits how to live their lives, but not constrained in doing so by specifically human needs, aims, and aspirations; it would be instructive to see, among other things, what morality would come down to in detail for them, and how relations between the species might be worked out (though of course they would be quite likely to work out very badly). It might have been good for humans to have had to take some non-humans more seriously than, as things are, they have occasion to do.

To be rational in this sense, then, rather than simply to be human, is a necessary condition for one's doings or non-doings to be a proper object of moral evaluation. Is it also a sufficient condition? Again the point is perhaps not very important; but for what it is worth, it seems reasonable to hold that it is not — at least in this sense, that it seems conceivable that, notwithstanding the rationality of some species of agents, questions of moral evaluation might not have arisen for them. For instance, there is the possibility, envisaged by Kant, of rational beings who would not only always see straight off what action it was that in fact was morally right, or required, but would always be thereby led to do it, and would never have the least inclination towards doing anything else. For them, at least moral exhortation and persuasion would be simply unnecessary; *ex hypothesi* there would be nothing in their doings to be condemned, and perhaps, if it was simply natural to them to act in that way, moral commendation also would be out of place. A great deal, at least, that is familiar to us in moral thought and discourse would not come up in their case; for there would be no occasion for it. It is perhaps also conceivable that the circumstances of life of some species of rational beings might have been such that no moral issues ever arose for them. If, for instance, though rational, they were all completely impassive, completely invulnerable, completely self-sufficient, not significantly affected in any way by anything that went on around them, and having to do with no sentient beings of any other sort, then it is perhaps hard to see how any of their doings could be judged morally better or worse than any alternatives. It would seem to make no difference of any morally assessable sort. However, it is surely of no great importance to decide this question; for we know well enough that human beings, who are in fact the only sort of rational beings we commonly encounter, are not like this, either by nature or with respect to their circumstances. So we may leave these rather fanciful speculations on one side, and move on to what we all actually know something about, that is, what may conveniently, if portentously, be called the 'human predicament.'

I had better make clear at once why I want to bring in, and indeed to start from, this perhaps archaic-looking topic. My idea is this. In general we evaluate things, it is to be supposed, for certain purposes; whenever, in any field, we rank or grade, commend or condemn, and so forth, we have — or should have, if there is to be any sense in what we are doing — some object in view, and quite possibly more than one. It is in fact risky to generalize about this, because particular cases differ so much among themselves. It might be objected, for instance, that while there will presumably be some pretty obvious 'object' in the evaluation of things that we use — for instance, to mark out the degree to which those things are good for what we propose to use them *for* — it is much less clear that we have any particular 'object' in evaluating, say, weather, or works of art. Still, at least evaluation is surely never just pointless; at the very least, even if we may sometimes have no practical purpose in view, it will be because we have some *preference* as between one thing and another that we bother at all to evaluate items of that kind. Further, it seems to me that to understand some species of evaluation (as contrasted perhaps with mastering it as a mere drill) is essentially a matter of grasping what its object is, what it is done *for;* and indeed if — *only* if — one understands this, can one be in any position to assess the appropriateness, or even relevance, of the standards and criteria employed.

Consider, for instance, the 'grading' of candidates in a school-leaving examination. Clearly, in considering how this is or should be done, it is essential to be clear as to what it is being done for. Is it the object, for instance, to determine and indicate how well candidates are judged to *have* done certain work at school? Or is it, differently, to indicate how well they are judged *likely* to do certain things in future, for instance in employment or at universities? Conceivably one might hold that these come to the same, on the ground that what a candidate has done is the only sound, or only assessable, indicator of what he may be expected to do; but if that is not so, clearly the two objects would make appropriate and relevant the employment of different criteria. Then again, it might be the object, or part of the object, to reward or reprove, encourage or stimulate, the examinees themselves; and this too would make 'grading' a different sort of exercise.

Now it is not impossible to raise the question: What is *moral* evaluation for? What is its point? Why do we distinguish between, say, actions as morally right or wrong, between people or qualities of character as good or bad? Why do we teach children to do this, by precept or example? Why do we think it worth doing? What are we trying to achieve, or bring about, by doing it? Well, it is by and large — with qualifications already noted — evaluation *of* the actions of rational beings. It does not seem plausible that in doing this we are simply, so to speak, disinterestedly awarding marks, for no particular reason or purpose, to ourselves or others. There is, it seems obvious here, some general practical end in view; and if so, it may seem manifest that the general object must be to bring it about, in some way or other, that rational beings act, in some respects or other, *better* than they would otherwise be liable to do. Put more pompously, the general object of moral evaluation must be to contribute in some respects, by way of the actions of rational beings, to the amelioration of the human predicament — that is, of the conditions in which *these* rational beings, humans, actually find themselves. Accordingly, I take it to be necessary to understanding in this case to consider, first, what it is in the human predicament that calls for amelioration, and second, what might reasonably be suggested (to put it guardedly) as the specific contribution of 'morality' to such amelioration. How are things liable to go wrong? And how exactly — or, perhaps, plausibly — can morality be understood as a contribution to their going better? These are the questions that I think worth asking. In thus talking, in archaic style, about the 'human predicament,' I believe, and in a sense hope, that I shall have nothing to say the truth of which will not be immediately obvious to everyone. There are some things nevertheless that it seems relevant to say; and in a sense it would not even matter if they were not true. For the present question is really what 'morality' can be seen as presupposing; and the answer to that is presumably independent of the question whether all that is presupposed is true.

It seems reasonable, and in the present context is highly relevant, to say, without necessarily going quite so far as Hobbes did, that the human predicament is inherently such that things are liable to go badly. This seems to be inherently so, but not completely hopelessly so; that is, there are circumstances, not in the least likely to change significantly or to be changed by our own efforts, which cannot but tend to make things go badly, but also something at least can be done, many different things in fact, to make them go at least somewhat better than they would do, if no such things were done at all.

In the first place, a human being as a certain kind of animal has what may be called biological needs. The life-span of humans is in any case limited; but if a person is to survive at all he must have air and water, usually shelter, and appropriate food, and he must not be subjected to gross physical damage. Apart from this there are countless other things which, while not absolute needs for every member of the species, can reasonably be regarded as indispensable enough, and indispensable for enough humans, to be called needs also. Then, in addition to and overlapping with the things that people need, there are the things that they want. (A man may not want something that he needs, if he does not know that he needs it, or even if he does know; and of course many things that we want are not things that we need.) Although there may be some things that almost every human beings wants (but does not absolutely need), there is obviously also almost endless personal diversity in wants, attributable to differences of circumstances, information, and individual character and aims, or to pure vagaries of taste and fancy. Furthermore, while it seems to be a necessary truth that, if one needs something, one is at least *prima facie* and in that respect better off if one has it

than if one does not, it is clear that people may want things which it would not be for their good to have, or indeed in any sense good that they should have; and sometimes they may know quite clearly that that is so. If we take a person's 'interests' to comprise those things which it is or would be actually for his good that he should have, it is evident that not only may he not know what his interests are, but he may not want to satisfy or pursue them even if he does know; and he may want to do or have things that it would not, and sometimes to his own knowledge would not, be in his interest to do or have. Attempts have sometimes been made to deny that a man may be a poor judge of his own interests, but surely wrongly. The motive, I think, has been apprehension of the practical consequences of allowing that a man might be a better judge of another's interests than that other person is of his own. It has been felt, understandably, that this, if admitted, might be taken as a pretext for a kind of paternalistic interference which, even if wholly well-intentioned, might be undesirable. But this, though understandable, is confused. If we wish to argue against the idea that a man may, quite in general, be properly compelled to act in a way which someone else thinks, but he does not, to be in his interest, we need not do so by trying to maintain that no one *could* be a better judge of his interests than he is himself. It is quite possible to maintain that, even if I do assess your interests better than you do, I am not necessarily entitled thereby to make you follow my judgement rather than your own.

Now some human needs, wants, and interests are, special and exceptional circumstances apart, just naturally satisfied by the human environment and situation, and others frustrated. For instance, there is naturally available in the atmosphere of the planet, without any intervention of ours, enough air for everybody to breathe (not always clean air, but that is another matter); and there are doubtless some things that people want to do, or perhaps would like to do, or wish that they could do, which are simply physically impossible — either completely so, for everybody, or impossible in certain conditions, or for certain people. But, uncontroversially, over an enormous range of needs, wants, and interests, these are neither just naturally satisfied, nor naturally, ineluctably frustrated. In an enormous range of cases, something both needs to be done, and also at least in principle could be done. And of course this is where practical problems arise.

Clearly, within the general area of theoretical possibility, what anyone can do, or could arrange that others should do, is limited by the availability of information, and also, no doubt one should add, of intelligence. Both in large matters of, for instance, national policy, and in small matters of purely private and personal concern, what can actually be done (except by accident) is not what could in technical theory be done, but only what is known, effectively realized, to be possible. At least as serious is the fact that the resources needed for doing things, again both in large matters and small, are practically always limited; not everything that is needed, or wanted, or would be advantageous can be done at the same time, or even could ever be done at all. This means, of course, that some 'satisfactions' must be postponed to others, with consequent problems about priorities; and some, no doubt, cannot possibly be secured at all.

This is the case, as one may put it, of attainable satisfactions competing for priority; but notoriously there are even less tractable forms of competition than this. In the first place, there is absolutely no reason to assume that the needs, wants, and interests of any one individual will just naturally form what might be called a consistent set, or coherent programme. We have noted already that a man may not want what he needs, often does not need what he wants, and may not want to get what it is in his interest that he should have; but of course it is also true that he may want things, not all of which it is practically, or even logically, possible that he should ever have. If so, there will be absolutely no reason to believe that his *total* satisfaction, meaning thereby satisfaction of *all* his needs, wants, and interests, is, in any order of priority, even logically possible, let alone practically. Then secondly, and even more notoriously, in practice people cannot but be often in competition with other people; practically at any rate, even if not in Utopian theory, it is often the case that the full or even partial satisfaction of one, or some, is attainable only at the expense of others — that is, by bringing about a situation which in some degree frustrates or does not wholly satisfy them. Nor, it seems, is this simply a practical difficulty of limited resources; for just as the wants, etc., of a single individual do not necessarily form a set such that satisfaction of all of them is possible even logically, the same may be true of the wants, etc., of pairs or of any larger groups of people. If, for instance, you want to exert absolute domination over

me, and I over you, it is not logically possible that both these wants should be fully satisfied; and similarly if, say, you want exclusive possession of some particular thing that I possess, and want too.

What emerges so far, then, from even the sketchiest survey of the human predicament is perhaps depressing enough. Though perhaps not many of the things people need, or want, or would be the better for having are just naturally, ineluctably, and absolutely unobtainable (I do not say that *none* are), it is also true that not many such things are just naturally available anyway, without anything in particular being done. Human knowledge and intelligence set limits of one sort to what *can* be done; and limits of another sort are set by limited resources. Given these limitations, there is no practical possibility of everyone's having everything that he wants, or would be the better for having, or even perhaps everything that he needs. But further, there is not merely a practical difficulty here, however insuperable; for, whether for an individual or for a group (or, for that matter, for groups of groups), there is no reason to believe that total satisfaction is even a logical possibility. People may have, both as individuals and as members of groups, wants and even interests the joint satisfaction of which is not logically possible.

But of course that is not all that may reasonably depress us. Even if what we have vaguely called total satisfaction is not a practical or even a logical possibility, there is reason to think that there is a practical possibility of a good deal of satisfaction — practical, that is, from the point of view of available resources and known technical feasibility. We have been assured by a variety of prophets, in the H. G. Wells or (in some moods) Bertrand Russell manner, that, notwithstanding the perplexing diversity of people's interests and wants, and the doubtless lesser variety of their actual needs, there exist both the resources and the technical capacity to go at least a very considerable way towards the general satisfaction of the inhabitants of our planet, and not only in grossly material respects; and, discounting a little the blue-skies fervour characteristic of such prophets, there is no reason wholly to disbelieve what they say. But of course there are snags; and these have to do with certain further facts about human beings.

We have already mentioned, as limiting factors, limited resources, limited information, limited intelligence. What we need now to bring in might be called limited rationality, and limited sympathies. In the first place it may be said — certainly with extreme vagueness, but still with pretty evident truth — that human beings in general are not just naturally disposed always to do what it would be best that they should do, even if they see, or are perfectly in a position to see, what that is. Even if they are not positively neurotic or otherwise maladjusted, people are naturally somewhat prone to be moved by short-run rather than long-run considerations, and often by the pursuit of more blatant, intense, and obtrusive satisfactions rather than of those cooler ones that on balance would really be better. While mostly 'rational' in the minimal sense mentioned above — that is, able in at least some degree to envisage practical alternatives, to deliberate, and to decide — they are not all just naturally, or indeed in any other way, rational in the more exacting sense of being regularly disposed to deliberate well and to act accordingly. And this is so, of course, even where a person has to consider no interests, wants, or needs but his own.

Next, limited sympathies. This may even be too mild a term for some of the things that I have in mind. One may say for a start, mildly, that most human beings have some natural tendency to be more concerned about the satisfaction of their own wants, etc., than those of others. A man who does not like being hungry, and who is naturally inclined to take such steps as he can to satisfy his hunger, may very well care less, even not at all, about the hunger of others, and may not care at all whether anything is done to satisfy them. Even if he does care to some extent about others, it is quite likely to be only about *some* others — family, friends, class, tribe, country, or 'race.' There is also, besides complete or comparative indifference, such a thing as active malevolence, perhaps even purely disinterested malevolence; a man will sometimes be not only unconcerned about, but actively malevolent towards, others whom he may see as somehow in competition with himself, and sometimes perhaps even towards some whose frustrations or sufferings are not even supposed to be for the advancement of any interest of his own. There are two obvious ways in which, consequentially, things in the human predicament are liable to go badly. For people are not simply confronted, whether as individuals or groups, with the problems of getting along satisfactorily in material conditions that may, in varying degrees, be ungenial or hostile. They are also highly vulnerable to other people; and they often need the help of

other people. But, given 'limited sympathies,' it cannot be assumed that needed help will naturally be forthcoming; and it cannot even be assumed that active malevolence will *not* be forthcoming. And perhaps above all, there may be the impossibility of trust. Whether, in pursuit of some end of my own, I need your help, or merely your non-interference, I may well be unable to trust you either to co-operate or to keep out of it, if I think that you are not only much less concerned about my ends and interests than your own, but possibly even actively hostile to my attainment of my ends. If so, then it may be impossible for either of us to do, either separately or together, things that would be advantageous to us both, and which perhaps we both clearly see would be advantageous to us both; and it may be necessary for us individually to do things, for instance in self-protection, the doing of which may be exceedingly laborious, wasteful, and disagreeable. It will be obvious that all this applies as fully to relations between groups as between individuals; and indeed that distrust and active hostility between groups has been, in the human predicament, as frequent and constant as between individuals, and vastly more damaging.

So far we have not, I think, said anything seriously disputable, or at all unfamiliar. It is obvious that human beings have, in general, an *interest* in the course of events in which they are involved: for, though they may indeed want some things which they would not be at all the better for having, they do have many entirely harmless and proper and reasonable wants; and they also have interests and actual needs, satisfaction of which may be absolutely necessary for their well-being. But the course of events is not at all likely, without their intervention, to go in a way at all satisfactory to them; and even with intervention, there is still so much that may go wrong. Resources are limited; knowledge, skills, information, and intelligence are limited; people are often not rational, either in the management of their own affairs or in the adjustment of their own affairs in relation to others. Then, finally, they are vulnerable to others, and dependent on others, and yet inevitably often in competition with others; and, human sympathies being limited, they may often neither get nor give help that is needed, may not manage to co-operate for common ends, and may be constantly liable to frustration or positive injury from directly hostile interference by other persons.

Thus it comes about that—as Hobbes of course most memorably insisted—there is in what may be called the human predicament a certain 'natural' tendency for things to go very badly; meaning thereby not, of course, in this connection, *morally* badly, but badly merely in the sense that, given the above-mentioned wholly indisputable facts about people and the circumstances in which they exist, there is the very evident possibility of very great difficulty in securing, for all or possibly even any of them, much that they want, much that it would be in their interest to have, even much that they need. And the facts that make this so are facts about the *human* predicament; there is probably no great interest in speculating about possible circumstances of other conceivable species of rational beings, but still it is worth bearing in mind that the facts we have so summarily surveyed are *contingent* facts. It is easy enough to see in general terms how very different the situation would be if the beings concerned were less vulnerable, less aggressive, less egotistical, less irrational, more intelligent, more self-sufficient, and more favoured by material circumstances.

With respect to the very general limitations we have mentioned, as making it the case that things are inherently liable to go badly for people, one might raise the question whether they can be ranked in any order of relative importance. It seems to me that they can be, though probably not quite uncontroversially.

Their relative prominence, of course, will vary to some extent from case to case. Sometimes poverty of resources will be most immediately conspicuous. If things go rather badly for the inhabitants of ice-fields, or deserts, or tropical jungles, it may be unnecessary to look any further for at any rate most of the explanation than to the extreme ungeniality of those physical environments. Sometimes lack of skills and knowledge will catch the eye, as in the case of people placed in intrinsically quite favourable circumstances which they lack the technical ability to make much use of. But in general it seems to me to be true, in two different ways, that more significant limits are set by other factors. It is only, after all, in comparatively unusual cases that the means of reasonable human existence are just ineluctably, physically unavailable (though it should not be forgotten that this may not always be the case); nor, one may well think (though possibly future generations will think differently), are many of the major ills of the human predicament more than partially attributable to sheer lack of knowledge and technical skills. One may well think that by far the most important matter is the poor use, or positive misuse, of resources and skills that for the most part are quite readily available; and it seems that this must be laid, in one way or another, at the door of limited rationality and limited sympathies. And in a sense these *must* always be the most important factors. For they determine what, of the things that *can* be done, *are* done; resources and skills constitute power, but power to do damage as well as to do good. Whether resources and skills are ample or very limited, it must in any case be a crucial question whether or not the use that is made of them is reasonable and humane.

But now, if limited rationality and limited sympathies are crucial, which is one to regard as the more important of the two? Perhaps it is not very sensible to attempt a definite answer to this question, if only because in practice these two factors are extraordinarily difficult to disentangle from one another. One might be inclined, pursuing much the same train of thought as in the last paragraph, to see limited sympathies as fundamental; for a man may be wholly rational, clear-headed, sane, and still, if he is not to act destructively towards others, it is essential that he should not simply see, but care, what becomes of them. Or again, if one society or group is not to oppress another, it is surely fundamental that it should not be either hostile or indifferent to that other's interests. Thus one may feel some sympathy with the common run of uplifting—if unpractical—discourses about the fundamental necessity for improvement of a 'change of heart.' But one may also feel, rightly, for two reasons, that such discourses over-simplify. In the first place, much that is most damagingly done seems really attributable, not to the malevolence of men, but to sheer folly and confusion of mind; some wars, for example, though not indeed all wars, may well seem not so much wicked as nearly insane, owing far more to short-sightedness, thoughtlessness, and muddle than to actual ill-will. So one may sometimes feel that there is plenty of good-will about, plenty of humane intentions, if only men were saner in seeing how to bring them to bear. But secondly, is it not the case that much failure of human sympathy is itself the direct offspring of un-reason? Racial hostility, for instance, is not merely—though of course

—a gross defect of human sympathy; it is also—in common no doubt with many other hatreds, hostilities, and fears—a gross deformation of rationality. If people were saner, their sympathies also would be less stunted and deformed; hearts would be in much better shape if heads were less tangled, and haunted, and befogged. Surely it has been a very common failing of moralists, professionally pre-occupied with the weakness of good-will in human affairs, enormously to under-rate the strength in that connection, not simply of ill-will, but of sheer unreason. It is possible conceptually to distinguish one from the other, and in practice sometimes to recognize one in the other's absence. But so often they go together, each playing into the other's hand, and perhaps not realistically to be ranked in any order of precedence.

Precedence, though, in what respect? It may well be the case that, as things are, rationality may be in shorter world supply than human sympathy, so that what we need more of at the moment is rationality. Nevertheless, there still seems to be a good case for the contention that something like (not, I hasten to say, exactly like) Kant's 'goodwill' is more fundamental still. If, for instance, I believe that you are both ready and able at any time to sacrifice me and my interests to the pursuit of your own, I shall not be reassured by any decrease in your muddleheadedness—unless, indeed, as might very well not be the case, in an un-muddled perspective the sacrifice of me would be seen to be irrational from your point of view. Rationality in fact seems, like intelligence and skill and resources, to be something that can be used to do harm (at least to some) as well as good; what is ultimately crucial is *how* it is to be used. Nothing in the end, then, seems to be more important, in the inherent liability to badness of the human predicament, than that limitation which I have called, vaguely enough, 'limited sympathies.'

Now, the general suggestion that (guardedly) I wish to put up for consideration is this: that the 'general object' of morality, appreciation of which may enable us to *understand* the basis of moral evaluation, is to contribute to betterment—or non-deterioration—of the human predicament, primarily and essentially by seeking to countervail 'limited sympathies' and their potentially most damaging effects. It is the proper business of morality, and the general object of moral evaluation, not of course to add to our available resources, nor—directly anyway—to our knowledge of how to make advantageous use of them, nor—again, not directly—to make us more rational in the judicious pursuit of our interests and ends; its proper business is to expand our sympathies, or, better, to reduce the liability to damage inherent in their natural tendency to be narrowly restricted. We may note at once that, if this is, as I think, in a sense the most important of the built-in tendencies of things to go wrong, the present suggestion fits well with the common idea that there is something peculiarly *important* about morality. But that is too vague to be much use. The only way, I suppose, to see whether there is anything much in this suggestion—to see whether it illuminates the nature of 'the moral point of view'—is to see what follows from this general supposition, how it works out, and whether what it would imply is closely consonant enough with what we already think we know about moral judgement. It must be remembered, of course, that quite different ways of looking at the matter might quite well issue in just the same implications, so that argument of this pattern is certainly not demonstrative. But we may give it a try, and see how persuasive we can make it look.

Suggestions for Further Reading

Blum, Lawrence. *Friendship, Altruism, and Morality.* Routledge and Kegan Paul, 1980. Contains a sustained critique on some aspects of rule-governed ethics such as the principles of universalizability and impartiality.

Foot, Philippa. *Virtues and Vices.* Blackwell's, 1978.

Goodpaster, K. E., ed. *Perspectives on Morality: Essays by William K. Frankena.* University of Notre Dame, 1976. Contains important essays on the subject matter of this chapter.

Hancock, Roger. *Twentieth Century Ethics.* New York: Columbia University Press, 1974.

Hare, R. M. *The Language of Morals.* Oxford University Press, 1952.

Hare, R. M. *Freedom and Reason.* Oxford University Press, 1961.

Hudson, W. D., ed. *The Is/Ought Question.* St. Martin's Press.

Hudson, W. D. *Modern Moral Philosophy.* 2nd ed. Macmillan, 1983. A clear, comprehensive survey of the issues discussed in this section.

Moore, G. E. *Principia Ethica.* Cambridge University, 1903. The book that started the major discussion of metaethics in the twentieth century.

Nowell-Smith, Patrick. *Ethics.* Penguin Books, 1954.

Pritchard, H. A. *Moral Obligation.* Oxford University Press, 1968.

Ross, David W. *The Right and the Good.* Oxford University Press, 1930.

Searle, John. "How to Derive 'Ought' from 'Is.'" *The Philosophical Review* 73, Jan. 1964.

Sellars, Wilfred, and John Hospers, eds. *Readings in Ethical Theory.* 2nd ed. New York: Prentice-Hall, 1970. The largest collection of essays on the problems discussed in this section.

Stevenson, C. L. *Ethics and Language.* Yale University Press, 1944.

Urmson, J. O. *The Emotive Theory of Ethics.* London: Huchinson, 1968.

Warnock, G. J. *The Object of Morality.* Methuen, 1971. The book that signaled the revival of ethical naturalism.

Warnock, Mary. *Ethics Since 1900.* Oxford University Press, 1960. A short, clear exposition of the history of ethics in the twentieth century.

Part IX

Moral Realism and the Challenge of Skepticism

Why should we not rather make the opposite assumption that all the particular moral judgments we intuitively make are likely to derive from discarded religious systems, from warped views of sex and bodily functions, or from customs necessary for the survival of the group in social and economic circumstances that now lie in the distant past?

PETER SINGER
"Sidgwick and Reflective Equilibrium,"
Monist, July 1974, vol. 58, no. 3, p. 516

In this Part of our work we continue our discussion of the justification of moral theories and beliefs begun in Parts II and VIII. Now we consider the problem in its most contemporary form by examining the comparison of ethical theories with scientific ones and asking whether contemporary epistemology throws any light on the issue of moral skepticism.

First we need to define some technical terms. Metaphysical realism is the view, to quote Michael Dummett, that some claims or statements about the world "possess an objective truth-value independently of our means of knowing it: they are true or false in virtue of a reality existing independently of us."[1] It follows from this that some statements about the world are true, and they are true whether or not we believe they are. The antirealist denies at least one part of this conjunct. Most people are realistic in this sense, that is, they believe that some of our claims about the universe are true whether or not anyone believes them and would be so even if no one believed them.

A moral realist is one who holds an analogous thesis about ethics: that there are moral facts and that they exist independently of whether we believe them. Recurring to our discussion in Part VIII, naturalists, non-naturalists, and supernaturalists are moral realists, while noncognitivists are antirealists who deny the possibility of the existence of moral facts.

However, one might reject emotivism and prescriptivism and still be an antirealist. This is where the skeptic comes in. The skeptic need not have a positive theory about morality in order to deny what the realist asserts. He or she might reject noncognitivism as an adequate account of morality, believing instead that cognitivism is the correct account of moral claims, but that in fact none of our moral theories are true. Spinoza said that good and evil are "nothing more but modes in which the imagination is affected in different ways, and, nevertheless, they are regarded by the ignorant as being special attributes of things,"[2] and J. L. Mackie, in our first reading, accepts the cognitivist's analysis of morality but denies that the criteria are satisfied: "The denial of objective values will have to be put forward . . . as an 'error theory,' a theory that although most people in making moral judgments implicitly claim, among other things, to be pointing to something objectively prescriptive, these claims are all false."[3] Moral skeptics, then, doubt or deny that any of our moral theories or judgments are true. A diagram of the positions look like this:

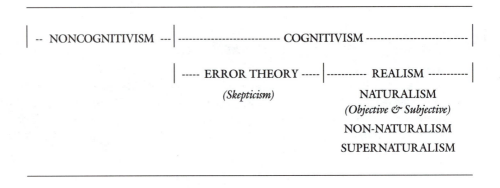

Mackie acknowledges the importance of the claims of realists in holding to objective values, but offers two arguments against such views: the argument from relativity or disagreement, and the argument from queerness. The argument from disagreement points out that there is no universal moral code to which all people everywhere adhere, which seems to indicate that morality is culturally dependent. The argument from queerness aims at showing that it is implausible to suppose that such things as values have an independent existence.

In this Part's second essay, David Brink takes issue with Mackie, arguing that the realist has a response to each of these points.

In our third reading, Gilbert Harman argues for an antirealist position by noting an asymmetry between scientific theories that require observations to confirm them and moral theories, which don't seem to be confirmed in the same way. Scientific theory is tested against the world, so that if a predicted observation occurs, our theory is confirmed, but if it doesn't occur, we feel some pressure to alter our theory. With regard to moral theories, we do not see 'rightness' or 'wrongness' in acts in the same way we identify a vapor trail in a cloud chamber as a proton. Moral insights occur because of our upbringing, not because of the way the world is. Hence, we may conclude that there are no moral facts in the way that there are scientific facts. This result Harman calls moral nihilism.

Harman next considers ways to offset this conclusion. One way would be if we could reduce moral facts to certain sociological and psychological facts. Harman examines this possibility and concludes that this reduction, at best, would have to be "complex, vague, and difficult to specify." It is doubtful whether there are any moral facts.

In our fourth reading, Nicholas Sturgeon takes issue with Harman on the disparity between scientific and moral facts. He argues that we often discover that moral facts "do appear relevant by perfectly ordinary standards to the explanation of moral beliefs and of a good deal else besides." There is a symmetry between scientific explanation and moral explanation, so that if we reject moral explanations of our moral observations, we must also reject scientific explanations of our scientific observations. So skepticism about morality entails skepticism about science, a result not welcome to most moral antirealists.

In our fifth reading, Evan K. Jobe argues that Sturgeon fails to establish his major theses: that moral qualities can play an essential role in the scientific explanation of human conduct and that moral realism is compatible with physicalism. Although Sturgeon has shown that this latter point is possible, it is another matter to show that it is plausible.

In our sixth reading, Bernard Williams sets forth a modified skepticism. He argues that there can be knowledge of specific ethical claims — those involving what he calls "thick ethical concepts," such as cowardice, brutality, gratitude, lying, promising, and the like — but philosophi-

cal reflection can destroy such knowledge by disturbing or replacing those concepts so that beliefs previously formed with those concepts can no longer be formed. Whereas reflection can destroy, it cannot create moral knowledge. Thus, reflective cultures such as ours are left with little moral knowledge, but instead have perhaps only some vague and unevenly held beliefs, such as "one has to have special reason to kill someone."

In our final reading, Bruce Russell takes up the issues of skepticism as discussed by Williams and others. He argues that there is no good reason to accept skepticism and that it is not clear how Williams made his case that reflection can destroy ethical knowledge.

Using recent work in epistemology by Alvin Plantinga, Russell argues that current arguments purporting to show that the sources of moral belief are unreliable are themselves unsound. With regard to Williams's special modified skepticism, Russell argues that while philosophical reflection may undermine some ethical beliefs by disturbing some of the wider cultural beliefs that support the culture's ethics, it is not clear that reflection would affect an "unshifting core" of such concepts. Certainty about ethical beliefs or knowledge would require a clearer understanding of the criteria for knowledge or justified beliefs that we now possess, but based on our current conceptions, it seems that we are within our epistemic rights in believing that the "unshifting core" of our morality is true.

In the third part of Russell's essay, he takes up a second form of ethical skepticism — practical skepticism as to whether ethical considerations necessarily give everyone an overriding reason to act ethically all of the time. Russell examines arguments against this kind of skepticism and concludes that they are unsound: The "problem that remains unsolved is to explain when and why moral requirements sometimes provide overriding reasons to act and sometimes do not."

Endnotes

[1] Michael Dummett, *Truth and Other Enigmas* (Harvard University Press, 1978), p. 146. Hilary Putnam puts it this way: "A realist (with respect to a given theory or discourse) holds that (1) sentences of that theory are true or false; and (2) what makes them true or false is something external—that is to say, it is not (in general) our data, actual or potential, or the structure of our minds, or our language, etc."

(Quoted in "The Many Moral Realisms," Geoffrey Sayre-McCord, *The Southern Journal of Philosophy*, XXIV (1986), supplement. I am indebted to this article in writing this introduction, although I have simplified Sayre-McCord's account.)

[2] Baruch Spinoza, *Ethics* (Haffner Press, 1949), p. 77.

[3] J. L. Mackie, *Ethics: Inventing Right and Wrong* (Penguin, 1977), p. 35.

IX.1 *The Subjectivity of Values*

J. L. MACKIE

J. L. Mackie (1917–1982) was a fellow in philosophy at University College, Oxford University. His work covers virtually every major area in philosophy. His book *Ethics: Inventing Right and Wrong,* from which this selection is taken, represents a classical skeptical position on moral values. Mackie disagrees with the noncognitivists who say that ethical language is meaningless. Moral statements make claims about the nature of reality—claims that there are moral facts. Unfortunately, these statements are all false; there are no objective values. Mackie presents two arguments that show why this is the conclusion to which rational people should come.

The first is the argument from relativity or disagreement, which says that since morals seem to be culturally dependent and vary over time and place, the burden of proof is on the person who contends that we should not take this diversity at face value. This argument indicates that there is no separate or supervenient reality. The second argument is the argument from queerness, which contends that if there were objective values, they would have to be very strange things indeed, but that there is no good reason to suppose that there are these queer objects. Thus, by the principle of parsimony (that is, do not multiply objects beyond necessity), we should conclude that there are no such objects.

Moral Scepticism

There are no objective values. This is a bald statement of the thesis of this chapter, but before arguing for it I shall try to clarify and restrict it in ways that may meet some objections and prevent some misunderstanding.

The statement of this thesis is liable to provoke one of three very different reactions. Some will think it not merely false but pernicious; they will see it as a threat to morality and to everything else that is worthwhile, and they will find the presenting of such a thesis in which purports to be a book on ethics paradoxical or even outrageous. Others will regard it as a trivial truth, almost too obvious to be worth mentioning, and certainly too plain to be worth much argument. Others again will say that it is meaningless or empty, that no real issue is raised by the question whether values are or are not part of the fabric of the world. But, precisely because there can be these three different reactions, much more needs to be said.

The claim that values are not objective, are not part of the fabric of the world, is meant to include not only moral goodness, which might be most naturally equated with moral value, but also other things that could be more loosely called moral values or disvalues — rightness and wrongness, duty, obligation, an action's being rotten and contemptible, and so on. It also includes non-moral values, notably aesthetic ones, beauty and various kinds of artistic merit. I shall not discuss these explicitly, but clearly much the same considerations apply to aesthetic and to moral values, and there would be at least some initial implausibility in a view that gave the one a different status from the other.

Since it is with moral values that I am primarily concerned, the view I am adopting may be called moral scepticism. But this name is likely to be misunderstood: 'moral scepticism' might also be used as a name for either of two first order views, or perhaps for an incoherent mixture of the two. A moral sceptic might be the sort of person who says 'All this talk of morality is tripe,' who rejects morality and will take no notice of it. Such a person may be literally rejecting all moral judgements; he is more likely to be making moral judgements of his own, expressing a positive moral condemnation of all that conventionally passes for morality; or he may be confusing these two logically incompatible views, and saying that he rejects all morality, while he is in fact rejecting only a particular morality that is current in the society in which he has grown up. But I am not at present concerned with the merits or faults of such a position. These are first order moral views, positive or negative: the person who adopts either of them is taking a certain practical, normative, stand. By contrast, what I am discussing is a second order view, a view about the status of moral values and the nature of moral valuing, about where and how they fit into the world. These first and second order views are not merely distinct but completely independent: one could be a second order moral sceptic without being a first order one, or again the other way round. A man could hold strong moral

views, and indeed ones whose content was thoroughly conventional, while believing that they were simply attitudes and policies with regard to conduct that he and other people held. Conversely, a man could reject all established morality while believing it to be an objective truth that it was evil or corrupt.

With another sort of misunderstanding moral scepticism would seem not so much pernicious as absurd. How could anyone deny that there is a difference between a kind action and a cruel one, or that a coward and a brave man behave differently in the face of danger? Of course, this is undeniable; but it is not to the point. The kinds of behaviour to which moral values and disvalues are ascribed are indeed part of the furniture of the world, and so are the natural, descriptive, differences between them; but not, perhaps, their differences in value. It is a hard fact that cruel actions differ from kind ones, and hence that we can learn, as in fact we all do, to distinguish them fairly well in practice, and to use the words 'cruel' and 'kind' with fairly clear descriptive meanings; but is it an equally hard fact that actions which are cruel in such a descriptive sense are to be condemned? The present issue is with regard to the objectivity specifically of value, not with regard to the objectivity of those natural, factual differences on the basis of which differing values are assigned.

Subjectivism

Another name often used, as an alternative to 'moral scepticism,' for the view I am discussing is 'subjectivism.' But this too has more than one meaning. Moral subjectivism too could be a first order, normative, view, namely that everyone really ought to do whatever he thinks he should. This plainly is a (systematic) first order view; on examination it soon ceases to be plausible, but that is beside the point, for it is quite independent of the second order thesis at present under consideration. What is more confusing is that different second order views compete for the name 'subjectivism.' Several of these are doctrines about the meaning of moral terms and moral statements. What is often called moral subjectivism is the doctrine that, for example, 'This action is right' *means* 'I approve of this action,' or more generally that moral judgements are equivalent to reports of the speaker's own feelings or attitudes. But the view I am now discussing is to be distinguished in two vital respects from any such doctrine as this. First, what I have called moral scepticism is a negative doctrine, not a positive one: it says what there isn't, not what there is. It says that there do not exist entities or relations of a certain kind, objective values or requirements, which many people have believed to exist. Of course, the moral sceptic cannot leave it at that. If his position is to be at all plausible, he must give some account of how other people have fallen into what he regards as an error, and this account will have to include some positive suggestions about how values fail to be objective, about what has been mistaken for, or has led to false beliefs about, objective values. But this will be a development of his theory, not its core: its core is the negation. Secondly, what I have called moral scepticism is an ontological thesis, not a linguistic or conceptual one. It is not, like the other doctrine often called moral subjectivism, a view about the meanings of moral statements. Again, no doubt, if it is to be at all plausible, it will have to give some account of their meanings, and I shall say something about this [later]. But this too will be a development of the theory, not its core.

It is true that those who have accepted the moral subjectivism which is the doctrine that moral judgements are equivalent to reports of the speaker's own feelings or attitudes have usually presupposed what I am calling moral scepticism. It is because they have assumed that there are no objective values that they have looked elsewhere for an analysis of what moral statements might mean, and have settled upon subjective reports. Indeed, if all our moral statements were such subjective reports, it would follow that, at least so far as we are aware, there are no objective moral values. If we were aware of them, we would say something about them. In this sense this sort of subjectivism entails moral scepticism. But the converse entailment does not hold. The denial that there are objective values does not commit one to any particular view about what moral statements mean, and certainly not to the view that they are equivalent to subjective reports. No doubt if moral values are not objective they are in some very broad sense subjective, and for this reason I would accept 'moral subjectivism' as an alternative name to 'moral scepticism.' But subjectivism in this broad sense must be distinguished

from the specific doctrine about meaning referred to above. Neither name is altogether satisfactory: we simply have to guard against the (different) misinterpretations which each may suggest.

The Multiplicity of Second Order Questions

The distinctions drawn in the last two sections rest not only on the well-known and generally recognized difference between first and second order questions, but also on the more controversial claim that there are several kinds of second order moral question. Those most often mentioned are questions about the meaning and use of ethical terms, or the analysis of ethical concepts. With these go questions about the logic of moral statements: there may be special patterns of moral argument, licensed, perhaps, by aspects of the meanings of moral terms — for example, it may be part of the meaning of moral statements that they are universalizable. But there are also ontological, as contrasted with linguistic or conceptual, questions about the nature and status of goodness or rightness or whatever it is that first order moral statements are distinctively about. These are questions of factual rather than conceptual analysis: the problem of what goodness is cannot be settled conclusively or exhaustively by finding out what the word 'good' means, or what it is conventionally used to say or to do.

Recent philosophy, biased as it has been towards various kinds of linguistic inquiry, has tended to doubt this, but the distinction between conceptual and factual analysis in ethics can be supported by analogies with other areas. The question of what perception is, what goes on when someone perceives something, is not adequately answered by finding out what words like 'see' and 'hear' mean, or what someone is doing in saying 'I perceive . . . ,' by analysing, however fully and accurately, any established concept of perception. There is a still closer analogy with colours. Robert Boyle and John Locke called colours 'secondary qualities,' meaning that colours as they occur in material things consist simply in patterns of arrangement and movement of minute particles on the surfaces of objects, which make them, as we would now say, reflect light of some frequencies better than others, and so enable these objects to produce colour sensations in us, but that colours as we see them do not literally belong to the surfaces of material things. Whether Boyle and Locke were right about this cannot be settled by finding out how we use colour words and what we mean in using them. Naïve realism about colours might be a correct analysis not only of our pre-scientific colour concepts but also of the conventional meanings of colour words, and even of the meanings with which scientifically sophisticated people use them when they are off their guard, and yet it might not be a correct account of the status of colours.

Error could well result, then, from a failure to distinguish factual from conceptual analysis with regard to colours, from taking an account of the meanings of statements as a full account of what there is. There is a similar and in practice even greater risk of error in moral philosophy. There is another reason, too, why it would be a mistake to concentrate second order ethical discussions on questions of meaning. The more work philosophers have done on meaning, both in ethics and elsewhere, the more complications have come to light. It is by now pretty plain that no simple account of the meanings of first order moral statements will be correct, will cover adequately even the standard, conventional, sense of the main moral terms; I think, none the less, that there is a relatively clear-cut issue about the objectivity of moral values which is in danger of being lost among the complications of meaning.

The Claim to Objectivity

If I have succeeded in specifying precisely enough the moral values whose objectivity I am denying, my thesis may now seem to be trivially true. Of course, some will say, valuing, preferring, choosing, recommending, rejecting, condemning, and so on, are human activities, and there is no need to look for values that are prior to and logically independent of all such activities. There may be widespread agreement in valuing, and particular value-judgements are not in general arbitrary or isolated: they typically cohere with others, or can be criticized if they do not, reasons can be given for them, and so on: but if all that the subjectivist is maintaining is that desires,

ends, purposes, and the like figure somewhere in the system of reasons, and that no ends or purposes are objective as opposed to being merely intersubjective, then this may be conceded without much fuss.

But I do not think that this should be conceded so easily. As I have said, the main tradition of European moral philosophy includes the contrary claim, that there are objective values of just the sort I have denied. I have referred already to Plato, Kant, and Sidgwick. Kant in particular holds that the categorical imperative is not only categorical and imperative but objectively so: though a rational being gives the moral law to himself, the law that he thus makes is determinate and necessary. Aristotle begins the *Nicomachean Ethics* by saying that the good is that at which all things aim, and that ethics is part of a science which he calls 'politics,' whose goal is not knowledge but practice; yet he does not doubt that there can be *knowledge* of what is the good for man, nor, once he has identified this as well-being or happiness, *eudaimonia,* that it can be known, rationally determined, in what happiness consists; and it is plain that he thinks that this happiness is intrinsically desirable, not good simply because it is desired. The rationalist Samuel Clarke holds that

> these eternal and necessary differences of things make it *fit and reasonable* for creatures so to act . . . even separate from the consideration of these rules being the *positive will* or *command of God;* and also antecedent to any respect or regard, expectation or apprehension, of any *particular private and personal advantage or disadvantage, reward or punishment,* either present or future . . .

Even the sentimentalist Hutcheson defines moral goodness as 'some quality apprehended in actions, which procures approbation . . . ,' while saying that the moral sense by which we perceive virtue and vice has been given to us (by the Author of nature) to direct our actions. Hume indeed was on the other side, but he is still a witness to the dominance of the objectivist tradition, since he claims that when we 'see that the distinction of vice and virtue is not founded merely on the relations of objects, nor is perceiv'd by reason,' this 'wou'd subvert all the vulgar systems of morality.' And Richard Price insists that right and wrong are 'real characters of actions,' not 'qualities of our minds,' and are perceived by the understanding; he criticizes the notion of moral sense on the ground that it would make virtue an affair of taste, and moral right and wrong 'nothing in the objects themselves'; he rejects Hutcheson's view because (perhaps mistakenly) he sees it as collapsing into Hume's.

But this objectivism about values is not only a feature of the philosophical tradition. It has also a firm basis in ordinary thought, and even in the meanings of moral terms. No doubt it was an extravagance for Moore to say that 'good' is the name of a non-natural quality, but it would not be so far wrong to say that in moral contexts it is used as if it were the name of a supposed non-natural quality, where the description 'non-natural' leaves room for the peculiar evaluative, prescriptive, intrinsically action-guiding aspects of this supposed quality. This point can be illustrated by reflection on the conflicts and swings of opinion in recent years between non-cognitivist and naturalist views about the central, basic, meanings of ethical terms. If we reject the view that it is the function of such terms to introduce objective values into discourse about conduct and choices of action, there seem to be two main alternative types of account. One (which has importantly different subdivisions) is that they conventionally express either attitudes which the speaker purports to adopt towards whatever it is that he characterizes morally, or prescriptions or recommendations, subject perhaps to the logical constraint of universalizability. Different views of this type share the central thesis that ethical terms have, at least partly and primarily, some sort of non-cognitive, non-descriptive, meaning. Views of the other type hold that they are descriptive in meaning, but descriptive of natural features, partly of such features as everyone, even the non-cognitivist, would recognize as distinguishing kind actions from cruel ones, courage from cowardice, politeness from rudeness, and so on, and partly (though these two overlap) of relations between the actions and some human wants, satisfactions, and the like. I believe that views of both these types capture part of the truth. Each approach can account for the fact that moral judgements are action-guiding or practical. Yet each gains much of its plausibility from the felt inadequacy of the other. It is a very natural reaction to any non-cognitive analysis of ethical terms to protest that there is more to ethics than this, something more external to the maker of moral judgements, more authoritative over both him and those of or to whom he speaks, and this reaction is likely to persist even when full allowance has been made

for the logical, formal, constraints of full-blooded prescriptivity and universalizability. Ethics, we are inclined to believe, is more a matter of knowledge and less a matter of decision than any non-cognitive analysis allows. And of course naturalism satisfies this demand. It will not be a matter of choice or decision whether an action is cruel or unjust or imprudent or whether it is likely to produce more distress than pleasure. But in satisfying this demand, it introduces a converse deficiency. On a naturalist analysis, moral judgements can be practical, but their practicality is wholly relative to desires or possible satisfactions of the person or persons whose actions are to be guided; but moral judgements seem to say more than this. This view leaves out the categorical quality of moral requirements. In fact both naturalist and non-cognitive analyses leave out the apparent authority of ethics, the one by excluding the categorically imperative aspect, the other the claim to objective validity or truth. The ordinary user of moral language means to say something about whatever it is that he characterizes morally, for example a possible action, as it is in itself, or would be if it were realized, and not about, or even simply expressive of, his, or anyone else's, attitude or relation to it. But the something he wants to say is not purely descriptive, certainly not inert, but something that involves a call for action or for the refraining from action, and one that is absolute, not contingent upon any desire or preference or policy or choice, his own or anyone else's. Someone in a state of moral perplexity, wondering whether it would be wrong for him to engage, say, in research related to bacteriological warfare, wants to arrive at some judgement about this concrete case, his doing this work at this time in these actual circumstances; his relevant characteristics will be part of the subject of the judgement, but no relation between him and the proposed action will be part of the predicate. The question is not, for example, whether he really wants to do this work, whether it will satisfy or dissatisfy him, whether he will in the long run have a pro-attitude towards it, or even whether this is an action of a sort that he can happily and sincerely recommend in all relevantly similar cases. Nor is he even wondering just whether to recommend such action in all relevantly similar cases. He wants to know whether this course of action would be wrong in itself. Something like this is the everyday objectivist concept of which talk about non-natural qualities is a philosopher's reconstruction.

The prevalence of this tendency to objectify values — and not only moral ones — is confirmed by a pattern of thinking that we find in existentialists and those influenced by them. The denial of objective values can carry with it an extreme emotional reaction, a feeling that nothing matters at all, that life has lost its purpose. Of course this does not follow; the lack of objective values is not a good reason for abandoning subjective concern or for ceasing to want anything. But the abandonment of a belief in objective values can cause, at least temporarily, a decay of subjective concern and sense of purpose. That it does so is evidence that the people in whom this reaction occurs have been tending to objectify their concerns and purposes, have been giving them a fictitious external authority. A claim to objectivity has been so strongly associated with their subjective concerns and purposes that the collapse of the former seems to undermine the latter as well.

This view, that conceptual analysis would reveal a claim to objectivity, is sometimes dramatically confirmed by philosophers who are officially on the other side. Bertrand Russell, for example, says that 'ethical propositions should be expressed in the optative mood, not in the indicative'; he defends himself effectively against the charge of inconsistency in both holding ultimate ethical valuations to be subjective and expressing emphatic opinions on ethical questions. Yet at the end he admits

> Certainly there *seems* to be something more. Suppose, for example, that some one were to advocate the introduction of bullfighting in this country. In opposing the proposal, I should *feel,* not only that I was expressing my desires, but that my desires in the matter are *right,* whatever that may mean. As a matter of argument, I can, I think, show that I am not guilty of any logical inconsistency in holding to the above interpretation of ethics and at the same time expressing strong ethical preferences. But in feeling I am not satisfied.

But he concludes, reasonably enough, with the remark: 'I can only say that, while my own opinions as to ethics do not satisfy me, other people's satisfy me still less.'

I conclude, then, that ordinary moral judgements include a claim to objectivity, an assumption that there are objective values in just the sense in which I am concerned to deny this. And I do not think it is going too far to say that this assumption has been incorporated in the basic, conventional, meanings of moral terms. Any analysis of the meanings of moral terms which omits this claim to objective, intrinsic, prescriptivity is to that extent incomplete; and this is true of any non-cognitive analysis, any naturalist one, and any combination of the two.

If second order ethics were confined, then, to linguistic and conceptual analysis, it ought to conclude that moral values at least are objective: that they are so is part of what our ordinary moral statements mean: the traditional moral concepts of the ordinary man as well as of the main line of western philosophers are concepts of objective value. But it is precisely for this reason that linguistic and conceptual analysis is not enough. The claim to objectivity, however ingrained in our language and thought, is not self-validating. It can and should be questioned. But the denial of objective values will have to be put forward not as the result of an analytic approach, but as an 'error theory', a theory that although most people in making moral judgements implicitly claim, among other things, to be pointing to something objectively prescriptive, these claims are all false. It is this that makes the name 'moral scepticism' appropriate.

But since this is an error theory, since it goes against assumptions ingrained in our thought and built into some of the ways in which language is used, since it conflicts with what is sometimes called common sense, it needs very solid support. It is not something we can accept lightly or casually and then quietly pass on. If we are to adopt this view, we must argue explicitly for it. Traditionally it has been supported by arguments of two main kinds, which I shall call the argument from relativity and the argument from queerness, but these can, as I shall show, be supplemented in several ways.

The Argument from Relativity

The argument from relativity has as its premise the well-known variation in moral codes from one society to another and from one period to another, and also the differences in moral beliefs between different groups and classes within a complex community. Such variation is in itself merely a truth of descriptive morality, a fact of anthropology which entails neither first order nor second order ethical views. Yet it may indirectly support second order subjectivism: radical differences between first order moral judgements make it difficult to treat those judgements as apprehensions of objective truths. But it is not the mere occurrence of disagreements that tells against the objectivity of values. Disagreement on questions in history or biology or cosmology does not show that there are no objective issues in these fields for investigators to disagree about. But such scientific disagreement results from speculative inferences or explanatory hypotheses based on inadequate evidence, and it is hardly plausible to interpret moral disagreement in the same way. Disagreement about moral codes seems to reflect people's adherence to and participation in different ways of life. The causal connection seems to be mainly that way round: it is that people approve of monogamy because they participate in a monogamous way of life rather than that they participate in a monogamous way of life because they approve of monogamy. Of course, the standards may be an idealization of the way of life from which they arise: the monogamy in which people participate may be less complete, less rigid, than that of which it leads them to approve. This is not to say that moral judgements are purely conventional. Of course there have been and are moral heretics and moral reformers, people who have turned against the established rules and practices of their own communities for moral reasons, and often for moral reasons that we would endorse. But this can usually be understood as the extension, in ways which, though new and unconventional, seemed to them to be required for consistency, of rules to which they already adhered as arising out of an existing way of life. In short, the argument from relativity has some force simply because the actual variations in the moral codes are more readily explained by the hypothesis that they reflect ways of life than by the hypothesis that they express perceptions, most of them seriously inadequate and badly distorted, of objective values.

But there is a well-known counter to this argument from relativity, namely to say that the items for which objective validity is in the first place to be claimed are not specific moral rules or codes but very general basic principles which are recognized at least implicitly to some extent in all society — such principles as provide the foundations of what Sidgwick has called different methods of ethics: the principle of universalizability, perhaps, or the rule that

one ought to conform to the specific rules of any way of life in which one takes part, from which one profits, and on which one relies, or some utilitarian principle of doing what tends, or seems likely, to promote the general happiness. It is easy to show that such general principles, married with differing concrete circumstances, different existing social patterns or different preferences, will beget different specific moral rules; and there is some plausibility in the claim that the specific rules thus generated will vary from community to community or from group to group in close agreement with the actual variations in accepted codes.

The argument from relativity can be only partly countered in this way. To take this line the moral objectivist has to say that it is only in these principles that the objective moral character attaches immediately to its descriptively specified ground or subject: other moral judgements are objectively valid or true, but only derivatively and contingently — if things had been otherwise, quite different sorts of actions would have been right. And despite the prominence in recent philosophical ethics of universalization, utilitarian principles, and the like, these are very far from constituting the whole of what is actually affirmed as basic in ordinary moral thought. Much of this is concerned rather with what Hare calls 'ideals' or, less kindly, 'fanaticism.' That is, people judge that some things are good or right, and others are bad or wrong, not because — or at any rate not only because — they exemplify some general principle for which widespread implicit acceptance could be claimed, but because something about those things arouses certain responses immediately in them, though they would arouse radically and irresolvably different responses in others. 'Moral sense' or 'intuition' is an initially more plausible description of what supplies many of our basic moral judgements than 'reason.' With regard to all these starting points of moral thinking the argument from relativity remains in full force.

The Argument from Queerness

Even more important, however, and certainly more generally applicable, is the argument from queerness. This has two parts, one metaphysical, the other epistemological. If there were objective values, then they would be entities or qualities or relations of a very strange sort, utterly different from anything else in the universe. Correspondingly, if we were aware of them, it would have to be by some special faculty of moral perception or intuition, utterly different from our ordinary ways of knowing everything else. These points were recognized by Moore when he spoke of non-natural qualities, and by the intuitionists in their talk about a 'faculty of moral intuition.' Intuitionism has long been out of favour, and it is indeed easy to point out its implausibilities. What is not so often stressed, but is more important, is that the central thesis of intuitionism is one to which any objectivist view of values is in the end committed: intuitionism merely makes unpalatably plain what other forms of objectivism wrap up. Of course the suggestion that moral judgements are made or moral problems solved by just sitting down and having an ethical intuition is a travesty of actual moral thinking. But, however complex the real process, it will require (if it is to yield authoritatively prescriptive conclusions) some input of this distinctive sort, either premises or forms of argument or both. When we ask the awkward question, how we can be aware of this authoritative prescriptivity, of the truth of these distinctively ethical premises or of the cogency of this distinctively ethical pattern of reasoning, none of our ordinary accounts of sensory perception or introspection or the framing and confirming of explanatory hypotheses or inference or logical construction or conceptual analysis, or any combination of these, will provide a satisfactory answer; 'a special sort of intuition' is a lame answer, but it is the one to which the clearheaded objectivist is compelled to resort.

Indeed, the best move for the moral objectivist is not to evade this issue, but to look for companions in guilt. For example, Richard Price argues that it is not moral knowledge alone that such an empiricism as those of Locke and Hume is unable to account for, but also our knowledge and even our ideas of essence, number, identity, diversity, solidity, inertia, substance, the necessary existence and infinite extension of time and space, necessity and possibility in general, power, and causation. If the understanding, which Price defines as the faculty within us that discerns truth, is also a source of new simple ideas of so many other sorts, may it not also be a power of immediately perceiving right and wrong, which yet are real characters of actions?

This is an important counter to the argument from queerness. The only adequate reply to it would be to show how, on empiricist foundations, we can construct an account of the ideas and beliefs and knowledge that we have of all these matters. I cannot even begin to do that here, though I have undertaken some parts of the task elsewhere. I can only state my belief that satisfactory accounts of most of these can be given in empirical terms. If some supposed metaphysical necessities or essences resist such treatment, then they too should be included, along with objective values, among the targets of the argument from queerness.

This queerness does not consist simply in the fact that ethical statements are 'unverifiable.' Although logical positivism with its verifiability theory of descriptive meaning gave an impetus to non-cognitive accounts of ethics, it is not only logical positivists but also empiricists of a much more liberal sort who should find objective values hard to accommodate. Indeed, I would not only reject the verifiability principle but also deny the conclusion commonly drawn from it, that moral judgements lack descriptive meaning. The assertion that there are objective values or intrinsically prescriptive entities or features of some kind, which ordinary moral judgements presuppose, is, I hold, not meaningless but false.

Plato's Forms give a dramatic picture of what objective values would have to be. The Form of the Good is such that knowledge of it provides the knower with both a direction and an overriding motive; something's being good both tells the person who knows this to pursue it and makes him pursue it. An objective good would be sought by anyone who was acquainted with it, not because of any contingent fact that this person, or every person, is so constituted that he desires this end, but just because the end has to-be-pursuedness somehow built into it. Similarly, if there were objective principles of right and wrong, any wrong (possible) course of action would have not-to-be-doneness somehow built into it. Or we should have something like Clarke's necessary relations of fitness between situations and actions, so that a situation would have a demand for such-and-such an action somehow built into it.

The need for an argument of this sort can be brought out by reflection on Hume's argument that 'reason'—in which at this stage he includes all sorts of knowing as well as reasoning—can never be an 'influencing motive of the will.' Someone might object that Hume has argued unfairly from the lack of influencing power (not contingent upon desires) in ordinary objects of knowledge and ordinary reasoning, and might maintain that values differ from natural objects precisely in their power, when known, automatically to influence the will. To this Hume could, and would need to, reply that this objection involves the postulating of value-entities or value-features of quite a different order from anything else with which we are acquainted, and of a corresponding faculty with which to detect them. That is, he would have to supplement his explicit argument with what I have called the argument from queerness.

Another way of bringing out this queerness is to ask, about anything that is supposed to have some objective moral quality, how this is linked with its natural features. What is the connection between the natural fact that an action is a piece of deliberate cruelty—say, causing pain just for fun—and the moral fact that it is wrong? It cannot be an entailment, a logical or semantic necessity. Yet it is not merely that the two features occur together. The wrongness must somehow be 'consequential' or 'supervenient'; it is wrong because it is a piece of deliberate cruelty. But just what *in the world* is signified by this 'because'? And how do we know the relation that it signifies, if this is something more than such actions being socially condemned, and condemned by us too, perhaps through our having absorbed attitudes from our social environment? It is not even sufficient to postulate a faculty which 'sees' the wrongness: something must be postulated which can see at once the natural features that constitute the cruelty, and the wrongness, and the mysterious consequential link between the two. Alternatively, the intuition required might be the perception that wrongness is a higher order property belonging to certain natural properties; but what is this belonging of properties to other properties, and how can we discern it? How much simpler and more comprehensible the situation would be if we could replace the moral quality with some sort of subjective response which could be causally related to the detection of the natural features on which the supposed quality is said to be consequential.

It may be thought that the argument from queerness is given an unfair start if we thus relate it to what are admittedly among the wilder products of philosophical fancy—Platonic Forms, non-natural qualities, self-evident relations of fitness, faculties of intuition, and the like. Is it equally forceful if applied to the terms in which everyday moral judgements are more likely to be expressed—though still . . . with a claim to objectivity—'you must do this,' 'you can't do that,' 'obligation,' 'unjust,' 'rotten,' 'disgraceful,' 'mean,' or talk about good reasons for or against possible actions? Admittedly not; but that is because the objective prescriptivity, the element a claim for whose authoritativeness is embedded in ordinary moral thought and language, is not yet isolated in these forms of speech, but is presented along with relations to desires and feelings, reasoning about the means to desired ends, interpersonal demands, the injustice which consists in the violation of what are in the context the accepted standards of merit, the psychological constituents of meanness, and so on. There is nothing queer about any of these, and under cover of them the claim for moral authority may pass unnoticed. But if I am right in arguing that it is ordinarily there, and is therefore very likely to be incorporated almost automatically in philosophical accounts of ethics which systematize our ordinary thought even in such apparently innocent terms as these, it needs to be examined, and for this purpose it needs to be isolated and exposed as it is by the less cautious philosophical reconstructions.

Patterns of Objectification

Considerations of these kinds suggest that it is in the end less paradoxical to reject than to retain the common-sense belief in the objectivity of moral values, provided that we can explain how this belief, if it is false, has become established and is so resistant to criticisms. This proviso is not difficult to satisfy.

On a subjectivist view, the supposedly objective values will be based in fact upon attitudes which the person has who takes himself to be recognizing and responding to those values. If we admit what Hume calls the mind's 'propensity to spread itself on external objects,' we can understand the supposed objectivity of moral qualities as arising from what we can call the projection or objectification of moral attitudes. This would be analogous to what is called the 'pathetic fallacy,' the tendency to read our feelings into their objects. If a fungus, say, fills us with disgust, we may be inclined to ascribe to the fungus itself a non-natural quality of foulness. But in moral contexts there is more than this propensity at work. Moral attitudes themselves are at least partly social in origin: socially established — and socially necessary — patterns of behaviour put pressure on individuals, and each individual tends to internalize these pressures and to join in requiring these patterns of behaviour of himself and of others. The attitudes that are objectified into moral values have indeed an external source, though not the one assigned to them by the belief in their absolute authority. Moreover, there are motives that would support objectification. We need morality to regulate interpersonal relations, to control some of the ways in which people behave towards one another, often in opposition to contrary inclinations. We therefore want our moral judgements to be authoritative for other agents as well as for ourselves: objective validity would give them the authority required. Aesthetic values are logically in the same position as moral ones; much the same metaphysical and epistemological considerations apply to them. But aesthetic values are less strongly objectified than moral ones; their subjective status, and an 'error theory' with regard to such claims to objectivity as are incorporated in aesthetic judgements, will be more readily accepted, just because the motives for their objectification are less compelling.

But it would be misleading to think of the objectification of moral values as primarily the projection of feelings, as in the pathetic fallacy. More important are wants and demands. As Hobbes says, 'whatsoever is the object of any man's Appetite or Desire, that is it, which he for his part calleth *Good*'; and certainly both the adjective 'good' and the noun 'goods' are used in non-moral contexts of things because they are such as to satisfy desires. We get the notion of something's being objectively good, or having intrinsic value, by reversing the direction of dependence here, by making the desire depend upon the goodness, instead of the goodness on the desire. And this is aided by the fact that the desired thing will indeed have features that make it desired, that enable it to arouse a desire or that make it such as to satisfy some desire that is already there. It is fairly easy to confuse the way in which a thing's desirability is indeed objective with its having in our

sense objective value. The fact that the word 'good' serves as one of our main moral terms is a trace of this pattern of objectification.

Similarly related uses of words are covered by the distinction between hypothetical and categorical imperatives. The statement that someone 'ought to' or, more strongly, 'must' do such-and-such may be backed up explicitly or implicitly by reference to what he wants or to what his purposes and objects are. Again, there may be a reference to the purposes of someone else, perhaps the speaker: 'You must do this' — 'Why?' — 'Because I want such-and-such.' The moral categorical imperative which could be expressed in the same words can be seen as resulting from the suppression of the conditional clause in a hypothetical imperative without its being replaced by any such reference to the speaker's wants. The action in question is still required in something like the way in which it would be if it were appropriately related to a want, but it is no longer admitted that there is any contingent want upon which its being required depends. Again this move can be understood when we remember that at least our central and basic moral judgements represent social demands, where the source of the demand is indeterminate and diffuse. Whose demands or wants are in question, the agent's, or the speaker's, or those of an indefinite multitude of other people? All of these in a way, but there are advantages in not specifying them precisely. The speaker is expressing demands which he makes as a member of a community, which he has developed in and by participation in a joint way of life; also, what is required of this particular agent would be required of any other in a relevantly similar situation; but the agent too is expected to have internalized the relevant demands, to act as if the ends for which the action is required were his own. By suppressing any explicit reference to demands and making the imperatives categorical we facilitate conceptual moves from one such demand relation to another. The moral uses of such words as 'must' and 'ought' and 'should,' all of which are used also to express hypothetical imperatives, are traces of this pattern of objectification.

It may be objected that this explanation links normative ethics too closely with descriptive morality, with the mores or socially enforced patterns of behaviour that anthropologists record. But it can hardly be denied that moral thinking starts from the enforcement of social codes. Of course it is not confined to that. But even when moral judgements are detached from the mores of any actual society they are liable to be framed with reference to an ideal community of moral agents, such as Kant's kingdom of ends, which but for the need to give God a special place in it would have been better called a commonwealth of ends.

Another way of explaining the objectification of moral values is to say that ethics is a system of law from which the legislator has been removed. This might have been derived either from the positive law of a state or from a supposed system of divine law. There can be no doubt that some features of modern European moral concepts are traceable to the theological ethics of Christianity. The stress on quasi-imperative notions, on what ought to be done or on what is wrong in a sense that is close to that of 'forbidden,' are surely relics of divine commands. Admittedly, the central ethical concepts for Plato and Aristotle also are in a broad sense prescriptive or intrinsically action-guiding, but in concentrating rather on 'good' than on 'ought' they show that their moral thought is an objectification of the desired and the satisfying rather than of the commanded. Elizabeth Anscombe has argued that modern, non-Aristotelian, concepts of *moral* obligation, *moral* duty, of what is *morally* right and wrong, and of the *moral* sense of 'ought' are survivals outside the framework of thought that made them really intelligible, namely the belief in divine law. She infers that 'ought' has 'become a word of mere mesmeric force,' with only a 'delusive appearance of content,'

and that we would do better to discard such terms and concepts altogether, and go back to Aristotelian ones.

There is much to be said for this view. But while we can explain some distinctive features of modern moral philosophy in this way, it would be a mistake to see the whole problem of the claim to objective prescriptivity as merely local and unnecessary, as a post-operative complication of a society from which a dominant system of theistic belief has recently been rather hastily excised. As Cudworth and Clarke and Price, for example, show, even those who still admit divine commands, or the positive law of God, may believe moral values to have an independent objective but still action-guiding authority. Responding to Plato's *Euthyphro* dilemma, they believe that God commands what he commands because it is in itself good or right, not that it is good or right merely because and in that he commands it. Otherwise God himself could not be called good. Price asks, 'What can be more preposterous, than to make the Deity nothing but will; and to exalt this on the ruins of all his attributes?' The apparent objectivity of moral value is a widespread phenomenon which has more than one source: the persistence of a belief in something like divine law when the belief in the divine legislator has faded out is only one factor among others. There are several different patterns of objectification, all of which have left characteristic traces in our actual moral concepts and moral language.

IX.2 *Moral Realism and the Sceptical Arguments from Disagreement and Queerness*

DAVID BRINK

David Brink teaches philosophy at the Massachusetts Institute of Technology and has written several articles on moral realism. In this essay he analyzes Mackie's two arguments against moral realism: the argument from relativity or disagreement, and the argument from queerness. Brink contends that Mackie has not made his case. The moral realist has a plausible response to both of them.

1. *Introduction*

The most important kind of challenge to moral realism or moral objectivism argues that there is a *special* problem with realism in ethics. I shall defend moral realism against two influential versions of this challenge recently formulated by J. L. Mackie in his book *Ethics: Inventing Right and Wrong*.[1] According to standards of argument which Mackie himself sets, neither his argument from disagreement nor his argument from queerness shows any special problem for moral realism. Let me explain why.

Moral realism is best explained as a special case of a global realist thesis. The general thesis common to realist claims about a variety of disciplines is a two-part metaphysical claim:

R: (a) there are facts of kind *x,* and
(b) these facts are logically independent of our evidence, i.e. those beliefs which are our evidence, for them.[2]

Moral realism is then obtained by substituting 'moral' for the variable '*x*.'

MR: (a) there are moral facts, and
(b) these facts are logically independent of our evidence, i.e. those beliefs which are our evidence, for them.

Moral realism claims that there are objective moral facts and implies that there are true moral propositions.

Moral scepticism is technically an epistemological doctrine and so is officially neutral with respect to the metaethical thesis of moral realism. Moral scepticism claims that we have no moral knowledge and this claim is compatible with the existence of objective moral facts and true moral propositions. But while moral realism and moral scepticism are compatible (we may just have no cognitive access to moral facts), the standard and most plausible reason for claiming that we have no moral knowledge is the belief that there are no moral facts. This must be why Mackie construes moral scepticism as an anti-realist thesis. I shall follow Mackie in this and treat moral scepticism as a denial of the existence of objective values.

There are two basic kinds of moral sceptic. The first kind applies general sceptical considerations to the special case of morality. On his view, there are no moral facts, but neither are there any other objective facts about the world. Of course, this first sort of sceptic is quite radical and has not been terribly influential as a source of moral scepticism. The second kind of moral sceptic claims that there is a special problem about realism in ethics, a problem which does not afflict realism about most other disciplines. This clearly has been the more popular and

Reprinted with permission from *Australasian Journal of Philosophy* 62 (1984):111–125.

philosophically influential version of moral scepticism. Mackie is this second kind of moral sceptic.

As this second kind of moral sceptic, Mackie complains that belief in the existence of objective values is no part of a plausible realist world-view. (*E:* p. 17) Mackie's sceptical arguments, therefore, cannot turn on the application of general sceptical considerations. If it can be shown that the moral realist's metaphysical and epistemological commitments are no less plausible than those of, say, the physical realist, then Mackie's sceptical arguments will have been answered.

Although it is possible to *defend* moral realism against sceptical arguments without establishing any kind of presumption in its favour, there are, as Mackie recognises, general considerations which require the moral sceptic to bear a certain burden of proof. First, this second version of moral scepticism concedes a presumption in favour of moral realism. If, as this second sort of scepticism assumes, realism is plausible about a wide range of disciplines, then there must be some special justification for taking a different view about the existence and nature of moral facts. Of course, this establishes only a very weak presumption of favour of moral realism, but it is one which the moral sceptic must rebut.

Moreover, belief in moral realism is supported by certain features of our moral practice. In moral deliberation and moral argument we search for answers to our moral questions, answers whose correctness we assume to be independent of our means of arriving at them. Of course, this presumption too is defeasible, but this takes some argument. As Mackie claims, moral scepticism must have the status of an error theory; it must explain how and why our commitment to the objectivity of moral values is mistaken. (*E:* p. 35)

Mackie distinguishes two arguments for the second version of moral scepticism. The first turns on the apparent unresolvability of many moral disputes and so is best thought of as an argument from disagreement, while the second turns on the mysterious character objective values would seem to have and so represents an argument from queerness. Mackie presses both of these arguments against moral realism and in favour of moral scepticism and subjectivism. In what follows, I shall examine and rebut Mackie's arguments from disagreement and queerness; I shall argue that neither argument establishes any special problem for moral realism.

Although these two arguments may not exhaust the arguments for the second version of moral scepticism, they are sufficiently important both historically and philosophically that successfully rebutting them will go a long way towards defending moral realism.

2. *Moral Objectivity*

Before discussing the details of the arguments from disagreement and queerness, we need to establish just which version of moral realism is or need be in question. In section 1 I described moral realism as the metaethical view that there are objective moral facts. However, in pressing the arguments from disagreement and queerness, Mackie employs a stronger or more committal version of moral realism according to which not only are there moral facts but also these moral facts are *objectively prescriptive*. (*E:* pp. 23, 26–7, 29, 40, 42; *HMT:* pp. 22, 53, 55, 134, 146; *MT:* pp. 102, 104, 115–16) Indeed, although both the argument from disagreement and the argument from queerness apply to my formulation of moral realism, some of the special appeal of the argument from queerness derives from the assumption that moral facts would have to be objectively prescriptive. (*E:* pp. 40–1; *HMT:* p. 61)

In claiming that moral facts would have to be objectively prescriptive, Mackie is claiming that moral realism requires the truth of *internalism*. Internalism is the *a priori* thesis that the recognition of moral facts itself either necessarily motivates or necessarily provides reasons for action. Internalism is an *a priori* thesis, because its proponents claim that the recognition of moral facts necessarily motivates or provides reasons for action no matter what the moral facts turn out to be. We can distinguish *motivational internalism* (MI) and *reasons internalism* (RI): MI holds that it is *a priori* that the recognition of moral facts itself necessarily motivates the agent to perform the moral action, while RI claims that it is *a priori* that the recognition of moral facts itself necessarily provides the agent with reason to perform the moral action. *Externalism*, by contrast, denies both MI and RI.

Although Mackie is unclear as between MI and RI, he clearly thinks that some version of internalism is required by moral realism. Both MI and RI make exceptionally strong claims. MI claims that — whatever the moral facts turn out to be and regardless of the psychological make-up of the agent — the mere recognition of a moral fact necessarily provides some motivation to perform the moral action, while RI claims that — whatever the moral facts turn out to be and regardless of the agent's interests or desires — the mere recognition of a moral fact necessarily provides the agent with at least some reason to perform the moral action. These claims are quite implausible, and it is unclear why moral realism is committed to either of them.

It is unlikely that the recognition of moral facts *necessarily* motivates or provides reasons for action; it is very unlikely that the recognition of moral facts *alone* necessarily motivates or provides reasons for action; and the mere recognition of moral facts almost certainly does not necessarily motivate or provide reasons for action *regardless of what the moral facts turn out to be*. Whether the recognition of moral facts motivates certainly depends upon what the moral facts are, and, at least on most plausible moral theories, whether recognition of these facts motivates is a matter of contingent (even if deep) psychological fact about the agent. Whether the recognition of moral facts provides reasons for action depends upon whether the agent has reason to do what morality requires. But this, of course, depends upon what morality requires, i.e. upon what the moral facts are, and, at least on standard theories of reasons for action, whether recognition of these facts provides reason for action will depend upon contingent (even if deep) facts about the agent's desires or interests. So, internalism is false; it is not something which we can know *a priori*, i.e. whatever the moral facts turn out to be, that the recognition of moral facts alone either necessarily motivates or necessarily provides reasons for action.

· It is hard to see why moral realism should be committed to the truth of internalism. Mackie claims both that moral realists have traditionally been internalists (*E:* p. 23) and that internalism is part of common sense moral thinking. (*E:* p. 35) But both claims seem false and would carry relatively little weight, even if true. Once we make clear the strength of the internalist claim — that we know *a priori* that *mere* recognition of moral facts *necessarily* motivates or provides reasons for action — it is less clear that the tradition of moral realism is a tra-

dition of internalism. In particular, although I cannot argue the claims here, I doubt that Plato, Hume, or Sidgwick is, as Mackie claims, an internalist. And, of course, even if many moral philosophers have thought that internalism is true, it would not follow that they were right. Nor does common sense moral thinking seem to support belief in internalism; in fact, it seems extremely unlikely that any belief so recherché could be part of common sense moral thinking. Even if belief in internalism were part of common sense moral thinking, it would be revisable, especially if it could be shown that belief in internalism plays a social role such that it would persist even if mistaken.

So no good reason has been produced for thinking that internalism is true or for thinking that moral realism requires internalism. This means that the moral realist can defend externalism. In particular, determination of the motivational and reason-giving power of moral facts will have to await specifications of the moral facts and of the desires and interests of agents. In defending moral realism against the arguments from disagreement and queerness, I will offer what I call a functionalist theory of moral value according to which moral facts are facts about human well-being and flourishing as a model specification of moral realist claims. This account illustrates the kind of justification of morality which the externalist can provide, for this functionalist theory implies that moral facts will *as a matter of fact at least typically* provide agents with reasons to do the morally correct thing.

3. The Argument from Disagreement

Mackie claims that the best explanation of inter- and intra-societal ethical disagreement is that there simply are no moral facts, only differences of attitude, commitment, or decision. (*E:* pp. 36–7) Of course, disagreement does not entail scepticism. Mackie recognises that we do not infer from the fact that there are disagreements in the natural sciences that the natural sciences are not objective disciplines. Nor do we make what might appear to be the more modest inference from the fact that there is a specific dispute in some subject that there is no fact of the matter on the particular issue in question. For example, no one concluded from the apparently quite deep disagreement among astronomers a short while ago about the existence of black holes that there was no fact of the matter concerning the existence of black holes. Mackie's claim is that disagreement in ethics is somehow more fundamental than disagreement in other disciplines. In particular, realism about a discipline requires that its disputes be resolvable at least in principle, and, while most scientific disputes do seem resolvable, many moral disputes do not.

Mackie imagines the moral realist replying that moral disputes are resolvable, because deep moral disagreements are not really cases of disagreement. Rather, they are cases in which 'disputants' apply antecedently shared moral principles under different empirical conditions. (*E:* p. 37) The resulting moral judgments are about different action types, so the 'disagreements' in question are really only apparent.

Mackie issues two rejoinders to this realist reply. His first rejoinder is that this realist response commits the realist to (a) claiming that necessity can only attach to general moral principles and (b) accepting the following counterfactual: '. . . if things had been otherwise, quite different sorts of actions would have been right.' (*E:* p. 37) (a) and (b), Mackie claims, imply that many action types will be right or wrong only contingently.

Although this rejoinder does raise some interesting questions about the modal status of moral facts, it in no way threatens moral realism. First, certainly some moral facts are contingent, and, even if this realist reply requires the contingency of some moral facts, this shows nothing about how many moral facts the realist must regard as contingent. But, secondly and more importantly, Mackie's modal issue is a red herring. The truth of moral realism turns on the existence of moral facts, not their modal status.

Mackie's second rejoinder to the realist reply is simply that some moral disputes are real disputes. Not all putative moral disagreements can be explained away as the application of antecedently shared moral principles in different circumstances. (*E:* p. 38)

Mackie is right that many moral disputes are genuine, and, if the realist had no account of these disputes, Mackie would have a strong argument against moral realism. But the realist can account for moral disputes.

As we have seen, not every apparent moral disagreement is a genuine dispute. But the realist need not maintain even that all genuine moral disputes are resolvable. He can maintain that some moral disputes have no uniquely correct answers. Moral ties are possible, and considerations, each of which is objectively valuable, may be incommensurable. So the moral realist need only maintain that most genuine moral disputes are resolvable.

Indeed, the realist can plausibly maintain that most genuine moral disputes are in principle resolvable. Mackie's discussion of the realist's reply shows that Mackie thinks moral disagreement is resolvable if and only if *antecedent* agreement on general moral principles obtains. This claim presupposes a one-way view of moral justification and argument according to which moral principles justify particular moral judgments but not vice versa. However, this view of moral justification is defective. As Goodman, Rawls, and other coherentists have argued, justification proceeds both from general principles to particular cases and from particular cases to general principles. Just as agreement about general moral principles may be exploited to resolve disagreement about particular moral cases, so agreement about particular moral cases may be exploited to resolve disagreement about general moral principles. Ideally, trade-offs among the various levels of generality of belief will be made in such a way as to maximise initial commitment, overall consistency, explanatory power, etc. A coherentist model of moral reasoning of this sort makes it much less plausible that disagreements over moral principles are in principle unresolvable.

Moreover, a great many moral disagreements depend upon disagreements over the non-moral facts. First, many disagreements over the non-moral facts result from culpable forms of ignorance of fact. Often, for moral or non-moral reasons, at least one disputant culpably fails to assess the non-moral facts correctly by being insufficiently imaginative in weighing the consequences for the relevant people of alternative actions or policies. This sort of error is especially important in moral disputes, since thought experiments (as opposed to actual tests) play such an important part in the assessment of moral theories. Thought experiments play a larger role in moral methodology than they do in scientific methodology, at least partly because it is often (correctly) regarded as immoral to assess moral theories by realising the relevant counterfactuals.

Secondly, many moral disagreements result from reasonable but nonetheless resolvable disagreements over the non-moral facts. The correct answers to moot moral questions often turn on certain non-moral facts about which reasonable disagreement is possible and which may in fact be known by no one. Correct answers to moral questions can turn at least in part upon correct answers to non-moral questions such as 'What (re)distribution of a certain class of goods would make the worst-off representative person in a particular society best-off?', 'Would public ownership of the means of production in the United States lead to an increase or decrease in the average standard of living?', 'What is the correct theory of human personality?', and 'What kind of life would my severely mentally retarded child lead (if I brought the pregnancy to term and raised the child), and how would caring for him affect my family and me?' However difficult and controversial these questions are, the issues which they raise are in principle resolvable. Moral disputes commonly do turn on disagreement over issues such as these, and, insofar as they do, moral disputes are clearly resolvable in principle.

Mackie argues that if moral realism were true, all moral disputes should be resolvable, and since many seem irresolvable, he concludes that moral realism is false. But the moral realist need only claim that *most genuine* moral disputes are *in principle* resolvable. Not all apparent moral disagreements are genuine, because some apparent moral disputes merely reflect the application of antecedently shared moral principles under different circumstances. Not every genuine moral dispute need be even in principle resolvable, since moral ties are possible and some objective moral values may be incommensurable. Of those genuine moral disputes which the realist is committed to treating as in principle resolvable, some depend upon antecedent disagreement over moral principles, while others depend upon disagreement over the non-moral facts. The realist can claim that antecedent disagreement over moral principles is in principle resolvable by coherence arguments and that disagreement over the non-moral facts is always in principle resolvable. The moral realist gives a plausible enough account of moral disagreement for us to say that Mackie has not shouldered the burden of proof for his claim that the falsity of moral realism is the best explanation of the nature of moral disagreement.

4. *The Argument from Queerness*

The rough idea behind the argument from queerness is that objective moral facts and properties would have to be so different from the sort of natural facts and properties for which we do have evidence that we have good *a posteriori* reason to reject moral realism. (*E*: pp. 38–42; *MT*: pp. 115–16) As I said in section 2, the argument from queerness is supposed to tell especially against the existence of moral facts conceived of as being objectively prescriptive. (*E*: pp. 40–1; *HMT*: p. 61) I claimed that in committing realism to objective prescriptivity Mackie is claiming that moral realism requires internalism. But I argued that internalism is implausible and that Mackie produces no good reason for committing realism to internalism. Instead, the realist can defend externalism; determination of whether agents have reason or motive to be moral will depend upon the content of morality and facts about agents. In explaining why objective values are not queer, I will offer a model specification of moral realism, which, together with plausible empirical assumptions, implies that agents generally do have reasons to be moral.

There are two limbs to the argument from queerness: one metaphysical, one epistemological. (*E*: p. 38) I turn to the metaphysical branch of the argument first. Mackie thinks that moral realism is a metaphysically queer doctrine, because he believes that moral facts or properties would have to be ontologically simple or independent. (*E*: p. 38) The assumption is that moral properties would have to be *sui generis*, that is, ontologically independent of natural properties with which we are familiar. Although it is not inconceivable that there should be *sui generis* moral properties, we have very good *a posteriori* evidence for the truth of materialism and for the falsity of ontological pluralism.

However, Mackie's crucial assumption that moral facts and properties would have to be *sui generis* is false; moral realism does not require ontological pluralism. The moral realist has at least two options on the assumption that materialism is true: he can claim that moral properties are identical with certain physical properties, or he can claim that moral properties supervene upon certain physical properties. Because moral properties and their instances could be realised in nonphysical as well as a variety of physical ways, neither moral properties nor their instances should be identified with physical properties or their instances. For this reason, it is best for the moral realist to claim that moral properties supervene upon physical properties.

Mackie recognises the realist's claim about the supervenience of moral facts and properties on physical facts and properties but claims that the alleged supervenient relation is also metaphysically queer:

> Another way of bringing out this queerness is to ask about anything that is supposed to have some objective moral quality, how this is linked with its natural features. What is the connection between the natural fact that an action is a case of deliberate cruelty—say, causing pain just for fun—and the moral fact that it is wrong? It cannot be an entailment, a logical or semantic necessity. Yet it is not merely that the two features occur together. The wrongness must somehow be 'consequential' or 'supervenient'; it is wrong because it is a piece of deliberate cruelty. But just what *in the world* is signified by this 'because'? (*E:* p. 41)

Although I do not think that Mackie has really motivated a metaphysical worry about moral supervenience, I shall defend moral realism against the charge of metaphysical queerness by adopting the strategy which Mackie mentions of finding partners in guilt—although once it is clear what sort of company the realist is keeping it would only be perverse to regard them as partners in *guilt*. I shall argue that the supervenient relation which the realist claims obtains between moral properties and natural or physical properties is neither uncommon nor mysterious.

Although it is an interesting question what the precise relation is between property identity and supervenience, it is fairly clear that one property can supervene upon another without those two properties being identical. A supervenient relation obtains

between two properties or sets of properties just in case the one property or set of properties is causally realised by the other property or set of properties; the former property or set of properties is the supervening property or set of properties, and the latter property or set of properties is the base property or set of properties. Supervenience implies that no change can occur in the supervening property without a change occurring in the base property, but it also asserts a claim of ontological dependence. Assuming, as Mackie does, that materialism is true, all properties ultimately supervene on material or physical base properties. Physical properties are basic then in the sense that all other properties are nothing over and above physical properties. Biological, social, psychological, and moral properties are all realised physically; they are simply different *kinds* of combinations and arrangements of matter which hang together explanatorily.

Supervenience is a relation of causal constitution or dependence. There is nothing strange and certainly nothing unique about the supervenience of moral properties on physical properties. Assuming materialism is true, mental states supervene on physical states, yet few think that mental states are metaphysically queer (and those that do do not think that supervenience makes them queer). Social facts such as unemployment, inflation, and exploitation supervene upon physical facts, yet no one supposes that social facts are metaphysically queer. Biological states such as being an organism supervene on physical states, yet no one supposes that organisms are queer entities. Macroscopic material objects such as tables supervene on microscopic physical particles, yet no one supposes that tables are queer entities. In short, it is difficult to see how the realist's use of supervenience in explaining the relationship between moral and physical properties makes his position queer. Moral properties are not ontologically simple or independent; but then neither are mental states, social facts, biological states, or macroscopic material objects. It is unlikely that moral properties are identical with physical properties; more properties could have been realised nonmaterially. But there is every reason to believe that in the actual world moral properties, like other natural properties, are realised materially.

This realist account of supervenience discharges an explanatory obligation which the argument from metaphysical queerness imposes. The details of the way in which moral properties supervene upon other natural properties are worked out differently by different moral theories. Determination of which account of moral supervenience is best will depend upon determination of which moral theory provides the best account of all our beliefs, both moral and non-moral. Although I obviously cannot do here what is needed to defend a particular account of moral supervenience, I will now offer a *model* specification of the moral realist's metaphysical claims.

When trying to determine the way in which moral properties supervene upon other natural properties, one might start by looking at plausible theories about other kinds of properties. Functional theories provide plausible accounts of a wide variety of kinds of properties; the nature of biological, psychological, social, and economic properties is profitably viewed in functional terms. Consider functionalist theories of mind as an example. Although functionalism is not without its critics, it is fair to say that there are no rival *theories* in the philosophy of mind today. What is essential to any particular mental state type, according to functionalism, is the causal role which that mental state plays in the activities which are characteristic of the organism as a whole. Mental states are identified and distinguished from other mental states in terms of the causal relations which they bear to sensory inputs, behavioural outputs, and other mental states. To take a hoary example, functionalist theories of mind claim that pain is identified and distinguished from other mental states by virtue of its tendency to result from tissue damage, to produce an injury-avoidance desire, and to issue in the appropriate injury-avoidance behaviour. The physical states which realise this functional state are the physical states upon which pain supervenes.

Similarly, the moral realist might claim that moral properties are functional properties. He might claim that what is essential to moral properties is the causal role which they play in the characteristic activities of human organisms. In particular, the realist might claim that moral properties are those which bear upon the maintenance and flourishing of human organisms. Maintenance and flourishing presumably consist in necessary conditions for survival, other needs associated with basic well-

being, wants of various sorts, and distinctively human capacities. People, actions, policies, states of affairs, etc. will bear good-making moral properties just insofar as they contribute to the satisfaction of these needs, wants, and capacities. People, actions, policies, states of affairs, etc. will bear bad-making moral properties just insofar as they fail to promote or interfere with the satisfaction of these needs, wants, and capacities. The physical states which contribute to or interfere with the satisfaction of these needs, wants, and capacities are the physical states upon which, on this functionalist theory, moral properties ultimately supervene.

Although I cannot and do not need to defend here this functionalist model, it is worth pointing out how this model addresses two issues of concern to Mackie, namely, the justifiability of morality and the decidability of moral disputes. In section 2 I argued that internalism is implausible and that determination of whether agents have motivation or reason to be moral depends upon the content of morality and facts about agents. If this functionalist account of moral value which I have proposed as a realist model is plausible, then there is reason to think that moral facts will at least typically provide agents with reasons for action. Everyone has reason to promote his own well-being, and everyone has reason to promote the well-being of others at least to the extent that his own well-being is tied up with theirs. Presumably, any plausible theory of human needs, wants, and capacities will show that the satisfaction of these desiderata for any given individual will depend to a large extent on the well-being of others. People have needs and desires for friendship and love and for the benefits of cooperative activity; they also have capacities for sympathy, benevolence, and social intercourse. In order to satisfy these social needs, desires, and capacities, agents must develop and maintain stable social dispositions, and this means that they will often have reason to benefit others even when they do not otherwise benefit by their action. So, although there may be cases in which maintaining or promoting human well-being involves no benefit to the agent, there is good reason to suppose that human well-being and agent well-being will by and large coincide. As this functionalist theory of value illustrates, externalism allows a strong justification of morality.

This functionalist theory of moral value also

helps to explain the nature of moral disagreement. Common sense and attention to the argument from disagreement tell us that moral disputes can be extremely difficult to resolve. This functionalist specification of moral realism explains why many moral disputes which are in principle resolvable are nonetheless so difficult to resolve even under favourable conditions. Because facts about human well-being and flourishing depend at least in part upon facts in such complex and controversial empirical disciplines as economics, social theory, and psychology, even disputants who share something like the functionalist theory of value and are well informed will often disagree about what morality requires.

In addition to the metaphysical complaint about 'what in the world' a supervenient relation is, Mackie lodges an epistemological complaint about how we could know when the appropriate supervenient relation obtains. (*E:* p. 41) We may know that certain natural facts or facts under a non-moral description obtain, but how do we know or go about finding out whether these physical facts realise any moral facts and, if so, which? Mackie claims that we could gain this kind of moral knowledge only if we had special faculties for the perception of moral facts of the sort ethical intuitionism ensures. But, Mackie argues, although moral intuitionism could have been true, there are good *a posteriori* grounds for believing that no such faculties exist. Therefore, barring the cognitive inaccessibility of moral facts, moral realism must be false. (*E:* pp. 38–9)

The epistemological belief that moral realism is committed to intuitionism rests at least in Mackie's case on the mistaken metaphysical assumption that moral values would have to be ontologically *sui generis*. If and only if moral facts were queer kinds of entities would we need some special faculty for cognitive access to them. But the realist denies that moral facts are *sui generis;* moral facts supervene on natural facts. One goes about discovering which natural facts moral facts supervene on by appeal to moral theories. (Of course, appeal to a particular moral theory is justified only if that theory coheres well with other moral and non-moral beliefs we hold.) For example, if the functionalist account of moral value sketched above can be defended, then we do know how to set about ascertaining which if any moral facts supervene on a particular set of natural facts. We ascertain whether the natural facts in question contribute to, interfere with, or are neutral

with respect to the maintenance and promotion of human well-being. Granted, in many cases this will be no easy task, since completion of the task will depend in part upon answers to controversial empirical questions in such fields as economics, social theory, and psychology. But all this shows is that moral knowledge is sometimes hard to come by, not that it is queer or mysterious.

Mackie might complain that both acceptance and application of moral theories must be guided by other moral commitments. Not only does acceptance of the functionalist theory of value depend upon its coherence with, among other things, other moral beliefs, but also the findings of such disciplines as economics, sociology, and psychology cannot fully determine the extension of 'human well-being and flourishing.' Even if the special sciences can tell us something about human needs, wants, and capacities, and the effective ways of realising them, these sciences cannot rank these components of the good or adjudicate conflicts among them. Some irreducibly normative questions must be answered in determining what constitutes human well-being and flourishing.

But if the fact that some or all of our moral judgments are theory-dependent in this way is supposed to present a genuine epistemological problem for the moral realist which is not simply the result of applying general sceptical considerations to the case of morality, Mackie must claim that theory-dependence is a feature peculiar to moral methodology. Is this claim at all plausible?

Here, as before, the moral realist can find quite respectable partners 'in guilt.' It is a commonplace in the philosophy of science that scientific methodology is profoundly theory-dependent. Assessments of theoretical simplicity, and theory confirmation as well as standards of experimental design and instrument improvement require appeal to the best available background theories in the relevant disciplines. For example, in theory confirmation there is an ineliminable comparative component. Theories count as well confirmed only if they have been tested against relevant rivals, and determination of which alternative theories are relevant or worth considering requires appeal to background bodies of accepted theory. Acceptance of normal scientific observations and judgments, as well as application of general methodological principles, is also theory-laden. For example, judgments about the acidity or alkalinity of a substance which are based on the results of litmus paper tests pre-suppose belief in the normality of the test conditions and acceptance of the relevant chemical theories explaining how litmus paper detects pH and how pH reflects acidity and alkalinity.

The fact that scientific method is heavily theory-dependent shows that science and ethics are on a par in being theory-dependent. Thus, the fact that moral commitments must be appealed to in the acceptance and application of moral theories poses *no special* epistemological problem for moral realism. Of course, although most of us do not draw non-realist conclusions from the theory-dependence of scientific method, one may wonder how the profoundly theory-dependent methodologies in science and ethics can be *discovery* procedures. The answer is that theory-dependent methodologies are discovery procedures just in case a sufficient number of background theories in the disciplines in question are approximately true. And I have been arguing that Mackie has provided no good reason for doubting that some of our moral background theories are approximately true.

Mackie might respond that the moral and scientific cases are not in fact on a par and that there is reason to doubt the approximate truth of our moral theories, because while there is a good deal of consensus about the truth of the scientific theories appealed to, say, in the making of pH judgments, there is a notable lack of consensus about which moral theories to appeal to in making moral judgments. There are at least three reasons, however, for dismissing this response. First, this response probably overstates both the degree of consensus about which scientific theories are correct and the degree of disagreement about which moral theories are correct. Secondly, the response probably also overstates the amount of antecedent agreement necessary to reach eventual moral agreement. Finally, this response just raises from a different perspective the argument from disagreement, and we saw that the moral realist has a plausible account of moral disputes.

These considerations show that moral realism is committed to nothing metaphysically or epistemologically queer. The realist holds that moral facts supervene upon other natural facts and that moral knowledge is acquired in the same theory-dependent way that other knowledge is. Moral realism is plausible enough both metaphysically and epistemologically to allow us to say that Mackie has again failed to shoulder the burden of proof.

---

5. *Conclusion*

Mackie follows an important sceptical tradition in attempting to show that there is a special problem about realism in ethics. He recognises that it is the sceptic who bears the burden of proof but claims that his arguments from disagreement and queerness satisfy this burden. I argued, however, that neither argument provides good reason for disbelieving moral realism; certainly neither argument successfully bears the sceptic's burden of proof. The moral realist has various resources with which to account for moral disputes, and neither his account of the supervenience of moral facts nor his account of the theory-dependence of moral knowledge is queer or uncommon. I also introduced and developed a functionalist theory of moral value according to which moral facts are facts about human well-being and flourishing. Although the truth of this functionalist theory is not essential to the defence of moral realism, it does provide a plausible model for a realist program in ethics. Mackie's arguments from disagreement and queerness do not exhaust the sceptical challenges to moral realism. But both arguments are sufficiently important that by successfully rebutting them we have gone a long way towards defending moral realism.[3]

Endnotes

[1] J. L. Mackie, *Ethics: Inventing Right and Wrong* (New York: Penguin Books, 1977) (hereinafter *E*). Mackie further discusses a number of features of these two arguments in *Hume's Moral Theory* (Boston: Routledge and Kegan Paul, 1980) (hereinafter *HMT*) and *The Miracle of Theism* (New York: Oxford University Press, 1982) (hereinafter *MT*). Parenthetical references in the text to *E*, *HMT*, or *MT* are to pages in these books.

[2] Cf. Michael Devitt, "Dummett's Anti-Realism," *Journal of Philosophy* 80 (1983): 75–76. For obvious reasons, the kind of dependence asserted in R is logical, not causal.

[3] I would like to thank Tom Arner, Richard Boyd, Norman Dahl, T. H. Irwin, David Lyons, John McDowell, Alan Sidelle, Nicholas Sturgeon, and readers for the *Australasian Journal of Philosophy* for helpful comments on earlier versions of this paper.

IX.3 *Moral Nihilism*

Gilbert Harman

Gilbert Harman is professor of philosophy at Princeton University and is the author of several works in ethics and epistemology, including *The Nature of Morality,* from which this selection is taken. Here Harman sets forth an antirealist position by nothing an asymmetry between scientific theories that require observations to confirm them and moral theories, which don't seem to be confirmed in the same way. Scientific theory is tested against the world, so that if a predicted observation occurs, our theory is confirmed, but if it doesn't occur, we feel some pressure to alter our theory. With regard to moral theories, we do not see 'rightness' or 'wrongness' in acts in the same way we identify a vapor trail in a cloud chamber as a proton. Moral insights occur because of our upbringing, not because of the way the world is. Hence, we may conclude that there are no moral facts in the way that there are scientific facts. This result Harman calls moral nihilism.

Harman next considers ways to offset this conclusion. One way would be if we could reduce moral facts to certain sociological and psychological facts. Harman examines this possibility and concludes that this reduction, at best, would have to be "complex, vague, and difficult to specify." It is doubtful whether there are any moral facts.

Ethics and Observation

The Basic Issue

Can moral principles be tested and confirmed in the way scientific principles can? Consider the principle that, if you are given a choice between five people alive and one dead or five people dead and one alive, you should always choose to have five people alive and one dead rather than the other way round. We can easily imagine examples that appear to confirm this principle. Here is one:

> You are a doctor in a hospital's emergency room when six accident victims are brought in. All six are in danger of dying but one is much worse off than the others. You can just barely save that person if you devote all of

your resources to him and let the others die. Alternatively, you can save the other five if you are willing to ignore the most seriously injured person.

It would seem that in this case you, the doctor, would be right to save the five and let the other person die. So this example, taken by itself, confirms the principle under consideration. Next, consider the following case:

> You have five patients in the hospital who are dying, each in need of a separate organ. One needs a kidney, another a lung, a third a heart, and so forth. You can save all five if you take a single healthy person and remove his heart, lungs, kidneys, and so forth, to distribute to these five patients. Just such a healthy person is in room 306. He is in the hospital for routine tests. Having seen his test results, you know that he is perfectly healthy and of the right tissue compatibility. If you do nothing, he will survive without incident; the

other patients will die, however. The other five patients can be saved only if the person in Room 306 is cut up and his organs distributed. In that case, there would be one dead but five saved.

The principle in question tells us that you should cut up the patient in Room 306. But in this case, surely you must not sacrifice this innocent bystander, even to save the five other patients. Here a moral principle has been tested and disconfirmed in what may seem to be a surprising way.

This, of course, was a "thought experiment." We did not really compare a hypothesis with the world. We compared an explicit principle with our feelings about certain imagined examples. In the same way, a physicist performs thought experiments in order to compare explicit hypotheses with his "sense" of what should happen in certain situations, a "sense" that he has acquired as a result of his long working familiarity with current theory. But scientific hypotheses can also be tested in real experiments, out in the world.

Can moral principles be tested in the same way, out in the world? You can observe someone do something, but can you ever perceive the rightness or wrongness of what he does? If you round a corner and see a group of young hoodlums pour gasoline on a cat and ignite it, you do not need to *conclude* that what they are doing is wrong; you do not need to figure anything out; you can *see* that it is wrong. But is your reaction due to the actual wrongness of what you see or is it simply a reflection of your moral "sense," a "sense" that you have acquired perhaps as a result of your moral upbringing?

Observation

The issue is complicated. There are no pure observations. Observations are always "theory laden." What you perceive depends to some extent on the theory you hold, consciously or unconsciously. You see some children pour gasoline on a cat and ignite it. To really see that, you have to possess a great deal of knowledge, know about a considerable number of objects, know about people: that people pass through the life stages infant, baby, child, adolescent, adult. You must know what flesh and blood animals are, and in particular, cats. You must have some idea of life. You must know what gasoline is,

what burning is, and much more. In one sense, what you "see" is a pattern of light on your retina, a shifting array of splotches, although even that is theory, and you could never adequately describe what you see in that sense. In another sense, you see what you do because of the theories you hold. Change those theories and you would see something else, given the same pattern of light.

Similarly, if you hold a moral view, whether it is held consciously or unconsciously, you will be able to perceive rightness or wrongness, goodness or badness, justice or injustice. There is no difference in this respect between moral propositions and other theoretical propositions. If there is a difference, it must be found elsewhere.

Observation depends on theory because perception involves forming a belief as a fairly direct result of observing something; you can form a belief only if you understand the relevant concepts and a concept is what it is by virtue of its role in some theory or system of beliefs. To recognize a child as a child is to employ, consciously or unconsciously, a concept that is defined by its place in a framework of the stages of human life. Similarly, burning is an empty concept apart from its theoretical connections to the concepts of heat, destruction, smoke, and fire.

Moral concepts — Right and Wrong, Good and Bad, Justice and Injustice — also have a place in your theory or system of beliefs and are the concepts they are because of their context. If we say that observation has occurred whenever an opinion is a direct result of perception, we must allow that there is moral observation, because such an opinion can be a moral opinion as easily as any other sort. In this sense, observation may be used to confirm or disconfirm moral theories. The observational opinions that, in this sense, you find yourself with can be in either agreement or conflict with your consciously explicit moral principles. When they are in conflict, you must choose between your explicit theory and observation. In ethics, as in science, you sometimes opt for theory, and say that you made an error in observation or were biased or whatever, or you sometimes opt for observation, and modify your theory.

In other words, in both science and ethics, general principles are invoked to explain particular cases and, therefore, in both science and ethics, the general principles you accept can be tested by appealing to particular judgments that certain things are right or wrong, just or unjust, and so forth; and these judgments are analogous to direct perceptual judgments about facts.

Observational Evidence

Nevertheless, observation plays a role in science that it does not seem to play in ethics. The difference is that you need to make assumptions about certain physical facts to explain the occurrence of the observations that support a scientific theory, but you do not seem to need to make assumptions about any moral facts to explain the occurrence of the so-called moral observations I have been talking about. In the moral case, it would seem that you need only make assumptions about the psychology or moral sensibility of the person making the moral observation. In the scientific case, theory is tested against the world.

The point is subtle but important. Consider a physicist making an observation to test a scientific theory. Seeing a vapor trail in a cloud chamber, he thinks, "There goes a proton." Let us suppose that this is an observation in the relevant sense, namely, an immediate judgment made in response to the situation without any conscious reasoning having taken place. Let us also suppose that his observation confirms his theory, a theory that helps give meaning to the very term "proton" as it occurs in his observational judgment. Such a confirmation rests on inferring an explanation. He can count his making the observation as confirming evidence for his theory only to the extent that it is reasonable to explain his making the observation by assuming that, not only is he in a certain psychological "set," given the theory he accepts and his beliefs about the experimental apparatus, but furthermore, there really was a proton going through the cloud chamber, causing the vapor trail, which he saw as a proton. (This is evidence for the theory to the extent that the theory can explain the proton's being there better than competing theories can.) But, if his having made that observation could have been equally well explained by his psychological set alone, without the need for any assumption about a proton, then the observation would not have been evidence for the existence of that proton and therefore would not have been evidence for the theory. His making the

observation supports the theory only because, in order to explain his making the observation, it is reasonable to assume something about the world over and above the assumptions made about the observer's psychology. In particular, it is reasonable to assume that there was a proton going through the cloud chamber, causing the vapor trail.

Compare this case with one in which you make a moral judgment immediately and without conscious reasoning, say, that the children are wrong to set the cat on fire or that the doctor would be wrong to cut up one healthy patient to save five dying patients. In order to explain your making the first of these judgments, it would be reasonable to assume, perhaps, that the children really are pouring gasoline on a cat and you are seeing them do it. But, in neither case is there any obvious reason to assume anything about "moral facts," such as that it really is wrong to set the cat on fire or to cut up the patient in Room 306. Indeed, an assumption about moral facts would seem to be totally irrelevant to the explanation of your making the judgment you make. It would seem that all we need assume is that you have certain more or less well articulated moral principles that are reflected in the judgments you make, based on your moral sensibility. It seems to be completely irrelevant to our explanation whether your intuitive immediate judgment is true or false.

The observation of an event can provide observational evidence for or against a scientific theory in the sense that the truth of that observation can be relevant to a reasonable explanation of why that observation was made. A moral observation does not seem, in the same sense, to be observational evidence for or against any moral theory, since the truth or falsity of the moral observation seems to be completely irrelevant to any reasonable explanation of why that observation was made. The fact that an observation of an event was made at the time it was made is evidence not only about the observer but also about the physical facts. The fact that you made a particular moral observation when you did does not seem to be evidence about moral facts, only evidence about you and your moral sensibility. Facts about protons can affect what you observe, since a proton passing through the cloud chamber can cause a vapor trail that reflects light to your eye in a way that, given your scientific training and psychological set, leads you to judge that what you see is a proton. But there does not seem to be any way in which the actual rightness or wrongness of a given situation can have any effect on your perceptual apparatus. In this respect, ethics seems to differ from science.

In considering whether moral principles can help explain observations, it is therefore important to note an ambiguity in the word "observation." You see the children set the cat on fire and immediately think, "That's wrong." In one sense, your observation is that what the children are doing is wrong. In another sense, your observation is your thinking that thought. Moral principles might explain observations in the first sense but not in the second sense. Certain moral principles might help to explain why it was *wrong* of the children to set the cat on fire, but moral principles seem to be of no help in explaining *your thinking* that that is wrong. In the first sense of "observation," moral principles can be tested by observation — "That this act is wrong is evidence that causing unnecessary suffering is wrong." But in the second sense of "observation," moral principles cannot clearly be tested by observation, since they do not appear to help explain observations in this second sense of "observation." Moral principles do not seem to help explain your observing what you observe.

Of course, if you are already given the moral principle that it is wrong to cause unnecessary suffering, you can take your seeing the children setting the cat on fire as observational evidence that they are doing something wrong. Similarly, you can suppose that your seeing the vapor trail is observational evidence that a proton is going through the cloud chamber, if you are given the relevant physical theory. But there is an important apparent difference between the two cases. In the scientific case, your making that observation is itself evidence for the physical theory because the physical theory explains the proton, which explains the trail, which explains your observation. In the moral case, your making your observation does not seem to be evidence for the relevant moral principle because that principle does not seem to help explain your observation. The explanatory chain from principle to observation seems to be broken in morality. The moral principle may "explain" why it is wrong for the children to set the cat on fire. But the wrongness of that act does not appear to help explain the act, which you observe, itself. The explanatory chain appears to be broken in such a way that neither the moral principle nor the wrongness of the act can help explain why you observe what you observe.

A qualification may seem to be needed here. Perhaps the children perversely set the cat on fire simply "because it is wrong." Here it may seem at first that the actual wrongness of the act does help explain why they do it and therefore indirectly helps explain why you observe what you observe just as a physical theory, by explaining why the proton is producing a vapor trail, indirectly helps explain why the observer observes what he observes. But on reflection we must agree that this is probably an illusion. What explains the children's act is not clearly the actual wrongness of the act but, rather, their belief that the act is wrong. The actual rightness or wrongness of their act seems to have nothing to do with why they do it.

Observational evidence plays a part in science it does not appear to play in ethics, because scientific principles can be justified ultimately by their role in explaining observations, in the second sense of observation — by their explanatory role. Apparently, moral principles cannot be justified in the same way. It appears to be true that there can be no explanatory chain between moral principles and particular observings in the way that there can be such a chain between scientific principles and particular observings. Conceived as an explanatory theory, morality, unlike science, seems to be cut off from observation.

Not that every legitimate scientific hypothesis is susceptible to direct observational testing. Certain hypotheses about "black holes" in space cannot be directly tested, for example, because no signal is emitted from within a black hole. The connection with observation in such a case is indirect. And there are many similar examples. Nevertheless, seen in the large, there is the apparent difference between science and ethics we have noted. The scientific realm is accessible to observation in a way the moral realm is not.

Ethics and Mathematics

Perhaps ethics is to be compared, not with physics, but with mathematics. Perhaps such a moral principle as "You ought to keep your promises" is confirmed or disconfirmed in the way (whatever it is) in which such a mathematical principle as "5 + 7 = 12" is. Observation does not seem to play the role in mathematics it plays in physics. We do not and cannot perceive numbers, for example, since we cannot be in causal contact with them. We do not even understand what it would be like to be in a causal contact with the number 12, say. Relations among numbers cannot have any more of an effect on our perceptual apparatus than moral facts can.

Observation, however, *is* relevant to mathematics. In explaining the observations that support a physical theory, scientists typically appeal to mathematical principles. On the other hand, one never seems to need to appeal in this way to moral principles. Since an observation is evidence for what best explains it, and since mathematics often figures in the explanations of scientific observations, there is indirect observational evidence for mathematics. There does not seem to be observational evidence, even indirectly, for basic moral principles. In explaining why certain observations have been made, we never seem to use purely moral assumptions. In this respect, then, ethics appears to differ not only from physics but also from mathematics.

In what follows, we will be considering a number of possible responses to the apparent fact that ethics is cut off from observational testing in a way that science is not. Some of these responses claim that there is a distinction of this sort between science and ethics and try to say what its implications are. Others deny that there is a distinction of this sort between science and ethics and argue that ethics is not really exempt from observational testing in the way it appears to be.

Nihilism and Naturalism

Moral Nihilism

We have seen that observational evidence plays a role in science and mathematics it does not seem to play in ethics. Moral hypotheses do not help explain why people observe what they observe. So ethics is problematic and nihilism must be taken seriously. Nihilism is the doctrine that there are no moral facts, no moral truths, and no moral knowledge. This doctrine can account for why reference to moral facts does not seem to help explain observations, on the grounds that what does not exist cannot explain anything.

An extreme version of nihilism holds that morality is simply an illusion: nothing is ever right or wrong, just or unjust, good or bad. In this version, we should abandon morality, just as an atheist abandons religion after he has decided that religious facts cannot help explain observations. Some extreme nihilists have even suggested that morality is merely a superstitious remnant of religion.

Such extreme nihilism is hard to accept. It implies that there are no moral constraints — that everything is permitted. As Dostoevsky observes, it implies that there is nothing wrong with murdering your father. It also implies that slavery is not unjust and that Hitler's extermination camps were not immoral. These are not easy conclusions to accept.

This, of course, does not refute extreme nihilism. Nihilism does not purport to reflect our ordinary views; and the fact that it is difficult to believe does not mean that it must be false. At one time in the history of the world people had difficulty in believing that the earth was round; nevertheless the earth was round. A truly religious person could not easily come to believe that God does not exist; that is no argument against atheism. Extreme nihilism is a possible view and it deserves to be taken seriously.

On the other hand, it is also worth pointing out that extreme nihilism is not an automatic consequence of the point that moral facts apparently cannot help explain observations. Although this is grounds for nihilism, there are more moderate versions of nihilism. Not all versions imply that morality is a delusion and that moral judgments are to be abandoned the way an atheist abandons religious judgments. Thus, a more moderate nihilism holds that the purpose of moral judgments is not to describe the world but to express our moral feelings or to serve as imperatives we address to ourselves and to others. In this view, morality is not undermined by its apparent failure to explain observations, because to expect moral judgments to be of help in explaining observations is to be confused about the function of morality. It is as if you were to expect to explain observations by exclaiming, "Alas!" or by commanding, "Close the door!"

Moderate nihilism is easier to accept than extreme nihilism. It allows us to keep morality and continue to make moral judgments. It does not imply that there is nothing wrong with murdering your father, owning slaves, or setting up extermination camps. Because we disapprove of these activities, we can, according to moderate nihilism, legitimately express our disapproval by saying that they are wrong.

Moderate nihilism, nevertheless, still conflicts with common sense, even if the conflict is less blatant. To assert, as even moderate nihilists assert, that there are no moral facts, no moral truths, and no moral knowledge is to assert something that runs counter to much that we ordinarily think and say. If someone suggests that it was wrong of members of the Oregon Taxpayers Union to have kidnapped Sally Jones in order to get at her father, Austin P. Jones, and you agree, you will express your agreement by saying, "That's *true!*" Similarly, in deciding what to do on a particular occasion, you say such things as this, "I *know* that I should not break my promise to Herbert, but I really would like to go to the beach today." We ordinarily do speak of moral judgments as true or false; and we talk as if we knew certain moral truths but not others.

Nihilism, then, extreme or moderate, is in conflict with ordinary ways of talking and thinking. Although such a conflict does not refute a theory, we must ask whether we can accommodate the point about ethics and observation without having to give up our ordinary views and endorsing some form of nihilism.

Reductions

Our previous discussion suggests the following argument for moral nihilism:

> Moral hypotheses never help explain why we observe anything. So we have no evidence for our moral opinions.

The argument depends upon this assumption:

> We can have evidence for hypotheses of a certain sort only if such hypotheses sometimes help explain why we observe what we observe.

But that assumption is too strong. Hypotheses about the average American citizen never help explain why we observe anything about a particular American, but we can obtain evidence for such hypotheses by obtaining evidence for hypotheses about American citizens. The reason is that facts about the average American citizen are definable in terms of facts about American citizens. Facts of the first sort are constructed out of and therefore reduc-

ible to facts of the second sort. Even if assumptions about moral facts do not directly help explain observations, it may be that moral facts can be reduced to other sorts of facts and that assumptions about these facts do help explain observations. In that case there could be evidence for assumptions about moral facts.

To take another example, we might be able to account for color perception without making the supposition that objects actually have colors. For we might be able to explain how objects whose surfaces have certain physical characteristics will reflect light of a particular wave length; this light then strikes the retina of an observer's eye, affecting him in a way that might be described by an adequate neurophysiological psychology. That is, we might be able to explain perception of color entirely in terms of the physical characteristics of the objects perceived and the properties of light together with an account of the perceptual apparatus of the observer. This would not prove that there are no facts about colors; it would only show that facts about colors are not additional facts, over and above physical and psychological facts. If we could explain color perception in this way, we would conclude that facts about color are somehow reducible to facts about the physical characteristics of perceived objects, facts about light, and facts about the psychology and perceptual apparatus of perceivers. We might consider whether moral facts are in a similar way constructible out of or reducible to certain other facts that can help explain our observations.

Ethical Naturalism: Functionalism

This is certainly a plausible suggestion for certain non-moral evaluative facts. Consider, for example, what is involved in something's being a good thing of its kind, a good knife, a good watch, or a good heart. Associated with these kinds of things are certain functions. A knife is something that is used for cutting; a watch is used to keep time; a heart is that organ that pumps the blood. Furthermore, something is a good thing of the relevant kind to the extent that it adequately fulfills its proper function. A good knife cuts well; a good watch keeps accurate time; a good heart pumps blood at the right pressure without faltering. Let us use the letter "K" to stand for a kind of thing. Then, for these cases, a good K is a K that adequately fulfills its function. It is a factual question whether or not something is a good K because it is a factual question whether or not Ks have that function and a factual question whether or not this given something adequately fulfills that function.

Moreover, a K ought to fulfill its function. If it does not do so, something has gone wrong. Therefore, it is a factual question whether a given K of this sort is as it ought to be and does what it ought to do, and it is a factual question whether anything is wrong with a K of this sort. A knife ought to be sharp, so that it will cut well. There is something wrong with a heart that fails to pump blood without faltering.

There are, of course, two somewhat different cases here, artifacts, such as watches and knives, and parts of natural systems, such as hearts. The functions of artifacts are determined by their makers and users. The functions of parts of natural systems are determined by their roles in sustaining those systems. In either case, though, it is a factual question what the relevant function of a K is.

Let us next consider a somewhat different range of cases: a good meal, a good swim, a good time. We might stretch a point and say that meals, swims, and times have functions or purposes; but it would be more accurate to say that they can answer to certain interests. We judge that particular meals, swims, or times are good inasmuch as they answer to the relevant interests. Where different sets of interests are relevant, we get ambiguity: "a good meal" may mean a nourishing meal or a tasty meal.

With this range of cases, "ought" and "wrong" are used as before. A good meal ought to be balanced (or tasty). There is something wrong with a steak that is not tender and juicy.

More complex cases involve roles that a person can have in one way or another: a good farmer, a good soldier, a good teacher, a good citizen, a good thief. A person is evaluated in terms of functions, roles, and various interests in a way that is hard to specify. Here too the words "ought" and "wrong" are relevant as before. During battle, we say, a soldier ought to obey his superior officers without question. It is wrong for a teacher to play favorites. A thief ought to wear gloves.

Some kinds of things are not associated with functions, purposes, or sets of interests; for example, rocks per se are not. Therefore, it does not make sense to ask apart from a specific context whether

something is a good rock. We can answer such a question only in relation to interests that we might have in possible uses of the rock. For example, it might be a good rock to use as a paperweight; but, if it is to be used as a doorstop, maybe it ought to be heavier.

The relevant evaluative judgments are factual. The facts are natural facts though somewhat complex facts. We judge that something is good or bad, that it is right or wrong, that it ought or ought not to have certain characteristics or do certain things, relative to a cluster of interests, roles, and functions. We can abbreviate this by saying that something X is good to the extent that it adequately answers to the relevant interests. To specify those interests is to specify what X is good as. Similarly, a person P ought to do D if and only if P's doing D would answer to the relevant interests.

This analysis is a realistic one for many cases and it suggests how evaluative facts might be constructed out of observable facts even when the evaluative facts themselves do not figure in explanations of observations. That my watch is a good one may not explain anything about my observations of it; but that it keeps fairly accurate time does help to explain its continual agreement with the announcements of the time on the radio and perhaps the goodness of my watch consists in facts of this sort.

But a problem manifests itself when this sort of analysis is applied in ethics. Consider the case in which you are a doctor who either can save five patients by cutting up the healthy patient in Room 306 and distributing his organs to the other patients or can do nothing and let the five other patients die. The problem is that in either case you would be satisfying certain interests and not others. The interests of the five dying patients conflict with the interests of the healthy patient in Room 306. The moral question is what you ought to do, taking all interests into account. As we saw earlier, our intuitive judgment is that you ought not to sacrifice the one patient in Room 306 to save the five other patients. Is this a factual judgment? If we suppose that it is a fact that you ought not to sacrifice the patient in Room 306, how is that fact related to facts that can help explain observations? It is not at all obvious how we can extend our analysis to cover this sort of case.

Actually, the problem is not peculiar to ethics. Is a heavy, waterproof, shockproof watch that can withstand a considerable amount of pressure a better or worse watch than a lighter, graceful, delicate watch without those features? Is one teacher better or worse than a second if the first teacher makes students unhappy while teaching them more?

To some extent, our difficulty in these cases lies in the vagueness of our standards for watches and teachers. Often we can resolve the vagueness by specifying relevant interests. The heavy watch is a better watch for deep-sea diving. The lighter watch is better for social occasions, out of the water. In the case of evaluating teachers, we must decide what we want from teachers — perhaps that their students should learn a certain minimal amount and, given that they learn at least that much, that they not be made miserable. But even given further specifications of our interests in watches and teachers in this way, there may be no fact of the matter as to which watch or teacher is better — not because these are not factual questions but because of vagueness of standards. Factual questions are still factual even when they cannot be answered because of vagueness. (Is a door open or shut if it is slightly ajar?) Furthermore, even in cases where we feel intuitively that one watch or teacher is clearly better, we may not be able to specify very clearly the interests, functions, and roles with reference to which one is better, as a watch or teacher, than the other. Still, it may well be a fact that one is better — a fact constructed in a way that we can only vaguely specify from facts of a sort that can help explain observations.

Similarly, it *may* be that moral facts, such as the fact that you ought not to sacrifice the healthy patient in Room 306 to save the five other patients, can be constructed in some way or other out of facts of a sort that can explain observations, even though we can only vaguely indicate relevant roles, interests, and functions.

That would vindicate ethical naturalism, which is the doctrine that moral facts are facts of nature. Naturalism as a general view is the sensible thesis that *all* facts are facts of nature. Of course, one can accept naturalism in general without being committed to ethical naturalism, since one can instead be a nihilist and deny that there are any moral facts at all, just as one might deny that there are any religious facts. Naturalists must be either ethical nihilists or ethical naturalists. The question is how do we decide between ethical nihilism and ethical naturalism, and there is no simple answer. If an analysis of moral facts as facts about functions, roles, and interests could be made plausible, that would be a powerful argument for ethical naturalism. But the relevant functions, roles, and interests can at best be only vaguely indicated, so the proposed analysis is difficult to evaluate. Nihilism remains a possibility.

Why Ethics Is Problematic

Although we are in no position to assume that nihilism, extreme or moderate, is correct, we are now in a position to see more clearly the way in which ethics is problematic. Our starting point in this chapter was that moral judgments do not seem to help explain observations. This led us to wonder whether there are moral facts, moral truths, and moral knowledge. We saw that there could be moral facts if these facts were reducible in some way or other to other facts of a sort that might help explain observations. For we noticed that there are facts about the average American citizen, even though such facts do not themselves help explain observations, because such facts are reducible to facts about American citizens that can help explain observations. Similarly, we noticed that we would not decide that there are no facts about colors even if we were able to explain color perception without appealing to facts about colors; we would instead suppose that facts about colors are reducible to facts about the physical surfaces of objects, the properties of light, and the neurophysiological psychology of observers. So, we concluded that we did not have to accept ethical nihilism simply because moral facts do not seem to help explain observations; instead we might hope for a naturalistic reduction of moral facts.

With this in mind, we considered the possibility that moral facts might be reduced to facts about interests, roles, and functions. We concluded that, if they were to be, the reduction would have to be complex, vague, and difficult to specify. Ethics remains problematic.

It is true that the reduction of facts about colors is also complex, vague, and difficult (probably impossible) to specify. But there is an important difference between facts about colors and moral facts. Even if we come to be able to explain color perception by appeal to the physical characteristics of surfaces, the properties of light, and the neurophysiological psychology of observers, we will still *sometimes* refer to the actual colors of objects in explaining color perception, if only for the sake of simplicity. For example, we will explain that something looks green because it is yellow and the light is blue. It may be that the reference to the actual color of the object in an explanation of this sort can be replaced with talk about the physical characteristics of the surface. But that would greatly complicate what is a simple and easily understood explanation. That is why, even after we come to be able to give explanations without referring to the actual colors of objects, we will still assume that objects have actual colors and that therefore facts about the actual colors of objects are somehow reducible to facts about physical characteristics of surfaces and so forth, even though we will (probably) not be able to specify the reduction in any but the vaguest way. We will continue to believe that objects have colors because we will continue to refer to the actual colors of objects in the explanations that we will in practice give. A similar point does not seem to hold for moral facts. There does not ever seem to be, even in practice, any point to explaining someone's moral observations by appeal to what is actually right or wrong, just or unjust, good or bad. It always seems to be more accurate to explain moral observations by citing facts about moral views, moral sensibility. So, the reasons we have for supposing that there are facts about

colors do not correspond to reasons for thinking that there are moral facts.

It is true that facts about the average American citizen never seem to help explain observations, even in practice. In this respect such facts are like moral facts. But there is this difference. We can give a *precise* reduction of facts about the average American citizen; we cannot for moral facts. We are willing to think that there are facts about the average American citizen because we can explicitly define these facts in terms of facts that are of a sort that can help to explain observations. The trouble with alleged moral facts is that, as far as we can see at present, there is no simple and precise way to define them in terms of natural facts.

We are willing to suppose that there are facts about color, despite our not knowing precisely how to reduce them, because in practice we assume that there are such facts in many of our explanations of color perception, even if in theory this assumption is dispensable. We are willing to suppose that there are facts about the average American citizen, despite our never using such an assumption to explain observations because we can precisely reduce these facts to facts of a sort that can help explain observations. Since moral facts seem to be neither precisely reducible nor useful even in practice in our explanations of observations, it remains problematic whether we have any reason to suppose that there are any moral facts.

IX.4 *Moral Explanations*

NICHOLAS STURGEON

Nicholas Sturgeon is professor of philosophy at Cornell University and the author of several articles in ethics. In this selection he takes issue with Harman on the disparity between scientific and moral facts. He argues that we often discover that moral facts "do appear relevant by perfectly ordinary standards to the explanation of moral beliefs and of a good deal else besides." There is a symmetry between scientific explanation and moral explanation, so that if we reject moral explanations of our moral observations, we must also reject scientific explanations of our scientific observations. Thus, skepticism about morality entails skepticism about science, a result not welcome to most moral antirealists.

There is one argument for moral skepticism that I respect even though I remain unconvinced. It has sometimes been called the argument from moral diversity or relativity, but that is somewhat misleading, for the problem arises not from the diversity of moral views, but from the apparent difficulty of *settling* moral disagreements, or even of knowing what would be required to settle them, a difficulty thought to be noticeably greater than any found in settling disagreements that arise in, for example, the sciences. This provides an argument for moral skepticism because one obviously possible explanation for our difficulty in settling moral disagreements is that they are really unsettleable, that there is no way of justifying one rather than another competing view on these issues; and a possible further explanation for the unsettleability of moral disagreements, in turn, is moral nihilism, the view that on these issues there just is no fact of the matter, that the impossibility of discovering and establishing moral truths is due to there not being any.

I am, as I say, unconvinced: partly because I think this argument exaggerates the difficulty we actually find in settling moral disagreements, partly because there are alternative explanations to be con-

sidered for the difficulty we do find. Under the latter heading, for example, it certainly matters to what extent moral disagreements depend on disagreements about other questions which, however disputed they may be, are nevertheless regarded as having objective answers: questions such as which, if any, religion is true, which account of human psychology, which theory of human society. And it also matters to what extent consideration of moral questions is in practice skewed by distorting factors such as personal interest and social ideology. These are large issues. Although it is possible to say some useful things to put them in perspective, it appears impossible to settle them quickly or in any a priori way. Consideration of them is likely to have to be piecemeal and, in the short run at least, frustratingly indecisive.

These large issues are not my topic here. But I mention them, and the difficulty of settling them, to show why it is natural that moral skeptics have hoped to find some quicker way of establishing their thesis. I doubt that any exist, but some have of course been proposed. Verificationist attacks on ethics should no doubt be seen in this light, and J. L. Mackie's recent "argument from queerness" is a clear instance.[1] The quicker response on which I shall concentrate, however, is neither of these, but instead an argument by Gilbert Harman designed to bring out the "basic problem" about morality, which in his view is "its apparent immunity from

Excerpted from *Morality, Reason and Truth*, eds. D. Copp and D. Zimmerman (Rowman and Allanheld, 1984). © 1984. Reprinted by permission of the publisher.

observational testing" and "the seeming irrelevance of observational evidence."[2] The argument is that reference to moral facts appears unnecessary for the *explanation* of our moral observations and beliefs.

Harman's view, I should say at once, is not in the end a skeptical one, and he does not view the argument I shall discuss as a decisive defense of moral skepticism or moral nihilism. Someone else might easily so regard it, however. For Harman himself regards it as creating a strong prima facie case for skepticism and nihilism, strong enough to justify calling it "the problem with ethics." And he believes it shows that the only recourse for someone who wishes to avoid moral skepticism is to find defensible reductive definitions for ethical terms; so skepticism would be the obvious conclusion to draw for anyone who doubted the possibility of such definitions. I believe, however, that Harman is mistaken on both counts. I shall show that his argument for skepticism either rests on claims that most people would find quite implausible (and so cannot be what constitutes, for *them,* the problem with ethics); or else becomes just the application to ethics of a familiar *general* skeptical strategy, one which, if it works for ethics, will work equally well for unobservable theoretical entities, or for other minds, or for an external world (and so, again, can hardly be what constitutes the distinctive problem with *ethics*). I have argued elsewhere, moreover, that one can in any case be a moral realist, and indeed an ethical naturalist, without believing that we are now or ever will be in possession of reductive naturalistic definitions for ethical terms.

I. The Problem with Ethics

Moral theories are often tested in thought experiments, against imagined examples; and, as Harman notes, trained researchers often test scientific theories in the same way. The problem, though, is that scientific theories can also be tested against the world, by observations or real experiments; and, Harman asks, "can moral principles be tested in the same way, out in the world?" (p. 4).

This would not be a very interesting or impressive challenge, of course, if it were merely a resurrection of standard verificationist worries about

whether moral assertions and theories have any testable empirical implications, implications statable in some relatively austere "observational" vocabulary. One problem with that form of the challenge, as Harman points out, is that there are no "pure" observations, and in consequence no purely observational vocabulary either. But there is also a deeper problem that Harman does not mention, one that remains even if we shelve worries about "pure" observations and, at least for the sake of argument, grant the verificationist his observational language, pretty much as it was usually conceived: that is, as lacking at the very least any obviously theoretical terminology from any recognized science, and of course as lacking any moral terminology. For then the difficulty is that moral principles fare just as well (or just as badly) against the verificationist challenge as do typical scientific principles. For it is by now a familiar point about scientific principles — principles such as Newton's law of universal gravitation or Darwin's theory of evolution — that they are entirely devoid of empirical implications when considered in isolation. We do of course base observational predictions on such theories and so test them against experience, but that is because we do *not* consider them in isolation. For we can derive these predictions only by relying at the same time on a large background of additional assumptions, many of which are equally theoretical and equally incapable of being tested in isolation.

A less familiar point, because less often spelled out, is that the relation of moral principles to observation is similar in *both* these respects. Candidate moral principles — for example, that an action is wrong just in case there is something else the agent could have done that would have produced a greater balance of pleasure over pain — lack empirical implications when considered in isolation. But it is easy to derive empirical consequences from them, and thus to test them against experience, if we allow ourselves, as we do in the scientific case, to rely on a background of other assumptions of comparable status. Thus, if we conjoin the act-utilitarian principle I just cited with the further view, also untestable in isolation, that it is always wrong deliberately to kill a human being, we can deduce from these two premises together the consequence that deliberately killing a human being always produces a lesser balance of pleasure over pain than some available alternative act; and this claim is one any positivist would have conceded we know, in principle at least, how to test. If we found it to be false, moreover, then we would be forced by this empirical test to abandon at least one of the moral claims from which we derived it.

It might be thought a worrisome feature of this example, however, and a further opening for skepticism, that there could be controversy about which moral premise to abandon, and that we have not explained how our empirical test can provide an answer to *this* question. And this may be a problem. It should be a familiar problem, however, because the Duhemian commentary includes a precisely corresponding point about the scientific case: that if we are at all cautious in characterizing what we observe, then the requirement that our theories merely be *consistent* with observation is a very weak one. There are always many, perhaps indefinitely many, different mutually inconsistent ways to adjust our views to meet this constraint. Of course, in practice we are often confident of how to do it: if you are a freshman chemistry student, you do not conclude from your failure to obtain the predicted value in an experiment that it is all over for the atomic theory of gases. And the decision can be equally easy, one should note, in a moral case. Consider two examples. From the surprising moral thesis that Adolf Hitler was a morally admirable person, together with a modest piece of moral theory to the effect that no morally admirable person would, for example, instigate and oversee the degradation and death of millions of persons, one can derive the testable consequence that Hitler did not do this. But he did, so we must give up one of our premises; and the choice of which to abandon is neither difficult nor controversial.

Or, to take a less monumental example, contrived around one of Harman's own, suppose you have been thinking yourself lucky enough to live in a neighborhood in which no one would do anything wrong, at least not in public; and that the modest piece of theory you accept, this time, is that malicious cruelty, just for the hell of it, is wrong. Then, as in Harman's example, "you round a corner and see a group of young hoodlums pour gasoline on a cat and ignite it." At this point, either your confidence in the neighborhood or your principle about cruelty has got to give way. But the choice is easy, if dispiriting, so easy as hardly to require thought. As Harman says, "You do not need to *conclude* that

what they are doing is wrong; you do not need to figure anything out; you can *see* that it is wrong" (p. 4). But a skeptic can still wonder whether this practical confidence, or this "seeing," rests in either sort of case on anything more than deeply ingrained conventions of thought—respect for scientific experts, say, and for certain moral traditions—as opposed to anything answerable to the facts of the matter, any reliable strategy for getting it right about the world.

Now, Harman's challenge is interesting partly because it does not rest on these verificationist doubts about whether moral beliefs have observational implications, but even more because what it does rest on is a partial answer to the kind of general skepticism to which, as we have seen, reflection on the verificationist picture can lead. Many of our beliefs are justified, in Harman's view, by their providing or helping to provide a reasonable *explanation* of our observing what we do. It would be consistent with your failure, as a beginning student, to obtain the experimental result predicted by the gas laws, that the laws are mistaken. But a better explanation, in light of your inexperience and the general success experts have had in confirming and applying these laws, is that you made some mistake in running the experiment. So our scientific beliefs can be justified by their explanatory role; and so too, in Harman's view, can mathematical beliefs and many commonsense beliefs about the world.

Not so, however, moral beliefs: they appear to have no such explanatory role. That is "the problem with ethics." Harman spells out his version of this contrast:

> You need to make assumptions about certain physical facts to explain the occurrence of the observations that support a scientific theory, but you do not seem to need to make assumptions about any moral facts to explain the occurrence of the so-called moral observations I have been talking about. In the moral case, it would seem that you need only make assumptions about the psychology or moral sensibility of the person making the moral observation. (p. 6)

More precisely, and applied to his own example, it might be reasonable, in order to explain your judging that the hoodlums are wrong to set the cat on fire, to assume "that the children really are pouring gasoline on a cat and you are seeing them do it." But there is no

> obvious reason to assume anything about "moral facts," such as that it is really wrong to set the cat on fire. . . . Indeed, an assumption about moral facts would seem to be totally ir- relevant to the explanation of your making the judgment you make. It would seem that all we need assume is that you have certain more or less well articulated moral principles that are reflected in the judgments you make, based on your moral sensibility. (p. 7)

And Harman thinks that if we accept this conclu- sion, suitably generalized, then, subject to one pos- sible qualification concerning reduction that I have discussed elsewhere, we must conclude that moral theories cannot be tested against the world as scien- tific theories can, and that we have no reason to be- lieve that moral facts are part of the order of nature or that there is any moral knowledge (pp. 23, 35).

My own view is that Harman is quite wrong, not in thinking that the explanatory role of our be- liefs is important to their justification, but in think- ing that moral beliefs play no such role. I shall have to say something about the initial plausibility of Harman's thesis as applied to his own example, but part of my reason for dissenting should be apparent from the other example I just gave. We find it easy (and so does Harman, p. 108) to conclude from the evidence not just that Hitler was not morally admir- able, but that he was morally depraved. But isn't it plausible that Hitler's moral depravity — the fact of his really having been morally depraved — forms part of a reasonable explanation of why we believe he was depraved? I think so, and I shall argue con- cerning this and other examples that moral beliefs very commonly play the explanatory role Harman denies them. Before I can press my case, however, I need to clear up several preliminary points about just what Harman is claiming and just how his argu- ment is intended to work.

II. *Observation and Explanation*

(1) For there are several ways in which Harman's argument invites misunderstanding. One results from his focusing at the start on the question of whether there can be moral *observations*. But this question turns out to be a side issue, in no way cen- tral to his argument that moral principles cannot be tested against the world. There are a couple of rea- sons for this, of which the more important by far is that Harman does not really require of moral facts, if belief in them is to be justified, that they figure in the explanation of moral observations. It would be enough, on the one hand, if they were needed for the explanation of moral beliefs that are not in any interesting sense observations. For example, Har- man thinks belief in moral facts would be vindicated if they were needed to explain our drawing the moral conclusions we do when we reflect on hypo- thetical cases, but I think there is no illumination in calling these conclusions observations. It would also be enough, on the other hand, if moral facts were needed for the explanation of what were clearly ob- servations, but not moral observations. Harman thinks mathematical beliefs are justified, but he does not suggest that there are mathematical observa- tions; it is rather that appeal to mathematical truths helps to explain why we make the physical observa- tions we do (p. 10). Moral beliefs would surely be justified, too, if they played such a role, whether or not there are any moral observations.

So the claim is that moral facts are not needed to explain our having any of the moral beliefs we do, whether or not those beliefs are observations, and are equally unneeded to explain any of the observa- tions we make, whether or not those observations are moral. In fact, Harman's view appears to be that moral facts aren't needed to explain anything at all: though it would perhaps be question-begging for him to begin with this strong a claim, since he grants that if there were any moral facts, then appeal to other moral facts — more general ones, for exam- ple — might be needed to explain *them* (p. 8). But he is certainly claiming, at the very least, that moral facts aren't needed to explain any nonmoral facts we have any reason to believe in.

(2) Other possible misunderstandings concern what is meant in asking whether reference to moral facts is *needed* to explain moral beliefs. One warning about this question I have dealt with in my discus- sion of reduction elsewhere; but another, about what Harman is clearly *not* asking, and about what sort of answer I can attempt to defend to the ques- tion he is asking, I can spell out here. For Harman's question is clearly not just whether there is *an* expla- nation of our moral beliefs that does not mention

moral facts. Almost surely there is. Equally surely, however, there is *an* explanation of our common-sense nonmoral beliefs that does not mention an external world: one which cites only our sensory experience, for example, together with whatever needs to be said about our psychology to explain why with that history of experience we would form just the beliefs we do. Harman means to be asking a question that will lead to skepticism about moral facts, but not to skepticism about the existence of material bodies or about well-established scientific theories of the world.

Harman illustrates the kind of question he is asking, and the kind of answer he is seeking, with an example from physics that it will be useful to keep in mind. A physicist sees a vapor trail in a cloud chamber and thinks, "There goes a proton." What explains his thinking this? Partly, of course, his psychological set, which largely depends on his beliefs about the apparatus and all the theory he has learned; but partly also, perhaps, the hypothesis that "there really was a proton going through the cloud chamber, causing the vapor trail, which he saw as a proton." We will *not* need this latter assumption, however, "if his having made that observation could have been equally well explained by his psychological set alone, without the need for any assumption about a proton" (p. 6). So for reference to moral facts to be *needed* in the explanation of our beliefs and observations, is for this reference to be required for an explanation that is somehow *better* than competing explanations. Correspondingly, reference to moral facts will be unnecessary to an explanation, in Harman's view, not just because we can find some explanation that does not appeal to them, but because *no* explanation that appeals to them is any better than some competing explanation that does not.

Now, fine discriminations among competing explanations of almost anything are likely to be difficult, controversial, and provisional. Fortunately, however, my discussion of Harman's argument will not require any fine discriminations. This is because Harman's thesis, as we have seen, is *not* that moral explanations lose out by a small margin; nor is it that moral explanations, though sometimes initially promising, always turn out on further examination to be inferior to nonmoral ones. It is, rather, that reference to moral facts always looks, right from the start, to be "completely irrelevant" to the explanation of any of our observations and beliefs. And my

argument will be that this is mistaken: that many moral explanations appear to be good explanations, or components in good explanations, that are not obviously undermined by anything else that we know. My suspicion, in fact, is that moral facts are needed in the sense explained, that they will turn out to belong in our best overall explanatory picture of the world, even in the long run, but I shall not attempt to establish that here. Indeed, it should be clear why I could not pretend to do so. For I have explicitly put to one side the issue (which I regard as incapable in any case of quick resolution) of whether and to what extent actual moral disagreements can be settled satisfactorily; but I assume it would count as a defect in any sort of explanation to rely on claims about which rational agreement proved unattainable. So I concede that it *could* turn out, for anything I say here, that moral explanations are all defective and should be discarded. What I shall try to show is merely that many moral explanations look reasonable enough to be in the running; and, more specifically, that nothing Harman says provides any reason for thinking they are not. This claim is surely strong enough (and controversial enough) to be worth defending.

(3) It is implicit in this statement of my project, but worth noting separately, that I take Harman to be proposing an *independent* skeptical argument—independent not merely of the argument from the difficulty of settling disputed moral questions, but also of other standard arguments for moral skepticism. Otherwise his argument is not worth separate discussion. For *any* of these more familiar skeptical arguments will of course imply that moral explanations are defective, on the reasonable assumption that it would be a defect in any explanation to rely on claims as doubtful as these arguments attempt to show all moral claims to be. But if *that* is why there is a problem with moral explanations, one should surely just cite the relevant skeptical argument, rather than this derivative difficulty about moral explanations, as the basic "problem with ethics," and it is that argument we should discuss. So I take Harman's interesting suggestion to be that there is a *different* difficulty that remains even if we put other arguments for moral skepticism aside and *assume,* for the sake of argument, that there are moral facts (for example, that what the children in his example are doing is really wrong): namely, that these assumed facts *still* seem to play no explanatory role.

This understanding of Harman's thesis crucially affects my argumentative strategy in a way to which I should alert the reader in advance. For it should be clear that assessment of this thesis not merely permits, but *requires,* that we provisionally assume the existence of moral facts. I can see no way of evaluating the claim that *even if* we assumed the existence of moral facts they would still appear explanatorily irrelevant, without assuming the existence of some, to see how they would look. So I do freely assume this in each of the examples I discuss in the next section. (I have tried to choose plausible examples, moreover, moral facts most of us would be inclined to believe in if we did believe in moral facts, since those are the easiest to think about; but the precise examples don't matter, and anyone who would prefer others should feel free to substitute her own.) I grant, furthermore, that if Harman were right about the outcome of this thought experiment—that even after we assumed these facts they still looked irrelevant to the explanation of our moral beliefs and other nonmoral facts—then we might conclude with him that there were, after all, no such facts. But I claim he is wrong: that once we have provisionally assumed the existence of moral facts they *do* appear relevant, by perfectly ordinary standards, to the explanation of moral beliefs and of a good deal else besides. Does this prove that there *are* such facts? Well of course it helps support that view, but here I carefully make no claim to have shown so much. What I *show* is that any remaining reservations about the existence of moral facts must be based on those *other* skeptical arguments, of which Harman's argument is independent. In short, there may still be a "problem with ethics," but it has *nothing* special to do with moral explanations.

III. *Moral Explanations*

Now that I have explained how I understand Harman's thesis, I turn to my arguments against it. I shall first add to my example of Hitler's moral character several more in which it seems plausible to cite moral facts as part of an explanation of nonmoral facts, and in particular of people's forming the moral opinions they do. I shall then argue that Harman gives us no plausible reason to reject or ignore these explanations; I shall claim, in fact, that the same is

true for his own example of the children igniting the cat. I shall conclude, finally, by attempting to diagnose the source of the disagreement between Harman and me on these issues.

My Hitler example suggests a whole range of extremely common cases that appear not to have occurred to Harman, cases in which we cite someone's moral character as part of an explanation of his or her deeds, and in which that whole story is then available as a plausible further explanation of someone's arriving at a correct assessment of that moral character. Take just one other example. Bernard DeVoto, in *The Year of Decision: 1846,* describes the efforts of American emigrants already in California to rescue another party of emigrants, the Donner Party, trapped by snows in the High Sierras, once their plight became known. At a meeting in Yerba Buena (now San Francisco), the relief efforts were put under the direction of a recent arrival, Passed Midshipman Selim Woodworth, described by a previous acquaintance as "a great busybody and ambitious of taking a command among the emigrants." But Woodworth not only failed to lead rescue parties into the mountains himself, where other rescuers were counting on him (leaving children to be picked up by him, for example), but had to be "shamed, threatened and bullied" even into organizing the efforts of others willing to take the risk; he spent time arranging comforts for himself in camp, preening himself on the importance of his position; and as a predictable result of his cowardice and his exercises in vainglory, many died who might have been saved, including four known still to be alive when he turned back for the last time in mid-March.

DeVoto concludes: "Passed Midshipman Woodworth was just no damned good."[3] I cite this case partly because it has so clearly the structure of an inference to a reasonable explanation. One can think of competing explanations, but the evidence points against them. It isn't, for example, that Woodworth was a basically decent person who simply proved too weak when thrust into a situation that placed heroic demands on him. He volunteered, he put no serious effort even into tasks that required no heroism, and it seems clear that concern for his own position and reputation played a much larger role in his motivation than did any concern for the people he was expected to save. If DeVoto is right about this evidence, moreover, it seems reasonable that part of the explanation of his believing that Woodworth was no damned good is just that Woodworth *was* no damned good.

DeVoto writes of course with more moral intensity (and with more of a flourish) than academic historians usually permit themselves, but it would be difficult to find a serious work of biography, for example, in which actions are not explained by appeal to moral character: sometimes by appeal to specific virtues and vices, but often enough also by appeal to a more general assessment. A different question, and perhaps a more difficult one, concerns the sort of example on which Harman concentrates, the explanation of judgments of right and wrong. Here again he appears just to have overlooked explanations in terms of moral character: a judge's thinking that it would be wrong to sentence a particular offender to the maximum prison term the law allows, for example, may be due in part to her decency and fair-mindedness, which I take to be moral properties if any are. But do moral features of the action or institution being judged ever play an explanatory role? Here is an example in which they appear to. An interesting historical question is why vigorous and reasonably widespread moral opposition to slavery arose for the first time in the eighteenth and nineteenth centuries, even though slavery was a very old institution; and why this opposition arose primarily in Britain, France, and in French- and English-speaking North America, even though slavery existed throughout the New World. There is a standard answer to this question. It is that chattel slavery in British and French America, and then in the United States, was much *worse* than previous forms of slavery, and much worse than slavery in Latin America. This is, I should add, a controversial explanation. But as is often the case with historical explanations, its proponents do not claim it is the whole story, and many of its opponents grant that there may be some truth in these comparisons, and that they may after all form a small part of a larger explanation. This latter concession is all I require for my example. Equally good for my purpose would be the more limited thesis which explains the growth of anti-slavery sentiment in the United States, between the Revolution and the Civil War, in part by saying that slavery in the United States became a more oppressive institution during that time. The appeal in these standard explanations is straightforwardly to moral facts.

What is supposed to be wrong with all these explanations? Harman says that assumptions about moral facts seem "completely irrelevant" in explaining moral observations and moral beliefs (p. 7), but on its more natural reading that claim seems pretty obviously mistaken about these examples. For it is natural to think that if a particular assumption is completely irrelevant to the explanation of a certain fact, then that fact would have obtained, and we could have explained it just as well, even if the assumption had been false. But I do not believe that Hitler would have done all he did if he had not been morally depraved, nor, on the assumption that he was not depraved, can I think of any plausible explanation for his doing those things. Nor is it plausible that we would all have believed he was morally depraved even if he hadn't been. Granted, there is a tendency for writers who do not attach much weight to fascism as a social movement to want to blame its evils on a single maniacal leader, so perhaps some of them would have painted Hitler as a moral monster even if he had not been one. But this is only a tendency, and one for which many people know how to discount, so I doubt that our moral belief really is overdetermined in this way. Nor, similarly, do I believe that Woodworth's actions were overdetermined, so that he would have done just as he did even if he had been a more admirable person. I suppose one could have doubts about DeVoto's objectivity and reliability; it is obvious he dislikes Woodworth, so perhaps he would have thought him a moral loss and convinced his readers of this no matter what the man was really like. But it is more plausible that the dislike is mostly based on the same evidence that supports DeVoto's moral view of him, and that very different evidence, at any rate, would have produced a different verdict. If so, then Woodworth's moral character is part of the explanation of DeVoto's belief about his moral character.

It is more plausible of course that serious moral opposition to slavery would have emerged in Britain, France, and the United States even if slavery hadn't been worse in the modern period than before, and worse in the United States than in Latin America, and that the American antislavery movement would have grown even if slavery had not become more oppressive as the nineteenth century progressed. But that is because these moral facts are offered as at best a partial explanation of these developments in moral opinion. And if they really *are* part of the explanation, as seems plausible, then it is also plausible that whatever effect they produced was not entirely overdetermined; that, for example, the growth of the antislavery movement in the United States would at least have been somewhat slower if slavery had been and remained less bad an institution. Here again it hardly seems "completely irrelevant" to the explanation whether or not these moral facts obtained.

It is more puzzling, I grant, to consider Harman's own example in which you see the children igniting a cat and react immediately with the thought that this is wrong. Is it true, as Harman claims, that the assumption that the children are really doing something wrong is "totally irrelevant" to any reasonable explanation of your making that judgment? Would you, for example, have reacted in just the same way, with the thought that the action is wrong, even if what they were doing *hadn't* been wrong, and could we explain your reaction equally well on this assumption? Now, there is more than one way to understand this counterfactual question, and I shall return below to a reading of it that might appear favorable to Harman's view. What I wish to point out for now is merely that there is a natural way of taking it, parallel to the way in which I have been understanding similar counterfactual questions about my own examples, on which the answer to it has to be simply: it depends. For to answer the question, I take it, we must consider a situation in which what the children are doing is not wrong, but which is otherwise as much like the actual situation as possible, and then decide what your reaction would be in that situation. But since what makes their action wrong, what its wrongness *consists* in, is presumably something like its being an act of gratuitous cruelty (or, perhaps we should add, of intense cruelty, and to a helpless victim), to imagine them not doing something wrong we are going to have to imagine their action different in this respect. More cautiously and more generally, if what they are actually doing is wrong, and if moral properties are, as many writers have held, supervenient on natural ones, then in order to imagine them not doing something wrong we are going to have to suppose their action different from the actual one in some of its natural features as well. So our question becomes: Even if the children had been doing something else, something just different enough not to

be wrong, would you have taken them even so to be doing something wrong?

Surely there is no one answer to this question. It depends on a lot about you, including your moral views and how good you are at seeing at a glance what some children are doing. It probably depends also on a debatable moral issue; namely, just *how* different the children's action would have to be in order not to be wrong. (Is unkindness to animals, for example, also wrong?) I believe we can see how, in a case in which the answer was clearly affirmative, we might be tempted to agree with Harman that the wrongness of the action was no part of the explanation of your reaction. For suppose you are like this. You hate children. What you especially hate, moreover, is the sight of children enjoying themselves; so much so that whenever you see children having fun, you immediately assume they are up to no good. The more they seem to be enjoying themselves, furthermore, the readier you are to fasten on any pretext for thinking them engaged in real wickedness. Then it is true that even if the children had been engaged in some robust but innocent fun, you would have thought they were doing something wrong; and Harman is perhaps right about you that the actual wrongness of the action you see is irrelevant to your thinking it wrong. This is because your reaction is due to a feature of the action that coincides only very accidentally with the ones that make it wrong. But, of course, and fortunately, many people aren't like this (nor does Harman argue that they are). It isn't true of them, in general, that if the children had been doing something similar, although different enough not to be wrong, they would still have thought the children were doing something wrong. And it isn't true either, therefore, that the wrongness of the action is irrelevant to the explanation of why they think it wrong.

Now, one might have the sense from my discussion of all these examples, but perhaps especially from my discussion of this last one, Harman's own, that I have perversely been refusing to understand his claim about the explanatory irrelevance of moral facts in the way he intends. And perhaps I have not been understanding it as he wishes. In any case, I agree, I have certainly not been understanding the crucial counterfactual questions, of whether we would have drawn the same moral conclusion even if the moral facts had been different, in the way he must intend. But I am not being perverse. I believe, as I have said, that my way of taking the question is the more natural one. And, more importantly: although there is, I grant, a reading of that question on which it will always yield the answer Harman wants — namely, that a difference in the moral facts would *not* have made a difference in our judgment — I do not believe this reading can support his argument. I must now explain why.

It will help if I contrast my general approach with his. I am approaching questions about the justification of belief in the spirit of what Quine has called "epistemology naturalized."[4] I take this to mean that we have in general no a priori way of knowing which strategies for forming and refining our beliefs are likely to take us closer to the truth. The only way we have of proceeding is to assume the approximate truth of what seems to us the best overall theory we already have of what we are like and what the world is like, and to decide in the light of *that* what strategies of research and reasoning are likely to be reliable in producing a more nearly true overall theory. One result of applying these procedures, in turn, is likely to be the refinement or perhaps even the abandonment of parts of the tentative theory with which we began.

I take Harman's approach, too, to be an instance of this one. He says we are justified in believing in those facts that we need to assume to explain why we observe what we do. But he does not think that our knowledge of this principle about justification is a priori. Furthermore, as he knows, we cannot decide whether one explanation is better than another without relying on beliefs we already have about the world. Is it really a better explanation of the vapor trail the physicist sees in the cloud chamber to suppose that a proton caused it, as Harman suggests in his example, rather than some other charged particle? Would there, for example, have been no vapor trail in the absence of that proton? There is obviously no hope of answering such questions without assuming at least the approximate truth of some quite far-reaching microphysical theory, and our knowledge of such theories is not a priori.

But my approach differs from Harman's in one crucial way. For among the beliefs in which I have enough confidence to rely on in evaluating explanations, at least at the outset, are some moral beliefs.

And I have been relying on them in the following way. Harman's thesis implies that the supposed moral fact of Hitler's being morally depraved is irrelevant to the explanation of Hitler's doing what he did. (For we may suppose that if it explains his doing what he did, it also helps explain, at greater remove, Harman's belief and mine in his moral depravity.) To assess this claim, we need to conceive a situation in which Hitler was *not* morally depraved and consider the question whether in that situation he would still have done what he did. My answer is that he would not, and this answer relies on a (not very controversial) moral view: that in any world at all like the actual one, only a morally depraved person could have initiated a world war, ordered the "final solution," and done any number of other things Hitler did. That is why I believe that, if Hitler hadn't been morally depraved, he wouldn't have done those things, and hence that the fact of his moral depravity is relevant to an explanation of what he did.

Harman, however, cannot want us to rely on any such moral views in answering this counterfactual question. This comes out most clearly if we return to his example of the children igniting the cat. He claims that the wrongness of this act is irrelevant to an explanation of your thinking it wrong, that you would have *thought* it wrong even if it wasn't. My reply was that in order for the action not to be wrong it would have had to lack the feature of deliberate, intense, pointless cruelty, and that if it had differed in this way you might very well *not* have thought it wrong. I also suggested a more cautious version of this reply: that since the action is in fact wrong, and since moral properties supervene on more basic natural ones, it would have had to be different in *some* further natural respect in order not to be wrong; and that we do not know whether if it had so differed you would still have thought it wrong. Both of these replies, again, rely on moral views, the latter merely on the view that there is *something* about the natural features of the action in Harman's example that makes it wrong, the former on a more specific view as to which of these features do this.

But Harman, it is fairly clear, intends for us *not* to rely on any such moral views in evaluating his counterfactual claim. His claim is not that if the action had not been one of deliberate cruelty (or had otherwise differed in whatever way would be required to remove its wrongness), you would still have thought it wrong. It is, instead, that if the action were one of deliberate, pointless cruelty, but this *did not make it wrong,* you would still have thought it was wrong. And to return to the example of Hitler's moral character, the counterfactual claim that Harman will need in order to defend a comparable conclusion about that case is not that if Hitler had been, for example, humane and fair-minded, free of nationalistic pride and racial hatred, he would still have done exactly as he did. It is, rather, that if Hitler's psychology, and anything else about his situation that could strike us as morally relevant, had been exactly as it in fact was, but this had *not constituted moral depravity,* he would still have done exactly what he did.

Now the antecedents of these two conditionals are puzzling. For one thing, both are, I believe, necessarily false. I am fairly confident, for example, that Hitler really was morally depraved; and since I also accept the view that moral features supervene on more basic natural properties, I take this to imply that there is no possible world in which Hitler has just the personality he in fact did, in just the situation he was in, but is not morally depraved. Any attempt to describe such a situation, moreover, will surely run up against the limits of our moral concepts — what Harman calls our "moral sensibility" — and this is no accident. For what Harman is asking us to do, in general, is to consider cases in which absolutely *everything* about the nonmoral facts that could seem morally relevant to us, in light of whatever moral theory we accept and of the concepts required for understanding that theory, is held fixed, but in which the moral judgment that our theory yields about the case is nevertheless mistaken. So it is hardly surprising that, using that theory and those concepts, we should find it difficult to conceive in any detail what such a situation would be like. It is especially not surprising when the cases in question are as paradigmatic in light of the moral outlook we in fact have as is Harman's example or is, even more so, mine of Hitler's moral character. The only way we could be wrong about this latter case (assuming we have the nonmoral facts right) would be for our whole theory to be hopelessly wrong, so radically mistaken that there could be no hope of straightening it out through adjustments from within.

But I do not believe we should conclude, as we might be tempted to, that we therefore know a priori that this is not so, or that we cannot understand these conditionals that are crucial to Harman's argument. Rather, now that we have seen how we have to understand them, we should grant that they are true: that if our moral theory were somehow hopelessly mistaken, but all the nonmoral facts remained exactly as they in fact are, then, since we do *accept* that moral theory, we would still draw exactly the moral conclusions we in fact do. But we should deny that any skeptical conclusion follows from this. In particular, we should deny that it follows that moral facts play no role in explaining our moral judgments.

For consider what follows from the parallel claim about microphysics, in particular about Harman's example in which a physicist concludes from his observation of a vapor trail in a cloud chamber, and from the microphysical theory he accepts, that a free proton has passed through the chamber. The parallel claim, notice, is *not* just that if the proton had not been there the physicist would still have thought it was. This claim is implausible, for we may assume that the physicist's theory is generally correct, and it follows from that theory that if there hadn't been a proton there, then there wouldn't have been a vapor trail. But in a perfectly similar way it is implausible that if Hitler hadn't been morally depraved we would still have thought he was: for we may assume that our moral theory also is at least roughly correct, and it follows from the most central features of that theory that if Hitler hadn't been morally depraved, he wouldn't have done what he did. The *parallel* claim about the microphysical example is, instead, that if there hadn't been a proton there, but there *had* been a vapor trail, the physicist would still have concluded that a proton was present. More precisely, to maintain a perfect parallel with Harman's claims about the moral cases, the antecedent must specify that although no proton is present, absolutely *all* the non-microphysical facts that the physicist, in light of his theory, might take to be relevant to the question of whether or not a proton is present, are exactly as in the actual case. (These macrophysical facts, as we may for convenience call them, surely include everything one would normally think of as an observable fact.) Of course, we shall be unable to imagine this without imagining that the physicist's theory is pretty badly mistaken; but I believe we should grant that, *if* the physicist's theory were somehow this badly mistaken, but all the macrophysical facts (including all the observable facts) were held fixed, then the physicist, since he does accept that theory, would still draw all the same conclusions that he actually does. That is, this conditional claim, like Harman's parallel claim about the moral cases, is true.

But no skeptical conclusions follow; nor can Harman, since he does not intend to be a skeptic about physics, think that they do. It does not follow, in the first place, that we have any reason to think the physicist's theory *is* generally mistaken. Nor does it follow, furthermore, that the hypothesis that a proton really did pass through the cloud chamber is not part of a good explanation of the vapor trail, and hence of the physicist's thinking this has happened. This looks like a reasonable explanation, of course, only on the assumption that the physicist's theory is at least roughly true, for it is this theory that tells us, for example, what happens when charged particles pass through a supersaturated atmosphere, what other causes (if any) there might be for a similar phenomenon, and so on. But, as I say, we have not been provided with any reason for not trusting the theory to this extent.

Similarly, I conclude, we should draw no skeptical conclusions from Harman's claims about the moral cases. It is true that if our moral theory were seriously mistaken, but we still believed it, and the nonmoral facts were held fixed, we would still make just the moral judgments we do. But *this* fact by itself provides us with no reason for thinking that our moral theory *is* generally mistaken. Nor, again, does it imply that the fact of Hitler's really having been morally depraved forms no part of a good explanation of his doing what he did and hence, at greater remove, of our thinking him depraved. This explanation will appear reasonable, of course, only on the assumption that our accepted moral theory is at least roughly correct, for it is this theory that assures us that only a depraved person could have thought, felt, and acted as Hitler did. But, as I say, Harman's argument has provided us with no reason for not trusting our moral views to this extent, and hence with no reason for doubting that it is sometimes moral facts that explain our moral judgments.

I conclude with three comments about my argument.

(1) I have tried to show that Harman's claim—that we would have held the particular moral beliefs we do even if those beliefs were untrue—admits of two readings, one of which makes it implausible, and the other of which reduces it to an application of a general skeptical strategy, a strategy which could as easily be used to produce doubt about microphysical as about moral facts. The general strategy is this. Consider any conclusion C we arrive at by relying both on some distinguishable "theory" T and on some body of evidence not being challenged, and ask whether we would have believed C even if it had been false. The plausible answer, *if* we are allowed to rely on T, will often be no: for if C had been false, then (according to T) the evidence would have had to be different, and in that case we wouldn't have believed C. (I have illustrated the plausibility of this sort of reply for all my moral examples, as well as for the microphysical one.) But the skeptic of course intends us *not* to rely on T in this way, and so rephrases the question: Would we have believed C even if it were false *but* all the evidence had been exactly as it in fact was? Now the answer has to be yes; and the skeptic concludes that C is doubtful. (It should be obvious how to extend this strategy of belief in other minds, or in an external world.) I am of course not convinced: I do not think answers to the rephrased question show anything interesting about what we know or justifiably believe. But it is enough for my purposes here that no such *general* skeptical strategy could pretend to reveal any problems peculiar to belief in *moral* facts.

(2) My conclusion about Harman's argument, although it is not exactly the same as, is nevertheless similar to and very much in the spirit of the Duhemian point I invoked earlier against verificationism. There the question was whether typical moral assertions have testable implications, and the answer was that they do, so long as you include additional moral assumptions of the right sort among the background theories on which you rely in evaluating these assertions. Harman's more important question is whether we should ever regard moral facts as relevant to the explanation of nonmoral facts, and in particular of our having the moral beliefs we do. But the answer, again, is that we should, so long as we are willing to hold the right sorts of *other* moral assumptions fixed in answering counterfactual questions. Neither answer shows morality to be on any shakier ground than, say, physics, for typical

microphysical hypotheses, too, have testable implications, and appear relevant to explanations, only if we are willing to assume at least the approximate truth of an elaborate microphysical theory and to hold this assumption fixed in answering counterfactual questions.

(3) Of course, this picture of how explanations depend on background theories, and moral explanations in particular on moral background theories, does show why someone already tempted toward moral skepticism on other grounds (such as those I mentioned at the beginning of this essay) might find Harman's claim about moral explanations plausible. To the extent that you already have pervasive doubts about moral theories, you will also find moral facts nonexplanatory. So I grant that Harman has located a natural symptom of moral skepticism; but I am sure he has neither traced this skepticism to its roots nor provided any independent argument for it. His claim (p. 22) that we do not *in fact* cite moral facts in explanation of moral beliefs and observations cannot provide such an argument, for that claim is false. So, too, is the claim that assumptions about moral facts seem irrelevant to such explanations, for many do not. The claim that we *should* not rely on such assumptions because they *are* irrelevant, on the other hand, unless it is supported by some independent argument for moral skepticism, will just be question-begging: for the principle test of whether they are relevant, in any situation in which it appears they might be, is a counterfactual question about what would have happened if the moral fact had not

obtained, and how we answer that question depends precisely upon whether we *do* rely on moral assumptions in answering it.

My own view I stated at the outset: that the only argument for moral skepticism with any independent weight is the argument from the difficulty of settling disputed moral questions. I have shown that anyone who finds Harman's claim about moral explanations plausible must already have been tempted toward skepticism by some other considerations, and I suspect that the other considerations will typically be the ones I sketched. So that is where discussion should focus. I also suggested that those considerations may provide less support for moral skepticism than is sometimes supposed, but I must reserve a thorough defense of that thesis for another occasion.

Endnotes

[1] J. L. Mackie, *Ethics: Inventing Right and Wrong* (Penguin, 1977), pp. 38–42.

[2] Gilbert Harman, *The Nature of Morality: An Introduction to Ethics* (Oxford University Press, 1977), pp. vii, viii. Unless otherwise indicated, parenthetical page references are to this work.

[3] Bernard DeVoto, *The Year of Decision: 1846* (Houghton Mifflin, 1942), p. 442.

[4] W. V. Quine, "Epistemology Naturalized," in *Ontological Relativity and Other Essays* (Columbia University Press, 1969), pp. 69–90. Also see "Natural Kinds" in the same book, pp. 114–138.

IX.5 A *Critique of Sturgeon's Defence of Moral Realism*

EVAN K. JOBE

Evan K. Jobe, until his recent retirement, taught philosophy at Texas Tech University. His publications include journal articles on scientific law, scientific explanation, the nature of time, and the nature of abstract objects. In this article he argues that Sturgeon in his defense of moral realism (see preceding article) has failed to make his case for certain theses, such as that moral qualities of persons can play an essential role in the scientific explanation of human conduct and that moral realism is compatible with physicalism.

Can a moral principle be tested and confirmed empirically? Can the fact that an event exhibits a moral quality play a role in explaining why a person observes the event as having that quality? Gilbert Harman, in attempting to point to a radical difference between scientific and moral facts, has endorsed a negative answer to these questions.[1] With Harman's discussion in mind, Nicholas Sturgeon takes the affirmative side in his "Moral Explanations," a potentially influential essay that is now beginning to appear in the textbook anthologies.[2] Sturgeon rounds out his defence of moral realism by further arguing that moral qualities of persons can play an essential role in the scientific explanation of human conduct. Finally, he attempts to enhance the appeal of moral realism by arguing for the plausibility of its compatibility with physicalism. While granting that Sturgeon's discussion is challenging and instructive I shall try to show that on all points mentioned here Sturgeon has failed to make a good case.

1. Can a Moral Principle Be Tested and Confirmed Empirically?

In support of the affirmative Sturgeon points out that when a moral principle is combined with one or more other principles of comparable status it may

be possible to derive an empirical consequence. In this respect morality is quite akin to science, since scientific principles are also normally testable only when conjoined to other scientific principles. As an example he cites the act-utilitarian principle that an action is wrong just in case there is something else the agent could have done that would have produced a greater net balance of pleasure over pain. He says:

> Thus, if we conjoin the act-utilitarian principle I have just cited with the further view, also untestable in isolation, that it is always wrong deliberately to kill a human being, we can deduce from these two premises together the consequence that deliberately killing a human being always produces a lesser balance of pleasure over pain than some available alternative act; and this claim is one any positivist would have conceded we know, in principle at least, how to test. If we found it to be false, moreover, then we would be forced by this empirical test to abandon at least one of the moral claims from which we derived it.[3]

While Sturgeon's claim here is clearly correct it is not at all sufficient to show that a principle can be tested and confirmed, for the procedure he describes is applicable to vast amounts of nonsense. To take an example, consider the principle (a) "If a person is happy on a Sunday then the Absolute is smiling on him at that time." When (a) is combined with a "comparable principle" such as (b) "If the Absolute smiles on a person on a given day then that person will be happy on the next day," we can deduce

Reprinted from "Sturgeon's Defence of Moral Realism," *Dialogue* XXIX (1990) by permission.

the consequence that if a person is happy on Sunday then he will be happy on Monday. So, if Jones, say, is happy on Sunday but not on Monday we can conclude that not both (a) and (b) can be true. But the test outcome does not in the slightest raise the probability of either component claim, and so we have no more reason than before for accepting either one. Oddly, with regard to his logically parallel examples Sturgeon goes on to discuss the problem of *which* moral statement is to be abandoned, as though the outcome as such gave us some reason for abandoning exactly one of the components.[4]

Perhaps it could be urged in Sturgeon's defence that he never explicitly claims that a moral principle can be tested *and confirmed* — he speaks only of testing. His point may have been rather that moral claims are subject to empirical falsification. To this I would reply, first, that his discussion forms part of a criticism of a presentation by Harman, who begins his book with the question "Can moral principles be tested and confirmed in the way scientific principles can?"[5] If Sturgeon is not addressing Harman's question his failure to say so is surprising. Second, Sturgeon is clearly attempting to defend his moral realism against the sceptic, and a prominent form of scepticism involves the denial that moral assertions, strictly speaking, have truth values. As the nonsensical example cited above shows, a testing outcome of the type described is not enough to guarantee even that the sentences in question possess a truth value. I conclude that Sturgeon's discussion fails as a rebuttal of either Harman's claim or that of the moral sceptic.

2. Can the Fact That an Event Exhibits a Moral Quality Play a Role in Explaining Why a Person Observes the Event as Having That Quality?

This question must be distinguished from the question whether a person's *acceptance* of a moral principle can help explain his observing an event as exhibiting a particular moral quality. Essentially this distinction is already drawn by Harman in his example that is the focus of much of Sturgeon's discussion of this question. Harman says:

If you round a corner and see a group of young hoodlums pour gasoline on a cat and ignite it, you do not need to *conclude* that what they are doing is wrong; you do not need to figure anything out; you can *see* that it is wrong. But is your reaction due to the actual wrongness of what you see or is it simply a reflection of your moral "sense," a "sense" that you have acquired as a result of your moral upbringing?[6]

Harman points out that the actual wrongness of the actions observed *seems* to be irrelevant to a scientific explanation of why the observer makes the judgment that the action is wrong, but he does not argue for this claim.[7] The alleged irrelevance does, of course, follow from Harman's own theory of the nature of morality, but he is presumably not presupposing the correctness of that theory at this point. I do not wish to defend Harman's theory, but I think that his claim here is correct. What I should like to do here is to inquire more closely into the reasons for its correctness.

The major problem in attempting to ascertain what is relevant to a scientific explanation of why we observe something to be the case is that at this point in the history of psychology and psycho-physics we lack any really detailed explanations of such matters. For example, we are currently unable to furnish a detailed scientific explanation of why at time t a person — Smith, say — makes the observational judgment that there is a cat lying on a mat in front of him. We do know enough, however, to see that the question just posed is itself quite unclear, for the event to be explained is the terminus of various causal chains, and the question gives no clear indication of just how far backward any such chain is to be pursued. An explanation of minimal scope in this respect might begin with the state of Smith's visual cortex resulting from the slightly earlier input from his optic nerves and trace the causal chain forward from the visual cortex into whatever other brain regions are involved in having the impression of seeing objects *as* in front of one, of seeing objects *as* a cat and a mat in a certain relation, etc. Now, it is precisely this part of Smith's observational judgment that we are currently least able to fill out in a satisfactory way, and indeed to do so would constitute a major scientific achievement.

Assuming the availability of such an explanation, however, it would be relatively easy to augment it so as to furnish the more extended explanation that begins not with events in Smith's visual cortex but rather with the pattern of his retinal stimulation at the time in question. Now, a still further account that pursues the visual causal chain backwards through Smith's corneas and outside his body might also be desired, and this last augmentation is the one we are scientifically best equipped to handle. It would involve such matters as details about the light entering his eyes and how its parameters depend on the properties of the surfaces from which it was reflected. The crucial thing to note is that this final step in completing the explanation need involve only such additional data as are required to explain the pattern of Smith's retinal stimulation, and any facts about the observed scene that are not relevant to explaining the pattern cannot be relevant to what we would ordinarily regard as a complete scientific explanation of Smith's observational judgment.

Now let us shift the example to the complex observational impression that Smith might have in seeing a group of children pour gasoline on a cat and set fire to it. His impression that such an event is occurring arouses his moral indignation, and among other properties that he attributes to the situation he believes to exist is that of moral wrongness. It is possible that his retinal stimulation is actually a causal consequence of some children's setting fire to a cat. It is also possible that it is caused by a scenario in which, say, some children are setting fire to a cushion in the form of a cat, perhaps for some good reason. The point is that a correct outside-the-skin explanation of Smith's observational impression can involve only those properties of the observed scenario that causally determine Smith's pattern of retinal stimulation. Now, the moral wrongness of the action in progress is surely causally irrelevant to that pattern of retinal stimulation. But any causal chain leading from the observed scene to Smith's final act of moral judgment must lead through that retinal pattern. Hence, the rightness or wrongness of the events before him is explanatorily irrelevant to Smith's moral judgment — or, as Harman calls it, Smith's moral observation. I tend to suppose that it was some such considerations of scientific plausibility that underlay Harman's claim of explanatory irrelevance. In any case, such considerations seem to furnish good grounds for the correctness of his claim.

Let us now take a look at Sturgeon's reasons for disagreeing with Harman's claim. Referring to Harman, he says:

> He claims that the wrongness of this act is irrelevant to an explanation of your thinking it wrong, that you would have *thought* it wrong even if it wasn't. My reply was that in order for the action not to be wrong it would have had to lack the feature of deliberate, intense, pointless cruelty, and that if it had differed in this way you might very well *not* have thought it wrong.[8]

To begin, it is incorrect to attribute to Harman the position that the observer *would* have thought it wrong even if it had not been. Harman's claim surely implies only that the observer *might* have made a judgment of moral wrongness in the absence of any wrongness attaching to the activity he was observing. Sturgeon's further point, I gather, is that the wrongness must be at least indirectly relevant by virtue of the relevance of the feature of deliberate, intense, pointless cruelty. But it is hard to see how this feature could be relevant to the observer's pattern of retinal stimulation. The hypothetical scenario of cushion burning cited earlier could serve as an example in which roughly the same optical impression would be produced but in which the element of cruelty is absent. The observer's moral observation would surely be the same in the two cases. As a more cautious variant of his reply Sturgeon suggests the following:

> [S]ince the action is in fact wrong, and since moral properties supervene on the more basic natural ones, it would have had to be different in *some* further natural respect in order not to be wrong; and that we do not know whether if it had so differed you would still have thought it wrong.[9]

Even granting that this is so, it is hard to see its relevance for the issue at hand. Suppose, for example, that the presence of a certain motive is (a) a causal factor for the observed action, thereby indirectly a causal factor for any observational impressions of that action, and thus further indirectly a causal factor for a moral judgment based on those impressions, and also (b) the aspect of the action that makes the action morally wrong. From this we can hardly conclude that the moral wrongness is itself a causal or explanatory factor for the moral judgment. Finally, Sturgeon concludes his discussion of this topic by setting forth what he thinks may be a fairer interpretation of Harman's position. Concerning Harman, he says:

> His claim is not that if the action had not been one of deliberate cruelty (or had otherwise differed in whatever way would be required to remove its wrongness), you would still have thought it wrong. It is, instead, that if the action were one of deliberate, pointless cruelty, but *this did not make it wrong,* you would still have thought it was wrong.[10]

Sturgeon discusses this interpretation at some length, but I shall not comment further, since I see no reason for attributing this view to Harman or to anyone else.

3. Can Moral Qualities of Persons Play an Essential Role in Explaining Human Conduct?

It should suffice to cite a couple of examples that Sturgeon uses as evidence for his affirmative answer to this question. One is drawn from Bernard De-Voto's account of the behaviour of a naval midshipman, Selim Woodworth, who in 1846 was put in charge of a rescue mission in the snowy High Sierra mountains of the United States. It turns out that instead of taking an active part in leading or even organizing rescue teams he focussed on his own comfort while glorying in the prestige of his official position — with the result that many lives were needlessly lost. Sturgeon cites DeVoto's pronouncement that Midshipman Woodworth was "no damned good," and adds: "I cite this case partly because it has so clearly the structure of an inference to a reasonable explanation. One can think of competing explanations, but the evidence points against them."[11] Another example concerns Hitler's moral depravity. Sturgeon says:

> [I]n any world at all like the actual one, only a morally depraved person could have initiated a world war, ordered the "final solution," and done any number of other things Hitler did. That is why I believe that, if Hitler hadn't been morally depraved, he wouldn't have done those things, and hence that the fact of his moral depravity is relevant to any explanation of what he did.[12]

In evaluating Sturgeon's thesis I shall not accord separate treatment to the properties of no-damned-goodness and moral depravity, each of which in the contexts cited appears to be a species of or a close approximation to the quality of *moral badness.* The question then comes down to whether a trait such as moral badness may properly enter into an explanation of the sorts of behaviour exhibited by Woodworth or Hitler.

The best explanations for human actions that we can in practice usually hope for are those citing specific beliefs and desires. But we do have explanations of a sort in terms of *dispositional* traits such as irascibility, stinginess, truthfulness, benevolence, etc. It seems initially plausible that alongside such traits there may be such a trait as *moral badness,* understood as the disposition to do morally bad things — things that are morally bad in the familiar sense in which actions and outcomes may be said to be morally bad. (I shall call this familiar sense of "morally bad" the "appraisive" sense of the term.) If moral badness in this ordinary appraisive sense enters into explanations of human actions it seems reasonable to suppose that it does so through its connection with moral badness in the dispositional sense suggested above. We need then to try to become as clear as possible about this possible connection.

In pursuing this inquiry we might first note an interesting ambiguity that can arise in describing a dispositional trait, for example, in saying that a person has a disposition to do things of type K. To take a specific case, suppose that Jones has a tendency to tell off-colour jokes whenever the opportunity arises. Now, it may well be that his Aunt Mathilde disapproves of such jokes. It then seems to be literally correct to say that Jones has a tendency to tell jokes that his Aunt Mathilde disapproves of. But this could be a misleading thing to say, for it could be taken in either of two ways that I am assuming are here inappropriate. It could mean (1) that Jones is motivated to take his Aunt Mathilde's potential disapproval into account in selecting the jokes he tells, or — strange to say — (2) that the property of being disapproved of by Aunt Mathilde is a property that actually enters into the regularities governing Jones's psychological functioning.

Let us return now to Midshipman Woodworth in Sturgeon's example. Consider a particular action of his, for example, his refusing to lead a rescue party into the mountains. Presumably, a relatively informative explanation of this could be given in terms of his immediate strong desire for safety and comfort and his weak desire to help others, combined with his belief that undertaking the mission would be dangerous and uncomfortable. A less informative explanation could be given in terms of dispositional traits such as selfishness and insensitivity — but these traits are surely implicitly related to certain underlying psychological mechanisms from which their explanatory relevance derives. Thus, it appears that his behaviour is fully explainable in purely psychological terms. It is true that a person like Woodworth who is selfish and insensitive is likely to do a lot of things that are morally bad. But there seems to be no reason at all to suppose that the property of moral badness in the ordinary appraisive sense enters into the psychological mechanisms governing the behaviour of such a person — any more than there is reason to suppose that the property of being disapproved of by Aunt Mathilde entered into the psychological processes involved in Jones's tendency to tell jokes of which his aunt disapproved. So, while citation of moral badness, understood as the disposition to do morally bad things, may have some low-grade explanatory value, we should not conclude that the quality of being morally bad in the ordinary appraisive sense has any explanatory role. Now consider the first misinterpretation of Jones's proclivity listed earlier. The analogous case with respect to moral badness would be one (presumably rare) in which a person is actually motivated to do certain things *because* of his belief that they are morally bad. But in such a case it would clearly be the *belief* in the moral badness, not the moral quality itself, that would be explanatorily relevant.

But Sturgeon's examples suggest further complications. Having a disposition to do morally bad things is itself a morally bad thing — in the appraisive sense — and persons who have such a disposition would frequently be judged as morally bad — in the appraisive sense. It is probably this fact that underlies the initial plausibility of Sturgeon's thesis that moral qualities of persons are explanatorily relevant to their behaviour. In any case, Sturgeon's argument in his Hitler example requires independent treatment, since it cannot plausibly be construed as implicitly invoking a dispositional mode of explanation. It is surely true that a person can be judged as morally bad for reasons other than his possession of some standing disposition. For example, it seems quite reasonable to say something of the form: "Anyone who would (freely and knowingly) do something of kind X is a morally bad person." And from this it follows that if a person is *not* morally bad then he would *not* do something of kind X. Now, in his Hitler example Sturgeon argues that if this last is true, then if a person does do something of kind X then his being morally bad is explanatorily relevant to his doing it. But the claimed entailment stands in need of justification, since there are logically parallel cases in which the corresponding entailment clearly does not hold. For example, it may be that anyone who would tell an off-colour joke is a person of whom Aunt Mathilde would not approve. It follows that if someone is a person of whom Aunt Mathilde *would* approve then he would *not* tell an off-colour joke. But it surely does not follow from this last that if Jones tells an off-colour joke then the property of being someone of whom Aunt Mathilde would not approve is relevant to explaining why Jones told the joke. Again, it appears that Sturgeon has set forth an initially very plausible but ultimately unsound case for the explanatory relevance of moral qualities as such.

---

4. *Does Sturgeon Make Plausible the Thesis That Ethical Properties Are Actually Physical Properties?*

Presumably because it is utterly implausible that ethical concepts are expressible in physical language, Sturgeon's approach here is to drive a wedge between being a physical property and being a property describable in the language of physics. He says: "Physicalism entails nothing in any case about whether even biology or psychology, let alone ethics, is reducible to physics."[13] He says that there are a number of reasons why this is the case, but he presents only an argument based on some prior work by Richard Boyd:

> If there are (as there appear to be) any continuous physical parameters, then there are continuum many states in the world, but there

are at most countably many predicates in any language, including that of even ideal physics; so there are more physical properties than there are physical expressions to represent them. Thus, although physicalism certainly entails that biological and psychological properties (and ethical properties, too, if there are any) are physical, nothing follows about whether we have any but biological or psychological or ethical terminology for representing these particular physical properties.[14]

The first thing to note here is that, in the light of quantum physics, it seems doubtful that any physical parameters do vary continuously. And so, while any real number within a certain range may be a *possible* value for a given parameter, only a countable (infinite but denumerable) number of such values is actually realized in the world. For the sake of argument, however, let us suppose that some physical systems do exhibit a strictly continuous variation in some of their physical parameters. To evaluate the significance of Sturgeon's point we need to look more closely at just what this would involve. Suppose, for example, that the temperature of point *a* varies continuously from, say, 50 to 51 degrees during a certain time interval. Since the number of real numbers between 50 and 51 is nondenumerably infinite it follows that point *a* runs through uncountably many *states,* each of which involves a pair of real numbers as magnitudes of temperature and the corresponding time. And for any such state it would be *permissible* to speak of a corresponding *property,* the property of being at a certain temperature at a certain time. So, if point *a* varies in temperature as indicated it can be said to instantiate a nondenumerable infinity of such "properties" during the time interval in question. But the language of mathematics can contain only a denumerably infinite number of distinct expressions and therefore cannot assign a distinct name to each of the nondenumerably infinite values in a finite interval such as that between 50 and 51. Thus, what Sturgeon is claiming is literally true: there are far more physical properties than there are physical predicates. It is therefore *logically possible* that those elusive entities, ethical properties, are tucked away among that nondenumerable set of properties that escape being pinned down by physical predicates. But we should keep in mind how broadly we must use the term

"property" here. Just as when we think of ethical properties we normally have in mind such qualities as goodness, rightness, justice, etc., so when we think of physical properties we normally have in mind such things as mass, velocity, electric field potential, etc. We do not tend to think of specific *degrees* of these as properties—but it is only in this sense that we have been given reason for saying that there is a nondenumerable infinity of physical properties. The question is whether the fact that physical parameters such as those mentioned are capable of taking on nondenumerably many *degrees of intensity* makes it more *plausible* than before that there is a physical niche for qualities such as goodness, rightness, justice, etc. Assuming that ethical naturalism is logically possible to begin with, it would surely have been rash to deny the bare possibility of such a niche even without the benefit of Sturgeon's discussion. Sturgeon has shown that this bare possibility is in fact demonstrable. But demonstrating that something is possible is not at all the same as showing why it should be considered plausible. Sturgeon has not, as far as I can see, given us any additional reason for supposing that moral realism is plausibly compatible with physicalism.

Endnotes

[1] Gilbert Harman, *The Nature of Morality: An Introduction to Ethics* (Oxford University Press, 1977), Chapter 1.

[2] Nicholas Sturgeon, "Moral Explanations," in *Morality, Reason, and Truth: New Essays on the Foundations of Ethics,* David Copp and David Zimmerman, eds. (Rowman and Allanheld, 1984), pp. 49–78. Reprinted (without notes) in *Ethical Theory: Classical and Contemporary Readings,* Louis Pojman, ed. (Wadsworth, 1989), pp. 437–448.

[3] Ibid., p. 51.

[4] Ibid., p. 52.

[5] Harman, *The Nature of Morality,* p. 3.

[6] Ibid., pp. 68–69.

[7] Ibid., pp. 7–9.

[8] Sturgeon, "Moral Explanations," p. 68.

[9] Ibid., pp. 68–69.

[10] Ibid., p. 69.

[11] Ibid., pp. 63–64.

[12] Ibid., p. 68.

[13] Ibid., pp. 59–60.

[14] Ibid., p. 60.

IX.6 *Ethics and the Limits of Philosophy*

BERNARD WILLIAMS

Bernard Williams is professor of philosophy at Oxford University and the University of California at Berkeley. He is the author of several works in moral philosophy and the philosophy of the mind. In this selection from his book, *Ethics and the Limits of Philosophy,* he argues that there can be knowledge of specific ethical claims — those involving what he calls "thick ethical concepts," such as cowardice, brutality, gratitude, lying, promising, and the like — but philosophical reflection can destroy such knowledge by disturbing or replacing those concepts so that beliefs previously formed with those concepts can no longer be formed. Whereas reflection can destroy, it cannot create moral knowledge. Thus, reflective cultures such as ours are left with little moral knowledge, but instead have perhaps only some vague and unevenly held beliefs, such as "one has to have special reason to kill someone."

So far I have not said much about objectivity, though earlier chapters have had a good deal to do with it. If an Archimedean point could be found and practical reason, or human interests, could be shown to involve a determinate ethical outlook, then ethical thought would be objective, in the sense that it would have been given an objective foundation. Those are possibilities — or they might have turned out to be possibilities — within the perspective of practical reason. Very often, however, discussions of objectivity come into moral philosophy from a different starting point, from an interest in comparing ethical beliefs with knowledge and claims to truth of other kinds, for instance with scientific beliefs. Here a rather different conception of objectivity is involved. It is naturally associated with such questions as what can make ethical beliefs true, and whether there is any ethical knowledge. It is in this field of comparisons that various distinctions between fact and value are located.

Discussions of objectivity often start from considerations about disagreement. This makes it seem as if disagreement were surprising, but there is no reason why that should be so (the earliest thinkers in the Western tradition found conflict at least as obvious a feature of the world as concord). The interest in disagreement comes about, rather, because neither agreement nor disagreement is universal. It is not that disagreement needs explanation and agreement does not, but that in different contexts disagreement requires different sorts of explanations, and so does agreement.

The way in which we understand a given kind of disagreement, and explain it, has important practical effects. It can modify our attitude to others and our understanding of our own outlook. In relation to other people, we need a view of what is to be opposed, rejected, and so forth, and in what spirit; for ourselves, disagreement can raise a warning that we may be wrong, and if truth or correctness is what we are after, we may need to reform our strategies.

Disagreement does not necessarily have to be overcome. It may remain an important and constitutive feature of our relations to others, and also be seen as something that is merely to be expected in the light of the best explanations we have of how such disagreement arises. There can be tension involved here, if we at once feel that the disagreement is about very important matters and that there is a good explanation of why the disagreement is only to be expected. The tension is specially acute when the disagreement is not only important but expresses itself in judgments that seem to demand assent from others. . . . ([T]here is a special problem for relativism, of trying to understand our outlook in a way that will accommodate both sides of the tension.)

Among types of disagreement, and the lessons that can be learned from them, there is a well-known polarity. At one extreme there is the situation of two children wanting one bun or two heroes wanting one slave girl. The disagreement is practical, and its explanation is not going to cast much doubt on the cognitive powers of the people involved. It may be said that this kind of case is so primitively practical that it hardly even introduces any judgment over which there is disagreement. Even at the most primitive level, of course, there is disagreement about *what is to be done,* but this is so near to desire and action that no one is going to think that the disagreement shows any failure of knowledge or understanding. It is simply that two people want incompatible things. But the conflict may well not remain as blank as that, and if the parties want to settle it by ordered speech rather than by violence, they will invoke more substantive judgments, usually of justice, and the children will talk about fairness or the heroes about precedence.

In their most basic form, at least, these disagreements need not make anyone think that someone has failed to recognize or understand something, or that they cannot speak the language. At the opposite pole of the traditional contrast are disagreements that do make one think this. What these typically are depends on the theory of knowledge favored by the commentator, but they often involve the observation under standard conditions of what the Oxford philosopher J. L. Austin used to call "middle-sized dry goods." An important feature of these examples is that the parties are assumed to share the same concepts and to be trained in the recognition of furniture, pens, pennies, or whatever.

Around these paradigms there have been formed various oppositions: between practical and theoretical, or value and fact, or *ought* and *is.* Each of these has been thought to represent a fundamental difference in what disagreement means, and they are often taken to suggest contrasting hopes for resolving it. But it is a mistake to suppose that these oppositions are different ways of representing just one distinction. Indeed, the two examples I have mentioned significantly fail to correspond to the

two ends of any one of these contrasts. The quarrel about the allocation of a good is certainly an example of the practical, but until one gets to the stage of taking seriously the claims of justice, it is not yet a disagreement about value. A disagreement in the perception of furniture is without doubt a disagreement about a matter of fact, but is not yet a disagreement about what is most often contrasted with the practical, namely the theoretical. To assemble these kinds of example into some one contrast requires more work. It has been done, characteristically, by reducing the evaluative to the practical and extending the factual to the theoretical. Both these maneuvers are of positivist inspiration, and they are both suspect. It is not surprising that some philosophers now doubt whether there is any basic distinction at all that can be constructed to the traditional pattern.

I accept that there is no one distinction in question here. I also accept that the more positivistic formulations that have gone into defining each side of such a distinction are misguided. Still I believe that in relation to ethics there is a genuine and profound difference to be found, and also — it is a further point — that the difference is enough to motivate some version of the feeling (itself recurrent, if not exactly traditional) that science has some chance of being more or less what it seems, a systematized theoretical account of how the world really is, while ethical thought has no chance of being everything it seems. The tradition is right, moreover, not only in thinking that there is such a distinction, but also in thinking that we can come to understand what it is through understanding disagreement. However, it is not a question of how much disagreement there is, or even of what methods we have to settle disagreement, though that of course provides many relevant considerations. The basic difference lies rather in our reflective understanding of the best hopes we could coherently entertain for eliminating disagreement in the two areas. It is a matter of what, under the most favorable conditions, would be the best explanation of the end of disagreement: the explanation — as I shall say from now on — of convergence.

The fundamental difference lies between the ethical and the scientific. I hope to explain why one end of the contrast should be labeled "the scientific" rather than, say, "the factual." The other end is labeled "the ethical" because the ethical is what we are considering, and it would require a good deal of discussion either to extend the field or to narrow it. It is not called "the evaluative" because that additionally covers at least the area of aesthetic judgment, which raises many questions of its own. It is not called "the normative," a term that covers only part of the interest of the ethical (roughly, the part concerned with rules) and also naturally extends to such things as the law, which again raises different questions. More significantly, it is not called "the practical." This would displace a large part of the problem, for a reason we have already noticed in considering prescriptions and the *is–ought* distinction. It is not hard to concede that there is a distinction between the practical and the nonpractical. There is clearly such a thing as practical reasoning or deliberation, which is not the same as thinking about how things are. It is *obviously* not the same, and this is why positivism thought it had validated the traditional distinction by reducing the evaluative to the practical. But the reduction is mistaken, and it makes the whole problem look easier than it is.

The basic idea behind the distinction between the scientific and the ethical, expressed in terms of convergence, is very simple. In a scientific inquiry there should ideally be convergence on an answer, where the best explanation of the convergence involves the idea that the answer represents how things are; in the area of the ethical, at least at a high level of generality, there is no such coherent hope. The distinction does not turn on any difference in whether convergence will actually occur, and it is important that this is not what the argument is about. It might well turn out that there will be convergence in ethical outlook, at least among human beings. The point of the contrast is that, even if this happens, it will not be correct to think it has come about because convergence has been guided by how things actually are, whereas convergence in the sciences might be explained in that way if it does happen. This means, among other things, that we understand differently in the two cases the existence of convergence or, alternatively, its failure to come about.

I shall come back to ways in which we might understand ethical convergence. First, however, we must face certain arguments suggesting that there is really nothing at all in the distinction, expressed in these terms. There are two different directions from which this objection can come. In one version, the notion of a convergence that comes about because

of how things are is seen as an empty notion. According to the other, the notion of such a convergence is not empty, but it is available as much in ethical cases as in scientific — that is to say, the notion has some content, but it does nothing to help the distinction.

I have already said that the point of the distinction and of its explanation in terms of convergence does not turn on the question whether convergence actually occurs. On the scientific side, however, it would be unrealistic to disconnect these ideas totally from the ways in which the history of Western science since the seventeenth century is to be understood. The conception of scientific progress in terms of convergence cannot be divorced from the history of Western science because it is the history of Western science that has done most to encourage it. It is quite hard to deny that that history displays a considerable degree of convergence; what has been claimed is that this appearance has no real significance because it is a cultural artifact, a product of the way in which we choose to narrate the history of science. Richard Rorty has written:

> It is less paradoxical . . . to stick to the classic notion of "better describing what was already there" for physics. This is not because of deep epistemological or metaphysical considerations, but simply because, when we tell our Whiggish stories about how our ancestors gradually crawled up the mountain on whose (possibly false) summit we stand, we need to keep some things constant throughout the story . . . Physics is the paradigm of "finding" simply because it is hard (at least in the West) to tell a story of changing universes against the background of an unchanging Moral law or poetic canon, but very easy to tell the reverse sort of story. [*Philosophy and the Mirror of Nature* (Princeton University Press, 1980), p. 344f]

There are two notable faults in such a description of scientific success and what that success means. One is its attitude to the fact that it is easy to tell one kind of story and hard to tell the other. *Why* is the picture of the world "already there," helping to control our descriptions of it, so compelling? This seems to require some explanation on Rorty's account, but it does not get one. If the reference to "the West" implies a cultural or anthropological explanation, it is totally unclear what it would be: totally unclear, indeed, what it could be, if it is not going itself to assume an already existing physical world in which human beings come into existence and develop their cultures.

The point that an assumption of this kind is going to lie behind any explanations of what we do leads directly to the second fault in Rorty's account: it is self-defeating. If the story he tells were true, then there would be no perspective from which he could express it in this way. If it is overwhelmingly convenient to say that science describes what is already there, and if there are no deep metaphysical or epistemological issues here but only a question of what is convenient (it is "simply because" of this that we speak as we do), then what everyone should be saying, including Rorty, is that science describes a world already there. But Rorty urges us not to say that, and in doing so, in insisting, as *opposed to* that, on our talking of what it is convenient to say, he is trying to reoccupy the transcendental standpoint outside human speech and activity, which is precisely what he wants us to renounce.

A more effective level of objection lies in a negative claim that Rorty and others make, that no convergence of science, past or future, could possibly be explained in any meaningful way by reference to the way the world is, because there is an insoluble difficulty with the notion of "the world" as something that can determine belief. There is a dilemma. On the one hand, "the world" may be characterized in terms of our current beliefs about what it contains; it is a world of stars, people, grass, or tables. When "the world" is taken in this way, we can of course say that our beliefs about the world are affected by the world, in the sense that for instance our beliefs about grass are affected by grass, but there is nothing illuminating or substantive in this — our conception of the world as the object of our beliefs can do no better than repeat the beliefs we take to represent it. If, on the other hand, we try to form some idea of a world that is prior to any description of it, the world that all systems of belief and representation are trying to represent, then we have an empty notion of something completely unspecified and unspecifiable. So either way we fail to have a notion of "the world" that will do what is required of it.

Each side of this dilemma takes all our representations of the world together, in the one case putting them all in and in the other leaving them all

out. But there is a third and more helpful possibility, that we should form a conception of the world that is "already there" in terms of some but not all of our beliefs and theories. In reflecting on the world that is there *anyway,* independent of our experience, we must concentrate not in the first instance on what our beliefs are about, but on how they represent what they are about. We can select among our beliefs and features of our world picture some that we can reasonably claim to represent the world in a way to the maximum degree independent of our perspective and its peculiarities. The resultant picture of things, if we can carry through this task, can be called the "absolute conception" of the world. In terms of that conception, we may hope to explain the possibility of our attaining the conception itself, and also the possibility of other, perspectival, representations.

This notion of an absolute conception can serve to make effective a distinction between "the world as it is independent of our experience" and "the world as it seems to us." It does this by understanding "the world as it seems to us" as "the world as it seems peculiarly to us"; the absolute conception will, correspondingly, be a conception of the world that might be arrived at by any investigators, even if they were very different from us. What counts as a relevant difference from us, and indeed what for various levels of description will count as "us," will, again, be explained on the basis of the conception itself; we shall be able to explain, for instance, why one kind of observer can make observations that another kind cannot make. It is centrally important that these ideas relate to science, not to all kinds of knowledge. We can *know* things whose content is perspectival: we can know that grass is green, for instance, though *green,* for certain, and probably *grass* are concepts that would not be available to every competent observer of the world and would not figure in the absolute conception. (As we shall see, people can know things even more locally perspectival than that.) The point is not to give an account of knowledge, and the contrast with value should be expressed not in terms of knowledge but of science. The aim is to outline the possibility of a convergence characteristic of science, one that could meaningfully be said to be a convergence on how things (anyway) are.

That possibility, as I have explained it, depends heavily on notions of explanation. The substance of the absolute conception (as opposed to those vacuous or vanishing ideas of "the world" that were offered before) lies in the idea that it could non-vacuously explain how it itself, and the various perspectival views of the world, are possible. It is an important feature of modern science that it contributes to explaining how creatures with our origins and characteristics can understand a world with properties that this same science ascribes to the world. The achievements of evolutionary biology and the neurological sciences are substantive in these respects, and their notions of explanation are not vacuous. It is true, however, that such explanations cannot themselves operate entirely at the level of the absolute conception, because what they have to explain are psychological and social phenomena, such as beliefs and theories and conceptions of the world, and there may be little reason to suppose that they, in turn, could be adequately characterized in nonperspectival terms. How far this may be so is a central philosophical question. But even if we allow that the explanations of such things must remain to some degree perspectival, this does not mean that we cannot operate the notion of the absolute conception. It will be a conception consisting of nonperspectival materials available to any adequate investigator, of whatever constitution, and it will also help to explain to us, though not necessarily to those alien investigators, such things as our capacity to grasp that conception. Perhaps more than this will turn out to be available, but no more is necessary in order to give substance to the idea of "the world" and to defeat the first line of objection to the distinction, in terms of possible convergence, between the scientific and the ethical.

The opposite line of objection urges that the idea of "converging on how things are" is available, to some adequate degree, in the ethical case as well. The place where this is to be seen is above all with those substantive or thick ethical concepts I have often mentioned. Many exotic examples of these can be drawn from other cultures, but there are enough left in our own: *coward, lie, brutality, gratitude,* and so forth. They are characteristically related to reasons for action. If a concept of this kind applies, this often provides someone with a reason for action, though that reason need not be a decisive one and may be outweighed by other reasons, as we saw with their role in practical reasoning in Chapter 1. Of course, exactly what reason for action is provided, and to whom, depends on the situation, in ways that may well be governed by this and by other ethical concepts, but some general connection with action is clear enough. We may say, summarily, that such concepts are "action-guiding."

At the same time, their application is guided by the world. A concept of this sort may be rightly or wrongly applied, and people who have acquired it can agree that it applies or fails to apply to some new situation. In many cases the agreement will be spontaneous, while in some other cases there is room for judgment and comparison. Some disagreement at the margin may be irresoluble, but this does not mean that the use of the concept is not controlled by the facts or by the user's perception of the world. (As with other concepts that are not totally precise, marginal disagreements can indeed help to show how their use *is* controlled by the facts.) We can say, then, that the application of these concepts is at the same time world-guided and action-guiding. How can it be both at once?

The prescriptivist account discussed in the last chapter gives a very simple answer to this question. Any such concept, on that account, can be analyzed into a descriptive and a prescriptive element: it is guided round the world by its descriptive content, but has a prescriptive flag attached to it. It is the first feature that allows it to be world-guided, while the second makes it action-guiding. Some of the difficulties with this picture concern the prescriptive element and how it is supposed to guide action in the relevant sense (telling yourself to do something is not an obvious model for recognizing that you have a reason to do it). But the most significant objection applies to the other half of the analysis. Prescriptivism claims that what governs the application of the concept to the world is the descriptive element and that the evaluative interest of the concept plays no part in this. All the input into its use is descriptive, just as all the evaluative aspect is output. It follows that, for any concept of this sort, you could produce another that picked out just the same features of the world but worked simply as a descriptive concept, lacking any prescriptive or evaluative force.

Against this, critics have made the effective point that there is no reason to believe that a descriptive equivalent will necessarily be available. How we "go on" from one application of a concept to another is a function of the kind of interest that the concept represents, and we should not assume that we could see how people "go on" if we did not share the evaluative perspective in which this kind of concept has its point. An insightful observer can indeed come to understand and anticipate the use of the concept without actually sharing the values of the people who use it: this is an important point, and I shall come back to it. But in imaginatively anticipating the use of the concept, the observer also has to grasp imaginatively its evaluative point. He cannot stand quite outside the evaluative interests of the community he is observing, and pick up the concept simply as a device for dividing up in a rather strange way certain neutral features of the world.

It is very plausible, and it is certainly possible, that there should be ethical concepts that make these demands on understanding. It does not need, in fact, to be much more than possible to play an important part in this argument, by reminding moral philosophy of what the demands made by an adequate philosophy of language or by the philosophy of social explanation may turn out to be. If it is not only possible but plausible, moral philosophy will be well advised to consider what must be said if it is true.

The sympathetic observer can follow the practice of the people he is observing; he can report, anticipate, and even take part in discussions of the use they make of their concept. But, as with some other concepts of theirs, relating to religion, for instance, or to witchcraft, he may not be ultimately identified with the use of the concept: it may not really be his. This possibility, of the insightful but not totally identified observer, bears on an important question, whether those who properly apply ethical concepts of this kind can be said to have ethical knowledge.

Let us assume, artificially, that we are dealing with a society that is maximally homogeneous and minimally given to general reflection; its members simply, all of them, use certain ethical concepts of this sort. (We may call it the "hypertraditional" society.) What would be involved in their having ethical knowledge? According to the best available accounts of propositional knowledge, they would have to believe the judgments they made; those judgments would have to be true; and their judgments would have to satisfy a further condition, which has been extensively discussed in the philosophy of knowledge but which can be summarized by saying that the first two conditions must be nonacci-

dentally linked: granted the way that the people have gone about their inquiries, it must be no accident that the belief they have acquired is a true one, and if the truth on the subject had been otherwise, they would have acquired a different belief, true in those different circumstances. Thus I may know, by looking at it, that the die has come up 6, and this roughly involves the claim that if it had come up 4, I would have come to believe, by looking at it, that it had come up 4 (the alternative situations to be considered have to be restricted to those moderately like the actual one). Taking a phrase from Robert Nozick, we can say that the third requirement—it involves a good deal more elaboration than I have suggested—is that one's belief should "track the truth."

The members of the hypertraditional society apply their thick concepts, and in doing so they make various judgments. If any of those judgments can ever properly be said to be true, then their beliefs can track the truth, since they can withdraw judgments if the circumstances turn out not to be what was supposed, can make an alternative judgment if it would be more appropriate, and so on. They have, each, mastered these concepts, and they can perceive the personal and social happenings to which the concepts apply. If there is truth here, their beliefs can track it. The question left is whether any of these judgments can be true.

An objection can be made to saying that they are. If they are true, the observer can correctly say that they are; letting *F* stand in for one of their concepts, he can say, "The headman's statement, 'The boy is *F*,' is true." Then he should be able to say, in his own person, "the boy is *F*." But he is not prepared to do that, since *F* is not one of his concepts.

How strong is this objection? It relies on the following principle: A cannot correctly say that B speaks truly in uttering S unless A could also say something tantamount to S. This may seem to follow from a basic principle about truth, the *disquotation principle,* to the effect that *P* is true if and only if P. But that principle cannot be applied so simply in deciding what can be said about other people's statements. For a naive example, we may imagine a certain school slang that uses special names for various objects, places, and institutions in the school. It is a rule that these words are appropriately used only by someone who is a member of the school, and this rule is accepted and understood by a group outside the school (it would have to be, if it were to be *that* rule at all). People know that if they use these terms in their own person they will be taken for members of the school, or else criticized, and so forth. Suppose that in this slang "Weeds" were the name of some school building. Under the imagined rules, an observer could not, entirely in his own person and not playing a role, properly say "Robertson is at Weeds." But he could say, "Smith said 'Robertson is at Weeds,'" and he could then add to that, "and what Smith said is true." (Indeed — though this is not necessary to the argument — it seems quite natural for him to go one step further than that and say, "Smith truly said that Robertson was at Weeds.")

In this simple case, it is of course true that the observer has other terms that refer to the same things as the slang terms. Presumably, so do the local users; but there are other examples in which this is not so, as with languages in which males and females use different names for the same thing. In the school case, both the observer and the locals have verbal means to factor out what makes a given slang statement true from what, as contrasted with that, makes it appropriate for a particular person to make it. Where the gender of the speaker determines the correct term that he or she should use, it is more complicated. In the case of the thick ethical concept, it is more complicated still, because the observer does not have a term that picks out just the same things as the locals' term picks out and, at the same time, is entirely independent of the interest that shapes their use. (He has, of course, an expression such as "what they call *F*," and the fact that he can use it, although it is not independent of their term, is important: his intelligent use of it shows that he can indeed understand their use of their term, although he cannot use it himself.)

Despite its differences from the simple case of school slang, however, we can see the case of the ethical concept as only a deeper example of the same thing. In both cases, there is a condition that has to be satisfied if one is to speak in a certain way, a condition satisfied by the locals and not by the observer, and in both cases it is a matter of belonging to a certain culture. When we compare those cases with each other, and both of them with the situation in which vocabulary is affected by the speaker's gender, we can understand why the observer is barred from saying just what the locals say, and we can also see that he is not barred from recognizing that what

they say can be true. The disquotation principle, then, does not lead to the conclusion that the locals' statements, involving their thick ethical concepts, cannot be true.

There is a different argument for the conclusion that the locals' statements may not be true. This claims, more bluntly, that they may be false: not because they can be mistaken in ways that the locals themselves could recognize, but because an entire segment of the local discourse may be seen from outside as involving a mistake. This possibility has been much discussed by theorists. Social anthropologists have asked whether ritual and magical conceptions should be seen as mistaken in our terms, or rather as operating at a different level, not commensurable with our scientific ideas. Whatever may be said more generally, it is hard to deny that magic, at least, is a causal conception, with implications that overlap with scientific conceptions of causality. To the extent this is so, magical conceptions can be seen from the outside as false, and then no one will have known to be true any statement claiming magical influence, even though he may have correctly used all the local criteria for claiming a given piece of magical influence. The local criteria do not reach to everything that is involved in such claims. In cases of this sort, the problem with conceding truth to the locals' statements is the opposite of the one discussed before. The earlier claim was that their notions were so different from the observer's that he could not assert what they asserted. Now the problem is that their statements may imply notions similar enough to some of his for him to deny what they assert.

We may see the local ethical statements in a way that raises this difficulty. On this reading, the locals' statements imply something that can be put in the observer's terms and is rejected by him: that it is *right,* or *all right,* to do things he thinks it is not right, or all right, to do. Prescriptivism sees things in this way. The local statements entail, together with their descriptive content, an all-purpose *ought.* We have rejected the descriptive half of that analysis — is there any reason to accept the other half?

Of course, there is a minimal sense in which the locals think it "all right" to act as they do, and they do not merely imply this, but reveal it, in the way they live. To say that they "think it all right" at this level is not to mention any further and disputable judgment of theirs; it is merely to record their practice. Must we agree that there is a judgment, to be expressed by using some universal moral notion, which they accept and the observer may very well reject?

I do not think we have to accept this idea. More precisely, I do not think we can decide whether to accept it until we have a more general picture of the whole question; this is not an issue that in itself can force more general conclusions on us. The basic question is how we are to understand the relations between practice and reflection. The very general kind of judgment that is in question here — a judgment using a very general concept — is essentially a product of reflection, and it comes into question when someone stands back from the practices of society and its use of these concepts and asks whether this is the right way to go on, whether these are good ways in which to assess actions, whether the kinds of character that are admired are rightly admired. In many traditional societies themselves there is some degree of reflective questioning and criticism, and this is an important fact. It is for the sake of the argument, to separate the issues, that I have been using the idea of the hypertraditional society where there is no reflection.

In relation to this society, the question now is: Does the practice of the society, in particular the judgments that members of the society make, imply answers to reflective questions about that practice, questions they have never raised? Some judgments made by members of a society do indeed have implications, which they have never considered, at a more general or theoretical level. This will be true of their magical judgments if those are taken as causal claims; it is true of their mathematical judgments and of their judgments about the stars. We may be at some liberty whether to construe what they are saying as expressing mathematical judgments or opinions about the stars; but if we do take them to be making those judgments and expressing those opinions, their statements will have more general implications. If what a statement expresses is an opinion about the stars, it follows that it can be contradicted by another opinion about the stars.

There are two different ways in which we can see the activities of the hypertraditional society. They depend on different models of ethical practice. One of them may be called an "objectivist" model. According to this, we shall see the members of the society as trying, in their local way, to find out the truth about values, an activity in which we and other human beings, and perhaps creatures who are not human beings, are all engaged. We shall then see their judgments as having these general implications, rather as we see primitive statements about the stars as having implications that can be contradicted by more sophisticated statements about the stars. On the other model we shall see their judgments as part of their way of living, a cultural artifact they have come to inhabit (though they have not consciously built it). On this, nonobjectivist, model, we shall take a different view of the relations between that practice and critical reflection. We shall not be disposed to see the level of reflection as implicitly already there, and we shall not want to say that their judgments have, just as they stand, these implications.

The choice between these two different ways of looking at their activities will determine whether we say that the people in the hypertraditional society have ethical knowledge. It is important to be quite clear what ethical knowledge is in question. It is knowledge involved in their making judgments in which they use their thick concepts. We are not considering whether they display knowledge *in using those concepts rather than some others*: this would be an issue at the reflective level. The question "does the society possess ethical knowledge?" is seriously ambiguous in that way. The collective reference to the society invites us to take the perspective in which its ethical representations are compared with other societies' ethical representations, and this is the reflective level, at which they certainly do not possess knowledge. There is another sense of the question in which it asks whether members of the society could, in exercising their concepts, express knowledge about the world to which they apply them, and the answer to that might be yes.

The interesting result of this discussion is that the answer will be yes if we take the nonobjectivist view of their ethical activities: various members of the society will have knowledge, when they deploy their concepts carefully, use the appropriate criteria, and so on. But on the objectivist view they do not have knowledge, or at least it is most unlikely that they do, since their judgments have extensive implications, which they have never considered, at a reflective level, and we have every reason to believe that, when those implications are considered, the traditional use of ethical concepts will be seriously affected.

The objectivist view, while it denies knowledge to the unreflective society, may seem to promise knowledge at the reflective level. Characteristically, it expects the demands of knowledge to be satisfied only by reflection. No doubt there are some ethical beliefs, universally held and usually vague ("one has to have a special reason to kill someone"), that we can be sure will survive at the reflective level. But they fall far short of any adequate, still less systematic, body of ethical knowledge at that level, and I think that the outcome of my earlier discussion of ethical theory has shown that, at least as things are, no such body of knowledge exists. Later I shall suggest that, so far as propositional knowledge of ethical truths is concerned, this is not simply a matter of how things are. Rather, at a high level of reflective generality there could be no ethical knowledge of this sort — or, at most, just one piece.

If we accept that there can be knowledge at the hypertraditional or unreflective level; if we accept the obvious truth that reflection characteristically disturbs, unseats, or replaces those traditional concepts; and if we agree that, at least as things are, the reflective level is not in a position to give us knowledge we did not have before — then we reach the notably un-Socratic conclusion that, in ethics, *reflection can destroy knowledge.* . . .

Another consequence, if we allow knowledge at the unreflective level, will be that not all propositional knowledge is additive. Not all pieces of knowledge can be combined into a larger body of knowledge. We may well have to accept that conclusion anyway from other contexts that involve perspectival views of the world. A part of the physical world may present itself as one color to one kind of observer, and another to another; to another, it may not exactly be a color at all. Call those qualities perceived by each kind of observer *A, B, C.* Then a skilled observer of one kind can know that the surface is *A*, of another kind that it is *B*, and so on, but there is no knowledge that it is *A* and *B* and *C.* This result would disappear if what *A* or *B* or *C* meant were something relational — if, when observers said "that is *A*" they meant "*A* to observers like us." It is very doubtful that this is the correct account. If it is not, the coherence of those pieces of knowledge is

secured at a different level, when the various perceived qualities are related to the absolute conception. Their relation to the conception is also what makes it clear that the capacities that produce these various pieces of knowledge are all forms of *perception.* Of course we have good reason to believe this before we possess any such theoretical conception, and certainly before we possess its details. This is because our everyday experience, unsurprisingly, reveals a good deal of what we are and how we are related to the world, and in this way leads us toward the theoretical conception.

Some think of the knowledge given by applying ethical concepts as something like perception. But we can now see a vital asymmetry between the case of the ethical concepts and the perspectival experience of secondary qualities such as colors. This asymmetry shows, moreover, that the distinction between the scientific and the ethical has wider implications. It is not merely a matter of distinguishing between an ideally nonperspectival science on the one hand and ethical concepts on the other. Not all perspectival concepts are ethical, and there are significant differences between ethical and other perspectival concepts, such as those of sense perception.

The main difference is that, in the case of secondary qualities, what explains also justifies; in the ethical case, this is not so. The psychological capacities that underly our perceiving the world in terms of certain secondary qualities have evolved so that the physical world will present itself to us in reliable and useful ways. Coming to know that these qualities constitute our form of perceptual engagement with the world, and that this mode of presentation works in a certain way, will not unsettle the system. In the ethical case, we have an analogy to the perceptual just to this extent, that there is local convergence under these concepts: the judgments of those who use them are indeed, as I put it before, world-guided. This is certainly enough to refute the simplest oppositions of fact and value. But if it is to mean anything for a wider objectivity, everything depends on what is to be said *next.* With secondary qualities, it is the explanation of the perspectival perceptions that enables us, when we come to reflect on them, to place them in relation to the perceptions of other people and other creatures; and that leaves everything more or less where it was, so far as our perceptual judgments are concerned. The question is whether we can find an ethical analogy to that. Here we have to go outside local judgments to a reflective or second-order account of them, and here the analogy gives out.

There is, first, a problem of what the second-order account is to be. An *explanation* of those local judgments and of the conceptual differences between societies will presumably have to come from the social sciences: cultural differences are in question. Perhaps no existing explanation of such things goes very deep, and we are not too clear how deep an explanation might go. But we do know that it will not look much like the explanation of color perception. The capacities it will invoke are those involved in finding our way around in a social world, not merely the physical world, and this, crucially, means *in some social world or other,* since it is certain both that human beings cannot live without a culture and that there are many different cultures in which they can live, differing in their local concepts.

In any case, an explanatory theory is not enough to deal with the problems of objectivity raised by the local ethical concepts. In the case of secondary qualities, the explanation also justifies, because it can show how the perceptions are related to physical reality and how they can give knowledge of that reality, which is what they purport to do. The question with them is: Is this a method of finding our way around the physical world? The theoretical account explains how it is. In the ethical case, this is not the kind of question raised by reflection. If we ask the question "is this a method of finding our way around the social world?" we would have to be asking whether it was a method of finding our way around some social world or other, and the answer to that must obviously be yes (unless the society were extremely disordered, which is not what we were supposing). The question raised is rather "is this a good way of living compared with others?"; or, to put it another way, "is this the best kind of social world?"

When these are seen to be the questions, the reflective account we require turns out to involve reflective *ethical* considerations. These are the considerations that some believe should take the form of an ethical theory. The reflective considerations will have to take up the job of justifying the local concepts once those have come to be questioned. An ethical theory might even, in a weak sense, pro-vide some explanations. It might rationalize some cultural differences, showing why one local concept rather than others was ethically appropriate in particular circumstances (we can recall here the possibilities and perils of indirect utilitarianism). But while it might explain why it was reasonable for people to have these various ethical beliefs, it would not be the sort of theory that could explain why they did or did not have them. It could not do something that explanations of perception can do, which is to generate an adequate theory of error and to account generally for the tendency of people to have what, according to its principles, are wrong beliefs.

If a wider objectivity were to come from all this, then the reflective ethical considerations would themselves have to be objective. This brings us back to the question whether the reflective level might generate its own ethical knowledge. If this is understood as our coming to have propositional knowledge of ethical truths, then we need some account of what "tracking the truth" will be. The idea that our beliefs can track the truth at this level must at least imply that a range of investigators could rationally, reasonably, and unconstrainedly come to converge on a determinate set of ethical conclusions. What are the hopes for such a process? I do not mean of its actually happening, but rather of our forming a coherent picture of how it might happen. If it is construed as convergence on a body of ethical truths which is brought about and explained by the fact that they are truths — this would be the strict analogy to scientific objectivity — then I see no hope for it. In particular, there is no hope of extending to this level the kind of world-guidedness we have been considering in the case of the thick ethical concepts. Discussions at the reflective level, if they have the ambition of considering all ethical experience and arriving at the truth about the ethical, will necessarily use the most general and abstract ethical concepts such as "right," and those concepts do not display world-guidedness (which is why they were selected by prescriptivism in its attempt to find a pure evaluative element from which it could *detach* world-guidedness).

I cannot see any convincing theory of knowledge for the convergence of reflective ethical thought on ethical reality in even a distant analogy to the scientific case. Nor is there a convincing analogy with mathematics, a case in which the notion of an independent reality is at least problematic. . . .

[T]here is the important point that every noncontradictory piece of mathematics is part of mathematics, though it may be left aside as too trivial or unilluminating or useless. But not every noncontradictory structure of ethical reflection can be part of one such subject, since bodies of ethical thought can conflict with one another in ways that not only lack the kinds of explanation that could form a credible theory of error, but have too many credible explanations of other kinds.

I do not believe, then, that we can understand reflection as a process that substitutes knowledge for beliefs attained in unreflective practice. We must reject the objectivist view of ethical life as in that way a pursuit of ethical truth. But this does not rule out all forms of objectivism. There is still the project of trying to give an objective grounding or foundation to ethical life. . . . Those ideas should be now freed from the Socratic requirement that they should provide a reason to *each* person to lead an ethical life rather than not. For the purposes we are now considering, it would be significant enough if such considerations could give us a schema of an ethical life that would be the best ethical life, the most satisfactory for human beings in general. The question to be answered is: Granted that human beings need to share a social world, is there anything to be known about their needs and their basic motivations that will show us what this world would best be?

I doubt that there will turn out to be a very satisfying answer. It is probable that any such considerations will radically underdetermine the ethical options even in a given social situation (we must remember that what we take the situation to be is itself, in part, a function of what ethical options we can see). Any ethical life is going to contain restraints on such things as killing, injury, and lying, but those restraints can take very different forms. Again, with respect to the virtues, which is the most natural and promising field for this kind of inquiry, we only have to compare Aristotle's catalogue of the virtues with any that might be produced now to see how pictures of an appropriate human life may differ in spirit and in the actions and institutions they call for. We also have the idea that there are many and various forms of human excellence which will not all fit together into one harmonious whole, so any determinate ethical outlook is going to represent some kind of specialization of human possibilities. That idea is deeply entrenched in any naturalistic or, again, historical conception of human nature — that is, in any adequate conception of it — and I find it hard to believe that it will be overcome by an objective inquiry, or that human beings could turn out to have a much more determinate nature than is suggested by what we already know, one that timelessly demanded a life of a particular kind.

The project of giving to ethical life an objective and determinate grounding in considerations about human nature is not, in my view, very likely to succeed. But it is at any rate a comprehensible project, and I believe it represents the only intelligible form of ethical objectivity at the reflective level. It is worth asking what would be involved in its succeeding. We should notice, first, how it would have to be human beings that were primarily the subject of our ethics, since it would be from their nature that its conclusions would be drawn. Here this project joins hands with contractualism, in seeing other animals as outside the primary constituency of ethics, and at most beneficiaries of it, while it expects less than contractualism does of our relations to extraterrestrials, who would be connected with it simply through the rules of mutual restraint that might figure in a nonaggression treaty.

If the project succeeded, it would not simply be a matter of agreement on a theory of human nature. The convergence itself would be partly in social and psychological science, but what would matter would be a convergence to which scientific conclusions provided only part of the means. Nor, on the other hand, would there be a convergence directly on ethical truths, as in the other objectivist model. One ethical belief might be said to be in its own right an object of knowledge at the reflective level, to the effect that a certain kind of life was best for human beings. But this will not yield other ethical truths directly. The reason, to put it summarily, is that the excellence or satisfactoriness of a life does not stand to beliefs involved in that life as premise stands to conclusion. Rather, an agent's excellent life is characterized by *having* those beliefs, and most of the beliefs will not be about that agent's dispositions or life, or about other people's dispositions, but about the social world. That life will involve, for instance, the agent's using some thick concepts rather than others. Reflection on the excellence of a life does not itself establish the truth of judgments using those concepts or of the agent's other ethical judgments. Instead it shows that there is good reason (granted the commitment to an ethical life) to live a life that involves those concepts and those beliefs.

The convergence that signaled the success of this project would be a convergence of practical reason, by which people came to lead the best kind of life and to have the desires that belonged to that life; convergence in ethical belief would largely be a part and consequence of that process. One very general ethical belief would, indeed, be an object of knowledge at that level. Many particular ethical judgments, involving the favored thick concepts, could be known to be true, but then judgments of this sort (I have argued) are very often known to be true anyway, even when they occur, as they always have, in a life that is not grounded at the objective level. The objective grounding would not bring it about that judgments using those concepts were true or could be known: this was so already. But it would enable us to recognize that certain of them were the best or most appropriate thick concepts to use. Between the two extremes of the one very general proposition and the many concrete ones, other ethical beliefs would be true only in the oblique sense that they were the beliefs that would help us to find our way around in a social world which—on this optimistic program—was shown to be the best social world for human beings.

This would be a structure very different from that of the objectivity of science. There would be a radical difference between ethics and science, even if ethics were objective in the only way in which it intelligibly could be. However, this does not mean that there is a clear distinction between (any) fact and (any) value; nor does it mean that there is no ethical knowledge. There is some, and in the less reflective past there has been more.

The problems I have discussed here are not merely hypothetical questions, of whether ethics might eventually turn out to be objective and, if so, how. They are problems about the nature of ethical thought, the way in which it can understand its own nature and the extent to which it can consistently appear to be what it really is. Those are serious problems on any showing, and would be so even if ethical thought turned out to be objective in the only way that is intelligible. We shall see them more distinctly when we have looked at them from a different angle, that of relativism.

IX.7 Two Forms of Ethical Skepticism

BRUCE RUSSELL

Bruce Russell is associate professor of philosophy at Wayne State University and the author of several articles on ethics and philosophy of religion. He provides the following remarks to introduce our next reading:

"Among our beliefs are certain moral or ethical beliefs about the rightness or wrongness of actions and the goodness or badness of persons, their dispositions, characters, motivations, and so on. I argue that general requirements for justified belief and knowledge cannot be used to show that justified ethical belief and knowledge are impossible.

"The first two sections of the paper are meant to allay doubts about the possibility of ethical knowledge and justified ethical belief, but the third section is meant to raise doubts as to whether people always have adequate reason to do what is morally required of them in circumstances in which most others are acting morally. Important arguments to show everyone has adequate reason are criticized, but examples are also given to show that moral requirements sometimes outweigh agent-centered considerations. The problem, which remains unsolved, lies in determining when moral requirements outweigh agent-centered considerations and when they do not, and in explaining why moral requirements sometimes outweigh agent-centered considerations but sometimes do not."

Metaethics is generally considered to be interested in questions about the nature of moral judgments and of how, if at all, they can be justified. One form of ethical skepticism doubts that it is possible to justify moral claims and principles or that there can be moral knowledge. Sections I and II below address such doubt by considering whether general requirements for justified belief and knowledge can be used to show that there can or cannot be justified moral belief and knowledge.

Another form of ethical skepticism grants that there can be justified moral belief and knowledge but doubts whether people always have most reason to do what they are morally required to do, even in circumstances in which most others are acting morally. Section III addresses this doubt, especially arguments to show that moral requirements do pro-

vide overriding reasons for action in circumstances in which most others are acting morally.

Hence, this paper is about two forms of ethical skepticism: the one that doubts whether it is possible for one to know or be justified in believing ethical claims, the other that doubts whether ethical requirements necessarily provide overriding reasons for action, even in what might be called moral environments. I will argue that the first, but not the second, sort of ethical skepticism is unfounded.

I. General Requirements on Justified Belief and Knowledge

"A person's noetic structure is the set of propositions he believes, together with certain epistemic relations that hold among him and these propositions."[1] Some of these beliefs are basic, not being believed on the basis of any other of the person's

Written for the first edition of this anthology. © Bruce Russell, 1988.

beliefs; others are nonbasic. Typically, moral propositions are contained in a person's noetic structure, propositions such as

1. It was wrong of the boys to set the cat on fire.
2. It is wrong to cause unnecessary (and unwanted) pain just for the fun of it.
3. A child who is about to undergo what would otherwise be painful surgery should be given an anesthetic before the operation.[2]

(1) would be basic if one just immediately formed that belief, say, on seeing the boys set the cat ablaze, although it might also be based on (2) plus the belief that the boys' setting the cat on fire is an instance of causing unnecessary (and unwanted) pain just for the fun of it. Whether (2) and (3) are basic or not for someone will also depend on whether the person holding them holds them on the basis of some other beliefs or not.

Presumably, *some* of our beliefs are *properly* basic. That can mean one of two things. First, it can mean that there is nothing unreasonable, irrational, or intellectually irresponsible, nor is there any defect in our noetic structure if we hold such beliefs without any evidence provided by others. Second, it can mean that those beliefs have sufficient warrant so that, if true, they constitute knowledge, even though they lack evidential support of our beliefs from others.[3] Some of our beliefs must be properly basic, for, as Alvin Plantinga has said,

> if you have evidence for every proposition you believe, then (granted certain plausible assumptions about the formal properties of the evidence relation) you will believe infinitely many propositions; and no one has time, these busy days, for that.[4]

If some of our beliefs are *properly* basic why aren't (1), (2), and (3)? Classical foundationalism (CF) is the view that a belief is properly basic for someone if and only if it is self-evident, incorrigible, or evident to the senses for that person. A proposition is self-evident if it is seen to be true upon grasping or understanding it. "1 + 1 = 2" and "no person is both six feet tall and not six feet tall at the same time" are self-evident propositions. A proposition is incorrigible for a person, roughly, if it is not possible for that person to believe that proposition and it be false. Propositions about one's own mental states (such as "I am in pain" and "I *seem* to see a tree") are generally considered to be incorrigible.

They are not necessarily self-evident because I don't know, for instance, that "I am in pain" is true simply upon understanding it. I must rely on my sensations, not just my understanding, to apprehend whether "I am in pain" is true or not. Propositions that are evident to the senses are perceptual propositions, "propositions whose truth or falsehood we can determine by looking or employing some other sense."[5] Could one show that (1), (2), and (3) are not properly basic for someone by arguing that classical foundationalism is true and that neither (1), (2), nor (3) are self-evident, incorrigible, or evident to the senses for that person?

It seems that one could not. Plantinga has argued that classical foundationalism is self-referentially incoherent because belief in it is neither self-evident, incorrigible, nor evident to the senses, and is not supported by beliefs that are.[6] Hence no one knows, or is justified in believing, that classical foundationalism is true according to its very own standard. Thus, it cannot be used to prove that (1), (2), and (3) are not properly basic.

Furthermore, at least (2) and (3) seem to be self-evident. In discussing self-evidence, Plantinga notes that there is an epistemic and a phenomenological component to self-evident propositions:

> A proposition *p* is self-evident to a person S only if S has *immediate* knowledge of *p*—that is, knows *p*, and does not know *p* on the basis of his knowledge of other propositions.[7]

Such a proposition also has a "luminous aura or glow when you bring it to mind or consider it." In Locke's terms it has an "evident luster" or "clarity and brightness" about it; in Descartes' terms, it is "clear and distinct." It is this phenomenological feature of self-evident propositions that compels or impels us to believe them. Surely, for most of us (2) and (3) are self-evident, and in the appropriate circumstances (1) would also be.[8] It is their apparent self-evidence that confers warrant on these propositions.[9]

So even if foundationalism were true, it could not be used to show that no moral beliefs are properly basic. In fact, insofar as it says that *if* a proposition is either self-evident or incorrigible or evident to the senses for someone, then it is properly basic, foundationalism can even be used to show that belief that (2) and (3), and so some moral beliefs, *are* properly basic. Since classical foundationalism seems to give sufficient conditions of proper basicality, many of us are perfectly justified in believing (2) and other moral propositions.[10]

Someone might object either that foundationalism, or the particular version of it I have considered, is false. She might hold that a person is justified in believing a proposition, or that a proposition is properly basic for that person, if and only if it coheres with the rest of her beliefs. Now many coherentists do not make clear what they mean by "coherence," and there are various suggestions as to what it does mean. Also, some people are "global" coherentists, holding that epistemic justification for *any* sort of belief depends on its coherence with others beliefs. Others are "local" coherentists, holding, for example, that epistemic justification depends on coherence, *except* in the case of perceptual beliefs or beliefs about our current mental states.

Against the global coherentists it can be argued that coherence is not necessary for justification because certain perceptual beliefs can be justified even if they do not cohere with other beliefs. For instance, suppose your spouse has told me that you are in South America and I form a coherent set of beliefs that includes the belief that you are in South America. Then I see you in the bright lights of the supermarket as I am trying to pick out a ripe avocado, and I form the belief that you are home right here in the United States. That belief is properly basic and I am justified in holding it despite the fact that it does not cohere with the rest of my beliefs.[11]

Against local coherentism it can be argued that, because it is a hybrid of foundationalism and coherentism, it lacks the appeal of generality that either global coherentism or foundationalism has. We need an explanation of why coherence is needed for some, but not other, types of belief to be warranted. Second, it would seem that we can be epistemically justified in holding apparently self-evident beliefs that do not cohere with others of our beliefs. Third, one would think that beliefs supported by perceptual beliefs or beliefs about our current mental states, but which are not themselves those sorts of beliefs, could be epistemically justified even if they did not cohere with others of our beliefs. For instance, beliefs that we arrive at through induction on observations (say, the belief that all swans are white) can be justified even if they fail to cohere with many of our other beliefs.

In general, coherentism, whether global or local, is mistaken because it ignores the fact that in certain circumstances reliable belief-producing mechanisms can confer warrant on beliefs, even if they do not cohere with others of our beliefs.

But even if coherentism were correct, it could not be used to show that no moral belief is, or can be, justified. That is so because the moral beliefs of some of us at least do cohere with the rest of our beliefs. So it seems that coherentism could even be used to show that some of our moral beliefs are justified.

Unfortunately, the conditions the coherentist offers for justified belief, or proper basicality, are neither necessary *nor sufficient*. They are not sufficient because one can imagine situations in which one's beliefs remain coherent, but fixed as one's experiences change. Suppose I hike up Skyline Ridge near Mt. Baker in Washington and form the beliefs typically produced by the experiences associated with hiking in mountainous terrain. I believe, for instance, that I am walking briskly along a trail through some woods, that the air is cool, and that the sun is shining at an oblique angle through the trees. Suppose, now, that I am riding home in the backseat of an automobile and my experiences are those one typically has when traveling along. But suppose, also, for some odd reason, that my beliefs remain those coherent ones I had while hiking down the mountain trail. Despite having the experience of seeing the paved road, the fences, the grassland beside the road, of smelling the cigar smoke in the car, and so on, I still believe that I am hiking down the shaded trail in the open air. Although my beliefs form a coherent set, the ones about my hiking down the shaded trail would not be justified and not properly basic. Hence, coherence is not sufficient for a belief to be justified for someone, and so moral beliefs are not justified simply because they cohere with other beliefs a person has.[12]

Perhaps neither the classical foundationalists nor the coherentists have it right concerning the conditions of justified belief or proper basicality. Perhaps reliabilism is correct: a belief that P is properly basic for a person S if and only if S's belief that P was reliably produced. One would then argue that moral beliefs, even if self-evident, are not reliably produced. From that it would follow that no moral beliefs are properly basic, and that self-evidence does not necessarily render a belief properly basic.

Must a belief be reliably produced to be properly basic, and is it true that moral beliefs are never reliably produced and are not supported by any beliefs that are? It would seem that reliability is not a necessary condition of justified belief. Suppose a mad scientist or a Cartesian demon produced experiences in us indistinguishable from the sensory experiences we now have, together with the corresponding perceptual beliefs that we normally form upon having those experiences. We would then be justified in holding those beliefs, even though they would all be false and not reliably produced, provided we did not have any reason to believe that they were not reliably produced.

At this point I need to distinguish between two notions of epistemic justification. In one sense a person is epistemically justified in believing a proposition if she has not violated any epistemic duties and if there is no defect in her noetic structure in virtue of her believing that proposition. In another sense a person is epistemically justified in believing a proposition only if that justification, or enough of it, would turn her true belief into knowledge. Someone may be epistemically justified in the first sense without being epistemically justified in the second.[13] The structure of my beliefs may in no way be flawed, and I may have violated no epistemic duties in forming them, but they may lack what has been called positive epistemic status, the stuff that is needed to turn true belief into knowledge.

In fact, that is just what seems to be true in the evil demon and mad scientist cases I described above. Although my beliefs about what there is in the external world would all be false, my noetic *structure* would not be defective. The relationships between my beliefs, and those between them and my experiences, need not be flawed in any way. And I could not be epistemically blamed, nor would I be negligent in holding those beliefs about the external world, because it is assumed that there is no way for me to find out that I am being systematically deceived. Still, even if some of my beliefs happened to be true (say, because the evil demon or the mad scientist inculcated them in me *thinking they were false*), I would not *know* they were. That is so because it would just be by accident that they were true and I believed them. If ninety-nine out of one hundred buildings that look like barns are really barn façades, but I do not realize that that is so and my ignorance is not epistemically culpable, then I do not know that the barn I am looking at is a barn, even if I am epistemically justified in the first sense in believing it is.

So one might maintain that reliability is a necessary condition of epistemic justification in the second sense; that is, of positive epistemic status, even if it is not a necessary condition of epistemic justification in the normative sense. One might then argue that moral beliefs do not have positive epistemic status because they are not reliably produced. In an oft-quoted passage, Peter Singer questions whether moral convictions derive "from discarded religious systems, from warped views of sex and bodily functions, or from customs necessary for the survival of the group in social and economic circumstances that now lie in the distant past."[14] The subsequent passage in his text suggests that moral convictions would lack epistemic warrant if they derived from such unreliable sources.

But how do we know that discarded religious systems, warped views of sex and bodily functions, and outmoded customs are unreliable sources of moral belief? Two answers come to mind. First, one might argue that nonmoral beliefs that derive from such origins are unreliable, and we know that they are by checking those beliefs against beliefs that derive from reliable sources. But even if we knew that the nonmoral beliefs that derive from such origins were often false, how would this justify us in concluding that moral beliefs deriving from those same origins are also often false? There are scientists who are reliable sources of truth in their specialities, but who could not tell you what type of fertilizer to use on your begonias. A reliable source of truth in one area may be unreliable in another, and vice versa.

Second, one might argue that because there is so much disagreement between different people's moral beliefs, we know that an unreliable mechanism must produce them. If there were a great deal of disagreement between perceivers as to the shapes of physical objects, we would think that perception is not a reliable source of beliefs about the shapes of objects.

There are two replies that can be given to this objection. First, in the case of perception, we might be able to construct an "error theory" to explain why the perceptions of certain perceivers were unreliable sources of beliefs about the shapes of objects, whereas others were not. That would render much of the disagreement innocuous. A similar thing might be done with respect to ethical disagreement. Perhaps moral beliefs that derive from discarded religious systems, warped views of sex and bodily functions, and so on, *are* unreliable. But that does not impugn the epistemic status of moral beliefs that do not stem from such sources. So why can't we claim positive epistemic status for the moral beliefs we have, or could form on reflection, that do not stem from these questionable sources?

The second reply is that if moral disagreement counts against the positive epistemic status of moral beliefs, then epistemological disagreement must count against the positive epistemic status of epistemiological beliefs, including the belief in reliabilism itself. If, because of epistemological disagreement, we are not justified in believing reliabilism is true, then we will not be able to depend on reliabilism to show that moral beliefs lack positive epistemic status.

Perhaps beliefs must satisfy some condition other than, or in addition to, those proposed by the classical foundationalist, the coherentist, and the reliabilist. In particular, one might hold that for any proposition to be justified, it must help explain, or enhance the explanation of, the occurrence of one or more of our observations, or be entailed or made likely by ones that do, in those cases in which an observation is an immediate judgment made by someone but not based on conscious reasoning.[15] One might then argue that no moral proposition helps explain, or enhances our explanation of, anything, and is not entailed or made likely by ones that do, and so conclude that no moral propositions are justified.

Some have argued that moral claims do help explain the occurrence of some of our observations.[16] However, I believe that either the explanatory requirement on justification is self-defeating or, in an extended sense, moral claims can help explain our moral observations.

According to Harman, an observation is an immediate judgment that is not based on conscious reasoning. If, on seeing my wife walking across campus or some boys setting a cat on fire, I immediately judge, "There's my wife" or "It's wrong of the boys to set that cat on fire," then I have made observations, the former empirical, the latter moral. Clearly, the explanatory requirement does not help explain the occurrence of any of our empirical, non-normative observations and is not entailed or made more likely by any empirical propositions. Observations are mental events, and the occurrence of a mental event is not going to be explained by an hy-

pothesis about what we are justified in believing, even if it might be explained in part by a proposition about what we *believe* we are justified in believing. Nor are any propositions about what is the case going to entail or make more likely an hypothesis about what we are justified in believing.

The explanatory requirement might in some sense be said to help explain certain epistemic intuitions — observations about which of our beliefs are justified and which not. For instance, the explanatory requirement might explain our intuition that we are justified in believing that all crows are black but not justified in believing that leprechauns exist. The explanatory requirement could be used to show that *what* we judge in these cases is true because the proposition that all crows are black helps explain why we have never observed a nonblack crow, whereas the proposition that leprechauns exist does not help explain any of our observations. (We think that propositions about the effects of alcohol consumption on perceptions or psychological suggestion better explain observations of leprechauns.) But in this sense of "explanation" moral theories could help "explain" moral observations. We immediately judge that it is wrong of the boys to set a cat on fire and obligatory for someone to save a drowning child when all he has to do is reach out his hand. Utilitarianism can be used to show that *what* we judge in these cases is true because burning the cat will produce more pain and failing to save the child more unhappiness in the world. But neither the explanatory requirement nor utilitarianism can explain why we make the epistemic or moral judgments we do, why those mental acts occur. Our *belief* that the explanatory requirement or utilitarianism is correct could help explain that, but the *truth* of what we believe cannot. Neither utilitarianism nor the explanatory requirement themselves helps explain why we immediately *judge* what we do, why those mental acts take place.

So moral theories can help explain moral intuitions as much, or as little, as the explanatory requirements helps explain epistemic intuitions. Either the explanatory requirement does not help explain anything (and is not entailed or made likely by propositions that do), and is then hoist on its own petard, or in an extended sense it does, but then so do certain moral theories. In either case it cannot be used to show that no moral claims are justified.

II. Williams's Arguments Against Ethical Knowledge

We have seen that if the sources of moral belief could be shown to be unreliable in the appropriate sense, then it could be shown that moral beliefs lack positive epistemic status and so cannot constitute knowledge. Whereas the arguments to show that the sources of moral belief are unreliable were unsuccessful, there are other recent arguments, which rest on general epistemic requirements, to show that there cannot be ethical knowledge and certainly not a systematic *body* of such knowledge comparable to that found in science. Bernard Williams has argued that there can be knowledge of specific ethical claims, those involving what he calls "thick ethical concepts," such as cowardice, brutality, gratitude, treachery, courage, lying, and promising.[17] But he thinks that reflection can destroy such knowledge by disturbing, unseating, or replacing those concepts so that beliefs previously formed with those concepts can no longer be formed. Williams further thinks that reflection cannot generate its own knowledge (p. 151), so that reflective cultures like our own are left with little ethical knowledge, perhaps with only some vague and universally held beliefs, such as "one has to have special reasons to kill someone" (p. 148) or a belief that a certain kind of life is the best for human beings (p. 154).

It is not clear how Williams thinks reflection can destroy ethical knowledge. Suppose someone in a traditional and unreflective society is convinced, say, that punishing a dog by not giving it water and food for two days is cruel or that a particular rape and beating was brutal. How does reflection disturb, unseat, or replace such concepts as cruelty or brutality in such a way as to destroy such knowledge?

Perhaps another example will help. Suppose some society thought it was unchaste for a woman to display her breasts in public. Suppose the notion of chastity was "driven from use" by some later reflective society because of that notion's association with discarded religious beliefs or warped views of sex and bodily functions. Then Williams's point, applied to this example, would seem to be that it was and still would be unchaste for a woman to show her breasts in public, but that only the traditional society would have knowledge that it was unchaste

because only the traditional society would have access to the relevant concept. If members of the later society could form the relevant belief, then that belief would still be true, but because they cannot, they lack the knowledge the earlier society possessed. Reflection has destroyed certain ethical knowledge, and even its possibility, by driving the relevant concept from use.

But whereas reflection might drive certain "thick" ethical concepts from use, there is no reason to think it will drive all such concepts from use. Even if reflection would affect the borders of such concepts as brutality, gratitude, and so on, how would it so totally undermine their use as to prevent beliefs being formed in terms of those concepts? There seems to be an unshifting core to such concepts, and reflection can do nothing to discredit their use. Hence, beliefs involving those concepts can still be formed in a reflective society and they will, or at least can, constitute knowledge.

Williams's argument that reflection cannot generate ethical knowledge is no more convincing than his argument that it destroys more specific ethical knowledge. Williams thinks that for someone to know anything, her belief must both be true and "track the truth."[18] The last condition implies that there must be a nonaccidental link between the truth of the belief and the subject's holding it. In order to have knowledge, she must hold it, in some sense, *because* it is true. It is further assumed that the relevant link is present only if the person would not hold the belief if it were false. Williams then argues that even if ethical beliefs that result from reflection were true, they would not track the truth and so would not constitute knowledge.

Both parts of Williams's argument are unconvincing. First, it does not seem true that for a belief to constitute knowledge it must track the truth in the way Williams requires. Let (D) be the proposition that I am not being systematically deceived by an evil demon. My belief (D) can constitute knowledge even though I would still believe (D) if such a demon were deceiving me.

Some might reject the intuition that is the basis of this counterexample to the conception of knowledge Williams employs. But there are other problems with that conception. Let (H) be the proposition that I am home in my study. Now according to the requirement that belief must track the truth to be knowledge, it is possible that I know the conjunction of (D) and (H), but not (H) itself. We can assume that if the conjunction were true I would believe it, but if it were false I would not — by virtue of the fact that I would not believe I am home in my study if I weren't. (Because of a deal the evil demon made with my wife, he never deceives me about whether I am home in my study or not.) Hence, the conjunction would track the truth, even though (D) would not. Thus, according to the conception of knowledge being considered, the conjunction could be known even though one of its conjuncts could not.[19] Most people would find it difficult to accept that one could know a conjunction, but not know one of its conjuncts.

Even if Williams were right in thinking a belief has to track the truth for it to be knowledge, he has not shown that reflective ethical beliefs do not track the truth. He argues that for reflective ethical beliefs to track the truth they "must at least imply that a range of investigators could rationally, reasonably, and unconstrainedly come to converge on a determinate set of ethical conclusions" (p. 151). He thinks that there is little hope of our forming "a coherent picture of how it might happen," let alone of its happening. Williams thinks that there is little hope of explaining any convergence in ethical beliefs by the fact that they are true. He seems to think that there is no such hope because (a) such reflective beliefs would be formed using "the most general and abstract ethical concepts such as 'right,'" (b) such concepts are not world-guided, and (c) convergence on the relevant ethical beliefs could be explained by their truth only if the concepts used in their expression were world-guided. A concept is world-guided just in case it "may be rightly or wrongly applied, and people who have acquired it can agree that it applies or fails to apply to some new situation" (p. 141). Its correct application is determined by features of the world and not simply by the desires and interests of those who use it.

Williams's argument seems to rest on the assumption that a reflective ethical belief can track the truth only if there can be free and rational convergence on that belief, whenever such convergence is due to its truth. One might wonder whether this assumption, when generalized to cover nonethical beliefs as well, is, like the explanatory requirement discussed above, self-defeating. There seems to be no more hope that the best explanation of convergence on Williams's assumption would be in terms

of its truth than that the best explanation of ethical convergence would be in terms of ethical truth. So by Williams's own lights, we have reason to think his assumption does not track the truth, and so we cannot know it is true. Hence, we cannot know that the conclusion reached on its basis is true.

But even if the assumption were correct, one would still have to accept the claim that there cannot be free and rational convergence on reflective ethical beliefs that is due to their truth to get Williams's conclusion. But why can't there be such convergence? Suppose people with diverse ethical beliefs, raised in diverse societies and with diverse religious and cultural heritages, came together to discuss ethical theory and ended up by agreeing on certain criteria of rightness and wrongness or goodness and badness. Although there will be competing psychological and sociological hypotheses to explain the emergence of such a convergence, it is possible that the best explanation of the convergence is that everyone came to recognize the truth about ethical matters. Since that is possible, contra Williams, it is reasonable to believe that there *can* be a relevant sort of convergence.

Williams said he saw no hope of "forming a coherent picture" of how the relevant sort of "convergence *might* emerge" (p. 151; my emphasis). I have tried to construct the relevant sort of picture. Suppose Williams replied that what he meant was that he saw no hope of the relevant sort of convergence emerging, while granting that it was logically possible. A belief that it is *unlikely* that the relevant sort of convergence will emerge seems as premature as the opposite belief that it is likely to emerge.

In his "Concluding Chapter" in *Reasons and Persons,* Derek Parfit is optimistic about the possibility of progress in ethics. He points out that nonreligious ethics has been studied by many people only since 1960, and he concludes that

> Belief in God, or in many gods, prevented free development of moral reasoning. Disbelief in God, openly admitted by a majority, is a very recent event, not yet completed. Because this event is so recent, Non-Religious Ethics is at a very early stage. We cannot yet predict whether, as in Mathematics, we will reach agreement. Since we cannot know how Ethics will develop, it is not irrational to have high hopes.[20]

To be confident that there can or cannot be justified ethical beliefs or knowledge, and bodies of such beliefs or knowledge (whether formed in terms of specific or general ethical concepts), we would have to know more about epistemology — more about the conditions of justified belief and knowledge in general, whether ethical or not. But based on what we do know, it seems possible for there to be justified ethical belief and knowledge, and even for there to be systematic bodies of such knowledge. Furthermore, it seems that the only way to make advances in epistemology is by appealing to epistemic intuitions and constructing and testing epistemological theories via those intuitions. Even forms of reliabilism (which, unlike other epistemological theories, often are not constructed to account for epistemic intuitions) must stand up to putative counterexamples. To avoid internal incoherence, epistemological theories, arrived at through their ability to account for certain epistemic intuitions and to avoid counterexamples, must not condemn the method of their own justification. But if the method of their own justification must not be condemned, then, without special argument, a similar method in ethics, in which ethical theories are arrived at through their ability to account for certain ethical intuitions and to avoid counterexamples, must not be condemned either.

III. *Moral Requirements and Reasons for Action*

What I have said so far might be seen as directed to someone who is an ethical skeptic in the sense that he doubts whether there is, or can be, ethical knowledge. But there is another sense in which one might be an ethical skeptic. This second sort of skeptic is skeptical about 'the force of ethical considerations,'[21] that is, she doubts whether ethical considerations necessarily give everyone some, or overriding, reason to act. One might grant that we know that it is wrong to torture children for the fun of it but still wonder whether there is any, or sufficient, reason for a particularly sadistic and clever person, who enjoys torturing children and knows he can get away with it, to refrain from torturing a child.

To answer this question adequately, one might think that one must first defend some theory of reasons for action. The four main categories into which such theories fall can be generated by considering two important distinctions. First, there is the distinction between agent-relative and agent-neutral theories of reasons for action; the former claims that only facts about actions involving some appropriate relationship or the agent (for example, being in *his* self-interest, benefiting those *he* cares about, being what *he* does or would under ideal circumstances prefer, and so on) constitute reasons for action, and the latter denies it. Second, there is the distinction between internalism and externalism; the former holds that all reasons for action depend on what people want or desire, or would want or desire under some ideal conditions, and the latter denies it. Ideal conditions will be those in which the person knows the relevant facts, is thinking clearly, and is free from distorting influences.

A person who thought that the only, or the supreme, reason for action depends on what a person wants, or would want if ideally situated, would be an agent-relative internalist. In his view, reasons for action would depend on the agent's desires alone. A person who thought that the only, or supreme, reason for action depends on what *anyone,* the agent or others, wants or would want, would be an agent-neutral internalist. In this view, unlike in agent-relative internalism, what other people want or would want gives an agent reason to act even if he does not (and would not, even if ideally situated) care about their desires. Someone who held that what is in a person's self-interest is independent of what she wants, or would want under ideal conditions, and that the only, or supreme, reason for action depends on what is in a person's self-interest, would be an agent-relative externalist. Finally, someone who held both that what is for someone's good is independent of what that person wants, or would want under ideal conditions, and that the only, or supreme, reason for action depends on what is for *anyone's* good — the agent's or others' — would be an agent-neutral externalist. In this view, unlike in agent-relative externalism, the good of others, as well as of the agent himself, would provide reasons for action.

Some of these views can be defeated by counterexamples. Consider the following example, which shows that agent-relative internalism is false. Suppose someone's strongest desire is to jump off a cliff. He has no reason for wanting this, but the desire survives reflection, cognitive psychotherapy, and so on. It is not true that what there is most reason for him to do is to jump off the cliff, and it is doubtful whether there is even *any* reason for this person to jump.[22] Hence, at least agent-relative internalist theories of what there is most reason to do are mistaken.

Of course, one might argue that this example only shows that self-interest should be understood in externalist terms. Still, what there is most reason to do is what is most in a person's self-interest. So the correct theory of reasons for action is a form of agent-relative externalism.

But the following example shows at least that agent-relative externalist reasons for action cannot be the *only* reasons for action. Suppose a callous individual is indifferent, and would remain indifferent even if ideally situated, between taking candy from a baby and spending his last two Canadian quarters on a candy bar before leaving Canada. Suppose, also, that it is no more in his interest to spend the money than to steal the candy, if interest and ideal preference are not identical. Surely the fact that the one alternative involves doing something wrong, namely, taking candy from a baby, is a reason for this person to refrain from that course of action and so to spend his quarters instead.

Of course, all this example shows is that *some* reasons for action are agent-neutral. One could still hold that agent-neutral reasons only serve as tie-breakers for determining what one should do when it is a toss-up from the standpoint of agent-relative considerations. But even this seems false if we consider the earlier example modified so that the man slightly prefers, and it is slightly more in his self-interest, to take the candy from the baby. Even here it seems that there is more reason for him to spend his quarters on a candy bar than to take the candy from the baby.

The real issue seems to be not whether moral reasons sometimes provide some, or even overriding, reasons for action, but whether they *always* provide overriding reasons for action. Is it *always* true that if a person is morally required to do something, then it would be contrary to reason for that person to refrain from doing it?

Authors in this collection have argued that morality is essentially social, that moral requirements are social constraints on the pursuit of agent-relative aims.[23] They have then argued that, in circum-stances in which enough others are willing to adhere to these social constraints, everyone has adequate reason to adhere to these constraints and so to do what morality requires. Reasons for the position that everyone has adequate reason to adhere to those constraints vary. David Gauthier holds that reason requires one to maximize considered preferences (that is, preferences formed under certain ideal conditions) and that one will do that best by being disposed to adhere to moral principles when enough others are so disposed. Given that one has that disposition, one will be required by reason to act morally, even when one knows that doing so will *not* maximize the satisfaction of considered preferences. Kurt Baier has argued that morality is a system of sanctioned social directives that is for the good of everyone alike, as compared to some appropriate benchmark. He then argues that everyone has equally good and sufficient reason to adhere to such a system when enough others also adhere to it. That is so because everyone has sufficient reason for adhering to some system, and someone could demand a better reason for adhering to an inequitable system only if he had a special reason to support his demand, which no one has.

Both Gauthier's and Baier's arguments assume that the entirety of morality is social and provides constraints on the pursuit of individual ends so that those ends can ultimately be better served. But it is doubtful whether morality is completely social in its nature. There are obligations to outsiders, people with whom social interaction is impossible or not mutually beneficial. Surely it is wrong to torture unwanted orphans or animals just for the fun of it, and it would be wrong to destroy some extraterrestrial society by sending it our nuclear wastes, even if we could never enter into social interaction with its members. But such actions would be wrong in views like Gauthier's and Baier's only if permitting them would, through contingent effects on the dispositions and motivations of people, damage social interaction with those who are capable of such interaction. There is a strong intuition that such actions would be wrong even if the benefits of social interaction were not affected by permitting them.

Further, the argument that rests on the view that, in noncooperative situations, reason requires one to maximize considered preference will fail insofar as all agent-relative internalist views are mistaken. However, a parallel argument could be constructed using some agent-relative externalist view of the nature of reasons for action. But another problem will still have to be faced: namely, the problem of showing that everyone (even sadistic and clever people) has sufficient reason to adhere to moral requirements in situations in which most others also so adhere, but in which the sadistic and clever person knows he can get away with violating those requirements, and in which that violation will (let us assume) both maximize the satisfaction of his considered preferences and best serve his self-interest. It seems that if a clever person is 'opaque' enough — can disguise his true motives well enough — then, according to the agent-relative conceptions of reasons for action, reason will require him to appear to be moral in order to take advantage of those who really are.[24] If so, he will not always have sufficient reason to do what morality requires, even in circumstances in which most others are moral people.

Baier's argument tries to meet this objection by claiming that everyone has sufficient reason to adhere to some system of social directives (because of the benefits of cooperation that will be enjoyed by everyone) and that no one has adequate reason for adhering to any system except the one that is for the good of everyone alike, as compared to some appropriate benchmark. But it is not clear that everyone has sufficient reason for adhering to some system of social directives. Why doesn't a very clever and egoistic person only have sufficient reason to get others to adhere and to pretend that he is adhering? Furthermore, even if everyone had sufficient reason to adhere to some system, why couldn't someone have sufficient reason to adhere to some social system that favored him and his loved ones more than it favored others and their loved ones? Of course, there is a sense in which he could not *in reason demand* that others adhere to that system, too. He could not give them grounds why they should adopt that social system rather than the one that favored them, or even the one that is for the good of everyone alike. It would not in any way be contrary to reason for them to adhere, or want to adhere, to some other social system. But if that can be said for them, it can also be said for the clever egoist. It is not in any way contrary to reason for him to adhere, or want others to adhere, to the system that favors him and those for whom he cares. A person cannot in reason demand a system of distributing slices of cake that favors him over others (say, he gets to cut the cake *and* select the first slice), but if he does not care about justice, it is in no way contrary to reason for him to want such a system adhered to, to try to get others to adhere to it as well, and to adhere to it himself if he can get away with it. This will be so even if everyone has the best possible reasons (that anyone can *in reason demand*) for adhering to some other system of distribution (say, one in which some person gets to slice the cake but selects his piece last).

The example involving taking candy from a baby shows that *sometimes* moral requirements outweigh agent-centered considerations. The example of the clever and sadistic person shows that *if* what a person has most reason to do is determined by what is most in his self-interest or by what best fulfills his considered preferences, then a person can have most reason to do what is wrong, even when others are acting morally. But since the example involving taking candy from a baby undercuts the conception (of what there is most reason to do) on which that conclusion rests, is there any reason to believe that it can be contrary to reason for a person to do what is morally required of him? What reason is there to believe that moral requirements are not *always* overriding?

Consider the following example. A young woman has her heart set on getting into medical school. If she gets in, through hard work and dedication she will graduate and become a good physician. However, even after much study she has been unable to score high enough on the MCATs to be admitted to any medical school. She finds herself with an opportunity to cheat that will ensure her an MCAT score that is high enough to gain admittance to some medical school and so to eventually fulfill her lifelong dream. Her patients will not be harmed by being treated by an incompetent physician because she will not be an incompetent physician once she receives the necessary training. At most the only person who will be harmed is the person denied admittance to medical school because this young woman will take one of the available places and so leave one less slot to be filled. Assume that this person will only be slightly harmed and that somehow the young woman knows all this. It would be wrong for this young woman to cheat to get into medical school, but why isn't it true that if she does not care about cheating, then what she has most reason to do is to cheat if she knows she can get away with it?

Consider another example. Suppose your son has robbed a rich man of some of his jewels, the police are after him, and he asks you to help him escape to Brazil. You know you can arrange things so that neither of you will get caught. You also know that if he is caught he will be sent to prison and his life will be ruined, but if he escapes, he will have a good life in Brazil. It would be wrong of you to help him escape, but why isn't it true that what you have most reason to do is to help your son escape justice?

The example involving taking candy from a baby suggests that sometimes moral requirements outweigh agent-centered considerations, but the above two examples suggest that sometimes they do not. A possible explanation is that the interests of others, as well as those of oneself and those for whom one cares, have weight. To counteract natural partiality, which overvalues agent-centered interests, morality in its rules overvalues the interests of those other than the agent and his favorites. Hence, morality can require, as in the cases of the young woman and the parent, that a person do what it is contrary to reason for her to do. On the other hand, what morality requires may be what reason requires, even if what morality requires is not what is most in the agent's interest or best fulfills his desires, and thus not what a person partial to himself and his favorites *believes* reason requires. The example involving taking candy from a baby makes this point.

Of course, the crucial element in this account is the claim that the interests of those other than the agent and his favorites give the agent some reason for action. I do not know of a convincing argument for that crucial claim, which is not based on examples like the one involving taking candy from a baby. Without such an argument many people will fall back on some agent-centered conception of reasons for action, and then, despite their resistance, they will be forced to conclude that, in many more cases than they would like to admit, what people have most reason to do is to act wrongly.

IV. *Summary and Unsolved Problems*

I have argued that general requirements on justified belief and knowledge cannot be used to show that justified ethical belief and knowledge are impossi- ble. Relying heavily on Alvin Plantinga's work, I ar- gued that many of the proposed general require- ments were mistaken, and then I added that even if they were not, they often could not be used in de- fense of the first sort of ethical skepticism, which doubts that there can be justified ethical belief or knowledge. But reliability survived as a necessary condition of knowledge and threatens ethical knowledge even if it does not threaten what I called epistemic justification in the normative sense. On the side of sufficiency, apparent self-evidence sur- vived as a warrant conferring property of beliefs, in- cluding ethical ones. A problem remains concerning the epistemic status of a belief that appears self-evi- dent, but is the result of an unreliable belief-produc- ing mechanism.[25]

The second sort of ethical skepticism, which doubts whether everyone always has adequate rea- son to do what morality requires, even in circum- stances in which most people are moral, is more plausible. Important arguments to show that it is false do not succeed. On the other hand, agent-rela- tive views that imply that moral considerations never provide overriding (or even any) reasons for action seem false, too. The problem, which remains unsolved, is to explain when and why moral re- quirements sometimes provide overriding reasons to act and sometimes do not.[26]

Endnotes

[1] See Alvin Plantinga, "Reason and Belief in God," in Alvin Plantinga and Nicholas Wolterstorff, eds. *Faith and Ratio- nality* (University of Notre Dame Press, 1983), p. 48 and "Coherentism and the Evidentialist Objection to Belief in God," in Robert Audi and William J. Wainwright, eds. *Ra- tionality, Religious Belief, and Moral Commitment* (Cornell University Press, 1986), p. 115.

[2] The first example is taken from Gilbert Harman, *The Nature of Morality* (Oxford University Press, 1977), pp. 4, 7–8; the second is from Plantinga, "Reason and Belief in God," *ibid.,* p. 56; and the third is from Renford Bambrough, *Moral Scepticism and Moral Knowledge* (Hu- manities Press, 1979), p. 15. Their purposes in bringing up these examples are diverse and don't always coincide with mine.

[3] A discussion of a parallel distinction concerning epistemic justification appears later in this reading.

[4] Plantinga, "Reason and Belief in God," p. 39. The assump- tions Plantinga has in mind are: (a) a proposition that gets all its warrant from itself has no warrant, (b) the gets-all-its- warrant-from relationship is transitive, and (c) warrant does not increase just by virtue of warrant transfer. If you

held a finite number of beliefs and each got all its warrant from some other belief, then each would get all its warrant from itself, which means that none of your beliefs would be warranted. But surely some are warranted and, as Plantinga has said, no one can hold infinitely many beliefs. So it is false that each belief gets all its warrant from other beliefs. A similar argument can be used to show that it is also false that each belief gets *some* of its warrant from other beliefs.

[5] See Plantinga, "Reason and Belief in God," p. 57 and pp. 55–58 for the above account of propositions that are self-evident, incorrigible, and evident to the senses.

[6] Plantinga, "Reason and Belief in God," esp. pp. 60–61.

[7] "Reason and Belief in God," p. 57.

[8] *Ibid.* for this entire paragraph. It should be noted that a proposition might be self-evident for one person but not for another. For instance, $12 \times 12 = 144$ is probably self-evident for you, but not for some six-year-olds. Also, a proposition might appear to be self-evident when it is not. Think of the following proposition, which leads to Russell's Paradoxes: for every property P there exists a set S such that X is a member of S if and only if X has P. Or for someone who has not considered that space itself might have causal properties, it might seem self-evident that if something happens in one place in the universe, then that same thing must happen in some other place in the universe if the conditions surrounding its occurrence are the same.

[9] See Plantinga, "Coherentism and the Evidentialist Objection," p. 123.

[10] Plantinga (in "Reason and Belief in God," p. 59) concedes, at least for the sake of argument, that classical foundationalism does offer sufficient conditions of proper basicality.

[11] Plantinga offers a similar critique of coherentism in "Coherentism and the Evidentialist Objection," pp. 137–38. Before rejecting coherentism, Plantinga first argues that the most charitable interpretation of coherentism sees it as offering a rival account to classical foundationalism of the conditions under which a belief is properly basic (*ibid.,* p. 125).

[12] Plantinga offers a variety of examples to show that coherence is not sufficient for warrant nondefectiveness (in my terms, for justified belief) in "Coherentism and the Evidentialist Objection," pp. 136–37).

[13] The distinction between these two types of justification can be gleaned from what Plantinga says in "Reason and Belief in God," p. 79 and in note 14. The distinction is made more clearly and explicitly by him in several unpublished papers on justification that he handed out at an NEH Summer Institute in Philosophy of Religion in 1986.

[14] Plantinga, "Sidgwick and Reflective Equilibrium," *Monist* 58 (1974):517.

[15] See Warren Quinn, "Truth and Explanation in Ethics," *Ethics* 96, 3(1986):524–44, esp. p. 526; and Gilbert Harman, *The Nature of Morality* (Oxford University Press, 1977), esp. p. 3–23.

[16] For instance, Nicholas Sturgeon, "Moral Explanations," in David Copp and David Zimmerman, eds. *Morality, Reason, and Truth* (Rowman and Allanheld, 1984), pp. 49–78; reprinted in Part IX.4 of this volume.

[17] Bernard Williams, *Ethics and the Limits of Philosophy* (Harvard University Press, 1985), pp. 129 and 140. Parenthetical pagination in the text refers to that book. This material is in Part IX.6 of this book.

[18] Williams in *Ethics and the Limits of Philosophy* cites Robert Nozick's work in *Philosophical Explanations* (Harvard University Press, 1981) in connection with this idea that knowledge must track the truth.

[19] The criticisms I offered of the Nozickian conception of knowledge that Williams accepts are taken from Plantinga's "Justification and Theism," an unpublished paper in which Plantinga criticizes Nozick's epistemological views. Objections like those Plantinga offers were raised by my colleague Michael McKinsey in conversation with me before I had read Plantinga's paper.

[20] Derek Parfit, *Reasons and Persons* (Oxford University Press, 1984), p. 454.

[21] Williams, *op. cit.,* p. 25.

[22] Parfit gives this example in *Reasons and Persons,* pp. 122–25.

[23] See the discussions in this volume by Gauthier and Kavka (Parts X.3 and X.4).

[24] Gauthier indirectly establishes this possibility in Chapter VI of *Morals By Agreement* (Oxford University Press, 1986). He argues that whether it is rational for you to constrain the pursuit of your ends depends on how many others are constraining pursuit of theirs, on how easily you can identify those who are, and on how easily others can identify you if you are not. He thinks that the values of the relevant variables are such as to make it rational to constrain pursuit of individual ends. But this leaves open the possibility that it is not rational to constrain such pursuit, even when most others are. For instance, if you were very clever so that others could not find you out and you did not care about those others, reason would require you to appear to be a "constrained maximizer" while taking advantage of others who really were.

[25] Plantinga suggests in "Coherentism and the Evidentialist Objection" that apparent self-evidence confers positive epistemic status on a belief only because the felt impulsion to believe, produced by the awareness of a self-evident proposition, is the result of a properly functioning cognitive mechanism. In the end he tries to account for foundationalist intuitions through a form of reliabilism, according to which a belief has positive epistemic status just in case it is the result of a properly functioning cognitive faculty operating in an environment for which it is suited.

[26] I am grateful to Keith Burgess-Jackson and Louis Pojman for their comments on and criticisms of an earlier draft of this paper.

Suggestions for Further Reading

Copp, David, and David Zimmerman, eds. *Morality, Reason, and Truth: New Essays on the Foundations of Ethics.* Rowman and Allanheld, 1984.

Darwell, Stephen. *Impartial Reason.* Cornell University Press, 1983.

Gewirth, Alan. *Reason and Morality.* University of Chicago Press, 1978.

Gillispie, Norman, ed. "Moral Realism," *Southern Journal of Philosophy* XXIV, Supplement, 1986. This volume contains an excellent collection of essays on moral realism, including a bibliography on the subject by Geoffrey Sayre-McCord.

Putnam, Hilary. *Reason, Truth, and History.* Cambridge University Press, 1981.

Railton, Peter. "Moral Realism," *Philosophical Review* 95, 1986.

Sayre-McCord, Geoffrey, ed. *Essays in Moral Realism.* Cornell University Press, 1988.

Werner, Richard. "Ethical Realism," *Ethics,* 93, 1983.

Part X

Morality and Self-Interest

One great difficulty must remain unsolved. Rather, I assert that it is intrinsically insoluble. There is no absolute coincidence between virtue and happiness. I cannot prove that it is always prudent to act rightly or that it is always happiest to be virtuous. My inability to prove those propositions arises, as I hold, from the fact that they are not true. This admission does nothing to diminish our belief in the surpassing importance of morality and of its essential connection with social welfare; and further, it does not diminish the intrinsic motives to virtue, inasmuch as those motives are not really based upon prudence. But I cannot go further.

LESLIE STEPHENS
The Science of Ethics, G. P. Putnam's Sons, 1882, p. 434

The Good is good for you.
Statement of Socratic Ethics

"Why should people in general be moral?" and "Why should I be moral?" These two questions should not be confused: the former asks for a justification for the institution of morality, whereas the latter asks for reasons why one personally should be moral, even when it does not appear to be in one's own interest. I once knew a student who cheated his way into medical school. He became a successful physician, a faithful church member, and a wise father. Suppose he even gave . of his largesse to support the institution of mo-

rality. It could still be said that he was not a completely moral man.

Thomas Hobbes's account in the *Leviathan* (Part III.1) offers a plausible justification of morality in general. Without a minimal morality, society is impossible. Without it we exist in a state of nature deprived of common laws, reliable expectations, and security of person and possessions. There is no incentive to mutual trust or cooperation, but only anarchic chaos as egoists try to maximize personal utility. The result is, in

Hobbes's words, a "war of all against all" in which individual life is "solitary, poor, nasty, brutish, and short."

Morality serves as an antidote to this state of nature and allows self-interested individuals to fulfill their needs and desires in a context of peace and cooperation. As such, morality is a mechanism for social control. It is in all of our interests to have a moral system that is generally adhered to, so that we can maximize our individual life plans. Unless there is general adherence to the moral point of view, society will break down.

This may be neither a full picture of morality nor a very inspiring one, but it is certainly part of the picture—the part with which virtually everyone agrees. Whatever more there is to morality and whether it is, as Kant said, "a jewel that shines by its own light," is another matter, one that has to do with a further question about morality.

This further question is, "Why should I be moral?" Why shouldn't I *appear* to be moral and promote morality in society, so that I can profit egoistically from the docility of the stupid public? Paul Taylor calls this the "ultimate question":

> There is one problem of moral philosophy that perhaps deserves, more than any other, to be called the Ultimate Question. It is the question of the rationality of the moral life itself. It may be expressed thus: Is the commitment to live by moral principles a decision grounded or is it in the final analysis, an arbitrary choice? (*Problems of Moral Philosophy*, Dickenson, 1978, p. 483)

The question was first raised over two millennia ago in Plato's dialogue, the *Republic*. Plato's brother, Glaucon, asks whether justice is something that is only a necessary evil. That is, he wants to know whether it is the case that it would be better if we could have complete freedom to indulge ourselves as we will; but since others could do the same, is it better to compromise and limit our acquisitive instincts? Our first reading

in Part X records a dialogue among Plato, Glaucon, their brother Adeimantus, and Socrates. They tell the story of a shepherd named Gyges who comes upon a ring, which at his behest makes him invisible. He uses it to escape the external sanctions of society—its laws and censure—and to serve his greed to the fullest. Glaucon asks whether it is not plausible to suppose that we all would do likewise. Then he offers a thought experiment that compares the life of the seemingly just (but unjust) man who is incredibly successful with the life of the seemingly unjust (but just) man who is incredibly unsuccessful. Which would we choose?

Socrates' answer to Glaucon and Adeimantus is that, in spite of appearances, we should choose the life of the so-called unsuccessful but just person because it is to our advantage to be moral. Socrates' answer depends on a notion of mental health. He contends that immorality corrupts the inner person, so that one is happy or unhappy in exact proportion to one's moral integrity.

In our second reading, Richard Taylor discusses these points at length and attempts to unravel the Socratic dilemma. He contrasts two views of morality (or "justice," as it is referred to in Plato's writings): the Socratic one, in which morality is seen as having objective existence in the nature of things apart from human desire, and the conative (that is, based in the will) one, which views morality as conventional, as a product of human need and desire. The answer to the Socratic dilemma depends on which view of morality is correct. Taylor believes that Socrates' solution to the dilemma is the wrong one, and that in reality the seemingly just (but unjust) person is the happier person.

Others besides Taylor see something puzzling in Socrates' solution, which seems to depend on a view of human nature that is different from our modern notion. Moreover, in many contemporary accounts of moral duty, one only has a duty to do some act A if one has sufficient reason to do A. But this seems to generate a paradox, the paradox of morality and advantage, which goes like this:

1. If it is morally right to do act A, then it must be reasonable to do act A.

2. If morality isn't based on good reasons, it must be delusory.

3. But self-interest is also founded on reason (prudence).

4. But sometimes the requirements of morality are incompatible with the requirements of self-interest.

5. But if morality is to be compelling, it should be in our self-interest.

6. Because morality is not always in our self-interest, one must wonder if it is not simply a delusion, an artifice to keep us in place. If it is a delusion, the rational person will be an egoist and promote morality for everyone else, but violate it whenever he can safely do so.

As David Gauthier puts it, "Morality is a system of principles such that it is advantageous for everyone if everyone accepts and acts on it, yet acting on the system of principles requires that some persons perform disadvantageous acts."

In our third reading, Gauthier uses a version of the Prisoner's Dilemma to show that it may sometimes be in our interest to be immoral. If we're all moral, we'll all do better than if all are prudent, but "any one man will always do better if he is prudent than if he is moral. There is no real paradox in supposing that morality is advantageous even though it requires the performance of disadvantageous acts." This tells us why *we* ought to be moral in general, but it doesn't tell us why *I* should be moral, why I should not act egoistically when it is in my self-interest to do so. Nevertheless, complete commitment to morality, which involves the special qualities of trustworthiness and fairness, may have certain advantages that prudent persons cannot attain, and these advantages are a function of the sacrifices that moral principles impose on their adherents.

In our fourth reading, Gregory Kavka attempts to resolve this paradox and reconcile prudence with morality. Beginning with an analysis of a Hobbesian approach to the problem (one similar to Gauthier's), Kavka argues that this sort of approach, while illuminating and partially correct, "cannot take us far enough" and ultimately is invalid because of its assumption of psychological egoism (compare with Part III of this volume), which assumes that all motivation must be self-interested.

What needs to be added to the Hobbesian picture is an account of internal sanctions, the kind of built-in constraints that are an important part of socialization. If one has been raised in a normal social context, one will feel deep psychic distress at the thought of harming others and deep psychic satisfaction at being moral. For these persons, the combination of internal and external sanctions may well bring prudence and morality close together. But this situation may not apply to persons not brought up in a moral context. Should this dismay us? No, we should not perceive "an immoralist's gloating that it does not pay him to be moral . . . as a victory over us. It is more like the pathetic boast of a deaf person that he saves money because it does not pay him to buy opera records."

Kavka deals with the following objections to his resolution of the paradox: (1) that morality often requires the sacrifice of one's life, and this cannot be in one's interest; (2) that morality requires powerful groups to treat weak groups fairly when it would be in the interest of the powerful to exploit the weak; and (3) that morality requires helping future generations, but there seems to be no self-interested reason to do so. A close examination of Kavka's careful discussion of these issues is rewarding. His conclusion is that "while it is normally prudent to be moral, it is sometimes rational to be moral even if it is not prudent."

The reader may want to read Bruce Russell's essay, "Two Forms of Ethical Skepticism" (Part IX.7), the second part of which discusses skepticism about justifying an answer to this question.

X.1 *Why Be Moral?*

PLATO

Plato (427-347 B.C.) lived in Athens and is the earliest philosopher for which extensive works still remain today. In a series of dialogues he immortalized his teacher, Socrates. Perhaps his greatest dialogue is the *Republic,* from which this reading is taken. The *Republic* is a classic treatise on political philosophy that centers on the concept of justice or moral rightness. In this work Plato, through his idealization of Socrates, argues there will only be justice when reason rules and the people are obedient to its commands. This utopia is possible only in an aristocracy in which the rulers are philosophers — philosopher-kings.

In our selection, Glaucon, who is Plato's older brother, asks Socrates whether justice is good in itself or only a necessary evil. Playing the devil's advocate, he puts forth the hypothesis that egotistic power-seeking, in which we have complete freedom to indulge ourselves, might be the ideal state of existence. However, the hypothesis continues, reason quickly shows us that others might seek the same power, which would interfere with our freedom and cause a state of chaos in which no one was likely to have any of one's desires fulfilled. So we compromise and limit our acquisitive instincts. Justice or a system of morality is simply the result of that compromise. It has no intrinsic value — it is better than chaos, but worse than undisturbed power. It is better to compromise and limit our acquisitive instincts.

To illustrate his point he tells the story of a shepherd named Gyges who comes upon a ring, which at his behest makes him invisible. He uses it to escape the external sanctions of society — its laws and censure — and to serve his greed to the fullest. Glaucon asks whether it is not plausible to suppose that we all would do likewise. Then he offers a thought experiment that compares the life of the seemingly just (but unjust) man who is incredibly successful with the life of the seemingly unjust (but just) man who is incredibly unsuccessful. Which would we choose?

We enter the dialogue in the second book of the *Republic.* Socrates has just shown that the type of egoism advocated by Thrasymachus is contradictory. It is Socrates who is speaking.

With these words I was thinking that I had made an end of the discussion; but the end, in truth, proved to be only a beginning. For Glaucon, who is always the most pugnacious of men, was dissatisfied at Thrasymachus's retirement; he wanted to have the battle out. So he said to me: Socrates, do you wish really to persuade us, or only to seem to have persuaded us, that to be just is always better than to be unjust?

I should wish really to persuade you, I replied, if I could.

Then you certainly have not succeeded. Let me ask you now: — How would you arrange goods — are there not some which we welcome for their own sakes, and independently of their consequences, as, for example, harmless pleasures and enjoyments, which delight us at the time, although nothing follows from them?

Reprinted from *The Dialogues of Plato,* translated by Benjamin Jowett (Charles Scribner's Sons, 1889).

I agree in thinking that there is such a class, I replied.

Is there not also a second class of goods, such as knowledge, sight, health, which are desirable not only in themselves, but also for their results?

Certainly, I said.

And would you not recognize a third class, such as gymnastic, and the care of the sick, and the physician's art; also the various ways of money-making—these do us good but we regard them as disagreeable; and no one would choose them for their own sakes, but only for the sake of some reward or result which flows from them?

There is, I said, this third class also. But why do you ask?

Because I want to know in which of the three classes you would place justice?

In the highest class, I replied, among those goods which he who would be happy desires both for their own sake and for the sake of their results.

Then the many are of another mind; they think that justice is to be reckoned in the troublesome class, among goods which are to be pursued for the sake of rewards and of reputation, but in themselves are disagreeable and rather to be avoided.

I know, I said, that this is their manner of thinking, and that this was the thesis which Thrasymachus was maintaining just now, when he censured justice and praised injustice. But I am too stupid to be convinced by him.

I wish, he said, that you would hear me as well as him, and then I shall see whether you and I agree. For Thrasymachus seems to me, like a snake, to have been charmed by your voice sooner than he ought to have been; but to my mind the nature of justice and injustice have not yet been made clear. Setting aside their rewards and results, I want to know what they are in themselves, and how they inwardly work in the soul. If you please, then, I will revive the argument of Thrasymachus. And first I will speak of the nature and origin of justice according to the common view of them. Secondly, I will show that all men who practice justice do so against their will, of necessity, but not as a good. And thirdly, I will argue that there is reason in this view, for the life of the unjust is after all better far than the life of the just—if what they say is true, Socrates, since I myself am not of their opinion. But still I acknowledge that I am perplexed when I hear the voices of Thrasymachus and myriads of others dinning in my ears; and, on the other hand, I have never yet heard the superiority of justice to injustice maintained by any one in a satisfactory way. I want to hear justice praised in respect of itself; then I shall be satisfied, and you are the person from whom I think that I am most likely to hear this; and therefore I will praise the unjust life to the utmost of my power, and my manner of speaking will indicate the manner in which I desire to hear you too praising justice and censuring injustice. Will you say whether you approve of my proposal?

Indeed I do; nor can I imagine any theme about which a man of sense would oftener wish to converse.

I am delighted, he replied, to hear you say so, and shall begin by speaking, as I proposed, of the nature and origin of justice.

They say that to do injustice is, by nature, good; to suffer injustice, evil; but that the evil is greater than the good. And so when men have both done and suffered injustice and have had experience of both, not being able to avoid the one and obtain the other, they think that they had better agree among themselves to have neither; hence there arise laws and mutual covenants; and that which is ordained by law is termed by them lawful and just. This they affirm to be the origin and nature of justice:—it is a mean or compromise, between the best of all, which is to do injustice and not be punished, and the worst of all, which is to suffer injustice without the power of retaliation; and justice, being at a middle point between the two, is tolerated not as a good, but as the lesser evil, and honoured by reason of the inability of men to do injustice. For no man who is worthy to be called a man would ever submit to such an agreement if he were able to resist; he would be mad if he did. Such is the received account, Socrates, of the nature and origin of justice.

Now that those who practice justice do so involuntarily and because they have not the power to be unjust will best appear if we imagine something of this kind: having given both to the just and the unjust power to do what they will, let us watch and see whither desire will lead them; then we shall discover in the very act the just and unjust man to be proceeding along the same road, following their interest, which all natures deem to be their good, and are only diverted into the path of justice by the force of law. The liberty which we are supposing may be most completely given to them in the form of such a power as is said to have been possessed by Gyges the ancestor of Croesus the Lydian. According to the tradition, Gyges was a shepherd in the service of the king of Lydia; there was a great storm, and an earthquake made an opening in the earth at the place where he was feeding his flock. Amazed at the sight, he descended into the opening, where, among other marvels, he beheld a hollow brazen horse, having doors, at which he stooping and looking in saw a dead body of stature, as appeared to him, more than human, and having nothing on but a gold ring; this he took from the finger of the dead and reascended. Now the shepherds met together, according to custom, that they might send their monthly report about the flocks to the king; into their assembly he came having the ring on his finger, and as he was sitting among them he chanced to turn the collet of the ring inside his hand, when instantly he became invisible to the rest of the company and they began to speak of him as if he were no longer present. He was astonished at this, and again touching the ring he turned the collet outwards and reappeared; he made several trials of the ring, and always with the same result — when he turned the collet inwards he became invisible, when outwards he reappeared. Whereupon he contrived to be chosen one of the messengers who were sent to the court; where as soon as he arrived he seduced the queen, and with her help conspired against the king and slew him, and took the kingdom. Suppose now that there were two such magic rings, and the just put on one of them and the unjust the other; no man can be imagined to be of such an iron nature that he would stand fast in justice. No man would keep his hands off what was not his own when he could safely take what he liked out of the market, or go into houses and lie with any one at his pleasure, or kill or release from prison whom he would, and in all respects be like a God among men. Then the actions of the just would be as the actions of the unjust; they would both come at last to the same point. And this we may truly affirm to be a great proof that a man is just, not willingly or because he thinks that justice is any good to him individually, but of necessity, for wherever any one thinks that he can safely be unjust, there he is unjust. For all men believe in their hearts that injustice is far more profitable to the individual than justice, and he who argues as I have been supposing, will say that they are right. If you could imagine any one obtaining this power of becoming invisible, and never doing any wrong or touching what was another's, he would be

thought by the lookers-on to be a most wretched idiot, although they would praise him to one another's faces, and keep up appearances with one another from a fear that they too might suffer injustice. Enough of this.

Now, if we are to form a real judgment of the life of the just and unjust, we must isolate them; there is no other way; and how is the isolation to be effected? I answer: Let the unjust man be entirely unjust, and the just man entirely just; nothing is to be taken away from either of them, and both are to be perfectly furnished for the work of their respective lives. First, let the unjust be like other distinguished masters of craft; like the skillful pilot or physician, who knows intuitively his own powers and keeps within their limits, and who, if he fails at any point, is able to recover himself. So let the unjust make his unjust attempts in the right way, and lie hidden if he means to be great in his injustice (he who is found out is nobody): for the highest reach of injustice is: to be deemed just when you are not. Therefore I say that in the perfectly unjust man we must assume the most perfect injustice; there is to be no deduction, but we must allow him, while doing the most unjust acts, to have acquired the greatest reputation for justice. If he have taken a false step he must be able to recover himself; he must be one who can speak with effect, if any of his deeds come to light, and who can force his way where force is required by his courage and strength, and command of money and friends. And at his side let us place the just man in his nobleness and simplicity, wishing, as Aeschylus says, to be and not to seem good. There must be no seeming, for if he seem to be just he will be honoured and rewarded, and then we shall not know whether he is just for the sake of justice or for the sake of honours and rewards; therefore, let him be clothed in justice only, and have no other covering; and he must be imagined in a state of life the opposite of the former. Let him be the best of men, and let him be thought the worst; then he will have been put to the proof; and we shall see whether he will be affected by the fear of infamy and its consequences. And let him continue thus to the hour of death; being just and seeming to be unjust. When both have reached the uttermost extreme, the one of justice and the other of injustice, let judgment be given which of them is the happier of the two.

Heavens! my dear Glaucon, I said, how energetically you polish them up for the decision, first one and then the other, as if they were two statues.

I do my best, he said. And now that we know what they are like there is no difficulty in tracing out the sort of life which awaits either of them. This I will proceed to describe; but as you may think the description a little too coarse, I ask you to suppose, Socrates, that the words which follow are not mine. — Let me put them into the mouths of the eulogists of injustice: they will tell you that the just man who is thought unjust will be scourged, racked, bound — will have his eyes burnt out; and, at last, after suffering every kind of evil, he will be impaled: Then he will understand that he ought to seem only, and not to be, just; the words of Aeschylus may be more truly spoken of the unjust than of the just. For the unjust is pursuing a reality; he does not live with a view to appearances — he wants to be really unjust and not to seem only: —

His mind has a soil deep and fertile.
Out of which spring his prudent counsels.[1]

In the first place, he is thought just, and therefore bears rule in the city; he can marry whom he will, and give in marriage to whom he will; also he can trade and deal where he likes, and always to his own advantage, because he has no misgivings about injustice; and at every contest, whether in public or private, he gets the better of his antagonists, and gains at their expense, and is rich, and out of his gains he can benefit his friends, and harm his enemies; moreover, he can offer sacrifices, and dedicate gifts to the gods abundantly and magnificently, and can honour the gods or any man whom he wants to honour in a far better style than the just, and therefore he is likely to be dearer than they are to the gods. And thus, Socrates, gods and men are said to unite in making the life of the unjust better than the life of the just.

I was going to say something in answer to Glaucon, when Adeimantus, his brother, interposed: Socrates, he said, you do not suppose that there is nothing more to be urged?

Why, what else is there? I answered.

The strongest point of all has not been even mentioned, he replied.

Well, then, according to the proverb, 'Let brother help brother' — if he fails in any part do you assist him; although I must confess that Glaucon has already said quite enough to lay me in the dust, and take from me the power of helping justice.

Nonsense, he replied. But let me add something more: There is another side to Glaucon's argument about the praise and censure of justice and injustice, which is equally required in order to bring out what I believe to be his meaning. Parents and tutors are always telling their sons and their wards that they are to be just; but why? not for the sake of justice, but for the sake of character and reputation; in the hope of obtaining for him who is reputed just some of those offices, marriages, and the like which Glaucon has enumerated among the advantages accruing to the unjust from the reputation of justice. More, however, is made of appearances by this class of persons than by the others; for they throw in the good opinion of the gods, and will tell you of a shower of benefits which the heavens, as they say, rain upon the pious; and this accords with the testimony of the noble Hesiod and Homer, the first of whom says, that the gods make the oaks of the just —

To bear acorns at their summit, and bees in the middle;
And the sheep are bowed down with the weight of their fleeces.[2]

and any other blessings of a like kind are provided for them. And Homer has a very similar strain; for he speaks of one whose fame is —

As the fame of some blameless king who, like a god,
Maintains justice; to whom the black earth brings forth
Wheat and barley, whose trees are bowed with fruit,
And his sheep never fail to bear, and the sea gives him fish.[3]

Still grander are the gifts of heaven which Musaeus and his son[4] vouchsafe to the just; they take them down into the world below, where they have the saints lying on couches at a feast, everlastingly drunk, crowned with garlands; their idea seems to be that an immortality of drunkenness is the highest meed of virtue. Some extend their rewards yet further; the posterity, as they say, of the faithful and just shall survive to the third and fourth generation. This is the style in which they praise justice. But about the wicked there is another strain; they bury them in a slough in Hades, and make them carry water in a sieve; also while they are yet living they bring them to infamy, and inflict upon them the punishments which Glaucon described as the portion of the just who are reputed to be unjust; nothing else does their invention supply. Such is their manner of praising the one and censuring the other.

Once more, Socrates, I will ask you to consider another way of speaking about justice and injustice, which is not confined to the poets, but is found in prose writers. The universal voice of mankind is always declaring that justice and virtue are honourable, but grievous and toilsome; and that the pleasures of vice and injustice are easy of attainment, and are only censured by law and opinion. They say also that honesty is for the most part less profitable than dishonesty; and they are quite ready to call wicked men happy, and to honour them both in public and private when they are rich or in any other way influential, while they despise and overlook those who may be weak and poor, even though acknowledging them to be better than the others. But most extraordinary of all is their mode of speaking about virtue and the gods: they say that the gods apportion calamity and misery to many good men, and good and happiness to the wicked. And mendicant prophets go to rich men's doors and persuade them that they have a power committed to them by the gods of making an atonement for a man's own or his ancestor's sins by sacrifices or charms, with rejoicings and feasts; and they promise to harm an enemy, whether just or unjust, at a small cost; with magic arts and incantations binding heaven, as they say, to execute their will. And the poets are the authorities to whom they appeal, now smoothing the path of vice with words of Hesiod: —

Vice may be had in abundance without trouble; the way is smooth and her dwelling-place is near. But before virtue the gods have set toil,[5]

and a tedious and uphill road: then citing Homer as a witness that the gods may be influenced by men; for he also says: —

The gods, too, may be turned from their purpose; and men pray to them and avert their wrath by sacrifices and soothing entreaties, and by libations and the odour of fat, when they have sinned and transgressed.[6]

And they produce a host of books written by Musaeus and Orpheus, who were children of the Moon and the Muses — that is what they say — according to which they perform their ritual, and persuade not only individuals, but whole cities, that expiations and atonements for sin may be made by sacrifices and amusements which fill a vacant hour, and are equally at the service of the living and the dead; the latter sort they call mysteries, and they redeem us from the pains of hell, but if we neglect them no one knows what awaits us.

He proceeded: And now when the young hear all this said about virtue and vice, and the way in which gods and men regard them, how are their minds likely to be affected, my dear Socrates, — those of them, I mean, who are quickwitted, and, like bees on the wing, light on every flower, and from all that they hear are prone to draw conclusions as to what manner of persons they should be and in what way they should walk if they would make the best of life? Probably the youth will say to himself in the words of Pindar —

Can I by justice or by crooked ways of deceit ascend a loftier tower which may be a fortress to me all my days?

For what men say is that, if I am really just and am not also thought just, profit there is none, but the pain and loss on the other hand are unmistakable. But if, though unjust, I acquire the reputation of justice, a heavenly life is promised to me. Since then, as philosophers prove, appearance tyrannizes over truth and is lord of happiness, to appearance I must devote myself. I will describe around me a picture and shadow of virtue to be the vestibule and exterior of my house; behind I will trail the subtle and crafty fox, as Archilochus, greatest of sages, recommends. But I hear some one exclaiming that the concealment of wickedness is often difficult; to which I answer, Nothing great is easy. Nevertheless, the argument indicates this, if we would be happy, to be the path along which we should proceed. With a view to concealment we will establish secret brotherhoods and political clubs. And there are professors of rhetoric who teach the art of persuading courts and assemblies; and so, partly by persuasion and partly by force, I shall make unlawful gains and not be punished. Still I hear a voice saying that the gods cannot be deceived, neither can they be compelled. But what if there are no gods? or, suppose them to have no care of human things — why in either case should we mind about concealment? And even if there are gods, and they do care about us, yet we know of them only from tradition and the genealogies of the poets; and these are the very persons who say that they may be influenced and turned by 'sacrifices and soothing entreaties and by offerings.' Let us be consistent then, and believe both or neither. If the poets speak truly, why then we had better be unjust, and offer of the fruits of injustice; for if we are just, although we may escape the vengeance of heaven, we shall lose the gains of injustice; but, if we are unjust, we shall keep the gains, and by our sinning and praying, and praying and sinning, the gods will be propitiated, and we shall not be punished. 'But there is a world below in which either we or our posterity will suffer for our unjust deeds.' Yes, my friend, will be the reflection, but there are mysteries and atoning deities, and these have great power. That is what mighty cities declare; and the children of the gods, who were their poets and prophets, bear a like testimony.

On what principle, then, shall we any longer choose justice rather than the worst injustice? When, if we only unite the latter with a deceitful regard to appearances, we shall fare to our mind both with gods and men, in life and after death, as the most numerous and the highest authorities tell us. Knowing all this, Socrates, how can a man who has any superiority of mind or person or rank or wealth, be willing to honour justice; or indeed to refrain from laughing when he hears justice praised? And even if there should be some one who is able to disprove the truth of my words, and who is satisfied that justice is best, still he is not angry with the unjust, but is very ready to forgive them, because he also knows that men are not just of their own free will; unless, peradventure, there be some whom the divinity within him may have inspired with a hatred of injustice, or who has attained knowledge of the truth — but no other man. He only blames injustice who, owing to cowardice or age or some weakness, has not the power of being unjust. And this is proved by the fact that when he obtains the power, he immediately becomes unjust as far as he can be.

The cause of all this, Socrates, was indicated by us at the beginning of the argument, when my brother and I told you how astonished we were to find that of all the professing panegyrists of justice — beginning with the ancient heroes of whom any memorial has been preserved to us, and ending with the men of our own time — no one has ever blamed injustice or praised justice except with a view to the glories, honours, and benefits which flow from them. No one has ever adequately described either in verse or prose the true essential nature of either of them abiding in the soul, and invisible to any human or divine eye; or shown that of all the things of a man's soul which he has within him, justice is the greatest good, and injustice the greatest evil. Had this been the universal strain, had you sought to persuade us of this from our youth upwards, we should not have been on the watch to keep one another from doing wrong, but every one would have been his own watchman, because afraid, if he did wrong, of harbouring in himself the greatest of evils. I dare say that Thrasymachus and others would seriously hold the language which I have been merely repeating, and words even stronger than these about justice and injustice, grossly, as I conceive, perverting their true nature. But I speak in this vehement manner, as I must frankly confess to you, because I want to hear from you the opposite side; and I would ask you to show not only the superiority which justice has over injustice, but what effect they have on the possessor of them which makes the one to be a good and the other an evil to him. And please, as Glaucon requested of you, to exclude reputations; for unless you take away from each of them his true reputation and add on the false, we shall say that you do not praise justice, but the appearance of it; we shall think that you are only exhorting us to keep injustice dark, and that you really agree with Thrasymachus in thinking that justice is another's good and the interest of the stronger, and that injustice is a man's own profit and interest, though injurious to the weaker. Now as you have admitted that justice is one of that highest class of goods which are desired indeed for their results, but in a far greater degree for their own sakes — like sight or hearing or knowledge or health, or any other real and natural and not merely conventional good — I would ask you in your praise of justice to regard one point only: I mean the essential good and evil which justice and injustice work in the possessors of them. Let others praise justice and censure injustice, magnifying the rewards and honours of the one and abusing the other; that is a manner of arguing which, coming from them, I am ready to tolerate, but from you who have spent your whole life in the consideration of this question, unless I hear the contrary from your own lips, I expect something better. And therefore, I say, not only prove to us that justice is better than injustice, but show what they either of them do to the possessor of them, which makes the one to be a good and the other an evil, whether seen or unseen by gods and men.

Endnotes

[1] *Seven Against Thebes*, 574.

[2] Hesiod, *Works and Days*, 230.

[3] Homer, *Od.* xix. 109.

[4] Eumolpus.

[5] Hesiod, *Works and Days*, 287.

[6] Homer, *Iliad*, ix. 493.

X.2 *On the Socratic Dilemma*

RICHARD TAYLOR

Until his recent retirement, Richard Taylor was professor of philosophy at Rochester University, and he is the author of several works on ethical issues, including *Good and Evil,* from which this selection is taken. Taylor takes up the dilemma presented by Glaucon in the *Republic* and tries to unravel it. He argues that Socrates' mistake is that he supposed that there is such a thing as justice (or goodness) *by nature,* rather than seeing that those concepts are relative to ordinary human feelings, needs, and desires. As such, the dilemma dissolves in favor of the man who has reached his goals.

The entire Socratic system rests on a presupposition, never really proved, that there is such a thing as natural justice or virtue, and that it is something good, not merely as a means to good things, but for its own sake. This claim is loaded with significance, and whether one accepts or rejects it will probably determine, more than anything else, his whole outlook on morality.

The Test

What is basically at issue here can be aptly illustrated with an experiment in the imagination suggested by, and in fact in its essentials the same as, one propounded by Socrates in Plato's *Republic*. The experiment is as follows.

Imagine two men, Mr. Adam and Mr. Brown — or, for short, A and B. Now, in your imagination, endow A with every virtue, and B with every vice. We suppose, for example, that A is honest and considerate of others, truthful in his dealings with them, that he is kind, modest, courageous when courage is called for, temperate in his indulgence of pleasures, and so on. We suppose, in short, that this man, A, is the paragon of moral excellence, in whatever we consider moral excellence to consist. Next, endow B with all the opposite qualities. B, we thus suppose, is dishonest and disregardful of others, mendacious in his dealings with his fellow, whenever this appears to him advantageous, cruel, vain, cowardly, and insatiable in his cravings of pleasures and possessions. We suppose, in short, that B is a model of moral corruption, a thief and murderer bound by no restraints whatever.

Let us suppose next, however, that each of these men is universally believed to be the opposite of what he in fact is. That is, A, even though he is the model of moral goodness, is erroneously believed

From *Good and Evil* (Macmillan, 1970). Reprinted by permission of Prometheus Books.

by everyone to be totally corrupt—to possess, that is, the very qualities that are in fact possessed by B; and B, in turn, even though he is the arch criminal and the exemplar of moral corruption, is erroneously believed by all to be the model of virtue—to possess, that is, the very qualities that are in fact possessed by A. Everyone has, in short, a total misconception of the character of each of these men.

What we are here imagining is not, it should be noted, entirely absurd, although it is admittedly not easy to see how such total misconceptions could ever really prevail for very long. If we admit, as all men must, that people are not always what they appear to be, then we must admit that it is at least possible that the contrast between what a man really is and what others think he is might be as complete as we are now imagining in the cases of A and B. Indeed, we know that good men have sometimes been put to death by others who erroneously thought they were wicked (Jesus is perhaps an example), and wicked men have gone to their graves with everyone singing their praises, never suspecting the baseness of their inner characters. In the examples we have imagined we are only supposing that this contrast between what a man is and what he appears to others to be is total and complete, and that the misconceptions are never discovered.

Continuing our imaginative experiment, then, we next suppose that each of these men, A and B, receives from his society the desert appropriate to what he is thought by that society to be. Thus, A, the good man, languishes in jail, with roaches and rats for his companions, and water and bread for his food. He dwells in dirt, and is spat on by his fellows, until eventually he is mercifully hanged. Why? Just because, as they suppose, he is wicked and evil, a thief and murderer, deserving of nothing else. He knows, of course, that he is none of these things, and is in fact the opposite, but his own witness to his character is not of much avail to him in these baneful circumstances.

The real thief and murderer, B, on the other hand (who has always managed to cover his tracks and conceal his true nature), walks through the world bathed in glory and leaving in his wake the admiration and praise of everyone. Medals are struck in his honor, public places inscribed with his name, and the highest offices thrust upon him—all of which tributes he exploits, of course, to further his own greedy ends, conveying always the false impression that his deepest interest is service to the public good. Parents point him out to their children as an object of emulation, and all vie for his approval. When he finally dies, full of years and loaded with honors, he receives a state funeral and the tribute of all who have heard his name. And why does he receive this enviable treatment at the hands of all? Simply because, as it seems to them, he clearly deserves it, considering his greatness, his goodness, and his devotion to the well-being of all. He of course knew otherwise, but nothing required him to correct the universally held misconception of himself that he had so skillfully created and he had, of course, every inducement to perpetuate it.

Now, with these two pictures before us, let us ask: Which of these two men is better off? One can find, in his answer to that straightforward question, the clearest indication of whether or not he really embraces the Socratic ethics. Our first man, A, possesses genuine moral goodness and the true beauty of a harmonious and well-governed inner life. He lacks only the usual consequences and rewards of such goodness. Our other man, B, possesses all the usual rewards of goodness and greatness, although he is really devoid of either, and his inner life is entirely base and corrupt. Which man, then, has what is truly worth having? Which has made his life really worthwhile? And if a wise man were given the choice between these two lives, with no third alternative offered, which, in the light of his wisdom, should he choose?

It will not do at this point to say that the situation just portrayed in imagination would not be likely ever to exist in fact. It will not do to say that our man B, for example, would surely be found out sooner or later and his rewards replaced with their opposites, nor will it do to insist that A's true nature, and the misconceptions that all have entertained concerning him, must surely be discovered before he is hanged and the injustices to him corrected and compensated. This would simply be cheating and refusing to face the challenge that the examples contain. It is not presupposed that situations like these often arise in the world, or even, that they ever arise. It is only claimed that it is possible, that things could happen this way, whether they ever do or not. And then our question is a fair one: suppose there *were* these two men, A and B, whose inner and outer lives were precisely as we have described them, which is the better life? Which man has the most, or is lacking least, of what an intelligent man, knowing the true worth of things, would want for himself?

The first man A, it is obvious, has nothing of any worth except real justice — provided, of course, that there is such a thing as justice. One could point to nothing else in his life as a thing of value. The dirt, the bugs, the obloquy, and the final pain of the gallows, cannot possibly be represented as things to be sought by anyone. Still, he *is* in fact, if not in appearance, a good and just man, provided such goodness and justice are something real and not just words that stand for nothing existing in nature. Man B, on the other hand, possesses everything that men seek — except, of course, justice or goodness. The honor, reward, praise, and esteem that he enjoys, his power, and his wealth can hardly be represented as things that men shun as evils. Still, he does utterly lack, in fact if not in appearance, justice and goodness, provided there really are such things as justice and goodness, and that these are not just philosophical abstractions.

Now if one supposes, with Socrates, that justice is something real, something that exists by nature and not just a conventional thing invented by men for the attainment of certain practical advantages, and that such justice is worth possessing for its own sake and not just for its consequences or rewards, then one cannot avoid saying that A is *better off* than B. For A, no matter what else he may lack — and he of course lacks everything else — does possess this, and this, according to Socrates, is worth possessing at *all* cost and sacrifice. If one further identifies such justice with a certain kind of harmonious inner life, an inner life wherein one's desires are under the governance of reason and intelligence, then one will affirm the same answer. For A does possess that inner life, he knows that there exist no real grounds for reproaching him, and nothing that men can do to him or to the externals of his life can divest him of that justice.

If, on the other hand, one supposes that justice is only a conventional thing, a set of practices and precepts invented by men for the achievement of certain desired results, then one can hardly avoid saying that B is better off. Indeed, his position is enviable beyond comparison, for he has all the rewards of justice without having to pay any of the price of a just life. He has all of the rewards of crime and none of the cost of it. He is, to be sure, bereft of justice, but in case there is no such thing as genuine justice, in case this is merely a concept of convention and not one of nature, then it follows that, by lack-

ing this, he lacks nothing real. And if, furthermore, the rational pursuit of what is by nature good, and the subordination of passion and desire to this rational end, is not something good for its own sake — in case, for example, there is no such natural good — then B, lacking this, again lacks nothing real. His reason and intelligence are subordinated to his desires, and as a result his desires are abundantly fulfilled. If, in view of all this, one concludes that B is better off, or even that his life is in the slightest to be preferred to A's life, then one can no longer pretend to give any credit to the ethics of Socrates. One cannot have it both ways. One cannot in sincerity nod approval of Socrates's highsounding theme, and at the same time give the slightest preference to the life and fate of Mr. B. And on the other hand, if one finds anything to be said in favor of A's life and fate, then he will find it very difficult to avoid the conclusions to which Socrates wants to lead him. For there is only one thing of any worth that A can possibly be said to possess, and that is justice. And because it is a justice that bears no fruit at all, and is insufficient to deflect any pain and misery to its possessor, it must be a natural justice, a kind of justice that contains its whole worth within itself, and not the kind of justice that is merely a tool for the attainment of certain desired ends.

It is doubtful whether many philosophers have faced this basic problem of ethics in terms of the contrast just illustrated. Most men seem to prefer to extol the idea of a true or natural justice, as opposed to a merely man-made justice, without considering what they are really committed to by such an idea. Plato faced the question quite clearly. Indeed, the imaginative experiment just elicited was probably his own invention, although he represents Socrates as its author in the *Republic*. In any case, justice was represented by Plato as a quality that could, at least imperfectly, be exemplified in societies, institutions, and laws, as well as in men. What Plato never seems to have doubted is that there is such a thing as true justice, that it is something that is not made by men, but something that can be discovered by men. At his hands it became detached from the physical world, which was reduced in his philosophy to a kind of shadow existence. Pure justice came to be thought of as something accessible only to the highest reaches of philosophical penetration, and he thought that the knowledge of it was the highest aspiration any man could set for himself. This thought has persisted, at least as a sentiment, for men still speak of justice and of moral goodness generally with a certain awe and reverence. It is, moreover, thought to be somewhat degrading to this noble idea to suggest that it might be a mere contrivance of men, something that is quite variable from one time and place to another, and something humanly fabricated for nothing more pretentious than the furtherance of certain utterly practical aims of social life.

Is There a Natural Justice?

Let us, then, face the question: Is there any such thing as justice, as it is typically represented in Socratic ethics? We can grant at once that there is such a thing as mental health, that men who possess it are in one clear sense good and those who lack it — who are, in contemporary terms, "mixed up" — are lacking in something of great value. But this is not what we are asking. This is, in my opinion, the most valuable contribution to ethics that Socrates made; that is, his identification of moral goodness with certain perfectly natural characteristics and relations of a man's inner life. But it is not the one that has endured. Most philosophers and moralists regard these as purely psychological observations, and rather archaic ones at that, having really nothing to do with philosophical ethics. I profoundly disagree with this appraisal, but because the Socratic reduction of morals to psychology is not the part of Socratic ethics that has endured in philosophical literature, it is not the aspect of Socratic ethics on which I shall dwell.

I want to consider only whether there is such a thing as justice, *by nature;* that is, whether the distinction between good and evil is, as Socrates always presupposed, a natural distinction rather than one that is drawn by men and is relative to ordinary human feelings, needs, and desires. Socrates thought that there is such a thing, and that it exists by nature and not by human contrivance or invention. By this he did not mean that justice is something automatically *produced* by nature — there is nothing automatic about a just man or a just government, for example — but that the justice or moral goodness of anything possessing it is an objective property of it

whose nature can be discerned by reason, that is, by philosophy. If there is a genuine justice or a genuine moral good independent of human invention, then all the seemingly paradoxical conclusions that Socrates drew do follow quite inevitably. He was, moreover, quite right in maintaining that philosophy is the most important endeavor a man can undertake, that philosophers ought to be honored above all other men, even though they might sometimes, as Socrates often did, make all those about them feel like wretched fools. For if there is such a thing as pure justice or pure moral goodness, and if philosophy is the only road to the discovery of it, then surely everything else is of subordinate importance. And if, moreover, no man ever pursues an unjust or immoral end except through ignorance, then it is of the greatest possible importance to each individual man to know what the true good is, or in other words, to pursue the philosophical life. He can neglect it only at his own peril.

But suppose we consider an alternative approach. Consider, first, that human nature is — as Socrates himself maintained — a combination of reason, or intelligence, and desire, or what I would prefer to call the will. That is to say, we not only discover, by reason and intelligence, that certain things are so; we also will that certain things should be other than they are. This is but another way of saying that human beings *pursue ends,* that they try to bring about certain states through their efforts. Thus, to take a humble example, a man might be exceedingly poor. By his intelligence he can understand that this is so. It is the fact that is given to him. But he is not apt to like the fact; we can suppose that he wants to be rich, or at least delivered from poverty. There is his end or goal, something that is *not* simply given to his intelligence, because it is a state of affairs that does not even exist and may never exist. It is an end or goal that is projected by his will; it is what he wills should be so, although in fact it is not so.

This model of human nature, then, as an amalgam of intelligence and will, yields an elementary distinction between *what is* and *what ought to be.* By our reason and intelligence, drawing from the testimony of our senses, we discover what is, but what *ought* to be is the declaration of the will. This is to say that what ought to be is a desideratum, the object of desire, or simply what is wanted by this or that man, by some group of men, or perhaps by all men. Thus, one can form in his mind a more or less accurate conception of things as they are. This is simply understanding, or the apprehension of truth, which is sometimes accurate and clear and at other times vague and inaccurate and infected with error. Along with such a conception of things as they are, one can form another conception of things as they should be. This simply means things as he would have them, things as he would want them to be. At this level, this quite clearly has nothing to do with understanding or the apprehension of truth. It has rather to do with the will. One finds that the world, or some large or small part of it, is such and such; he wills that it should be otherwise; and this latter finds expression by his declaring that something, which does not exist, ought to exist. Or one perhaps finds that the world, or some large or small part of it, is such and such, and he wills that it should be precisely so. That is, he finds that the world or some part of it, as it is, is precisely such as to promise fulfillment of his aims and aspirations. In that case he declares that what is — the world as he finds it — is what ought to be. In either case, it is clear that one's declaration of what ought to be is the expression not of his reason or intelligence, but of his will — that is, of his desires, aims, and aspirations, whatever these might be.

One can from this same point of view see how the distinction between good and evil arises. Men do not look out at the world and at human practices and institutions and simply find that, among other things, some are good, some bad, and some a mixture of both. This is simply superficial. Nor does a man of great intellect and rational penetration manage to make these distinctions any better. Good and evil are not, as Socrates sometimes thought, elusive or deeply hidden properties of things that only a philosopher can hope to discern. The reason they are so hard to discern, even by a philosopher, is apparently that they are not qualities of things at all, just considered by themselves and independent of human needs and feelings. Men pronounce things good to the extent that those things appear to promise satisfaction of their needs or the fulfillment of their aims and goals, whatever these might be. They pronounce things bad to the extent that they appear threatening, either as obstacles to what we happen to want, or as sources of just what we do not want. The distinction between good and evil is therefore relative to goals, ends, and wants — in a word, to the will — and has no meaning except in relation to this. To convince oneself of this, one needs only to consider how such a distinction could ever even arise for a race of beings entirely devoid of will, whatever might be their endowments of reason and intelligence. Such a race of beings would have no ends and goals, no aspirations, would want nothing, and would shun nothing. How, then, could they pronounce some things good and others bad? How, indeed, could they even form an understanding of such a distinction? Everything, it would seem, would be on a dead level for such beings, nothing would offer any promise, and nothing any threat, for they would have no aims for which promise of fulfillment or threat of frustration would have any bearing.

Looking at things in this light, one can at once see both the truth and the error in Socrates' contention that no man voluntarily pursues evil or does injustice. Socrates evidently regarded this as a significant and somewhat surprising philosophical insight, filled with implications for ethics, and many since him have struggled to reconcile what appears so paradoxical in it with what at the same time appears quite impeccably true. Socrates, as we have seen, inferred from this thesis that all wrongdoing must be the product of ignorance, and forthwith concluded that the kind of ignorance involved must be ignorance of what is really good. This is in a sense true, but not in the sense that the good of which the wrongdoer is ignorant is some good existing by nature and independently of his own wants and needs. Thus, if we consider again the thirsty traveler who comes to a well and wants to drink from it, not knowing that it is poisoned, we can indeed say that his undertaking *that* immediate end is a product of his ignorance. He does not know that the well is poisoned, and that drinking from it would therefore be something bad. But this quite clearly presupposes that he wants to live, that he therefore does not want to be poisoned. The poisonous character of the well is not bad, considered by itself; it is bad only in relation to the fact that the man's desire to live greatly outweighs his desire to drink, however thirsty he might be. Good and evil, in this simple example, are quite clearly relative to a man's needs — that is, to his aims and purposes — and in isolation from these have no significance at all.

So when Socrates said that no man can voluntarily pursue an end that is evil, knowing that it is evil, he was quite right, but not in the sense that these words first suggest. The claim must not be understood to mean that any man, knowing what is good, must seek it, or that a wise man cannot fail to be just, and so on, for that is plainly contrary to what everyone knows to be true. All that the claim means, really, is that men do pursue goals, that they want to attain certain things by their actions; in short, that they want to achieve those ends that they do in fact want—and this is a trivial truth, a mere tautology. For if the good, for this or that man, is simply the object of his desire or will, then we are told nothing on being told that every man seeks the good—in other words, that every man desires that which he desires—and that one can fail to desire the good only from ignorance. Such ignorance is not ignorance of whether something is or is not in fact good, for good and evil are not, by themselves, facts to begin with. The kind of ignorance in question can be only an ignorance of certain real features of a situation that, if known, would affect one's desires with respect to it.

The philosophical theory underlying the foregoing remarks is, of course, very superficial as presented, and it would not take much acumen to riddle it with difficulties. No attempt will be made at this point to develop it, however, for my purpose has only been to suggest that there are alternatives to the Socratic conception of ethics and, in particular, to the idea that good and evil must be natural and not merely conventional things or, as some would now express it, that good and evil must be "objective." What is true by nature, I shall maintain as we get more deeply into the subject, is that men do have needs and desires, that they are desiderative or goal-seeking creatures. I have found it convenient to express this conception of human nature by saying that men are *conative* beings. Such a conception does not by itself make anything good or evil by nature, but it nevertheless provides the natural foundation for the distinction between good and evil and, indeed, for every moral distinction.

X.3 *Morality and Advantage*

DAVID GAUTHIER

David Gauthier is professor of philosophy at the University of Pittsburgh and the author of several works in ethics, including *Morality by Agreement*. In this article he examines the relationship of morality to prudence and advantage. Morality, if generally adhered to, leads to everyone's advantage but requires that some persons perform disadvantageous acts.

Gauthier uses a version of the Prisoner's Dilemma to show that it may sometimes be in our interest to be immoral. If we're all moral, we'll all do better than if we all are prudent, but "any one man will always do better if he is prudent than if he is moral. There is no real paradox in supposing that morality is advantageous even though it requires the performance of disadvantageous acts." This tells us why *we* ought to be moral in general, but it doesn't tell us why *I* should be moral, why I should not act egoistically when it is in my self-interest to do so. Nevertheless, complete commitment to morality, which involves the special qualities of trustworthiness and fairness, may have certain advantages that prudent persons cannot attain and that these advantages are a function of the sacrifices that moral principles impose on their adherents.

I

Hume asks, rhetorically, "what theory of morals can ever serve any useful purpose, unless it can show, by a particular detail, that all the duties which it recommends, are also the true interest of each individual?"[1] But there are many to whom this question does not seem rhetorical. Why, they ask, do we speak the language of morality, impressing upon our fellows their duties and obligations, urging them with appeals to what is right and good, if we could speak to the same effect in the language of prudence, appealing to considerations of interest and advantage? When the poet, Ogden Nash, is moved by the muse to cry out:

> O Duty,
> Why hast thou not the visage of a sweetie
> or a cutie?[2]

Reprinted with permission from *Philosophical Review* 76 (1967): 460-75.

we do not anticipate the reply:

> O Poet,
> I really am a cutie and I think you ought to
> know it.

The belief that duty cannot be reduced to interest, or that morality may require the agent to subordinate all considerations of advantage, is one which has withstood the assaults of contrary-minded philosophers from Plato to the present. Indeed, were it not for the conviction that only interest and advantage can motivate human actions, it would be difficult to understand philosophers contending so vigorously for the identity, or at least compatibility, of morality with prudence.

Yet if morality is not true prudence it would be wrong to suppose that those philosophers who have sought some connection between morality and advantage have been merely misguided. For it is a truism that we should all expect to be worse off if men were to substitute prudence, even of the most enlightened kind, for morality in all of their deliberations. And this truism demands not only some connection between morality and advantage, but a seemingly paradoxical connection. For if we should all expect to suffer, were men to be prudent instead of moral, then morality must contribute to advantage in a unique way, a way in which prudence — following reasons of advantage — cannot.

Thomas Hobbes is perhaps the first philosopher who tried to develop this seemingly paradoxical connection between morality and advantage. But since he could not admit that a man might ever reasonably subordinate considerations of advantage to the dictates of obligation, he was led to deny the possibility of real conflict between morality and prudence. So his argument fails to clarify the distinction between the view that claims of obligation reduce to considerations of interest and the view that claims of obligation promote advantage in a way in which considerations of interest cannot.

More recently, Kurt Baier has argued that "being moral is following rules designed to overrule self-interest whenever it is in the interest of everyone alike that everyone should set aside his interest."[3] Since prudence is following rules of (enlightened) self-interest, Baier is arguing that morality is designed to overrule prudence when it is to everyone's advantage that it do so — or, in other words, that morality contributes to advantage in a way in which prudence cannot.[4]

Baier does not actually demonstrate that morality contributes to advantage in this unique and seemingly paradoxical way. Indeed, he does not ask how it is possible that morality should do this. It is this possibility which I propose to demonstrate.

II

Let us examine the following proposition, which will be referred to as "the thesis": *Morality is a system of principles such that it is advantageous for everyone if everyone accepts and acts on it, yet acting on the system of principles requires that some persons perform disadvantageous acts.*

What I wish to show is that this thesis *could be true,* that morality could possess those characteristics attributed to it by the thesis. I shall not try to

show that the thesis is true — indeed, I shall argue in Section V that it presents at best an inadequate conception of morality. But it is plausible to suppose that a modified form of the thesis states a necessary, although not a sufficient, condition for a moral system.

Two phrases in the thesis require elucidation. The first is "advantageous for everyone." I use this phrase to mean that *each* person will do better if the system is accepted and acted on than if *either* no system is accepted and acted on *or* a system is accepted and acted on which is similar, save that it never requires any person to perform disadvantageous acts.

Clearly, then, the claim that it is advantageous for everyone to accept and act on the system is a very strong one; it may be so strong that no system of principles which might be generally adopted could meet it. But I shall consider in Section V one among the possible ways of weakening the claim.

The second phrase requiring elucidation is "disadvantageous acts." I use this phrase to refer to acts which, in the context of their performance, would be less advantageous to the performer than some other act open to him in the same context. The phrase does not refer to acts which merely impose on the performer some short-term disadvantage that is recouped or outweighed in the long run. Rather it refers to acts which impose a disadvantage that is never recouped. It follows that the performer may say to himself, when confronted with the requirement to perform such an act, that it would be better *for him* not to perform it.

It is essential to note that the thesis, as elucidated, does not maintain that morality is advantageous for everyone in the sense that each person will do *best* if the system of principles is accepted and acted on. Each person will do better than if no system is adopted, or than if the one particular alternative mentioned above is adopted, but not than if any alternative is adopted.

Indeed, for each person required by the system to perform some disadvantageous act, it is easy to specify a better alternative — namely, the system modified so that it does not require *him* to perform any act disadvantageous to himself. Of course, there is no reason to expect such an alternative to be better than the moral system for everyone, or in fact for anyone other than the person granted the special exemption.

A second point to note is that each person must gain more from the disadvantageous acts performed by others than he loses from the disadvantageous acts performed by himself. If this were not the case, then some person would do better if a system were adopted exactly like the moral system save that it never requires *any* person to perform disadvantageous acts. This is ruled out by the force of "advantageous for everyone."

This point may be clarified by an example. Suppose that the system contains exactly one principle. Everyone is always to tell the truth. It follows from the thesis that each person gains more from those occasions on which others tell the truth, even though it is disadvantageous to them to do so, than he loses from those occasions on which he tells the truth even though it is disadvantageous to him to do so.

Now this is not to say that each person gains by telling others the truth in order to ensure that in return they tell him the truth. Such gains would merely be the result of accepting certain short-term disadvantages (those associated with truth-telling) in order to reap long-term benefits (those associated with being told the truth). Rather, what is required by the thesis is that those disadvantages which a person incurs in telling the truth, when he can expect neither short-term nor long-term benefits to accrue to him from truth-telling, are outweighed by those advantages he receives when others tell him the truth when they can expect no benefits to accrue to them from truth-telling.

The principle enjoins truth-telling in those cases in which whether one tells the truth or not will have no effect on whether others tell the truth. Such cases include those in which others have no way of knowing whether or not they are being told the truth. The thesis requires that the disadvantages one incurs in telling the truth in these cases are less than the advantages one receives in being told the truth by others in parallel cases; and the thesis requires that this holds for everyone.

Thus we see that although the disadvantages imposed by the system on any person are less than the advantages secured him through the imposition of disadvantages on others, yet the disadvantages are real in that incurring them is *unrelated* to receiving the advantages. The argument of long-term prudence, that I ought to incur some immediate disadvantage *so that* I shall receive compensating advantages later on, is entirely inapplicable here.

III

It will be useful to examine in some detail an example of a system which possesses those characteristics ascribed by the thesis to morality. This example, abstracted from the field of international relations, will enable us more clearly to distinguish, first, conduct based on immediate interest; second, conduct which is truly prudent; and third, conduct which promotes mutual advantage but is not prudent.

A and *B* are two nations with substantially opposed interests, who find themselves engaged in an arms race against each other. Both possess the latest in weaponry, so that each recognizes that the actual outbreak of full scale war between them would be mutually disastrous. This recognition leads *A* and *B* to agree that each would be better off if they were mutually disarming instead of mutually arming. For mutual disarmament would preserve the balance of power between them while reducing the risk of war.

Hence *A* and *B* enter into a disarmament pact. The pact is advantageous for both if both accept and act on it, although clearly it is not advantageous for either to act on it if the other does not.

Let *A* be considering whether or not to adhere to the pact in some particular situation, whether or not actually to perform some act of disarmament. *A* will quite likely consider the act to have disadvantageous consequences. *A* expects to benefit, not by its own acts of disarmament, but by *B*'s acts. Hence if *A* were to reason simply in terms of immediate interest, *A* might well decide to violate the pact.

But *A*'s decision need be neither prudent nor reasonable. For suppose first that *B* is able to determine whether or not *A* adheres to the pact. If *A* violates, then *B* will detect the violation and will then consider what to do in the light of *A*'s behavior. It is not to *B*'s advantage to disarm alone; *B* expects to gain, not by its own acts of disarmament, but by *A*'s acts. Hence *A*'s violation, if known to *B*, leads naturally to *B*'s counterviolation. If this continues, the effect of the pact is entirely undone, and *A* and *B* return to their mutually disadvantageous arms race. *A*, foreseeing this when considering whether or not to adhere to the pact in the given situation, must therefore conclude that the truly prudent course of action is to adhere.

Now suppose that *B* is unable to determine whether or not *A* adheres to the pact in the particular situation under consideration. If *A* judges adherence to be in itself disadvantageous, then it will decide, both on the basis of immediate interest and on the basis of prudence, to violate the pact. Since *A*'s decision is unknown to *B*, it cannot affect whether or not *B* adheres to the pact, and so the advantage gained by *A*'s violation is not outweighed by any consequent loss.

Therefore if *A* and *B* are prudent they will adhere to their disarmament pact whenever violation would be detectable by the other, and violate the pact whenever violation would not be detectable by the other. In other words, they will adhere openly and violate secretly. The disarmament pact between *A* and *B* thus possesses two of the characteristics ascribed by the thesis to morality. First, accepting the pact and acting on it is more advantageous for each than making no pact at all. Second, in so far as the pact stipulates that each must disarm even when disarming is undetectable by the other, it requires each to perform disadvantageous acts — acts which run counter to considerations of prudence.

One further condition must be met if the disarmament pact is to possess those characteristics ascribed by the thesis to a system of morality. It must be the case that the requirement that each party perform disadvantageous acts be essential to the advantage conferred by the pact; or, to put the matter in the way in which we expressed it earlier, both *A* and *B* must do better to adhere to this pact than to a pact which is similar save that it requires no disadvantageous acts. In terms of the example, *A* and *B* must do better to adhere to the pact than to a pact which stipulates that each must disarm only when disarming is detectable by the other.

We may plausibly suppose this condition to be met. Although *A* will gain by secretly retaining arms itself, it will lose by *B*'s similar acts, and its losses may well outweigh its gains. *B* may equally lose more by *A*'s secret violations than it gains by its own. So, despite the fact that prudence requires each to violate secretly, each may well do better if both adhere secretly than if both violate secretly. Supposing this to be the case, the disarmament pact is formally analogous to a moral system, as characterized by the thesis. That is, acceptance of and adherence to the pact by *A* and *B* is more advantageous for each, either than making no pact at all or than acceptance of and adherence to a pact requir-

ing only open disarmament, and the pact requires each to perform acts of secret disarmament which are disadvantageous.

Some elementary notation, adapted for our purpose from the mathematical theory of games, may make the example even more perspicuous. Given a disarmament pact between *A* and *B*, each may pursue two pure strategies — adherence and violation. There are, then, four possible combinations of strategies, each determining a particular outcome. These outcomes can be ranked preferentially for each nation; we shall let the numerals 1 to 4 represent the ranking from first to fourth preference. Thus we construct a simple matrix,[5] in which *A*'s preferences are stated first:

		B	
		adheres	*violates*
	adheres	2,2	4,1
A	violates	1,4	3,3

The matrix does not itself show that agreement is advantageous to both, for it gives only the rankings of outcomes given the agreement. But it is plausible to assume that *A* and *B* would rank mutual violation on a par with no agreement. If we assume this, we can then indicate the value to each of making and adhering to the pact by reference to the matrix.

The matrix shows immediately that adherence to the pact is not the most advantageous possibility for either, since each prefers the outcome, if it alone violates, to the outcome of mutual adherence. It shows also that each gains less from its own violations than it loses from the other's, since each ranks mutual adherence above mutual violation.

Let us now use the matrix to show that, as we argued previously, public adherence to the pact is prudent and mutually advantageous, whereas private adherence is not prudent although mutually advantageous. Consider first the case when adherence — and so violation — are open and public.

If adherence and violation are open, then each knows the strategy chosen by the other, and can adjust its own strategy in the light of this knowledge — or, in other words, the strategies are interdependent. Suppose that each initially chooses the strategy of adherence. *A* notices that if it switches to violation it gains — moving from 2 to 1 in terms of preference ranking. Hence immediate interest dictates such a switch. But it notices further that if it switches, then *B* can also be expected to switch — moving from 4 to 3 on its preference scale. The eventual outcome would be stable, in that neither could benefit from switching from violation back to adherence. But the eventual outcome would represent not a gain for *A* but a loss — moving from 2 to 3 on its preference scale. Hence prudence dictates no change from the strategy of adherence. This adherence is mutually advantageous; *A* and *B* are in precisely similar positions in terms of their pact.

Consider now the case when adherence and violation are secret and private. Neither nation knows the strategy chosen by the other, so the two strategies are independent. Suppose *A* is trying to decide which strategy to follow. It does not know *B*'s choice. But it notices that if *B* adheres, then it pays *A* to violate, attaining 1 rather than 2 in terms of preference ranking. If *B* violates, then again it pays *A* to violate, attaining 3 rather than 4 on its preference scale. Hence, no matter which strategy *B* chooses, *A* will do better to violate, and so prudence dictates violation.

B of course reasons in just the same way. Hence each is moved by considerations of prudence to violate the pact, and the outcome assigns each rank 3 on its preference scale. This outcome is mutually disadvantageous to *A and B,* since mutual adherence would assign each rank 2 on its preference scale.

If *A* and *B* are both capable only of rational prudence, they find themselves at an impasse. The advantage of mutual adherence to the agreement when violations would be secret is not available to them, since neither can find it in his own overall interest not to violate secretly. Hence, strictly prudent nations cannot reap the maximum advantage possible from a pact of the type under examination.

Of course, what *A* and *B* will no doubt endeavor to do is eliminate the possibility of secret violations of their pact. Indeed, barring additional complications, each must find it to his advantage to make it possible for the other to detect his own violations. In other words, each must find it advantageous to ensure that their choice of strategies is interdependent, so that the pact will always be prudent for each to keep. But it may not be possible for them to ensure this, and to the extent that they cannot, prudence will prevent them from maximizing mutual advantage.

IV

We may now return to the connection of morality with advantage. Morality, if it is a system of principles of the type characterized in the thesis, requires that some persons perform acts genuinely disadvantageous to themselves, as a means to greater mutual advantage. Our example shows sufficiently that such a system is possible, and indicates more precisely its character. In particular, by an argument strictly parallel to that which we have pursued, we may show that men who are merely prudent will not perform the required disadvantageous acts. But in so violating the principles of morality, they will disadvantage themselves. Each will lose more by the violations of others than he will gain by his own violations.

Now this conclusion would be unsurprising if it were only that no man can gain if he alone is moral rather than prudent. Obviously such a man loses, for he adheres to moral principles to his own disadvantage, while others violate them also to his disadvantage. The benefit of the moral system is not one which any individual can secure for himself, since each man gains from the sacrifices of others.

What is surprising in our conclusion is that no man can ever gain if he is moral. Not only does he not gain by being moral if others are prudent, but he also does not gain by being moral if others are moral. For although he now receives the advantage of others' adherence to moral principles, he reaps the disadvantage of his own adherence. As long as his own adherence to morality is independent of what others do (and this is required to distinguish morality from prudence), he must do better to be prudent.

If all men are moral, all will do better than if all are prudent. But any one man will always do better if he is prudent than if he is moral. There is no real paradox in supposing that morality is advantageous, even though it requires the performance of disadvantageous acts.

On the supposition that morality has the characteristics ascribed to it by the thesis, is it possible to answer the question "Why should we be moral?" where "we" is taken distributively, so that the question is a compendious way of asking, for each person, "Why should I be moral?" More simply, is it possible to answer the question "Why should I be moral?"

I take it that this question, if asked seriously, demands a reason for being moral other than moral reasons themselves. It demands that moral reasons be shown to be reasons for acting by a noncircular argument. Those who would answer it, like Baier, endeavor to do so by the introduction of considerations of advantage.

Two such considerations have emerged from our discussion. The first is that if all are moral, all will do better than if all are prudent. This will serve to answer the question "Why should we be moral?" if this question is interpreted rather as "Why should we all be moral—rather than all being something else?" If we must all be the same, then each person has a reason—a prudential reason—to prefer that we all be moral.

But, so interpreted, "Why should we be moral?" is not a compendious way of asking, for each person, "Why should I be moral?" Of course, if everyone is to be whatever I am, then I should be moral. But a general answer to the question "Why should I be moral?" cannot presuppose this.

The second consideration is that any individual always does better to be prudent rather than moral, provided his choice does not determine other choices. But in so far as this answers the question "Why should I be moral?" it leads to the conclusion "I should not be moral." One feels that this is not the answer which is wanted.

We may put the matter otherwise. The individual who needs a reason for being moral which is not itself a moral reason cannot have it. There is nothing surprising about this; it would be much more surprising if such reasons could be found. For it is more than apparently paradoxical to suppose that considerations of advantage could ever of themselves justify accepting a real disadvantage.

V

I suggested in Section II that the thesis, in modified form, might provide a necessary, although not a sufficient, condition for a moral system. I want now to consider how one might characterize the man who would qualify as moral according to the thesis—I shall call him the "moral" man—and then ask what would be lacking from this characterization, in terms of some of our commonplace moral views.

The rationally prudent man is incapable of moral behavior, in even the limited sense defined by the thesis. What difference must there be between the prudent man and the "moral" man? Most simply, the "moral" man is the prudent but trustworthy man. I treat trustworthiness as the capacity which enables its possessor to adhere, and to judge that he ought to adhere, to a commitment which he has made, without regard to consideration of advantage.

The prudent but trustworthy man does not possess this capacity completely. He is capable of trustworthy behavior only in so far as he regards his *commitment* as advantageous. Thus he differs from the prudent man just in the relevant respect; he accepts arguments of the form "If it is advantageous for me to agree to do *x,* and I do agree to do *x,* then I ought to do *x,* whether or not it then proves advantageous for me to do *x.*"

Suppose that *A* and *B,* the parties to the disarmament pact, are prudent but trustworthy. *A,* considering whether or not secretly to violate the agreement, reasons that its advantage in making and keeping the agreement, provided *B* does so as well, is greater than its advantage in not making it. If it can assume that *B* reasons in the same way, then it is in a position to conclude that it ought not to violate the pact. Although violation would be advantageous, consideration of this advantage is ruled out by *A*'s trustworthiness, given the advantage in agreeing to the pact.

The prudent but trustworthy man meets the requirements implicitly imposed by the thesis for the "moral" man. But how far does this "moral" man display two characteristics commonly associated with morality—first, a willingness to make sacrifices, and second, a concern with fairness?

Whenever a man ignores his own advantage for reasons other than those of greater advantage, he may be said to make some sacrifice. The "moral" man, in being trustworthy, is thus required to make certain sacrifices. But these are extremely limited. And—not surprisingly, given the general direction of our argument—it is quite possible that they limit the advantages which the "moral" man can secure.

Once more let us turn to our example. *A* and *B* have entered into a disarmament agreement and, being prudent but trustworthy, are faithfully carrying it out. The government of *A* is now informed by its scientists, however, that they have developed an effective missile defense, which will render *A* invulnerable to attack by any of the weapons actually or potentially at *B*'s disposal, barring unforeseen technological developments. Furthermore, this defense can be installed secretly. The government is now called upon to decide whether to violate its agreement with *B,* install the new defense, and, with the arms it has retained through its violation, establish its dominance over *B.*

A is in a type of situation quite different from that previously considered. For it is not just that *A* will do better by secretly violating its agreement. *A* reasons not only that it will do better to violate no matter what *B* does, but that it will do better if both violate than if both continue to adhere to the pact. *A* is now in a position to gain from abandoning the agreement; it no longer finds mutual adherence advantageous.

We may represent this new situation in another matrix:

		B	
		adheres	*violates*
	adheres	3,2	4,1
A			
	violates	1,4	2,3

We assume again that the ranking of mutual violation is the same as that of no agreement. Now had this situation obtained at the outset, no agreement would have been made, for *A* would have had no reason to enter into a disarmament pact. And of course had *A* expected this situation to come about, no agreement — or only a temporary agreement — would have been made; *A* would no doubt have risked the short-term dangers of the continuing arms race in the hope of securing the long-run benefit of predominance over *B* once its missile defense was completed. On the contrary, *A* expected to benefit from the agreement, but now finds that, because of its unexpected development of a missile defense, the agreement is not in fact advantageous to it.

The prudent but trustworthy man is willing to carry out his agreements, and judges that he ought to carry them out, in so far as he considers them advantageous. *A* is prudent but trustworthy. But is *A* willing to carry out its agreement to disarm, now that it no longer considers the agreement advantageous?

If *A* adheres to its agreement in this situation, it makes a sacrifice greater than any advantage it receives from the similar sacrifices of others. It makes a sacrifice greater in kind than any which can be re-

quired by a mutually advantageous agreement. It must, then, possess a capacity for trustworthy behavior greater than that ascribed to the merely prudent but trustworthy man (or nation). This capacity need not be unlimited; it need not extend to a willingness to adhere to any commitment no matter what sacrifice is involved. But it must involve a willingness to adhere to a commitment made in the expectation of advantage, should that expectation be disappointed.

I shall call the man (or nation) who is willing to adhere, and judges that he ought to adhere, to his prudentially undertaken agreements even if they provide disadvantageous to him, the trustworthy man. It is likely that there are advantages available to trustworthy men which are not available to merely prudent but trustworthy men. For there may be situations in which men can make agreements which each expects to be advantageous to him, provided he can count on the others' adhering to it whether or not their expectation of advantage is realized. But each can count on this only if all have the capacity to adhere to commitments regardless of whether the commitment actually proves advantageous. Hence, only trustworthy men who know each other to be such will be able rationally to enter into, and so to benefit from, such agreements.

Baier's view of morality departs from that stated in the thesis in that it requires trustworthy, and not merely prudent but trustworthy, men. Baier admits that "a person might do better for himself by following enlightened self-interest rather than morality." This admission seems to require that morality be a system of principles which each person may expect, initially, to be advantageous to him, if adopted and adhered to by everyone, but not a system which actually is advantageous to everyone.

Our commonplace moral views do, I think, support the view that the moral man must be trustworthy. Hence, we have established one modification required in the thesis, if it is to provide a more adequate set of conditions for a moral system.

But there is a much more basic respect in which the "moral" man falls short of our expectations. He is willing to temper his single-minded pursuit of advantage only by accepting the obligation to adhere to prudentially undertaken commitments. He has no real concern for the advantage of others, which would lead him to modify his pursuit of advantage when it conflicted with the similar pursuits of others. Unless he expects to gain, he is unwilling to accept restrictions on the pursuit of advantage which are intended to equalize the opportunities open to all. In other words, he has no concern with fairness.

We tend to think of the moral man as one who does not seek his own well-being by means which would deny equal well-being to his fellows. This marks him off clearly from the "moral" man, who differs from the prudent man only in that he can overcome the apparent paradox of prudence and obtain those advantages which are available only to those who can display real restraint in their pursuit of advantage.

Thus a system of principles might meet the conditions laid down in the thesis without taking any account of considerations of fairness. Such a system would contain principles for ensuring increased advantage (or expectation of advantage) to everyone, but no further principle need be present to determine the distribution of this increase.

It is possible that there are systems of principles which, if adopted and adhered to, provide advantages which strictly prudent men, however rational, cannot attain. These advantages are a function of the sacrifices which the principles impose on their adherents.

Morality may be such a system. If it is, this would explain our expectation that we should all be worse off were we to substitute prudence for morality in our deliberations. But to characterize morality as a system of principles advantageous to all is not to answer the question "Why should I be moral?" nor is it to provide for those considerations of fairness which are equally essential to our moral understanding.

Endnotes

[1] David Hume, *An Enquiry Concerning the Principles of Morals*, sec. ix, pt. ii.

[2] Ogden Nash, "Kind of an Ode to Duty."

[3] Kurt Baier, *The Moral Point of View: A Rational Basis of Ethics* (Ithaca, 1958), p. 314. [This passage does not appear in the abridged edition. But cf. "Moralities are systems of principles whose acceptance by everyone as overruling the dictates of self-interest is in the interest of everyone alike. . . ."]

[4] That this, and only this, is what he is entitled to claim may not be clear to Baier, for he supposes his account of morality to answer the question "Why should we be moral?" interpreting "we" distributively. This, as I shall argue in Sec. IV, is quite mistaken.

[5] Those familiar with the theory of games will recognize the matrix as a variant of the Prisoner's Dilemma. In a more formal treatment, it would be appropriate to develop the relation between morality and advantage by reference to the Prisoner's Dilemma. This would require reconstructing the disarmament pact and the moral system as proper games. Here I wish only to suggest the bearing of game theory on our enterprise.

X.4 A Reconciliation Project

Gregory Kavka

Gregory Kavka is professor of philosophy at the University of California at Irvine and the author of several works in ethical and political theory, including issues related to the arms race.

In this article, Kavka attempts to resolve the paradox of prudence and morality. Beginning with an analysis of a Hobbesian approach to the problem, he argues that this sort of approach, while illuminating and partially correct, "cannot take us far enough" and ultimately is invalid because of its assumption of psychological egoism. What needs to be added to the Hobbesian picture is an account of internal sanctions, the kind of built-in constraints that are an important part of socialization. If one has been raised in a normal social context, one will feel deep psychic distress at the thought of harming others and deep psychic satisfaction at being moral. For these persons, the combination of internal and external sanctions may well bring prudence and morality close together. Although this condition may not apply to persons not brought up in a moral context, this should not alarm us. We should not perceive "an immoralist's gloating that it does not pay him to be moral . . . as a victory over us. It is more like the pathetic boast of a deaf person that he saves money because it does not pay him to buy opera records."

Clarifying the nature of the relationship between ethical and self-interested conduct is one of the oldest problems of moral philosophy. As far back as Plato's *Republic,* philosophers have approached it with the aim of reconciling morality and self-interest by showing that moral behavior is required by, or at least is consistent with, rational prudence. Let us call this undertaking the Reconciliation Project. In modern times this project is generally viewed as doomed to failure. It is believed that unless we make an outdated and implausible appeal to divine sanctions, we cannot expect to find agreement between moral and prudential requirements.

Can this negative verdict on the Reconciliation Project be avoided? Before we can deal with this question, we must distinguish among versions of the project along four dimensions. The *audience* dimension concerns to whom our arguments about coincidence of duty and interest are addressed. Sometimes it is supposed that a successful version of the Reconciliation Project must be capable of converting to virtue a hardened cynic or immoralist such as Thrasymachus. This is too much to ask. Immoralists are not likely to understand or appreciate the benefits of living morally, nor are they usually the sort of people who will listen to, or be swayed by, abstract rational arguments. A more modest aim is to speak convincingly to the puzzled ordinary person, such as Glaucon, who fears that in following the path of morality he is being irrational and is harming himself, but who is willing to listen to and ponder arguments to the contrary. We shall here be concerned with versions of the Reconciliation Project having this more modest aim.

A second dimension concerns the sort of *agent* for whom morality and self-interest are supposed to coincide. Versions of the Reconciliation Project that are ambitious along this dimension might attempt to demonstrate such coincidence in the case of all actual human beings, or even all possible human beings. More restrained versions would concentrate

From *Morality, Reason and Truth*, eds. D. Copp and D. Zimmerman (Rowman and Allanheld, 1984). Copyright © 1984. Reprinted by permission of the publisher.

on more limited classes, such as persons without severe emotional disturbances or persons capable of self-assessment and love for others. The audience and agent dimensions of the Reconciliation Project are related. If one's aim in pursuing the project is to create or strengthen moral motivation, one would normally choose an agent class that just encompasses one's audience, so as to convince one's listeners that it pays *them* (promotes their own interests) to be moral, while at the same time exposing one's argument to the fewest possible objections. But if one aims at promoting theoretical understanding, one's agent class may be broader or narrower than one's audience. One may, for example, seek to convince reflective persons of goodwill that it pays everyone to be moral. Agent and audience classes need not even overlap; one might argue to sophisticated theorists that morality pays for the unsophisticated, who could not be expected successfully to disguise their immoralities.

The third dimension of the Reconciliation Project is the *social* one. Whether morality pays is partly a function of others' responses to one's immoralities. Are morality and prudence supposed to coincide, then, in all imaginable social environments, all feasible ones, all (or most) actual ones, some feasible ones, or some imaginable ones? Different answers to this question yield importantly different versions of the Reconciliation Project.

Fourth and finally, if we say that morality and prudence coincide, does this mean that (i) each individual ethical act is prudent or (ii) that there are sufficient prudential reasons for adopting a moral way of life and acting in accordance with moral rules? This question concerns the nature of the objects or entities to be reconciled and calls attention to the *object* dimension of the Reconciliation Project. Reconciling all particular acts of duty with prudence is so unpromising a task as to have been largely shunned by the major philosophical exponents of the project. (Although, as we shall see below, much depends on whether prudential evaluations of acts are undertaken prospectively or retrospectively.) Thus Plato argues the prudential advantages of moral dispositions or ways of life, while Hobbes focuses on providing a prudential grounding for moral rules.

Taking note of the object dimension allows us to clarify the Reconciliation Project by answering a preliminary objection to it. According to this objection, the project mut fail because supposedly moral actions are not really moral if they are motivated by prudential concerns. We may, however, accept this observation about motivation and moral action without damaging the Reconciliation Project properly construed. For that project is not committed to morality and prudence being identical, or to moral and prudential motives or reasons for action being the same. Rather, prudence and morality are supposed to be reconcilable in two senses. They recommend the same courses of conduct (where conduct is described in some motive-neutral way). Further, it is consistent with the requirements of prudence to adopt and live a moral way of life, even though this involves developing a pattern of motivation in which nonprudential considerations play an important role. Thus the Reconciliation Project survives the preliminary objection because it concerns, along its object dimension, acts or rules of action or ways of life, rather than motives or reasons for action.

Still, the Reconciliation Project is hopeless if we adopt very stringent interpretations of it along most or all of its four dimensions. We cannot expect to convince a clever immoralist that it pays everyone to act morally on every specific occasion in any sort of society. But why should we consider only such extreme versions of the project? Taking account of the dimensions of variation of the Reconciliation Project, I propose instead to discuss some less extreme versions (and modifications) of it to see to what extent they can be carried out and why they fail when they do. In the course of this investigation, I hope partly to vindicate the rationality of being moral and to clarify further the relationship between morality, prudence, and rationality.

I begin by sketching a Hobbesian version of the Reconciliation Project that presupposes psychological egoism and relies exclusively on external sanctions (social rewards and punishments) to reconcile obligation and interest. This Hobbesian approach provides considerable illumination, but it suffers from serious defects. To correct some of these, I consider the significance of internal (self-imposed psychological) sanctions. Next, I take up the two most intractable objections to all forms of the project. These concern the obligation to die for others, and those duties owed by members of strong groups to members of weak groups who are apparently not in a position to reciprocate benefits bestowed on them. Finally, I note how the recognition of nonegoistic motives transforms the Reconciliation Project. Throughout, my remarks are largely programmatic. I sketch alternatives, problems, and general strategies for solving problems and leave much detail to be filled in later. I hope nonetheless to say enough to show that the Reconciliation Project is still philosophically interesting and important.

I. The Hobbesian Strategy

As a starting point, let us consider Hobbes's version of the Reconciliation Project. In seeking to reconcile duty and interest, Hobbes is limited by two self-imposed restrictions: He rules out appeal to religious sanctions, and he leaves no place for internal sanctions (such as guilt feelings) in his account of human psychology. Hence, Hobbes is reduced to arguing his case solely in terms of external sanctions; that is, social rewards and punishments. He does, however, marshall these relatively meager resources to good advantage.

The core of Hobbes's view is that the general rules of conduct that a farsighted prudent man concerned with his own survival, security, and well-being would follow are essentially the rules of traditional morality. The function of these rules is to promote peace, cooperation, and mutual restraint for the benefit of all parties. The rules therefore forbid killing, assault, and robbery, and they require keeping one's agreements, settling disputes by arbitration, providing aid to others when the cost to one is small and the benefit to them is large, and so on. The self-interested individual, if sufficiently rational and farsighted, will follow these rules because doing so is the best (and only reliable) way to ensure peaceful and cooperative relations with others. The person, for example, who wastes on luxuries what others need to survive is not likely to be helped by others if he later falls into want; nor will his person and property ever be safe from the desperate acts of the needy. The dangers of hostile reactions by others that confront the habitual assailant, thief, or contract-breaker are even more obvious. And while people may try to conceal their violations of moral rules, the long-run dangers of exposure and retaliation by others are great. Thus, argues Hobbes, morality is superior to immorality as a general policy, from the viewpoint of rational prudence.

One may agree that normally morality is a more prudent general policy than immorality but raise doubts about its prudential rationality in two special circumstances: when one is confident that a violation would go undiscovered and unpunished, and when others are not willing to reciprocate restraint. In the first case, it appears that one would benefit by *offensively* violating moral rules; that is, by not complying with them when others are complying. In the second case, prudence seems to call for a *defensive* violation—for noncompliance motivated by the belief that others are not complying and the desire not to put oneself at a disadvantage. Hobbes recognizes and attempts to deal with both cases.

Hobbes's argument against offensive violations of moral rules is presented in his famous reply to the Fool. He acknowledges that such violations will in some cases turn out, *in retrospect,* to best serve the agent's interests. But because they risk serious external sanctions (such as the withdrawal of all future cooperation by others), they are never *prospectively* rational. Since the consequences of failure are horrible and the chances of failure are not precisely calculable, it is not a rational gamble to offensively violate moral rules. Underlying this Hobbesian argument is an intuition about rational prudence that is reflected in the usual connotation of the word *prudence*. To be prudent is to play it safe and not take large, uncontrollable risks. It is not implausible to suppose that rational pursuit of one's own interests requires being prudent in this sense when one's vital interest are at stake.

To develop this point, let us follow decision theorists in drawing a distinction between choices under *risk* and under *uncertainty*. In the former cases, one has reliable knowledge of the probabilities that the various possible outcomes would follow the different available courses of action. In choices under uncertainty, one lacks such knowledge. Rawls contends that rationality requires that, when making vitally important choices under uncertainty, one follow a Maximin Strategy—choose the act with the best worst outcome. I have argued elsewhere for using a Disaster Avoidance Strategy in such circumstances—choosing the alternative that maximizes one's chances of avoiding all unacceptable outcome. Both strategies favor playing it safe in the sense of aiming at avoidance (or minimization) of the risk of unacceptable outcomes.

Now suppose we view choices among actions in the real world as made under uncertainty. (This is plausible for the most part, given our limited understanding of the complex factors that determine the consequences of our actions.) If, as Hobbes suggests, offensive violators risk the application of serious external sanctions, offensive violations would be irrational according to both the Maximin and Disaster Avoidance viewpoints. For the offensive violator accepts, under uncertainty, an unnecessary (or greater than necessary) risk of suffering disastrous consequences. So if either Rawls's analysis of rational prudential choice under uncertainty of my own is correct, Hobbes's argument against offensive violations under uncertainty is largely vindicated.

The considerations just presented attempt in effect to reconcile the requirements of morality and prudence as applied to (a certain class of) particular actions. They may serve, that is, as part of a Reconciliation Project focusing along the object dimension on *acts*. They function ever more effectively as part of an argument for the coincidence of *rules* of morality and prudence. We can imagine someone claiming that living by some rule such as the following would better serve one's interests than following moral rules: "Follow the moral rules except when you believe (or confidently believe) you can get away with violating them." But if one lives by this sort of rule, one is likely to undergo the risks inherent in offensive violations on a good number of occasions. And even if one is cautious in selecting the occasions, the risk of getting caught and suffering serious sanctions on one or more occasions will be substantial and much greater than the chance of getting caught on one particular occasion. Hence, insofar as rational prudence requires avoiding or minimizing risks of suffering serious sanctions, it would not recommend a policy of clever "compromise" between moral and immoral conduct as exemplified in this rule.

We have seen that Hobbes tries to reconcile duty and prudence in the case of offensive violations by denying that such violations are prudential. The opposite tack is adopted for defensive violations. These, Hobbes claims, are not contrary to moral duty. Agents are not obligated to follow the constraints of traditional morality unless others are reciprocating their restraint. To comply with moral rules unilaterally is to render oneself prey to others, and this, Hobbes urges, one is not required to do.

The governing principle of Hobbesian morality, then, is what I call the Copper Rule: "Do unto others as they *do* unto you." This principle enunciates a less glittering moral ideal than the familiar Golden Rule, which requires us to treat others well regardless of whether they treat us well in return. In thus opting for a reciprocal rather than unilateral interpretation of moral requirements, is Hobbes abandoning traditional morality?

To answer this question, we must distinguish between two aspects of morality — practice morality and ideal morality. Practice morality encompasses the standards of conduct actually expected of, and generally practiced by, persons living within a given moral tradition. It is roughly the part of morality concerned with *requirements,* those standards for which people are blamed, criticized, or punished for failing to live up to. Ideal morality refers to standards of moral excellence that a tradition sets up as models to aspire to and admire. Praise, honor, and respect are the rewards of those who live by its higher, more demanding standards. But, in general, people are not blamed for falling short of such ideals, or even for not aiming at them.

Now there surely are important strands of unilateralism in the ideal morality of the Western tradition. The Golden Rule, the admonition to love thine enemy, and the principle of turning the other cheek, all concern treating well even those who do not reciprocate. But if we turn to practice, and the standards of conduct that are actually treated as moral requirements, we find Copper Rule reciprocity to be a reasonable summary of much of what we observe. For practice morality allows us considerable leeway to engage in otherwise forbidden conduct toward those who violate moral constraints, especially when this is necessary for protection. Thus individuals may kill in self-defense, society may deprive criminals of their liberty, contracts may be broken when reciprocal fulfillment cannot be expected, and so forth.

We may then, without committing Hobbes to absurdity, attribute to him the claim that, in practice, traditional moral rules contain exception clauses allowing for defensive "violations" of the main clauses of the rule, if these are aimed at other violators. In adopting this pruned-down conception of moral requirements, Hobbes has abandoned the ambitious dream of achieving a reconciliation between ideal morality and prudence. But he has avoided one telling objection to the Reconciliation Project: that morality requires us (as prudence does not) to sacrifice our interests to the immoral, who will be all too ready to take advantage of such a sacrifice. Note, however, that the companion objection that morality sometimes requires us to sacrifice our interests for others who are moral is not dealt with by the Copper Rule interpretation of morality. Forms of this objection will be considered later.

As we have seen, Hobbes treats offensive and defensive violations of moral rules quite differently. In the former case, he reconciles prudence to morality by altering cynical interpretations of what prudence demands, while in the latter case he reconciles morality to prudence by offering a nonstandard interpretation of morality. Yet in each case he draws our attention to the oft-neglected social dimension of the Reconciliation Project. His discussion of defensive violations suggests that under certain conditions — anarchy or general noncompliance with traditional moral rules — moral and prudential requirements coincide, but only as a result of the effective loosening or disappearance of the former. Hence, *how* duty and interest are reconciled is a function of the social environment. In arguing for the imprudence of offensive violations of moral rules, Hobbes presupposes threats of external sanctions that are serious enough to make such violations a bad gamble. Therefore, his argument does not apply to imaginary situations in which society rewards immoral actions, or even certain real ones in which it ignores serious immoralities when they are committed by members of some privileged groups.

Suppose, then, that our aim is to reconcile prudence with traditional moral requirements (without the exception clauses); that is, do not kill or steal, aid the needy when the costs are small, and so on. Hobbes suggests that this reconciliation is possible only in a certain sort of social environment — one we may call *punitive*. In a punitive environment, serious violators of moral norms are sought out, apprehended, and given stiff punishments frequently enough to make immorality a bad prudential risk. As a result, there is general compliance with moral rules and little need for one to undertake defensive violations. In a punitive social environment, offensive violations of moral rules are irrational and defensive ones are unnecessary. If an actual social environment is punitive, the Reconciliation Project seems to have succeeded with respect to it. And if such an environment is feasible but nonactual, those who wish people to act morally but fear the distracting influence of self-interest will have some reason to create it.

Let us now briefly summarize the Hobbesian approach to the Reconciliation Project, which is based on external sanctions. It consists first of proposing specific interpretations of that project along two of the four dimensions. With respect to the object dimension, it focuses on rules or policies rather than on individual acts. (Although the reply to the Fool fits within an act version of the project as well.) And it presupposes a punitive social environment, avoiding the dubious claim that duty and interest coincide in any social context. Further, it provides a novel interpretation of moral requirements — the Copper Rule or reciprocal interpretation — and it rests on a "playing it safe" theory of rational prudential choice under uncertainty. All of these aspects of the Hobbesian strategy make contributions to the interpretation and development of the Reconciliation Project. None is without plausibility. However, there are two fatal objections that the Hobbesian Strategy cannot adequately answer.

The first concerns punitive social environments. These are beneficial in discouraging immoral conduct, but they have costs. To render immorality a bad risk solely via threats of punishments, such punishments must be made very heavy and/or very probable. In a society of significant size, doing the latter would normally require a massive policing establishment with large monetary costs (borne by the citizens), interferences with personal liberty and privacy (searches, eavesdropping, surveillance), and dangers of police power and influence over the political and economic institutions of society. Heavy penalties also have social costs — monetary costs of supporting prisons, lessened chances of reconciliation between offenders and society, dangers of gross injustice if the innocent might sometimes be punished, and so on. In short, we must accept trade-offs between various things that we value and the deterrence of serious immorality. And it may not always be possible for society, by use of external sanctions alone, to ensure that "crime does not pay" without sacrificing too much in the way of individual liberty, privacy, and protection from excessive state and police power.

Our second objection concedes that immorality generally does not pay, and even allows, that immorality is prudentially irrational under genuine uncertainty. However, *some* opportunities for immoral gain may present themselves under risk; that is, the probabilities of detection and punishment may be reliably known. In these situations, maximizing expected personal utility is arguably the most rational course, and this may imply engaging in an offensive violation. A slumlord, for example, may have relatively precise statistical data that allow him to estimate reliably the odds of his getting caught and punished if he hires a professional arsonist to burn one of his buildings so that he can collect the insurance. If the chances of arrest and conviction are low and the return is high, the crime may have positive expected value for him, and it will be prudentially rational for him to undertake it. The rules of a system of rational self-interest will be formulated to allow agents to take advantage of such situations.

These two objectives reveal that while external sanctions alone can take us, via the Hobbesian Strategy, some considerable way toward reconciling duty and interest, they cannot take us far enough. We at least need some device other than a punitive social environment that can alter the calculations or dispositions of the slumlord and other potential criminals. The obvious candidates here are internal sanctions, psychic structures that punish immorality and reward virtue. Unlike external sanctions, these are relatively free of problems concerning evasion and detection, since one's conscience follows one everywhere, and they do not threaten privacy and democracy as do secret police forces. In the next session, I will explore how their inclusion may extend and strengthen the Hobbesian arguments for the coincidence for morality and prudence.

II. *Internal Sanctions*

Internal sanctions come in two varieties, negative and positive. The negative sanctions are guilt feelings and related forms of psychic distress that most of us are subject to feel when we believe we have done wrong. We develop the tendency to experience such feelings under such circumstances as part of the socialization process we undergo in growing up. It is no mystery why society nurtures and encourages the development of this tendency; it benefits others to the extent that it inhibits or deters misconduct by the individual. And once one possesses the ten-

dency, it imposes extra—and relatively certain—costs on immorality, costs which may tip the prudential balance in favor of restraint. Arson may not be the most rational option for our slumlord, for example, if in addition to prison he risks, with high probability, significant guilt feelings over endangering the lives of tenants or over cheating his insurance company. With internal sanctions operating along with external sanctions in this way, the social environment need not be so punitive as to keep serious immorality within tolerable limits.

There is no entirely satisfactory label for the positive internal sanctions, the agreeable feelings that typically accompany moral action and the realization that one has acted rightly, justly, or benevolently. So let us opt for the vague term "the satisfactions of morality." Moral people have long testified as to the strength and value of such satisfactions, often claiming that they are the most agreeable satisfactions we can attain. This last claims goes beyond what is necessary for our purposes. All we need to assert is that there are special significant pleasures or satisfactions that accompany regular moral action and the practice of a moral way of life that are not available to (unreformed) immoralists and others of their ilk. For if this is so, then the forgoing of these potential satisfactions must be charged as a significant opportunity cost of choosing an immoral way of life.

Can an individual have it both ways, enjoying the psychic benefits of morality while living an immoral life? He could, perhaps, if he lived immorally while sincerely believing he was not. Certain fanatics who selflessly devote themselves to false moral ideals, such as purifying the human race by eugenics or pleasing God by destroying nonbelievers, might fall in this category. Of more concern in the present context, however, is the individual who adopts morality as a provisional way of life or policy while planning to abandon it if a chance to gain much by immorality should arise later. This person, we would say, is not truly moral, and it is hard to believe that he would perceive himself to be, so long as his motives are purely prudential and his commitment to morality is only conditional. In any case, we would not expect him to experience the satisfactions of morality in the same way, or to the same degree, as the genuinely moral individual who is aware of the (relative) purity of his motives and the nature and depth of his commitment.

Note that if this is so we have arrived at a paradox of self-interest: *being* purely self-interested will not always best serve one's interests. For there may be certain substantial personal advantages that accrue only to those who are not purely self-interested, such as moral people. Thus it may be rational for you, as a purely self-interested person, to cease being one if you can, to transform yourself into a genuinely moral person. And once you are such a person, you will not be disposed to act immorally, under risk, whenever so doing promises to maximize personal expected utility.

The lesson of this paradox, and the opportunity cost of being immoral, does not apply, though, to those (if any) who are no longer capable of learning to enjoy the satisfactions of living a moral life. Further, some people may still be capable of developing an appreciation of these satisfactions, but the transition costs of moving to this state from their present immoral condition may outweigh the advantages gained. For people such as these, especially those who are immune from guilt feelings, the prudential argument for being moral must essentially rest on external sanctions. And with respect to some individuals, such as hardened but cautious immoralists or clever psychopaths, the argument may fail.

Thus we must acknowledge a restriction of the Reconciliation Project along its agent dimension. It is too much to claim that it pays one to be moral, irrespective of one's psychological characteristics. Rather, the argument from internal sanctions supports the prudential rationality of living a moral life for the two classes of people constituting the vast majority of humankind: First, those who are already endowed with conscience and moral motivations, so that they experience the satisfactions of living morally and are liable to suffering guilt feelings when they do wrong. Second, those who are capable of developing into moral persons without excessive costs — immoralists who are not fully committed to that way of life, and children.

Should we be dismayed that the Reconciliation Project may not encompass, along its agent dimension, those incapable of enjoying the satisfactions of morality? This depends upon our aims in pursuing the project and the audience to whom its arguments are addressed. Insofar as our aim is to reassure the ordinary good man that he is not harming himself by being moral, or to encourage parents who want to do the best for their children to give them moral

education, we need not worry. And if we seek theoretical illumination, we achieve more by recognizing the variation along the agent dimension than by denying it. Only if our aim were the hopeless one of convincing dedicated immoralists to be moral, by using rational arguments, would we be in difficulty. Am I confessing, then, that we are helpless in the face of the immoralist? No, we are not helpless in the practical sense, for we can use external sanctions to restrain immoralists. Nor should we perceive an immoralist's gloating that it does not pay him to be moral (because the satisfactions of morality are not for him) as a victory over us. It is more like the pathetic boast of a deaf person that he saves money because it does not pay him to buy opera records.

III. *The Ultimate Sacrifice*

We have seen how the recognition of internal sanctions allows us to deal with two objections that undermine the Hobbesian external-sanctions approach to the Reconciliation Project. Two difficult objections remain, however, even when internal sanctions are taken into account. The first is that morality sometimes requires the sacrifice of one's life, and this cannot be in one's interests. The second is that morality requires powerful groups to treat weak groups fairly and decently, while it better serves the interests of the powerful group's members not to do so.

The objection concerning death runs as follows. In certain circumstances, morality requires of us that we give up our lives to protect others. We are bound by obligations of fair play, gratitude, and perhaps consent to fight in just wars of national defense. Fulfilling these obligations costs many people their lives. Extreme situations can also arise in civilian life in which morality requires one to accept one's own death. If gangsters credibly threaten to kill me unless I kill an innocent person, I must refrain. If I am a loser in a fair and necessary lifeboat lottery, I am morally bound to abide by the outcome. If half of the expedition's necessary food supply is lost as a result of my recklessness, I must be the first to agree to go without food on the long return trip so that others may survive. And so on. In each of these cases, however, self-interest seems to counsel taking the opposite course. Where there is life there is hope, and even if the likely cost of saving my life is to suffer severe internal and external sanctions (such as imprisonment, depression, and guilt for the military deserter), that cost must be less than the premature loss of my life, since such loss would deprive me of all future enjoyments and frustrate all of my main plans and desires.

In response to this objection, let us first note that there are fates worse than death. And for some people, living with the knowledge that one has preserved one's life at the cost of the lives of others, the sacrifice of one's principles, or the desertion of a cause one loves may be such a fate. In addition, society is aware of the heavy value that people place on the continuation of their own lives and typically responds by using heavy external sanctions to encourage appropriate life-risking behavior in defense of society. Thus infantry officers may stand behind their own lines and shoot those who retreat, thereby rending advance a safer course than retreat. (Even if advance is virtually suicidal, death with honor at the hands of the enemy may be a lesser evil than death with dishonor at the hands of one's own officers.) On the positive side, those who risk or lose their lives in battle are often offered significant rewards by their fellow citizens—medals, honors, praise, and material compensation for themselves or their families.

The upshot of this is that in a substantial number of cases the sacrifice of one's life for moral ends may be consistent with the requirements of prudence because it constitutes the lesser of two extreme personal evils. It would, however, be disingenuous to suggest that this is so in most, much less all, cases. Officers cannot shoot all deserters or retreaters, nor are courts likely to sentence to death those who cheat in lifeboat lotteries. And relatively few are so committed to morality that they could not eventually recover, at least partially, from the negative psychic effects of abandoning principle to preserve their lives. So we must concede that self-interest and morality will frequently, or usually, recommend divergent courses of action when there is a stark choice between immoral action and certain death.

Does this concession destroy the Reconciliation Project? Only if we have in mind a version of the project that focuses, along the object dimension, on acts. If instead we consider, as we have been, whether adopting the moral *way of life* is consistent with prudence, the answer may well be different. In adopting or pursuing a moral way of life, we are, it is true, running a *risk* of sacrificing our lives imprudently. For the requirements of morality may sometimes call for us to give up (or risk) our lives. And if we do develop the habits and dispositions appropriate to the moral life, we are likely (or at least more likely than otherwise) to live up to these requirements at the cost of our lives, if we find ourselves in appropriate circumstances. Notice, however, that in assessing this risk and weighing it against the advantages of the moral life, we must consider how likely we are to find ourselves in such circumstances.

Now this depends, in turn, on our view of what the substantive rules of morality require of us. If they demand that one right all wrongs and fight all injustices anywhere at any time with all the means one possesses and regardless of the personal cost, the likelihood that one would be morally obligated to lay down (or seriously risk) one's life at some time or another is obviously large. But surely on any reasonable conception they require much less than this. Perhaps you are obligated to give up your life (i) to protect your country in a just war; (ii) to protect those to whom you owe special duties of protection (your children, your passengers if you are a ship's captain); (iii) to protect those you owe immense debts of gratitude (your parents); (iv) to avoid seriously violating the rights of innocent others (as in the gangster threat situation); (v) to save others from dangers that your misconduct, recklessness, or negligence has created; (vi) to keep important agreements you have made (such as accepting employment as a bodyguard); or (vii) to save the lives of large numbers of innocent people when you are the only one who can do so. And perhaps there are other specific duties of sacrifice that I have left off this list. But as a whole, the duties are limited to special and quite unlikely circumstances. (Military service is the only seriously life-endangering-required activity that is at all likely to confront a significant segment of the population. Presumably such service is morally obligatory only if the war is just, which frequently is not the case. Further, in most wars the percentage of those serving who are killed is rather low.)

Now if the chances are small that you will ever confront a situation in which you are morally obligated to surrender your life, it may well pay you to adopt a moral way of life, even if doing so increases the likelihood that you would sacrifice your life in such a situation. For the relatively certain external and internal benefits of the moral life should far outweigh the very unlikely loss of one's life. Further, it is worth noting that many immoral lifestyles — crime, debauchery, deception of all those around you — may have much higher premature death rates than the moral life. Insofar as adoption of a moral way of life ensures that you will not lapse into one of these alternatives, it may even on balance increase your life expectancy.

The argument, then, is that adopting a moral way of life carries at most a very small net risk to one's life. Since it provides significant benefits with high probability, it is a reasonable prudential choice. It is useful in understanding this argument to compare adopting a moral way of life with two other activities that are not generally thought to be imprudent: joining the military and entering into a long-term love relationship, such as by marrying or having children. These undertakings are like becoming moral in the main respect relevant to our argument. They are likely to involve or produce changes in one's motivational structure that would render one more likely to risk or sacrifice one's life in certain circumstances, such as when your loved ones or comrades in arms are in danger. (In addition, military service carries a nonnegligible risk of finding yourself in precisely these circumstances.) But this feature of these undertakings is not usually thought to render them ineligible choices from a prudential perspective. Why, then, should the same feature render becoming moral a generally imprudent course of conduct? This activity, like entering a long-term love relationship, promises very large external and internal rewards while involving a relatively tiny risk of loss of life. The gamble is hardly more foolish in the case of virtue than in the case of love.

IV. *Group Immorality*

Human beings, as has often been remarked, are social creatures. We need one another for a variety of practical and emotional reasons — for help in securing satisfaction of our material needs, for physical protection, for companionship, for love, and so on. The above arguments that duty and interest coincide all rest on this fact. Individuals need the help rather than the hostility of society to prosper, and in the process of social learning they internalize norms of conscience that further fuse their interests with those of the social group. However, one does not require the aid or cooperation of *all* others, only of a sufficient number of those with whom one is likely to come in contact. This fact generates the most telling objection to the Reconciliation Project: That it is not in the interests of powerful *groups* and their members to treat decently and to help, as morality demands, the members of weak groups, who are apparently not in a position to return good for good and evil for evil.

It is clear that when we consider relations among groups, our earlier tools for reconciling interest and obligation cannot be used in the same way. External sanctions operate effectively, to the extent they do, because it is in the general interest of society and its members to restrain individuals from harming others. But if there is a split between groups in society, there may be no effective sanction against members of a dominant group harming members of a powerless group. For the others in the dominant group may condone, or even approve, such conduct, while the members of the powerless group are too weak to punish the offenders. And if the norms of the dominant group allow, or even encourage, mistreatment of the powerless group — as throughout history they often have — even well-socialized members of the dominant group may carry out such mistreatment without suffering substantial guilt feelings.

This objection shows that there cannot be a satisfactory solution to the Reconciliation Project if the project is strictly interpreted along the social and degree dimensions. That is, we cannot hope to show that in all historically actual (much less all conceivable) social circumstances it has been (or would be) in the interests of all groups and their members to act morally toward members of other groups. Instead, particular cases of supposed divergence of group duty and interest must be considered on an ad hoc basis, and the most we can reasonably aspire to is the presentation of arguments that make it plausible that obligation and interest coincide in *actual* present circumstances. This will not ease the anxiety of moralists who seek a noncontingent guarantee that interest and duty will never diverge. But it could suffice to convince the attentive moral individual, or group leader, that he or she is not being foolish in acting morally, or in leading his or her group in a moral direction.

Before discussing the three most important specific instances of the objection before us, it should be pointed out that whether there is hope of reconciling group interest and duty depends on what we take the demands of duty to be. In the case of individuals, we saw that a unilateralist-idealistic interpretation of moral requirements might render the Reconciliation Project impossible. Similarly, if we interpret morality as requiring rich and powerful groups to share so much with the poor and weak as to create absolute equality, there is very little prospect that duty and interest can be reconciled. But it is far from obvious that morality demands this much. What morality does clearly require is that the rich and powerful refrain from actively harming the poor and weak, and that the former aid the latter when the costs of giving are small and the benefits of receiving are large. We shall see that with this modest interpretation of the obligations of the powerful, reconciling their obligations with their interests may be possible.

Let us turn to our examples, the first concerning justice within a society. Why should rich and powerful groups in a nation allow the poor opportunities for education, employment, and advancement and provide social-welfare programs that benefit the poor as morality requires? Why shouldn't they simply oppress and exploit the poor? There are several reasons why, in modern times, it is most probably in the long-term interest of the rich and powerful to treat the domestic poor well. First, some rich individuals, and more likely some of their children, may be poor at some time in the future and thus benefit from programs to help the poor. Second, offering opportunities to members of all groups widens the pool of talent available to fill socially useful jobs, which should provide long-run economic benefits to members of all groups. Third, and most important, there is the reason that has impressed social theorists from Hobbes to Rawls: Decent treatment of all promotes social stability and cohesion and discourages revolution. This reason is especially important in contemporary times, when ideals of human dignity, equality, and justice are known and espoused virtually everywhere, and when revolution is frequently proposed as a legitimate means of attaining such ideals.

Taken together, these reasons constitute a strong case, on prudential grounds, for decent treatment of the domestic poor by a nation's dominant groups. In fact, if we apply Disaster Avoidance reasoning, it turns out that the third reason alone shows that good treatment of the poor is prudentially rational. For if the poor find the status quo unacceptable and apply such reasoning, they will revolt. Thus Hobbes writes, "Needy men and hardy, not contented with their present condition, . . . are inclined to . . . stir up trouble and sedition; for there is no . . . such hope to mend an ill game as by causing a new shuffle." The rich, being aware of this, will (if they follow a Disaster Avoidance strategy) seek to prevent the poor from falling into such unacceptable circumstances. For the rich thereby maximize their chances of obtaining an outcome acceptable to them: preservation of something resembling the status quo.

What about a wealthy and powerful nation aiding poor, weak nations? Is this in the long-run interest of the former as well as the latter? In a world of advanced technology, international markets, ideological conflicts among powerful nations, and nuclear weapons, it most probably is. In competition with other powerful nations, allies — even poor nations — are useful for political, economic, and military reasons. And economic development of poor nations should, in the long run, produce economic benefits for richer nations, such as by providing markets and reliable supplies of various raw and finished goods. Most important, continued poverty in the Third World is likely to produce continued political turmoil, civil wars, and regional wars between nations. In a world armed to the teeth with nuclear weapons, and with more and more nations acquiring such weapons, the long-run danger of rich developed countries being drawn into a devastating military conflict started by a desperate poor nation, or some desperate group within such a nation, is far from negligible.

The above arguments about domestic and international justice suggest there is, after all, a form of reciprocity between powerful and weak groups because of interdependencies between the two in economic and security matters. The poor cannot return the aid of the rich in kind, but they can offer their talents, their purchasing power, and so on. If not treated well, they cannot directly punish the rich and powerful, but they can stir up serious trouble for them if they are willing to experience such trouble themselves. Thus they are able, and likely, to return good for good and evil for evil to the rich in the long run, and it will be rational for the rich to act accordingly.

Even this form of reciprocity is not available, however, to deal with our third and most puzzling example — the treatment of future generations. Future generations (beyond the next few) are powerless to act upon us, since they will not exist until after we are dead. Yet we have substantial power to determine the quality of their lives by influencing their numbers and the nature of the social and natural environment into which they will be born. Given this absolute asymmetry in power to affect one another, how can it be in our interest to act morally toward future generations? Morality requires us, at a minimum, to leave our descendants with enough resources to allow future people to live decent lives. But this would necessitate having a lower material standard of living than we could obtain by depleting resources and contaminating the environment whenever it is convenient to do so. If future generations cannot punish us for ruthlessly exploiting the earth in this way, doesn't rational prudence require it of us?

The supporter of the Reconciliation Project can come some considerable way toward answering even this objection. He might point out first that misuse of resources and damage to the environment will often produce substantial negative effects within our own lifetimes. So, for the most part, it is in our own interests to follow conservation policies that will turn out to benefit future generations. This reply will take us only so far, however. For there are policies whose benefits are experienced now and most of whose costs will be borne generations later (such as building nuclear power plants without having solved the long-term waste storage problem). Also, optimal *rates* of use of scarce nonrenewable resources will vary greatly depending upon how long we care about the resource lasting. Hence, there is a far from perfect overlap between the resource and environmental policies likely to most benefit present people and those likely to ensure a decent life for future generations.

A more promising argument begins from the fact that most people care very deeply about the happiness of their own children and grandchildren, and hence their own happiness would be diminished by contemplating the prospect of these descendants having to live in a resource-depleted world. Further, they realize that their children's and grandchildren's happiness will in turn be affected by the prospects for happiness of *their* children and grandchildren, and so forth. Hence, the happiness of present people is linked, generation by generation, to the prospects for happiness of some likely members of distant future generations. This "chain-connection" argument has considerable force, but it falls short of constituting a full solution to the problem before us. This is because the perceived happiness of one's children and grandchildren is only one component of the well-being or happiness of the typical parent. And the perceived happiness of *their* children and grandchildren is, in turn, only one component of the happiness of one's children and grandchildren. So there is a multiplier effect over generations that quickly diminishes the influence on a present person's happiness of the prospects for happiness of his later descendants. And we must seek some other device to link living peoples' interests firmly with those of distant future generations.

The most promising such device is an appeal to our need to give meaning to our lives and endeavors. I have suggested elsewhere that one strong reason we have for providing future people with the means to survive and prosper is that this is our best hope for the successful continuation of certain human enterprises that we value (and may have contributed to) — science, the arts and humanities, morality, religion, democratic government. Similarly, Ernest Partridge has argued that human beings have a psychological need for "self-transcendence"; that is, a need to contribute to projects that are outside themselves and that will continue after their deaths. Those without such goals are unlikely to find meaning in their lives, especially during the middle and later stages of life, when people typically reflect on their own mortality. Thus Partridge says, "We need the future, *now*."

There is a great deal of truth in this argument, but there are some limits to what it can show. It cannot reconcile the interests and obligations to posterity of the narcissist who has no self-transcending goals and is incapable of developing them. However, this need not worry us anymore than did the corresponding remark made earlier about the person no longer capable of becoming moral. The self-transcending life may be the happier life for the vast majority who still can live it, and these people have good prudential reasons for doing so. The more important problem is that not all self-transcending concerns need be directed toward the distant future. They may involve goals that do not extend much beyond one's lifetime (such as the prosperity of one's children or the eventual rise to power of one's favorite political movement). Such goals may give meaning to one's life without supplying reasons to provide for the welfare of distant generations. Perhaps, though, it is a psychological fact that enterprises that promise to continue into the indefinite future are better able to provide meaning in our lives, or to provide consolation for our mortality. If so, there would be powerful prudential reasons for one's adopting self-transcending concerns of unlimited temporal scope, and for protecting the social and natural environments for future generations.

These are the best arguments I can think of for a coincidence of self-interest and our obligations to posterity. Many (including myself at times) will find them only partly convincing. Does this lack of complete conviction indicate that we should abandon the Reconciliation Project? No. Instead, we may broaden our interpretation of that project.

V. The Wider Project

The general strategy I have followed in outlining a defense of the Reconciliation Project has been to restrain the project's ambitions where necessary. Thus the scope of the project has been narrowed in several ways. It applies to ways of life rather than particular actions and to practice morality rather than ideal morality. It succeeds with respect to most people and groups in actual social circumstances, but not with respect to all people and groups in all actual or possible circumstances. It may not convince the skeptical immoralist to change his ways, but it provides good reasons for moral people not to regret (or abandon) their way of life and for loving parents to raise their children to be moral.

However, to understand better the relationship between morality, rationality, and self-interest, we must briefly consider an important *widening* of the Reconciliation Project. For that project may be viewed as but a specific instance of a more general project: reconciling morality with the requirements of practical rationality. Given two special assumptions—the truth of Psychological Egoism and the

interpretation of practical rationality as the efficient pursuit of the agent's ends (whatever they may be)—this Wider Reconciliation Project would collapse into our original version concerning morality and self-interest. But the first of these assumptions is surely false; on any construal that does not render all motives self-interested by definition, people sometimes do have unselfish aims and possess and act upon non-self-interested motives. As a result, the question of whether moral requirements are consistent with the rational pursuit of the actual ends that people have is both distinct from and more important than the question of whether these requirements cohere with the demands of prudence.

Would shifting our focus to the Wider Reconciliation Project render irrelevant all we have said about the original project? If self-interested concerns played only an insignificant role in human motivation, it would. But clearly this is not the case. In fact, while Psychological Egoism is false, I would venture to propose that a milder doctrine, which I call Predominant Egoism, is probably true. Predominant Egoism says that human beings are, as a matter of fact, predominantly self-interested in the following sense. At least until they have achieved a satisfactory level of security and well-being, people's self-interested concerns tend to override their other-regarding, idealistic, and altruistic motives in determining their actions. Further, those nonselfish concerns that are sufficiently powerful to move people to acts that seriously conflict with self-interest tend to be limited in scope, such as to the well-being of family and friends and the advancement of specific favored projects or institutions.

Now if it is true that people are predominantly self-interested, in this sense, many or most of their strongest motives and dearest ends are self-interested ones. And the above arguments about reconciling duty and interest will be highly relevant to the task of reconciling duty and the rational pursuit of people's actual ends. But in carrying out this Wider Reconciliation Project, there would be a new resource to appeal to—the altruistic and nonselfish ends that most everyone actually has to some degree. The presence of these ends may extend the range of cases in which the requirements of reason and morality coincide beyond those in which prudence and morality coincide.

Consider again our relationship to future generations. Most of us do have significant nonselfish concerns about the well-being of our children and grandchildren and the survival and prospering of the human species. So we have reason to provide for these things *over and above* the contribution that our awareness of such provision makes to our own psychic well-being. This further strengthens both the chain-connection and self-transcendence arguments for reconciling practical rationality with our duties to posterity. For it shows that in carrying out such duties we are fulfilling ends of ours not previously considered (that is, non-selfish ends) in addition to contributing to our own happiness.

The recognition of nonselfish ends also provides a fresh perspective on the sustenance of moral motivation over generations. We suggested earlier that parents seeking to promote their children's interests would have good reasons to raise their children to be moral. This suggestion would have little significance if we were operating upon an assumption of the truth of Psychological Egoism. (For then the only relevant question would be whether it is in a *parent's* interest to raise his or her children to be moral.) Since, however, concern for the well-being of one's children is among the strongest and most universal of non-self-interested human concerns, the suggestion is crucial to our understanding of how morality is rationally passed on from generation to generation. Typical parents who care strongly for the well-being of their children and care

somewhat for the well-being of others have three significant reasons for raising those children to be moral: This will likely benefit the children (in accordance with our earlier arguments that being moral usually pays), it will likely benefit others who are affected by the children, and it will likely benefit the parents themselves (because their children will treat them better). And when children grow up as moral beings possessing consciences and the potential to experience the satisfactions of morality, it is, we have argued, most always in their interest to continue to live a moral life. Further, they, as parents, will have the same reasons for raising their children to be moral as their parents had for raising them in this manner. Thus morality can be seen to be potentially self-sustaining from generation to generation, without even taking into account socializing influences on the child from outside the family.

In raising children to be moral, and in providing for future generations, some of the ends that we seek to achieve are non-self-interested ones. Given the content of moral rules and their connection with protecting the interests of others, many morally required actions will satisfy ends of this kind. As a result, the Wider Reconciliation Project should be successful in more cases than the original project. We may restate this crucial point: While it is normally prudent to be moral, it is sometimes rational to be moral even if it is not prudent.

Suggestions for Further Reading

Baier, Kurt. *The Moral Point of View.* Cornell University Press, 1958.

Frankena, William. *Thinking About Morality.* University of Michigan Press, 1980.

Gauthier, David, ed. *Morality and Rational Self-Interest.* Prentice-Hall, 1970.

Gauthier, David. *Morality by Agreement.* Clarendon Press, 1986.

Hospers, John. *Human Conduct: An Introduction to the Problems of Ethics.* Harcourt Brace Jovanovich, 1961.

Nielsen, Kai. "Is 'Why Should I Be Moral?' an Absurdity?" *Australasian Journal of Philosophy* 36, 1958.

Nielsen, Kai. "Why Should I Be Moral?" *Methodos* XV, no. 59–60, 1963. This comprehensive article appears in several anthologies.

Phillips, D.Z. "Does It Pay to Be Good?" *Proceedings of the Aristotelian Society* 65, 1964–1965.

Richards, David. *A Theory of Reasons for Action.* Oxford University Press, 1971.

Part XI

Religion and Ethics

Does God love goodness because it is good, or is it good because God loves it?

God is like a cosmic gardener — he tends and protects individual morality, he nourishes it and helps it bloom. Some people, like a hothouse orchid or a fancy rose, do seem to need religion for their morality to have a purpose or justification. Others are like the Queen Anne's Lace — able to withstand almost anything on their own. And many are borderline QAL, who need just that extra bit of fertilizer to break into bloom — and God provides it. But mankind could do as well. The relationship between God and morality is as simple as that — God is a parent, gardener, and so on. He strengthens and cushions individual morality, he gives motivation (in the form of the outcomes: heaven or hell), and justice and order in a sometimes extremely chaotic world. But morality exists apart from God, and as hard as it is for some to accept it, could survive and even flourish in a world without God.

LAURA BURRELL
Sophomore, University of Mississippi

Does morality depend on religion, and are religious ethics essentially different from secular ethics? These questions are related, but not the same. Unlike many religions found in the ancient world, Judaism, Islam, and Christianity are ethical monotheisms. They not only promise salvation to the faithful, but they tie ethical responsibility into the matrix of salvation in a very close way, either by making the moral life a necessary condition for God's favor, or a consequence of it.

The first question is whether moral standards themselves depend on God for their valid-ity or whether there is an autonomy of ethics, so that even God is subject to the moral order. As Socrates asks in our first reading from the *Euthyphro*, "Do the gods love holiness because it is holy, or is it holy because the gods love it?" According to one theory, called the *divine command theory*, ethical principles are simply the commands of God. They derive their validity from the fact that God commanded them, and they *mean* 'Commanded by God.' Without God, there would be no universally valid morality. As Dostoyevski wrote in *Brothers Karamazov*, "If God doesn't exist, everything is permissible." Without God we have moral nihilism.

We can analyze the divine command theory into three separate theses: (1) morality (that is, rightness and wrongness) originates with God; (2) moral rightness simply means willed by God and moral wrongness means against the will of God; and (3) no further reasons for action are necessary. Essentially, morality is based on divine will, not on independently existing reasons for action.

There are many modified versions of the divine command theory that drop or qualify one or more of the three theses, but the strongest form includes all three theses.

The opposing viewpoint—we will call it the *autonomy of ethics* position—denies all three theses: morality does not originate with God (although the way God created us may affect the specific nature of morality); rightness and wrongness are based on something other than simply God's will (for example, the flourishing of the creation, the perfection of rational beings); and there are reasons for acting one way or the other that may be known independently of God's will. In sum, ethics are autonomous and even God must keep the moral law, which exists independently of God—as the laws of mathematics and logic do.

God, of course, *knows* what is right—better than we do—but, in principle, we act morally for the same reasons that God does. We both follow moral reasons that are independent of God. If there is no God (in this account), nothing is changed. Morality is left intact, and if we choose to be moral, we have the very same duties as we would have if we were theists.

The motivation for the divine command theory is to preserve or do justice to the omnipotence or sovereignty of God. God somehow is thought to be less sovereign or necessary to our lives if he is not the source of morality. When the believer asks what the will of God is, the question

is a direct appeal to a personal will, not to an independently existing rule.

One problem with the divine command theory is that it would seem to make redundant the attribution of 'goodness' to God. When we say, "God is good," we think that we are ascribing a property to God; but if 'good' simply meant 'that which God commands or wills,' then we are not attributing any property to God. Our statement then merely means 'God wills what God wills,' which is a tautology. A second problem is that if God's arbitrary fiat (in the sense of not being based on reasons) is the sole criterion for right and wrong, it would seem to be logically possible for such heinous acts as rape, killing of the innocent for the fun of it, and gratuitous cruelty to become morally good actions—if God suddenly decided to command us to do these things. But then, wouldn't morality be reduced to the right of the powerful, to Nietzsche's "might makes right?"

The second problem related to the matter of religion and morality is the degree to which religious morality and nonreligious morality are in *content* and *form* similar to each other. The problem also relates to the adequacy of motivation. According to some, secularity offers insufficient incentive to live a moral life, or, at least, an altruistic life. Since 'ought' implies 'can,' we conclude that secular ethics is less altruistic than religious ethics.

As our second reading shows, Immanuel Kant, who held to the autonomy of ethics, believed there could be no difference between valid religious ethics and valid philosophical ethics. God and humanity both must obey the same rational principles, and reason is sufficient to guide us to these principles.

Kant's system exalts ethics as an intrinsic good; indeed, doing one's duty for no other reason but that it is one's duty is the highest good there is. As such, it is related to religion, to our duty to God. God loves the virtuous, and finally will reward the virtuous with happiness in proportion to their virtue. In fact, God and immortality are necessary postulates of ethics.

Immortality is a necessary postulate in this way: We are commanded by the moral law to be morally perfect. Since 'ought' implies 'can,' we must be *able* to reach moral perfection. But we cannot attain perfection in this life, for the task is an infinite one. So there must be an afterlife in which we continue to make progress toward this ideal.

God is a necessary postulate in that there must be someone to enforce the moral law. That is, to be completely justified the moral law must end in a just recompense of happiness in accordance to virtue. The good must be rewarded by happiness in proportion to their virtue, and the evil in proportion to their vice. This harmonious correlation of virtue and happiness does not happen in this life, so it must happen in the next life. So there must be a God, acting as judge and enforcer of the moral law, without which the moral law would be unjustified.

Kant is not saying that we can *prove* that God exists or that we ought to be moral *in order* to be happy. Rather, the idea of God serves as a completion of our ordinary idea of ethics.

In our third reading, Bertrand Russell disagrees with Kant about the need for God in order to have an adequate morality. One can be moral, and, within the limits of thoughtful stoic resignation, even happy. The world is absurd, a godless tragedy in which "Nature, omnipotent but blind, in the revolutions of her secular hurryings through the abysses of space, has brought forth at last a child, subject still to her power, but gifted with sight, with knowledge of good and evil, with the capacity of judging all the works of his unthinking Mother." It is this conscious power of moral evaluation that makes the child superior to his omnipotent mother. People are free to think, to evaluate, to create, and to live committed to ideals. So in spite of suffering, despair, and death,

human beings are free. Life has the meaning that we give it.

In "Religion and the Queerness of Morality," George Mavrodes picks up on the Kantian theme and criticizes Russell's secular view as puzzling. If there is no God, then doesn't secular ethics suffer from a certain inadequacy? Mavrodes argues that Russell's world of secular morality cannot satisfactorily answer the question, Why should I be moral? For, on its account, the common goods at which morality in general aims are often just those goods that we sacrifice in carrying out our moral obligations. Why should we sacrifice our welfare for our moral duty?

Another oddity about secular ethics is that it is superficial, not deeply rooted. it seems to lack the metaphysical basis that a Platonic or Judeo-Christian worldview affords. "Values and obligations cannot be deep in such a [secular] world. What is deep in a Russellian world must be such things as matter and energy, or perhaps natural law, chance, or chaos. If it really were a fact that one had obligations in a Russellian world, then something would be laid upon man that might cost a man everything but that went no further than man. And that difference from a Platonic world seems to make all the difference."

Mavrodes outlines how a religious morality can meet these desiderata, and, if we are inclined to believe that morality is not queer, how it can provide some evidence for the religious worldview.

Kai Nielsen's article, "Ethics Without God," was written twenty years before Mavrodes' paper on the queerness of morality, and it anticipates some of his arguments. Nielsen's thesis is that even if "God is dead," it really doesn't matter as far as our morality is concerned. First, with the loss of faith all our essential moral values are left intact. We still can be happy, find security and emotional peace, experience love and friendship, and enjoy creative work and a rich variety of experiences. Second, both the secular and the religious bases of ethics involve an objective rationale that contains central principles, such as benevolence and respect for persons and justice. Our common nature and quest for the good life is all the grounding that ethics needs. It is true that morality sometimes calls for the sacrifice of nonmoral goods. It would be nice if this were not the case, but life is sometimes difficult. Nielsen notes that both secular ethics and religion have a difficult time with evil, for it is the central hindrance to religious belief for many.

XI.1 *Morality and Religion*

PLATO

We have already encountered the writings of Plato (427–347 B.C.) in our readings in Parts I and X. Here we find his mentor, Socrates, engaged in a dialogue with the self-righteously religious Euthyphro, who is going to court to report his father for having killed a slave. In the course of the discussion Socrates raises the question that has come to be known as the question of the divine command theory of ethics: Is the good good because God loves it, or does God love the good because it is good?

SOCRATES: But shall we . . . say that whatever all the gods hate is unholy, and whatever they all love is holy: while whatever some of them love, and others hate, is either both or neither? Do you wish us now to define holiness and unholiness in this manner?

EUTHYPHRO: Why not, Socrates?

SOCRATES: There is no reason why I should not, Euthyphro. It is for you to consider whether that definition will help you to instruct me as you promised.

EUTHYPHRO: Well, I should say that holiness is what all the gods love, and that unholiness is what they all hate.

SOCRATES: Are we to examine this definition, Euthyphro, and see if it is a good one? Or are we to be content to accept the bare assertions of other men, or of ourselves, without asking any questions? Or must we examine the assertions?

EUTHYPHRO: We must examine them. But for my part I think that the definition is right this time.

SOCRATES: We shall know that better in a little while, my good friend. Now consider this question. Do the gods love holiness because it is holy, or is it holy because they love it?

EUTHYPHRO: I do not understand you, Socrates.

SOCRATES: I will try to explain myself: we speak of a thing being carried and carrying, and being led and leading, and being seen and seeing; and you understand that all such expressions mean different things, and what the difference is.

EUTHYPHRO: Yes, I think I understand.

SOCRATES: And we talk of a thing being loved, and, which is different, of a thing loving?

EUTHYPHRO: Of course.

SOCRATES: Now tell me: is a thing which is being carried in a state of being carried, because it is carried, or for some other reason?

EUTHYPHRO: No, because it is carried.

Reprinted from the *Euthyphro*, translated by William Jowett (Charles Scribner's Sons, 1889).

SOCRATES: And a thing is in a state of being led, because it is led, and of being seen, because it is seen?

EUTHYPHRO: Certainly.

SOCRATES: Then a thing is not seen because it is in a state of being seen; it is in a state of being seen because it is seen: and a thing is not led because it is in a state of being led; it is in a state of being led because it is led: and a thing is not carried because it is in a state of being carried; it is in a state of being carried because it is carried. Is my meaning clear now, Euthyphro? I mean this: if anything becomes or is affected, it does not become because it is in a state of becoming; it is in a state of becoming because it becomes; and it is not affected because it is in a state of being affected: it is in a state of being affected because it is affected. Do you not agree?

EUTHYPHRO: I do.

SOCRATES: Is not that which is being loved in a state, either of becoming, or of being affected in some way by something?

EUTHYPHRO: Certainly.

SOCRATES: Then the same is true here as in the former cases. A thing is not loved by those who love it because it is in a state of being loved. It is in a state of being loved because they love it.

EUTHRYPHRO: Necessarily.

SOCRATES: Well, then, Euthyphro, what do we say about holiness? Is it not loved by all the gods, according to your definition?

EUTHYPHRO: Yes.

SOCRATES: Because it is holy, or for some other reason?

EUTHYPHRO: No, because it is holy.

SOCRATES: Then it is loved by the gods because it is holy: it is not holy because it is loved by them?

EUTHYPHRO: It seems so.

SOCRATES: But then what is pleasing to the gods is pleasing to them, and is in a state of being loved by them, because they love it?

EUTHYPHRO: Of course.

SOCRATES: Then holiness is not what is pleasing to the gods, and what is pleasing to the gods is not holy, as you say, Euthyphro. They are different things.

EUTHYPHRO: And why, Socrates?

SOCRATES: Because we are agreed that the gods love holiness because it is holy: and that it is not holy because they love it. Is not this so?

EUTHYPHRO: Yes.

SOCRATES: And that what is pleasing to the gods because they love it, is pleasing to them by reason of this same love: and that they do not love it because it is pleasing to them.

EUTHYPHRO: True.

SOCRATES: Then, my dear Euthyphro, holiness, and what is pleasing to the gods, are different things. If the gods had loved holiness because it is holy, they would also have loved what is pleasing to them because it is pleasing to them; but if what is pleasing to them had been pleasing to them because they loved it, then holiness too would have been holiness, because they loved it. But now you see that they are opposite things, and wholly different from each other. For the one is of a sort to be loved because it is loved: while the other is loved, because it is of a sort to be loved. My question, Euthyphro, was, What is holiness? But it turns out that you have not explained to me the essence of holiness; you have been content to mention an attribute which belongs to it, namely, that all the gods love it. You have not yet told me what is its essence. Do not, if you please, keep from me what holiness is; begin again and tell me that. Never mind whether the gods love it, or whether it has other attributes: we shall not differ on that point. Do your best to make it clear to me what is holiness and what is unholiness.

XI.2 *God and Immortality as Necessary Postulates of Morality*

IMMANUEL KANT

Immanuel Kant (1724–1804) was professor of philosophy at the University of Königsberg and is generally recognized as one of the greatest philosophers and, especially, moral philosophers, in the history of Western civilization. In this section from his *Critique of Practical Reason,* he argues that religion is indirectly confirmed by our knowledge of the moral law. The moral law is the highest good (*summum bonum*) — to be moral is to carry out one's duty to God. God loves the virtuous, and finally will reward the virtuous with happiness in proportion to their virtue. In fact, God and immortality are necessary postulates of ethics.

Immortality is necessary in this way: We are commanded by the moral law to be morally perfect. Since 'ought' implies 'can,' we must be *able* to reach moral perfection. But we cannot attain perfection in this life, for the task is an infinite one. So there must be an afterlife in which we continue to make progress toward this ideal.

God is a necessary postulate in that there must be someone to enforce the moral law. That is, to be completely justified the moral law must result in a just distribution of happiness in accordance to virtue. The good must be rewarded by happiness in proportion to their virtue, and the evil in proportion to their vice. This harmonious correlation of virtue and happiness does not happen in this life, so it must happen in the next life. So there must be a God, acting as judge and enforcer of the moral law, without which the moral law would be unjustified.

The ideal of moral perfection rewarded by perfect happiness is the highest good (the *summum bonum*) in its complete manifestation.

The Immortality of the Soul as a Postulate of Pure Practical Reason

The realization of the *summum bonum* in the world is the necessary object of a will determinable by the moral. But in this will the *perfect accordance* of the mind with the moral law is the supreme condition of the *summum bonum.* This then must be possible, as well as its object, since it is contained in the command to promote the latter. Now, the perfect accordance of the will with the moral law is *holiness,* a perfection of which no rational being of the sensible world is capable at any moment of his existence.

Since, nevertheless, it is required as practically necessary, it can only be found in a *progress in infinitum* toward that perfect accordance, and on the principles of pure practical reason it is necessary to assume such a practical progress as the real object of our will.

Now, this endless progress is only possible on the supposition of an *endless* duration of the *existence* and personality of the same rational being (which is called the immortality of the soul). The *summum bonum,* then, practically is only possible on the supposition of the immortality of the soul; consequently this immortality, being inseparably connected with the moral law, is a postulate of pure practical reason (by which I mean a *theoretical* proposition, not demonstrable as such, but which is an inseparable result of an unconditional *a priori practical* law).

Reprinted from *Critique of Practical Reason,* translated by T. K. Abbott (Longmans, Green, 1873).

This principle of the moral destination of our nature, namely, that it is only in an endless progress that we can attain perfect accordance with the moral law, is of the greatest use, not merely for the present purpose of supplementing the impotence of speculative reason, but also with respect to religion. In default of it, either the moral law is quite degraded from its *holiness,* being made out to be *indulgent,* and conformable to our convenience, or else men strain their notions of their vocation and their expectation to an unattainable goal, hoping to acquire complete holiness of will, and so they lose themselves in fantastical *theosophic* dreams, which wholly contradict self-knowledge. In both cases the unceasing *effort* to obey punctually and thoroughly a strict and inflexible command of reason, which yet is not ideal but real, is only hindered. For a rational but finite being, the only thing possible is an endless progress from the lower to higher degrees of moral perfection. The *Infinite* Being, to whom the condition of time is nothing, sees in this to us endless succession a whole of accordance with the moral law; and the holiness which His command inexorably requires, in order to be true to His justice in the share which He assigns to each in the *summum bonum,* is to be found in a single intellectual intuition of the whole existence of rational beings. All that can be expected of the creature in respect of the hope of this participation would be the consciousness of his tried character, by which, from the progress he has hitherto made from the worse to the morally better, and the immutability of purpose which has thus become known to him, he may hope for a further unbroken continuance of the same, however long his existence may last, even beyond this life, and thus he may hope, not indeed here, nor in any imaginable point of his future existence, but only in the endlessness of his duration (which God alone can survey) to be perfectly adequate to his will (without indulgence or excuse, which do not harmonize with justice).

The Existence of God as Postulate of Pure Practical Reason

In the foregoing analysis the moral law led to a practical problem which is prescribed by pure reason alone, without the aid of any sensible motives, namely, that of the necessary completeness of the first and principal element of the *summum bonum,* viz. Morality; and as this can be perfectly solved only in eternity, to the postulate of *immortality.* The same law must also lead us to affirm the possibility of the second element of the *summum bonum,* viz. Happiness proportioned to that morality, and this on grounds as disinterested as before, and solely from impartial reason; that is, it must lead to the supposition of the existence of a cause adequate to this effect; in other words, it must postulate the *existence of God,* as the necessary condition of the possibility of the *summum bonum* (an object of the will which is necessarily connected with the moral legislation of pure reason). We proceed to exhibit this connexion in a convincing manner.

Happiness is the condition of a rational being in the world with whom *everything goes according to his wish and will*; it rests, therefore, on the harmony of physical nature with his whole end, and likewise with the essential determining principle of his will. Now the moral law as a law of freedom commands by determining principles, which ought to be quite independent on nature and on its harmony with our faculty of desire (as springs). But the acting rational being in the world is not the cause of the world and of nature itself. There is not the least ground, therefore, in the moral law for a necessary connexion between morality and proportionate happiness in a being that belongs to the world as part of it, and therefore dependent on it, and which for that reason cannot by his will be a cause of his nature, nor by his own power make it thoroughly harmonize, as far as his happiness is concerned, with his practical principles. Nevertheless, in the practical problem of pure reason, i.e. the necessary pursuit of the *summum bonum,* such a connexion is postulated as necessary: we ought to endeavour to promote the *summum bonum,* which, therefore, must be possible. Accordingly, the existence of a cause of all nature, distinct from nature itself, and containing the principle of this connexion, namely, of the exact harmony of happiness with morality, is also *postulated.* Now, this supreme cause must contain the principle of the harmony of nature, not merely with a law of the will of rational beings, but with the conception of this *law,* in so far as they make it the *supreme determining principle of the will,* and consequently not merely with the form of morals, but with their morality as their motive, that is, with their moral character. Therefore, the *summum bonum* is possible in the world only on the supposition of a Supreme Being having a causality corresponding to moral character. Now a being that is capable of acting on the conception of laws is an *intelligence* (a rational being), and the causality of such a being according to this conception of laws is his *will*; therefore the supreme cause of nature, which must be presupposed as a condition of the *summum bonum,* is a being which is the cause of nature by *intelligence* and *will,* consequently its author, that is God. It follows that the postulate of the possibility of the *highest derived good* (the best world) is likewise the postulate of the reality of a *highest original good,* that is to say, of the existence of God. Now it was seen to be a duty for us to promote the *summum bonum*; consequently it is not merely allowable, but it is a necessity connected with duty as a requisite, that we should presuppose the possibility of this *summum bonum*; and as this is possible only on condition of the existence of God, it inseparably connects the supposition of this with duty; that is, it is morally necessary to assume the existence of God.

It must be remarked here that this moral necessity is *subjective,* that is, it is a want, and to *objective,* that is, itself a duty, for there cannot be a duty to suppose the existence of anything (since this concerns only the theoretical employment of reason). Moreover, it is not meant by this that it is necessary to suppose the existence of God *as a basis of all obligation in general* (for this rests, as has been sufficiently proved, simply on the autonomy of reason itself). What belongs to duty here is only the endeavour to realize and promote the *summum bonum* in the world, the possibility of which can therefore be postulated; and as our reason finds it not conceivable except on the supposition of a supreme intelligence, the admission of this existence is therefore connected with the consciousness of our duty, although the admission itself belongs to the domain of speculative reason. Considered in respect of this alone, as a principle of explanation, it may be called a *hypothesis,* but in reference to the intelligibility of an object given us by the moral law (the *summum bonum*), and consequently of a requirement for practical purposes, it may be called *faith,* that is to say a pure *rational faith,* since pure reason (both in its theoretical and its practical use) is the sole source form which it springs. . . .

The doctrine of Christianity, even if we do not yet consider it as a religious doctrine, gives, touching this point, a conception of the *summum bonum*

(the kingdom of God), which alone satisfies the strictest demand of practical reason. The moral law is holy (unyielding) and demands holiness of morals, although all the moral perfection to which man can attain is still only virtue, that is, a rightful disposition arising from *respect* for the law, implying consciousness of a constant propensity to transgression, or at least a want of purity, that is, a mixture of many spurious (not moral) motives of obedience to the law, consequently a self-esteem combined with humility. In respect, then, of the holiness which the Christian law requires, this leaves the creature nothing but a progress *in infinitum,* but for that very reason it justifies him in hoping for an endless duration of his existence. The *worth* of a character *perfectly* accordant with the moral law is infinite, since the only restriction on all possible happiness in the judgment of a wise and all-powerful distributor of it is the absence of conformity of rational beings to their duty. But the moral law of itself does not *promise* any happiness, for according to our conceptions of an order of nature in general, this is not necessarily connected with obedience to the law. Now Christian morality supplies this defect (of the second indispensable element of the *summum bonum*) by representing the world, in which rational beings devote themselves with all their soul to the moral law, as a *kingdom of God,* in which nature and morality are brought into a harmony foreign to each of itself, by a holy Author who makes the derived *summum bonum* possible. *Holiness* of life is prescribed to them as a rule even in this life, while the welfare proportioned to it, namely, *bliss,* is represented, as attainable only in an eternity; because the *former* must always be the pattern of their conduct in every state, and progress toward it is already possible and necessary in this life; while the *latter,* under the name of happiness, cannot be attained at all in this world (so far as our own power is concerned), and therefore is made simply an object of hope. Nevertheless, the Christian principle of *morality* itself is not theological (so as to be heteronomy), but is autonomy of pure practical reason, since it does not make the knowledge of God and His will the foundation of these laws, but only of the attainment of the *summum bonum,* on condition of following these laws, and it does not even place the proper *spring* of this obedience in the desired results, but solely in the conception of duty, as that of which the faithful observance alone constitutes the worthiness to obtain those happy consequences.

In this manner the moral laws lead through the conception of the *summum bonum* as the object and final end of pure practical reason to *religion,* that is, to the *recognition of all duties as divine commands, not as sanctions, that is to say, arbitrary ordinances of a foreign will and contingent in themselves,* but as essential *laws* of every free will in itself, which, nevertheless, must be regarded as commands of the Supreme Being, because it is only from a morally perfect (holy and good) and at the same time all-powerful will, and consequently only through harmony with this will, that we can hope to attain the *summum bonum* which the moral law makes it our duty to take as the object of our endeavours. Here again, then, all remains disinterested and founded merely on duty; neither fear nor hope being made the fundamental springs, which if taken as principles would destroy the whole moral worth of actions. The moral law commands me to make the highest possible good in a world the ultimate object of all my conduct. But I cannot hope to effect this otherwise than by the harmony of my will with that of a holy and good Author of the world; and although the conception of the *summum bonum* is a whole, in which the greatest happiness is conceived as combined in the most exact proportion with the highest degree of moral perfection (possible in creatures), includes *my own happiness,* yet it is not this that is the determining principle of the will which is enjoined to promote the *summum bonum,* but the moral law, which, on the contrary, limits by strict conditions my unbounded desire of happiness.

Hence also morality is not properly the doctrine how we should *make* ourselves happy, but how we should become *worthy* of happiness. It is only when religion is added that there also comes in the hope of participating some day in happiness in proportion as we have endeavoured to be not unworthy of it.

A man is *worthy* to possess a thing or a state when his possession of it is in harmony with the *summum bonum.* We can now easily see that all worthiness depends on moral conduct, since in the conception of the *summum bonum* this constitutes the condition of the rest (which belongs to one's state), namely, the participation of happiness. Now it follows from this that *morality* should never be treated as a *doctrine of happiness,* that is, an instruction how to become happy; for it has to do simply with the rational condition (*conditio sine qua non*) of happiness, not with the means of attaining it. But

when morality has been completely expounded (which merely imposes duties instead of providing rules for selfish desires), then first, after the moral desire to promote the *summum bonum* (to bring the kingdom of God to us) has been awakened, a desire founded on a law, and which could not previously arise in any selfish mind, and when for the behoof of this desire the step to religion has been taken, then this ethical doctrine may be also called a doctrine of happiness because the *hope* of happiness first begins with religion only.

We can also see from this that, when we ask what is *God's ultimate end* in creating the world, we must not name the *happiness* of the rational beings in it, but the *summum bonum,* which adds a further condition to that wish of such beings, namely, the condition of being worthy of happiness, that is, the *morality* of these same rational beings, a condition which alone contains the rule by which only they can hope to share in the former at the hand of a *wise* Author. For as *wisdom* theoretically considered signifies *the knowledge of the summum bonum,* and practically *the accordance of the will with the summum bonum,* we cannot attribute to a supreme independent wisdom an end based merely on *goodness.* For we cannot conceive the action of this goodness (in respect of the happiness of rational beings) as suitable to the highest original good, except under the restrictive conditions of harmony with the holiness[1] of His will. Therefore those who placed the end of creation in the glory of God (provided that this is not conceived anthropomorphically as a desire to be praised) have perhaps hit upon the best expression. For nothing glorifies God more than that which is the most estimable thing in the world, respect for His command, the observance of the holy duty that His law imposes on us, when there is added thereto His glorious plan of crowning such a beautiful order of things with corresponding happiness. If the latter (to speak humanly) make Him worthy of love, by the *former* He is an object of adoration. Even men can never acquire respect by benevolence alone, though they may gain love, so that the greatest beneficence only procures them honour when it is regulated by worthiness.

That in the order of ends, man (and with him every rational being) is *an end in himself,* that is, that he can never be used merely as a means by any (not even by God) without being at the same time an end also himself, that therefore *humanity* in our person must be *holy* to ourselves, this follows now of itself because he is the *subject of the moral law,* in other words, of that which is holy in itself, and on account of which and in agreement with which alone can anything be termed holy. For this moral law is founded on the autonomy of his will, as a free will which by its universal laws must necessarily be able to agree with that to which it is to submit itself.

Endnote

[1] In order to make these characteristics of these conceptions clear, I add the remark that whilst we ascribe to God various attributes, the quality of which we also find applicable to creatures, only that in Him they are raised to the highest degree, e.g. power, knowledge, presence, goodness, &c., under the designations of omnipotence, omniscience, omnipresence, &c., there are three that are ascribed to God exclusively, and yet without the addition of greatness, and which are all moral. He is the *only holy,* the *only blessed,* the *only wise,* because these conceptions already imply the absence of limitation. In the order of these attributes He is also the *holy lawgiver* (and creator), the *good governor* (and preserver), and the *just judge,* three attributes which include everything by which God is the object of religion, and in conformity with which the metaphysical perfections are added of themselves in the reason.

XI.3 *A Free Man's Worship*

BERTRAND RUSSELL

Bertrand Russell (1872–1970), once a student and a tutor at Cambridge University, is one of the most significant philosophers and social critics of the twentieth century. In this essay written in 1903, he disagrees with Kant on the need for religion as the culmination of ethics. We can be both moral and happy without God. The world is absurd, a godless tragedy in which "Nature, omnipotent but blind, in the revolutions of her secular hurryings through the abysses of space, has brought forth at last a child, subject still to her power, but gifted with sight, with knowledge of good and evil, with the capacity of judging all the works of his unthinking Mother." It is this conscious power of moral evaluation that makes the child superior to his omnipotent Mother. He has the capacity to reason, to evaluate, to create, and to live committed to ideals. So in spite of suffering, despair, and death, human beings are free and life may be meaningful.

To Dr. Faustus in his study Mephistopheles told the history of the Creation, saying:

'The endless praises of the choirs of angels had begun to grow wearisome; for, after all, did he not deserve their praise? Had he not given them endless joy? Would it not be more amusing to obtain undeserved praise, to be worshipped by beings whom he tortured? He smiled inwardly, and resolved that the great drama should be performed.

'For countless ages the hot nebula whirled aimlessly through space. At length it began to take shape, the central mass threw off planets, the planets cooled, boiling seas and burning mountains heaved and tossed, from black masses of cloud hot sheets of rain deluged the barely solid crust. And now the first germ of life grew in the depths of the ocean, and developed rapidly in the fructifying warmth into vast forest trees, huge ferns springing from the damp mould, sea monsters breeding, fighting, devouring, and passing away. And from the monsters, as the play unfolded itself, Man was born, with the power of thought, the knowledge of good and evil, and the cruel thirst for worship. And Man saw that all is passing in this mad, monstrous world, that all is struggling to snatch, at any cost, a few brief moments of life before Death's inexorable decree. And Man said: "There is a hidden purpose, could we but fathom it, and the purpose is good; for we must reverence something, and in the visible world there is nothing worthy of reverence." And Man stood aside from the struggle, resolving that God intended harmony to come out of chaos by human efforts. And when he followed the instincts which God had transmitted to him from his ancestry of beasts of prey, he called it Sin, and asked God to forgive him. But he doubted whether he could be justly forgiven, until he invented a divine Plan by which God's wrath was to have been appeased. And seeing the present was bad, he made it yet worse, that thereby the future might be better. And he gave God thanks for the strength that enabled him to forgo even the joys that were possible. And God smiled; and when he saw that Man had become perfect in renunciation and worship, he sent another sun through the sky, which crashed into Man's sun; and all returned again to nebula.

"Yes," he murmured, "it was a good play; I will have it performed again.'"

Such, in outline, but even more purposeless, more void of meaning, is the world which Science presents for our belief. Amid such a world, if anywhere, our ideals henceforward must find a home. That Man is the product of causes which had no prevision of the end they were achieving; that his origin, his growth, his hopes and fears, his loves and his beliefs, are but the outcome of accidental collocations of atoms; that no fire, no heroism, no intensity of thought and feeling, can preserve an individual life beyond the grave; that all the labours of the ages, all the devotion, all the inspiration, all the noonday brightness of human genius, are destined to extinction in the vast death of the solar system, and that the whole temple of Man's achievement must inevitably be buried beneath the debris of a universe in ruins — all these things, if not quite beyond dispute, are yet so nearly certain, that no philosophy which rejects them can hope to stand. Only within the scaffolding of these truths, only on the firm foundation of unyielding despair, can the soul's habitation henceforth be safely built.

How, in such an alien and inhuman world, can so powerless a creature as Man preserve his aspirations untarnished? A strange mystery it is that Nature, omnipotent but blind, in the revolutions of her secular hurryings through the abysses of space, has brought forth at last a child, subject still to her power, but gifted with sight, with knowledge of good and evil, with the capacity of judging all the works of his unthinking Mother. In spite of Death, the mark and seal of the parental control, Man is yet free, during his brief years, to examine, to criticize, to know, and in imagination to create. To him alone, in the world with which he is acquainted, this freedom belongs; and in this lies his superiority to the resistless forces that control his outward life.

The savage, like ourselves, feels the oppression of his impotence before the powers of Nature; but having in himself nothing that he respects more than Power, he is willing to prostrate himself before his gods, without inquiring whether they are worthy of his worship. Pathetic and very terrible is the long history of cruelty and torture, of degradation and human sacrifice, endured in the hope of placating the jealous gods: surely, the trembling believer thinks, when what is most precious has been freely given, their lust for blood must be appeased, and more will not be required. The religion of Moloch — as such creeds may be generically called — is in essence the cringing submission of the slave, who dare not, even in his heart, allow the thought that his master deserves no adulation. Since the independence of ideals is not yet acknowledged, Power may be freely worshipped, and receive an unlimited respect, despite its wanton infliction of pain.

But gradually, as morality grows bolder, the claim of the ideal world begins to be felt; and worship, if it is not to cease, must be given to gods of another kind than those created by the savage. Some, though they feel the demands of the ideal, will still consciously reject them, still urging that naked Power is worthy of worship. Such is the attitude inculcated in God's answer to Job out of the whirlwind: the divine power and knowledge are paraded, but of the divine goodness there is no hint. Such also is the attitude of those who, in our own day, base their morality upon the struggle for survival, maintaining that the survivors are necessarily the fittest. But others, not content with an answer so repugnant to the moral sense, will adopt the position which we have become accustomed to regard as specially religious, maintaining that, in some hidden manner, the world of fact is really harmonious with the world of ideals. Thus Man creates God, all-powerful and all-good, the mystic unity of what is and what should be.

But the world of fact, after all, is not good; and, in submitting our judgement to it, there is an element of slavishness from which our thoughts must be purged. For in all things it is well to exalt the dignity of Man, by freeing him as far as possible from the tyranny of non-human Power. When we have realized that Power is largely bad, that Man, with his knowledge of good and evil, is but a helpless atom in a world which has no such knowledge, the choice is again presented to us: Shall we worship Force, or shall we worship Goodness? Shall our God exist and be evil, or shall he be recognized as the creation of our own conscience?

The answer to this question is very momentous, and affects profoundly our whole morality. The worship of Force, to which Carlyle and Nietzsche and the creed of Militarism have accustomed us, is the result of failure to maintain our own ideals against a hostile universe: it is itself a prostrate submission to evil, a sacrifice of our best to Moloch. If strength indeed is to be respected, let us respect rather the strength of those who refuse that false 'recognition of facts' which fails to recognize that facts are often bad. Let us admit that, in the world we know, there are many things that would be better otherwise, and that the ideals to which we do and must adhere are not realized in the realm of matter. Let us preserve our respect for truth, for beauty, for the ideal of perfection which life does not permit us to attain, though none of these things meet with the approval of the unconscious universe. If Power is bad, as it seems to be, let us reject it from our hearts. In this lies Man's true freedom: in determination to worship only the God created by our own love of the good, to respect only the heaven which inspires the insight of our best moments. In action, in desire, we must submit perpetually to the tyranny of outside forces; but in thought, in aspiration, we are free, free from our fellow men, free from the petty planet on which our bodies impotently crawl, free even, while we live, from the tyranny of death. Let us learn, then, that energy of faith which enables us to live constantly in the vision of the good; and let us descend, in action, into the world of fact, with that vision always before us.

When first the opposition of fact and ideal grows fully visible, a spirit of fiery revolt, of fierce hatred of the gods, seems necessary to the assertion of freedom. To defy with Promethean constancy a hostile universe, to keep its evil always in view, always actively hated, to refuse no pain that the malice of Power can invent, appears to be the duty of all who will not bow before the inevitable. But indignation is still a bondage, for it compels our thoughts to be occupied with an evil world; and in the fierceness of desire from which rebellion springs there is a kind of self-assertion which it is necessary for the wise to overcome. Indignation is a submission of our thoughts, but not of our desires; the Stoic freedom in which wisdom consists is found in the submission of our desires, but not of our thoughts. From the submission of our desires springs the virtue of resignation; from the freedom of our thoughts springs the whole world of art and philosophy, and the vision of beauty by which, at last, we half reconquer the reluctant world. But the vision of beauty is possible only to unfettered contemplation, to thoughts not weighted by the load of eager wishes; and thus Freedom comes only to those who no longer ask of life that it shall yield them any of those personal goods that are subject to the mutations of Time.

Although the necessity of renunciation is evidence of the existence of evil, yet Christianity, in preaching it, has shown a wisdom exceeding that of the Promethean philosophy of rebellion. It must be admitted that, of the things we desire, some, though they prove impossible, are yet real goods; others, however, as ardently longed for, do not form part of a fully purified ideal. The belief that what must be renounced is bad, though sometimes false, is far less often false than untamed passion supposes; and the creed of religion, by providing a reason for proving that it is never false, has been the means of purifying our hopes by the discovery of many austere truths.

But there is in resignation a further good element: even real goods, when they are unattainable, ought not to be fretfully desired. To every man comes, sooner or later, the great renunciation. For the young, there is nothing unattainable; a good thing desired with the whole force of a passionate will, and yet impossible, is to them not credible. Yet, by death, by illness, by poverty, or by the voice of duty, we must learn, each one of us, that the world was not made for us, and that, however beautiful may be the things we crave, Fate may nevertheless forbid them. It is the part of courage, when misfortune comes, to bear without repining the ruin of our hopes, to turn away our thoughts from vain regrets. This degree of submission to Power is not only just and right: it is the very gate of wisdom.

But passive renunciation is not the whole of wisdom; for not by renunciation alone can we build a temple for the worship of our own ideals. Haunting foreshadowings of the temple appear in the realm of imagination, in music, in architecture, in the untroubled kingdom of reason, and in the golden sunset magic of lyrics, where beauty shines and glows, remote from the touch of sorrow, remote from the fear of change, remote from the failures and disenchantments of the world of fact. In the contemplation of these things the vision of heaven will shape itself in our hearts, giving at once a touchstone to judge the world about us, and an inspiration by which to fashion to our needs whatever is not incapable of serving as a stone in the sacred temple.

Except for those rare spirits that are born without sin, there is a cavern of darkness to be traversed before that temple can be entered. The gate of the cavern is despair, and its floor is paved with the gravestones of abandoned hopes. There Self must die; there the eagerness, the greed of untamed desire must be slain, for only so can the soul be free from the empire of Fate. But out of the cavern the Gate of Renunciation leads again to the daylight of wisdom, by whose radiance a new insight, a new joy, a new tenderness, shine forth to gladden the pilgrim's heart.

When, without the bitterness of impotent rebellion, we have learnt both to resign ourselves to the outward rule of Fate and to recognize that the non-human world is unworthy of our worship, it becomes possible at last so to transform and refashion the unconscious universe, so to transmute it in the crucible of imagination, that a new image of shining gold replaces the old idol of clay. In all the multiform facts of the world—in the visual shapes of trees and mountains and clouds, in the events of the life of Man, even in the very omnipotence of Death—the insight of creative idealism can find the reflection of a beauty which its own thoughts first made. In this way mind asserts its subtle mastery over the thoughtless forces of Nature. The more evil the material with which it deals, the more thwarting

to untrained desire, the greater is its achievement in inducing the reluctant rock to yield up its hidden treasures, the prouder its victory in compelling the opposing forces to swell the pageant of its triumph. Of all the arts, Tragedy is the proudest, the most triumphant; for it builds its shining citadel in the very centre of the enemy's country, on the very summit of his highest mountain; from its impregnable watchtowers, his camps and arsenals, his columns and forts, are all revealed; within its walls the free life continues, while the legions of Death and Pain and Despair, and all the servile captains of tyrant Fate, afford the burghers of that dauntless city new spectacles of beauty. Happy those sacred ramparts, thrice happy the dwellers on that all-seeing eminence. Honour to those brave warriors who, through countless ages of warfare, have preserved for us the priceless heritage of liberty, and have kept undefiled by sacrilegious invaders the home of the unsubdued.

But the beauty of Tragedy does but make visible a quality which, in more or less obvious shapes, is present always and everywhere in life. In the spectacle of Death, in the endurance of intolerable pain, and in the irrevocableness of a vanished past, there is a sacredness, an overpowering awe, a feeling of the vastness, the depth, the inexhaustible mystery of existence, in which, as by some strange marriage of pain, the sufferer is bound to the world by bonds of sorrow. In these moments of insight, we lose all eagerness of temporary desire, all struggling and striving for petty ends, all care for the little trivial things that, to a superficial view, make up the common life of day by day; we see, surrounding the narrow raft illumined by the flickering light of human comradeship, the dark ocean on whose rolling waves we toss for a brief hour; from the great night without, a chill blast breaks in upon our refuge; all the loneliness of humanity amid hostile forces is concentrated upon the individual soul, which must struggle alone, with what of courage it can command, against the whole weight of a universe that cares nothing for its hopes and fears. Victory, in this struggle with the powers of darkness, is the true baptism into the glorious company of heroes, the true initiation into the overmastering beauty of human existence. From that awful encounter of the soul with the outer world, renunciation, wisdom, and charity are born; and with their birth a new life begins. to take into the inmost shrine of the soul the irresistible forces whose puppets we seem to be—Death and change, the irrevocableness of the past, and the powerlessness of Man before the blind hurry of the universe from vanity to vanity—to feel these things and know them is to conquer them.

This is the reason why the Past has such magical power. The beauty of its motionless and silent pictures is like the enchanted purity of late autumn, when the leaves, though one breath would make them fall, still glow against the sky in golden glory. The Past does not change or strive; like Duncan, after life's fitful fever it sleeps well; what was eager and grasping, what was petty and transitory, has faded away, the things that were beautiful and eternal shine out of it like stars in the night. Its beauty, to a soul not worthy of it, is unendurable; but to a soul which has conquered Fate it is the key of religion.

The life of Man, viewed outwardly, is but a small thing in comparison with the forces of Nature. The slave is doomed to worship Time and Fate and Death, because they are greater than anything he finds in himself, and because all his thoughts are of things which they devour. But, great as they are, to think of them greatly, to feel their passionless splendour, is greater still. and such thought makes us free men; we no longer bow before the inevitable in Oriental subjection, but we absorb it, and make it a part of ourselves. To abandon the struggle for private happiness, to expel all eagerness of temporary desire, to burn with passion for eternal things—this is emancipation, and this is the free man's worship. And this liberation is effected by a contemplation of Fate; for Fate itself is subdued by the mind which leaves nothing to be purged by the purifying fire of Time.

United with his fellow men by the strongest of all ties, the tie of a common doom, the free man finds that a new vision is with him always, shedding over every daily task the light of love. The life of Man is a long march through the night, surrounded by invisible foes, tortured by weariness and pain, towards a goal that few can hope to reach, and where none may tarry long. One by one, as they march, our comrades vanish from our sight, seized by the silent orders of omnipotent Death. Very brief is the time in which we can help them, in which their happiness or misery is decided. Be it ours to shed sunshine on their path, to lighten their sorrows by the balm of sympathy, to give them the pure joy of a never-tiring affection, to strengthen failing courage, to instil faith in hours of despair. Let us not weigh in grudging scales their merits and demerits, but let us think only of their need—of the sorrows, the difficulties, perhaps the blindnesses, that make the misery of their lives; let us remember that they are fellow-sufferers in the same darkness, actors in the same tragedy with ourselves. And so, when their day is over, when their good and their evil have become eternal by the immortality of the past, be it ours to feel that, where they suffered, where they failed, no deed of ours was the cause; but wherever a spark of the divine fire kindled in their hearts, we were ready with encouragement, with sympathy, with brave words in which high courage glowed.

Brief and powerless is Man's life; on him and all his race the slow, sure doom falls pitiless and dark. Blind to good and evil, reckless of destruction, omnipotent matter rolls on its relentless way; for Man, condemned today to lose his dearest, tomorrow himself to pass through the gate of darkness, it remains only to cherish, ere yet the blow fall, the lofty thoughts that ennoble his little day; disdaining the coward terrors of the salve of Fate, to worship at the shrine that his own hands have built; undismayed by the empire of chance, to preserve a mind free from the wanton tyranny that rules his outward life; proudly defiant of the irresistible forces that tolerate, for a moment, his knowledge and his condemnation, to sustain alone, a weary but unyielding Atlas, the world that his own ideals have fashioned despite the trampling march of unconscious power.

XI.4 *Religion and the Queerness of Morality*

GEORGE MAVRODES

George Mavrodes is professor of philosophy at the University of Michigan. In this reading he follows up the Kantian idea of the need for God in ethics, if ethics is to be completely justified. He criticizes Russell's secular view as puzzling, for if there is no God, secular ethics suffers from a certain inadequacy. Mavrodes argues that Russell's world of secular morality cannot satisfactorily answer the question, Why should I be moral? For, on its account, the common goods at which morality in general aims are often just those goods that we sacrifice in carrying out our moral obligations. Why should we sacrifice our welfare for our moral duty?

Another oddity about secular ethics is that it is superficial, not deeply rooted. It seems to lack the metaphysical basis that a Platonic or Judeo-Christian worldview affords. Values and obligations are not as deep in a secular world. Mavrodes outlines how a religious morality can meet these desiderata, and, if we are inclined to believe that morality is not queer, how it can provide some evidence for the religious worldview.

Many arguments for the existence of God may be construed as claiming that there is some feature of the world that would somehow make no sense unless there was something else that had a stronger version of that feature or some analogue of it. So, for example, the cosmological line of argument may be thought of as centering upon the claim that the way in which the world exists (called "contingent" existence) would be incomprehensible unless there were something else—that is, God—that had a stronger grip upon existence (that is, "necessary" existence).

Now, a number of thinkers have held a view something like this with respect to morality. They have claimed that in some important way morality is dependent upon religion—dependent, that is, in such a way that if religion were to fail, morality would fail also. And they have held that the dependence was more than psychological, that is, if religion were to fail, it would somehow be *proper* (perhaps logically or perhaps in some other way) for morality to fail also. One way of expressing this theme is Dostoevsky's "If there is no God, then everything is permitted," a sentiment that in this century has been prominently echoed by Sartre. But perhaps the most substantial philosophical thinker of the modern period to espouse this view, though in a rather idiosyncratic way, was Immanuel Kant, who held that the existence of God was a necessary postulate of 'practical' (that is, moral) reason.

On the other hand, it has recently been popular for moral philosophers to deny this theme and to maintain that the dependence of morality on religion is, at best, merely psychological. Were religion to fail, so they apparently hold, this would grant no sanction for the failure of morality. For morality stands on its own feet, whatever those feet may turn out to be.

Now, the suggestion that morality somehow depends on religion is rather attractive to me. It is this suggestion that I wish to explore in this paper, even though it seems unusually difficult to formulate clearly the features of this suggestion that make it attractive. I will begin by mentioning briefly some aspects that I will not discuss.

From *Rationality, Religious Belief and Moral Commitment: New Essays in the Philosophy of Religion*, eds. R. Audi and W. Wainwright (Cornell University Press, 1986). Copyright © 1986 by Cornell University. Reprinted by permission of the publisher and author.

First, beyond this paragraph I will not discuss the claim that morality cannot survive psychologically without the support of religious belief. At least in the short run, this proposal seems to me false. For there certainly seem to be people who reject religious belief, at least in the ordinary sense, but who apparently have a concern with morality and who try to live a moral life. Whether the proposal may have more force if it is understood in a broader way, as applying to whole cultures, epochs, and so forth, I do not know.

Second, I will not discuss the attempt to define some or all moral terms by the use of religious terms, or vice versa. But this should not be taken as implying any judgment about this project.

Third, beyond this paragraph I shall not discuss the suggestion that moral statements may be entailed by religious statements and so may be "justified" by religious doctrines or beliefs. It is popular now to hold that no such alleged entailment can be valid. But the reason usually cited for this view is the more general doctrine that moral statements cannot be validly deduced from nonmoral statements, a doctrine usually traced to Hume. Now, to my mind the most important problem raised by this general doctrine is that of finding some interpretation of it that is both significant and not plainly false. If it is taken to mean merely that there is *some* set of statements that entails no moral statement, then it strikes me as probably true, but trivial. At any rate, we should then need another reason to suppose that religious statements fall in this category. If, on the other hand, it is taken to mean that one can divide the domain of statements into two classes, the moral and the nonmoral, and that none of the latter entail any of the former, then it is false. I, at any rate, do not know a version of this doctrine that seems relevant to the religious case and that has any reasonable likelihood of being true. But I am not concerned on this occasion with the possibly useful project of deducing morality from religion, and so I will not pursue it further. My interest is closer to a move in the other direction, that of deducing religion from morality. (I am not quite satisfied with this way of putting it and will try to explain this dissatisfaction later on.)

For the remainder of this discussion, then, my project is as follows. I will outline one rather common nonreligious view of the world, calling attention to what I take to be its most relevant features.

Then I shall try to portray some sense of the odd status that morality would have in a world of that sort. I shall be hoping, of course, that you will notice that this odd status is not the one that you recognize morality to have in the actual world. But it will perhaps be obvious that the "world-view" amendments required would move substantially toward a religious position.

First, then, the nonreligious view. I take a short and powerful statement of it from a 1903 essay by Bertrand Russell, "A Free Man's Worship."

> That man is the product of causes which had no prevision of the end they were achieving; that his origin, his growth, his hopes and fears, his loves and his beliefs are but the outcome of accidental collocations of atoms; that no fire, no heroism, no intensity of thought and feeling, can preserve an individual life beyond the grave; that all the labors of the ages, all the devotion, all the inspiration, all the noonday brightness of human genius, are destined to extinction in the vast death of the solar system, and that the whole temple of man's achievement must inevitably be buried beneath the debris of a universe in ruins — all these things, if not quite beyond dispute, are yet so nearly certain that no philosophy which rejects them can hope to stand. Only within the scaffolding of these truths, only on the firm foundation of unyielding despair, can the soul's habitation henceforth be safely built.[1]

For convenience, I will call a world that satisfies the description given here a "Russellian world." But we are primarily interested in what the status of morality would be in the actual world if that world should turn out to be Russellian. I shall therefore sometimes augment the description of a Russellian world with obvious features of the actual world.

What are the most relevant features of a Russellian world? The following strike me as especially important: (1) Such phenomena as minds, mental activities, consciousness, and so forth are the products of entities and causes that give no indication of being mental themselves. In Russell's words, the causes are "accidental collocations of atoms" with "no prevision of the end they were achieving." Though not stated explicitly by Russell, we might add the doctrine, a commonplace in modern science, that mental phenomena — and indeed life itself — are comparative latecomers in the long history of the earth. (2) Human life is bounded by physical death and each individual comes to a permanent end at his physical death. We might add to this the observation that the span of human life is comparatively short, enough so that in some cases we can, with fair confidence, predict the major consequences of certain actions insofar as they will affect a given individual throughout his whole remaining life. (3) Not only each individual but also the human race as a species is doomed to extinction "beneath the debris of a universe in ruins."

So much, then, for the main features of a Russellian world. Because the notion of benefits and goods plays an important part in the remainder of my discussion, I want to introduce one further technical expression — "Russellian benefit." A Russellian benefit is one that could accrue to a person in a Russellian world. A contented old age would be, I suppose, a Russellian benefit, as would a thrill of sexual pleasure or a good reputation. Going to heaven when one dies, though a benefit, is not a Russellian benefit. Russellian benefits are only the benefits possible in a Russellian world. But one can have Russellian benefits even if the world is not Russellian. In such a case there might, however, also be other benefits, such as going to heaven.

Could the actual world be Russellian? Well, I take it to be an important feature of the actual world that human beings exist in it and that in it their actions fall, at least sometimes, within the sphere of morality — that is, they have moral obligations to act (or to refrain from acting) in certain ways. And if they do not act in those ways, then they are properly subject to a special and peculiar sort of adverse judgment (unless it happens that there are special circumstances that serve to excuse their failure to fulfill the obligations). People who do not fulfill their obligations are not merely stupid or weak or unlucky; they are morally reprehensible.

Now, I do not have much to say in an illuminating manner about the notion of moral obligation, but I could perhaps make a few preliminary observations about how I understand this notion. First, I take it that morality includes, or results in, judgments of the form "*N* ought to do (or to avoid doing) _____" or "It is *N*'s duty to do (or to avoid doing) _____." That is, morality ascribes to particular people an obligation to do a certain thing on a certain occasion. No doubt morality includes

other things as well — general moral rules, for example. I shall, however, focus on judgments of the sort just mentioned, and when I speak without further qualification of someone's having an obligation I intend it to be understood in terms of such a judgment.

Second, many authors distinguish prima facie obligations from obligations "all things considered." Probably this is a useful distinction. For the most part, however, I intend to ignore prima facie obligations and to focus upon our obligations all things considered, what we might call our "final obligations." These are the obligations that a particular person has in some concrete circumstance at a particular place and time, when all the aspects of the situation have been taken into account. It identifies the action that, if not done, will properly subject the person to the special adverse judgment.

Finally, it is, I think, a striking feature of moral obligations that a person's being unwilling to fulfill the obligation is irrelevant to having the obligation and is also irrelevant to the adverse judgment in case the obligation is not fulfilled. Perhaps even more important is the fact that, at least for some obligations, it is also irrelevant in both these ways for one to point out that he does not see how fulfilling the obligations can do him any good. In fact, unless we are greatly mistaken about our obligations, it seems clear that in a Russellian world there are an appreciable number of cases in which fulfilling an obligation would result in a loss of good to ourselves. On the most prosaic level, this must be true of some cases of repaying a debt, keeping a promise, refraining from stealing, and so on. And it must also be true of those rarer but more striking cases of obligation to risk death or serious injury in the performance of a duty. People have, of course, differed as to what is good for humans. But so far as I can see, the point I have been making will hold for any candidate that is plausible in a Russellian world. Pleasure, happiness, esteem, contentment, self-realization, knowledge — all of these can suffer from the fulfillment of a moral obligation.

It is not, however, a *necessary* truth that some of our obligations are such that their fulfillment will yield no net benefit, within Russellian limits, to their fulfiller. It is not contradictory to maintain that, for every obligation that I have, a corresponding benefit awaits me within the confines of this world and this life. While such a contention would not be contradictory, however, it would neverthe-less be false. I discuss below one version of this con-tention. At present it must suffice to say that a per-son who accepts this claim will probably find the remainder of what I have to say correspondingly less plausible.

Well, where are we now? I claim that in the ac-tual world we have some obligations that, when we fulfill them, will confer on us no net Russellian ben-efit—in fact, they will result in a Russellian loss. If the world is Russellian, then Russellian benefits and losses are the only benefits and losses, and also then we have moral obligations whose fulfillment will re-sult in a net loss of good to the one who fulfills them. I suggest, however, that it would be very strange to have such obligations—strange not sim-ply in the sense of being unexpected or surprising but in some deeper way. I do not suggest that it is strange in the sense of having a straightforward log-ical defect, of being self-contradictory to claim that we have such obligations. Perhaps the best thing to say is that were it a fact that we had such obligations, then the world that included such a fact would be absurd—we would be living in a crazy world.

Now, whatever success I may have in this paper will in large part be a function of my success (or lack thereof) in getting across a sense of that absurdity, that queerness. On some accounts of morality, in a Russellian world there would not be the strangeness that I allege. Perhaps, then, I can convey some of that strangeness by mentioning those views of mo-rality that would eliminate it. In fact, I believe that a good bit of their appeal is just the fact that they do get rid of this queerness.

First, I suspect that morality will not be queer in the way I suggest, even in a Russellian world, if judgments about obligations are properly to be an-alyzed in terms of the speaker rather than in terms of the subject of the judgment. And I more than sus-pect that this will be the case if such judgments are analyzed in terms of the speaker's attitude or feeling toward some action, and/or his attempt or inclina-tion to incite a similar attitude in someone else. It may be, of course, that there is something odd about the supposition that human beings, con-sciousness, and so forth, could arise at all in a Russellian world. A person who was impressed by that oddity might be attracted toward some "tele-ological" line of reasoning in the direction of a more religious view. But I think that this oddity is not the one I am touching on here. Once given the existence of human beings with capacities for feelings and at-titudes, there does not seem to be anything further that is queer in the supposition that a speaker might have an attitude toward some action, might express that attitude, and might attempt (or succeed) in in-citing someone else to have a similar attitude. Any-one, therefore, who can be satisfied with such an analysis will probably not be troubled by the queer-ness that I allege.

Second, for similar reasons, this queerness will also be dissipated by any account that understands judgments about obligations purely in terms of the feelings, attitudes, and so forth of the subject of the judgment. For, given again that there are human be-ings with consciousness, it does not seem to be any additional oddity that the subject of a moral judg-ment might have feelings or attitudes about an ac-tual or prospective action of his own. The assump-tion that morality is to be understood in this way takes many forms. In a closely related area, for exam-ple, it appears as the assumption—so common now that it can pass almost unnoticed—that guilt could not be anything other than guilt *feelings,* and that the "problem" of guilt is just the problem generated by such feelings.

In connection with our topic here, however, we might look at the way in which this sort of analysis enters into one plausible-sounding explanation of morality in a Russellian world, an explanation that has a scientific flavor. The existence of morality in a Russellian world, it may be said, is not at all absurd because its existence there can be given a perfectly straightforward explanation: morality has a survival value for a species such as ours because it makes pos-sible continued cooperation and things of that sort. So it is no more absurd that people have moral obli-gations than it is absurd that they have opposable thumbs.

I think that this line of explanation will work only if one analyzes obligations into feelings, or be-liefs. I think it is plausible (though I am not sure it is correct) to suppose that everyone's having feelings of moral obligation might have survival value for a species such as Man, given of course that these feel-ings were attached to patterns of action that con-tributed to such survival. And if that is so, then it is not implausible to suppose that there may be a sur-vival value for the species even in a moral feeling that leads to the death of the individual who has it. So far so good. But this observation, even if true, is not relevant to the queerness with which I am here concerned. For I have not suggested that the existence of moral feelings would be absurd in a Russellian world; it is rather the existence of moral *obligations* that is absurd, and I think it important to make the distinction. It is quite possible, it seems to me, for one to feel (or to believe) that he has a certain obligation without actually having it, and also vice versa. Now, beliefs and feelings will presumably have some effect upon actions, and this effect may possibly contribute to the survival of the species. But, so far as I can see, the addition of actual moral obligations to these moral beliefs and feelings will make no further contribution to action nor will the actual obligations have an effect upon action in the absence of the corresponding feelings and beliefs. So it seems that neither with nor without the appropriate feelings will moral obligations contribute to the survival of the species. Consequently, an "evolutionary" approach such as this cannot serve to explain the existence of moral obligations, unless one rejects my distinction and equates the obligations with the feelings.

And finally, I think that morality will not be queer in the way I allege, or at least it will not be as queer as I think, if it should be the case that every obligation yields a Russellian benefit to the one who fulfills it. Given the caveat expressed earlier, one can perhaps make some sense out of the notion of a Russellian good or benefit for a sentient organism in a Russellian world. And one could, I suppose, without further queerness imagine that such an organism might aim toward achieving such goods. And we could further suppose that there were certain actions — those that were "obligations" — that would, in contrast with other actions, actually yield such benefits to the organism that performed them. And finally, it might not be too implausible to claim that an organism that failed to perform such an action was defective in some way and that some adverse judgment was appropriate.

Morality, however, seems to require us to hold that certain organisms (namely, human beings) have in addition to their ordinary properties and relations another special relation to certain actions. This relation is that of being "obligated" to perform those actions. And some of those actions are pretty clearly such that they will yield only Russellian losses to the one who performs them. Nevertheless,

we are supposed to hold that a person who does not perform an action to which he is thus related is defective in some serious and important way and an adverse judgment is appropriate against him. And that certainly does seem odd.

The recognition of this oddity — or perhaps better, this absurdity — is not simply a resolution to concern ourselves only with what "pays." Here the position of Kant is especially suggestive. He held that a truly moral action is undertaken purely out of respect for the moral law and with no concern at all for reward. There seems to be no room at all here for any worry about what will "pay." But he also held that the moral enterprise needs, in a deep and radical way, the postulate of a God who can, and will, make happiness correspond to virtue. This postulate is "necessary" for practical reason: Perhaps we could put this Kantian demand in the language I have been using here, saying that the moral enterprise would make no sense in a world in which that correspondence ultimately failed.

I suspect that what we have in Kant is the recognition that there cannot be, in any "reasonable" way, a moral demand upon me, unless reality itself is committed to morality in some deep way. It makes sense only if there is a moral demand on the world too and only if reality will in the end satisfy that demand. This theme of the deep grounding of morality is one to which I return briefly near the end of this paper.

The oddity we have been considering is, I suspect, the most important root of the celebrated and somewhat confused question, "Why should I be moral?" Characteristically, I think, the person who asks that question is asking to have the queerness of that situation illuminated. From time to time there are philosophers who make an attempt to argue — perhaps only a halfhearted attempt — that being moral really is in one's interest after all. Kurt Baier, it seems to me, proposes a reply of this sort. He says:

> Moralities are systems of principles whose acceptance by everyone as overruling the dictates of self-interest is in the interest of everyone alike though following the rules of a morality is not of course identical with following self-interest. . . .
>
> The answer to our question 'Why should we be moral?' is therefore as follows: We should be moral because being moral is

following rules designed to overrule self-interest whenever it is in the interest of everyone alike that everyone should set aside his interest.[2]

As I say, this seems to be an argument to the effect that it really is in everyone's interest to be moral. I suppose that Baier is here probably talking about Russellian interests. At least, we must interpret him in that way if his argument is to be applicable in this context, and I will proceed on that assumption. But how exactly is the argument to be made out?

It appears here to begin with a premise something like

(A) It is in everyone's best interest (including mine, presumably) for everyone (including me) to be moral.

This premise itself appears to be supported earlier by reference to Hobbes. As I understand it, the idea is that without morality people will live in a "state of nature," and life will be nasty, brutish, and short. Well, perhaps so. At any rate, let us accept (A) for the moment. From (A) we can derive

(B) It is in my best interest for everyone (including me) to be moral.

And from (B) perhaps one derives

(C) It is in my best interest for me to be moral.

And (C) may be taken to answer the question, "Why should I be moral?" Furthermore, if (C) is true, then moral obligation will at least not have the sort of queerness that I have been alleging.

Unfortunately, however, the argument outlined above is invalid. The derivation of (B) from (A) *may* be all right, but the derivation of (C) from (B) is invalid. What does follow from (B) is

(C') It is in my best interest for me to be moral *if everyone else is moral.*

The argument thus serves to show that it is in a given person's interest to be moral only on the assumption that everyone else in the world is moral. It might, of course, be difficult to find someone ready to make that assumption.

There is, however, something more of interest in this argument. I said that the derivation of (B) from (A) may be all right. But in fact is it? If it is not all right, then this argument would fail even if everyone else in the world were moral. Now (A) can be

interpreted as referring to "everyone's best interest" ("the interest of everyone alike," in Baier's own words) either collectively or distributively; that is, it may be taken as referring to the best interest of the whole group considered as a single unit, or as referring to the best interest of each individual in the group. But if (A) is interpreted in the collective sense, then (B) does not follow from it. It may not be in *my* best interest for everyone to act morally, even if it is in the best interest of the group as a whole, for the interest of the group as a whole may be advanced by the sacrificing of my interest. On this interpretation of (A), then, the argument will not answer the question "Why should I be moral?" even on the supposition that everyone else is moral.

If (A) is interpreted in the distributive sense, on the other hand, then (B) does follow from it, and the foregoing objection is not applicable. But another objection arises. Though (A) in the collective sense has some plausibility, it is hard to imagine that it is true in the distributive sense. Hobbes may have been right in supposing that life in the state of nature would be short, etc. But some lives are short anyway. In fact, some lives are short just because the demands of morality are observed. Such a life is not bound to have been shorter in the state of nature. Nor is it bound to have been less happy, less pleasurable, and so forth. In fact, does it not seem obvious that *my* best Russellian interest will be further advanced in a situation in which everyone else acts morally but I act immorally (in selected cases) than it will be in case everyone, including me, acts morally? It certainly seems so. It can, of course, be observed that if I act immorally then so will other people, perhaps reducing my benefits. In the present state of the world that is certainly true. But in the present state of the world it is also true, as I observed earlier, that many other people will act immorally *anyway,* regardless of what I do.

A more realistic approach is taken by Richard Brandt.[3] He asks, "Is it *reasonable* for me to do my duty if it conflicts seriously with my personal welfare?" After distinguishing several possible senses of this question, he chooses a single one to discuss further, presumably a sense that he thinks important. As reformulated, the question is now: "Given that doing x is my duty and that doing some conflicting act y will maximize my personal welfare, will the performance of x instead of y satisfy my reflective preferences better?" And the conclusion to which he comes is that "the correct answer may vary from one person to another. It depends on what kind of person one is, what one cares about." And within Russellian limits Brandt must surely be right in this. But he goes on to say, "It is, of course, no defense of one's failure to do one's duty, before others or society, to say that doing so is not 'reasonable' for one in this sense." And this is just to bring the queer element back in. It is to suppose that besides "the kind of person" I am and my particular pattern of "cares" and interests there is something else, my duty, which may go against these and in any case properly overrides them. And one feels that there must be some sense of "reasonable" in which one can ask whether a world in which that is true is a reasonable world, whether such a world makes any sense.

This completes my survey of some ethical or metaethical views that would eliminate or minimize this sort of queerness of morality. I turn now to another sort of view, stronger I think than any of these others, which accepts that queerness but goes no further. And one who holds this view will also hold, I think, that the question "Why should I be moral?" must be rejected in one way or another. A person who holds this view will say that it is simply a fact that we have the moral obligations that we do have, and that is all there is to it. If they sometimes result in a loss of good, then that too is just a fact. These may be puzzling or surprising facts, but there are lots of puzzling and surprising things about the world. In a Russellian world, morality will be, I suppose, an "emergent" phenomenon; it will be a feature of certain effects though it is not a feature of their causes. But the wetness of water is an emergent feature, too. It is not a property of either hydrogen or oxygen. And there is really nothing more to be said; somewhere we must come to an end of reasons and explanations. We have our duties. We can fulfill them and be moral, or we can ignore them and be immoral. If all that is crazy and absurd — well, so be it. Who are we to say that the world is not crazy and absurd?

Such a view was once suggested by William Alston in a criticism of Hasting Rashdall's moral argument for God's existence. Alston attributed to Rashdall the view that "God is required as a locus for the moral law." But Alston then went on to ask, "Why could it not just be an ultimate fact about the universe that kindness is good and cruelty bad? This seems to have been Plato's view." And if we rephrase

Alston's query slightly to refer to obligations, we might be tempted to say, "Why not indeed?"

I say that this is perhaps the strongest reply against me. Since it involves no argument, there is no argument to be refuted. And I have already said that, so far as I can see, its central contention is not self-contradictory. Nor do I think of any other useful argument to the effect that the world is not absurd and crazy in this way. The reference to Plato, however, might be worth following for a moment. Perhaps Plato did think that goodness, or some such thing related to morality, was an ultimate fact about the world. But a Platonic world is not very close to a Russellian world. Plato was not a Christian, of course, but his worldview has very often been taken to be congenial (especially congenial compared to some other philosophical views) to a religious understanding of the world. He would not have been satisfied, I think, with Russell's "accidental collocations of atoms," nor would he have taken the force of the grave to be "so nearly certain." The idea of the Good seems to play a metaphysical role in his thought. It is somehow fundamental to what *is* as well as to what ought to be, much more fundamental to reality than are the atoms. A Platonic man, therefore, who sets himself to live in accordance with the Good aligns himself with what is deepest and most basic in existence. Or to put it another way, we might say that whatever values a Platonic world imposes on a man are values to which the Platonic world itself is committed, through and through.

Not so, of course, for a Russellian world. Values and obligations cannot be deep in such a world. They have a grip only upon surface phenomena, probably only upon man. What is deep in a Russellian world must be such things as matter and energy, or perhaps natural law, chance, or chaos. If it really were a fact that one had obligations in a Russellian world, then something would be laid upon man that might cost a man everything but that went no further than man. And that difference from a Platonic world seems to make all the difference.

This discussion suggests, I think, that there are two related ways in which morality is queer in a Russellian world. Or maybe they are better construed as two aspects of the queerness we have been exploring. In most of the preceding discussion I have been focusing on the strangeness of an overriding demand that does not seem to conduce to the *good* of the person on whom it is laid. (In fact, it does not even promise his good.) Here, however, we focus on the fact that this demand — radical enough in the human life on which it is laid — is *superficial* in a Russellian world. Something that reaches close to the heart of my own life, perhaps even demanding the sacrifice of that life, is not deep at all in the world in which (on a Russellian view) that life is lived. And that, too, seems absurd.

This brings to an end the major part of my discussion. If I have been successful at all you will have shared with me to some extent in the sense of the queerness of morality, its absurdity in a Russellian world. If you also share the conviction that it cannot in the end be absurd in that way, then perhaps you will also be attracted to some religious view of the world. Perhaps you also will say that morality must have some deeper grip upon the world than a Russellian view allows. And, consequently, things like mind and purpose must also be deeper in the real world than they would be in a Russellian world. They must be more original, more controlling. The accidental collocation of atoms cannot be either primeval or final, nor can the grave be an end. But of course that would be only a beginning, a sketch waiting to be filled in.

We cannot here do much to fill it in further. But I should like to close with a final, and rather tentative suggestion, as to a direction in which one might move in thinking about the place of morality in the world. It is suggested to me by certain elements in my own religion, Christianity.

I come more and more to think that morality, while a fact, is a twisted and distorted fact. Or perhaps better, that it is a barely recognizable version of another fact, a version adapted to a twisted and distorted world. It is something like, I suppose, the way in which the pine that grows at timberline, wind blasted and twisted low against the rock, is a version of the tall and symmetrical tree that grows lower on the slopes. I think it may be that the related notions of sacrifice and gift represent (or come close to representing) the fact, that is, the pattern of life, whose distorted version we know here as morality. Imagine a situation, an "economy" if you will, in which no one ever buys or trades for or seizes any good thing. But whatever good he enjoys is either one which he himself has created or else one which he receives as a free and unconditional gift. And as soon as he has tasted it and seen that it is good he stands ready to give it away in his turn as soon as the

opportunity arises. In such a place, if one were to speak either of his rights or his duties, his remark might be met with puzzled laughter as his hearers struggled to recall an ancient world in which those terms referred to something important.

We have, of course, even now some occasions that tend in this direction. Within some families perhaps, or even in a regiment in desperate battle, people may for a time pass largely beyond morality and live lives of gift and sacrifice. On those occasions nothing would be lost if the moral concepts and the moral language were to disappear. But it is probably not possible that such situations and occasions should be more than rare exceptions in the daily life of the present world. Christianity, however, which tells us that the present world is "fallen" and hence leads us to expect a distortion in its important features, also tells us that one day the redemption of the world will be complete and that then all things shall be made new. And it seems to me to suggest an "economy" more akin to that of gift and sacrifice than to that of rights and duties. If something like that should be true, then perhaps morality, like the Marxist state, is destined to wither away (unless perchance it should happen to survive in hell).

Christianity, then, I think is related to the queerness or morality in one way and perhaps in two. In the first instance, it provides a view of the world in which morality is not an absurdity. It gives morality a deeper place in the world than does a Russellian view and thus permits it to "make sense." But in the second instance, it perhaps suggests that morality is not the deepest thing, that it is provisional and transitory, that it is due to serve its use and then to pass away in favor of something richer and deeper. Perhaps we can say that it begins by inverting the quotation with which I began and by telling us that, since God exists, not everything is permitted; but it may also go on to tell us that, since God exists, in the end there shall be no occasion for any prohibition.

Endnotes

[1] Bertrand Russell, *Mysticism and Logic* (New York: Barnes & Noble, 1917), pp. 47–48.

[2] Kurt Baier, *The Moral Point of View* (Ithaca: Cornell University Press, 1958), p. 314.

[3] Richard Brandt, *Ethical Theory* (Englewood Cliffs, N.J.: Prentice Hall, 1959), pp. 375–78.

XI.5 *Ethics Without God*

Kai Nielsen

Kai Nielsen is professor of philosophy at Calgary University in Canada. This
article was written twenty years before Mavrodes' paper on the queerness of
morality, but it anticipates some of Mavrodes' arguments. Nielsen's thesis is
that even if "God is dead," it really doesn't matter as far as our morality is
concerned. First, with the loss of faith all our essential moral values are left
intact. We still can be happy, find security and emotional peace, experience
love and friendship, and enjoy creative work and a rich variety of experiences.
Second, both the secular and the religious bases of ethics involve an objective
rationale that contains central principles, such as benevolence and respect for
persons and justice. Our common nature and quest for the good life is all the
grounding that ethics needs. It is true that morality sometimes calls for
sacrifice of nonmoral goods. It would be nice if this were not the case, but life
is sometimes difficult. Nielsen notes that both secular ethics and religion have
a difficult time with evil.

There certainly are fundamental difficulties and perhaps even elements of incoherence in Christian
ethics, but what can a secular moralist offer in its
stead? Religious morality — and Christian morality
in particular — may have its difficulties, but secular
morality, religious apologists argue, has still greater
difficulties. It leads, they claim, to ethical scepticism,
nihilism, or, at best, to a pure conventionalism.
Such apologists could point out that if we look at
morality with the cold eye of an anthropologist we
will — assuming we are clearheaded — find morality
to be nothing more than the often conflicting *mores*
of the various tribes spread around the globe. If we
eschew the kind of insight that religion can give us,
we will have no Archimedean point in accordance
with which we can decide how it is that we ought to
live and die. If we look at ethics from such a purely
secular point of view, we will discover that it is constituted by tribal conventions, conventions which
we are free to reject if we are sufficiently free from
ethnocentrism. We can continue to act in accordance with them or we can reject them and adopt a
different set of conventions; but whether we act in

accordance with the old conventions or forge "new
tablets," we are still acting in accordance with certain conventions. Relative to them certain acts are
right or wrong, reasonable or unreasonable, but we
cannot justify these fundamental moral conventions
themselves or the ways of life which they partially
codify.

When these points are conceded, theologians
are in a position to press home a powerful apolo-
getic point. When we become keenly aware, they argue, of the true nature of such conventionalism and
when we become aware that there is no overarching
purpose that men were destined to fulfill, the myriad purposes, the aims and goals humans create for
themselves, will be seen not to be enough. When we
realize that life does not have a meaning — that is, a
significance — which is there to be found, but that
we human beings must by our deliberate decisions
give it whatever meaning it has, we will (as Sartre so
well understood) undergo estrangement and despair. We will drain our cup to its last bitter drop
and feel our alienation to the full. Perhaps there are
human purposes, purposes to be found *in* life, and
we can and do have them even in a Godless world,
but without God there can be no one overarching
purpose, no one basic scheme of human existence,
in virtue of which we could find a meaning for our
grubby lives. It is this overall sense of meaning that

From "Ethics Without Religion," *The Ohio University Review* VI (1964): 48–51; 57–62. Reprinted by permission of
the publisher.

man so ardently strives for, but it is not to be found in a purely secular worldview. You secularists, a new Pascal might argue, must realize, if you really want to be clearheaded, that no purely human purposes are ultimately worth striving for. What you humanists can give us by way of a scheme of human existence will always be a poor second-best and not what the human heart most ardently longs for.

The considerations for and against an ethics not rooted in a religion are complex and involuted; a fruitful discussion of them is difficult, for in considering the matter our passions, our anxieties, our (if you will) ultimate concerns are involved, and they tend to blur our vision, enfeeble our understanding, of what exactly is at stake. But we must not forget that what is at stake here is just what kind of ultimate commitments or obligations a man could have without evading any issue, without self-deception or without delusion. I shall be concerned to display and assess, to make plain but also to weigh, some of the most crucial considerations for and against a purely secular ethic. While I shall in an objective fashion try to make clear what the central issues are, I shall also give voice to my reflective convictions on this matter. I shall try to make evident my reasons for believing that we do not need God or any religious conception to support our moral convictions. I shall do this, as I think one should in philosophy, by making apparent the dialectic of the problem (by bringing to the fore the conflicting and evolving considerations for and against) and by arguing for what I take to be their proper resolution.

I am aware that Crisis Theologians would claim that I am being naive, but I do not see why purposes of purely human devising are not ultimately worth striving for. There is much that we humans prize and would continue to prize even in a Godless world. Many things would remain to give our lives meaning and point even after "the death of God."

Take a simple example. All of us *want* to be happy. But in certain bitter or sceptical moods we question what happiness is or we despairingly ask ourselves whether anyone can really be happy. Is this, however, a sober, sane view of the situation? I do not think that it is. Indeed we cannot adequately define "happiness" in the way that we can "bachelor," but neither can we in that way define "chair," "wind," "pain," and the vast majority of words in everyday discourse. For words like "bachelor," "triangle," or "father" we can specify a consistent set of properties that all the things and only the things denoted by these words have, but we cannot do this for "happiness," "chair," "pain," and the like. In fact, we cannot do it for the great majority of our words. Yet there is no greater loss here. Modern philosophical analysis has taught us that such an essentially Platonic conception of definition is unrealistic and unnecessary.[1] I may not be able to define "chair" in the way that I can define "bachelor," but I understand the meaning of "chair" perfectly well. In normal circumstances, at least, I know what to sit on when someone tells me to take a chair. I may not be able to define "pain," but I know what it is like to be in pain, and sometimes I can know when others are in pain. Similarly, though I cannot define "happiness" in the same way that I can define "bachelor," I know what it is like to be happy, and I sometimes can judge with considerable reliability whether others are happy or sad. "Happiness" is a slippery word, but it is not so slippery that we are justified in saying that nobody knows what happiness is.

A man could be said to have lived a happy life if he had found lasting sources of satisfaction in his life and if he had been able to find certain goals worthwhile and to achieve at least some of them. He could indeed have suffered some pain and anxiety, but his life must, for the most part, have been free from pain, estrangement, and despair, and must, on balance, have been a life which he has liked and found worthwhile. But surely we have no good grounds for saying that no one achieves such a balance or that no one is ever happy even for a time. We all have some idea of what would make us happy and of what would make us unhappy; many people, at least, can remain happy even after "the death of God." At any rate, we need not strike Pascalian attitudes, for even in a purely secular world there are permanent sources of human happiness for anyone to avail himself of.

What are they? What are these relatively permanent sources of human happiness that we all want or need? What is it which, if we have it, will give us the basis for a life that could properly be said to be happy? We all desire to be free from pain and want. Even masochists do not seek pain for its own sake; they endure pain because this is the only psychologically acceptable way of achieving something else (usually sexual satisfaction) that is so gratifying to them that they will put up with the pain to achieve it. We all want a life in which sometimes we can enjoy ourselves in which we can attain our fair share of some of the simple pleasures that we all desire. They are not everything in life, but they are important, and our lives would be impoverished without them.

We also need security and emotional peace. We need and want a life in which we will not be constantly threatened with physical or emotional harassment. Again this is not the only thing worth seeking, but it is an essential ingredient in any adequate picture of the good life.

Human love and companionship are also central to a significant or happy life. We prize them, and a life which is without them is most surely an impoverished life, a life that no man, if he would take the matter to heart, would desire. But I would most emphatically assert that human love and companionship are quite possible in a Godless world, and the fact that life will some day inexorably come to an end and cut off love and companionship altogether enhances rather than diminishes their present value.

Furthermore, we all need some sort of creative employment or meaningful work to give our lives point, to save them from boredom, drudgery, and futility. A man who can find no way to use the talents he has or a man who can find no work which is meaningful to him will indeed be a miserable man. But again there is work—whether it be as a surgeon, a farmer, or a fisherman—that has a rationale even in a world without God. And poetry, music, and art retain their beauty and enrich our lives even in the complete absence of God or the gods.

We want and need art, music, and the dance. We find pleasure in travel and conversation and in a rich variety of experiences. The sources of human enjoyment are obviously too numerous to detail. But all of them are achievable in a Godless universe. If some can be ours, we can attain a reasonable measure of happiness. Only a Steppenwolfish personality beguiled by impossible expectations and warped by irrational guilts and fears can fail to find happiness in the realization of such ends. But to be free of impossible expectations people must clearly recognize that there is no "one big thing" or, for that matter, "small thing" which would make them permanently happy; almost anything permanently and exclusively pursued will lead to that nausea that Sartre has so forcefully brought to our attention. But we can, if we are not too sick and if our situation is not too precarious, find lasting sources of human happiness in a purely secular world.

It is not only happiness for ourselves that can give us something of value, but there is the need to do what we can to diminish the awful sum of human misery in the world. I have never understood those who say that they find contemporary life meaningless because they find nothing worthy of devoting their energies to. Throughout the world there is an immense amount of human suffering, suffering that can, through a variety of human efforts, be partially alleviated. Why can we not find a meaningful life in devoting ourselves, as did Doctor Rieux in Albert Camus' *The Plague,* to relieving somewhat the sum total of human suffering? Why cannot this give our lives point, and for that matter an over-all rationale? It is childish to think that by human effort we will someday totally rid the world of suffering and hate, of deprivation and sadness. This is a permanent part of the human condition. But specific bits of human suffering can be alleviated. The plague is always potentially with us, but we can destroy the Nazis and we can fight for racial and social equality throughout the world. And as isolated people, as individuals in a mass society, we find people turning to us in dire need, in suffering and in emotional deprivation, and we can as individuals respond to those people and alleviate or at least acknowledge that suffering and deprivation. A man who says, "If God is dead, nothing matters," is a spoilt child who has never looked at his fellow men with compassion.

Yet, it might be objected, if we abandon a Judaeo-Christian *Weltanschauung,* there can, in a secular world, be no "one big thing" to give our lives an overall rationale. We will not be able to see written in the stars the final significance of human effort. There will be no architectonic purpose to give our lives such a rationale. Like Tolstoy's Pierre in *War and Peace,* we desire *somehow* to gather the sorry scheme of things entire into one intelligible explanation so that we can finally crack the riddle of human destiny. We long to understand why it is that men suffer and die. If it is a factual answer that is wanted when such a question is asked, it is plain enough. Ask any physician. But clearly this is not what people who seek such answers are after. They want some *justification* for suffering; they want some way of showing that suffering is after all for a good purpose. It can, of course, be argued that suffering sometimes is a good thing, for it occasionally gives us insight and at times even brings about in the man who suffers a capacity to love and to be kind. But there is plainly an excessive amount of human suffering—the suffering of children in childrens' hospitals, the suffering of people devoured by cancer, and the sufferings of millions of Jews under the Nazis—for which there simply is no justification. Neither the religious man nor the secularist can explain, that is justify, such suffering and find some overall "scheme of life" in which it has some place, but only the religious man needs to do so. The secularist understands that suffering is not something to be justified but simply to be struggled against with courage and dignity. And in this fight, even the man who has been deprived of that which could give him some measure of happiness can still find or make for himself a meaningful human existence. . . .

The dialectic of our problem has not ended. The religious moralist might acknowledge that human happiness is indeed plainly a good thing while contending that secular morality, where it is consistent and reflective, will inevitably lead to some variety of egoism. An individual who recognized the value of happiness and self-consciousness might, if he were free of religious restraints, ask himself why he should be concerned with the happiness and self-awareness of *others,* except where their happiness and self-awareness would contribute to his own good. We must face the fact that sometimes, as the world goes, people's interests clash. Sometimes the common good is served only at the expense of some individual's interests. An individual must therefore, in such a circumstance, sacrifice what will make him happy for the common good. Morality requires this sacrifice of us, *when it is necessary* for the common good; morality, any morality, exists in part at least to adjudicate between the conflicting interests and demands of people. It is plainly evident that everyone cannot be happy all the time and that sometimes one person's happiness or the happiness of a group is at the expense of another person's happiness. Morality requires that we attempt to distribute happiness as evenly as possible. We must be fair: each person is to count for one and none is to count for more than one. Whether we like a person or not, whether he is useful to his society or not, his interests, and what will make him happy, must also be considered in any final decision as to what ought to be done. The requirements of justice make it necessary that

each person be given equal consideration. I cannot justify my neglect of another person in some matter of morality simply on the grounds that I do not like him, that he is *not* a member of my set, or that he is *not* a productive member of society. The religious apologist will argue that behind these requirements of justice as fairness there lurks the ancient religious principle that men are creatures of God, each with an infinite worth, and thus men are never to be treated only as means but as persons deserving of respect in their own right. They have an infinite worth simply as persons.

My religious critic, following out the dialectic of the problem, should query: why should you respect someone, why should you treat all people equally, if doing this is not in your interest or not in the interests of your group? No purely secular justification can be given for so behaving. My critic now serves his *coup de grâce*: the secularist, as well as the "knight of faith," acknowledges that the principle of respect for persons is a precious one—a principle that he is unequivocally committed to, but the religious man alone can *justify* adherence to this principle. The secularist is surreptitiously drawing on Christian inspiration when he insists that all men should be considered equal and that people's rights must be respected. For a secular morality to say all it wants and needs to say, it must, at this crucial point, be parasitical upon a God-centered morality. Without such a dependence on religion, secular morality collapses into egoism.

It may well be the case that, as a historical fact, our moral concern for persons came from our religious conceptions, but it is a well-known principle of logic that the validity of a belief is independent of its origin. What the religious moralist must do is to show that only on religious grounds could such a principle of respect for persons be justifiably asserted. But he has not shown that this is so; and there are good reasons for thinking that it is not so. Even if the secularist must simply subscribe to the Kantian principle, "Treat every man as an end and never as a means only," as he must subscribe to the claim, "Happiness is good," it does not follow that he is on worse ground than the religious moralist, for the religious moralist too, as we have seen, must simply subscribe to his ultimate moral principle, "Always do what God wills." *In a way,* the religious moralist's position here is simpler than the secularist's, for he needs only the fundamental moral principle that he ought to do what God wills. The secularist appears to need at least two fundamental principles. But in another and more important way the religious moralist's position is more complex, for he must subscribe to the extraordinarily obscure notion that man is a creature of God and as such has infinite worth. The Kantian principle may in the last analysis simply require subscription, but it is not inherently mysterious. To accept it does not require a crucifixion of the intellect. And if we are prepared simply to commit ourselves to one principle, why not to two principles, neither of which involves any appeal to conceptions whose very intelligibility is seriously in question?

The above argument is enough to destroy the believer's case here. But need we even make those concessions? I do not think so. There is a purely secular rationale for treating people fairly, for regarding them as persons. Let me show how this is so. We have no evidence that men ever lived in a pre-social state of nature. Man, as we know him, is an animal with a culture; he is part of a community, and the very *concept* of community implies binding principles and regulations—duties, obligations and rights. Yet, by an exercise in imagination, we could conceive, in broad outline at any rate, what it would be like to live in such a pre-social state. In such a state no one would have any laws or principles to direct his behaviour. In that sense man would be completely free. But such a life, as Hobbes graphically depicted, would be a clash of rival egoisms. Life in that state of nature would, in his celebrated phrase, "be nasty, brutish and short." Now if men were in such a state and if they were perfectly rational egoists, what kind of community life would they choose, given the fact that they were, very roughly speaking, nearly equal in strength and ability? (That in communities as we find them men are not so nearly equal in power is beside the point, for our *hypothetical* situation.) Given that they all start from scratch and have roughly equal abilities, it seems to me that it would be most reasonable, even for rational egoists, to band together into a community where each man's interests were given equal consideration, where each person was treated as deserving of respect. Each rational egoist would want others to treat him with respect, for his very happiness is contingent upon that; and he would recognize, if he

were rational, that he could attain the fullest cooperation of others only if other rational egoists knew or had good grounds for believing that their interests and their persons would also be respected. Such cooperation is essential for each egoist if all are to have the type of community life which would give them the best chance of satisfying their own interests to the fullest degree. Thus, even if men were thorough egoists, we would still have rational grounds for subscribing to a principle of respect for persons. That men are not thoroughly rational, do not live in a state of nature, and are not thorough egoists, does not gainsay the fact that we have rational grounds for regarding social life, organized in accordance with such a principle, as being objectively better than a social life which ignored this principle. The point here is that even rational egoists could see that this is the best possible social organization where men are nearly equal in ability.

Yet what about the world we live in—a world in which, given certain extant social relationships, men are not equal or even nearly equal in power and opportunity? What reason is there for an egoist who is powerfully placed to respect the rights of others, when they cannot hurt him? We can say that his position, no matter how strong, might change and he might be in a position where he would need his rights protected, but this is surely not a strong enough reason for respecting those rights. To be moral involves respecting those rights, but our rational egoist may not propose to be moral. In considering such questions we reach a point in reasoning at which we must simply *decide* what sort of person we shall strive to become. But, as I have said, the religious moralist reaches the same point. He too must make a decision of principle, but the principle he adopts is a fundamentally incoherent one. He not only must decide, but his decision must involve the acceptance of an absurdity.

It is sometimes argued by religious apologists that only if there is a God who can punish men will we be assured that naturally selfish men will be fair and considerate of others. Without this punitive sanction or threat men would go wild. Men will respect the rights of others only if they fear a wrathful and angry God. Yet it hardly seems to be the case that Christians, with their fear of hell, have been any better at respecting the rights of others than non-Christians. A study of the Middle Ages or the conquest of the non-Christian world makes this plain enough. And even if it were true (as it is not) that Christians were better in this respect than non-Christians, it would not show that they had a superior moral reason for their behavior, for in so acting and in so reasoning, they are not giving a morally relevant reason at all but are simply acting out of fear for their own hides. Yet Christian morality supposedly takes us beyond the clash of the rival egoisms of secular life.

In short, Christian ethics has not been able to give us a sounder ground for respecting persons than we have with a purely secular morality. The Kantian principle of respect for persons is actually bound up in the very idea of morality, either secular or religious, and there are good reasons, of a perfectly mundane sort, why we should have the institution of morality as we now have it, namely, that our individual welfare is dependent on having a device which equitably resolves social and individual conflicts. Morality has an objective rationale in complete independence of religion. Even if God is dead, it doesn't really matter.

It is in just this last thrust, it might be objected, that you reveal your true colors and show your own inability to face a patent social reality. At this point the heart of your rationalism is very irrational. For millions of people "the death of God" means very much. It really does matter. In your somewhat technical sense, the concept of God may be chaotic or unintelligible, but this concept, embedded in our languages—embedded in "the stream of life"—has an enormous social significance for many people. Jews and Christians, if they take their religion to heart, could not but feel a great rift in their lives with the loss of God, for they have indeed organized a good bit of their lives around their religion. Their very life-ideals have grown out of these, if you will, myth-eaten concepts. What should have been said is that if "God is dead" it matters a lot, but we should stand up like men and face this loss and learn to live in the Post-Christian era. As Nietzsche so well knew, to do this involves a basic reorientation of one's life and not just an intellectual dissent to a few statements of doctrine.

There is truth in this and a kind of "empiricism about man" that philosophers are prone to neglect. Of course it does matter when one recognizes that one's religion is illusory. For a devout Jew or Christian to give up his God most certainly is important and does take him into the abyss of a spiritual crisis. But in saying that it doesn't *really* matter I was implying what I have argued for in this essay, namely, that if a believer loses his God but can keep his nerve, think the matter over, and thoroughly take it to heart, life can still be meaningful and morality yet have an objective rationale. Surely, for good psychological reasons, the believer is prone to doubt this argument, but if he will only "hold on to his brains" and keep his courage, he will come to see that it is so. In this crucial sense it remains true that if "God is dead" it doesn't really matter.

Endnote

[1] This is convincingly argued in Michael Scriven's essay "Definitions, Explanations, and Theories," in Herbert Feigl, Michael Scriven, and Grover Maxwell, eds. *Minnesota Studies in the Philosophy of Science,* III (Minneapolis, 1958), pp. 99–195.

Suggestions for Further Reading

Adams, Robert M. "A Modified Divine Command Theory of Ethical Wrongness," in *The Virtue of Faith.* Oxford University Press, 1987.

Helm, Paul, ed. *The Divine Command Theory of Ethics.* Oxford University Press, 1979. Contains valuable articles by Frankena, Rachels, Quinn, Adams, and Young.

Kant, Immanuel. *Religion Within the Bounds of Reason Alone,* tr. T. M. Greene and H. H. Hudson. HarperCollins, 1960.

Kierkegaard, Soren. *Fear and Trembling,* tr. Howard and Edna Hong. Princeton University Press, 1983.

Mitchell, Basil. *Morality: Religious and Secular.* Oxford University Press, 1980.

Mouw, Richard J. *The God Who Commands.* University of Notre Dame Press, 1990.

Nielsen, Kai. *Ethics Without God.* Pemberton Books, 1973. A very accessible defense of secular morality.

Outka, Gene, and J. P. Reeder, eds. *Religion and Morality: A Collection of Essays.* Anchor Books, 1973. Contains Robert M. Adams's "A Modified Divine Command Theory of Ethical Wrongness."

Pojman, Louis, ed. *Ethical Theory: Classical and Contemporary Readings.* Wadsworth, 1989. Part XI contains important essays by Kant, Russell, Mavrodes, and Nielsen.

————. "Ethics: Religious and Secular." *The Modern Schoolman* LXX (Nov. 1992).

Robinson, Richard. *An Atheist's Values.* Clarendon Press, 1964.

Quinn, Philip. *Divine Commands and Moral Requirements.* Clarendon Press, 1978.

Ward, Keith. *Ethics and Christianity.* Allen & Unwin, 1970.

Part XII

Justice

Justice, [Aristotle] said, consists in treating equals equally and unequals
unequally but in proportion to their relevant differences. This involves, first,
the idea of impartiality. . . . Impartiality implies a kind of equality — not that
all cases should be treated alike but that the onus rests on whoever would treat
them differently to distinguish them in relevant ways. . . . That is what is really
meant by the right to equal consideration — to be treated alike unless relevant
differences have been proved."

STANLEY BENN

"Justice," in *The Encyclopedia of Philosophy*, ed. Paul Edwards, Macmillan, 1967, vol. 3, p. 299

It is only from the selfishness and confined generosity of men, along with the scanty provision
nature has made for his wants, that justice derives its origin.

DAVID HUME

A Treatise of Human Nature, Oxford University Press, 1739

Problems of justice typically arise, as David
Hume pointed out over two centuries ago, when
in situations of scarcity we seek to adjudicate between competing claims for limited goods.[1]
Consider this example. If one hundred candidates apply for a highly desirable position, what
are the correct moral and legal criteria by which
to decide who should get the job? Should the selection be based on merit? Contribution? Individual need? Previous effort? Likely contribution
to society or the company? Should race and sex
be taken into consideration? If in the past blacks

and women have been systematically discriminated against, should affirmative action programs involve reverse discrimination, prescribing
that blacks and women with inferior credentials
be hired before white males?

Or consider the use of kidney dialysis machines in a county hospital that can afford only
five such machines, but has a waiting list of
twenty needy people. How should we decide
which five should be treated? Should it be by lottery? By a first-come-first-served policy? By utilitarian considerations (for example, two of the

candidates are leading professionals who contribute greatly to the social good)? Or by a complex set of factors (including age, health, responsibilities, and merit)?

Theories of justice may be divided into *formal* and *material* types. A formal theory of justice gives a definition of 'justice' without filling in any content. Material theories of justice specify the relevant content to be inserted into the formulas. The classical principle of formal justice, based on Book V of Aristotle's *Nicomachean Ethics*, is that equals should be treated equally and unequals unequally. The formula is one of proportionality:

$$\frac{A \text{ has } X \text{ of } P}{B \text{ has } Y \text{ of } P} = \frac{A \text{ should have } X \text{ of } Q}{B \text{ should have } Y \text{ of } Q}$$

That is, if person A has X units more (less) of a relevant property than person B, then A should receive X units more (less) in the way of reward or punishment than B. For example, if A has worked 8 hours and B only 4 hours at the same job, A should receive twice the amount of wages than B.

The formal or proportionality principle is used in law in the guise of the rule — the rule of precedent — that like cases should be decided in like manner. This principle applies both to retributive justice, in which punishment for an offense is in question ("an eye for an eye, a tooth for a tooth, a life for a life"), and to commutative justice, in which obligation is based on a promise or contract that demands fulfillment. In this section we will concentrate on the most well-known type of justice, distributive justice — the distribution of goods and services.

The formal principle of justice is similar to the principle of universalizability, which we discussed in Part VIII of this work. It requires that impartial and consistent standards be applied to sexual ethics: It is wrong for women, but permissible for men, to engage in premarital heterosexual intercourse. But this seems unjust, for gender seems an irrelevant difference. If it is all right for Jack to engage in premarital sex, then it is also all right for Jill to engage in premarital sex; but if it is immoral for Jill to engage in premarital sex, it is also immoral for Jack. The principle doesn't tell us whether some act is right or wrong, but simply calls for consistency. If we were content to live only with the formal principle, we might treat people very badly and still be considered just. As one of his players once said of Vince Lombardi, the former coach of football's Green Bay Packers, "He treated us all equally — like dogs."

Some philosophers, such as Stanley Benn (quoted at the beginning of this Part), believe that the formal principle of equal treatment for equals implies a kind of *presumption* of equal treatment of people. But there are problems with this viewpoint.

As Joel Feinberg points out, sometimes the presumption is instead for unequal treatment of people. Suppose that a father suddenly decides to share his fortune, and he divides it in two and gives half each to his oldest son and his neighbor's oldest son.[2] We should say that this kind of impartiality is misguided and, in reality, unjust. We need to specify the respect in which people are equal and so deserve the same kind of treatment, and this seems to be a material problem, not a purely formal one. In other words, Benn confuses an *exceptive principle* ("Treat all people alike except when there are relevant differences among them") that is formal with a *presumptive principle* ("Treat all people alike *until it can be shown* that there are relevant differences among them").

The formal principle does not tell us which qualities determine which kinds of distribution or goods or treatment. Thus, material principles are needed to supplement the formal definition. Aristotle's own material principle involved merit: Each person is to be given what he or she deserves. So, a coach could justly treat his players like dogs only if they were doglike. Otherwise, he should treat them more humanely.

Other philosophers have argued for principles besides merit. In our third reading, Nicholas

Rescher lists seven "canons" of distributive justice: people are to be treated (1) as equals; or according to their (2) needs, (3) merit or ability, (4) effort or sacrifices, (5) contribution, or (6) economic usefulness; or according to (7) the public good.

Rescher analyzes each of these "canons," including their strengths and weaknesses, and concludes that none of them is sufficient in itself as a criterion for distributive justice. Rescher argues for a complex, multifaceted approach to this issue. Different types of situations require giving predominance to different material principles. For example, with regard to wages, a person's just desert is to be measured in terms of productivity or contribution, but when it comes to public welfare, human need is the overriding consideration. The question is, how do we decide which particular "canon" of justice applies in any given situation?

Material theories of justice may be further divided into patterned and nonpatterned types of justice. A patterned principle chooses some trait(s) that indicates how the proper distribution is to be accomplished. It has the form:

To each according to _____:

To quote from Robert Nozick's *Anarchy, State and Utopia*: "Let us call a principle of distribution *patterned* if it specifies that a distribution is to vary along with some natural dimension, weighted sum of natural dimensions, or lexicographic ordering of natural dimensions." In our fourth reading, Nozick rejects patterned types of principles, such as those of Rescher, because such an attempt to regulate distribution constitutes a violation of liberty. He illustrates this point by considering how a great basketball player, Wilt Chamberlain, can justly upset the patterned balance. Suppose that we have reached a patterned situation of justice based on equality. Imagine that there is a great demand to watch Chamberlain play basketball and that people are

willing to pay him an extra 25 cents per ticket in order to see him play. If one million people pay to see him play during the year, the additional gate receipts add up to $250,000. Chamberlain thus takes home a great deal more than our patterned formula allows, but he seems to have a right to this. Nozick's point is that, in order to maintain a pattern, one must either "continually interfere to stop people from transferring resources as they wish to, or continually interfere to take from some persons resources that others for some reason chose to transfer to them."

Nozick argues for a libertarian view of nonpatterned justice, which he calls the "theory of entitlement." A distribution is just if everyone has that to which he is entitled. To determine what people are entitled to, we must understand what the original position of holdings or possessions was and what constitutes a just transfer of holdings. Borrowing from John Locke's theory of property rights, he argues that we have a right to any possession so long as ownership does not worsen the position of anyone else.

In our fifth reading, John Rawls's "A Liberal Theory of Justice," we have quite a different theory of nonpatterned justice. Rawls agrees that patterned versions of justice are faulty, but he disagrees with libertarian views like Nozick's. Instead, he presents a version of the social contract that is broadly Kantian, in which a theory of just procedures takes the place of substantive principles. Rawls asks us to imagine being behind a "veil of ignorance" in which we have very little, if any, knowledge of who we are, and he then asks us to choose the general principles that will govern our social policies. Rawls argues that the principles that rational people will choose are those that maximize individual freedom, that arrange social and economic inequalities in ways that are to everyone's advantage, and that guarantee equal opportunity in attaining privileged positions.

There is an enormous literature on Rawls's work. Some of these works are cited in the

Suggestions for Further Reading at the end of this Part.

In our sixth reading, Wallace Matson in his "Justice: A Funeral Oration" by a series of imaginative tales contrasts natural justice (the authentic type) over against paternalistic justice. The former is "bottom-up" and based on voluntary agreements, while the latter is "top-down," based on the will of government. In the former freedom is the starting point and property the necessary good; while in the latter equality is the goal and the government effectively owns all property. The mistake of paternalistic or top-down justice is to suppose that the love and egalitarianism of the family can be extended to society at large. Matson illustrates the tension between these two motifs that exists in the philosophy of John Rawls, who with his first principle of liberty expresses bottom-up justice, but with his second difference principle—which distributes all inequalities in favor of the parties that are worst off—expresses top-down, paternalistic justice.

Finally, Thomas Nagel examines the moral status of equality as a political value, comparing it with the competing values of individual rights and utility. Comparing liberal equality, especially Rawls's theory, with radical equality and these with libertarian and utilitarian considerations, he concludes that no one value is absolute, but that "a plausible social morality will show the influence of them all." Nevertheless, Nagel's own view is that the urgency of basic individual needs procures a presumption in favor of equality over the other values, all things being roughly equal.

Endnotes

[1] To be precise, we are speaking here primarily of distributive justice.

[2] See Joel Feinberg, *Social Philosophy* (Englewood Cliffs, N.J.: Prentice-Hall, 1973), pp. 100f.

XII.1 *Formal Justice*

ARISTOTLE

Aristotle (384–322 B.C.) — Greek physician, tutor to Alexander the Great, and one of the most important philosophers who ever lived — wrote importantly on every major subject in philosophy. This selection, from his *Nicomachean Ethics*, is the most influential essay ever written on the subject of justice. Justice requires that equals should be treated equally and unequals unequally. The formula is one of proportionality:

$$\frac{\text{A has X of P}}{\text{B has Y of P}} = \frac{\text{A should have X of Q}}{\text{B should have Y of Q}}$$

That is, if person A has X units more (less) of a relevant property than person B, then A should receive X units more (less) in the way of reward or punishment than B. This is a purely formal theory of justice (that is, it does not specify what "P" stands for in the equation), but Aristotle thought that merit was the proper material content that should go into the equation. For example, if A has 10 units of merit and B only 5 units, then A should receive twice the reward as B.

Chapter I

Prefatory remarks. The different senses of Justice ascertained from those of Injustice.

Now the points for our inquiry in respect of Justice and Injustice are what kind of actions are their object-matter and what kind of a mean state Justice is and between what points the abstract principle of it, i.e. the Just, is a mean. And our enquiry shall be, if you please, conducted in the same method as we have observed in the foregoing parts of this Treatise.

We see then that all men mean by the term Justice a moral state such that in consequence of it men have the capacity of doing what is just and actually do it and wish it: similarly also with respect to Injustice, a moral state such that in consequence of it men do unjustly and wish what is unjust: let us also be content then with these as a ground-work sketched out.

I mention the two because the same does not hold with regard to States whether of mind or body as with regard to Sciences or Faculties: I mean that whereas it is thought that the same Faculty or Science embraces contraries a State will not: from health, for instance, not the contrary acts are done but the healthy ones only; we say a man walks healthily when he walks as the healthy man would.

However of the two contrary states the one may be frequently known from the other, and oftentimes the states from their subject-matter: if it be seen clearly what a good state of body is then is it also seen what a bad state is, and from the things which belong to a good state of body the good state itself is seen and vice versa. If, for instance, the good state is firmness of flesh it follows that the bad state is flabbiness of flesh; and whatever causes firmness of flesh is connected with the good state.

It follows moreover in general that if of two contrary terms the one is used in many senses so also will the other be; as, for instance, if 'the Just' then also 'the Unjust.' Now Justice and Injustice do seem to be used respectively in many senses but, because the line of demarcation between these is very fine and minute, it commonly escapes notice that they

Reprinted from *Nicomachean Ethics*, translated by D.P. Chase (Oxford University Press, 1877).

are thus used, and it is not plain and manifest as where the various significations of terms are widely different: for in these last the visible difference is great; for instance the word κλεις is used equivocally to denote the bone which is under the neck of animals and the instrument with which people close doors.

Let it be ascertained then in how many senses the term 'Unjust man' is used. Well, he who violates the law and he who is a grasping man and the unequal man are all thought to be Unjust: and so manifestly the Just man will be the law-abiding and the equal man. 'The Just' then will be the lawful and the equal, and 'the Unjust' the unlawful and the unequal.

Well, since the Unjust man is also a grasping man, he will be so, of course, with respect to good things, but not of every kind only those which are the subject-matter of good and bad fortune and which are in themselves always good but not always to the individual. Yet men pray for and pursue these things: this they should not do, but pray that things which are in the abstract good may be so also to them, and choose what is good for themselves.

But the Unjust man does not always choose actually the greater part but even sometimes the less; as in the case of things which are simply evil: still, since the less evil is thought to be in a manner a good and the grasping is after good, therefore even in this case he is thought to be a grasping man i.e. one who strives for more good than fairly falls to his share: of course he is also an unequal man this being an inclusive and common term.

Chapter II

Of Justice in that sense in which it is coextensive with Virtue.

We said that the violator of Law is Unjust, and the keeper of the Law Just: further it is plain that all Lawful things are in a manner Just, because by Lawful we understand what have been defined by the legislative power and each of these we say is Just. The Laws too give directions on all points, aiming either at the common good of all or that of the best or that of those in power (taking for the standard real goodness or adopting some other estimate); in

one way we mean by Just those things which are apt to produce and preserve happiness and its ingredients for the social community.

Further, the Law commands the doing the deeds not only of the brave man (as not leaving the ranks nor flying nor throwing away one's arms) but those also of the perfectly self-mastering man, as abstinence from adultery and wantonness; and those of the meek man, as refraining from striking others or using abusive language: and in like manner in respect of the other virtues and vices commanding some things and forbidding others, rightly if it is a good law, in a way somewhat inferior, if it is one made at haphazard.

Now this Justice is in fact perfect Virtue, yet not simply so but, as exercised toward one's neighbour: and for this reason Justice is thought oftentimes to be the best of the Virtues, and

'neither Hesper nor the Morning-star
So worthy of our admiration':

and in a proverbial saying we express the same;

'All virtue is in Justice comprehended.'

And it is in a special sense perfect Virtue because it is the practice of perfect Virtue. And perfect it is because he that has it is able to practise his virtue towards his neighbour and not merely on himself; I mean there are many who can practise virtue in the regulation of their own personal conduct who are wholly unable to do it in transactions with their neighbour. And for this reason that saying of Bias is thought to be a good one

'Rule will show what a man is';

for he who bears Rule is necessarily in contact with others, i.e., in a community. And for this same reason Justice alone of all the Virtues is thought to be a good to others because it has immediate relation to some other person, inasmuch as the Just man does what is advantageous to another either to his ruler or fellow-subject. Now he is the basest of men who practises vice not only in his own person but towards his friends also; but he the best who practises virtue not merely in his own person but towards his neighbour, for this is a matter of some difficulty.

However, Justice in this sense is not a part of Virtue but is coextensive with Virtue; nor is the Injustice which answers to it a part of Vice but coextensive with Vice. Now wherein Justice in this sense differs from Virtue appears from what has been said: it is the same really but the point of view is not the same: in so far as it has respect to one's neighbour it is Justice, in so far as it is such and such a moral state it is simply Virtue.

Vice, having the same name because the definition is in the same genus; for both have their force in dealings with others, but the one acts upon honour or wealth or safety, or by whatever one name we can include all these things, and is actuated by pleasure attendant on gain, while the other acts upon all things which constitute the sphere of the good man's action.

Chapter III

That there is particular Injustice and therefore particular Justice.

But the object of our enquiry is Justice in the sense in which it is a part of Virtue (for there is such a thing, as we commonly say), and likewise with respect to particular Injustice. And of the existence of this last the following consideration is a proof: there are may vices by practising which a man acts unjustly, of course, but does not grasp at more than his share of good; if, for instance, by reason of cowardice he throws away his shield or by reason of illtemper he uses abusive language or by reason of stinginess does not give a friend pecuniary assistance; but whenever he does a grasping action it is often in the way of none of these vices certainly not in all of them, still in the way of some vice or other (for we blame him), and in the way of Injustice. There is then some kind of Injustice distinct from that co-extensive with Vice and related to it as a part to a whole, and some 'Unjust' related to that which is coextensive with violation of the law as a part to a whole.

Again, suppose one man seduces a man's wife with a view to gain and actually gets some advantage by it, and another does the same from impulse of lust at an expense of money and damage; this latter will be thought to be rather destitute of self-mastery than a grasping man and the former Unjust but not destitute of self-mastery: now why? plainly because of his gaining.

Again all other acts of Injustice we refer to some particular depravity, as, if a man commits adultery, to abandonment to his passions; if he deserts his comrade, to cowardice; if he strikes another, to anger; but, if he gains by the act, to no other vice than to Injustice.

Thus it is clear that there is a kind of Injustice different from and beside that which includes all

Chapter IV

The Justice coextensive with Virtue is dismissed from further consideration.

Now that there is more than one kind of Justice, and that there is one which is distinct from and beside that which is co-extensive with Virtue, is plain: we must next ascertain what it is and what are its characteristics.

Well, the Unjust has been divided into the unlawful and the unequal and the Just accordingly into the lawful and the equal: the aforementioned Injustice is in the way of the unlawful. And as the unequal and the more are not the same but differing as part to whole (because all more is unequal but not all unequal more), so the Unjust and the Injustice we are now in search of are not the same with, but other than, those before mentioned, the one being the parts the other the wholes; for this particular Injustice is a part of the Injustice co-extensive with Vice and likewise this Justice of the Justice co-extensive with Virtue. So that what we have now to speak of is the particular Justice and Injustice and likewise the particular Just and Unjust.

Here then let us dismiss any further consideration of the Justice ranking as coextensive with Virtue (being the practice of Virtue in all its bearings towards others), and of the co-relative Injustice (being similarly the practice of Vice). It is clear too that we must separate off the Just and the Unjust involved in these: because one may pretty well say that most lawful things are those which naturally result in action from Virtue in its fullest sense, because the law enjoins the living in accordance with each Virtue and forbids living in accordance with each Vice. And the producing causes of Virtue in all its bearings are those enactments which have been made respecting education for society.

By the way, as to individual education, in respect of which a man is simply good without reference to others, whether it is the province of politics or some other science we must determine at a future time: for it may be it is not the same thing to be a good man and a good citizen in every case.

Chapter V

The division of Particular Justice into two species.

Now of the Particular Justice and the Just involved in it one species is that which is concerned in the distributions of honour or wealth or such other things as are to be shared among the members of the social community (because in these one man as compared with another may have either an equal or an unequal share), and the other is that which is Corrective in the various transactions between man and man.

And of this latter there are two parts, because of transactions some are voluntary and some involuntary; voluntary, such as selling buying use bail borrowing deposit hiring: and this class is called voluntary because the origination of these transactions is voluntary.

The involuntary again are either such as affect secrecy: as theft adultery poisoning pimping kidnapping of slaves assassination false witness; or accompanied with open violence; as insult bonds death plundering maiming foul language slanderous abuse.

Chapter VI

That Distributive Justice implies four proportional terms.

Well the unjust man we have said is unequal and the abstract 'Unjust' unequal: further it is plain that there is some mean of the unequal, that is to say the equal or exact half (because in whatever action there is the greater and the less there is also the equal, i.e. the exact half). If then the Unjust is unequal the Just is equal, which all must allow without further proof:

and as the equal is a mean the Just must be also a mean. Now the equal implies two terms at least: it follows then that the Just is both a mean and equal, and these to certain persons; and, in so far as it is a mean, between certain things (that is the greater and the less), and, so far as it is equal, between two, and in so far as it is just it is so to certain persons. The Just then must imply four terms at least, for those to which it is just are two and the terms representing the things are two.

And there will be the same equality between the terms representing the persons as between those representing the things: because as the latter are to one another so are the former: for if the persons are not equal they must not have equal shares; in fact this is the very source of all the quarrelling and wrangling in the world when either they who are equal have and get awarded to them things not equal, or, being not equal, those things which are equal. Again the necessity of this equality of ratios is shown by the common phrase 'according to rate,' for all agree that the Just in distributions ought to be according to some rate, but what that rate is to be all do not agree; the Democrats are for freedom Oligarchs for wealth others for nobleness of birth and the Aristocratic party for virtue.

The Just, then, is a certain proportionable thing. For proportion does not apply merely to number in the abstract but to number generally, since it is equality of ratios and implies four terms at least; (that this is the case in what may be called discrete proportion is plain and obvious, but it is true also in continual proportion for this uses the one term as two and mentions it twice; thus $A : B : C$ may be expressed $A : B : : B : C$. In the first B is named twice; and so, if, as in the second, B is actually written twice, the proportionals will be four:) and the Just likewise implies four terms at the least, and the ratio between the two pairs of terms is the same because the persons and the things are divided similarly. It will stand then thus, $A : B : : C : D$, and then permutando $A : C : : B : D$, and then (supposing C and D to represent things) $A + C : B + D : : A : B$. The distribution in fact consisting in putting together these terms thus: and if they are put together so as to preserve this same ratio the distribution puts them together justly. So then the joining together of the first and third and second and fourth proportionals is the Just in distribution, and this Just is the mean relatively to that which violates the proportionate, for the proportionate is a mean and the Just is proportionate. Now mathematicians call this kind of proportion geometrical: for in geometrical proportion the whole is to the whole as each part to each part. Furthermore this proportion is not continual because the person and thing do not make up one term.

The Just then is this proportionate and the Unjust that which violates the proportionate; and so there comes to be the greater and the less: which in fact is the case in actual transactions, because he who acts unjustly has the greater share, and he who is treated unjustly has the less, of what is good: but in the case of what is bad this is reversed: for the less evil compared with the greater comes to be reckoned for good because the less evil is more choiceworthy than the greater and what is choiceworthy is good and the more so the greater good.

This then is the one species of the Just.[1]

Endnote

[1] Aristotle goes on to discuss "corrective justice," which arises in transactions like contracts. — Ed. note.

XII.2 *Justice as Convention*

DAVID HUME

David Hume (1711–1776), a Scottish empiricist, was one of the greatest philosophers of the Enlightenment. In this essay he describes justice as a human convention caused by the intersection of people's tendencies toward "selfishness and limited generosity" with conditions of scarcity in the world. Eliminate any of these conditions and justice would disappear. Hume also discusses the problem of equality in relation to justice.

1

. . . I have already observed that justice takes its rise from human conventions; and that these are intended as a remedy to some inconveniences, which proceed from the concurrence of certain *qualities* of the human mind with the *situation* of external objects. The qualities of the mind are *selfishness* and *limited generosity*. And the situation of external objects is their *easy change*, joined to their *scarcity* in comparison of the wants and desires of men. But however philosophers may have been bewildered in those speculations, poets have been guided more infallibly, by a certain taste or common instinct, which in most kinds of reasoning goes further than any of that art and philosophy, with which we have been yet acquainted. They easily perceived, if every man had a tender regard for another, or if nature supplied abundantly all our wants and desires, that the jealousy of interest, which justice supposes, could no longer have place; nor would there be any occasion for those distinctions and limits of property and possession, which at present are in use among mankind. Increase to a sufficient degree the benevolence of man, or the bounty of nature, and you render justice useless, by supplying its place with much nobler virtues, and more valuable blessings. The selfishness of men is animated by the few possessions we have, in proportion to our wants; and it is to restrain this selfishness, that men have been obliged to separate themselves from the

Excerpted from *A Treatise on Human Nature* (1739).

community, and to distinguish between their own goods and those of others.

Nor need we have recourse to the fictions of poets to learn this; but beside the reason of the thing, may discover the same truth by common experience and observation. It is easy to remark, that a cordial affection renders all things common among friends; and that married people in particular mutually lose their property, and are unacquainted with the *mine* and *thine*, which are so necessary, and yet cause such disturbance in human society. The same effect arises from any alteration in the circumstances of mankind; as when there is such a plenty of anything as satisfies all the desires of men. In which case the distinction of property is entirely lost, and everything remains in common. This we may observe with regard to air and water, though the most valuable of all external objects; and may easily conclude, that if men were supplied with everything in the same abundance or if *everyone* had the same affection and tender regard for *everyone* as for himself, justice and injustice would be equally unknown among mankind.

Here then is a proposition, which, I think, may be regarded as certain, *that it is only from the selfishness and confined generosity of men, along with the scanty provision nature has made for his wants, that justice derives its origin*. If we look backward we shall find that this proposition bestows an additional force on some of those observations which we have already made on this subject.

First, we may conclude from it, that a regard to public interest, or a strong extensive benevolence, is not our first and original motive for the observation of the rules of justice; since it is allowed, that if men were endowed with such a benevolence, these rules would never have been dreamed of.

Secondly, we may conclude from the same principle, that the sense of justice is not founded on reason, or on the discovery of certain connexions and relations of ideas, which are eternal, immutable, and universally obligatory. For since it is confessed, that such an alteration as that above-mentioned, in the temper and circumstances of mankind, would entirely alter our duties and obligations, it is necessary upon the common system, *that the sense of virtue is derived from reason*, to show the change which this must produce in the relations and ideas. But it is evident, that the only cause, why the extensive gen-

erosity of man, and the perfect abundance of everything, would destroy the very idea of justice, is because they render it useless; and that, on the other hand, his confined benevolence, and his necessitous condition, give rise to that virtue, only by making it requisite to the public interest, and to that of every individual. It was therefore a concern for our own, and the public interest, which made us establish the laws of justice; and nothing can be more certain, than that it is not any relation of ideas, which gives us this concern, but our impressions and sentiments, without which everything in nature is perfectly indifferent to us, and can never in the least affect us. The sense of justice, therefore, is not founded on our ideas, but on our impressions.

Thirdly, we may further confirm the foregoing proposition, *that those impressions, which give rise to this sense of justice, are not natural to the mind of man, but arise from artifice and human conventions*. For since any considerable alteration of temper and circumstances destroys equally justice and injustice; and since such an alteration has an effect only by changing our own and the public interest; it follows, that the first establishment of the rules of justice depends on these different interests. But if men pursued the public interest naturally, and with a hearty affection, they would never have dreamed of restraining each other by these rules; and if they pursued their own interest, without any precaution, they would run head-long into every kind of injustice and violence. These rules, therefore, are artificial, and seek their end in an oblique and indirect manner; nor is the interest, which gives rise to them, of a kind that could be pursued by the natural and inartificial passions of men.

To make this more evident, consider, that though the rules of justice are established merely by interest, their connexion with interest is somewhat singular, and is different from what may be observed on other occasions. A single act of justice is frequently contrary to *public interest*; and were it to stand alone, without being followed by other acts, may, in itself, be very prejudicial to society. When a man of merit of a beneficent disposition, restores a great fortune to a miser, or a seditious bigot, he has acted justly and laudably, but the public is a real sufferer. Nor is every single act of justice, considered apart, more conducive to private interest, than to public; and it is easily conceived how a man may impoverish himself by a single instance of integrity, and have reason to wish that with regard to that single act, the laws of justice were for a moment suspended in the universe. But however single acts of justice may be contrary, either to public or private interest, it is certain, that the whole plan or scheme is highly conducive, or indeed absolutely requisite, both to the support of society, and the well-being of every individual. It is impossible to separate the good from the ill. Property must be stable, and must be fixed by general rules. Though in one instance the public be a sufferer, this momentary ill is amply compensated by the steady prosecution of the rule, and by the peace and order, which it establishes in society. And even every individual person must find himself a gainer, on balancing the account; since, without justice, society must immediately dissolve, and everyone must fall into that savage and solitary condition, which is infinitely worse than the worst situation that can possibly be supposed in society. When therefore men have had experience enough to observe that whatever may be the consequence of any single act of justice performed by a single person, yet the whole system of actions, concurred in by the whole society, is infinitely advantageous to the whole, and to every part; it is not long before justice and property take place. Every member of society is sensible of this interest. Everyone expresses this sense to his fellows, along with the resolution he has taken of squaring his actions by it, on condition that others will do the same. No more is requisite to induce any one of them to perform an act of justice, who has the first opportunity. This becomes an example to others. And thus justice establishes itself by a kind of convention or agreement; that is, by a sense of interest, supposed to be common to all and where every single act is performed in expectation that others are to perform the like. Without such a convention no one would ever have dreamed that there was such a virtue as justice, or have been induced to conform his actions to it. Taking any single act, my justice may be pernicious in every respect; and it is only upon the supposition, that others are to imitate my example, that I can be induced to embrace that virtue; since nothing but this combination can render justice advantageous, or afford me any motives to conform myself to its rules.

2

If we examine the *particular* laws by which justice is directed and property determined we shall still be presented with the same conclusion. The good of mankind is the only object of all these laws and regulations. Not only it is requisite for the peace and interest of society that men's possessions should be separated but the rules, which we follow in making the separation are such as can best be contrived to serve further the interests of society.

We shall suppose that a creature possessed of reason but unacquainted with human nature, deliberates with himself that rules of justice or property would best promote public interest, and establish peace and security among mankind. His most obvious thought would be, to assign the largest possessions to the most extensive virtue, and give everyone the power of doing good, proportioned to his inclination. In a perfect theocracy where a being infinitely intelligent governs by particular volitions, this rule would certainly have place and might serve to the wisest purposes. But were mankind to execute such a law, so great is the uncertainty of merit, both from its natural obscurity, and from the self-conceit of each individual, that no determinate rule of conduct would ever result from it; and the total dissolution of society must be the immediate consequence. Fanatics may suppose *that dominion is founded on grace*, and *that saints alone inherit the earth*, but the civil magistrate very justly puts these sublime theorists on the same footing with common robbers, and teaches them by the severest discipline that a rule which, in speculation, may seem the most advantageous to society, may yet be found in practice totally pernicious and destructive.

That there were *religious* fanatics of this kind in England, during the civil wars, we learn from history; though it is probable, that the obvious *tendency* of these principles excited such horror in mankind, as soon obliged the dangerous enthusiasts to renounce, or at least conceal their tenets. Perhaps the *levellers*, who claimed an equal distribution of property, were a kind of *political* fanatics which arose from the religious species and more openly avowed their pretensions; as carrying a more plausible appearance, of being practicable in themselves as well as useful to human society.

It must, indeed, be confessed that nature is so liberal to mankind that, were all her presents equally divided among the species, and improved by art and industry, every individual would enjoy all the necessaries, and even most of the comforts of life, nor would ever be liable to any ills, but such as might accidentally arise from the sickly frame and constitution of his body. It must also be confessed that wherever we depart from this equality, we rob the poor of more satisfaction than we add to the rich, and that the slight gratification of a frivolous vanity in one individual frequently costs more than bread to many families, and even provinces. It may appear withal, that the rule of equality, as it would be highly *useful*, is not altogether *impracticable*, but has taken place, at least in an imperfect degree, in some republics, particularly that of Sparta, where it was attended, it is said, with the most beneficial consequences. Not to mention that the Agrarian laws, so frequently claimed in Rome, and carried into execution in many Greek cities, proceeded all of them from a general idea of the utility of this principle.

But historians and even common sense may inform us, that, however specious these ideas of *perfect* equality may seem, they are really, at bottom, *impracticable*; and were they not so, would be extremely *pernicious* to human society. Render possessions ever so equal, men's different degrees of art, care, and industry will immediately break that equality. Or if you check these virtues, you reduce society to the most extreme indigence; and instead of preventing want and beggary in a few, render it unavoidable to the whole community. The most rigorous inquisition too is requisite to watch every inequality on its first appearance; and the most severe jurisdiction to punish and redress it. But besides that so much authority must soon degenerate into tyranny and be exerted with great partialities; who can possibly be possessed of it in such a situation as is here supposed? Perfect equality of possessions destroying all subordination weakens extremely the authority of magistracy and must reduce all power nearly to a level, as well as property.

We may conclude, therefore, that in order to establish laws for the regulation of property we must be acquainted with the nature and situation of man; must reject appearances, which may be false, though specious; and must search for those rules, which are, on the whole, most *useful* and *beneficial*. Vulgar sense and slight experience are sufficient for this purpose; where men give not way to too selfish avidity or too extensive enthusiasm. . . .

XII.3 *Distributive Justice*

Nicholas Rescher

Nicholas Rescher is professor of philosophy at the University of Pittsburgh and has written prolifically in philosophy. In this essay he discusses seven candidates for material principles of distributive justice: people are to be treated (1) as equals; or according to their (2) needs, (3) merit or ability, (4) effort or sacrifices, (5) contribution, or (6) economic usefulness; or according to (7) the public good.

Rescher analyzes each of these candidates, including their strengths and weaknesses, and concludes that none of them is sufficient in itself as a criterion of distributive justice. Rescher argues for a complex, multifaceted approach to this issue. Different types of situations require giving predominance to different material principles. For example, with regard to wages, a person's just desert is to be measured in terms of productivity or contribution; but when it comes to public welfare, human need is the overriding consideration. The question is, how do we decide which particular "canon" of justice applies in any given situation?

In the course of the long history of discussions on the subject, distributive justice has been held to consist, wholly or primarily, in the treatment of all people:

1. as equals (except possibly in the case of certain "negative" distributions such as punishments)

2. according to their needs

3. according to their ability or merit or achievements

4. according to their efforts and sacrifices

5. according to their actual productive contribution

6. according to the requirements of the common good, or the public interest, or the welfare of mankind, or the greatest good of a greater number

7. according to a valuation of their socially useful services in terms of their scarcity in the essentially economic terms of supply and demand

Correspondingly, seven "canons" of distributive justice result, depending upon which of these factors is taken as the ultimate or primary determination of individual claims; namely, the canons of equality, need, ability, effort, productivity, public utility, and supply and demand. Brief consideration must be given to each of these proposed conceptions of justice.[1]

The Canon of Equality

This canon holds that justice consists in the treatment of people as equals. Here we have the *egalitarian* criterion of (idealistic) democratic theorists. The shortcomings of this canon have already been canvassed in considerable detail . . . to the effect that the principle is oblivious to the reality of differential claims and desert. It is vulnerable to all the same lines of objection which hold against the type of just-wage principle advocated by G. B. Shaw — to let all who contribute to the production of the social-economic product share in it equally.

Reprinted with permission from *Distributive Justice* (Bobbs-Merrill, 1966).

Moreover, the specification of the exact way in which equality is to be understood is by no means so simple and straightforward as it seems on first view. Is one, for example, to think of the type of fixed constant equality that is at issue in a sales tax, or the "equal burden" type of differential equality at issue in a graduated income tax; and more generally, is the "equality" at issue strict equality, equality of sacrifice, equality of opportunity-and-risk, equality of rights, or equality of "consideration," etc.?

A rule of strict equality violates the most elemental requisites of the concept of justice itself: justice not only requires the equal treatment of equals, as the canon at issue would certainly assure, but also under various circumstances requires the converse, the (appropriately measured) unequal treatment of unequals, a requisite which the canon violates blatantly. In any distribution among individuals whose legitimate claims with respect to this distribution are diverse, the treatment of people as equals without reference to their differential claims outrages rather than implements our sense of justice.

The Canon of Need

This canon holds that justice consists in the treatment of people according to their needs. Here we have the *socialistic* principle of the idealistic socialistic and communist theoreticians: "to each according to his needs."[2] Basically this principle is closely allied with the preceding one, and is, like it, one of *rectification*: recognizing that as things stand, men come into the world with different possessions and opportunities as well as differences in natural endowments, the principle professes to treat them, not equally, but so as to *make* them as equal as possible.

Regarding this principle, it has been said:

If the task of distribution were entirely independent of the process of production, this rule would be ideal [from the standpoint of justice]; for it would treat men as equal in those respects in which they are equal; namely, as beings endowed with the dignity and the potencies of personality; and it would treat them as unequal in those respects in which they are unequal; that is, in their desires and capacities.[3]

This limitation of the rule is of itself too narrow. The principle does recognize inequalities, but it recognizes only one sort; it rides roughshod not only over the matter of productive contributions but over all other ways of grounding legitimate claims (e.g., those based on kinship, on [nonproductive] services rendered, on contracts and compacts, etc.) that make for relevant differences, i.e., inequalities, among the potential recipients of a distribution. Nor, for that matter, is the principle as clear-cut as it seems on first view: by the time anything like an adequate analysis of "need" has been provided, the principle covers a wide-ranging area. For example, are we to interpret the "needs" at issue as *real* needs or as *felt* needs?

The Canon of Ability and/or Achievement

This canon holds that justice consists in the treatment of people according to their abilities. Here we have the *meritarian* criterion going back to Aristotle and echoed by the (Jeffersonian) theorists of a "natural aristocracy of ability." Natural ability, however, is a latent quality which subsists in the mode of potentiality. It represents natural endowments that can be cultivated to varying degrees and may or may not become operative and actually put to work. To allocate rewards with reference solely to innate ability, unqualified by considerations of how the abilities in question are used or abused, would be to act in a way that is patently unjust. Moreover, a question can validly be raised as to the propriety of having natural ability — which is, after all, wholly a "gift of the gods" and in no way a matter of desert — count as the sole or even the primary basis of claims.

This objection might be countered by granting that it may hold for *natural* (or innate) ability, but that it fails to be applicable when the "ability" at issue is an *acquired* ability, or perhaps even more aptly, a *demonstrated* ability of the persons at issue, as determined by their achievements. This is the criterion naturally used in giving grades to students and prizes to tennis plays (where need, for instance, and effort are deliberately discounted). But in this case the canon becomes transformed, in its essentials, into the Canon of Productivity, which will be dealt with below.

The Canon of Effort

This canon holds that justice consists in the treatment of people according to their efforts and sacrifices on their own behalves, or perhaps on behalf of their group (family, society, fellowmen). Here we have the *puritanical* principal espoused by theorists of a "Puritan ethic," who hold that God helps (and men should help) those who help themselves. Burke lauded the "natural society" in which "it is an invariable law that a man's acquisitions are in proportion to his labors." Think also of the historic discussions of a just wage and the traditional justification of differential wage scales. On the question of wages, classical socialists such as Fourier and St. Simon argued that the wage should be inversely proportioned to the intrinsic pleasantness (interest, appeal, prestige) of the task. (Presumably, thus, the policeman walking the beat shall receive more than the captain sitting at headquarters.) But the difficulties of this standpoint lie on the surface, e.g., the difficulty of maintaining morale and discipline in a setting in which the claims of ability and responsibility go unrecognized.

Moreover, the principle ignores the fact that effort is of its very nature a many-sided thing: it can be either fruitful or vain, well-directed or misguided, properly applied or misapplied, availing or unavailing, etc. To allocate rewards by effort as such without reference to its nature and direction is to ignore a key facet of just procedure — to fail to make a distinction that makes a difference. Also, to reward by effort rather than achievement is socially undesirable: it weakens incentive and encourages the inefficient, the untalented, the incompetent.

The Canon of Productivity

This canon holds that justice consists in the treatment of people according to their actual productive contribution to their group. Here we have the essentially economic principle of the social-welfare-minded *capitalistic* theoreticians. The claim-bases at issue here are primarily those traditionally considered in economics: services rendered, capital advanced, risks run, and the like. Much is to be said on behalf of this principle as a *restricted* rule, governing the division of proceeds and profits resulting from a common productive enterprise; but it is clearly defective as a general principle of distributive justice, simply because it is an overly limited single-factor criterion. The principle is prepared to put aside all considerations not only of unmerited claims in general, but also of merited claims when merited through extra-productive factors such as need and effort.

Yet one cannot fail to be impressed by the appeal to justice of such an argument as the following:

> When men of equal productive power are performing the same kind of labour, superior amounts of product do represent superior amounts of effort. . . . If men are unequal in productive power their products are obviously not in proportion to their efforts. Consider two men whose natural physical abilities are so unequal that they can handle with equal effort shovels differing in capacity by fifty per cent. Instances of this kind are innumerable in industry. If these two men are rewarded according to productivity, one will get fifty per cent more compensation than the other. Yet the surplus received by the more fortunate man does not represent any action or quality for which he is personally responsible. It corresponds to no larger output of personal effort, no superior exercise of will, no greater personal desert.[4]

Note here the criticism of a (restricted) purely economic application of the principle by an appeal to one's sense of justice. If such an appeal is to be given but the slightest (even if not ultimately decisive) weight, as I think it must, then the canon in question must *a fortiori* be at once abandoned as an exclusive and exhaustive general principle of distributive justice.

The Canon of Social Utility

This canon holds that justice consists in the treatment of people according to the best prospects for advancing the common good, or the public interest, or the welfare of mankind, or the greater good of a greater number. The theory has two basic variants, according as one resorts to a distinction between the common good of men considered *collectively*, as constituting a social group with some sort of life of its own, or merely *distributively*, as an aggregation of separate individuals. In the former case we have the "public interest," expedientialist variant of the canon with roots going back to Hebraic theology, Stoic philosophy, and Roman jurisprudence (*pro bono publico*). In the second case we have the *utilitarian* and more modern, individualistic version of the canon.

The same fundamental criticism (already dwelt upon at considerable length in our preceding discussion) can be deployed against both versions of the theory: an individual's *proper share viewed from the angle of the general good* cannot be equated with his *just share* pure and simple, because there is no "pre-established harmony" to guarantee that all of the individual's legitimate claims (the authoritative determinants of his just share) be recognized and acceded to when "the *general* good" becomes the decisive criterion. And insofar as these legitimate claims are disallowed—or *could* be disallowed—in a patently unjust (though socially advantageous) way, the principle of the primacy of the general good exhibits a feature which precludes its acceptance as a principle of justice.

The Canon of Supply and Demand

This canon holds that justice consists in the treatment of people according to a valuation of their socially useful—or perhaps merely desired—contributions, these being evaluated not on the basis of the value of the product (as with the Canon of Productivity, above), but on the basis of relative scarcity of the service. Here we have the essentially economic principle of the more hard-boiled "play of the market" school of laissez-faire theoreticians. The train dispatcher would thus deserve a larger part of the proceeds of the joint operation than the conductor, the general manager more than the section foreman, the buyer more than the salesgirl, because—while in each case both kinds of contribution are alike essential to the enterprise—the former type of labour calls for skills that are relatively scarcer, being less plentifully diffused throughout the working population. Such valuation then rests not upon the relative extent or intrinsic merit of the

contribution made, but upon the fact that that contribution is viewed by the community as necessary or desirable, and can either be made successfully by fewer people, or else involves such expenditures, risks, hardships, or hazards that fewer people are willing to undertake the task. (Throughout recent years successful entertainers have been remunerated more highly than successful physicians—and on this principle, justly so.)

As a criterion of justice, this canon suffers from the general defects as does the Canon of Productivity which it seeks to qualify. Not only does it put aside any accommodation of unmerited claims, but also any claims based upon factors (such as individual need and expenditure of effort) which have no basis in the making of a productive contribution to felt social needs.

Our Own Position: The Canon of Claims

One and the same shortcoming runs through all of the above canons of distributive justice: they are all *monistic*. They all recognize but one solitary, homogeneous mode of claim production (be it need, effort, productivity, or whatever), to the exclusion of all others. A single specific ground of claim establishment is canonized as uniquely authoritative, and all the others dismissed. As a result, these canons all suffer the aristocratic fault of hyperexclusiveness. As we see it, they err not so much in commission as in omission.

To correct this failing requires that we go from a concept of claim establishment that is monistic and homogeneous to one that is pluralistic and heterogeneous. To do so we put forward, as representing (in essentials) our own position on the issue of distributive justice, the Canon of Claims: Distributive justice consists in the treatment of people *according to their legitimate claims*, positive and negative. This canon shifts the burden to—and thus its implementation hinges crucially upon—the question of the nature of legitimate claims, and of the machinery for their mutual accommodation in cases of plurality, and their reconciliation in cases of conflict. To say this is not a criticism of the principle, but simply the recognition of an inevitable difficulty which must be encountered by any theory of distributive justice at the penalty of showing itself grossly inadequate.

The Canon of Claims plainly avoids the fault of overrestrictiveness: indeed, it reaches out to embrace all the other canons. From its perspective each canon represents one particular sort of ground (need, effort, productivity, etc.) on whose basis certain legitimate claims — upon whose accommodation it insists — can be advanced. The evaluation of these claims in context, and their due recognition under the circumstances, is in our view the key element of distributive justice.

We must be prepared to take such a multifaceted approach to claims because of the propriety of recognizing different kinds of claims-grounds as appropriate types of distribution. Our society inclines to the view that in the case of wages, desert is to be measured according to productivity of contribution qualified by supply-and-demand considerations; in the case of property income, by productivity considerations; in public-welfare distributions, by need qualified to avoid the demoralization inherent in certain types of means-tests; and in the negative distributions of taxation, by ability-to-pay qualified by social-utility considerations. The list could be extended and refined at great length but is already extensive enough to lend support to our pluralistic view of claims.

One important consequence of our canon must be noted. With it, the concept of justice is no solitarily self-sufficient ultimate, but becomes dependent upon the articulation of certain coordinate ideas, namely, those relating to claims and their establishment. The unraveling of the short thesis that distributive justice requires (in general) the accommodation of legitimate claims is but the preface of a long story about claims, a story for which there is neither need nor space here. Moreover, since claims themselves are not (at any rate, not in general) established by considerations of abstract justice, but are in large part grounded in positive law, the heavy dependence of justice upon a body of positive law may be seen. Where abstract justice might countenance various alternative divisions, the law specifies one particular procedure that underwrites a certain specific set of claims. That law shall embody considerations of justice is a trite thesis, but that there is a converse requirement resulting in mutual dependence is less frequently observed.

In espousing the Canon of Claims we may note that the search for a canon of distributive justice is carried back to the Roman jurists' view that the definitive principle of justice is inherent in the dictum *suum cuique tribuens* — "giving each his own." To the question *What is his own?* we have given the answer *What he deserves!*; that is, a share ideally equal — or at any rate generally proportional — to his legitimate claims.

Endnotes

[1] All of these canons except number 3 (the Canon of Ability) are competently and instructively discussed from an essentially economic point of view — from the special angle of the idea of a just wage or income — in Chapter 14 of John A. Ryan, *Distributive Justice*, 3rd ed. (New York: Macmillan, 1942).

[2] The formula "From each according to his abilities; to each according to his needs" was first advanced by the early French socialists of the Utopian school, and was officially adopted by German socialists in the Gotha Program of 1875.

[3] Ryan, *Distributive Justice*, p. 181.

[4] Ryan, *Distributive Justice*, pp. 183–84.

XII.4 A *Libertarian Theory of Justice*

ROBERT NOZICK

Robert Nozick is professor of philosophy at Harvard University and the author of several works in political philosophy and epistemology. In this essay from his *Anarchy, State, and Utopia*, Nozick distinguishes between two types of material principles of justice: patterned and nonpatterned. A patterned principle chooses some trait(s) that indicate how the proper distribution is to be accomplished. It has the form:

> To each according to _____.

"Let us call a principle of distribution *patterned* if it specifies that a distribution is to vary along with some natural dimension, weighted sum of natural dimensions, or lexicographic ordering of natural dimensions." Nozick rejects patterned types of principle, such as those of Rescher, because such an attempt to regulate distribution constitutes a violation of liberty.

Nozick argues for a libertarian view of nonpatterned justice that he calls the "theory of entitlement." A distribution is just if everyone has that to which he is entitled. To determine what people are entitled to, we must understand what the original position of holdings or possessions was and what constitutes a just transfer of holdings. Borrowing from John Locke's theory of property rights (cf. Part XIII.1), he argues that we have a right to any possession so long as ownership does not worsen the position of anyone else.

The minimal state is the most extensive state that can be justified. Any state more extensive violates people's rights. Yet many persons have put forth reasons purporting to justify a more extensive state. It is impossible within the compass of this book to examine all the reasons that have been put forth. Therefore, I shall focus upon those generally acknowledged to be most weighty and influential, to see precisely wherein they fail. In this chapter we consider the claim that a more extensive state is justified, because [it is] necessary (or the best instrument) to achieve distributive justice; in the next chapter we shall take up diverse other claims.

The term "distributive justice" is not a neutral one. Hearing the term "distribution," most people presume that some thing or mechanism uses some principle or criterion to give out a supply of things. Into this process of distributing shares some error may have crept. So it is an open question, at least, whether *re*distribution should take place; whether we should do again what has already been done once, though poorly. However, we are not in the position of children who have been given portions of pie by someone who now makes last minute adjustments to rectify careless cutting. There is no *central* distribution, no person or group entitled to control all the resources, jointly deciding how they are to be doled out. What each person gets, he gets from others who give to him in exchange for something, or as a gift. In a free society, diverse persons control different resources, and new holdings arise out of the voluntary exchanges and actions of persons. There is no more a distributing or distribution of shares than there is a distributing of mates in a society in which persons choose whom they shall marry. The total result is the product of many individual decisions which the different individuals involved are entitled to make. Some uses of the term "distribution," it is true, do not imply a previous distributing appropriately judged by some criterion (for example, "probability distribution"); nevertheless, despite the title of this chapter, it would be best to use a terminology that clearly is neutral. We shall speak of people's holdings; a principle of justice in holdings describes (part of) what justice tells us (requires) about holdings. I shall state first what I take to be the correct view about justice in holdings, and then turn to the discussion of alternative views.

The Entitlement Theory

The subject of justice in holdings consists of three major topics. The first is the *original acquisition of holdings*, the appropriation of unheld things. This includes the issues of how unheld things may come to be held, the process, or processes, by which unheld things may come to be held, the things that may come to be held by these processes, the extent of what comes to be held by a particular process, and so on. We shall refer to the complicated truth about this topic, which we shall not formulate here, as the principle of justice in acquisition. The second topic concerns the *transfer of holdings* from one person to another. By what processes may a person transfer holdings to another? How may a person acquire a holding from another who holds it? Under this topic come general descriptions of voluntary exchange, and gift and (on the other hand) fraud, as well as reference to particular conventional details fixed upon in a given society. The complicated truth about this subject (with placeholders for conventional details) we shall call the principle of justice in transfer. (And we shall suppose it also includes principles governing how a person may divest himself of a holding, passing it into an unheld state.)

If the world were wholly just, the following inductive definition would exhaustively cover the subject of justice in holdings.

1. A person who acquires a holding in accordance with the principle of justice in acquisition is entitled to that holding.

2. A person who acquires a holding in accordance with the principle of justice in transfer, from someone else entitled to the holding, is entitled to the holding.

3. No one is entitled to a holding except by (repeated) applications of 1 and 2.

The complete principle of distributive justice would say simply that a distribution is just if everyone is entitled to the holdings they possess under the distribution.

A distribution is just if it arises from another just distribution by legitimate means. The legitimate means of moving from one distribution to another are specified by the principle of justice in transfer. The legitimate first "moves" are specified by the principle of justice in acquisition.[1] Whatever arises from a just situation by just steps is itself just. The means of change specified by the principle of justice in transfer preserve justice. As correct rules of inference are truth-preserving and any conclusion deduced via repeated application of such rules from only true premises is itself true, so the means of transition from one situation to another specified by the principle of justice in transfer are justice-preserving, and any situation actually arising from repeated transitions in accordance with the principle from a just situation is itself just. The parallel between justice-preserving transformations and truth-preserving transformations illuminates where it fails as well as where it holds. That a conclusion could have been deduced by truth-preserving means from premises that are true suffices to show its truth. That from a just situation a situation *could* have arisen via justice-preserving means does *not* suffice to show its justice. The fact that a thief's victims voluntarily *could* have presented him with gifts does not entitle the thief to his ill-gotten gains. Justice in holdings is historical; it depends upon what actually has happened. We shall return to this point later.

Not all actual situations are generated in accordance with the two principles of justice in holdings: the principle of justice in acquisition and the principle of justice in transfer. Some people steal from others, or defraud them, or enslave them, seizing their product and preventing them from living as they choose, or forcibly exclude others from competing in exchanges. None of these are permissible modes of transition from one situation to another. And some persons acquire holdings by means not sanctioned by the principle of justice in acquisition. The existence of past injustice (previous violations of the first two principles of justice in holdings) raises the third major topic under justice in holdings: the rectification of injustice in holdings. If past injustice has shaped present holdings in various ways, some identifiable and some not, what now, if anything, ought to be done to rectify these injustices? What obligations do the performers of injustice have toward those whose position is worse than it would have been had the injustice not been done? Or, than it would have been had compensation been paid promptly? How, if at all, do things change if the beneficiaries and those made worse off are not the direct parties in the act of injustice, but, for example, their descendants? Is an injustice done to someone whose holding was itself based upon an unrectified injustice? How far back must one go in wiping clean the historical slate of injustices? What may victims of injustice permissibly do in order to rectify the injustices being done to them, including the many injustices done by persons acting through their government? I do not know of a thorough or theoretically sophisticated treatment of such issues. Idealizing greatly, let us suppose theoretical investigation will produce a principle of rectification. This principle uses historical information about previous situations and injustices done in them (as defined by the first two principles of justice and rights against interference), and information about the actual course of events that flowed from these injustices, until the present, and it yields a description (or descriptions) of holdings in the society. The principle of rectification presumably will make use of its best estimate of subjunctive information about what would have occurred (or a probability distribution over what might have occurred, using the expected value) if the injustice had not taken place. If the actual description of holdings turns out not to be one of the descriptions yielded by the principle, then one of the descriptions yielded must be realized.[2]

The general outlines of the theory of justice in holdings are that the holdings of a person are just if he is entitled to them by the principles of justice in acquisition and transfer, or by the principle of rectification of injustice (as specified by the first two principles). If each person's holdings are just, then the total set (distribution) of holdings is just. To turn these general outlines into a specific theory we would have to specify the details of each of the three principles of justice in holdings: the principle of acquisition of holdings, the principle of transfer of holdings, and the principle of rectification of violations of the first two principles. I shall not attempt that task here. (Locke's principle of justice in acquisition is discussed below.)

Historical Principles and End-Result Principles

The general outlines of the entitlement theory illuminate the nature and defects of other conceptions of distributive justice. The entitlement theory of justice in distribution is *historical*; whether a distribution is just depends upon how it came about. In contrast, *current time-slice principles* of justice hold that the justice of a distribution is determined by how things are distributed (who has what) as judged by some *structural* principle(s) of just distribution. A utilitarian who judges between any two distributions by seeing which has the greater sum of utility and, if the sums tie, applies some fixed equality criterion to choose the more equal distribution would hold a current time-sliced principle of justice. As would someone who had a fixed schedule of trade-offs between the sum of happiness and equality. According to a current time-slice principle, all that needs to be looked at, in judging the justice of a distribution, is who ends up with what; in comparing any two distributions one need look only at the matrix presenting the distributions. No further information need be fed into a principle of justice. It is a consequence of such principles of justice that any two structurally identical distributions are equally just. (Two distributions are structurally identical if they present the same profile, but perhaps have different persons occupying the particular slots. My having ten and your having five, and my having five and your having ten are structurally identical distributions.) Welfare economics is the theory of current time-slice principles of justice. The subject is conceived as operating on matrices representing only current information about distribution. This, as well as some of the usual conditions (for example, the choice of distribution is invariant under relabeling of columns), guarantees that welfare economics will be a current time-slice theory, with all of its inadequacies.

Most persons do not accept current time-slice principles as constituting the whole story about distributive shares. They think it relevant in assessing the justice of a situation to consider not only the distribution it embodies, but also how that distribution came about. If some persons are in prison for murder or war crimes, we do not say that to assess the justice of the distribution in the society we must look only at what this person has, and that person has, and that person has, . . . at the current time. We think it relevant to ask whether someone did something so that he *deserved* to be punished, deserved to have a lower share. Most will agree to the relevance of further information with regard to punishments and penalties. Consider also desired things. One traditional socialist view is that workers are entitled to the product and full fruits of their labor; they have earned it; a distribution is unjust if it does not give the workers what they are entitled to. Such entitlements are based upon some past history. No socialist holding this view would find it comforting to be told that because the actual distribution A happens to coincide structurally with the one he desires D, A therefore is no less just than D; it differs only in that the "parasitic" owners of capital received under A what the workers are entitled to under D, and the workers receive under A what the owners are entitled to under D, namely very little. This socialist rightly, in my view, holds onto the notions of earning, producing, entitlement, desert, and so forth, and he rejects current time-slice principles that look only to the structure of the resulting set of holdings. (The set of holdings resulting from what? Isn't it implausible that how holdings are produced and come to exist has no effect at all on who should hold what?) His mistake lies in his view of what entitlements arise out of what sorts of productive processes.

We construe the position we discuss too narrowly by speaking of *current* time-slice principles. Nothing is changed if structural principles operate upon a time sequence of current time-slice profiles and, for example, give someone more now to counterbalance the less he has had earlier. A utilitarian or an egalitarian or any mixture of the two over time will inherit the difficulties of his more myopic comrades. He is not helped by the fact that *some* of the information others consider relevant in assessing a distribution is reflected, unrecoverably, in past matrices. Henceforth, we shall refer to such unhistori-

cal principles of distributive justice, including the current time-slice principles, as *end-result principles* or *end-state principles*.

In contrast to end-result principles of justice, *historical principles* of justice hold that past circumstances or actions of people can create differential entitlements or differential deserts to things. An injustice can be worked by moving from one distribution to another structurally identical one, for the second, in profile the same, may violate people's entitlements or deserts; it may not fit the actual history.

Patterning

The entitlement principles of justice in holdings that we have sketched are historical principles of justice. To better understand their precise character, we shall distinguish them from another subclass of the historical principles. Consider, as an example, the principle of distribution according to moral merit. This principle requires that total distributive shares vary directly with moral merit; no person should have a greater share than anyone whose moral merit is greater. (If moral merit could be not merely ordered but measured on an interval or ratio scale, stronger principles could be formulated.) Or consider the principle that results by substituting "usefulness to society" for "moral merit" in the previous principle. Or instead of "distribute according to moral merit," or "distribute according to usefulness to society," we might consider "distribute according to the weighted sum of moral merit, usefulness to society, and need," with the weights of the different dimensions equal. Let us call a principle of distribution patterned if it specifies that a distribution is to vary along with some natural dimension, weighted sum of natural dimensions, or lexicographic ordering of natural dimensions. And let us say a distribution is patterned if it accords with some patterned principle. (I speak of natural dimensions, admittedly without a general criterion for them, because for any set of holdings some artificial dimensions can be gimmicked up to vary along with the distribution of the set.) The principle of distribution in accordance with moral merit is a patterned historical principle, which specifies a patterned distribution. "Distribute according to I.Q."

is a patterned principle that looks to information not contained in distributional matrices. It is not historical, however, in that it does not look to any past actions creating differential entitlements to evaluate a distribution; it requires only distributional matrices whose columns are labeled by I.Q. scores. The distribution in a society, however, may be composed of such simple patterned distributions, without itself being simply patterned. Different sectors may operate different patterns, or some combination of patterns may operate in different proportions across a society. A distribution composed in this manner, from a small number of patterned distributions, we also shall term "patterned." And we extend the use of "pattern" to include the overall designs put forth by combinations of end-state principles.

Almost every suggested principle of distributive justice is patterned: to each according to his moral merit, or needs, or marginal product, or how hard he tries, or the weighted sum of the foregoing, and so on. The principle of entitlement we have sketched is *not* patterned.[3] There is no one natural dimension or weighted sum or combination of a small number of natural dimensions that yields the distributions generated in accordance with the principle of entitlement. The set of holdings that results when some persons receive their marginal products, others win at gambling, others receive a share of their mate's income, others receive gifts from foundations, others receive interest on loans, others receive gifts from admirers, others receive returns on investment, others make for themselves much of what they have, others find things, and so on, will not be patterned. Heavy strands of patterns will run through it; significant portions of the variance in holdings will be accounted for by pattern-variables. If most people most of the time choose to transfer some of their entitlement to others only in exchange for something from them, then a large part of what many people hold will vary with what they held that others wanted. More details are provided by the theory of marginal productivity. But gifts to relatives, charitable donations, bequests to children, and the like, are not best conceived, in the first instance, in this manner. Ignoring the strands of pattern, let us suppose for the moment that a distribution actually arrived at by the operation of the principle of entitlement is random with respect to any pattern. Though the resulting set of holdings will be unpatterned, it will not be incomprehensible, for it can be seen as arising from the operation of a small number of principles. These principles specify how an initial distribution may arise (the principle of acquisition of holdings) and how distributions may be transformed into others (the principle of transfer of holdings). The process whereby the set of holdings is generated will be intelligible, though the set of holdings itself that results from this process will be unpatterned.

The writings of F.A. Hayek focus less than is usually done upon what patterning distributive justice requires. Hayek argues that we cannot know enough about each person's situation to distribute to each according to his moral merit (but would justice demand we do so if we did have this knowledge?); and he goes on to say, "Our objection is against all attempts to impress upon society a deliberately chosen pattern of distribution, whether it be an order of equality or of inequality."[4] However, Hayek concludes that in a free society there will be distribution in accordance with value rather than moral merit; that is, in accordance with the perceived value of a person's actions and services to others. Despite his rejection of a patterned conception of distributive justice, Hayek himself suggests a pattern he thinks justifiable: distribution in accordance with the perceived benefits given to others, leaving room for the complaint that a free society does not realize exactly this pattern. Stating this patterned strand of a free capitalist society more precisely, we get "To each according to how much he benefits others who have the resources for benefiting those who benefit them." This will seem arbitrary unless some acceptable initial set of holdings is specified, or unless it is held that the operation of the system over time washes out any significant effects from the initial set of holdings. As an example of the latter, if almost anyone would have bought a car from Henry Ford, the supposition that it was an arbitrary matter who held the money then (and so bought) would not place Henry Ford's earnings under a cloud. In any event, *his* coming to hold it is not arbitrary. Distribution according to benefits to others *is* a major patterned strand in a free capitalist society, as Hayek correctly points out, but it is only a strand and does not constitute the whole pattern of a system of entitlements (namely, inheritance, gifts for arbitrary reasons, charity, and so on) or a standard that one should insist society fit. Will people tolerate for long a system yielding distributions that they believe are unpatterned?[5] No doubt people will not long accept a distribution they believe is *unjust*. People want their society to be and to look just. But must the look of justice reside in a resulting pattern rather than in the underlying generating principles? We are in no position to conclude that the inhabitants of a society embodying an entitlement conception of justice in holdings will find it unacceptable. Still, it must be granted that were people's reasons for transferring some of their holdings to others always irrational or arbitrary, we would find this disturbing. (Suppose people always determined what holdings they would transfer, and to whom, by using a random device.) We feel more comfortable upholding the justice of an entitlement system if most of the transfers under it are done for reasons. This does not mean necessarily that all deserve what holdings they receive. It means only that there is a purpose or point to someone's transferring a holding to one person rather than to another; that usually we can see what the transferrer thinks he's gaining, what cause he thinks he's serving, what goals he thinks he's helping to achieve, and so forth. Since in a capitalist society people often transfer holdings to others in accordance with how much they perceive these others benefiting them, the fabric constituted by the individual transactions and transfers is largely reasonable and intelligible.[6] (Gifts to loved ones, bequests to children, charity to the needy also are nonarbitrary components of the fabric.) In stressing the large strand of distribution in accordance with benefit to others, Hayek shows the point of many transfers, and so shows that the system of transfer of entitlements is not just spinning its gears aimlessly. The system of entitlements is defensible when constituted by the individual aims of individual transactions. No overarching aim is needed, no distributional pattern is required.

To think that the task of a theory of distributive justice is to fill in the blank in "to each according to his _____" is to be predisposed to search for a pattern; and the separate treatment of "from each according to his _____" treats production and distribution as two separate and independent issues. On an entitlement view these are *not* two separate questions. Whoever makes something, having bought or contracted for all other held resources used in the process (transferring some of his holdings for these cooperating factors), is entitled to it.

The situation is *not* one of something's getting made, and there being an open question of who is to get it. Things come into the world already attached to people having entitlements over them. From the point of view of the historical entitlement conception of justice in holdings, those who start afresh to complete "to each according to his _____" treat objects as if they appeared from nowhere, out of nothing. A complete theory of justice might cover this limit case as well; perhaps here is a use for the usual conceptions of distributive justice.[7]

So entrenched are maxims of the usual form that perhaps we should present the entitlement conception as a competitor. Ignoring acquisition and rectification, we might say:

> From each according to what he chooses to do, to each according to what he makes for himself (perhaps with the contracted aid of others) and what others choose to do for him and choose to give him of what they've been given previously (under this maxim) and haven't yet expended or transferred.

This, the discerning reader will have noticed, has its defects as a slogan. So as a summary and great simplification (and not as a maxim with any independent meaning) we have:

> *From each as they choose, to each as they are chosen.*

How *Liberty Upsets Patterns*

It is not clear how those holding alternative conceptions of distributive justice can reject the entitlement conception of justice in holdings. For suppose a distribution favored by one of these nonentitlement conceptions is realized. Let us suppose it is your favorite one and let us call this distribution D_1; perhaps everyone has an equal share, perhaps shares vary in accordance with some dimension you treasure. Now suppose that Wilt Chamberlain is greatly in demand by basketball teams, being a great gate attraction. (Also suppose contracts run only for a year, with players being free agents.) He signs the following sort of contract with a team: In each home game, twenty-five cents from the price of each ticket of admission goes to him. (We ignore the question of whether he is "gouging" the owners, letting them look out for themselves.) The season starts, and people cheerfully attend his team's games; they buy their tickets, each time dropping a separate twenty-five cents of their admission price into a special box with Chamberlain's name on it. They are excited about seeing him play; it is worth the total admission price to them. Let us suppose that in one season one million persons attend his home games, and Wilt Chamberlain winds up with $250,000, a much larger sum than the average income and larger even than anyone else has. Is he entitled to this income? Is this new distribution D_2, unjust? If so, why? There is *no* question about whether each of the people was entitled to the control over the resources they held in D_1, because that was the distribution (your favorite) that (for the purposes of argument) we assumed was acceptable. Each of these persons *chose* to give twenty-five cents of their money to Chamberlain. They could have spent it on going to the movies, or on candy bars, or on copies of *Dissent* magazine, or of *Monthly Review*. But they all, at least one million of them, converged on giving it to Wilt Chamberlain in exchange for watching him play basketball. If D_1 was a just distribution, and people voluntarily moved from it to D_2 transferring parts of their shares they were given under D_1 (what was it for if not to do something with?), isn't D_2 also just? If people were entitled to dispose of the resources to which they were entitled (under D_1), didn't this include their being entitled to give it to, or exchange it with, Wilt Chamberlain? Can anyone else complain on grounds of justice? Each other person already has his legitimate share under D_1. Under D_1, there is nothing that anyone has that anyone else has a claim of justice against. After someone transfers something to Wilt Chamberlain, third parties *still* have their legitimate shares; *their* shares are not changed. By what process could such a transfer among two persons give rise to a legitimate claim of distributive justice on a portion of what was transferred, by a third party who had no claim of justice on any holding of the others *before* the transfer?[8] To cut off objections irrelevant here, we might imagine the exchanges occurring in a socialist society, after hours: After playing whatever basketball he does in his daily work, or doing whatever other daily work he does, Wilt Chamberlain decides to put in *overtime* to earn additional money. (First his work quota is set; he works

time over that.) Or imagine it is a skilled juggler people like to see, who puts on shows after hours.

Why might someone work overtime in a society in which it is assumed their needs are satisfied? Perhaps because they care about things other than needs. I like to write in books that I read, and to have easy access to books for browsing at odd hours. It would be very pleasant and convenient to have the resources of Widener Library in my backyard. No society, I assume, will provide such resources close to each person who would like them as part of his regular allotment (under D_1). Thus, persons either must do without some extra things that they want, or be allowed to do something extra to get some of these things. On what basis could the inequalities that would eventuate be forbidden? Notice also that small factories would spring up in a socialist society, unless forbidden. I melt down some of my personal possessions (under D_1) and build a machine out of the material. I offer you, and others, a philosophy lecture once a week in exchange for your cranking the handle on my machine, whose products I exchange for yet other things, and so on. (The raw materials used by the machine are given to me by others who possess them under D_1, in exchange for hearing lectures.) Each person might participate to gain things over and above their allotment under D_1. Some persons even might want to leave their job in socialist industry and work full time in this private sector. [In any case] I wish merely to note how private property even in means of production would occur in a socialist society that did not forbid people to use as they wished some of the resources they are given under the socialist distribution D_1. The socialist society would have to forbid capitalist acts between consenting adults.

The general point illustrated by the Wilt Chamberlain example and the example of the entrepreneur in a socialist society is that no end-state principle or distributional patterned principle of justice can be continuously realized without continuous interference with people's lives. Any favored pattern would be transformed into one unfavored by the principle, by people choosing to act various ways; for example, by people exchanging goods and services with other people, or giving things to other people, things the transferrers are entitled to under the favored distributional pattern. To maintain a pattern one must either continually interfere to stop people from transferring resources as they wish to, or continually (or periodically) interfere to take from some persons resources that others for some reason chose to transfer to them. (But if some time limit is to be set on how long people may keep resources others voluntarily transfer to them, why let them keep these resources for *any* period of time? Why not have immediate confiscation?) It might be objected that all persons voluntarily will choose to refrain from actions which would upset the pattern. This presupposes unrealistically (1) that all will most want to maintain the pattern (are those who don't, to be "reeducated" or forced to undergo "self-criticism"?), (2) that each can gather enough information about his own actions and the ongoing activities of others to discover which of his actions will upset the pattern, and (3) that diverse and far-flung persons can coordinate their actions to dovetail into the pattern. Compare the manner in which the market is neutral among persons' desires, as it reflects and transmits widely scattered information via prices, and coordinates persons' activities.

It puts things perhaps a bit too strongly to say that every patterned (or end-state) principle is liable to be thwarted by the voluntary actions of the individual parties transferring some of their shares they receive under the principle. For perhaps some *very* weak patterns are not so thwarted. Any distributional pattern with any egalitarian component is overturnable by the voluntary actions of individual persons over time; as is every patterned condition with sufficient content so as actually to have been proposed as presenting the central core of distributive justice. Still, given the possibility that some weak conditions or patterns may not be unstable in this way, it would be better to formulate an explicit description of the kind of interesting and contentful patterns under discussion, and to prove a theorem about their instability. Since the weaker the patterning, the more likely it is that the entitlement system itself satisfies it, a plausible conjecture is that any patterning either is unstable or is satisfied by the entitlement system. . . .

Redistribution and Property Rights

Apparently, patterned principles allow people to choose to expend upon themselves, but not upon others, those resources they are entitled to (or rather, receive) under some favored distributional pattern D_1. For if each of several persons chooses to expend some of his D_1 resources upon one other person, then that other person will receive more than his D_1 share, disturbing the favored distributional pattern. Maintaining a distributional pattern is individualism with a vengeance! Patterned distributional principles do not give people what entitlement principles do, only better distributed. For they do not give the right to choose what to do with what one has; they do not give the right to choose to pursue an end involving (intrinsically, or as a means) the enhancement of another's position. To such views, families are disturbing; for within a family occur transfers that upset the favored distributional pattern. Either families themselves become units to which distribution takes place, the column occupiers (on what rationale?), or loving behavior is forbidden. We should note in passing the ambivalent position of radicals toward the family. Its loving relationships are seen as a model to be emulated and extended across the whole society, at the same time that it is denounced as a suffocating institution to be broken and condemned as a focus of parochial concerns that interfere with achieving radical goals. Need we say that it is not appropriate to enforce across the wider society the relationships which are voluntarily undertaken? Incidentally, love is an interesting instance of another relationship that is historical, in that (like justice) it depends upon what actually occurred. An adult may come to love another because of the other's characteristics; but it is the other person, and not the characteristics, that is loved. The love is not transferable to someone else with the same characteristics, even to one who "scores" higher for these characteristics. And the love endures through changes of the characteristics that gave rise to it. One loves the particular person one actually encountered. Why love is historical, attaching to persons in this way and not to characteristics, is an interesting and puzzling question.

Proponents of patterned principles of distributive justice focus upon criteria for determining who is to receive holdings; they consider the reasons for which someone should have something, and also the total picture of holdings. Whether or not it is better to give than to receive, proponents of patterned principles ignore giving altogether. In considering the distribution of goods, income, and so forth, their theories are theories of recipient justice; they completely ignore any right a person might have to give something to someone. Even in exchanges where each party is simultaneously giver and recipient, patterned principles of justice focus only upon the recipient role and its supposed rights. Thus discussions tend to focus on whether people (should) have a right to inherit, rather than on whether people (should) have a right to bequeath or on whether persons who have a right to hold also have a right to choose that others hold in their place. I lack a good explanation of why the usual theories of distributive justice are so recipient oriented; ignoring givers and transferrers and their rights is of a piece with ignoring producers and their entitlements. But why is it *all* ignored?

Patterned principles of distributive justice necessitate *re*distributive activities. The likelihood is small that any actual freely-arrived-at set of holdings fits a given pattern; and the likelihood is nil that it will continue to fit the pattern as people exchange and give. From the point of view of an entitlement theory, redistribution is a serious matter indeed, involving, as it does, the violation of people's rights. (An exception is those takings that fall under the principle of the rectification of injustices.) From other points of view, also, it is serious.

Taxation of earnings from labor is on a par with forced labor. Some persons find this claim obviously true: taking the earnings of *n* hours labor is like taking *n* hours from the person; it is like forcing the person to work *n* hours for another's purpose. Others find the claim absurd. But even these, *if* they object to forced labor, would oppose forcing unemployed hippies to work for the benefit of the needy. And they would also object to forcing each person to work five extra hours each week for the benefit of the needy. But a system that takes five hours' wages in taxes does not seem to them like one that forces someone to work five hours, since it offers the person forced a wider range of choice in activities than does taxation in kind with the particular labor specified. (But we can imagine a gradation of systems of forced labor, from one that specifies a particular activity, to one that gives a choice among two activities, to . . . ; and so on up.) Furthermore, people envisage a system with something like a proportional tax on everything above the amount necessary for basic needs. Some think this does not force someone to work extra hours, since there is no fixed number of extra hours he is forced to work, and

since he can avoid the tax entirely by earning only enough to cover his basic needs. This is a very uncharacteristic view of forcing for those who *also* think people are forced to do something *whenever* the alternatives they face are considerably worse. However, *neither* view is correct. The fact that others intentionally intervene, in violation of a side constraint against aggression, to threaten force to limit the alternatives, in this case to paying taxes or (presumably the worse alternative) bare subsistence, makes the taxation system one of forced labor and distinguishes it from other cases of limited choices which are not forcings.

The man who chooses to work longer to gain an income more than sufficient for his basic needs prefers some extra goods or services to the leisure and activities he could perform during the possible nonworking hours; whereas the man who chooses not to work the extra time prefers the leisure activities to the extra goods or services he could acquire by working more. Given this, if it would be illegitimate for a tax system to seize some of a man's leisure (forced labor) for the purpose of serving the needy, how can it be legitimate for a tax system to seize some of a man's goods for that purpose? Why should we treat the man whose happiness requires certain material goods or services differently from the man whose preferences and desires make such goods unnecessary for his happiness? Why should the man who prefers seeing a movie (and who has to earn money for a ticket) be open to the required call to aid the needy, while the person who prefers looking at a sunset (and hence need earn no extra money) is not? Indeed, isn't it surprising that redistributionists choose to ignore the man whose pleasures are so easily attainable without extra labor, while adding yet another burden to the poor unfortunate who must work for his pleasures? If anything, one would have expected the reverse. Why is the person with the nonmaterial or nonconsumption desire allowed to proceed unimpeded to his most favored feasible alternative, whereas the man whose pleasures or desires involve material things and who must work for extra money (thereby serving whomever considers his activities valuable enough to pay him) is constrained in what he can realize? Perhaps there is no difference in principle. And perhaps some think the answer concerns merely administrative convenience. (These questions and issues will not disturb those who think that forced labor to serve the needy or to realize some favored end-state pattern is acceptable.) In a fuller discussion we would have (and want) to extend our argument to include interest, entrepreneurial profits, and so on. Those who doubt that this extension can be carried through, and who draw the line here at taxation of income from labor, will have to state rather complicated patterned *historical* principles of distributive justice, since end-state principles would not distinguish *sources* of income in any way. It is enough for now to get away from end-state principles and to make clear how various patterned principles are dependent upon particular views about the sources or the illegitimacy or the lesser legitimacy of profits, interest, and so on; which particular views may well be mistaken.

What sort of right over others does a legally institutionalized end-state pattern give one? The central core of the notion of a property right in X, relative to which other parts of the notion are to be explained, is the right to choose which of the constrained set of options concerning X shall be realized or attempted. The constraints are set by other principles or laws operating in the society; in our theory, by the Lockean rights people possess (under the minimal state). My property rights in my knife allow me to leave it where I will, but not in your chest. I may choose which of the acceptable options involving the knife is to be realized. This notion of property helps us to understand why earlier theorists spoke of people as having property in themselves and their labor. They viewed each person as having a right to decide what would become of himself and what he would do, and as having a right to reap the benefits of what he did.

This right of selecting the alternative to be realized from the constrained set of alternatives may be held by an *individual* or by a *group* with some procedure for reaching a joint decision; or the right may be passed back and forth, so that one year I decide what's to become of X, and the next year you do (with the alternative of destruction, perhaps, being excluded). Or, during the same time period, some types of decisions about X may be made by me, and others by you. And so on. We lack an adequate, fruitful, analytical apparatus for classifying the *types* of constraints on the set of the options among which choices are to be made, and the *types* of ways decision powers can be held, divided, and amalgamated. A *theory* of property would, among other things, contain such a classification of constraints and decision modes, and from a small number of principles would follow a host of interesting statements about the *consequences* and effects of certain combinations of constraints and modes of decision.

When end-result principles of distributive justice are built into the legal structure of a society, they (as do most patterned principles) give each citizen an enforceable claim to some portion of the total social product; that is, to some portion of the sum total of the individually and jointly made products. This total product is produced by individuals laboring, using means of production others have saved to bring into existence, by people organizing production or creating means to produce new things or things in a new way. It is on this batch of individual activities that patterned distributional principles give each individual an enforceable claim. Each person has a claim to the activities and the products of other persons, independently of whether the other persons enter into particular relationships that give rise to these claims, and independently of whether they voluntarily take these claims upon themselves, in charity or in exchange for something.

Whether it is done through taxation on wages or on wages over a certain amount, or through seizure of profits, or through there being a big *social pot* so that it's not clear what's coming from where and what's going where, patterned principles of distributive justice involve appropriating the actions of other persons. Seizing the results of someone's labor is equivalent to seizing hours from him and directing him to carry on various activities. If people force you to do certain work, or, unrewarded work, for a certain period of time, they decide what you are to do and what purposes your work is to serve apart from your decisions. This process whereby they take this decision from you makes them a *part owner* of you; it gives them a property right in you. Just as having such partial control and power of decision, by right, over an animal or inanimate object would be to have a property right in it.

End-state and most patterned principles of distributive justice institute (partial) ownership by others of people and their actions and labor. These principles involve a shift from the classical liberals' notion of self-ownership to a notion of (partial) property rights in *other* people.

Considerations such as these confront end-state and other patterned conceptions of justice with the question of whether the actions necessary to achieve the selected pattern don't themselves violate moral side constraints. Any view holding that there are moral side constraints on actions, that not all moral considerations can be built into end-states that are to be achieved . . . must face the possibility that some of its goals are not achievable by any morally permissible available means. An entitlement theorist will face such conflicts in a society that deviates from the principles of justice for the generation of holdings, if and only if the only actions available to realize the principles themselves violate some moral constraints. Since deviation from the first two principles of justice (in acquisition and transfer) will involve other persons' direct and aggressive intervention to violate rights, and since moral constraints will not exclude defensive or retributive action in such cases, the entitlement theorist's problem rarely will be pressing. And whatever difficulties he has in applying the principle of rectification to persons who did not themselves violate the first two principles are difficulties in balancing the conflicting considerations so as correctly to formulate the complex principle of rectification itself; he will not violate moral side constraints by applying the principle. Proponents of patterned conceptions of justice, however, often will face head-on clashes (and poignant ones if they cherish each party to the clash) between moral side constraints on how individuals may be treated and their patterned conception of justice that presents an end-state or other pattern that *must* be realized.

May a person emigrate from a nation that has institutionalized some end-state or patterned distributional principle? For some principles (for example, Hayek's) emigration presents no theoretical problem. But for others it is a tricky matter. Consider a nation having a compulsory scheme of minimal social provision to aid the neediest (or one organized so as to maximize the position of the worst-off group); no one may opt out of participating in it. (None may say, "Don't compel me to contribute to others and don't provide for me via this compulsory mechanism if I am in need.") Everyone above a certain level is forced to contribute to aid the needy. But if emigration from the country were allowed, anyone could choose to move to another country that did not have compulsory social provision but otherwise was (as much as possible) identical. In such a case, the person's *only* motive for leaving would be to avoid participating in the compulsory scheme of social provision. And if he

does leave, the needy in his initial country will receive no (compelled) help from him. What rationale yields the result that the person be permitted to emigrate, yet forbidden to stay and opt out of the compulsory scheme of social provision? If providing for the needy is of overriding importance, this does militate against allowing internal opting out; but it also speaks against allowing external emigration. (Would it also support, to some extent, the kidnapping of persons living in a place without compulsory social provision, who could be forced to make a contribution to the needy in your community?) Perhaps the crucial component of the position that allows emigration solely to avoid certain arrangements, while not allowing anyone internally to opt out of them, is a concern for fraternal feelings within the country. "We don't want anyone here who doesn't contribute, who doesn't care enough about the others to contribute." That concern, in this case, would have to be tied to the view that forced aiding tends to produce fraternal feelings between the aided and the aider (or perhaps merely to the view that the knowledge that someone or other voluntarily is not aiding produces unfraternal feelings).

Locke's Theory of Acquisition

Before we turn to consider other theories of justice in detail, we must introduce an additional bit of complexity into the structure of the entitlement theory. This is best approached by considering Locke's attempt to specify a principle of justice in acquisition. Locke views property rights in an unowned object as originating through someone's mixing his labor with it. This gives rise to many questions. What are the boundaries of what labor is mixed with? If a private astronaut clears a place on Mars, has he mixed his labor with (so that he comes to own) the whole planet, the whole uninhabited universe, or just a particular plot? Which plot does an act bring under ownership? The minimal (possibly disconnected) area such that an act decreases entropy in that area, and not elsewhere? Can virgin land (for the purposes of ecological investigation by high-flying airplane) come under ownership by a Lockean process? Building a fence around a territory presumably would make one the owner of only the fence (and the land immediately underneath it).

Why does mixing one's labor with something make one the owner of it? Perhaps because one owns one's labor, and so one comes to own a previously unowned thing that becomes permeated with what one owns. Ownership seeps over into the rest. But why isn't mixing what I own with what I don't own a way of losing what I own rather than a way of gaining what I don't? If I own a can of tomato juice and spill it in the sea so that its molecules (made radioactive, so I can check this) mingle evenly throughout the sea, do I thereby come to own the sea, or have I foolishly dissipated my tomato juice? Perhaps the idea, instead, is that laboring on something improves it and makes it more valuable; and anyone is entitled to own a thing whose value he has created. (Reinforcing this, perhaps, is the view that laboring is unpleasant. If some people made things effortlessly, as the cartoon characters in *The Yellow Submarine* trail flowers in their wake, would they have lesser claim to their own products whose making didn't *cost* them anything?) Ignore the fact that laboring on something may make it less valuable (spraying pink enamel paint on a piece of driftwood that you have found). Why should one's entitlement extend to the whole object rather than just to the *added value* one's labor has produced? (Such reference to value might also serve to delimit the extent of ownership; for example, substitute "increases the value of" for "decreases entropy in" in the above entropy criterion.) No workable or coherent value-added property scheme has yet been devised, and any such scheme presumably would fall to objections (similar to those) that fell the theory of Henry George.

It will be implausible to view improving an object as giving full ownership to it, if the stock of unowned objects that might be improved is limited. For an object's coming under one person's ownership changes the situation of all others. Whereas previously they were at liberty (in Hohfeld's sense) to use the object, they now no longer are. This change in the situation of others (by removing their liberty to act on a previously unowned object) need not worsen their situation. If I appropriate a grain of sand from Coney Island, no one else may now do as they will with *that* grain of sand. But there are plenty of other grains of sands left for them to do the same with. Or if not grains of sand, then other things. Alternatively, the things I do with the grain of sand I appropriate might improve the position of others, counterbalancing their loss of liberty to use

that grain. The crucial point is whether appropriation of an unowned object worsens the situation of others.

Locke's proviso that there be "enough and as good left in common for others" . . . is meant to ensure that the situation of others is not worsened. (If this proviso is met is there any motivation for his further condition of nonwaste?) It is often said that this proviso once held but now no longer does. But there appears to be an argument for the conclusion that if the proviso no longer holds, then it cannot ever have held so as to yield permanent and inheritable property rights. Consider the first person Z for whom there is not enough and as good left to appropriate. The last person Y to appropriate left Z without his previous liberty to act on an object, and so worsened Z's situation. So Y's appropriation is not allowed under Locke's proviso. Therefore the next to last person X to appropriate left Y in a worse position, for X's act ended permissible appropriation. Therefore X's appropriation wasn't permissible. But then the appropriator two from last, W, ended permissible appropriation and so, since it worsened X's position, W's appropriation wasn't permissible. And so on back to the first person A to appropriate a permanent property right.

This argument, however, proceeds too quickly. Someone may be made worse off by another's appropriation in two ways: first, by losing the opportunity to improve his situation by a particular appropriation of any one; and second, by no longer being able to use freely (without appropriation) what he previously could. A *stringent* requirement that another not be made worse off by an appropriation would exclude the first way if nothing else counterbalances the diminution in opportunity, as well as the second. A *weaker* requirement would exclude the second way, though not the first. With the weaker requirement, we cannot zip back so quickly from Z to A, as in the above argument; for though person Z can no longer *appropriate*, there may remain some for him to *use* as before. In this case Y's appropriation would not violate the weaker Lockean condition. (With less remaining that people are at liberty to use, users might face more inconvenience, crowding, and so on; in that way the situation of others might be worsened, unless appropriation stopped far short of such a point.) It is arguable that no one legitimately can complain if the weaker provision is satisfied. However, since this is less clear than in the case of the more stringent proviso,

Locke may have intended this stringent proviso by "enough and as good" remaining, and perhaps he meant the nonwaste condition to delay the end point from which the argument zips back.

Is the situation of persons who are unable to appropriate (there being no more accessible and useful unowned objects) worsened by a system allowing appropriation and permanent property? Here enter the various familiar social considerations favoring private property: it increases the social product by putting means of production in the hands of those who can use them most efficiently (profitably); experimentation is encouraged, because with separate persons controlling resources, there is no one person or small group whom someone with a new idea must convince to try it out; private property enables people to decide on the pattern and types of risks they wish to bear, leading to specialized types of risk bearing; private property protects future persons by leading some to hold back resources from current consumption for future markets; it provides alternate sources of employment for unpopular persons who don't have to convince any one person or small group to hire them, and so on. These considerations enter a Lockean theory to support the claim that appropriation of private property satisfies the intent behind the "enough and as good left over" proviso, *not* as a utilitarian justification of property. They enter to rebut the claim that because the proviso is violated no natural right to private property can arise by a Lockean process. The difficulty in working such an argument to show that the proviso is satisfied is in fixing the appropriate baseline for comparison. Lockean appropriation makes people no worse off than they would be *how*? This question of fixing the baseline needs more detailed investigation than we are able to give it here. It would be desirable to have an estimate of the general economic importance of original appropriation in order to see how much leeway there is for differing theories of appropriation and of the location of the baseline. Perhaps this importance can be measured by the percentage of all income that is based upon untransformed raw materials and given resources (rather than upon human actions), mainly rental income representing the unimproved value of land, and the price of raw material *in situ*, and by the percentage of current wealth which represents such income in the past.

We should note that it is not only persons favoring *private* property who need a theory of how property rights legitimately originate. Those believing in collective property, for example those believing that a group of persons living in an area jointly own the territory, or its mineral resources, also must provide a theory of how such property rights arise; they must show why the persons living there have rights to determine what is done with the land and resources there that persons living elsewhere don't have (with regard to the same land and resources).

The Proviso

Whether or not Locke's particular theory of appropriation can be spelled out so as to handle various difficulties, I assume that any adequate theory of justice in acquisition will contain a proviso similar to the weaker of the ones we have attributed to Locke. A process normally giving rise to a permanent bequeathable property right in a previously unowned thing will not do so if the position of others no longer at liberty to use the thing is thereby worsened. It is important to specify *this* particular mode of worsening the situation of others, for the proviso does not encompass other modes. It does not include the worsening due to more limited opportunities to appropriate (the first way above, corresponding to the more stringent condition), and it does not include how I "worsen" a seller's position if I appropriate materials to make some of what he is selling, and then enter into competition with him. Someone whose appropriation otherwise would violate the proviso still may appropriate provided he compensates the others so that their situation is not thereby worsened; unless he does compensate these others, his appropriation will violate the proviso of the principle of justice in acquisition and will be an illegitimate one. A theory of appropriation incorporating this Lockean proviso will handle correctly the cases (objections to the theory lacking the proviso) where someone appropriates the total supply of something necessary for life.

A theory which includes this proviso in its principle of justice in acquisition must also contain a more complex principle of justice in transfer. Some reflection of the proviso about appropriation constrains later actions. If my appropriating all of a certain substance violates the Lockean proviso, then so does my appropriating some and purchasing all the rest from others who obtained it without otherwise violating the Lockean proviso. If the proviso excludes someone's appropriating all the drinkable water in the world, it also excludes his purchasing it all. (More weakly, and messily, it may exclude his charging certain prices for some of his supply.) This proviso (almost?) never will come into effect; the more someone acquires of a scarce substance which others want the higher the price of the rest will go, and the more difficult it will become for him to acquire it all. But still, we can imagine, at least, that something like this occurs: someone makes simultaneous secret bids to the separate owners of a substance, each of whom sells assuming he can easily purchase more from the other owners; or some natural catastrophe destroys all of the supply of something except that in one person's possession. The total supply could not be permissibly appropriated by one person at the beginning. His later acquisition of it all does not show that the original appropriation violated the proviso (even by a reverse argument similar to the one above that tried to zip back from Z to A). Rather, it is the combination of the original appropriation *plus* all the later transfers and actions that violates the Lockean proviso.

Each owner's title to his holding includes the historical shadow of the Lockean proviso on appropriation. This excludes his transferring it into an agglomeration that does violate the Lockean proviso and excludes his using it in a way, in coordination with others or independently of them, so as to violate the proviso by making the situation of others worse than their baseline situation. Once it is known that someone's ownership runs afoul of the Lockean proviso, there are stringent limits on what he may do with (what it is difficult any longer unreservedly to call) "his property." Thus a person may not appropriate the only water hole in a desert and charge what he will. Nor may he charge what he will if he possesses one, and unfortunately it happens that all the water holes in the desert dry up, except for his. This unfortunate circumstance, admittedly no fault of his, brings into operation the Lockean proviso and limits his property rights. Similarly, an owner's property right in the only island in an area does not allow him to order a castaway from a shipwreck off his island as a trespasser, for this would violate the Lockean proviso.

Notice that the theory does not say that owners do have these rights, but that the rights are overridden to avoid some catastrophe. (Overridden rights do not disappear; they leave a trace of a sort absent in the cases under discussion.) There is no such external (and *ad hoc?*) overriding. Considerations internal to the theory of property itself, to its theory of acquisition and appropriation, provide the means for handling such cases. The results, however, may be coextensive with some condition about catastrophe, since the baseline for comparison is so low as compared to the productiveness of a society with private appropriation that the question of the Lockean proviso being violated arises only in the case of catastrophe (or a desert-island situation).

The fact that someone owns the total supply of something necessary for others to stay alive does *not* entail that his (or anyone's) appropriation of anything left some people (immediately or later) in a situation worse than the baseline one. A medical researcher who synthesizes a new substance that effectively treats a certain disease and who refuses to sell except on his terms does not worsen the situation of others by depriving them of whatever he has appropriated. The others easily can possess the same materials he appropriated; the researcher's appropriation or purchase of chemicals didn't make those chemicals scarce in a way so as to violate the Lockean proviso. Nor would someone else's purchasing the total supply of the synthesized substance from the medical researcher. The fact that the medical researcher uses easily available chemicals to synthesize the drug no more violates the Lockean proviso than does the fact that the only surgeon able to perform a particular operation eats easily obtainable food in order to stay alive and to have the energy to work. This shows that the Lockean proviso is not an "end-state principle"; it focuses on a particular way that appropriative actions affect others, and not on the structure of the situation that results.

Intermediate between someone who takes all of the public supply and someone who makes the total supply out of easily obtainable substances is someone who appropriates the total supply of something in a way that does not deprive the others of it. For example, someone finds a new substance in an out-of-the-way place. He discovers that it effectively treats a certain disease and appropriates the total supply. He does not worsen the situation of others; if he did not stumble upon the substance no one else would have, and the others would remain without it. However, as time passes, the likelihood increases that others would have come across the substance; upon this fact might be based a limit to his property right in the substance so that others are not below their baseline position; for example, its bequest might be limited. The theme of someone worsening another's situation by depriving him of something he otherwise would possess may also illuminate the example of patents. An inventor's patent does not deprive others of an object which would not exist if not for the inventor. Yet patents would have this effect on others who independently invent the object. Therefore, these independent inventors, upon whom the burden of proving independent discovery may rest, should not be excluded from utilizing their own invention as they wish (including selling it to others). Furthermore, a known inventor drastically lessens the chances of actual independent invention. For persons who know of an invention usually will not try to reinvent it, and the notion of independent discovery here would be murky at best. Yet we may assume that in the absence of the original invention, sometime later someone else would have come up with it. This suggests placing a time limit on patents, as a rough rule of thumb to approximate how long it would have taken, in the absence of knowledge of the invention, for independent discovery.

I believe that the free operation of a market system will not actually run afoul of the Lockean proviso. (Recall that crucial to our story in Part I of how a protective agency becomes dominant and a *de facto* monopoly is the fact that it wields force in situations of conflict, and is not merely in competition, with other agencies. A similar tale cannot be told about other businesses.) If this is correct, the proviso will not play a very important role in the activities of protective agencies and will not provide a significant opportunity for future state action. Indeed, were it not for the effects of previous *illegitimate* state action, people would not think of the possibility of the proviso's being violated as of more interest than any other logical possibility. (Here I make an empirical historical claim; as does someone who disagrees with this.) This completes our indication of the complication in the entitlement theory introduced by the Lockean proviso.

Endnotes

[1] Applications of the principles of justice in acquisition may also occur as part of the move from one distribution to another. You may find an unheld thing now and appropriate

it. Acquisitions also are to be understood as included when, to simplify, I speak only of transitions by transfers.

[2] If the principle of rectification of violations of the first two principles yields more than one description of holdings, then some choice must be made as to which of these is to be realized. Perhaps the sort of considerations about distributive justice and equality that I argue against play a legitimate role in *this* subsidiary choice. Similarly, there may be room for such considerations in deciding which otherwise arbitrary features a statute will embody, when such features are unavoidable because other considerations do not specify a precise line; yet a line must be drawn.

[3] One might try to squeeze a patterned conception of distributive justice into the framework of the entitlement conception, by formulating a gimmicky obligatory "principle of transfer" that would lead to the pattern. For example, the principle that if one has more than the mean income one must transfer everything one holds above the mean to persons below the mean so as to bring them up (but not over) the mean. We can formulate a criterion for a "principle of transfer" to rule out such obligatory transfers, or we can say that no correct principle of transfers, no principle of transfers in a free society will be like this. The former is probably the better course, though the latter also is true.

Alternatively, one might think to make the entitlement conception instantiate a pattern, by using matrix entries that express the relative strength of a person's entitlements as measured by some real-valued function. But even if the limitation to natural dimensions failed to exclude this function, the resulting edifice would *not* capture our system of entitlements to *particular* things.

[4] F. A. Hayek, *The Constitution of Liberty* (Chicago: University of Chicago Press, 1960), p. 87.

[5] This question does not imply that they will tolerate any and every patterned distribution. In discussing Hayek's views, Irving Kristol has recently speculated that people will not long tolerate a system that yields distributions patterned in accordance with value rather than merit. (" 'When Virtue Loses All Her Loveliness'—Some Reflections on Capitalism and 'The Free Society,' " *The Public Interest*, [Fall 1970]: 3–15.) Kristol, following some remarks of Hayek, equates the merit system with justice. Since some case can be made for the external standard of distribution in accordance with benefit to others, we ask about a weaker (and therefore more plausible) hypothesis.

[6] We certainly benefit because economic incentives operate to get others to spend much time and energy to figure out how to serve us by providing things we will want to pay for. It is not mere paradox mongering to wonder whether capitalism should be criticized for most rewarding and hence encouraging, not individuals like Thoreau who go about their own lives, but people who are occupied with serving others and winning them as customers. But to defend capitalism one need not think businessmen are the finest human types. (I do not mean to join here the general maligning of businessmen, either.) Those who think the finest should acquire the most can try to convince their fellows to transfer resources in accordance with *that* principle.

[7] Varying situations continuously from that limit situation to our own would force us to make explicit the underlying rationale of entitlements and to consider whether entitlement considerations lexicographically precede the considerations of the usual theories of distributive justice, so that

the *slightest* strand of entitlement outweighs the considerations of the usual theories of distributive justice.

8 Might not a transfer have instrumental effects on a third party, changing his feasible options? (But what if the two parties to the transfer independently had used their holdings in this fashion?) I discuss this question below, but note here that this question concedes the point for distributions of ultimate intrinsic noninstrumental goods (pure utility experience, so to speak) that are transferable. It also might be objected that the transfer might make a third party more envious because it worsens his position relative to someone else. I find it incomprehensible how this can be thought to involve a claim of justice. . . .

Here and elsewhere in this chapter, a theory which incorporates elements of pure procedural justice might find what I say acceptable, *if* kept in its proper place; that is, if background institutions exist to ensure that satisfaction of certain conditions on distributive shares. But if these institutions are not themselves the sum or invisible-hand result of people's voluntary (nonaggressive) actions, the constraints they impose require justification. At no point does *our* argument assume any background institutions more extensive than those of the minimal night-watchman state, a state limited to protecting persons against murder, assault, theft, fraud, and so forth.

XII.5 A *Liberal Theory of Justice*

JOHN RAWLS

John Rawls is professor of philosophy at Harvard University and the author of several works in moral and political theory. In this essay from his important work, *A Theory of Justice*, we have quite a different theory of nonpatterned justice from that of Nozick's. He presents a theory of just procedures, so that whatever results from these processes is itself just. Rawls asks us to imagine being behind a "veil of ignorance" in which we have very little, if any, knowledge of who we are, and he then asks us to choose the general principles that will then govern our social policies. Rawls argues that the following principles, or something very close to them, will be chosen by rational beings:

I. Special Conception of Justice

  1. Each person is to have an equal right to the most extensive basic liberty that is compatible with a similar liberty for others.

  2. Social and economic inequalities are to be arranged so that they are both (a) reasonably expected to be to everyone's advantage, and (b) attached to positions and offices open to all.

II. General Conception of Justice

  All social values — liberty and opportunity, income and wealth, and the bases of self-respect — are to be distributed equally unless an unequal distribution of any or all of these values is to everyone's advantage.

My aim is to present a conception of justice which generalizes and carries to a higher level of abstraction the familiar theory of the social contract as

Excerpted by permission of the publishers from *A Theory of Justice* by John Rawls, Cambridge, MA: The Belknap Press of Harvard University Press. Copyright © 1971 by the President and Fellows of Harvard College and the author.

found, say, in Locke, Rousseau, and Kant. In order to do this we are not to think of the original contract as one to enter a particular society or to set up a particular form of government. Rather, the guiding idea is that the principles of justice for the basic structure of society are the object of the original agreement. They are the principles that free and rational persons concerned to further their own interests would accept in an initial position of equality as defining the fundamental terms of their association. These principles are to regulate all further agreements; they specify the kinds of social cooperation that can be entered into and the forms of government that can be established. This way of regarding the principles of justice I shall call justice as fairness.

Thus we are to imagine that those who engage in social cooperation choose together, in one joint act, the principles which are to assign basic rights and duties and to determine the division of social benefits. Men are to decide in advance how they are to regulate their claims against one another and what is to be the foundation charter of their society. Just as each person must decide by rational reflection what constitutes his good—that is, the system of ends which it is rational for him to pursue—so a group of persons must decide once and for all what is to count among them as just and unjust. The choice which rational men would make in this hypothetical situation of equal liberty, assuming for the present that this choice problem has a solution, determines the principles of justice.

In justice as fairness the original position of equality corresponds to the state of nature in the traditional theory of the social contract. This original position is not, of course, thought of as an actual historical state of affairs, much less as a primitive condition of culture. It is understood as a purely hypothetical situation characterized so as to lead to a certain conception of justice. Among the essential features of this situation is that no one knows his place in society, his class position or social status, nor does any one know his fortune in the distribution of natural assets and abilities, his intelligence, strength, and the like. I shall even assume that the parties do not know their conceptions of the good or their special psychological propensities. The principles of justice are chosen behind a veil of ignorance. This ensures that no one is advantaged or disadvantaged in the choice of principles by the outcome of natural chance or the contingency of social circumstances. Since all are similarly situated and no one is able to design principles to favor his particular condition, the principles of justice are the result of a fair agreement or bargain. For given the circumstances of the original position, the symmetry of everyone's relations to each other, this initial situation is fair between individuals as moral persons;

that is, as rational beings with their own ends and capable, I shall assume, of a sense of justice. The original position is, one might say, the appropriate initial status quo, and thus the fundamental agreements reached in it are fair. This explains the propriety of the name "justice as fairness"; it conveys the idea that the principles of justice are agreed to in an initial situation that is fair. The name does not mean that the concepts of justice and fairness are the same, any more than the phrase "poetry as metaphor" means that the concepts of poetry and metaphor are the same.

Justice as fairness begins, as I have said, with one of the most general of all choices which persons might make together, namely, with the choice of the first principles of a conception of justice which is to regulate all subsequent criticism and reform of institutions. Then, having chosen a conception of justice, we can suppose that they are to choose a constitution and a legislature to enact laws, and so on, all in accordance with the principles of justice initially agreed upon. Our social situation is just if it is such that by this sequence of hypothetical agreements we would have contracted into the general system of rules which defines it. Moreover, assuming that the original position does determine a set of principles (that is, that a particular conception of justice would be chosen), it will then be true that whenever social institutions satisfy these principles those engaged in them can say to one another that they are cooperating on terms to which they would agree if they were free and equal persons whose relations with respect to one another were fair. They could all view their arrangements as meeting the stipulations which they would acknowledge in an initial situation that embodies widely accepted and reasonable constraints on the choice of principles. The general recognition of this fact would provide the basis for a public acceptance of the corresponding principles of justice. No society can, of course, be a scheme of cooperation which men enter voluntarily in a literal sense; each person finds himself placed at birth in some particular position in some particular society, and the nature of this position materially affects his life prospects. Yet a society satisfying the principles of justice as fairness comes as close as a society can to being a voluntary scheme, for it meets the principles which free and equal persons would assent to under circumstances that are fair. In this sense its members are autonomous and the obligations they recognize self-imposed.

One feature of justice as fairness is to think of the parties in the initial situation as rational and mutually disinterested. This does not mean that the parties are egoists; that is, individuals with only certain kinds of interests, say in wealth, prestige, and domination. But they are conceived as not taking an interest in one another's interests. They are to presume that even their spiritual aims may be opposed, in the way that the aims of those of different religions may be opposed. Moreover, the concept of rationality must be interpreted as far as possible in the narrow sense, standard in economic theory, of taking the most effective means to given ends. I shall modify this concept to some extent . . . , but one must try to avoid introducing into it any controversial ethical elements. The initial situation must be characterized by stipulations that are widely accepted.

In working out the conception of justice as fairness one main task clearly is to determine which principles of justice would be chosen in the original position. To do this we must describe this situation in some detail and formulate with care the problem of choice which it presents. It may be observed, however, that once the principles of justice are thought of as arising from an original agreement in a situation of equality, it is an open question whether the principle of utility would be acknowledged. Offhand it hardly seems likely that persons who view themselves as equals, entitled to press their claims upon one another, would agree to a principle which may require lesser life prospects for some simply for the sake of a greater sum of advantages enjoyed by others. Since each desires to protect his interests, his capacity to advance his conception of the good, no one has a reason to acquiesce in an enduring loss for himself in order to bring about a greater net balance of satisfaction. In the absence of strong and lasting benevolent impulses, a rational man would not accept a basic structure merely because it maximized the algebraic sum of advantages irrespective of its permanent effects on his own basic rights and interests. Thus it seems that the principle of utility is incompatible with the conception of social cooperation among equals for mutual advantage. It appears to be inconsistent with the idea of reciprocity implicit in the notion of a well-ordered society. Or, at any rate, so I shall argue.

I shall maintain instead that the persons in the initial situation would choose two rather different principles: the first requires equality in the assignment of basic rights and duties, while the second holds that social and economic inequalities; for example, inequalities of wealth and authority; are just only if they result in compensating benefits for everyone, and in particular for the least advantaged members of society. These principles rule out justifying institutions on the grounds that the hardships of some are offset by a greater good in the aggregate. It may be expedient but it is not just that some should have less in order that others may prosper. But there is no injustice in the greater benefits earned by a few provided that the situation of persons not so fortunate is thereby improved. The intuitive idea is that since everyone's well-being depends upon a scheme of cooperation without which no one could have a satisfactory life, the division of advantages should be such as to draw forth the willing cooperation of everyone taking part in it, including those less well situated. Yet this can be expected only if reasonable terms are proposed. The two principles mentioned seem to be a fair agreement on the basis of which those better endowed, or more fortunate in their social position, neither of which we can be said to deserve, could expect the willing cooperation of others when some workable scheme is a necessary condition of the welfare of all. Once we decide to look for a conception of justice that nullifies the accidents of natural endowment and the contingencies of social circumstance as counters in quest for political and economic advantage, we are led to these principles. They express the result of leaving aside those aspects of the social world that seem arbitrary from a moral point of view.

The problem of the choice of principles, however, is extremely difficult. I do not expect the answer I shall suggest to be convincing to everyone. It is, therefore, worth noting from the outset that justice as fairness, like other contract views, consists of two parts: (1) an interpretation of the initial situation and of the problem of choice posed there, and (2) a set of principles which, it is argued, would be agreed to. One may accept the first part of the theory (or some variant thereof), but not the other, and conversely. The concept of the initial contractual situation may seem reasonable although the particular principles proposed are rejected. To be sure, I want to maintain that the most appropriate conception of this situation does lead to principles of justice contrary to utilitarianism and perfectionism, and therefore that the contract doctrine provides an alternative to these views. Still, one may dispute this contention even though one grants that the contractarian method is a useful way of studying ethical theories and of setting forth their underlying assumptions.

Justice as fairness is an example of what I have called a contract theory. Now there may be an objection to the term "contract" and related expressions, but I think it will serve reasonably well. Many words have misleading connotations which at first are likely to confuse. The terms "utility" and "utilitarianism" are surely no exception. They too have unfortunate suggestions which hostile critics have been willing to exploit; yet they are clear enough for those prepared to study utilitarian doctrine. The same should be true of the term "contract" applied to moral theories. As I have mentioned, to understand it one has to keep in mind that it implies a certain level of abstraction. In particular, the content of the relevant agreement is not to enter a given society or to adopt a given form of government, but to accept certain moral principles. Moreover, the undertakings referred to are purely hypothetical: a contract view holds that certain principles would be accepted in a well-defined initial situation.

The merit of the contract terminology is that it conveys the idea that principles of justice may be conceived as principles that would be chosen by rational persons, and that in this way conceptions of justice maybe explained and justified. The theory of justice is a part, perhaps the most significant part, of the theory of rational choice. Furthermore, principles of justice deal with conflicting claims upon the advantages won by social cooperation; they apply to the relations among several persons or groups. The word "contract" suggests this plurality as well as the condition that the appropriate division of advantages must be in accordance with principles acceptable to all parties. The condition of publicity for principles of justice is also connoted by the contract phraseology. Thus, if these principles are the outcome of an agreement, citizens have a knowledge of the principles that others follow. It is characteristic of contract theories to stress the public nature of political principles. Finally there is the long tradition of the contract doctrine. Expressing the tie with this line of thought helps to define ideas and accords with natural piety. There are then several advantages in the use of the term "contract." With due precautions taken, it should not be misleading.

A final remark. Justice as fairness is not a complete contract theory. For it is clear that the contractarian idea can be extended to the choice of more or less an entire ethical system; that is, to a system including principles for all the virtues and not only for justice. Now for the most part I shall consider only principles of justice and others closely related to them; I make no attempt to discuss the virtues in a systematic way. Obviously if justice as fairness succeeds reasonably well, a next step would be to study the more general view suggested by the name "rightness as fairness." But even this wider theory fails to embrace all moral relationships, since it would seem to include only our relations with other persons and to leave out of account how we are to conduct ourselves toward animals and the rest of nature. I do not contend that the contract notion offers a way to approach these questions, which are certainly of the first importance; and I shall have to put them aside. We must recognize the limited scope of justice as fairness and of the general type of view that it exemplifies. How far its conclusions must be revised once these other matters are understood cannot be decided in advance.

The Original Position and Justification

I have said that the original position is the appropriate initial status quo which insures that the fundamental agreements reached in it are fair. This fact yields the name "justice as fairness." It is clear, then, that I want to say that one conception of justice is more reasonable than another, or justifiable with respect to it, if rational persons in the initial situation would choose its principles over those of the other for the role of justice. Conceptions of justice are to be ranked by their acceptability to persons so circumstanced. Understood in this way the question of justification is settled by working out a problem of deliberation: we have to ascertain which principles it would be rational to adopt given the contractual situation. This connects the theory of justice with the theory of rational choice.

If this view of the problem of justification is to succeed, we must, of course, describe in some detail the nature of this choice problem. A problem of rational decision has a definite answer only if we know the beliefs and interests of the parties, their relations with respect to one another, the alternatives between which they are to choose, the procedure whereby they make up their minds, and so on. As the circumstances are presented in different ways, correspondingly different principles are accepted. The concept of the original position, as I shall refer to it, is that of the most philosophically favored interpretation of this initial choice situation for the purposes of a theory of justice.

But how are we to decide what is the most favored interpretation? I assume, for one thing, that there is a broad measure of agreement that principles of justice should be chosen under certain conditions. To justify a particular description of the initial situation one shows that it incorporates these commonly shared presumptions. One argues from widely accepted but weak premises to more specific conclusions. Each of the presumptions should by itself be natural and plausible; some of them may seem innocuous or even trivial. The aim of the contract approach is to establish that taken together they impose significant bounds on acceptable principles of justice. The ideal outcome would be that these conditions determine a unique set of principles; but I shall be satisfied if they suffice to rank the main traditional conceptions of social justice.

One should not be misled, then, by the somewhat unusual conditions which characterize the original position. The idea here is simply to make vivid to ourselves the restrictions that it seems reasonable to impose on arguments for principles of justice, and therefore on these principles themselves. Thus it seems reasonable and generally acceptable that no one should be advantaged or disadvantaged by natural fortune or social circumstances in the choice of principles. It also seems widely agreed that it should be impossible to tailor principles to the circumstances of one's own case. We should ensure further that particular inclinations and aspirations, and persons' conceptions of their good, do not affect the principles adopted. The aim is to rule out those principles that it would be rational to propose for acceptance, however little the chance of success, only if one knew certain things that are irrelevant from the standpoint of justice. For example, if a man knew that he was wealthy, he might find it rational to advance the principle that various taxes for welfare measures be counted unjust; if he knew that he was poor, he would most likely propose the contrary principle. To represent the desired restrictions one imagines a situation in which everyone is deprived of this sort of information. One excludes the knowledge of those contingencies which sets men at odds and allows them to be guided by their prejudices. In this manner the veil of ignorance is arrived at in a natural way. This concept should cause no difficulty if we keep in mind the constraints on arguments that it is meant to express. At any time we can enter the original position, so to speak, simply by following a certain procedure; namely, by arguing for principles of justice in accordance with these restrictions.

It seems reasonable to suppose that the parties in the original position are equal. That is, all have the same rights in the procedure for choosing principles; each can make proposals, submit reasons for their acceptance, and so on. Obviously the purpose of these conditions is to represent equality between human beings as moral persons, as creatures having a conception of their good and capable of a sense of justice. The basis of equality is taken to be similarity in these two respects. Systems of ends are not ranked in value; and each man is presumed to have the requisite ability to understand and to act upon whatever principles are adopted. Together with the veil of ignorance, these conditions define the principles of justice as those which rational persons concerned to advance their interests would consent to as equals when none are known to be advantaged or disadvantaged by social and natural contingencies.

There is, however, another side to justifying a particular description of the original position. This is to see if the principles which would be chosen match our considered convictions of justice or extend them in an acceptable way. We can note whether applying these principles would lead us to make the same judgments about the basic structure of society which we now make intuitively and in which we have the greatest confidence; or whether, in cases where our present judgments are in doubt and given with hesitation, these principles offer a resolution which we can affirm on reflection. There are questions which we feel sure must be answered in a certain way. For example, we are confident that religious intolerance and racial discrimination are unjust. We think that we have examined these things with care and have reached what we believe is an impartial judgment not likely to be distorted by an excessive attention to our own interests. These convictions are provisional fixed points which we presume any conception of justice must fit. But we have much less assurance as to what is the correct distribution of wealth and authority. Here we may be looking for a way to remove our doubts. We can check an interpretation of the initial situation, then, by the capacity of its principles to accommodate our firmest convictions and to provide guidance where guidance is needed.

In searching for the most favored description of this situation we work from both ends. We begin by describing it so that it represents generally shared and preferably weak conditions. We then see if these conditions are strong enough to yield a significant set of principles. If not, we look for further premises equally reasonable. But if so, and these principles match our considered convictions of justice, then so far well and good. But presumably there will be discrepancies. In this case we have a choice. We can either modify the account of the initial situation or we can revise our existing judgments, for even the judgments we take provisionally as fixed points are liable to revision. By going back and forth, sometimes altering the conditions of the contractual circumstances, at others withdrawing our judgments and conforming them to principle, I assume that eventually we shall find a description of the initial situation that both expresses reasonable conditions and yields principles which match our considered judgments duly pruned and adjusted. This state of affairs I refer to as reflective equilibrium. It is an equilibrium because at last our principles and judgments coincide; and it is reflective since we know to what principles our judgments conform and the premises of their derivation. At the moment everything is in order. But this equilibrium is not necessarily stable. It is liable to be upset by further examination of the conditions which should be imposed on the contractual situation and by particular cases which may lead us to revise our judgments. Yet for the time being we have done what we can to render coherent and to justify our convictions of social justice. We have reached a conception of the original position.

I shall not, of course, actually work through this process. Still, we may think of the interpretation of the original position that I shall present as the result of such a hypothetical course of reflection. It represents the attempt to accommodate within one scheme both reasonable philosophical conditions on principles as well as our considered judgments of justice. In arriving at the favored interpretation of the initial situation there is no point at which an appeal is made to self-evidence in the tra-

ditional sense either of general conceptions or particular convictions. I do not claim for the principles of justice proposed that they are necessary truths or derivable from such truths. A conception of justice cannot be deduced from self-evident premises or conditions on principles; instead, its justification is a matter of the mutual support of many considerations, of everything fitting together into one coherent view.

A final comment. We shall want to say that certain principles of justice are justified because they would be agreed to in an initial situation of equality. I have emphasized that this original position is purely hypothetical. It is natural to ask why, if this agreement is never actually entered into, we should take any interest in these principles, moral or otherwise. The answer is that the conditions embodied in the description of the original position are ones that we do in fact accept. Or if we do not, then perhaps we can be persuaded to do so by philosophical reflection. Each aspect of the contractual situation can be given supporting grounds. Thus what we shall do is to collect together into one conception a number of conditions on principles that we are ready upon due consideration to recognize as reasonable. These constraints express what we are prepared to regard as limits on fair terms of social cooperation. One way to look at the idea of the original position, therefore, is to see it as an expository device which sums up the meaning of these conditions and helps us to extract their consequences. On the other hand, this conception is also an intuitive notion that suggests its own elaboration, so that led on by it we are drawn to define more clearly the standpoint from which we can best interpret moral relationships. We need a conception that enables us to envision our objective from afar: the intuitive notion of the original position is to do this for us. . . .

Two Principles of Justice

I shall now state in a provisional form the two principles of justice that I believe would be chosen in the original position. In this section I wish to make only the most general comments, and therefore the first formulation of these principles is tentative. As we go on I shall run through several formulations and approximate step by step the final statement to be given much later. I believe that doing this allows the exposition to proceed in a natural way.

The first statement of the two principles reads as follows:

> First: each person is to have an equal right to the most extensive basic liberty compatible with a similar liberty for others.
>
> Second: social and economic inequalities are to be arranged so that they are both (a) reasonably expected to be to everyone's advantage, and (b) attached to positions and offices open to all.

There are two ambiguous phrases in the second principle, namely "everyone's advantage" and "open to all." Determining their sense more exactly will lead to a second formulation of the principle. . . .

By way of general comment, these principles primarily apply, as I have said, to the basic structure of society. They are to govern the assignment of rights and duties and to regulate the distribution of social and economic advantages. As their formulation suggests, these principles presuppose that the social structure can be divided into two more or less distinct parts, the first principle applying to the one, the second to the other. They distinguish between those aspects of the social system that define and secure the equal liberties of citizenship and those that specify and establish social and economic inequalities. The basic liberties of citizens are, roughly speaking, political liberty (the right to vote and to be eligible for public office) together with freedom of speech and assembly; liberty of conscience and freedom of thought; freedom of the person along with the right to hold (personal) property; and freedom from arbitrary arrest and seizure as defined by the concept of the rule of law. These liberties are all required to be equal by the first principle, since citizens of a just society are to have the same basic rights.

The second principle applies, in the first approximation, to the distribution of income and wealth and to the design of organizations that make use of differences in authority and responsibility, or chains of command. While the distribution of wealth and income need not be equal, it must be to everyone's advantage, and at the same time, positions of authority and offices of command must be accessible to all. One applies the second principle by holding positions open, and then, subject to this constraint, arranges social and economic inequalities so that everyone benefits.

These principles are to be arranged in a serial order with the first principle prior to the second. This ordering means that a departure from the institutions of equal liberty required by the first principle cannot be justified by, or compensated for, by greater social and economic advantages. The distribution of wealth and income, and the hierarchies of authority, must be consistent with both the liberties of equal citizenship and equality of opportunity.

It is clear that these principles are rather specific in their content, and their acceptance rests on certain assumptions that I must eventually try to explain and justify. A theory of justice depends upon a theory of society in ways that will become evident as we proceed. For the present, it should be observed that the two principles (and this holds for all formulations) are a special case of a moral general conception of justice that can be expressed as follows:

> All social values — liberty and opportunity, income and wealth, and the bases of self-respect — are to be distributed equally unless an unequal distribution of any, or all, of these values is to everyone's advantage.

Injustice, then, is simply inequalities that are not to the benefit of all. Of course, this conception is extremely vague and requires interpretation.

As a first step, suppose that the basic structure of society distributes certain primary goods, that is, things that every rational man is presumed to want. These goods normally have a use whatever a person's rational plan of life. For simplicity, assume that the chief primary goods at the disposition of society are rights and liberties, powers and opportunities, income and wealth. (Later on . . . the primary good of self-respect has a central place.) These are the social primary goods. Other primary goods such as health and vigor, intelligence and imagination, are natural goods; although their possession is influenced by the basic structure, they are not so directly under its control. Imagine, then, a hypothetical initial arrangement in which all the social primary goods are equally distributed: everyone has similar rights and duties, and income and wealth are evenly shared. This state of affairs provides a benchmark for judging improvements. If certain inequalities of wealth and organizational powers would make everyone better off than in this hypothetical starting situation, then they accord with the general conception.

Now it is possible, at least theoretically, that by giving up some of their fundamental liberties men are sufficiently compensated by the resulting social and economic gains. The general conception of justice imposes no restrictions on what sort of inequalities are permissible; it only requires that everyone's position be improved. We need not suppose anything so drastic as consenting to a condition of slavery. Imagine instead that men forgo certain political rights when the economic returns are significant and their capacity to influence the course of policy by the exercise of these rights would be marginal in any case. It is this kind of exchange which the two principles as stated rule out; being arranged in serial order they do not permit exchanges between basic liberties and economic and social gains. The serial ordering of principles expresses an underlying preference among primary social goods. When this preference is rational so likewise is the choice of these principles in this order.

In developing justice as fairness I shall, for the most part, leave aside the general conception of justice and examine instead the special case of the two principles in serial order. The advantage of this procedure is that from the first the matter of priorities is recognized and an effort made to find principles to deal with it. One is led to attend throughout to the conditions under which the acknowledgement of the absolute weight of liberty with respect to social and economic advantages, as defined by the lexical order of the two principles, would be reasonable. Offhand, this ranking appears extreme and too special a case to be of much interest; but there is more justification for it than would appear at first sight. Or at any rate, so I shall maintain. Furthermore, the distinction between fundamental rights and liberties and economic and social benefits marks a difference among primary social goods that one should try to exploit. It suggests an important division in the social system. Of course, the distinctions drawn and the ordering proposed are bound to be at best only approximations. There are surely circumstances in which they fail. But it is essential to depict clearly the main lines of a reasonable conception of justice; and under many conditions, anyway, the two principles in serial order may serve well enough. When necessary we can fall back on the more general conception.

The fact that the two principles apply to institutions has certain consequences. Several points illustrate this. First of all, the rights and liberties referred to by these principles are those that are defined by the public rules of the basic structure. Whether men are free is determined by the rights and duties established by the major institutions of society. Liberty is a certain pattern of social forms. The first principle simply requires that certain sorts of rules, those defining basic liberties, apply to everyone equally and that they allow the most extensive liberty compatible with a like liberty for all. The only reason for circumscribing the rights defining liberty and making men's freedom less extensive than it might otherwise be is that these equal rights as institutionally defined would interfere with one another.

Another thing to bear in mind is that when principles mention persons, or require that everyone gain from an inequality, the reference is to representative persons holding the various social positions, or offices, or whatever, established by the basic structure. Thus in applying the second principle I assume that it is possible to assign an expectation of well-being to representative individuals holding these positions. This expectation indicates their life prospects as viewed from their social station. In general, the expectations of representative persons depend upon the distribution of rights and duties throughout the basic structure. When this changes, expectations change. I assume, then, that expectations are connected: by raising the prospects of the representative man in one position we presumably increase or decrease the prospects of representative men in other positions. Since it applies to institutional forms, the second principle (or rather the first part of it) refers to the expectations of representative individuals. As I shall discuss below, neither principle applies to distributions of particular goods to particular individuals who may be identified by their proper names. The situation where someone is considering how to allocate certain commodities to needy persons who are known to him is not within the scope of the principles. They are meant to regulate basic institutional arrangements. We must not assume that there is much similarity from the standpoint of justice between an administrative allotment of goods to specific persons and the appropriate design of society. Our common sense intuitions for the former may be a poor guide to the latter.

Now the second principle insists that each person benefit from permissible inequalities in the basic structure. This means that it must be reasonable for each relevant representative man defined by this structure, when he views it as a going concern, to prefer his prospects with the inequality, to his prospects without it. One is not allowed to justify differences in income or organizational powers on the ground that the disadvantages of those in one position are outweighed by the greater advantages of those in another. Much less can infringements of liberty be counterbalanced in this way. Applied to the basic structure, the principle of utility would have us maximize the sum of expectations of representative men (weighted by the number of persons they represent, on the classical view); and this would permit us to compensate for the losses of some by the gains of others. Instead, the two principles require that everyone benefit from economic and social inequalities.

The Reasoning Leading to the Two Principles of Justice

It will be recalled that the general conception of justice as fairness requires that all primary social goods will be distributed equally unless an unequal distribution would be to everyone's advantage. No restrictions are placed on exchanges of these goods and therefore a lesser liberty can be compensated for by greater social and economic benefits. Now looking at the situation from the standpoint of one person selected arbitrarily, there is no way for him to win special advantages for himself. Nor, on the other hand, are there grounds for his acquiescing in special disadvantages. Since it is not reasonable for him to expect more than an equal share in the division of social goods, and since it is not rational for him to agree to less, the sensible thing for him to do is to acknowledge as the first principle of justice one requiring an equal distribution. Indeed, this principle is so obvious that we would expect it to occur to anyone immediately.

Thus, the parties start with a principle of establishing equal liberty for all, including equality of opportunity, as well as an equal distribution of income and wealth. But there is no reason why this acknowledgment should be final. If there are inequalities in the basic structure that work to make everyone better off in comparison with the benchmark of initial equality, why not permit them? The immediate gain which a greater equality might allow can be regarded as intelligently invested in view of its future return. If, for example, these inequalities set up various incentives which succeed in eliciting more productive efforts, a person in the original position may look upon them as necessary to cover the costs of training and to encourage effective performance. One might think that ideally individuals should want to serve one another. But since the parties are assumed not to take an interest in one another's interests, their acceptance of these inequalities is only the acceptance of the relations in which men stand in the circumstances of justice. They have no grounds for complaining of one another's motives. A person in the original position would, therefore, concede the justice of these inequalities. Indeed, it would be shortsighted of him not to do so. He would hesitate to agree to these regularities only if he would be dejected by the bare knowledge or perception that others were better situated; and I have assumed that the parties decide as if they are not moved by envy. In order to make the principle regulating inequalities determinate, one looks at the system from the standpoint of the least advantaged representative man. Inequalities are permissible when they maximize, or at least all contribute to, the long-term expectations of the least fortunate group in society.

Now this general conception imposes no constraints on what sorts of inequalities are allowed, whereas the special conception, by putting the two principles in serial order (with the necessary adjustments in meaning), forbids exchanges between basic liberties and economic and social benefits. I shall not try to justify this ordering here. . . . But roughly, the idea underlying this ordering is that if the parties assume that their basic liberties can be effectively exercised, they will not exchange a lesser liberty for an improvement in economic well-being. It is only when social conditions do not allow the effective establishment of these rights that one can concede their limitation; and these restrictions can be granted only to the extent that they are necessary to prepare the way for a free society. The denial of equal liberty can be denied only if it is necessary to raise the level of civilization so that in due course these freedoms can be enjoyed. Thus in adopting a serial order we are in effect making a special assumption in the original position, namely, that the parties know that the conditions of their society, whatever they are, admit the effective realization of the equal liberties. The serial ordering of the two principles of justice eventually comes to be reasonable if the general conception is consistently followed. This lexical ranking is the long-run tendency of the general view. For the most part I shall assume that the requisite circumstances for the serial order obtain.

It seems clear from these remarks that the two principles are at least a plausible conception of justice. The question, though, is how one is to argue for them more systematically. Now there are several things to do. One can work out their consequences for institutions and note their implications for fundamental social policy. In this way they are tested by a comparison with our considered judgments of justice. . . . But one can also try to find arguments in their favor that are decisive from the standpoint of the original position. In order to see how this might be done, it is useful as a heuristic device to think of the two principles as the maximin solution to the problem of social justice. There is an analogy between the two principles and the maximin rule for choice under uncertainty. This is evident from the fact that the two principles are those a person would choose for the design of a society in which his enemy is to assign him his place. The maximin rule tells us to rank alternatives by their worst possible outcomes; we are to adopt the alternative the worst outcome of which is superior to the worst outcomes of the others. The persons in the original position do not, of course, assume that their initial place in society is decided by a malevolent opponent. As I note below, they should not reason from false premises. The veil of ignorance does not violate this idea, since an absence of information is not misinformation. But that the two principles of justice would be chosen if the parties were forced to protect themselves against such a contingency explains the sense in which this conception is the maximin solution. And this analogy suggests that if the original position has been described so that it is rational for the parties to adopt the conservative attitude expressed by this rule, a conclusive argument can indeed be constructed for these principles. Clearly the maximin rule is not, in general, a suitable guide for choices under uncertainty. But it is attractive in situations marked by certain special features. My aim,

then, is to show that a good case can be made for the two principles based on the fact that the original position manifests these features to the fullest possible degree, carrying them to the limit, so to speak.

Consider the gain-and-loss table below. It represents the gains and losses for a situation which is not a game of strategy. There is no one playing against the person making the decision; instead he is faced with several possible circumstances which may or may not obtain. Which circumstances happen to exist does not depend upon what the person choosing decides or whether he announces his moves in advance. The numbers in the table are monetary values (in hundreds of dollars) in comparison with some initial situation. The gain (g) depends upon the individual's decision (d) and the circumstances (c). Thus $g = f(d,c)$. Assuming that there are three possible decisions and three possible circumstances, we might have this gain-and-loss table.

DECISIONS	CIRCUMSTANCES		
	c_1	c_2	c_3
d_1	-7	8	12
d_2	-8	7	14
d_3	5	6	8

The maximin rule requires that we make the third decision. For in this case the worst that can happen is that one gains five hundred dollars, which is better than the worst for the other actions. If we adopt one of these we may lose either eight or seven hundred dollars. Thus, the choice of d_3 maximizes $f(d,c)$ for that value of c which for a given d, minimizes f. The term "maximin" means the *maximum minimorum*; and the rule directs our attention to the worst that can happen under any proposed course of action, and to decide in the light of that.

Now there appear to be three chief features of situations that give plausibility to this unusual rule. First, since the rule takes no account of the likelihoods of the possible circumstances, there must be some reason for sharply discounting estimates of these probabilities. Offhand, the most natural rule of choice would seem to be to compute the expectation of monetary gain for each decision and then to adopt the course of action with the highest prospect. (This expectation is defined as follows: let us suppose that g_{ij} represent the numbers in the gain-and-loss table, where i is the row index and j is the column index; and let $p_j j = 1, 2, 3$, be the likelihoods of the circumstances, with $\Sigma p_i = 1$. Then the expectation for the ith decision is equal to $\Sigma p_j g_{ij}$.) Thus it must be, for example, that the situation is one in which a knowledge of likelihoods is impossible, or at best extremely insecure. In this case it is unreasonable not to be skeptical of probabilistic calculations unless there is no other way out, particularly if the decision is a fundamental one that needs to be justified to others.

The second feature that suggests the maximin rule is the following: the person choosing has a conception of the good such that he cares very little, if anything, for what he might gain above the minimum stipend that he can, in fact, be sure of by following the maximin rule. It is not worthwhile for him to take a chance for the sake of a further advantage, especially when it may turn out that he loses much that is important to him. This last provision brings in the third feature; namely, that the rejected alternatives have outcomes that one can hardly accept. The situation involves grave risks. Of course, these features work most effectively in combination. The paradigm situation for following the maximin rule is when all three features are realized to the highest degree. This rule does not, then, generally apply, nor of course is it self-evident. Rather, it is a maxim, a rule of thumb, that comes into its own in special circumstances. Its application depends upon the qualitative structure of the possible gains and losses in relation to one's conception of the good, all this against a background in which it is reasonable to discount conjectural estimates of likelihoods.

It should be noted, as the comments on the gain-and-loss table say, that the entries in the table represent monetary values and not utilities. This difference is significant since for one thing computing expectations on the basis of such objective values is not the same thing as computing expected utility and may lead to different results. The essential point, though, is that in justice as fairness the parties do not know their conception of the good and cannot estimate their utility in the ordinary sense. In any case, we want to go behind de facto preferences generated by given conditions. Therefore expectations are based upon an index of primary goods and the parties make their choice accordingly. The entries in the example are in terms of money and not utility to indicate this aspect of the contract doctrine.

Now, as I have suggested, the original position has been defined so that it is a situation in which the maximin rule applies. In order to see this, let us review briefly the nature of this situation with these three special features in mind. To begin with, the veil of ignorance excludes all but the vaguest knowledge of likelihoods. The parties have no basis for determining the probable nature of their society, or their place in it. Thus they have strong reasons for being wary of probability calculations if any other course is open to them. They must also take into account the fact that their choice of principles should seem reasonable to others, in particular their descendants, whose rights will be deeply affected by it. There are further grounds for discounting that I shall mention as we go long. For the present it suffices to note that these considerations are strengthened by the fact that the parties know very little about the gain-and-loss table. Not only are they unable to conjecture the likelihoods of the various possible circumstances, they cannot say much about what the possible circumstances are, much less enumerate them and foresee the outcome of each alternative available. Those deciding are much more in the dark than the illustration by a numerical table suggests. It is for this reason that I have spoken of an analogy with the maximin rule.

Several kinds of arguments for the two principles of justice illustrate the second feature. Thus, if we can maintain that these principles provide a workable theory of social justice, and that they are compatible with reasonable demands of efficiency, then this conception guarantees a satisfactory minimum. There may be, on reflection, little reason for trying to do better. Thus much of the argument . . . is to show, by their application to the main questions of social justice, that the two principles are a satisfactory conception. These details have a philosophical purpose. Moreover, this line of thought is practically decisive if we can establish the priority of liberty, the lexical ordering of the two principles. For this priority implies that the persons in the original position have no desire to try for greater gains at the expense of the equal liberties. The minimum assured by the two principles in lexical order is not one that the parties wish to jeopardize for the sake of greater economic and social advantages. . . .

Finally, the third feature holds if we can assume that other conceptions of justice may lead to institutions that the parties would find intolerable. For example, it has sometimes been held that under some conditions the utility principle (in either form) justifies, if not slavery or serfdom, at any rate serious infractions of liberty for the sake of greater social benefits. We need not consider here the truth of this claim, or the likelihood that the requisite conditions obtain. For the moment, this contention is only to illustrate the way in which conceptions of justice may allow for outcomes which the parties may not be able to accept. And having the ready alternative of the two principles of justice which secure a satisfactory minimum, it seems unwise, if not irrational, for them to take a chance that these outcomes are not realized.

So much, then, for a brief sketch of the features of situations in which the maximin rule comes into its own and of the way in which the arguments for the two principles of justice can be subsumed under them. . . .

The Final Formulation of the Principles of Justice

. . . I now wish to give the final statement of the two principles of justice for institutions. For the sake of completeness, I shall give a full statement including earlier formulations.

First Principle Each person is to have an equal right to the most extensive total system of equal basic liberties compatible with a similar system of liberty for all.

Second Principle Social and economic inequalities are to be arranged so that they are both

a. to the greatest benefit of the least advantaged, consistent with the just savings principle, and

b. attached to offices and positions open to all under conditions of fair equality of opportunity.

First Priority Rule (The Priority of Liberty) The principles of justice are to be ranked in lexical order

and therefore liberty can be restricted only for the sake of liberty. There are two cases:

a. a less extensive liberty must strengthen the total system of liberty shared for all;

b. a less than equal liberty must be acceptable to those with the lesser liberty.

Second Priority Rule (The Priority of Justice over Efficiency and Welfare) The second principle of justice is lexically prior to the principle of efficiency and to that of maximizing the sum of advantages; and fair opportunity is prior to the different principle. There are two cases:

a. an inequality of opportunity must enhance the opportunities of those with the lesser opportunity;

b. an excessive rate of saving must on balance mitigate the burden of those bearing this hardship.

General Conception All social primary goods — liberty and opportunity, income and wealth, and the bases of self-respect — are to be distributed equally unless an unequal distribution of any or all of these goods is to the advantage of the least favored.

By way of comment, these principles and priority rules are no doubt incomplete. Other modifications will surely have to be made, but I shall not further complicate the statement of the principles. It suffices to observe that when we come to nonideal theory, we do not fall back straightway upon the general conception of justice. The lexical ordering of the two principles, and the valuations that this ordering implies, suggest priority rules which seem to be reasonable enough in many cases. By various examples I have tried to illustrate how these rules can be used and to indicate their plausibility. Thus the ranking of the principles of justice in ideal theory reflects back and guides the application of these principles to nonideal situations. It identifies which limitations need to be dealt with first. The drawback of the general conception of justice is that it lacks the definite structure of the two principles in serial order. In more extreme and tangled instances of nonideal theory there may be no alternative to it. At some point the priority of rules for nonideal cases will fail; and indeed, we may be able to find no satisfactory answer at all. But we must try to postpone the day of reckoning as long as possible, and try to arrange society so that it never comes. . . .

The Kantian Interpretation

Kant held, I believe, that a person is acting autonomously when the principles of his action are chosen by him as the most adequate possible expression of his nature as a free and equal rational being. The principles he acts upon are not adopted because of his social position or natural endowments, or in view of the particular kind of society in which he lives or the specific things that he happens to want. To act on such principles is to act heteronomously. Now the veil of ignorance deprives the persons in the original position of the knowledge that would enable them to choose heteronomous principles. The parties arrive at their choice together as free and equal rational persons knowing only that those circumstances obtain which give the rise to the need for principles of justice.

To be sure, the argument for these principles does add in various ways to Kant's conception. For example, it adds the feature that the principles chosen are to apply to the basic structure of society; and premises characterizing this structure are used in deriving the principles of justice. But I believe that this and other additions are natural enough and remain fairly close to Kant's doctrine, at least when all of his ethical writings are viewed together. Assuming, then, that the reasoning in favor of the principles of justice is correct, we can say that when persons act on these principles they are acting in accordance with principles that they would choose as rational and independent persons in an original position of equality. The principles of their actions do not depend upon social or natural contingencies, nor do they reflect the bias of the particulars of their plan of life or the aspirations that motivate them. By acting from these principles persons express their nature as free and equal rational beings subject to the general conditions of human life. For to express one's nature as a being of a particular kind is to act on the principles that would be chosen if this nature were the decisive determining element. Of course, the choice of the parties in the original position is subject to the restrictions of that situation. But when we knowingly act on the principles of justice in the ordinary course of events, we deliberately assume the limitations of the original position. One reason for doing this, for persons who can do so and want to, is to give expression to one's nature.

The principles of justice are also categorical imperatives in Kant's sense. For by a categorical imperative Kant understands a principle of conduct that applies to the person in virtue of his nature as a free and equal rational being. The validity of the principle does not presuppose that one has a particular desire or aim. Whereas a hypothetical imperative by contrast does assume this: it directs us to take certain steps as effective means to achieve a specific end. Whether the desire is for a particular thing, or whether it is for something more general, such as certain kinds of agreeable feelings or pleasures, the corresponding imperative is hypothetical. Its applicability depends upon one's having an aim which one need not have as a condition of being a rational human individual. The argument for the two principles of justice does not assume that the parties have particular ends, but only that they desire certain primary goods. These are things that it is rational to want whatever else one wants. Thus given human nature, wanting them is part of being rational; and while each is presumed to have some conception of the good, nothing is known about his final ends. The preference for primary goods is derived, then, from only the most general assumptions about rationality and the conditions of human life. To act from the principles of justice is to act from categorical imperatives in the sense that they apply to us whatever in particular our aims are. This simply reflects the fact that no such contingencies appear as premises in their derivation.

We may note also that the motivational assumption of mutual disinterest accords with Kant's notion of autonomy, and gives another reason for this condition. So far this assumption has been used to characterize the circumstances of justice and to provide a clear conception to guide the reasoning of the parties. We have also seen that the concept of benevolence, being a second-order notion, would not work out well. Now we can add that the assumption of mutual disinterest is to allow for freedom in the choice of a system of final ends. Liberty in adopting a conception of the good is limited only by principles that are deduced from a doctrine which imposes no prior constraints on these conceptions. Presuming mutual disinterest in the original position carries out this idea. We postulate that the parties have opposing claims in a suitably general sense. If their ends were restricted in some specific way, this would appear at the outset as an arbitrary restriction on freedom. Moreover, if the parties were conceived as altruists, or as pursuing certain kinds of pleasures, then the principles chosen would apply, as far as the argument would have shown, only to persons whose freedom was restricted to choices compatible with altruism or hedonism. As the argument now runs, the principles of justice cover all persons with rational plans of life, whatever their content, and these principles represent the appropriate restrictions on freedom. Thus it is possible to say that the constraints on conceptions of the good are the result of an interpretation of the contractual situation that puts no prior limitations on what men may desire. There are a variety of reasons, then, for the motivational premise of mutual disinterest. This premise is not only a matter of realism about the circumstances of justice or a way to make the theory manageable. It also connects up with the Kantian idea of autonomy. . . .

The original position may be viewed, then, as a procedural interpretation of Kant's conception of autonomy and the categorical imperative. The principles regulative of the kingdom of ends are those that would be chosen in this position, and the description of this situation enables us to explain the sense in which acting from these principles expresses our nature as free and equal rational persons. No longer are these notions purely transcendent and lacking explicable connections with human conduct, for the procedural conception of the original position allows us to make these ties. . . .

XII.6 *Justice:* A *Funeral Oration*

Wallace Matson

Wallace Matson until his recent retirement was professor of philosophy at the
University of California at Berkeley and is the author of several books
including *A New History of Philosophy* (1987) and *The Existence of God* (1965).
He submitted the following abstract of his essay:

Philosophers such as John Rawls have filched the name Justice from
rendering-each-his-due and bestowed it on doling-out-pleasure-experiences-
equally-all-around, the doling to be done by philosopher kings. These thinkers
either do not perceive or do not care about the incompatibility of pseudojustice with liberty.

After sketching a generic account of the origin of the concept of justice in
bargaining situations, not (necessarily) between equals, I offer speculations as
to why pseudojustice has been able to usurp its prestige among intellectuals,
and whether there is any chance of a revival of the genuine article.

The auncient Ciuilians do say justice is a wille perpetuall and constant, which gyueth to euery man his right.

— Sir Thomas Elyot, 1531

TAX JUSTICE: IT'S IN YOUR INTEREST!
. . . The military budget seems to have replaced human needs as a priority. . . . UC employees have a right to a job and a living wage. . . . To insure this right, AFSCME is asking UC employees to support the *Split Roll Tax Initiative*, which will redistribute the benefits of Proposition 13 among residents and renters, while taking a fair share from commerce. Along with other tax equality measures . . . this will put the state budget back on its feet. . . .
PUBLIC EMPLOYEES NEED TAX JUSTICE IN CALIFORNIA!
— From a manifesto handed out in Berkeley, 1982

Reprinted from *Social Philosophy and Policy* 1 (1983) by permission of the author.

1. *Threnody*

Is it any longer possible to talk seriously about justice and rights? Are these words corrupted and debased beyond redemption? There is no need to multiply examples of how anything that any pressure group has the chutzpah to lay claim to forthwith becomes a right, *nemine contradicente*. Nor is this Newspeak restricted to the vulgar. The President of the Pacific Division of the American Philosophical Association has granted permission to misuse words like *rights* and *justice* if you do so in the service of desirable political ends.[1] Our most universally acclaimed theoretician of justice has shown at length that justice is a will perpetual and constant to forcibly take goods from those who have earned them and give them to those who have not;[2] and the leading light of Anglo-American jurisprudence has constructed a 'straightforward' argument proving that a citizen's right to equal protection of the laws is fully satisfied if only the bureaucrat denying him or her a public benefit on racial grounds shows 'respect and concern' while processing the forms.[3]

Linguistic entropy makes it as futile to try to rehabilitate mutilated words as to put toothpaste back in the tube. The semantic battle has been lost; and with it a lot more than perspicuous speech. From Plato onward ideologues have sought to capture the vocabulary of justice, the paradigm of OK words, and tie it to schemes aiming at doing away with rights and justice. Now they have brought it off. A single generation has witnessed the movement of enlightened thought away from the position that any discrimination in treatment based merely on race is a grievous wrong, all the way to a consensus that forgetting about race and treating people as individuals is proof positive of racism, and people who advocate it should be ostracized and deprived of the protection of the First Amendment. It took the Supreme Court hardly a decade to discover that the Civil Rights Act of 1964, which in the plainest and clearest language ever seen in a statute condemned racial quotas, really encouraged or even mandated them. Scarcely less abrupt has been the transformation of admiration and fostering of excellence into the vice of elitism. The deepest philosophico-legal thinker of the western United States has preached against the immorality of requiring any applicant for any job to possess qualifications for it.[4] At the other end of the country lives another heavyweight moralist who can imagine no worse injustice than paying smart people more than dumb people.[5]

Why then am I writing about justice? What can arguments accomplish anyway? The windmills of the *Zeitgeist* ("spirit of the times" — ED.) keep right on turning. I write also about the interpretation of Parmenides (5th century B.C.). The one activity is likely to produce about as much change in the world as the other.

2. A Tale of the South Seas

The island of Alpha is not on any chart and is claimed by no nation. It is a delightful place with abundant vegetation which when properly cultivated yields delicious groceries. The lagoon abounds in succulent fish. There are plenty of materials for shelter, clothing, whatever you need or desire and know how to make.

A, the sole inhabitant, who arrived on Alpha quite by accident, works a not excessively fatiguing forty-hour week producing all he wants save companionship, and being satisfied, makes no attempt to attract rescuers.

In this situation, Aristotle has told us, no questions of just and unjust can arise. One cannot be unjust to oneself "except metaphorically," and there is no one else for A to be unjust to, or vice versa.

Beta is an island near Alpha but quite unlike it: barren, plagued by vermin. It too has but one inhabitant, B, who also arrived by accident. B lives at the brink of starvation, laboriously scratching the soil to grow the single, foul-tasting, barely edible plant found on the island.

A and B do not communicate nor even know of each other's existence.

The condition of B is pitiable, but there is no more cause for talk of injustice on Beta than on Alpha. Can it be said, however, that the state of affairs consisting of A on Alpha and B on Beta is an unjust state of affairs? A and B are certainly unequal, which condition benefits neither of them, and it has been said that injustice is simply inequalities that are not to the advantage of all. Nevertheless, it would be bizarre to contend that the situation contains injustice. B's condition is unfortunate but not unjust (nor just either). The mere coexistence of A without interaction cannot add a new moral dimension.

So let us add some interaction and see what happens.

There are no materials on Beta for making a boat or raft, and the strait between the islands is shark-infested. So B cannot go to Alpha. And A has no incentive to go to Beta. But now a volcano emerges from the sea, and when it has cooled there is a land bridge making Alpha and Beta one island.

Let us consider the time interval when B can enter the Alpha district but has not actually done so. We have then a single territory containing two inhabitants, one of whom is in possession of fewer goods than the other. Is this a condition of injustice?

The difference is only that now it is feasible to equalize the conditions of A and B whereas previously it was not. If there is injustice it consists in the unequal possessions of A and B and can be remedied by taking from A and giving to B. But then it cannot be the case that the injustice arose when the islands became connected; it must rather have existed previously but only at that moment become remediable. (Murder is murder whether or not it can be punished.) But this would be contrary to our conclusion that no injustice arose from the mere comparison of the two conditions.

None of this will surprise us. We knew that justice is a social concept; so as long as A and B were incommunicado the notion had no application. If we now arrange for them to meet and converse, no injustice can be deemed to have arisen here either. How could it? B is now conscious of being worse off than A, and will no doubt feel envy, will want to share in A's bounty. B may even complain of "unjust fate," but that can only be poetry. The change has been only in knowledge; and the previous absence of injustice did not depend on ignorance.

Various things may happen when B sets foot on Alpha territory. Let us consider some of the possibilities.

Case I. Suppose the Alpha territory is a land of such abundance that it cannot be exploited by A alone; there are resources that A does not need and cannot make use of. It is no injustice if B now appropriates some or all of these goods. Nothing has been taken to which A has established any claim, nor has A been harmed.

But what if A regards B as a threat or nuisance? Would injustice be committed if A chased B out of the area or took even more drastic measures? It is hard to see what the charge could be based on, if A and B have held no converse. On a right to be let alone if one is behaving peaceably? But what if A is a lady and B is a tiger? — a possibility not ruled out by any of our suppositions. Is it not permissible to drive tigers away from one's vicinity, even if in fact the tiger has only peaceable intentions? If so, how is the situation changed if instead of a tiger one is confronted with another human being of unknown intent?

Case II. Zucchini does not grow wild in Alpha; all that there is has been cultivated by A, but there is more of it than A can possibly make use of. Would injustice arise if B should appropriate some of the surplus without A's consent? Hardly, for the surplus does not constitute a good for A, even though he produced it. Whatever happens to it is a matter of indifference as far as A is concerned; and if A is not made any worse off there can be no injustice.

Case III. Is the moral situation altered if the produce with which B absconds is something necessary for A's dinner? Well, again, if B is a tiger, we should not want to say that it is guilty of injustice, however inconvenient its conduct may be for A. And how should it differ if B is human? Both the tiger and the man are hungry, perceive an opportunity to eat, and take it. If they do fight it out, "like animals," no question of justice arises. But if A and B are human (as we shall henceforth assume) they may have an alternative not generally available to the brute creature: they can communicate, talk things over, and reach some settlement of the question "Who gets what?" that is more advantageous for one or the other or both than direct and, perhaps, uncertain combat.

3. *Intermission*

There are in Alpha two classes of things: those which exist, or exist in altered form, or in the place where they are, because of the labor of A; and those that do not, but would be just as they are even if A had never been there. The first class of things consists of cultivated plants, constructed shelter, utensils, fish hooks, woodpiles, and the like. Call them the Artifacts. It is characteristic of human beings to labor to produce artifacts. The essence of life — any kind of life — consists in doing, acting; production of things is one important kind of doing. This means, in the human case, experiencing a need or at least a desire for something; picturing to oneself the advantage of possessing that thing; making a plan to bring it into existence or into one's possession; and expending effort to that end according to a developed pattern of skill. We speak of this in terms of the Will and its satisfaction. When all goes well we end up having what we want, and sometimes we are better off thereby. Not to be able to carry out one's own projects in this way but to serve only the interests of others, is so far not to live a human life. Extreme deprivation of this kind is slavery.

Most projects are recognized to be more or less chancy. The compassing of material ends may be frustrated by droughts, earthquakes, diseases, wild beasts, etc. Any animal can be viewed as a device for sorting out its dinner and other necessities from an environment in which the constituents occur more or less at random. And the whole process may be got through successfully and then at the last moment the desired product is snatched away, as with the Old Man in Hemingway's story. None of these frustrations is literally immoral. Tigers are not murderers and coyotes are not thieves.

To a certain extent the same attitude may be taken to other human beings, if they are strangers, not in one's group: forces of nature to be coped with as best one can. It is different, however, within the tribe. That is a group within which it is taken for granted that at least some cooperation will be extended.

People may help one another because they are forced to by threats or punishment, but that negates essential humanity. Voluntary assistance must be based on some community of goals.

4. The Tale Continued

Case IV. Let us now suppose that A and B confer. Let us suppose further that A has not produced any more artifacts than he can himself use and consume, but he has been so skillful and industrious that his production comprises considerably more than he requires for mere survival. Let us refer to the difference between A's total store and what he needs for bare survival as A's quasi-surplus.

This is what A has to bargain with. It seems that he cannot concede more than it to B, for if he does he cannot survive, so he might as well fight. A's aim in negotiating will be to give up as little of the quasi-surplus as possible to B, and to get in exchange for it as much as he can from B.

What can B bargain with? He has no surplus at all; indeed, to make the situation even starker we may assume that the earthquake destroyed Beta so that B is entirely destitute. This would, however, merely increase A's problem, for if no bargain can be struck, B will fight, which we assume A wants to avoid. Let us suppose that B can survive only if ceded 150% of A's quasi-surplus. Does it follow that there must be war to the death? No, fortunately, because if B pitches in and helps, the production of artifacts in Alpha may increase to the point where both A and B can survive. In other words, B can contribute his labor even if he lacks material resources. It turns out, then, that A can cede more than his quasi-surplus as long as the excess is made up by the added effort.

The upshot is that both A and B may be individually better off for making an agreement to share goods and labor than either one would have been if they fought winner-take-all.

Perhaps truce would be a better word than agreement for the arrangement that A and B set up. For the question of course arises, What is to prevent either party from violating the provisions of the pact when he sees fit? And the answer can only be: Nothing. We can expect no more than that each party will abide by the pact as long as it is in his interest to do so. But it was in the interest of both parties to conclude the treaty in the first place; it remains in the interest of each party to see to it that the other one remains in the same situation; and it will not be impossible in general for him to do so. Covenants without the sword are but words, true; but each of our covenantors has and retains his sword.

Even in this simplified situation the particulars of the compact might take indefinitely many different forms, depending on the amount of A's armaments and other resources in relation to B's, their bargaining skills, and their preferences. They might agree to pool their resources (notwithstanding A's initial advantage) and share alike; or erect a fence across the island not henceforth to be crossed by either without the other's permission; or agree that B should go to work for A five days in seven at a fixed wage. Or B might consent to become A's slave. What any such compact is, though, is an acquiescence of wills in the restriction of their own future objects. For A to cede a shovel to B is for A to renounce the satisfaction of any future desire he might have to dig with that particular shovel. B in his turn denies himself liberty to kill, disable, or maim A.

The transaction is fraught with momentous consequences. *First*, there are now obligations—bonds—between A and B; to this extent at least they form a community. They have set up rules, and they ought to abide by them. This ought, to be sure, is a prudential ought: the sanction, the consequence of nonconformity, is that the truce will be called off, and the parties will again be in danger of physical attack by each other, which they both want to avoid. To avoid resumption of war over minor infractions of the truce conditions, they may agree on methods of restitution. There will be problems about determining when a rule has been violated, as there are in tennis without an umpire, but they need not be insurmountable.

Second, A and B have invented property, at least if there are any clauses in the treaty specifying that any artifacts or other objects, or parcels of land, are to be off limits to one party without the consent of the other. Ownership is acknowledged, exclusive control of use or access.

But was there not already property before the truce? What about the artifacts A had labored to produce? Were not they, at least, already his?

John Locke's argument is that a man owns his own body; therefore he owns the labor of his body; therefore whatever he "mixes" that labor with becomes *pro tanto* an extension of his body; therefore he owns it too. The argument gets off to a bad start: "I own my own body" may look like a truism but it hardly is. It is a question of fact whether one has acknowledged, exclusive control of the use of one's body, and there are people for whom the answer is No. No doubt that is not as it should be; but we are talking of how things are. And while it is true that before B appeared on the scene A had exclusive control of the use of his own body, the exclusive control was not acknowledged. It takes two to make property.

When A and B draw up their treaty there is no limitation in principle to what they may agree to be the property of one and of the other, or to be held in common or left subject to subsequent claim. There is nothing about the axe that A has laboriously constructed from scratch that makes it his property, or property at all: no more than a tree that he plans to cut down, perhaps, some time next year and saw into boards. Nevertheless, there is something more than sentiment making the relation between a man and that with which he has "mixed his labor" particularly intimate and fit to be legitimized, as it were, by acknowledgment of ownership. Labor need not be unpleasant always, but it is generally engaged in not for its own sake but because some comprehensive plan requires it; the agent envisages some end, the production of something, the enjoyment of which is viewed a good in itself; he plans how to get it; and realizing that work is indispensable, he works. To deprive a man of some good thing that he got by luck, without effort, is indeed to frustrate him; but to take away the product of his labor is to do double damage. He has undergone the hardship of toil, and in vain. He would not have put up with the drudgery if he had known of the outcome in advance. So it is impossible to suppose that anyone would voluntarily forgo the enjoyment—which means the ownership—of what he has mixed his labor with, unless in exchange for some other good perceived as of at least equivalent value. This means that in the terms of the truce between A and B, possession of their respective artifacts will be guaranteed to them unless they receive compensation. And since A and B begin their negotiations with each in physical possession of his artifacts, it is, to be sure, as if they had property to begin with. Moreover, this concern that each has for what he produces shapes the form that their agreement will take. It is to the continuing interest of each that each should keep on producing things. Therefore the truce will contain provisions for maintaining production, which must recognize and respect the producer's ownership of his product or allow compensation if it is to be taken from him; otherwise there could remain no motive to keep it going, unless sheer fear, which is incompatible with the primary aim of the agreement.

And so, *third* and finally, we see in this agreement the genesis of rights and justice. The truce once agreed to will remain in force only as long as both parties find its continuance to their advantage. Now, some truces are made for stipulated, definite periods of time, but not this one, since the motive for making it is to avoid combat altogether. Hence it has no expiration date and cannot be abrogated by mutual consent. Breaking it is a unilateral act of war and will provoke the indignation of the other party, who was willing to continue it and was living up to it. This is enough to generate the use of moral language, supposing it has not up to now been current. One has a *right* to have the terms adhered to; failure to observe the terms on which one has agreed is *injustice*. Even if derelictions in this regard are initially only violations of a prudential ought, they are very serious, as tending to bring about the dissolution of community. Moreover the prudence they offend against is primarily not that of the agent himself but of his fellow citizen; in consequence of which objections are bound to take on a moral tone.

Thomas Hobbes held that to enter into society is to give up at least some rights, whereas I am claiming that there are no rights outside community. This is perhaps a verbal point, but hardly of no consequence. Hobbes's Right of Nature, an absolute "right to all things," is anomalous in that it has no correlative duty. In the state of nature I have the right to appropriate your shovel or hit you over the head, but that does not mean that you have any duty to submit or to refrain from doing the same to me. The sense of "right" in this context, then, seems to be only "not subject to moral censure," or as a hockey player not in the penalty box has a right to pass the puck. But this is at least a misleading way of speaking; the thought is more straightforwardly conveyed simply by saying that before any agreements have been made, questions of right and wrong in the moral sense cannot arise.

The objection might be raised that this truce cannot be the origin of justice and rights, for it might be asked of the truce itself, Is it a just agreement? Does it not, or could it not, infringe on the rights of a party?

But it is a logical point about justice that injustice cannot be suffered voluntarily, as Aristotle saw. And the truce is not only concluded but maintained voluntarily.

This reply may be thought unsatisfactory on the ground that the parties are not equal in their bargaining positions. Hence one (A) may get the better of the bargain, i.e. be in a better position after concluding it than the other party (B). Indeed, as I admitted, one form the agreement might take would be for B to make himself A's slave. But this or any other inequitable arrangement would be manifestly unjust. And it is not only absurd but morally repugnant to suggest that a slave would be behaving unjustly, violating his master's rights, if he subsequently rebelled (broke the truce). Furthermore, no such desperate engagement could be voluntarily undertaken.

I answer: First, the view that any inequality is *ipso facto* unjust is mere dogma. It is certainly not self-evidently true, for *prima facie* it is not unjust to pay travel money and honoraria to learned persons who participate in enlightening conferences on justice. The objection based on slavery is more serious. I do not assert with complete confidence that a person might voluntarily agree to become a slave. In practice there are, of course, degrees of slavery; but I suppose the concept is of one whose will is entirely subordinate to another's, one who never makes plans of his own and carries them out. Galley slavery must approximate this condition. If that is so, then the question whether one can voluntarily become a slave seems to be the same as whether the will can voluntarily negate itself permanently. If as I maintain the essence of life is the exertion of will, then the slave is as good as dead.

But not quite. Where there is life there is hope. Probably the only circumstances in which one would choose slavery would be where the only alternative was death. And a choice's being between unpleasant alternatives does not make it no choice. If the terms of our truce involve my becoming your slave, then we form a community within which you have a right to all my services and I have no right to pursue any interest of mine independent of yours; and *within that community* I act unjustly if I do anything for myself. But let us not forget that according to the view being presented I may choose at any time to abrogate the truce and bring the community to an end. In practice, then, a community consisting of one master and one slave is likely to be unstable, the slave always on the lookout for the opportune moment to get out of that status. In other words, it is a sort of degenerate case of community, hardly distinguishable from a lull in a state of war.

5. *Morals of the Story*

A novelist would tell the tale differently, but to much the same effect. Actual people in this sort of situation, if not murderously inclined or forced by extreme scarcity to eliminate competition, will come to some agreement, perhaps tacit, of the form "I'll let you alone if you let me alone; and I'll help you out from time to time if you reciprocate." Appropriation by one of things the other had made, or even just found, would be regarded as stealing and if serious would lead to conflict.

That is to say, they would establish a community and a system of justice based on agreement. This can be called justice "from the bottom up": it is not imposed on them by any superior force, for there isn't any. It comes from their mutual apprehension of necessary conditions for human beings, each with his own interests and plans, to dwell in close proximity without fighting. It can fittingly be called natural, being a direct consequence of what human life is about, the expression of human capabilities in achieving planned goals in those universal and unavoidable circumstances of existence of a semigregarious species.

However, there is, as we have seen, no constraint on the particular form of the truce. It must represent what the parties to it, not in some hypothetical and abstract condition but in concrete circumstances of their existence, can agree on as preferable to direct physical confrontation. In particular it does not presuppose equality of power in the bargaining situation, or of talents or industry, or of luck, or of the distribution of goods that result, or of anything except that all parties have equal rights to insist on the equal observance of those clauses of the treaty in which their particular interests are safeguarded. Nevertheless, natural justice if it does not (necessarily) start from an initial position of equality and does not guarantee eventual achievement of it, yet facilitates betterment of the individual's position through effort. That is what its main purpose is: to make it possible for plans to be carried out without arbitrary interference and frustration by fellow members of the community. Even in our story, destitute B will probably be able to come to terms with prosperous A that will make it possible for him through hard work to approach A's level of luxurious consumption. Remember: the harsher the terms A attempts to impose on B, the greater danger he runs of B's abrogating the truce.

The story is not a myth of the origin of government; it is Lockean, not Hobbist. There is no Sovereign set up to whom all owe deference and who has a monopoly of power wherewith to coerce the intractable; there are only the individuals with whatever resources they happen to command. As Locke noted, such an arrangement will be attended with certain inconveniences showing, for example, a need for impartial umpires and arbitrators. How it might come about (after a few more castaways had landed) that a central authority would be set up, and what its functions would or should be, is another topic. But the institutions and conceptions of right and justice would antedate the formation of such an authority, the operations of which would be liable to criticism from the standpoint of justice. So much seems incontrovertible; the Hobbesian contention to the contrary is paradoxical and carries no conviction.

Lest this analysis be regarded as excessively hard-boiled, note that the conception of justice as observance of rules agreed on from the motive of self-interest by no means precludes the existence and importance in the community of interactions in which the requirements of justice are voluntarily held in abeyance: love and charity. Indeed it is what makes them possible: one cannot simultaneously make love and war.

Finally we observe that nothing precludes the extension of the truce to later arrivals. The conditions may have to be modified for their benefit; the arrival of a third castaway would so perturb the relations of A and B that there might have to be a new constitutional convention, as it were. But not for every new immigrant; as population grows we may expect the weight of existing agreement to impose itself on latecomers in a take-it-or-leave-it fashion.

And what is the bearing of this story and its morals on actual human affairs? This: We have been examining the kinds of relations other than out-and-out no-holds-barred conflict that can subsist between human beings; we have concluded that peace might be based on agreement; that the agreement cannot be expected to outlast its advantageousness to all parties; that the terms of agreement define what justice is, and what the rights of the parties are, within the community of those in agreement — in particular and most importantly it creates the rights of property. The normative character of the rights so specified is derived from the fact — so we have contended — that persons wishing each to attain his own goals in the context of association with other persons, would agree to them.

However, we have been assuming that human plans to achieve particular separate goals sometimes lead to conflict; and that conflict if serious will be settled by force unless the rivals can arrive at some compromise. But is it the case that human animals are necessarily motivated by individual "selfish" interests? Is it not possible — maybe sometimes actual — that they could as it were submerge their own interests into one big interest, the general welfare, the pursuit of which would involve only peaceful cooperation?

6. *South Seas* Tale II

B, oppressed by the harsh terms of the truce with A but impotent to revolt, has thought of a way out. Every week he spends the one afternoon he has to himself in collecting branches and vines from the little forest plot that A has not claimed. At last one day, having secretly made a raft, he scratches in the sand an insulting note to A and paddles off into the open sea.

After many hardships he struggles onto the shore of another island. From between the palms a majestic bearded figure appears.

Alas, B thinks to himself, here we go again. More truce terms!

But no. "Welcome to Gamma, O stranger" the figure intones in a kindly voice. "I am G. You must be hungry and thirsty. Won't you join us for dinner?"

At the groaning board B is introduced to the other islanders: F, an old man confined to a wheelchair; H, a mature and handsome woman; J, a lad of seventeen or so; and two children, K and L.

Over the coffee and liqueurs B deems the time opportune for discussing their future arrangements. "I'm grateful for your tacit temporary truce," he begins, "and hope you can make it permanent."

"Truce? What ever do you mean?"

"Why, the usual — I won't try to kill you as long as you don't — "

Consternation and alarm among the Gammanians. H grasps K and L protectively in her arms. Desperately trying to scurry out of the way, F overturns his wheelchair. J grabs a silver candlestick and advances menacingly on B but is restrained by G, who at last restores a modicum of calm.

B then explains how things are done on Alpha. The Gammanians weep at the sad tale. H comforts him that he has arrived finally in a civilized community.

"But how can you get along without a truce?" B is still puzzled. "Don't you have your individual interests and goals, and don't you have to have some means of reconciling the conflicts to which they inevitably give rise?"

"Well," the youthful J begins to reply, "Sometimes I — "

But G cuts him off. "Not at all. We have only one goal, which is the good life for us all. Each of us helps to achieve it in any way that he or she can, and each gets all the help he or she needs from all the rest. From each according to his ability; to each according to his need."

"Just like one big happy family," B muses, dimly recalling childhood scenes.

"Of course," says G. "That's what we are — a family!"

"But what happens if you have different ideas about what your needs are?"

A suggestion of a frown appears on J's face, and he seems to exchange a significant glance with H;

but G replies: "Oh, sometimes there is some perplexity about that, but when there is, we handle it democratically."

"You mean, you have a discussion and then vote on the different proposals?"

"Not exactly," says G. "I listen to what everybody has to say, and then I explain what the wise thing to do is. As everybody here is rational, they all concur, and that's that. — From now on, we all want you to feel that you are one of the family. — You must be tired. H will make your bed in the dormitory. Tomorrow after breakfast J will show you the woodpile and get you started — I take it you know something about woodchopping? — "

And so they lived happily ever after.

7. *Another Batch of Morals*

Within the family — I mean the "traditional" family as found (say) in the novels of Jane Austin and Samuel Butler — there is little concern for justice in the sense of giving each member his or her rights. Ordinarily there is one "breadwinner," the father, who is the sole or at least principal source of income, most of which is disbursed for the common benefit of all. Where it is used to buy things for individuals, the principle of distribution is need not merit; the snaggle-toothed daughter must have her orthodontia before the musical prodigy acquires a Steinway. And if the old folks and infants are helpless and only a drain on resources, their needs must nevertheless be provided. Competitiveness plays no part, or at least it is deplored when it does. This is called Love.

Most philosophers now writing experienced family life more or less along these lines when they were young, or at least were able to view it close up. And it may seem a more satisfactory way to order relations between people than "justice" with its stern judgments and devil-take-the-hindmost attitude. The transition from the warm nurturing environment of the family to the cold and impersonal rat-race in which the independent individual is caught up may be as traumatic as birth itself. That is doubtless one reason why the family is preferred by so many to the treaty as the proper model for human relationships.

Another is that it is inherently equalitarian. Within the ideal family all members are equal in a number of respects. There is no distinction of rich and poor; if one member has more expended on him, it is not so that he can enjoy a higher "standard of living." One does not have higher status than another or receive more deference. (Again, this is the ideal; but it is why we feel that something is wrong in the household where Cinderella lives.) Parents are careful to treat all their children fairly, which means dividing up benefits equally unless one has greater need than other; the notion of "earning" hardly enters except in comparatively trivial ways mostly concerned with putative training for the rat-race to come; and even here the experts tend to deprecate it. Granted that intrafamilial conflicts, notably sibling rivalry, have always occurred, they are — or used to be — considered superficial and due to immaturity. Universal brotherhood has been taken as synonymous with the elimination of human conflicts.

"Why can't the whole human race, or at least the whole nation, be like that?" the philosopher asks, and so do the plain man and woman. The plain man is likely to answer, "Because family relations are based on affection, which won't stretch that far." So do some philosophers, e.g. Hobbes in commenting on the perpetual state of war "in many places of *America*, except the government of small Families, the concord whereof dependeth on naturall lust".[6] But many others, of whom the first and greatest was Plato, have maintained that the project is not impossible; all that is needed is a salutary revision of education and institutional arrangements, whereupon paternal, maternal, filial, fraternal, and sororal affection will become the cement binding together a completely unified and, therefore, happy social order in which everyone cares for everyone else.

These philosophers base their optimism on the belief that so-called human nature is all nurture, there is no limit to how outlooks and motivations can be altered by training. This is held as a dogma by many social thinkers, like creationism among fundamentalists. But also like creationism, it is an empirical question whether it is true. A lot of evidence is in, all of it adverse: the utter failure of every attempt whether on a large scale or small, to produce the requisite changes (with the doubtful and minor exception of Israeli kibbutzim). The explanation of this dismal history is provided by the science of sociobiology. But is it altogether regrettable that human beings cannot be improved to fill the bill? If we

scrutinize the family model more closely we may find that it has less pleasant aspects.

If there is no conflict within the ideal family, it is because there is only one will, or only one that counts: father's. Husband and wife being "one flesh," the woman's will is held to coincide with her man's. ("Man's happiness is: I will. Woman's happiness is: He wills." — Nietzsche.) The children are under tutelage, their wills are being formed, and are not to be regarded as competent in their own right. When in adolescence they begin to develop wills of their own and assert them, that is the well-known revolt against parental authority and the first step in exit from the familial hearth.

The totalitarian implications, when the family is held up as a model for emulation by the larger community, are obvious. If they are not seen immediately it is because within the family the will of the father is (sometimes) not regarded as merely the expression of the de facto dominant family member, but as the voice of Reason. "Father knows best." His macrocosmic analogue, then, is not looked upon as a vulgar tyrant but as the Philosopher King. And all his subjects, that is, all the children of the Philosopher Father's extended family, agree entirely with him insofar as they are rational — and that is all that matters, of course. Who wants to be irrational? Nevertheless, there is no getting around the fact that the expanded family, unlike the microcosm, must maintain its "children" in tutelage not for fifteen or twenty years but for all their lives. They cannot be allowed to grow up; all their important decisions must be made for them from above.

This has not bothered philosophers from Plato to Pol Pot who saw themselves as the loving fathers. It is, however, a stumbling block to Professor John Rawls (to his credit), and accounts for some incoherencies in his philosophy, as I shall explain presently.

Now, what will the conception of justice be according to the family model?

The short answer to this question is that there will be no such conception, although the word will be retained for propaganda effect. As we saw, there is little use for a notion of justice within the real family; and this will carry over. However, let us go the long way around to this conclusion.

The first thing to notice is that the adjective in the phrase "distributive justice" now receives emphasis. On the agreement model of justice the question of *distributing* anything hardly arises. The main idea of justice from the bottom up is that people are to keep what they produce unless they voluntarily exchange it for what others have made. It is no part of the agreement model that there will be a Master Distributor at all, distinct from the producers. That is one reason for calling it justice from the bottom up.

It is otherwise with the family model. In the (real) family there is a divorce between production and acquisition on the one hand and distribution on the other. With unimportant exceptions property is held in common; where all can make use of it as they do; where they cannot it is distributed (by Father, or at least according to his will) without special consideration for who in particular made, earned, or acquired it. The *fundamentum distributionis* being need, things will be thought of as rightly distributed when they go to the neediest; or if they are such that one member's need for them is no greater than another's, when the distribution is fair, that is, equal.

Second, fathers are *ex officio* utilitarians. The loving father's aim is that all his dependents should be happy, and equally so. He is a "good provider" and what he provides is satisfactions. That does not mean of course that he caters to every whim; he does not "spoil" his dependents. He may on occasion be judgmental and punishing, but it is for their own good; when he birches the unruly offspring it really does hurt him more than the wailing lad. If family members are in trouble, he is automatically on their side and will do all he can to get them out of it regardless of whether it is "their own fault."

Magnified to the scale of society this concern becomes what in contemporary jargon is called "compassion." Anyone who is hard up for whatever reason is to have his or her needs met at the expense of all who are not hard up. And so in this regard the paternalistic society will equate justice with compassion (a term which itself has undergone a curious transformation — one hardly tends to picture sleek politicians and bureaucrats as "suffering with" the objects of their solicitude). It is held that need entails the right to its fulfillment.

Natural justice on the other hand has no conceptual connection to utility, only a factual one. The idea of justice is that people should get what they deserve, what they have earned, and to find out what fits this specification it is not relevant to calculate the consequences of the award. But since the prospect of enjoying the fruits of one's labors is by and large the most potent incentive to labor, and

labor by and large is what produces goods that satisfy desires, the observance of natural justice promotes utility demonstrably better for all concerned than "compassionate" redistribution.

Third, the characteristic concern of the father for his dependents is positive in the sense that it is not enough for him to keep them from harm, he must actively promote their welfare. Writ large, this means that the Philosopher King has not discharged his duty to his subjects when he has prevented or redressed wrongdoing among them; he must improve them, make them positively better off than they were, even if he knows that in so doing some inconveniences are regrettably bound to occur. Thus Dr. Goebbels mused:

> There can be no peace in Europe until the last Jews are eliminated from the continent.

> That, of course, raises a large number of exceedingly delicate questions. What is to be done with the half-Jews? What with those related to Jews? In-laws of Jews? Persons married to Jews? Evidently we still have quite a lot to do and undoubtedly a multitude of personal tragedies will ensue within the framework of the solution of this problem. But that is unavoidable. . . . We are doing a good work in proceeding radically and consistently. The task we are assuming today will be an advantage and a boon to our descendants.[7]

In contrast, the partisan of natural justice does not suppose that the reign of justice and the millennium are necessarily one and the same thing. Justice is no doubt desirable for its own sake, but its main value is instrumental: it is one important condition for the productive release of human energy. And in a way the negative is primary: all that the champion of justice is called upon to do is to eliminate *in*justice; once that has been done he can rest and allow those whom he has liberated from its shadow to go about the task of making a better world.

In sum: Every society must have some recognized rules for deciding questions of ownership. In a social structure based on agreement the rules will be those of natural justice, justice from the bottom up, providing for initial ownership and subsequent voluntary exchange of the products of one's own labor. In a paternalistic society, on the other hand, such considerations will not be decisive or paid much attention. The term "justice" will nevertheless be retained on account of its favorable associations to refer to the principles observed by the persons who have the power, authority, and wisdom to redistribute the goods taken from the producers and put into a common pot. These principles will emphasize the satisfaction of needs, the most urgent getting the highest priority. Where needs are equal, distribution will be equal as far as possible. Moreover the distribution is to be handled in such a way that a harmonious social pattern is produced, a "better world." This last principle applies especially to the distribution of intangibles such as status. A person will be said to have a "right" to X if and only if the distribution pattern assigns X to that person.

This is artificial justice or justice from the top down.

8. *Illustration: Affirmative Action*

Philosophy is sometimes said to have no practical consequences. If so, the theory of justice is not philosophy, for whether one holds one view or another of justice makes an enormous difference in practice: As an example, let us consider the ways in which justice from the bottom up and from the top down deal with the problem of racial discrimination in employment.

First, justice from the bottom up:

In a society recognizing this norm, citizens may make whatever agreements they choose, for any reason or none, as long as they do not infringe on the rights of other citizens. So if I am a Ruritanian widgetmaker, a manufacturer of widgets who detests Ruritanians may legitimately refuse to hire me. And if there are many more of his sort, we Ruritanian widgetmakers will be at a disadvantage, we will be discriminated against just because we are Ruritanians, and that is bad. But happily the problem will solve itself. We will offer our services to non-Ruritanophobe entrepreneurs for wages lower than the bigots must pay; and if we really are just as good workers, our unbiased employers will be put at a competitive advantage over the prejudiced ones. In the not very long run, then, the gap between Ruritanian and non-Ruritanian wage levels will disappear. And in the somewhat longer run the very idea of this sort of discrimination will begin to look silly, and we will be welcomed as fellow club members and sons-in-law by the former meanies. At any rate

this is the pattern that has hitherto manifested itself time and again in the United States. It is well to note in this connection that slavery in the Southern states was, and South African apartheid is, imposed by government edict, i.e. they are interferences with freedom of contract.

Justice from the top down takes a different approach. Everybody is equal to everybody else (dogma), therefore, Ruritanians are just as good at making widgets as anyone else (non sequitur); therefore, if Ruritanian representation in the widget industry is not equal to the statistical expectation, it must be the work of prejudice (non sequitur), which if sincerely denied must be an unconscious aversion (absurdity). This is sin, which must be put down by force, viz. the imposition of a pro-Ruritanian quota (called something else) on widgetmakers. This will, of course, have two effects: it will disrupt the widget industry, already reeling from Japanese competition; and it will exacerbate resentment against Ruritanians.

9. *Some Paradoxes*

The derivation of some main tenets of contemporary liberal (another word-corpse) opinion from the family model will no doubt strike some people as absurd, on the ground that liberals hold the old-fashioned family to be a pernicious institution which must be abolished or at least drastically overhauled. But hostility of derivative to original is hardly unheard of. Christianity with its anti-Semitism is after all in origin a Jewish sect. Nazism was a kind of socialism. And no one can deny that Plato's Republic is paternalistic; yet Plato was the first to propose the abolition of the family in order to eliminate emotional competition with his extended political family. Totalitarian liberalism finds no embarrassment in this.

It is otherwise, however, with John Rawls. The celebrated Difference Principle, that "social and economic inequalities are to be arranged so that they are . . . to the greatest benefit of the least advantaged," and its elaboration are all easily deducible from the family model. But we must not forget that there is another Rawlsian Principle of Justice, that of equal liberties — "each person is to have an equal right to the most extensive basic liberty compatible with a similar liberty for others" — which comes first and is required to be satisfied before one even starts thinking about fulfilling the Difference Principle. The sincerity of Rawls's advocacy of liberty, at least political liberty, and his rejection of a constitution where the Philosopher King runs everything, cannot be called in question. And that is why Rawls bases his philosophy on consent of self-interested parties; as we have seen, that is what generates a free society. But Rawls hedges his commitment. The personages behind the veil of ignorance are deprived of all flesh and blood, what is left being only the abstract Voice of Reason, which might as well be a single Rational Person wishing equal happiness for all — which as we have also seen is central to the paternalistic model.

Rawls's theory thus turns out, unsurprisingly, to be a confection of incompatible elements. The principle of equal liberties is bottom-up, but the difference principle is top-down. It would be humanly impossible to instantiate both principles simultaneously: the redistribution required by the second can only be brought about by force, thereby contravening the equal liberties. Rawls like many thinkers of today has failed to see what was so clear to Locke and his contemporaries, that without property rights there can be no rights at all. For government, not being producer of anything, has to be supported out of citizens' property. So if government has complete control of property there can be no limit on its power. In particular, as the economist Milton Friedman has emphasized, the dissenter from official policy has no base of operations or even of livelihood.

Perhaps the blindness of Rawls and so many others to this point, so obvious both in theory and in practice, results from their having convinced themselves that if ever *they* were in power, of course *they* would never abuse their position by clobbering the opposition, but would behave as exemplary liberals.

10. *In Aeternam?*

We have compared two conceptions that claim the name justice.

One is that of rendering every man his due. A man's due is what he has acquired by his own efforts and not taken from some other man without consent. A community in which this conception is realized will be one in which the members agree not to interfere in the legitimate endeavors of each other to achieve their individual goals, and to help each other to the extent that the conditions for doing so are mutually satisfactory. These agreements obtain at the level of the individual citizens, for which reason I call this conception justice from the bottom up. ("Up": there may develop a hierarchical arrangement with those at the top having special duties of enforcing the agreements; but if so, the decision concerning which agreements to enforce will not originate with them.) Such a community will be one giving the freest possible rein to all its members to develop their particular capacities and use them to carry out their plans for their own betterment. If this activity is The Good for Man (and I hold with the Philosopher that it is), then it is appropriate to call the associated conception of justice natural.

The other conception holds justice to be the satisfaction of needs so as to bring everyone as far as possible onto the same plateau of pleasurable experience. The view of human life underlying it is that life consists of two separable phases, production and consumption; the consumption phase is where The Good lies; there is ultimately no reason why any individual should have any more or less of this Good than any other individual; and the problem of how to secure the requisite production is merely technical. Society based on this conception must be structured as a hierarchy of authority, in order to solve the problem of production and to administer justice, i.e. to adjust the satisfaction quanta. Thus I have called this justice from the top down (though of course I don't think it is really justice at all).

Justice from the top down as I have described it does not sound attractive. I have tried to account for the fact that, nevertheless, it commands the enthusiastic support of so many clever men and women and is everywhere on the march by showing its emotional basis in the structure of the family, an institution that has been felt to be, at its best, a warm, conflict-free, loving refuge from fear and anxiety. Many people do not really *want* to grow up, and when they do they yearn for a return to blissful dependence in the family or even in the stage of development previous to that. I do not think it can be controverted that this is part of the explanation for the popularity of top-down justice; but nor can it be the whole, for such a complex phenomenon must be due to many factors. Among them are genuine compassion for the unfortunate and altruistic desire to help them; fantasies of omnipotence, to which powerless academic intellectuals are exceptionally liable; and envy. What the proportions are, is anybody's guess.

As there is no hope of lessening the influence of these emotions in human affairs, the triumph of the top-down cannot be stemmed unless there are yet more powerful emotions to pit against them. What might they be? I can think of three possibilities: the desire that everyone has that he himself should be given his due, and the concomitant outrage, with which more and more people are becoming acquainted, when the top-down authority denies it; revulsion witnessing the actual, practical effects of top-down justice, e.g. in Cambodia; and finally the life force itself, Spinoza's *conatus*, the endeavor of each thing to persevere in its being, and not (except in parasites) by sucking forever but by getting proper solid nourishment. I *hope* these are strong enough to prevail and show this funeral oration to have been premature: Justice is not dead, only mugged by intellectual hoods.

Endnotes

[1] Joel Feinberg, *Rights, Justice, and the Bounds of Liberty* (Princeton: Princeton University Press, 1980), 141, 153. I am indebted to Max Hocutt for this reference.

[2] John Rawls, *A Theory of Justice* (Cambridge, MA: Harvard University Press, 1971), 277–280 *et passim*.

[3] Ronald Dworkin, *Taking Rights Seriously* (Cambridge: Harvard University Press, 1977), 227–229.

[4] Richard Wasserstrom, "A Defense of Programs of Preferential Treatment," in Vincent Barry, ed., *Applying Ethics* (Belmont, CA: Wadsworth, 1982), 332 f.

[5] Thomas Nagel, *Mortal Questions* (New Rochelle, N.Y: Cambridge University Press, 1979), 99 f.

[6] *Leviathan*, Chapter 13.

[7] *The Goebbels Diaries*, ed. and trans. Louis P. Lochner (Westport, CT.: Greenwood, 1971), 135 (March 7, 1942).

XII.7 *Equality*

THOMAS NAGEL

Thomas Nagel is professor of philosophy at New York University and is the author of several works in ethics. In this essay he argues that although values are neither physical nor mental, they have an objective status in that they provide reasons for acting that are independent of anyone's personal situation. Values presume an impartial perspective—a view from nowhere. For example, the evil of pain is a reason for us to want it eliminated, even if we are not ourselves suffering. We do not need *additional* reasons for wanting it removed from the sufferer. Nagel concedes that there are no conclusive arguments in favor of his thesis that values are objective, but he contends that there are reasons to accept this thesis as the best explanation of our moral sentiments. This thesis increases in cogency indirectly as we defeat objections to it, which is what Nagel does in the latter portion of his essay.

In this essay, Nagel analyzes the concept of equality as a moral and political value and compares it with two competing political values, liberty and utility. A complete plausible social morality will include all three. The appeal of equality is that it, as against utilitarianism, treats individuals in their separateness as distinct persons, and, as against libertarianism, it appeals to our intuitions that the urgency of basic need puts special demands upon us. He concludes with an argument for equal treatment based on impersonal concern for others based on an impersonal concern for oneself, a view described at length in reading IV.6, "The View from Nowhere."

I

It is difficult to argue for the intrinsic social value of equality without begging the question. Equality can be defended up to a point in terms of other values like utility and liberty. But some of the most difficult questions are posed when it conflicts with these.

Contemporary political debate recognizes four types of equality: political, legal, social, and economic. The first three cannot be defined in formal terms. Political equality is not guaranteed by granting each adult one vote and the right to hold public office. Legal equality is not guaranteed by granting everyone the right to a jury trial, the right to bring suit for injuries, and the right to counsel. Social equality is not produced by the abolition of titles and official barriers to class mobility. Great substantive inequalities in political power, legal protection, social esteem and self-respect are compatible with these formal conditions. It is a commonplace that real equality of every kind is sensitive to economic factors. While formal institutions may guarantee a minimum social status to everyone, big differences in wealth and income will produce big distinctions above that—distinctions that may be inherited as well.

So the question of economic equality cannot be detached from the others, and this complicates the issue, because the value of the other types of equality may be of a very different kind. To put it somewhat paradoxically, their value may not be strictly egalitarian. It may depend on certain rights, like the right to fair treatment by the law, that must be impartially protected, and that cannot be protected without a measure of substantive equality. Rights

Reprinted from *Mortal Questions* (Cambridge University Press, 1979) by permission.

are in an extended sense egalitarian, because everyone is supposed to have them; but this is not a matter of distributive justice. The equal protection of individual rights is usually thought to be a value independent of utility and of equality in the distribution of advantages. Later I shall comment on the relation among these values, but for now let us assume their distinctness. This means that the defense of economic equality on the ground that it is needed to protect political, legal, and social equality may not be a defense of equality *per se* — equality in the possession of benefits in general. Yet the latter is a further moral idea of great importance. Its validity would provide an independent reason to favor economic equality as a good in its own right. If, *per impossibile*, large economic inequalities did not threaten political, legal, and social equality, they would be much less objectionable. But there might still be something wrong with them.

In addition to the arguments that depend on its relation to other types of equality, there is at least one nonegalitarian, instrumental argument for economic equality itself, on grounds of utility. The principle of diminishing marginal utility states that for many goods, a particular further increment has less value to someone who already possesses a significant amount of the good than to someone who has less.[1] So if the total quantity of such a good and the number of recipients remains constant, an equal distribution of it will always have greater total utility than a less equal one.

This must be balanced against certain costs. First, attempts to reduce inequality may also reduce the total quantity of goods available, by affecting incentives to work and invest. For example, a progressive income tax and diminishing marginal utility make it more expensive to purchase the labor of those whose services are most in demand. Beyond a certain point, the pursuit of equality may sacrifice overall utility, or even the welfare of everyone in society.

Second, the promotion of equality may require objectionable means. To achieve even moderate equality it is necessary to restrict economic liberty, including the freedom to make bequests. Greater equality may be attainable only by more general coercive techniques, including ultimately the assignment of work by public administration instead of private contracts. Some of these costs may be unacceptable not only on utilitarian grounds but because

they violate individual rights. Opponents of the goal of equality may argue that if an unequal distribution of benefits results from the free interactions and agreements of persons who do not violate each other's rights, then the results are not objectionable, provided they do not include extreme hardship for the worst off.

II

So there is much to be said about the instrumental value and disvalue of equality; the question of its intrinsic value does not arise in isolation. Yet the answer to that question determines what instrumental costs are acceptable. If equality is in itself good, then producing it may be worth a certain amount of inefficiency and loss of liberty.

There are two types of argument for the intrinsic value of equality, communitarian and individualistic. According to the communitarian argument, equality is good for a society taken as a whole. It is a condition of the right kind of relations among its members, and of the formation in them of healthy fraternal attitudes, desires, and sympathies. This view analyzes the value of equality in terms of a social and individual ideal. The individualistic view, on the other hand, defends equality as a correct *distributive* principle — the correct way to meet the conflicting needs and interests of distinct people, whatever those interests may be, more or less. It does not assume the desirability of any particular kinds of desires, or any particular kinds of interpersonal relations. Rather it favors equality in the distribution of human goods, whatever these may be — whether or not they necessarily include goods of community and fraternity.

Though the communitarian argument is very influential, I am going to explore only the individualistic one, because that is the type of argument that I think is more likely to succeed. It would provide a moral basis for the kind of liberal egalitarianism that seems to me plausible. I do not have such an argument. This essay is a discussion of the form such an argument would have to take, what its starting points should be, and what it must overcome.

A preference for equality is at best one component in a theory of social choice, or choice involving numbers of people. Its defense does not require the rejection of other values with which it may come into conflict. However, it is excluded by theories of social choice which make certain other values dominant. Egalitarianism may once have been opposed to aristocratic theories, but now it is opposed in theoretical debate by the adherents of two non-aristocratic values: utility and individual rights. I am going to examine the dispute in order to see how equality might be shown to have a value that can resist these to some extent, without replacing them.

Though I am interested in the most general foundation for such a principle, I shall begin by discussing a more specialized egalitarian view, the position of John Rawls.[2] It applies specifically to the design of the basic social institutions, rather than to distributive choices, and perhaps it cannot be extended to other cases. But it is the most developed liberal egalitarian view in the field, and much debate about equality focuses on it. So I will initially pose the opposition between equality, utility, and rights in terms of his positions. Later I shall explain how my own egalitarian view differs from his

Rawls's theory assigns more importance to equal protection of political and personal liberties than to equality in the distribution of other benefits. Nevertheless it is strongly egalitarian in this respect also. His principle of distribution for general goods, once equality in the basic liberties is secure, is that inequalities are justified only if they benefit the worst-off group in the society (by yielding higher productivity and employment, for example).

This so-called Difference Principle is used not to determine allocation directly, but only for the assessment of economic and social institutions, which in turn influence the allocation of goods. While it is counted a good thing for anyone to be made better off, the value of improving the situation of those who are worse off takes priority over the value of improving the situation of those who are better off. This is largely independent of the relative quantities of improvement involved, and also of the relative numbers of persons. So given a choice between making a thousand poor people somewhat better off and making two thousand middle class people considerably better off, the first choice would be preferred. It should be added that people's welfare for these purposes is assessed in terms of overall life prospects, not just prosperity at the moment.

This is a very strong egalitarian principle, though it is not the most radical we can imagine. It is constructed by adding to the general value of improvement a condition of priority to the worst off. A more egalitarian position would hold that some inequalities are bad even if they benefit the worst off, so that a situation in which *everyone* is worse off may be preferable if the inequalities are reduced enough. So long as the argument remains individualistic such a position could seem attractive only for reasons stemming from the connection between economic and social equality.[3]

Later I shall discuss Rawls's arguments for the view, and offer some additional ones, but first let me say something about the two positions to which it is naturally opposed, and against which it has to be defended. They are positions that do not accord intrinsic value to equality but admit other values whose pursuit or protection may require the acceptance of considerable inequality. Those values, as I have said, are utility and individual rights.

From a utilitarian point of view, it does not make sense to forgo greater benefits for the sake of lesser, or benefits to more people for the sake of fewer, just because the benefits to the worst off will be greater. It is better to have more of what is good and less of what is bad, no matter how they are distributed.

According to a theory of individual rights, it is wrong to interfere with people's liberty to keep or bequeath what they can earn merely in order to prevent the development of inequalities in distribution. It may be acceptable to limit individual liberty to prevent grave evils, but inequality is not one of those. Inequalities are not wrong if they do not result from wrongs of one person against another. They must be accepted if the only way to prevent them is to abridge individual rights to the kind of free action that violates no one else's rights.

Both types of theory point out the costs of pursuing distributive equality, and deny that it has independent value that outweighs these costs. More specifically, the pursuit of equality is held to require the illegitimate sacrifice of the rights or interests of some individuals to the less important interests of others. These two theories are also radically opposed to one another. Together with egalitarianism they form a trio of fundamentally different views about how to settle conflicts among the interests of different people.

III

What is the nature of the dispute between them? The units about which the problem arises are individual persons, individual human lives. Each of them has a claim to consideration. In some sense the distinctness of these claims is at the heart of the issue. The question is whether (a) the worst off have a prior claim, or (b) the enforcement of that claim would ignore the greater claim of others not among the worst off, who would benefit significantly more if a less egalitarian policy were adopted instead, or (c) it would infringe the claims of other persons to liberty and the protection of their rights.

Now this looks like a dispute about the value of equality. But it can also be viewed as a dispute about *how* people should be treated equally, not about whether they should be. The three views share an assumption of moral equality between persons, but differ in their interpretations of it. They agree that the moral claims of all persons are, at a sufficiently abstract level, the same, but disagree over what these are.[4]

The defender of rights locates them in the freedom to do certain things without direct interference by others. The utilitarian locates them in the requirement that each person's interests be fully counted as a component in the calculation of utility used to decide which states of affairs are best and which acts or policies are right. The egalitarian finds them in an equal claim to actual or possible advantages. The issue remains acute even though most social theories do not fall squarely into one of these categories, but give primacy to one interpretation of moral equality and secondary status to the others.

All three interpretations of moral equality attempt to give equal weight, in essential respects, to each person's point of view. This might even be described as the mark of an enlightened ethic, though some theories that do not share it still qualify as ethical. If the opposition of views about distributive equality can be regarded as a disagreement about the proper interpretation of this basic requirement of moral equality, that provides a common reference against which the opposing positions may be measured. It should be possible to compare the quality of their justifications, instead of simply registering their mutual incompatibility.

What it means to give equal weight to each person's point of view depends on what is morally essential to that point of view, what it is in each of us that must be given equal weight. It also depends on how the weights are combined. And these two aspects of the answer are interdependent. Let us consider each of the positions from this point of view.

IV

The moral equality of utilitarianism is a kind of majority rule: each person's interests count once, but some may be outweighed by others. It is not really a majority of *persons* that determines the result, but a majority of interests suitably weighted for intensity. Persons are equal in the sense that each of them is given a 'vote' weighted in proportion to the magnitude of his interests. Although this means that the interests of a minority can sometimes outweigh the interests of a majority, the basic idea is majoritarian because each individual is accorded the same (variable) weight and the outcome is determined by the largest total.

In the simplest version, all of a person's interests or preferences are counted, and given a relative weight depending on their weight for him. But various modifications have been suggested. One doubt voiced about utilitarianism is that it counts positively the satisfaction of evil desires (sadistic or bigoted ones, for example). Mill employed a distinction between higher and lower pleasures, and gave priority to the former. (Could there be a corresponding distinction for pains?) Recently, Thomas Scanlon has argued that any distributive principle, utilitarian or egalitarian, must use some objective standard of interest, need, or urgency distinct from mere subjective preference to avoid unacceptable consequences. Even if the aim is to maximize the total of some quantity of benefit over all persons, it is necessary to pick a single measure of that quantity that applies fairly to everyone, and pure preference is not a good measure. "The fact that someone would be willing to forgo a decent diet in order to build a monument to his god does not mean that his claim on others for aid in his project has the same strength as a claim for aid in obtaining enough to eat (even assuming that the sacrifices required of others would be the same)."[5]

Even if a standard of objectivity is introduced, the range of morally relevant interests can still be quite broad, and it will vary from person to person. The individual as moral claimant continues to be more or less the whole person. On the other hand, anyone's claims can in principle be completely outvoted by the claims of others. In the final outcome a given individual's claims may be met hardly at all, though they have been counted in the majoritarian calculation used to arrive at that outcome.

Utilitarianism takes a generous view of individual moral claims and combines them aggregatively. It applies the resulting values to the assessment of overall results or states of affairs, and derives the assessment of actions from this as a secondary result. One is to do what will tend to promote the results that appear best from a point of view that combines all individual interests. The moral equality of utilitarianism consists in letting each person's interests contribute in the same way to determining what in sum would be best overall.

V

Rights are very different, both in structure and in content. They are not majoritarian or in any other way aggregative, and they do not provide an assessment of overall results. Instead, they determine the acceptability of actions directly. The moral equality of persons under this conception is their equal claim against each other not to be interfered with in specified ways. Each person must be treated equally in certain definite respects by each other person.

In a sense, these claims are not combined at all. They must be respected individually. What anyone may do is restricted to what will not violate the rights of anyone else. Since the designated aspect of each person's point of view sets this limit *by itself*, the condition is a kind of unanimity requirement.

Rights may be absolute, or it may be permissible to override them when a significant threshold is reached in the level of harm that can be prevented by doing so. But however they are defined, they must be respected in every case where they apply. They give every person a limited veto over how others may treat him.

This kind of unanimity condition is possible only for rights that limit what one person may do to another. There cannot in this sense be rights to *have* certain things — a right to medical care, or to a decent standard of living, or even a right to life. The language of rights is sometimes used in this way, to indicate the special importance of certain human goods. But I believe that the true moral basis of such claims is the priority of more urgent over less urgent individual needs, and this is essentially an egalitarian principle. To preserve distinctions I shall use the term 'right' only for a claim that gives its possessor a kind of veto power, so that if everyone has the right, that places a condition of unanimous acceptability, in this respect, on action. There can be no literal right to life in that sense, because there are situations in which any possible course of action will lead to the death of someone or other; and if everyone had a right to stay alive, nothing would be permissible in those situations.[6]

Rights of the kind I am considering escape this problem because they are agent-centered. A right not to be killed, for example, is not a right that everyone do what is required to insure that you are not killed. It is merely a right not to be killed, and it is correlated with other people's duty not to *kill* you.

Such an ethic does not enjoin that violations of rights be minimized. That would be to count them merely as particularly grave evils in the assessment of outcomes. Instead, rights limit action directly: each person is forbidden to violate directly the rights of others even if he could reduce the overall number of violations of rights indirectly by violating a few himself. It is hard to account for such agent-centered restrictions. One thing to say about them by way of interpretation is that they represent a higher degree of moral inviolability than principles requiring us to do whatever will minimize the violation of rights. For if that were the principle, then violation of the right would not always be wrong. The moral claim of a right not to be murdered even to prevent several other murders is stronger than the claim which merely counts murder as a great evil, for the former prohibits murders that the latter would permit. That is true even though the latter might enable one to prevent more murders than the former. But this does not go very far toward explaining agent-centered rights. A serious account would have to consider not only the protected interests but the relation between the agent and the person he is constrained not to treat in certain ways, even to achieve very desirable ends. The concern with what one is doing to whom, as opposed to the concern with what happens, is an important primary source of ethics that is poorly understood.

Having noted that rights yield an assessment in the first instance of actions rather than of outcomes, we can see that they also define individual moral claims more narrowly than does utilitarianism, and combine them differently. The utilitarian constructs an impersonal point of view in which those of all individuals are combined to give judgments of utility, which in turn are to guide everyone's actions. For a defender of rights, the respects in which each person is inviolable present a direct and *independent* limit to what any other person may do to him. There is no single combination of viewpoints which yields a common goal for everyone, but each of us must limit our actions to a range that is not unacceptable to anyone else in certain respects. Typically, the range of what may be done because it violates no rights is rather large.

For this reason the morality of rights tends to be a limited, even a minimal morality. It leaves a great deal of human life ungoverned by moral restrictions or requirements. That is why, if unsupplemented, it leads naturally to political theories of limited government, and, in the extreme, to the libertarian theory of the minimal state. The justification of broad government action to promote all aspects of the general welfare requires a much richer set of moral requirements.[7]

This type of limited morality also has the consequence that the numbers of people on either side of an issue do not count. In a perfectly unanimous morality the only number that counts is one. If moral acceptability is acceptability in a certain respect from each person's point of view, then even if in other respects one course of action is clearly more acceptable to most but not all of the people involved, no further moral requirement follows.[8]

The moral equality of rights, then, consists in assigning to each person the same domain of interests with respect to which he may not be directly interfered with by anyone else.

VI

Oddly enough, egalitarianism is based on a more obscure conception of moral equality than either of the less egalitarian theories. It employs a much richer version of each person's point of view than does a theory of rights. In that respect it is closer to

utilitarianism. It also resembles utilitarianism formally, in being applied first to the assessment of outcomes rather than of actions. But it does not combine all points of view by a majoritarian method. Instead, it establishes an order of priority among needs and gives preference to the most urgent, regardless of numbers. In that respect it is closer to rights theory.

What conception of moral equality is at work here, i.e. what equal moral claim is being granted to everyone and how are these claims combined? Each individual's claim has a complex form: it includes more or less all his needs and interests, but in an order of relative urgency or importance. This determines both which of them are to be satisfied first and whether they are to be satisfied before or after the interests of others. Something close to unanimity is being invoked. An arrangement must be acceptable first from the point of view of everyone's most basic claims, then from the point of view of everyone's next most basic claims, etc. By contrast with a rights theory, the individual claims are not limited to specific restrictions on how one may be treated. They concern whatever may happen to a person, and in appropriate order of priority they include much more than protection from the most basic misfortunes. This means that the order of priority will not settle all conflicts, since there can be conflicts of interest even at the most basic level, and therefore unanimity cannot be achieved. Instead, one must be content to get as close to it as possible.

One problem in the development of this idea is the definition of the order of priority: whether a single, objective standard of urgency should be used in construing the claims of each person, or whether his interests should be ranked at his own estimation of their relative importance. In addition to the question of objectivity, there is a question of scale. Because moral equality is equality between persons, the individual interests to be ranked cannot be momentary preferences, desires, and experiences. They must be aspects of the individual's life taken as a whole: health, nourishment, freedom, work, education, self-respect, affection, pleasure. The determination of egalitarian social policy requires some choice among them, and the results will be very different depending on whether material advantages or individual liberty and self-realization are given priority.

But let me leave these questions aside. The essential feature of an egalitarian priority system is that it counts improvements to the welfare of the worse off as more urgent than improvements to the welfare of the better off. These other questions must be answered to decide who is worse off and who is better off, and how much, but what makes a system egalitarian is the priority it gives to the claims of those whose overall life prospects put them at the bottom, irrespective of numbers of overall utility. Each individual with a more urgent claim has priority, in the simplest version of such a view, over each individual with a less urgent claim. The moral equality of egalitarianism consists in taking into account the interests of each person, subject to the same system of priorities of urgency, in determining what would be best overall.

VII

It is obvious that the three conceptions of moral equality with which we are dealing are extremely different. They define each person's equal moral claim differently, and they derive practical conclusions from sets of such claims in different ways. They seem to be radically opposed to one another, and it is very difficult to see how one might decide among them.

My own view is that we do not have to. A plausible social morality will show the influence of them all. This will certainly not be conceded by utilitarians or believers in the dominance of rights. But to defend liberal egalitarianism it is not necessary to show that moral equality *cannot* be interpreted in the ways that yield rights or utilitarianism. One has only to show that an egalitarian interpretation is also acceptable. The result then depends on how these disparate values combine.

Though my own view is somewhat different from that of Rawls, I shall begin by considering his arguments, in order to explain why another account seems to me necessary.[9] He gives two kinds of argument for his position. One is intuitive and belongs to the domain of ordinary moral reasoning. The other is theoretical and depends on the construction by which Rawls works out his version of the social contract and which he calls the Original Position. I shall begin with two prominent examples of the first kind of argument and then go on to a brief consideration of the theoretical construction.

One point Rawls makes repeatedly is that the natural and social contingencies that influence welfare—talent, early environment, class background—are not themselves deserved. So differences in benefit that derive from them are morally arbitrary.[10] They can be justified only if the alternative would leave the least fortunate even worse off. In that case everyone benefits from the inequalities, so the extra benefit to some is justified as a means to this. A less egalitarian principle of distribution, whether it is based on rights or on utility, allows social and natural contingencies to produce inequalities justified neither because everyone benefits nor because those who get more deserve more.

The other point is directed specifically against utilitarianism. Rawls maintains that utilitarianism applies to problems of social choice—problems in which the interests of many individuals are involved—a method of decision appropriate for one individual.[11] A single person may accept certain disadvantages in exchange for greater benefits. But no such compensation is possible when one person suffers the disadvantages and another gets the benefits.

So far as I can see, neither of these arguments is decisive. The first assumes that inequalities need justification, that there is a presumption against permitting them. Only that would imply that undeserved inequalities are morally arbitrary in an invidious sense, unless otherwise justified. If they were arbitrary only in the sense that there were no reasons for or against them, they would require no justification, and the aim of avoiding them could provide no reason to infringe on anyone's rights. In any case the utilitarian has a justification to offer for the inequalities that his system permits: that the sum of advantages is greater than it would be without the inequality. But even if an inequality were acceptable only if it benefited everyone, that would not have to imply anything as strong as the Difference Principle. More than one deviation from equality may benefit everyone to some extent, and it would require a specific egalitarian assumption to prefer the one that was most favorable to the worst off.

The second argument relies on a diagnosis of utilitarianism that has recently been challenged by Derek Parfit.[12] But even if the diagnosis is correct, it does not supply an argument for equality, for it does not say why this method of summation is not acceptable for the experiences of many individuals. It certainly cannot be justified simply by extension from the individual case, but it has enough *prima facie* appeal to require displacement by some better alternative. It merely says that more of what is good is better than less, and less of what is bad is better than more. Someone might accept this conclusion without having reached it by extending the principle of individual choice to the social case. There is no particular reason to think that the principle will be either the same or different in the two cases.

In Utilitarianism intrapersonal compensation has no special significance. It acquires significance only against the background of a refusal *in general* to accept the unrestricted summation of goods and evils — a background to which it provides the exception. This background must be independently justified. By itself, the possibility of intrapersonal compensation neither supports nor undermines egalitarian theories. It implies only that *if* an egalitarian theory is accepted, it should apply only across lives rather than within them. It is a reason for taking individual human lives, rather than individual experiences, as the units over which any distributive principle should operate. But it could serve this function for antiegalitarian as well as for egalitarian views. This is the reverse of Rawls's argument: no special distributive principle should be applied *within* human lives because that would be to extend to the individual the principle of choice appropriate for society. Provided that condition is met, intrapersonal compensation is neutral among distributive principles.

Next let me consider briefly Rawls's contractarian argument. Though he stresses that his theory is about the morality of social institutions, its general ideas about equality can I think be applied more widely. The Original Position, his version of the social contract, is a constructed unanimity condition which attributes to each person a schematic point of view that abstracts from the differences between people, but allows for the main categories of human interest. The individual is expected to choose principles for the assessment of social institutions on the assumption that he may be anyone, but without assuming that he has an equal chance of being anyone, or that his chance of being in a certain situation is proportional to the number of people in that situation.

The resulting choice brings out the priorities that are generally shared, and combines interests ranked by these priorities without regard to the numbers of people involved. The principles unanimously chosen on the basis of such priorities grant to each person the same claim to have his most urgent needs satisfied prior to the less urgent needs of anyone else. Priority is given to individuals who, taking their lives as a whole, have more urgent needs, rather than to the needs that more individuals have.

There has been much controversy over whether the rational choice under the conditions of uncertainty and ignorance that prevail in the Original Position would be what Rawls says it is, or even whether any choice could be rational under those conditions. But there is another question that is prior. Why does what it would be rational to agree to under those conditions determine what is right?

Let us focus this question more specifically on the features of the Original Position that are responsible for the egalitarian result. There are two of them. One is that the choice must be unanimous, and therefore everyone must be deprived of all information about his conception of the good or his position in society. The other is that the parties are not allowed to choose as if they had an equal chance of being anyone in the society, because in the absence of any information about probabilities it is not, according to Rawls, rational to assign some arbitrarily, using the Principle of Insufficient Reason. The Original Position is constructed by subtracting information without adding artificial substitutes. This results directly in the maximin strategy of choice, which leads to principles that favor the worst off in general and impose even more stringent equality in the basic liberties.

Suppose Rawls is right about what it would be rational to choose under those conditions. We must then ask why a unanimous choice under conditions of ignorance, without an assumption that one has an equal chance of being anyone in the society, correctly expresses the constraints of morality. Other constructions also have a claim to counting all persons as moral equals. What makes these conditions of unanimity under ignorance the right ones? They insure that numbers do not count[13] and urgency does, but that is the issue. A more fundamental type of argument is needed to settle it.

VIII

The main question is whether a kind of unanimity should enter into the combination of different points of view when evaluative judgments are being made about outcomes. This is an issue between egalitarian and utilitarian theories, both of which concern themselves with outcomes. Rights theories are opposed to both, because although they use a kind of unanimity condition, it is a condition on the acceptability of actions rather than of outcomes. In defending an interpretation of moral equality in terms of unanimity applied in the assessment of outcomes, I am therefore denying that either utilitarianism or rights theories, or both, represent the whole truth about ethics.

As I have said, acceptance of egalitarian values need not imply total exclusion of the others. Egalitarians may allow utility independent weight, and liberal egalitarians standardly acknowledge the importance of certain rights, which limit the means that may be used in pursuing equality and other ends.[14] I believe that rights exist and that this agent-centered aspect of morality is very important. The recognition of individual rights is a way of accepting a requirement of unanimous acceptability when weighing the claims of others in respect to what one may do. But a theory based exclusively on rights leaves out too much that is morally relevant, even if the interests it includes are among the most basic. A moral view that gives no weight to the value of overall outcomes cannot be correct.[15]

So let me return to the issue of unanimity in the assessment of outcomes. The essence of such a criterion is to try in a moral assessment to include each person's point of view separately, so as to achieve a result which is in a significant sense acceptable to each person involved or affected. Where there is conflict of interests, no result can be completely acceptable to everyone. But it is possible to assess each result from each point of view to try to find the one that is least unacceptable to the person to whom it is most unacceptable. This means that any other alternative will be more unacceptable to someone than this alternative is to anyone. The preferred alternative is in that sense the least unacceptable, considered from each person's point of view separately. A radically egalitarian policy of giving absolute priority to the worst off, regardless of numbers, would result from always choosing the least unacceptable alternative, in this sense.

This ideal of individual acceptability is in fundamental opposition to the aggregative ideal, which constructs a special moral point of view by combining those of individuals into a single conglomerate viewpoint distinct from all of them. That is done in

utilitarianism by adding them up. Both the separate and the conglomerate methods count everyone fully and equally. The difference between them is that the second moves beyond individual points of view to something more comprehensive than any of them, though based on them. The first stays closer to the points of view of the individuals considered.

It is this ideal of acceptability to each individual that underlies the appeal of equality. We can see how it operates even in a case involving small numbers. Suppose I have two children, one of which is normal and quite happy, and the other of which suffers from a painful handicap. Call them respectively the first child and the second child. I am about to change jobs. Suppose I must decide between moving to an expensive city where the second child can receive special medical treatment and schooling, but where the family's standard of living will be lower and the neighborhood will be unpleasant and dangerous for the first child — or else moving to a pleasant semirural suburb where the first child, who has a special interest in sports and nature, can have a free and agreeable life. This is a difficult choice on any view. To make it a test for the value of equality, I want to suppose that the case has the following feature: the gain to the first child of moving to the suburb is substantially greater than the gain to the second child of moving to the city. After all, the second child will also suffer from the family's reduced standard of living and the disagreeable environment. And the educational and therapeutic benefits will not make him happy but only less miserable. For the first child, on the other hand, the choice is between a happy life and a disagreeable one. Let me add as a feature of the case that there is no way to compensate either child significantly for its loss if the choice favoring the other child is made. The family's resources are stretched, and neither child has anything else to give up that could be converted into something of significant value to the other.

If one chose to move to the city, it would be an egalitarian decision. It is more urgent to benefit the second child, even though the benefit we can give him is less than the benefit we can give the first child. This urgency is not necessarily decisive. It may be outweighed by other considerations, for equality is not the only value. But it is a factor, and it depends on the worse off position of the second child. An improvement in his situation is more important than an equal or somewhat greater improvement in the situation of the first child.

Suppose a third child is added to the situation, another happy, healthy one, and I am faced with the same choice in allocation of indivisible goods. The greater urgency of benefiting the second child remains. I believe that this factor is essentially unchanged by the addition of the third child. It remains just as much more urgent to benefit the second child in this case as it was when there were only two children.[16]

The main point about a measure of urgency is that it is done by pairwise comparison of the situations of individuals. The simplest method would be to count *any* improvement in the situation of someone worse off as more urgent than any improvement in the situation of someone better off; but this is not especially plausible. It is more reasonable to accord greater urgency to large improvements somewhat higher in the scale than to very small improvements lower down. Such a modified principle could still be described as selecting the alternative that was least unacceptable from each point of view. This method can be extended to problems of social choice involving large numbers of people. So long as numbers do not count it remains a type of unanimity criterion, defined by a suitable measure of urgency. The problem of justifying equality then becomes the problem of justifying the pursuit of results that are acceptable to each person involved.

Before turning to a discussion of this problem, let me say why I think that even if it were solved, it would not provide the foundation for a correct egalitarian theory. It seems to me that no plausible theory can avoid the relevance of numbers completely. There may be some disparities of urgency so great that the priorities persist whatever numbers are involved. But if the choice is between preventing severe hardship for some who are very poor and deprived, and preventing less severe but still substantial hardship for those who are better off but still struggling for subsistence, then it is very difficult for me to believe that the numbers do not count, and that priority of urgency goes to the worse off however many more there are of the better off. It might be suggested that this is a case where equality is outweighed by utility. But if egalitarian urgency is itself sensitive to numbers in this way, it does not seem that any form of unanimity criterion could explain the foundation of the view. Nor does any alternative foundation suggest itself.

IX

For a view of the more uncompromising type, similar in structure to that of Rawls, we need an explanation of why individual pairwise comparison to find the individually least unacceptable alternative is a good way to adjudicate among competing interests. What would it take to justify this method of combining individual claims? I think the only way to answer this question is to ask another: what is the source of morality? How do the interests of others secure a hold on us in moral reasoning, and does this imply a way in which they must be considered in combination?

I have a view about the source of other-regarding moral reasons that suggests an answer to this question. The view is not very different from the one I defended in *The Possibility of Altruism*,[17] and I will only sketch it here. I believe that the general form of moral reasoning is to put yourself in the other people's shoes. This leads to acceptance of an impersonal concern for them corresponding to the impersonal concern for yourself that is needed to avoid a radical incongruity between your attitudes from the personal and impersonal standpoints, i.e. from inside and outside your life. Some considerable disparity remains, because the personal concerns remain in relation to yourself and your life: they are not to be replaced or absorbed by the impersonal ones that correspond to them.[18] (One is also typically concerned in a personal way for the interests of certain others to whom one is close.) But we derive moral reasons by forming in addition a parallel impersonal concern corresponding to the interests of all other individuals. It will be as strong or as weak, as comprehensive or as restricted, as the impersonal concern we are constrained by the pressures of congruency to feel about ourselves. In a sense, the requirement is that you love your neighbor as yourself: but only as much as you love yourself when you look at yourself from outside, with fair detachment.

The process applies separately to each individual and yields a set of concerns corresponding to the individual lives. There may be disparities between a person's objective interests and his own subjectively perceived interests or wishes, but apart from this, his claims enter the impersonal domain of reasons unchanged, as those of an individual. They do not come detached from him and go into a big hopper with all the others. The impersonal concern of ethics is an impersonal concern for oneself and all others as individuals. It derives from the necessary generalization of an impersonal concern for one's own life and interests, and the generalization preserves the individualistic form of the original.

For this reason the impersonal concern that results is fragmented: it includes a separate concern for each person, and it is realized by looking at the world from each person's point of view separately and individually, rather than by looking at the world from a single comprehensive point of view. Imaginatively one must split into all the people in the world, rather than turn oneself into a conglomeration of them.

This, it seems to me, makes pairwise comparison the natural way to deal with conflicting claims. There may be cases where the policy chosen as a result will seek to maximize satisfaction rather than equalizing it, but this will only be where all individuals have an equal chance of benefiting, or at least not a conspicuously unequal chance.[19] At the most basic level, the way to choose from many separate viewpoints simultaneously is to maintain them intact and give priority to the most urgent individual claims.

As I have said equality is only one value and this is only one method of choice. We can understand a radically egalitarian system just as we can understand a radical system of rights, but I assume neither is correct. Utility is a legitimate value, and the majoritarian or conglomerate viewpoint on which it depends is an allowable way of considering the conflicting interests of numbers of different people at once. Still, the explanation of egalitarian values in terms of separate assessment from each point of view is a step toward understanding; and if it does not imply that these values are absolute, that is not necessarily a drawback.

Endnotes

[1] This is obviously not true of things in which interest varies greatly, like recordings of bird songs, or horror comic books.

[2] John Rawls, *A Theory of Justice* (Cambridge, Mass.: Harvard University Press, 1971).

[3] The argument would be that improvements in the well-being of the lower class as a result of material productivity spurred by wage differentials are only apparent: damage to their self-respect outweighs the material gains. And even in-

equalities that genuinely benefit the worst off may destroy nondistributive values like community or fraternity. See Christopher Ake, 'Justice as Equality', *Philosophy & Public Affairs*, V, no. 1 (Fall 1975), 69–89, esp. 76–7.

[4] This way of looking at the problem was suggested to me by a proposal of Rawls (personal communication, January 31, 1976): Suppose we distinguish between the equal treatment of persons and their (equal) right to be treated as equals. (Here persons are *moral* persons.) The *latter* is more basic: Suppose the Original Position represents the latter *re* moral persons when they agree on principles and suppose they *would* agree on *some* from of equal treatment. What more is needed?

[5] T.M. Scanlon, 'Preference and Urgency', *Journal of Philosophy* LXXII, no. 19 (Nov. 6, 1975), 659-60.

[6] There may be circumstances in which nothing is permissible—true moral dilemmas in which every possible course of action is wrong. But these arise only from the clash of distinct moral principles and not from the application of one principle. See chapter 5, above.

[7] The issue over the *extent* of morality is one of the deepest in ethical theory. Many have felt it an objection to utilitarianism that it makes ethics swallow up everything, leaving only one optimal choice, or a small set of equally optimal alternatives, permissible for any person at any time. Those who offer this objection differ over the size and shape of the range of choices that should be left to individual inclination after the ethical boundaries have been drawn.

[8] John Taurek has recently defended essentially this position in his paper, 'Should the Numbers Count?' *Philosophy & Public Affairs* VI, no. 4 (Summer 1977), 293–316. He holds that given a choice between saving one life and saving five others, one is not required to save the five: one may save either the one or the five. I believe that he holds this because there is at least one point of view from which saving the five is not the better choice. Taurek does believe that some moral requirements derive from special rights and obligations, but in cases like this, where there are fundamental conflicts of interest, it is impossible to define a condition of universal acceptability, and the choice is therefore not governed by any moral requirement.

[9] Some of my comments are developed in 'Rawls on Justice', *Philosophical Review* LXXXIII (1973), 220–33.

[10] Rawls, *Theory of Justice*, pp. 74, 104.

[11] Rawls, *Theory of Justice*, pp. 27, 187.

[12] 'Later Selves and Moral Principles', in *Philosophy & Personal Relations*, ed. A. Montefiore (London: Routledge and Kegan Paul, 1973). Parfit suggests that utilitarianism could express the dissolution of temporally extended individuals into experiential sequences rather than the conflation of separate individuals into a mass person.

[13] Since the Difference Principle is applied not to individuals but to social classes, conflicts of interest within the worst off or any other groups are absorbed in a set of average expectations. This means that the numbers count in a sense *within* a social class, in determining which policy benefits it most on average. But numbers do not count in determining priority among classes in the urgency of their claims. That is why the problems of this conception of social justice are similar to those of a more individually tailored egalitarianism.

14 Such a view is defended by Ronald Dworkin in *Taking Rights Seriously* (Cambridge, Mass.: Harvard University Press, 1977).

15 I have said more about this in 'Libertarianism Without Foundations,' *Yale Law Journal* LXXXV, (1975), a review of Robert Nozick, *Anarchy, State, and Utopia* (New York: Basic Books, 1974).

16 Note that these thoughts do not *depend* on any idea of personal identity over time, though they can *employ* such an idea. All that is needed to evoke them is a distinction between persons at a time. The impulse to distributive equality arises so long as we can distinguish between two experiences being had by two persons and their being had by one person. The criteria of personal identity over time merely determine the size of the units over which a distributive principle operates. That, briefly, is what I think is wrong with Parfit's account of the relation between distributive justice and personal identity.

17 Oxford: Clarendon Press, 1970.

18 In this respect my present view differs from the one in *The Possibility of Altruism.*

19 I leave aside the question when the equality of chances can be counted as real enough to supersede the inequality of actual outcomes. Perhaps that applies only to certain kinds of outcomes, and certain ways of determining chances.

Suggestions for Further Reading

Bedau, Hugo, ed. *Justice and Equality*. Prentice Hall, 1971.

Benn, Stanley. "Justice," in *The Encyclopedia of Philosophy*. Macmillan, 1967.

Daniels, Norman, ed. *Reading Rawls*. Basic Books, 1975.

Nagel, Thomas. *Equality and Partiality*. Oxford University Press, 1991.

Nielsen, Kai. "Radical Egalitarian Justice: Justice as Equality," *Social Theory and Practice*, vol. 5, no. 2, 1979.

Nozick, Robert. *Anarchy, State, and Utopia*. Basic Books, 1974.

Okin, Susan Moller. *Justice, Gender, and the Family*. Basic Books, 1989.

Rawls, John. *A Theory of Justice*. Harvard University Press, 1971.

Rawls, John. *Political Liberalism*. Columbia University Press, 1993.

Reiman, Jeffrey. *Justice and Modern Moral Philosophy*. Yale University Press, 1990.

Rescher, Nicholas. *Distributive Justice*. Bobbs-Merrill, 1966.

Sandel, Michael. *Liberalism and the Limits of Justice*. Cambridge University Press, 1988.

Sterba, James. *The Demands of Justice*. University of Notre Dame Press, 1980.

Sterba, James, ed. *Justice: Alternative Political Perspectives*. Wadsworth, 1980.

Sterba, James. *How to Make People Just*. Rowman & Littlefield, 1988.

Veatch, Robert M. *The Foundations of Justice*. Oxford University Press, 1986.

Walzer, Michael. *Spheres of Justice*. Oxford University Press, 1983.

Part XIII
Rights

We hold these truths to be self-evident, that all men are created equal, that they are endowed by their Creator with certain inalienable Rights, that among these are Life, Liberty, and the Pursuit of Happiness.

Declaration of Independence of the United States of America, July 4, 1776

Natural rights is simple nonsense: natural and imprescriptible rights, rhetorical nonsense, — nonsense upon stilts. . . . Right is a child of law; from real laws come real rights, but from imaginary law, from "laws of nature," come imaginary rights. . . . A natural right is a son that never had a father.

JEREMY BENTHAM
"Anarchical Fallacies," *The Works of Jeremy Bentham,* ed. John Bowring, vol. 2, 1843

Human rights have been the centerpiece of political theory for over two centuries. They were the justification for the American and French Revolutions in the eighteenth century and for a succession of revolutions for political independence in the nineteenth and twentieth centuries, as well as the motivation for the civil rights movement in the 1960s and the women's movement in the 1970s.

Natural rights are said to be the moral basis of positive law and the grounds for welfare rights and foreign aid, but the exact set of such universal rights varies. The United Nations Declaration on Human Rights includes free education and paid holidays. Other groups extend rights to animals, to corporations, and to forests. Nevertheless, almost all rights systems grant human beings the rights of life, liberty, property, and the pursuit of happiness.

Rights are important to our lives. We are ready to defend them, to demand their recognition and enforcement, and to complain of injustice when they are not complied with. We use them as vital premises in arguments that proscribe courses of action (for example, "Please stop smoking in this public place, for we non-smokers have a right to clean air"). Eventually, when we receive no redress for violations of our rights, we even consider civil disobedience.

It is because of their importance that we need to ask: What precisely are rights? Where do rights come from? And are there any natural rights, rights that do not depend on social contract, prior moral duties, utilitarian outcomes, or ideals?

Although there is a great deal of variation in defining 'rights' in the literature, for our purposes we can say that a right is a claim against others that at the same time includes a liberty on one's own behalf.[1] J. L. Mackie captures this combination when he writes, "A right, in the most important sense, is a conjunction of a freedom and a claim-right. That is, if someone, A, has the moral right to do X, not only is he entitled to do X if he chooses — he is not morally required not to do X — but he is also protected in his doing of X — others are morally required not to interfere or prevent him."[2] Rights are typically relational in that we have them against other people: If I have a right against you regarding X, you have a duty to me regarding X. For example, if you have promised to pay me $10 for cutting your lawn and I have done so I have a right to that $10 and you have a duty to pay up.

Rights give us special advantage. If you have a right, then others require special justification for overriding or limiting your right; and conversely, if you have a right, you have a justification for limiting the freedom of others in regard to exercising that right.

Next we should distinguish among the basic types of rights that we will encounter in this part of our work:

1. Natural rights: those rights, if any, that humans (or other beings) have simply by nature of what they are. According to the Declaration of Independence, God bestows these rights upon us.

2. Human rights: this is an ambiguous term. Sometimes it means 'natural rights,' at other times it means rights that humans have, and at still other times it means moral rights.

3. Moral rights: those rights that are justified by a given moral system. They may be derivative of duties or ideals or utilitarian outcomes.

4. Positive rights: those rights that society affords its members, including *legal rights,* such as the right of a woman to have an abortion or the right to vote.

5. Prima facie rights: presumptive rights that may not necessarily be an *actual right* in a given situation. My right to hear loud music may be overridden by your right to peace and quiet.[3]

6. Absolute rights: rights that cannot be overridden. For example, for those who hold that justice is an absolute right, my right to fair treatment may not be overridden by utilitarian considerations.

Many take natural rights for granted. In his book, *Taking Rights Seriously,* even so capable a philosopher as Ronald Dworkin simply assumes that we have rights without argument:

> Some philosophers, of course, reject the idea that citizens have rights apart from what the law happens to give them. Bentham thought that the idea of moral rights was "nonsense on stilts." But that view has never been part of our orthodox political theory, and politicians of both parties appeal to the rights of the people to justify a great part of what they want to do. I shall not be concerned, in this essay, to defend the thesis that citizens have moral rights against their governments. (*Taking Rights Seriously,* Harvard University Press, 1977, p. 184)

This attitude seems philosophically unsatisfying. We want to know what the nature of rights is, whether we have any human rights, and what they are. We want, as philosophical beings, to have a justification for our rights claims. Consider, for instance, two claims: (1) "I have a right to smoke wherever I please" and (2) "I have a right to be treated justly." What distinguishes (2) from (1)? Why do at least most of us accept (2), but not (1), as a valid right? Are all rights simply legal rights? Or are rights simply relative to cultural tastes? Consider Arthur Danto's view that they are simply what our peers will let us get away with:

> In the afterwash of 1968, I found myself a member of a group charged with working out disciplinary procedures for acts against my university. It was an exemplary group from the perspective of representation so urgent at the time: administrators, tenured and nontenured faculty, graduate and undergraduate students, men and women, whites and blacks. We all wondered, nevertheless, what right we had to do what was asked of us, and a good bit of time went into expressing our insecurities. Finally, a man from the law school said, with the tried patience of someone required to explain what should be plain as day and in a tone of voice I can still hear: "This is the way it is with rights. You want 'em, so you say you got 'em, and if nobody says you don't then you do." In the end he was right. We worked a code out which nobody liked, but in debating it the community acknowledged the rights. ("Constructing an Epistemology of Human Rights: A Pseudo Problem?" in *Human Rights,* ed. E. Paul, F. Miller, and J. Paul. Blackwell, 1984, p. 30)

But apply this to Gangster Gus, who extorts "protection" money from all the local businesses, claiming that he has a right to do so. When challenged, he quotes Danto: "This is the way it is with rights. You want 'em, so you say you got 'em, and if nobody says you don't then you do." He might just as well have said, "Might makes right." We should be able to do better than this or else drop rights language altogether.

We must first consider what is meant by 'natural rights' and by what is often used as its synonym, 'human rights.' By a 'natural right' we mean a right that is ours simply by the nature of things, independent of any other reason or moral duty or ideal. This notion, which may be traced back to the Stoics and was explicit in the late Middle Ages, became prominent in the seventeenth century with the works of Hugo Grotius (1583–1645) and John Locke (1632–1704). For Locke, the author of our first reading, humans possess rights by nature (namely, life, liberty, and property) that society must recognize if it is to be legitimate. They are bestowed on us by God. Because these rights are a gift of God, they are 'inalienable' or 'imprescriptible'; that is, we do not give them to people, nor can we take them away or even give our own rights away (for example, we cannot give away our right to freedom by selling ourselves into slavery). They become the proper basis of all specific rights, such as the right to vote, to be protected by the Law, to sell property, to work, and to be educated. Let us call this position the natural law theory of rights. Here is a contemporary expression of this theory:

> The human person possesses rights because of the very fact that it is a person, a whole, master of itself and of its acts, and which consequently is not merely a means to an end, but an end, an end which must be treated as such. The dignity of the human person? The expression means nothing if it does not signify that by virtue of natural law, the human person has the right to be respected, is the subject of rights, possesses rights. These are things which are owed to man because of the very fact that he is man. (Jacques Maritain, *The Rights of Man,* London, Charles Scribner's, 1944, p. 37)

Most philosophers who deny natural rights do not deny that we have rights. They simply deny that they are in the nature of things, as the natural law theorists affirm. These antinaturalists state that all rights are derivable from something else, such as law, moral duty, utilitarian outcomes, or ideals. Let us look at each of these possibilities:

1. Some philosophers, including the legal positivist John Austin, Jeremy Bentham, and, in our readings, Alasdair MacIntyre argue that all rights (as well as their correlative duties) are institutional in the way that legal rights are. We referred to these earlier as *positive rights,* those actually recognized by organized society. As MacIntyre writes:

> [C]laims to the possession of rights . . . presuppose the existence of a socially established set of rules. Such sets of rules only come into existence at particular historical periods under particular social circumstances. They are in no way universal features of the human condition . . .
> [T]he existence of particular types of social institution or practice is a necessary condition for the notion of a claim to the possession of a right being an intelligible type of human performance.

2. Duty-based (deontological) ethical theories, such as those of Kant, Ross, or Frankena, hold that rights are simply entailments of moral obligations. Since I have a duty to pay you back the money I borrowed, you have a corresponding right to the money. However, some duties do not generate rights. For example, I have a duty to share my abundance with the poor and needy, but no one poor and needy person has a right to it. If you are poor, you cannot properly demand $50 from me, for there may be others equally poor to whom I choose to give the money. It is duty that is primary to the moral system, and rights are but correlates to duties. To have a right means simply that one is the *beneficiary* of someone else's duty. For this reason, it is misleading to speak of human rights as a separate subject apart from a duty-based moral system.

3. Goal-based theories, such as the utilitarianism of John Stuart Mill, argue that rights are derivable from our understanding of utility. We will all be happier if we have certain of our interests protected, especially our interest in noninterference.

4. A variation on this theme is the view of Kurt Baier and Richard Brandt that rights are those claims and liberties that would be included in an ideal moral system, which need not be a utilitarian one. They are moral features that should be assigned to us even though they may be missing. Hence, we may assert that blacks had a *right* to freedom from slavery before the Emancipation Proclamation, even though the majority of people in the southern United States, as well as the law, failed to recognize that right. It is in this light that we may interpret the rights enumerated in the United Nations Universal Declaration of Human Rights, such as the right to free education and paid holidays. These are ideals that we should strive to realize.

To philosophers who hold to natural rights, these antinaturalist views seem like a profanation of rights, an undermining of rights' power and presence. In order to counter this tendency to treat 'rights' as second-class citizens in our moral repertoire, Joel Feinberg in our second reading uses a thought experiment in which he asks you to imagine a place, Nowheresville, that is quite nice but lacks rights. Having all the other benefits a good society could offer except this one thing, Feinberg argues, leaves Nowheresville in bad shape, for rights are logically connected with claims. In Nowheresville people cannot make moral claims, and in this way they are deprived of a certain self-respect and dignity. Rights are valid moral claims that give us inherent dignity. "To think of oneself as the holder of rights is not to be unduly but properly proud, to have that minimal self-respect that is necessary to be worthy of the love and esteem of others. To respect a person then, or to think of him as possessed of human dignity, simply *is* to think of him as a potential maker of claims." As such, rights are necessary to an adequate moral theory.

Our third reading is Ronald Dworkin's "Taking Rights Seriously," in which he argues that collective goals of the State (such as prosperity, administrative convenience, and political efficiency) are not a sufficient justification for denying individuals their rights. Rights are like trump cards that prevail over all other political considerations. This article is especially important for its discussion of the relation of rights to civil disobedience.

In our fourth reading, Alan Gewirth goes further than Feinberg and Dworkin, arguing that rights are the basis of morality and can be proven rationally. After clearly defining human rights ("rights which all persons equally have simply insofar as they are human") and critically surveying previous attempts to justify the belief in the existence of these rights, Gewirth presents an argument that claims to demonstrate that such rights exist. Starting from the premise that "I do X for end or purpose E," which entails "E is good," he constructs an argument showing that on the basis of "generic features" of action, freedom, and purposiveness, we can conclude that there are universal human rights.

Gewirth's argument is succinct and precise. It constitutes a challenge to antinatural rights philosophers.

In our final reading, Alasdair MacIntyre criticizes rights-based moral theories — much in the spirit of Bentham — as nonsense on stilts. Natural rights no more exist than do unicorns and witches. He then analyzes Gewirth's rationalistic version of a defense of human rights and argues that Gewirth has committed a logical mistake of deriving a right from a need.

In order to provide a concrete example of the way rights-language is used in our world, I have included a copy of the United Nations Universal Declaration of Human Rights at the end of this Part of our book.

Endnotes

[1] For a more comprehensive treatment of the nature of a right, see Carl Wellman, *A Theory of Rights* (Rowman and Allanheld, 1985), Chapter 2, and James Nickel, *Making Sense of Human Rights* (University of California Press, 1987), Chapter 2. Wellman develops Wesley Hohfeld's fourfold meaning of a 'right' in terms of claim, liberty, power, and immunity.

[2] J. L. Mackie, "Can There Be a Right-Based Moral Theory?" *Midwest Studies in Philosophy* 3 (1978).

[3] We need to distinguish a "prima facie right" from some act being "prima facie the right thing to do." A person may have a prima facie right to be a miser, but it may not be the morally right thing to do.

XIII.1 *Natural Rights*

JOHN LOCKE

John Locke (1632–1704) was a famous English philosopher and physician. His *Two Treatises,* from which this selection is taken, was an important factor in the development of parliamentary government in England and in the struggle for independence in the United States. Locke's ideas are reflected in the Declaration of Independence. All humans, being created by God, possess equal natural rights (that is, in the state of nature they possess life, liberty, and property) that society must recognize if it is to be legitimate. These natural rights are bestowed on us by God. Because these rights are a gift of God, they are 'inalienable' or 'imprescribable,' that is, we do not give them to people, nor can we take them away or even give our own rights away (for example, we cannot give away our right to freedom by selling ourselves into slavery). They become the proper basis of all specific rights.

Chapter II
Of the State of Nature

4. To understand political power aright, and derive it from its original, we must consider what state all men are naturally in, and that is a state of perfect freedom to order their actions and dispose of their possessions and persons as they think fit, within the bounds of the law of nature, without asking leave, or depending upon the will of any other man.

A state also of equality, wherein all the power and jurisdiction is reciprocal, no one having more than another; there being nothing more evident than that creatures of the same species and rank, promiscuously born to all the same advantages of nature, and the use of the same faculties, should also be equal one amongst another without subordination or subjection, unless the Lord and Master of them all should by any manifest declaration of His will set one above another, and confer on him by an evident and clear appointment an undoubted right to dominion and sovereignty.

5. This equality of men by nature the judicious Hooker looks upon as so evident in itself and be- yond all question, that he makes it the foundation of that obligation to mutual love amongst men on which he builds the duties they owe one another, and from whence he derives the great maxims of justice and charity. His words are: —

> The like natural inducement hath brought men to know that it is no less their duty to love others than themselves; for seeing those things which are equal must needs all have one measure, if I cannot but wish to receive good, even as much at every man's hands as any man can wish unto his own soul, how should I look to have any part of my desire herein satisfied, unless myself be careful to satisfy the like desire, which is undoubtedly in other men weak, being of one and the same nature? To have anything offered them repug- nant to this desire, must needs in all respects grieve them as much as me, so that, if I do harm, I must look to suffer, there being no reason that others should show greater mea- sures of love to me than they have by me showed unto them. My desire, therefore, to be loved of my equals in nature as much as possible may be, imposeth upon me a natural duty of bearing to themward fully the like affection; from which relation of equality be- tween ourselves and them that are as our-

From *Two Treatises,* 1690.

selves, what several rules and canons natural reason hath drawn for direction of life no man is ignorant. (Eccl. Pol., lib. i)

6. But though this be a state of liberty, yet it is not a state of license; though man in that state have an uncontrollable liberty to dispose of his person or possessions, yet he has not liberty to destroy himself, or so much as any creature in his possession, but where some nobler use than its bare preservation calls for it. The state of nature has a law of nature to govern it, which obliges everyone; and reason, which is that law, teaches all mankind who will but consult it, that, being all equal and independent, no one ought to harm another in his life, health, liberty, or possessions. For men being all the workmanship of one omnipotent and infinitely wise Maker — all the servants of one sovereign Master, sent into the world by His order, and about His business — they are His property, whose workmanship they are, made to last during His, not one another's pleasure; and being furnished with like faculties, sharing all in one community of nature, there cannot be supposed any such subordination among us, that may authorize us to destroy one another, as if we were made for one another's uses, as the inferior ranks of creatures are for ours. Everyone, as he is bound to preserve himself, and not to quit his station willfully, so, by the like reason, when his own preservation comes not in competition, ought he, as much as he can, to preserve the rest of mankind, and not, unless it be to do justice on an offender, take away or impair the life, or what tends to the preservation of the life, the liberty, health, limb, or goods of another.

7. And that all men be restrained from invading others' rights, and from doing hurt to one another, and the law of nature be observed, which willeth the peace and preservation of all mankind, the execution of the law of nature is in that state put into every man's hand, whereby everyone has a right to punish the transgressors of that law to such a degree as may hinder its violation. For the law of nature would, as all other laws that concern men in this world, be in vain if there were nobody that, in the state of nature, had a power to execute that law, and thereby preserve the innocent and restrain offenders. And if anyone in the state of nature may punish another for any evil he has done, everyone may do so. For in that state of perfect equality, where naturally there is no superiority or jurisdiction of one over another, what any may do in prosecution of that law, everyone must needs have a right to do.

8. And thus in the state of nature one man comes by a power over another; but yet no absolute or arbitrary power, to use a criminal, when he has got him in his hands, according to the passionate heats or boundless extravagance of his own will; but only to retribute to him so far as calm reason and conscience dictate what is proportionate to his transgression, which is so much as may serve for reparation and restraint. For these two are the only reasons why one man may lawfully do harm to another, which is that we call punishment. In transgressing the law of nature, the offender declares himself to live by another rule than that of common reason and equity, which is that measure God has set to the actions of men, for their mutual security; and so he becomes dangerous to mankind, the tie which is to secure them from injury and violence being sighted and broken by him. Which, being a trespass against the whole species, and the peace and safety of it, provided for by the law of nature, every man upon this score, by the right he hath to preserve mankind in general, may restrain, or, where it is necessary, destroy things noxious to them, and so may bring such evil on anyone who hath transgressed that law, as may make him repent the doing of it, and thereby deter him, and by his example others, from doing the like mischief. And in this case, and upon this ground, every man hath a right to punish the offender, and be executioner of the law of nature.

9. I doubt not but this will seem a very strange doctrine to some men: but before they condemn it, I desire them to resolve me by what right any prince or state can put to death or punish an alien, for any crime he commits in their country. 'Tis certain their laws, by virtue of any sanction they receive from the promulgated will of the legislative, reach not a stranger: they speak not to him, nor, if they did, is he bound to hearken them. The legislative authority, by which they are in force over the subjects of that commonwealth, hath no power over him. Those who have the supreme power of making laws in England, France, or Holland, are to an Indian but like the rest of the world — men without authority. And, therefore, if by the law of nature every man hath not a power to punish offenses against it, as he

soberly judges the case to require, I see not how the magistrates of any community can punish an alien of another country; since in reference to him they can have no more power than what every man naturally may have over another.

10. Besides the crime which consists in violating the law, and varying from the right rule of reason, whereby a man so far becomes degenerate, and declares himself to quit the principles of human nature, and to be a noxious creature, there is commonly injury done, and some person or other, some other man receives damage by his transgression, in which case he who hath received any damage, has, besides the right of punishment common to him with other men, a particular right to seek reparation from him that has done it. And any other person who finds it just, may also join with him that is injured, and assist him in recovering from the offender so much as many make satisfaction for the harm he has suffered.

11. From these two distinct rights — the one of punishing the crime for restraint and preventing the like offense, which right of punishing is in everybody; the other of taking reparation, which belongs only to the injured party — comes it to pass that the magistrate, who by being magistrate hath the common right of punishing put into his hands, can often, where the public good demands not the execution of the law, remit the punishment of criminal offenses by his own authority, but yet cannot remit the satisfaction due to any private man for the damage he has received. That he who has suffered the damage has a right to demand in his own name, and he alone can remit. The damnified person has this power of appropriating to himself the goods or service of the offender, by right of self-preservation, as every man has a power to punish the crime, to prevent its being committed again, by the right he has of preserving all mankind, and doing all reasonable things he can in order to that end. And thus it is that every man in the state of nature has a power to kill a murderer, both to deter others from doing the like injury, which no reparation can compensate, by the example of the punishment that attends it from everybody, and also to secure men from the attempts of a criminal who having renounced reason, the common rule and measure God hath given to mankind, hath by the unjust violence and slaughter he hath committed upon one, declared war against all mankind, and therefore may be destroyed as a lion

or a tiger, one of those wild savage beasts with whom men can have no society nor security. And upon this is grounded that great law of nature. "Whoso sheddeth man's blood, by man shall his blood be shed." And Cain was so fully convinced that everyone had a right to destroy such a criminal, that after the murder of his brother he cries out, "Every one that findeth me shall slay me;" so plain was it writ in the hearts of mankind.

12. By the same reason may a man in the state of nature punish the lesser breaches of that law. It will perhaps be demanded, With death? I answer, each transgression may be punished to that degree, and with so much severity, as will suffice to make it an ill bargain to the offender, give him cause to repent, and terrify others from doing the like. Every offense that can be committed in the state of nature, may in the state of nature be also punished equally, and as far forth as it may, in a commonwealth. For though it would be beside my present purpose to enter here into the particulars of the law of nature, or its measures of punishment, yet it is certain there is such a law, and that, too, as intelligible and plain to a rational creature and a studier of that law as the positive laws of commonwealth; nay, possibly plainer, as much as reason is easier to be understood than the fancies and intricate contrivances of men, following contrary and hidden interests put into words; for truly so are a great part of the municipal laws of countries, which are only so far right as they are founded on the law of nature, by which they are to be regulated and interpreted.

13. To this strange doctrine — viz., that in the state of nature everyone has the executive power of the law of nature — I doubt not but it will be objected that it is unreasonable for men to be judges in their own cases, that self-love will make men partial to themselves and their friends. And on the other side, that ill-nature, passion, and revenge will carry them too far in punishing others; and hence nothing but confusion and disorder will follow; and that therefore God hath certainly appointed government to restrain the partiality and violence of men. I easily grant that civil government is the proper remedy for the inconveniences of the state of nature, which must certainly be great where men may be judges in their own case, since 'tis easy to be imagined that he who was so unjust as to do his brother an injury, will scarce be so just as to condemn himself for it. But I shall desire those who make this objection, to re-

member that absolute monarchs are but men, and if government is to be the remedy of those evils which necessarily follow from men's being judges in their own cases, and the state of nature is therefore not to be endured, I desire to know what kind of government that is, and how much better it is than the state of nature, where one man commanding a multitude, has the liberty to be judge in his own case, and may do to all his subjects whatever he pleases, without the least question or control of those who execute his pleasure; and in whatsoever he doth, whether led by reason, mistake, or passion, must be submitted to, which men in the state of nature are not bound to do one to another? And if he that judges, judges amiss in his own or any other case, he is answerable for it to the rest of mankind.

14. 'Tis often asked as a mighty objection, Where are, or ever were there, any men in such a state of nature? To which it may suffice as an answer at present: That since all princes and rulers of independent governments all through the world are in a state of nature, 'tis plain the world never was, nor ever will be, without numbers of men in that state. I have named all governors of independent communities, whether they are or are not in league with others. For 'tis not every compact that puts an end to the state of nature between men, but only this one of agreeing together mutually to enter into one community, and make one body politic; other promises and compacts men may make one with another, and yet still be in the state of nature. The promises and bargains for truck, etc., between the two men in Soldania, in or between a Swiss and an Indian, in the woods of America, are binding to them, though they are perfectly in a state of nature in reference to one another. For truth and keeping of faith belong to men as men, and not as members of society.

15. To those that say there were never any men in the state of nature, I will not only oppose the authority of the judicious Hooker—(Eccl. Pol., lib. i., sect. 10), where he says, "The laws which have been hitherto mentioned," i.e., the laws of nature, "do bind men absolutely, even as they are men, although they have never any settled fellowship, and never any solemn agreement amongst themselves what to do or not to do; but forasmuch as we are not by ourselves sufficient to furnish ourselves with competent store of things needful for such a life as our nature doth desire—a life fit for the dignity of

man—therefore to supply those defects and imperfections which are in us, as living single and solely by ourselves, we are naturally induced to seek communion and fellowship with others; this was the cause of men's uniting themselves at first in politic societies"—but I moreover affirm that all men are naturally in that state, and remain so, till by their own consents they make themselves members of some politic society; and I doubt not, in the sequel of this discourse, to make it very clear.

Chapter V
Of Property

25. Whether we consider natural reason, which tells us that men being once born have a right to their preservation, and consequently to meat and drink and such other things as nature affords for their subsistence; or revelation, which gives us an account of those grants God made of the world to Adam, and to Noah and his sons, 'tis very clear that God, as King David says, Psalm cxv. 16, "has given the earth to the children of men," given it to mankind in common. But this being supposed, it seems to some a very great difficulty how anyone should ever come to have a property in anything. I will not content myself to answer that if it be difficult to make out property upon a supposition that God gave the world to Adam and his posterity in common, it is impossible that any man but one universal monarch should have any property upon a supposition that God gave the world to Adam and his heirs in succession, exclusive of all the rest of his posterity. But I shall endeavor to show how men might come to have a property in several parts of that which God gave to mankind in common, and that without any express compact of all the commoners.

26. God, who hath given the world to men in common, hath also given them reason to make use of it to the best advantage of life and convenience. The earth and all that is therein is given to men for the support and comfort of their being. And though all the fruits it naturally produces, and beasts it feeds, belong to mankind in common, as they are produced by the spontaneous hand of nature; and nobody has originally a private dominion exclusive of the rest of mankind in any of them as they are

thus in their natural state; yet being given for the use of men, there must of necessity be a means to appropriate them some way or other before they can be of any use or at all beneficial to any particular man. The fruit or venison which nourishes the wild Indian, who knows no enclosure, and is still a tenant in common, must be his, and so his, i.e., a part of him, that another can no longer have any right to it, before it can do any good for the support of his life.

27. Though the earth and all inferior creatures be common to all men, yet every man has a property in his own person; this nobody has any right to but himself. The labor of his body and the work of his hands we may say are properly his. Whatsoever, then, he removes out of the state that nature hath provided and left it in, he hath mixed his labor with, and joined to it something that is his own, and thereby makes it his property. It being by him removed from the common state nature placed it in, it hath by this labor something annexed to it that excludes the common right of other men. For this labor being the unquestionable property of the laborer, no man but he can have a right to what that is once joined to, at least where there is enough, and as good left in common for others.

28. He that is nourished by the acorns he picked up under an oak, or the apples he gathered from the trees in the wood, has certainly appropriated them to himself. Nobody can deny but the nourishment is his. I ask, then, When did they begin to be his — when he digested, or when he ate, or when he boiled, or when he brought them home, or when he picked them up? And 'tis plain if the first gathering made them not his, nothing else could. That labor put a distinction between them and common; that added something to them more than nature, the common mother of all, had done, and so they became his private right. And will anyone say he had no right to those acorns or apples he thus appropriated, because he had not the consent of all mankind to make them his? Was it a robbery thus to assume to himself what belonged to all in common? If such a consent as that was necessary, man had starved, notwithstanding the plenty God had given him. We see in commons which remain so by compact that 'tis the taking any part of what is common and removing it out of the state nature leaves it in, which begins the property; without which the common is of no use. And the taking of this or that part does not depend on the express consent of all the commoners. Thus the grass my horse has bit, the turfs my servant has cut, and the ore I have dug in any place where I have a right to them in common with others, become my property without the assignation or consent or anybody. The labor that was mine removing them out of that common state they were in, hath fixed my property in them.

29. By making an explicit consent of every commoner necessary to anyone's appropriating to himself any part of what is given in common. Children or servants could not cut the meat which their father or master had provided for them in common without assigning to everyone his peculiar part. Though the water running in the fountain be everyone's, yet who can doubt but that in the pitcher is his only who drew it out? His labor hath taken it out of the hands of Nature where it was common, and belonged equally to all her children, and hath thereby appropriated it to himself.

30. Thus this law of reason makes the deer that Indian's who hath killed it; it is allowed to be his goods who hath bestowed his labor upon it, though, before, it was the common right of everyone. And amongst those who are counted the civilized part of mankind, who have made and multiplied positive laws to determine property, this original law of nature for the beginning of property, in what was before common, still takes place, and by virtue thereof, what fish anyone catches in the ocean, that great and still remaining common of mankind; or what ambergris anyone takes up here is by the labor that removes it out of that common state nature left it in, made his property who takes that pains about it. And even amongst us, the hare that anyone is hunting is thought his who pursues her during the chase. For being a beast that is still looked upon as common, and no man's private possession, whoever has employed so much labor about any of that kind as to find and pursue her has thereby removed her from the state of nature wherein she was common, and hath began a property.

31. It will perhaps be objected to this, that if gathering the acorns, or other fruits of the earth, etc., makes a right to them, then anyone may engross as much as he will. To which I answer, Not so. The same law of nature that does by this means give us property, does also bound that property too. "God has given us all things richly" (1 Tim. vi. 17), is the voice of reason confirmed by inspiration. But

how far has He given it us? To enjoy. As much as anyone can make use of to any advantage of life before it spoils, so much he may by his labor fix a property in; whatever is beyond this, is more than his share, and belongs to others. Nothing was made by God for man to spoil or destroy. And thus considering the plenty of natural provisions there was a long time in the world, and the few spenders, and to how small a part of that provision the industry of one man could extend itself, and engross it to the prejudice of others — especially keeping within the bounds, set by reason, of what might serve for his use — there could be then little room for quarrels or contentions about property so established.

32. But the chief matter of property being now not the fruits of the earth, and the beasts that subsist on it, but the earth itself, as that which takes in and carries with it all the rest, I think it is plain that property in that, too, is acquired as the former. As much land as a man tills, plants, improves, cultivates, and can use the product of, so much is his property. He by his labor does as it were enclose it from the common. Nor will it invalidate his right to say, everybody else has an equal title to it; and therefore he cannot appropriate, he cannot enclose, without the consent of all his fellow-commoners, all mankind. God, when He gave the world in common to all mankind, commanded man also to labor, and the penury of his condition required it of him. God and his reason commanded him to subdue the earth, i.e., improve it for the benefit of life, and therein lay out something upon it that was his own, his labor. He that, in obedience to this command of God, subdued, tilled, and sowed any part of it, thereby annexed to it something that was his property, which another had no title to, nor could without injury take from him.

33. Nor was this appropriation of any parcel of land, by improving it, any prejudice to any other man, since there was still enough and as good left; and more than the yet unprovided could use. So that in effect there was never the less left for others because of his enclosure for himself. For he that leaves as much as another can make use of, does as good as take nothing at all. Nobody could think himself injured by the drinking of another man, though he took a good draught, who had a whole river of the same water left him to quench his thirst; and the case of land and water, where there is enough of both, is perfectly the same.

34. God gave the world to men in common; but since He gave it them for their benefit, and the greatest conveniences of life they were capable to draw from it, it cannot be supposed He meant it, should always remain common and uncultivated. He gave it to the use of the industrious and rational (and labor was to be his title to it), not to the fancy or covetousness of the quarrelsome and contentious. He that had as good left for his improvement as was already taken up, needed not complain, ought not to meddle with what was already improved by another's labor; if he did, it is plain he desired the benefit of another's pains, which he had no right to, and not the ground which God had given him in common with others to labor on, and whereof there was as good left as that already possessed, and more than he knew what to do with, or his industry could reach to.

XIII.2 *The Nature and Value of Rights*

JOEL FEINBERG

Joel Feinberg is professor of philosophy at the University of Arizona and the
author of several works in ethical, legal, and political theory. In this essay he
begins with a thought experiment in which he asks you to imagine
Nowheresville, a world very much like our own. Although it has all the other
benefits a good society could offer, including moral duties and benevolence,
Nowheresville is still missing something important—rights. The people of
Nowheresville cannot make moral claims or righteous demands when they are
discriminated against, and in this way they are deprived of a certain self-
respect and dignity. Rights are valid moral claims that give us inherent dignity,
and as such they are necessary to an adequate moral theory.

1

I would like to begin by conducting a thought experiment. Try to imagine Nowheresville—a world
very much like our own except that no one, or
hardly any one (the qualification is not important),
has *rights*. If this flaw makes Nowheresville too ugly
to hold very long in contemplation, we can make it
as pretty as we wish in other moral respects. We can,
for example, make the human beings in it as attractive and virtuous as possible without taxing our
conceptions of the limits of human nature. In particular, let the virtues of moral sensibility flourish.
Fill this imagined world with as much benevolence,
compassion, sympathy, and pity as it will conveniently hold without strain. Now we can imagine
men helping one another from compassionate motives merely, quite as much or even more than they
do in our actual world from a variety of more complicated motives.

This picture, pleasant as it is in some respects,
would hardly have satisfied Immanuel Kant. Benevolently motivated actions do good, Kant admitted,
and therefore are better, *ceteris paribus,* than malevo-
lently motivated actions; but no action can have su-

preme kind of worth—what Kant called "moral
worth"—unless its whole motivating power derives
from the thought that it is *required by duty.* Accordingly, let us try to make Nowheresville more appealing to Kant by introducing the idea of duty into it,
and letting the sense of duty be a sufficient motive
for many beneficent and honorable actions. But
doesn't this bring our original thought experiment
to an abortive conclusion? If duties are permitted
entry into Nowheresville, are not rights necessarily
smuggled in along with them?

The question is well-asked, and requires here a
brief digression so that we might consider the so-
called "doctrine of the logical correlativity of rights
and duties." This is the doctrine that (i) all duties
entail other people's rights and (ii) all rights entail
other people's duties. Only the first part of the doctrine, the alleged entailment from duties to rights,
need concern us here. Is this part of the doctrine
correct? It should not be surprising that my answer
is: "In a sense yes and in a sense no." Etymologically,
the word "duty" is associated with actions that are
due someone else, the payments of debts *to* creditors, the keeping of agreements with promises, the
payment of club dues, or legal fees, or tariff levies to
appropriate authorities or their representatives. In
this original sense of "duty," all duties are correlated
with the rights of those *to* whom the duty is owed.
On the other hand, there seem to be numerous
classes of duties, both of a legal and non-legal kind,

Reprinted with permission from *The Journal of Value Inquiry* 4(1970):243–257.

that are *not* logically correlated with the rights of other persons. This seems to be a consequence of the fact that the word "duty" has come to be used for *any* action understood to be *required*, whether by the rights of others, or by law, or by higher authority, or by conscience, or whatever. When the notion of requirement is in clear focus it is likely to seem the only element in the idea of duty that is essential, and the other component notion — that a duty is something *due* someone else — drops off. Thus, in this widespread but derivative usage, "duty" tends to be used for any action we feel we *must* (for whatever reason) do. It comes, in short, to be a term of moral modality merely; and it is no wonder that the first thesis of the logical correlativity doctrine often fails.

Let us then introduce duties into Nowheresville, but only in the sense of actions that are, or believed to be, morally mandatory, but not in the older sense of actions that are due others and can be claimed by others as their right. Nowheresville now can have duties of the sort imposed by positive law. A legal duty is not something we are implored or advised to do merely; it is something the law, or an authority under the law, *requires* us to do whether we want to or not, under pain of penalty. When traffic lights turn red, however, there is no determinate person who can plausibly be said to claim our stopping as his due, so that the motorist owes it to *him* to stop, in the way a debtor owes it to his creditor to pay. In our own actual world, of course, we sometimes owe it to our *fellow motorists* to stop; but that kind of right-correlated duty does not exist in Nowheresville. There, motorists "owe" obedience to the Law, but they owe nothing to one another. When they collide, no matter who is at fault, no one is accountable to anyone else, and no one has any sound grievance or "right to complain."

When we leave legal contexts to consider moral obligations and other extra-legal duties, a greater variety of duties-without-correlative-rights present themselves. Duties of charity, for example, require us to contribute to one or another of a large number of eligible recipients, no one of whom can claim our contribution from us as his due. Charitable contributions are more like gratuitous services, favours, and gifts than like repayments of debts or reparations; and yet we do have duties to be charitable. Many persons, moreover, in our actual world believe that they are required by their own consciences

to do more than that "duty" that *can* be demanded of them by their prospective beneficiaries. I have quoted elsewhere the citation from H. B. Acton of a character in a Malraux novel who "gave all his supply of poison to his fellow prisoners to enable them by suicide to escape the burning alive which was to be their fate and his." This man, Acton adds, "probably did not think that [the others] had more of a right to the poison than he had, though he thought it his duty to give it to them."[1] I am sure that there are many actual examples, less dramatically heroic than this fictitious one, of persons who believe, rightly or wrongly, that they *must do* something (hence the word "duty") for another person in excess of what that person can appropriately demand of him (hence the absence of "right").

Now the digression is over and we can return to Nowheresville and summarize what we have put in it thus far. We now find spontaneous benevolence in somewhat larger degree than in our actual world, and also the acknowledged existence of duties of obedience, duties of charity, and duties imposed by exacting private consciences, and also, let us suppose, a degree of conscientiousness in respect to those duties somewhat in excess of what is to be found in our actual world. I doubt that Kant would be fully satisfied with Nowheresville even now that duty and respect for law and authority have been added to it; but I feel certain that he would regard their addition at least as an improvement. I will now introduce two further moral practices into Nowheresville that will make the world very little more appealing to Kant, but will make it appear more familiar to us. These are the practices connected with the notions of *personal desert* and what I call a *sovereign monopoly of rights*.

When a person is said to deserve something good from us what is meant in parts is that there would be a certain propriety in our giving that good thing to him in virtue of the kind of person he is, perhaps, or more likely, in virtue of some specific thing he has done. The propriety involved here is a much weaker kind than that which derives from our having promised him the good thing or from his having qualified for it by satisfying the well-advertised conditions of some public rule. In the latter case he could be said not merely to deserve the good thing but also to have a *right* to it, that is to be in a position to demand it as his due; and of course we will not have that sort of thing in Nowheresville.

That weaker kind of propriety which is mere desert is simply a kind of *fittingness* between one party's character or action and another party's favorable response, much like that between humor and laughter, or good performance and applause.

The following seems to be the origin of the idea of deserving good or bad treatment from others: A master or lord was under no obligation to reward his servant for especially good service; still a master might naturally feel that there would be a special fittingness in giving a gratuitous reward as a grateful response to the good service (or conversely imposing a penalty for bad service). Such an act while surely fitting and proper was entirely supererogatory. The fitting response in turn from the rewarded servant should be gratitude. If the deserved reward had not been given him he should have had no complaint, since he only *deserved* the reward, as opposed to having a *right* to it, or a ground for claiming it as his due.

The idea of desert has evolved a good bit away from its beginnings by now, but nevertheless, it seems clearly to be one of those words J. L. Austin said "never entirely forget their pasts."[2] Today servants qualify for their wages by doing their agreed upon chores, no more and no less. If their wages are not forthcoming, their contractual rights have been violated and they can make legal claim to the money that is their due. If they do less than they agreed to do, however, their employers may "dock" them, by paying them proportionately less than the agreed upon fee. This is all a matter of right. But if the servant does a splendid job, above and beyond his minimal contractual duties, the employer is under no further obligation to reward him, for this was not agreed upon, even tacitly, in advance. The additional service was all the servant's idea and done entirely on his own. Nevertheless, the morally sensitive employer may feel that it would be exceptionally appropriate for him to respond, freely on *his* own, to the servant's meritorious service, with a reward. The employee cannot demand it as his due, but he will happily accept it, with gratitude, as a fitting response to his desert.

In our age of organized labor, even this picture is now archaic; for almost every kind of exchange of service is governed by hard bargained contracts so that even bonuses can sometimes be demanded as a matter of right, and nothing is given for nothing on either side of the bargaining table. And perhaps that

is a good thing; for consider an anachronistic instance of the earlier kind of practice that survives, at least as a matter of form, in the quaint old practice of "tipping." The tip was originally conceived as a reward that has to be earned by "zealous service." It is not something to be taken for granted as a standard response to *any* service. That is to say that its payment is a *"gratuity,"* not a discharge of obligation, but something given apart from, or in addition to, anything the recipient can expect as a matter of right. That is what tipping originally meant at any rate, and tips are still referred to as "gratuities" in the tax forms. But try to explain all that to a New York cab driver! If he has *earned* his gratuity, by God, he has it coming, and there had better be sufficient acknowledgement of his desert or he'll give you a piece of his mind! I'm not generally prone to defend New York cab drivers, but they do have a point here. There is the making of a paradox in the queerly unstable concept of an "earned gratuity." One can understand how "desert" in the weak sense of "propriety" or "mere fittingness" tends to generate a stronger sense in which desert is itself the ground for a claim of right.

In Nowheresville, nevertheless, we will have only the original weak kind of desert. Indeed, it will be impossible to keep this idea out if we allow such practices as teachers grading students, judges awarding prizes, and servants serving benevolent but class-conscious masters. Nowheresville is a reasonably good world in many ways, and its teachers, judges, and masters will generally try to give students, contestants, and servants the grades, prizes, and rewards they deserve. For this the recipients will be grateful; but they will never think to complain, or even feel aggrieved, when expected responses to desert fail. The masters, judges, and teachers don't *have* to do good things, after all, for *anyone*. One should be happy that they *ever* treat us well, and not grumble over their occasional lapses. Their hoped for responses, after all, are *gratuities,* and there is no wrong in the omission of what is merely gratuitous. Such is the response of persons who have no concept of *rights,* even persons who are proud of their own deserts.[3]

Surely, one might ask, rights have to come in somewhere, if we are to have even moderately complex forms of social organization. Without rules that confer rights and impose obligations, how can we have ownership of property, bargains and deals, promises and contracts, appointments and loans, marriages and partnerships? Very well, let us introduce all of these social and economic practices into Nowheresville, but *with one big twist*. With them I should like to introduce the curious notion of a "sovereign right-monopoly." You will recall that the subjects in Hobbes's *Leviathan* had no rights whatever against their sovereign. He could do as he liked with them, even gratuitously harm them, but this gave them no valid grievance against him. The sovereign, to be sure, had a certain duty to treat his subjects well, but this duty was owed not to the subjects directly, but to God, just as we might have a duty to a person to treat his property well, but of course no duty to the property itself but only to its owner. Thus, while the sovereign was quite capable of *harming* his subjects, he could commit no wrong against them that they could complain about, since they had no prior claims against his conduct. The only party *wronged* by the sovereign's mistreatment of his subjects was God, the supreme lawmaker. Thus, in repenting cruelty to his subjects, the sovereign might say to God, as David did after killing Uriah, "to Thee only have I sinned."[4]

Even in the *Leviathan,* however, ordinary people had ordinary rights *against one another.* They played roles, occupied offices, made agreements, and signed contracts. In a genuine "sovereign right-monopoly," as I shall be using that phrase, they will do all those things too, and thus incur genuine obligations toward one another; but the obligations (here is the twist) will not be owed directly *to* promises, creditors, parents, and the like, but rather to God alone, or to the members of some elite, or to a single sovereign under God. Hence, the rights correlative to the obligations that derive from these transactions are all owned by some "outside" authority.

As far as I know, no philosopher has ever suggested that even our role and contract obligations (in this, our actual world) are all owed directly to a divine intermediary, but some theologians have approached such extreme moral occasionalism. I have in mind the familiar phrase in certain widely distributed religious tracts that "it takes three to marry," which suggests that marital vows are not made between bride and groom directly but between each spouse and God, so that if one breaks his vow, the other cannot rightly complain of being wronged, since only God could have claimed performance of the marital duties as his *own* due; and hence God alone had a claim-right violated by the nonperformance. If John breaks his vow to God, he might then properly repent in the words of David: "To Thee only have I sinned."

In our actual world, very few spouses conceive of their mutual obligations in this way; but their small children, at a certain stage in their moral upbringing, are likely to feel precisely this way toward *their* mutual obligations. If Billy kicks Bobby and is punished by Daddy, he may come to feel contrition for his naughtiness induced by his painful estrangement from the loved parent. He may then be happy to make amends and sincere apology to *Daddy*; but when Daddy insists that he apologize to his wronged brother, that is another story. A direct apology to Billy would be a tacit recognition of Billy's status as a right-holder against him, someone he can wrong as well as harm, and someone to whom he is directly accountable for his wrongs. This is a status Bobby will happily accord Daddy; but it would imply a respect for Billy that he does not presently feel, so he bitterly resents according it to him. On the "three-to-marry" model, the relations between each spouse and God would be like those between Bobby and Daddy; respect for the other spouse as an independent claimant would not even be necessary; and where present, of course, never sufficient.

The advocates of the "three-to-marry" model who conceive it either as a description of our actual institution of marriage or a recommendation of what marriage ought to be, may wish to escape this embarrassment by granting rights to spouses in capacities other than as promisees. They may wish to say, for example, that when John promises God that he will be faithful to Mary, a right is thus conferred not only on God as promisee but also on Mary herself as third-party beneficiary, just as when John contracts with an insurance company and names Mary as his intended beneficiary, she has a right to the accumulated funds after John's death, even though the insurance company made no promise to her. But this seems to be an unnecessarily cumbersome complication contributing nothing to our understanding of the marriage bond. The life insurance transaction is necessarily a three party relation, involving occupants of three distinct offices, no two of whom alone could do the whole job. The transaction, after all, is defined as the purchase by the customer (first office) from the vendor (second office) of protection for a beneficiary (third office) against the customer's untimely death. Marriage, on the other hand, in this our actual world, appears to be a binary relation between a husband and wife, and even though third parties such as children, neighbors, psychiatrists, and priests may sometimes be helpful and even causally necessary for the survival of the relation, they are not logically necessary to our *conception* of the relation, and indeed many married couples do quite well without them. Still I am not now purporting to describe our actual world, but rather trying to contrast it with a counterpart world of the imagination. In *that* world, it takes three to make almost *any* moral relation and all rights are owned by God or some sovereign under God.

There will, of course, be delegated authorities in the imaginary world, empowered to give commands to their underlings and to punish them for their disobedience. But the commands are all given in the name of the right-monopoly who in turn are the only persons to whom obligations are owed. Hence, even intermediate superiors do not have claim-rights against their subordinates but only legal *powers* to create obligations in the subordinates *to* the monopolistic right-holders, and also the legal *privilege* to impose penalties in the name of that monopoly.

2

So much for the imaginary "world without rights." If some of the moral concepts and practices I have allowed into that world do not sit well with one another, no matter. Imagine Nowheresville with all of these practices if you can, or with any harmonious subset of them, if you prefer. The important thing is not what I've let into it, but what I have kept out. The remainder of this paper will be devoted to an analysis of what precisely a world is missing when it does not contain rights and why that absence is morally important.

The most conspicuous difference, I think, between the Nowheresvillians and ourselves has something to do with the activity of *claiming*. Nowheresvillians, even when they are discriminated against invidiously, or left without the things they need, or otherwise badly treated, do not think to leap to their feet and make righteous demands against one another though they may not hesitate to resort to force and trickery to get what they want. They have no notion of rights, so they do not have a notion of what is their due; hence they do not claim before they take. The conceptual linkage between personal rights and claiming has long been noticed by legal writers and is reflected in the standard usage in which "claim-rights" are distinguished from other mere liberties, immunities, and powers, also sometimes called "rights," with which they are easily confused. When a person has a legal claim-right to X, it must be the case (i) that he is at liberty in respect to X, i.e. that he has no duty to refrain from or relinquish X, and also (ii) that his liberty is the ground of other people's *duties* to grant him X or not to interfere with him in respect to X. Thus, in the sense of claim-rights, it is true by definition that rights logically entail other people's duties. The paradigmatic examples of such rights are the creditor's right to be paid a debt by his debtor, and the landowner's right not to be interfered with by anyone in the exclusive occupancy of his land. The creditor's right against his debtor, for example, and the debtor's duty to his creditor, are precisely the same relation seen from two different vantage points, as inextricably linked as the two sides of the same coin.

And yet, this is not quite an accurate account of the matter, for it fails to do justice to the way claim-rights are somehow prior to, or more basic than, the duties with which they are necessarily correlated. If Nip has a claim-right against Tuck, it is because of this fact that Tuck has a duty to Nip. It is only because something from Tuck is *due* Nip (directional element) that there is something Tuck *must do* (modal element). This is a relation, moreover, in which Tuck is bound and Nip is free. Nip not only *has* a right, but he can choose whether or not to exercise it, whether to claim it, whether to register complaints upon its infringement, even whether to release Tuck from his duty, and forget the whole thing. If the personal claim-right is also backed up by criminal sanctions, however, Tuck may yet have a duty of obedience to the law from which no one, not even Nip, may release him. He would even have such duties if he lived in Nowheresville; but duties subject to acts of claiming, duties derivative from the contingent upon the personal rights of others, are unknown and undreamed of in Nowheresville.

Many philosophical writers have simply identified rights with claims. The dictionaries tend to define "claims," in turn as "assertions of right," a dizzying piece of circularity that led one philosopher to complain — "We go in search of rights and are directed to claims, and then back again to rights in bureaucratic futility."[5] What then is the relation between a claim and a right?

As we shall see, a right *is* a kind of claim, and a claim is "an assertion of right," so that a formal definition of either notion in terms of the other will not get us very far. Thus if a "formal definition" of the usual philosophical sort is what we are after, the game is over before it has begun, and we can say that the concept of a right is a "simple, undefinable, unanalysable primitive." Here as elsewhere in philosophy this will have the effect of making the commonplace seem unnecessarily mysterious. We would be better advised, I think, not to attempt definition of either "right" or "claim," but rather to use the idea of a claim in informal elucidation of the idea of a right. This is made possible by the fact that *claiming* is an elaborate sort of rule-governed *activity*. A claim is that which is claimed, the object of the act of claiming. . . . If we concentrate on the whole activity of claiming, which is public, familiar, and open to our observation, rather than on its upshot alone, we may learn more about the generic nature of rights than we could ever hope to learn from a formal definition, even if one were possible. Moreover, certain facts about rights more easily, if not solely, expressible in the language of claims and claiming are essential to a full understanding not only of what rights are, but also why they are so vitally important.

Let us begin then by distinguishing between: (i) making claim to . . . , (ii) claiming that . . . , and (iii) having a claim. One sort of thing we may be doing when we claim is to *make claim to something*. This is "to petition or seek by virtue of supposed right; to demand as due." Sometimes this is done by an acknowledged right-holder when he serves notice that he now wants turned over to him that which has already been acknowledged to be his, something borrowed, say, or improperly taken from him. This is often done by turning in a chit, a receipt, an I.O.U., a check, an insurance policy, or a deed, that is, a *title* to something currently in the possession of someone else. On other occasions, making claim is making application for titles or rights themselves, as when a mining prospector stakes a claim to mineral rights, or a householder to a tract of land in the public domain, or an inventor to his patent rights. In the one kind of case, to make claim is to exercise rights one already has by presenting title; in the other kind of case it is to apply for the title itself, by showing that one has satisfied the conditions specified by a rule for the ownership of title and therefore that one can demand it as one's due.

Generally speaking, only the person who has a title or who has qualified for it, or someone speaking in his name, can make claim to something as a matter of right. It is an important fact about rights (or claims), then, that they can be claimed only by those who have them. Anyone can claim, of course, *that* this umbrella is yours, but only you or your representative can actually claim the umbrella. If Smith owes Jones five dollars, only Jones can claim the five dollars as his own, though any bystander can *claim that* it belongs to Jones. One important difference then between *making legal claim to* and *claiming that* is that the former is a legal performance with direct legal consequences whereas the latter is often a mere piece of descriptive commentary with no legal force. Legally speaking, *making claim to* can itself make things happen. This sense of "claiming," then, might well be called "the performative sense." The legal power to claim (performatively) one's right or the things to which one has a right seems to be essential to the very notion of a right. A right to which one could not make claim (i.e. not even for recognition) would be a very "imperfect" right indeed!

Claiming that one has a right (what we can call "propositional claiming" as opposed to "performative claiming") is another sort of thing one can do with language, but it is not the sort of doing that characteristically has legal consequences. To claim that one has rights is to make an assertion that one has them, and to make it in such a manner as to demand or insist that they be recognized. In this sense of "claim" many things in addition to rights can be claimed, that is, many other kinds of proposition can be asserted in the claiming way. I can claim, for example, that you, he, or she has certain rights, or that Julius Caesar once had certain rights; or I can claim that certain statements are true, or that I have certain skills, or accomplishments, or virtually anything at all. I can claim that the earth is flat. What is essential to *claiming that* is the manner of assertion. One can assert without even caring very much whether anyone is listening, but part of the point of propositional claiming is to *make sure* people listen. When I claim to others that I know something, for example, I am not merely asserting it, but rather "obtruding my putative knowledge upon their attention, demanding that it be recognized, that appropriate notice be taken of it by those concerned. . . ."[6] Not every truth is properly assertable, much less claimable, in every context. To claim that something is the case in circumstances that justify no more than calm assertion is to behave like a boor. (This kind of boorishness, I might add, is probably less common in Nowheresville.) But not to claim in the appropriate circumstances that one has a right is to be spiritless or foolish. A list of "appropriate circumstances" would include occasions when one is challenged, when one's possession is denied, or seems insufficiently acknowledged or appreciated; and of course even in these circumstances, the claiming should be done only with an appropriate degree of vehemence.

Even if there are conceivable circumstances in which one would admit rights diffidently, there is no doubt that their characteristic use and that for which they are distinctively well suited, is to be claimed, demanded, affirmed, insisted upon. They are especially sturdy objects to "stand upon," a most useful sort of moral furniture. Having rights, of course, makes claiming possible; but it is claiming that gives rights their special moral significance. This feature of rights is connected in a way with the customary rhetoric about what it is to be a human being. Having rights enables us to "stand up like men," to look others in the eye, and to feel in some fundamental way the equal of anyone. To think of oneself as the holder of rights is not to be unduly but properly proud, to have that minimal self-respect that is necessary to be worthy of the love and esteem of others. Indeed, respect for persons (this is an intriguing idea) may simply be respect for their rights, so that there cannot be the one without the other; and what is called "human dignity" may simply be the recognizable capacity to assert claims. To respect a person then, or to think of him as possessed of human dignity, simply *is* to think of him as a potential maker of claims. Not all of this can be packed into a definition of "rights"; but these are *facts* about the possession of rights that argue well

their supreme moral importance. More than anything else I am going to say, these facts explain what is wrong with Nowheresville.

We come now to the third interesting employment of the claiming vocabulary, that involving not the verb "to claim" but the substantive "a claim." What is to *have a claim* and how is this related to rights? I would like to suggest that *having a claim consists in being in a position to claim, that is, to make claim to* or *claim that.* If this suggestion is correct it shows the primacy of the verbal over the nominative forms. It links claims to a kind of activity and obviates the temptation to think of claims as *things,* on the model of coins, pencils, and other material possessions which we can carry in our hip pockets. To be sure, we often make or establish our claims by presenting titles, and these typically have the form of receipts, tickets, certificates, and other pieces of paper or parchment. The title, however, is not the same thing as the claim; rather it is the evidence that establishes the claim as valid. On this analysis, one might have a claim without ever claiming that to which one is entitled, or without even knowing that one has the claim; for one might simply be ignorant of the fact that one is in a position to claim; or one might be unwilling to exploit that position for one reason or another, including fear that the legal machinery is broken down or corrupt and will not enforce one's claim despite its validity.

Nearly all writers maintain that there is some intimate connection between having a claim and having a right. Some identify right and claim without qualification; some define "right" as justified or justifiable claim, others as recognized claim, still others as valid claim. My own preference is for the latter definition. Some writers, however, reject the identification of rights with valid claims on the ground that all claims as such are valid, so that the expression "valid claim" is redundant. These writers, therefore, would identify rights with claims *simpliciter.* But this is a very simple confusion. All claims, to be sure, are *put forward* as justified, whether they are justified in fact or not. A claim conceded even by its maker to have no validity is not a claim at all, but a mere demand. The highwayman, for example, *demands* his victim's money; but he hardly makes claim to it as rightfully his own.

But it does not follow from this sound point that it is redundant to qualify claims as justified (or as I prefer, valid) in the definition of a right; for it remains true that not all claims put forward as valid really are valid; and only the valid ones can be acknowledged as rights.

If having a valid claim is not redundant, i.e. if it is not redundant to pronounce *another's* claim valid, there must be such a thing as having a claim that is not valid. What would this be like? One might accumulate just enough evidence to argue with relevance and cogency that one has a right (or ought to be granted a right), although one's case might not be overwhelmingly conclusive. In such a case, one might have strong enough argument to be entitled to a hearing and given fair consideration. When one is in this position, it might be said that one "has a claim" that deserves to be weighed carefully. Nevertheless, the balance of reasons may turn out to militate against recognition of the claim, so that the claim, which one admittedly had, and perhaps still does, is not a valid claim or right. "Having a claim" in this sense is an expression very much like the legal phrase "having a *prima facie* case." A plaintiff establishes a *prima facie* case for the defendant's liability when he establishes grounds that will be sufficient for liability unless outweighed by reasons of a different sort that may be offered by the defendant. Similarly, in the criminal law, a grand jury returns an indictment when it thinks that the prosecution has sufficient evidence to be taken seriously and given a fair hearing, whatever countervailing reasons may eventually be offered on the other side. That initial evidence, serious but not conclusive, is also sometimes called a *prima facie* case. In a parallel *"prima facie* sense" of "claim," having a claim to X is not (yet) the same as having a right to X, but is rather having a case of at least minimal plausibility that one has a right to X, a case that does establish a right, not to X, but to a fair hearing and consideration. Claims, so conceived, differ in degree: some are stronger than others. Rights, on the other hand, do not differ in degree; no one right is more of a right than another.[7]

Another reason for not identifying rights with claims *simply* is that there is a well-established usage in international law that makes a theoretically interesting distinction between claims and rights. Statesmen are sometimes led to speak of "claims" when they are concerned with the natural needs of deprived human beings in conditions of scarcity.

Young orphans *need* good upbringings, balanced diets, education, and technical training everywhere in the world; but unfortunately there are many places where these goods are in such short supply that it is impossible to provision all who need them. If we persist, nevertheless, in speaking of these needs as constituting rights and not merely claims, we are committed to the conception of a right which is an entitlement *to* some good, but not a valid claim *against* any particular individual; for in conditions of scarcity there may be no determinate individuals who can plausibly be said to have a duty to provide the missing goods to those in need. J. E. S. Fawcett therefore prefers to keep the distinction between claims and rights firmly in mind. "Claims," he writes, "are needs and demands in movement, and there is a continuous transformation, as a society advances [towards greater abundance] of economic and social claims into civil and political rights . . . and not all countries or all claims are by any means at the same stage in the process."[8] The manifesto writers on the other side who seem to identify needs, or at least basic needs, with what they call "human rights," are more properly described, I think, as urging upon the world community the moral principle that *all* basic human needs ought to be recognized as *claims* (in the customary *prima facie* sense) worthy of sympathy and serious consideration right now, even though, in many cases, they cannot yet plausibly be treated as *valid* claims, that is, as grounds of any other people's duties. This way of talking avoids the anomaly of ascribing to all human beings now, even those in pre-industrial societies, such "economic and social rights" as "periodic holidays with pay."[9]

Still for all of that, I have a certain sympathy with the manifesto writers, and I am even willing to speak of a special "manifesto sense" of "right," in which a right need not be correlated with another's duty. Natural needs are real claims if only upon hypothetical future beings not yet in existence. I accept the moral principle that to have an unfulfilled need is to have a kind of claim against the world, even if against no one in particular. A natural need for some good as such, like a natural desert, is always a reason in support of a claim to that good. A person in need, then, is always "in a position" to make a claim, even when there is no one in the corresponding position to do anything about it. Such claims, based on need alone, are "permanent possibilities of rights," the natural seed from which rights grow. When manifesto writers speak of them as if already actual rights, they are easily forgiven, for this is but a powerful way of expressing the conviction that they ought to be recognized by states here and now as potential rights and consequently as determinants of *present* aspirations and guides to *present* policies. That usage, I think, is a valid exercise of rhetorical license.

I prefer to characterize rights as valid claims rather than justified ones, because I suspect that justification is rather too broad a qualification. "Validity," as I understand it, is justification of a peculiar and narrow kind, namely justification within a system of rules. A man has a legal right when the official recognition of his claim (as valid) is called for by the governing rules. This definition, of course, hardly applies to moral rights, but that is not because the genus of which moral rights are a species is something other than *claims*. A man has a moral right when he has a claim the recognition of which is called for—not (necessarily) by legal rules—but by moral principles, or the principles of an enlightened conscience.

There is one final kind of attack on the generic identification of rights with claims, and it has been launched with great spirit in a recent article by H. J. McCloskey, who holds that rights are not essentially claims at all, but rather entitlements. The springboard of his argument is his insistence that rights in their essential character are always *rights to*, not *rights against*:

> My right to life is not a right against anyone. It is my right and by virtue of it, it is normally permissible for me to sustain my life in the face of obstacles. It does give rise to rights against others *in the sense* that others have or may come to have duties to refrain from killing me, but it is essentially a right of mine, not an infinite list of claims, hypothetical and actual, against an infinite number of actual, potential, and as yet nonexistent human beings . . . Similarly, the right of the tennis club member to play on the club courts is a right to play, not a right against some vague group of potential or possible obstructors.[10]

The argument seems to be that since rights are essentially rights *to,* whereas claims are essentially claims *against,* rights cannot be claims, though they can be grounds for claims. The argument is doubly defective though. First of all, contrary to McCloskey, rights (at least legal claim-rights) *are* held *against* others. McCloskey admits this in the case of *in personam* rights (what he calls "special rights") but denies it in the case of *in rem* rights (which he calls "general rights"):

> Special rights are sometimes against specific individuals or institutions—e.g. rights created by promises, contracts, etc. . . . but these differ from . . . characteristic . . . general rights where the right is simply a right to . . . [11]

As far as I can tell the only reason McCloskey gives for denying that *in rem* rights are against others is that those against whom they would have to hold make up an enormously multitudinous and "vague" group, including hypothetical people not yet even in existence. Many others have found this a paradoxical consequence of the notion of *in rem* rights, but I see nothing troublesome in it. If a general rule gives me a right of noninterference in a certain respect against everybody, then there are literally hundreds of millions of people who have a duty toward me in that respect; and if the same general rule gives the same right to everyone else, then it imposes on me literally hundreds of millions of duties—or duties towards hundreds of millions of people. I see nothing paradoxical about this, however. The duties, after all, are negative; and I can discharge all of them at a stroke simply by minding my own business. And if all human beings make up one moral community and there are hundreds of millions of human beings, we should expect there to be hundreds of millions of moral relations holding between them.

McCloskey's other premise is even more obviously defective. There is no good reason to think that all *claims* are "essentially" *against,* rather than *to.* Indeed most of the discussion of claims above has been of claims *to,* and we have seen, the law finds it useful to recognize claims *to* (or "mere claims") that are not yet qualified to be claims *against,* or rights (except in a "manifesto sense" of "rights").

Whether we are speaking of claims or rights, however, we must notice that they seem to have two dimensions, as indicated by the prepositions "to" and "against," and it is quite natural to wonder whether either of these dimensions is somehow more fundamental or essential than the other. All rights seem to merge *entitlements to* do, have, omit, or be something with *claims against* others to act or refrain from acting in certain ways. In some statements of rights the entitlement is perfectly determinate (e.g., *to* play tennis) and the claim vague (e.g. *against* "some vague group of potential or possible obstructors"); but in other cases the object of the claim is clear and determinate (e.g. *against* one's parents), and the entitlement general and indeterminate (e.g. to be given a proper upbringing). If we mean by "entitlement" that *to* which one has a right and by "claim" something directed at those against whom the right holds (as McCloskey apparently does), then we can say that all claim-rights necessarily involve both, though in individual cases the one element or the other may be in sharper focus.

In brief conclusion: To have a right is to have a claim against someone whose recognition as valid is called for by some set of governing rules or moral principles. To have a *claim* in turn, is to have a case meriting consideration, that is, to have reasons or grounds that put one in a position to engage in performative and propositional claiming. The activity of claiming, finally, as much as any other thing, makes for self-respect and respect for others, gives a sense to the notion of personal dignity, and distinguishes this otherwise morally flawed world from the even worse world of Nowheresville.

Endnotes

[1] H. B. Acton, "Symposium of 'Rights'," *Proceedings of the Aristotelian Society,* Supplementary Volume 24 (1950): 107–108.

[2] J. L. Austin, "A Plea for Excuses," *Proceedings of the Aristotelian Society,* Vol. 57 (1956–57).

[3] For a fuller discussion of the concept of personal desert see my "Justice and Personal Desert," in C. J. Chapman, ed. *Nomos VI, Justice* (New York: Atherton Press, 1963), pp. 69–97.

[4] II Sam. 11. Cited with approval by Thomas Hobbes in *The Leviathan,* Part II, Chapter 21.

[5] H. B. Acton, *op. cit.*

[6] G. J. Warnock, "Claims to Knowledge," *Proceedings of the Aristotelian Society,* Supplementary Volume 36 (1962): 21.

[7] This is the important difference between rights and mere claims. It is analogous to the difference between *evidence* of guilt (subject to degrees of cogency) and conviction of guilt (which is all or nothing). One can "have evidence" that is not conclusive just as one can "have a claim" that is not valid. "Prima-facieness" is built into the sense of "claim," but the notion of a "prima-facie right" makes little sense. On the latter point see A. I. Melden, *Rights and Right Conduct* (Oxford: Basil Blackwell, 1959), pp. 18–20, and Herbert Morris, "Persons and Punishment," *The Monist* 52 (1968): 498–99.

[8] J. E. S. Fawcett, "The International Protection of Human Rights," in D. D. Raphael, ed. *Political Theory and the Rights of Man* (Bloomington: Indiana University Press, 1967), pp. 125 and 128.

[9] As declared in Article 24 of *The Universal Declaration of Human Rights* adopted on December 10, 1948, by the General Assembly of the United Nations.

[10] H. J. McCloskey, "Rights," *Philosophical Quarterly* 15 (1965): 118.

[11] *Loc. cit.*

XIII.3 *Taking Rights Seriously*

RONALD DWORKIN

Ronald Dworkin is professor of jurisprudence at Oxford University and professor of law at New York University. He is the author of several works in philosophy of law, most recently *Law's Empire* (Fontana, 1986). In this article he argues that collective goals of the State (such as prosperity, administrative convenience, and political efficiency) are not a sufficient justification for denying individuals their rights. Rights are like trump cards that prevail over all other political considerations. This article is especially important for its discussion of the relation of rights to civil disobedience.

1. *The Rights of Citizens*

The language of rights now dominates political debate in the United States. Does the Government respect the moral and political rights of its citizens? Or does the Government's foreign policy, or its race policy, fly in the face of these rights? Do the minorities whose rights have been violated have the right to violate the law in return? Or does the silent majority itself have rights, including the right that those who break the law be punished? It is not surprising that these questions are now prominent. The concept of rights, and particularly the concept of rights against the Government, has its most natural use when a political society is divided, and appeals to co-operation or a common goal are pointless.

The debate does not include the issue of whether citizens have *some* moral rights against their Government. It seems accepted on all sides that they do. Conventional lawyers and politicians take it as a point of pride that our legal system recognizes, for example, individual rights of free speech, equality, and due process. They base their claim that our law deserves respect, at least in part, on that fact, for

they would not claim that totalitarian systems deserve the same loyalty.

Some philosophers, of course, reject the idea that citizens have rights apart from what the law happens to give them. Bentham thought that the idea of moral rights was 'nonsense on stilts.' But that view has never been part of our orthodox political theory, and politicians of both parties appeal to the rights of the people to justify a great part of what they want to do. I shall not be concerned, in this essay, to defend the thesis that citizens have moral rights against their governments; I want instead to explore the implications of that thesis for those, including the present United States Government, who profess to accept it.

It is much in dispute, of course, what *particular* rights citizens have. Does the acknowledged right to free speech, for example, include the right to participate in nuisance demonstrations? In practice the Government will have the last word on what an individual's rights are, because its police will do what its officials and courts say. But that does not mean that the Government's view is necessarily the correct view; anyone who thinks it does must believe that men and women have only such moral rights as Government chooses to grant, which means that they have no moral rights at all.

All this is sometimes obscured in the United States by the constitutional system. The American Constitution provides a set of individual *legal* rights in the First Amendment, and in the due process, equal protection, and similar clauses. Under present legal practice the Supreme Court has the power to declare an act of Congress or of a state legislature void if the Court finds that the act offends these provisions. This practice has led some commentators to suppose that individual moral rights are fully protected by this system, but that is hardly so, nor could it be so.

The Constitution fuses legal and moral issues, by making the validity of a law depend on the answer to complex moral problems, like the problem of whether a particular statute respects the inherent equality of all men. This fusion has important consequences for the debates about civil disobedience; I have described these elsewhere and I shall refer to them later. But it leaves open two prominent questions. It does not tell us whether the Constitution, even properly interpreted, recognizes all the moral rights that citizens have, and it does not tell us whether, as many suppose, citizens would have a duty to obey the law even if it did invade their moral rights.

Both questions become crucial when some minority claims moral rights which the law denies, like the right to run its local school system, and which lawyers agree are not protected by the Constitution. The second question becomes crucial when, as now, the majority is sufficiently aroused so that Constitutional amendments to eliminate rights, like the right against self-incrimination, are seriously proposed. It is also crucial in nations, like the United Kingdom, that have no constitution of a comparable nature.

Even if the Constitution were perfect, of course, and the majority left it alone, it would not follow that the Supreme Court could guarantee the individual rights of citizens. A Supreme Court decision is still a legal decision, and it must take into account precedent and institutional considerations like relations between the Court and Congress, as well as morality. And no judicial decision is necessarily the right decision. Judges stand for different positions on controversial issues of law and morals and, as the fights over Nixon's Supreme Court nominations showed, a President is entitled to appoint judges of his own persuasion, provided that they are honest and capable.

So, though the constitutional system adds something to the protection of moral rights against the Government, it falls far short of guaranteeing these rights, or even establishing what they are. It means that, on some occasions, a department other than the legislature has the last word on these issues, which can hardly satisfy someone who thinks such a department profoundly wrong.

It is of course inevitable that some department of government will have the final say on what law will be enforced. When men disagree about moral rights, there will be no way for either side to prove its case, and some decision must stand if there is not to be anarchy. But that piece of orthodox wisdom must be the beginning and not the end of a philosophy of legislation and enforcement. If we cannot insist that the Government reach the right answers about the rights of its citizens, we can insist at least that it try. We can insist that it take rights seriously, follow a coherent theory of what these rights are, and act consistently with its own professions. I shall try to show what that means, and how it bears on the present political debates.

2. *Rights and the Right to Break the Law*

I shall start with the most violently argued issue. Does an American ever have the moral right to break a law? Suppose someone admits a law is valid; does he therefore have a duty to obey it? Those who try to give an answer seem to fall into two camps. The conservatives, as I shall call them, seem to disapprove of any act of disobedience; they appear satisfied when such acts are prosecuted, and disappointed when convictions are reversed. The other group, the liberals, are much more sympathetic to at least some cases of disobedience; they sometimes disapprove of prosecutions and celebrate acquittals. If we look beyond these emotional reactions, however, and pay attention to the arguments the two parties use, we discover an astounding fact. Both groups give essentially the same answer to the question of principle that supposedly divides them.

The answer that both parties give is this. In a democracy, or at least a democracy that in principle respects individual rights, each citizen has a general moral duty to obey all the laws, even though he would like some of them changed. He owes that duty to his fellow citizens, who obey laws that they do not like, to his benefit. But this general duty cannot be an absolute duty, because even a society that is in principle just may produce unjust laws and policies, and a man has duties other than his duties to the State. A man must honour his duties to his God and to his conscience, and if these conflict with his duty to the State, then he is entitled, in the end, to do what he judges to be right. If he decides that he must break the law, however, then he must submit to the judgment and punishment that the State imposes, in recognition of the fact that his duty to his fellow citizens was overwhelmed but not extinguished by his religious or moral obligation.

Of course this common answer can be elaborated in very different ways. Some would describe the duty to the State as fundamental, and picture the dissenter as a religious or moral fanatic. Others would describe the duty to the State in grudging terms, and picture those who oppose it as moral heroes. But these are differences in tone, and the position I described represents, I think, the view of most of those who find themselves arguing either for or against civil disobedience in particular cases.

I do not claim that it is everyone's view. There must be some who put the duty to the State so high that they do not grant that it can ever be overcome. There are certainly some who would deny that a man ever has a moral duty to obey the law, at least in the United States today. But these two extreme positions are the slender tails of a bell curve, and all those who fall in between hold the orthodox position I described — that men have a duty to obey the law but have the right to follow their consciences when it conflicts with that duty.

But if that is so, then we have a paradox in the fact that men who give the same answer to a question of principle should seem to disagree so much, and to divide so fiercely, in particular cases. The paradox goes even deeper, for each party, in at least some cases, takes a position that seems flatly inconsistent with the theoretical position they both accept. This position was tested, for example, when someone evaded the draft on grounds of conscience, or encouraged others to commit this crime. Conservatives argued that such men must be prosecuted, even though they are sincere. Why must they be prosecuted? Because society cannot tolerate the decline in respect for the law that their act constitutes and encourages. They must be prosecuted, in short, to discourage them and others like them from doing what they have done.

But there seems to be a monstrous contradiction here. If a man has a right to do what his conscience tells him he must, then how can the State be justified in discouraging him from doing it? Is it not wicked for a state to forbid and punish what it acknowledges that men have a right to do?

Moreover, it is not just conservatives who argue that those who break the law out of moral conviction should be prosecuted. The liberal is notoriously opposed to allowing racist school officials to go slow on desegregation, even though he acknowledges that these school officials think they have a moral right to do what the law forbids. The liberal does not often argue, it is true, that the desegregation laws must be enforced to encourage general respect for law. He argues instead that the desegregation laws must be enforced because they are right. But his position also seems inconsistent: can it be right to prosecute men for doing what their conscience requires, when we acknowledge their right to follow their conscience?

We are therefore left with two puzzles. How can two parties to an issue of principle, each of which thinks it is in profound disagreement with the other, embrace the same position on that issue? How can it be that each side urges solutions to particular problems which seem flatly to contradict the position of principle that both accept? One possible answer is that some or all of those who accept the common position are hypocrites, paying lip service to rights of conscience which in fact they do not grant.

There is some plausibility in this charge. A sort of hypocrisy must have been involved when public officials who claim to respect conscience denied Muhammed Ali the right to box in their states. If Ali, in spite of his religious scruples, had joined the Army, he would have been allowed to box even though, on the principles these officials say they honour, he would have been a worse human being for having done so. But there are few cases that seem so straightforward as this one, and even here the officials did not seem to recognize the contradiction between their acts and their principles. So we must search for some explanation beyond the truth that men often do not mean what they say.

The deeper explanation lies in a set of confusions that often embarrass arguments about rights. These confusions have clouded all the issues I mentioned at the outset and have crippled attempts to develop a coherent theory of how a government that respects rights must behave.

In order to explain this, I must call attention to the fact, familiar to philosophers, but often ignored in political debate, that the word 'right' has different force in different contexts. In most cases when we say that someone has 'right' to do something, we imply that it would be wrong to interfere with his doing it, or at least that some special grounds are needed for justifying any interference. I use this strong sense of right when I say that you have the right to spend your money gambling, if you wish, though you ought to spend it in a more worthwhile way. I mean that it would be wrong for anyone to interfere with you even though you propose to spend your money in a way that I think is wrong.

There is a clear difference between saying that someone has a right to do something in this sense and saying that it is the 'right' thing for him to do, or that he does no 'wrong' in doing it. Someone may have the right to do something that is the wrong thing for him to do, as might be the case with gambling. Conversely, something may be the right thing for him to do and yet he may have no right to do it, in the sense that it would not be wrong for someone to interfere with his trying. If our army captures an enemy soldier, we might say that the right thing for him to do is to try to escape, but it would not follow that it is wrong for us to try to stop him. We might admire him for trying to escape, and perhaps even think less of him if he did not. But there is no suggestion here that it is wrong of us to stand in his way; on the contrary, if we think our cause is just, we think it right for us to do all we can to stop him.

Ordinarily this distinction, between the issues of whether a man has a right to do something and whether it is the right thing for him to do, causes no trouble. But sometimes it does, because sometimes we say that a man has a right to do something when we mean only to deny that it is the wrong thing for him to do. Thus we say that the captured soldier has a 'right' to try to escape when we mean, not that we do wrong to stop him, but that he has no duty not to make the attempt. We use 'right' this way when we speak of someone having the 'right' to act on his own principles, or the 'right' to follow his own conscience. We mean that he does no wrong to proceed on his honest convictions, even though we disagree with these convictions, and even though, for policy or other reasons, we must force him to act contrary to them.

Suppose a man believes that welfare payments to the poor are profoundly wrong, because they sap enterprise, and so declares his full income-tax each year but declines to pay half of it. We might say that he has a right to refuse to pay, if he wishes, but that the Government has a right to proceed against him for the full tax, and to fine or jail him for late payment if that is necessary to keep the collection system working efficiently. We do not take this line in most cases; we do not say that the ordinary thief has a right to steal, if he wishes, so long as he pays the penalty. We say a man has the right to break the law, even though the State has a right to punish him, only when we think that, because of his convictions, he does no wrong in doing so.[1]

These distinctions enable us to see an ambiguity in the orthodox question: Does a man ever have a right to break the law? Does that question mean to ask whether he ever has a right to break the law in the strong sense, so that the Government would do wrong to stop him, by arresting and prosecuting him? Or does it mean to ask whether he ever does the right thing to break the law, so that we should all respect him even though the Government should jail him?

If we take the orthodox position to be an answer to the first — and most important — question, then the paradoxes I described arise. But if we take it as an answer to the second, they do not. Conservatives and liberals do agree that sometimes a man does not do the wrong thing to break a law, when his conscience so requires. They disagree, when they do, over the different issue of what the State's response should be. Both parties do think that sometimes the State should prosecute. But this is not inconsistent with the proposition that the man prosecuted did the right thing in breaking the law.

The paradoxes seem genuine because the two questions are not usually distinguished, and the orthodox position is presented as a general solution to the problem of civil disobedience. But once the distinction is made, it is apparent that the position has been so widely accepted only because, when it is applied, it is treated as an answer to the second question but not the first. The crucial distinction is obscured by the troublesome idea of a right to conscience; this idea has been at the centre of most recent discussions of political obligation, but it is a red herring drawing us away from the crucial political questions. The state of a man's conscience may be decisive, or central, when the issue is whether he does something morally wrong in breaking the law; but it need not be decisive or even central when the issue is whether he has a right, in the strong sense of that term, to do so. A man does not have the right, in that sense, to do whatever his conscience demands, but he may have the right, in that sense, to do something even though his conscience does not demand it.

If that is true, then there has been almost no serious attempt to answer the questions that almost everyone means to ask. We can make a fresh start by stating these questions more clearly. Does an American ever have the right, in a strong sense, to do something which is against the law? If so, when? In order to answer these questions put in that way, we must try to become clearer about the implications of the idea, mentioned earlier, that citizens have at least some rights against their government.

I said that in the United States citizens are supposed to have certain fundamental rights against their Government, certain moral rights made into legal rights by the Constitution. If this idea is significant, and worth bragging about, then these rights must be rights in the strong sense I just described. The claim that citizens have a right to free speech must imply that it would be wrong for the Government to stop them from speaking, even when the Government believes that what they will say will cause more harm than good. The claim cannot mean, on the prisoner-of-war analogy, only that citizens do no wrong in speaking their minds, though the Government reserves the right to prevent them from doing so.

This is a crucial point, and I want to labour it. Of course a responsible government must be ready to justify anything it does, particularly when it limits the liberty of its citizens. But normally it is a sufficient justification, even for an act that limits liberty, that the act is calculated to increase what the philosophers call general utility — that it is calculated to produce more over-all benefit than harm. So, though the New York City government needs a justification for forbidding motorists to drive up Lexington Avenue, it is sufficient justification if the proper officials believe, on sound evidence, that the gain to the many will outweigh the inconvenience to the few. When individual citizens are said to have rights against the Government, however, like the right of free speech, that must mean that this sort of justification is not enough. Otherwise the claim would not argue that individuals have special protection against the law when their rights are in play, and that is just the point of the claim.

Not all legal rights, or even Constitutional rights, represent moral rights against the Government. I now have the legal right to drive either way on Fifty-seventh Street, but the Government would do no wrong to make that street one-way if it thought it in the general interest to do so. I have a Constitutional right to vote for a congressman every two years, but the national and state governments would do no wrong if, following the amendment procedure, they made a congressman's term four years instead of two, again on the basis of a judgment that this would be for the general good.

But those Constitutional rights that we call fundamental like the right of free speech, are supposed to represent rights against the Government in the strong sense; that is the point of the boast that our legal system respect the fundamental rights of the citizen. If citizens have a moral right of free speech, then governments would do wrong to repeal the First Amendment that guarantees it, even if they were persuaded that the majority would be better off if speech were curtailed.

I must not overstate the point. Someone who claims that citizens have a right against the Government need not go so far as to say that the State is *never* justified in overriding that right. He might say, for example, that although citizens have a right to free speech, the Government may override that right when necessary to protect the rights of others, or to prevent a catastrophe, or even to obtain a clear and major public benefit (though if he acknowledged this last as a possible justification he would be treating the right in question as not among the most important or fundamental). What he cannot do is to say that the Government is justified in overriding a right on the minimal grounds that would be sufficient if no such right existed. He cannot say that the Government is entitled to act on no more than a judgment that its act is likely to produce, overall, a benefit to the community. That admission would make his claim of a right pointless, and would show him to be using some sense of 'right' other than the strong sense necessary to give his claim the political importance it is normally taken to have.

But then the answers to our two questions about disobedience seem plain, if unorthodox. In our society a man does sometimes have the right, in the strong sense, to disobey a law. He has that right whenever that law wrongly invades his rights against the Government. If he has a moral right to free speech, that is, then he has a moral right to break any law that the Government, by virtue of his right, had no right to adopt. The right to disobey the law is not a separate right, having something to do with conscience, additional to other rights against the Government. It is simply a feature of these rights against the Government, and it cannot be denied in principle without denying that any such rights exist.

These answers seem obvious once we take rights against the Government to be rights in the strong sense I described. If I have a right to speak my mind on political issues, then the Government does wrong to make it illegal for me to do so, even if it thinks this is in the general interest. If, nevertheless, the Government does make my act illegal, then it does a further wrong to enforce that law against me. My right against the Government means that it is wrong for the Government to stop me from speaking; the Government cannot make it right to stop me just by taking the first step.

This does not, of course, tell us exactly what rights men do have against the Government. It does not tell us whether the right of free speech includes the right of demonstration. But it does mean that passing a law cannot affect such rights as men do have, and that is of crucial importance, because it dictates the attitude that an individual is entitled to take toward his personal decision when civil disobedience is in question.

Both conservatives and liberals suppose that in a society which is generally decent everyone has a duty to obey the law, whatever it is. That is the source of the 'general duty' clause in the orthodox position, and though liberals believe that this duty can sometimes be 'overridden,' even they suppose, as the orthodox position maintains, that the duty of obedience remains in some submerged form, so that a man does well to accept punishment in recognition of that duty. But this general duty is almost incoherent in a society that recognizes rights. If a

man believes he has a right to demonstrate, then he must believe that it would be wrong for the Government to stop him, with or without benefit of a law. If he is entitled to believe that, then it is silly to speak of a duty to obey the law as such, or of a duty to accept the punishment that the State has no right to give.

Conservatives will object to the short work I have made of their point. They will argue that even if the Government was wrong to adopt some law, like a law limiting speech, there are independent reasons why the Government is justified in enforcing the law once adopted. When the law forbids demonstration, then, so they argue, some principle more important than the individual's right to speak is brought into play, namely the principle of respect for law. If a law, even a bad law, is left unenforced, then respect for law is weakened, and society as a whole suffers. So an individual loses his moral right to speak when speech is made criminal, and the Government must, for the common good and for the general benefit, enforce the law against him.

But this argument, though popular, is plausible only if we forget what it means to say that an individual has a right against the State. It is far from plain that civil disobedience lowers respect for law, but even if we suppose that it does, this fact is irrelevant. The prospect of utilitarian gains cannot justify preventing a man from doing what he has a right to do, and the supposed gains in respect for law are simply utilitarian gains. There would be no point in the boast that we respect individual rights unless that involved some sacrifice, and the sacrifice in question must be that we give up whatever marginal benefits our country would receive from overriding these rights when they prove inconvenient. So the general benefit cannot be a good ground for abridging rights, even when the benefit in question is a heightened respect for law.

But perhaps I do wrong to assume that the argument about respect for law is only an appeal to general utility. I said that a state may be justified in overriding or limiting rights on other grounds, and we must ask, before rejecting the conservative position, whether any of these apply. The most important — and least well understood — of these other grounds invokes the notion of *competing rights* that would be jeopardized if the right in question were not limited. Citizens have personal rights to the State's protection as well as personal rights to be free from the State's interference, and it may be necessary for the Government to choose between these two sorts of rights. The law of defamation, for example, limits the personal right of any man to say what he thinks, because it requires him to have good grounds for what he says. But this law is justified, even for those who think that it does invade a personal right, by the fact that it protects the right of others not to have their reputations ruined by a careless statement.

The individual rights that our society acknowledges often conflict in this way, and when they do it is the job of government to discriminate. If the Government makes the right choice, and protects the more important at the cost of the less, then it has not weakened or cheapened the notion of a right; on the contrary it would have done so had it failed to protect the more important of the two. So we must acknowledge that the Government has a reason for limiting rights if it plausibly believes that a competing right is more important.

May the conservative seize on this fact? He might argue that I did wrong to characterize his argument as one that appeals to the general benefit, because it appeals instead to competing rights, namely the moral right of the majority to have its laws enforced, or the right of society to maintain the degree of order and security it wishes. These are the rights, he would say, that must be weighed against the individual's right to do what the wrongful law prohibits.

But this new argument is confused, because it depends on yet another ambiguity in the language of rights. It is true that we speak of the 'right' of society to do what it wants, but this cannot be a 'competing right' of the sort that may justify the invasion of a right against the Government. The existence of rights against the Government would be jeopardized if the Government were able to defeat such a right by appealing to the right of a democratic majority to work its will. A right against the Government must be a right to do something even when the majority thinks it would be wrong to do it, and even when the majority would be worse off for having it done. If we now say that society has a right to do whatever is in the general benefit, or the right to preserve whatever sort of environment the majority wishes to live in, and we mean that these are the sort of rights that provide justification for

overruling any rights against the Government that may conflict, then we have annihilated the latter rights.

In order to save them, we must recognize as competing rights only the rights of other members of the society as individuals. We must distinguish the 'rights' of the majority as such, which cannot count as a justification for overruling individual rights, and the personal rights of members of a majority, which might well count. The test we must use is this. Someone has a competing right to protection, which must be weighed against an individual right to act, if that person would be entitled to demand that protection from his government on his own title, as an individual, without regard to whether a majority of his fellow citizens joined in the demand.

It cannot be true, on this test, that anyone has a right to have all the laws of the nation enforced. He has a right to have enforced only those criminal laws, for example, that he would have a right to have enacted if they were not already law. The laws against personal assault may well fall into that class. If the physically vulnerable members of the community—those who need police protection against personal violence—were only a small minority, it would still seem plausible to say that they were entitled to that protection. But the laws that provide a certain level of quiet in public places, or that authorize and finance a foreign war, cannot be thought to rest on individual rights. The timid lady on the streets of Chicago is not entitled to just the degree of quiet that now obtains, nor is she entitled to have boys drafted to fight in wars she approves. There are laws—perhaps desirable laws— that provide these advantages for her, but the justification for these laws, if they can be justified at all, is the common desire of a large majority, not her personal right. If, therefore, these laws do abridge someone else's moral right to protest, or his right to personal security, she cannot urge a competing right to justify the abridgement. She has no personal right to have such laws passed, and she has no competing right to have them enforced either.

So the conservative cannot advance his argument much on the ground of competing rights, but he may want to use another ground. A government, he may argue, may be justified in abridging the personal rights of its citizens in an emergency, or when a very great loss may be prevented, or perhaps, when some major benefit can clearly be secured. If the nation is at war, a policy of censorship may be justified even though it invades the right to say what one thinks on matters of political controversy. But the emergency must be genuine. There must be what Oliver Wendell Holmes described as a clear and present danger, and the danger must be one of magnitude.

Can the conservative argue that when any law is passed, even a wrongful law, this sort of justification is available for enforcing it? His argument might be something of this sort. If the Government once acknowledges that it may be wrong — that the legislature might have adopted, the executive approved, and the courts left standing, a law that in fact abridges important rights — then this admission will lead not simply to a marginal decline in respect for law, but to a crisis of order. Citizens may decide to obey only those laws they personally approve, and that is anarchy. So the Government must insist that whatever a citizen's rights may be before a law is passed and upheld by the courts, his rights thereafter are determined by that law.

But this argument ignores the primitive distinction between what may happen and what will happen. If we allow speculation to support the justification of emergency or decisive benefit, then, again, we have annihilated rights. We must, as Learned Hand said, discount the gravity of the evil threatened by the likelihood of reaching that evil. I know of no genuine evidence to the effect that tolerating some civil disobedience, out of respect for the moral position of its authors, will increase such disobedience, let alone crime in general. The case that it will must be based on vague assumptions about the contagion of ordinary crimes, assumptions that are themselves unproved, and that are in any event largely irrelevant. It seems at least as plausible to argue that tolerance will increase respect for officials and for the bulk of the laws they promulgate, or at least retard the rate of growing disrespect.

If the issue were simply the question whether the community would be marginally better off under strict law enforcement, then the Government would have to decide on the evidence we have, and it might not be unreasonable to decide, on balance, that it would. But since rights are at stake, the issue is the very different one of whether tolerance would

destroy the community or threaten it with great harm, and it seems to me simply mindless to suppose that the evidence makes that probable or even conceivable.

The argument from emergency is confused in another way as well. It assumes that the Government must take the position either that a man never has the right to break the law, or that he always does. I said that any society that claims to recognize rights at all must abandon the notion of a general duty to obey the law that holds in all cases. This is important, because it shows that there are no short cuts to meeting a citizen's claim to right. If a citizen argues that he has a moral right not to serve in the Army, or to protest in a way he finds effective, then an official who wants to answer him, and not simply bludgeon him into obedience, must respond to the particular point he makes, and cannot point to the draft law or a Supreme Court decision as having even special, let alone decisive, weight. Sometimes an official who considers the citizen's moral arguments in good faith will be persuaded that the citizen's claim is plausible, or even right. It does not follow, however, that he will always be persuaded or that he always should be.

I must emphasize that all these propositions concern the strong sense of right, and they therefore leave open important questions about the right thing to do. If a man believes he has the right to break the law, he must then ask whether he does the right thing to exercise that right. He must remember that reasonable men can differ about whether he has a right against the Government, and therefore the right to break the law, that he thinks he has; and therefore that reasonable men can oppose him in good faith. He must take into account the various consequences his act will have, whether they involve violence, and such other considerations as the context makes relevant; he must not go beyond the rights he can in good faith claim, to acts that violate the rights of others.

On the other hand, if some official, like a prosecutor, believes that the citizen does *not* have the right to break the law, then *he* must ask whether he does the right thing to enforce it. . . . In Chapter 8 I argue that certain features of our legal system, and in particular the fusion of legal and moral issues in our Constitution, mean that citizens often do the right thing in exercising what they take to be moral rights to break the law, and that prosecutors often do the right thing in failing to prosecute them for it. I will not anticipate those arguments here; instead I want to ask whether the requirement that Government take its citizens' rights seriously has anything to do with the crucial question of what these rights are.

3. *Controversial Rights*

The argument so far has been hypothetical: if a man has a particular moral right against the Government, that right survives contrary legislation or adjudication. But this does not tell us what rights he has, and it is notorious that reasonable men disagree about that. There is wide agreement on certain clearcut cases; almost everyone who believes in rights at all would admit, for example, that a man has a moral right to speak his mind in a non-provocative way on matters of political concern, and that this is an important right that the State must go to great pains to protect. But there is great controversy as to the limits of such paradigm rights, and the so-called 'anti-riot' law involved in the famous Chicago Seven trial of the last decade is a case in point.

The defendants were accused of conspiring to cross state lines with the intention of causing a riot. This charge is vague — perhaps unconstitutionally vague — but the law apparently defines as criminal emotional speeches which argue that violence is justified in order to secure political equality. Does the right of free speech protect this sort of speech? That, of course, is a legal issue, because it invokes the free-speech clause of the First Amendment of the Constitution. But it is also a moral issue, because, as I said, we must treat the First Amendment as an attempt to protect a moral right. It is part of the job of governing to 'define' moral rights through statutes and judicial decisions, that is, to declare officially the extent that moral rights will be taken to have in law. Congress faced this task in voting on the anti-riot bill, and the Supreme Court has faced it in countless cases. How should the different departments of government go about defining moral rights?

They should begin with a sense that whatever they decide might be wrong. History and their descendants may judge that they acted unjustly when they thought they were right. If they take their duty seriously, they must try to limit their mistakes, and they must therefore try to discover where the dangers of mistake lie.

They might choose one of two very different models for this purpose. The first model recommends striking a balance between the rights of the individual and the demands of society at large. If the Government *infringes* on a moral right (for example, by defining the right of free speech more narrowly than justice requires), then it has done the individual a wrong. On the other hand, if the Government *inflates* a right (by defining it more broadly than justice requires) then it cheats society of some general benefit, like safe streets, that there is no reason it should not have. So a mistake on one side is as serious as a mistake on the other. The course of government is to steer to the middle, to balance the general good and personal rights, giving to each its due.

When the Government, or any of its branches, defines a right, it must bear in mind, according to the first model, the social cost of different proposals and make the necessary adjustments. It must not grant the same freedom to noisy demonstrations as it grants to calm political discussion, for example, because the former causes much more trouble than the latter. Once it decides how much of a right to recognize, it must enforce its decision to the full. That means permitting an individual to act within his rights, as the Government has defined them, but not beyond, so that if anyone breaks the law, even on grounds of conscience, he must be punished. No doubt any government will make mistakes, and will regret decisions once taken. That is inevitable. But this middle policy will ensure that errors on one side will balance out errors on the other over the long run.

The first model, described in this way, has great plausibility, and most laymen and lawyers, I think, would respond to it warmly. The metaphor of balancing the public interest against personal claims is established in our political and judicial rhetoric, and this metaphor gives the model both familiarity and appeal. Nevertheless, the first model is a false one, certainly in the case of rights generally regarded as important, and the metaphor is the heart of its error.

The institution of rights against the Government is not a gift of God, or an ancient ritual, or a national sport. It is a complex and troublesome practice that makes the Government's job of securing the general benefit more difficult and more expensive, and it would be a frivolous and wrongful practice unless it served some point. Anyone who professes to take rights seriously, and who praises our Government for respecting them, must have some sense of what that point is. He must accept, at the minimum, one or both of two important ideas. The first is the vague but powerful idea of human dignity. This idea, associated with Kant, but defended by philosophers of different schools, supposes that there are ways of treating a man that are inconsistent with recognizing him as a full member of the human community, and holds that such treatment is profoundly unjust.

The second is the more familiar idea of political equality. This supposes that the weaker members of a political community are entitled to the same concern and respect of their government as the more powerful members have secured for themselves, so that if some men have freedom of decision whatever the effect on the general good, then all men must have the same freedom. I do not want to defend or elaborate these ideas here, but only to insist that anyone who claims that citizens have rights must accept ideas very close to these.[2]

It makes sense to say that a man has a fundamental right against the Government, in the strong sense, like free speech, if that right is necessary to protect his dignity, or his standing as equally entitled to concern and respect, or some other personal value of like consequence. It does not make sense otherwise.

So if rights make sense at all, then the invasion of a relatively important right must be a very serious matter. It means treating a man as less than a man, or as less worthy of concern than other men. The institution of rights rests on the conviction that this is a grave injustice, and that it is worth paying the incremental cost in social policy or efficiency that is necessary to prevent it. But then it must be wrong to say that inflating rights is as serious as invading them. If the Government errs on the side of the individual, then it simply pays a little more in social efficiency than it has to pay; it pays a little more, that is, of the same coin that it has already decided must be spent. But if it errs against the individual it inflicts an insult upon him that, on its own reckoning, it is worth a great deal of that coin to avoid.

So the first model is indefensible. It rests, in fact, on a mistake I discussed earlier, namely the confusion of society's rights with the rights of members of society. 'Balancing' is appropriate when the Government must choose between competing claims of right — between the Southerner's claim to freedom of association, for example, and the black man's claim to an equal education. Then the Government can do nothing but estimate the merits of the competing claims, and act on its estimate. The first model assumes that the 'right' of the majority is a competing right that must be balanced in this way; but that, as I argued before, is a confusion that threatens to destroy the concept of individual rights. It is worth noticing that the community rejects the first model in that area where the stakes for the individual are highest, the criminal process. We say that it is better that a great many guilty men go free than that one innocent man be punished, and that homily rests on the choice of the second model for government.

The second model treats abridging a right as much more serious than inflating one, and its recommendations follow from that judgment. It stipulates that once a right is recognized in clear-cut cases, then the Government should act to cut off that right only when some compelling reason is presented, some reason that is consistent with the suppositions on which the original right must be based. It cannot be an argument for curtailing a right, once granted, simply that society would pay a further price for extending it. There must be something special about that further cost, or there must be some other feature of the case, that makes it sensible to say that although great social cost is warranted to protect the original right, this particular cost is not necessary. Otherwise, the Government's failure to extend the right will show that its recognition of the right in the original case is a sham, a promise that it intends to keep only until that becomes inconvenient.

How can we show that a particular cost is not worth paying without taking back the initial recognition of a right? I can think of only three sorts of grounds that can consistently be used to limit the definition of a particular right. First, the Government might show that the values protected by the original right are not really at stake in the marginal case, or are at stake only in some attenuated form. Second, it might show that if the right is defined to include the marginal case, then some competing right, in the strong sense I described earlier, would be abridged. Third, it might show that if the right were so defined, then the cost to society would not be simply incremental, but would be of a degree far beyond the cost paid to grant the original right, a degree great enough to justify whatever assault on dignity or equality might be involved.

It is fairly easy to apply these grounds to one group of problems the Supreme Court faced, imbedded in constitutional issues. The draft law provided an exemption for conscientious objectors, but this exemption, as interpreted by the draft boards, has been limited to those who object to *all* wars on *religious* grounds. If we suppose that the exemption is justified on the ground that an individual has a moral right not to kill in violation of his own principles, then the question is raised whether it is proper to exclude those whose morality is not based on religion, or whose morality is sufficiently complex to distinguish among wars. The Court held, as a matter of Constitutional law, that the draft boards were wrong to exclude the former, but competent to exclude the latter.

None of the three grounds I listed can justify either of these exclusions as a matter of political morality. The invasion of personality in forcing men to kill when they believe killing immoral is just as great when these beliefs are based on secular grounds, or take account of the fact that wars differ in morally relevant ways, and there is no pertinent difference in competing rights or in national emergency. There are differences among the cases, of course, but they are insufficient to justify the distinction. A government that is secular on principle cannot prefer a religious to a nonreligious morality as such. There are utilitarian arguments in favour of limiting the exception to religious or universal grounds—an exemption so limited may be less expensive to administer, and may allow easier discrimination between sincere and insincere applicants. But these utilitarian reasons are irrelevant, because they cannot count as grounds for limiting a right.

What about the anti-riot law, as applied in the Chicago trial? Does the law represent an improper limitation of the right to free speech, supposedly protected by the First Amendment? If we were to apply the first model for government to this issue, the argument for the anti-riot law would look strong. But if we set aside talk of balancing as inappropriate, and turn to the proper grounds for limiting a right, then the argument becomes a great deal weaker. The original right of free speech must suppose that it is an assault on human personality to stop a man from expressing what he honestly believes, particularly on issues affecting how he is governed. Surely the assault is greater, and not less, when he is stopped from expressing those principles of political morality that he holds most passionately, in the face of what he takes to be outrageous violations of these principles.

It may be said that the anti-riot law leaves him free to express these principles in a non-provocative way. But that misses the point of the connection between expression and dignity. A man cannot express himself freely when he cannot match his rhetoric to his outrage, or when he must trim his sails to protect values he counts as nothing next to those he is trying to vindicate. It is true that some political dissenters speak in ways that shock the majority, but it is arrogant for the majority to suppose that the orthodox methods of expression are the proper ways to speak, for this is a denial of equal concern and respect. If the point of the right is to protect the dignity of dissenters, then we must make judgments about appropriate speech with the personalities of the dissenters in mind, not the personality of the 'silent' majority for whom the anti-riot law is no restraint at all.

So the argument fails, that the personal values protected by the original right are less at stake in this marginal case. We must consider whether competing rights, or some grave threat to society, nevertheless justify the anti-riot law. We can consider these two grounds together, because the only plausible competing rights are rights to be free from violence, and violence is the only plausible threat to society that the context provides.

I have no right to burn your house, or stone you or your car, or swing a bicycle chain against your skull, even if I find these to be natural means of expression. But the defendants in the Chicago trial were not accused of direct violence; the argument runs that the acts of speech they planned made it likely that others would do acts of violence, either in support of or out of hostility to what they said. Does this provide a justification?

The question would be different if we could say with any confidence how much and what sort of violence the anti-riot law might be expected to prevent. Will it save two lives a year, or two hundred, or two thousand? Two thousand dollars of property, or two hundred thousand, or two million? No one can say, not simply because prediction is next to impossible, but because we have no firm understanding of the process by which demonstration disintegrates into riot, and in particular of the part played by inflammatory speech, as distinct from poverty, police brutality, blood lust, and all the rest of human and economic failure. The Government must try, of course, to reduce the violent waste of lives and property, but it must recognize that any attempt to locate and remove a cause of riot, short of a reorganization of society, must be an exercise in speculation, trial, and error. It must make its decisions under conditions of high uncertainty, and the institution of rights, taken seriously, limits its freedom to experiment under such conditions.

It forces the Government to bear in mind that preventing a man from speaking or demonstrating offers him a certain and profound insult, in return for a speculative benefit that may in any event be achieved in other if more expensive ways. When lawyers say that rights may be limited to protect other rights, or to prevent catastrophe, they have in mind cases in which cause and effect are relatively clear, like the familiar example of a man falsely crying 'Fire!' in a crowded theater.

But the Chicago story shows how obscure the causal connections can become. Were the speeches of Hoffman or Rubin necessary conditions of the riot? Or had thousands of people come to Chicago for the purposes of rioting anyway, as the Government also argues? Were they in any case sufficient conditions? Or could the police have contained the violence if they had not been so busy contributing to it, as the staff of the President's Commission on violence said they were?

These are not easy questions, but if rights mean anything, then the Government cannot simply assume answers that justify its conduct. If a man has a right to speak, if the reasons that support that right extend to provocative political speech, and if the effects of such speech on violence are unclear, then the Government is not entitled to make its first attack on that problem by denying that right. It may be that abridging the right to speak is the least expensive course, or the least damaging to police morale, or the most popular politically. But these are utilitarian arguments in favor of starting one place rather than another, and such arguments are ruled out by the concept of rights.

This point may be obscured by the popular belief that political activists look forward to violence and 'ask for trouble' in what they say. They can hardly complain, in the general view, if they are taken to be the authors of the violence they expect, and treated accordingly. But this repeats the confusion I tried to explain earlier between having a right and doing the right thing. The speaker's motives may be relevant in deciding whether he does the right thing in speaking passionately about issues that may inflame or enrage the audience. But if he has a right to speak, because the danger in allowing him to speak is speculative, his motives cannot count as independent evidence in the argument that justifies stopping him.

But what of the individual rights of those who will be destroyed by a riot, of the passer-by who will be killed by a sniper's bullet or the shopkeeper who will be ruined by looting? To put the issue in this way, as a question of competing rights, suggests a principle that would undercut the effect of uncertainty. Shall we say that some rights to protection are so important that the Government is justified in doing all it can to maintain them? Shall we therefore say that the Government may abridge the rights of others to act when their acts might simply increase the risk, by however slight or speculative a margin, that some persons' right to life or property will be violated?

Some such principle is relied on by those who oppose the Supreme Court's recent liberal rulings on police procedure. These rulings increase the chance that a guilty man will go free, and therefore marginally increase the risk that any particular member of the community will be murdered, raped, or robbed. Some critics believe that the Court's decisions must therefore be wrong.

But no society that purports to recognize a variety of rights, on the ground that a man's dignity or equality may be invaded in a variety of ways, can accept such a principle. If forcing a man to testify against himself, or forbidding him to speak, does the damage that the rights against self-incrimination and the right of free speech assume, then it would be contemptuous for the State to tell a man that he must suffer this damage against the possibility that other men's risks of loss may be marginally reduced. If rights make sense, then the degrees of their importance cannot be so different that some count not at all when others are mentioned.

Of course the Government may discriminate and may stop a man from exercising his right to speak when there is a clear and substantial risk that his speech will do great damage to the person or property of others, and no other means of preventing this are at hand, as in the case of the man shouting 'Fire!' in a theater. But we must reject the suggested principle that the Government can simply ignore rights to speak when life and property are in question. So long as the impact of speech on these other rights remains speculative and marginal, it must look elsewhere for levers to pull.

4. *Why Take Rights Seriously?*

I said at the beginning of this essay that I wanted to show what a government must do that professes to recognize individual rights. It must dispense with the claim that citizens never have a right to break its law, and it must not define citizens' rights so that these are cut off for supposed reasons of the general good. Any Government's harsh treatment of civil disobedience, or campaign against vocal protest, may therefore be thought to count against its sincerity.

One might well ask, however, whether it is wise to take rights all that seriously after all. America's genius, at least in her own legend, lies in not taking any abstract doctrine to its logical extreme. It may be time to ignore abstractions, and concentrate instead on giving the majority of our citizens a new sense of their Government's concern for their welfare, and of their title to rule.

That, in any event, is what former Vice-President Agnew seemed to believe. In a policy statement on the issue of 'weirdos' and social misfits, he said that the liberals' concern for individual rights was a headwind blowing in the face of the ship of state. That is a poor metaphor, but the philosophical point it expresses is very well taken. He recognized, as many liberals do not, that the majority cannot travel as fast or as far as it would like if it recognizes the rights of individuals to do what, in the majority's terms, is the wrong thing to do.

Spiro Agnew supposed that rights are divisive, and that national unity and a new respect for law may be developed by taking them more skeptically.

But he is wrong. America will continue to be divided by its social and foreign policy, and if the economy grows weaker again the divisions will become more bitter. If we want our laws and our legal institutions to provide the ground rules within which these issues will be contested then these ground rules must not be the conqueror's law that the dominant class imposes on the weaker, as Marx supposed the law of a capitalist society must be. The bulk of the law — that part which defines and implements social, economic, and foreign policy — cannot be neutral. It must state, in its greatest part, the majority's view of the common good. The institution of rights is therefore crucial, because it represents the majority's promise to the minorities that their dignity and equality will be respected. When the divisions among the groups are most violent, then this gesture, if law is to work, must be most sincere.

The institution requires an act of faith on the part of the minorities, because the scope of their rights will be controversial whenever they are important, and because the officers of the majority will act on their own notions of what these rights really are. Of course these officials will disagree with many of the claims that a minority makes. That makes it all the more important that they take their decisions gravely. They must show that they understand what rights are, and they must not cheat on the full implications of the doctrine. The Government will not re-establish respect for law without giving the law some claim to respect. It cannot do that if it neglects the one feature that distinguishes law from ordered brutality. If the Government does not take rights seriously, then it does not take law seriously either.

Endnotes

[1] It is not surprising that we sometimes use the concept of having a right to say that others must not interfere with an act and sometimes to say that the act is not the wrong thing to do. Often, when someone has *no* right to do something, like attacking another man physically, it is true *both* that it is the wrong thing to do and that others are entitled to stop it, by demand, if not by force. It is therefore natural to say that someone has a right when we mean to deny *either* of these consequences, as well as when we mean to deny both.

[2] He need not consider these ideas to be axiomatic. He may, that is, have reasons for insisting that dignity or equality are important values, and these reasons may be utilitarian. He may believe, for example, that the general good

will be advanced, *in the long run,* only if we treat indignity or inequality as very great injustices, and never allow our *opinions* about the general good to justify them. I do not know of any good arguments for or against this sort of 'in-stitutional' utilitarianism, but it is consistent with my point, because it argues that we must treat violations of dignity and equality as special moral crimes, beyond the reach of ordinary utilitarian justification.

XIII.4 *Epistemology of Human Rights*

ALAN GEWIRTH

Alan Gewirth is professor emeritus of philosophy at the University of Chicago and the author of *Reason of Morality* and several essays in moral theory. He believes that rights are the basis of morality and can be proven rationally. After clearly defining human rights ("rights which all persons equally have simply insofar as they are human") and critically surveying previous attempts to justify the belief in the existence of these rights, Gewirth sets forth an argument that claims to demonstrate that such rights exist. Starting from the premise that "I do X for end or purpose E," which entails "E is good," he constructs an argument showing that on the basis of "generic features" of action, freedom, and purposiveness, we can conclude that there are universal human rights.

Gewirth's argument is succinct and precise. It constitutes a challenge to antinatural-rights philosophers to show where his argument goes wrong.

Human rights are rights which all persons equally have simply insofar as they are human. But are there any such rights? How, if at all, do we know that there are?

It is with this question of knowledge, and the related question of existence, that I want to deal in this paper.

I. *Conceptual Questions*

The attempt to answer each of these questions, however, at once raises further, more directly conceptual questions. In what sense may human rights be said to exist? What does it mean to say that there *are* such rights or that persons have them? This question, in turn, raises a question about the nature of human rights. What is the meaning of the expression "human rights"?

Within the limits of the present paper I cannot hope to deal adequately with the controversial issues raised by these conceptual questions. But we may make at least a relevant beginning by noting that, in terms of Hohfeld's famous classification of four different kinds of rights,[1] the human rights are primarily claim-rights, in that they entail correlative duties of other persons or groups to act or to refrain from acting in ways required for the right-holders' having that to which they have rights.

It will help our understanding of this and other aspects of human rights if we note that the full structure of a claim-right is given by the following formula:

A has a right to X against B by virtue of Y.

There are five main elements here: first, the *Subject* (A) of the right, the person or persons who have the

Reprinted with permission from *Human Rights,* eds. Ellen Paul, Fred Miller, and Jeffrey Paul (Blackwell, 1984).

right; second, the *Nature* of the right; third, the *Object* (X) of the right, what it is a right to; fourth, the *Respondent* (B) of the right, the person or persons who have the correlative duty; fifth, the *Justifying Basis* or *Ground* (Y) of the right. (I capitalize each of these elements for the sake of emphasis and for easier recognition in what follows).

Let us now briefly analyze the human rights in terms of these five elements. Each element involves controversial questions about the interpretation of human rights, but for the present purposes I shall have to be content with a brief summary. The Subjects of the human rights are all human beings equally. The Respondents of the human rights are also all human beings, although in certain respects governments have special duties to secure the rights. The Objects of the human rights, what they are rights to, are certain especially important kinds of goods. I shall subsequently argue that these goods consist in the necessary conditions of human action, and that it is for this reason that the human rights are supremely mandatory. It is also largely because the human rights have these Objects that they are uniquely and centrally important among all moral concepts, since no morality, together with the goods, virtues, and rules emphasized in diverse moralities, is possible without the necessary goods of action that are the Objects of human rights.

Let us, now, turn to the Nature of human rights, which was one of the conceptual questions I raised at the outset. This Nature is often expressed by formulations that are common to all claim-rights: that rights are entitlements, or justified claims, or the moral property of individuals. While recognizing some merit in each of these formulations, I wish to suggest another that is at once more comprehensive and more specifically tied to human rights. Such rights are *personally oriented, normatively necessary moral requirements*. Let me briefly elucidate the point of each part of this definition. The point of calling the human rights *personally oriented* is to bring out that they are requirements that are owed to distinct Subjects or individuals for the good of those individuals. This feature distinguishes human rights from utilitarian and collectivist norms where rights, if upheld at all, are consequential upon or instrumental to the fulfillment of aggregative or collective goals. The point of saying that the rights are *normatively necessary* is to indicate that compliance with them is morally mandatory.

Such mandatoriness distinguishes the human rights from virtues and other goods whose moral status may be supererogatory, such as generosity or charity. Finally, in saying that the human rights are *moral requirements,* I wish to indicate three distinct but related aspects of human rights: they are requirements, first, in the sense of necessary needs; second, in the sense of justified entitlements; and third, in the sense of claims or demands made on or addressed to other persons. These three aspects involve the relations, respectively, between the Subjects and the Objects of the rights, between Objects and their Justifying Basis, and between Subjects and their Respondents.

What has been said so far, then, is that the Nature of human rights consists in personally oriented, normatively necessary moral requirements that every human have the necessary goods of action. From this it follows that the Justifying Basis or Ground of human rights is a normative moral principle that serves to prove or establish that every human morally ought, as a matter of normative necessity, to have the necessary goods as something to which he is personally entitled, which he can claim from others as his due.

These considerations have a direct bearing on one of the other conceptual questions I raised at the outset, about what it means for human rights to exist. The existence in question is not, in any straightforward way, empirical. Although Thomas Jefferson wrote that all humans "are endowed by their Creator with certain inalienable rights," it is not the case that humans are born having rights in the sense in which they are born having legs. At least, their having legs is empirically verifiable, but this is not the case with their having moral rights. The having or existence of human rights consists in the first instance not in the having of certain physical or mental attributes, but rather in certain justified moral requirements, in the three senses of "requirement" mentioned above.

There is, indeed, a sense in which the existence of human rights may be construed as consisting in certain positive institutional conditions. In this sense, human rights exist, or persons have human rights, when and insofar as there is social recognition and legal enforcement of all persons' equal entitlement to the aforementioned Objects, i.e. the necessary goods of action. But this positivist interpretation of the existence of human rights is posterior to a normative moral interpretation, since, as we have seen, the rights are in the first instance justified moral requirements. In the phrase, "there are human rights," "there are" is ambiguous as between positive and normative meanings. In the sense of "existence" that is relevant here, the existence of human rights is independent of whether they are guaranteed or enforced by legal codes or are socially recognized. For if the existence of human rights depended on such recognition or enforcement, it would follow that there were no human rights prior to or independent of these positive enactments.

The primary relevant sense of the existence of human rights, then, is the normatively moral justificatory one. In this sense, for human rights to exist, or for all persons to have human rights, means that there are conclusive moral reasons that justify or ground the moral requirements that constitute the Nature of human rights, such that every human can justifiably claim or demand, against all other humans or, in relevant cases, against governments, that he have or possess the necessary conditions of human action.

From this it follows that the epistemological question I raised at the outset is crucial to answering the ontological question of whether there are any human rights. That human rights exist, or that persons have human rights, is a proposition whose truth depends on the possibility, in principle, of constructing a body of moral justificatory argument from which that proposition follows as a logical consequence. This consideration also entails the epistemological point that to know or ascertain whether there are human rights requires not the scrutiny of legal codes or the empirical observation of social conditions but rather the ability, in principle, to construct such a moral argument.

The qualification "in principle" must be emphasized here. I am not saying that the very existence of human rights as a certain kind of morally justified norm is contingent on the actual success of this or that philosophical justificatory exercise. The existence of human rights depends on the existence of certain moral justificatory reasons; but these reasons may exist even if they are not explicitly ascertained. Because of this, it is correct to say that all persons had human rights even in ancient Greece, whose leading philosophers did not develop the relevant reasons. Thus, the existence of moral reasons is in important respects something that is discov-

ered rather than invented. The failure of this or that attempt at discovery does not, of itself, entail that there is nothing there *to be* discovered.

The epistemological structure suggested by these considerations is unilinear and foundationalist, since the existence of human rights is held to follow from justificatory moral reasons and ultimately from a supreme moral principle. An alternative, coherentist structure would involve that the existence of human rights is not to be established in any such unilinear way but rather by a sequence of interrelated reasons that may themselves include judgments about the existence of human rights. This latter structure, however, besides being more complicated, may be convicted of vicious circularity, including the difficulty that it may not serve to convince those who on purportedly rational grounds have denied the existence of human rights. I shall deal below with some further aspects of this question.

There have, of course, been philosophers, such as Bentham and Marx, who on various other grounds have denied the very possibility of constructing a moral justificatory argument for human rights. Hence, they have denied that human rights exist in what I have said is the primary sense of such existence. Among the grounds they have given for this denial is the moral one that human rights are excessively individualistic or egoistic, so that their espousal leads, in Bentham's words, to overriding what is "conducive to the happiness of society,"[2] and, in Marx's words, to separating man from the values of "community" and "degrading the sphere in which man functions as a species-being."[3] I shall not deal further with these criticisms here, except to note that they involve the epistemological question of whether a rational justification can be given of a moral principle that holds that all persons equally have certain moral rights. Such a principle should be able to accommodate the social emphasis of thinkers like Bentham and Marx while avoiding their excesses.

In the remainder of this paper, then, I want to do two main things. First, I shall conduct a brief critical examination of some of the main recent attempts on the part of moral philosophers to work out an affirmative answer to the epistemological question of whether the existence of human rights can be known, proved, or established. In criticizing each of these attempted answers, I shall elicit certain conditions that must be satisfied by a successful answer to the question. Second, I shall give my own answer and shall indicate why I think it fulfills these conditions.

II. *Prior Attempts at Justification: Conditions for Success*

Before considering the answers given by other philosophers, we should note that arguments for human rights are sometimes identical with arguments for distributive justice, or at least are presented in the context of arguments for distributive justice. The reason for this is that the concepts of rights and of distributive justice are closely related. One of the most traditional definitions of justice is that it consists in giving each person his due, and this is largely equivalent to giving each person what he has a right to. Hence, rights are the substantive content of what, according to many conceptions of justice, ought to be distributed to persons. The universality of human rights is further brought out in the definition's reference to "each person." This definition as such, however, does not include the additional, formal idea of the *equal* distribution of rights. But many traditional conceptions of justice do, of course, incorporate this further element of equality.

The answers I shall consider to the epistemological question of human rights will also coincide in part, then, with answers that have been given in arguments for egalitarian justice, which involve especially that all persons have a right to be treated equally in certain basic respects.

One traditional answer is intuitionist. Thus, Thomas Jefferson held it to be "self-evident" that all humans equally have certain rights, and Robert Nozick has peremptorily asserted that "individuals have rights." Such assertion is not, of course, an argument for the existence of human rights; it would not serve at all to convince the many persons throughout history who have had different intuitions on this question. Hence, this answer fails to satisfy *the condition of providing an argument.*

The remaining answers to be considered do provide arguments of various sorts. One argument is "formal." It holds that all persons ought to be treated alike unless there is some good reason for treating them differently. The 'ought' contained in this principle is held to entail that all persons have a *right* to be treated alike, and hence to be treated as equals. This in turn is held to entail that all persons have rights to equal consideration. This principle is based on the still more general principle that cases which are of the same kind ought to be treated in the same way, and being human is held to be such a kind.

The formal principle raises many difficult problems of interpretation. In particular, it leaves unspecified what constitutes a "good reason" for treating persons differently, that is, what sub-kinds are relevant to differential treatment; and, of course, very many differences, including intelligence, sex, religion, color, economic class, have been held to be thus relevant. The principle, then, can eventuate not only in egalitarianism but also in drastic inegalitarianism of many different sorts. Hence, the argument fails to satisfy what I shall call *the condition of determinacy,* since it may serve to justify mutually opposed allocations of rights.

The next three answers I shall consider bring in certain contents. One is the argument of Joel Feinberg, who sets forth the "interest principle" that "the sorts of things who *can* have rights are precisely those who have (or can have) interests." Now, waiving the murkiness of the concept of "interests," I think this principle is true as far as it goes; but it does not, of itself, go far enough to provide an adequate basis for human rights. Feinberg's arguments for the principle establish at most that it gives a necessary rather than a sufficient condition for having rights. More generally, he does not show just how the having of interests serves to ground the having of rights. Surely, not every case of having an interest is a case of having a right to the satisfaction of the interest. Hence, the argument does not fulfill what I shall call *the condition of sufficiency,* of providing a sufficient ground for the ascription of rights. Moreover, since animals may have interests and humans may have unequal interests, the "interest principle" does not justify either rights that belong only to humans or rights that belong to all humans equally. Hence the argument does not satisfy *the condition of adequate egalitarian premises,* since it does not establish *equality* of rights among all humans.

Another answer that tries to base human rights on human needs or interests was given by William Frankena. He held that humans "are capable of enjoying a good life in a sense in which other animals are not. . . . As I see it, it is the fact that all men are similarly capable of enjoying a good life in this sense that justifies the *prima facie* requirement that they be treated as equals." The sense in question is one which Frankena identifies as "the happy or satisfactory life."

It will be noted that this argument moves from an "is" ("the fact that all men are similarly capable . . .") to an "ought" ("the requirement that they be treated as equals"). The argument does not fulfill *the condition of logical derivability of "ought" from "is."* For it fails to show how the factual similarity adduced by Frankena justifies the normative egalitarian obligation he upholds. One might accept the factual antecedent and yet deny the normative consequent, on the ground, for example, that the value of some person's happiness or goodness of life is greatly superior to that of other persons, so that their rights to happiness or to certain modes of treatment are not equal. In addition, the argument may also fail to satisfy the condition of justified egalitarian premises, for it still remains to be shown that all humans are equal (or even sufficiently similar) in their capacity for enjoying happiness in the sense intended by Frankena.

His argument, also, does not satisfy *the condition of a rational justification of the criterion of relevance.* It fails to show why the factual characteristics in respect of which humans are *equal* or *similar* are decisively relevant to how they ought to be treated, as against those factual characteristics in respect of which humans are *unequal* or *dissimilar,* such as the capacity to reason or to attain command over others or to control their appetites or to produce valued commodities or to work toward long-range goals, and so forth. Hence, the degree to which some factual characteristic is distributed among persons cannot of itself be the justifying ground for the allocation of rights.

A more direct way of deriving rights from needs is to *define* human rights as justified claims to the fulfillment of important needs. This, in effect, is what is done by Susan Moller Okin when she defines a human right as "a claim to something (whether a freedom, a good, or a benefit) of crucial importance for human life." She lists three kinds of important human needs — to basic physical goods, to physical security, to being treated with respect. She then says, "Using the definition of human

rights given above . . . we can logically infer three fundamental human rights from these three needs."

This definitional way of inferring the existence of human rights suffers from at least two difficulties. First, just because human rights are *defined* as claims to important goods, this does not prove that anyone *has* such claims, in the sense that these claims *ought* to be fulfilled. Since human rights, as claim-rights, entail correlative duties, how does the *definition* of human rights as claims to the fulfillment of important needs serve to ground the substantive assertion that persons have duties to fulfill these needs? Why should any person who is reluctant to accept this duty regard Okin's definition as a sufficient justifying ground? Her argument, then, does not fulfill *the condition of rationally necessary acceptability to all rational persons.*

A related difficulty is that Okin's definition takes sides on controverted substantive issues about human rights. Some philosophers have held, for example, that the only human rights are the rights to freedom, which require only duties of noninterference on the part of Respondents. Why, then, should they accept Okin's definition as a basis for the positive duties she attributes to Respondents? For this reason, her argument does not satisfy *the condition of an adequate account of the Objects of rights.*

Let us next consider a fifth answer to the epistemological question. This is H. L. A. Hart's famous presuppositional argument. He says: "If there are any moral rights at all, it follows that there is at least one natural right, the equal right of all men to be free." His point is that all special moral rights are grounded either in Respondents' freely choosing to create their obligations or in the fairness of having an equal distribution of freedom among persons who subject themselves to mutual restrictions. Hence, Hart's argument for the equal natural right of all humans to freedom is that this right is presupposed by all or at least some of the most important special moral rights.

This argument suffers from at least three difficulties. First, it does not satisfy what I shall call *the condition of justified premises.* Hart has not adequately established that there *are* the special moral rights that figure in the antecedent of his initial statement. He appeals especially to the rights created by promises. But it is not self-evident that an act of saying, "I promise," taken by itself, generates any rights or duties. If there is indeed such generation, it is because there is presupposed a background institution defined by certain rules. Hence, there must be a prior justification of this institution as authorizing the generation of valid rights and duties. Here, however, Hart's argument fails to satisfy the condition of determinacy. For there may be morally wrong institutions, so that even though they are constituted by certain rules, these do not authorize valid rights and duties. Hart, however, has not provided this more general justification of the institutions he invokes. Hence, since his implicit appeal to institutions may yield morally wrong as well as morally right results, his premise is not morally determinate.

A further difficulty of Hart's argument is that, like Feinberg's argument, it does not fulfill the condition of justified egalitarian premises. If special moral rights are to be used to show that there is an *equal* right of *all* men to be free, then such universal equality must be found in the special rights themselves. But Hart has not shown that all men equally derive rights from the transactions of promising, consenting, and imposing mutual restrictions. He presupposes, without any justificatory argument, the very egalitarianism he seeks to establish. A believer in basic human inequality, such as Nietzsche, would deny that all men are equal with regard to the special rights. Hence, Hart's argument does not establish the egalitarian universalism he upholds.

A sixth argument for equality of rights is the procedural one given in Rawls's famous theory of justice. He justifies this equality by arguing that if the constitutional structure of a society were to be chosen by persons who are "in an initial position of equality" and who choose from behind a "veil of ignorance" of all their particular qualities, the principles of justice they would choose would provide that each person must have certain basic, equal rights.

Amid its many complexities, this by now familiar argument fails to satisfy three important conditions. One is *the condition of truth*: persons are not in fact equal in power and ability, nor are they ignorant of all their particular qualities. Hence, to assume that they are (in some sort of "original position"), and to base on this equality and ignorance one's ascription of equal rights, is to argue from a false premise. In making this point I do not overlook that arguments based on counterfactual assumptions may be cogent and even powerful. But the cogency of Rawls's assumptions is reduced because of their

exceptional extensiveness and the direct use he makes of them to justify an egalitarian conclusion. His argument also fails to satisfy the condition of rationally necessary acceptability to all rational persons, to which I have previously referred. For the total ignorance of particulars that Rawls ascribes to his equal persons has no independent rational justification. Hence, no reason is given as to why actual rational persons, who know their particular characteristics, should accept the equality of rights that is based on their assumed ignorance. In addition, Rawls's argument does not satisfy *the condition of non-circularity*, since he attains his egalitarian result only by putting into his premises an equality (of power and ignorance) which cannot itself be justified.

The seventh and final argument for equal human rights that I shall consider here is based on the doctrine that all humans are equal in dignity or worth. Thus the United Nations Universal Declaration of Human Rights (1948), in its first Article, says: "All human beings are born free and equal in dignity and rights." It is important to consider what is meant here by "dignity." Presumably, dignity is not an "empirical" characteristic in the way the having of interests or the capacity for feeling physical pain is empirically ascertainable. The sense of "dignity" in which all humans are said to have equal dignity is not the same as that in which it may be said of some person that he lacks dignity or that he behaves without dignity, where what is meant is that he is lacking in decorum, is too raucous or obsequious, or is not "dignified." This kind of dignity is one that humans may occurrently exhibit, lack, or lose, whereas the dignity in which all humans are said to be equal is a characteristic that belongs permanently and inherently to every human as such.

One difficulty with the attempt to derive human rights from such inherent dignity is that the two expressions, "A has human rights" and "A has inherent dignity" may seem to be equivalent, so that the latter simply reduplicates the former. Thus, for example, Jacques Maritain wrote: "The dignity of the human person? The expression means nothing if it does not signify that by virtue of natural law, the human person has the right to be respected, is the subject of rights, possesses rights." If, however, the two expressions are thus equivalent in meaning, the attribution of dignity adds nothing substantial to the attribution of rights, and someone who is doubtful about the latter attribution will be equally doubtful about the former. Thus, the argument for rights based on inherent dignity, so far, does not satisfy the condition of non-circularity.

It is essential, then, to consider whether the attribution of inherent dignity can have a status independent of and logically prior to the attribution of rights. An important doctrine of this sort was set forth by Kant, who based his attribution of dignity (*Würde*) to the rational being on his autonomy or freedom, his capacity for self-legislation, for acting according to laws he gives to himself. Now, Kant held that such autonomy is not an empirical characteristic since it applies only to rational beings as things-in-themselves and, hence, as not subject to the deterministic laws of natural phenomena. This doctrine, however, involves all the difficulties of the distinction between phenomena and noumena, including the cognitive non-ascertainability of the latter. Hence, the Kantian derivation of rights from inherent dignity does not satisfy *the condition of empirical reference* as regards the characteristics of humans to which one appeals.

There is more to be said on this matter of the relation of human rights to human dignity, but I shall be able to make my view of this relation clearer after I have set forth my own positive doctrine.

This concludes my examination of seven recent attempts to give justificatory arguments for equal human rights. The examination has indicated that a successful argument must satisfy at least twelve conditions: providing an argument, determinacy, sufficiency, adequate egalitarian premises, logical derivability of "ought" from "is," rational justification of the criterion of relevance, rationally necessary acceptability to all rational persons, adequate account of the Objects of rights, justified premises, truth, non-circularity, and empirical reference.

III. The Justificatory Argument for Human Rights

I now wish to present my own answer to the justificatory or epistemological question of human rights. It will be recalled that the Justifying Basis or Ground of human rights must be a normative moral principle that serves to prove or establish that every person morally ought to have the necessary goods of action as something to which he or she is entitled. The epistemological question, hence, comes down to whether such a moral principle can be rationally justified.

It is important to note that not all moral principles will serve for this purpose. Utilitarian, organicist, and elitist moral principles either do not justify any moral rights at all, or justify them only as ancillary to and contingent upon various collective goals, or do make rights primary but not as equally distributed among all humans. Hence, it will be necessary to show how the moral principle that justifies equal human rights is superior, in point of rational cogency, to these other kinds of moral principles.

Now, there are well-known difficulties in the attempt to provide a rational justification of any moral principle. Obviously, given some high-level moral principle, we can morally justify some specific moral rule or particular moral judgment or action by showing how its rightness follows from the principle. But how can we justify the basic principle itself? Here, by definition, there is no higher or more general moral principle to be appealed to as an independent variable. Is it the case, then, that justification comes to a stop here? This would mean that we cannot rationally adjudicate between *conflicting* moral principles and ways of life and society, such as those epitomized, for example, by Kant's categorical imperative, Bentham's utilitarianism, Kierkegaard's theological primacy, Stirner's egoism, Nietzsche's exaltation of the superman, Spencer's doctrine of the survival of the fittest, and so on.

The Problem of the Independent Variable

One of the central problems here is that of the independent variable. Principles serve as independent variables for justifying lower-level rules and judgments; but what is the independent variable for justifying principles themselves? Another way to bring out this problem in relation to morality is to contrast particular empirical statements and particular moral judgments. Consider, on the one hand, such a statement as "Mrs. Jones *is* having an abortion," and, on the other hand, "Mrs. Jones *ought* to have an abortion." We know, at least in principle, how to go about checking the truth of the first statement, namely, by referring to certain empirical facts that serve as the independent variables for the statement to be checked against. But how do we go about checking the truth of the second statement, that Mrs. Jones *ought* to have an abortion? Indeed, what would it *mean* for the second statement to be true? What is the independent variable for *it* to be checked against? For the first statement to be true means that it corresponds to certain empirical facts. But with regard to a judgment like "Mrs. Jones *ought* to have an abortion," what facts would *it* have to correspond to in order to be true? Is there any moral '*ought*' in the world, in the way in which the factual '*is*' is in the world, serving as the independent variable for testing or confirming the relevant statements? If not, then is the moral judgment in no sense either true or false?

The problem we have reached, then, is whether there is any non-question-begging answer to the problem of the independent variable in morality. I now want to suggest that there is. To see this, we must recall that all moral precepts, regardless of their greatly varying contents, are concerned with how persons ought to *act* toward one another. Think, for example, of the Golden Rule: "*Do* unto others as you would have them do unto you." Think also of Kant's categorical imperative: "*Act* in such a way that the maxim of your action can be a universal law." Similarly, Bentham tells us to *act* so as to maximize utility; Nietzsche tells us to *act* in accord with the ideals of the superman; Marx tells us to *act* in accord with the interests of the proletariat; Kierkegaard tells us to *act* as God commands, and so forth.

The independent variable of all morality, then, is human *action*. This independent variable cuts across the distinctions between secular and religious moralities, between egalitarian and elitist moralities, between deontological and teleological moralities, and so forth.

But how does this independent variable of action help us to resolve the difficulties of moral justification? Surely we can't take the various rival moral principles and justify one of them as against the others simply by checking it against the fact of human action. Moreover, since if action is to be genuinely the non-question-begging independent variable of morality, it must fit *all* moral principles, how does action enable us to justify *one* moral principle *as against* its rivals?

The answer to these questions is given by the fact that action has what I have called a *normative*

structure, in that, logically implicit in action, there are certain evaluative and deontic judgments, certain judgments about goods and rights made by agents; and when these judgments are subjected to certain morally neutral rational requirements, they entail a certain supreme moral principle. Hence, if any agent denies the principle, he can be shown to have contradicted himself, so that his denial, and the actions stemming from it, cannot be rationally justifiable. Thus, together with action, the most basic kind of reason, deductive rationality, also serves as an independent variable for the justification of the supreme principle of morality.

Why Action Gives the Principle a Rationally Necessary Acceptability

It is important to note that because the principle is grounded in the generic features of action, it has a certain kind of *material necessity*. It will be recalled that some of the justificatory arguments for rights examined above failed because they did not satisfy the condition that they be acceptable to all rational persons as a matter of rational necessity. For example, why must any rational person accept Rawls's starting point in the "veil of ignorance"? Why, for that matter, is it rationally necessary for any rational person to accept the Golden Rule or any other moral principle that has hitherto been propounded?

The condition of rationally necessary acceptability is fulfilled, however, when the independent variable of the argument is placed in the generic features of action. For this involves that, simply by virtue of being an agent, one logically must accept the argument and its conclusion that all persons equally have certain moral rights. Now, being an actual or prospective agent is not an optional or variable condition for any person, except in the sense that he may choose to commit suicide or, perhaps, to sell himself into slavery; and even then the steps he intentionally takes toward these goals involve agency on his part. Hence, if there are moral rights and duties that logically accrue to every person simply by virtue of being an actual or prospective agent, the argument that traces this logical sequence will necessarily be rationally acceptable to every agent: he will have to accept the argument on pain of self-contradiction.

There is a sense in which this grounding of the moral principle in action involves a foundationalist conception of justification. For, as we shall see, the argument begins with a statement attributable to any agent, that he performs some purposive action. This statement is based on the agent's direct awareness of what he is doing, and it leads, in a unilinear sequence, to his statement that he and all other agents have certain rights and correlative duties. I need not be concerned, in the present context, with further epistemological issues about the certainty or trustworthiness of the rational agent's direct awareness or about any presumed "data" on which this awareness might be based.

The argument's unilinearity, with its concomitant avoidance of circularity, is an important asset. In this regard, the justificatory procedure I shall follow does not have the defects of Rawls's method of "reflective equilibrium," according to which "considered" moral judgments and general moral principles are reciprocally tested against and adjusted to one another. There are at least two difficulties with this method. First, the "considered moral judgments" of one person or group may differ markedly from those of another person or group, so that they do not provide a firm or consistent basis for justifying a moral principle. Second, the argument is circular since the principle is justified by the very judgments that it is in turn adduced to justify.

My argument, in contrast, begins not from variable moral judgments but from statements that must be accepted by every agent because they derive from the generic features of purposive action. Hence, my argument is not "foundationalist" in the sense that it begins from *moral* or *evaluative* statements that are taken to be self-justifying or self-evident. The present argument is one in which statements about actions, and not statements about values or duties, are taken as the basic starting point. And these statements entail, in a noncircular sequence, certain judgments about the existence of human rights.

The Argument for Equal Human Rights

I shall, now, give a brief outline of the rational line of argument that goes from action, through its normative structure, to the supreme principle of morality, and thence to equal human rights. In my book, *Reason and Morality,* I have presented a full statement of the argument, so that for present purposes I shall stress only certain main points.

To begin with, we must note certain salient characteristics of action. In ordinary as well as scientific language, the word 'action' is used in many different senses: we talk, for example, about physical action at a distance, about the action of the liver, and so forth. But the meaning of 'action' that is relevant here is that which is the common object of all moral and other practical precepts, such as the examples I gave before. Moral and other practical precepts, as we have seen, tell persons to *act* in many different ways. But amid these differences, the precepts all assume that the persons addressed by them can control their behaviour by their unforced choice with a view to achieving whatever the precepts require. All actions as envisaged by moral and other practical precepts, then, have two *generic features*. One is *voluntariness* or *freedom,* in that the agents control or can control their behavior by their unforced choice while having knowledge of relevant circumstances. The other generic feature is *purposiveness* or *intentionality,* in that the agents aim to attain some end or goal which constitutes their reason for acting; this goal may consist either in the action itself or in something to be achieved by the action.

Now, let us take an agent A, defined as an actual or prospective performer of actions in the sense just indicated. When he performs an action, he can be described as saying or thinking:

(1) "I do X for end or purpose E."

Since E is something he unforcedly chooses to attain, he thinks E has sufficient value to merit his moving from quiescence to action in order to attain it. Hence, from his standpoint, (1) entails

(2) "E is good."

Note that (2) is here presented in quotation marks, as something said or thought by the agent A. The kind of goodness he here attributes to E need not be moral goodness; its criterion varies with whatever purpose E the agent may have in doing X. But what it shows already is that, in the context of action, the 'Fact-Value gap' is already bridged, for by the very *fact* of engaging in action, every agent must implicitly accept for himself a certain *value*-judgment about the value or goodness of the purposes for which he acts.

Now, in order to act for E, which he regards as good, the agent A must have the proximate necessary conditions of action. These conditions are closely related to the generic features of action that I mentioned before. You will recall that these generic features are voluntariness or freedom and purposiveness or intentionality. But when purposiveness is extended to the general conditions required for success in achieving one's purposes, it becomes a more extensive condition which I shall call *well-being*. Viewed from the standpoint of action, then, well-being consists in having the various substantive conditions and abilities, ranging from life and physical integrity to self-esteem and education, that are required if a person is to act either at all or with general chances of success in achieving the purposes for which he acts. So freedom and well-being are the necessary conditions of action and of successful action in general. Hence, from the agent's standpoint, from (2) "E is good" there follows

(3) "My freedom and well-being are necessary goods."

This may also be put as

(4) "I must have freedom and well-being."

where this 'must' is a practical-prescriptive requirement, expressed by the agent, as to his having the necessary conditions of his action.

Now from (4) there follows

(5) "I have rights to freedom and well-being.

To show that (5) follows from (4), let us suppose that the agent were to deny (5). In that case, because of the correlativity of rights and strict 'oughts,' he would also have to deny

(6) "All other persons ought at least to refrain from removing or interfering with my freedom and well-being."

By denying (6), he must accept

(7) "It is not the case that all other persons ought at least to refrain from removing or interfering with my freedom and well-being."

By accepting (7), he must also accept

(8) "Other persons may (i.e. it is permissible that other persons) remove or interfere with my freedom and well-being."

And by accepting (8), he must accept

(9) "I may not (i.e. it is permissible that I not) have freedom and well-being."

But (9) contradicts (4), which said "I must have freedom and well-being." Since every agent must accept (4), he must reject (9). And since (9) follows from the denial of (5), "I have rights to freedom and well-being," every agent must also reject that denial. Hence, every agent logically must accept (5) "I have rights to freedom and well-being."

What I have shown so far, then, is that the concept of a right, as a justified claim or entitlement, is logically involved in all action as a concept that signifies for every agent his claim and requirement that he have, and at least not be prevented from having, the necessary conditions that enable him to act in pursuit of his purposes. I shall sometimes refer to these rights as *generic rights,* since they are rights that the generic features of action and of successful action characterize one's behavior.

It must be noted, however, that, so far, the criterion of these rights that every agent must claim for himself is only prudential, not moral, in that the criterion consists for each agent in his own needs of agency in pursuit of his own purposes. Even though the right-claim is addressed to all other persons as a correlative 'ought'-judgment, still its justifying criterion for each agent consists in the necessary conditions of his own action.

To see how this prudential right-claim also becomes a moral right, we must go through some further steps. Now, the sufficient as well as necessary reason or justifying condition for which every agent must hold that he has rights to freedom and well-being is that he is a prospective purposive agent. Hence, he must accept

(10) "I have rights to freedom and well-being because I am a prospective purposive agent,"

where this "because" signifies a sufficient as well as necessary justifying condition.

Suppose some agent were to reject (10), and were to insist, instead, that the only reason he has the generic rights is that he has some more restrictive characteristic R. Examples of R would include: being an American, being a professor, being an *Übermensch,* being male, being a capitalist or a proletarian, being white, being named "Wordsworth Donisthorpe," and so forth. Thus, the agent would be saying

(11) "I have rights to freedom and well-being *only* because I am R,"

where "R" is something more restrictive than being a prospective purposive agent.

Such an agent, however, would contradict himself. For he would then be in the position of saying that if he did *not* have R, he would *not* have the generic rights, so that he would have to accept

(12) "I do not have rights to freedom and well-being."

But we saw before that, as an agent, he *must* hold that he has rights to freedom and well-being. Hence, he must drop his view that R alone is the sufficient justifying condition of his having the generic rights, so that he must accept that simply being a prospective purposive agent is a sufficient as well as a necessary justifying condition of his having rights to freedom and well-being. Hence, he must accept (10).

Now by virtue of accepting (10), the agent must also accept

(13) "All prospective purposive agents have rights to freedom and well-being."

(13) follows from (10) because of the principle of universalization. If some predicate P belongs to some subject S because that subject has some general quality Q (where this 'because' signifies a sufficient reason), then that predicate logically must belong to every subject that has Q. Hence, since the predicate of having the generic rights belongs to the original agent because he is a prospective purposive agent, he logically must admit that every purposive agent has the generic rights.

At this point the rights become moral ones, and not only prudential, on that meaning of "moral" where it has both the formal component of setting forth practical requirements that are categorically obligatory, and the material component that those requirements involve taking favorable account of the interests of persons other than or in addition to the agent or the speaker. When the original agent now says that *all* prospective purposive agents have rights to freedom and well-being, he is logically committed to respecting and hence taking favorable account of the interests of all other persons with regard to their also having the necessary goods or conditions of action.

Since all other persons are actual or potential recipients of his action, every agent is logically committed to accepting

(14) "I ought to act in accord with the generic rights of my recipients as well as of myself."

This requirement can also be expressed as the general moral principle:

(15) "Act in accord with the generic rights of your recipients as well as of yourself."

I shall call this the Principle of Generic Consistency (*PGC*), since it combines the formal consideration of consistency with the material consideration of the generic features and rights of action. As we have seen, every agent, on pain of contradiction and hence of irrationality, must accept this principle as governing all his interpersonal actions.

This, then, completes my argument for equal human rights. Its central point can be summarized in two main parts. In the first part (steps 1 to 9), I have argued that every agent logically must hold or accept that he has rights to freedom and well-being as the necessary conditions of his action, as conditions that he *must* have; for if he denies that he has these rights, then he must accept that other persons may remove or interfere with his freedom and well-being, so that he *may not* have them; but this would contradict his belief that he *must* have them. In the second part (steps 10 to 14), I have argued that the agent logically must accept that all other prospective purposive agents have the same rights to freedom and well-being as he claims for himself.

Since all humans are actual, prospective, or potential agents, the rights in question belong equally to all humans. Thus, the argument fulfills the specifications for human rights that I mentioned at the outset: that both the Subjects and the Respondents of the rights are all human equally, that the Objects of the rights are the necessary goods of human action, and that the Justifying Basis of the rights is a valid moral principle.

How the Argument Fulfills the Conditions of Justification

It will also be recalled that in my critique of previous attempts to answer the epistemological question of human rights I listed twelve conditions that the attempts had collectively failed to satisfy. I do not have the time now to do any more than to indicate very briefly how my own argument satisfies each of these conditions. The condition of providing an argument is obviously satisfied. The remaining eleven conditions, which concern the requirements for a successful argument justifying or proving the existence of human rights, may be divided into four groups. First, the conditions of justified premises, truth, and empirical reference are fulfilled by my argument because I begin from actual, empirically discriminable agents who pursue their purposes and know the relevant circumstances of their action. Second, the argument also fulfills the conditions of adequate egalitarian premises and rational justification of the criterion of relevance, because the agents are equal as having purposes and it is this having of purposes which has been shown to be relevant to their claiming of rights. Third, the argument has fulfilled the conditions of non-circularity and logical derivability of 'ought' from 'is,' because it has shown how the claiming of rights with their correlative 'ought' logically follows from being a purposive agent, while at the same time such agency has not been defined in terms of claiming or having rights. Fourth, the argument fulfills the remaining conditions of determinacy, sufficiency, rationally necessary acceptability to all rational persons, and adequate account of the Objects of rights. For the argument has shown how every agent's needs for the necessary goods of action provide a sufficient basis for his claiming rights to their fulfillment; and the opposites of these rights are not derivable from the argument in question. Moreover — and the importance of this must again be stressed — the argument is necessarily acceptable to all rational person qua agents because it is logically grounded in the generic features that characterize all actions and agents.

Some Objections to the Argument

Many questions may be raised about this argument. They include objections made on behalf of egoists, amoralists, "fanatics," radical social critics, and historians, as well as charges that the idea of prudential rights [as found in step (5) above] makes no sense and that the argument's egalitarian conclusion is not in fact justified. I have dealt with these objections elsewhere.

I wish, now, to consider two further objections against the first nine steps of my argument as given above. These steps culminate in the assertion that every agent logically must hold or accept that he has rights to freedom and well-being as the necessary conditions of his action. One objection bears on the Objects of these rights. My argument moves from step (4), "I must have freedom and well-being," to step (5), "I have rights to freedom and well-being." The argument is that if the agent denies (5) then he also has to deny (4). It may be objected, however, that this argument entails that whenever some person holds that he must have something X, he also has to hold that he has a right to X. But this, to put it mildly, is implausible. If someone thinks that he *must* have a ten-speed bicycle, or the love of some woman, it surely does not follow that he thinks, let alone has to think, that he has a *right* to these Objects.

My reply to this objection is that it overlooks an important restriction. My argument is confined to *necessary contents* — to what is necessarily connected with being an agent, and hence to the necessary goods of action. Hence the argument excludes the kinds of *contingent reasons* that figure in the objection. Persons do, of course, desire many particular things, and they may even feel that they *must* have some of these. But there is a difference between a 'must' that is concerned with Objects that are, strictly speaking, dispensable, and a 'must' whose Objects are the necessary conditions of action. The latter Objects, unlike the former, have an ineluctableness within the context of action that reflects the rational necessity to which the argument must be confined if its culminating obligatoriness is to be justified. I shall deal with this further below, in connection with the dialectically necessary method.

A second objection bears on the Subjects of the rights. In my argument above I held that if the agent denies (5), "I have rights to freedom and well-being," then, because of the correlativity of rights and strict 'oughts,' he must also deny (6), "All other persons ought at least to refrain from removing or interfering with my freedom and well-being." I, then, showed that the denial of (6) entails a statement (9) which contradicts another statement (4) which every agent must accept, so that to avoid self-contradiction every agent must accept (5). It may be objected, however, that a statement like (6) may be accepted on grounds other than the acceptance of a rights-statement like (5). The grounds may be utilitarian or of some other non-rights sort. Consider, for example, (6a), "All persons ought to refrain from removing or interfering with the well-being of trees (or animals, or fine old buildings)." One may accept this without having to accept (5a), "Trees (or animals, or fine old buildings) have rights to well-being." In other words, one may accept that one *ought not to harm* certain entities without accepting that these entities have *rights* to non-harm. But since my argument above depended on the logical equivalence between a statement (5) that upholds rights and a statement (6) that upholds the 'ought' of not harming, the objection is that the need to accept (6) does not entail the need to accept (5). If it did, we should have to accept that trees, animals, and even old buildings have rights.

My answer to this objection is that it misconstrues the criterion of the 'ought' in (6). This 'ought' is not upheld on general utilitarian grounds or on other general grounds not primarily related to its beneficiary. Rather, it is upheld as signifying something that is due or owed to the beneficiary, something to which he is entitled by virtue of its being required for all his purposive actions. Thus the 'ought' in (6) has a specificity and stringency

which are not captured in (6a). Hence, my argument does not entail that entities other than human purposive agents have rights, since its 'ought' involves the more specific requirement of something that is owed or due. This more specific 'ought' can pertain only to human purposive agents as its beneficiaries. And such a strict 'ought,' unlike other 'oughts' that are looser or less specific, is correlative with a rights-judgment.

Endnotes

1 Wesley N. Hohfeld, *Fundamental Legal Conceptions* (New Haven: Yale University Press, 1964), 36ff.

2 Jeremy Bentham, *A Critical Examination of the Declaration of Rights*, by B. Parekh, ed. *Bentham's Political Thought* (New York: Barnes and Noble, 1973), 271.

3 Karl Marx, *On the Jewish Question*, in R. C. Tucker, ed. *The Marx-Engels Reader*, 2nd ed. (New York: W. W. Norton, 1978), 43.

XIII.5 A *Critique of Gewirth and the Notion of Rights*

ALASDAIR MACINTYRE

Alasdair MacIntyre is professor of philosophy at the University of Notre Dame and the author of several works in ethics and philosophy of religion. His work, *After Virtue,* is one of the most widely discussed books on ethics in recent years. In this section from *After Virtue,* MacIntyre criticizes rights-based moral theories — much in the spirit of Bentham — as nonsense on stilts. Natural rights no more exist than do unicorns and witches. He then analyzes Gewirth's rationalistic version of a defense of human rights and argues that Gewirth has committed the logical mistake of deriving a right from a need.

[. . . Analytic philosophers revived the Kantian project demonstrating that the] authority and objectivity of moral rules is precisely that authority and objectivity which belongs to the exercise of reason. Hence their central project was, indeed is, that of

showing that any rational agent is logically committed to the rules of morality in virtue of his or her rationality.

The example which I have chosen is that made by Alan Gewirth in *Reason and Morality* (1978). I choose Gewirth's book because it is not only one of the most recent of such attempts, but also because it deals carefully and scrupulously with objections and

Excerpted with permission from *After Virtue* (University of Notre Dame, 1981).

criticism that have been made of earlier writers. Moreover Gewirth adopts what is at once a clear and a strict view of what reason is: in order to be admitted as a principle of practical reason, a principle must be analytic; and in order for a conclusion to follow from premises of practical reason, it must be demonstrably entailed by those premises. There is none of the looseness and vagueness about what constitutes 'a good reason' which had weakened some earlier analytic attempts to exhibit morality as rational.

The key sentence of Gewirth's book is: 'Since the agent regards as necessary goods the freedom and well-being that constitute the generic features of his successful action, he logically must also hold that he has rights to these generic features and he implicitly makes a corresponding rights-claim' (p. 63). Gewirth's argument may be spelled out as follows. Every rational agent has to recognise a certain measure of freedom and well-being as prerequisites for his exercise of rational agency. Therefore each rational agent must will, if he is to will at all, that he possess that measure of these goods. This is what Gewirth means when he writes in the sentence quoted of 'necessary goods.' And there is clearly no reason to quarrel with Gewirth's argument so far. It turns out to be the next step that is at once crucial and questionable.

Gewirth argues that anyone who holds that the prerequisites for his exercise of rational agency are necessary goods is logically committed to holding also that he has a right to these goods. But quite clearly the introduction of the concept of a right needs justification both because it is at this point a concept quite new to Gewirth's argument *and* because of the special character of the concept of a right.

It is first of all clear that the claim that I have a right to do or have something is a quite different type of claim from the claim that I need or want or will be benefited by something. From the first — if it is the only relevant consideration — it follows that others ought not to interfere with my attempts to do or have whatever it is, whether it is for my own good or not. From the second it does not. And it makes no difference what kind of good or benefit is at issue.

Another way of understanding what has gone wrong with Gewirth's argument is to understand why this step is so essential to his argument. It is of course true that if I claim a right in virtue of my possession of certain characteristics, then I am logically committed to holding that anyone else with the same characteristics also possess this right. But it is just this property of necessary universalisability that does not belong to claims about either the possession of or the need or desire for a good, even a universally necessary good.

One reason why claims about goods necessary for rational agency are so different from claims to the possession of rights is that the latter in fact presuppose, as the former do not, the existence of a socially established set of rules. Such sets of rules only come into existence at particular historical periods under particular social circumstances. They are in no way universal features of the human condition. Gewirth readily acknowledges that expressions such as 'a right' in English and cognate terms in English and other languages only appeared at a relatively late point in the history of the language toward the close of the middle ages. But he argues that the existence of such expressions is not a necessary condition for the embodiment of the concept of a right in forms of human behaviour; and in this at least he is clearly right. But the objection that Gewirth has to meet is precisely that those forms of human behaviour which presuppose notions of some ground to entitlement, such as the notion of a right, always have a highly specific and socially local character, and that the existence of particular types of social institution or practice is a necessary condition for the notion of a claim to the possession of a right being an intelligible type of human performance. (As a matter of historical fact such types of social institution or practice have not existed universally in human societies.) Lacking any such social form, the making of a claim to a right would be like presenting a check for payment in a social order that lacked the institution of money. Thus Gewirth has illicitly smuggled into his argument a conception which does not in any way belong, as it must do if his case is to succeed, to the minimal characterisation of a rational agent.

By 'rights' I do not mean those rights conferred by positive law or custom on specified classes of person; I mean those rights which are alleged to belong to human beings as such and which are cited as a reason for holding that people ought not to be interfered with in their pursuit of life, liberty and happiness. They are the rights which were spoken of in the eighteenth century as natural rights or as the rights of man. Characteristically in that century they were defined negatively, precisely as rights *not* to be interfered with. But sometimes in that century and much more often in our own positive rights — rights to due process, to education or to employment are examples — are added to the list. The expression 'human rights' is now commoner than either of the eighteenth-century expressions. But whether negative or positive and however named they are supposed to attach equally to all individuals, whatever their sex, race, religion, talents or deserts, and to provide a ground or a variety of particular moral stances.

It would of course be a little odd that there should be such rights attaching to human beings simply *qua* human beings in light of the fact, which I alluded to in my discussion of Gewirth's argument, that there is no expression in any ancient or medieval language correctly translated by our expression 'a right' until near the close of the Middle Ages: the concept lacks any means of expression in Hebrew, Greek, Latin or Arabic, classical or medieval, before about 1400, let alone in Old English, or in Japanese even as late as the mid-nineteenth century. From this it does not of course follow that there are no natural or human rights; it only follows that no one could have known that there were. And this at least raises certain questions. But we do not need to be distracted into answering them, for the truth is plain: there are no such rights, and belief in them is one with belief in witches and in unicorns.

The best reason for asserting so bluntly that there are no such rights is indeed of precisely the same type as the best reason which we possess for asserting that there are no witches and the best reason which we possess for asserting that there are no unicorns: every attempt to give good reasons for believing that there *are* such rights has failed. The eighteenth-century philosophical defenders of natural rights sometimes suggest that the assertions which state that men possess them are self-evident truths; but we know that there are no self-evident truths. Twentieth-century moral philosophers have sometimes appealed to their and our intuitions; but one of the things that we ought to have learned from the history of moral philosophy is that the introduction of the word 'intuition' by a moral philosopher is always a signal that something has gone badly wrong with an argument. In the United Nations declaration on human rights of 1949 what has since become the normal U.N. practice of not giving good reasons for *any* assertions whatsoever is followed with great rigour. And the latest defender of such rights, Ronald Dworkin (*Taking Rights Seriously*, 1976) concedes that the existence of such rights cannot be demonstrated, but remarks on this point simply that it does not follow from the fact that a statement cannot be demonstrated that it is not true (p. 81). Which is true, but could equally be used to defend claims about unicorns and witches.

Natural or human rights then are fictions — just as is utility — but fictions with highly specific properties. In order to identify them it is worth noticing briefly once more the other moral fiction which emerges from the eighteenth century's attempts to reconstruct morality, the concept of utility. When Bentham first turned 'utility' into a quasi-technical term, he did so, as I have already noticed, in a way that was designed to make plausible the notion of summing individual prospects of pleasure and pain. But, as John Stuart Mill and other utilitarians expanded their notion of the variety of aims which human beings pursue and value, the notion of its being possible to sum all those experiences and activities which give satisfaction became increasingly implausible for reasons which I suggested earlier. The objects of natural and educated human desire are irreducibly heterogeneous and the notion of summing them either for individuals or for some population has no clear sense. But if utility is thus not a clear concept, then to use it as if it is, to employ it as if it could provide us with a rational criterion, is indeed to resort to a fiction.

A central characteristic of moral fictions which comes clearly into view when we juxtapose the concept of utility to that of rights is now identifiable: they purport to provide us with an objective and impersonal criterion, but they do not. And for this reason alone there would have to be a gap between their purported meaning and the uses to which they are actually put. Moreover we can now understand a little better how the phenomenon of incommensurable premises in modern moral debate arises. The concept of rights was generated to serve one set of purposes as part of the social invention of the autonomous moral agent; the concept of utility was devised for quite another set of purposes. And both were elaborated in a situation in which substitute artifacts for the concepts of an older and more traditional morality were required, substitutes that had to have a radically innovative character if they were to give even an appearance of performing their new social functions. Hence when claims invoking rights are matched against claims appealing to utility or when either or both are matched against claims based on some traditional concept of justice, it is not surprising that there is no rational way of deciding which type of claim is to be given priority or how one is to be weighed against the other. Moral incommensurability is itself the product of a particular historical conjunction.

This provides us with an insight important for understanding the politics of modern societies. For what I described earlier as the culture of bureaucratic individualism results in their characteristic overt political debates being between an individualism which makes its claims in terms of rights and forms of bureaucratic organisation which make their claims in terms of utility. But if the concept of rights and that of utility are a matching pair of incommensurable fictions, it will be the case that the moral idiom employed can at best provide a semblance of rationality for the modern political process, but not its reality. The mock rationality of the debate conceals the arbitrariness of the will and power at work in its resolution.

Appendix

Universal Declaration of Human Rights

Whereas Member States have pledged themselves to achieve, in co-operation with the United Nations, the promotion of universal respect for and observance of human rights and fundamental freedoms.

Whereas a common understanding of these rights and freedoms is of the greatest importance for the full realisation of this pledge,

Now, therefore, the General Assembly, Proclaim this Universal Declaration of Human Rights as a common standard of achievement for all peoples and all nations, to the end that every individual and every organ of society, keeping this Declaration constantly in mind, shall strive by teaching and education to promote respect for these rights and freedoms and by progressive measures, national and international, to secure their universal and effective recognition and observance, both among the peoples of Member States themselves

Adopted on December 10, 1948 by the General Assembly of the United Nations at the Palais de Chaillot, Paris.

and among the peoples of territories under their jurisdiction.

Article 1

All human beings are born free and equal in dignity and rights. They are endowed with reason and conscience and should act towards one another in a spirit of brotherhood.

Article 2

1. Everyone is entitled to all the rights and freedoms set forth in this Declaration, without distinction of any kind, such as race, colour, sex, language, religion, political or other opinion, national or social origin, property, birth or other status.

2. Furthermore, no distinction shall be made on the basis of the political, jurisdictional or international status of the country or territory to which a person belongs, whether it be independent, trust, non-self-governing or under any other limitation of sovereignty.

Article 3

Everyone has the right to life, liberty and security of person.

Article 4

No one shall be held in slavery or servitude; slavery and the slave trade shall be prohibited in all their forms.

Article 5

No one shall be subjected to torture or to cruel, inhuman or degrading treatment or punishment.

Article 6

Everyone has the right to recognition everywhere as a person before the law.

Article 7

All are equal before the law and are entitled without any discrimination to equal protection of the law. All are entitled to equal protection against any discrimination in violation of this Declaration and against any incitement to such discrimination.

Article 8

Everyone has the right to an effective remedy by the competent national tribunals for acts violating the fundamental rights granted him by the constitution or by law.

Article 9

No one shall be subjected to arbitrary arrest, detention or exile.

Article 10

Everyone is entitled in full equality to a fair and public hearing by an independent and impartial tribunal, in the determination of his rights and obligations and of any criminal charge against him.

Article 11

1. Everyone charged with a penal offence has the right to be presumed innocent until proved guilty according to law in a public trial at which he has had all the guarantees necessary to his defence.

2. No one shall be held guilty of any penal offence on account of any act or omission which did not constitute a penal offence, under national or international law, at the time when it was committed. Nor shall a heavier penalty be imposed than the one that was applicable at the time the penal offence was committed.

Article 12

No one shall be subjected to arbitrary interference with his privacy, family, home or correspondence, nor to attacks upon his honour and reputation. Everyone has the right to the protection of the law against such interference or attacks.

Article 13

1. Everyone has the right to freedom of movement and residence within the borders of each State.

2. Everyone has the right to leave any country, including his own, and to return to his country.

Article 14

1. Everyone has the right to seek and to enjoy in other countries asylum from persecution.

2. This right may not be invoked in the case of prosecutions genuinely arising from non-political crimes or from acts contrary to the purposes and principles of the United Nations.

Article 15

1. Everyone has the right to a nationality.

2. No one shall be arbitrarily deprived of his nationality nor denied the right to change his nationality.

Article 16

1. Men and women of full age, without any limitation due to race, nationality or religion, have the right to marry and to found a family. They are entitled to equal rights as to marriage, during marriage and at its dissolution.

2. Marriage shall be entered into only with the free and full consent of the intending spouses.

3. The family is the natural and fundamental group unit of society and is entitled to protection by society and the State.

Article 17

1. Everyone has the right to own property alone as well as in association with others.

2. No one shall be arbitrarily deprived of his property.

Article 18

Everyone has the right to freedom of thought, conscience and religion; this right includes freedom to change his religion or belief, and freedom, either alone or in community with others and in public or private, to manifest his religion or belief in teaching, practice, worship and observance.

Article 19

Everyone has the right to freedom of opinion and expression; this right includes freedom to hold opinions without interference and to seek, receive and impart information and ideas through any media and regardless of frontiers.

Article 20

1. Everyone has the right to freedom of peaceful assembly and association.

2. No one may be compelled to belong to an association.

Article 21

1. Everyone has the right to take part in the government of his country, directly or through freely chosen representatives.

2. Everyone has the right of equal access to public service in his country.

3. The will of the people shall be the basis of the authority of government; this will shall be expressed in periodic and genuine elections which shall be by universal and equal suffrage and shall be held by secret vote or by equivalent free voting procedures.

Article 22

Everyone, as a member of society, has the right to social security and is entitled to realisation, through national effort and international co-operation and in accordance with the organisation and resources of each State, of the economic, social and cultural rights indispensable for his dignity and the free development of his personality.

Article 23

1. Everyone has the right to work, to free choice of employment, to just and favourable conditions of work and to protection against unemployment.

2. Everyone, without any discrimination, has the right to equal pay for equal work.

3. Everyone who works has the right to just and favourable remuneration ensuring for himself and his family an existence worthy of human dignity, and supplemented, if necessary, by other means of social protection.

4. Everyone has the right to form and to join trade unions for the protection of his interests.

Article 24

Everyone has the right to rest and leisure, including reasonable limitation of working hours and periodic holidays with pay.

Article 25

1. Everyone has the right to a standard of living adequate for the health and well-being of

himself and of his family, including food, clothing, housing and medical care and necessary social services, and the right to security in the event of unemployment, sickness, disability, widowhood, old age or other lack of livelihood in circumstances beyond his control.

2. Motherhood and childhood are entitled to special care and assistance. All children, whether born in or out of wedlock, shall enjoy the same social protection.

Article 26

1. Everyone has the right to education. Education shall be free, at least in the elementary and fundamental stages. Elementary education shall be compulsory. Technical and professional education shall be made generally available and higher education shall be equally accessible to all on the basis of merit.

2. Education shall be directed to the full development of the human personality and to the strengthening of respect for human rights and fundamental freedoms. It shall promote understanding, tolerance and friendship among all nations, racial or religious groups, and shall further the activities of the United Nations for the maintenance of peace.

3. Parents have a prior right to choose the kind of education that shall be given to their children.

Article 27

1. Everyone has the right freely to participate in the cultural life of the community, to enjoy the arts and to share in scientific advancement and its benefits.

2. Everyone has the right to the protection of the moral and material interests resulting from any scientific, literary or artistic production of which he is the author.

Article 28

Everyone is entitled to a social and international order in which the rights and freedoms set forth in this Declaration can be fully realised.

Article 29

1. Everyone has duties to the community in which alone the free and full development of his personality is possible.

2. In the exercise of his rights and freedoms, everyone shall be subject only to such limitations as are determined by law solely for the purpose of securing due recognition and respect for the rights and freedoms of others and of meeting the just requirements of morality, public order and the general welfare in a democratic society.

3. These rights and freedoms may in no case be exercised contrary to the purposes and principles of the United Nations.

Article 30

Nothing in this Declaration may be interpreted as implying for any State, group or person any right to engage in any activity or to perform any act aimed at the destruction of any of the rights and freedoms set forth herein.

Suggestions for Further Reading

Dworkin, Ronald. *Taking Rights Seriously*. Harvard University Press, 1977.

Gewirth, Alan. *Human Rights*. University of Chicago Press, 1982.

Hohfeld, Wesley Newcomb. *Fundamental Legal Conceptions*. Yale University Press, 1919, especially pp. 35–64.

Lomasky, Loren. *Persons, Rights, and Moral Community*. Oxford University Press, 1987.

Lyons, David, ed. *Rights*. Wadsworth, 1979. Contains a good collection of articles.

Nickel, James. *Making Sense of Human Rights*. University of California Press, 1987.

Paul, Ellen, Fred Miller, and Jeffrey Paul, eds. *Human Rights*. Blackwell, 1984. Contains a good recent collection.

Pennock, J. R. and J. W. Chapman, eds. *Human Rights*. New York University Press, 1981.

Waldron, Jeremy, ed. *Theories of Rights*. Oxford University Press, 1984. Contains nine important essays, especially those of Vlastos, Dworkin, Mackie, and Raz.

Wellman, Carl. *A Theory of Rights*. Rowman and Allanheld, 1985.

A Glossary of Ethical Terms

Absolute A moral absolute is a universally binding principle; it can never be overridden by another principle. Utilitarianism is a type of system with only one ethical absolute principle— "Do that action which maximizes utility." Kant's system has several absolutes, whereas other deontological systems may have only a few broad absolutes, such as "Never cause unnecessary harm." Sometimes *ethical absolutism* refers to the notion that there is only one correct answer to every moral problem. Diametrically opposed to ethical absolutism is ethical relativism, which says that the validity of ethical principles is dependent on social acceptance. In between these polar opposites is ethical objectivism. *See* Objectivism; Relativism.

Aretaic ethics (Greek *arete*, virtue) The theory, first presented by Aristotle, that the basis of ethical assessment is character. Rather than seeing the heart of ethics in actions or duties, it focuses on the character and dispositions of the agent. Whereas *deontological* and *teleological* ethical systems emphasize *doing*, aretaic or virtue ethics emphasize *being* — being a certain type of person who will no doubt manifest his or her being in appropriate actions. *See* Part VII (text).

Categorical imperative The categorical imperative commands actions that are necessary of themselves without reference to other ends. This is contrasted with *hypothetical imperatives*, which command actions not for their own sakes but for some other good. For Kant, moral duties command categorically. They represent the injunctions of reason, which endows them with universal validity and objective necessity. *See* Hypothetical imperative.

Deontological ethics Deontological (Greek *deon*, duty) ethical systems see certain features in the moral act itself as having intrinsic value. These are contrasted with *teleological systems*, which see the ultimate criterion of morality in some nonmoral value that results from actions. For example, for the deontologist, telling the truth is the right thing to do even when it may cause pain or harm, and lying is the wrong thing to do even when it may produce good consequences. *See* Teleological ethics; Part V (text).

Egoism There are two types of egoism. Psychological egoism, a *descriptive* theory about human motivation, holds that people always act to satisfy their perceived best interest. Ethical egoism is a *prescriptive* or normative theory about how people *ought* to act. They ought to act according to their perceived best interests. *See* Part III (text).

Emotivism This is a version of *noncognitivism*, which holds that moral judgments do not have truth values but are expressions of our attitudes. They express our feelings and serve as a mechanism to persuade others to act as we desire. A. J. Ayer, a prominent emotivist, holds that the moral judgment that murder is wrong reduces to the emotional expression "Murder — Boo!" *See* Part VIII.2, VIII.3 (text).

Hedonic (Greek *hedone*, pleasure) Possessing pleasurable or painful quality. Sometimes "hedon" is used to stand for a quantity of pleasure.

Hedonism Psychological hedonism is the theory that motivation is to be explained exclusively in terms of desire for pleasure and aversion from pain. Ethical hedonism is the theory that pleasure is the only intrinsic positive value and pain or "unpleasant consciousness" the only thing that has negative intrinsic value or intrinsic disvalue. All other values are derived from these two. *See* Part IV (text).

Hedonistic paradox The apparent contradiction arising from the doctrine that pleasure is the only thing worth seeking and the fact that whenever one seeks pleasure, it is not found. Pleasure normally arises as an accompaniment of satisfaction of desire whenever one reaches one's goal.

Heteronomy of the will This is Kant's term for the determination of the will on nonrational grounds. It is contrasted with *autonomy of the will* where the will is guided by reason.

Hypothetical imperative Hypothetical imperatives command actions because they are useful for the attainment of some end that one may or may not desire to obtain. Ethicists who view moral duties to be dependent on consequences would view moral principles as hypothetical imperatives. They have the form: If you want X, do action A (for example, If you want to live in peace, do all in your power to prevent violence). This is contrasted with the *categorical imperative*. *See* Categorical imperative.

Intuitionism This is the ethical theory that the good or the right thing to do can be known directly via the intuition. In our readings, G. E. Moore (Part VIII.2) and W.D. Ross (Part VI.2) exemplify different versions of this view. Moore is an intuitionist about the good, defining it as a simple, unanalyzable property, and Ross is an intuitionist about what is right.

Naturalism The theory that ethical terms are defined through factual terms in that ethical terms refer to natural properties. Ethical hedonism is one version of ethical naturalism, for it states that the good that is at the basis of all ethical judgment refers to the experience of pleasure. Other naturalists, like Geoffrey Warnock, speak of the content of morality in terms of promoting human flourishing or ameliorating the human predicament. *See* Part VIII (text).

Noncognitivism This is the theory that ethical judgments have no truth value but express attitudes or prescriptions. *See* Emotivism; Prescriptivism; Part VIII (text).

Objectivism This is the view that moral principles have objective validity whether or not people recognize them as such; that is, moral rightness or wrongness does not depend on social approval but on independent considerations. Objectivism differs from absolutism in that it allows that all or many of its principles are overridable in given situations. *See* Part II.

Prescriptivism The noncognitivist theory, set forth by R.M. Hare (Part VIII.5) that claims that although moral judgments do not have truth values, they are more than mere expressions of attitudes. Moral judgments are universal prescriptions. For example, the judgment that Mary should have an abortion implies that *anyone* in relevantly similar circumstances as Mary should have an abortion.

Relativism There are two main types of relativism: cultural and ethical. Cultural relativism is a descriptive thesis, stating that there is enormous variety of moral beliefs across cultures. It is neutral as to whether this is the way things ought to be. Ethical relativism, on the other hand, is an evaluative thesis that holds that the truth of a moral judgment depends on whether a culture recognizes the principle in question. *See* Part II (text).

Supererogatory (Latin *supererogatus* — beyond the call of duty) A supererogatory act is one that is not required by moral principles but contains enormous value. Supererogatory acts are those that are beyond the call of duty, such as risking one's life to save a stranger. Although most moral systems allow for the possibility of supererogatory acts, some theories (most versions of classical utilitarianism) deny that there can be such acts.

Teleological ethics Teleological ethical theories place the ultimate criterion of morality in some nonmoral value (for example, happiness or welfare) that results from acts. Whereas *deontological* ethical theories ascribe intrinsic value to features of the acts themselves, teleological theories see only instrumental value in the acts but intrinsic value in the consequences of those acts. Both ethical egoism and utilitarianism are teleological theories. *See* Deontological ethics; Parts III, V (text).

Universalizability This principle, found explicitly in Kant's and R.M. Hare's philosophy and implicitly in most ethicists' works, states that if some act is right (or wrong) for one person in a situation, it is right (or wrong) for any relevantly similar person in that kind of situation. It is a principle of consistency that aims to eliminate irrelevant considerations from ethical assessment. *See* Prescriptivism.

Utilitarianism The theory that the right action is that which maximizes utility. Sometimes "utility" is defined in terms of *pleasure* (Jeremy Bentham), *happiness* (J.S Mill), *ideals* (G. E. Moore and H. Rashdall), or *interests* (R. B. Perry). Its motto, which characterizes one version of utilitarianism, is "The Greatest Happiness for the Greatest Number." Utilitarians further divide into *act* and *rule* utilitarians. Act utilitarians hold that the right act in a situation is that which results (or is most likely to result) in the best consequences, whereas rule utilitarians hold that the right act is that which conforms to the set of rules which in turn will result in the best consequences (relative to other sets of rules). *See* Part V (text).